PHILIP'S

ENCYCLOPEDIC

WORLD ATLAS

COUNTRIES OF THE WORLD
Text
Keith Lye

WORLD CITIES
Cartography by Philip's

Page 230, Dublin: The town plan of Dublin is based on Ordnance Survey
Ireland by permission of the Government Permit Number 8097. ©
Ordnance Survey Ireland and Government of Ireland.

Ordnance Survey® **Page 231, Edinburgh, and page 235, London:**
This product includes mapping data licensed from
Ordnance Survey® with the permission of the Controller of Her Majesty's
Stationery Office. © Crown copyright 2006. All rights reserved. Licence
number 100011710.

Vector data courtesy of Gräfe and Unser Verlag GmbH, München, Germany
(city-centre maps of Bangkok, Beijing, Cape Town, Jerusalem, Mexico City, Moscow,
Singapore, Sydney, Tokyo and Washington D.C.)
The following city maps utilize base data supplied courtesy of
MapQuest.com, Inc. (© MapQuest)
(Las Vegas, New Orleans, Orlando)

All satellite images in this section courtesy of NPA Group, Edenbridge,
Kent (www.satmaps.com)

Published in Great Britain in 2006
by Philip's,
a division of Octopus Publishing Group Limited,
2–4 Heron Quays, London E14 4JP

Copyright © 2006 Philip's

Cartography by Philip's

ISBN-13 978–0–540–08947–5
ISBN-10 0–540–08947–8

A CIP catalogue record for this book is available from the British Library.

Printed in Hong Kong

Details of other Philip's titles and services can be found on our website at:
www.philips-maps.co.uk

PHILIP'S

ENCYCLOPEDIC

WORLD ATLAS

4 Contents

Contents 5

6 Contents

Contents 7

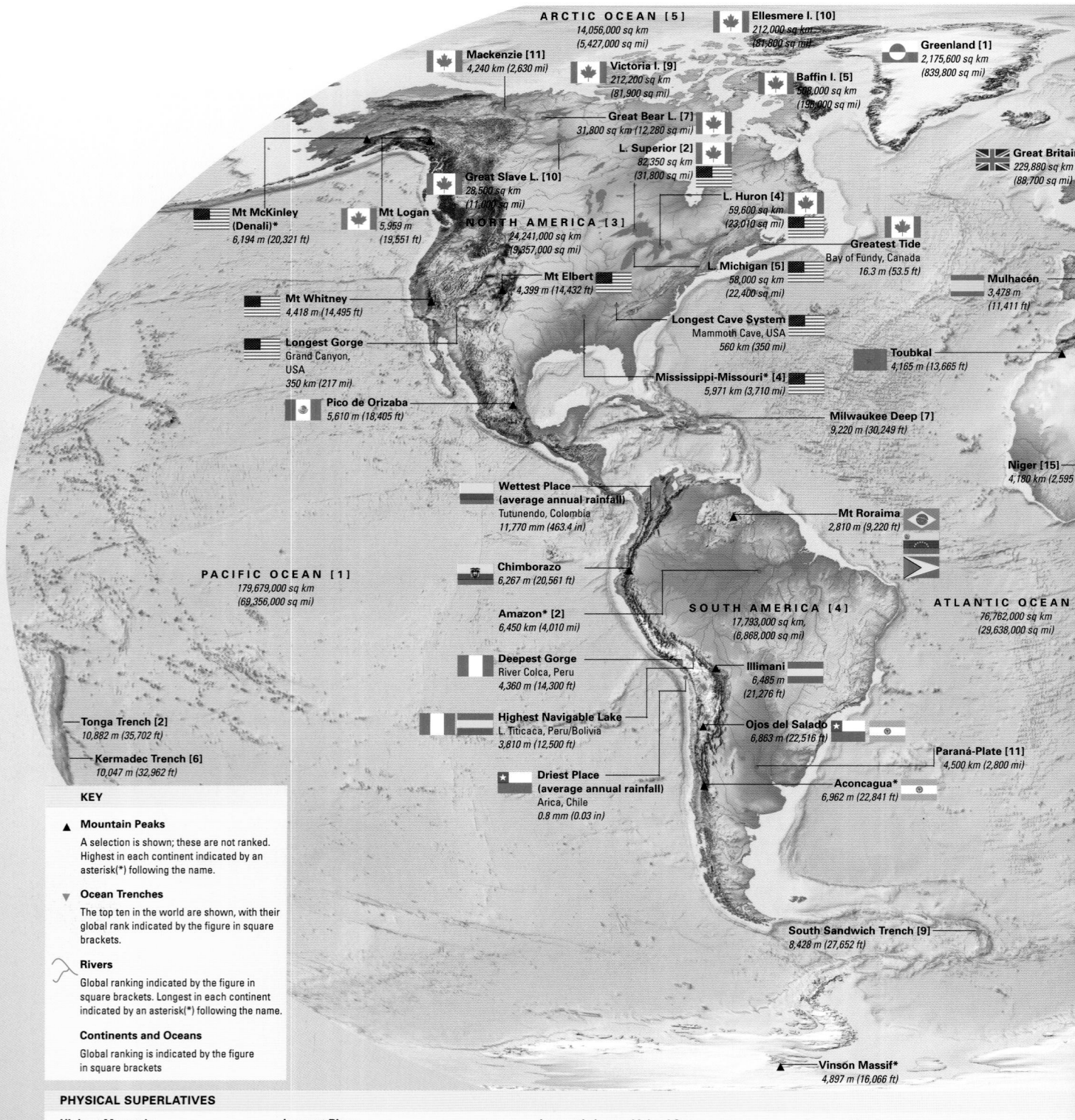

ARCTIC OCEAN [5]
14,056,000 sq km
(5,427,000 sq mi)

Ellesmere I. [10]
212,000 sq km
181,800 sq mi

Greenland [1]
2,175,600 sq km
(839,800 sq mi)

Mackenzie [11]
4,240 km (2,630 mi)

Victoria I. [9]
212,200 sq km
(81,900 sq mi)

Baffin I. [5]
508,000 sq km
(196,000 sq mi)

Great Bear L. [7]
31,800 sq km (12,280 sq mi)

L. Superior [2]
82,350 sq km
(31,800 sq mi)

Great Britain
229,880 sq km
(88,700 sq mi)

Great Slave L. [10]
28,500 sq km
(11,000 sq mi)

L. Huron [4]
59,600 sq km
(23,010 sq mi)

Mt McKinley
(Denali)*
6,194 m (20,321 ft)

Mt Logan
5,959 m
(19,551 ft)

NORTH AMERICA [3]
24,241,000 sq km
(9,357,000 sq mi)

Greatest Tide
Bay of Fundy, Canada
16.3 m (53.5 ft)

L. Michigan [5]
58,000 sq km
(22,400 sq mi)

Mulhacén
3,478 m
(11,411 ft)

Mt Elbert
4,399 m (14,432 ft)

Mt Whitney
4,418 m (14,495 ft)

Longest Cave System
Mammoth Cave, USA
560 km (350 mi)

Toubkal
4,165 m (13,665 ft)

Longest Gorge
Grand Canyon,
USA
350 km (217 mi)

Mississippi-Missouri* [4]
5,971 km (3,710 mi)

Milwaukee Deep [7]
9,220 m (30,249 ft)

Pico de Orizaba
5,610 m (18,405 ft)

Niger [15]
4,180 km (2,595

Wettest Place
(average annual rainfall)
Tutunendo, Colombia
11,770 mm (463.4 in)

Mt Roraima
2,810 m (9,220 ft)

PACIFIC OCEAN [1]
179,679,000 sq km
(69,356,000 sq mi)

Chimborazo
6,267 m (20,561 ft)

Amazon* [2]
6,450 km (4,010 mi)

SOUTH AMERICA [4]
17,793,000 sq km,
(6,868,000 sq mi)

ATLANTIC OCEAN
76,762,000 sq km
(29,638,000 sq mi)

Deepest Gorge
River Colca, Peru
4,360 m (14,300 ft)

Illimani
6,485 m
(21,276 ft)

Highest Navigable Lake
L. Titicaca, Peru/Bolivia
3,810 m (12,500 ft)

Ojos del Salado
6,863 m (22,516 ft)

Paraná-Plate [11]
4,500 km (2,800 mi)

Tonga Trench [2]
10,882 m (35,702 ft)

Kermadec Trench [6]
10,047 m (32,962 ft)

Driest Place
(average annual rainfall)
Arica, Chile
0.8 mm (0.03 in)

Aconcagua*
6,962 m (22,841 ft)

KEY

▲ **Mountain Peaks**
A selection is shown; these are not ranked.
Highest in each continent indicated by an
asterisk(*) following the name.

▽ **Ocean Trenches**
The top ten in the world are shown, with their
global rank indicated by the figure in square
brackets.

〰 **Rivers**
Global ranking indicated by the figure in
square brackets. Longest in each continent
indicated by an asterisk(*) following the name.

Continents and Oceans
Global ranking is indicated by the figure
in square brackets

South Sandwich Trench [9]
8,428 m (27,652 ft)

Vinson Massif*
4,897 m (16,066 ft)

PHYSICAL SUPERLATIVES

Highest Mountains	Longest Rivers	Largest Lakes and Inland Seas	Largest Islands
1 Everest, Asia 8,850 m (29,035 ft)	1 Nile, Africa 6,670 km (4,140 mi)	1 Caspian Sea, Asia 371,000 sq km (143,000 sq mi)	1 Greenland, N. America 2,175,600 sq km (839,800 sq mi)
2 K2 (Godwin Austen), Asia 8,611 m (28,251 ft)	2 Amazon, S. America 6,450 km (4,010 mi)	2 Lake Superior, N. America 82,350 sq km (31,800 sq mi)	2 New Guinea, Oceania 821,030 sq km (317,000 sq mi)
3 Kanchenjunga, Asia 8,598 m (28,208 ft)	3 Yangtze, Asia 6,380 km (3,960 mi)	3 Lake Victoria, Africa 68,000 sq km (26,000 sq mi)	3 Borneo, Asia 744,360 sq km (287,400 sq mi)
4 Lhotse, Asia 8,516 m (27,939 ft)	4 Mississippi-Missouri, N. America 5,971 km (3,710 mi)	4 Lake Huron, N. America 59,600 sq km (23,010 sq mi)	4 Madagascar, Africa 587,040 sq km (226,660 sq mi)
5 Makalu, Asia 8,481 m (27,824 ft)	5 Yenisey-Angara, Asia 5,550 km (3,445 mi)	5 Lake Michigan, N. America 58,000 sq km (22,400 sq mi)	5 Baffin Island, N. America 508,000 sq km (196,100 sq mi)
6 Cho Oyu, Asia 8,201 m (26,906 ft)	6 Huang He, Asia 5,464 km (3,395 mi)	6 Lake Tanganyika, Africa 33,000 sq km (13,000 sq mi)	6 Sumatra, Asia 473,600 sq km (182,860 sq mi)
7 Dhaulagiri, Asia 8,172 m (26,811 ft)	7 Ob-Irtysh, Asia 5,410 km (3,360 mi)	7 Great Bear Lake, N. America 31,800 sq km (12,280 sq mi)	7 Honshu, Asia 230,500 sq km (88,980 sq mi)
8 Manaslu, Asia 8,156 m (26,758 ft)	8 Congo, Africa 4,670 km (2,900 mi)	8 Lake Baikal, Asia 30,500 sq km (11,780 sq mi)	8 Great Britain, Europe 229,880 sq km (88,700 sq mi)
9 Nanga Parbat, Asia 8,126 m (26,660 ft)	9 Mekong, Asia 4,500 km (2,795 mi)	9 Lake Malawi/Nyasa, Africa 29,600 sq km (11,430 sq mi)	9 Victoria Island, N. America 212,200 sq km (81,900 sq mi)
10 Annapurna, Asia 8,078 m (26,502 ft)	10 Amur, Asia 4,442 km (2,760 mi)	10 Great Slave Lake, N. America 28,500 sq km (11,000 sq mi)	10 Ellesmere Island, N. America 212,000 sq km (81,800 sq mi)

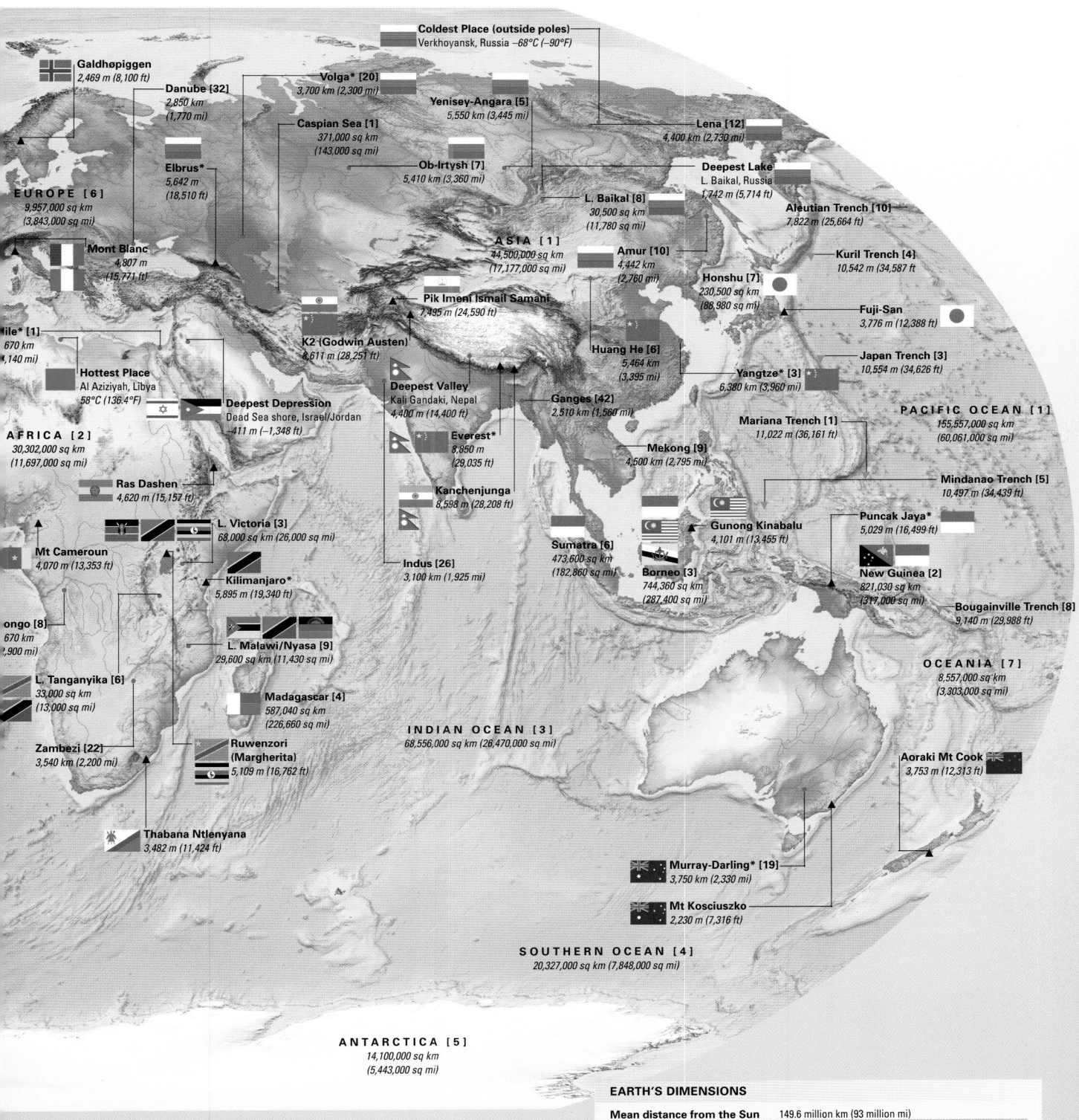

INSIDE THE EARTH

Layer	Density (water = 1)	Temperature		State	Thickness	
Crust (continental)	2.8	<500°C	(930°F)	Solid	c. 40 km	(c. 25 mi)
Crust (oceanic)	2.9	<1,100°C	(2,010°F)	Solid	c. 7 km	(c. 4 mi)
Upper mantle	4.3	<1,400°C	(2,550°F)	Molten	c. 900 km	(c. 560 mi)
Lower mantle	5.5	<1,700°C	(3,090°F)	Solid	c. 1,900 km	(c. 1,180 mi)
Outer core	10.0	<2,300°C	(7,170°F)	Molten	c. 2,200 km	(c. 1,370 mi)
Inner core	13.5	<5,500°C	(9,930°F)	Solid	c. 1,300 km	(c. 810 mi)

EARTH'S DIMENSIONS

Mean distance from the Sun	149.6 million km (93 million mi)
Average speed around the Sun	108,000 km/h (66,600 mph)
Age	4,600 million years
Mass	5.9×10^{21} tonnes
Density (water = 1)	5.52
Volume	$1,083,230 \times 10^6$ cu km ($260,000 \times 10^6$ cu mi)
Area	510 million sq km (197 million sq mi)
Land surface	149 million sq km (58 million sq mi) = 29.3% of total area
Water surface	361 million sq km (139 million sq mi) = 70.7% of total area
Equatorial circumference	40,074 km (24,901 mi)
Polar circumference	40,008 km (24,860 mi)
Equatorial diameter	12,756 km (7,926 mi)
Polar diameter	12,714 km (7,900 mi)

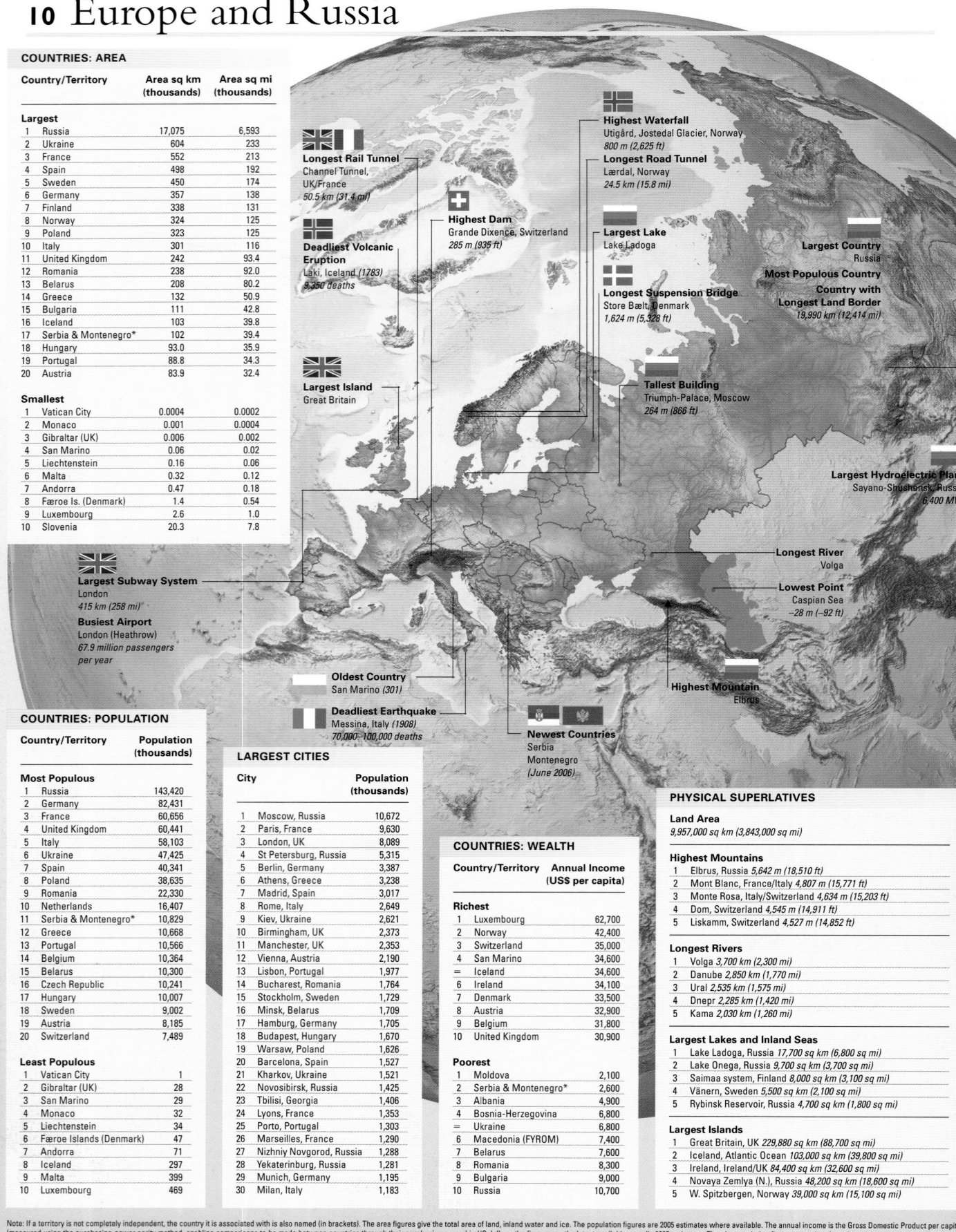

COUNTRIES: AREA

Country/Territory	Area sq km (thousands)	Area sq mi (thousands)
Largest		
1 Russia	17,075	6,593
2 Ukraine	604	233
3 France	552	213
4 Spain	498	192
5 Sweden	450	174
6 Germany	357	138
7 Finland	338	131
8 Norway	324	125
9 Poland	323	125
10 Italy	301	116
11 United Kingdom	242	93.4
12 Romania	238	92.0
13 Belarus	208	80.2
14 Greece	132	50.9
15 Bulgaria	111	42.8
16 Iceland	103	39.8
17 Serbia & Montenegro*	102	39.4
18 Hungary	93.0	35.9
19 Portugal	88.8	34.3
20 Austria	83.9	32.4
Smallest		
1 Vatican City	0.0004	0.0002
2 Monaco	0.001	0.0004
3 Gibraltar (UK)	0.006	0.002
4 San Marino	0.06	0.02
5 Liechtenstein	0.16	0.06
6 Malta	0.32	0.12
7 Andorra	0.47	0.18
8 Færoe Is. (Denmark)	1.4	0.54
9 Luxembourg	2.6	1.0
10 Slovenia	20.3	7.8

COUNTRIES: POPULATION

Country/Territory	Population (thousands)
Most Populous	
1 Russia	143,420
2 Germany	82,431
3 France	60,656
4 United Kingdom	60,441
5 Italy	58,103
6 Ukraine	47,425
7 Spain	40,341
8 Poland	38,635
9 Romania	22,330
10 Netherlands	16,407
11 Serbia & Montenegro*	10,829
12 Greece	10,668
13 Portugal	10,566
14 Belgium	10,364
15 Belarus	10,300
16 Czech Republic	10,241
17 Hungary	10,007
18 Sweden	9,002
19 Austria	8,185
20 Switzerland	7,489
Least Populous	
1 Vatican City	1
2 Gibraltar (UK)	28
3 San Marino	29
4 Monaco	32
5 Liechtenstein	34
6 Færoe Islands (Denmark)	47
7 Andorra	71
8 Iceland	297
9 Malta	399
10 Luxembourg	469

LARGEST CITIES

City	Population (thousands)
1 Moscow, Russia	10,672
2 Paris, France	9,630
3 London, UK	8,089
4 St Petersburg, Russia	5,315
5 Berlin, Germany	3,387
6 Athens, Greece	3,238
7 Madrid, Spain	3,017
8 Rome, Italy	2,649
9 Kiev, Ukraine	2,621
10 Birmingham, UK	2,373
11 Manchester, UK	2,353
12 Vienna, Austria	2,190
13 Lisbon, Portugal	1,977
14 Bucharest, Romania	1,764
15 Stockholm, Sweden	1,729
16 Minsk, Belarus	1,709
17 Hamburg, Germany	1,705
18 Budapest, Hungary	1,670
19 Warsaw, Poland	1,626
20 Barcelona, Spain	1,527
21 Kharkov, Ukraine	1,521
22 Novosibirsk, Russia	1,425
23 Tbilisi, Georgia	1,406
24 Lyons, France	1,353
25 Porto, Portugal	1,303
26 Marseilles, France	1,290
27 Nizhniy Novgorod, Russia	1,288
28 Yekaterinburg, Russia	1,281
29 Munich, Germany	1,195
30 Milan, Italy	1,183

COUNTRIES: WEALTH

Country/Territory	Annual Income (US$ per capita)
Richest	
1 Luxembourg	62,700
2 Norway	42,400
3 Switzerland	35,000
4 San Marino	34,600
= Iceland	34,600
6 Ireland	34,100
7 Denmark	33,500
8 Austria	32,900
9 Belgium	31,800
10 United Kingdom	30,900
Poorest	
1 Moldova	2,100
2 Serbia & Montenegro*	2,600
3 Albania	4,900
4 Bosnia-Herzegovina	6,800
= Ukraine	6,800
6 Macedonia (FYROM)	7,400
7 Belarus	7,600
8 Romania	8,300
9 Bulgaria	9,000
10 Russia	10,700

PHYSICAL SUPERLATIVES

Land Area
9,957,000 sq km (3,843,000 sq mi)

Highest Mountains
1 Elbrus, Russia 5,642 m (18,510 ft)
2 Mont Blanc, France/Italy 4,807 m (15,771 ft)
3 Monte Rosa, Italy/Switzerland 4,634 m (15,203 ft)
4 Dom, Switzerland 4,545 m (14,911 ft)
5 Liskamm, Switzerland 4,527 m (14,852 ft)

Longest Rivers
1 Volga 3,700 km (2,300 mi)
2 Danube 2,850 km (1,770 mi)
3 Ural 2,535 km (1,575 mi)
4 Dnepr 2,285 km (1,420 mi)
5 Kama 2,030 km (1,260 mi)

Largest Lakes and Inland Seas
1 Lake Ladoga, Russia 17,700 sq km (6,800 sq mi)
2 Lake Onega, Russia 9,700 sq km (3,700 sq mi)
3 Saimaa system, Finland 8,000 sq km (3,100 sq mi)
4 Vänern, Sweden 5,500 sq km (2,100 sq mi)
5 Rybinsk Reservoir, Russia 4,700 sq km (1,800 sq mi)

Largest Islands
1 Great Britain, UK 229,880 sq km (88,700 sq mi)
2 Iceland, Atlantic Ocean 103,000 sq km (39,800 sq mi)
3 Ireland, Ireland/UK 84,400 sq km (32,600 sq mi)
4 Novaya Zemlya (N.), Russia 48,200 sq km (18,600 sq mi)
5 W. Spitzbergen, Norway 39,000 sq km (15,100 sq mi)

Map labels

Longest Rail Tunnel
Channel Tunnel, UK/France
50.5 km (31.4 mi)

Deadliest Volcanic Eruption
Laki, Iceland (1783)
9,350 deaths

Highest Dam
Grande Dixence, Switzerland
285 m (935 ft)

Highest Waterfall
Utigård, Jostedal Glacier, Norway
800 m (2,625 ft)

Longest Road Tunnel
Lærdal, Norway
24.5 km (15.8 mi)

Largest Lake
Lake Ladoga

Longest Suspension Bridge
Store Bælt, Denmark
1,624 m (5,328 ft)

Largest Country
Russia

Most Populous Country

Country with Longest Land Border
19,990 km (12,414 mi)

Tallest Building
Triumph-Palace, Moscow
264 m (866 ft)

Largest Island
Great Britain

Largest Hydroelectric Plant
Sayano-Shushensk, Russia
6,400 MW

Largest Subway System
London
415 km (258 mi)

Busiest Airport
London (Heathrow)
67.9 million passengers per year

Oldest Country
San Marino (301)

Deadliest Earthquake
Messina, Italy (1908)
70,000–100,000 deaths

Newest Countries
Serbia
Montenegro
(June 2006)

Longest River
Volga

Lowest Point
Caspian Sea
−28 m (−92 ft)

Highest Mountain
Elbrus

Note: If a territory is not completely independent, the country it is associated with is also named (in brackets). The area figures give the total area of land, inland water and ice. The population figures are 2005 estimates where available. The annual income is the Gross Domestic Product per capita (measured using the purchasing-power parity method, enabling comparisons to be made between countries through their purchasing power) in US dollars; the figures are the latest available, usually 2005 estimates. The city population figures are taken from the most recent census or estimate available, and as far as possible are the population of the metropolitan area or urban agglomeration (for example, greater New York or Paris).
*In June 2006, Serbia and Montenegro formally declared their independence and are now separate sovereign states.

COUNTRIES: AREA

Country/Territory	Area sq km (thousands)	Area sq mi (thousands)
Largest		
1 China	9,597	3,705
2 India	3,287	1,269
3 Kazakhstan	2,725	1,052
4 Saudi Arabia	2,150	830
5 Indonesia	1,905	735
6 Iran	1,648	636
7 Mongolia	1,567	605
8 Pakistan	796	307
9 Turkey	775	299
10 Burma (= Myanmar)	677	261
11 Afghanistan	652	252
12 Yemen	528	204
13 Thailand	513	198
14 Turkmenistan	488	188
15 Uzbekistan	447	173
16 Iraq	438	169
17 Japan	378	146
18 Vietnam	332	128
19 Malaysia	330	127
20 Oman	310	119
Smallest		
1 Macau (China)	0.02	0.007
2 Maldives	0.30	0.12
3 Gaza Strip (OPT)	0.36	0.14
4 Singapore	0.68	0.26
5 Bahrain	0.69	0.27
6 Hong Kong (China)	1.1	0.42
7 Brunei	5.8	2.2
8 West Bank (OPT)	5.9	2.3
9 Cyprus	9.3	3.6
10 Lebanon	10.4	4.0

COUNTRIES: POPULATION

Country/Territory	Population (thousands)
Most Populous	
1 China	1,306,314
2 India	1,080,264
3 Indonesia	241,974
4 Pakistan	162,420
5 Bangladesh	144,320
6 Japan	127,417
7 Philippines	87,857
8 Vietnam	83,536
9 Turkey	69,661
10 Iran	68,018
11 Thailand	65,444
12 South Korea	48,423
13 Burma (= Myanmar)	42,909
14 Afghanistan	29,929
15 Nepal	27,677
16 Uzbekistan	26,851
17 Saudi Arabia	26,418
18 Iraq	26,075
19 Malaysia	23,953
20 North Korea	22,912
Least Populous	
1 Maldives	349
2 Brunei	372
3 Macau (China)	449
4 Bahrain	688
5 Cyprus	780
6 Qatar	863
7 East Timor	1,041
8 Gaza Strip (OPT)	1,376
9 Bhutan	2,232
10 Kuwait	2,336

LARGEST CITIES

City	Population (thousands)
1 Mumbai (Bombay), India	18,336
2 Delhi, India	15,334
3 Kolkata (Calcutta), India	14,299
4 Jakarta, Indonesia	13,194
5 Shanghai, China	12,665
6 Dhaka, Bangladesh	12,560
7 Tokyo, Japan	12,064
8 Karachi, Pakistan	11,819
9 Beijing, China	10,849
10 Manila, Philippines	10,677
11 Seoul, South Korea	9,888
12 Tianjin, China	9,346
13 Istanbul, Turkey	8,953
14 Tehran, Iran	7,352
15 Hong Kong, China	7,182
16 Chennai (Madras), India	6,915
17 Bangkok, Thailand	6,604
18 Bangalore, India	6,532
19 Yokohama, Japan	6,427
20 Lahore, Pakistan	6,373
21 Hyderabad, India	6,145
22 Wuhan, China	6,003
23 Baghdad, Iraq	5,910
24 Riyadh, Saudi Arabia	5,514
25 Ahmedabad, India	5,171
26 Ho Chi Minh City, Vietnam	5,030
27 Chongqing, China	4,975
28 Shenyang, China	4,916
29 Pune, India	4,485
30 Singapore City, Singapore	4,372

COUNTRIES: WEALTH

Country/Territory	Annual Income (US$ per capita)
Richest	
1 Hong Kong (China)	36,800
2 Japan	30,400
3 Singapore	29,700
4 United Arab Emirates	29,100
5 Taiwan	26,700
6 Qatar	26,000
7 Brunei	23,600
8 Israel	22,200
9 Kuwait	22,100
10 Cyprus	21,600
Poorest	
1 East Timor	400
2 Gaza Strip (OPT)	600
3 Afghanistan	800
= Yemen	800
5 West Bank (OPT)	1,100
6 Tajikistan	1,200
7 Bhutan	1,400
8 Nepal	1,500
9 North Korea	1,800
= Burma (= Myanmar)	1,800

Largest Subway System
Tokyo
281 km (174.5 mi)

Busiest Airport
Tokyo (Haneda)
63.2 million passengers
per year

Longest Rail Tunnel
Sei-kan, Japan
53.9 km (33.5 mi)

Longest Suspension Bridge
Akashi-kaikyo, Japan
1,991 m (6,533 ft)

Longest River
Yangtze

Largest Country
China

**Country with
Longest Land Border**
22,147 km (13,753 mi)

Oldest Country
(221 BC)

Most Populous Country

Largest Lake
Caspian Sea

Lowest Point
Dead Sea
–418 m (–1,371 ft)

Largest Desert
Saudi Arabia
2,331,000 sq km (900,000 sq mi)

Tallest Building
Taipei 101, Taiwan
510 m (1,673 ft)

**Longest Road
Tunnel**
Hsuehshan, Taiwan
12.9 km (8.0 mi)

Largest Island
Borneo

Highest Dam
Rogun, Tajikistan
335 m (1,099 ft)

**Highest
Mountain**
Everest

**Largest Hydroelectric
Plant**
Ertan, China
3,300 MW

Deadliest Earthquake
Shanxi, China (1556)
830,000 deaths

Newest Country
East Timor
(May 2002)

Deadliest Volcanic Eruption
Tambora, Indonesia (1815)
92,000 deaths

Highest Waterfall
Dudhsagar,
Khandepar River,
India
600 m (1,964 ft)

PHYSICAL SUPERLATIVES

Land Area
44,500,000 sq km (17,177,000 sq mi)

Highest Mountains
1 Everest, China/Nepal 8,850 m (29,035 ft)
2 K2 (Godwin Austen), China/Kashmir 8,611 m (28,251 ft)
3 Kanchenjunga, India/Nepal 8,598 m (28,208 ft)
4 Lhotse, China/Nepal 8,516 m (27,939 ft)
5 Makalu, China/Nepal 8,481 m (27,824 ft)

Longest Rivers
1 Yangtze 6,380 km (3,960 mi)
2 Yenisey–Angara 5,550 km (3,445 mi)
3 Huang He 5,464 km (3,395 mi)
4 Ob–Irtysh 5,410 km (3,360 mi)
5 Mekong 4,500 km (2,795 mi)

Largest Lakes and Inland Seas
1 Caspian Sea, W. Central Asia 371,000 sq km (143,000 sq mi)
2 Lake Baikal, Russia 30,500 sq km (11,780 sq mi)
3 Tonlé Sap, Cambodia 20,000 sq km (7,700 sq mi)
4 Lake Balkhash, Kazakhstan 18,500 sq km (7,100 sq mi)
5 Aral Sea, Kazakhstan/Uzbekistan 17,160 sq km (6,625 sq mi)

Largest Islands
1 Borneo, S. E. Asia 744,360 sq km (287,400 sq mi)
2 Sumatra, Indonesia 473,600 sq km (182,860 sq mi)
3 Honshu, Japan 230,500 sq km (88,980 sq mi)
4 Sulawesi (Celebes), Indonesia 189,000 sq km (73,000 sq mi)
5 Java, Indonesia 126,700 sq km (48,900 sq mi)

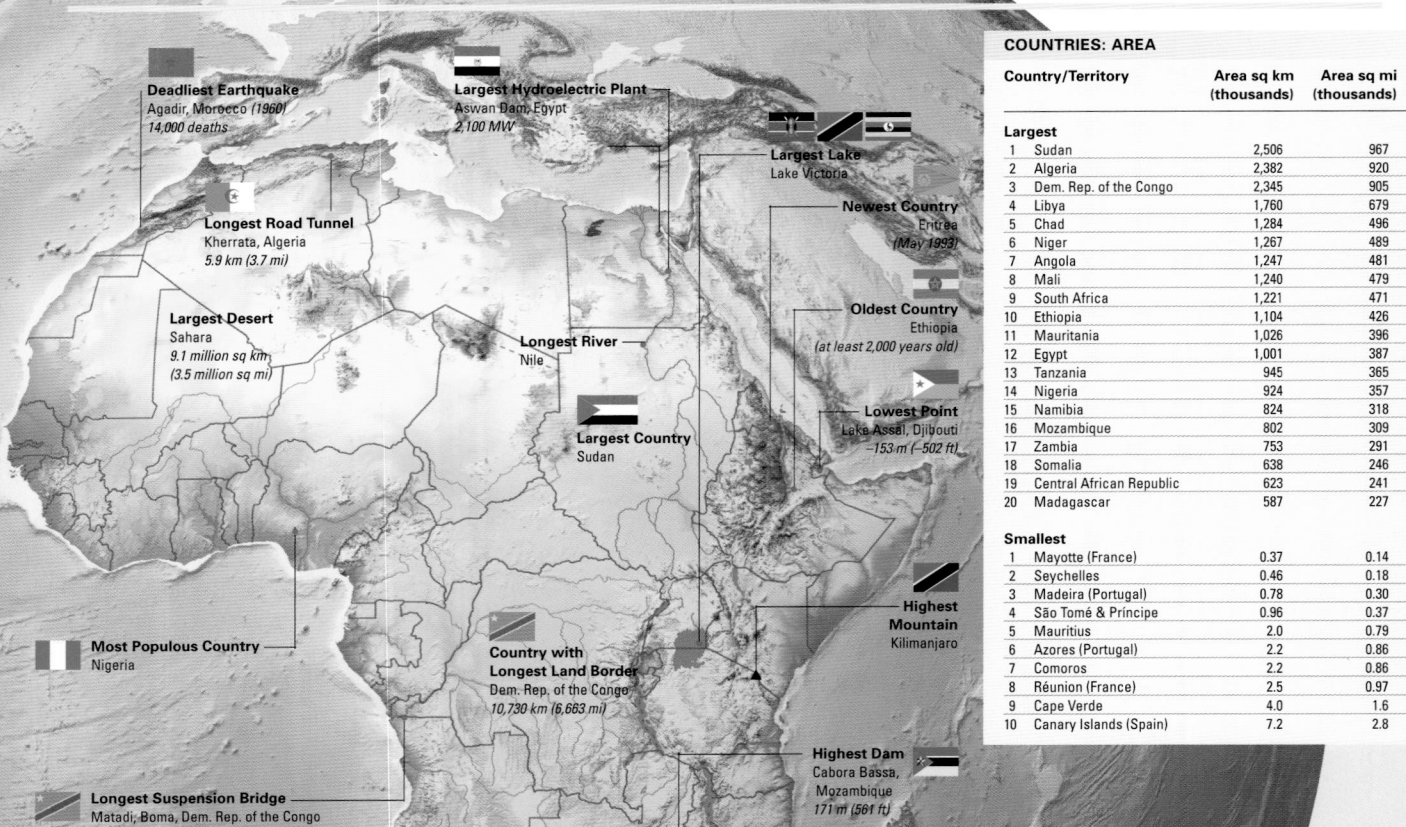

Deadliest Earthquake
Agadir, Morocco *(1960)*
14,000 deaths

Largest Hydroelectric Plant
Aswan Dam, Egypt
2,100 MW

Largest Lake
Lake Victoria

Newest Country
Eritrea
(May 1993)

Longest Road Tunnel
Kherrata, Algeria
5.9 km (3.7 mi)

Oldest Country
Ethiopia
(at least 2,000 years old)

Largest Desert
Sahara
9.1 million sq km
(3.5 million sq mi)

Longest River
Nile

Lowest Point
Lake Assal, Djibouti
−153 m (−502 ft)

Largest Country
Sudan

Highest Mountain
Kilimanjaro

Most Populous Country
Nigeria

Country with Longest Land Border
Dem. Rep. of the Congo
10,730 km (6,663 mi)

Highest Dam
Cabora Bassa,
Mozambique
171 m (561 ft)

Longest Suspension Bridge
Matadi, Boma, Dem. Rep. of the Congo
520 m (1,706 ft)

Largest Island
Madagascar

Highest Waterfall
Tugela, Tugela River, South Africa
947 m (3,110 ft)

Busiest Airport
Johannesburg
14 million passengers per year

Tallest Building
Carlton Centre Office Tower,
Johannesburg
223 m (732 ft)

Longest Rail Tunnel
Hex River, South Africa
13.4km (8.6 mi)

COUNTRIES: AREA

Country/Territory	Area sq km (thousands)	Area sq mi (thousands)
Largest		
1 Sudan	2,506	967
2 Algeria	2,382	920
3 Dem. Rep. of the Congo	2,345	905
4 Libya	1,760	679
5 Chad	1,284	496
6 Niger	1,267	489
7 Angola	1,247	481
8 Mali	1,240	479
9 South Africa	1,221	471
10 Ethiopia	1,104	426
11 Mauritania	1,026	396
12 Egypt	1,001	387
13 Tanzania	945	365
14 Nigeria	924	357
15 Namibia	824	318
16 Mozambique	802	309
17 Zambia	753	291
18 Somalia	638	246
19 Central African Republic	623	241
20 Madagascar	587	227
Smallest		
1 Mayotte (France)	0.37	0.14
2 Seychelles	0.46	0.18
3 Madeira (Portugal)	0.78	0.30
4 São Tomé & Príncipe	0.96	0.37
5 Mauritius	2.0	0.79
6 Azores (Portugal)	2.2	0.86
7 Comoros	2.2	0.86
8 Réunion (France)	2.5	0.97
9 Cape Verde	4.0	1.6
10 Canary Islands (Spain)	7.2	2.8

PHYSICAL SUPERLATIVES

Land Area
30,302,000 sq km (11,697,000 sq mi)

Highest Mountains
1 Kilimanjaro, Tanzania 5,895 m (19,340 ft)
2 Mt Kenya, Kenya 5,199 m (17,057 ft)
3 Ruwenzori (Margherita), Uganda/
  Dem. Rep. of the Congo 5,109 m (16,762 ft)
4 Ras Dashen, Ethiopia 4,620 m (15,157 ft)
5 Meru, Tanzania 4,565 m (14,977 ft)

Longest Rivers
1 Nile 6,670 km (4,140 mi)
2 Congo 4,670 km (2,900 mi)
3 Niger 4,180 km (2,595 mi)
4 Zambezi 3,540 km (2,200 mi)
5 Oubangi/Uele 2,250 km (1,400 mi)

Largest Lakes and Inland Seas
1 Lake Victoria 68,000 sq km (26,000 sq mi)
2 Lake Tanganyika 33,000 sq km (13,000 sq mi)
3 Lake Malawi/Nyasa 29,600 sq km (11,430 sq mi)
4 Lake Chad 25,000 sq km (9,700 sq mi)
5 Lake Turkana 8,500 sq km (3,300 sq mi)

Largest Islands
1 Madagascar 587,040 sq km (226,660 sq mi)
2 Socotra 3,600 sq km (1,400 sq mi)
3 Réunion 2,500 sq km (965 sq mi)
4 Tenerife 2,350 sq km (900 sq mi)
5 Mauritius 1,865 sq km (720 sq mi)

COUNTRIES: WEALTH

Country/Territory	Annual Income (US$ per capita)
Richest	
1 Madeira (Portugal)	22,700
2 Canary Islands (Spain)	19,900
3 Azores (Portugal)	15,000
4 Mauritius	13,300
5 South Africa	11,900
6 Botswana	10,100
7 Libya	8,400
8 Seychelles	7,800
= Namibia	7,800
10 Tunisia	7,600
Poorest	
1 Comoros	600
= Malawi	600
= Somalia	600
4 Burundi	700
= Liberia	700
= Tanzania	700
7 Congo	800
= Dem. Rep. of the Congo	800
= Ethiopia	800
= Sierra Leone	800

LARGEST CITIES

City	Population (thousands)
1 Cairo, Egypt	11,146
2 Lagos, Nigeria	11,135
3 Kinshasa, Dem. Rep. of the Congo	5,717
4 Alexandria, Egypt	3,760
5 Casablanca, Morocco	3,743
6 Abidjan, Ivory Coast	3,516
7 Algiers, Algeria	3,260
8 Johannesburg, South Africa	2,950
9 Cape Town, South Africa	2,930
10 Addis Ababa, Ethiopia	2,899
11 Kano, Nigeria	2,884
12 Luanda, Angola	2,839
13 Nairobi, Kenya	2,818
14 Khartoum, Sudan	2,742
15 Dar es Salaam, Tanzania	2,683
16 Durban / eThekwini, South Africa	2,391
17 Ibadan, Nigeria	2,375
18 Dakar, Senegal	2,313
19 Tunis, Tunisia	2,063
20 Douala, Cameroon	1,980
21 Accra, Ghana	1,970
22 Rabat, Morocco	1,859
23 Antananarivo, Madagascar	1,808
24 Tripoli, Libya	1,733
25 Yaoundé, Cameroon	1,727
26 Pretoria / Tshwane, South Africa	1,590
27 Harare, Zimbabwe	1,527
28 Conakry, Guinea	1,465
29 Lusaka, Zambia	1,450
30 Bamako, Mali	1,379

COUNTRIES: POPULATION

Country/Territory	Population (thousands)
Most Populous	
1 Nigeria	128,772
2 Egypt	77,506
3 Ethiopia	73,053
4 Dem. Rep. of the Congo	60,086
5 South Africa	44,344
6 Sudan	40,187
7 Tanzania	36,766
8 Kenya	33,830
9 Morocco	32,726
10 Algeria	32,532
11 Uganda	27,269
12 Ghana	21,030
13 Mozambique	19,407
14 Madagascar	18,040
15 Ivory Coast	17,298
16 Cameroon	16,380
17 Burkina Faso	13,925
18 Zimbabwe	12,747
19 Mali	12,292
20 Malawi	12,159
Least Populous	
1 Seychelles	81
2 São Tomé & Príncipe	187
3 Mayotte (France)	194
4 Azores (Portugal)	236
5 Madeira (Portugal)	241
6 Western Sahara	273
7 Cape Verde	418
8 Djibouti	477
9 Equatorial Guinea	536
10 Comoros	671

PHYSICAL SUPERLATIVES

Land Area
8,557,000 sq km (3,303,000 sq mi)

Highest Mountains
1. Puncak Jaya, Indonesia 5,029 m (16,499 ft)
2. Puncak Trikora, Indonesia 4,730 m (15,518 ft)
3. Puncak Mandala, Indonesia 4,702 m (15,427 ft)
4. Mt Wilhelm, Papua New Guinea 4,508 m (14,790 ft)
5. Mauna Kea, USA (Hawai'i) 4,205 m (13,796 ft)

Longest Rivers
1. Murray–Darling 3,750 km (2,330 mi)
2. Darling 3,070 km (1,905 mi)
3. Murray 2,575 km (1,600 mi)
4. Murrumbidgee 1,690 km (1,050 mi)
5. Lachlan 1,370 km (850 mi)

Largest Lakes and Inland Seas
1. Lake Eyre, Australia 8,900 sq km (3,400 sq mi)
2. Lake Torrens, Australia 5,800 sq km (2,200 sq mi)
3. Lake Gairdner, Australia 4,800 sq km (1,900 sq mi)
4. Lake Mackay, Australia 3,490 sq km (1,380 sq mi)
5. Lake Amadeus, Australia 1,032 sq km (400 sq mi)

Largest Islands
1. New Guinea, Indon./Papua NG 821,030 sq km (317,000 sq mi)
2. New Zealand (S.), Pacific Ocean 150,500 sq km (58,100 sq mi)
3. New Zealand (N.), Pacific Ocean 114,700 sq km (44,300 sq mi)
4. Tasmania, Australia 67,800 sq km (26,200 sq mi)
5. New Britain, Papua NG 37,800 sq km (14,600 sq mi)

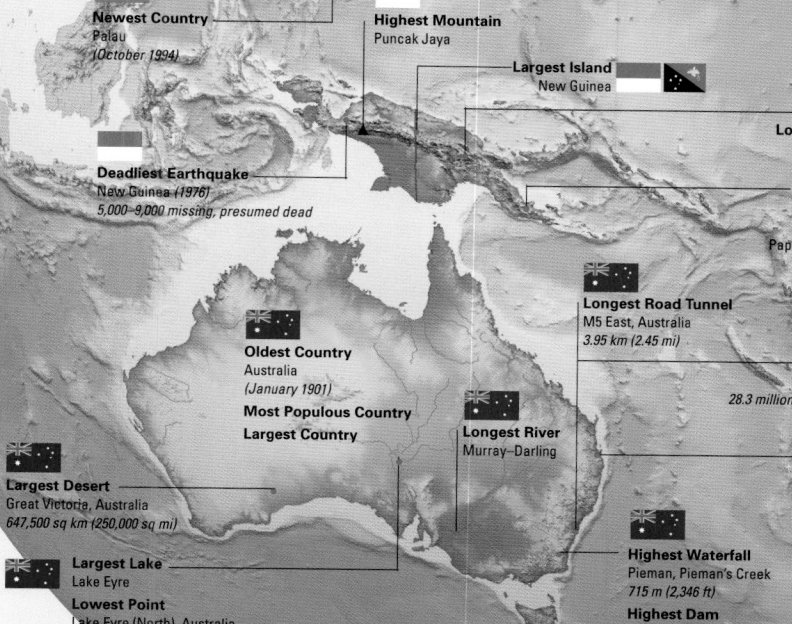

Newest Country
Palau
(October 1994)

Highest Mountain
Puncak Jaya

Largest Island
New Guinea

Country with Longest Land Border
Papua New Guinea
820 km (509 mi)

Deadliest Earthquake
New Guinea (1976)
5,000–9,000 missing, presumed dead

Deadliest Volcanic Eruption
Mt Lamington,
Papua New Guinea (1951)
2,942 deaths

Longest Road Tunnel
M5 East, Australia
3.95 km (2.45 mi)

Busiest Airport
Sydney
28.3 million passengers per year

Oldest Country
Australia
(January 1901)

Most Populous Country
Largest Country

Longest River
Murray–Darling

Tallest Building
Q1 Tower, Gold Coast
275 m (902ft)

Largest Desert
Great Victoria, Australia
647,500 sq km (250,000 sq mi)

Largest Lake
Lake Eyre

Lowest Point
Lake Eyre (North), Australia
−16 m (−52 ft)

Highest Waterfall
Pieman, Pieman's Creek
715 m (2,346 ft)

Highest Dam
Dartmouth
180 m (591 ft)

Largest Hydroelectric Plant
Snowy Mountains
3,800 MW

Longest Rail Tunnel
Kaimai, New Zealand
8.9 km (5.5 mi)

COUNTRIES: AREA

	Country/Territory	Area sq km (thousands)	Area sq mi (thousands)
1	Australia	7,741	2,989
2	Papua New Guinea	463	179
3	New Zealand	271	104
4	Solomon Islands	28.9	11.2
5	New Caledonia (France)	18.6	7.2
6	Fiji Islands	18.3	7.1
7	Vanuatu	12.2	4.7
8	French Polynesia (France)	4.0	1.5
9	Samoa	2.8	1.1
10	Kiribati	0.73	0.28
11	Fed. States of Micronesia	0.70	0.27
12	Tonga	0.65	0.25
13	Guam (US)	0.55	0.21
14	Northern Mariana Islands (US)	0.46	0.18
15	Palau	0.46	0.18
16	Cook Is. (NZ)	0.24	0.09
17	American Samoa (US)	0.20	0.08
18	Wallis & Futuna Islands (France)	0.20	0.08
19	Marshall Islands	0.18	0.07
20	Tuvalu	0.03	0.01
21	Nauru	0.02	0.008

COUNTRIES: POPULATION

	Country/Territory	Population (thousands)
1	Australia	20,090
2	Papua New Guinea	5,545
3	New Zealand	4,035
4	Fiji Islands	893
5	Solomon Islands	538
6	French Polynesia (France)	270
7	New Caledonia (France)	216
8	Vanuatu	206
9	Samoa	177
10	Guam (US)	169
11	Tonga	112
12	Fed. States of Micronesia	108
13	Kiribati	103
14	Northern Mariana Is. (US)	80
15	Marshall Islands	59
16	American Samoa (US)	58
17	Cook Islands (NZ)	21
18	Palau	20
19	Wallis & Futuna Is. (France)	16
20	Nauru	13
21	Tuvalu	12

COUNTRIES: WEALTH

	Country/Territory	Annual Income (US$ per capita)
1	Australia	32,000
2	New Zealand	24,100
3	Guam (US)	21,000
4	French Polynesia (France)	17,500
5	New Caledonia (France)	15,000
6	Northern Mariana Is. (US)	12,500
7	Palau	9,000
8	American Samoa (US)	8,000
9	Fiji Islands	6,000
10	Samoa	5,600
11	Nauru	5,000
12	Cook Islands (NZ)	5,000
13	Wallis & Futuna Is. (France)	3,800
14	Vanuatu	2,900
15	Papua New Guinea	2,400
16	Tonga	2,300
17	Fed. States of Micronesia	2,000
18	Solomon Islands	1,700
19	Marshall Islands	1,600
20	Tuvalu	1,100
21	Kiribati	800

LARGEST CITIES

	City	Population (thousands)
1	Sydney, Australia	4,388
2	Melbourne, Australia	3,663
3	Brisbane, Australia	1,769
4	Perth, Australia	1,484
5	Auckland, New Zealand	1,152
6	Adelaide, Australia	1,137

Antarctica

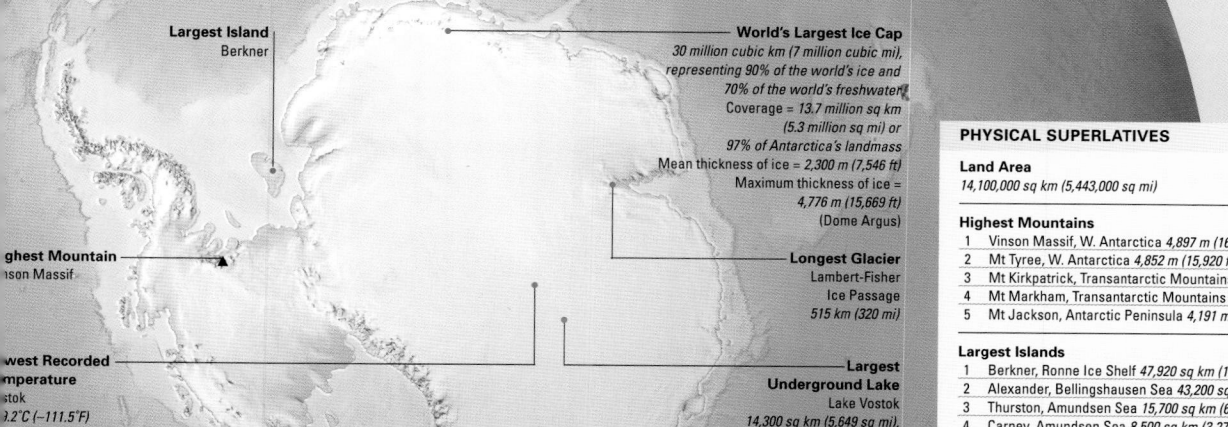

Largest Island
Berkner

World's Largest Ice Cap
30 million cubic km (7 million cubic mi),
representing 90% of the world's ice and
70% of the world's freshwater
Coverage = 13.7 million sq km
(5.3 million sq mi) or
97% of Antarctica's landmass
Mean thickness of ice = 2,300 m (7,546 ft)
Maximum thickness of ice =
4,776 m (15,669 ft)
(Dome Argus)

Longest Glacier
Lambert-Fisher
Ice Passage
515 km (320 mi)

Highest Mountain
Vinson Massif

Lowest Recorded Temperature
Vostok
−89.2°C (−111.5°F)

Largest Underground Lake
Lake Vostok
14,300 sq km (5,649 sq mi),
at a depth of 4.0 km (2.5 mi)
below the ice surface

PHYSICAL SUPERLATIVES

Land Area
14,100,000 sq km (5,443,000 sq mi)

Highest Mountains
1. Vinson Massif, W. Antarctica 4,897 m (16,066 ft)
2. Mt Tyree, W. Antarctica 4,852 m (15,920 ft)
3. Mt Kirkpatrick, Transantarctic Mountains 4,528 m (14,855 ft)
4. Mt Markham, Transantarctic Mountains 4,349 m (14,268 ft)
5. Mt Jackson, Antarctic Peninsula 4,191 m (13,751 ft)

Largest Islands
1. Berkner, Ronne Ice Shelf 47,920 sq km (18,500 sq mi)
2. Alexander, Bellingshausen Sea 43,200 sq km (16,630 sq mi)
3. Thurston, Amundsen Sea 15,700 sq km (6,045 sq mi)
4. Carney, Amundsen Sea 8,500 sq km (3,275 sq mi)
5. Roosevelt, Ross Ice Shelf 7,500 sq km (2,890 sq mi)

Highest Mountain
Mt McKinley (Denali)

Largest Island
Greenland

Largest Lake
Lake Superior

Tallest Building
Sears Tower, Chicago
442 m (1,450 ft)

Longest Road Tunnel
Ted Williams, Boston
4.2 km (2.6 mi)

Longest Rail Tunnel
Mount MacDonald, Canada
14.6 km (9.1 mi)

Largest Country
Canada

Largest Hydroelectric Plant
Grand Coulee, United States
6,809 MW

Largest Subway System
New York,
370 km (230 mi)

Oldest Country
United States
(July 1776)

Most Populous Country
Country with Longest Land Border
12,034 km (7,473 mi)

Busiest Airport
Atlanta (Hartsfield)
85.9 million passengers per year

Highest Waterfall
Yosemite, Yosemite Creek,
United States
739 m (2,425 ft)

Newest Country
Antigua & Barbuda
(November 1981)

Lowest Point
Death Valley, United States
–86 m (–282 ft)

Largest Desert
Great Basin, United States
492,100 sq km (190,000 sq mi)

Deadliest Volcanic Eruption
Mt Pelée, Martinique *(1902)*
29,025 deaths

Longest River
Mississippi–Missouri

Highest Dam
Manuel M. Torres, Mexico
261 m (856 ft)

Deadliest Earthquake
Guatemala City, Guatemala *(1976)*
23,000 deaths

COUNTRIES: AREA

Country/Territory	Area sq km (thousands)	Area sq mi (thousands)
Largest		
1 Canada	9,971	3,850
2 United States of America	9,629	3,718
3 Greenland (Denmark)	2,176	840
4 Mexico	1,958	756
5 Nicaragua	130	50.2
6 Honduras	112	43.3
7 Cuba	111	42.8
8 Guatemala	109	42.0
9 Panama	75.5	29.2
10 Costa Rica	51.1	19.7
11 Dominican Republic	48.5	18.7
12 Haiti	27.8	10.7
13 Belize	23.0	8.9
14 El Salvador	21.0	8.1
15 Bahamas	13.9	5.4
16 Jamaica	11.0	4.2
17 Puerto Rico (US)	8.9	3.4
18 Trinidad & Tobago	5.1	2.0
19 Guadeloupe (France)	1.7	0.66
20 Martinique (France)	1.1	0.43
Smallest		
1 Bermuda (UK)	0.05	0.02
2 Anguilla (UK)	0.10	0.04
3 Montserrat (UK)	0.10	0.04
4 Virgin Islands (UK)	0.15	0.06
5 Aruba (Netherlands)	0.19	0.07
6 Cayman Islands (UK)	0.26	0.10
7 St Kitts & Nevis	0.26	0.10
8 Grenada	0.34	0.13
9 Virgin Islands (US)	0.35	0.13
10 St Vincent & the Grenadines	0.39	0.15

COUNTRIES: POPULATION

Country/Territory	Population (thousands)
Most Populous	
1 United States of America	295,734
2 Mexico	106,203
3 Canada	32,805
4 Guatemala	14,655
5 Cuba	11,347
6 Dominican Republic	8,950
7 Haiti	8,122
8 Honduras	6,975
9 El Salvador	6,705
10 Nicaragua	5,465
11 Costa Rica	4,016
12 Puerto Rico (US)	3,917
13 Panama	3,039
14 Jamaica	2,732
15 Trinidad & Tobago	1,089
16 Guadeloupe (France)	449
17 Martinique (France)	433
18 Bahamas	302
19 Belize	279
20 Barbados	279
Least Populous	
1 Montserrat (UK)	9
2 Anguilla (UK)	13
3 Turks & Caicos Is. (UK)	21
4 Virgin Islands (UK)	23
5 St Kitts & Nevis	39
6 Cayman Islands (UK)	44
7 Greenland (Denmark)	56
8 Bermuda (UK)	65
9 Dominica	69
10 Antigua & Barbuda	69

LARGEST CITIES

City	Population (thousands)
1 Mexico City, Mexico	19,013
2 New York, USA	17,800
3 Los Angeles, USA	11,789
4 Chicago, USA	8,308
5 Philadelphia, USA	5,149
6 Toronto, Canada	5,060
7 Miami, USA	4,919
8 Dallas-Fort Worth, USA	4,146
9 Boston, USA	4,032
10 Washington, USA	3,934
11 Guadalajara, Mexico	3,905
12 Detroit, USA	3,903
13 Houston, USA	3,823
14 Monterrey, Mexico	3,517
15 Montréal, Canada	3,511
16 Atlanta, USA	3,500
17 Guatemala City, Guatemala	3,242
18 San Francisco, USA	3,229
19 Phoenix, USA	2,907
20 Seattle, USA	2,712
21 San Diego, USA	2,674
22 Santo Domingo, Dom. Rep.	2,563
23 Minneapolis–St Paul, USA	2,389
24 San Juan, Puerto Rico	2,357
25 Havana, Cuba	2,192
26 Vancouver, Canada	2,125
27 Port-au-Prince, Haiti	2,090
28 St Louis, USA	2,078
29 Baltimore, USA	2,076
30 Tampa–St Petersburg, USA	2,062

PHYSICAL SUPERLATIVES

Land Area
24,241,000 sq km (9,357,000 sq mi)

Highest Mountains
1 Mt McKinley (Denali), USA (Alaska) *6,194 m (20,321 ft)*
2 Mt Logan, Canada *5,959 m (19,551 ft)*
3 Pico de Orizaba, Mexico *5,610 m (18,405 ft)*
4 Mt St Elias, Canada/USA *5,489 m (18,008 ft)*
5 Popocatépetl, Mexico *5,452 m (17,887 ft)*

Longest Rivers
1 Mississippi–Missouri *5,971 km (3,710 mi)*
2 Mackenzie *4,240 km (2,630 mi)*
3 Missouri *4,088 km (2,540 mi)*
4 Mississippi *3,782 km (2,350 mi)*
5 Yukon *3,185 km (1,980 mi)*

Largest Lakes and Inland Seas
1 Lake Superior, Canada/USA *82,350 sq km (31,800 sq mi)*
2 Lake Huron, Canada/USA *59,600 sq km (23,010 sq mi)*
3 Lake Michigan, USA *58,000 sq km (22,400 sq mi)*
4 Great Bear Lake, Canada *31,800 sq km (12,280 sq mi)*
5 Great Slave Lake, Canada *28,500 sq km (11,000 sq mi)*

Largest Islands
1 Greenland, Atlantic Ocean *2,175,600 sq km (839,800 sq mi)*
2 Baffin Island, Canada *508,000 sq km (196,100 sq mi)*
3 Victoria Island, Canada *212,200 sq km (81,900 sq mi)*
4 Ellesmere Island, Canada *212,000 sq km (81,800 sq mi)*
5 Cuba, Caribbean Sea *110,860 sq km (42,800 sq mi)*

COUNTRIES: WEALTH

Country/Territory	Annual Income (US$ per capita)
Richest	
1 United States of America	41,800
2 Virgin Islands (UK)	38,500
3 Bermuda (UK)	36,000
4 Canada	32,800
5 Cayman Islands (UK)	32,300
6 Aruba (Netherlands)	28,000
7 Greenland (Denmark)	20,000
8 Bahamas	18,800
9 Puerto Rico (US)	18,500
10 Barbados	17,300
Poorest	
1 Haiti	1,600
2 Nicaragua	2,800
3 Honduras	2,900
= St Vincent & the Grenadines	2,900
5 Cuba	3,300
6 Montserrat (UK)	3,400
7 Jamaica	4,300
= Guatemala	4,300
9 Grenada	5,000
10 El Salvador	5,100

COUNTRIES: AREA

	Country/Territory	Area sq km (thousands)	Area sq mi (thousands)
1	Brazil	8,514	3,287
2	Argentina	2,780	1,074
3	Peru	1,285	496
4	Colombia	1,139	440
5	Bolivia	1,099	424
6	Venezuela	912	352
7	Chile	757	292
8	Paraguay	407	157
9	Ecuador	284	109
10	Guyana	215	83

COUNTRIES: POPULATION

	Country/Territory	Population (thousands)
1	Brazil	186,113
2	Colombia	42,954
3	Argentina	39,538
4	Peru	27,926
5	Venezuela	25,375
6	Chile	15,981
7	Ecuador	13,364
8	Bolivia	8,858
9	Paraguay	6,348
10	Uruguay	3,416

LARGEST CITIES

	City	Population (thousands)
1	São Paulo, Brazil	18,333
2	Buenos Aires, Argentina	13,349
3	Rio de Janeiro, Brazil	11,469
4	Lima, Peru	8,180
5	Bogotá, Colombia	7,594
6	Santiago, Chile	5,623
7	Belo Horizonte, Brazil	5,304
8	Pôrto Alegre, Brazil	3,795
9	Recife, Brazil	3,527
10	Brasília, Brazil	3,341
11	Salvador, Brazil	3,331
12	Caracas, Venezuela	3,276
13	Fortaleza, Brazil	3,261
14	Medellín, Colombia	3,236
15	Curitiba, Brazil	2,871
16	Campinas, Brazil	2,640
17	Cali, Colombia	2,583
18	Guayaquil, Ecuador	2,387
19	Valencia, Venezuela	2,330
20	Maracaibo, Venezuela	2,182
21	Belém, Brazil	2,097
22	Barranquilla, Colombia	1,918
23	Goiânia, Brazil	1,878
24	Asunción, Paraguay	1,750
25	Manaus, Brazil	1,673
26	Santos, Brazil	1,634
27	Córdoba, Argentina	1,592
28	La Paz, Bolivia	1,533
29	Quito, Ecuador	1,514
30	Montevideo, Uruguay	1,353

Tallest Building
Parque Central Torre Este, Caracas
221 m (725 ft)

Oldest Country
Colombia
(July 1810)

Longest Road Tunnel
Fernando Gómez Martínez, Colombia
4.5 km (2.9 mi)

Deadliest Volcanic Eruption
Nev. del Ruiz, Colombia (1985)
25,000 deaths

Longest Suspension Bridge
Puente de Angostura, Venezuela
712 m (2,336 ft)

Highest Waterfall
Angel, Caroni River, Venezuela
980 m (3,212 ft)

Newest Country
Suriname
(November 1975)

Deadliest Earthquake
Western Peru (1970)
66,000 deaths

Largest Lake
Lake Titicaca

Longest River
Amazon

Largest Country
Brazil

Most Populous Country

Country with Longest Land Border
14,691 km (9,123 mi)

Longest Rail Tunnel
Tunelão, Brazil
8.7 km (5.4 mi)

Highest Mountain
Aconcagua

Largest Hydroelectric Plant
Itaipu, Brazil/Paraguay
12,600 MW

Largest Desert
Patagonian, Argentina
673,400 sq km (260,000 sq mi)

Largest Island
Tierra del Fuego

Lowest Point
Valdés Peninsula
−40 m (−131 ft)

PHYSICAL SUPERLATIVES

Land Area
17,793,000 sq km (6,868,000 sq mi)

Highest Mountains
Aconcagua, Argentina 6,962 m (22,841 ft)
Bonete, Argentina 6,872 m (22,546 ft)
Ojos del Salado, Argentina/Chile 6,863 m (22,516 ft)
Pissis, Argentina 6,779 m (22,241 ft)
Mercedario, Argentina/Chile 6,770 m (22,211 ft)

Longest Rivers
Amazon 6,450 km (4,010 mi)
Paraná–Plate 4,500 km (2,800 mi)
Purus 3,350 km (2,080 mi)
Madeira 3,200 km (1,990 mi)
São Francisco 2,900 km (1,800 mi)

Largest Lakes and Inland Seas
Lake Titicaca, Bolivia/Peru 8,300 sq km (3,200 sq mi)
Lake Poopo, Bolivia 2,800 sq km (1,100 sq mi)
Lake Mar Chiquita, Argentina 2,000 sq km (780 sq mi)
Lake General Carrera (Buenos Aires), Argentina/Chile 1,850 sq km (720 sq mi)
Lake Argentino, Argentina 1,470 sq km (575 sq mi)

Largest Islands
Tierra del Fuego, Argentine/Chile 47,000 sq km (18,100 sq mi)
Chiloe, Chile 8,400 sq km (3,235 sq mi)
Falkland Is. (East), Atlantic Ocean 6,800 sq km (2,600 sq mi)
Wellington, Chile 5,560 sq km (2,140 sq mi)
Riesco, Chile 5,110 sq km (1,970 sq mi)

COUNTRIES: WEALTH

	Country/Territory	Annual Income (US$ per capita)
1	Argentina	13,600
2	Chile	11,300
3	Uruguay	10,000
4	Brazil	8,500
5	French Guiana (France)	8,300
6	Colombia	7,100
7	Venezuela	6,400
8	Peru	6,000
9	Paraguay	4,900
10	Suriname	4,700

COUNTRIES OF THE WORLD

KEY
- ■ ● City or town
- ★ Capital city
- ✈ Major airport
- △ Highest point in country
- ∿ International boundary
- ⌒ Railway
- ⌒ Road
- ∿ River

Introduced in January 2002, this flag replaces that of the Mujaheddin ('holy warriors'), who defeated Afghanistan's socialist government but lost power at the end of 2001. The flag is the 19th different design used by the country since 1901.

The Islamic Republic of Afghanistan is a landlocked country bordered by Turkmenistan, Uzbekistan, Tajikistan, China, Pakistan, and Iran. The main regions are the northern plains, the central highlands, and the south-western lowlands.

The central highlands, comprising most of the Hindu Kush and its foothills, with peaks rising to more than 6,400 m [21,000 ft], cover nearly three-quarters of the land. Many Afghans live in the deep valleys of the highlands. The River Kabul flows east to the Khyber Pass border with Pakistan.

Much of the south-west is desert, while the northern plains contain most of the country's limited agricultural land. Grasslands cover much of the north, while the vegetation in the dry south is sparse.

Trees are rare in both regions. But forests of such coniferous trees as pine and fir grow on the higher mountain slopes, with cedars lower down. Alder, ash, juniper, oak and walnut grow in the mountain valleys.

Area	652,090 sq km [251,772 sq mi]
Population	28,514,000
Capital (population)	Kabul (1,565,000)
Government	Transitional regime
Ethnic groups	Pashtun (Pathan) 44%, Tajik 25%, Hazara 10%, Uzbek 8%, others 8%
Languages	Pashtu, Dari/Persian (both official), Uzbek
Religions	Islam (Sunni Muslim 84%, Shiite Muslim 15%), others
Currency	Afghani = 100 puls
Website	www.afghan-web.com

CLIMATE

The height of the land and the country's remote position have a great effect on the climate. In winter, northerly winds bring cold, snowy weather in the mountains, but summers are hot and dry. The rainfall decreases to the south with temperatures higher throughout the year.

HISTORY

In ancient times, the area was invaded by Aryans, Persians, Greeks and Macedonians, and warrior armies from central Asia. Arab armies introduced Islam in the late 7th century. It has always occupied a strategic position, because the Khyber Pass was both the gateway to India and the back door to Russia.

Its modern history began in 1747, when local tribes united for the first time, though a civil war was fought between 1819 and 1835 as factions struggled for power. In 1839, British troops invaded Afghanistan, in an attempt to reduce Russian influence. Over the next 80 years, Britain fought three Anglo-Afghan wars to maintain control over the region. The British finally withdrew in 1921, when Afghanistan became independent.

POLITICS

In 1964, Afghanistan adopted a democratic constitution, but the country's ruler, King Zahir, and the legislature failed to agree on reforms. Muhammad Daoud Khan, the king's cousin, seized power in 1973 and abolished the monarchy. He ruled as president until 1978, when he was killed during a left-wing coup. The new regime's socialist policies conflicted with Islam and provoked a rebellion.

On 25 December 1987, Soviet troops invaded Afghanistan to support the left-wing regime. The Soviet occupation led to a protracted civil war. Various Muslim groups united behind the banner of the Mujaheddin ('holy warriors') to wage a guerrilla campaign, financed by the United States and aided by Pakistan. Soviet forces withdrew in 1989.

By 1992, the Mujaheddin had overthrown the government. The fundamentalist Muslim Taliban ('students') became the dominant group and, by 2000, the Taliban regime controlled 90% of the land.

In October 2001, the Taliban regime refused to hand over Saudi-born Osama bin Laden, the man suspected of masterminding the attacks on New York City and Washington D.C. on 11 September 2001. This led to international action being taken against Afghanistan, with the United States to the fore. The objective was to destroy both bin Laden's terrorist organization, al Qaida, and the Taliban. In November, the Taliban regime collapsed and a coalition government was set up, led by Hamid Karzai, who was sworn into office in 2002. Later that year, more than 1,000 people died in an earthquake in northern Afghanistan.

Despite ongoing conflict, a draft constitution was approved in January 2004. The first democratic elections for president were held in October 2004, won by Hamid Karzai. September 2005 saw parliamentary and provincial elections.

ECONOMY

Afghanistan is one of the world's poorest countries. About 60% of the people are farmers, many of whom are semi-nomadic herders. Wheat is the chief crop. Natural gas is produced, together with some coal, copper, gold, precious stones and salt. There are few factories. Exports include karakul skins (which are used to make hats and jackets), carpets, dried fruit and nuts.

KABUL

Capital of Afghanistan situated on the River Kabul in the eastern part of the country. It is strategically located in a high mountain valley in the Hindu Kush. The city was taken by Genghis Khan in the 13th century. Later it became part of the Mogul Empire, from 1526 to 1738. It has been the capital since 1776 and was occupied by the British during the Afghan Wars in the 19th century. Following the Soviet invasion in 1979, Kabul was the scene of bitter fighting. Unrest continued into the mid-1990s as rival Muslim groups fought for control. Industries include textiles, leather goods, and furniture.

***Great Mosque of Herat**, known as the Majsjid-i-Jami, or the Friday Mosque, built in the 13th century during the Timurid dynasties*

Albania's official name, Shqiperia, means 'Land of the Eagle', and the black double eagle was the emblem of the 15th-century hero Skanderbeg. A star placed above the eagle in 1946 was removed in 1992 when a non-Communist government was formed.

Area 28,748 sq km [11,100 sq mi]
Population 3,545,000
Capital (population) Tirana (300,000)
Government Multiparty republic
Ethnic groups Albanian 95%, Greek 3%, Macedonian, Vlachs, Gypsy
Languages Albanian (official)
Religions Many people say they are non-believers; of the believers, 70% follow Islam and 30% follow Christianity (Orthodox 20%, Roman Catholic 10%)
Currency Lek = 100 qindars
Website www.parlament.al

The Republic of Albania lies in the Balkan Peninsula. It faces the Adriatic Sea in the west and is bordered by Serbia and Montenegro, Macedonia and Greece. About 70% of the land is mountainous, with the highest point, Korab, reaching 2,764 m [9,068 ft] on the Macedonian border. Most Albanians live in the west on the coastal lowlands – the main farming region. Albania lies in an earthquake zone and severe earthquakes occur occasionally.

CLIMATE

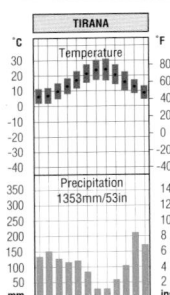

The coastal areas of Albania have a typical Mediterranean climate, with fairly dry, sunny summers and cool, moist winters. The mountains have a severe climate, with heavy winter snow.

HISTORY

Albania was originally part of a region called Illyria. In 167 BC, it became part of the Roman Empire. When the Roman Empire broke up in AD 395, much of Albania became part of the Byzantine Empire. The country was subsequently conquered by Goths, Bulgarians, Slavs and Normans, although southern Albania remained part of the Byzantine Empire until 1204.

Much of Albania became part of the Serbian Empire in the 14th century and in the 15th century, a leader named Skanderbeg, now regarded as a national hero, successfully led the Albanians against the invading Ottoman Turks. But after his death in 1468, the Turks took over the country. Albania was part of the Ottoman Empire until 1912, when Albania declared its independence.

Italy invaded Albania in 1939, but German forces took over the country in

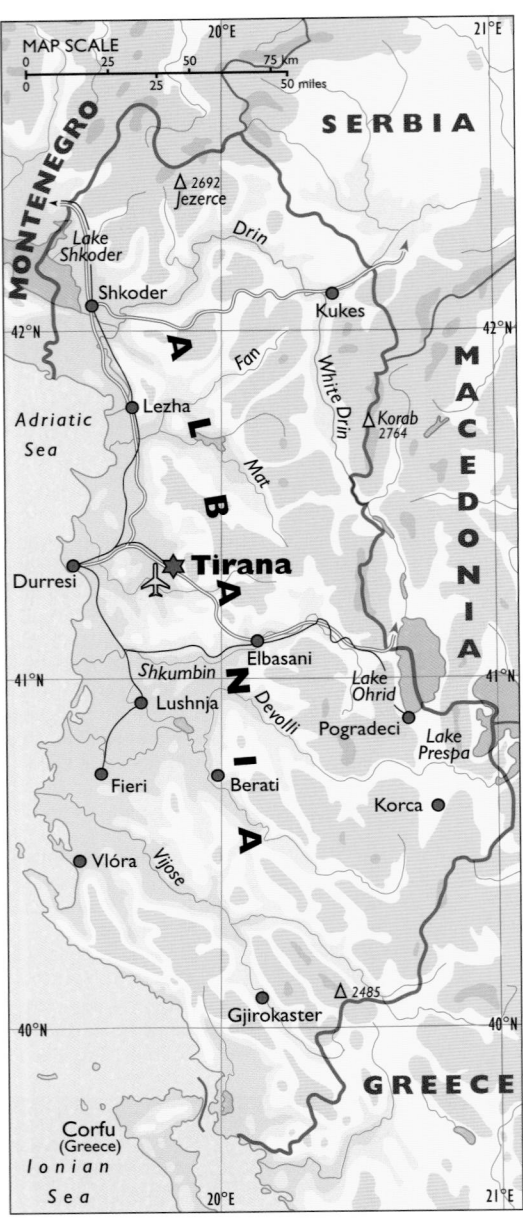

TIRANA (TIRANË)

Capital of Albania situated on the banks of the River Ishm in central Albania. Tirana's geographical position on the fertile forested land between the Adriatic and eastern Albania played a major part in its development from settlement to capital city. The city was founded in the early 17th century by the Ottoman Turks and became the capital in 1920. In 1946 the communists came to power and the industrial sector of the city was developed. Industries include metal goods, agricultural machinery and textiles. Places of interest include Skanderbeg Square with the main historical buildings. Also the 18th century Haxhi Ethem Bey Mosque; Art Gallery (Albanian); National Museum of History.

1943. At the end of World War II, an Albanian People's Republic was formed under the Communist leaders who had led the partisans against the Germans. Pursuing a modernization programme on rigid Stalinist lines, the regime of Enver Hoxha at various times associated politically and economically with Yugoslavia (to 1948), the Soviet Union (1948–61) and China (1961–77), before following a fiercely independent policy. After Hoxha died in 1985, his successor, Ramiz Alia, continued the dictator's austere policies, but by the end of the decade, even Albania was affected by the sweeping changes in Eastern Europe.

POLITICS

In 1990, the more progressive wing of the Communist Party, led by Ramiz Alia, won the struggle for power. The new government instituted a wide programme of reform, including the legalization of religion, the encouragement of foreign investment, the introduction of a free market for peasants' produce, and the establishment of pluralist democracy. The Communists comfortably retained their majority in 1991 elections, but the government was brought down two months later by a general strike. An interim coalition 'national salvation' committee took over, but collapsed within six months.

Elections in 1992 finally brought to an end the last Communist regime in Europe when the non-Communist Democratic Party won power. In 1997, amid a financial crisis caused by the collapse of fraudulent pyramid-selling schemes, fresh elections took place. The socialist-led government that took power was re-elected in 2001. The stability of the region was threatened when Albanian-speaking Kosovars and Macedonians, many favouring the creation of a Greater Albania, fought with government forces in north-western Macedonia.

ECONOMY

Albania is Europe's poorest country. Some 62% of the population are employed in agriculture. Major crops include fruits, maize, olives, potatoes, sugar beet, vegetables and wheat. Livestock farming and the fishing industry are also important.

Private ownership has been encouraged since 1991, but change has been slow. Albania has some minerals, such as chromite, copper and nickel, which are exported. There is also some oil, brown coal and hydroelectricity, and a few heavy industries.

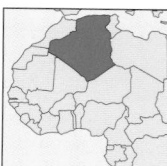

The star and crescent and the colour green on Algeria's flag are traditional symbols of the Islamic religion. The liberation movement which fought for independence from French rule from 1954 used this flag. It became the national flag when Algeria became independent in 1962.

The People's Democratic Republic of Algeria is Africa's second largest country after Sudan. Most Algerians live in the north, on the fertile coastal plains and hill country. South of this region lie high plateaux and ranges of the Atlas Mountains. Four-fifths of Algeria is in the Sahara, the world's largest desert.

CLIMATE

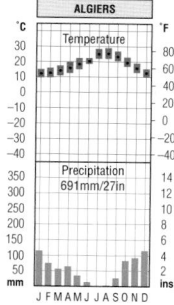

The coast has a Mediterranean climate, with warm and dry summers and mild and moist winters. The northern highlands have warmer summers and colder winters. The arid Sahara is hot by day and cool by night. Annual rainfall is less than 200 mm [8 in].

HISTORY

In early times, the region came under such rulers as the Phoenicians, Carthaginians, Romans and Vandals. Arabs invaded the area in the AD 600s, converting the local Berbers to Islam and introducing Arabic. Intermarriage has made it difficult to distinguish Arabs from Berbers by ancestry, though Berber dialects are still spoken. A law, effective from July 1998 making Arabic the only language allowed in public life, met with much opposition in Berber-speaking areas.

POLITICS

Algeria experienced French colonial rule and colonization by settlers, finally achieving independence in 1962, following years of bitter warfare between nationalist guerrillas and French armed forces. After independence, the socialist FLN (National Liberation Party) formed a one-party government. Opposition parties were permitted in 1989.

An Algerian *camel train crosses the desert*

ALGIERS

Capital and largest city of Algeria, north Africa's chief port on the Mediterranean. Founded by the Phoenicians, it has been ruled by Romans, Berber Arabs, Turks and Muslim Barbary pirates. In 1830 the French made Algiers the capital of the colony of Algeria. In World War II it was the headquarters of the Allies and seat of the French provisional government. During the 1950s and 1960s it was a focus for the violent struggle for independence. The old city is based round a 16th-century Turkish citadel. The 11th-century Sidi Abderrahman Mosque is a major destination for pilgrims.

In 1991, a Muslim party, the FIS (Islamic Salvation Front) won an election. The FLN cancelled the election results and declared a state of emergency. Terrorist activities mounted and, between 1991 and 1999, about 100,000 people were killed. A proposal to ban political parties based on religion was approved in a referendum in 1996. In 1999, Abdelaziz Boutflika, the candidate thought to be favoured by the army, was elected president. The scale of the violence was reduced. In 2005, the government agreed to accept the demands of the Berber community, including official recognition of the Berber language. In September an amnesty for Islamist guerrillas was approved in a referendum.

ECONOMY

Algeria is a developing country, whose main income is from its two main natural resources, oil and natural gas. Its natural gas reserves are among the world's largest. Oil and gas account for around two-thirds of the country's total revenues and more than 90% of the exports. Algeria's crude oil refining capacity is the biggest in Africa. About 16% of the population are employed in agriculture.

Area 2,381,741 sq km [919,590 sq mi]
Population 32,129,000
Capital (population) Algiers (Alger, 1,722,000)
Government Socialist republic
Ethnic groups Arab-Berber 99%
Languages Arabic and Berber (both official), French
Religions Sunni Muslim 99%
Currency Algerian dinar = 100 centimes
Website www.algeria-un.org

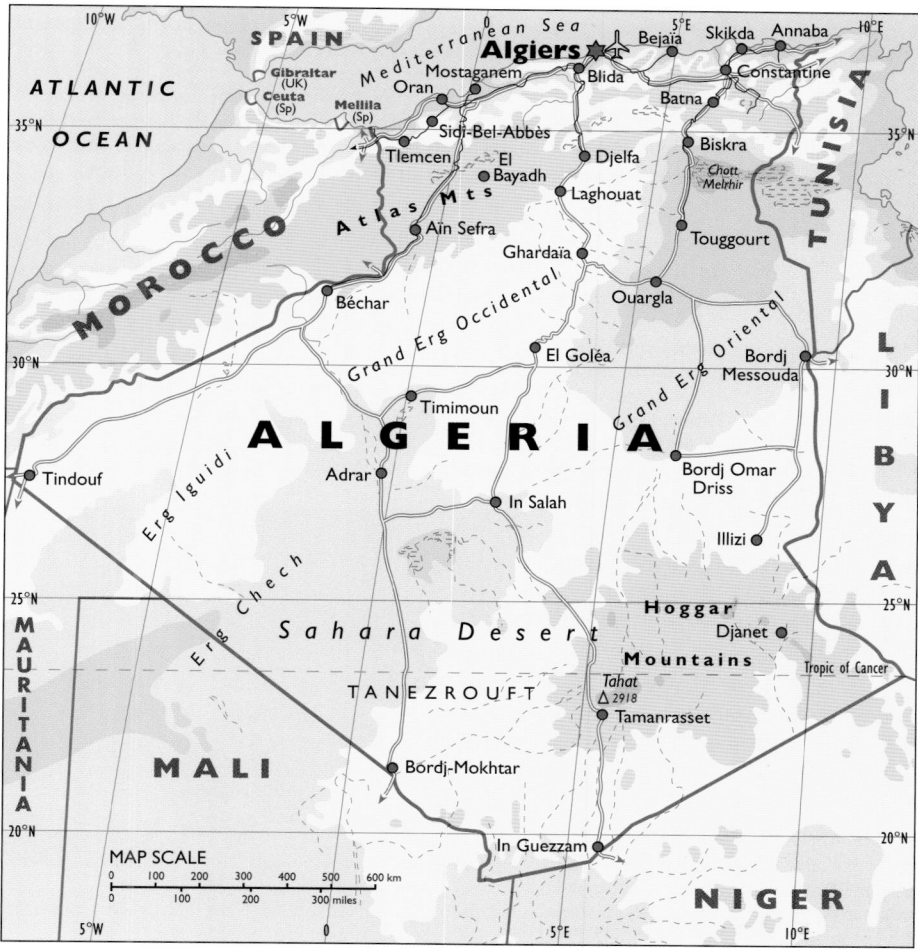

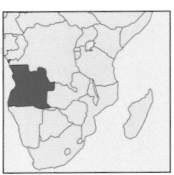

The flag is based on the flag of the MPLA (the Popular Movement for the Liberation of Angola) during the independence struggle. The emblem includes a star symbolizing socialism, one half of a gearwheel to represent industry, and a machete symbolizing agriculture.

Area 1,246,700 sq km [481,351 sq mi]
Population 10,979,000
Capital (population) Luanda (2,250,000)
Government Multiparty republic
Ethnic groups Ovimbundu 37%,
Kimbundu 25%, Bakongo 13%, others 25%
Languages Portuguese (official),
many others
Religions Traditional beliefs 47%,
Roman Catholic 38%, Protestant 15%
Currency Kwanza = 100 lwei
Website www.angola.org

The Republic of Angola is a large country, more than twice the size of France, on the south-western coast of Africa. The majority of the country is part of the plateau that forms most of southern Africa, with a narrow coastal plain in the west.

Angola has many rivers. In the north-east, several rivers flow northwards to become tributaries of the River Congo, while in the south, some rivers, including the Cubango (Okavango) and the Cuanda, flow south-eastwards into inland drainage basins in the interior of Africa.

CLIMATE

Angola has a tropical climate, with temperatures of over 20°C [68°F] all year round, though upland areas are cooler. The coastal regions are dry, increasingly so to the south of Luanda, but the rainfall increases to the north and east. The rainy season is between November and April. Tropical forests flourish in the north, but the vegetation along the coast is sparse, with semi-desert in the south.

HISTORY

Bantu-speaking peoples from the north settled in Angola around 2,000 years ago. In the late 15th century, Portuguese navigators, seeking a route to Asia around Africa, explored the coast and, in the early 16th century, the Portuguese set up bases.

Angola became important as a source of slaves for Brazil, Portugal's huge colony in South America. After the decline of the slave trade, Portuguese settlers began to develop the land. The Portuguese population increased gently in the 20th century.

In the 1950s, local nationalists began to demand independence. In 1956, the MPLA (Popular Movement for the Liberation of Angola) was founded with support from the Mbundu and mestizos (people of African and European descent). The MPLA led a revolt in Luanda in 1961, but it was put down by Portuguese troops.

Other opposition groups developed. In the north, the Kongo set up the FNLA (Front for the Liberation of Angola), while, in 1966, southern peoples, including many Ovimbundu, formed UNITA

Oil rig *in Luanda harbour; with the US and China as key customers the oil industry of Angola has been a major boon to the economy*

(National Union for the Total Independence of Angola).

POLITICS

The Portuguese agreed to grant Angola independence in 1975, after which rival nationalist forces began a struggle for power. A long-running civil war developed between the government forces, who received aid from the Soviet Union and Cuba, the FNLA in the north and UNITA in the south. As the war developed, both the FNLA and UNITA turned to the West for support, while UNITA received support from South Africa. FNLA guerrilla activity ended in 1984, but UNITA took control of large areas. Economic progress was hampered not only by the vast spending on defence and security, but also by the MPLA government's austere Marxist policies.

In 1991, a peace accord was agreed and multiparty elections were held, in which the MPLA, which had renounced Marxism-Leninism, won a majority with Jose Eduardo Dos Santos, president since 1979, retaining power. But UNITA's leaders rejected the election result and civil war resumed in 1994. In 1997, the government invited UNITA leader, Jonas Savimbi, to join a coalition but he refused.

Savimbi was killed in action in February 2002, raising hopes of peace and the army and rebels signed a cease-fire to end conflict. Angola then started the lengthy process of rebuilding its devastated infrastructure with thousands of refugees to be resettled and landmines to be cleared.

ECONOMY

Angola is a developing country, where 70% of the people are poor farmers, although agriculture contributes only about 9% of the gross domestic product. The main food crops include cassava, maize, sweet potatoes and beans, while bananas, coffee, palm products, seed cotton and sugar cane are grown for export. Cattle are the leading livestock, but sheep and goats are raised in drier areas.

Despite the poverty of most of its people and its low per capita GNP, Angola has much economic potential. It has oil reserves near Luanda and in the enclave of Cabinda, which is separated from Angola by a strip of land belonging to the Democratic Republic of Congo. Oil and mineral fuels are the leading exports.

Other resources include diamonds (the second most important export), copper and manganese. Angola also has a growing industrial sector. Manufactures include cement, chemicals, processed food and textiles.

LUANDA

Capital, chief port, and largest city of Angola, on the Atlantic coast. Luanda was first settled by the Portuguese in 1575. Its economy thrived on the shipment of more than 3 million slaves to Brazil until the abolition of slavery in the 19th century. Today, it exports crops from the province of Luanda.

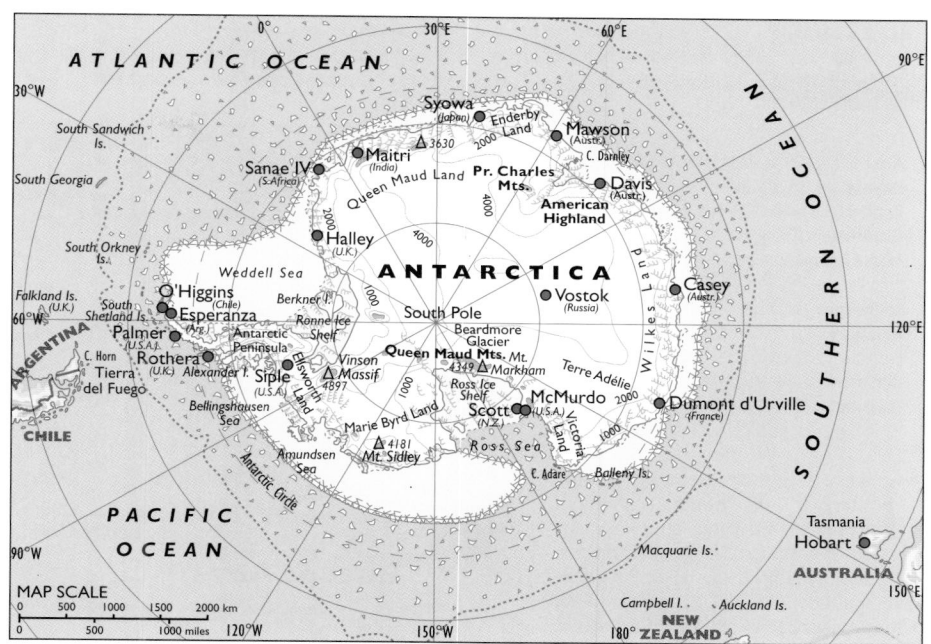

Antarctica is the fifth-largest continent (larger than Europe or Australasia), covering almost 10% of the world's total land area. Surrounding the South Pole, it is bordered by the Antarctic Ocean and the southern sections of the Atlantic, Pacific and Indian Oceans. Almost entirely within the Antarctic Circle, it is of great strategic and scientific interest.

No people live there permanently, though scientists frequently stay for short periods to conduct research and exploration. Seven nations lay claim to sectors of it. Covered by an ice-sheet with an average thickness of c. 1,800 m [5,900 ft], it contains c. 90% of the world's ice and more than 70% of its fresh water and plays a crucial role in the circulation of the atmosphere and ocean, and hence in determining the planetary climate.

LAND

Resembling an open fan, with the Antarctic Peninsula as a handle, the continent is a snowy desert covering approximately 14.2 million sq km [5.5 million sq mi]. The land is a high plateau with an average elevation of 1,800 m [6,000 ft] and rising to 4,897 m [16,066 ft] in the Vinson Massif. Mountain ranges occur near the coasts.

The interior, or South Polar Plateau, lies beneath c. 2,000 m [6,500 ft] of snow, accumulated over tens of thousands of years. Mineral deposits exist in the mountains, but their recovery is not practicable. Coal may be plentiful, but the value of known deposits of copper, nickel, gold, and iron will not repay the expense, both financial and environmental, of their extraction and export.

SEAS AND GLACIERS

Antarctic rivers are frozen, inching towards the sea, and instead of lakes there are large bodies of ice along the coasts. The great Beardmore Glacier creeps down from the South Polar Plateau, and eventually becomes part of the Ross Ice Shelf. The southernmost part of the Atlantic is the portion of the Antarctic Ocean known as the Weddell Sea.

CLIMATE AND VEGETATION

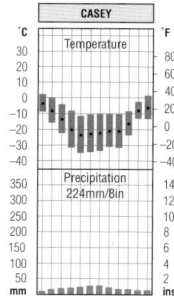

The coldest, windiest, highest (on average), and driest continent. During summer, more solar radiation reaches the surface at the South Pole than is received at the Equator in an equivalent period.

Mostly uninhabitable, Antarctica is cold all year, with only a few coastal areas free from snow or ice in summer (December to February). On most of the continent the temperature remains below freezing, and in August it has been recorded at nearly -90°C [-130°F]. Precipitation is generally 18–38cm [7–15in] of snow a year, but it melts at a slower rate, allowing a build-up over the centuries.

Mosses manage to survive on rocks along the outer rim of the continent. Certain algae grow on the snow, and others appear in pools of fresh water when melting occurs.

HISTORY

Antarctic islands were sighted first in the 18th century, and in 1820 Nathaniel Palmer reached the Antarctic Peninsula. Between 1838 and 1840, US explorer Charles Wilkes discovered enough of the coast to prove that a continent existed, and the English explorer James Clark Ross made coastal maps. Towards the end of the 19th century, exploration of the interior developed into a race for the South Pole. Roald Amundsen reached the Pole on 14 December 1911, a month before Captain Robert Scott. The aeroplane brought a new era of exploration, and Richard E. Byrd became the best-known of the airborne polar explorers.

ANTARCTIC TREATY

The Antarctic Treaty in 1961 set aside the area for peaceful uses only, guaranteeing freedom of scientific investigation, banning waste disposal and nuclear testing, and suspending the issue of territorial rights. By 1990 the original 12 signatories had grown to 25, with a further 15 nations granted observer status in subsequent deliberations. But the Treaty itself was threatened by wrangles between different countries, government agencies and international pressure groups.

Finally in July 1991, the belated agreement of the UK and the USA assured unanimity on a new accord to ban all mineral exploration for a further 50 years. This can only be rescinded if all the present signatories, plus a majority of any future adherents, agree. While the treaty has always lacked a formal mechanism for enforcement, it is firmly underwritten by public concern generated by the efforts of environmental pressure groups such as Greenpeace, which has been foremost in the campaign to have Antarctica declared as a 'World Park'.

The continent appears to be under threat from global warming. Some scientists believe this was the cause of the break-up of ice shelves along the Antarctic peninsula. Rising temperatures have also disturbed the breeding patterns of the Adelie penguins.

Area 14 million sq km [280,000 sq km ice-free, 13.72 million sq km ice-covered] 5,405,430 sq mi [108,108 sq mi ice-free, 5,297,322 sq mi ice-covered]
Government The Antarctic Treaty
Websites www.antarctica.ac.uk; www.aad.gov.au

Paradise Bay in Antarctica; the bay is home to penguins, seals and whales

The 'celeste' (sky blue) and white stripes were the symbols of independence around the city of Buenos Aires, where an independent government was set up in 1810. It became the national flag in 1816. The gold May Sun was added two years later.

Area 2,780,400 sq km [1,073,512 sq mi]
Population 39,145,000
Capital (population) Buenos Aires (2,965,000)
Government Federal republic
Ethnic groups European 97%, Mestizo, Amerindian
Languages Spanish (official)
Religions Roman Catholic 92%, Protestant 2%, Jewish 2%, others
Currency Peso = 10,000 australs
Website www.sectur.gov.ar

The Argentine Republic is the largest of South America's Spanish-speaking countries. Its western boundary lies in the Andes, with basins, ridges and peaks of more than 6,000 m [19,685 ft] in the north. South of latitude 27°S, the ridges merge into a single high cordillera, with Aconcagua, at 6,962 m [22,849 ft], the tallest mountain in the western hemisphere.

In the south, the Andes are lower, with glaciers and volcanoes. Eastern Argentina is a series of alluvial plains, from the Andean foothills to the sea. The Gran Chaco in the north slopes down to the Paraná River, from the high desert of the Andean foothills to lowland swamp forest. Between the Paraná and Uruguay rivers is Mesopotamia, a fertile region. Further south are the damp and fertile pampa grasslands. Thereafter, the pampa gives way to the dry, windswept plateaux of Patagonia towards Tierra del Fuego.

CLIMATE

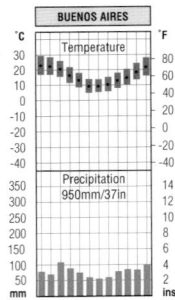

The climate varies from subtropical in the north to temperate in the south. Rainfall is abundant in the north-east, but is lower to the west and south. Patagonia is a dry region, crossed by rivers that rise in the Andes.

HISTORY

Spanish explorers first reached the coast in 1516, landing on the shores of the Rio de la Plata. They were soon followed by others in search of gold and silver. Early prosperity, based on stock raising and farming, combined with stable government, was boosted from 1870 by a massive influx of European immigrants, particularly Italians and Spaniards, for whom Argentina was a viable alternative to the United States. They settled lands recently cleared of Native Americans, often organized by huge land companies.

Development of a good railway network to the ports, plus steamship services to Europe, and, from 1877, refrigerated vessels, helped to create the strong meat, wool and wheat economy that carried Argentina into the 20th century. Before the Great Depression in the 1930s, Argentina was one of the world's more prosperous nations.

POLITICS

The collapse in the economy during the Great Depression led to a military coup in 1930. This started a long period of military intervention in the politics of the country.

From 1976, the 'dirty war', saw the torture, wrongful imprisonment and murder ('disappearance') of up to 15,000 people by the military with 2 million people fleeing the country. In 1982, the government, blamed for the poor state of the economy, launched an invasion of the Falkland Islands (Islas Malvinas), which they had claimed since 1820. Britain regained the islands by sending an expeditionary force. After losing the conflict Argentina's President Galtieri resigned. Constitutional government was restored in 1983 though the army remained influential.

In 1999, Argentina and Britain signed an agreement concerning the Falkland Islands, the first since 1982. This meant that Argentines were allowed to visit the Falkland Islands and erect a memorial to their war dead, with Argentina agreeing to allow flights from the Falkland Islands to Chile.

In December 2001, violent protests broke out when the government introduced severe austerity measures, with the peso devalued and policies aimed at restoring the economy announced. The economy finally began to grow again in 2003 and 2004.

ECONOMY

An 'upper-middle-income' developing country and one of the richest in South America in terms of natural resources, especially its fertile farmland. The economic base is mainly agricultural. Chief products are beef, maize and wheat. Sheep are raised in drier parts of the country, while other crops include citrus fruits, cotton, flax, grapes, potatoes, sorghum, sugar cane, sunflower seeds and tea.

Oilfields in Patagonia and the Piedmont make Argentina almost self-sufficient in oil and natural gas, these are a valuable export.

BUENOS AIRES

Capital of Argentina, on the estuary of the Río de la Plata, 240 km [150 mi] from the Atlantic Ocean. Originally founded by Spain in 1536, it was refounded in 1580 after being destroyed by the indigenous population. It became a separate federal district and capital of Argentina in 1880. Buenos Aires later developed as a commercial centre for beef, grain and dairy products. It is the seat of the National University (1821). The people of Buenos Aires are known as Portenos and are of multinational origins, with Italian and German names actually outnumbering Spanish. The city is renowned for its vibrant nightlife, with people rarely eating before 9pm and indeed many staying out until dawn. Industries include meat processing, flour milling, textiles, metal works, car assembly.

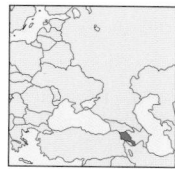
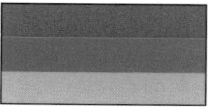

Armenia's flag was first used between 1918 and 1922, when the country was an independent republic. It was readopted on 24 August 1990. The red represents the blood shed in the past, the blue the land of Armenia, and the orange the courage of the people.

YEREVAN

Capital of Armenia, on the River Razdan, southern Caucasus. One of the world's oldest cities, it was capital of Armenia from as early as the 7th century (though under Persian control). A crucial crossroads for caravan routes between India and Transcaucasia, it is the site of a 16th-century Turkish fortress. It is a traditional wine-making centre. Industries include chemicals, plastics, cables, tyres, metals, vodka.

Area 29,800 sq km [11,506 sq mi]
Population 2,991,000
Capital (population) Yerevan (1,249,000)
Government Multiparty republic
Ethnic groups Armenian 93%, Russian 2%, Azeri 1%, others (mostly Kurds) 4%
Languages Armenian (official)
Religions Armenian Apostolic 94%
Currency Dram = 100 couma
Website www.armeniaforeignministry.com

The Republic of Armenia is a landlocked country in south-western Asia. Mostly consisting of a rugged plateau, criss-crossed by long faults. Movements along the faults cause earth tremors and occasionally major earthquakes. Armenia's highest point is Mount Aragats, at 4,090 m [13,149 ft] above sea level. The lowest land is in the north-west, where the capital Yerevan is situated. The largest lake is Ozero (Lake) Sevan.

The vegetation in Armenia ranges from semi-desert to grassy steppe, forest, mountain pastures and treeless tundra at the highest levels. Oak forests are found in the south-east, with beech being the most common tree in the forests of the north-east. Originally it was a much larger kingdom centred on Mount Ararat incorporating present-day northeast Turkey and parts of north west Iran.

CLIMATE

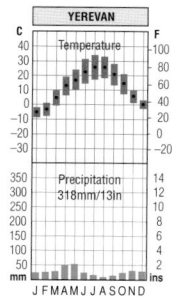

The height of the land, which averages 1,500 m [4,920 ft] gives rise to severe winters and cool summers. The highest peaks are snow-capped, but the total yearly rainfall is low, between and 200 and 800 mm [8 and 31 in].

HISTORY

Armenia was an advanced ancient kingdom, considered to be one of the original sites of iron and bronze smelting. A nation was established in the 6th century BC and Alexander the Great expelled the Persians in 330 BC. In 69 BC Armenia was incorporated into the Roman Empire. In AD 303, Armenia became the first country to adopt Christianity as its state religion. From 886 to 1046 Armenia was an independent kingom. From the 11th to 15th centuries the Mongols were the greatest power in the region. By the 16th century Armenia was controlled by the Ottoman Empire. Despite religious discrimination, the Armenians generally prospered under Turkish rule. Eastern Armenia was the battleground between the rival Ottoman and Persian empires. In 1828 Russia acquired Persian Armenia and (with many promises of religious tolerance) many Armenians moved to the Russian-controlled area. In Turkish Armenia, British promises of protection encouraged nationalist movements. The Turkish

response was uncompromising killing about 200,000 in 1896 alone. In the Russian sector, a process of Russification was enforced.

During World War I, Armenia was the battleground for the Turkish and Russian armies. Armenians were accused of aiding the Russians and Turkish atrocities intensified. More than 600,000 Armenians were killed by Turkish troops and 1.75 million were deported to Syria and Palestine. The Armenian Autonomous Republic was set up in the area held by Russia in 1918, but the western part of historic Armenia remained in Turkey, and the north-west was held by Iran. In 1920, Armenia became a Communist republic. In 1922, it became, with Azerbaijan and Georgia, part of the Transcaucasian Republic within the Soviet Union. But the three territories became separate Soviet Socialist Republics in 1936. Earthquakes in 1984 and 1988 killed more than 80,000 people and destroyed many cities.

After the break-up of the Soviet Union in 1991, Armenia became an independent republic and joined the Commonwealth of Independent States (CIS).

POLITICS

Armenia has long disputed the status of Nagorno-Karabakh, an area enclosed by Azerbaijan where the majority of the people are Armenians. In 1992, Armenia occupied the territory between its eastern border and Nagorno-Karabakh. A cease-fire in 1994 left Armenia in control of about 20% of Azerbaijan's land area. With Azerbaijan and its ally Turkey blockading its borders, Armenia became increasingly dependent on Iran and Georgia for access to the outside world.

In 1998 Robert Kocharian former leader of Nagorno-Karabakh, became president. In 1999, gunmen stormed parliament and killed the prime minister.

A 9th-century church stands on Lake Sevan, an alpine freshwater lake near the border with Azerbaijan

ECONOMY

The World Bank classifies Armenia as a 'lower-middle-income' economy. Conflict with Azerbaijan in the early 1990s and the earthquakes have damaged the economy, but since 1992 the government has encouraged free enterprise.

Poverty, corruption and political assassinations contributed to Armenia losing 20% of its population in the 1990s. The country is highly industrialized with production dominated by mining and chemicals. Copper is the chief metal, but gold, lead and zinc are also mined. Agriculture is the second-largest sector, with cotton, tobacco, fruit and rice the main products.

AZORES

The Azores is a group of nine large and several small islands rising from the Mid-Atlantic Ridge in the North Atlantic Ocean. They are mostly mountainous, of relatively recent volcanic origin and lie about 1,200 km [745 mi] west of Lisbon. They have been Portuguese since the mid-15th century.
From 1938 until 1978, they were governed as three districts of Portugal, becoming an autonomous region in 1976. Farming and fishing are the main occupations.

Area 2,247 sq km [868 sq mi]
Population 243,000
Capital (population) Ponta Delgada (21,000)
Government Autonomous region of Portugal
Ethnic groups Azorean
Languages Portuguese (official)
Religion Roman Catholic
Currency Euro = 100 cents
Website www.drtacores.pt

BERMUDA

Bermuda comprises some 150 small islands, the coral caps of ancient volcanoes rising from the floor of the North Atlantic Ocean. Uninhabited when discovered in 1503 by the Spaniard Juan Mermúdez, the islands were taken over by the British over a century later, with slaves brought from Virginia. Bermuda is Britain's oldest overseas territory, but has a long tradition of self-government.
Tourism is the mainstay of the economy, but the islands are a tax haven for overseas companies.

Area 53 sq km [21 sq mi]
Population 65,000
Capital (population) Hamilton (1,000)
Government Parliamentary British overseas territory with internal self-government
Ethnic groups Black 55%, White 34%, others
Languages English (official), Portuguese
Religion Anglican 23%, Roman Catholic 15%, African Methodist Episcopal 11%, others
Currency Bermudian dollar = 100 cents
Website www.bermudatourism.com

CANARY ISLANDS

The Canary Islands are seven large islands and many small volcanic islands situated off southern Morocco, with the main islands being Fuertaventura, Gran Canaria, Lanzarote and Tenerife. The climate is subtropical, dry at sea level, wetter in the mountains. Claimed by Portugal in 1341, they were ceded to Spain in 1479. Two Spanish provinces since 1927. The statute of autonomy was granted in 1982. Tourism is the most important source of income. Farming and fishing are also key earners.

Area 7,447 sq km [2,875 sq mi]
Population 1,672,689
Capital Santa Cruz (Tenerife), Las Palmas (Gran Canaria)
Government Constitutional monarchy
Ethnic groups Spanish
Languages Spanish (official)
Religion Roman Catholic
Currency Euro = 100 cents
Website www.canarias.org

CAPE VERDE

The Republic of Cape Verde consists of ten large and five small islands, divided into the Barlavento (windward) and Sotavento (leeward) groups. They are volcanic and mainly mountainous, with steep cliffs and rocky headlands. The highest point is on the island of Fogo, an active volcano standing at 2,829 m [9,281 ft]). The climate is tropical, being hot for most of the year and mainly dry at sea level. The higher ground is cooler.

Area 4,033 sq km [1,557 sq mi]
Population 415,000
Capital (population) Praia (95,000)
Government Multiparty republic
Ethnic groups Creole (mulatto) 71%, African 28%
Languages Portuguese and Crioulo
Religion Roman Catholic and Protestant
Currency Cape Verde escudo = 100 centavos
Website www.caboverde.com

Portuguese since the 15th century, Verde included Portuguese Guinea (now Guinea-Bissau) until 1879, when the mainland territory was separated. It was populated with slaves from Africa, and used chiefly as a provisioning station and assembly point for slaves in the trade from West Africa. In 1991, the ruling party was soundly trounced in the country's first multiparty elections by a newly legalized opposition party, the Movement for Democracy (MPD). The former ruling African Independence Party (PAICV) regained power in 2001.
Bananas, beans, coffee, fruit, groundnuts, maize and sugar cane are grown on the wetter, higher ground, when they are not ruined by endemic droughts. Cape Verde's exports comprise fish and fish preparations and bananas. Economic problems, include high unemployment levels and the arrival of thousands of Angolan refugees. Cape Verde became fully independent in 1975.

FALKLAND ISLANDS

The Falkland Islands (Islas Malvinas) lie 480 km [300 mi] to the west of Argentina and consist of two main islands, and more than 200 small ones.
Discovered in 1592 by the English navigator John Davis, the Falklands were first occupied nearly 200 years later by the French (East) and the British (West). The French interest, bought by Spain in 1770, was assumed by Argentina in 1806. The British, who had withdrawn in 1774, returned in 1832. They dispossessed the Argentinian settlers and founded a settlement of their own, one that became a colony in 1892.
In 1982, Argentinian forces invaded the islands, but two months later, after armed conflict and the loss of 255 British and over 1,000 Argentines, the United Kingdom regained possession. In 1999, a formal agreement between Britain and Argentina permitted Argentinians to visit the islands. The majority of the population lives in Stanley and everywhere outside the town is known as the Camp, from the Spanish word for countryside. The economy is dominated by sheep-farming, though an offshore fishery now provides much needed income.

Area 12,173 sq km [4,700 sq mi]
Population 2,967
Capital (population) Stanley (2,000)
Government Overseas British territory
Ethnic groups British
Languages English (official)
Religions Anglican
Currency Falkland pound = 100 pence
Website www.falklandislands.com

MADEIRA

Madeira is the largest of the group of volcanic islands lying 550 km [350 mi] west of the Moroccan coast. Porto Santo, the uninhabited Islas Selvagens (not shown on the map) and the Desertas complete the group. The island of Madeira makes up more than 90% of the total area.
With a warm climate and fertile soils, the Madeira Islands are known for their rich exotic plant life. The abundance of species is all the more surprising because rainfall is confined to the winter months. The present name, meaning 'wood', was given by the Portuguese when they first saw the forested islands in 1419. The forests were largely destroyed and a farming industry was established. Spain held the islands between 1580 and 1640, while Britain occupied the islands twice early in the 19th century. Thereafter it came under the rule of Portugal and in 1974 was granted autonomy.
Major crops include bananas, maize, mangoes, oranges and sugar cane. Grapes are grown to make Madeira wine. Fishing is important, as is tourism. Madeira is also known for its hand embroidery and wickerwork crafted from willow.

Area 794 sq km [307 sq mi]
Population 253,482
Capital (population) Funchal (5,618)
Government Autonomous region of Portugal
Ethnic groups Portuguese
Languages Portuguese (official)
Religions Roman Catholic
Currency Euro = 100 cents
Website www.madeiratourism.org

Atlantic Islands 25

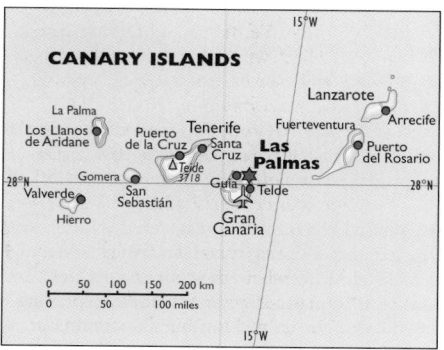

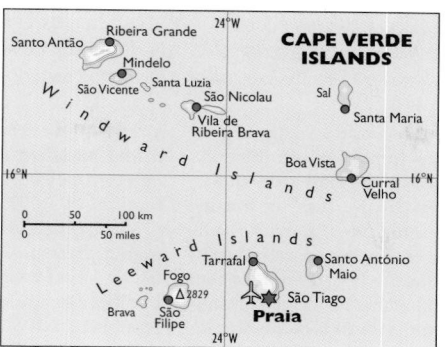

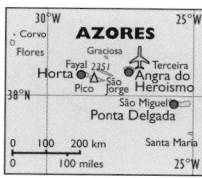

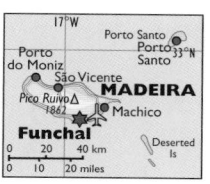

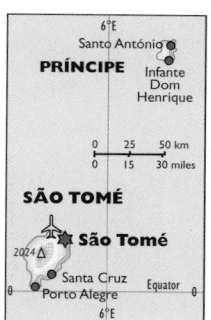

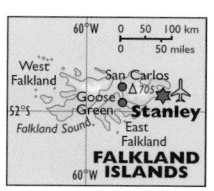

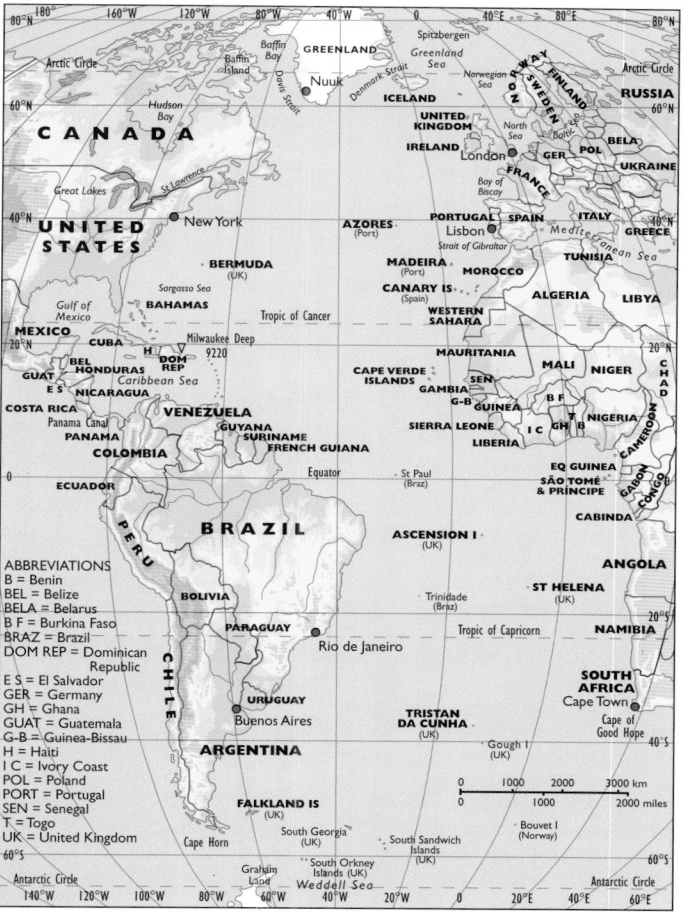

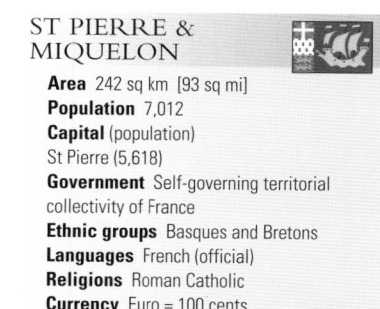

ST PIERRE & MIQUELON

Area 242 sq km [93 sq mi]
Population 7,012
Capital (population)
St Pierre (5,618)
Government Self-governing territorial collectivity of France
Ethnic groups Basques and Bretons
Languages French (official)
Religions Roman Catholic
Currency Euro = 100 cents
Website www2.st-pierre-et-miquelon.info

A group of eight small islands in the Gulf of St Lawrence, south west of Newfoundland, Canada. Miquelon is the largest island. The group was claimed for France in 1535, and since 1985 has been a 'territorial collectivity', sending delegates to the French parliament. Fishing is the most important activity, and has led to disputes with Canada.

SÃO TOMÉ & PRÍNCIPE

Area 964 sq km [372 sq mi]
Population 187,410
Capital (population)
São Tomé (5,618)
Government Republic
Ethnic groups Mestico, Angolares, Forros, Servicais, Tongas, Europeans (primarily Portuguese)
Languages Portuguese (official)
Religions Roman Catholic
Currency Dobra = 100 céntimos
Website www.saotome.st

In the Gulf of Guinea, 300 km [200 mi] off the west coast of Africa. São Tome is the largest of two volcanic and mountainous islands, the vegetation is mainly tropical rainforest. They were discovered in 1471. The Portuguese established plantations in the late 18th century. The islands became independent in 1975. Cocoa, coffee, bananas, and coconuts are grown on plantations, and their export is the republic's major source of income.

ST HELENA

South Atlantic island, 1,920 km [1,190 mi] from the coast of west Africa Discovered by the Portuguese in 1502, it was captured by the Dutch in 1633 and passed to the British East India Company in 1659. It became a British crown colony in 1834 and is chiefly known as the place of Napoleon I's exile. It is now a UK dependent territory and administrative centre for the islands of Ascension and Tristan da Cunha. The main employer on the island is the St Helena government. It's industry includes the servicing of ships and the export of fish and handicrafts.

Area 122 sq km [47 sq mi]
Population 5,000
Capital (population) Jamestown (884)
Government British overseas territory
Ethnic groups Britsih
Languages English (official)
Religion Anglican
Currency Pound sterling = 100 pence
Website www.sainthelena.gov.sh

TRISTAN DA CUNHA

Tristan da Cunha is one of a group of four islands in the south Atlantic Ocean, between South Africa and South America. The group was discovered in 1506 by the Portuguese and annexed by Britain in 1816. In 1961, Tristan, suffered a volcanic eruption that caused the evacuation to Britain of the entire population. However one year later the islanders voted overwhelmingly to return to their remote home. It is the world's most isolated settlement and is administered from St Helena.

Area 98 sq km [38 sq mi]
Population 273
Capital (population) Edinburgh of the Seven Seas (273)
Government British overseas territory
Ethnic groups British
Languages English (official)
Religions Anglican
Currency Pound sterling = 100 pence
Website www.tristandc.com

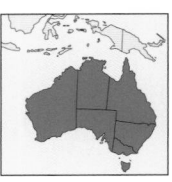

The national flag (above left) was adopted in 1901. It includes the British Union Flag, revealing Australia's historic links with Britain. In 1995, the Australian government put the flag used by the country's Aboriginal people (below left) on the same footing as the national flag.

Australia is the world's sixth-largest country. The huge Western Plateau makes up 66% of its land area, and is mainly flat and dry. Off the coast of north-east Queensland lies the Great Barrier Reef. The Great Dividing Range extends down the entire east coast and into Victoria. The mountains of Tasmania are a southerly extension of the range. The highlands separate the east coastal plains from the Central Lowlands and include Australia's highest peak, Mount Kosciuszko, in New South Wales. The capital, Canberra, lies in the foothills. The south-east lowlands are drained by the Murray and Darling, Australia's two longest rivers. Lake Eyre is the continent's largest lake. It lies on the edge of the Simpson Desert and is a dry salt flat for most of the year. Alice Springs lies in the heart of the continent, close to Ayers Rock (Uluru).

Much of the Western Plateau is desert, although areas of grass and low shrubs are found on its margins. The grasslands of the Central Lowlands are used to raise livestock. The north has areas of savanna and rainforest. In dry areas, acacias are common. Eucalyptus grows in wetter regions.

CLIMATE

Only 10% of Australia has an average annual rainfall greater than 1,000 mm [39 in]. These areas include some of the tropical north (where Darwin is situated), the north-east coast, and the south-east. The coasts are usually warm and many parts of the south and south-west, including Perth, enjoy a Mediterranean climate of dry summers and moist winters. The interior is dry and many rivers are only seasonal.

HISTORY

Native Australians (Aborigines) entered the continent from south-east Asia more than 50,000 years ago. They settled throughout the country and remained isolated from the rest of the world until the first European explorers, the Dutch, arrived in the 17th century. The Dutch did not settle. In 1770 British explorer Captain James Cook reached Botany Bay and claimed the east coast for Great Britain. In 1788 Britain built its first settlement (for convicts) on the site of present-day Sydney. The first free settlers arrived three years later.

In the 19th century, the economy developed rapidly, based on mining and sheep-rearing. At this time the continent was divided into colonies, which later were to become states. In 1901 the states of Queensland, Victoria, Tasmania, New South Wales, South Australia and Western Australia, federated to create the Commonwealth of Australia. In 1911 Northern Territory joined the federation. A range of progressive social welfare policies were adopted, such as old-age pensions in 1909. The federal capital was established in 1927 at Canberra, Australian Capital Territory. Australia fought as a member of the Allies in both world wars. The Battle of the Coral Sea in 1942 prevented a full-scale attack on the continent.

POLITICS

Post-1945 Australia steadily realigned itself with its Asian neighbours. Robert Menzies, Australia's longest-serving prime minister, oversaw many economic and social reforms and dispatched Australian troops to the Vietnam War. In 1977 Prime Minister Gough Whitlam was removed from office by the British governor general. He was succeeded by Malcolm Fraser. In 1983 elections, the Labour Party defeated Fraser's Liberal Party, and Bob Hawke became prime minister. His shrewd handling of industrial disputes and economic recession helped him win

a record four terms in office. In 1991 Hawke was forced to resign as leader and was succeeded by Paul Keating. Backed by a series of opinion polls, Keating proposed that Australia should become a republic by 2001.

Keating won the 1993 general election and persevered with his free market reforms. In 1996 elections, Keating was defeated by a coalition led by John Howard. In 1998 Howard narrowly secured a second term in office. In a referendum of 1999 Australia voted against becoming a republic. In 2000 Sydney hosted the 28th Summer Olympic Games, nicknamed the 'Friendly Games'.

The historic maltreatment of Native Australians remains a contentious political issue. In 1993 the government passed the Native Title Act

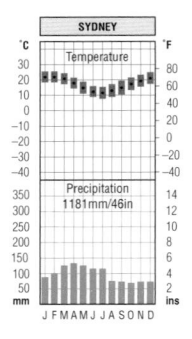
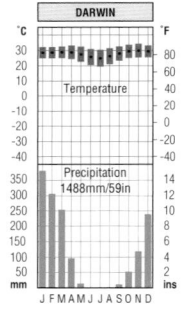
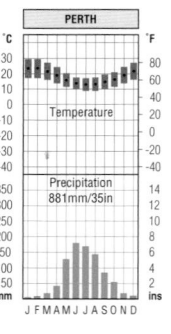
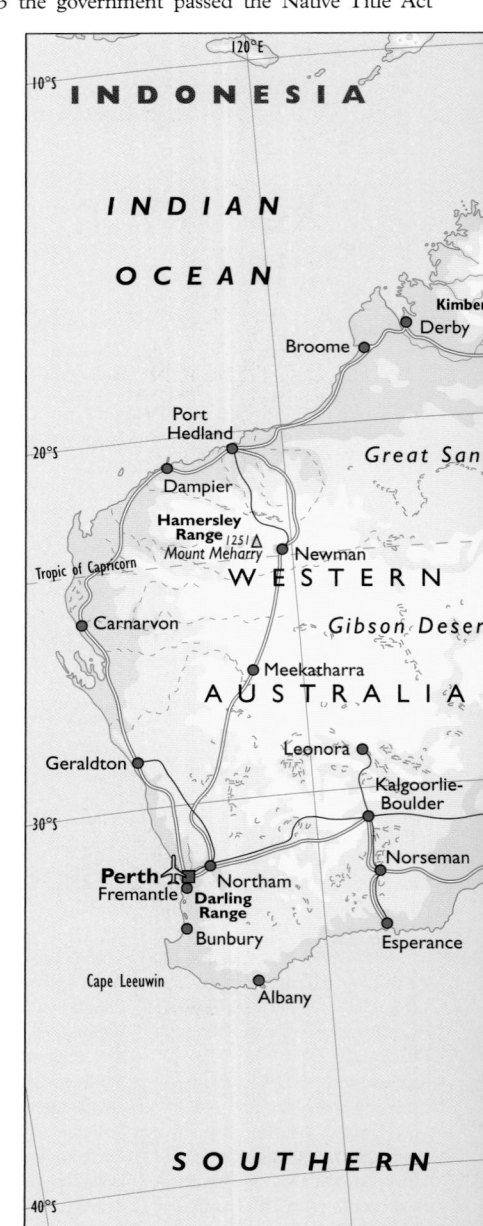

Area 7,741,229 sq km [2,988,885 sq mi]
Population 19,913,000
Capital (population) Canberra (309,000)
Government Federal constitutional monarchy
Ethnic groups Caucasian 92%, Asian 7%, Aboriginal 1%
Languages English (official)
Religions Roman Catholic 26%, Anglican 26%, other Christian 24%, non-Christian 24%
Currency Australian dollar = 100 cents
Website www.australia.gov.au

GREAT BARRIER REEF

The world's largest tropical coral reef, in the Coral Sea off the north east coast of Queensland. It was first explored by James Cook in 1770. It forms a natural breakwater and is up to 800 m [2,600 ft] wide. The reef is separated from the mainland by a shallow lagoon, 11–24 km [7–15 mi] wide. At 2,000 km [1,250 mi] in length, with an area of approximately 207,000 sq km [80,000 sq mi] the reef is the largest natural feature on earth. A World Heritage Area since 1981 it is the world's biggest tropical marine reserve. and home to 360 species of hard corals.

which restored to Native Australians land rights over their traditional hunting and sacred areas. In January 2002, eastern Australia suffered devastating bush fires.

Howard secured a fourth term in 2004 elections and vowed to stay leader of the Liberal Party for as long as the members want him.

In recent years Australia has brokered peace deals in the more troubled spots of the Pacific such as Papua New Guinea and the Solomon Islands.

ECONOMY

Australia is a prosperous country. Originally an agrarian economy, although crops grow on only 6% of the land. The country remains a major producer and exporter of farm products, particularly cattle, wheat and wool. Grapes grown for winemaking are also important. Australia is rich in natural resources and is a major producer of minerals, such as bauxite, coal, copper, diamonds, gold, iron ore, manganese, nickel, silver, tin, tungsten and zinc. Some oil and natural gas is also produced.

The majority of Australia's imports are manufactured products. They include machinery and other capital goods required by factories. The country has a highly developed manufacturing sector; the major products include consumer goods, notably foodstuffs and household articles. Tourism is a vital industry.

CANBERRA

Capital of Australia on the River Molonglo, Australian Capital Territory, south-eastern Australia. Settled in the early 1820s, it was chosen in 1908 as the new site for Australia's capital (succeeding Melbourne). The transfer of all governmental agencies was not completed until after World War II. Canberra has the Australian National University (1946), Royal Australian Mint (1965), Royal Military College and Stromlo Observatory. The new Parliament House was opened in 1988. Other important buildings include the National Library, National Museum, and National Gallery. Tidbinbilla Nature Reserve is located just outside the city.

MAP SCALE

0   200   400   600   800   1000 km

0   200   400   600 miles

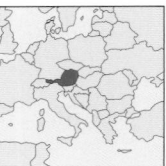

According to legend, the colours on Austria's flag date back to a battle in 1191, during the Third Crusade, when an Austrian duke's tunic was stained with blood, except under his swordbelt, where it remained white. The flag was officially adopted in 1918.

Area 83,859 sq km [32,378 sq mi]
Population 8,175,000
Capital (population) Vienna (1,560,000)
Government Federal republic
Ethnic groups Austrian 90%, Croatian, Slovene, others
Languages German (official)
Religions Roman Catholic 78%, Protestant 5%, Islam and others 17%
Currency Euro = 100 cents
Website www.austria.info

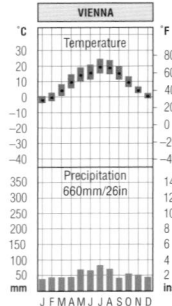

The picturesque village of Mitteldorf *in the high alpine region of the Tyrol, western Austria, is popular with winter and summer visitors alike*

The Republic of Austria is a landlocked country in the heart of Europe. About three-quarters of the land is mountainous. Northern Austria contains the valley of the River Danube, and the Vienna Basin. This is Austria's main farming region.

Southern Austria contains ranges of the Alps, which rise to their highest point of 3,797 m [12,457 ft] at Grossglockner.

CLIMATE

The climate is influenced both by westerly and easterly winds. The moist westerly winds bring rain and snow. They also moderate the temperatures. Dry easterly winds bring very cold weather during the winter, and hot weather during the summer.

HISTORY

Following the collapse of the Roman Empire, of which Austria, south of the Danube formed a part, the area was invaded and settled by waves of Asian, Germanic and Slav peoples. In the late 8th century, Austria came under the rule of Charlemagne, but in the 10th century, the area was overrun by Magyars.

VIENNA (WIEN)

Capital of Austria, on the River Danube. Vienna flourished under the Romans, but after they left in the 5th century it fell to a succession of eastern European invaders. The first Habsburg ruler was installed in 1276. It was the seat of the Holy Roman Empire 1558–1806. Occupied by the French during the Napoleonic Wars, it was later chosen as the site of the Congress of Vienna. Capital of the Austro-Hungarian Empire, it was the cultural and social centre of 19th-century Europe under Emperor Franz Joseph. After World War II, it was occupied (1945–55) by joint Soviet-Western forces. Historic buildings include St Stephen's Cathedral (12th-C), the Schönbrunn, and the Hofburg.

In 955, the German king Otto I brought Austria under his rule, and in 962 it became part of what later became known as the Holy Roman Empire. German emperors ruled the area until 1806, when the Holy Roman Empire broke up. The Habsburg ruler of the Holy Roman Empire became Emperor Francis I of Austria. In 1867, Austria and Hungary set up the powerful dual monarchy of Austria-Hungary.

Austria-Hungary was allied to Germany in World War I, but the defeated empire collapsed in 1918. Austria's present boundaries derive from the Versailles Treaty, signed in France in June 1919. In 1933, the Christian Socialist Chancellor Engelbert Dollfuss ended parliamentary democracy and ruled as a dictator. He was assassinated in 1934 due to his opposition to the Austrian Nazi Party's aim of uniting Austria and Germany.

The *Anschluss* (union with Germany) was achieved by the German invasion in March 1938. Austria became a province of the Third Reich called Ostmark until the defeat of the Axis powers in 1945.

POLITICS

After World War II, Austria was occupied by the Allies, Britain, France and the United States and it paid reparations for a 10-year period. After agreeing to be permanently neutral, Austria became an independent federal republic in 1955.

In 1994, two-thirds of the people voted in favour of joining the European Union and the country became a member in 1995. Austria became a centre of controversy in 1999, when the extreme right-wing Freedom Party, led by Jörg Haider, who had described Nazi Germany's employment policies as 'sound', came second in national elections. In February 2000, a coalition government was formed consisting of equal numbers of ministers from the conservative People's Party, which had come third in the elections, and the Freedom Party. However, the Freedom Party suffered a setback in 2001 when its vote fell in city elections in Vienna.

ECONOMY

Austria is a prosperous country with plenty of hydroelectric power, some oil and gas, and reserves of lignite (brown coal). The country's leading economic activity is manufacturing metals and metal products, including iron and steel, vehicles, machinery, machine tools and ships. Craft industries, making such things as fine glassware, jewellery and porcelain are also important. Dairy and livestock farming are the leading agricultural activities. Major crops include barley, potatoes, rye, sugar beet and wheat.

Azerbaijan's flag was adopted in 1991. Light blue is a traditional Turkic colour. At the centre of the red stripe is a white crescent and star, traditional symbols of Islam. The points of the star represent the eight groups of people in Azerbaijan.

The Republic of Azerbaijan lies in eastern Transcaucasia, bordering the Caspian Sea to the east. The Caucasus Mountains are in the north and include Azerbaijan's highest peak, Mount Bazar-Dyuzi, at 4,466 m [14,652 ft]. Another highland region including the Little Caucasus Mountains and part of the rugged Armenian plateau, lies in the south-west.

Between these regions lies a broad plain drained by the River Kura, its eastern part (south of the capital Baku) lies below sea level. Azerbaijan also includes the Nakhichevan Autonomous Republic on the Iran frontier, an area cut off from the rest of Azerbaijan by Armenian territory.

Forests grow on the mountains, while the lowlands comprise grassy steppe or semi-desert.

Area 86,600 sq km [33,436 sq mi]
Population 7,868,000
Capital (population) Baku (1,792,000)
Government Federal multiparty republic
Ethnic groups Azeri 90%, Dagestani 3%, Russian, Armenian, others
Languages Azerbaijani (official), Russian, Armenian
Religions Islam 93%, Russian Orthodox 2%, Armenian Orthodox
Currency Azerbaijani manat = 100 gopik
Website www.president.az

CLIMATE

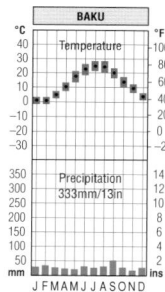

Azerbaijan has hot summers and cool winters. The plains have low rainfall ranging from *c.* 130 to 380 mm [5 to 15 in] a year. The uplands have much higher rainfall as does the subtropical south east coast.

HISTORY

In ancient times, the area now called Azerbaijan was invaded many times. Arab armies introduced Islam in 642, but most modern Azerbaijanis are descendants of Persians and Turkic peoples who migrated to the area from the east by the 9th century.

Azerbaijan was ruled by the Mongols between the 13th and 15th centuries and then by the Persian Safavid dynasty. By the early 19th century it was under Russian control.

After the Russian Revolution of 1917, attempts were made to form a Transcaucasian Federation made up of Armenia, Azerbaijan and Georgia. When this failed, Azerbaijanis set up an independent state. But Russian forces occupied the area in 1920. In 1922, the Communists set up a Transcaucasian Republic consisting of Armenia, Azerbaijan and Georgia, and placed it under Russian control. In 1936, the areas became separate Soviet Socialist Republics within the Soviet Union.

POLITICS

Following the break-up of the Soviet Union in 1991, Azerbaijan became independent. In 1992, Abulfaz Elchibey became president in Azerbaijan's first contested election. In 1993 Elchibey fled and Heydar Aliev, former head of the Communist Party and the KGB in Azerbaijan, assumed the presidency. He was elected later that year and Azerbaijan joined the Commonwealth of Independent States (CIS).

Economic progress was slow, partly because of the conflict with Armenia over the enclave of Nagorno-Karabakh, a region in Azerbaijan where the majority of people are Christian Armenians. A cease-fire in 1994 left Armenia in control of about 20% of Azerbaijan's land area. Talks held in 2001 in an attempt to resolve the dispute proved fruitless and sporadic fighting continues.

In 1998 Aliev was re-elected president. In 2001 Azerbaijan joined the Council of Europe. In 2003, Aliev's son Ilham Aliev became president. His government was re-elected in 2005, despite charges of fraud.

ECONOMY

In the mid-1990s, the World Bank classified Azerbaijan as a 'lower- middle-income' economy. Yet, by the late 1990s, the oil reserves in the Baku area on the Caspian Sea, and in the sea itself, held great promise. Oil extraction and manufacturing, including oil refining and the production of chemicals, machinery and textiles, are now the most valuable sources of revenue.

Large areas of land are irrigated and crops include cotton, fruit, grains, tea, tobacco and vegetables. Fishing is still important although the Caspian Sea is becoming increasingly polluted. Private enterprise is now encouraged.

BAKU

Capital of Azerbaijan, a port on the west coast of the Caspian Sea. A trade and craft centre in the Middle Ages, Baku prospered under the Shirvan shahs in the 15th century. Commercial oil production began in the 1870s. At the beginning of the 20th century, Baku lay at the centre of the world's largest oilfield. Industries include oil processing and equipment, shipbuilding, electrical machinery, chemicals.

Baku *the rigs of this forest of derricks have produced oil for more than a century*

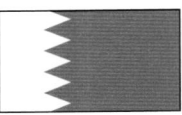

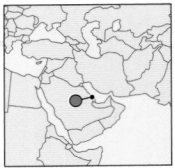

Red and white are traditional colours of the Gulf States. The white historically identified friendly Arab states. The five steps in the serration denote the five Pillars of Islam.

Area 694 sq km [268 sq mi]
Population 678,000
Capital (population) Manama (140,000)
Government Constitutional hereditary monarchy
Ethnic groups Bahraini 62%, others
Languages Arabic, English, Farsi, Urdu
Religions Muslim (Shi'a and Sunni) 81%, Christian 9%, other
Currency Bahraini dinar = 1000 fils
Website www.bahrain.gov.bh

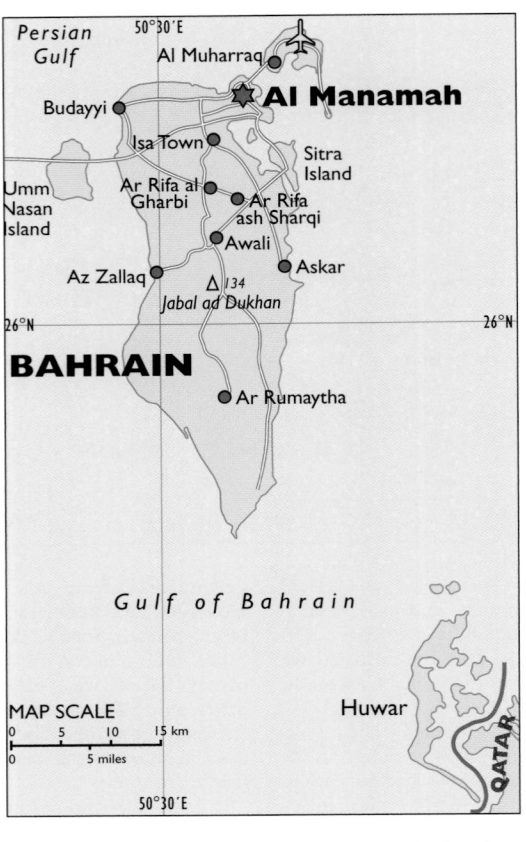

The Kingdom of Bahrain, a former Emirate and now a constitutional hereditary monarchy, is an archipelago consisting of more than 30 islands in the Persian Gulf. The largest of the islands, also called Bahrain, makes up seven-eighths of the country. Causeways link the island of Bahrain to the second largest island of Al Muharraq to the north-east and also to the Arabian peninsula.

Sandy, desert plains make up most of this small, low-lying island country. In the northern coastal areas of Bahrain, freshwater springs provide water for drinking and also for irrigation.

CLIMATE

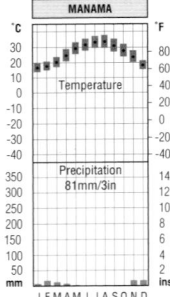

Bahrain has a humid climate. Winters are mild, with temperatures ranging from about 10°C [50°F] to 27°C [80°F]. Summers are hot and humid, with temperatures often soaring to more than 38°C [100°F]. The average annual rainfall is low. Northern Bahrain is the wettest area, with about 80 mm [3 in] a year. The rain occurs mainly in winter and rainfall is almost non-existent in summer months.

HISTORY

Bahrain was part of a trading civilization called Dilmun, which prospered between about 2000 and 1800 BC. This civilization was linked to the Sumerian, Babylonian and Assyrian civilizations to the north, and with the Indus Valley civilization in what is now Pakistan. Bahrain later came under Islamic Arab influence of the from the 7th century.

Portugal seized the archipelago from its Arab rulers in 1521, but the Persians conquered the islands in 1603, holding them against attacks by the Portuguese and Omanis. However, in 1782, the Al Khalifah Arabs from Saudi Arabia took over the islands and they have ruled ever since.

In the early 19th century, Britain helped Bahrain to prevent annexation by Saudi Arabian invaders. As a result, Bahrain agreed to let Britain take control of its foreign affairs. Bahrain effectively became a British protectorate, though it was not called one. In the 1920s and 1930s, the Bahrainis established welfare systems, which were later funded by revenue from oil, which was discovered in 1932.

Political reforms began in the 1950s and, in 1970, the Emir turned over some of his power to a Council of State, which became a Cabinet. Britain withdrew from the Persian Gulf region in 1971 and Bahrain became fully independent.

POLITICS

Bahrain adopted a new constitution in 1973. This created a National Assembly with 30 elected members. However, relations between the National Assembly and the ruling Al Khalifa family were difficult and the National Assembly was dissolved in 1975. The country was then ruled by the Emir and his cabinet, headed by the prime minister, the Emir's appointee.

MANAMA (AL-MANAMAH)

Capital of Bahrain, on the north coast of Bahrain Island, in the Persian Gulf. It was made a free port in 1958, and a deepwater harbour was built in 1962. It is the country's principal port and commercial centre. Industries include oil refining, banking, boatbuilding.

In February 2002, a new constitution changed the country from an Emirate into a constitutional hereditary monarchy and the ruler Sheikh Hamad bin Isa Al-Khalifa became king. Elections for a new directly elected House of Deputies took place later that year, with women allowed to vote for the first time. The 40-member House of Deputies together with a second chamber, a Shura Council, consisting of experts appointed by the king, made up the National Assembly, Bahrain's first parliament since 1975.

Political problems in recent years have included tensions between the Sunni Muslims and the Shiite majority. During the First Gulf War, Bahrain supported Iraq against Iran and, in 1996, Bahrain accused Iran of supporting an underground Shiite organization. Relations with Iran improved in 2002–4.

The fact that the US Fifth Fleet uses Bahrain as its headquarters in the Persian Gulf has provoked terrorist incidents. Although the people have more freedom than others in the region, opposition groups continue to press for further progress, including greater powers for the elected House of Deputies. The opposition groups organized large public rallies in 2005.

ECONOMY

The people of Bahrain enjoy one of the highest standards of living in the Persian Gulf. The average life expectancy at birth (2005 estimate) is 74 years and free medical services are available. Adult literacy is at 89%.

Bahrain's prosperity is based on oil, although the country lacks major reserves. Petroleum and petroleum products accounted for 68% of the exports in 2002. However, when oil production waned in the 1970s, Bahrain diversified its economy. Its aluminium smelting plant is the Gulf's largest non-oil industrial complex and aluminium, in all forms, accounted for 15% of the exports in 2002. Textiles and clothing accounted for another 8%.

In the late 1990s, industry, commerce and services employed 79% of the workforce, government 20% and agriculture 1%. Bahrain is a major banking and financial centre, and it is home to numerous multinational companies that operate in the Gulf region. In 2003, work began on a complete renovation of the old port of Manama. Construction, fishing and transport are important and a tourist industry is developing.

Bangladesh adopted this flag in 1971, following the country's break from Pakistan. The green is said to represent the fertility of the land. The red disc is the sun of independence. It commemorates the blood shed during the struggle for freedom.

The People's Republic of Bangladesh is one of the world's most densely populated countries. Apart from the hilly regions in the far north-east and south-east, most of the land is flat and covered by fertile alluvium spread over the land by the Ganges, Brahmaputra and Meghna rivers. These rivers overflow when they are swollen by the annual monsoon rains. Floods also occur along the coast, 575 km [357 mi] long, when tropical cyclones (the name for hurricanes in this region) drive seawater inland. These periodic storms cause great human suffering. The world's most devastating tropical cyclone ever recorded occurred in Bangladesh in 1970, when an estimated 1 million people were killed. Most of Bangladesh is cultivated, but forests cover about 16% of the land. They include bamboo forests in the north-east and mangrove forests in the swampy Sundarbans region in the south-west, which is a sanctuary for the Royal Bengal tiger.

CLIMATE

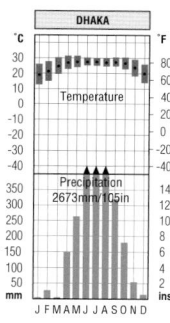

Bangladesh has a tropical monsoon climate. Dry northerly winds blow during the winter, but, in summer, moist winds from the south bring monsoon rains. In 1998, around two-thirds of the entire country was submerged, causing extensive damage. In December 2004, Bangladesh emerged relatively unscathed by the tsunami in the Indian Ocean.

HISTORY

For 300 years after the mid-8th century AD, Buddhist rulers governed eastern Bengal, the area that now makes up Bangladesh. In the 13th century, Muslims from the north extended their rule into Bengal and, in 1576, the area became part of the Muslim Mughal Empire which was ruled by the emperor Akbar. This empire, which also included India, Pakistan and Afghanistan, began to break up in the early 18th century. Europeans, who had first made contact with the area in the 16th century, began to gain influence.

The East India Company, chartered by the English government in 1600 to develop trade in Asia, became the leading trade power in Bengal by the mid-18th century. In 1757, following the defeat of the nawab of Bengal in the Battle of Plessey, the East India Company effectively ruled Bengal. Discontent with the company led to the Sepoy Rebellion in 1857. In 1958,

Area 143,998 sq km [55,598 sq mi]
Population 141,340,000
Capital (population) Dhaka (3,839,000)
Government Multiparty republic
Ethnic groups Bengali 98%, tribal groups
Languages Bangali (official), English
Religions Islam 83%, Hinduism 16%
Currency Taka =100 paisas
Website www.bangladeshonline.com

DHAKA (DACCA)

Capital of Bangladesh, a port on the Ganges delta, eastern Bangladesh. Its influence grew as the 17th century Mogul capital of Bengal. In 1765 it came under British control. At independence (1947) it was made capital of the province of East Pakistan. Severely damaged during the war of independence from Pakistan, it became capital of Bangladesh (1971). Sights include the Dakeshwari Temple, Bara Katra Palace (1644) and mosques. It is in the centre of the world's largest jute-producing area. Industries include engineering, textiles, printing, glass, chemicals.

the British government took over the East India Company and its territory became known as British India.

POLITICS

In 1947, British India was partitioned between the mainly Hindu India and the Muslim Pakistan. Pakistan consisted of two parts, West and East Pakistan, which were separated by about 1,600 km [1,000 mi] of Indian territory. Differences developed between West and East Pakistan, since people in the east felt themselves victims of ethnic and economic discrimination by the Urdu and Punjabi-speaking peoples of the west.

In 1971, resentment turned to war when Bengali irregulars, aided by Indian troops, established the independent nation of 'Free Bengal', with Sheikh Mujibur Rahman as head of state. The Sheikh's assassination in 1975 – in one of the four military coups in the first 11 years of independence – led finally to a takeover by General Zia Rahman, who created an Islamic state before he, too, was assassinated in 1981. General Ershad took over in a coup in 1982. He resigned as army chief in 1986 to become a civilian president.

By 1990, protests from supporters of his two predecessors toppled Ershad from power and, after the first free parliamentary elections since independence, a coalition government was formed in 1991. Many problems arose in the 1990s, including the increasing strength of Muslim fundamentalism and the consequences of cyclone damage. In 1996, Sheikh Hasina Wajed of the Awami League became prime minister, but, in 1999, she was defeated by Khaleda Zia, leader of the Nationalist Party.

ECONOMY

Bangladesh is one of the world's poorest countries. Its economy depends mainly on agriculture, which employs more than half of the workforce. Rice is the chief crop and Bangladesh is the world's fourth largest producer.

Other important crops include jute, sugar cane, tobacco and wheat. Jute processing is the leading manufacturing industry and jute is the leading export. Other manufactures include leather, paper and textiles.

***Young Bangladeshi women** in an after-school reading group*

In September 1991, Belarus adopted a red and white flag, replacing the flag used in the Soviet era. In June 1995, following a referendum vote to improve relations with Russia, it was replaced with a design similar to the old flag, but without the hammer and sickle.

Area 207,600 sq km [80,154 sq mi]
Population 10,311,000
Capital (population) Minsk (1,677,000)
Government Multiparty republic
Ethnic groups Belarusian 81%,
Russian 11%, Polish, Ukrainian, others
Languages Belarusian, Russian
(both official)
Religions Eastern Orthodox 80%,
others 20%
Currency Belarusian rouble = 100 kopecks
Website www.mfa.gov.by/eng

A baker serves customers at a bakery in Minsk

The Republic of Belarus is a land-locked country in Eastern Europe, formerly part of the Soviet Union. The land is low-lying and mostly flat. In the south, much of the land is marshy. This area contains Europe's largest marsh and peat bog, the Pripet Marshes.

A hilly region extends rom north-east to south-west and includes the highest point in Belarus, situated near the capital Minsk. This hill reaches a height of 346 m [1,135 ft] above sea level. Over 1,000 lakes, mostly small, dot the landscape. Forests cover large areas. Belarus and Poland jointly control a remnant of virgin forest, which contains a herd of rare wisent (European bison). This is the Belovezha Forest, which is known as theBialowieza Forest in Poland.

CLIMATE

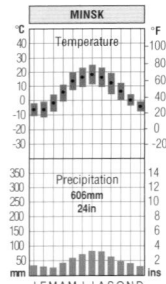

The climate of Belarus is affected by both the moderating influence of the Baltic Sea and continental conditions to the east. The winters are cold and the summers warm.

HISTORY

Slavic people settled in what is now Belarus about 1,500 years ago. In the 9th century, the area became part of the first East Slavic state, Kievan Rus, which became a major European power in the 10th and 11th centuries. Mongol invaders captured the eastern part of Kievan Rus in the 13th century, while Germanic tribes threatened from the west. Belarus allied itself with Lithuania, which also became a powerful state. In 1386, the Lithuanian Grand Duke married the queen of Poland and Lithuanian-Polish kings ruled both countries until 1569, when Lithuania with Belarus merged with Poland. In the 18th century, Russia took most of eastern Poland, including Belarus. Yet the people of Belarus continued to maintain their individuality.

Following the Russian Revolution of 1917, a Communist government replaced tsarist rule in Russia, and, in March 1918, Belarus became an independent, non-Communist republic. Later that year, Russian Communists invaded Belarus, renaming it Byelorussia, a name derived from the Russian *Belaya Rus*, or White Russia. They established a Communist government there in 1919, and in 1922, the country became a founder republic of the Soviet Union. In 1939, Russia occupied what is now western Belarus, which had been part of Poland since 1919. Nazi troops occupied the area between 1941 and 1944, during which one in four citizens died. Byelorussia became a founding member of the United Nations in 1945.

POLITICS

In 1990, the Byelorussian parliament declared that its laws took precedence over those of the Soviet Union. On 25 August 1991, many observers were very surprised that this most conservative and Communist-dominated of parliaments declared its independence. This quiet state of the Soviet Union played a supporting role in its deconstruction and the creation of the Commonwealth of Independent States (CIS). In September 1991, the republic changed its name back from the Russian form of Byelorussia to Belarus, its Belarusian form.

The Communists retained control in Belarus after independence. A new constitution introduced in 1994 led to presidential elections that brought Alexander Lukashenko to power. This enabled economic reform to get under way, though the country remained pro-Russian. Lukashenko favoured a union with Russia and, in 1999, signed a union treaty committing the countries to setting up a confederal state. However, Russia insisted that a referendum would have to take place before any merger took place. In 2001, Lukashenko was re-elected president amid accusations of electoral fraud. A referendum in 2004 showed overwhelming support for the removal of the two-term limit on Lukashenko's rule Western observers alleged fraud saying that the vote was neither free nor fair.

In 2005 Belarus was listed by the US as Europe's last remaining outpost of tyranny.

ECONOMY

The World Bank classifies Belarus as an 'upper-middle-income' economy. Like other former republics of the Soviet Union, it faces many problems in turning from Communism to a free-market economy.

Under Communist rule, many manufacturing industries were set up, making such things as chemicals, trucks and tractors, machine tools and textiles. Farming is important and major products include barley, eggs, flax, meat, potatoes and other vegetables, rye and sugar beet. Leading exports include machinery and transport equipment, chemicals and food products.

MINSK

Capital of Belarus, on the River Svisloch. Founded *c.* 1060, it was under Lithuanian and Polish rule before becoming part of Russia in 1793. During World War II Minsk was almost completely destroyed and only a few historical buildings were left standing. The city was rebuilt as the showplace city of a modern republic. In 1974 Minsk was awarded the Soviet title of 'Hero City' for its sufferings in World War II and speedy reconstruction. In 1991, Minsk became the administrative centre of the newly formed CIS. Industries include textiles, machinery, motor vehicles, electronic goods.

Belgium's national flag was adopted in 1830, when the country won its independence from the Netherlands. The colours came from the arms of the province of Brabant, in central Belgium, which rebelled against Austrian rule in 1787.

The Kingdom of Belgium is a densely populated country in western Europe. Behind the 63 km [39 mi] long coastline on the North Sea, lie its coastal plains. Some low-lying areas, called polders, are protected from the sea by dykes (sea walls).

Central Belgium consists of low plateaux and the only highland region is the Ardennes in the south-east. The Ardennes, reaching a height of 694 m [2,277 ft], consists largely of moorland, peat bogs and woodland. The country's chief rivers are the Schelde, which flows through Tournai, Gent (or Ghent) and Antwerp in the west, and the Sambre and the Meuse, which flow between the central plateau and the Ardennes.

Area 30,528 sq km [11,787 sq mi]
Population 10,348,000
Capital (population) Brussels (136,000)
Government Federal constitutional monarchy
Ethnic groups Belgian 89% (Fleming 58%, Walloon 31%), others
Languages Dutch, French, German (all official)
Religions Roman Catholic 75%, others 25%
Currency Euro = 100 cents
Website www.belgium.be

CLIMATE

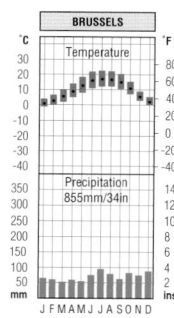

The moderating effects of the sea give much of Belgium a temperate climate, with mild winters and cool summers. Moist winds from the Atlantic Ocean bring significant amounts of rainfall throughout the year, especially in the Ardennes. During January and February, much snow falls in the Ardennes, where temperatures are more extreme. Brussels has mild winters and warm summers.

HISTORY

Due to its strategic position, Belgium has often been called the 'cockpit of Europe'. In the Middle Ages, the area was split into small states, but, with the Netherlands and Luxembourg, it was united and made prosperous by the dukes of Burgundy in the 14th and 15th centuries. Later, at various times, Belgium, came under Austrian, Spanish and French rule.

From 1815, following the Napoleonic Wars, Belgium and the Netherlands were united as the 'Low Countries' but, in 1830, a National Congress proclaimed independence from the Dutch. In 1831, Prince Leopold of Saxe-Coburg became Belgium's king.

The division between Belgium and the Netherlands rested on history rather than geography. Belgium was a mainly Roman Catholic country while the Netherlands was mainly Protestant. Both were neutral in foreign policy, but both were occupied by the Nazis from 1940 until September 1944.

After World War II, Belgium achieved rapid economic progress, first through collaboration with the Netherlands and Luxembourg, which formed a customs union called Benelux, and later as a founder member of what is now the European Union. In 1960, Belgium granted independence to the Belgian Congo (now the Democratic Republic of the Congo) and, in 1962, its supervision of Ruanda-Urundi (now Rwanda and Burundi) was ended.

POLITICS

Belgium has always been an uneasy marriage of two peoples: the majority Flemings, who speak a language closely related to Dutch, and the Walloons, who speak French. The dividing line between the two communities runs east–west, just south of Brussels, although the capital is officially bilingual.

Since the inception of the country, the Flemings have caught up and overtaken the Walloons in cultural influence as well as in numbers. In 1971, the constitution was revised and three economic regions were established: Flanders (Vlaanderen), Wallonia (Wallonie) and Brussels. However, tensions remained.

In 1993, Belgium adopted a federal system of government, with each of the three regions being granted its own regional assembly. Further changes in 2001 gave the regions greater tax-raising powers, plus responsibility for agriculture and the promotion of trade. Elections under this system were held in 1995 and 1999. Since 1995, the Chamber of Deputies has had 150 members, and the Senate 71. The regional assembly of Flanders had 118 deputies, while the assemblies of Brussels and Wallonia had 75 each.

Historic buildings *line a canal in Bruges; the city's name is derived from Bryggja, which means landing stage in Old Norse*

ECONOMY

Belgium is a major trading nation, with a highly developed economy. Almost 75% of its trade is with other EU nations.

With few natural resources it must import a large percentage of the raw materials required for industry. Its main products include chemicals, processed food and steel. The steelworks lie near to ports because they are powered by petroleum. In 2002, parliament voted to phase out the use of nuclear energy by 2025.

Agriculture employs less than 2% of the people, but Belgian farmers produce most of the food needed by the people. The chief crops are barley and wheat, but the most valuable activities are dairy farming and livestock rearing.

BRUSSELS (BRUXELLES)

Capital of Belgium and of Brabant province, central Belgium. During the Middle Ages, it achieved prosperity through the wool trade and became capital of the Spanish Netherlands. In 1830 it became capital of newly independent Belgium. Places of interest include a 13th-century cathedral, the town hall, splendid art nouveau buildings, and academies of fine arts. The main commercial, financial, cultural, and administrative centre of Belgium, it is also the headquarters of the European Union (EU) and of the North Atlantic Treaty Organization (NATO). Industries include textiles, chemicals, electronic equipment, electrical goods, brewing.

Above the shield is a mahogany tree, beside it stand two woodcutters denoting the two main ethnic groups of Belize. A ring of 50 laurel leaves marks the year 1950, start of the liberation struggle. The country's motto is also shown - Sub umbra floreo (I flourish in the shade).

Area 8,867 sq miles [22,966 sq km]
Population 273,000
Capital (population) Belmopan (8,000)
Government Constitutional monarchy
Ethnic groups Mestizo 49%, Creole 25%, Mayan Indian 11%, Garifuna 6%, others 9%
Languages English (official), Spanish, Creole
Religions Roman Catholic 50%, Protestant 27%, others
Currency Belizean dollar = 100 cents
Website www.belize.gov.bz

Belize is a monarchy whose head of state is Britain's monarch. It lies on the Caribbean Sea in central America. A governor-general represents the monarch, while an elected government, headed by a prime minister, rules the country day-to-day.

Behind the swampy coastal plain in the south, the land rises to the low Maya Mountains, which reach 1,120 m [3,675 ft] at Victoria Peak. Northern Belize is mostly low lying and swampy. The main river, the River Belize, flows across the centre of the country. Rainforest covers large areas. A barrier reef stretches 297 km (185 mi) along the coast, the longest of its kind in the Western Hemisphere.

CLIMATE

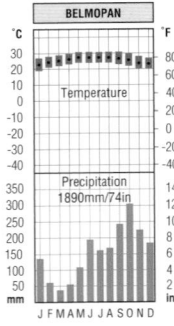

Belize has a humid tropical climate with high temperatures all year. Average rainfall ranges from 1,300 mm [52 in] in the north to over 3,800 mm [150 in] in the south. It is occasionally hit by hurricanes, a storm in 2001 killed 22 and left 12,000 homeless.

HISTORY

Between 300 BC and AD 1000 Belize was part of the Maya Empire. In the 16th century Spain claimed the area but did not settle. The first European settlement was founded by shipwrecked soldiers in 1638. Over the next 150 years Britain gradually took control of Belize and established sugar plantations using slave labour.

In 1862 Belize became the colony of British Honduras. Renamed Belize in 1973 it gained full independence in 1981. Guatemala, which had claimed the area since the early 19th century, opposed Belize's independence and British troops remained to prevent a possible invasion.

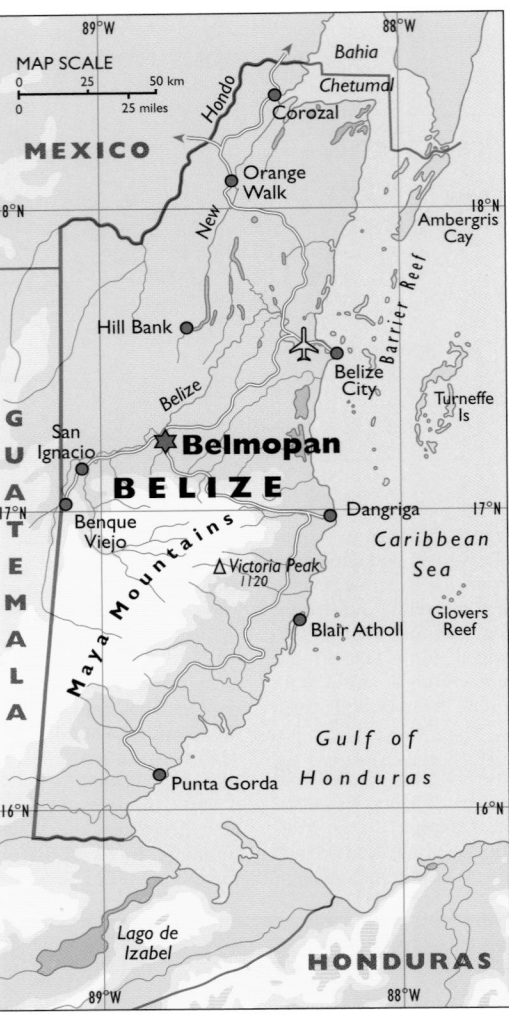

Mangrove forest and delta *on Caribbean coast of Belize; mangroves are important for providing a habitat for wildlife*

BELMOPAN

Capital of Belize, on the River Belize. It replaced Belize City, 80 km [50 mi] upstream, as capital in 1971, the latter having been largely destroyed by a hurricane in 1961. The building of Belmopan began in 1966 and was completed in 1971. As an inland city temperatures are high in the daytime but much cooler at night. In its centre are the National Assembly Building and the majority of central government offices. Residents are mostly government employees and their families. As the city is relatively new, inhabitants originate from other areas of the country, with just a small indigenous population.

POLITICS

In 1983, Guatemala reduced its claim to the southern half of Belize. Improved relations in the early 1990s led Guatemala to recognize Belize's independence and in 1992, Britain agreed to withdraw its troops from the country. Mayan land rights remain a contentious political issue.

High levels of unemployment are a major problem as is a growing involvement in the South American drug trade which has brought with it increasing levels of violent crime

ECONOMY

The World Bank classifies Belize as a 'lower-middle-income' developing country. Tourism is the mainstay of the economy and in recent years cruise ships have called there, bringing extra income. Agriculture is still important, with cane sugar the chief commercial crop and export. Other crops include bananas, beans, citrus fruits, maize and rice. Forestry is of longstanding importance, even featuring on the flag. Fishing is the second biggest earner.

MAYA

Outstanding culture of classic American civilization, occupying south Mexico and north Central America. The civilization divides into three periods. The pre-classic era was from 1000 BC to AD 300. The classic era, when it was at its height, was from the 3rd to the 9th centuries. The Maya built great temple cities. They were skilful potters and weavers and productive farmers. They worshipped gods and ancestors and blood sacrifice was an important element of religion. The post-classic era extended from AD 100 to 1500 when the Maya civilization declined. Much was destroyed after the Spanish conquest in the 16th century.

Benin 35

The colours on this flag, used by Africa's oldest independent nation, Ethiopia, symbolize African unity. Benin adopted this flag after independence in 1960. A flag with a red (Communist) star replaced it between 1975 and 1990, after which Benin dropped its Communist policies.

The Republic of Benin, formerly called Dahomey, is one of Africa's smallest countries. It extends north-south for about 620 km [390 mi]. The coastline on the Bight of Benin, which is about 100 km [62 mi] long, is lined by lagoons. It lacks natural harbours and the harbour at Cotonou, the main port and commercial centre, is artificial.

Behind the coastal lagoons is a flat plain. Beyond this plain is a marshy depression, but the land rises to a low plateau in central Benin. The highest land is in the north-west.

Savanna covers most of northern Benin. The north is home to many typical savanna animals, such as buffaloes, elephants and lions. The north has two national parks, the Penjari and the 'W', which Benin shares with Burkina Faso and Niger.

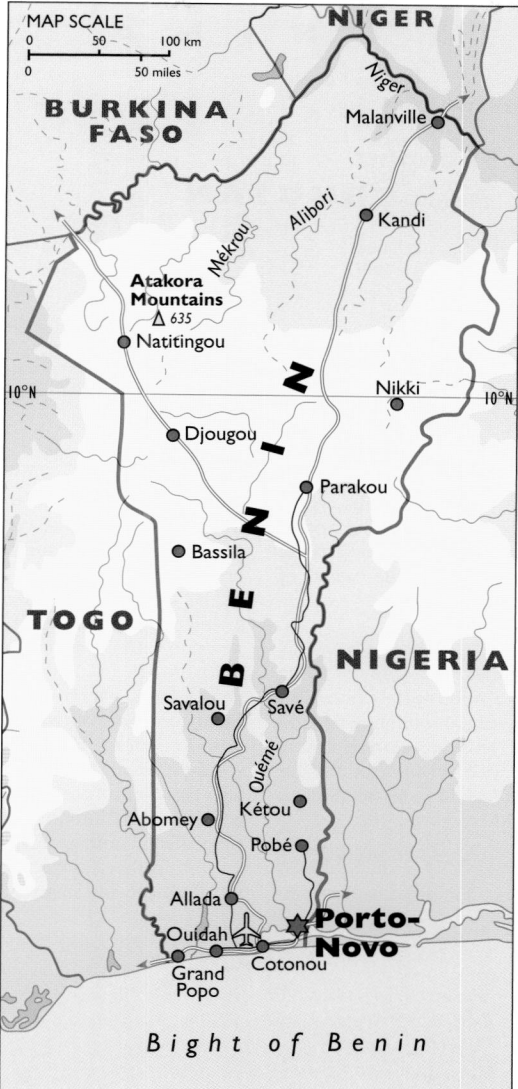

MAP SCALE

Area 112,622 sq km [43,483 sq mi]
Population 7,250,000
Capital (population) Porto-Novo (233,000)
Government Multiparty republic
Ethnic groups Fon, Adja, Bariba, Yoruba, Fulani
Languages French (official), Fon, Adja, Yoruba
Religions Traditional beliefs 50%, Christianity 30%, Islam 20%
Currency CFA franc = 100 centimes
Website www.gouv.bj/en/

CLIMATE

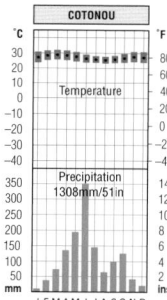

Benin has a hot, wet climate. The average annual temperature on the coast is 25°C [77°F], while the average annual rainfall is 1,330 mm [52 in]. The forested inland plains are wetter than the coast, but the rainfall decreases to the north, which has rainy summer season and a very dry winter.

HISTORY

The ancient kingdom of Dahomey, a prominent West African kingdom which developed in the 15th century, had its capital at Abomey in what is now south-western Benin. In the 17th century, the kings of Dahomey became involved in supplying slaves to European slave traders, including the Portuguese, who shipped many Dahomeans to the Americas. The shoreline of present-day Benin became part of what was called the Slave Coast. Many slaves were shipped to Brazil. Traces of the culture and religion of the slaves still survive in parts of the Americas, For example, the voodoo cult in Haiti originated in Dahomey.

PORTO-NOVO

Capital of Benin, a port on the Gulf of Guinea near the border with Nigeria. Settled by 16th-century Portuguese traders, it later became a shipping point for slaves to America. It was made the country's capital at independence in 1960, but Cotonou is assuming increasing importance. Today it is a market for the surrounding agricultural region.

After slavery was ended in the 19th century, France began to gain influence in the area. Around 1851, France signed a treaty with the kingdom of Dahomey and, in the 1890s, the area, which also included some other small African states, became a French colony. From 1904, they ruled Dahomey as part of a huge region called French West Africa, which also included what are now Burkina Faso, Guinea, Ivory Coast, Mauritania, Mali, Niger and Senegal. Dahomey became an overseas territory of France in 1946 and a self-governing nation in the French Community in 1958. Full independence was achieved in 1960.

POLITICS

Dahomey suffered from instability and unrest in the early years of independence. The first president, Hubert Maga, was removed in 1963 in a military coup led by General Christophe Soglo. A presidential council was set up in 1970 and Hubert Maga became one of three rotating presidents. But this regime was overthrown in 1973 by a coup led by Lt-Col Matthieu Kérékou. In 1975, Kérékou announced that the country would be renamed Benin after the powerful state known for its magnificent sculptures in south-western Nigeria. Benin became a Marxist-Leninist People's Republic and, in 1977, it became a one-party state. This regime, headed by President Kérékou, held power until 1989, when, following the lead of several East European countries in abandoning Communism, Kérékou announced that his country would also abandon Marxism-Leninism and, instead, follow liberal economic policies.

In 1990, a new democratic constitution with a presidential system was introduced. Presidential elections were held in 1991 and Nicéphore Soglo, a former World Bank executive and prime minister, defeated Kérékou. However, in 1996, Kérékou defeated Soglo and returned to power. Kérékou, who was re-elected in 2001, worked to restore Benin's fragile economy. Many observers have praised Benin's transition from a Marxist-Leninist state into one of Africa's most stable democracies.

ECONOMY

Benin is a poor developing country. About half of the population depends on agriculture, but farming is largely at subsistence level. The main food crops include beans, cassava, millet, rice, sorghum and yams. The chief cash crops are cotton, palm oil and palm kernels. Forestry is also important.

Benin produces some oil, but manufacturing remains on a small scale. It depends heavily upon Nigeria for trade.

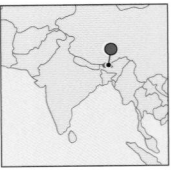

The dragon dates to the 17th century. The jewels in the dragon's claws represent Bhutan's wealth. The white symbolizes purity. The gold represents the secular power of the Druk Gyalpo (Dragon King), and the orange, the spiritual power of Buddhism.

Area 47,000 sq km [18,147 sq mi]
Population 2,186,000
Capital (population) Thimphu (35,000)
Government Constitutional monarchy
Ethnic groups Bhutanese 50%,
Nepalese 35%
Languages Dzongkha (official)
Religions Buddhism 75%, Hinduism 25%
Currency Ngultrum = 100 cetrum
Website www.bhutan.gov.bt

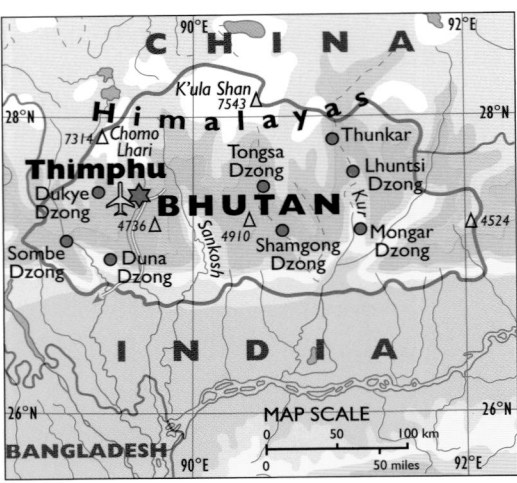

MAP SCALE

The Kingdom of Bhutan is a small, landlocked country in the eastern Himalayas, between India and the Tibetan plateau of China. Southern Bhutan, along the border with India, is the lowest land region, ranging between about 50 and 900 m [160 to 2,950 ft] above sea level. North of the plains is a mountainous region between about 1,500 and 4,250 m [4,920 to 13,940 ft]. The northernmost region lies in the Great Himalayan range, reaching more than 7,300 m [23,950 ft]. Most people live in the fertile valleys of rivers which flow generally from north to south.

CLIMATE

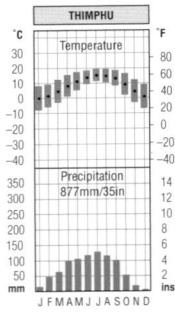

The altitude determines the climate. The southern plains have a subtropical, rainy climate, with an average annual rainfall of around 5,000 mm [197 in]. Dense vegetation covers much of the region, with savanna in the far south. Central Bhutan has a moderate climate, though winters are cold.

HISTORY

Around 1,200 years ago Tibetan invaders settled in the area. In the early 17th century, Bhutan became a separate state when a Tibetan lama (Buddhist monk), who was both a spiritual and temporal ruler, took power. The country was divided into districts ruled by governors and fort commanders. The 19th century was plagued by civil wars in which rival governors battled for power. In 1907, Bhutan became a monarchy when Ugyen Wangchuk, the powerful governor of Tongsa district, made himself Maharajah (now King) and set up the country's first effective central government. The monarch was hereditary and the Maharajah's successors have ruled the country ever since.

In 1910, Britain took control of Bhutan's foreign affairs in 1910, but it did not interfere in internal affairs. This treaty was renewed with newly independent India in 1949. India also returned some parts of Bhutan which had been annexed by Britain and agreed to help Bhutan develop its economy and, later, its defence.

THIMPHU

Bhutan's capital is located in the west of the country. The city is modern in age only (established in 1952) as all new buildings are built following traditional designs. Among its sights are the Memorial Chorten (dedicated to the king's late father Jigme Dorji Wangchuck) and the Tashicho Dzong a 350-year-old structure built by Shabdrung Ngawang Namgyal and refurbished in 1961 to house government departments and ministries.

Buddhist monks chanting and drumming
during the Wangdi Tsechu Festival at Wangdue Phodrang Dzong

POLITICS

Bhutan's remote but strategic position cut it off from the outside world for centuries and it only began to open up to outsiders in the 1970s. The roots of reform go back to 1952 when Jigme Dorji Wangchuk succeeded to the throne and a national assembly was established to advise the king. Slavery was abolished in 1958 and, in 1959, Bhutan admitted several thousand refugees after China had annexed Tibet. The first cabinet was set up in 1968.

In 1972, King Jigme Dorji Wangchuk died and was succeeded by his son, Jigme Singye Wangchuk. The new king continued Bhutan's policy of slow modernization. The first foreign tourists were admitted in 1974, although tourism was restricted to people on prepackaged or guided tours. Independent travel was discouraged as Bhutan sought to preserve its majority Buddhist culture. A television service was not introduced until 1999.

The king gave up some of the monarch's absolute powers in 1998, giving up his role as head of the government. Instead, he ruled in conjunction with the government, a National Assembly and a royal advisory council. In 2005, the government published a new draft constitution, which would make Bhutan a democracy with a parliament consisting of two elected houses. The parliament would have the right to impeach the king by a two-thirds vote.

Ethnic conflict has marred Bhutan's recent history. In 1986, a new law came into force making citizenship dependent on length of residence in Bhutan. Many ethnic Nepalis living in the south were made illegal immigrants, while other measures emphasizing Buddhist culture further antagonized the minority Nepalis. This led to violence in 1990, causing many Nepalis to flee. In 2005 the king announced that he would step down in 2008, when democratic elections would be held.

ECONOMY

Bhutan is a poor country. The rugged terrain makes the building of roads and other infrastructure difficult. Agriculture, mainly subsistence farming, cattle rearing and forestry, accounts for 93% of the workforce. Barley, rice and wheat are the chief food crops. Other products include citrus fruits, dairy products and maize. Industry is small scale, some coal is mined in the south.

The country's economy is closely linked to that of India with nearly 90% of Bhutan's total exports going to India. Bhutan has considerable hydroelectric power potential and electricity is exported to India. However, economic development is hampered by Bhutan's desire to maintain its traditional culture. The controls placed by the government on outside groups have inevitably restricted foreign investment.

This flag, which has been Bolivia's national and merchant flag since 1888, dates back to 1825 when Bolivia became independent. The red stands for Bolivia's animals and the courage of the army, the yellow for its mineral resources, and the green for its agricultural wealth.

The Republic of Bolivia is a landlocked country in South America. It can be divided into two regions. The west is dominated by two parallel ranges of the Andes Mountains. The western cordillera forms Bolivia's border with Chile. The eastern range runs through the heart of Bolivia. Between the two, lies the Altiplano. The Altiplano is the most densely populated region of Bolivia and the site of its famous ruins, it includes the seat of government, La Paz, close to Lake Titicaca. Sucre, the legal capital, lies in the Andean foothills.

The east is a relatively unexplored region of lush, tropical rainforest, inhabited mainly by Native South Americans. In the south-east lies the Gran Chaco.

The windswept Altiplano is a grassland region. The semi-arid Gran Chaco is a largely unpopulated vast lowland plain, drained by the River Madeira, a tributary of the Amazon. The region is famous for its quebracho trees which are a major source of tannin.

Area 1,098,581 sq km [424,162 sq mi]
Population 8,724,000
Capital (population) La Paz (seat of government, 940,000); Sucre (legal capital/seat of judiciary, 177,000)
Government Multiparty republic
Ethnic groups Mestizo 30%, Quechua 30%, Aymara 25%, White 15%
Languages Spanish, Aymara, Quechua (all official)
Religions Roman Catholic 95%
Currency Boliviano = 100 centavos
Website www.bolivia.com

CLIMATE

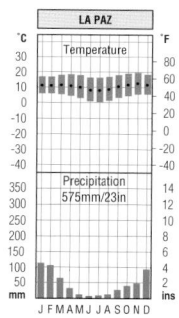

Bolivia's climate varies greatly according the to altitude with the highest Andean peaks permanently covered in snow. In contrast, the eastern plains have a humid tropical climate. The main rainy season takes place between December and February.

HISTORY

American Indians have lived in Bolivia for at least 10,000 years. The main groups today are the Aymara and Quechua people.

When Spanish soldiers arrived in the early 16th century, Bolivia was part of the Inca empire. Following the defeat of the Incas, Spain ruled from 1532 to 1825, when Antonio José de Sucre, one of revolutionary leader Simón Bolívar's generals, defeated the Spaniards.

Since independence, Bolivia has lost much territory to its neighbours. In 1932, Bolivia fought with Paraguay for control of the Gran Chaco region. Bolivia lost and most of this area passed to Paraguay in 1938.

POLITICS

Following the Chaco War, Bolivia entered a long period of instability. It had ten presidents, six of whom were members of the military, between 1936 and 1952, when the Revolutionary Movement replaced the military. The new government launched a series of reforms, which included the break-up of large estates and the granting of land to Amerindian farmers. Another military uprising occurred in 1964, heralding another period of instability.

Elections were held in 1980, but the military again intervened until 1982, when civilian government was restored. Presidential elections were held in 1989, 1993 and 1997, when General Hugo Bánzer Suárez, who had ruled as a dictator in the 1970s, became president. In 2005, Evo Morales, a left-wing Aymaran Indian and peasant leader, was elected president.

ECONOMY

Bolivia is one of the poorest countries in South America. It has several natural resources, including tin, silver and natural gas, but the chief activity is agriculture, which employs 47% of the people. Potatoes, wheat and a grain called quinoa are important crops on the Altiplano, while bananas, cocoa, coffee and maize are grown at the lower, warmer levels.

Manufacturing is small-scale and the main exports are mineral ores and fossil fuels. Coca, which is used to make cocaine, is exported illegally. In 2002–3, the production of coca plummeted, causing social unrest. In 2004, the people voted in favour of a government plan to export natural gas via a port in Peru.

LA PAZ

Administrative capital and largest city of Bolivia, in the west of the country. Founded by the Spanish in 1548 on the site of an Inca village, it was one of the centres of revolt in the War of Independence (1809–24). Located at 3,600 m [12,000 ft] in the Andes, it is the world's highest capital city. Industries include chemicals, tanning, flour-milling, electrical equipment, textiles, brewing and distilling.

Plaza San Francisco *in La Paz, with the 16th century Iglesia de San Francisco in the background*

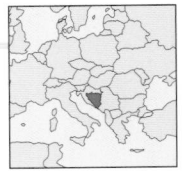

A new flag was adopted in 1998, as the previous flag was thought to be synonymous with the wartime Muslim regime. The blue background and white stars represent the country's links with the EU. The triangle stands for the three ethnic groups in the country.

Area 51,197 sq km [19,767 sq mi]
Population 4,008,000
Capital (population) Sarajevo (529,000)
Government Federal republic
Ethnic groups Bosnian 48%, Serb 37%, Croat 14%
Languages Bosnian, Serbian, Croatian
Religions Islam 40%, Serbian Orthodox 31%, Roman Catholic 15%, others 14%
Currency Convertible marka = 100 convertible pfenniga
Website www.fbihvlada.gov.ba/engleski/

Bosnia-Herzegovina is one of the five republics to emerge from the former Federal People's Republic of Yugoslavia. Much of the country is mountainous or hilly, with an arid limestone plateau in the south-west. The River Sava, which forms most of the northern border with Croatia, is a tributary of the River Danube. Because of the country's odd shape, the coastline is limited to a short stretch of 20 km [13 mi] on the Adriatic coast.

CLIMATE

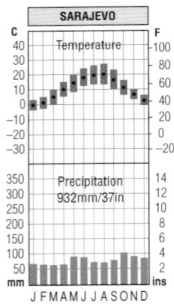

The coast benefits from a Mediterranean climate. Summers are dry and sunny, while winters are moist and mild. Inland, the weather is more severe, with hot, dry summers and bitterly cold, snowy winters. The north experiences the most severe weather.

HISTORY

Slavs settled in the area that is now Bosnia-Herzegovina around 1,400 years ago. In the late 15th century, the area was taken by the Ottoman Turks. In 1878, the dual monarchy of Austria-Hungary gained temporary control over Bosnia-Herzegovina and it formally took over the area in 1908. The assassination of Archduke Franz Ferdinand of Austria-Hungary in Sarajevo, in June 1914, was the catalyst for the start of World War I. In 1918, Bosnia-Herzegovina became part of the Kingdom of the Serbs, Croats and Slovenes, renamed Yugoslavia in 1929. Germany occupied Yugoslavia during World War II, and Bosnia-Herzegovina came under a puppet regime in Croatia. A Communist government took over in Yugoslavia in 1945, and a new constitution in 1946 made the country a federal state, with Bosnia-Herzegovina as one of its six constituent republics.

Under Communism, Bosnia-Herzegovina was a potentially explosive area due to its mix of Bosnian Muslims, Orthodox Christian Serbs and Roman Catholic Croats, as well as Albanian, gypsy and Ukrainian minorities. The ethnic and religious differences started to exert themselves after the death of Yugoslavia's president Josip Broz Tito in 1980, and increasing indications that Communist economic policies were not working.

POLITICS

Free elections were held in 1990 and non-Communists won a majority, with a Muslim, Alija Izetbegovic, as president. In 1991, Croatia and Slovenia declared themselves independent republics and seceded from Yugoslavia. Bosnia-Herzegovina held a referendum on independence in 1992. Most Bosnian Serbs boycotted the vote, but the Muslims and Croats voted in favour and Bosnia-Herzegovina proclaimed its independence. War then broke out.

At first, the Muslim-dominated government allied itself uneasily with the Croat minority, but it was at once under attack by local Serbs, supported by their co-nationals from beyond Bosnia-Herzegovina's borders. In their 'ethnic cleansing' campaign, heavily equipped Serb militias drove poorly-armed Muslims from towns they had long inhabited. By early 1993, the Muslims controlled less than a third of the former federal republic, and even the capital, Sarajevo, became disputed territory, with constant shelling.

The Muslim-Croat alliance rapidly disintegrated and refugees approached the million mark. Tougher economic sanctions on Serbia in April 1993 had little effect on the war in Bosnia. A small UN force attempted to deliver relief supplies to civilians and maintain 'safe' Muslim areas to no avail.

In 1995, the warring parties agreed to a solution to the conflict, the Dayton Peace Accord - the dividing of the country into two self-governing provinces, one Bosnian Serb and the other Muslim-Croat, under a central, unified, multi-ethnic government. A NATO-led force helped stabilize the country, this was replaced in 2004 by a European force when problems were no longer political.

ECONOMY

The economy of Bosnia-Herzegovina, was shattered by the war in the early 1990s. Manufactures include electrical equipment, machinery and transport equipment, and textiles. Farm products include fruits, maize, tobacco, vegetables and wheat, but the country has to import food.

Old Bridge, Mostar *built in 1566 and destroyed in November 1993, when it was shelled by Bosnian Croat troops, it reopened in 2004*

SARAJEVO

Capital of Bosnia-Herzegovina, on the River Miljacka. It fell to the Turks in 1429, and flourished as a commercial centre in the Ottoman Empire. Passing to the Austro-Hungarian Empire in 1878, the city was a centre of Serb and Bosnian resistance to Austrian rule. In June 1914 a Serb nationalist assassinated Austrian Archduke Franz Ferdinand in the city, an act that precipitated World War I. In 1991 Sarajevo became the focal point of the civil war between Bosnian-Serb troops and Bosnian government forces. The city lay under prolonged siege, often without water, electricity, or basic medical supplies. After the 1995 Dayton Peace Accord, it in effect became a Bosnian city, though with a reduced population as many Serbs fled.

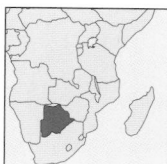

The black-and-white zebra stripe in the centre of Botswana's flag symbolizes racial harmony. The blue represents rainwater, because water supply is the most vital need in this dry country. This flag was adopted in 1966, when Botswana became independent from Britain.

The Republic of Botswana is a landlocked country which lies in the heart of southern Africa. The majority of the land is flat or gently rolling, with an average height of about 1,000 m [3,280 ft]. More hilly country lies in the east. The Kalahari, a semi-desert area covers much of Botswana.

Most of the south has no permanent streams. But large depressions occur in the north. In one, the Okavango River, which flows from Angola, forms a large delta, an area of swampland. Another depression contains the Makgadikgadi Salt Pans. During floods, the Botletle River drains from the Okavango Swamps into the Makgadikgadi Salt Pans.

CLIMATE

Temperatures are high during the summer which runs from October to April, but the winter months are much cooler. Night-time temperatures in winter sometimes drop below freezing. The average rainfall ranges from over 400 mm [16 in] in the east to less than 200 mm [8 in] in the south-west.

Gaborone, the capital of Botswana, lies in the wetter eastern part of the country, where the majority of the population lives. The rainy season occurs during summer, between the months of November and March. Frosts sometimes occur in parts of the east when the temperature drops below freezing.

HISTORY

The earliest inhabitants of the region were the San, who are also called Bushmen. They had a nomadic way of life, hunting wild animals and collecting plant foods.

The Tswana, who speak a Bantu language, now form the majority of the population. They are cattle owners, who settled in eastern Botswana more than 1,000 years ago. Their arrival led the San to move into the Kalahari region. Today, the San form a tiny minority, most of whom live in permanent settlements and work on cattle ranches.

POLITICS

Britain ruled the area as the Bechuanaland Protectorate between 1885 and 1966. When the country became independent, it adopted the name of Botswana. Since then, unlike many African countries, Botswana has been a stable multiparty democracy.

The economy has undergone a steady process of diversification under succes-

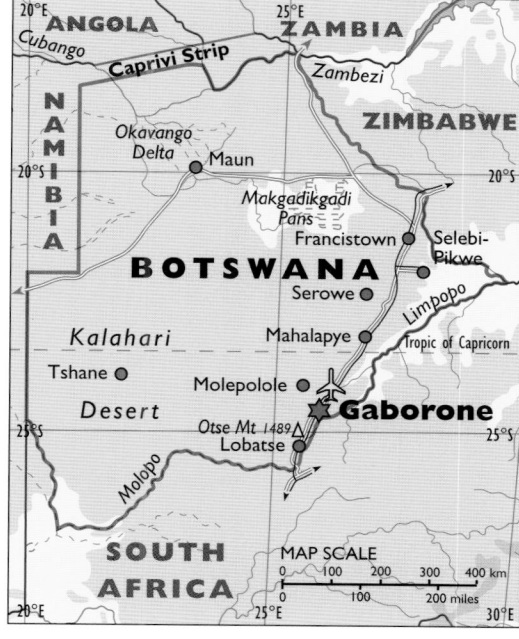

Area 581,730 sq km [224,606 sq mi]
Population 1,562,000
Capital (population) Gaborone (186,000)
Government Multiparty republic
Ethnic groups Tswana (or Setswana) 79%, Kalanga 11%, Basarwa 3%, others
Languages English (official), Setswana
Religions Traditional beliefs 85%, Christianity 15%
Currency Pula = 100 thebe
Website www.gov.bw

sive presidents. Botswana's first president, Sir Seretse Khama, who died in 1980, and his successor, Sir Ketumile Masire, who served from 1980 until 1998, when he retired in favour of Festus Mogae. Despite a severe drought, the economy expanded and the government introduced major social programmes. Tourism also grew as huge national parks and reserves were established. However, by the early 2000s, Botswana had the world's highest rate of HIV infection – around one in five of the population had the virus. The average life expectancy fell from 60 to 40 years. Botswana does however have one of Africa's most progressive programmes in place to deal with the disease.

ECONOMY

In 1966, Botswana was one of Africa's poorest countries, depending on meat and live cattle for its exports. But the discovery of minerals, including coal, cobalt, copper and nickel, has helped to diversify the economy. The mining of diamonds at Orapa, started in 1971 and was the chief factor in the transformation of the economy. By 1997, Botswana had become the world's leading producer, overtaking Australia and the Democratic Republic of the Congo. Diamonds accounted for about 74% of Botswana's exports, followed by copper-nickel matte, textiles and meat products. Another major source of income comes from tourists, the majority of whom come from South Africa, which continues to have a great influence on Botswana.

The development of mining and tourism has reduced the relative importance of farming, though agriculture still employs about a fifth of the population. The most important type of farming is livestock raising, particularly cattle, which are mostly reared in the wetter east. Crops include beans, maize, millet, sorghum and vegetables.

GABORONE

Capital of Botswana, close to the border with South Africa. First settled in the 1890s, it served as the administrative headquarters of the former Bechuanaland Protectorate. In 1966 it became the capital of an independent Botswana.

Elephant searching for food in Chobe National Park

The Federative Republic of Brazil is the world's fifth largest country. Structurally, it has two main regions. In the north is the vast Amazon basin, once an inland sea and now drained by a river system that carries one-fifth of the world's running water. The largest area of river plain is in the upper part of the basin, along the frontiers with Bolivia and Peru. Downstream, the flood plain is relatively narrow.

The Brazilian Highlands make up the country's second main region and consist largely of hard crystalline rock dissected into rolling uplands. They include the heartland (Mato Grosso) and the whole western flank of the country from the bulge to the border with Uruguay. The undulating plateau of the northern highlands carries poor soils.

The typical vegetation is thorny scrub which, in the south, merges into wooded savanna. Conditions are better in the south, where rainfall is more reliable. More than 60% of the population lives in the four southern and south-eastern states, the most developed part of Brazil, though accounting only for 17% of Brazil's total area.

CLIMATE

Manaus has high temperatures all through the year. The rainfall is heavy, though the period from June to September is drier than the rest of the year. The capital, Brasília, and the city Rio de Janeiro also have tropical climates, with much more marked dry seasons than Manaus. The far south has a temperate climate. The north-eastern interior is the driest region, with an average annual rainfall of only 250 mm [10 in] in places. The rainfall is also unreliable and severe droughts are common in this region.

The Amazon basin contains the world's largest rainforests, which the Brazilians call the selvas. The forests contain an enormous variety of plant and animal species. But many species are threatened by loggers and those who wish to exploit the forests. The destruction of the forest is also ruining the lives of the last surviving groups of Amazonian Indians.

Forests grow on the north-eastern coasts, but the dry interior has large areas of thorny scrub. The south-east contains fertile farmland and large ranches.

HISTORY

The Portuguese explorer Pedro Alvarez Cabral claimed Brazil for Portugal in 1500. While Spain was occupied in western South America, the first Portuguese colonists settled in the north-east in the 1530s. They were followed by other settlers, missionaries, explorers and prospectors who gradually penetrated the country during the 17th and 18th centuries. They found many groups of Amerindians, some of whom lived semi-nomadic lives, hunting, fishing and gathering fruits, while others lived in farming villages, growing cassava and other crops.

The Portuguese enslaved many Amerindians who were used for plantation work, while others were driven into the interior. The Portuguese also introduced about 4 million African slaves, notably in the sugarcane-growing areas in the north-east. For many decades following the early settlements, Brazil was mainly a sugar-producing colony, with most plantations centred on the rich coastal plains of the north-east. These areas later produced cotton, cocoa, rice and other crops. In the south, colonists penetrated the interior in search of slaves and minerals, especially gold and diamonds. The city of Ouro Preto in Minas Gerais was built and Rio de Janeiro grew as a port for the area.

Initially little more than a group of rival provinces, Brazil began to unite in 1808, when the Portuguese royal court, transferred from Lisbon to Rio de Janeiro. The eldest son of King Joas VI of Portugal was chosen as the 'Perpetual Defender' of Brazil by a national congress. In 1822, he proclaimed the independence of the country and was chosen as the constitutional emperor with the title of Pedro I. He became increasingly unpopular and was forced to abdicate in 1831. He was succeeded by his five-year-old son, Pedro II, who officially took office in 1841. Pedro's liberal policies included the gradual abolition of slavery.

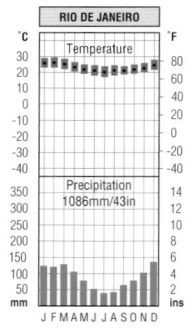

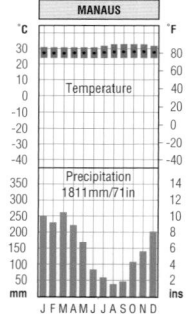

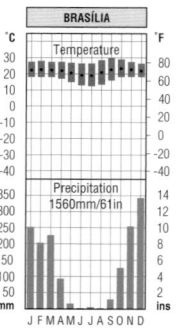

Aerial view of Rio de Janeiro, with the Brazilian Highlands in the background and the Christ the Redeemer (Cristo Redentor) statue to the fore; the statue measures 38 m (125 ft)

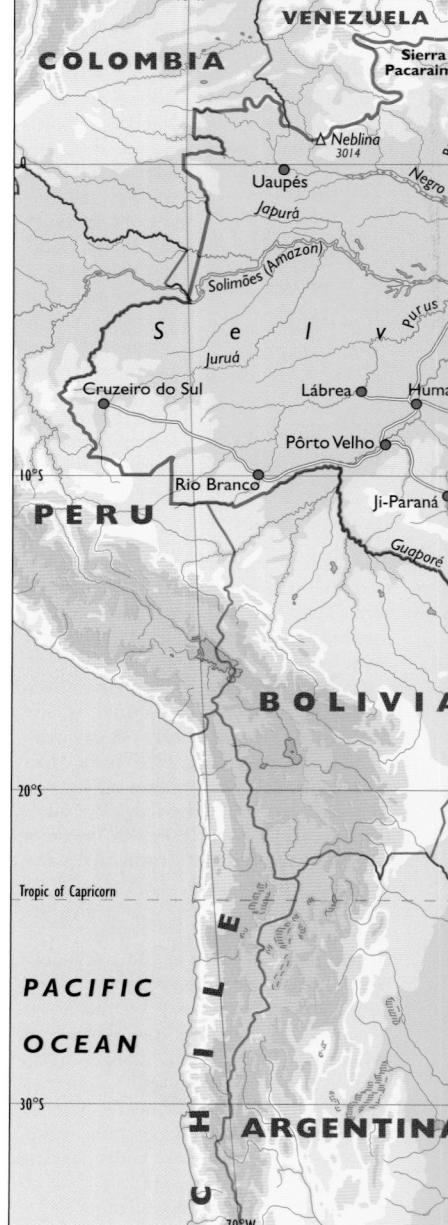

During the 19th century, São Paulo state became the centre of a huge coffee-growing industry. While the fortunes made in mining helped to develop Rio de Janeiro, profits from coffee were invested in the city of São Paulo. Immigrants from Italy and Germany settled in the south, introducing farming in the fertile valleys, in co-existence with the cattle ranchers and gauchos of the plains. The second half of the 19th century saw the development of the wild rubber industry in the Amazon basin, where the city of Manaus, with its world-famous opera house, served as a centre and market. Although Manaus lies 1,600 km [1,000 mi] from the mouth of the Amazon, rubber from the hinterland could be shipped out directly to world markets in ocean-going steamers. Brazil enjoyed a virtual monopoly of the rubber trade until the early 20th century, when Malaya began to compete, later with massive success.

A federal system was adopted for the United States of Brazil in the 1881 constitution and Brazil became a republic in 1889. Until 1930, the country experienced very strong economic expansion and prospered, but social unrest in 1930 resulted in a major revolt. From then on the country was under the control of President Getulio Vargas, who estab-lished a strong corporate state similar to that of fascist Italy, although Brazil entered World War II on the side of the Allies. Democracy, often corrupt, prevailed from 1956, 1964 and 1985. In between there were five military presidents of illiberal regimes.

POLITICS

A new constitution came into force in October 1988 – the eighth since Brazil became independent from Portugal in 1822. The constitution transferred powers from the president to the congress and paved the way for a return to democracy. In 1989, Fernando Collor de Mello was elected to cut inflation and combat corruption. But he made little progress and in 1992, with inflation soaring, his vice-president, Itamar Franco, took over as president. He served until 1994 when the Social Democrat Fernando Henrique Cardoso, a former finance minister, was elected president.

In elections in 2002, Luiz Inácio Lula da Silva, leader of the left-wing Workers' Party, was elected president. Popularly known as 'Lula', he had promised many social reforms. In office, he proved to be a pragmatist, following moderate economic policies. In 2005, his government was damaged by corruption charges.

ECONOMY

Brazil's total volume of production is one of the largest in the world, but many people, including poor farmers and residents of the *favelas* (city slums), do not share in the country's fast economic growth. Widespread poverty, together with high inflation and unemployment, cause political problems.

Industry is the most valuable activity, employing about 20% of the workforce. Brazil is among the world's top producers of bauxite, chrome, diamonds, gold, iron ore, manganese and tin. Its manufactures include aircraft, cars, chemicals, processed food, raw sugar, iron and steel, paper and textiles.

Agriculture employs 28% of workers. Coffee is a major export. Other leading products include bananas, citrus fruits, cocoa, maize, rice, soya beans and sugar cane. Brazil is the top producer of eggs, meat and milk in South America.

Forestry is a major industry, though the exploitation of the rainforests, with 1.5% to 4% of Brazil's forest being destroyed every year, is a disaster for the entire world.

Area 8,514,215 sq km [3,287,338 sq mi]
Population 184,101,000
Capital (population) Brasilia (2,016,000)
Government Federal republic
Ethnic groups White 55%, Mulatto 38%, Black 6%, others 1%
Languages Portuguese (official)
Religions Roman Catholic 80%
Currency Real = 100 centavos
Website www.turismo.gov.br

BRASÍLIA

Capital city, located in west central Brazil. Although the city was originally planned in 1891, building did not start until 1956. The city was laid out in the shape of an aircraft, and Oscar Niemeyer designed the modernist public buildings. It was inaugurated as the capital in 1960, in order to develop Brazil's interior.

This flag, first adopted in 1878, uses the colours associated with the Slav people. The national emblem, incorporating a lion – a symbol of Bulgaria since the 14th century – was first added to the flag in 1947. It is now added only for official government occasions.

Area 110,912 sq km [42,823 sq mi]
Population 7,518,000
Capital (population) Sofia (1,139,000)
Government Multiparty republic
Ethnic groups Bulgarian 84%, Turkish 9%, Gypsy 5%, Macedonian, Armenian, others
Languages Bulgarian (official), Turkish
Religions Bulgarian Orthodox 83%, Islam 12%, Roman Catholic 2%, others
Currency Lev = 100 stotinki
Website www.government.bg/English

BALKAN MOUNTAINS

Major mountain range of the Balkan Peninsula, extending from eastern Serbia through central Bulgaria to the Black Sea. The range is a continuation of the Carpathian Mountains. It is rich in minerals and forms a climatic barrier for the interior. The highest pass is Shipka Pass, c. 1,270 m [4,166 ft], and the highest peak is Botev, 2,375 m [7,793 ft].

The Republic of Bulgaria is a country in the Balkan Peninsula, facing the Black Sea in the east. There are two main lowland regions. The Danubian lowlands in the north consists of a plateau that descends to the Danube, which forms much of the boundary with Romania. The other lowland region is the warmer valley of the River Maritsa, where cotton, fruits, grains, rice, tobacco and vines are grown.

Separating the two lowland areas are the Balkan Mountains (Stara Planina), rising to heights of over 2,000 m [6,500 ft]. North of the capital Sofia (Sofiya), the Balkan Mountains contain rich mineral veins of iron and non-ferrous metals.

In south-facing valleys overlooking the Maritsa Plain, plums, tobacco and vines are grown. A feature of this area is Kazanluk, from which attar of roses is exported worldwide to the cosmetics industry. South and west of the Maritsa Valley are the Rhodope (or Rhodopi) Mountains, which contain lead, zinc and copper ores.

CLIMATE

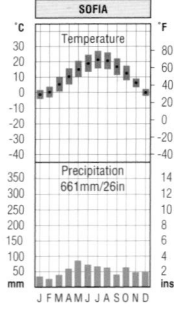

The average temperature in Sofia is 15°-21° C (60-70° F) in the summer and between -1° and 5° C (30°-40° F) in the winter. Other regions experience more extreme ranges of temperature but winters are rarely severe. Rainfall is moderate all through the year.

HISTORY

Most of the Bulgarian people are descendants of Slavs and nomadic Bulgar tribes who arrived from the east in the 6th and 7th centuries. A powerful Bulgar kingdom was set up in 681, but the country became part of the Byzantine Empire in the 11th century.

Ottoman Turks ruled Bulgaria from 1396 and ethnic Turks still form a sizeable minority in the country. In 1879, Bulgaria became a monarchy, and in 1908 became fully independent. Bulgaria was an ally of Germany in World War I (1914–18) and again in World War II (1939–45). In 1944, Soviet troops invaded Bulgaria. After the war, the monarchy was abolished and the country became a Communist ally of the Soviet Union.

SOFIA (SOFIJA)

Capital of Bulgaria and Sofia province, in west central Bulgaria, at the foot of the Vitosha Mountains. Known for its hot mineral springs, Sofia was founded by the Romans in the 2nd century ad. From 1018 to 1185, it was ruled by the Byzantine Empire (as Triaditsa). Sofia passed to the second Bulgarian Empire (1186–1382), and then to the Ottoman Empire (1382–1878). In 1877, Sofia was captured by Russia and chosen as the capital of Bulgaria by the Congress of Berlin. Industries include steel, machinery, textiles, rubber, chemicals, metallurgy, leather goods, food processing.

POLITICS

In the period after World War II, and especially under President Zhikov from 1954, Bulgaria became all too dependent on the Soviet Union. In 1990, the Communist Party held on to power under increasing pressure by ousting Zhikov, renouncing its leading role in the nation's affairs and changing its name to the Socialist Party, before winning the first free elections since the war, albeit unconvincingly and against confused opposition. With improved organization, the Union of Democratic Forces defeated the old guard in the following year and began the unenviable task of making the transition to a free-market economy. Subsequent governments faced numerous problems, including inflation, food shortages, rising unemployment, strikes, a large foreign debt, a declining manufacturing industry, increased prices for raw materials, and a potential drop in the expanding tourist industry. In 2001, the former king, Siméon Saxe-Coburg-Gotha, who had left Bulgaria in 1948 when the monarchy was abolished, became prime minister. He left office when his party lost the elections in 2005.

ECONOMY

According to the World Bank, Bulgaria in the 1990s was a 'lower-middle-income' developing country. Bulgaria has some deposits of minerals, including brown coal, manganese and iron ore. Manufacturing is the leading economic activity, though problems arose in the early 1990s, because much industrial technology was outdated. The main products are chemicals, processed foods, metal products, machinery and textiles. Manufactures are the leading exports. Bulgaria trades mainly with countries in Eastern Europe.

Wheat and maize are the chief crops of Bulgaria. Fruit, oilseeds, tobacco and vegetables are also important. Livestock farming, particularly the rearing of dairy and beef cattle, sheep and pigs, is an important source of revenue.

Rila Monastery, founded in 10th century it is listed as a UNESCO World Heritage Site

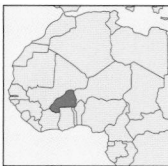

AFRICA

Burkina Faso 43

This flag was adopted in 1984, when Upper Volta was renamed Burkino Faso.
The red, green and yellow colours used on this flag symbolize the desire for African unity.
This is because they are used on the flag of Ethiopia, Africa's oldest independent country.

The Democratic People's Republic of Burkina Faso is a landlocked country, a little larger than the United Kingdom, in West Africa. But Burkina Faso has only one-sixth of the population of the UK. Burkina Faso consists of a plateau, between about 300 m and 700 m [650–2,300 ft] above sea level. The plateau is cut by several rivers. Most of the rivers flow south into Ghana or east into the River Niger. During droughts, some of the rivers stop flowing, becoming marshes.

The northern part of the country is covered by savanna, consisting of grassland with stunted trees and shrubs. It is part of a region called the Sahel, where the land merges into the Sahara Desert. Overgrazing of the land and deforestation are common problems in the Sahel, causing desertification in many areas of the country.

Woodlands border the rivers and parts of the south-east region are swampy. The south-east contains the 'W' National Park, which Burkina Faso shares with Benin and Niger, and the Arly Park. A third wildlife area is the Po Park situated south of Ouagadougou.

Area 274,000 sq km [105,791 sq mi]
Population 13,575,000
Capital (population) Ouagadougou (637,000)
Government Multiparty republic
Ethnic groups Mossi 40%, Gurunsi, Senufo, Lobi, Bobo, Mande, Fulani
Languages French (official), Mossi, Fulani
Religions Islam 50%, traditional beliefs 40%, Christianity 10%
Currency CFA franc = 100 centimes
Website www.burkinaembassy-usa.org

The French conquered the Mossi capital of Ouagadougou in 1897 and they made the area a protectorate. In 1919, the area became a French colony called Upper Volta. In 1947, Upper Volta gained semi-autonomy within the French Union, and in 1958 became an autonomous republic within the French Community.

CLIMATE

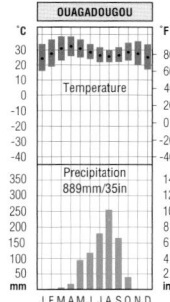

Burkina Faso has three main seasons. From October to February, it is relatively cool and dry. From March to April, it is hot and dry, while it is hot and humid from May to September.

HISTORY

The people of Burkina Faso are divided into two main groups. The Voltaic group includes the Mossi, who form the largest single group, and the Bobo. The other main group is the Mande family. Burkina Faso also contains some Fulani herders and Hausa traders, who are related to the people of northern Nigeria. In early times, the ethnic groups in Burkina Faso were divided into kingdoms and chiefdoms. The leading kingdom, which was ruled by an absolute monarch called the Moro Naba, was that of the Mossi. It has existed since the 13th century. The semi-autonomous states fiercely resisted domination by the larger Mali and Songhai Empires.

POLITICS

Upper Volta achieved independence in 1960 and adopted a strong presidential form of government. Persistent drought and austerity measures led to a military coup in 1966. Civilian rule partially returned in 1970 but the military, led by Sangoule Lamizana, regained power in 1974. Lamizana became president after elections in 1978, but was overthrown in 1980. Parliament and the constitution were suspended and a series of military regimes ensued. In 1983 Thomas Sankara gained power in a bloody coup.

In 1984, as a symbolic break from the country's colonial past, Sankara changed Upper Volta's name to Burkina Faso 'land of the incorruptible'. In 1987, Sankara was assassinated and Captain Blaise Campaore seized power. Campaore became president in unopposed elections in 1991. Elections in 1992 were the first multiparty ballots since 1978. In 1998 elections, Campaore gained a landslide victory. More than 7% of the population have HIV, the second highest rate of infection in Africa (after Uganda).

ECONOMY

Burkina Faso is one of the world's 20 poorest countries and has become extremely dependent on foreign aid. Approximately 90% of the people earn their living by farming or by raising livestock. Grazing land covers around 37% of the land and farmland covers around 10%.

Most of Burkina Faso is dry with thin soils. The country's main food crops are beans, maize, millet, rice and sorghum. Cotton, groundnuts and shea nuts, whose seeds produce a fat used to make cooking oil and soap, are grown for sale abroad. Livestock is also important.

The country has few resources and manufacturing is on a small scale. There are deposits of manganese, zinc, lead and nickel in the north of the country, but exploitation awaits improvements to the transport system. Many young men work abroad in Ghana and Ivory Coast. The money they send to their families is important to the country's economy.

OUAGADOUGOU

Capital city lying in the centre of Burkina Faso. Ouagadougou was founded in the late 11th century as capital of the Mossi empire, it remained the centre of Mossi power until captured by the French in 1896. Industries include handicrafts, textiles, food processing, groundnuts, vegetable oil.

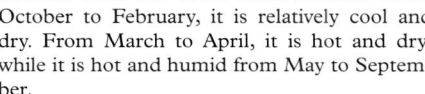

Families of alluvial gold diggers work in precarious conditions on the Yako site, about 100 km away from Ouagadougou

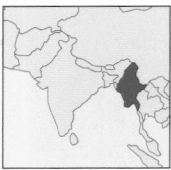

The colours on the flag were adopted in 1948 when Burma gained independence from Britain. The socialist symbol, added in 1974, includes a ring of 14 stars representing the country's 14 states. The gearwheel represents industry, the rice plant agriculture.

Area 676,578 sq km [261,227 sq mi]
Population 42,720,000
Capital (population) Rangoon (2,513,000)
Government Military regime
Ethnic groups Burman 68%, Shan 9%, Karen 7%, Rakhine 4%, Chinese, Indian, Mon
Languages Burmese (official), minority ethnic groups have their own languages
Religions Buddhism 89%, Christianity, Islam
Currency Kyat = 100 pyas
Website www.burmaproject.org

The Union of Burma is now officially known as the Union of Myanmar; its name was changed in 1989. Mountains border the country in the east and west, with the highest mountains in the north. Burma's highest mountain is Hkakabo Razi, which is 5,881 m [19,294 ft] high. Between these ranges is central Burma, which contains the fertile valleys of the Irrawaddy and Sittang rivers. The Irrawaddy delta on the Bay of Bengal is one of the world's leading rice-growing areas. Burma also includes the long Tenasserim coast in the south-east.

CLIMATE

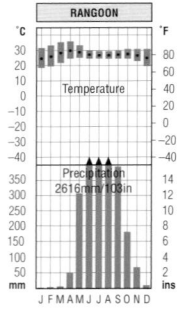

Burma has a tropical monsoon climate. There are three seasons. The rainy season runs from late May to mid-October. A cool, dry season follows, between late October and the middle part of February. The hot season lasts from late February to mid-May, though temperatures remain high during the humid rainy season.

HISTORY

Conflict between the Burmans and Mons dominated Burma's early history. In 1044 the Burman King Anawratha unified the Irrawaddy delta region. In 1287 Kublai

RANGOON (YANGON)

Capital of Burma (Myanmar), a seaport on the Rangoon (Yangon) River. The name Yangon means 'end of strife', Rangoon is the anglicized version. The site of a Buddhist shrine, it became capital in 1886, when the British annexed the country. Heavy fighting took place there in World War II between British and Japanese forces. It is the country's chief trade centre.

Khan conquered the Burman capital, Pagan. Burma was divided: the Shan controlled north Burma, while the resurgent Mons held the south. In the 16th century, the Burmans subjugated the Shan. In 1758 Alaungapaya reunified Burma, defeating the Mons kingdom and establishing the Konbaung dynasty.

Wars with British India marked much of the 19th century. The first war in 1824 resulted in the British gaining the coastal regions of Tenasserim and Arakan. The second war in 1852 saw the British gain control of the Irrawaddy delta. British India annexed Burma in the third war of 1885. In 1937 Burma gained limited self-government. Helped by the Burmese Independent Army, led by Aung San, Japan conquered the country in 1942. The installation of a puppet regime led Aung San to form a resistance movement. In 1947 Aung San was murdered. Burma achieved independence in 1948.

POLITICS

The socialist AFPFL government, led by U Nu, faced secessionist revolts by communists and Karen tribesmen. In 1958 U Nu invited General Ne Win to re-establish order. Civilian rule returned in 1960, but in 1962 Ne Win mounted a successful coup. His military dictatorship faced mass insurgency. In 1974 Ne Win became president. Mass demonstrations forced Ne Win to resign in 1988, but the military retained power under the guise of the State Law and Order Restoration Council (SLORC), led by General Saw Muang. In 1989 the country's name changed to Myanmar. The National League for Democracy (NLD), led by Aung San Suu Kyi, won elections in 1990, but SLORC annulled the result and placed Aung San Suu Kyi under house arrest. In 1997 SLORC became the State Peace and Development Council (SPDC). In 1998, NLD calls for the reconvening of Parliament led to mass detention of political opponents by the SPDC. In 2002 the SPDC released Aung San Suu Kyi from house arrest. She was arrested again in 2003.

In 2004 a United Nations report criticized the regime for holding more than 1,800 political detainees and for its failure to release opposition leader Aung San Suu Kyi from house arrest.

In November 2005 Burma announced that it was moving the seat of government to Pyinmana 400 km (250 mi) north of Rangoon, with immediate effect. Officials would not commit to whether this new site would become the capital with officials saying that everything would be made public at the appropriate time. The reason given for the move was that Pyinmana is in the centre of the country

ECONOMY

Agriculture is the main activity, employing 66% of the workforce. The chief crop is rice. Groundnuts, maize, plantains, pulses, seed cotton, sesame seeds and sugar cane are also produced. Forestry is important and teak is a major product. Fish and shellfish are another industry. The varied natural resources are mostly underdeveloped, but it is famous for its precious stones, especially rubies. Burma is almost self-sufficient in oil and natural gas.

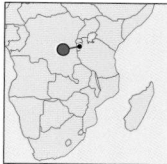

This flag was adopted in 1967 when Burundi became a republic. It has three red stars rimmed in green, symbolizing the nation's motto of 'Unité, Travail, Progrès'. The green represents hope for the future, the red the struggle for independence, and the white the desire for peace.

The Republic of Burundi is a small country in east-central Africa. A section of the Great Rift Valley, lies in the west. It contains part of Lake Tanganyika, whose shoreline is 772 m [2,533 ft] above sea level. East of the Rift Valley is a mountain zone, rising to 2,670 metres [8,760 ft]. The land descends to the east in a series of steppe-like plateaux. Burundi forms part of the Nile-Congo watershed and contains the headwaters of the River Kagera, the most remote source of the Nile.

Grassland covers much of Burundi, because much of the original forest has been cleared by farming and overgrazing. New forests are now being planted to halt the loss of soil fertility caused by erosion.

CLIMATE

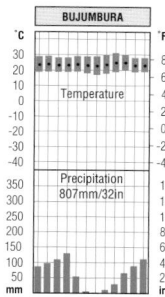

Bujumbura has an average annual temperature of 23°C [73°F]. June to August and December-January are dry, but the rest of the year rainy. The mountains and the central plateaux are distinctly cooler and wetter than the Rift Valley floor, but the rainfall decreases to the east.

HISTORY

The first known inhabitants of the area were the Twa, a pygmy group of hunting and gathering people, who now make up just 1% of the population. Around 1,000 years ago, a Bantu-speaking, iron-using farming people from the west, the Hutu, began to settle, pushing the Twa into remote areas. A third group, the cattle-owning Tutsi from the north-east, arrived around 600 years ago. They gradually took control of the area and, although in the minority, formed the ruling class. The Tutsi created a feudal state, making the Hutu serfs. The explorers Richard Burton and John Hanning Speke visited the area in 1858 in their quest to find the source of the Nile.

A powerful Tutsi kingdom under Mwami (king) Rugamba, that developed in the late 18th century, had broken up by the 1880s. Germany conquered what are now Burundi and Rwanda, in the late 1890s. The area, called Ruanda-Urundi, became part of German East Africa. But after Germany's defeat in World War I, Belgium took control.

In 1961, the people of Urundi voted to become a monarchy under Mwami Mwambutsa IV, who had ruled since 1915, while the people of Ruanda voted to become a republic.

POLITICS

The two territories finally became fully independent as Burundi and Rwanda on 1 July 1962. Since then, Burundi has suffered great conflict caused by ethnic rivalry between the Hutu majority and the Tutsi. Around 300,000 people have perished with many thousands displaced or as refugees. In 1965, Mwambutsa refused to appoint a Hutu prime minis-

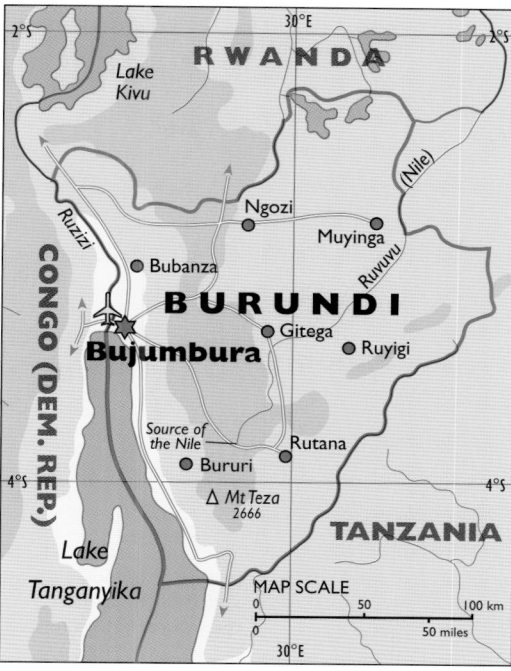

Area 27,834 sq km [10,747 sq mi]
Population 6,231,000
Capital (population) Bujumbura (235,000)
Government Republic
Ethnic groups Hutu 85%, Tutsi 14%, Twa (Pygmy)
Languages French, Kirundi (both official)
Religions Roman Catholic 62%, traditional beliefs 23%, Islam 10%, Protestant 5%
Currency Burundi franc = 100 centimes
Website www.burundi-embassy-berlin.com

ter, although the Hutu were in the majority. An attempted coup was brutally put down. In 1966, Mwambutsa was deposed by his son who became Mwami Ntare V, but Tutsi prime minister Michel Micombero deposed Ntare and declared Burundi to be a republic, with himself as president.

Between 1966 and 1972, most Hutu and some Tutsi were removed from high office. This culminated in a rebellion, when between 100,000 and 200,000 mostly Hutu were killed. In 1976, Jean-Baptiste Bagaza, a Tutsi, deposed Micombero. In 1981, Burundi became a one-party state, but Bagaza was deposed in 1987 by a coup led by Pierre Buyoya. Another uprising in 1988 led to the slaughter of thousands of Hutus.

In 1992, a new constitution gave the country a multiparty system and, in 1993, Melchior Ndadaye, a Hutu, beat Buyoya in presidential elections. But supporters of Bagaza assassinated Ndadaye. In 1994, the new president, Cyprien Ntaryamira, a Hutu, was killed in a plane crash, together with the Rwandan president, causing more ethnic violence. In 1996, Buyoya staged another coup and suspended the constitution. In 1999, peace talks began which led, in 2001, to the setting up of a transitional, power-sharing government. However, some Hutu rebel groups refused to sign the cease-fire. In 2003, Domitien Ndayizeye succeeded Buyoya as president, under the power-sharing agreement. In 2004, the disarming of rebels and soldiers began. In 2005, the people voted in favour of the new power-sharing constitution and hopes were high of an end to the conflict.

ECONOMY

Burundi is one of the world's poorest countries. 94% of the people depend on farming, mainly at subsistence level. The main food crops are bananas, beans, cassava, maize and sweet potatoes. Cattle, goats and sheep are raised and fish is important.

The economy depends on coffee and tea, which account for 90% of foreign exchange earnings, and cotton.

BUJUMBURA

Capital and chief port of Burundi, east -central Africa, at the north-east end of Lake Tanganyika. Founded in 1899 as part of German East Africa, it was the capital of Ruanda-Urundi after World War I and remained capital of Burundi upon independence in 1962.

In-patients prepare food *at the state hospital in Buhiga, Burundi, which is supported by Médecins Sans Frontières*

Red is the traditional colour of Cambodia. The blue symbolizes the water resources that are so important to the people, three-quarters of whom depend on farming for a living. The silhouette is the historic temple at Angkor Wat.

Area 181,035 sq km [69,898 sq mi]
Population 13,363,000
Capital (population) Phnom Penh (1,000,000)
Government Constitutional monarchy
Ethnic groups Khmer 90%, Vietnamese 5%, Chinese 1%, others
Languages Khmer (official), French, English
Religions Buddhism 95%, others 5%
Currency Riel = 100 sen
Website www.cambodia.gov.kh

The Kingdom of Cambodia is a country in South-east Asia. Low mountains border the country except in the south-east. But most of Cambodia consists of plains drained by the River Mekong, which enters Cambodia from Laos in the north and exits through Vietnam in the south-east. The north-west contains Tonlé Sap (or Great Lake). In the dry season, this lake drains into the River Mekong. But in the wet season, the level of the Mekong rises and water flows in the opposite direction from the river into Tonlé Sap – the lake then becomes the largest freshwater lake in Asia.

CLIMATE

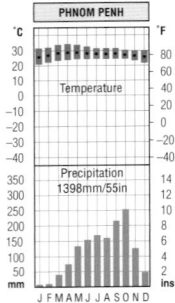

Cambodia has a tropical monsoon climate, with high temperatures all through the year. The dry season, when winds blow from the north or north-east, runs from November to April. During the rainy season, from May to October, moist winds blow from the south or south-east. The high humidity and heat often make conditions unpleasant. The rainfall is heaviest near the coast, and rather lower inland.

HISTORY

From 802 to 1431,.the Hindu-Buddhist Khmer people ruled a great empire. Its zenith came in the reign of Suryavarman II (1113–50), who built the great funerary temple of Angkor Wat. Together with Angkor Thom, the Angkor site contains the world's largest group of religious buildings. The wealth of the kingdom rested on fish from the lake and rice from the flooded lowlands, for which an extensive system of irrigation channels and strong reservoirs was developed. Thai forces captured Angkor in 1431 and forests covered the site. Following its rediscovery in 1860, it has been gradually restored and is now a major tourist attraction.

France ruled the country from 1863 as part of Indo-China until it achieved independence in 1954. In a short period of stability during the late 1950s and 1960s, the country developed its small-scale agricultural resources and rubber plantations. It remained predominantly rural, but achieved self-sufficiency in food, with some exports.

PHNOM PENH (PHNUM PÉNH)

Capital of Cambodia, in the south of the country, a port at the confluence of the rivers Mekong and Tonlé Sap. Founded in the 14th century, the city was the capital of the Khmers after 1434. In 1865, it became the capital of Cambodia. Occupied by the Japanese during World War II, it was extensively damaged during the Cambodian civil war. After the Khmer Rouge took power in 1975, the population was drastically reduced when many of its inhabitants were forcibly removed to work in the countryside. Industries include rice milling, brewing, distilling.

POLITICS

In 1969, US planes bombed North Vietnamese targets in Cambodia. In 1970, King Norodom Sihanouk was overthrown and Cambodia became a republic. Under assault from South Vietnamese troops, the Communist Vietnamese withdrew deep into Cambodia. US raids ended in 1973, but fighting continued as Cambodia's Communists in the Khmer Rouge fought against the government. The Khmer Rouge, led by Pol Pot, were victorious in 1975. They began a reign of terror, murdering government officials and educated people. Up to 2 million people were estimated to have been killed. After the overthrow of Pol Pot by Vietnamese forces in 1979, civil war raged between the puppet government of the People's Republic of Kampuchea (Cambodia) and the US-backed government of Democratic Kampuchea, a coalition of Prince Sihanouk, the Khmer Liberation Front, and the Khmer Rouge, who, from 1982, claimed to have abandoned their Communist ideology.

The Silver Pagoda, *Phnom Penh, lies inside the Royal Palace complex. It draws its name from the over 5000 silver tiles which cover the floor*

Devastated by war and denied almost any aid, Cambodia continued to decline. It was only the withdrawal of Vietnamese troops in 1989, sparking fear of a Khmer Rouge revival, that forced a settlement. In October 1991, a UN-brokered peace plan for elections in 1993 was accepted by all parties. A new constitution was adopted in September 1993, restoring democracy and the monarchy. Sihanouk again became king. However, the Khmer Rouge continued hostilities and were banned in 1994. In 1997, Hu Sen, the second prime minister, engineered a coup against Prince Norodom Ranariddh (Sihanouk's son), the first prime minister Ranariddh went into exile but returned in 1998. Elections in 1998 resulted in victory for Hu Sen, but Ranariddh alleged electoral fraud. A coalition government was formed in December 1998, with Hu Sen as prime minister. In 2001, the government set up a court to try leaders of the Khmer Rouge. In 2004, Sihanouk abdicated due to ill health and was succeeded by his son Prince Norodom Sihamoni.

ECONOMY

Cambodia is a poor country whose economy has been wrecked by war. By 1986, it was only able to supply 80% of its needs. Recovery has been slow. Farming is the main activity and rice, rubber and maize important. Tourism is increasing – the impressive Angkor temples are a major attraction.

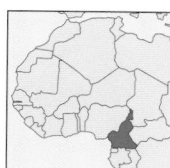

Cameroon uses the colours that appear on the flag of Ethiopia, Africa's oldest independent nation. These colours symbolize African unity. The flag is based on the tricolour adopted in 1957. The design with the yellow liberty star dates from 1975.

The Republic of Cameroon in West Africa got its name from the Portuguese word *camarões*, or prawns. This name was used by Portuguese explorers who fished for prawns along the coast. Behind the narrow coastal plains on the Gulf of Guinea, the land rises to a series of plateaux. In the north, the land slopes down towards the Lake Chad (Tchad) basin. The mountain region in the south-west of the country includes Mount Cameroon, a volcano which erupts from time to time. The vegetation varies greatly from north to south. The deserts in the north merge into dry and moist savanna in central Cameroon, with dense tropical rainforests in the humid south.

YAOUNDÉ

Capital of Cameroon, West Africa. Located in beautiful hills on the edge of dense jungle, German traders founded it in 1888. During World War I, it was occupied by Belgian troops, and later acted as capital (1921–60) of French Cameroon. Since independence, it has grown rapidly as a financial and administrative centre with strong Western influences. It is the site of the University of Cameroon (1962). The city also serves as a market for the surrounding region, notably in coffee, cacao, and sugar.

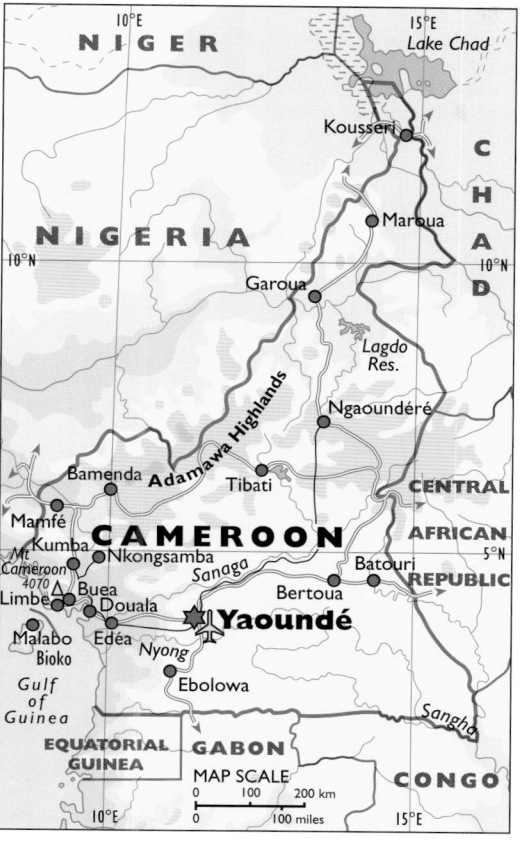

Area 475,442 sq km [183,568 sq mi]
Population 16,064,000
Capital (population) Yaoundé (649,000)
Government Multiparty republic
Ethnic groups Cameroon Highlanders 31%, Bantu 27%, Kirdi 11%, Fulani 10%, others
Languages French and English (both official), many others
Religions Christianity 40%, traditional beliefs 40%, Islam 20%
Currency CFA franc = 100 centimes
Website www.camnet.cm

English-speaking people, Cameroon became the 52nd member of the Commonwealth. In 2002, the International Court of Justice gave Cameroon sovreignty over the disputed oil-rich Bakassi peninsula. But Nigeria failed to reach the deadline for the handover of the area in 2004.

Presidential elections in 2004 saw Paul Biya win a new seven-year term with more than 70% of the vote. The result was accepted by Commonwealth observers, but opposition parties alleged widespread fraud.

ECONOMY

Like most countries in tropical Africa, Cameroon's economy is based on agriculture, which employs 73% of the people. The chief food crops include cassava, maize, millet, sweet potatoes and yams.

Cameroon is fortunate in having some oil, the country's chief export, and bauxite. Although Cameroon has few manufacturing and processing industries, its mineral exports and its self-sufficiency in food production make it one of the wealthier countries in tropical Africa. Another important industry is forestry, ranking second among the exports, after oil. Other exports are cocoa, coffee, aluminium and cotton.

CLIMATE

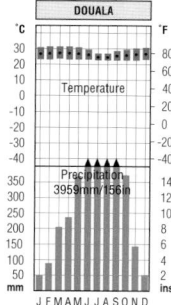

The rainfall is heavy, especially in the highlands. The rainiest months near the coast are from June to September. The rainfall decreases to the north and the far north has a hot, dry climate. Temperatures are high on the coast, whereas the inland plateaux are cooler.

HISTORY

Among the early inhabitants of Cameroon were groups of Bantu-speaking people. (There are now more than 160 ethnic groups, each with their own language.) In the late 15th century, Portuguese explorers, who were seeking a sea route to Asia around Africa, reached the Cameroon coast. From the 17th century, southern Cameroon was a centre of the slave trade, but slavery was ended in the early 19th century. In 1884, the area became a German protectorate. Germany lost Cameroon during World War I (1914–18). The country was then divided into two parts, one ruled by Britain and the other by France.

POLITICS

In 1960, French Cameroon became the independent Cameroon Republic. In 1961, after a vote in British Cameroon, part of the territory joined the Cameroon Republic to become the Federal Republic of Cameroon. The other part joined Nigeria. In 1972, Cameroon became a unitary state called the United Republic of Cameroon. It adopted the name Republic of Cameroon in 1984, but the country had two official languages. Opposition parties were legalized in 1992, and Paul Biya was elected president in 1993 and 1997. In 1995, partly to placate the

Woman cleaning fish *in Rey Bouba, home of the Mond people, Province du Nord region; the region covers much of the northern half of the country*

Canada's flag, with its simple 11-pointed maple leaf emblem, was adopted in 1965 after many attempts to find an acceptable design. The old flag, used from 1892, was the British Red Ensign, but this flag became unpopular with Canada's French community.

A vast confederation of ten provinces and three territories, Canada is the world's second largest country after Russia, with an even longer coastline – about 250,000 km [155,000 mi]. It is sparsely populated because it contains vast areas of virtually unoccupied mountains, cold forests, tundra and polar desert in the north and west. About 80% of the population of Canada lives within about 300 km [186 mi] of the southern border.

Forests of cedars, hemlocks and other trees grow on the western mountains, with firs and spruces at the higher levels. The mountain forests provide habitats for bears, deer and mountain lions, while the sure-footed Rocky Mountain goats and bighorn sheep roam above the tree line (the upper limit of tree growth).

The interior plains were once grassy prairies. While the drier areas are still used for grazing cattle, the wetter areas are used largely for growing wheat and other cereals. North of the prairies are the boreal forests which, in turn merge into the treeless tundra and Arctic wastelands in the far north. The lowlands in south-eastern Canada contain forests of deciduous trees, such as beech, hickory, oak and walnut.

fall of 250 mm to 500 mm [10–20 in]. The rainfall in south-eastern Canada ranges from around 800 mm [31 in] in southern Ontario to about 1,500 mm [59 in] on the coasts of Newfoundland and Nova Scotia. Heavy snow falls in eastern Canada in winter.

HISTORY

Canada's first people, ancestors of the Native Americans, arrived in North America from Asia around 40,000 years ago. Later arrivals were the Inuit (Eskimos), who also came from Asia. Norse voyagers and fishermen were probably the first to visit Canada, but John Cabot's later discovery of North America in 1497 led to the race to annex lands and wealth, with France and Britain the main contenders.

The creation of the British Commonwealth in 1931 made Canada a sovereign nation under the crown. Canada is now a constitutional monarchy. Under the Constitution Act of 1982, Queen Elizabeth II is head of state and a symbol of the close ties between Canada and Britain. The British monarch is represented by an appointed governor-general, but the country is ruled by a prime minister, and an elected, two-chamber parliament.

CLIMATE

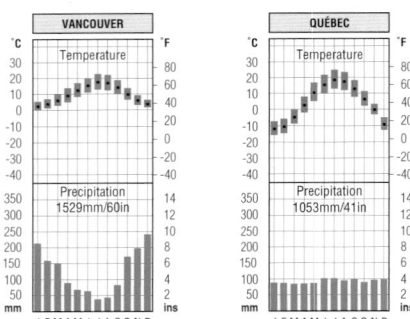

Canada has a cold climate. In winter, temperatures fall below freezing point throughout most of the country. But the south-western coast has a relatively mild climate. Along the Arctic Circle, the temperatures are, on average, below freezing for seven months a year. By contrast, hot winds from the Gulf of Mexico warm southern Ontario and the St Lawrence River lowlands in summer. As a result, southern Ontario has a frost-free season of nearly six months.

The coasts of British Columbia are wet, with an average annual rainfall of more than 2,500 mm [98 in] in places. The prairies however are arid or semi-arid, with an average annual rain-

Area 9,970,610 sq km [3,849,653 sq mi]
Population 32,508,000
Capital (population) Ottawa (774,000)
Government Federal multiparty constitutional monarchy
Ethnic groups British origin 28%, French origin 23%, other European 15%, Amerindian/Inuit 2%, others
Languages English and French (both official)
Religions Roman Catholic 46%, Protestant 36%, Judaism, Islam, Hinduism
Currency Canadian dollar = 100 cents
Website http://canada.gc.ca

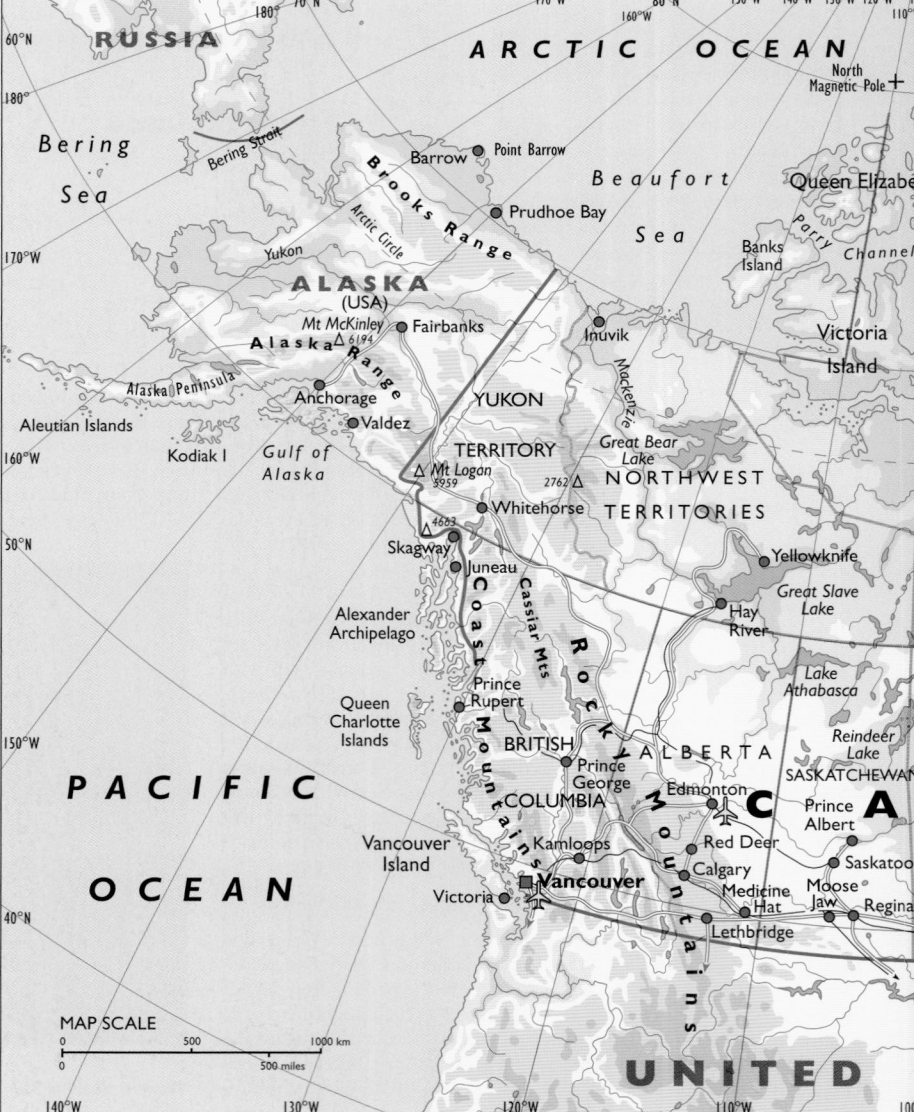

POLITICS

Canada combines the cabinet system with a federal form of government, with each province having its own government. The federal government can reject any law passed by a provincial legislature, though this seldom happens in practice. The territories are self-governing, but the federal government plays a large part in their administration.

Canada and the United States of America have the largest bilateral trade flow in the world. Economic co-operation was further enhanced in 1993 when Canada, the United States and Mexico set up NAFTA (North American Free Trade Agreement).

A constant problem facing those who want to maintain the unity of Canada is the persistence of French culture in Québec, which has fuelled a separatist movement seeking to turn the province into an independent French-speaking republic. More than two-thirds of the population of Québec are French speakers. In 1994, the people of Québec voted the separatist Parti Québécois into provincial office. The incoming prime minister announced that independence for Québec would be the subject of a referendum in 1995. In that referendum, 49.4% voted 'Yes' (for separation) while 50.5% voted 'No'.

Provincial elections in 1998 resulted in another victory for the Parti Québécois. But while the separatist party won 75 out of the 125 seats in the provincial assembly, it won only 43% of the popular vote, compared with 44% for the anti-secessionist Liberal Party and 12% for the floating

Toronto City Hall, *designed by Finnish architect Viljo Revell, it opened in 1965*

Action Démocratique de Québec. Also significant was a ruling by Canada's highest court that, under Canadian law, Québec does not have the right to secede unilaterally. The court ruled that, should a clear majority of the people in the province vote by 'a clear majority' to a 'clear question' in favour of independence, the federal government and the other provinces would have to negotiate Québec's secession.

Other problems involve the rights of the aboriginal Native Americans and the Inuit, who together numbered about 470,000 in 1991. In 1999, a new Inuit territory was created. Called Nunavut, it is made up of 64% of the former North-west Territories, and covers 2,201,400 sq km [649,965 sq mi]. The population in 1991 was about 25,000, 85% of whom were Inuit. Nunavut, whose capital is Iqaluit (formerly Frobisher Bay), will depend on future aid, but its mineral reserves and the prospects of an ecotourist industry hold out promise for the future.

ECONOMY

Canada is a highly developed and prosperous country. Although farmland covers only 8% of the country, Canadian farms are highly productive. Canada is one of the world's leading producers of barley, wheat, meat and milk. Forestry and fishing are other important industries. It is rich in natural resources, especially oil and natural gas. Canada exports minerals, including copper, gold, iron ore, uranium and zinc. Manufacturing is important, mainly in the cities where 79% of the population lives. Canada processes farm and mineral products. It also produces cars, chemicals, electronic goods, machinery, paper and timber products.

Tourism is an important source of income with both winter and summer popular tourist seasons.

OTTAWA

Capital of Canada, in south-east Ontario, on the Ottawa River and the Rideau Canal. Founded in 1826 as Bytown, it acquired its present name in 1854. Queen Victoria chose it as capital of the United Provinces in 1858, and in 1867 it became the national capital of the Dominion of Canada. Industries include glass-making, printing, publishing, sawmilling, pulp-making, clocks and watches.

ANGUILLA

Most northerly of the Leeward Islands. Settled in the 17th century by English colonists, it became part of the St Kitts-Nevis-Anguilla group. Declared independent in 1967, it re-adopted British colonial status in 1980, and is now a self-governing dependency. The economy of the flat, coral island is based on fishing and tourism.

Area 96 sq km [37 sq mi]
Population 13,000
Capital The Valley (1,169)
Government Overseas territory of the UK
Ethnic groups Black 90%, Mixed 5%, White 3%
Languages English
Religions Anglican 29%, Methodist 24%, Protestant 30%, Roman Catholic 6%
Currency East Caribbean dollar = 100 cents
Website www.anguilla-vacation.com

ANTIGUA & BARBUDA

Part of the Lesser Antilles in the Leeward Islands. Antigua is atypical of the Leeward Islands as it has no rivers or forests. Barbuda, by contrast, is a wooded, low coral atoll. Only 1,400 people live on the game reserve island of Barbuda, where lobster fishing is the main occupation, and none on the rocky island of Redondo. Antigua and Barbuda gained internal self-government in 1967, and independence in 1981. The islands are dependent on tourism.

Area 442 sq km [171 sq mi]
Population 68,000
Capital St John's (22,634)
Government Constitutional monarchy
Ethnic groups Black, British, others
Languages English, Local dialects
Religions Christian
Currency East Caribbean dollar = 100 cents
Website www.antigua-barbuda.org

ARUBA

Dutch island in the Caribbean, off the coast of north-west Venezuela. First inhabited by Caquetios Indians from the Arawak tribe. It was part of the Netherlands Antilles until 1986. Independence was revoked in 1990, at Aruba's request, and it is now an autonomous part of the Netherlands. Oil refining, phosphates and tourism are the key earners.

Area 193 sq km [75 sq mi]
Population 71,000
Capital Oranjestad (26,355)
Government Parliamentary democracy
Ethnic groups Mixed White/Caribbean Amerindian 80%
Languages Dutch (official), Papiamento, English, Spanish
Religions Roman Catholic 82%, Protestant 8%
Currency Aruban guilder/florin = 100 cents
Website www.aruba.com

BAHAMAS

Small independent state in the West Indies including over 700 islands, of which 14 serve as the main hub. The largest island is Grand Bahama. Mainly limestone and coral, the rocky terrain provides little chance for agricultural development. Most of the islands are low, flat, and riverless with mangrove swamps. The land is at its highest at Mount Alvernia on Cat Island with a measurement of 63 m (206 ft). The longest known underwater cave and cavern system in the world is situated in Lucayan National Park on Grand Bahama. The climate of the islands is subtropical with temperatures averaging 21–32°C [70–90°F].

In 1964, Britain granted limited self-government to the Bahamas. They became a Commonwealth in 1969, with independence in 1973. Income is from tourism, fishing, salt and rum.

Area 13,878 sq km [5,358 sq mi]
Population 297,000
Capital Nassau (210,832)
Government Constitutional parliamentary democracy
Ethnic groups Black 85%, White 12%, others
Languages English (official), Creole
Religions Baptist 35%, Anglican 15%, Roman Catholic 14%, Pentecostal 8%, Church of God 5%, Methodist 4%, others
Currency Bahamian dollar = 100 cents
Website www.bahamas.gov.bs

CARIBBEAN SEA

Extension of the northern Atlantic Ocean linked to the Gulf of Mexico by the Yucatán Channel and to the Pacific Ocean by the Panama Canal. The first European to discover the Caribbean was Columbus in 1492, who named it after the Carib. It soon lay on the route of many Spanish expeditions and became notorious for piracy, particularly after other European powers established colonies in the West Indies. With the opening of the Panama Canal (1914) its strategic importance increased. Area: c.2.64 million sq km (1,020,000sq mi).

Dutch buildings in central Oranjestad, Aruba

Caribbean Islands 51

BARBADOS

Island state in the Windward Islands, West Indies. Barbados' warm climate encouraged the growth of its two largest industries: sugar cane and tourism. It was settled by the British in 1627, and dominated by British plantation owners (using African slave labour until the abolition of slavery) for the next 300 years. It gained independence in 1966.

Area 430 sq km [166 sq mi]
Population 277,000
Capital Bridgetown (80,000)
Government Parliamentary democracy
Ethnic groups Black 90%, Asian, White
Languages English
Religions Protestant 67%, Roman Catholic 4%
Currency Barbadian dollar = 100 cents
Website www.barbados.org

CAYMAN ISLANDS

British dependency in the West Indies, comprising Grand Cayman, Little Cayman, and Cayman Brac, 325 km (200 mi) north-west of Jamaica, in the Caribbean Sea. The islands are riverless and the coasts mostly protected by offshore reefs. They were discovered by Columbus in 1503, and

Area 264 sq km [102 sq mi]
Population 42,000
Capital Georgetown (20,600)
Government Overseas territory of the UK
Ethnic groups Mixed 40%, White 20%, Black 20%
Languages English
Religions Protestant, Roman Catholic
Currency Caymanian dollar = 100 cents
Website www.gov.ky

ceded to Britain in the 17th century. The islanders voted against independence in 1962. Tourism, international finance, turtle and shark fishing, are major sources of revenue.

DOMINICA

An independent island nation in the east Caribbean Sea, it is the largest of the Windward Islands. The present population are mainly the descendants of African slaves. Dominica is mountainous and heavily forested, and the climate is tropical. It boasts the Morne Trois Pitons National Park – established in 1975 and declared a World Heritage Site in 1997. The park plays host to the Boiling Lake and the Valley of Desolation as well as many other lakes and waterfalls and is centred on the Morne Trois Pitons volcano which rises to 1,342 m (4,403 ft).

Area 751 sq km [290 sq mi]
Population 70,000
Capital Roseau (20,000)
Government Parliamentary democracy
Ethnic groups Black, Mixed black and European, European, Syrian, Carib Amerindian
Languages English (official), French patois
Religions Roman Catholic 77%, Protestant 15%
Currency East Caribbean dollar = 100 cents
Website www.avirtualdominica.com

Dominica achieved complete independence as a republic within the Commonwealth in 1978. It is one of the poorest Caribbean countries. Agriculture dominates the economy. In recent years the island has benefitted greatly from being the location for Hollywood films.

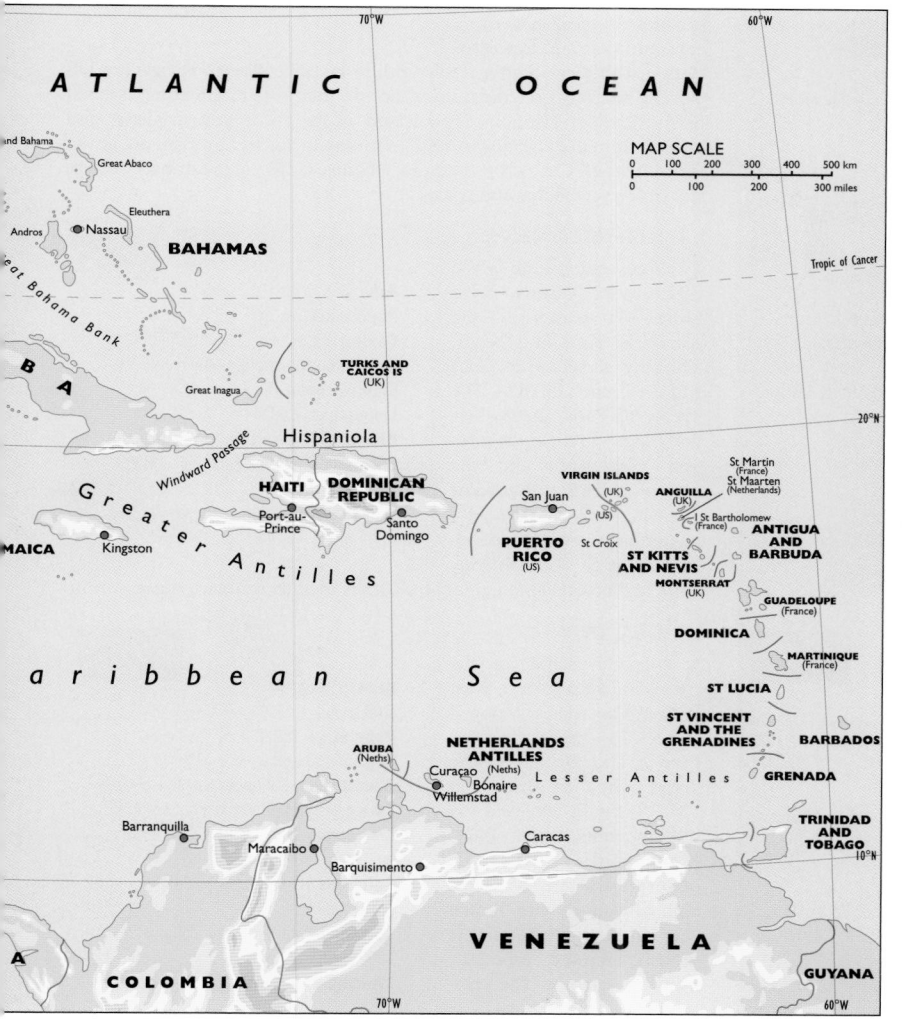

A cannon rusts at the ruins of Fort Shirley, overlooking Prince Rupert Bay, Dominica

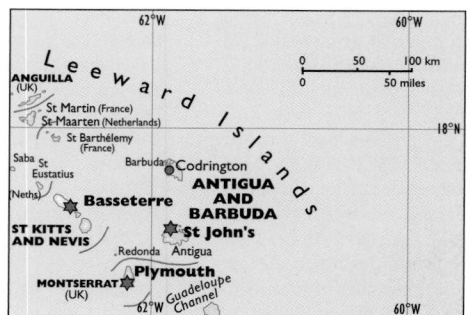

GRENADA

Independent island nation in the south east Caribbean Sea, the most southerly of the Windward Islands, 160 km [100 mi] north of Venezuela. It consists of Grenada and the smaller islands of the Southern Grenadines dependency. It is volcanic in origin, with a ridge of mountains running north–south. The climate is tropical with occasional hurricanes. The agrarian economy is based on cocoa, bananas, sugar, spices, and citrus fruits. It depends greatly on tourism.

Area 344 sq km [133 sq mi]
Population 101,400
Capital St George's (8,000)
Government Constitutional monarchy
Ethnic groups Black 82%, others
Languages English (official), French patois
Religions Roman Catholic 53%, Protestant 47%
Currency East Caribbean dollar = 100 cents
Website www.grenadagrenadines.com

GUADELOUPE

French overseas department (since 1946), consisting of the islands of Basse-Terre, Grande-Terre and several smaller islands in the Leeward Islands. The Island of Saint Martin is shared with the Netherlands Antilles. Discovered in 1493 by Columbus and settled by France in 1635. Guadeloupe was briefly held by Britain and Sweden, but reverted to French rule in 1816. The chief crops are sugar cane and bananas. Industries include distilling and tourism.

Area 1,705 sq km [658 sq mi]
Population 440,000
Capital Basse-Terre (14,000)
Government Overseas department of France
Ethnic groups Black or mulatto 90%, White 5%
Languages English (official), Spanish, Creole
Religions Roman Catholic 95%, Hindu and pagan African 4%
Currency Euro = 100 cents
Website www.guadeloupe.pref.gouv.fr

MARTINIQUE

Island in the Windward group of the Lesser Antilles. Martinique was inhabited by Carib Indians until they were displaced by French settlers after 1635. The island became a permanent French possession after the Napoleonic Wars. Of volcanic origin, it is the largest of the Lesser Antilles. In 1902, a volcanic eruption completely destroyed the original capital, St Pierre.

Area 1,102 sq km [425 sq mi]
Population 426,000
Capital Fort de France (100,000)
Government Overseas department of France
Ethnic groups African and African-White-Indian mixture 90%
Languages French, Creole patois
Religions Roman Catholic 85%, Protestant 10%
Currency Euro = 100 cents
Website www.martinique.org

MONTSERRAT

Montserrat is one of the Leeward Islands in the Lesser Antilles. It is dominated by an active volcano in the Soufrière Hills. The British colonized in 1632. It formed part of the Leeward Island colony from 1871 until 1956, when it became a separate, dependent territory of the UK. In 1995, a volcanic eruption destroyed the capital Plymouth and most of the population fled. Many have since returned. Revenue comes from tourism, offshore finance and cotton.

Area 102 sq km [40 sq mi]
Population 9,000
Capital Brades Estate (interim)
Government Overseas territory of the UK
Ethnic groups Black, White
Languages English
Religions Christian
Currency East Caribbean dollar = 100 cents
Website www.gov.ms

NETHERLANDS ANTILLES

Group of five main islands (and part of a sixth) in the West Indies. The islands were settled by the Spanish in 1527 and captured by the Dutch in 1634. They were granted internal self-government in 1954. The group includes Aruba, Bonaire, Curaçao, Saba, Saint Eustatius, and the southern half of Saint Maarten. Oil refining, petrochemicals, and tourism provide revenue.

Area 800 sq km [309 sq mi]
Population 216,000
Capital Willemstad (Curacao) (130,000)
Government Autonomous country within the Kingdom of the Netherlands
Ethnic groups Mixed Black 85%, others
Languages Papiamento 65%, English 16%, Dutch 7% (official)
Religions Roman Catholic 72%, others
Currency Netherlands Antillean guilder = 100 cents
Website www.gov.an

PUERTO RICO

The Commonwealth of Puerto Rico is the easternmost island in the Greater Antilles. The land is mountainous, with a narrow coastal plain. the highest point is Cerro de Punta (4,389 ft [1,338 m]). The climate is hot and wet. Ceded by Spain to the US in 1898, Puerto Rico became a self-governing commonwealth in free association with the US after a referendum in 1952. Puerto Ricans are US citizens, but pay no federal taxes, nor do they vote in US congressional or presidential elections. The island is the most industrialized and urbanized in the Caribbean, and manufacturing and tourism are growing industries. Cash crops include bananas, coffee, sugar, tobacco, tropical fruits, vegetables and spices.

Area 3,459 sq mi [8,959 sq km]
Population 3,916,632
Capital (population) San Juan (433,733)
Government Commonwealth
Ethnic groups White 80%, black 8%, others
Languages Spanish, English
Religions Roman Catholic 85%, others 15%
Currency US dollar = 100 cents
Website www.gotopuertorico.com

ST KITTS & NEVIS

Self-governing state in the Leeward Islands, West Indies. It comprises the islands St Kitts and Nevis. The English settled in 1623 and the French in 1624. The Treaty of Paris (1783) settled Anglo-French disputes over possession, and the islands gained self-government in 1967. Nevis held a referendum on independence from St Kitts in May 1998 and is still campaigning. Industries include tourism, sugar, cotton.

Area 261 sq km [101 sq mi]
Population 39,000
Capital Basseterre (St Kitts) (18,000)
Government Constitutional monarchy
Ethnic groups Black
Languages English
Religions Anglican, Roman Catholic
Currency East Caribbean dollar = 100 cents
Website www.stkittsnevis.net

ST LUCIA

Volcanic island in the Windward group, West Indies. The island changed hands 14 times between France and Britain before being ceded to Britain in 1814. It finally achieved full self-government in 1979. Mountainous (the twin peton peaks are a scenic highlight), lush and forested, its tourist income is growing rapidly, especially from cruise ships. The principal export is bananas.

Area 539 sq km [208 sq mi]
Population 162,000
Capital Castries
Government Parliamentary democracy
Ethnic groups Black 90%
Languages English (official), French patois
Religions Roman Catholic 68%, Protestant
Currency East Caribbean dollar = 100 cents
Website www.stlucia.gov.lc

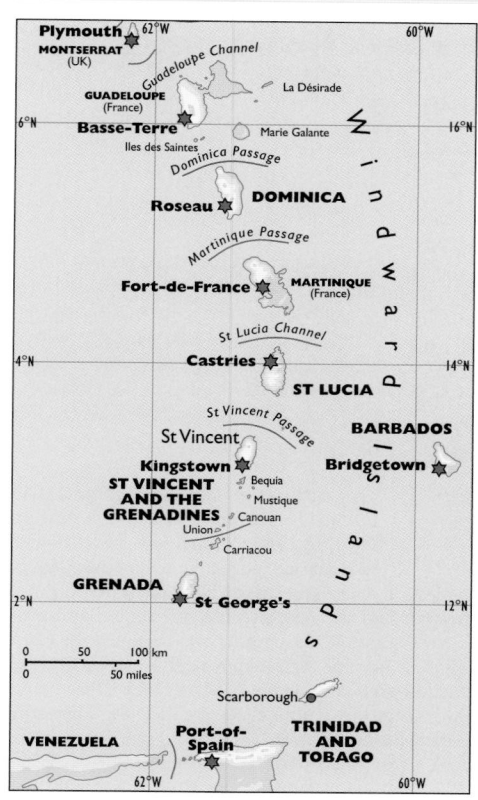

WINDWARD ISLANDS

Southern group of the Lesser Antilles islands, southeast West Indies. They extend from the Leeward Islands to the northeast coast of Venezuela. The principal islands are Martinique, Grenada, Dominica, St Lucia and St Vincent and the Grenadines group. The islands, volcanic in origin, are mountainous and forested. Tropical crops are grown, including sugar cane, bananas, spices, limes and cacao, but tourism is the leading industry. The islands were inhabited by the indigenous Carib until colonization began in the 17th century. The next two centuries witnessed a struggle for control between France and Britain. Britain eventually controlled all the islands, with the exception of Martinique.

ST VINCENT & GRENADINES

Island state of the Windward Islands, between St Lucia and Grenada comprising the volcanic island of St Vincent and five islands of the Grenadine group, including Mustique. In 1783 the British deported most of the native Carib population, who were replaced by African slave labour. St Vincent was part of the British Windward Islands colony (1880-1958) and of the West Indies Federation (1958–62). It gained self-government in 1969 and full independence in the Commonwealth in 1979.

Area 388 sq km [150 sq mi]
Population 117,000
Capital Kingstown
Government Parliamentary democracy
Ethnic groups Black 66%, Mixed 19%
Languages English, French patois
Religions Anglican 47%, Methodist 28%, Roman Catholic 13%
Currency East Caribbean dollar = 100 cents
Website www.svgtourism.com

TURKS & CAICOS

Turks and Caicos are two island groups of the British West Indies that include more than 40 islands, eight of which are inhabited. Grand Turk is the capital island and home of the government, while Providenciales is the most developed of the islands and their centre of tourism. Discovered in 1512 by Ponce de León, the islands were British from 1766. They were then administered via Jamaica from 1873–1959, and a separate Crown Colony from 1973. Most food products are imported. Exports include salt, sponges, and shellfish. The main sources of income are tourism and offshore banking.

Area 430 sq km [166 sq mi]
Population 19,000
Capital Cockburn Town (Grand Turk)
Government Overseas territory of the UK
Ethnic groups Black 90%
Languages English (official)
Religions Baptist 40%, Methodist 16%, Anglican 18%, Church of God 12%
Currency US dollar = 100 cents
Website www.turksandcaicosislands.gov.tc

BRITISH VIRGIN ISLANDS

British colony in the West Indies. It is a group of 36 islands, which form part of the Antilles between the Caribbean Sea and the Atlantic Ocean. Tortola is the commercial centre and capital island, it is also home to the highest point in the group, Mount Sage – 521 m (1,709 ft). First settled in the 17th century, the islands formed part of the Leeward Islands colony until 1956. The chief economic activity is tourism, though construction, rum production, and offshore banking are also important. Livestock farming is the leading form of agriculture.

Area 151 sq km [58 sq mi]
Population 22,000
Capital Road Town (Tortola)
Government Overseas territory of the UK
Ethnic groups Black 84%
Languages English (official)
Religions Protestant 86%, Roman Catholic 10%
Currency US dollar = 100 cents
Website www.bvitourism.com

US VIRGIN ISLANDS

Group of 68 islands in the Lesser Antilles. Chief islands are St Croix, St John and St Thomas. Spanish from 1553, the islands were Danish until 1917, when the USA bought them for US$25 million, to protect the northern approaches to the newly completed Panama Canal. The islands' residents are now US citizens. Tourism is the biggest earner, though on St Croix there is an oil refinery and an aluminium plant.

Area 347 sq km [134 sq mi]
Population 125,000
Capital Charlotte Amalie (St Thomas)
Government Unincorporated territory of the US
Ethnic groups Black 76%, White 13%
Languages English 75%, Spanish or Spanish Creole 17%, French or French Creole 7%
Religions Baptist 42%, Roman Catholic 34%
Currency US dollar = 100 cents
Website www.usvi.net

The red, yellow and green colours on this flag were originally used by Ethiopia, Africa's oldest independent nation. They symbolize African unity. The blue, white and red recall the flag of France, the country's colonial ruler. This flag was adopted in 1958.

The Central African Republic is a remote landlocked country in central Africa. It lies on a plateau, mostly 600–800 m (1,970–2,620 ft) above sea level, forming a watershed between the headwaters of two river systems. In the south, the rivers flow into the navigable River Ubangi (a tributary of the Congo). The Ubangi and the Bomu form much of its southern border. In the north, most rivers are headwaters of the River Chari, which flows north into Lake Chad.

Wooded savanna covers much of the country, with open grasslands in the north and rainforests in the south west. The country has many forest and savanna animals, such as buffalo, leopards, lions and elephants, and many bird species. About 6% of the land is protected in national parks and reserves, but tourism is on a small scale because of the republic's remoteness.

CLIMATE

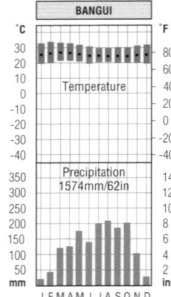

The climate is warm throughout the year, with an average annual rainfall in Bangui totalling 1,574 mm [62 in]. The north is drier, with an average annual rainfall total of about 800 mm [31 in].

HISTORY

Little is known of the country's early history. Between the 16th and 19th centuries, the population was greatly reduced by slavery, and the country is still thinly populated. France first occupied the area in 1887, and in 1894 established the colony of Ubangi-Shari at Bangui. In 1906 the colony was united with Chad, and in 1910 was subsumed into French Equatorial Africa (which included Chad, Congo and Gabon). Forced-labour rebellions occurred in 1928, 1935 and 1946. During World War II Ubangi-Shari supported the Free French. Post-1945 the colony received representation in the French parliament. In 1958 the colony voted to become a self-governing republic within the French community, and became the Central African Republic.

POLITICS

In 1960 Central African Republic declared independence, but the next six years saw a deterioration in the economy, and increasing government corruption

Area 622,984 sq km [240,534 sq mi]
Population 3,742,000
Capital (population) Bangui (553,000)
Government Multiparty republic
Ethnic groups Baya 33%, Banda 27%, Mandjia 13%, Sara 10%, Mboum 7% Mbaka 4%, others
Languages French (official), Sangho
Religions Traditional beliefs 35%, Protestant 25%, Roman Catholic 25%, Islam 15%
Currency CFA franc = 100 centimes
Website www.banguinet.net

BANGUI

Capital of the Central African Republic, on the River Ubangi, near the border with the Democratic Republic of Congo. Founded in 1889 by the French, it is the nation's chief port for international trade. Places of interest include the triumphal arch dedicated to Jean-Bédel Bokassa, the Boganda Museum and the central market. Industries include textiles, shoes, food processing, beer and soap.

and inefficiency under President David Dacko. It became a one-party state in 1962. In 1966 Colonel Jean Bédel Bokassa assumed power in a bloodless coup. He abrogated the constitution and dissolved the National Assembly.

In 1976 Bokassa transformed the republic into an empire, and proclaimed himself Emperor Bokassa I. The country was renamed the Central African Empire. His rule became increasingly brutal, and in 1979 he was deposed in a French-backed coup led by Dacko. Dacko, faced with continuing unrest, was replaced by André Kolingba in 1981. The army quickly banned all political parties.

The country adopted a new, multiparty constitution in 1991. Elections were held in 1993. An army rebellion in 1996 was finally put down in 1997 with the assistance of French troops. An attempted coup in 2001 was put down, with Libyan help, by President Ange-Félix Patassé, who had served as president since 1993. But a coup in 2003 brought General François Bozize to power and Patassé went into exile in Togo. A new constitution was introduced in 2004, followed by elections in 2005 which were won by General Bozize.

ECONOMY

The World Bank classifies the Central African Republic as a 'low-income' developing country. Approximately 10% of the land is cultivated and over 80% of the workforce are engaged in subsistence agriculture. The main food crops are bananas, maize, manioc, millet and yams. Coffee, cotton, timber and tobacco are the main cash crops

Diamonds, the only major mineral resource, are the most valuable single export. Manufacturing is on a very small scale. Products include beer, cotton fabrics, footwear, leather, soap and sawn timber. The Central African Republic's development has been greatly impeded by its remote position, its poor transport system and its untrained workforce. The country is heavily dependent on aid, especially from France.

UBANGI (OUBANGI)

The River Ubangi is a major tributary of the River Congo in central Africa, beginning at the junction of the Mbomou and Uele rivers. The Ubangi defines the boundary between the Central African Republic and the Democratic Republic of the Congo (DRC), passing through Bangui, after which it forms the boundary between the DRC and the Republic of Congo before emptying into the River Congo. It is an important artery for river boats between Bangui and Brazzaville.

A family of BaAka pygmies, an indigenous hunter-gatherer group located throughout Cameroon and the Central African Republic, prepare a meal outside their hut

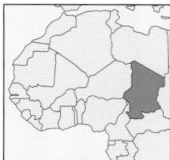

Chad's flag was adopted in 1959 as the country prepared for independence in 1960. The blue represents the sky, the streams in southern Chad, and hope. The yellow symbolizes the sun and the Sahara in the north. The red represents national sacrifice.

Chad is Africa's fifth largest country. It is more than twice as big as France (the former colonial power). Southern Chad is crossed by rivers that flow into Lake Chad, on the western border with Nigeria. The capital, Ndjamena, lies on the banks of the River Chari. Beyond a large depression (north east of Lake Chad) are the Tibesti Mountains, which rise steeply from the sands of the Sahara Desert. The mountains contain Chad's highest peak, Emi Koussi, at 3,415 m [11,204 ft]. The far south contains forests, while central Chad is a region of savanna, merging into the dry grasslands of the Sahel. Plants are rare in the northern desert. Droughts are common in north central Chad. Long droughts, over-grazing, and felling for firewood have exposed the Sahel's soil and wind erosion is increasing desertification.

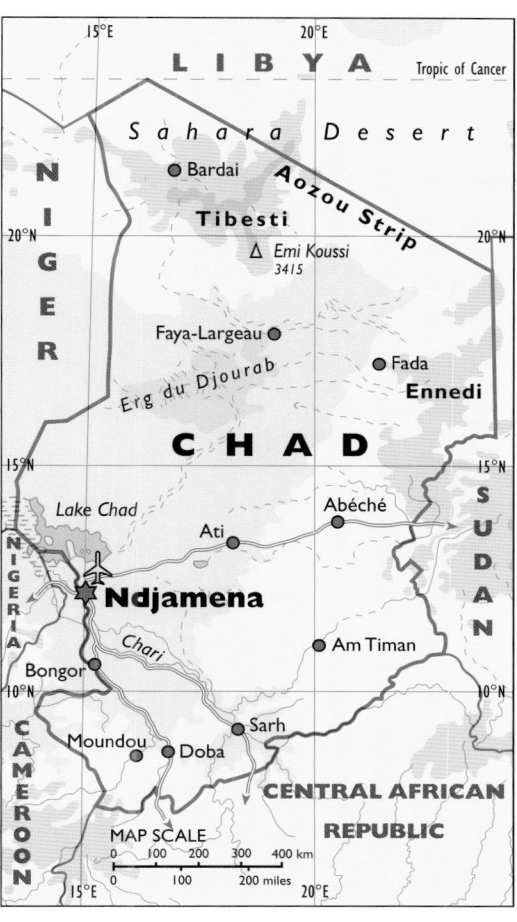

Villagers register to be tested for sleeping sickness at Danmadja village

Area 1,284,000 sq km [495,752 sq mi]
Population 9,539,000
Capital (population) Ndjamena (530,000)
Government Multiparty republic
Ethnic groups 200 distinct groups: mostly Muslim in the north and centre; mostly Christian or animist in the south
Languages French and Arabic (both official), many others
Religions Islam 51%, Christianity 35%, animist 7%
Currency CFA franc = 100 centimes
Website www.chadembassy.org

NDJAMENA

Capital of Chad, a port on the River Chari. Founded by the French in 1900, it was known as Fort Lamy until 1973. Ndjamena grew rapidly after independence in 1960. An important market for the surrounding region, which produces livestock, dates, and cereals. The main industry is meat processing.

POLITICS

In 1958 Chad gained autonomous status within the French Community, and in 1960 achieved full independence. Divisions between north and south rapidly surfaced. In 1965, President François Tombalbaye declared a one-party state and the north Muslims, led by the Chad National Liberation Front (Frolinat), rebelled. By 1973 the government, helped by the French, quashed the revolt. In 1980 Libya occupied northern Chad. In 1982, two leaders of Frolinat, Hissène Habré and Goukouni Oueddi, formed rival regimes. Splits soon emerged and Libya's bombing of Chad in 1983 led to the deployment of 3000 French troops. Libyan troops retreated, retaining only the uranium-rich Aozou Strip. A ceasefire took effect in 1987. In 1990, Habré was removed in a coup led by Idriss Déby. In 1994, the Aozou Strip was awarded to Chad. In 1996, a new democratic constitution was adopted and multi-party elections confirmed Déby as president. He was re-elected in 2001. In 2002 a peace treaty, signed by the government and the Movement for Democracy and Justice, ended three years of civil war. In 2004-5, Chad forces clashed with pro-Sudanese militia as the conflict in Sudan's Darfur province spilled over the border.

ECONOMY

Chad is one of the world's poorest countries, though its gold, uranium and oil reserves could be exploited to improve the situation but this has been hampered by a poor infrastructure. Agriculture dominates the economy, more than 80% of the workforce are engaged in farming, mainly at subsistence level. Groundnuts, millet, rice and sorghum are major crops in the wetter south. The most valuable crop is cotton.

CLIMATE

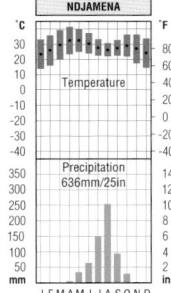

Central Chad has a hot tropical climate. There is a marked dry season from November to April. The south is wetter, with an average annual rainfall of about 1000 mm [39 in]. Conversely, the hot northern desert has an average annual rainfall of less than 130 mm [5 in].

HISTORY

Chad straddles two, often conflicting worlds: the north, populated by nomadic or semi-nomadic Muslim peoples, such as Arabs and Tuaregs; and the dominant south, where a sedentary population practise Christianity or traditional religions, such as animism. Lake Chad was an important watering point for the trans-Saharan caravans. Around AD 700 North African nomads founded the Kanem Empire. In the 14th century, the kingdom of Bornu expanded to incorporate Kanem. In the late 19th century the region fell to Sudan.

The first major European explorations were by the French in 1890. The French defeated the Sudanese in 1900, and in 1908 Chad became the largest province of French Equatorial Africa. In 1920 it became a separate colony.

LAKE CHAD (TCHAD)

North-central African lake, mainly in Chad, partly in Nigeria, Cameroon and Niger. The chief tributary is the River Chari. The lake has no outlet. The surface area varies by season from 10,000 to 26,000 sq km [3,861–10,000 sq mi]; maximum depth 7.6 m (25 ft).

Chile's flag was adopted in 1817. It was designed in that year by an American serving in the Chilean army who was inspired by the US Stars and Stripes. The white represents the snow-capped Andes, the blue the sky, and the red the blood of the nation's patriots.

Area 756,626 sq km [292,133 sq mi]
Population 15,824,000
Capital (population) Santiago (4,789,000)
Government Multiparty republic
Ethnic groups Mestizo 95%, Amerindian 3%
Languages Spanish (official)
Religions Roman Catholic 89%, Protestant 11%
Currency Chilean peso = 100 centavos
Website www.chileangovernment.cl

The Republic of Chile stretches 4,260 km [2,650 mi] from north to south, while the maximum east-west distance is only 430 km [270 mi]. The Andes mountains form Chile's eastern borders with Argentina and Bolivia. Ojos del Salado, at 6,863 m [22,516 f], is the second-highest peak in South America. Easter Island lies 3,500 km [2,200 mi] off Chile's west coast.

Western Chile contains three main land regions. In the north is the sparsely populated Atacama Desert, stretching 1,600 km [1,000 mi] south from the Peruvian border. The Central Valley, which contains the capital, Santiago, Valparaíso and Concepción, is by far the most densely populated region. In the south, the land has been heavily glaciated, the coastal uplands have been worn into islands, while the inland valleys are arms of the sea.

In the far south, the Strait of Magellan separates the Chilean mainland from Tierra del Fuego. Punta Arenas is the world's southernmost city.

CLIMATE

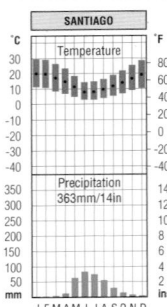

Chile is divided into three main climate zones. The Atacama Desert in the north has an arid climate, but temperatures are moderated by the cold Peru Current. Central Chile has a Mediterranean climate with hot, dry summers and mild, moist winters. The south has a cool and stormy climate prone to alpine conditions.

HISTORY

Amerindian people reached the southern tip of South America at least 8,000 years ago. In 1520, the Portuguese navigator Ferdinand Magellan became the first European to sight Chile. The country became a Spanish colony in the 1540s. Under Spain, the economy in the north was based on mining, while huge ranches, or *haciendas*, were set up in central Chile. After Chile became independent in 1818,

SANTIAGO

Capital of Chile, in central region on the River Mapocho, 90 km [55 mi] from Atlantic coast. Founded in 1541, it was destroyed by an earthquake in 1647. Most of the architecture dates from after 1850. It is the administrative, commercial, and cultural centre, accounting for nearly a third of the population.

mining continued to flourish in the north, while Valparaíso developed as a port exporting produce from central Chile to California and Australia. During a war (1879–83), it gained mineral-rich areas from Peru and Bolivia. Industrial growth, fuelled by revenue from nitrate exports, began in the early 20th century.

POLITICS

After World War II, Chile faced economic problems, partly caused by falls in world copper prices. A Christian Democrat was elected president in 1964, but was replaced by Salvador Allende Gossens in 1970. Allende's administration, the world's first democratically elected Marxist government, was overthrown in a CIA-backed coup in 1973. General Augusto Pinochet Ugarte took power as a dictator, banning all political activity in a repressive regime. A new constitution took effect from 1981, allowing for an eventual return to democracy. Elections took place in 1989. President Patrico Aylwin took office in 1990, but Pinochet secured continued office as commander-in-chief of the armed forces. Eduardo Frei was elected president in 1993 and he was succeeded by a socialist, Ricardo Lagos, who narrowly defeated a conservative candidate in January 2000. In 1999, General Pinochet, who was visiting Britain for medical treatment, was faced with extradition to Spain to answer charges that he had presided over acts of torture when he was Chile's dictator. In 2000, he was allowed to return to Chile where, in 2001, he was found to be too ill to stand trial. New charges were brought against him in 2004 and, in 2005 he was placed under house arrest.

ECONOMY

The World Bank classifies Chile as a 'lower-middle-income' developing country. Mining is important. Minerals dominate Chile's exports. The most valuable activity is manufacturing. Products include processed foods, metals, iron and steel, wood products and textiles.

Agriculture employs 18% of the workforce. The chief crop is wheat. Beans, fruits, maize and livestock products are also important. Chile's fishing industry is one of the world's largest.

Map labels

PERU
BOLIVIA
Arica
Iquique
Tropic of Capricorn
Antofagasta
△ 6739
Ojos del Salado △ 6863
Copiapó
PACIFIC
OCEAN
La Serena
ARGENTINA
Viña del Mar
Valparaíso
△ Aconcagua 6960
Santiago
Rancagua
Talca
Talcahuano
Chillán
Concepción
Temuco
Valdivia
Puerto Montt
Chiloé I.
Quellón
Chonos Archipelago
△ 3048
Wellington I.
△ 3600
Puerto Natales
Magellan's Strait
Punta Arenas
Tierra del Fuego
ATLANTIC OCEAN
Cape Horn
Atacama Desert
Andes
CHILE
PATAGONIA

MAP SCALE
0   250   500 km
0   250 miles

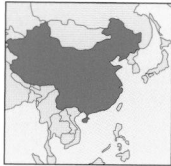

China's flag was adopted in 1949, when the country became a Communist People's Republic. Red is the traditional colour of both China and Communism. The large star represents the Communist Party programme. The smaller stars symbolize the four main social classes.

The People's Republic of China is the world's third largest country. Most people live on the eastern coastal plains, in the highlands or the fertile valleys of the rivers Huang He and Yangtze, Asia's longest river, at 6,380 km [3,960 mi].

Western China includes the bleak Tibetan plateau, bounded by the Himalayas. Everest, the world's highest peak, lies on the Nepal-Tibet border. Other ranges include the Tian Shan and Kunlun Shan. China also has deserts, such as the Gobi.

Large areas in the west are covered by sparse grasses or desert. The most luxuriant forests are in the south-east, such as the bamboo forest habitat of the rare giant panda.

CLIMATE

The capital, Beijing, in north-east China, has cold winters and warm summers, with moderate rainfall. Shanghai, in the east-central region, has milder winters and more rain. The south-east region has a wet, sub-tropical climate. In the west, the climate is more cold and severe.

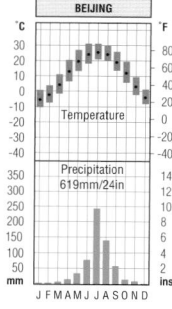
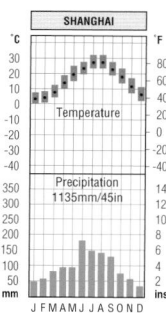
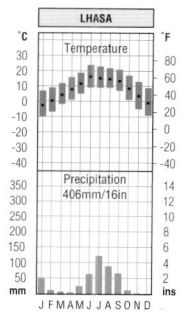

HISTORY

The first documented dynasty was the Shang (1523–1030 BC), when bronze casting was perfected. The Zhou dynasty (1030–221 BC) was the age of Chinese classical literature, in particular Confucius and Lao Tzu. China was unified by Qin Shihuangdi, whose tomb near Xian contains the famous terracotta army. The Qin dynasty (221–206 BC) also built the

majority of the Great Wall. The Han dynasty (202 BC–AD 220) developed the Empire, a bureaucracy based on Confucianism, and also introduced Buddhism. China then split into three kingdoms (Wei, Shu, and Wu) and the influence of Buddhism and Taoism grew. The T'ang dynasty from 618–907 was a golden era of artistic achievement, especially in poetry and fine art. Genghis Khan conquered most of China in the 1210s and established the Mongol empire. Kublai Khan founded the Yüan dynasty (1271–1368), an era of dialogue with Europe. The Ming dynasty (1368–1644) re-established Chinese rule and is famed for its fine porcelain. The Manchu Qing dynasty (1644–1912) began by vastly extending the empire, but the 19th century was marked by foreign interventions, such as the Opium War (1839–42), when Britain occupied Hong Kong. Popular disaffection culminated in the Boxer Rebellion (1900). The last Emperor (Henry Pu Yi) was overthrown in a revolution led by Sun Yat-sen and a republic established (1912).

China rapidly fragmented between a Beijing government supported by warlords, and Sun Yat-sen's nationalist Kuomintang government in Guangzhou. The Communist Party of China initially allied with the Kuomintang. In 1926, the Kuomintang, led by Chiang Kai-shek, emerged victorious and turned on their Communist allies. In 1930 a rival communist government was established, but was uprooted by Kuomintang troops and began the Long March (1934). Japan, taking advantage of the turmoil, established the puppet state of Manchukuo (1932). Chiang was forced to ally with the Communists. Japan launched a full-scale invasion in 1937, and conquered much of north and east China. From 1941 Chinese forces, with Allied support, began to regain territory. At the end of World War II, civil war resumed: nationalists supported by the USA and Communists by Russia. The Communists, with greater popular support, triumphed and the Kuomintang fled to Taiwan.

Area 9,596,961 sq km [3,705,387 sq mi]
Population 1,298,848,000
Capital (population) Beijing (7,362,000)
Government Single-party Communist republic
Ethnic groups Han Chinese 92%, many others
Languages Mandarin Chinese (official)
Religions Atheist (official)
Currency Renminbi yuan = 10 jiao = 100 fen
Website www.china.org.cn/english

BEIJING (PEKING)

Capital of the People's Republic of China, between the Pei and Hun rivers, north-east China. A settlement since 1000 BC, Beijing served as China's capital from 1421 to 1911. After the establishment of the Chinese Republic (1911–12), Beijing remained the political centre of China. The seat of government was transferred to Nanking in 1928. Beijing ('northern capital') became known as Pei-p'ing ('northern peace'). Occupied by the Japanese in 1937, it was restored to China in 1945 and came under Communist control in 1949. Its name was restored as capital of the People's Republic. The city comprises two walled sections: the Inner (Tatar) City, including the Forbidden City (imperial palace complex), and the Outer (Chinese) city. Beijing is the political, cultural, educational, financial, and transport centre of China. Heavy industry expanded after the end of the Civil War, and products now include textiles, iron, and steel.

The Forbidden City in Beijing *– home to the imperial palace during the Ming and Qing dynasties (15th to early 20th century) and now a UNESCO listed World Heritage Site*

POLITICS

Mao Zedong established the People's Republic of China on 1 October 1949. In 1950 China seized Tibet. Domestically, Mao began to collectivize agriculture and nationalize industry. In 1958 the Great Leap Forward planned to revolutionize industrial production. The Cultural Revolution (1966–76) mobilized Chinese youth against bourgeois culture. By 1971 China had a seat on the UN security council and its own nuclear capability. Following Mao's death (1976), a power struggle developed between the Gang of Four and moderates led by Deng Xiaoping; the latter emerged victorious. Deng began a process of modernization, forging closer links with the West. In 1989 a pro-democracy demonstration was crushed in Tiananmen Square. In 1997 Jiang Zemin succeeded Deng as paramount leader and in 2002 was succeeded by Hu Jintao. Providing that the country's leaders continue to follow their pragmatic path, many experts predict a major economic blossoming for China in the 21st century.

ECONOMY

By 2005, China had the world's sixth largest economy. However as its population is almost 1.3 billion China remains a poor country. The government announced in 2004 that it planned to slow down the country's rapid economic growth to help the rural poor, who had become relatively worse off as China's industries expanded.

Agriculture still employs nearly half of the population, but while less than 3% of the country can be cultivated, China has practised intensive farming for thousands of years and, as a result, is largely self-sufficient in food. However, the threat of floods and drought remain, despite government initiatives in soil conservancy, afforestation, together with irrigation and drainage projects. The crops grown vary according to the climate. The warm southeast has a long growing season and two to three crops can be grown on the same plot of land in a single year. Major crops in the area include rice, tea and sweet potatoes. In the north, with its cooler climate and shorter growing season, wheat is the chief crop, together with maize and sorghum. Western China is largely arid and barren and crops are grown only around isolated oases. However, nomadic pastoralists, such as the Uighurs in Xinjiang, raise goats, horses and sheep.

China leads the world in the production of rice, sweet potatoes and wheat. It also ranks among the top five producers of bananas, barley, natural rubber, sesame seed, sorghum, soya beans, sugar cane and tea. Livestock are also important. China leads the world in producing eggs, goats, horses and mules. It also ranks among the top five producers of beef and veal, cattle, poultry meat, sheep and wool.

The Badaling section of the Great Wall is one of the best preserved sections

MACAU (MACAO)

Former Portuguese overseas province in south-east China, 64 km [40 mi] west of Hong Kong, on the River Pearl estuary; it consists of the 6 sq km [2 sq mi] Macau Peninsula and the islands of Taipa and Colôane. The city of Santa Nome de Deus de Macao (co-extensive with the peninsula) connects via a narrow isthmus to the Chinese province of Guangzhou. Vasco da Gama discovered Macau in 1497, and the Portuguese colonized the island in 1557. In 1849, Portugal declared it a free port. In 1887, the Chinese government recognized Portugal's right of 'perpetual occupation'. Competition from Hong Kong and the silting of Macau's harbour led to the port's decline at the end of the 19th century. In 1974, Macau became a Chinese province under Portuguese administration. It returned to China in 1999 though China promised that its socialist economic system will not be practised there. Gambling and tourism are dominant in the economy. Other industries include textiles, electronics and plastics. Macau has a population of 455,000 of whom 50% are Buddhist and 15% Catholic. Cantonese is spoken by nearly 90% of the population.

Largo do Senado Square, the main square in Macau and the centre for many of the celebrations held throughout the year, especially Chinese New Year which takes place in late January

HONG KONG
(XIANGGANG SPECIAL ADMINISTRATIVE REGION)

Former British Crown Colony off the coast of south-east China; the capital is Victoria on Hong Kong Island. Hong Kong comprises: Hong Kong Island, ceded to Britain by China in 1842; the mainland peninsula of Kowloon, acquired in 1860; the New Territories on the mainland, leased for 99 years in 1898; and some 230 islets in the South China Sea. The climate is subtropical, with hot, dry summers. In 1984, the UK and China signed a Joint Declaration in which it was agreed that China would resume sovereignty over Hong Kong in 1997. It also provided that Hong Kong would become a special administrative region, with its existing social and economic structure unchanged for 50 years. It would remain a free port. The last British governor, Chris Patten (1992–97), introduced a legislative council. The handover to China completed on 1 July 1997, and Chief Executive Tung Chee-hwa was sworn in and a provisional legislative council appointed. Hong Kong is a vital international financial centre with a strong manufacturing base.

Hong Kong from Victoria Peak; the Peak is the highest mountain on Hong Kong Island (552 m/1811 ft) and a key attraction, it can be reached via a funicular tram and is home to the Peak Tower

The yellow on Colombia's flag depicts the land, which is separated from the tyranny of Spain by the blue, symbolizing the Atlantic Ocean. The red symbolizes the blood of the people who fought to make the country independent. The flag has been used since 1806.

Area 1,138,914 sq km [439,735 sq mi]
Population 42,311,000
Capital (population) Bogotá (6,545,000)
Government Multiparty republic
Ethnic groups Mestizo 58%, White 20%, Mulatto 14%, Black 4%
Languages Spanish (official)
Religions Roman Catholic 90%
Currency Colombian peso = 100 centavos
Website www.gobiernoenlinea.gov.co/ingles

Colombia is the only South American country to have coastlines on both the Pacific Ocean and the Caribbean Sea. Cartagena is the main Caribbean port. Colombia is dominated by three ranges of the Andean Mountains. On the edge of the western Cordillera lies the city of Cali. The Central Cordillera is a chain of volcanoes that divide the valleys of the rivers Magdalena and Cauca. It includes the city of Medellín. The eastern Cordillera contains the capital, Bogotá, at 2,800 m [9,200 ft]. East of the Andes lie plains drained by headwaters of the Amazon and Orinoco rivers.

Vegetation varies from dense rainforest in the south east to tundra in the snow-capped Andes. Coffee plantations line the western slopes of the eastern Cordillera. The ancient forests of the Caribbean lowlands have mostly been cleared. Savanna (*llanos*) covers the north eastern plains.

CLIMATE

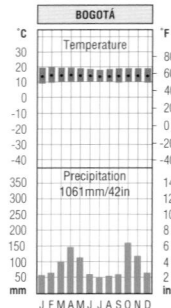

Altitude greatly affects the climate. The Pacific lowlands have a tropical, rainy climate, but Bogotá has mild annual temperatures. The lowlands of the Caribbean and the Magdalena valley both have dry seasons.

HISTORY

The pre-Colombian Chibcha civilization lived undisturbed in the eastern cordillera for thousands of years. In 1525 the Spanish established the first European settlement at Santa Marta. By 1538 conquistador Gonzalo Jiménez de Quesada conquered the Chibcha and established the city of Bogotá. Colombia became part of the New Kingdom of Granada, whose territory also included Ecuador, Panama, and Venezuela.

In 1819 Simón Bolívar defeated the Spanish at Boyacá, and established Greater Colombia. Bolivar became presi-

Coffee plants *in a plantation near Armenia, Colombia; the economy of this area is based heavily on the growing of coffee and bananas*

dent. In 1830, Ecuador and Venezuela gained independence. In 1885, the Republic of Colombia was formed. Differences between republican and federalist factions proved irreconcilable and the first civil war from 1899–1902 killed nearly 100,000 people. In 1903, aided by the United States, Panama gained independence. The second civil war (La Violencia, 1949–57) was even more bloody.

POLITICS

In 1957 Liberal and Conservative parties formed a National Front Coalition, which held power until 1974. Throughout the 1970s, Colombia's illegal trade in cocaine grew steadily, creating wealthy drug barons. In the 1980s, armed cartels (such as the Cali) destabilized Colombia with frequent assassinations of political and media figures.

A new constitution in 1991 protected human rights. Social Conservative Party (PSC) leader Andrés Pastrana Arango won the 1998 presidential elections and, in an effort to end the 30-year guerrilla war, negotiated with the Revolutionary Armed Forces of Colombia (FARC) and the National Liberation Army (ELN). Pastrana granted FARC a safe haven in southeast Colombia.

In 1999, the worst earthquake in Colombia's history killed more than 1,000 people and left thousands homeless. In 2002 Pastrana declared war on FARC, sending the army into FARC's 'safe haven'. Alvaro Uribe defeated Pastrana in 2002 presidential elections. Uribe promised even tougher action against terrorism.

ECONOMY

Colombia is a lower-middle income developing country. It is the world's second-largest coffee producer. Other crops include bananas, cocoa, and maize. Colombia also exports coal, oil, emeralds, and gold. In 1997 a collapse in the world coffee and banana markets led to a budget deficit. In 1998 Colombia devalued the peso, triggering the longest strike (20 days) in Colombia's history.

BOGOTÁ

Capital of Colombia, in the centre of the country on a fertile plateau. Bogotá was founded in 1538 by the Spanish on the site of a Chibcha Indian settlement. In 1819 it became the capital of Greater Colombia, part of which later formed Colombia. Today, it is a centre for culture, education and finance. Industries include tobacco, sugar, flour, textiles, engineering, chemicals.

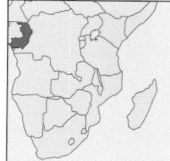

Congo's red flag, with the national emblem of a crossed hoe and mattock (a kind of pick-axe), was dropped in 1990, when the country officially abandoned the Communist policies it had followed since 1970. This new flag was adopted in its place.

The Republic of Congo lies on the River Congo in west-central Africa. The Equator runs through the centre of the country. Congo has a narrow coastal plain on which stands its main port, Pointe Noire, which itself lies on the Gulf of Guinea. Behind the plain are forested highlands through which the River Niari has carved a fertile valley. To the east lies Malebo (formerly Stanley) Pool, a large lake where the River Congo widens.

Central Congo consists of luxuriant savanna. Tree species include the valuable okoumé and mahogany. The north contains large swamps in the tributary valleys of the Congo and Ubangi rivers..

Area 342,000 sq km [132,046 sq mi]
Population 2,998,000
Capital (population) Brazzaville (938,000)
Government Military regime
Ethnic groups Kongo 48%, Sangha 20%, Teke 17%, M'bochi 12%
Languages French (official), many others
Religions Christianity 50%, animist 48%, Islam 2%
Currency CFA franc = 100 centimes
Website www.congo-site.com

BRAZZAVILLE

Capital and largest city of the Congo, West Africa, on the River Congo, below Stanley Pool. Founded in 1880, it was capital of French Equatorial Africa (1910–58) and a base for Free French forces in World War II. It has a university (1972) and a cathedral. It is a major port, connected by rail to the main Atlantic seaport of Pointe-Noire.

CLIMATE

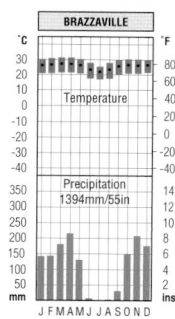

Most of the country has a humid, equatorial climate, with rain throughout the year. Brazzaville has a dry season between June and September. The narrow treeless coastal plain is drier and cooler than the rest of the country, because the cold Benguela current flows northwards along the coast.

HISTORY

The Loango and Bakongo kingdoms dominated the Congo when the first European arrived in 1482. Between the 15th and 18th centuries, part of Congo belonged to the huge Kongo kingdom, whose centre lay to the south. Portuguese explorers reached the coast of Congo in the 15th century and the area soon became a trading region, the main commodities being slaves and ivory. The slave trade continued until the 19th century.

European exploration of the interior did not occur until the late 19th century. In 1880 Pierre Savorgnan de Brazza explored the area and it became a French protectorate. It became known as Middle Congo, a country within French Equatorial Africa, which also included Chad, Gabon, and Ubangi-Shari (now called Central African Republic). In 1910 Brazzaville became the capital of French Equatorial Africa. In 1960 the Republic of Congo gained independence.

POLITICS

In 1964 Congo adopted Marxism-Leninism as the state ideology. The military, led by Marien Ngouabi, seized power in 1968. Ngouabi created the Congolese Workers Party (PCT) and was assassinated in 1977. The PCT retained power under Colonel Denis Sassou-Nguesso. In 1990 it renounced Marxism and Sassou-Nguesso was deposed. The Pan-African Union for Social Democracy (UPADS), led by Pascal Lissouba, won multi-party elections in 1992. However, in 1997, Sassou-Nguesso, assisted by his personal militia and also by troops from Angola, launched an uprising which overthrew Lissouba, who fled the country, taking refuge in Burkina Faso. But forces loyal to Lissouba fought back, starting a civil war. Cease-fires were agreed in 1999 and, in 2002, Sassou-Nguesso was elected president, winning 89% of the vote. A peace accord was signed in 2003.

ECONOMY

The World Bank classifies Congo as a 'lower-middle-income' developing country. Agriculture is the most important activity, employing about 60% of the workforce. But many farmers function merely at a subsistence level. The chief food crops include bananas, cassava, maize, plantains, rice and yams, while the leading cash crops include cocoa, coffee and sugar cane.

Congo's main exports are oil (which makes up 90% of the total) and timber. Manufacturing is relatively unimportant at the moment, hampered as it is by poor transport links. Inland, rivers form the main lines of communication, and Brazzaville is linked to the port of Pointe-Noire by the Congo-Ocean Railway.

Pygmy chimpanzees, Brazzaville; *also known as bonobos, these chimpanzees are said to be man's closest relative and are unique to the Congo Basin; they are now an endangered species and it is feared that they will be hunted to extinction*

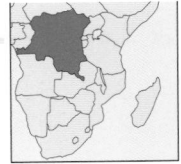

The Democratic Republic of the Congo adopted a new flag in 1997 after Laurent Kabila rose to power. The blue represents the UN's role in securing independence for the country, and the six small stars represent the original provinces of the independent state.

Democratic Republic of Congo is Africa's third-largest country. It is dominated by the River Congo. North-central Congo consists of a high plateau. In the east, the plateau rises to 5,109 m [16,762 ft] in the Ruwenzori mountains. Lakes Albert and Edward form much of Congo's border with Uganda. Lake Kivu lies along its border with Rwanda. Lake Tanganyika forms the border with Tanzania. All the lakes lie in an arm of the Great Rift Valley. Dense equatorial rainforests grow in the north, with savanna and swamps in the south.

CLIMATE

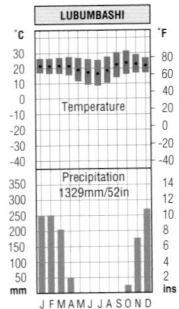

Much of Congo has an equatorial climate with high temperatures and heavy rainfall throughout the year. The south has a more subtropical climate.

HISTORY

From the 14th century, large Bantu kingdoms emerged. In 1482, a Portuguese navigator became the first European to reach the mouth of the River Congo. In the 19th century, ivory and slave traders formed powerful states. Henry Morton Stanley's explorations from 1874–77 established the route of the Congo. In 1878, King Leopold II of Belgium employed Stanley to found colonies along the Congo. In 1885, Leopold established the Congo Free State. His empire grew, and concessionaires gained control of the lucrative rubber trade. In 1908, Belgium established direct control as the colony of Belgium Congo. European companies exploited African labour to develop copper and diamond mines.

POLITICS

In 1960, the Republic of the Congo gained independence and Patrice Lumumba became prime minister. Joseph Mobutu, commander in chief of the Congolese National Army, seized power later that year. Lumumba was imprisoned and later murdered. In 1964, Belgium Congo plunged into civil war and Belgian troops intervened. In 1965, Mobutu proclaimed himself president and began a campaign of 'Africanization': Leopoldville became Kinshasa in 1966; the country and river renamed Zaïre in 1971; Katanga became Shaba in 1972; and Mobutu adopted the name Mobutu Sese Seko. Zaïre became a one-party state. Mobutu was re-elected unopposed in 1974 and 1977, finally accepting opposition parties in 1990, though elections were repeatedly deferred. In 1995, mil-

lions of Hutus fled from Rwanda into east Zaïre, to escape possible Tutsi reprisals. In 1996 rebels, led by Laurent Kabila, overthrew Mobuto. Zaïre became the Democratic Republic of Congo. In 1998, Congo descended into civil war between government forces, and Tutsi-dominated Congolese Rally for Democracy (RCD). The Lusaka Peace Agreement (1999) brought a cease-fire and 5,500 UN peace-keeping troops, but fighting continued. By 2001 the civil war had claimed more than 2.5 million lives. In 2001, Kabila was assassinated. He was succeeded by his son Joseph Kabila who, under a peace agreement, was installed as interim president of a transitional government in 2003. Unrest continued into 2005 with large swathes of the country still beyond the control of the government.

ECONOMY

Congo is a low-income developing country. It is the world's leading producer of cobalt and the second-largest producer of diamonds. Agriculture employs 71% of the workforce, mainly at subsistence level. Palm oil is the most vital cash crop.

KINSHASA

Capital of Democratic Republic of Congo, Kinshasa is a port on the River Congo and is located directly opposite Brazzaville, the capital of Republic of Congo. Founded in 1881, it replaced Boma as the capital of the Belgian Congo in 1923. Its name was changed in 1966. The city's population is greater than that of the rest of the country put together. It is known for its vibrancy and for being an important centre for music. Industries include tanning, chemicals, brewing, and textiles.

Area 2,344,858 sq km [905,350 sq mi]
Population 58,318,000
Capital (population) Kinshasa (4,665,000)
Government Single-party republic
Ethnic groups Over 200; the largest are Mongo, Luba, Kongo, Mangbetu-Azande
Languages French (official), tribal languages
Religions Roman Catholic 50%, Protestant 20%, Islam 10%, others
Currency Congolese franc = 100 centimes
Website www.monuc.org

Costa Rica's flag is based on the blue-white-blue pattern of the Central American Federation (1823–39). This Federation consisted of Costa Rica, El Salvador, Guatemala, Honduras and Nicaragua. The red stripe, which was adopted in 1848, reflects the colours of France.

The Republic of Costa Rica in Central America is bordered by Nicaragua to the north and Panama to the south. It has coastlines on both the Pacific Ocean and on the Caribbean Sea. Central Costa Rica consists of mountain ranges and plateaux with many volcanoes. The Meseta Central, where the capital, San José is situated, and the Valle del General in the south-east, have rich, volcanic soils and are the most thickly populated parts of Costa Rica.

The highlands descend to the Caribbean lowlands and the Pacific Coast region, with its low mountain ranges. San José stands at about 1,170 m [3,840 ft] above sea level.

Evergreen forests cover around 50% of Costa Rica. Oaks grow in the highlands, palm trees along the Caribbean coast and mangrove swamps are common on the Pacific coast.

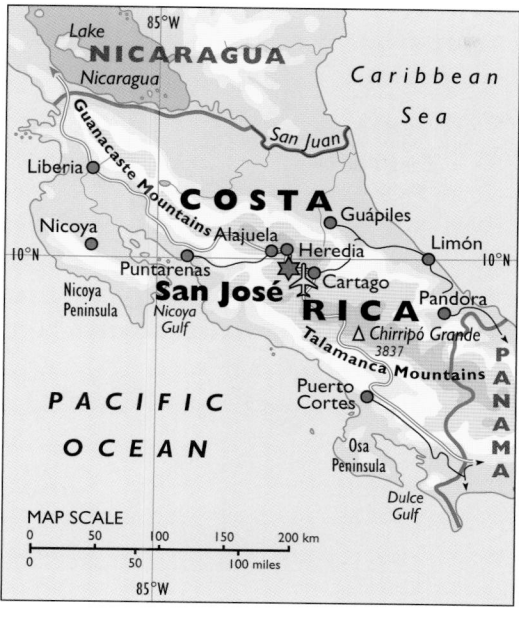

Area 51,100 sq km [19,730 sq mi]
Population 3,957,000
Capital (population) San José (337,000)
Government Multiparty republic
Ethnic groups White (including Mestizo) 94%, Black 3%, Amerindian 1%, Chinese 1%, others
Languages Spanish (official), English
Religions Roman Catholic 76%, Evangelical 14%
Currency Costa Rican colón = 100 céntimos
Website www.visitcostarica.com

CLIMATE

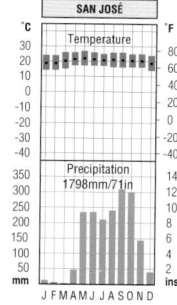

The Meseta Central benefits from a pleasant climate and an average annual temperature of 20°C [68° F], compared with more than 27°C [81° F] on the coast. The coolest months are December and January. The north-east trade winds bring heavy rain to the Caribbean coast. There is only half as much rainfall in the the highlands and on the Pacific coastlands as occurs on the Caribbean coast.

HISTORY

Christopher Columbus reached the Caribbean coast in 1502 and named the land Costa Rica, Spanish for 'rich coast'. Rumours of treasure attracted many Spaniards to settle in the country from 1561.

Spain ruled the country until 1821, when Spain's Central American colonies broke away to join the Mexican empire in 1822. In 1823, the Central American states broke with Mexico and set up the Central American Federation, the members being Costa Rica, Guatemala, Honduras, Nicaragua, and El Salvador. Later, this large union broke up and Costa Rica became fully independent in 1838. From the late 19th century, Costa Rica experienced a number of revolutions, with both periods of dictatorship and democracy. In 1917–19 General Tinoco formed a dictatorship then in 1948, following a revolt, the armed forces were abolished.

POLITICS

Jose Figueres Ferrer served as president from 1953 to 1958 and again from 1970 to 1974. In 1987 President Oscar Arias Sanchez was awarded the Nobel Peace Prize for his efforts to end the civil wars in Central America.

In 2002 Abel Pancho won the presidential elections. Costa Rica's image was tarnished in 2004 when three former presidents were imprisoned on charges of corruption. Despite this, Costa Rica is seen as an example of political stability in the region and continues to maintain this without having to resort to armed forces.

ECONOMY

Costa Rica is classified by the World Bank as a 'lower-middle-income' developing country. It is one of the most prosperous countries in Central America. There are high educational standards, and a high average life expectancy of 78 years.

Agriculture employs 24% of the workforce. Major crops include coffee, pineapples, bananas and sugar. Other crops include beans, citrus fruits, cocoa, potatoes, rice and maize. Cattle ranching is important.

The country's resources include its forests, but it lacks minerals apart from some bauxite and manganese. Manufacturing is increasing with electronics to the fore. It also has hydropower.

Tourism is a fast-growing industry with eco-tourism gaining in importance. The United States is Costa Rica's chief trading partner.

SAN JOSÉ

Capital and largest city of Costa Rica, in central Costa Rica, capital of San José province. Founded around 1736, it succeeded Cartago as capital in 1823, and soon became the centre of a prosperous coffee trade. Products include coffee, sugar cane, cacao, vegetables, fruit, tobacco.

Mountain village of Zarcero, *Alajuela in Central Valley, famed for the multi-formed topiary of its main square*

64 Croatia

Croatia adopted a red, white and blue flag in 1848. Under Communist rule, a red star appeared at the centre. In 1990, the red star was replaced by the present coat of arms, which symbolizes the various parts of the country.

Area 56,538 sq km [21,829 sq mi]
Population 4,497,000
Capital (population) Zagreb (779,000)
Government Multiparty republic
Ethnic groups Croat 90%, Serb 5%, others
Languages Croatian 96%
Religions Roman Catholic 88%, Orthodox 4%, Islam 1%, others
Currency Kuna = 100 lipas
Website www.vlada.hr/default.asp?ru=2

The Republic of Croatia was part of Yugoslavia until becoming independent in 1991. The region bordering the Adriatic Sea is called Dalmatia. It includes the coastal ranges, which contain large areas of bare limestone, reaching 1,913 m [6,276 ft] at Mount Troglav. Other highlands lie in the north-east. Most of the rest of the country consists of the fertile Pannonian Plains, which are drained by Croatia's two main rivers, the Drava and the Sava.

CLIMATE

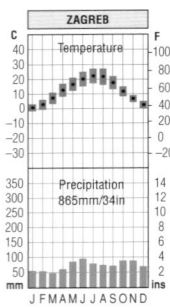

The coastal area has a climate akin to that of the Mediterranean, with hot, dry summers and mild, moist winters. Inland, the climate becomes more continental. Winters are cold, while temperatures often soar to 38°C [100°F] in the summer months.

HISTORY

Slav people settled in the area around 1,400 years ago. In 803, Croatia became part of the Holy Roman Empire. In 1102, the king of Hungary also became king of Croatia, creating a union that lasted 800 years. In 1526, much of Croatia and Hungary came under the Ottoman Turks. At about the same time, the Austrian Habsburgs gained control of the rest of Croatia. In 1699, the Habsburgs drove out the Turks and Croatia again came under Hungarian rule. In 1809, Croatia became part of the Illyrian provinces of Napoleon I of France, but the Habsburgs took over in 1815.

In 1867, Croatia became part of the dual monarchy of Austria-Hungary and in 1868 Croatia signed an agreement with Hungary guaranteeing Croatia some of its historic rights. During World War I, Austria-Hungary fought on the side of the defeated Axis powers, and, in 1918, the empire was broken up. Croatia declared its independence and joined with neighbouring states to form the Kingdom of the Serbs, Croats and Slovenes. Serbian domination provoked Croatian opposition. In 1929, the king changed the country's name to Yugoslavia and began to rule as a dictator. He was assassinated in 1934 by a Bulgarian employed by a Croatian terrorist group, provoking more hostility between Croats and Serbs.

Germany occupied Croatia in World War II. After the war, Communists took power in Yugoslavia, with Josip Broz Tito as its leader. After Tito's death in 1980, economic and ethnic rivalries threatened stability. In the early 1990s, Yugoslavia split into five nations. One of them, Croatia, declared itself independent in 1991.

POLITICS

After Serbia supplied arms to Serbs living in Croatia, war broke out between the two republics, causing great damage, large-scale movements of refugees and disruption of the economy, including the vital tourist industry.

In 1992, the United Nations sent a peace-keeping force to Croatia, effectively ending the war with Serbia. However, in 1992, war broke out in Bosnia-Herzegovina and Bosnian Croats occupied parts of the country. In 1994, Croatia helped to end the Croat-Muslim conflict in Bosnia-Herzegovina and, in 1995, after retaking some areas occupied by Serbs, it contributed to the drawing up of the Dayton Peace Accord, which ended the civil war.

Croatia's arch-nationalist president, Franco Tudjman, died in December 1999. In January 2000, Tudjman's Croatian Democratic Union was defeated in a general election by a more liberal, westward-leaning alliance of Social Democrats and Social Liberals. Stipe Mesic, the last head of state of the former Yugoslavia before it disintegrated in 1991, was elected president. In 2000, the government announced that it would prosecute suspected war criminals and co-operate with the war crimes tribunal in The Hague.

ECONOMY

The wars of the early 1990s disrupted Croatia's economy. Tourism on the Dalmatian coast had been a major industry and is making a gradual return. The manufacturing industries are the chief exports. Manufactures include cement, chemicals, refined oil and oil products, ships, steel and wood products.

Agriculture is important and major farm products include fruits, livestock, maize, soya beans, sugar beet and wheat.

Dubrovnik harbour and old city; *built in the 13th century, the town remains unspoilt*

ZAGREB

Capital of Croatia, on the River Sava. Founded in the 11th century, it became capital of the Hungarian province of Croatia and Slavonia during the 14th century. The city was an important centre of the 19th-century Croatian nationalist movement. In 1918 it was the meeting place of the Croatian Diet (parliament), which severed all ties with Austria-Hungary. In World War II, Zagreb was the capital of the Axis-controlled, puppet Croatian state. It was wrested from Axis control in 1945, and became capital of the Croatian Republic of Yugoslavia. Following the break-up of Yugoslavia in 1992, Zagreb remained capital of the newly independent state of Croatia. The city has many places of historical interest, including a Gothic cathedral and a Baroque archiepiscopal palace. Zagreb has a university (founded 1669) and an Academy of Arts and Sciences (1861).

Cuba's flag, the 'Lone Star' banner, was designed in 1849, but it was not adopted as the national flag until 1901, after Spain had withdrawn from the country. The red triangle represents the Cuban people's bloody struggle for independence.

The Republic of Cuba is the largest island country in the Caribbean Sea. It consists of one large island, Cuba, the Isle of Youth (Isla de la Juventud) and about 1,600 small islets. Mountains and hills cover about a quarter of Cuba. The highest mountain range, the Sierra Maestra in the south-east, reaches 2,000 m [6,562 ft] above sea level at the Pico Real del Turquino. The rest of the land consists of gently rolling country or coastal plains, crossed by fertile valleys that have been carved by the short, mostly shallow and narrow rivers.

Farmland covers about half of Cuba amnd 66% of this is given over to sugar cane. Pine forests still grow, especially in the south east. Mangrove swamps line some coastal areas.

CLIMATE

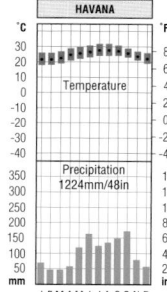

Cuba lies in the tropics. But sea breezes moderate the temperature, warming the land in winter and cooling it in summer.

HISTORY

In 1492 Christopher Columbus discovered the island and Spaniards began to settle there from 1511. Spanish rule ended in 1898, when the United States defeated Spain in the Spanish-American War. The United States ruled Cuba from 1898 until 1902, when the people elected Tomás Estrada Palma as president of the independent Republic of Cuba, though American influence remained strong. In 1933, an army sergeant named Fulgencio Batista seized power and ruled as dictator. However, under a new constitution, he was elected president in 1940, serving until 1944. He again seized power in 1952 and became dictator once more, but, on 1 January 1959, he fled Cuba following the overthrow of his regime by a revolutionary force led by a young lawyer, Fidel Castro. Many Cubans who were opposed to Castro left the country, settling in the United States.

POLITICS

The United States opposed Castro's policies, so he turned to the Soviet Union for assistance. In 1962, the US learned that nuclear missile bases armed by the Soviet Union had been established in Cuba. The US ordered the Soviet Union to remove the missiles and bases. After a few days, during which many people feared that a world war might break out, the Soviet Union agreed to American demands.

Cuba's relations with the Soviet Union remained strong until 1991, when the Soviet Union was broken up. The loss of Soviet aid greatly damaged Cuba's economy and the new situation undermined Castro's considerable social achievements. However, in February 1993, elections showed a high level of support for his left-wing policies. In 1998, hopes of a thaw in relations with the United States were raised when the US government announced that it was lifting the ban on flights to Cuba. The Pope, making his first visit to Cuba, criticized the 'unjust and ethically unac-ceptable' US blockade on Cuba. In 2000, the United States lifted its food embargo on Cuba. The last Russian base in Cuba closed in 2002. In 2004, following a United States crackdown on currency and travel, Cuba declared that US dollars would no longer be accepted as payments for goods and services.

HAVANA (LA HABANA)

Capital of Cuba, on the north west coast. It is the largest city and port in the West Indies. Havana was founded by the Spanish explorer Diego Velázquez in 1515, and moved to its present site in 1519. It became Cuba's capital at the end of the 16th century. Industries include oil refining, textiles, sugar and cigars.

Area 110,861 sq km [42,803 sq mi]
Population 11,309,000
Capital (population) Havana (2,192,000)
Government Socialist republic
Ethnic groups Mulatto 51%, White 37%, Black 11%
Languages Spanish (official)
Religions Christianity
Currency Cuban peso = 100 centavos
Website www.cubagob.gov.cu/ingles/

ECONOMY

The World Bank classifies Cuba as a 'lower-middle-income' country. Sugar cane remains Cuba's outstandingly important cash crop, accounting for more than 60% of the country's exports. It is grown on more than half of the island's cultivated land and Cuba is one of the world's top ten producers of the product. Before 1959, the sugar cane was grown on large estates, many of them owned by US companies. Following the Revolution, they were nationalized and the Soviet Union and Eastern European countries replaced the United States as the main market. The other main crop is tobacco, which is grown in the north-west. Cattle raising, milk production and rice cultivation have also been encouraged to help diversify the economy, and the Castro regime has devoted considerable efforts to improving the quality of rural life, making standards of living more homogeneous throughout the island.

Minerals and concentrates rank second to sugar among Cuba's exports, followed by fish products, tobacco and tobacco products, including the famous cigars, and citrus fruits. In the 1990s, Cuba sought to increase its trade with Latin America and China. Tourism is a major source of income, but the industry was badly hit following the terrorist attacks on the United States in 2001.

Vintage cars line the street near the Capitol building, Havana

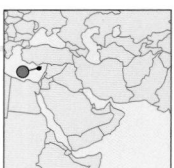

Area 9,251 sq km [3,572 sq mi]
Population 776,000
Capital (population) Nicosia (198,000)
Government Multiparty republic
Ethnic groups Greek Cypriot 77%, Turkish Cypriot 18%, others
Languages Greek and Turkish (both official), English
Religions Greek Orthodox 78%, Islam 8%
Currency Cypriot pound = 100 cents
Website www.cyprus.gov.cy

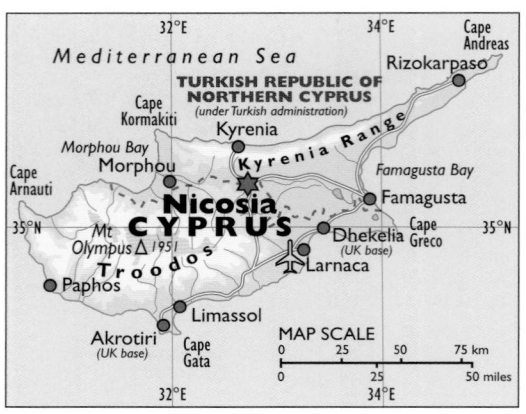

The Republic of Cyprus is an island nation which lies in the north-eastern Mediterranean Sea. Geographers regard it as part of Asia, but it resembles southern Europe in many ways. Cyprus has scenic mountain ranges, including the Kyrenia Range in the north and the Troodos Mountains in the south, which rise to 1,951 m [6,401 ft] at Mount Olympus.

The island also contains fertile lowlands used extensively for agriculture, including the broad Mesaoria Plain. Pine forests grow on the mountain slopes.

CLIMATE

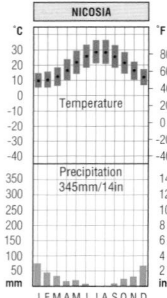

Cyprus experiences hot, dry summers and mild, wet winters. Summers are hotter than those further west in the Mediterranean as Cyprus lies close to the hot mainland of south-western Asia.

HISTORY

The history of Cyprus dates back to 7000 BC. Greeks settled on Cyprus around 3,200 years ago. By 1050 BC Cyprus was fully established as a Greek island having embraced the language and culture of Greece. In 333 BC it became part of the empire of Alexander the Great and in 58 BC part of the Roman Empire. From AD 330, the island was under the Byzantine empire.

Cyprus was defeated in 1191 by Richard the Lionheart and the island was sold to the Knights Templar. Catholicism became the official religion. The island was under Venetian control from 1489 and fortifications were added to the towns of Nicosia and Famagusta. In the 1570s, it became part of the Turkish Ottoman Empire and Islam was introduced.

Turkish rule continued until 1878 when Cyprus was leased to Britain although it was still part of the Ottoman Empire. When the Ottomans entered World War I in 1914, on the side of Germany, the island was annexed by Britain. It was proclaimed a Crown colony in 1925.

In the 1950s, Greek Cypriots, who made up four-fifths of the population, led by Greek Orthodox Archbishop Makarios, began a campaign for enosis (union) with Greece. A secret guerrilla force called EOKA attacked the British who exiled Makarios.

POLITICS

Cyprus became an independent country in 1960 with Makarios as president. Britain retained two military bases. The constitution of Cyprus provided for power-sharing between the Greek and Turkish Cypriots. But the constitution proved unworkable and fighting broke out. In 1964 the UN sent in a peace-keeping force.

In 1974, Cypriot forces led by Greek officers overthrew Makarios. This led Turkey to invade northern Cyprus, a territory occupying about 40% of the island. Many Greek Cypriots fled from the north, which, in 1983, was proclaimed an independent state called the Turkish Republic of Northern Cyprus. However, the only country to recognise its status was Turkey. The UN regards Cyprus as a single nation under the Greek-Cypriot government in the south. It is estimated that more than 30,000 Turkish troops are deployed in northern Cyprus. Despite UN-brokered peace negotiations, there are still frequent border clashes between the two communities.

In 2002, the European Union invited Cyprus to become a member. In April 2004, the people voted on a UN plan to reunify the island. The Turkish Cypriots voted in favour of the plan, but the Greek Cypriots voted against. As a result of this, only the south was admitted to membership of the EU on 1 May 2004.

ECONOMY

Cyprus got its name from the Greek word kypros, meaning copper, but little copper remains. The chief minerals are asbestos and chromium. The most valuable activity in Cyprus is tourism.

Industry employs 37% of the workforce and manufactures include cement, clothes, footwear, tiles and wine. In the early 1990s, the United Nations reclassified Cyprus as a developed rather than developing country, though the economy of the Turkish-Cypriot north lags behind that of the more prosperous Greek-Cypriot south.

Interior of Asinou Church, *Troodos Region; the church is filled with frescoes from the 12th century and is one of the 10 monuments in the area to be listed as a UNESCO World Heritage Site*

NICOSIA (LEVKOSÍA)

Capital of Cyprus, in the centre of the island. Known to the ancients as Ledra, the city was later held by Byzantines, French crusaders and Venetians. The Ottoman Turks occupied the city from 1571 to 1878, when it passed to Britain. It is now divided into Greek and Turkish sectors by a UN-maintained 'Green Line' and is the only divided city in Europe. Industries include cigarettes, textiles, footwear.

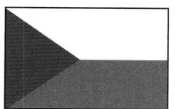

After independence, on 1 January 1993, the Czech Republic adopted the former flag of Czechoslovakia. It features the red and white of Bohemia in the west, together with the blue of Moravia and Slovakia. Red, white and blue are the colours of Pan-Slavic liberation.

The Czech Republic is the western three-fifths of the former country of Czechoslovakia. It contains two regions: Bohemia in the west and Moravia in the east. Mountains border much of the country in the west. The Bohemian basin in the north-centre is a fertile lowland region, with Prague, the capital city, as its main centre. Highlands cover much of the centre of the country, with lowlands in the south-east. Some rivers, such as the Elbe (Labe) and Oder (Odra) flow north into Germany and Poland. In the south, rivers flow into the Danube Basin.

Area 30,450 sq km [78,866 sq mi]
Population 10,246,000
Capital (population) Prague (1,193,000)
Government Multiparty republic
Ethnic groups Czech 81%, Moravian 13%, Slovak 3%, Polish, German, Silesian, Gypsy, Hungarian, Ukrainian
Languages Czech (official)
Religions Atheist 40%, Roman Catholic 39%, Protestant 4%, Orthodox 3%, others
Currency Czech koruna = 100 haler
Website www.czech.cz

CLIMATE

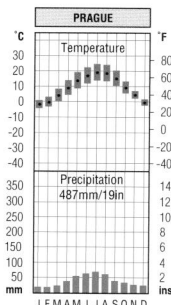

The climate of the Czech Republic is influenced by its landlocked position in east-central Europe. The country experiences a humid continental climate, with warm summers and cold winters. The average rainfall is moderate, with 500 mm to 750 mm [20 in to 30 in] annually in lowland areas.

HISTORY

The ancestors of the Czech people began to settle in what is now the Czech Republic around 1,500 years ago. Bohemia, in the west, became important in the 10th century as a kingdom within the Holy Roman Empire. By the 14th century, Prague was one of Europe's major cultural cities. Religious wars in the first half of the 15th century led many Czech people to become Protestants. From 1526, the Roman Catholic Habsburgs from Austria began to rule the area, but, in 1618, a Czech Protestant rebellion started the Thirty Years' War. From 1620, most Czechs were made to convert to Catholicism and adopt German as their language.

Czech nationalism grew throughout the 19th century. During World War I, Czech nationalists advocated the creation of an independent nation. At the end of the war, when Austria-Hungary collapsed, the new republic of Czechoslovakia was founded. The 1920s and 1930s were generally a period of stability and economic progress, but problems arose concerning the country's minority groups. Many Slovaks wanted a greater degree of self-government, while Germans living in Sudetenland, in western Czechoslovakia, were unhappy under Czech rule.

In 1938, Sudetenland was turned over to Germany and, in March 1939, Germany occupied the rest of the country. By 1945, following the Nazi defeat, a coalition government, including Czech Communists, was formed to rule the country. In 1948, Communist leaders seized control and made the country an ally of the Soviet Union in the Cold War. In 1968, the Communist government introduced reforms, which were known as the 'Prague spring'. However, Russian and other East European troops invaded and suppressed the reform group.

POLITICS

When democratic reforms were introduced in the Soviet Union in the 1980s, the Czechs also demanded change. In 1989, the Federal Assembly elected Václav Havel, a noted playwright and dissident, as the country's president and, in 1990, free elections were held. The smooth transition from Communism to democracy was called the 'Velvet Revolution'. The road to a free-market economy was not easy, with resulting inflation, falling production, strikes and unemployment, though tourism has partly made up for some of the economic decline. Political problems also arose when Slovaks began to demand independence. Finally, on 1 January 1993, the more statist Slovakia broke away from the free-market Czech Republic. However, the split was generally amicable and border adjustments were negligible. The Czechs and Slovaks maintained a customs union and other economic ties. Meanwhile the Czech government continued to develop ties with Western Europe when it became a member of NATO in 1992. On 1 May 2004 the Czech Republic became a member of the European Union.

ECONOMY

Under Communist rule the Czech Republic became one of the most industrialized parts of Eastern Europe. The country has deposits of coal, uranium, iron ore, magnesite, tin and zinc. Manufactures include such products as chemicals, iron and steel and machinery, but the country also has light industries making such things as glassware and textiles for export. Manufacturing employs about 40% of the Czech Republic's entire workforce.

Farming is important. The main crops include barley, fruit, hops for beer-making, maize, potatoes, sugar beet, vegetables and wheat. Cattle and other livestock are raised. The country was admitted into the Organization for Economic Co-operation and Development (OECD) in 1995.

PRAGUE (PRAHA)

Capital of the Czech Republic, on the River Vltava. Founded in the 9th century, it grew rapidly after Wenceslaus I established a German settlement in 1232. In the 14th century it was the capital of Bohemia. It was the capital of the Czechoslovak Republic (1918–93). Occupied in World War II by the Germans it was liberated by Soviet troops in 1945. Prague was the centre of Czech resistance to the Soviet invasion of 1968. Sights include Hradcany Castle and Charles Bridge. An important commercial centre, industries include engineering, iron and steel.

Stare Mesto, Prague; *the beautiful Old Town dates back to the 13th century*

Denmark's flag is called the Dannebrog, or 'the spirit of Denmark'. It may be the oldest national flag in continuous use. It represents a vision thought to have been seen by the Danish King Waldemar II before the Battle of Lyndanisse, which took place in Estonia in 1219.

Area 43,094 sq km [16,639 sq mi]
Population 5,413,000
Capital (population) Copenhagen (488,000)
Government Parliamentary monarchy
Ethnic groups Scandinavian, Inuit, Faeroese, German
Languages Danish (official), English, Faerose
Religions Evangelical Lutheran 95%
Currency Danish krone = 100 øre
Website http://denmark.dk

The Kingdom of Denmark is the smallest country in Scandinavia. It consists of a peninsula called Jutland (Jylland), which is joined to Germany, and more than 400 islands, 89 of which are inhabited. The land is flat and mostly covered by rocks dropped there by huge ice sheets during the last Ice Age. The highest point in Denmark is on Jutland and is only 173 m [568 ft].

CLIMATE

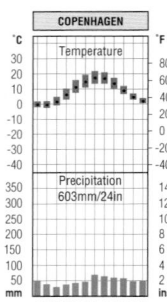

Denmark has a cool but pleasant climate. During cold spells in the winter The Sound between Sjælland and Sweden may freeze over. Summers are warm. Rainfall occurs throughout the year.

HISTORY

Danish Vikings terrorized much of Western Europe for about 300 years after AD 800. Danish kings ruled England in the 11th century. Control of the entrances to the Baltic Sea contributed to the power of Denmark in the Middle Ages, when the kingdom dominated its neighbours and expanded its territories to include Norway, Iceland, Greenland and the Faroe Islands. The link with Norway was broken in 1814, and with Iceland in 1944. But Greenland and the Faroes retained connections with Denmark. The granite island of Bornholm, off the southern tip of Sweden, also remains a Danish possession. This island was occupied by Germany in World War II, but it was liberated by the Soviet Union and returned to Denmark in 1946. Denmark was also occupied by Germany in 1940, but it was liberated in 1945. The Danes then set about rebuilding their industries and restoring their economy.

POLITICS

Denmark is a generally comfortable mixture of striking political opposites. The Lutheran tradition and the cradle of Hans Christian Andersen's fairy tales coexist with open attitudes to pornography and one of the highest illegitimacy rates in the West.

The country is one of the 'greenest' of the developed nations, with a pioneering Ministry of Pollution. In 1991, it became the first government anywhere to fine industries for emissions of carbon dioxide, the primary 'greenhouse' gas.

It joined the North Atlantic Treaty Organization (NATO) in 1949, and in 1973 it joined the European Community (now the European Union). However, it remains one of the European Union's least enthusiastic members and was one of the four countries that did not adopt the euro, the single EU currency, on 1 January 2002. In 1972, in order to join the EC, Denmark had become the first Scandinavian country to break away from the other major economic grouping in Europe, the European Free Trade Association (EFTA), but it continued to co-operate with its five Scandinavian partners through the consultative Nordic Council which was set up in 1953.

The Danes enjoy some of the world's highest living standards, although the cost of welfare provisions was high. The election of a Liberal-Conservative coalition in 2001 led to cutbacks. Under Prime Minister Anders Fogh Rasmussen, who won a second term in 2005, the government also tightened immigration controls, causing criticism by the UN High Commissioner for Refugees.

Denmark granted home rule to the Faeroe Islands in 1948, although in 1998, the government of the Faeroes announced plans for independence. In 1979, home rule was also granted to Greenland, which demonstrated its new-found independence by withdrawing from the European Community in 1985. Denmark is a constitutional monarchy, with a hereditary monarch, and its constitution was amended in 1953 to allow female succession to the throne.

ECONOMY

Denmark has few mineral resources, though there is now some oil and natural gas from the North Sea. It is one of Europe's wealthiest industrial nations. Farming employs only 4% of workers, but it is highly scientific and productive with.dairy farming and pig and poultry breeding chief areas.

From a firm agricultural base, Denmark has developed a wide range of industries. Some, including brewing, meat canning, fish processing, pottery, textiles and furniture making, use Danish products, but others, such as shipbuilding, oil refining, engineering and metal-working, depend on imported raw materials. Copenhagen is the chief industrial centre and draws more than a million tourists each year. At the other end of the scale is Legoland, the famous miniature town of plastic bricks, built at Billand, north-west of Vejle in eastern Jutland. It was here that Lego was created before it became the world's best-selling construction toy and a prominent Danish export.

COPENHAGEN (KØBENHAVN)

Capital and chief port of Denmark on east Sjælland and north Amager Island, in the Øresund. A trading and fishing centre by the early 12th century, it became Denmark's capital in 1443. It has a 17th-century stock exchange, the Amalienborg palace (home of the royal family) and the Christianborgs Palace. Other sights include the Tivoli Amusement Park and the Little Mermaid sculpture. The commercial and cultural centre of the nation, it has shipbuilding, chemical and brewing industries.

Egeskor Castle, Fuenen

FAEROE ISLANDS

The Faeroe (or Faroe) Islands are an autonomous region of Denmark. Situated in the North Atlantic Ocean between Iceland and the Shetland Islands, the region consists of 18 islands, 17 of which are inhabited. The main islands are Streymoy, on which the capital Tórshavn stands, Vágar, Suduroy and Sandoy. The islands have rugged coasts with abundant bird life. Most people live on the small coastal lowlands.

CLIMATE Winters are mild under the influence of the North Atlantic Drift, the extension of the warm Gulf Stream. Summers are cool and the weather is often overcast. Fogs are common and winds are often strong.

HISTORY Irish monks settled on the islands in the 6th century AD, though most of the islanders today are descendants of Vikings. The Faeroe Islands were part of the Kingdom of Norway from the 11th century until 1380. The islands came under Danish control when Norway joined the Kingdom of Denmark. British troops occupied the islands during World War II (1939–45), but they reverted to Danish control after the war.

POLITICS The Danes granted the islands self-government in 1948, making them a self-governing overseas administrative division of Denmark, with Denmark responsible for defence and foreign relations. The islands have their own parliament, consisting of 32 members elected on a proportional basis from the seven constituencies. The parliament elects the leader of the majority group as prime minister. Two members are elected to the Danish parliament.

In 2001, a planned referendum on independence was cancelled when the Danish government stated that it would cut off all financial aid to the islands within four years of independence.

ECONOMY The people enjoy a high standard of living. Fishing is the main activity and the country has benefited, since the 1990s, from increased production, together with high export prices. Faeroese fishermen have traditionally hunted pilot whales, but animal rights activists have called for the abandonment of the cull.

The government hopes to diversify the economy and explore the prospects of offshore oil and gas fields. The islands benefit from a Danish subsidy which accounts for 15% of the GDP. Tourism is also important, along with the production of wool.

Area 1,399 sq km [545.3 sq mi]
Population 46,962
Capital (population) Torshavn (17.939)
Government Self-governing overseas administrative division of Denmark
Ethnic groups Scandinavian
Languages Faroese, Danish
Religions Evangelical Lutheran
Currency Danish krone = 100 ore
Website www.visit-faroeislands.com

TÓRSHAVN

Capital city in the centre of the Faeroe Islands. In 800, Norwegian settlers replaced an Irish settlement on the islands. Tórshavn became the central meeting place. Christianity was introduced in about 1000. The isles came under Norwegian rule in 1035 and under Danish rule in 1816. Tórshavn became the seat of government in 1856. The Faeroese seafishing trade started in Tórshavn. Since 1974 the town has joined with Kaldbak, Hoyvík, Argir and Kollafjørur.

GREENLAND

Situated in the north-west Atlantic Ocean and lying mostly within the Arctic Circle, Greenland is regarded by geographers as the world's largest island. It is almost three times larger than the second largest island, New Guinea.

An ice sheet, the world's second largest after Antarctica, covers more than 85% of its area with an average depth of 1,500 m [5,000 ft]. Settlement is confined to the rocky south west coast.

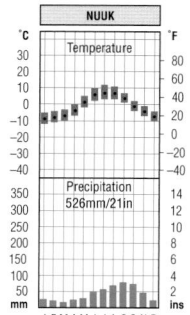

CLIMATE The south west coast, where the capital Nuuk (Godthåb) is situated, is warmed by Atlantic currents, even so, it has more than seven months with average temperatures below freezing.

HISTORY European discovery of Greenland is credited to Erik the Red, who settled in 982, founding a colony that lasted more than 500 years. Greenland became a Danish possession in 1380 and an integral part of the Danish kingdom in 1953.

POLITICS It was taken into the EC in 1973, despite a majority of Greenlanders voting against this. In 1979, after another referendum, home rule was introduced, with full internal self-government in 1981. In 1985, Greenland withdrew from the EC, halving the Community's land area.

ECONOMY Greenland still relies heavily on Danish aid and Denmark is its main trading partner. The chief rural occupations are sheep-rearing and fishing, with shrimps, prawns and molluscs being exported. The only major manufacturing industry is fish canning, which has drawn many Inuit to the towns. Few Inuit now follow the traditional life of nomadic hunting.

Most Greenlanders live between the primitive and the modern. Yet a nationalist mood prevails, buoyed by rich fish stocks, lead and zinc from Uummannaq in the north-west, untapped uranium in the south and possible oil in the east. In addition, an adventure-orientated tourist industry is expanding. In 1997, the nationalist resurgence led to Greenland making Inuit name forms official.

Area 2,166,086 sq km [836,330 sq mi]
Population 56,375
Capital (population) Nuuk (13,400)
Government Self-governing overseas administrative division of Denmark
Ethnic groups Greenlander 88% (Inuit and Greenland-born whites), Danish and others 12%
Languages Greenlandic (East Inuit), Danish, English
Religions Evangelical Lutheran
Currency Danish krone = 100 ore
Website http://dk.nanoq.gl

NUUK (DANISH, GODTHÅB)

Capital and largest town of Greenland, at the mouth of a group of fjords on the south-west coast. Founded in 1721, it is Greenland's oldest Danish settlement. Places of interest include the Greenlandic National Museum and Archives, the Katuaq Cultural Centre (with the island's only cinema) and Niels Lynges' House.

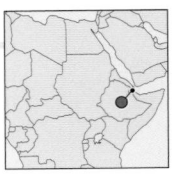

Based on the banner of the African People's League for Independence. Blue is the colour of the Issas people and also the sky and the sea. Green is for the Afars people and symbolizes fertile earth. The white triangle signifies peace and equality, the red star is a symbol of unity.

Area 23,200 sq km [8,958 sq mi]
Population 467,000
Capital (population) Djibouti (317,000)
Government Multiparty republic
Ethnic groups Somali 60%, Afar 35%
Languages Arabic and French (both official)
Religions Islam 94%, Christianity 6%
Currency Djiboutian franc = 100 centimes
Website www.presidence.dj

The Republic of Djibouti is a small country on the north-east coast of Africa, the capital is also Djibouti. Djibouti occupies a strategic position around the Gulf of Tadjoura, where the Red Sea meets the Gulf of Aden. Behind the coastal plain lie the Mabla Mountains, rising to Moussa Ali at 2,028 m [6,654 ft]. Djibouti contains the lowest point on the African continent, Lake Assal, at 155 m [509 ft] below sea level.

Nearly 90% of the land is semi-desert, and shortage of pasture and water make farming difficult.

CLIMATE

Djibouti has one of the world's hottest and driest climates with summer temperatures regularly exceeding 42°C [100°F]. Average annual rainfall is only 130 mm [5 in]. In the wooded Mabla Mountains, the average annual rainfall reaches 500 mm [20 in].

HISTORY

Islam arrived in the 9th century. The subsequent conversion of the Afars led to conflict with Christian Ethiopians who lived in the interior. By the 19th century, Somalian Issas moved north and occupied much of the Afars' traditional grazing land.

France gained influence in 1862, with its interest centered around Djibouti, the French commercial rival to the port of Aden. French Somaliland was established in 1888.

A referendum in 1967 saw 60% of the electorate vote to retain links with France, though most Issas favoured independence. The country was renamed the French Territory of the Afars and Issas.

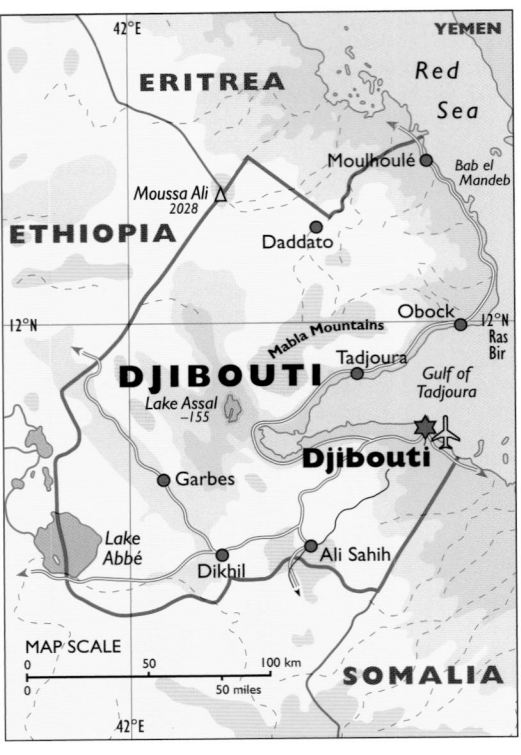

POLITICS

In 1977 the Republic of Djibouti gained full independence, and Hassan Gouled Aptidon of the Popular Rally for Progress (RPP) was elected president. He declared a one-party state in 1981. Protests against the Issas-dominated regime forced the adoption of a multi-party constitution in 1992. The Front for the Restoration of Unity and Democracy (FRUD), supported primarily by Afars, boycotted 1993 elections, and Aptidon was re-elected for a fourth six-year term. FRUD rebels continued an armed campaign for political representation. In 1996, government and FRUD forces signed a peace agreement, recognizing FRUD as a political party.

In 1999, Ismael Omar Gelleh succeeded Aptidon as president in the country's first multi-party presidential elections. He pursues a policy of closer links with France, which still has a strong military presence in Djibouti. In addition it is forging closer ties with the United States, with the only US military base in sub-Saharan Africa stationed there.

ECONOMY

Djibouti is a poor nation, heavily reliant on food imports and revenue from the capital city. A free-trade zone, it has no major resources and manufacturing is on a very small scale. The only important activity is livestock raising, and 50% of the population are pastoral nomads.

Its location at the mouth of the Red Sea is of great economic importance as it serves as a vital trans-shipment point.

Travertine vents on Lake Abbé in the south-west of Djibouti on the border with Ethiopia; the vents are formed by a calcium-rich flow from below the lake and they expel unpleasant sulphurous gases; the lake is heavily salted and therefore totally undrinkable

GULF OF ADEN

A body of water that makes up the western arm of the Arabian Sea, meeting the Red Sea at the Babu l-Mandeb strait. The gulf runs in a west–east direction, between Yemen and Somalia, meeting Djibouti at the western end. It is about 900 km [560 mi] long, and 500 km [310 mi] wide at the eastern end, between Ra's Asir of Somalia and the city of al-Mukalla in Yemen. The Gulf of Aden is an important route for commercial shipping.

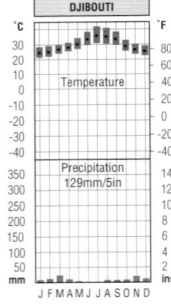

DJIBOUTI (JIBUTI)

Capital of Djibouti, on the western shore of an isthmus in the Gulf of Tadjoura, north-east Africa. Founded in 1888, it became capital in 1892, and a free port in 1949. Ethiopian emperor Menelik II built a railway from Addis Ababa, and Djibouti became the chief port for handling Ethiopian trade. While Eritrea was federated with Ethiopia (1952–93), it lost this status to the Red Sea port of Assab. Now home to two-thirds of the country's population.

RED SEA

Narrow arm of the Indian Ocean between north-east Africa and the Arabian Peninsula, connected to the Mediterranean by the Gulf of Suez and the Suez Canal. With the building of vessels too large for the canal and the construction of pipelines, the Red Sea's importance as a trade route has diminished. Its widest point is 320 km [200 mi]. It covers an area of 438,000 sq km [169,000 sq mi].

Dominican Republic

Blue represents liberty, red stands for blood shed during the struggle for liberation, the white cross is a symbol of sacrifice. The coat of arms features a Bible open at the Gospel of St John, symbolizing the Trinitarian movement that led the movement for independence.

Area 48,511 sq km [18,730 sq mi]
Population 8,834,000
Capital (population) Santo Domingo (2,061,000)
Government Multiparty republic
Ethnic groups Mulatto 73%, White 16%, Black 11%
Languages Spanish (official)
Religions Roman Catholic 95%
Currency Dominican peso = 100 centavos
Website www.dominicanrepublic.com

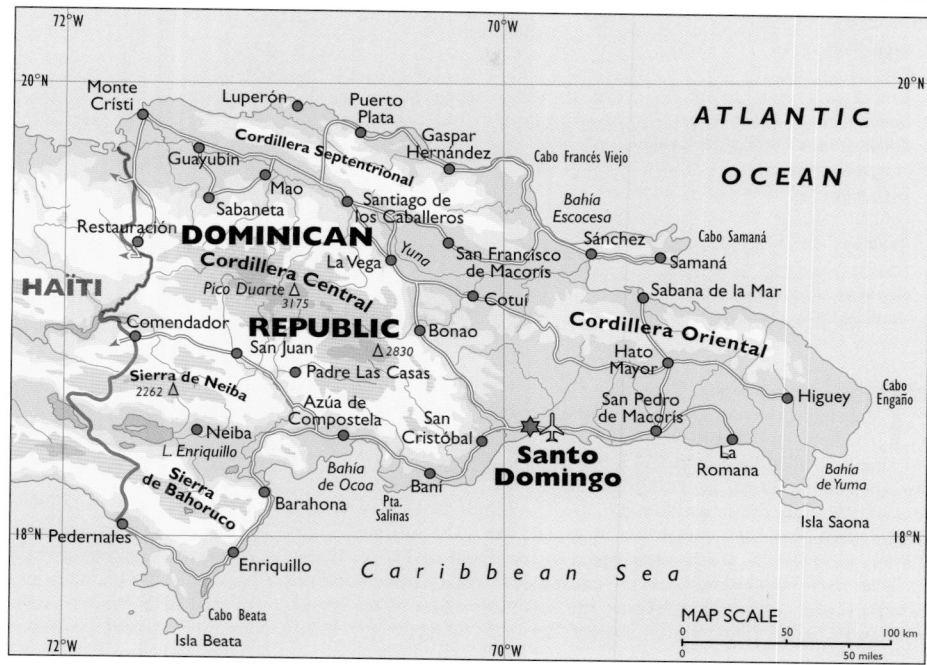

The Dominican Republic is the second largest of the Caribbean nations in both area and population, it shares the island of Hispaniola with Haiti, the Dominican Republic occupying the eastern two-thirds. Of the steep-sided mountains that dominate the island, the country includes the northern Cordillera Septentrional, the huge Cordillera Central, which rises to Pico Duarte, at 3,175 m [10,414 ft] the highest peak in the Caribbean, and the southern Sierra de Baoruco. Between them and to the east lie fertile valleys and lowlands, including the Vega Real and the coastal plains where the main sugar plantations are found.

CLIMATE

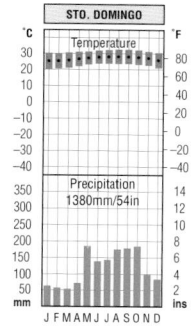

Typical of the Caribbean region, the climate is humid and hot throughout the year close to sea level, while cooler conditions prevail in the mountains. Rainfall is heavy, especially in the north-east.

HISTORY

Christopher Columbus 'discovered' the island on 5 December 1492. Its Amerindian population was soon to be decimated. The city of Santo Domingo, now the capital and chief port, was founded by Columbus' brother Bartholomew four years later and is the oldest in the Americas. For a long time a Spanish colony, Hispaniola was initially the centrepiece of their empire, but was later to become a poor relation.

In 1795, it became French, then Spanish again in 1809. But in 1821, when it was called Santo Domingo, it won its independence. Haiti held the territory from 1822 until 1844 when, on restoring sovereignty, it became the Dominican Republic.

Growing American influence culminated in occupation between 1916 and 1924. This was followed by a period of corrupt dictatorship. From 1930 until his assassination in 1961, the country was ruled by Rafael Trujillo, one of Latin America's best-known dictators, who imprisoned or killed many of his opponents. A power struggle developed between the military, the upper class, those who wanted the country to become a democracy and others who favoured making it a Communist regime.

Boats moored in Bayahibe Bay, on the south-east coast

POLITICS

In 1962 Juan Bosch became president, but was ousted in 1963. Bosch supporters tried to seize power in 1965, but were met with strong military opposition. This led to US military intervention in 1965. In 1966, a new constitution was adopted and Joaquín Balaguer was elected president (1966–78, 1986–96). Elections have been known to be violent and the United States has kept a watchful eye.

Leonel Fernández was elected president for a second time in 2004. He had campaigned on a ticket that promised to tackle inflation and once in office he introduced austerity measures, that included cuts to state spending.

ECONOMY

The World Bank describes the Dominican Republic as a 'lower-middle-income' developing country. In the 1990s, industrial growth that exploited the country's huge hydroelectric potential, mining and tourism has augmented the traditional agricultural economy, though the country is far from being politically stable. Agriculture is a major activity. Leading crops include avocados, bananas, beans, mangoes, oranges, plantains, rice, sugar cane and tobacco.

Gold and nickel are mined. Sugar refining is a major industry, with the bulk of the production exported to the United States. Leading exports are ferronickel, sugar, coffee, cocoa and gold. Its main trading partner is the United States.

SANTO DOMINGO (formerly CIUDAD TRUJILLO, 1936–61)

Capital and chief port of the Dominican Republic, on the south coast, on the River Ozama. Founded in 1496, it is the oldest continuous European settlement in the Americas. It was the seat of the Spanish viceroys in the early 1500s, and base for the Spaniards' conquering expeditions until it was devastated by an earthquake in 1562. It houses more than a third of the country's population, many of whom work in the sugar industry.

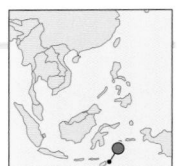

Yellow represents the vestiges of East Timor's colonial past. Black stands for the darkness to be overcome, while red recalls the struggle for liberation. The five-pointed star is the guiding light of peace.

Area 14,874 sq km [5,743 sq mi]
Population 1,019,000
Capital (population) Dili (52,000)
Government Multiparty republic
Ethnic groups Austronesian (Malayo-Polynesian), Papuan
Languages Tetum, Portuguese (both official), Indonesian, English
Religions Roman Catholic 90%, Muslim 4%, Protestant 3%
Currency US dollar = 100 cents
Website www.timor-leste.gov.tl

The Democratic Republic of Timor-Leste is a small island nation in South-east Asia. It became part of Indonesia in 1975, but it became independent in 2002, ending almost 500 years of foreign domination. The Timor Sea separates East Timor from Australia, which lies about 500 km [310 mi] away. East Timor occupies the north-eastern part of the island of Timor. It also includes some small islands and the enclave of Oscùsso-Ambeno on the north-western coast of West Timor, the Indonesian part of the island. The land is largely mountainous, rising to about 2,960 metres [9,711 ft].

CLIMATE

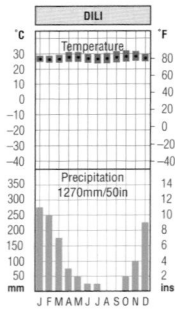

East Timor has a monsoon climate, with high temperatures throughout the year. The average temperature is more than 24°C [75°F], although the mountainous zone is cooler. The monsoon extends from November to May. The average annual rainfall is less than 1,500 mm [59 in]. The mountainous zone is wetter, with a shorter dry period of four months.

HISTORY

Europeans first visited the island of Timor in the 16th century and, following skirmishing between the Dutch and the Portuguese, East Timor came under Portuguese rule by treaties in 1859 and 1893. Japan occupied Timor between 1942 and 1945 during World War II, but the Portuguese returned after Japan was defeated. Following a coup in Portugal in 1974, the new government announced that its colonies should prepare for independence. The Portuguese withdrew from East Timor in August 1975 and Fretilin (the Revolutionary Front for an Independent East Timor) declared the territory independent, but in December 1975, Indonesia seized the territory.

The territory became the 27th province of Indonesia named Timor Timur. Indonesian rule proved oppressive and guerrilla resistance grew. In 1999, Indonesia agreed to let the people of East Timor vote on independence or local autonomy in a UN-supervised referendum. The people voted by almost 99% for independence. East Timor declared itself independent. However, pro-Indonesian militias, who were widely believed to have the backing of the Indonesian government, caused massive destruction until an international peace-keeping force restored order. It has been estimated that 1,400 people were killed and 250,000 were displaced.

POLITICS

East Timor gained full independence on 20 May 2002 and became the 191st member of the United Nations in September. The UN set up a Mission of Support in East Timor to help the Timorese authorities. The country's first president, a ceremonial head of state, was Xanana Gusmao who took 82.6% of the votes in a presidential election in April 2002. Gusmao was the former leader of the separatist guerrilla fighters and had been jailed by the Indonesians between 1992 and 1999.

Following independence, the new government replaced the UN-supervised transitional government and, in 2005, the United Nations withdrew the last of its troops. Some Australian troops remained to train an East Timorese army. East Timor has an elected National Parliament, which elects the country's head of state.

A major problem arising in independent East Timor was the bringing to trial of individuals responsible for atrocities committed during the country's violent transition. An Indonesian court tried people for human rights abuses in East Timor in 1999, while a joint Indonesian and East Timorese Truth and Friendship Commission was established to heal the wounds of the past. Some organizations have criticized the Truth and Friendship Commission, arguing that it is an attempt to bury the past rather than providing justice. However, the governments of East Timor and Indonesia have argued that it is important for the two countries to build a strong relationship between them.

Under emergency powers aimed at curbing gang violence, the police and the army came under the president's control in May 2006.

ECONOMY

Agriculture is the main activity. Arable farms cover 5% of the land and coffee is widely grown. Crops include bananas, cassava, maize, rice, soya beans and sweet potatoes. Coffee, sandalwood and marble are exported.

Following independence, the new country, with its shattered economy and infrastructure, was heavily dependent on foreign aid. However, offshore oil and gas deposits hold out hope for future development. Production of natural gas began in 2004. The oil and gas deposits are located under the Timor Sea and, following independence, East Timor denounced the maritime boundary given to Australia by Indonesia because it gave Australia control over what was probably the richest oil field region.

In 2005, Australia agreed on a division of the expected revenues on the oil and gas deposits, while East Timor agreed to postpone discussions on the disputed maritime boundary.

Rock outcrops *south of Baucau*

DILI

Capital of East Timor, on the north coast of Timor. Originally settled in 1520 by the Portuguese, who made it the capital of Portuguese Timor in 1596. Occupied by the Japanese during World War II. Occupied by Indonesian forces from 1975, but finally independent in 2002. The city retains links with its Portuguese past but has been rebuilt after the massive destruction of 1999.

Ecuador's flag was created by a patriot, Francisco de Miranda, in 1806. The armies of Simón Bolívar, the South American general, won victories over Spain, and flew this flag. At the centre is Ecuador's coat of arms, showing a condor over Mount Chimborazo.

The Republic of Ecuador straddles the Equator on the west coast of South America. Three ranges of the high Andes Mountains form the backbone of the country. Between the towering, snow-capped peaks of the mountains, some of which are volcanoes, lie a series of high plateaux, or basins. Nearly half of Ecuador's population lives on these plateaux.

West of the Andes lie the flat coastal lowlands, which border the Pacific Ocean and average 100 km [60 mi] in width. The eastern alluvial lowlands, often called the Oriente, are drained by headwaters of the River Amazon.

CLIMATE

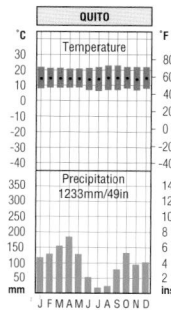

The climate in Ecuador is greatly influenced by the altitude. The coastal lowlands are hot, despite the cooling effect of the cold offshore Peru Current. The Andes have spring temperatures throughout the year, while the eastern lowlands are hot and humid. The rainfall is heaviest in the eastern lowlands and the northern coastal lowlands.

HISTORY

The Inca people of Peru conquered much of what is now Ecuador in the late 15th century. They introduced their language, Quechua, which is widely spoken today. In 1532 a colony was founded by the Spaniards in the territory, which was then called Quito. The country became independent in 1822, following the defeat of a Spanish force by an army led by General Antonio Jose de Sucre in a battle near Quito. Ecuador became part of Gran Colombia, a confederation which also included Colombia and Venezuela. Ecuador became a separate nation in 1830.

In 1832, Ecuador annexed the volcanic Galapagos Islands, which lie 970 km [610 mi] west of Ecuador, of which they form a province. The archipelago, which contains six main islands and more than 50 smaller ones, later became world-famous through the writings of Charles Darwin, who visited the islands in 1835. His descriptions of the unique endemic flora and fauna gave him crucial evidence for his theory of natural selection.

QUITO

Capital of Ecuador, at 2,850 m [9,260 ft], Quito lies almost on the Equator. The site was first settled by Quito Native Americans, and was captured by the Incas in 1487. It was taken by Spain in 1534, and liberated in 1822 by Antonio José de Sucre. A cultural and political centre, it is the site of the Central University of Ecuador (1787). In 1979 the historic centre of the city was declared a World Heritage Site by UNESCO. Products include textiles and handicrafts.

Area 283,561 sq km [109,483 sq mi]
Population 13,213,000
Capital (population) Quito (1,616,000)
Government Multiparty republic
Ethnic groups Mestizo 65%, Amerindian 25%, White 7%, Black 3%
Languages Spanish (official), Quechua
Religions Roman Catholic 95%
Currency US dollar = 100 cents
Website www.vivecuador.com

POLITICS

The failure of successive governments to tackle the country's many social and economic problems caused great instability in Ecuador throughout the 20th century. A war with Peru in 1941 led to loss of territory and border disputes flared up again in 1995, though the two countries eventually signed a peace treaty in January 1998.

Military regimes ruled the country between 1963 and 1966 and again from 1976 to 1979. However, under a new constitution introduced by the second of these military juntas and approved by a national referendum, civilian government was restored. Civilian governments have ruled Ecuador since multiparty elections in 1979. But the volatile character of politics here was evident throughout the 1980s and 1990s. For example, a state of emergency, albeit of short duration, was declared in 1986 and, in 1995, the vice-president was forced to leave the country after accusations that he had bribed opposition deputies.

In 1996, the president was deposed on the grounds of mental incompetence and, in 1998, accusations of fraud marred the victory of President Jamil Mahaud of the centre-right Popular Democracy Party. The early years of the 21st century were marked by political instability as successive presidents faced opposition from the military and public demonstrations. In 2000, economic problems made Ecuador adopt the US dollar as its sole unit of currency.

ECONOMY

The World Bank classifies Ecuador as a 'lower-middle-income' developing country. Agriculture employs 10% of the populous. Bananas, cocoa and coffee are all important export crops. Other products in the hot coastal lowlands include citrus fruits, rice and sugar cane, while beans, maize and wheat are important in the highlands. Cattle are raised for dairy products and meat, while fishing is important in the coastal waters. Forestry is a major activity. Ecuador produces balsa wood and such hardwoods as mahogany.

Mining is important with oil and oil products now playing a major part in the economy. Ecuador started to export oil in the early 1970s and is a member of the Organization of Petroleum Exporting Countries.

Manufactures include cement, Panama hats, paper products, processed food and textiles. Major exports are food and live animals, and mineral fuels. Ecuador's main trading partners are the United States and Colombia.

Women at a cooperative in Gualacea knit wool sweaters for export

A flag consisting of three bands of red, white and black, the colours of the Pan-Arab movement, was adopted in 1958. The present design has a gold eagle in the centre. This symbolizes Saladin, the warrior who led the Arabs in the 12th century.

Area 1,001,449 sq km [386,659 sq mi]
Population 76,117,000
Capital (population) Cairo (6,801,000)
Government Republic
Ethnic groups Egyptians/Bedouins/Berbers 99%
Languages Arabic (official), French, English
Religions Islam (mainly Sunni Muslim) 94%, Christian (mainly Coptic Christian) and others 6%
Currency Egyptian pound = 100 piastres
Website www.egypt.gov.eg/english/default.asp

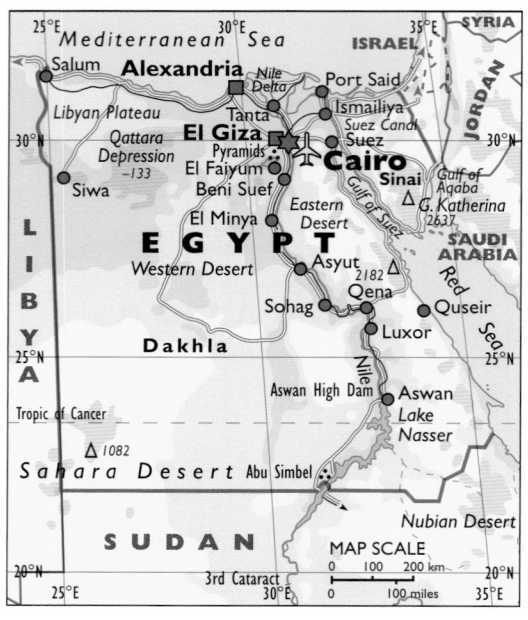

The Arab Republic of Egypt is Africa's second largest country by population after Nigeria. Most of Egypt is desert. Almost all the people live either in the Nile Valley and its fertile delta or along the Suez Canal, the artificial waterway between the Mediterranean and Red seas. This canal shortens the sea journey between the United Kingdom and India by 9,700 km [6,027 mi]. Recent attempts have been made to irrigate parts of the Western Desert.

Apart from the Nile Valley, Egypt has three other main regions. The Western and Eastern deserts are part of the Sahara. The Sinai Peninsula (Es Sina), to the east of the Suez Canal, is very mountainous and contains Egypt's highest peak, Gebel Katherina (2,637 m [8,650 ft]); few people live in this area.

CLIMATE

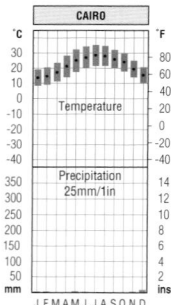

Egypt has a desert climate and is one of the world's sunniest countries. The low rainfall occurs in winter, if at all. Winters are mild, but summers hot. Conditions become unpleasant when hot and dusty winds blow from the deserts into the Nile Valley.

HISTORY

Ancient Egypt, which was founded about 5,000 years ago, was one of the great early civilizations. Throughout the country, pyramids, temples and richly decorated tombs are memorials to its great achievements. After Ancient Egypt declined, the country came under successive foreign rulers. Arabs occupied Egypt in AD 639-42. They introduced the Arabic language and Islam. Their influence was so great that many Egyptians now regard themselves as Arabs.

Egypt came under British rule in 1882, but it gained partial independence in 1922, becoming a monarchy.

CAIRO (AL-QAHIRAH)

Capital of Egypt and port on the River Nile. The largest city in Africa, Cairo was founded in 969 by the Fatimid dynasty and subsequently fortified by Saladin. Medieval Cairo became capital of the Mamluk empire, but declined under Turkish rule. During the 20th century it grew dramatically in population and area. Nearby are world-famous archaeological sites, the sphinx and the Pyramids of Giza. Old Cairo is a world heritage site containing over 400 mosques and other fine examples of Islamic art and architecture. Its five universities include the world's oldest, housed in the mosque of Al Azhar (972) and the centre of Shiite Koranic study.

POLITICS

In 1952, following a military revolution led by General Muhammad Naguib, the monarchy was abolished and Egypt became a republic. Naguib became president, but he was overthrown in 1954 by Colonel Gamal Abdel Nasser. President Nasser sought to develop Egypt's economy, and he announced a major project to build a new dam at Aswan to provide electricity and water for irrigation. When Britain and the United States failed to provide finance for building the dam, Nasser seized the Suez Canal Company in July 1956. In retaliation, Israel, backed by British and French troops, invaded the Sinai Peninsula and the Suez Canal region. However, under international pressure, they were forced to withdraw. Construction of the Aswan High Dam began in 1960 and it was fully operational by 1968.

In 1967, Egypt lost territory to Israel in the Six-Day War and Nasser tendered his resignation, but the people refused to accept it. After his death in 1970, Nasser was succeeded by his vice-president, Anwar el-Sadat. In 1973, Egypt launched a surprise attack in the Sinai Peninsula, but its troops were finally forced back to the Suez Canal. In 1977, Sadat began a peace process when he visited Israel and addressed the Knesset (Israel's parliament). Finally, in 1979, Egypt and Israel signed a peace treaty under which Egypt regained the Sinai Peninsula. However, extremists opposed contacts with Israel and, in 1981, Sadat was assassinated. He was succeeded as president by Hosni Mubarak.

In the 1990s, attacks on foreign visitors severely damaged tourism, despite efforts to curb the activities of Islamic extremists. In 1997, terrorists killed 58 foreign tourists near Luxor. Unrest continued in the 21st century. In 2005, Mubarak was victorious in the first contested presidential elections, but members of the banned Muslim Brotherhood, standing as independents, made gains in parliament.

ECONOMY

Egypt is Africa's second most industrialized country after South Africa, but remains a developing country. The people are poor, farming employs 34% of the workers. Most *fellahin* (peasants) grow food crops such as beans, maize, rice, sugar cane and wheat, but cotton is the chief cash crop. Egypt depends increasingly on the Nile. Its waters are seasonal, and control and storage have become essential in the last 100 years. The Aswan High Dam is the greatest Nile dam, and the water behind it in Lake Nasser makes desert reclamation possible. The electricity produced is important for industrial development. Another vital export prospect is natural gas.

Feluccas on the Nile *at Aswan in southern Egypt*

El Salvador 75

This flag was adopted in 1912, replacing the earlier 'Stars and Stripes'. The blue and white stripes are featured on the flags of several central American countries which gained their independence from Spain at the same time in 1821.

El Salvador is the smallest and most densely populated country in Central America. It has a narrow coastal plain along the Pacific Ocean. The majority of the interior is mountainous with many extinct volcanic peaks, overlooking a heavily populated central plateau. Earthquakes are common; in 1854, an earthquake destroyed the capital, San Salvador. In October 1986, another earthquake killed 400 people and caused widespread damage.

Grassland and some virgin forests of original oak and pine are found in the highlands. The central plateau and valleys have areas of grass and deciduous woodland, while tropical savanna or forest cover the coastal regions.

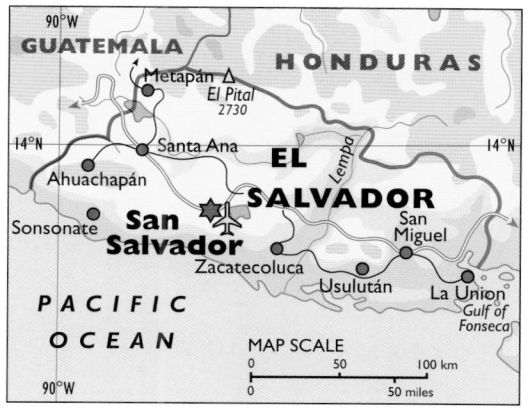

Area 21,041 sq km [8,124 sq mi]
Population 6,588,000
Capital (population) San Salvador (473,000)
Government Republic
Ethnic groups Mestizo 90%, White 9%, Amerindian 1%
Languages Spanish (official)
Religions Roman Catholic 83%
Currency US dollar = 100 cents
Website www.elsalvadorturismo.gob.sv

CLIMATE

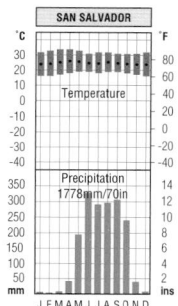

The coast has a hot tropical climate. Inland, the climate is moderated by altitude. The centre region has similar temperatures by day, but nights are cooler. Rain falls most afternoons between May and October.

HISTORY

In 1524–26 Spanish explorer Pedro de Alvarado conquered Native American tribes such as the Pipil, and the region became part of the Spanish Viceroyalty of Guatemala. Independence was achieved in 1821, and in 1823 El Salvador joined the Central American Federation. The federation dissolved in 1839.

El Salvador declared independence in 1841, but was continually subject to foreign interference (especially from Guatemala and Nicaragua). It was at this time that El Salvador's coffee plantations developed.

POLITICS

Following a collapse in the world coffee market, Maximiliano Hernández Martínez seized power in a palace coup in 1931. In 1944 a general strike overthrew his brutal dictatorship. After a period of progressive government, a military junta headed by Julio Adalberto Rivera from 1962 to 1967 and Fidel Sánchez Hernández from 1967 to 1972 seized power. Honduras' discriminatory immigration laws exacerbated tension on the

border between the two countries. The 'Soccer War' of 1969 broke out following an ill-tempered World Cup qualifying match. Within four days, El Salvador captured much of Honduras. A cease-fire occurred and the troops withdrew.

In the 1970s, the repressive National Republican Alliance (ARENA) regime compounded El Salvador's problems of overpopulation, unequal distribution of wealth, and social unrest. Civil war broke out in 1979 between US-backed government forces and the Farabundo Marti National Liberation Front (FMLN). The 12-year war claimed 75,000 lives and caused mass homelessness. A cease-fire held from 1992, and the FMLN became a recognized political party. In 1993 a UN Truth Commission led to the removal of senior army officers for human rights abuses, and the decommissioning of FMLN arms. Armando Calderón Sol became president in 1994 elections; Francisco Flores succeeded him in 1999.

In 2001, massive earthquakes killed about 1,200 people and left one million homeless. Tony Saca won 2004 presidential elections to become the fourth successive ARENA president.

ECONOMY

El Salvador is a lower-middle-income developing country. Farmland and pasture account for approximately 60% of land use. El Salvador is the world's 10th largest producer of coffee. Its reliance on the crop caused economic structural imbalance. Sugar and cotton grow on the coastal lowlands. Fishing is important, but manufacturing is on a small scale. The civil war devastated the economy. Between 1993 and 1995, El Salvador received more than US$100 million of credit from the International Monetary Fund.

__Volcan Santa Ana__ (Ilamatepec); at 2381 m (7,812 ft) Santa Ana is the highest volcano in El Salvador, its last eruption in 2005 killed two and caused the evacuation of thousands

SAN SALVADOR

Capital and largest city of El Salvador in central El Salvador. Founded in 1524 near the volcano of San Salvador, which rises to 1,885 m [6,184 ft] and last erupted in 1917. The city has frequently been damaged by earthquakes. The main industry is the processing of the coffee which is grown on the rich volcanic soils of the area. Other manufactures – beer, textiles, and tobacco.

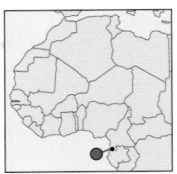

Green is for agriculture, white is peace and red is for blood shed in the fight for independence. Blue represents the Atlantic. The tree on the coat of arms is the tree under which the 1843 treaty with Spain was signed. The six stars represent the mainland and the five islands.

Area 28,051 sq km [10,830 sq mi]
Population 523,000
Capital (population) Malabo (30,000)
Government Multiparty republic (transitional)
Ethnic groups Bubi (on Bioko), Fang (in Rio Muni)
Languages Spanish and French (both official)
Religions Christianity
Currency CFA franc = 100 centimes
Website www.ceiba-guinea-ecuatorial.org

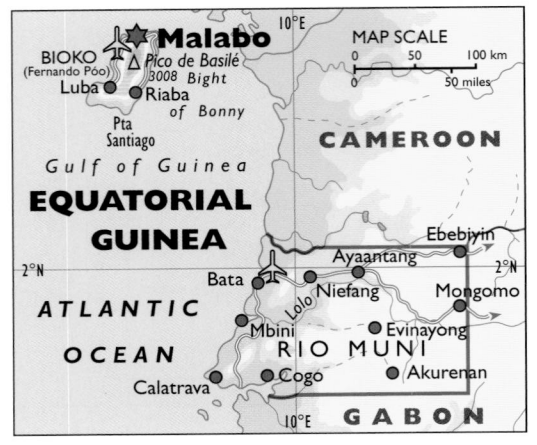

The Republic of Equatorial Guinea is located in west-central Africa and is one of the smallest countries on the African continent. It consists of a mainland territory between Cameroon and Gabon, called Río Muni (Mbini), and five islands in the Bight of Biafra (Bonny), the largest of which is Bioko (Fernando Póo).

Bioko is a volcanic island with fertile soils and a steep rocky coast. Malabo's harbour is part of a submerged volcano. Bioko is mountainous, rising to a height of 3,008 m [9,869 ft] at the Pico de Santa Isabel. It has varied vegetation with trees such as teak, mahogany, oak, walnut and rosewood, and grasslands at higher levels.

Mainland Río Muni (90% of all land) consists mainly of hills and plateaux behind the coastal plains. Its main river, the Lolo, rises in Gabon. Dense forest covers most of Río Muni and provides a habitat for animals such as lions, gazelles and elephants .

CLIMATE

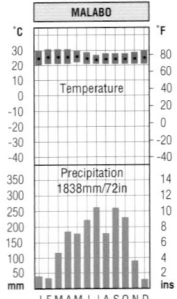

Situated on the equator, Equatorial Guinea has a tropical climate. High temperatures and high humidity are the norm with an average annual temperature of 25° C [77° F]. Bioko has heavy rainfall and there is a dry season from December to February. Río Muni has a similar climate to Bioko, though rainfall diminishes inland.

HISTORY

In 1472 Portuguese navigator Fernão do Pó sighted the largest island of Bioko. In 1778, Portugal ceded the islands and commercial mainland rights to Spain in exchange for some Brazilian territories. Yellow fever hit Spanish settlers on Bioko, and they withdrew in 1781. In 1827, Spain leased bases on Bioko to Britain, and the British settled some freed slaves. Descendants of these former slaves (*Fernandinos*) remain on the island. Spain returned in the mid-19th century and developed plantations on Bioko.

In 1956, the islands became the Overseas Provinces in the Gulf of Guinea. In 1959, the territory was divided into two provinces, Fernando Póo and Río Muni, and named Spanish Guinea. The two territories reunified in 1963 and became the Autonomous Territories of Equatorial Guinea. In 1968 the territory gained independence as the Republic of Equatorial Guinea.

POLITICS

In 1969 as a result of social unrest caused by factors such as ethnic conflict and economic problems, President Francisco Macías Nguema annulled the constitution. A military dictatorship ensued with up to 100,000 refugees fleeing to neighbouring countries. Nguema's dictatorship endured from 1968 to 1979 during which time more than 40,000 people were killed.

In 1979, Lieutenant-Colonel Teodoro Obiang Nguema Mbasogo deposed Nguema in a military coup. A 1991 referendum voted to set up a multi-party democracy, consisting of the ruling Equatorial Guinea Democratic Party (PDGE) and ten opposition parties. The main parties and most of the electorate boycotted elections in 1993, and the PDGE formed a government. In 1996 elections, again boycotted by most opposition parties, President Obiang claimed 99% of the vote. Human rights organisations accuse his regime of routine arrests and torture of opponents and the president is seen to control all the political parties.

In 2004 a coup attempt by foreign mercenaries was foiled and the leaders were arrested.

ECONOMY

Equatorial Guinea is a poor country. Agriculture employs around 60% of the people, though many farmers live at subsistence level, making little contribution to the economy. The main food crops are bananas, cassava and sweet potatoes. The chief cash crop is cocoa, grown on Bioko, though this has been hit by a worldwide dip in cocoa prices.

Oil has been produced off Bioko since 1966. By 2002 it accounted for more than 80% of exports. Despite the rapid expansion of the economy and massive increase in revenue, a UN human rights report stated that 65% of the people still live in 'extreme poverty'.

The government has promised that agriculture will benefit from the large amounts of revenue gained from oil, but this has yet to materialise. Other natural resources that have yet to be developed include titanium, iron ore, manganese and uranium. The country has forfeited much aid from the World Bank and the IMF due to corruption and mismanagement.

Cocoa (Theobroma cacao)

COCOA
Cocoa is the basic ingredient of chocolate. Also a drink obtained from the seeds of the tropical American evergreen tree Theobroma cacao. The seeds are crushed and some fatty substances are removed to produce cocoa powder. The cocoa industry is a key employer in Equatorial Guinea. Family Sterculiaceae.

MALABO
Seaport capital of Equatorial Guinea, on Bioko island, in the Gulf of Guinea in west central Africa. Founded in 1827 as a British base to suppress the slave trade, it was known as Santa Isabel until 1973. Malabo stands on the edge of a volcanic crater that acts as a natural harbour. Industries include fish processing, hardwoods, cocoa, coffee.

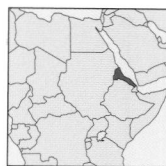

Based on the flag of the EPLF, the red triangle symbolizes blood shed in the fight for freedom, the blue triangle represents the Red Sea, the green triangle stands for agriculture. From 1952–9 Eritrea's flag bore a green wreath and olive branch in the centre of a field of United Nations' blue.

The State of Eritrea occupies a strategic geopolitical position on the Red Sea in north-eastern Africa. The coastal plain extends inland between 16 and 64 km [10–40 mi]. Inland are mountains. In the south-west, the mountains descend to the Danakil Desert. This desert contains Eritrea's lowest point at 75 m [246 ft] below sea level.

CLIMATE

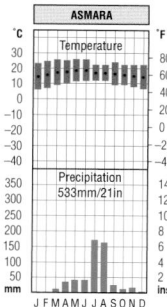

The temperature ranges from 16°C [61°F] in the highlands to 27°C [81°F] on the coastal plain. Rainfall on the coastal plain is between 150 and 250 mm [6-10 in] with up to 610 mm [24 in] in the highlands. The rainy season is from June to September.

HISTORY

The first settlers were from Africa, followed by others from the Arabian peninsula. Between AD 50 and 600, Eritrea was part of the Ethiopian kingdom of Axum. The people of Axum were converted to Christianity in the 4th century, but Muslims gained control of the area in the 7th century, introducing Islam to the coastal areas. Christianity survived inland.

In the 16th century, the Ottoman Empire took over the coastal area. Italy made Eritrea a colony in 1890. In 1935, Italy also conquered Ethiopia. During World War II, a British force drove the Italians out off north-eastern Africa. After the war, a British military administration ruled Eritrea.

In 1950, the UN made Eritrea a self-governing part of Ethiopia. Ethiopian rule proved unpopular and, in 1958, Eritrean nationalists formed the Eritrean Liberation Front (ELF). War broke out in 1961 between the ELF and the Ethiopians. In 1962, Ethiopia declared Eritrea to be a province, sparking off a war of independence.

The Eritrean People's Liberation Front (EPLF) was formed in 1970, replacing the ELF as the main anti-Ethiopian organization. In 1974, Ethiopian Emperor Haile Selassie was overthrown and a military government took power. EPLF victories gradually weakened Ethiopia's government. and the regime collapsed in 1991. The EPLF then formed a provisional government.

POLITICS

Eritrea declared independence in 1993, with Isaias Afewerki as president. The ruling People's Front for Democracy and Justice is the only party permitted in the country. The government has been criticized for the repression of opposition and closing the private press in 2001. Eritrea's relations with Ethiopia deteriorated in 1998 over a border dispute around the town of Badme, on Eritrea's south-western border. The conflict erupted into violence when

Area 45,405 sq miles [117,600 sq km]
Population 4,447,000
Capital (population) Asmara (358,000)
Government Transitional government
Ethnic groups Tigrinya 50%, Tigre and Kunama 40%, Afar 4%, Saho 3% and others
Languages Afar, Arabic, Tigre and Kunama, Tigrinya
Religions Islam, Coptic Christian, Roman Catholic
Currency Nakfa = 100 cents
Website www.shabait.com

ASMARA (ASMERA)

Capital of Eritrea, north-east Africa. Occupied by Italy in 1889 then their colonial capital and main base for the invasion of Ethiopia (1935–6). In the 1950s, the US built Africa's biggest military communications centre here. Absorbed by Ethiopia in 1952, it was the main garrison in the fight against independence-seeking Eritrean rebels. In 1993 it became the capital of independent Eritrea.

Ethiopia bombed Asmara airport, and Eritrea attacked Mekele in northern Ethiopia. The conflict continued into 2000. A cease-fire was agreed and a peace plan drawn up. UN observers arrived to help find a settlement. In 2001, the two countries agreed to a UN-proposed mediator to demarcate the border. In 2003, the boundary commission ruled that Badme lies in Eritrea. Tension continued and, in late 2005, Eritrea ordered UN peace-keeping troops to leave the country.

ECONOMY

One of Africa's poorest countries, half the population lives below the poverty line and life expectancy is 52 years. Since 1993, the economy has been set back by droughts, border conflict, and high population increase. The main activity is farming, mostly at subsistence level. Agriculture employs 80% of the workforce.

St Michael's Catholic Church, Keren, Anseba province; this Romanesque church is the oldest Catholic church in Eritrea

Estonia's flag was used between 1918 and 1940, when the country was an independent republic. It was readopted in June 1988. The blue is said to symbolize the sky, the black Estonia's black soil, and the white the snow that blankets the land in winter.

Area 45,100 sq km [17,413 sq mi]
Population 1,342,000
Capital (population) Tallinn (418,000)
Government Multiparty republic
Ethnic groups Estonian 65%, Russian 28%, Ukranian 2%, Belarusian 2%, Finnish 1%
Languages Estonian (official), Russian
Religions Lutheran, Russian and Estonian Orthodox, Methodist, Baptist, Roman Catholic
Currency Estonian kroon = 100 senti
Website www.riik.ee/en

The Republic of Estonia is the smallest of the three states on the east coast of the Baltic Sea, which were formerly part of the Soviet Union, but became independent in the early 1990s. Estonia consists of a generally flat plain which was covered by ice sheets during the Ice Age. The land is strewn with moraine (rocks deposited by the ice).

The country is dotted with more than 1,500 small lakes. Water, including the large Lake Peipus (Ozero Chudskoye) and the River Narva, makes up much of Estonia's eastern border with Russia. Estonia has more than 800 islands, which together comprise about a tenth of the country. The largest island is Saaremaa (Sarema).

Farmland and pasture account for more than 33% of land use.

CLIMATE

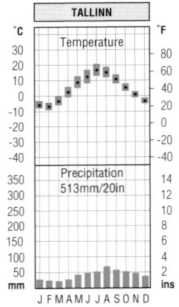

Despite its position to the north, Estonia has a fairly mild climate due to its proximity to the sea. Sea winds tend to warm the land during winter and cool it in summer. Rainfall averages from 480 to 580 mm (19-23 in).

HISTORY

The ancestors of the Estonians, who are related to the Finns, settled in the area several thousand years ago. Divided into several separate states, they were vulnerable to Viking attacks, but in the early 13th century, German crusaders, known as the Teutonic Knights, introduced Christianity. Germany took control of the southern part of Estonia and Denmark took control of the north. The Danes sold the north to the Germans in 1324 and Estonia became part of the Holy Roman Empire.

In 1561, Sweden took over northern Estonia and Poland ruled the south. Sweden controlled the entire country from 1625 until 1721 but, following the victory of Peter the Great over Sweden in the Great Northern War (1700–21), the area became part of the Russian Empire. On 24 February 1918, Estonia declared its independence. A democratic form of government was established in 1919. However, a fascist coup in 1934 ended democratic rule.

TALLINN

Capital and largest city of Estonia, on the Gulf of Finland, opposite Helsinki. Founded in 1219 by the Danes, it became a member of the Hanseatic League in 1285. It passed to Sweden in 1561, and was ceded to Russia in 1721. Developed in the 19th century for Russia's Baltic Fleet, it remains a major port and industrial centre. It was badly damaged in World War II. Tourism is increasing. Industries include machinery, cables, paper.

POLITICS

In 1939, Germany and the Soviet Union agreed to take over large areas of eastern Europe, and it was agreed that the Soviet Union would take over Estonia. The Soviet Union forcibly annexed the country in 1940. Germany invaded Estonia in 1941, but the Soviet Union regained control in 1944 when the country became the Estonian Soviet Socialist Republic. Many Estonians opposed Soviet rule and were deported to Siberia. About 100,000 Estonians settled in the West.

Resistance to Soviet rule was fuelled in the 1980s when the Soviet leader Mikhail Gorbachev began to introduce reforms and many Estonians called for independence. In 1990, the Estonian parliament declared Soviet rule invalid and called for a gradual transition to full independence. The Soviet Union regarded this action as illegal, but finally the Soviet State Council recognized the Estonian parliament's proclamation of independence in September 1991, shortly before the Soviet Union itself was dissolved in December 1991.

Since independence, Estonia has sought to increase links with Europe. It was admitted to the Council of Europe in 1993; has been a member of the World Trade Organization since 1999, and a member of NATO and the European Union since 2004. But despite the fact that it had the highest standard of living among the 15 former Soviet republics, Estonia has found the change to a free-market economy hard-going.

Other problems facing Estonia include crime, rural under-development and the status of its non-Estonian citizens, including Russians who make up about 30% of the population. In the country's first free elections in 1992, only Estonians were permitted to vote and all Russians were excluded. Tension on this issue continued through the 1990s as dual citizenship was outlawed, while restrictions imposed on Russians applying for Estonian citizenship included having to pass an Estonian language test.

ECONOMY

Manufacturing is Estonia's most valuable activity. The timber industry is among the most important industries, alongside metal-working, shipbuilding, clothing, textiles, chemicals and food processing. Food processing is based primarily on extremely efficient dairy farming and pig breeding, but oats, barley and potatoes are suited to the cool climate and the average soils.

Like the other two Baltic states, Estonia is not rich in natural resources, though its oil shale is an important mineral deposit; enough gas is extracted to supply St Petersburg, Russia's second largest city. The leading exports are mineral fuels and chemical products, followed by food, textiles and cloth, and wood and paper products. Finland and Russia are the leading trading partners.

A street in the Old Town *of Tallinn, with the spire of St Nicholas Church in the background*

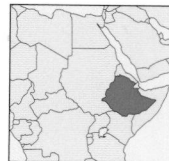

The tricolour flag of Ethiopia first appeared in 1897. The central pentangle was introduced in 1996, and represents the common will of the country's 68 ethnic groups, and the present sequence was adopted in 1914.

ADDIS ABABA (AMHARIC, 'NEW FLOWER')

Capital and largest city in Ethiopia, located on a plateau at 2,440 m [8,000 ft] in the highlands of Shewa province. Addis Ababa was made capital of Ethiopia in 1889. It is the headquarters of the African Union (AU). It is the main centre for the country's vital coffee trade. Industries include food, tanning, textiles, wood products.

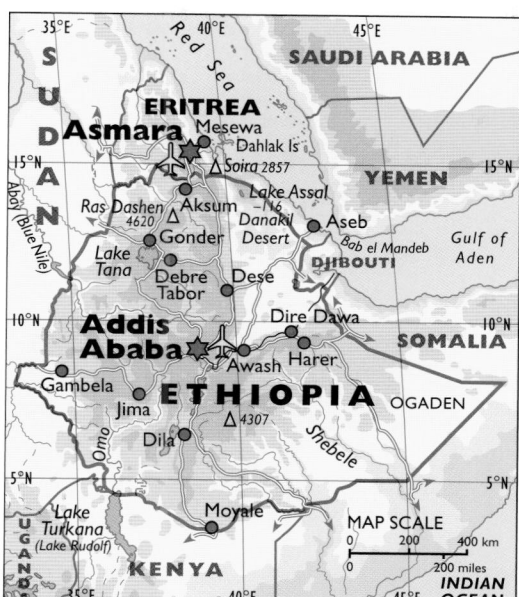

Area 1,104,300 sq km [426,370 sq mi]
Population 67,851,000
Capital (population) Addis Ababa (2,424,000)
Government Federation of nine provinces
Ethnic groups Oromo 40%, Amhara and Tigre 32%, Sidamo 9%, Shankella 6%, Somali 6% , others
Languages Amharic (official), many others
Religions Islam 47%, Ethiopian Orthodox 40%, traditional beliefs 12%
Currency Birr = 100 cents
Website www.mfa.gov.et

Ethiopia is dominated by the Ethiopian Plateau, a block of volcanic mountains. Its average height is 1,800 m to 2,450 m [6,000 ft to 8,000 ft], rising in the north to 4620m [15,157ft], at Ras Dashen. The Great Rift Valley bisects the plateau. The Eastern Highlands include the Somali Plateau and the desert of the Ogaden Plateau. The Western Highlands include the capital, Addis Ababa, the Blue Nile (Abbay) and its source, Lake Tana (Ethiopia's largest lake). The Danakil Desert forms Ethiopia's border with Eritrea.

Grass, farmland, and trees cover most of the highlands. Semi-desert and tropical savanna cover parts of the lowlands. Dense rainforest grows in the south-west.

CLIMATE

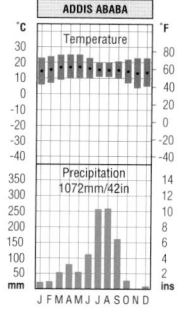

Ethiopia's climate is greatly affected by altitude. Addis Ababa, at 2,450 m [8,000 ft], has an average annual temperature of 20°C [68°F]. Rainfall is generally more than 1,000 mm [39 in], with a rainy season from April to September. The ne and sw lowlands are extremely hot and arid with less than 500 mm [20 in] rainfall, and frequent droughts.

HISTORY

According to legend, Menelik I, son of King Solomon and the Queen of Sheba, founded Ethiopia in about 1000 BC. In AD 321, the northern kingdom of Axum introduced Coptic Christianity. Judaism flourished in the 6th century. The expansion of Islam led to the isolation of Axum and the kingdom fragmented in the 16th century.

In 1855, Kasa reestablished unity, and proclaimed himself Negus (Emperor) Theodore, thereby founding the modern state. European intervention marked the late 19th century, and Menelik II became emperor with Italian support. He expanded the empire, made Addis Ababa his capital in 1889, and defeated an Italian invasion in 1895. In 1930, Menelik II's grandnephew, Ras Tafari Makonnen, was crowned Emperor Haile Selassie I. In 1935, Italian troops invaded Ethiopia (Abyssinia). In 1936, Italy combined Ethiopia with Somalia and Eritrea to form Italian East Africa. During World War II, British and South African forces recaptured Ethiopia, and Haile Selassie was restored as emperor in 1941.

In 1952, Eritrea federated with Ethiopia. The 1960s witnessed violent demands for Eritrean secession and economic equality. In 1962 Ethiopia annexed Eritrea.

POLITICS

In 1974, following famine in Ethiopia, Haille Selassie was killed. The monarchy was then abolished by the Provisional Military Administrative Council (PMAC). Military rule was repressive, and civil war broke out. The new PMAC leader, Mengistu Mariam, recaptured territory in Eritrea and the Ogaden with Soviet military assistance.

In 1984–5 widespread famine received global news coverage and 10,000 Falashas were airlifted to Israel. In 1987, Mengistu established the People's Democratic Republic of Ethiopia.

In 1991, the Tigrean-based Ethiopian People's Revolutionary Democratic Front (EPRDF) and the Eritrean People's Liberation Front (EPLF) brought down Mengistu. In 1995 the Federal Democratic Republic of Ethiopia was created, with Meles Zenawi as prime minister. A border war with Eritrea occurred in 1998-2000. Elections in 2005 led to protests and a crack-down on the opposition and press.

ECONOMY

Having been afflicted by drought and civil war in the 1970s and 1980s, Ethiopia is now one of the world's poorest countries. Agriculture is the main activity. Unfortunately the heavy reliance on agriculture in a drought-prone country has had dire consequences for the wealth of the nation.

A 2004 UN report stated that Ethiopia remained on the brink of disaster, with spiralling population growth, slow economic growth and environmental degradation. Coffee is the leading cash crop and export.

A group of women return from Lake Tana to Chache and Alua with jugs full of water

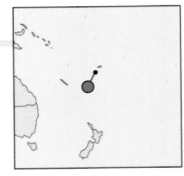

A modified version of the colonial flag, it includes the UK flag and the shield of the coat of arms. The light blue represents the Pacific. Each quarter of the St George cross features a product or symbol of Fiji: sugar cane, coconut palm, bananas, dove of peace and lion with cocoa pod.

Area 18,274 sq km [7,056 sq mi]
Population 881,000
Capital (population) Suva (70,000)
Government Republic
Ethnic groups Fijian 51% (predominantly Melanesian with a Polynesian admixture), Indian 44%, others
Languages English (official), Fijian, Hindustani
Religions Christian 52% (Methodist 37%, Roman Catholic 9%), Hindu 38%, Muslim 8%, others
Currency Fiji dollar = 100 cents
Website www.fiji.gov.fj

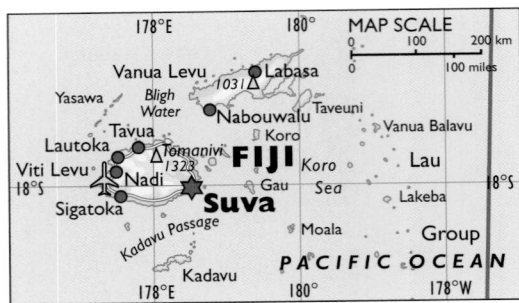

The Republic of Fiji Islands consists of more than 800 Melanesian islands situated in the South Pacific Ocean. The larger ones are mountainous and volcanic, and they are surrounded by coral reefs. There are also fertile coastal plains and river valleys. The rest of the islands are low, sandy coral atolls.. Easily the biggest islands are Viti Levu (meaning 'Big Island'), with the capital Suva on its south coast, and Vanua Levu ('Big Land'), which is just over half the size of the larger island.

Tropical forests cover more than half of the area of the islands.

Palm trees; *coconuts produced by the palm trees of Fiji are of great economic import to the islands*

CLIMATE

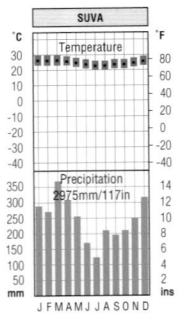

Fiji has a tropical oceanic climate, with southeast trade winds blowing throughout the year, Average temperatures vary between 16°C [60°F] and 32°C [90°F]. The average annual rainfall in Suva is 3,000 mm [118 in]. Heavy rains occur, especially between November and April. Much of the rain comes in short, heavy showers often after a sunny morning. But rains may last all day during the rainy season.

HISTORY

Melanesians, possibly from Indonesia, settled on the islands thousands of years ago, while a small group of Polynesians also reached the islands about 1,900 years ago. In 1643. the Dutch navigator Abel Janszoon Tasman became the first European to reach the islands. The British Captain James Cook arrived on Vatoa, one of the southern islands in 1774. Christian missionaries began to arrive in the 1830s.

Following conflict between various Fijian tribes in the mid-19th century, a local Christian chief named Cacobau, took control of western Fiji after having helped to restore peace there, while another Christian. Ma'afu. controlled the east. In 1871, European settlers named Cacobau king of Fiji and, in 1874, Fiji, at the request of Cacobau and other chiefs, became a British crown colony. In the late 19th century, European traders, missionaries and escaped convicts from Australia also settled in Fiji and, between 1879 and 1916, the British brought in more than 60,000 indentured labourers to work on the sugar plantations.

POLITICS

Fiji finally became independent on 10 October 1970, with Ratu Sir Kamisese Mara as prime minister. Fiji suffers today from its colonial past. Until the late 1980s, the Indian workers and their descendants out-

numbered the native Fijians. Mixing between the two groups was minimal and the ethnic Indians were second-class citizens in terms of electoral representation, economic opportunity and land ownership. However, they played an important role in the economy. The constitution adopted on independence was intended to ease racial tension. But, in 1987, two military coups led by Lt-Colonel Sitiveni Rabuka, overthrew the elected (and first) Indian majority government, although it had been led by an ethnic Fijian, Timoci Bavadra. The leaders suspended the constitution and set up a Fijian-dominated republic outside the Commonwealth.

The country returned to civilian rule in 1990. However, in 1992, elections were held under a new constitution guaranteeing Melanesian supremacy and Rabuka became prime minister. However, thousands of ethnic Indians had already emigrated before these elections, taking their valuable skills with them and causing severe economic problems. Fiji was readmitted to the Commonwealth in 1997 after it had introduced a non-discriminatory constitution. Peaceful elections in 1999 led to victory for the Fiji Labour Party, whose leader, an ethnic Indian, Mahendra Chaudhry, became prime minister, defeating Rabuka.

In May 2000, ethnic Fijians, led by businessman George Speight, seized parliament and held the prime minister, his cabinet and several MPs hostage. They were eventually disarmed and arrested, but Chaudhry was dismissed as prime minister. The army appointed an ethnic Fijian, Laisenia Qarase, leader of the nationalist Fiji United Party, as the new prime minister. His party won the elections in 2001 and the ethnic Indian Fijian Labour Party became the official opposition. Following the 2000 coup, the Commonwealth again expelled Fiji, but it was readmitted in 2002. In 2004, George Speight was sentenced to death but Fiji's president commuted the sentence to life imprisonment. In 2004, Fiji sent soldiers to Iraq for peace-keeping duties.

ECONOMY

Fiji is one of the more developed of the Pacific island states, But agriculture, which employs 70% of the population, remains the mainstay of its economy. Sugar cane, copra and ginger are the main cash crops, and fish and timber are also exported. Other crops include bananas, cassava, coconuts, sweet potatoes and rice.

Fiji mines gold, one of the main exports, silver and limestone, but sugar processing makes up one-third of industrial activity. Other manufactures include beer, cement and cigarettes. Tourism is another important activity, with 300,000 to 400,000 visitors arriving annually. However, ethnic and political tensions have slowed the development of the tourist industry.

The leading markets for Fiji's exports are Australia, the United Kingdom, the United States and Japan. Imports come from Australia, New Zealand, the United States and Japan. Fiji is heavily dependent on foreign aid.

SUVA

Seaport on the south-east coast of Viti Levu Island, in the south-west Pacific Ocean, capital of Fiji. It is the manufacturing and trade centre of the islands, with an excellent harbour. Exports include tropical fruits, copra, and gold.

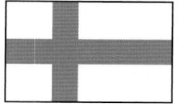

The flag of Finland was adopted in 1918, after the country had become an independent republic in 1917, following a century of Russian rule. The blue represents Finland's many lakes; the white symbolizes the blanket of snow which masks the land in winter.

The Republic of Finland (Suomi) has four geographical regions. In the south and west, on the Gulfs of Bothnia and Finland, is a low, narrow coastal strip, where most Finns live. The capital and largest city, Helsinki, is here. The Åland Islands lie in the entrance to the Gulf of Bothnia. Most of the interior is a beautiful wooded plateau, with more than 60,000 lakes. The Saimaa area is Europe's largest inland water system. A third of Finland lies within the Arctic Circle; this 'land of the midnight sun' is called Lappi (Lapland).

Forests (birch, pine, and spruce) cover 60% of Finland. The vegetation becomes more and more sparse to the north, until it merges into Arctic tundra.

CLIMATE

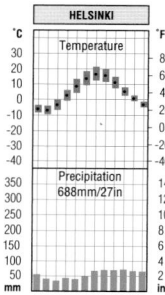

Finland has short, warm summers; Helsinki's July average is 17°C [63°F]. In Lapland, the temperatures are lower, and in June the sun never sets. Winters are long and cold; Helsinki's January average is 26°C [21°F]. The North Atlantic Drift keeps the Arctic coasts free of ice.

HISTORY

In the 8th century, Finnish-speaking settlers forced the Lapps to the north. Between 1150 and 1809, Finland was under Swedish rule. The close links between the countries continue today. Swedish remains an official language in Finland and one of the legacies of this period is a Swedish-speaking minority of 6% of the total population. In some localities on the south and west coasts, Swedish speakers are in the majority and Åland, an island closer to the Swedish coast than to Finland, is a self-governing province. Many towns use both Finnish and Swedish names. For example, Helsinki is Helsingfors, and Turku is Åbo in Swedish. Finnish bears little relation to the Swedish or any other Scandinavian language. It is closest to Magyar, the language of Hungary.

Lutheranism arrived in the 16th century. Wars between Sweden and Russia devastated Finland. Following the Northern War (1700–21), Russia gained much Finnish land. In the Napoleonic Wars, Russia conquered Finland and in 1809, it became an independent grand duchy of the Russian Empire, though the Russian tsar was its grand duke. Nationalist feelings developed during the 19th century, but in 1899 Russia sought to enforce its culture on the Finns. In 1903, the

Area	338,145 sq km [130,558 sq mi]

Area 338,145 sq km [130,558 sq mi]
Population 5,215,000
Capital (population) Helsinki (549,000)
Government Multiparty republic
Ethnic groups Finnish 93%, Swedish 6%
Languages Finnish and Swedish (both official)
Religions Evangelical Lutheran 89%
Currency Euro = 100 cents
Website www.government.fi

Russian governor suspended the constitution and became dictator, though following much resistance, self-government was restored in 1906. Finland proclaimed its independence in 1917, after the Russian Revolution and the collapse of the Russian Empire and, in 1919, it adopted a republican constitution. During World War I, the Soviet Union declared war on Finland and took the southern part of Karelia, where 12% of the Finnish people lived. Finland allied itself to Germany and Finnish troops regained southern Karelia. But at the end of the war, Russia regained southern Karelia and other parts of Finland. It also had to pay massive reparations to the Soviet Union.

After World War II, Finland pursued a policy of neutralism acceptable to the Soviet Union and this continued into the 1990s until the collapse of the Soviet Union. Finland also strengthened its links with other north European countries and became an associate member of the European Free Trade Association (EFTA) in 1961. Finland became a full member of EFTA in 1986, in a decade when its economy was growing at a faster rate than that of Japan.

POLITICS

In 1992, along with most of its fellow EFTA members, Finland, which had no longer any need to be neutral, applied for membership of the European Union (EU). In 1994, the Finnish people voted in favour of joining the EU and the country officially joined on 1 January 1995. On 1 January 2002 the euro became Finland's official sole unit of currency. Finland has also discussed the possibility of joining NATO. However, polls since the events of 11 September 2001 suggest that the majority of Finns favour non-alliance.

ECONOMY

Forests are Finland's most valuable resource. Forestry accounts for 35% of exports. The chief manufactures are wood and paper products. Post-1945 the economy has diversified. Engineering, shipbuilding and textile industries have grown. Farming employs only 9% of workforce. The economy has slowly recovered from the recession caused by the collapse of the Soviet bloc.

HELSINKI

Capital of Finland, in the south of the country, on the Gulf of Finland. Founded in 1550 by Gustavus I (Vasa), it became the capital in 1812. It has two universities (1849, 1908), a cathedral (1852), museums and art galleries. The commercial and administrative centre of the country, it is Finland's largest port. Industries include shipbuilding, engineering, food processing, ceramics, textiles.

The colours of this flag originated during the French Revolution of 1789. The red and blue are said to represent Paris, while the white represented the monarchy. The present design was adopted in 1794, and is meant to symbolize republican principles.

Area 551,500 sq km [212,934 sq mi]
Population 60,424,000
Capital (population) Paris (2,152,000)
Government Multiparty republic
Ethnic groups Celtic, Latin, Arab, Teutonic, Slavic
Languages French (official)
Religions Roman Catholic 85%, Islam 8%, others
Currency Euro = 100 cents
Website www.elysee.fr

The Republic of France is the largest country in Western Europe. The scenery is extremely varied. The Vosges Mountains overlook the Rhine Valley in the north-east, the Jura Mountains and the Alps form the borders with Switzerland and Italy in the south-east, while the Pyrenees straddle France's border with Spain. The only large highland area entirely within France is the Massif Central between the Rhône-Saône Valley and the basin of Aquitaine. This dramatic area, covering one-sixth of the country, has peaks rising to more than 1,800 m [5,900 ft]. Volcanic activity dating back 10 to 30 million years ago appears in the form of steep-sided volcanic plugs. Brittany (Bretagne) and Normandy (Normande) form a scenic hill region. Fertile lowlands cover most of northern France, including the densely populated Paris Basin. Another major lowland area, the Aquitanian Basin, is in the south-west, while the Rhône-Saône Valley and the Mediterranean lowlands are in the south-east.

CLIMATE

The climate varies from west to east and from north to south. The west comes under the moderating influence of the Atlantic Ocean, giving generally mild weather. To the east, summers are warmer and winters colder. The climate also becomes warmer as one travels from north to south. The Mediterranean Sea coast experiences hot, dry summers and mild, moist winters. The Alps, Jura and Pyrenees mountains have snowy winters. Winter sports centres are found in all three areas. Large glaciers occupy high valleys in the Alps.

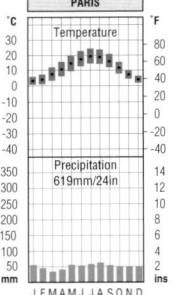
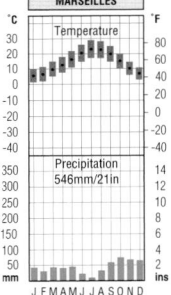
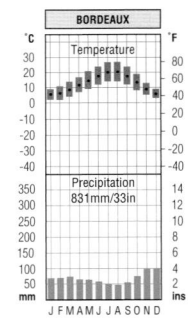

HISTORY

The Romans conquered France (then called Gaul) in the 50s BC. Roman rule began to decline in the 5th century AD and, in 486, the Frankish realm (as France was by then called) became independent under a Christian king, Clovis. In 800, Charlemagne, who had been king of the Franks since 768,

Cottage in field of lavender, Provence

became emperor of the Romans. Through conquest, his empire extended from central Italy to Denmark, and from eastern Germany to the Atlantic Ocean. However, in 843, the empire was divided into three parts and the area of France contracted.

After the Norman invasion of England in 1066, large areas of France came under English rule. By 1453, after the Hundred Years' War, France drove most of the English out. In this war, the French kings lost much power to French nobles, but Louis XI, who reigned from 1461 to 1483, laid the foundations for absolute rule by French kings.

France later became a powerful monarchy, but the French Revolution (1789–99) ended absolute rule by French kings. In 1799 Napoleon Bonaparte took power and fought a series of brilliant military campaigns before his final defeat in 1815. The monarchy was restored until 1848, when the Second Republic was founded. In 1852, Napoleon's nephew became Napoleon III, but the Third Republic was established in 1875.

France was the scene of much fighting during World War I (1914–18) and World War II (1939–45), causing great loss of life and much damage to the economy.

Post-war aid from the United States started a revival in its economy, but Communist-led strikes often crippled production. France also faced growing support for independence movements in its overseas empire. After a bitter war, France withdrew from French Indo-China in 1954 and then faced a long and costly struggle in Algeria, finally ending with Algeria's independence in 1962. The problems in Algeria caused considerable unrest in France in the 1950s and, in 1958, De Gaulle was recalled to power as prime minister. His government prepared a new constitution, establishing the Fifth Republic. It gave the president greater executive powers and reduced the power of parliament. The Electoral College elected De Gaulle as president for a seven-year term.

De Gaulle gave independence to many of its overseas territories and made France a major player in an alliance of western European nations. In 1957, France became a founder member of the European Economic Community (EEC). De Gaulle opposed British membership in 1963, considering that Britain's links with the United States would give it too much influence in Europe's economy, but his popularity waned in the late 1960s when huge student demonstrations and workers' strikes paralyzed the country and he resigned as president in 1969. His successor, Georges Pompidou, changed course in foreign affairs by re-establishing closer contacts with the United States and supporting the entry of Britain into the EEC.

POLITICS

Rapid urban growth has resulted in overcrowding and the growth of poorly built new districts to house immigrants, especially those from Spain and North Africa. The 4 million underprivileged workers from the Maghreb became a major political issue in the 1990s, leading to political successes in some areas for the extreme right. In France, as in most other countries, there also remains a disparity between the richer and the poorer regions. Other problems faced by France include unemployment, pollution and the growing number of elderly people.

A socialist government under Lionel Jospin was elected in 1997. He increased the minimum wage, shortened the working week, and adopted the euro. However, in 2002 centre-right parties won a resounding victory and Jean-Pierre Raffarin replaced Jospin as Prime Minister.

France has a long record of independence in foreign affairs and in 2003 it angered the US and some of its allies in the EU by opposing the invasion of Iraq, arguing that the UN weapons inspectors should be given more time to search for weapons of mass destruction in Iraq. France's stance angered some US congressmen who called for a boycott of French goods. The number of US tourist to France also fell.

PARIS

The capital of France is situated on the River Seine. When the Romans took Paris in 52 BC, it was a small village on the Ile de la Cité on the Seine. Under their rule it became an important administrative centre. During the 14th century Paris rebelled against the Crown and declared itself an independent commune. It suffered further civil disorder during the Hundred Years' War. In the 16th century, it underwent fresh expansion, its architecture strongly influenced by the Italian Renaissance. In the reign of Louis XIII, Cardinal Richelieu established Paris as the cultural and political centre of Europe. The French Revolution began in Paris when the Bastille was stormed by crowds in 1789. Under Emperor Napoleon I the city began to assume its present-day form. The work of modernization was continued under Napoleon III, when Baron Haussmann was commissioned to plan the boulevards, bridges and parks. Although occupied during the Franco-Prussian War (1870–71) and again in World War II, Paris was not badly damaged. The city proper consists of the Paris department, Ville de Paris. Its many famous buildings and landmarks include the Eiffel Tower, Arc de Triomphe, the Louvre, Notre Dame and the Pompidou Centre. Paris is an important European cultural, commercial and communications centre and is noted for its fashion industry and for the manufacture of luxury articles.

A resounding 'no' vote in the referendum on the European constitution in May 2005 led to the resignation of Raffarin and further decline in the relationship between Jacques Chirac and Tony Blair over the UK rebate and Common Agricultural Policy subsidies for French farmers.

ECONOMY

France is one of the world's most developed countries. It has the world's fourth largest economy. Its natural resources include its fertile soil, together with deposits of bauxite, coal, iron ore, oil and natural gas, and potash. France is also one of the world's top manufacturing nations and it has often innovated in bold and imaginative ways. The TGV, Concorde and hypermarkets are all typical examples. Paris is a world centre of fashion industries, but France has many other industrial towns and cities. Major manufactures include aircraft, cars, chemicals, electronic products, machinery, metal products, processed food, steel and textiles.

Agriculture employs about 2% of the people, but France is the largest producer of farm products in Western Europe, producing most of the food it needs. Wheat is a leading crop and livestock farming is of major importance. The food-processing industry is well known, especially for its cheeses, such as Brie and Camembert, and its top-quality wines from areas such as Alsace, Bordeaux, Burgundy, Champagne and the Loire valley. Fishing and forestry are leading industries. France is a popular year-round destination both for its beaches and for its mountains.

MONACO

The tiny Principality of Monaco consists of a narrow strip of coastline and a rocky peninsula on the French Riviera. Like the rest of the Riviera, it has mild, moist winters and dry, sunny summers. Average temperatures range from 10°C [50°F] in January to 24°C [75°F] in July. The average annual rainfall is about 800 mm [31 in].

The Genoese from northern Italy gained control of Monaco in the 12th century and, from 1297, it has been ruled for most of the time by the Genoese Grimaldi family. Monaco attracted little attention until the late 19th century when it developed into a major tourist resort. World attention was focused on Monaco in 1956 when Prince Rainier III of Monaco married the actress Grace Kelly. Their son, Prince Albert, became ruler upon Rainier's death in 2005. The country's wealth comes mainly from banking, finance, gambling and tourism. There are three casinos, a marine museum, a zoo and botanical gardens. It also stages the Monte Carlo Rally and the Monaco Grand Prix. Manufactures include chemicals, electronic goods and plastics. In 2001, France threatened to break its ties with Monaco unless it revised its legal system and prevented money laundering.

Area 1 sq km [0.4 sq mi]
Population 32,000
Capital (population) Monaco (30,000)
Government Constitutional monarchy
Religions Roman Catholic 62%, Protestant 30%
Currency Euro = 100 cents
Website www.visitmonaco.com

French Guiana flies the French flag. The colours originated during the French Revolution of 1789. The red and blue are said to represent Paris, while the white represented the monarchy. The present design was adopted in 1794, and is meant to symbolize republican principles.

Area 90,000 sq km [34,749 sq mi]
Population 191,000
Capital (population) Cayenne (51,000)
Government Overseas department of France
Ethnic groups Black or Mulatto 66%, East Indian/Chinese and Amerindian 12%, White 12%, others 10%
Languages French (official)
Religions Roman Catholic
Currency Euro = 100 cents
Website www.guyane.pref.gouv.fr

French Guiana is a French overseas department and the smallest country in mainland South America. The coastal plain is swampy in places, but dry areas are cultivated, particularly near the capital Cayenne. The River Maroni forms the border with Suriname, and the River Oyapock its eastern border with Brazil. Inland lies a plateau, with the low Tumuchumac Mountains in the south. Most of the rivers run north towards the Atlantic Ocean.

Rainforest covers approximately 90% of the land and contains valuable hardwood species. Mangrove swamps line parts of the coast; other areas are covered by tropical savanna.

CAYENNE

Capital and chief port of French Guiana, on the Atlantic coast. Founded in 1643 and named after an Indian Chief. Places of interest include the cathedral, the ruined 17th century Fort Cépérou, Hôtel de Ville and museums of local history.

do. The French were the first settlers in 1604 and French merchants founded Cayenne in 1637. The area became a French colony in the late 17th century, with a plantation economy dependent on African slaves. It remained French except for a brief period in the early 19th century. Slavery was abolished in 1848, and Asian labourers were introduced to work the land. From the time of the French Revolution, France used the colony as a penal settlement, and between 1852 and 1945 the country was notorious for the harsh treatment of prisoners. Captain Alfred Dreyfus was imprisoned on Devil's Island.

POLITICS

In 1946, French Guiana became an overseas department of France, and in 1974 it also became an administrative region. An independence movement developed in the 1980s, but most of the people want to retain links with France and continue to obtain financial aid to develop their territory.

CLIMATE

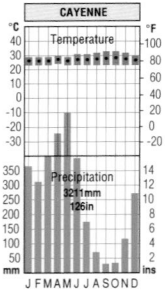

French Guiana has a hot equatorial climate with high temperatures throughout the year. Rainfall is heavy, especially between December and June, but it is dry between August and October. North-east trade winds blow across the country constantly.

HISTORY

The first people to live in what is now French Guiana were Amerindians. Today only a few of them survive in the interior. The first Europeans to explore the coast arrived in 1500 and they were followed by adventurers seeking El Dora-

ECONOMY

Although it has rich forest and mineral resources, such as bauxite (aluminium ore), French Guiana is a developing country with high unemployment. It depends greatly on France for money to run its services and the government is the country's biggest employer. Since 1975, Kourou has been the European Space Agency's rocket-launching site and has earned money for France by sending communications satellites into space.

The main industries are fishing, forestry, gold mining and agriculture. Crops include bananas, cassava, rice and sugar cane. French Guiana's main exports are shrimps, timber, and rosewood essence.

DEVIL'S ISLAND (ÎLE DU DIABLE)

The smallest island of the three Iles du Salut off the coast of French Guiana. A notorious French penal colony from 1852 to 1945 and most famous for the prison and the harsh treatment of its inmates whether they be political prisoners or murderers. Few prisoners made it off the island due to the high levels of disease and escape was almost impossible. The publicity surrounding the case of Captain Alfred Dreyfus in 1894 brought the horrors of this prison to the fore.

The launch of the third Ariane space rocket, seen from a beach in Kourou, French Guiana

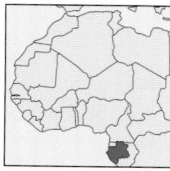

Gabon's flag was adopted in 1960 when the country became independent from France. The central yellow stripe symbolizes the Equator which runs through Gabon. The green stands for the country's forests. The blue symbolizes the sea.

RIVER OGOOUÉ (OGOWE)

The main river of Gabon, its basin drains nearly the entire country. Some of its tributaries can be found in Cameroon the Republic of Congo, and Equatorial Guinea. The Ogooué is about 900 km [560 mi] in length, rising in the north-west of the Bateke Plateau. It empties into the Gulf of Guinea, south of Port Gentil. The delta is approximately 100 km [62 mi] long and 100 km wide. The total waterbasin is 223,856 sq km [86,431sq mi], and is largely made up of forest.

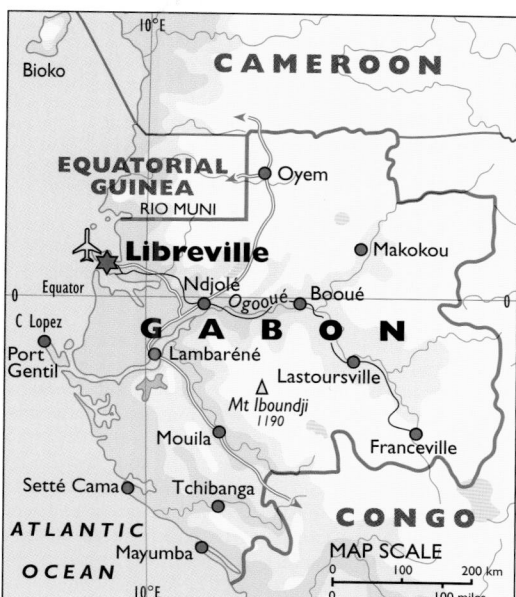

Area 267,668 sq km [103,347 sq mi]
Population 1,355,000
Capital (population) Libreville (362,000)
Government Multiparty republic
Ethnic groups Bantu tribes: Fang, Bandjabi, Bapounou, Eshira, Myene, Nzebi, Obamba and Okande
Languages French (official), Fang, Myene, Nzebi, Bapounou/Eschira, Bandjabi
Religions Christianity 75%, animist, Islam
Currency CFA franc = 100 centimes
Website www.senat.ga

The Gabonese Republic lies on the Equator in west-central Africa. In area, it is a little larger than the United Kingdom, with a coastline 800 km [500 mi] long. Behind the narrow, partly lagoon-lined coastal plain, the land rises to hills, plateaux and mountains divided by deep valleys carved by the River Ogooué and its tributaries.

Dense rainforest covers about 75% of Gabon, with tropical savanna in the east and south. The forests teem with wildlife, and Gabon has several national parks and wildlife reserves.

CLIMATE

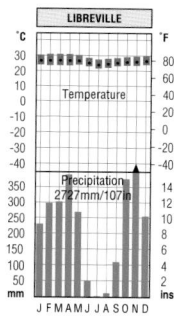

Most of Gabon has an equatorial climate. There are high temperatures and humidity throughout the year. The rainfall is heavy and the skies are often cloudy.

HISTORY

Explorers from Portugal reached the Gabon coast in the 1470s, and the area later became a source of slaves.

In 1839 France established the first European settlement. In 1849 freed slaves founded Libreville. Gabon became a French colony in the 1880s and achieved full independence in 1960.

Léon Mba was Gabon's first president from 1960 to 1967. In 1964, an attempted coup was put down when French troops intervened and crushed the revolt. In 1967, following the death of Léon Mba, Bernard-Albert Bongo, who later renamed himself El Hadj Omar Bongo, became president. He made Gabon a one-party state in 1968.

POLITICS

Free elections took place in 1990. The Gabonese Democratic Party (PDG) won a majority in the National Assembly. President Bongo, of the PDG, won the presidential elections in 1993, although accusations of fraud and corruption led to riots in Libreville. The international community condemned Bongo for his harsh suppression of popular demonstrations. He was re-elected in 1998. In 2003, constitutional changes enabled Bongo to stand as president as many times as he wished. In November 2005 he was again elected president and despite the pre-emptive protestations of the opposition, the elections were deemed free and fair by international observers.

ECONOMY

Gabon's abundant natural resources include its forests, oil and gas deposits near Port Gentil, together with manganese and uranium. These mineral deposits make Gabon one of Africa's wealthier countries.

However, agriculture still employs about 75% of the workforce, most farmers producing little more than they need to support their families. Crops include bananas, cassava, maize, and sugar cane. Cocoa and coffee are grown for export. Other exports include oil, manganese, timber and wood products, uranium.

LIBREVILLE

Capital and largest city of Gabon, at the mouth of the River Gabon, on the Gulf of Guinea. Founded by the French in 1843, and named Libreville (French for Freetown) in 1849, it was initially a refuge for escaped slaves. The city expanded with the development of the country's minerals and is now also an administrative centre. Places of interest include the Musée des Arts et Traditions, the French cultural centre, the presidential palace, St Marie's Cathedral, the Eglise St Michel with its carved wooden columns, Nkembo, the Arboretum de Sibang and two cultural villages. Other industries include timber (hardwoods), palm oil and rubber.

Timber stored at Owendo, *a suburb of Libreville*

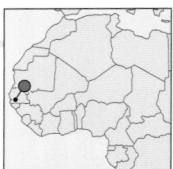

The colours represent features of the Gambian landscape. Green symbolizes the land and agricultural produce. Blue stands for the River Gambia, a vital trade route. Red represents the hot African sun. The two white bands stand for peace and unity.

The Republic of the Gambia is the smallest country in mainland Africa. It consists of a narrow strip of land bordering the River Gambia. The Gambia is almost entirely enclosed by Senegal, except along the short Atlantic coastline. The land is flat near the sea.

Mangrove swamps line the river banks. Much tropical savanna has been cleared for farming. The Gambia is rich in wildlife and has six national parks and reserves as well as several forest parks.

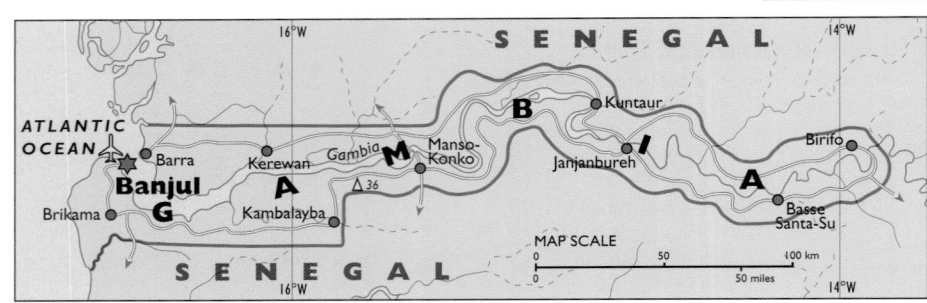

CLIMATE

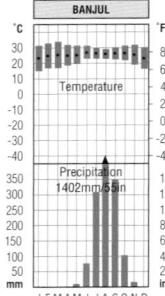

The Gambia has hot and humid summers, but winter temperatures (November to May) drop to around 16°C [61°F]. In the summer, moist winds heading south-west bring rain, which is heaviest on the coast.

HISTORY

Portuguese mariners reached Gambia's coast in 1455, when the area was part of the Mali empire. In the 16th century, Portuguese and English slave traders operated in the area. English traders bought rights to trade on the River Gambia in 1588, and in 1664 the English established a settlement on an island in the river estuary. In 1765, the British founded a colony called Senegambia, which included parts of present-day Gambia and Senegal. In 1783, Britain handed this colony over to France.

During the 1860s and 1870s, Britain and France discussed the exchange of the Gambia for some other French territory. No agreement was reached and Britain made the Gambia a British colony in 1888. It remained under British rule intil it achieved full independence in 1965 with Dawda Jawara as prime minister. In 1970 the Gambia became a republic.

POLITICS

Relations between the French-speaking Senegalese and the English-speaking Gambians form a major political issue. In 1981, an attempted coup in the Gambia was put down with the help of Senegalese troops. In 1982, The Gambia and Senegal set up a defence alliance, called the Confederation of Senegambia, though this alliance was later dissolved in 1989.

In 1992, Jawara was re-elected as president for a fifth term. In July 1994, he was overthrown in a military coup and fled into exile. The coup was led by Yahya Jammeh who was elected president in 1996. His regime faced charges of political repression. In 2001, Jammeh lifted the ban on opposition parties and was re-elected, though he is still criticized for impingeing press freedom.

ECONOMY

Agriculture is the main activity, employing more than 80% of the workforce. However, the government announced in 2004 that large oil reserves had been discovered. The main food crops include cassava, millet and sorghum, but groundnuts and groundnut products are the chief exports.

The money sent home by Gambians living abroad is important for the economy. Tourism is a growing industry.

Batik for sale outside Gena Bes batik showroom and workshop, Bakau

Area 11,295 sq km [4,361 sq mi]
Population 1,547,000
Capital (population) Banjul (42,000)
Government Military regime
Ethnic groups Mandinka 42%, Fula 18%, Wolof 16%, Jola 10%, Serahuli 9%, others
Languages English (official), Mandinka, Wolof, Fula
Religions Islam 90%, Christianity 9%, traditional beliefs 1%
Currency Dalasi = 100 butut
Website www.gambia.gm

MANGROVE

Common name for any one of 120 species of tropical trees or shrubs found in marine swampy areas. Also known as coastal woodland, tidal forest and mangrove forest.Its stilt-like aerial roots, which arise from the branches and hang down into the water, produce a thick undergrowth, useful in the reclaiming of land along tropical coasts. Even within the same delta the composition of the mangrove can vary substantially according to the conditions of salinity, tidal system and substrate (soil foundation). Some species have roots that rise up out of the water. It grows to a height of 20 m [70 ft].

BANJUL

Capital of the Gambia, the city lies on St Mary's Island, where the River Gambia enters the Atlantic Ocean. It was founded as a trading post by the British in 1816 and originally named Bathurst after Henry Bathurst, the secretary of the British Colonial Office. Banjul is Gambia's chief port and commercial centre. The main industry is groundnut processing, though tourism is growing rapidly.

The Republic of Georgia adopted a new flag in 2004. The flag had been in use some 500 years before as that of the medieval Georgian kingdom. It was subsequently used as the official symbol of the political party - United National Movement.

Georgia is located on the borders of Europe and Asia, facing the Black Sea. The land is rugged with the Caucasus Mountains forming its northern border. The highest mountain in this range, Mount Elbrus (5,642 m [18,506 ft]), lies over the border in Russia.

Lower ranges run through southern Georgia, through which pass the borders with Turkey and Armenia. The Black Sea coastal plains are in the west. In the east a low plateau extends into Azerbaijan. The main river in the east is the River Kura, on which the capital Tbilisi stands.

Area 69,700 sq km [26,911 sq mi]
Population 4,694,000
Capital (population) Tbilisi (1,268,000)
Government Multiparty republic
Ethnic groups Georgian 70%, Armenian 8%, Russian 6%, Azeri 6%, Ossetiam 3%, Greek 2%, Abkhaz 2%, others
Languages Georgian (official), Russian
Religions Georgian Orthodox 65%, Islam 11%, Russian Orthodox 10%, Amenian Apostolic 8%
Currency Lari = 100 tetri
Website www.parliament.ge

CLIMATE

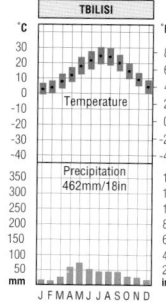

The Black Sea plains have hot summers and mild winters, when the temperature seldom drops below freezing. Rainfall is heavy, but inland Tbilisi has moderate rainfall, with the heaviest rains in the spring and early summer.

HISTORY

The first Georgian state was set up nearly 2,000 years ago and, by the 3rd century BC, most of what is now Georgia was united as a single kingdom. For much of its history, Georgia was ruled by various conquerors. For example, between about 60 BC and the 11th century, the area was ruled successively by Romans, Persians, Byzantines, Arabs and Seljuk Turks. Christianity was introduced in AD 330 and most Georgians are now members of the Georgian Orthodox Church. Georgia freed itself from foreign rule in the 11th and 12th centuries, but Mongol armies invaded in the 13th century. From the 16th to the 18th centuries, Iran and the Turkish Ottoman Empire struggled for control of the area.

In the late 18th century, Georgia sought the protection of Russia and, by the early 19th century was part of the Russian Empire. After the Russian Revolution of 1917, Georgia declared itself independent and was recognized by the League of Nations. However, Russian troops invaded in 1921, making Georgia part of the Soviet regime. From 1922, Georgia, Armenia and Azerbaijan were linked, forming the Transcaucasian Republic. But, in 1936, the territories became separate republics within the Soviet Union. Renowned for their longevity, the people of Georgia are famous for producing Josef Stalin, who was born in Gori, 65 km [40 mi] north-west of the capital Tbilisi. Stalin ruled the Soviet Union from 1929 until his death in 1953.

POLITICS

A maverick among the Soviet republics, Georgia was the first to declare its independence after the Baltic states (April 1991) and deferred joining the Commonwealth of Independent States (CIS) until 1993.

In 1991, Zviad Gamsakhurdia, a non-Communist who had been democratically elected president of Georgia in 1990, found himself holed up in Tbilisi's KGB headquarters, under siege from rebel forces. They represented widespread opposition to his government's policies, ranging from the economy to the imprisonment of his opponents. In January 1992, following the break-up of the Soviet Union, Gamsakhurdia fled the country and a military council took power.

Georgia contains three regions of minority peoples: South Ossetia, in north-central Georgia, where civil war broke out in the early 1990s, with nationalists demanding the right to set up their own governments; Abkhazia in the north-west, which proclaimed its sovereignty in 1994 with fierce fighting continuing until the late 1990s; Adjaria (or Adzharia) in the south-west, whose autonomy was recognized in Georgia's constitution in 2000.

In March 1992, Eduard Shevardnadze, former Soviet Foreign Minister, was named head of state and was elected, unopposed, later that year. He was re-elected in 1995 and 2000, but Georgia faced mounting problems, which threatened its stability. In 2001, Georgia and Abkhazia signed a peace accord and agreed to the safe return of refugees. In 2002, Russian and Georgian troops attacked Chechen rebels in Pankisi Gorge in north-eastern Georgia. US officials believed that Taliban fighters and other Islamic terrorists had also moved into this region. In 2004, Mikhail Saakashvili was elected president, but his authority was challenged by separatists in the three minority regions. 2005 saw an agreement by Russia to withdraw troops from its two remaining bases by the end of 2008.

ECONOMY

Georgia is a developing country. Agriculture is important. Major products include barley, citrus fruits, grapes for wine-making, maize, tea, tobacco and vegetables. Food processing, and silk- and perfume-making are other important activities. Sheep and cattle are reared.

Barite (barium ore), coal, copper and manganese are mined, and tourism is a major industry on the Black Sea coast. Georgia's mountains have huge potential for generating hydroelectric power, but most of Georgia's electricity is generated in Russia or Ukraine.

TBILISI (TIFLIS)

Largest city and capital of Georgia, on the upper River Kura. It was founded in the 5th century ad, and ruled successively by the Iranians, Byzantines, Arabs, Mongols, and Turks, before coming under Russian rule in 1801. Tbilisi's importance lies in its location on the trade route between the Black Sea and Caspian Sea. It is now the administrative and economic focus of modern Transcaucasia. Industries include chemicals, petroleum products, locomotives, electrical equipment.

The historic Tbilisi Baths, *housed in subterranean caverns with brick domes*

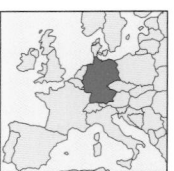

This flag, adopted by the Federal Republic of Germany (West Germany) in 1949, became the flag of the reunified Germany in 1990. The red, black and gold colours date back to the Holy Roman Empire. They are associated with the struggle for a united Germany from the 1830s.

Area 357,022 sq km [137, 846 sq mi]
Population 82,425,000
Capital (population) Berlin (3,387,000)
Government Federal multiparty republic
Ethnic groups German 92%, Turkish 3%, Serbo-Croatian, Italian, Greek, Polish, Spanish
Languages German (official)
Religions Protestant (mainly Lutheran) 34%, Roman Catholic 34%, Islam 4%, others
Currency Euro = 100 cents
Website www.deutschland.de

The Federal Republic of Germany lies in the heart of Europe. It is the fifth-largest country in Europe. Germany divides into three geographical regions: the north German plain, central highlands, and the south Central Alps. The rivers Elbe, Weser, and Oder drain the fertile northern plain, which includes the industrial centres of Hamburg, Bremen, Hanover, and Kiel. In the east, lies the capital, Berlin, and the former East German cities of Leipzig, Dresden and Magdeburg. North-west Germany (especially the Rhine, Ruhr and Saar valleys) is Germany's industrial heartland. It includes the cities of Cologne, Essen, Dortmund, Düsseldorf and Duisburg.

The central highlands include the Harz Mountains and the cities of Munich, Frankfurt, Stuttgart, Nuremberg and Augsburg.

Southern Germany rises to the Bavarian Alps on the border with Switzerland and Germany's highest peak, Zugspitze, (2,963 m [9,721 ft]). The Black Forest, overlooking the Rhine valley, is a major tourist attraction. The region is drained by the River Danube.

CLIMATE

Germany has a temperate climate. The north-west is warmed by the North Sea. The Baltic lowlands in the north-east are cooler. In the south, the climate becomes more continental.

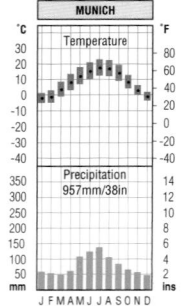

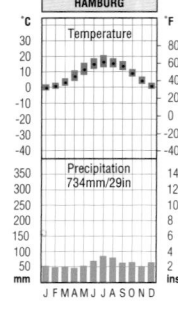

HISTORY

Around 3,000 years ago, various tribes from northern Europe began to settle in what is now Germany, occupying the valleys of the Rhine and the Danube. The Romans called this region Germania after the Germani, the name of one of the tribes. In the 5th century, the Germanic tribes attacked the Roman Empire and plundered Rome. The western part of the Roman Empire split up into several kingdoms, the largest of which was the Kingdom of the Franks.

In 486, Clovis, a Frankish king, extended his rule to include Gaul (now France) and western Germany, introducing Christianity and other Roman practices. Frankish ruler, Charlemagne, came to power in 768 and established his capital at Aachen. From 962, much of the German Empire became part of what was later known as the Holy Roman Empire under King Otto II of Germany.

In 1517, a German monk, Martin Luther, began to criticize many of the practices and teachings of the Roman Catholic Church. A Protestant movement called the Reformation soon attracted much support. By the early 17th century, the

Cologne Cathedral; although the foundation stone was laid in 1248 the building was not completed until 1880

people of Germany were deeply divided by political and religious rivalries. The Thirty Years' War, which began in 1618 and lasted for 30 years, ravaged much of the country with Germany losing territory to France and Sweden, and itself being split into hundreds of states and free cities. It took almost 200 years for Germany to recover

In the 17th century, the Hohenzollern family began to assume importance in eastern Germany, gradually extending their power and building a professional civil service and army.

Prussia stayed out of the Napoleonic wars until 1806, but following defeats by Napoleon, lost its territories west of the Elbe. Prussia did help defeat Napoleon's armies at the battles of Leipzig (1813) and Waterloo (1815) and following the Napoleonic wars, gained the Rhineland, Westphalia and much of Saxony.

In the early 1860s, the Prussian king, Wilhelm I, appointed Otto von Bismarck as prime minister. Bismarck set about strengthening Prussian power through three short wars. One conflict led to the acquisition of Schleswig-Holstein from Denmark, another led to the annexation of territory from Austria. The third was the Franco-Prussian War (1870–1), following which victorious Germany was granted Alsace and part of Lorraine. In 1871, Wilhelm I was crowned the first Kaiser of the new German Empire and Bismarck became the chancellor and head of government. Bismarck sought to consolidate German power and avoid conflict with Austria-Hungary and Russia, but was forced to resign in 1890 when Wilhelm II wanted to establish his own authority and extend Germany's influence in the world. Wilhelm's ambitions led Britain and France to establish the Entente Cordiale in 1904, with Britain and Russia signing a similar agreement in 1907. This left Europe divided, with Germany, Austria-Hungary and Italy forming the Triple Alliance.

After Germany and its allies were defeated in World War I, Germany became a republic and lost territories. Overseas, it lost its colonies. Germany's humiliation under the terms of the Versailles Treaty caused much resentment, made worse by the economic collapse of 1922–23. Support grew for the Nazi Party and its leader Adolf Hitler, who became chancellor in 1933. Hitler's order to invade Poland in 1939 triggered off World War II. His armies were finally defeated in 1945 and the country left in ruins. Germany was obliged to transfer the area east of the Oder and Neisse rivers to Poland and the Soviet Union. German-speaking inhabitants were expelled and the remainder of Germany was occupied by the four victorious Allied powers. In 1948, West Germany, consisting of the American, British and French zones, was proclaimed the Federal Republic of Germany with its provisional capital at Bonn, while the Soviet zone became the German Democratic Republic with its capital in East Berlin.

POLITICS

The post-war partition of Germany together with its geographical position, made it a central hub of the Cold War, which ended with the collapse of Communism in the late 1980s, early 1990s. The reunification of Germany came on 3 October 1990. West Germany, had become a showpiece of the West through its phenomenal recovery and sustained growth, the so-called 'economic miracle'. It played a major part, together with France, in the revival of Western Europe through the development of the European Community (now the European Union). Although East Germany had achieved the highest standard of living in the Soviet bloc, it was short of the levels of the EU members.

Following reunification, the new country adopted the name the Federal Republic of Germany. Massive investment was needed to rebuild the East's industrial base and transport system, meaning increased taxation. In addition, the new nation found itself funnelling aid into Eastern Europe. Germany led the EU in recognizing the independence of Slovenia, Croatia and the former Soviet republics. There were also social effects. While Germans in the West resented added taxes and the burden imposed by the East, easterners resented what many saw as the overbearing attitudes of westerners. Others feared a revival of the far right, with neo-Nazis and other right-wingers protesting against the increasing numbers of immigrant workers.

The creation of a unified state was far more complicated, expensive and lengthy an undertaking than envisaged when the Berlin Wall came down. In 1998, the centre-right government of Helmut Kohl, who had presided over reunification, was defeated by the left-of-centre Social Democratic Party (SPD), led by Gerhard Schröder. Schröder led an SPD-Green Party coalition which set about tackling Germany's high unemployment and a sluggish economy. Following the attacks on the United States on 11 September 2001, Schröder announced Germany's support for the campaign against terrorism, although Germany opposed the invasion of Iraq in 2003. In 2005, Schröder was narrowly defeated in elections. A broad left-right coalition was set up. The conservative Angela Merkel became Chancellor.

ECONOMY

Despite the problems associated with reunification, Germany has the world's third largest economy after the United States and Japan. The foundation of the 'economic miracle' that led to Germany's astonishing post-war recovery was manufacturing.

Germany's industrial strength was based on its coal reserves, though oil-burning and nuclear generating plants have become increasingly important since the 1970s. Lower Saxony has oilfields, while southern Germany also obtains power from hydroelectric plants. The country has supplies of potash and rock salt, together with smaller quantities of copper, lead, tin, uranium and zinc. The leading industrial region is the Ruhr, which produces iron and steel, together with major chemical and textiles industries. Germany is the world's third largest producer of cars, while other manufactures include cameras, electronic equipment, fertilizers, processed food, plastics, scientific instruments, ships, tools, and wood and pulp products.

Agriculture employs 2.4% of the workforce, but Germany imports about a third of its food. Barley, fruits, grapes, oats, potatoes, rye, sugar beet, vegetables and wheat are grown. Beef and dairy cattle are raised, together with pigs, poultry and sheep.

BERLIN

Capital and largest city of Germany, on the River Spree, north east Germany. Berlin was founded in the 13th century. It became the residence of the Hohenzollerns and the capital of Brandenburg, and later of Prussia. It rose to prominence as a manufacturing town and became the capital of the newly formed state of Germany in 1871. Virtually destroyed at the end of World War II, Berlin was divided into four sectors; British, French, US, and Soviet. On the formation of East Germany, the Soviet sector became East Berlin, the rest West Berlin. In 1961 East Germany erected the Berlin Wall, which divided the city until 1989. On the reunification of Germany in 1990, East Berlin and West Berlin amalgamated. Sights include the Brandenberg Gate, the Kaiser Wilhelm Memorial Church, and the Victory Column in the Tiergarten. Parts of the Berlin Wall remain as a monument.

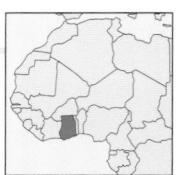

Ghana's flag has red, green and yellow bands like the flag of Ethiopia, Africa's oldest independent nation. These colours symbolize African unity. The black star is a symbol of African freedom. Ghana's flag was adopted when the country became independent in 1957.

Area 238,533 sq km [92,098 sq mi]
Population 20,757,000
Capital (population) Accra (949,000)
Government Republic
Ethnic groups Akan 44%, Moshi-Dagomba 16%, Ewe 13%, Ga 8%, Gurma 3%, Yoruba 1%
Languages English (official), Akan, Moshi-Dagomba, Ewe, Ga
Religions Christianity 63%, traditional beliefs 21%, Islam 16%
Currency Cedi = 100 pesewas
Website www.ghana.gov.gh

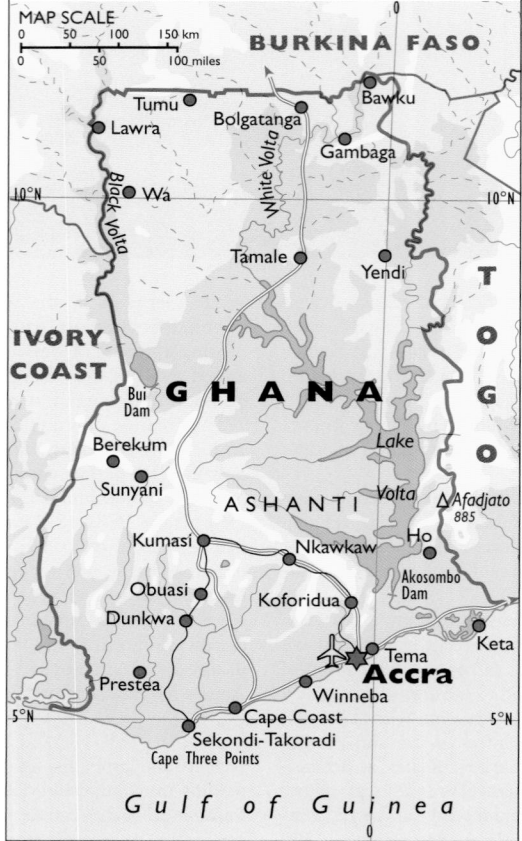

The Republic of Ghana faces the Gulf of Guinea in West Africa. This hot country, just north of the Equator, was formerly called the Gold Coast. Behind the thickly populated southern coastal plains, which are lined with lagoons, lies a plateau region in the south-west.

Northern Ghana is drained by the Black and White Volta Rivers, which flow into Lake Volta. This lake, which has formed behind the Akosombo Dam, is one of the world's largest artificially created lakes.

Rainforests grow in the south-west. To the north, the forests merge into savanna (tropical grassland with some woodland). More open grasslands dominate in the far north.

CLIMATE

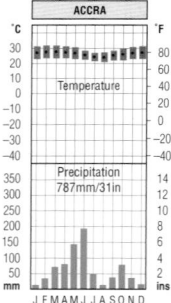

Ghana has a tropical climate. A cool offshore current reduces temperatures on the coast, and the north is hotter. The heaviest rains occur in the south-west. There are marked dry seasons in northern and eastern Ghana.

HISTORY

Ghana was a great African empire which flourished to the north-west of present-day Ghana between the AD 300s and 1000s. Modern Ghana was the first country in the Commonwealth to be ruled by black Africans.

Portuguese explorers reached the area in 1471 and named it the Gold Coast. The area became a centre of the slave trade in the 17th century. The slave trade was ended in the 1860s and the British gradually took control of the area. The country became independent in 1957, when it was renamed Ghana.

POLITICS

After independence, attempts were made to develop the economy by creating large state-owned manufacturing industries. But debt and corruption, together with falls in the price of cocoa, the chief export, caused economic problems. This led to instability and frequent coups. In 1981, power was invested in a Provisional National Defence Council, led by Flight-Lieutenant Jerry Rawlings.

The government steadied the economy and introduced several new policies, including the relaxation of government controls. In 1992, a new constitution was introduced which allowed for multiparty elections. Rawlings was re-elected later that year, and served until his retirement in 2000. The economy expanded in the 1990s, largely because the govern-

ment followed World Bank policies. When Rawlings retired, the opposition leader, John Agyekum Kufuor, leader of the New Patriotic Party, was elected president, defeating Rawlings' vice-president. He was re-elected in 2004.

ECONOMY

The World Bank classifies Ghana as a 'low-income' developing country. Most people are poor and farming employs 59% of the population. Food crops include cassava, groundnuts, maize, millet, plantains, rice and yams. But cocoa is the most valuable export crop. Timber and gold are also exported. Other valuable crops include tobacco, coffee, coconuts and palm kernels.

Many small factories produce goods, such as beverages, cement and clothing, for local consumption. The aluminium smelter at Tema, a port near Accra, is the country's largest factory. There are plans to construct around 600 km [378 mi] of pipeline which will form part of the West African Gas Pipeline Project. The aim is to lessen the dependence of electricity production on hydroelectric stations.

The wives of a Nankani chief use natural pigments and dung to decorate the huts within their compound; one of the women uses an earth-based pigment to paint a frieze of crocodile reliefs

ACCRA

Capital and largest city of Ghana, on the Gulf of Guinea. Occupied by the Ga people since the 15th century, it became the capital of Britain's Gold Coast colony in 1875. Today it is a major port and economic centre and is increasingly popular with tourists. Industries include engineering, timber, textiles, chemicals. The principal export is cacao.

Blue and white became Greece's national colours during the war of independence (1821–9). The nine horizontal stripes on the flag, which was finally adopted in 1970, represent the nine syllables of the battle cry 'Eleutheria i thanatos' ('Freedom or Death').

The Hellenic Republic, the official name of Greece, is a rugged country lying at the southern end of the Balkan Peninsula. Olympus (Ólimbos), at 2,917 m [9,570 ft], is the highest peak. Nearly a fifth of the land area is made up of around 2,000 islands, mainly in the Aegean Sea, east of the main peninsula, but also in the Ionian Sea to the west. Only 154 are inhabited. The island of Crete is structurally related to the main Alpine fold mountain system to which the mainland Pindos Range belongs.

CLIMATE

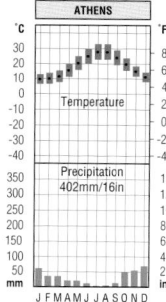

Low-lying areas in Greece have mild, moist winters and hot, dry summers. The east coast has more than 2,700 hours of sunshine a year and only about half of the rainfall of the west. The mountains have a more severe climate, with snow on the higher slopes in winter.

HISTORY

Around 2,500 years ago, Greece became the birthplace of Western civilization. Crete was the centre of the Minoan civilization, an early Greek culture, between about 3000 and 1400 BC. Following the end of the related Mycaenean period on the mainland (1580-100 BC), a 'dark age' lasted until about 800 BC. In about 750 BC, the Greeks began to colonize the Mediterranean, creating wealth through trade. The city-state of

Area 131,957 sq km [50,949 sq mi]
Population 10,648,000
Capital (population) Athens (772,000)
Government Mulktiparty republic
Ethnic groups Greek 98%
Languages Greek (official)
Religions Greek Orthodox 98%
Currency Euro = 100 cents
Website www.culture.gr

Athens reached its peak in the 461-431 BC, but in 338 BC Macedonia became the dominant power. In 334–331 BC, Alexander the Great conquered south-western Asia. Greece became a Roman province in 146 BC and, in AD 365, part of the Byzantine Empire. In 1453, the Turks defeated the Byzantine Empire. But between 1821 and 1829, the Greeks defeated the Turks. The country became an independent monarchy in 1830.

After World War II (1939–45), when Germany had occupied Greece, a civil war broke out between Communist and nationalist forces. This war ended in 1949. and a military dictatorship took power in 1967. The monarchy was abolished in 1973 and democratic government restored in 1974.

POLITICS

Greece joined the European Community in 1981. But despite efforts to develop the economy, Greece remains one of the poorest countries in the European Union. The euro became the sole unit of currency on 1 January 2002. Relations with Turkey have long been difficult. In 1999, the two countries helped each other when both were hit by major earthquakes. In 2000, Greece and Turkey signed agreements aimed at improving relations between them and indeed Greece has been supportive of Turkey's bid to join the EU, believing that membership would bring a much-needed element of stability to the region.

ECONOMY

Manufacturing is important. Products include processed food, cement, chemicals, metal products, textiles and tobacco. Lignite, bauxite and chromite are mined.

Farmland and grazing land cover about 75% of the land. Major crops include barley, grapes for wine-making, dried fruits, olives, potatoes, sugar beet and wheat. Poultry, sheep, goats, pigs and cattle are raised.

The vital tourist industry is based on the warm climate, beautiful scenery, and the historical sites dating back to the days of classical Greece. The successful hosting of the Olympic Games in 2004 brought a vital boost to the economy.

ATHENS (ATHÍNAI)

Capital and largest city of Greece, situated on the Saronic Gulf. The ancient city was built around the Acropolis, a fortified citadel, and was the greatest artistic and cultural centre in ancient Greece, gaining importance after the Persian Wars (500–449 BC). Athens prospered under Cimon and Pericles during the 5th century BC and provided a climate in which the great classical works of philosophy and drama were created. The most noted artistic treasures are the Parthenon (438 BC), the Erechtheum (406 BC), and the Theatre of Dionysus (500 BC, the oldest of the Greek theatres). Modern Athens and its port of Piraeus form a major Mediterranean transport and economic centre. Overcrowding and severe air pollution are damaging the ancient sites and the tourist industry.

Epidauros, *theatre whose construction was started in the mid-late 4th century BC; the excavation and restoration were eventually completed in 1963*

Guatemala's flag was adopted in 1871, but its origins go back to the days of the Central American Federation (1823–39), which was set up after the break from Spain in 1821. The Federation included Costa Rica, El Salvador, Guatemala, Honduras and Nicaragua.

Area 108,889 sq km [42,042 sq mi]
Population 14,281,000
Capital (population) Guatemala City (1,007,000)
Government Republic
Ethnic groups Ladino (mixed Hispanic and Amerindian) 55%, Amerindian 43%, others 2%
Languages Spanish (official), Amerindian languages
Religions Christianity, indigenous Mayan beliefs
Currency US dollar; Quetzal = 100 centavos
Website www.visitguatemala.com/site/home/index_3.html

The Central American republic of Guatemala contains a densely populated fertile mountain region. The capital, Guatemala City, is situated here. The highlands run east–west and contain many volcanoes. Guatemala is subject to frequent earthquakes and volcanic eruptions. Tajumulco, an inactive volcano, is the highest peak in Central America, at 4,211 m [13,816 ft].

South of the highlands lie the Pacific coastal lowlands. North of the highlands is the thinly populated Caribbean plain and the vast Petén tropical forest. Guatemala's largest lake, Izabal, drains into the Caribbean Sea.

Hardwoods, such as mahogany, rubber, palm, and chicozapote (from which chicle, used in chewing gum, is obtained), grow in the tropical forests in the north, with mangrove swamps on the coast. Oak and willow grow in the highlands, with fir and pine at higher levels. Much of the Pacific plains is farmland.

CLIMATE

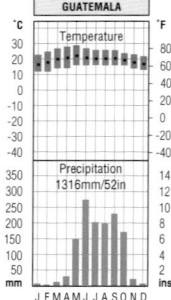

Guatemala lies in the tropics. The lowlands are hot and wet, with the central mountain region being cooler and drier. Guatemala City, at about 1,500 m [5,000 ft] above sea level, has a pleasant, warm climate, with a marked dry season between November and April.

HISTORY

Between AD 300 and 900, the Quiché branch of the Maya ruled much of Guatemala, but inexplicably abandoned their cities on the northern plains. The Quiché ruins at Tikal are the tallest temple pyramids in the Americas.

In 1523–24, the Spanish conquistador Pedro de Alvarado defeated the native tribes. In 1821, Guatemala became independent. From 1823–39, it formed part

of the Central American Federation. Various dictatorial regimes interfered in the politics of other Central American states, arousing resentment and leading to the creation of the Central American Court of Justice. In 1941, Guatemala nationalized the German-owned coffee plantations. After World War II, Guatemala embarked on further nationalization of plantations.

In 1960, the mainly Quiché Guatemalan Revolutionary National Unity Movement (URNG) began a guerrilla war that claimed more than 200,000 lives. During the 1960s and 1970s, terrorism and political assassinations beset Guatemala. In 1976, an earthquake devastated Guatemala City, killing more than 22,000 people.

POLITICS

Guatemala has a long-standing claim over Belize, but this was reduced in 1983 to the southern fifth of the country. In 1985, Guatemala elected its first civilian president for 15 years. Alvaro Arzú Irigoyen became president in 1996 elections, and a peace agreement with the URNG ended 35 years of civil war. Alfonso Portillo became president in 1999 elections, despite admitting to killing two men.

In 2004, US$35 million was paid in damages to victims of the civil war, 93% of the acts of violence during the civil war were found to have been perpetrated by the security forces.

ECONOMY

Guatemala is classified as a 'lower-middle-income' developing country. It is thought that up to 75% live below the poverty line. Agriculture employs nearly half the workforce and coffee, sugar, bananas and beef are the leading exports. Other important crops include cardomon and cotton, while maize is the chief food crop. However, Guatemala still has to import food to feed the people. Tourism and manufacturing are growing in importance. Manufactures include textiles, wood products, processed farm products, and handicrafts.

GUATEMALA CITY (CIUDAD GUATEMALA)

The capital of Guatemala lies on a plateau in the Sierra Madre. It is the largest city in Central America. Founded in 1776, the city was the capital of the Central American Federation from 1823–39. It was badly damaged by earthquakes in 1917–18 and 1976. Industries include mining, furniture, textiles, handicrafts.

Temple at Tikal, located in the Tikal National Park, a major site of the Mayan civilization; the park was inscribed as a UNESCO World Heritage Site in 1979

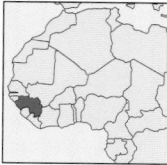

Guinea's flag was adopted when the country became independent from France in 1958. It uses the colours of the flag of Ethiopia, Africa's oldest nation, which symbolize African unity. The red represents work, the yellow justice and the green solidarity.

The Republic of Guinea, which faces the Atlantic Ocean in West Africa, can be divided into four regions: an alluvial coastal plain, which includes the capital, Conakry; the highland region of the Fouta Djallon, the source of one of Africa's longest rivers, the Niger; the north-east savanna; and the south-east Guinea Highlands, which rise to 1,752 m [5,748 ft] at Mount Nimba.

Mangrove swamps grow along parts of the coast. Inland, the Fouta Djallon is largely open grassland. North eastern Guinea is tropical savanna, with acacia and shea scattered across the grassland. Rainforests of ebony, mahogany, and teak grow in the Guinea Highlands.

Area 245,857 sq km [94,925 sq mi]
Population 9,246,000
Capital (population) Conakry (1,232,000)
Government Multiparty republic
Ethnic groups Peuhl 40%, Malinke 30%, Soussou 20%, others 10%
Languages French (official)
Religions Islam 85%, Christianity 8%, traditional beliefs 7%
Currency Guinean franc = 100 cauris
Website www.guinee.gov.gn

CLIMATE

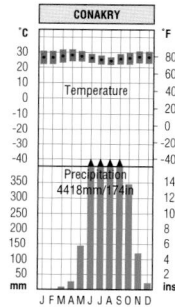

Guinea has a tropical climate. Conakry on the coast has heavy rains during its relatively cool season between May and November. Hot, dry harmattan winds blow south-westwards from the Sahara in the dry season. The Fouta Djalon is cooler than the coast. The driest region is in the north-east. This region and the south-eastern highlands have greater temperature variations than on the coast.

HISTORY

The north-east Guinea plains formed part of the medieval Empire of Ghana. The Malinke formed the Mali Empire, which dominated the region in the 12th century. The Songhai Empire supplanted the Malinke in the 15th century.

Portuguese explorers arrived in the mid-15th century and the slave trade began soon afterwards. From the 17th century, other European slave traders became active in Guinea. In the early 18th century, the Fulani embarked on a *jihad* (holy war) and gained control of the Fouta Djallon. Following a series of wars, France won control in the mid-19th century and, in 1891, it made Guinea a French colony. France exploited its bauxite deposits and mining unions developed.

In 1958, Guinea voted to become an independent republic and France severed all aid. Its first president, Sékou Touré (1958–84), adopted a Marxist programme of reform and embraced Pan-Africanism. Opposition parties were banned, and dissent brutally suppressed. In 1970, Portuguese Guinea (now Guinea-Bissau) invaded Guinea. Conakry later acted as the headquarters for independence movements in Guinea-Bissau. A military coup followed Touré's death in 1984, and Colonel Lansana Conté established the Military Committee for National Recovery (CMRN). Conté improved relations with the West and introduced free-enterprise policies.

CONAKRY

Capital city of Guinea, Conakry is located on Tombo Island, in the Atlantic Ocean and is connected to the mainland via a causeway. Founded in 1884 and occupied by French forces in 1887, it is Guinea's largest city. A major port and the administrative and commercial centre of Guinea, its economy revolves largely round the port, from where it exports alumina and bananas. Manufactures include food products, automobiles and beverages. The city is noted for its botanical garden. The Marché Madina, one of the largest markets in west Africa, is also worth a visit as are the cathedral and national museum.

POLITICS

Civil unrest forced the introduction of a multiparty system in 1992. Elections in 1993 confirmed Conté as president, amid claims of voting fraud. In February 1996, Conté foiled an attempted military coup. He was re-elected in 1998.

By 2000, Guinea was home to about 500,000 refugees from the wars in neighbouring Sierra Leone and Liberia. In 2000, rebel incursions from these countries killed more than 1,000 people, caused massive population displacement, and threatened to destablilize Guinea. Conté was re-elected in 2003, though the poll was boycotted by the opposition. His ailing health brings into question whether he will survive the full term. The president survived an assassination attempt in 2005 when shots were fired at his car.

ECONOMY

The World Bank classifies Guinea as a 'low-income' developing country. It is the world's second-largest producer of bauxite which accounts for 90% of its exports. Guinea has 25% of the world's known reserves of bauxite.

Other natural resources include diamonds, gold, iron ore and uranium. Due to the mining industry, the rail and road infrastructure is improving. Agriculture (mainly at subsistence level) employs 78% of the workforce. Major crops include bananas, cassava, coffee, palm kernels, pineapples, rice and sweet potatoes. Cattle and other livestock are raised in highland areas.

A Guinean fisherman *repairs a fishing net in Conakry*

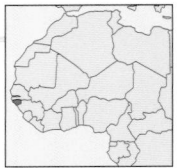

Red symbolizes the blood shed in the liberation struggle; yellow is for the hot African sun; green represents the fertile land and hope for the future. The black star stands for the African continent, paying homage to the flag of Ghana, the first African colony to gain independence.

Area 36,125 sq km [13,948 sq mi]
Population 1,388,000
Capital (population) Bissau (200,000)
Government Interim government
Ethnic groups Balanta 30%, Fula 20%, Manjaca 14%, Mandinga 13%, Papel 7%
Languages Portuguese (official),Crioulo
Religions Traditional beliefs 50%, Islam 45%, Christianity 5%
Currency CFA franc = 100 centimes
Website www.republica-da-guine-bissau.org

The Republic of Guinea-Bissau is a small country in West Africa. The land is mostly low-lying, with a broad, swampy, coastal plain and many flat offshore islands, including the Bijagós Archipelago. Mangrove forests line the coasts, and dense rainforest covers much of the coastal plain.

CLIMATE

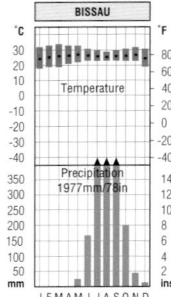

The country has a tropical climate, with its dry season from December to May and its rainy season from June to November.

HISTORY

It was first visited by Portuguese navigators in 1446. From the 17th to the early 19th century, Portugal used the coast as a slave-trading base. Portugal appointed a governor to administer Guinea-Bissau and the Cape Verde Islands in 1836, but in 1879 the territories separated and Guinea-Bissau became a colony, then called Portuguese Guinea. Development was slow, partly because the territory did not attract settlers on the same scale as Portugal's much healthier African colonies of Angola and Mozambique.

In 1956, African nationalists in Portuguese Guinea and Cape Verde founded the African Party for the Independence of Guinea and Cape Verde (PAIGC). Because Portugal seemed determined to hang on to its overseas territories, the PAIGC began a guerrilla war in 1963. By 1968, it held two-thirds of the country. In 1972, a rebel National Assembly, elected by the people in the PAIGC-controlled areas, voted to make the country independent as Guinea-Bissau.

POLITICS

In 1974, it formally achieved independence (followed by Cape Verde in 1975). The independent nation faced many problems arising from its under-developed economy and its lack of trained

BISSAU

Capital of Guinea-Bissau, near the mouth of the River Geba, western Africa. Established by the Portuguese as a slave-trading centre in 1687, Bissau became a free port in 1869. It replaced Bonama as capital in 1941. The port has recently been improved. Industries include oil processing.

personnel. Guinea-Bissau's leaders favoured union with Cape Verde. This objective was abandoned in 1980, when an army coup, led by Major João Vieira, overthrew the government. The Revolutionary Council which took over opposed unification with Cape Verde; it concentrated on national policies and socialist reforms.

In 1991, the PAIGC voted to introduce a multiparty system. The PAIGC won the 1994 elections, and Vieira was elected president. In 1998 an army rebellion sparked a civil war. The army rebels took power in 1999, but elections were held in 1999–2000. Kumba Ialá became president in 2000 but was overthrown in a coup in 2003. Civilian government was restored in 2004 when parliamentary elections were held.

ECONOMY

Guinea-Bissau is a poor country. Agriculture employs more than 70% of the workforce, but most farming is at subsistence level. Major crops include beans, coconuts, groundnuts, maize and rice. Fishing is also important.

BIJAGOS ARCHIPELAGO

Formed by the prehistoric delta of the Rio Grande de Buba and the Rio Geba, the Bijagos Archipelago consists of 88 islands and islets spread over 10,000 sq km [4,000 sq mi]. The rainy season brings fresh water into the coastal zone, while coastal currents from north and south meet, making the delta region vulnerable yet biologically rich. Between the islands, extensive mud flats are drained by a network of canals and creeks as the tide recedes. The characteristic vegetation of the islands are the palm groves. The tidal areas form a unique mosaic of mangroves and tidal flats. Hippos have adapted to life in sea water, while otters coexist with manatees, for whom the archipelago forms one of the most important strongholds in the region. Two species of dolphin live here. Reptiles include two species of crocodile and four species of marine turtle, including the green turtle for which the Bijagos Archipelago is the most important breeding site in West Africa. The archipelago is inhabited almost exclusively by the Bijagos ethnic group.

A fisherman tips his boat over to empty it of water, on a beach of the Bijagos Island

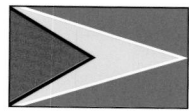

Guyana's flag was adopted in 1966 when the country became independent from Britain. The colours symbolize the people's energy in building a new nation (red), their perseverance (black), minerals (yellow), rivers (white), and agriculture and forests (green).

The Co-operative Republic of Guyana borders the Atlantic Ocean. It is the only English-speaking country in mainland South America and. The coastal plain, where the majority lives, is between 3 and 48 km [2–30 mi] wide, much of it below sea level. Dykes prevent flooding. Inland is hilly and forested and this terrain makes up Guyana's largest region. The land rises to 2,810 m [9,219 ft] in the Pakaraima Mountains, part of the Guiana Highlands on Guyana's western border. Other highlands are in the south and south-west. Guyana has impressive waterfalls, such as the King George VI Falls (488 m [1,601 ft], the Great Falls (256 m [840 ft]), and Kaieteur Falls (226 m [741 ft]).

The coastal plain is largely farmed, but wet savanna covers some areas. Inland, rainforests, rich in plant and animal species, cover about 85% of the country. Savanna occurs in the south-west.

CLIMATE

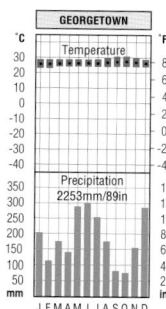

Guyana has a hot, humid equatorial climate. Rainfall ranges from 2,280 mm [90 in] on the coast to 3,560 mm [140 in] in the rainforest region. The rainfall decreases to the west and south.

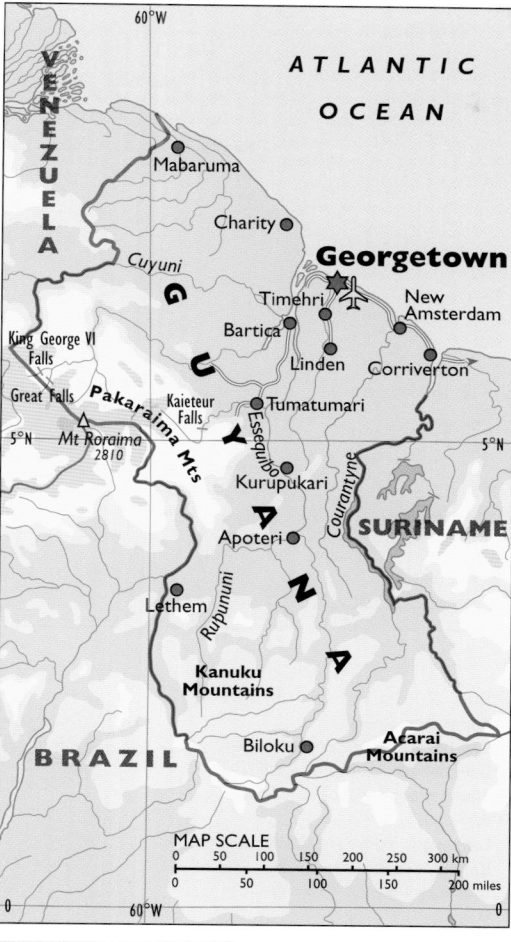

Area 214,969 sq km [83,000 sq mi]
Population 706,000
Capital (population) Georgetown (150,000)
Government Multiparty republic
Ethnic groups East Indian 50%, Black 36%, Amerindian 7%, others
Languages English (official), Creole, Hindi, Urdu
Religions Christianity 50%, Hinduism 35%, Islam 10%, others
Currency Guyanese dollar = 100 cents
Website www.guyana-tourism.com

Progressive People's Party (PPP) led by East Indian Cheddi Jagan won the elections. Britain then sent in troops and set up an interim administration. The constitution was restored in 1957, when the PPP split into a mostly Indian party, led by Jagan, and another group, led by a black lawyer, Forbes Burnham. Burnham's party, the more moderate People's National Congress (PNC), consisted mainly of the descendants of Africans. In 1961, British Guiana became self-governing, with Jagan as prime minister. Riots, strikes and racial coflict broke out in the early 1960s. Elections in 1964 were won by the PNC and its ally, the United Force and Burnham became prime minister

POLITICS

British Guiana became independent as Guyana on 26 May 1966 with Burnham as prime minister. In 1970, Guyana became a republic but remained a member of the Commonwealth. In 1980 Burnham became president and served in that post until his death in 1985. He was succeeded by the prime minister Desmond Hoyte, but, in 1992, the PPP won the elections and Ched di Jagan was elected president. On his death in 1997, he was succeeded by his wife Janet, who herself retired on health grounds in 1999. Her successor, Bharrat Jagdeo, a former finance minister, was re-elected in 2001 when the PPP won both the presidential and parliamentary elections. Venezuela continues to claim Guyanese territory west of the Essequibo river, while Suriname is in dispute with Guyana over the headwaters of the Corentyne River, which forms part of the border between the two countries. Guyana also has a long-standing dispute with Suriname over their sea boundary, which runs through a potentially important offshore oilfield.

HISTORY

The first inhabitants of Guyana were Arawak, Carib and Warrau Amerindians. The Dutch founded a settlement in what is now Guyana in 1581 and, in 1620, the Dutch West India Company began to set up armed bases and to import African slaves to work on the sugar plantations. However, between 1780 and 1813, the territory changed hands between the Dutch, French and British. Britain occupied Guyana in 1814 during the Napoleonic Wars, and, in 1831, Britain founded the colony of British Guiana. After slavery was abolished in 1834, many former slaves set up their own farms with East Indian and Chinese labourers introduced to replace them. Gold was discovered in 1879. In 1889, Venezuela claimed part of the territory, but its claims were over-ruled by an international arbitration tribunal. In 1953, the left-wing Guyanese

GEORGETOWN
Capital and largest city of Guyana, at the mouth of the River Demerara. Founded in 1781 by the British, it was the capital of the united colonies of Essequibo and Demerara and was known as Stabroek during the brief Dutch occupation from 1784. Renamed Georgetown in 1812. Industries: shipbuilding, brewing.

ECONOMY

Guyana is a poor developing country. Its resources include gold, bauxite (aluminium ore) and other minerals, its forests and fertile soils. Agriculture and mining are the chief activities. The leading crops are sugar cane and rice, but citrus fruits, cocoa, coffee and plantains are also important. Farmers also produce beef, pork, poultry and dairy products. Fishing and forestry are other activities

Kaieteur Falls *on the Potaro River; the falls have a drop of 226 m (741 ft) and are considered to be amongst the most powerful falls on Earth*

Blue represents Haitians of African and French descent. Red represents blood shed in the struggle for independence. The coat of arms features a liberty cap on a royal palm tree and two cannons flanked by flags with a scroll reading l'Union Fait la Force (Strength in Unity).

The Republic of Haiti occupies the western third of Hispaniola, the Caribbean's second largest island. The country's culture is associated with exciting music with strong rhythms and voodoo which is practised by around 80% of the people. The land is mainly rugged, with mountain chains forming peninsulas in the north and south. The highest peak, 2,680 metres [8,793 ft] is in Massif de la Selle in the south-east. Between the peninsulas is the Golfe de la Gonâve, which contains the large Isle de la Gonâve. Haiti's long coastline, which extends about 1,770 km [1,100 miles], is deeply indented.

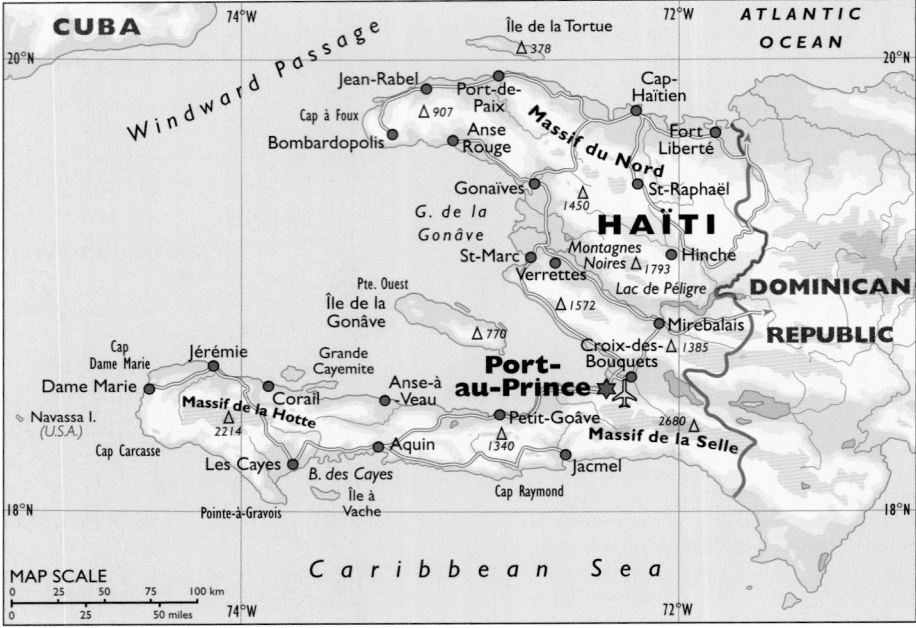

CLIMATE

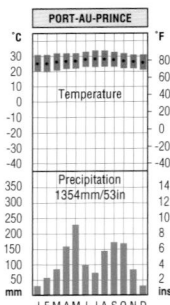

Haiti has a hot, humid tropical climate. Annual rainfall in the northern highlands is about 2,000 mm [79 in], more than twice that of the southern coast. The country is subject to tropical storms, which cause great damage.

HISTORY

In 1496, Spain established a settlement at Santo Domingo, now capital of the neighbouring Dominican Republic. This was the first European settlement in the Western Hemisphere. The local Arawak Amerindians were annihilated by Spanish settlers in barely 25 years. Spain ceded to the western part of Hispaniola to France in 1697. This area became Haiti. With an economy based on sugar cultivation and forestry, Haiti soon became prosperous.

In 1801, former slave Toussaint Louverture, led a revolt and proclaimed himself governor-general. A French force failed to conquer the interior of Haiti and the country became independent in 1804. Another former slave, Jean-Jacques

Area 27,750 sq km [10,714 sq mi]
Population 7,656,000
Capital (population) Port-au-Prince (917,000)
Government Multiparty republic
Ethnic groups Black 95%, Mulatto/White 5%
Languages French and Creole (both official)
Religions Roman Catholic 80%, Voodoo
Currency Gourde = 100 centimes
Website www.haititourisme.org

PORT-AU-PRINCE

Capital of Haiti, a port on the south-east shore of the Gulf of Gonâve, on the west coast of Hispaniola. Founded by the French in 1749, Port-au-Prince became the capital of Haiti in 1770. Industries include tobacco, textiles, cement, coffee, sugar.

A young market vendor hauls a wheelbarrow full of empty tin cans near the Marche des Bossales, Port-au-Prince's main market

1994. But he stood down in 1995 and was succeeded by René Préval. Violence and poverty still prevailed and, in 1999, Préval dissolved parliament and declared that he would rule by decree. But in the elections of 2000, Aristide again became president amid accusations of electoral irregularities, surviving an attempted coup in 2001. In 2003, voodoo was recognized as a religion. In 2004, rebels seized several towns and cities in an anti-government uprising. Aristide fled the country, accusing the United States of forcing him into exile. An interim president, Boniface Alexandre, was sworn in as president and an interim government, led by prime minister Gerald Latortue, a former foreign secretary and UN official, took control and a UN peace-keeping force arrived. Floods in May 2004 caused major loss of life in Haiti and the Dominican Republic, while, later that year, Hurricane Jeanne killed nearly 3,000 people in the north-west. In 2005, Hurricane Denis killed at least 45 people. Money-laundering, corruption and drug-trafficking are rife. Haiti is considered to be the transshipment point for cocaine en route to the United States.

Dessalines declared himself emperor. In 1915, following conflict between black and mulatto Haitians, the United States invaded the country to protect its interests. The troops withdrew in 1934, although the United States maintained control over the economy until 1947.

In 1956, François Duvalier ('Papa Doc') seized power in a military coup. He was elected president in 1957. Duvalier established a brutal dictatorship. He died in 1971 and his son Jean Claude Duvalier ('Baby Doc') became president. Like his father, Baby Doc used a murderous militia, the Tontons Macoutes, to conduct a reign of terror and maintain rule. In 1986, popular unrest forced Baby Doc to flee and a military regime took over.

POLITICS

The country's first multiparty elections were held in December 1990, the winner was radical Roman Catholic priest, Father Jean-Bertrand Aristide, who promised sweeping reforms. Aristide was re-elected in

ECONOMY

Haiti is the poorest country in the Western Hemisphere and 80% of the people live below the poverty line. Agriculture is the occupation of two-thirds of the people, but coffee is the only significant cash crop.

Honduras officially adopted its present flag in 1866. It is based on the flag of the Central American Federation, set up in 1823 and consisting of Costa Rica, El Salvador, Guatemala, Honduras, and Nicaragua. Honduras left the Federation in 1838.

The Republic of Honduras is the second largest country in Central America. It has two coastlines. The north Caribbean coast extends for about 600 km [375 mi], its deep offshore waters prompted the Spanish to name the country Honduras (Spanish for 'depths'); and a narrow, 80 km [50 mi] long, Pacific outlet to the Gulf of Fonseca. Along the north coast are vast banana plantations. To the east lies the Mosquito Coast. The Cordilleras highlands form 80% of Honduras, and include the capital, Tegucigalpa.

Pine forests cover 75% of Honduras. The northern coastal plains contain rainforest and tropical savanna. The Mosquito Coast contains mangrove swamps and dense forests. Mahogany and rosewood forest grow on lower mountain slopes.

Area 112,088 sq km [43,277 sq mi]
Population 6,824,000
Capital (population) Tegucigalpa (850,000)
Government Republic
Ethnic groups Mestizo 90%, Amerindian 7%, Black (including Black Carib) 2%, White 1%
Languages Spanish (official), Amerindian dialects
Religions Roman Catholic 97%
Currency Honduran lempira = 100 centavos
Website www.letsgohonduras.com

CLIMATE

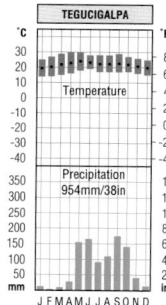

The climate is tropical, though the uplands, where the capital Tegucigalpa is situated, are cooler than the coastal plains. The heaviest rainfall occurs from November to May. The coast is often battered by hurricanes. In October 1998, Honduras and Nicaragua were hit by Hurricane Mitch, which caused floods and mudslides.

HISTORY

From AD 400 to 900, the Maya civilization flourished. The Spanish discovered the magnificent ruins at Copán in western Honduras in 1576, but these were covered in dense forest and were only rediscovered in 1839. Columbus sighted the coast in 1502. Pedro de Alvarado founded the first Spanish settlements in 1524. The Spanish gradually subdued the native population and established gold and silver mines.

In 1821 Honduras gained independence, and formed part of the Mexican Empire. From 1823 to 1838, Honduras was a member of the Central American Federation. Throughout the rest of the 19th century, Honduras was subject to continuous political interference, especially from Guatemala. Britain controlled the Mosquito Coast.

In the 1890s, American companies developed plantations in Honduras to grow bananas, which soon became the country's chief source of income. The companies exerted great political influence and the country became known as a 'banana republic', a name that was later applied to several other Latin American nations.

After World War II, demands grew for greater national autonomy and workers' rights. A military coup overthrew the Liberal government in 1963. In 1969, Honduras fought the short 'Soccer War' with El Salvador. The war was sparked off by the treatment of fans during a World Cup soccer series. Though the real reason was that Honduras had forced Salvadoreans in Honduras to give up land.

TEGUCIGALPA

Capital and largest city of Honduras, located in the mountainous central Cordilleras. Founded in the 16th century by the Spanish as a silver and gold mining town, it became the national capital in 1880. Industries include sugar, textiles, chemicals, cigarettes.

POLITICS

Civilian government returned in 1982. During the 1980s, Honduras allowed US-backed Contra rebels from Nicaragua to operate in Honduras against Nicaragua's left-wing Sandinista government. Honduras was heavily dependent on US aid. Popular demonstrations against the Contras, led to the declaration of a state of emergency in 1988. A ceasefire was then signed in Nicaragua, after which the Contra bases were closed down.

In 1992 Honduras signed a treaty with El Salvador, settling the disputed border. Liberal Party leader Carlos Flores became president in 1997 elections. In 1998, Hurricane Mitch killed more than 5,500 people and left 14 million people homeless. Human rights organisations estimated that 'death squads', often backed by the police, killed more than 1,000 street children in 2000. National Party leader Ricardo Maduro became president in 2001 elections.

ECONOMY

Honduras is the least industrialized country in Central America, and the poorest developing nation in the Americas. It has very few mineral resources, other than silver, lead and zinc.

Agriculture dominates the economy, forming 78% of exports and employing 38% of the workforce. Bananas and coffee are the leading exports, and maize the principal food crop. Cattle are raised in the mountain valleys and on the southern Pacific plains.

Fishing and forestry are also important. There are vast timber resources. Lack of an adequate transport infrastructure hampers development.

Stela in the ruins of Copan, to the west of Honduras; the great Mayan civilization once thrived in the area and it has been designated a UNESCO World Heritage Site

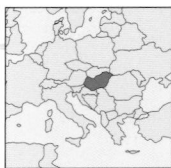

Hungary's flag was adopted in 1919. A state emblem was added in 1949 and removed in 1957. The colours of red, white and green had been used in the Hungarian arms since the 15th century. The tricolour design became popular during the 1848 rebellion against Habsburg rule.

Area 93,032 sq km [35,920 sq mi]
Population 10,032,000
Capital (population) Budapest (1,819,000)
Government Multiparty republic
Ethnic groups Magyar 90%, Gypsy, German, Serb, Romanian, Slovak
Languages Hungarian (official)
Religions Roman Catholic 68%, Calvinist 20%, Lutheran 5%, others
Currency Forint = 100 fillér
Website www.magyarorszag.hu/angol

The Republic of Hungary is a land-locked country in central Europe. The land is mostly low-lying and drained by the Danube (Duna) and its tributary, the Tisza. Most of the land east of the Danube belongs to a region called the Great Plain (Nagyalföld), which covers about half of Hungary.

West of the Danube is a hilly region, with some low mountains, called Transdanubia. This region contains the country's largest lake, Balaton. In the north-west is a small, fertile and mostly flat region called the Little Plain (Kisalföld).

Much of Hungary's original vegetation has been cleared. Large forests remain in the scenic northeastern highlands

CLIMATE

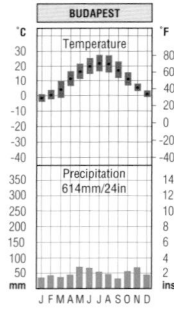

Hungary lies far from the moderating influence of the sea. As a result, summers are warmer and sunnier, and the winters colder than in Western Europe.

HISTORY

Magyars first arrived in the area from the east in the 9th century. In the 11th century, Hungary's first king, Stephen I, made Roman Catholicism the official religion. Hungary became a powerful kingdom, but in 1526 it was defeated by Turkish forces, who later occupied much of Hungary. In the late 17th century, the Austrian Habsburgs conquered Hungary. In 1867, Austria granted Hungary equal status in a 'dual monarchy', called Austria-Hungary. In 1914, a Bosnian student killed Archduke Franz Ferdinand, the heir to the Austria-Hungary throne. This led to World War I, when Austria-Hungary fought alongside Germany. Defeat in 1918 led to nearly 70% of its territory being apportioned by the Treaty of Versailles to Czechoslovakia, Yugoslavia and Romania. Some 2.6 million Hungarians live in these countries today.

The government hoped to regain these territories by siding with Hitler's Germany in World War II, but the Germansoccupied the country in 1944 and later that year the Red Army invaded. Elections were held in 1945 and, in 1946, the country was declared a republic. Although the small-holders had won a clear majority of the votes in the 1945 elections, the Communists gradually took control even after failing to win a majority of the votes cast in new elections in 1947.

POLITICS

Hungary became a Communist state in 1949, with a constitution based on that of the Soviet Union. The first leader of the Communist government was Mathias Rákosi, who was replaced in 1953 by Imre Nagy. Nagy sought to relax Communist policies and was forced from office in 1955. He was replaced by Rákosi in 1956 and this led to a major uprising in which many Hungarians were killed or imprisoned. Nagy and his co-workers were executed for treason in 1958.

Janos Kádár came to power in the wake of the suppression, but his was

a relatively progressive leadership, including an element of political reform and a measure of economic liberalism. However, in the late 1970s, the economic situation worsened and new political parties started to appear.

Kádár resigned in 1989 and the central Committee of the Socialist Workers' Party (the Communist Party) agreed to sweeping reforms, including the introduction of a pluralist system and a democratic parliament, which had formally been little more than a rubber-stamp assembly. The trial of Imre Nagy and his co-workers was declared unlawful and their bodies were reburied with honour in June 1989.

Szechenyi Baths, *Budapest; early-20th-century neo-Baroque thermal baths*

In 1990, Hungarians voted into office a centre-right coalition headed by the Democratic Forum. In 1994, the Hungarian Socialist Party (made up of ex-Communists) won a majority and governed in coalition with the Alliance of Free Democrats. However, in elections in 1998, Victor Orbán, leader of the Fidesz-Hungarian Civic

BUDAPEST
Capital of Hungary, on the River Danube. It was created in 1873 by uniting the towns of Buda (capital of Hungary since the 14th century) and Pest on the opposite bank. It became one of the two capitals of the Austro-Hungarian Empire. In 1918, it was declared capital of an independent Hungary. Budapest was the scene of a popular uprising against the Soviet Union in 1956. The old town contains a remarkable collection of buildings, including Buda Castle, the parliament building, the National Museum, and Roman remains.

Party, became prime minister. In 2002, the Socialists and the Free Democrat coalition, led by Peter Medgyessy, won a majority in parliament. Hungary became a member of NATO and the EU in 2004.

ECONOMY

Under communism the economy was transformed from agrarian to industrial. The new factories were owned by the government, as was most of the land. From the late 1980s, the government worked to increase private ownership. This change of policy caused many problems, including inflation and high rates of unemployment.

Manufacturing is the most valuable activity. The major products include aluminium made from local bauxite, chemicals, electrical and electronic goods, processed food, iron and steel, and vehicles. Agriculture remains important, major crops include grapes, maize, potatoes, sugar beet, and wheat.

Iceland 99

Iceland's flag dates from 1915. It became the official flag in 1944, when Iceland became fully independent. The flag, which uses Iceland's traditional colours, blue and white, is the same as Norway's flag, except that the blue and red colours are reversed.

The Republic of Iceland, in the North Atlantic Ocean, though deemed part of Europe, is closer to Greenland than Scotland. Iceland sits astride the Mid-Atlantic Ridge, the geological boundary between Europe and North America. The island is slowly getting wider as the ocean is stretched apart by the forces of plate tectonics.

Iceland has around 200 volcanoes and eruptions are frequent. An eruption under the Vatnajökull ice cap in 1996 created a subglacial lake which subsequently burst, causing severe flooding. Geysers and hot springs are other volcanic features. During the thousand years that Iceland has been settled, between 150 and 200 volcanic eruptions have occurred. Ice caps and glaciers cover about one-eighth of the land. The only habitable regions are the coastal lowlands.

Vegetation is sparse or non-existent on 75% of the land. Treeless grassland or bogs cover some areas. Deep fjords fringe the coast.

Area	103,000 sq km [39,768 sq mi]
Population	294,000
Capital (population)	Reykjavik (108,000)
Government	Multiparty republic
Ethnic groups	Icelandic 97%, Danish 1%
Languages	Icelandic (official)
Religions	Evangelical Lutheran 87%, other Protestant 4%, Roman Catholic 2%, others
Currency	Icelandic króna = 100 aurar
Website	www.icetourist.is

CLIMATE

Although it lies far to the north, Iceland's climate is moderated by the warm waters of the Gulf Stream. The port of Reykjavik is ice-free all the year round.

REYKJAVIK climate chart
Temperature / Precipitation 779mm/31in

HISTORY

Iceland was colonized by Vikings from Norway in AD 874 and the population grew as more settlers arrived from Norway and from the Viking colonies in the British Isles. In 930, the settlers founded the oldest, and what is thought to be the world's first, parliament (the Althing). One early settler was Erik the Red, a Viking who sailed to Greenland in about 982 and founded another colony there in about 985.

Iceland was an independent country until 1262 when, following a series of civil wars, the Althing recognized the rule of the king of Norway. When Norway united with Denmark in 1380, Iceland came under the rule of Danish kingdoms. Life on Iceland was never easy. The Black Death, which swept the island in 1402, claimed two-thirds of the population, while, in the late 18th century, volcanic eruptions destroyed crops, farmland and livestock, causing a famine. Then, during the Napoleonic Wars in the early 19th century, food supplies from Europe failed to reach the island and many people starved.

When Norway was separated from Denmark in 1814, Iceland remained under Danish rule. In the late 19th century, the invention of motorized craft, which changed the fishing industry, led to mounting demands for self-government. In 1918, Iceland was acknowledged as a sovereign state, but remained united with Denmark through a common monarch. During World War II, when Germany occupied Denmark, British and American troops landed in Iceland to protect it from invasion by the Germans. Finally, following a referendum in which 97% of the people voted to cut all ties with Denmark, Iceland became a fully independent republic on 17 June 1944.

REYKJAVÍK

Capital of Iceland, a port on the south-west coast. Founded in 870, it was the island's first permanent settlement. It expanded during the 18th century, and became the capital in 1918. During World War II, it served as a British and US air base. Tourism is now important. Industries include food processing, fishing, textiles, metallurgy, printing and publishing, and shipbuilding.

POLITICS

Fishing, on which Iceland's economy is based, is a major political issue. From 1975, Iceland extended its territorial waters to 200 nautical miles, causing skirmishes between Icelandic and British vessels. The issue was resolved in 1977 when Britain agreed not to fish in the disputed waters. Another problem developed in the late 1980s when Iceland reduced the allowable catches in its waters, because overfishing was causing the depletion of fishing stocks, especially of cod. The reduction of the fish catch led to a slowdown in the economy and, eventually, to a recession, though the economy recovered in the mid-1990s when the conservation measures appeared to have been successful. Iceland left the International Whaling Commission in 1992, because of its alleged anti-whaling policy. It rejoined in 2002, but in 2003 undertook its first whale hunt for 15 years, stating that it was a scientific catch to study the impact of whales on fish stocks.

Iceland has no armed forces of its own. However, it joined NATO in 1949 and, under a NATO agreement, the United States maintains a base on the island, which remains a political issue.

ECONOMY

Iceland has few resources other than the fishing grounds which surround it. Fishing and fish processing are major industries which dominate Iceland's overseas trade. Overfishing is an economic problem. Barely 1% of the land is used to grow crops, mainly root vegetables and fodder for livestock, but, 23% of the country is used for grazing sheep and cattle. Iceland is self-sufficient in meat and dairy products. Fruit and vegetables are grown in greenhouses heated by water from hot springs. Manufacturing is important and includes aluminium, cement, clothing, electrical equipment, fertilizers and processed foods. Geothermal power is a key energy source.

Hallgrimskirkja, Reykjavik; named after 17th-century hymn writer Hallgrímur Pétursson the church was finally completed in 1986; the statue is of Leifur Eiríksson, the first European to discover America (1000 AD)

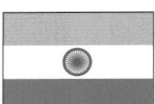

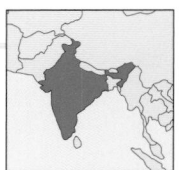

The Indian flag was adopted shortly after the country gained independence from Britain in 1947. The saffron (orange) represents renunciation, the white is for truth and the green symbolizes mankind's relationship with nature. The central wheel represents dynamism and change.

The Republic of India, the world's seventh largest country, extends from high in the Himalayas, through the Tropic of Cancer, to the warm waters of the Indian Ocean at Cape Comorin. India is the world's second most populous nation after China, and the largest democracy. The north contains the mountains and foothills of the Himalayan range. Rivers such as the Brahmaputra and Ganges (Ganga) rise in the Himalayas and flow across the fertile northern plains. Southern India consists of a large plateau called the Deccan which is bordered by two mountain ranges, the Western Ghats and the Eastern Ghats.

The Karakoram Range in the far north has permanently snow-covered peaks. The eastern Ganges delta has mangrove swamps. Between the gulfs of Kutch and Cambay are the deciduous forest habitats of the last of India's wild lions. The Ghats are clad in heavy rainforest.

An independence movement began in India after the Sepoy Rebellion of 1857–9 and, in 1885, the Indian National Congress was founded. In 1906, Indian Muslims, concerned that Hindus formed the majority of the members of the Indian National Congress, founded the Muslim League. In 1920, Mohandas K. Gandhi, a former lawyer, became leader of the Indian National Congress which soon became a mass movement. Gandhi's policy of non-violent disobedience proved highly effective, and in response Britain began to introduce political reforms. In the 1930s, the Muslim League called for the establishment of a Muslim state, called Pakistan.

In 1947, it was agreed that British India be partitioned into the mainly Hindu India and the Muslim Pakistan. Both countries became independent in August 1947, but the events were marred by mass slaughter as Hindus and Sikhs fled from Pakistan, and Muslims flocked to Pakistan from India. In the boundary disputes and reshuffling of minority populations that followed, some 1 million lives were lost. Since 1947–8, events have done little to promote good relations between the countries.

CLIMATE

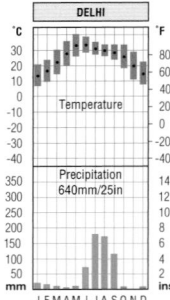

India has three seasons. The weather during the cool season, from October to February, is mild in the northern plains, but southern India remains hot, though temperatures are a little lower than for the rest of the year. Temperatures on the northern plains sometimes soar to 49°C [120°F] during the hot season from March to the end of June. Monsoon season starts in the middle of June and continues into September. At this time, moist south-easterly winds from the Indian Ocean bring heavy rains to India. Darjeeling in the north-east has an average annual rainfall of 3,040 mm [120 in], but parts of the Great Indian Desert in the north-west have only 50 mm [2 in] of rain a year. The monsoon rains are essential for India's farmers. If they arrive late, crops may be ruined. If the rainfall is considerably higher than average, floods may cause great destruction.

HISTORY

India's early settlers were scattered across the subcontinent in Stone Age times. The first of its many civilizations began to flourish in the Indus Valley in what is now Pakistan and western India around 4,500 years ago, and in the Ganges Valley from about 1500 BC, when Aryan people arrived in India from central Asia. The earlier, darker-skinned people, the Dravidians, moved southwards, ahead of the Aryans, and their descendants are now the main inhabitants of southern India.

India was the birthplace of several major religions including Hinduism, Buddhism and Sikhism. Islam was introduced from about AD 1000. The Muslim Mughal empire was founded in 1526. From the 17th century Britain began to gain influence and from 1858 to 1947, India was ruled as part of the British empire.

Taj Mahal, Agra; *built in 1632–48 by the Emperor Shah Jahan as a tomb for his wife, the white marble building is an outstanding example of Mughal architecture*

NEW DELHI

Capital of India, in the north of the country, on the River Yamuna in Delhi Union Territory. Planned by the British architects Edwin Lutyens and Herbert Baker, it was constructed in 1912–29 to replace Calcutta (now Kolkata) as the capital of British India. Whereas Old Delhi is primarily a commercial centre, New Delhi has an administrative function. Places of interest include the Coronation Durbar Site, the Crafts Museum and Humayun's Tomb. Industries include textile production, chemicals, machine tools, plastics, electrical appliances, and traditional crafts.

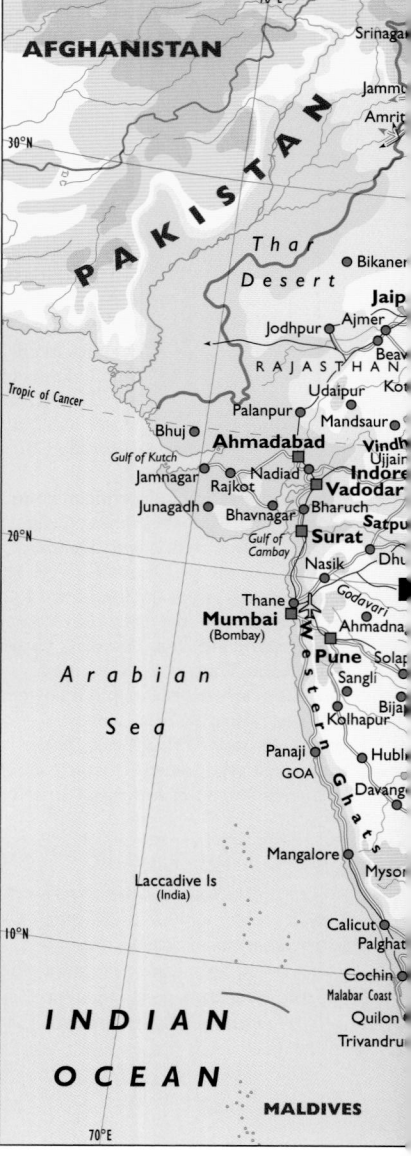

POLITICS

Gandhi was assassinated in 1948 by a Hindu extremist who hated him for his tolerant attitude towards Muslims. The country adopted a new constitution in 1948 making it a democratic republic within the Commonwealth, and elections were held in 1951 and 1952. India's first prime minister was Jawaharlal Nehru. The government sought to develop the economy and raise living standards at home, while, on the international stage, Nehru won great respect for his policy of non-alignment and neutrality. The disputed status of Kashmir was then India's thorniest security problem.

In 1966, Nehru's daughter, Indira Gandhi, took office. Her Congress Party lost support because of food shortages, unemployment and other problems. In 1971, India helped the people of East Pakistan achieve independence from West Pakistan to become Bangladesh. India tested its first atomic bomb in 1974, but pledged to use nuclear power for peaceful purposes only. In 1977, Mrs

Area 3,287,263 sq km [1,269,212 sq mi]
Population 1,065,071,000
Capital (population) New Delhi (295,000)
Government Multiparty federal republic
Ethnic groups Indo-Aryan (Caucasoid) 72%, Dravidian (Aboriginal) 25%, others (mainly Mongoloid) 3%
Languages Hindi, English,Telugu, Bengali, Marathi, Tamil, Urdu, Gujurati, Malayalam, Kannada, Oriya, Punjabi, Assamese, Kasmiri, Sindhi and Sanskrit (all official)
Religions Hinduism 82%, Islam 12%, Christianity 2%, Sikhism 2%, Buddhism and others
Currency Indian rupee = 100 paisa
Website www.tourisminindia.com

Gandhi lost her seat in parliament and her Congress Party was defeated by the Janata Party, a coalition led by Morarji R. Desai. Disputes in the Janata Party led to Desai's resignation in 1979 and, in 1980, Congress-I (the I standing for Indira) won the elections. Mrs Gandhi again became prime minister, but her government faced many problems. One problem was that many Sikhs wanted more control over the Punjab, and Sikh radicals began to commit acts of violence to draw attention to their cause. In 1984, armed Sikhs occupied the sacred Golden Temple, in Amritsar. In response, Indian troops attacked the temple, causing much damage and deaths. In October, 1984, two of Mrs Gandhi's Sikh guards assassinated her. Her son, Rajiv, was chosen to succeed her as prime minister, but, in 1989, Congress lost its majority in parliament and Rajiv resigned as prime minister, then during elections in 1991, he was assassinated by Tamil extremists.

India is a vast country with an enormous diversity of cultures. It has more than a dozen major languages, and many minor languages. Hindi, the national language, and the Dravidian languages of the south (Kannada, Tamil, Telugu and Malayam) are Indo-European. Sino-Tibetan languages are spoken in the north and east, while smaller groups speak residual languages in forested hill refuges.

Hinduism is all-pervasive and Buddhism is slowly reviving in the country of its origin. Jainism is strong in the merchant towns around Mount Abu in the Aravallis hills north of Ahmadabad. Islam has contributed many mosques and monuments, the Taj Mahal being the best known and India retains a large Muslim minority. The Punjab's militant Sikhs now seek separation. However, India's most intractable problem remains the divided region of Kashmir, the subject of a long conflict between India and Pakistan. However, in 2004 and 2005, both countries sought ways of easing the tension, including the opening up of cross-border transport services. In February 2006 India and Pakistan re-opened a second rail link connecting Munabao in Rajasthan with Khokrapar, a border town in Pakistan's Sindh province. Against this a wave of violence by Islamic militants occurred in Kashmir; the prime minister Manmohan Singh said that this would not halt peace efforts.

On 11th July 2006 more than 180 people died with over 700 injured in co-ordinated terrorist bomb attacks on moving trains and in stations in Mumbai.

ECONOMY

According to the World Bank, India is a 'low-income' developing country. Despite initiatives, its socialist policies have failed to raise the living standards of the poor. In the 1990s, the government introduced private enterprise policies to stimulate growth.

Farming employs 64% of the workforce. The main crops are rice, wheat, millet, sorghum, peas and beans. India has more cattle than any other country. Milk is produced but Hindus do not eat beef. India has reserves of coal, iron ore and oil, and manufacturing has expanded greatly since 1947 to include high-tech goods, iron and steel, machinery, refined petroleum, textiles, jewellery and transport equipment. India has begun to capitalize on its large numbers of fluent English speakers, with many working in call centres for multinational businesses. Another important provider of income is the large cinema industry, the most famous of which is the Hindi Bollywood.

CHRISTMAS ISLAND

Area 135 sq km [52 sq mi]
Population 2,771
Capital (population) The Settlement (1,508)
Government Territory of Australia
Ethnic groups Chinese 70%, European 20%, Malay 10%
Languages English (official), Chinese, Malay
Religions Buddhist 36%, Muslim 25%, Christian 18%, others
Currency Australian dollar = 100 cents
Website www.christmas.net.au

Island in the east Indian Ocean 320 km [200 mi] south of Java. Named by Captain William Mynors when he landed on Christmas Day 1643. Once under British rule, it was annexed to Australia in 1958. It has important lime phosphate deposits. The Australian Government has agreed to support a commercial space-launching site to aid the economy. Two-thirds of the island is national park making it good for bird-watching.

COCOS ISLANDS

Area 14 sq km [5.4 sq mi]
Population 628
Capital (population) West Island (120)
Government Territory of Australia
Ethnic groups Europeans, Cocos Malays
Languages Malay (Cocos dialect), English
Religions Sunni Muslim 80%, others
Currency Australian dollar = 100 cents
Website www.cocos-tourism.cc

Cocos (Keeling) Islands is made up of 27 coral islands. The islands are located 2,750 km (1,700 mi) north-west of Perth. The climate is consistent with the temperature remaining at 29°C [84°F] all year round no matter what the season. The average annual rainfall is 2,000 mm (74 in). Discovered in 1609 by Captain William Keeling, but uninhabited until the 19th century, the islands were annexed by the UK in 1857 and transferred to the Australian Government in 1955. Only two of the islands are inhabited and their population is split along ethnic lines, with ethnic Europeans on West Island and ethnic Malays on Home Island. Most food and other necessities are imported from Australia. Coconuts are the sole cash crop and there is a small tourist industry.

COMOROS

The Union des Isles Comoros, consists of three large volcanic islands and some smaller ones, at the northern end of the Mozambique Channel. The three major islands are Grande Comore (site of the capital), Anjouan, and Mohéli. They are mountainous, with tropical climate and fertile soil.

Area 2,170 sq km [838 sq mi]
Population 652,000
Capital (population) Moroni (30,000)
Government Independent republic
Ethnic groups Antalote, Cafre, Makoa, Oimatsaha, Sakalava
Languages Arabic and French (both official), Shikomoro
Religions Sunni Muslim 98%, Roman Catholic 2%
Currency Comoran franc = 100 centimes
Website www.arab.net/comoros

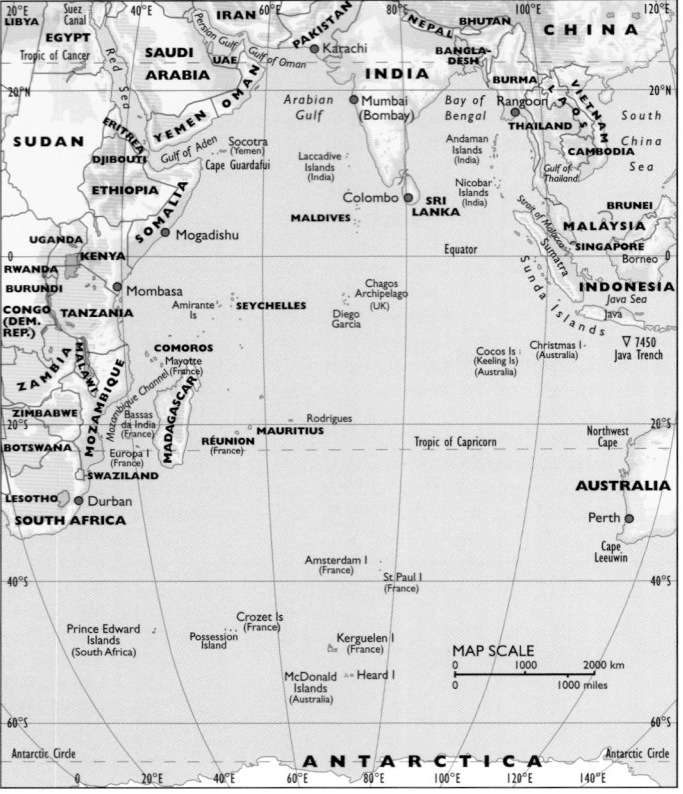

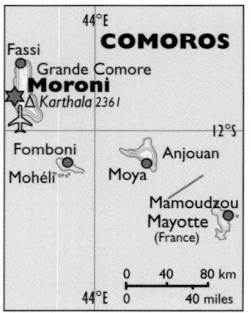

Grand Comore Island, Comoros; a man taps water from a baobab tree, which acts as a natural water reservoir

France took over one of the islands, Mayotte, in 1843 and, in 1886, the other islands came under French protection. The Comoros became independent in 1974, but the people of Mayotte opted to remain French. In the late 1990s, separatists on Anjouan and Mohéli islands sought to secede, but in 2004 each of the large islands was granted autonomy with its own president and legislature. The Comoros is a poor country. It exports cloves, perfume oils, coconuts, copra and vanilla.

MALDIVES

The Republic of the Maldives, Asia's smallest independent country, comprises some 1,200 low-lying coral islands grouped into 26 atolls, 202 of the islands are inhabited. They are scattered along a broad north–south line in the Indian Ocean about 640 km [400 mi] south west of Sri Lanka.

Area 298 sq km [115 sq mi]
Population 339,000
Capital (population) Malé (74,000)
Government Republic
Ethnic groups South Indians, Sinhalese, Arabs
Languages Maldivian Dhivehi (dialect of Sinhala, script derived from Arabic), English
Religion Sunni Muslim
Currency Rufiyaa = 100 laari
Website www.maldivesinfo.gov.mv

HISTORY AND POLITICS The islands are prone to flooding. They have a tropical climate and the monsoon season is from April to October.

Sri Lanka settled the islands in about 500 BC. From the 14th century, the ad-Din dynasty ruled the Maldives. In 1518, the Portuguese claimed the islands. From 1665 to 1886, the Maldives were a dependency of Ceylon (Sri Lanka).

They became a British protectorate in 1887. In 1965 they achieved independence as a sultanate and then became a republic when the sultan was deposed in 1968. Maumoon Abdul Gayoom has served as president since 1978. In 1982, the Maldives joined the Commonwealth. In 1988, Indian troops helped suppress an attempted coup.

A tsunami struck the islands in December 2004 killing 82 people.

Political parties are banned, though political activity is permitted, at least nominally. The president is chosen in a yes-no referendum. The voters are presented with just one candidate, chosen on their behalf by parliament. President Gayoom came under increasing pressure from human rights groups to ease up on his autocratic style of governance. There was anti-government violence on the streets. As a result of this he announced in 2005 that he planned to introduce a multiparty democracy.

ECONOMY The chief crops are bananas, coconuts, copra, mangoes, sweet potatoes and spices, but much food is imported. Fishing is important and the leading export is the bonito (Maldives tuna). Since 1972 the growth in tourism boosted foreign reserves, but the Maldives remain one of the world's poorest countries.

MAYOTTE

A French administered archipelago in the Indian Ocean to the east of the Comoros. The two major islands are Grande Terre and Petite Terre (Pamanzi). Grande Terre includes the new capital, Mamoudzou. Pamanzi is the site of the old capital, Dzaoudzi.

Mayotte has a tropical climate. It is generally hot and humid. The rainy season is from November to May, during northeastern monsoon. The dry season, from May to November, is cooler.

Area 373 sq km [144 sq mi]
Population 173,300
Capital (population) Mamoudzou (4,000)
Government Territorial collectivity of France
Ethnic groups Comorian (mixture of Bantu, Arab and Malagasy) 92%
Languages Mahorian (a Swahili dialect), French (official)
Religions Muslim 97%, Christian (mostly Roman Catholic)
Currency Euro = 100 cents
Website http://ctt.mayotte.free.fr/anglais/Eaccueil.htm

HISTORY AND POLITICS Mayotte was a French colony from 1843 to 1914 when it was attached to the Comoro group and collectively achieved administrative autonomy as a French Overseas Territory. In 1974, the rest of the Comoros became independent while Mayotte voted to remain a French dependency. In 1976 it became an overseas collectivity of France.

ECONOMY The economy is primarily agricultural, the chief products being bananas and mangoes.

RÉUNION

Area 2,510 sq km [969 sq mi]
Population 766,000
Capital (population) St-Denis (122,000)
Government Overseas department of France
Ethnic groups French, African, Malagasy, Chinese, Pakistani, Indian
Languages French (official), Creole
Religions Roman Catholic 86%, Hindu, Muslim, Buddhist
Currency Euro = 100 cents
Website www.la-reunion-tourisme.com/gb_entree.htm

The Department of Réunion is a volcanic island in the Mascarene group lying about 700 km [440 mi] east of Madagascar in the Indian Ocean. It has a mountainous, wooded centre, surrounded by a fertile coastal plain. The climate is tropical, but the temperature moderates with elevation. It is cool and dry from May to November and hot and rainy from November to April.

HISTORY AND POLITICS Discovered in 1513 by the Portuguese, France claimed Réunion in 1638. It became a French department in 1946. The island became part of an administrative region in 1973. There is increasing pressure on France for independence.

ECONOMY Sugar cane dominates the economy, though vanilla, perfume oils and tea also produce revenue. Tourism is the big hope for the future, but unemployment is high and the island relies on French aid.

SEYCHELLES

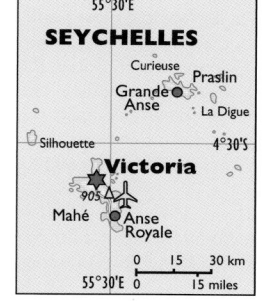

Area 455 sq km [176 sq mi]
Population 81,000
Capital (population) Victoria (24,000)
Government Republic
Ethnic groups French, African, Indian, Chinese, and Arab
Languages Creole 92%, English 5% (both official)
Religions Roman Catholic 82%, Anglican 6%, others
Currency Seychelles rupee = 100 cents
Website www.virtualseychelles.sc

The Republic of Seychelles includes a group of four large and 36 small granitic islands, plus a wide scattering of coralline islands, 14 of them inhabited, lying to the south and west. The islands experience a tropical oceanic climate.

Formerly part of the British Indian Ocean Territory (BIOT), Farquhar, Des Roches and Aldabra (famous for its unique wildlife) were returned to the Seychelles in 1976. The BIOT now consists only of the Chagos Archipelago, with Diego Garcia, the largest island, supporting a US Navy base.

HISTORY AND POLITICS French from 1756 and British from 1814, the islands gained their independence in 1976. A year later, a coup resulted in the setting up of a one-party socialist state that several attempts failed to remove. Multiparty elections were held in 1992 and France-Albert René, who had been elected president unopposed in 1979 and 1984, was re-elected president under a new constitution adopted in 1993. René was again re-elected president in 1998, but in 2004 he stepped down in favour of vice-president James Michel.

ECONOMY The Seychelles produces copra, cinnamon and tea, although rice is imported. Fishing and luxury tourism are the two main industries, with much fish produced for export.

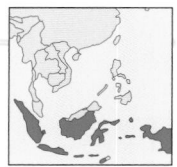

This flag was adopted in 1945, when Indonesia proclaimed itself independent from the Netherlands. The colours, which date back to the Middle Ages, were adopted in the 1920s by political groups in their struggle against Dutch rule.

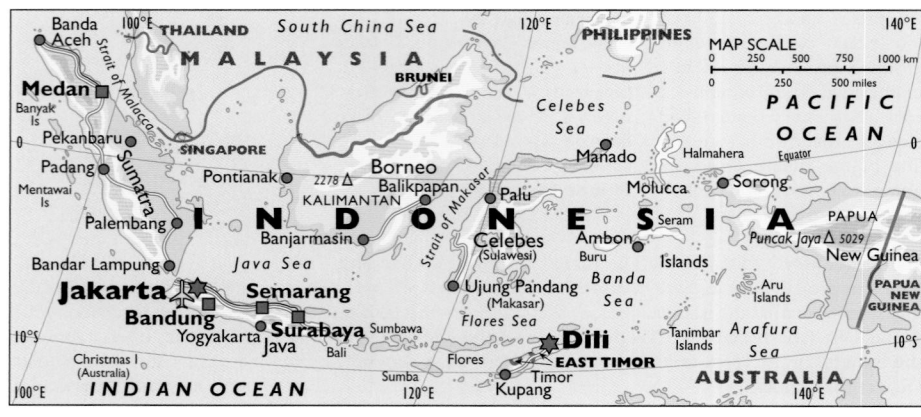

The Republic of Indonesia, in South-east Asia, consists of about 13,600 islands, less than 6,000 of which are inhabited. The island of Java covers only 7% of the country's area but it contains more than half of Indonesia's population. Three-quarters of the country is made up of five main areas: the islands of Sumatra, Java and Sulawesi (Celebes), together with Kalimantan (southern Borneo and Papua (western New Guinea). The islands are mountainous and many have extensive coastal lowlands. Indonesia contains more than 200 volcanoes, but the highest peak is Puncak Jaya, which reaches 5,029 m [16,503 ft] above sea level, is in West Papua.

CLIMATE

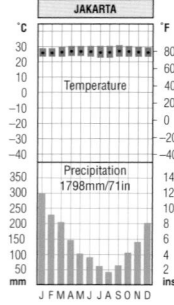

Indonesia has a hot and humid monsoon climate. Only Java and the Sunda Islands have a relatively dry season. From December to March, moist prevailing winds blow from mainland Asia. Between mid-June and October, dry prevailing winds blow from Australia.

HISTORY

From the 8th century, the empire of Sri Vijaya, which was centred on Palembang, held sway until it was replaced in the 14th century by the kingdom of Madjapahit, whose centre was east-central Java. Indonesia is the world's most populous Muslim nation, though Islam was introduced as recently as the 15th century. The area came under the domination of the Dutch East India Company in the 17th century. The Dutch government took over the islands in 1799. Japan occupied the islands in World War II and Indonesia declared its independence in 1945. The Dutch finally recognized Indonesia's independence in 1949.

POLITICS

Indonesia's first president, the anti-Western Achmed Sukarno, plunged his country into chaos. In 1962, Indonesia invaded Dutch New Guinea (now West Papua), and between 1963 and 1966 Sukarno sought to destabilize the Federation of Malaysia through incursions into northern Borneo. In 1967, Sukarno was toppled by General Suharto, following Sukarno's suppression of an alleged Communist-inspired uprising that cost 80,000 lives. Suharto's military regime, with US help, achieved significant economic growth, though corruption was rife. In 1975, Indonesian troops invaded East Timor, opposed by the local people. Suharto was forced to

JAKARTA

Capital of Indonesia, on the north-west coast of Java. Founded in 1619 as Batavia by the Dutch as a fort and trading post, it became the headquarters of the Dutch East India Company. It became the capital after Indonesia gained its independence in 1949. Industries include ironworking, printing and timber.

stand down in 1998 and his deputy, Bacharuddin Jusuf Habibie, succeeded him. In June 1999, Habibie's ruling Golkar Party was defeated in elections and, in October, the parliament elected Abdurrahman Wahid as president. However, Wahid, charged with corruption and general incompetence, was dismissed in 2001 and succeeded by the vice-president, Megawati Sukarnoputri (daughter of President Sukarno).

In the early 21st century, Indonesia faced many problems. East Timor seceded in 2002, while secessionist groups in Aceh province, northern Sumatra, and the Free Papua Movement in West Papua also demanded independence. Muslim-Christian clashes broke out in the Moluccas at the end of 1999, while indigenous Dyaks in Kalimantan clashed with immigrants from Madura.

In December 2004, more than 120,000 people were killed in Indonesia by a tsunami. Worst hit was Aceh, though the tragedy was followed by peace talks in 2005, ending the separatist conflict.

ECONOMY

The World Bank describes Indonesia as a 'lower-middle-income' developing country. Agriculture employs more than 40% of the workforce and rice is the main food crop. Bananas, cassava, coconuts, groundnuts, maize, spices and sweet potatoes are also grown. Major cash crops include coffee, palm oil, rubber, sugar cane, tea and tobacco. Fishing and forestry are also important.

There are important mineral reserves, including oil and natural gas. Bauxite, coal, iron ore, nickel and tin are also mined.

Borobudur Buddha; *the statue is part of the Borobudur Stupa on Java, the stupa represents the Buddhist cosmos*

Area 735,354 sq mi [1,904,569 sq km]
Population 238,453,000
Capital (population) Jakarta (9,374,000)
Government Multiparty republic
Ethnic groups Javanese 45%, Sundanese 14|%, Madurese 7%, coastal Malays 7%, approximately 300 others
Languages Bahasa Indonesian (official), many others
Religions Islam 88%, Roman Catholic 3%, Hinduism 2%, Buddhism 1%
Currency Indonesian rupiah = 100 sen
Website www.indonesiamission-ny.org

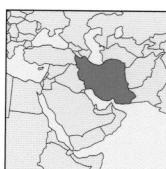

Iran's flag was adopted in 1980 by the country's Islamic government. The white stripe contains the national emblem, which is the word for Allah (God) in formal Arabic script. The words Allah Akbar (God is Great) is repeated 11 times on both the green and red stripes.

The Islamic Republic of Iran contains a barren central plateau which covers about half the country. It includes the Great Salt Desert (Dasht-e-Kavir) and the Great Sand Desert (Dasht-e-Lut). The Elburz Mountains (Alborz), which border the plateau to the north, contain Iran's highest peak, Damavand (5,604 m [18,386 ft]). North of the Elburz Mountains are the fertile, densely populated lowlands around the Caspian Sea, with a mild climate and abundant rainfall. Bordering the plateau to the west are the Zagros Mountains which separate the central plateau from the Khuzistan Plain, a region of sugar plantations and oil fields, which extends to the Iraqi border.

CLIMATE

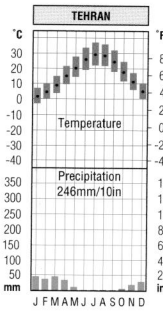

Much of Iran has a severe, dry climate, with hot summers and cold winters. Rain falls only about 30 days a year in Tehran and the annual temperature range is of more than 25°C [45°F]. The lowlands are generally milder.

HISTORY

Ancient Persia was a powerful empire. It flourished from 550 BC, when its king, Cyrus the Great, conquered the Medes, to 331 BC, when the empire was conquered by Alexander the Great. Arab armies introduced Islam in AD 641 and made Iran a great centre of learning.

Britain and Russia competed for influence in the area in the 19th century, and in the early 20th century the British began to develop the country's oil resources. In 1925, the Pahlavi family took power. Reza Khan became shah (king) and worked to modernize the country. Persia was renamed Iran in 1935. The Pahlavi Dynasty ended in 1979 when religious leader, Ayatollah Ruhollah Khomeini, made Iran an Islamic republic.

POLITICS

Iran and Iraq fought over disputed borders from 1980–8, the war led to a great reduction in Iran's vital oil production, but output returned to its mid-1970s levels by 1994. Ayatollah Khomeini died in 1989 but his views and anti-Western attitudes continued to dominate. In 1997, the liberal Mohammad Khatami, was elected president, but conservative clerics

Area 1,648,195 sq km [636,368 sq mi]
Population 69,019,000
Capital (population) Tehran (7,723,000)
Government Islamic Republic
Ethnic groups Persian 51%, Azeri 24%, Gilaki and Mazandarani 8%, Kurd 7%, Arab 3%, Lur 2%, Baluchi 2%, Turkmen 2%
Languages Persian, Turkic 26%, Kurdish
Religions Islam (Shi'ite Muslim 89%)
Currency Iranian rial = 100 dinars
Website www.netiran.com

TEHRAN

Capital of Iran, 105 km [65 mi] south of the Caspian Sea. Strategically placed on the edge of the plains, in the foothills of the country's highest mountains. In 1788, it replaced Isfahan as the capital of Persia. In the early 20th century, the old fortifications were demolished and a planned city established by the Shah. Now Iran's industrial, commercial, administrative and cultural centre.

made actual reform difficult with spiritual leader, Ayatollah Al Khameni, retaining much power. Khatami was re-elected in 2001, but the clerical establishment and institutions such as the judiciary and the Expediency Council, still blocked most of his reformist plans and he was left isolated. Between 2003 and 2005 the United States accused Iran of developing nuclear weapons, a charge Iran denied.

In 2005 Mahmoud Ahmadinejad, former mayor of Tehran, was voted in as president. Upon election he promised a period of peace and moderation, however, his subsequent statements that Israel should be wiped off the map and that the Holocaust was but a myth did little to endear him with the West. His promise to proceed with a nuclear programme for Iran continued to cause concern and in 2006 he announced that Iran had successfully enriched uranium and should now be deemed a nuclear power.

ECONOMY

Iran's prosperity is based on its oil which accounts for 95% of the country's exports. Oil revenues have been used to develop a manufacturing sector, but agriculture still accounts for 25% of the gross domestic product, even though farms cover only a tenth of the land. The main crops are wheat and barley. Livestock farming and fishing are also important.

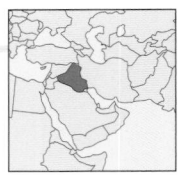

Iraq's flag was adopted in 1963, when the country was planning to federate with Egypt and Syria. It uses the four Pan-Arab colours. The three green stars symbolize the three countries. Iraq retained these stars even though the union failed to come into being.

Area 438,317 sq km [169,234 sq mi]
Population 25,375,000
Capital (population) Baghdad (4,865,000)
Government Republic
Ethnic groups Arab 77%, Kurdish 19%, Assyrian and others
Languages Arabic (official), Kurdish (official in Kurdish areas), Assyrian, Armenian
Religions Islam 97%, Christianity and others
Currency New Iraqi dinar
Website www.un.int/iraq/homepage.htm

The Republic of Iraq is a south-west Asian country at the head of the Persian Gulf. Deserts cover western and south-western Iraq, with part of the Zagros Mountains in the north-east, where farming can be practised without irrigation. Western Iraq contains a large slice of the Hamad (or Syrian) Desert, but essentially comprises lower valleys of the rivers Euphrates (Nahr al Furat) and Tigris (Nahr Dijlah). The region is arid, but has fertile alluvial soils. The Euphrates and Tigris join south of Al Qurnah, to form the Shatt al Arab. The Shatt al Arab's delta is an area of irrigated farmland and marshes. This waterway is shared with Iran.

CLIMATE

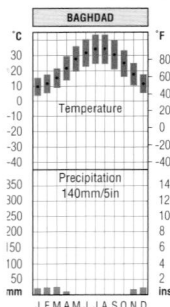

The climate of Iraq varies from temperate in the north to subtropical in the south and east. Baghdad, in central Iraq, has cool winters, with occasional frosts, and hot summers. Rainfall is generally low.

HISTORY

Mesopotamia was the home of several great civilizations, including Sumer, Babylon and Assyria. It later became part of the Persian Empire. Islam was introduced in AD 637 and Baghdad became the brilliant capital of the powerful Arab Empire. However, Mesopotamia declined after the Mongols invaded it in 1258. From 1534, Mesopotamia became part of the Turkish Ottoman Empire. Britain invaded the area in 1916. In 1921, Britain renamed the country Iraq and set up an Arab monarchy. Iraq finally became independent in 1932.

By the 1950s, oil dominated Iraq's economy. In 1952, Iraq agreed to take 50% of the profits of the foreign oil companies. This revenue enabled the government to pay for welfare services and development projects. But many Iraqis felt that they should benefit more from their oil.

Since 1958, when army officers killed the king and made Iraq a republic, the country has undergone turbulent times. In the 1960s, the Kurds, who live in northern Iraq, Iran, Turkey, Syria and Armenia, asked for self-rule. The govern-

ment rejected their demands and war broke out. A peace treaty was signed in 1975, but conflict continued.

POLITICS

In 1979, Saddam Hussein became Iraq's president. Under his leadership, Iraq invaded Iran in 1980, starting an eight-year war. During this war, Iraqi Kurds supported Iran and the Iraqi government attacked Kurdish villages with poison gas.

In 1990, Iraqi troops occupied Kuwait, but an international force drove them out in 1991. Since 1991, Iraqi troops have attacked Shi'ite Marsh Arabs and Kurds. In 1996, the government aided the forces of the Kurdish Democratic Party in an offensive against the Patriotic Union of Kurdistan, a rival Kurdish faction. In 1998, Iraq's failure to permit UNSCOM, the UN body charged with disposing of Iraq's deadliest weapons, access to all suspect sites led to Western bombardment of military sites. Periodic bombardment and economic sanctions continued, but Iraq was allowed to export a limited amount of oil in exchange for food and medicines.

The threat of war mounted after the terrorist attacks on the United States in 2001 and the rejection by Iraq in 2002 of the return of UN weapons inspectors. In 2002 and 2003, presure mounted on Iraq to dispose of its alleged weapons of mass destruction. Its failure to do so led to a coalition force, headed by the United States and the UK, to invade Iraq and overthrow the Saddam regime in March–April 2003. The coalition forces rapidly achieved their main objectives, but violence continued even after the capture of Saddam Hussein in December 2003.

Although largely boycotted by the Sunni Arabs, who make up a fifth of the population, elections took place in Iraq in 2005, but this still in an atmosphere of constant battle as civil order was still in disarray with daily attacks on civilians, Iraqi security forces and international agencies.

ECONOMY

Civil war and war damage in 1991 and 2003, UN sanctions, and economic mismanagement have all contributed to economic chaos. Oil remains Iraq's main resource, but a UN trade embargo in 1990 halted oil exports. Farmland covers around a fifth of the land. Products include barley, cotton, dates, fruit, livestock, wheat and wool. Iraq still has to import food. Industries include oil refining and the manufacture of petrochemicals and consumer goods.

Visitors climb the spiral stairway of the 9th-century mosque minaret at Samarra, Iraq

BAGHDAD

Capital of Iraq, on the River Tigris. Established in 762 as capital of the Abbasid caliphate, it became a centre of Islamic civilization and focus of caravan routes between Asia and Europe. It was almost destroyed by the Mongols in 1258. In 1921 Baghdad became the capital of newly independent Iraq. Notable sites include the 13th-century Abbasid Palace. In 1991 and 2003 Baghdad was badly damaged by bombing in the two Gulf Wars. Industries include building materials, textiles, tanning, bookbinding.

Ireland's flag was adopted in 1922 after the country had become independent from Britain, though nationalists had used it as early as 1848. Green represents Ireland's Roman Catholics, orange the Protestants, and the white a desire for peace between the two.

The Republic of Ireland consists of a large lowland region surrounded by a broken rim of low mountains. The lowlands include peat bogs. The uplands include the Mountains of Kerry with Carrauntoohill, Ireland's highest peak (1,041 m [3,415 ft]). The River Shannon is the longest in the Ireland, flowing through three large lakes, loughs Allen, Ree and Derg. Forests cover approximately 5% of Ireland. Much of the land is under pasture and a very small percentage is set aside for crops.

Area 70,273 sq km [27,132 sq mi]
Population 3,970,000
Capital (population) Dublin (482,000)
Government Multiparty republic
Ethnic groups Irish 94%
Languages Irish (Gaelic) and English (both official)
Religions Roman Catholic 92%, Protestant 3%
Currency Euro = 100 cents
Website www.irlgov.ie

DUBLIN (BAILE ÁTHA CLIATH)

Capital of the Republic of Ireland, at the mouth of the River Liffey on Dublin Bay. In 1014, Brian Boru recaptured it from the Danish. In 1170, it was taken by the English and became the seat of colonial government. Dublin suffered much bloodshed in nationalist attempts to free Ireland from English rule. Strikes beginning in 1913 finally resulted in the Easter Rising (1916). Dublin was the centre of the late 19th-century Irish literary renaissance. It is now the commercial and cultural centre of the Republic. Notable sites include Christ Church Cathedral (1053), St Patrick's Cathedral (1190), Trinity College (1591), and the Abbey Theatre (1904).

1916, republicans launched what was called the Easter Rebellion in Dublin, but the uprising was crushed. The republicans took over the Sinn Féin movement in 1918. They won a majority of Ireland's seats in the British parliament, but instead of going to London, they set up the Dáil Éireann (House of Representatives) in Dublin and declared Ireland an independent republic in January 1919.

In 1920, the British parliament passed the Government of Ireland Act, partitioning Ireland. The six Ulster counties accepted the Act, but fighting broke out in southern Ireland. In 1921, a treaty was agreed allowing southern Ireland to become a self-governing dominion, called the Irish Free State, within the British Commonwealth. With one Irish group accepting the treaty and another group, wanting complete independence civil war occurred between 1922 and 1923.

CLIMATE

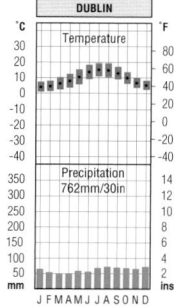

Ireland has a mild, damp climate influenced by the Gulf Stream current which warms the west coast, with Dublin in the east somewhat cooler. Rain occurs thoughout the year.

HISTORY

Celts settled in Ireland from about 400 BC. They were followed by the Vikings, Normans and the English. Vikings raided Ireland from the 790s, establishing settlements in the 9th century. But Norse domination was ended in 1014 when they were defeated by Ireland's king, Brian Boru. The Normans arrived in 1169 and, gradually, Ireland came under English influence.

In 1801, the Act of Union created the United Kingdom of Great Britain and Ireland. But Irish discontent intensified in the 1840s when a potato blight caused a famine in which a million people died and nearly a million emigrated. Britain was blamed for not having done enough to help. In 1905, Arthur Griffith founded Sinn Féin ('We Ourselves'), a movement advocating self-government for Ireland. Another secret organization, the Irish Republican Brotherhood, was also active in the early 20th century and its supporters became known as republicans. In

POLITICS

Ireland became a republic in 1949 and has subsequently played an independent role in Europe, joining the EEC in 1973 and, unlike Britain, adopting the euro as its currency in 2002. The government of Ireland has worked with British governments in attempts to solve the problems of Northern Ireland. In 1998, it supported the creation of a Northern Ireland Assembly, the setting up of north–south political structures, and the amendment of the 1937 constitution removing from it the republic's claim to Northern Ireland. A referendum showed strong support for the proposals and the amendments to the constitution. The 1998 Good Friday Agreement in Northern Ireland, aimed to end the long-standing conflict, it met with much support but ran into difficulties when the underground Irish Republican Army (IRA) refused to disarm. In July 2005 the IRA issued a statement of full disarmament.

ECONOMY

Aided by EU grants, farming is now relatively prosperous and includes cattle and dairy, sheep, pigs, potatoes and barley. Manufacturing is now the leading activity, with high-tech industries producing chemicals and pharmaceuticals, electronic equipment, machinery, paper and textiles. Tourism and racehorses are important industries.

Hore Abbey ruins at Cashel, County Tipperary, founded in 1266 by Cistercians

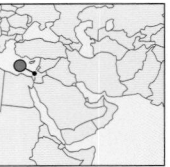

Israel's flag was adopted when the Jewish state declared itself independent in 1948. The blue and white stripes are based on the tallit, a Hebrew prayer shawl. The ancient, six-pointed Star of David is in the centre. The flag was designed in America in 1891.

Area 20,600 sq km [7,954 sq mi]
Population 6,199,000
Capital (population) Jerusalem (685,000)
Government Multiparty republic
Ethnic groups Jewish 80%, Arab and others 20%
Languages Hebrew and Arabic (both official)
Religions Judaism 80%, Islam (mostly Sunni) 14%, Christianity 2%, Druze and others 2%
Currency New Israeli shekel = 100 agorat
Website www.mfa.gov.il/MFA

The State of Israel is a small country in the eastern Mediterranean. The fertile Mediterranean plains are the most densely populated region. Inland lie the Judaeo-Galilean highlands, a series of ranges that extend from northern Israel to the northern tip of the Negev Desert in the south. To the east lie part of the Great Rift Valley, River Jordan, Sea of Galilee and the Dead Sea, whose shoreline is 418 m [1,371 ft] below sea level, the world's lowest point on land.

CLIMATE

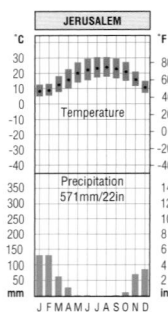

Northern Israel enjoys a typical Mediterranean climate, with hot, dry, summers and mild winters when heavy rains may occur, though generally on a small number of days. The average annual rainfall decreases west to east with only 70 mm [2.5 in] in the Dead Sea region. The driest region is the Negev Desert, where the average annual rainfall ranges from 200 mm [8 in] in the north to 50 mm [2 in] at the resort of Eilat on the Gulf of Aqaba. The most unpleasant conditions occur when hot dry khamsin winds blow from the Arabian peninsula, especially in early and late summer.

HISTORY

Israel is part of the ancient region of Palestine, which, because of its location at a crossroad of cultures, has long been a centre of conflict. Between about 1800 and 1500 BC, a group of people called Hebrews or Israelites settled in what was then known as the Land of Canaan. Later, Hebrews settled in Egypt, but they returned to Canaan in the 13th century BC. The southern group of Hebrews established a state called Judah and they

became known as Jews. Their capital was Jerusalem. The area later came under the Persians and, from 63 BC, the Romans. Following the suppression of Jewish revolts, the Romans drove the Jews out of Jerusalem and most Jews fled from Palestine. Muslim Arabs moved into the area in the AD 600s.

Most modern Israelis are descendants of Jewish immigrants who began to settle from the 1880s. Britain ruled Palestine from 1917. Large numbers of Jews escaping Nazi persecution arrived in the 1930s, provoking an Arab uprising against British rule. In 1947, the UN agreed to partition Palestine into an Arab and a Jewish state. Fighting broke out after Arabs rejected the plan.

The State of Israel came into being in May 1948, but fighting continued into 1949. Other Arab-Israeli wars were fought in 1956, 1967 and 1973. The Six Day War in 1967 led to the acquisition by Israel of the West Bank and East Jerusalem. Israel also occupied the Gaza Strip, the Sinai Peninsula (Egyptian) and the Golan Heights (Syrian). In 1982, Israel invaded Lebanon to destroy the stronghold of the PLO (Palestine Liberation Organization), but they left in 1985.

POLITICS

In 1978 Israel signed a treaty with Egypt leading to the return of the Sinai Peninsula to Egypt in 1979. Conflict continued between Israel and the PLO. In 1993, the PLO and Israel agreed to establish Palestinian self-rule in the Gaza Strip and in Jericho on the West Bank. The agreement was extended in 1995 to include more

Houses on the side of Mount of Olives, *Jerusalem; the mount is of historical importance to Jews and they have long sought to be buried there, as a result of this it is home to more than 150,000 graves, including the tomb of Zechariah the prophet*

JERUSALEM

Jerusalem is a sacred site for Christians, Jews and Muslims. It is capital of Israel, though the UN does not recognize this status and East Jerusalem is also claimed as the intended capital of a future Palestinian state. Jerusalem has repeatedly been occupied and destroyed throughout history. Jews were expelled from Jerusalem by the Romans (AD 135). It was occupied by the Ottoman Turks from the Middle Ages until 1917, when it became the capital of the British-mandated territory of Palestine. In 1948, it was divided between Jordan (east) and Israel (west). In 1967, the Israeli army captured the Old City of East Jerusalem and the united city became the capital of Israel. The Old City was the political and religious centre of the Jews in Biblical times and the Western (Wailing) Wall is the last remaining part of the holy Jewish Temple of Biblical times. Muslims believe that the Prophet Muhammad rose to Heaven from the site now occupied by the Dome of the Rock. For Christians, the principal site is the Church of the Sepulchre, which occupies the place believed to be Calvary (Golgotha), where Jesus was crucified.
Jerusalem is located on a ridge which forms part of the watershed that divides the Mediterranean plains to the west from the Jordan River and the Dead Sea to the east. Government and service industries, including tourism, are the main employers. Other light industrial activities include diamond cutting, the manufacture of clothing and shoes, printing and a variety of high-tech industries.

than 30% of the West Bank. Israel's prime minister, Yitzhak Rabin, who had been seeking a 'land for peace' settlement, was assassinated in 1995 and in 1996 the right-wing hardliner Binyamin Netanyahu became prime minister.

In 1999 the left-wing Ehud Barak won elections, promising to resume the peace process. Many problems remained, particularly the extension of Jewish settlements in the occupied areas and attacks on Israel by the militant Islamic group, Hezbollah, based in southern Lebanon. In 2001, Ariel Sharon, former general and leader of the right-wing Likud, was elected prime minister adopting a hardline policy against the Palestinians. In 2003, Western powers pressed Israel to adopt a 'road map' that would lead to the creation of two states, Israel and a democratic Palestine. In late 2004 the death of Palestinian leader Yasser Arafat held out hope that moderate policies might lead to the creation of a Palestinian state. Israel forcibly evicted Israeli settlers from Gaza and four settlements on the West Bank in August 2005. However, tension and conflict continued, making negotiations extremely difficult.

In late 2005, Sharon formed a new political party, Kadima. Its aim was to impose a peace settlement should negotiations with the Palestinian National Authority prove unsuccessful. However, before his party could

WEST BANK

Region west of River Jordan, north-west of the Dead Sea. Designated an Arab district in the 1947 UN plan for the partition of Palestine. Administered by Jordan after the first Arab-Israeli War (1948), but captured by Israel in the Six-Day War (1967). In 1988, Jordan passed its claim to the West Bank to the PLO. The 1994 Israeli-Palestinian Accord gave the Palestinian National Authority (PNA) limited autonomy in the West Bank. Difficulties resulting particularly from the growth of Israeli settlements and security disputes halted progress towards any Israeli withdrawal.

The golden Dome of the Rock mosque in Jerusalem's Old City is seen behind the controversial security barrier separating Jerusalem from the West Bank

be tested at the polls, he suffered a severe stroke. Ehud Olmert became the Kadima leader and, in elections in 2006, Kadima won most seats. Following lengthy talks with other parties, Olmert became prime minister heading a coalition government.

ECONOMY

The State of Israel has a high standard of living. Agriculture employs less than 3% of the population, but farming is highly efficient. Major products include beef, citrus fruits, cotton, dairy products and poultry. However, manufacturing accounts for around 38% of the gross domestic product. Israel produces a wide range of manufactures, including many high-technology projects. Machinery and equipment, computer software, cut diamonds, agricultural products, chemicals, textiles and clothing are exported. The United States is Israel's leading trading partner. Tourism is another major activity.

GAZA STRIP

Region bordering the Mediterranean Sea. From 1920, the region was part of the British Mandate of Palestine. It came under the control of Egypt, under the cease-fire arrangements following the Arab-Israeli War (1948). Israel seized the area during the Six-Day War (1967) when it became an Occupied Territory. But it came under the control of the Palestinian National Authority in 2005, when Israel withdrew all its settlers and armed forces. Palestinian Arabs make up the bulk of the population. Agriculture is important and exports include citrus fruits, flowers and textiles.

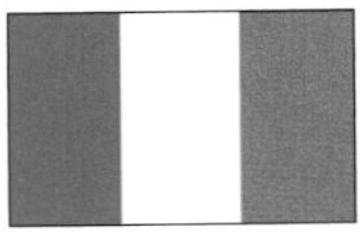

The Italian flag is based on the military standard carried by the French Republican National Guard when Napoleon invaded Italy in 1796, causing great changes in Italy's map. It was finally adopted as the national flag after Italy was unified in 1861.

Area 301,318 sq km [116,339 sq mi]
Population 58,057,000
Capital (population) Rome (2,460,000)
Government Multiparty republic
Ethnic groups Italian 94%, German, French, Albanian, Slovene, Greek
Languages Italian (official),German, French, Slovene
Religions Roman Catholic
Currency Euro = 100 cents
Website www.enit.it

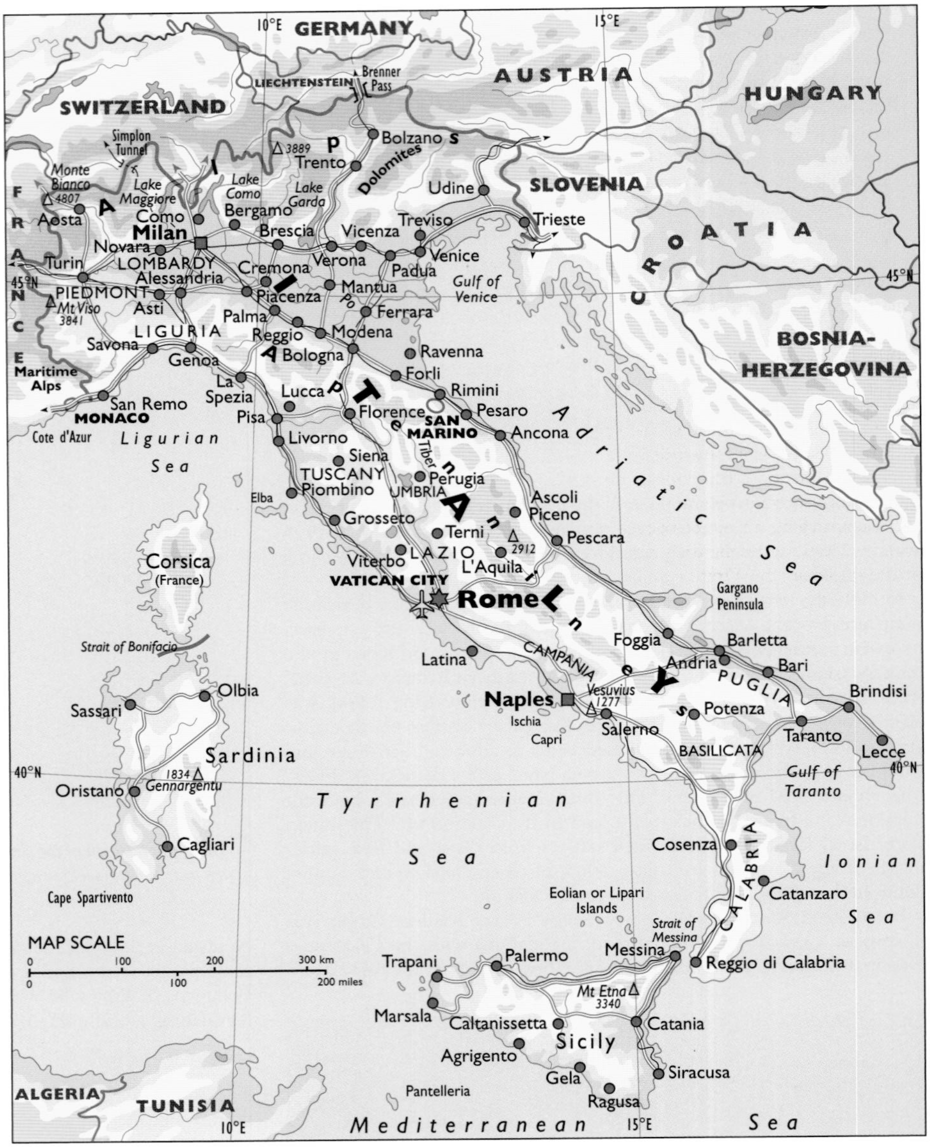

The Republic of Italy is bordered to the north by the Alps which overlook the northern plains, Italy's most fertile and densely populated region, drained by the River Po. The Apennines (Appennini), which form the backbone of southern Italy, reach their highest peaks (3,000 m [9,800 ft]), in the Gran Sasso Range overlooking the the central Adriatic Sea, near Pescara. Limestones are the most common rocks. Between the mountains are long, narrow basins, some with lakes.

Southern Italy contains a string of volcanoes, stretching from Vesuvius, near Naples (Nápoli), through the Lipari Islands, to Mount Etna on Sicily. Traces of volcanic activity are found throughout Italy. Ancient lava flows cover large areas and produce fertile soils. Italy is still subject to earthquakes and volcanic eruptions. Sicily is the largest island in the Mediterranean. Sardinia is more isolated from the mainland and its rugged, windswept terrain and lack of resources have set it apart.

CLIMATE

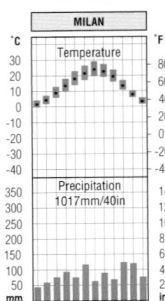

The north has cold, snowy winters, but warm and sunny summer months. Rainfall is plentiful, with brief but powerful thunderstorms in summer. Southern Italy has mild, moist winters and warm, dry summers.

HISTORY

Magnificent ruins throughout Italy testify to the glories of the ancient Roman Empire, which was founded in 753 BC. It reached its peak in the AD 100s and finally collapsed in the 400s, although the Eastern Roman Empire (the Byzantine Empire), survived another 1,000 years.

In the Middle Ages, Italy was split into many tiny states.and they made a huge contribution to the revival of art and learning, known as the Renaissance. Cities, such as Florence and Venice, testify to the artistic achievements of this period.

The struggle for unification (the Risorgimento) began early in the 19th century, but little progress was made until an alliance between France and Piedmont (then part of the Kingdom of Sardinia) drove Austria from Lombardy in 1859. Tuscany, Parma and Modena joined

Capalbio, *Tuscany; located on the coast in the province of Grosseto, the area that is now Capalbio was first settled in Etruscan times, around 900 BC*

ROME (ROMA)

Capital of Italy, on the River Tiber, west central Italy. Founded in the 8th century BC. The Roman Republic was founded around 500 BC. By the 3rd century BC, Rome ruled most of Italy and began to expand overseas. In the 1st century AD, the city was transformed as successive emperors built temples, palaces, public baths, arches, and columns. It remained the capital of the Roman Empire until AD 330. In the 5th century, Rome was sacked during the Barbarian invasions, and its population fell rapidly. In the Middle Ages, Rome became the seat of the papacy. In 1527, it was sacked by the army of Charles V. The city flourished once more in the 16th and 17th centuries. Italian troops occupied it in 1870, and in 1871 it became the capital of a unified Italy. The 1922 Fascist march on Rome brought Mussolini to power; he did much to turn Rome into a modern capital city.

Piedmont-Lombardy in 1860, and the Papal States, Sicily, Naples – including most of the southern peninsula – and Romagna were brought into the alliance. King Victor Emmanuel II was proclaimed ruler of a united Italy the following year. Venetia was acquired from Austria in 1866 and Rome was finally annexed in 1871. Since then, Italy has been a unified state, though the pope and his successors disputed the takeover of the Papal States. This dispute was resolved in 1929, when Vatican City was established as a fully independent state.

Since unification, the population has doubled, and though the rate of increase is notoriously slow today, the rapid growth of population, in a poor country attempting to develop its resources, forced millions of Italians to emigrate during the first quarter of the 20th century. Large numbers settled in the United States, South America and Australia. More recently, large numbers of Italians have moved into northern Europe for similar reasons.

In 1915, Italy entered World War I alongside the Allies (Britain, France and Russia). After the war, Italy was given nearly 23,000 sq km [9,000 sq mi] of territory that had belonged to Austria-Hungary. Benito Mussolini (Il Duce) became prime minister of Italy in 1922 and, from 1925 ruled as a dictator. In 1936, Italian forces invaded Ethiopia, while military personnel were sent to support the rebellion of General Franco in Spain. Italy agreed to fight alongside Germany in the event of war, though did not enter World War II until June 1940. During the war, Italy lost much of its colonial empire to the Allies and, in late 1943, declared war on Germany. Mussolini was captured and shot by partisans in 1945, when he tried to escape to Switzerland.

Italy became a republic in 1946 following a referendum. Allied troops left in 1947. Italy was a founder member of NATO in 1949, and of the EEC, now the European Union, in 1957. After the establishment of the EEC, Italy's economy began to expand. Much of the economic development took place in the industrialized north. Central Italy is less developed and represents a transition zone between the developed north and the poor agrarian south known as the Mezzogiorno.

POLITICS

In 1992, the old political establishment was driven from office with several prominent leaders accused of links to organized crime and some imprisoned. In 1996, the left-wing Olive Tree alliance led by Romano Prodi took office, but Prodi was forced to resign in 1998 following his rejection of demands made by his Communist allies. He was replaced by Massimo D'Alemo, the first former Communist to become prime minister. His attempts to create a two-party system in Italy failed in 1999.

By the late 1990s, it had the world's sixth largest economy and, on 1 January 2002, the euro became its currency. In 2001, Italy moved towards the political right when a coalition of centre-right parties won a substantial majority in parliament. Media tycoon Silvio Berlusconi, who had briefly served as prime minister in 1994 and who had spent several years fighting tax evasion charges, became prime minister.

ECONOMY

Fifty years ago, Italy was a mainly agricultural society. Today it is a major industrial power. It imports most of the raw materials used in industry. Industries include cars, chemicals, processed food, machinery, textiles. Major crops include grapes for wine-making, and olives, citrus fruits, sugar beet and vegetables. Cattle, pigs, poultry and sheep are raised.

VATICAN CITY

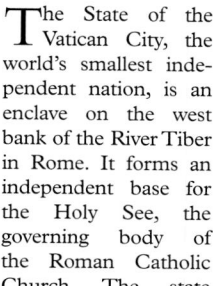

The State of the Vatican City, the world's smallest independent nation, is an enclave on the west bank of the River Tiber in Rome. It forms an independent base for the Holy See, the governing body of the Roman Catholic Church. The state includes St Peter's Square, St Peter's Basilica and Vatican Palace. The Vatican treasures include Michelangelo's frescoes in the Sistine Chapel and attract tourists from all over the world. The Vatican Library contains a priceless collection of both Christian and pre-Christian manuscripts. The popes have lived in the Vatican almost continuously since the 5th century. Sustained by investment income and voluntary contributions, the Vatican City is all that remains of the Papal States which, until 1870, occupied most of central Italy. In 1929, Mussolini recognized the Vatican's independence in return for papal recognition of the kingdom of Italy.

The population, including 100 Swiss Guards, the country's armed force, is entirely of unmarried males. The Commission appointed by the Pope to administer the affairs of the Vatican controls a radio station, the Pope's summer palace at Castel Gandolfo, and several churches in Rome. Vatican City has its own newspaper, police and railway stations, and issues its own stamps and coins.

Area 0.44 sq km [0.17 sq mi]
Population 921
Capital (population) Vatican City (921)
Government Ecclesiastical
Ethnic groups Italian, Swiss, others
Languages Italian, Latin, French, others
Religions Roman Catholic
Currency Euro = 100 cents
Website www.vatican.va

SAN MARINO

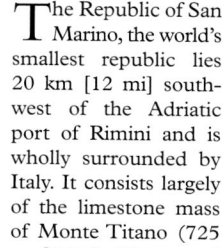

The Republic of San Marino, the world's smallest republic lies 20 km [12 mi] southwest of the Adriatic port of Rimini and is wholly surrounded by Italy. It consists largely of the limestone mass of Monte Titano (725 m [2,382 ft]) around which cluster wooded mountains, pastures, fortresses and medieval villages. San Marino has pleasant, mild summers and cool winters.

The republic was named after St Marinus, the stonemason saint who is said to have first established a community here in 301 AD. It has a friendship and co-operation treaty with Italy dating back to 1862 and uses Italian currency, but issues its own stamps, which are an important source of revenue. The state is governed by an elected council and has its own legal system. San Marino has no armed forces and its police are from the Italian constabulary. Most of the people live in the medieval city of San Marino, which receives more than 3 million tourists a year.

Chief occupations are tourism, limestone quarrying, ceramics, textiles and wine-making. The customs union with Italy makes San Marino an easy conduit for the illegal export of currency and certain kinds of tax evasion for Italians.

Area 61 sq km [24 sq mi]
Population 27,000
Capital (population) San Marino (2,395)
Government Republic
Ethnic groups Sanmarinese, Italian
Languages Italian (official)
Religions Roman Catholic
Currency Euro = 100 cents
Website www.visitsanmarino.com

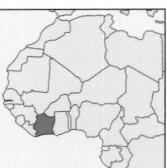

This flag was adopted in 1960 when the country became independent from France. It combines elements from the French tricolour and the Pan-African colours. Orange represents the northern savanna, white is for peace and unity and green for the forests in the south.

Area 322,463 sq km [124,503 sq mi]
Population 17,328,000
Capital (population) Yamoussoukro (107,000)
Government Multiparty republic
Ethnic groups Akan 42%, Voltaiques 18%, Northern Mandes 16%, Krous 11%, Southern Mandes 10%
Languages French (official), many native dialects
Religions Islam 40%, Christianity 30%, traditional beliefs 30%
Currency CFA franc = 100 centimes
Website www.afrika.no/index/Countries/C_te_d_Ivoire/index.html

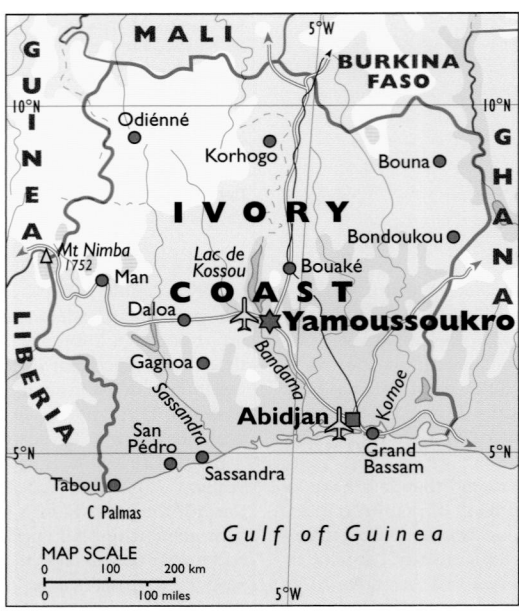

YAMOUSSOUKRO

Capital of Ivory Coast since 1983. Originally a small Baouké tribal village and birthplace of Ivory Coast's first president, Félix Houphouët-Boigny, it developed rapidly into the administrative and transport centre of Ivory Coast. Yamoussoukro's Our Lady of Peace Cathedral (consecrated by Pope John Paul II in 1990) is the world's largest Christian church.

The Republic of the Ivory Coast, in West Africa, is officially known as Côte d'Ivoire. The south-east coast is bordered by sand bars that enclose lagoons, on one of which the former capital and chief port of Abidjan is situated. But the south-western coast is lined by rocky cliffs. Behind the coast is a coastal plain, but the land rises inland to high plains. The highest land is an extension of the Guinea Highlands in the north-west, along the borders with Liberia and Guinea. Most of the country's rivers run north–south.

CLIMATE

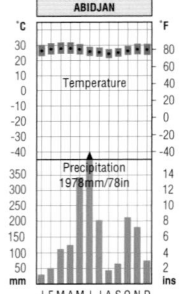

Ivory Coast has a hot and humid tropical climate, with high temperatures throughout the year. There are two distinct rainy seasons in the south of the country: between May and July, and from October to November. Inland, the rainfall decreases. Northern Ivory Coast has a dry season and only one rainy season. As a result, the forests in central Ivory Coast thin out to the north, giving way to savanna.

HISTORY

The region that is now Ivory Coast came under successive black African rulers until the late 15th century, when Europeans, attracted by the chance to trade in slaves and such local products as ivory, began to establish contacts along the coast. French missionaries reached the area in 1637 and, by the end of the 17th century, the French had set up trading posts on the coast. In 1842, France brought the Grand-Bassam area under its protection and Ivory Coast became a French colony in 1893. From 1895, it was ruled as part of French West Africa, a massive union which also included Benin, Burkina Faso, Guinea, Mali, Mauritania, Niger and Senegal. In 1946, Ivory Coast became a territory in the French Union. The port of Abidjan was built in the early 1950s, but the country achieved autonomy in 1958.

POLITICS

Ivory Coast became fully independent in 1960. Its first president, Félix Houphouët-Boigny, became the longest serving head of state in Africa with an uninterrupted period in office that ended with his death in 1993. Houphouët-Boigny was a paternalistic, pro-Western leader, who made his country a one-party state. In 1983, the National Assembly agreed to move the capital from Abidjan to Yamoussoukro, Houphouët-Boigny's birthplace. Visitors to Abidjan, where most of the country's Europeans live, are usually impressed by the city's general air of prosperity, but the cost of living for local people is high and there are great social and regional inequalities. Despite its political stability since independence, the country faces such economic problems as variations in the price of its export commodities, unemployment and high foreign debt.

Following the death of Houphouët-Boigny in 1993, the Speaker of the National Assembly, Henri Konan Bédié, proclaimed himself president. He was re-elected president in 1995. However, in December 1999, Bédié was overthrown during an army mutiny and a new administration was set up by General Robert Guei. Presidential elections, held after a new constitution was adopted in 2000, resulted in defeat for Guei by a veteran politician, Laurent Gbago. However, conflict began in 2002. By 2004 the country was divided into the government-held south and the rebel-held, mainly Muslim, north.

ECONOMY

Ivory Coast is one of Africa's more prosperous countries. Its free-market economy has proved attractive to foreign investors, especially French firms, while France has given much aid. It has an agrarian economy, which employs about three-fifths of the workforce. The chief farm products are cocoa, coffee, and cotton and make up nearly half the value of the total exports. Food crops include cassava, maize, plantains, rice, vegetables and yams. Manufactures include processed farm products, timber and textiles.

Biankouma, Pays Yacouba; *this old village in the mountainous west of the country is noted for its impeccable round huts*

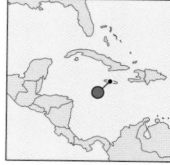

Jamaica 113

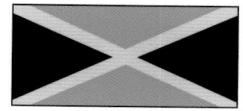

A committee of Jamaica's House of Representatives designed the national flag. the gold represents Jamaica's sunshine and natural resources; the green symbolizes agriculture and hope for the future; the black is for the hardships faced and overcome by its people.

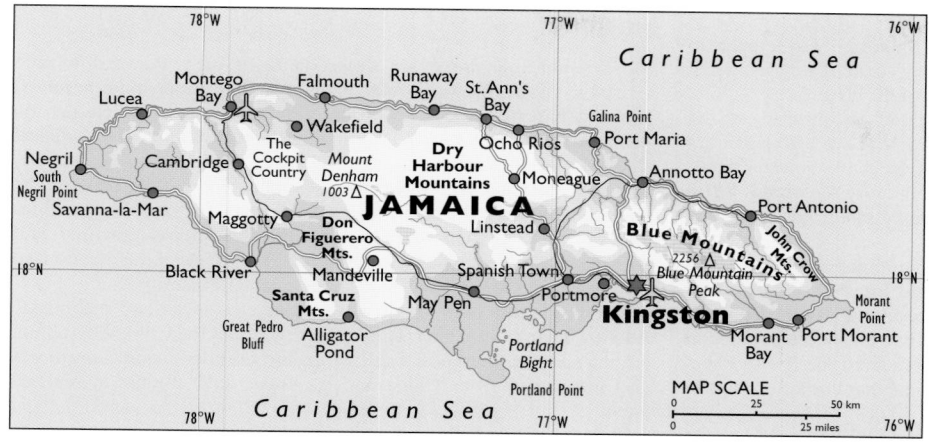

Area 10,990 sq km [4,244 sq mi]
Population 2,713,000
Capital (population) Kingston (104,000)
Government Constitutional monarchy
Ethnic groups Black 91%, Mixed 7%, East Indian
Languages English (official), patois English
Religions Protestant 61%, Roman Catholic 4%
Currency Jamaican dollar = 100 cents
Website www.jis.gov.jm

Jamaica is the third largest Caribbean island. It is a parliamentary democracy, with the monarch of the UK as its head of state. The coastal plain is narrow and discontinuous. Inland are hills, plateaux and mountains. The country's central range culminates in the Blue Mountain Peak (2,256 m [7,402 ft]). The Cockpit Country in the northwest of the island is an inaccessible limestone area, known for its many deep depressions, (cockpits). Jamaica is a lush, green island.

CLIMATE

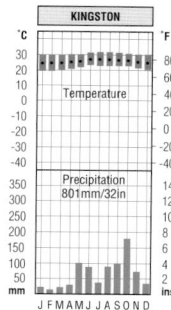

The climate is hot and humid. Temperatures range from 25°C [77°F] in January to 27°C [81°F] in July. Moist south-east trade winds bring rain to the more temperate highlands. Annual rainfall on the northern slopes may reach 5,000 mm [200 in]. But the sheltered south coast is much drier, about 750 mm [30 in] per year. The island is prone to periodic hurricanes.

HISTORY

In 1509, Spaniards occupied the island. Soon, the local Arawak Amerindian population had died out. The Spaniards imported African slaves to work the sugar plantations. The British took the island in 1655 and, with sugar as its staple product, it became a prized possession. The African slaves were the forefathers of much of the present population. But the plantations on which they worked disappeared when the sugar market collapsed in the 19th century.

In 1865, after 200 years of having their own elected body to help the British rule the island, Jamaica came under direct British rule as a crown colony, following the Moranty Bay rebellion. This peasant uprising, led by Baptist deacon Paul Bogle, was staged by freed slaves who were suffering acute hardship, but it was put down by British troops. In the

1930s, Jamaican leaders called for more power and riots took place in 1938, with people protesting against unemployment and Britain's racial policies. In that year, the People's National Party (PNP) was founded. In 1944, Britain granted Jamaica a new constitution, providing for an elected House of Representatives. In 1958, the island became a member of the British-sponsored Federation of the West Indies, but it withdrew in 1961.

POLITICS

Jamaica became an independent nation and a member of the British Commonwealth in 1962. It joined the Organization of American States in 1969. In the 1970s, economic problems developed. Michael Manley, leader of the PNP, became prime minister in 1972 and he pursued socialist policies, advocating a policy of non-alignment. The PNP won a second term in office in 1976. It nationalized businesses and sought closer ties with Cuba. In 1980, the Jamaica Labour Party (JLP), led by Edward Seaga defeated the PNP in elections. Seaga privatized much state-owned business and distanced Jamaica from Cuba. His moderate policies led to increased investment and better relations with Western countries. In 1989, the PNP defeated the JLP and Manley was returned to power as prime minister. However, Manley broadly followed Seaga's moderate policies. Manley retired on health grounds in 1992 and was succeeded by Percival J Patterson. The PNP was re-elected in 1993, 1998 and 2002.

Jamaica faces many problems, including drug trafficking. It has become a major transshipment point for cocaine being transported from South America to North America and Europe. Cannabis is produced in Jamaica. Corruption and money-laundering are major concerns. Price and tax increases led to riots in 1999, while in 2001, gun battles occurred with 27 people killed when the police searched for drugs in a poor district of Kingston. The murder rate in 2004 was 1,145. This figure was attributed by the police to street-gang violence.

In 2004 Hurricane Ivan destroyed thousands of homes, described as the worst natural disaster in living memory.

KINGSTON

Capital and largest city of Jamaica. It was founded in 1693. It rapidly developed into Jamaica's commercial centre, based on the export of raw cane sugar, bananas and rum. In 1872 it became the island's capital. Kingston is the cultural heart of Jamaica, the home of calypso and reggae music.

Bog Walk Gorge, *St Catherine; the gorge is located between Spanish Town and Linstead and takes its name from the Spanish 'Boca de Agua' meaning 'water's mouth'*

ECONOMY

Jamaica is a developing country. Agriculture employs about 20% of the workforce. The chief crop is sugar cane, other products include allspice, bananas, citrus fruits, cocoa, coconuts, coffee, milk, poultry, vegetables and yams. The country's chief resource is bauxite (aluminium ore) and Jamaica is one of the world's top producers. Cement, chemicals, cigars, clothing and textiles, fertilizers, machinery, molasses and petroleum products are also produced. Service industries account for 60% of the gross domestic product. Tourism brings in vital revenue.

Japan's flag was officially adopted in 1870, although Japanese emperors had used this simple design for many centuries. The flag shows a red sun on a white background. The geographical position of Japan is expressed in its name 'Nippon' or 'Nihon', meaning 'source of the Sun'.

Japan is an island nation in north-eastern Asia containing four large islands – Honshu, Hokkaido, Kyushu and Shikoku – which make up more than 98% of the country. Thousands of small islands, including the Ryukyu island chain, make up the rest of the country.

The four main islands are mainly mountainous, while many of the small islands are the tips of volcanoes rising from the sea bed. Japan has more than 150 volcanoes, about 60 of which are active. Volcanic eruptions, earthquakes and tsunamis often occur, because the islands lie on an unstable part of Earth where the continental plates are constantly moving.

Throughout Japan, complex folding and faulting has produced an intricate mosaic of landforms. Mountains and forested hills alternate with small basins and coastal lowlands, covered by alluvium deposited there by the short rivers that rise in the uplands. Most of the population lives on the coastal plains, one being the stretch from the Kanto Plain, where Tokyo is situated, along the narrow plains that border the southern coasts of Honshu, to northern Kyushu.

The pattern of landforms is further complicated by the presence of volcanic cones and calderas. The highest mountain in Japan, Fuji-san (3,776 m [12,388 ft]), is a long dormant volcano which last erupted in 1707. It is considered sacred, and is visited by thousands of pilgrims every year.

CLIMATE

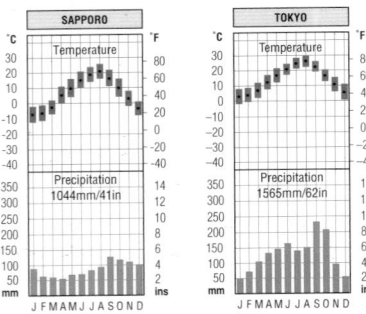

The climate of Japan varies greatly. Hokkaido in the north has cold, snowy winters. At Sapporo, temperatures below –20°C [4°F] have been recorded between December and March. Summers are warm, with temperatures often exceeding 30°C [86°F]. Rain falls throughout the year. Tokyo has the higher rainfall and temperatures while the southern islands of Shikoku and Kyushu in the south have warm temperate climates with hot summers and cold winters.

Area 377,829 sq km [145,880 sq mi]
Population 127,333,000
Capital (population) Tokyo (8,130,000)
Government Constitutional monarchy
Ethnic groups Japanese 99%, Chinese, Korean, Brazilian and others
Languages Japanese (official)
Religions Shintoism and Buddhism 84% (most Japanese consider themselves to be both Shinto and Buddhist), others
Currency Yen = 100 sen
Website http://web-japan.org

HISTORY

Most modern Japanese are descendants of early immigrants who arrived in successive waves from the Korean Peninsula and other parts of the Asian mainland. The earliest zone of settlement included the northern part of Kyushu Island and the coastlands of Setonaikai (Inland Sea). By the 5th century AD, Japan was divided among numerous clans, of which the largest and most powerful was the Yamato. The Yamato ruled from the area which now contains the city of Nara. Shinto, a polytheistic religion based on nature worship, was practised, and the Japanese imperial dynasty established. The chiefs of the Yamato clan are regarded as ancestors of the Japanese imperial family.

The 5th century AD was a time when new ideas and technology reached Japan from China. The Japanese adopted the Chinese system of writing and their methods of calculating the calendar. Confucianism was also introduced from China and, in about 552, Buddhism reached Japan.

From the early 12th century, political power passed increasingly to military aristocrats. Government was conducted in the name of the

emperor by warrior leaders called *shoguns*. Civil warfare between rival groups of feudal lords was endemic over long periods, but, under the rule of the Tokugawa *shoguns*, between 1603 and 1867, Japan enjoyed a great period of peace and prosperity. Military families (the feudal lords and their retainers, or *samurai*) formed a powerful elite. During the *shogun* era, a code of conduct called *bushido* ('the way of the warrior') was developed for the *samurai*, it stressed military skills and fearlessness, frugality, kindness, honesty and filial piety. The *samurai's* supreme obligation was, above all, to his feudal lord.

European contact began with the arrival of Portuguese sailors in 1543, then in 1549 a Spanish missionary came to convert the Japanese to Christianity. The Japanese put an end to missionary work in the 1630s when they ordered all Christian missionaries to leave the country, and forced Japanese converts to give up their faith. The only Europeans allowed to stay were Dutch traders, as they were not involved in missionary work. Japan only opened its ports to Western trade again in 1854 after American intervention.

The Meiji period from 1867 to 1912 was marked by the adoption of Western ideas and technology. An educational system and a telegraph network were set up, railways built and modern systems of banking and taxation introduced. In addition the samurai was abolished and a modern army and navy established.

In 1889, Japan introduced its first constitution under which the emperor became head of state and supreme commander of the army and navy. The emperor appointed government ministers, responsible to him. The constitution also allowed for a parliament, called the Diet, with two houses.

From the 1890s, Japan began to build up an overseas empire. In 1894–5, Japan fought China over the control of Korea. Under the Treaty of Shimonoseki (1895), Japan took Taiwan. Korea was made an independent territory, leaving it open to Japanese influence. Rivalry with Russia led to the Russo-Japanese War (1904–5). Under the Treaty of Portsmouth, Japan gained the Liaodong peninsula, which Russia had leased from China, while Russia recognized the supremacy of Japan's interests in Korea. Thus Japan was established as a world power.

In World War I Japan supported the Allies. After the war Japan's foreign policy strongly supported the maintenance of world peace, becoming a founding member of the League of Nations in 1920. The army seized Manchuria in 1931 and made it a puppet state called Manchukuo, they then extended their influence into other parts of northern China. In 1933, after the League of Nations condemned its actions in Manchuria Japan was forced to rescind its membership

During the 1930s, and especially after the outbreak of war between Japan and China in 1937, militarist control of Japan's government grew steadily. By the end of 1938, when Japan controlled most of eastern China, there was talk of bringing all of eastern Asia under Japanese control. In September 1939, Japan occupied the northern part of French Indo-China and, later that month, signed an agreement with Italy and Germany, assuring their co-operation in building a 'new world order', and acknowledging Japan's leadership in Asia.

In 1941 Japan launched a surprise attack on the American naval base

TOKYO

Capital of Japan, on east-central Honshu, at the head of Tokyo Bay. The modern city divides into distinct districts: Kasumigaseki, Japan's administrative centre; Marunouchi, its commercial centre; Ginza, its shopping and cultural centre; the west shore of Tokyo Bay, its industrial centre. Modern Tokyo also serves as the country's educational centre with more than 100 universities. Founded in the 12th century as Edo, it became capital of the Tokugawa shogunate in 1603. In 1868, the Japanese Reformation re-established imperial power, and the last shogun surrendered Edo Castle. Emperor Meiji renamed the city Tokyo, and it replaced Kyoto as the capital of Japan. In 1923, an earthquake and subsequent fire claimed more than 150,000 lives and necessitated the city's reconstruction. In 1944–5, intensive US bombing destroyed more than half of Tokyo, and another modernization and restoration programme began. Industries include electronics, cameras, car manufacture, metals, chemicals, textiles.

of Pearl Harbor, in Hawaii, an action that drew the United States into World War II. On 6 August 1945, American bombers dropped the first atomic bomb on Hiroshima. The USSR declared war on Japan and invaded Manchuria and Korea. On 9 August, the Americans dropped an atomic bomb on Nagasaki. World War II ended on 2 September 1945 when Japan officially surrendered.

POLITICS

The Allies occupied Japan in August 1945. Under a new constitution, power was transferred from the emperor to the people. The army and navy were abolished and the country renounced war as a political weapon. The emperor became a constitutional monarch.

Japan signed a Treaty of Peace that took effect on 28 April 1952. The Allied occupation ended on that day. When, in 1956, the Soviet Union and Japan agreed to end the state of war between them, Japan became a member of the UN.

The conservative Liberal-Democratic Party was formed in 1955, made up of rival Japanese parties. The LDP controlled Japan's government until the 1990s, when a series of coalition governments were formed. A true opposition party emerged in the late 1990s, when the Democratic Party of Japan united with several small parties. The country underwent a serious economic crisis in 1997. In 2001, the LDP chose Junichiro Koizumi as prime minister. Koizumi promised drastic reforms to revive the economy. He won a landslide victory in September 2005 after calling a snap election when his plans to privatise Japan's postal system were defeated in the upper house. After this victory his government announced plans to continue his reform programme and also to revise Japan's pacifist constitution.

ECONOMY

Japan has the world's second highest GDP after the United States. The most important sector of the economy is industry, though Japan has to import most of the raw materials and fuels it needs for its industries. Its success is based on the use of the latest technology, a skilled and hardworking labour force, vigorous export policies and a comparatively small spend on defence. Manufactures dominate its exports which include machinery, electrical and electronic equipment, vehicles and transport equipment, iron and steel, chemicals, textiles and ships. Japan is one of the world's top fishing nations and fish is an important source of protein. Only 15% of the land can be farmed due to its rugged nature yet the country produces about 70% of the food it requires. Rice is the chief crop, taking up about half of the farmland. Other major products include fruits, sugar beet, tea and vegetables.

Mount Fuji *with cherry blossoms; a dormant volcano that has long been worshipped as a sacred mountain it is surrounded by five lakes*

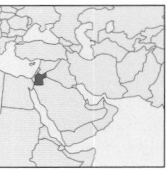

The green, white and black on this flag are the colours of the three tribes who led the Arab Revolt against the Turks in 1917; red is the colour of the Hussein Dynasty. The star was added in 1928. Its seven points represent the first seven verses of the Koran.

Area 89,342 sq km [34,495 sq mi]
Population 5,611,000
Capital (population) Amman (1,148,000)
Government Constitutional monarchy
Ethnic groups Arab 98% (Palestinians 50%)
Languages Arabic (official)
Religions Islam (mostly Sunni) 94%, Christianity (mostly Greek Orthodox) 6%
Currency Jordanian dinar = 1,000 fils
Website www.tourism.jo

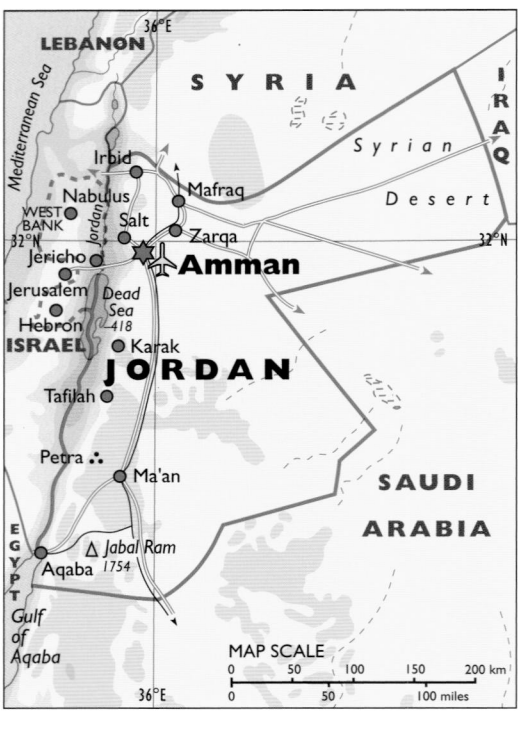

The Hashemite Kingdom of Jordan is an Arab country in south-western Asia. The Great Rift Valley in the west contains the River Jordan and the Dead Sea. East of the Rift Valley is the Transjordan Plateau, where most Jordanians live. To the east and south lie vast areas of desert. Jordan has a short coastline on an arm of the Red Sea, the Gulf of Aqaba. The country's highest peak is Jabal Ram (1,754 m [5,755 ft]).

CLIMATE

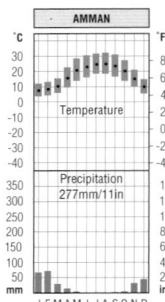

About 90% of Jordan has a desert climate, with an average annual rainfall of less than 200 mm [8 in]. Summers are hot, winters can be cold, with snow on higher areas. The north-west is the wettest area, with an average annual rainfall of 800 mm [31 in] in higher areas.

HISTORY

Jordan was first settled by Semitic peoples about 4,000 years ago, and later conquered by Egyptian, Assyrian, Chaldean, Persian and Roman forces. The area fell to Muslim Arabs in AD 636, the Arab culture they introduced survives to this day.

By the end of the 12th century, Christian crusaders controlled parts of western Jordan, but were driven out by the great Muslim warrior Saladin in 1187. The Egyptian Mamelukes overthrew Saladin's successors in 1250 and ruled until 1517, when the area was conquered by the Ottoman Turks. Jordan stagnated under their rule, but the opening of a railway in 1908 stimulated the economy. Arab and British forces defeated the Turks during World War I and after the war, the area east of the River Jordan was awarded to Britain by the League of Nations.

Britain created a territory called Transjordan, east of the River Jordan in 1921. It then became self-governing in 1923, but Britain retained control of its defences, finances and foreign affairs. This territory became fully independent as Jordan in 1946.

Since the creation of the State of Israel in 1948 Jordan has suffered from instability arising from Arab-Israeli conflict. After the first Arab-Israeli War (1948-9), Jordan acquired the West Bank, which was officially incorporated into the state in 1950. This crucial area, including East Jerusalem, was lost to Israel in the

war of 1967, causing many Palestinians to seek refuge in Jordan. In the 1970s, Palestinian guerrillas using Jordan as a base became a challenge to the authority of King Hussein's government. After a short civil war, the Palestinian leadership fled.

POLITICS

In 1988 King Hussein suddenly renounced all responsibility for the West Bank, thereby recognizing that the Palestine Liberation Organization, not Jordan, was the legitimate representative of the Palestinian people. Palestinians were still in the majority and the refugees, numbering around 900,000, placed a huge burden on an already weak economy. Jordan was further undermined by the 1991 Gulf War when, despite its official neutrality, the pro-Iraq, anti-Western stance of the Palestinians in Jordan damaged prospects of trade and aid deals with Europe and the United States, Jordan's vital economic links with Israel having already been severed. A ban on political parties was removed in 1991, and martial law lifted after 21 years. Multiparty elections were held in 1993 and, in 1994, Jordan and Israel signed a peace treaty, ending a 40-year-long state of war. The treaty restored some land in the south to Jordan.

King Hussein, who had commanded great respect for his role in Middle Eastern affairs, died in 1999. He was succeeded by his eldest son who became King Abdullah II. Following the path of his father, Abdullah sought to further the Israeli-Palestinian peace process. He also worked to consolidate his country's relations with other nations in the region. Despite local opposition to the invasion of Iraq in 2003, he supported the US-led war on terrorism and worked to improve relations with Israel. However, in November 2005 suicide bombers killed 57 in Amman and terrorist group al-Qaida claimed responsibility.

ECONOMY

Classified as a 'lower-middle-income' developing country, Jordan's economy depends substantially on aid. Less than 6% of the land is farmed. It has an oil refinery and manufactures include pharmaceuticals, cement, ceramics, fertilizers, shoes and textiles. Service industries, including tourism, employ more than 70% of the workforce.

AMMAN

Capital and largest city of Jordan. Known as Rabbath-Ammon, it was the chief city of the Ammonites in biblical times. Ptolemy II Philadelphus renamed it Philadelphia. A new city was built on seven hills from 1875, and it became the capital of Trans-Jordan in 1921. From 1948 it grew rapidly, partly as a result of the influx of Palestinian refugees. Industries include cement, textiles, tobacco, and leather.

The facade of the treasury (El-Khazneh), Petra; *an amazing rock-carved city created by the Nabateans over 2000 years ago*

Kazakhstan's flag was adopted on 4 June 1992, about six months after it had become independent. The blue represents cloudless skies, while the golden sun and the soaring eagle represent love of freedom. A vertical strip of gold ornamentation is on the left.

The Republic of Kazakhstan is a large country in west-central Asia. In the west, the Caspian Sea lowlands include the Karagiye Depression, which reaches 132 m [433 ft] below sea level. The lowlands extend eastwards through the Aral Sea area. The north contains high plains, but the highest land is along the eastern and southern borders. These areas include parts of the Altai and Tian Shan mountain ranges.

Eastern Kazakhstan contains several freshwater lakes, the largest of which is Lake Balkhash (Balqash Köl). The water in the rivers has been used for irrigation, causing ecological problems. The Aral Sea, deprived of water, shrank from 66,900 sq km [25,830 sq mi] in 1960, to 33,642 sq km [12,989 sq mi] in 1993. Areas which once provided fish have dried up and are now barren desert.

Kazakhstan has very little woodland. Grassy steppe covers much of the north, while the south is desert or semi-desert. Large, dry areas between the Aral Sea and Lake Balkhash have become irrigated farmland.

Area 2,724,900 sq km [1,052,084 sq mi]
Population 15,144,000
Capital (population) Astana (322,000)
Government Multiparty republic
Ethnic groups Kazakh 53%, Russian 30%, Ukranian 4%, German 2%, Uzbek 2%
Languages Kazakh (official), Russian, the former official language, is widely spoken
Religions Islam 47%, Russian Orthodox 44%
Currency Tenge = 100 tiyn
Website www.kz

CLIMATE

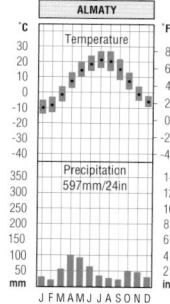

The extreme climate reflects position in the heart of Asia, far from the influence of the oceans. Winters are cold and snow covers the land for about 100 days, on average, at Almaty (Alma Ata). Rainfall is generally quite low.

HISTORY

From the late 15th century, the Kazakhs built up a large nomadic empire ruled by *khans*. But Kazakh power declined in the 17th century. In the early 18th century, Russia became influential in the area. In 1731, the Kazakhs in the west accepted Russian rule to gain protection from attack from neighbouring peoples. By the mid-1740s, Russia ruled most of the region and, in the early 19th century, Russia abolished the *khanates*. They also encouraged Russians and Ukrainians to settle in Kazakhstan.

After the Russian Revolution of 1917, many Kazakhs wanted independence, but the Communists prevailed and in 1936 Kazakhstan became a republic of the Soviet Union, called the Kazakh Soviet Socialist Republic. During and after World War II, the Soviet government moved many people from the west into Kazakhstan. From the 1950s, people were encouraged to work on a 'Virgin Lands' project, which involved bringing large areas of grassland under cultivation.

POLITICS

Reforms in the Soviet Union in the 1980s led to the break-up of the country in December 1991. Kazakhstan kept contacts with Russia and most of the former Soviet republics by joining the Commonwealth of Independent States (CIS), and in 1995 Kazakhstan announced that its army would unite with that of Russia. In December 1997, the government moved the capital from Alma Ata to Aqmola (later renamed Astana), a town in the Russian-dominated north. It was hoped that this move would bring some Kazakh identity to the area.

Under Soviet rule, Kazakhstan was a dumping ground and test bed. The rocket-launching site at Baykonur (Bayqongyr) suffered great environmental damage, including the shrinking of the Aral Sea by 70%. But Kazakhstan has emerged as a powerful entity, wealthier and more diversified than other Asian republics. It could provide the 'new order' between East and West. It is the only former Soviet republic whose ethnic population is almost outnumbered by another group (the Russians), and its Muslim revival is relatively muted. Its first elected president, Nursultan Nazarbayev, a former Communist leader, introduced many reforms, including a multiparty system. However, he has been criticized for his authoritarian rule and the elections of 2004 and 2005, were widely considered to be flawed.

ECONOMY

The World Bank classifies Kazakhstan as a 'lower-middle-income' developing country. Livestock farming, especially sheep and cattle, is an important activity, and major crops include barley, cotton, rice and wheat.

The country is rich in mineral resources, including coal and oil reserves, together with bauxite, copper, lead, tungsten and zinc. Manufactures include chemicals, food products, machinery and textiles. The first major pipeline transporting oil direct from the Caspian opened in 2001, the pipeline runs through Russia. To reduce dependence on Russia, Kazakhstan signed an agreement in 1997 to build a new pipeline to China.

Produce market,
Almaty; a vast array of vibrantly coloured fruit and vegetables being sold by the producers themselves in the town's central market

ASTANA
(formerly AQMOLA)

Capital of Kazakhstan, on the River Ishim in the steppes of north-central Kazakhstan. Under Soviet rule, Aqmola functioned as capital of the Virgin Lands. From 1961 to 1993 it was known as Tselinograd, and from 1993 to 1998 as Aqmola.

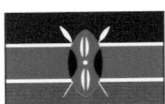

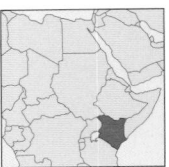

Kenya's flag dates from 1963, when the country became independent. It is based on the flag of KANU (Kenya African National Union), the political party which led the nationalist struggle. The Masai warrior's shield and crossed spears represent the defence of freedom.

Area 580,367 sq km [224,080 sq mi]
Population 32,022,000
Capital (population) Nairobi (2,143,000)
Government Multiparty republic
Ethnic groups Kikuyu 22%, Luhya 14%, Luo 13%, Kalenjin 12%, Kamba 11%, others
Languages Kiswahili and English (both official)
Religions Protestant 45%, Roman Catholic 33%, traditional beliefs 10%, Islam 10%
Currency Kenyan shilling = 100 cents
Website www.kenya.go.ke

The Republic of Kenya is located in East Africa straddling the Equator. Behind the narrow coastal plain on the Indian Ocean, the land rises to high plains and highlands, broken by volcanic mountains, including Mount Kenya, the highest peak at 5,199 m [17,057 ft].

Crossing the country is an arm of the Great Rift Valley with several lakes including Baringo, Magadi, Naivasha, Nakuru and, on the northern frontier, Lake Turkana (formerly Lake Rudolf).

CLIMATE

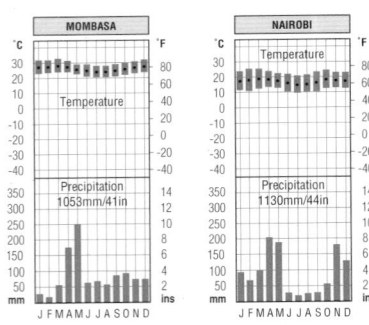

The coast is hot and humid, but inland the climate is moderated by the height of the land. The thickly populated southwestern highlands have summer temperatures 10°C [18°F] lower than the coast. Nights can be cool, but temperatures stay above zero. The main rainy season is from April to May. Only 15% of the country has a reliable rainfall of 800 mm [31 in].

HISTORY

The Kenyan coast has been an important trading centre for more than 2,000 years. Early Arab traders carried goods from eastern Asia and exchanged them for items from the local people. Portuguese explorer Vasco da Gama reached the coast in 1498. Later, the Portuguese competed with the Arabs for control of the coast.

The British took control of the coast in 1895, soon extending their influence inland with many Britons setting up large farms. Opposition to British rule mounted in the 1940s, and, in 1953, a secret movement called Mau Mau launched an armed struggle. Mau Mau was eventually defeated, but Kenya finally gained independence in 1963. Kenya's first president was nationalist veteran Jomo Kanyatta.

POLITICS

Many Kenyan leaders felt that the division of the population into 40 ethnic groups might lead to instability. They argued that Kenya should have a strong central government and, as a result, Kenya has been a one-party state for much of the time since independence. Multiparty democracy was restored in the early 1990s with elections in 1992, 1997 and 2002.

In the 1960s, attempts by Kenya, Tanzania and Uganda to collaborate collapsed due to the deep differences between the political and economic policies of the countries. Hopes were revived in 1999, when a new East African Community was created. Its aim was to establish a customs union, a common market, a monetary union, and, ultimately, a political union.

Jomo Kanyatta died in 1978 and was succeeded by the vice-president Daniel arap Moi, who stood down in 2002 after having been criticized for his autocratic rule, as well as corruption. The veteran Mwai Kibaki was elected president in 2002, promising to stamp out corruption. But by 2005 he was widely criticized for failing to fulfill his election pledge.

ECONOMY

According to the United Nations, Kenya is a 'low-income' developing country. Agriculture employs about 80% of the people, but many Kenyans are subsistence farmers. The chief food crop is maize. Bananas, beans, cassava and sweet potatoes are also grown. The main cash crops are coffee and tea. Manufactures include chemicals, leather, footwear, processed food, petroleum products and textiles.

NAIROBI

Capital and largest city of Kenya, in the south central part of the country. Founded in 1899, Nairobi replaced Mombasa as the capital of the British East Africa Protectorate in 1905. Nairobi has a national park (1946), a university (1970) and several institutions of higher education. It is an administrative and commercial centre. Industries: cigarettes, textiles, chemicals, food processing, furniture, glass.

Bare tree *by Lake Turkana, Loyangalani; situated to the north of Kenya, crossing the border with Ethiopia at its northernmost tip; the lake measures 6,750 sq km (2,606 sq mi)*

The flag of the Democratic People's Republic of Korea (North Korea) has been flown since Korea was split into two states in 1948. The colours are traditional ones in Korea. The design, with the red star, indicates that North Korea is a Communist country.

PYONGYANG

Capital of North Korea, in the west of the country, on the River Taedong. An ancient city, it was the capital of the Choson, Koguryo and Koryo kingdoms. In the 16th and 17th centuries, it came under both Japanese and Chinese rule. Pyongyang's industry developed during the Japanese occupation from 1910–45. It became the capital of North Korea in 1948. During the Korean War (1950–3), it suffered considerable damage.

Area 120,538 sq km [46,540 sq mi]
Population 22,698,000
Capital (population) Pyongyang (2,725,000)
Government Single-party people's republic
Ethnic groups Korean 99%
Languages Korean (official)
Religions Buddhism and Confucianism (religious freedom now an illusion created by government-sponsored religious groups)
Currency North Korean won = 100 chon
Website www.korea-dpr.com

The Democratic People's Republic of Korea occupies the northern part of the Korean Peninsula extending south from north-eastern China. Mountains form the heart of the country. The highest peak, Paektu-san (2,744 m [9,003 ft]) is on the northern border. East of the mountains lie the eastern coastal plains, which are densely populated, as are the coastal plains to the west which contain the capital, Pyongyang. Another small highland region in the south-east borders South Korea.

The coastal plains are mostly farmed, but some patches of chestnut, elm, and oak woodland survive on the hilltops. The mountains contain forests of such trees cedar, fir, pine, and spruce.

CLIMATE

North Korea has a fairly severe climate, with bitterly cold winters when winds blow from across central Asia, bringing snow. Rivers freeze over and sea-ice may b lock harbours on the coast. In summer, moist winds from the oceans bring rain.

HISTORY

North Korea's history is described on page 120 [see Korea, South]. North Korea was created in 1945, when the peninsula, a Japanese colony since 1910, was divided in two. Soviet forces occupied the north, with US forces in the south. Soviet occupation led to a Communist government being established in 1948 under the leadership of Kim Il Sung.

The Korean War began in June 1950 when North Korean troops invaded the south. North Korea, aided by China and the Soviet Union, fought with South Korea, which was supported by troops from the United States and other UN members. The war ended in July 1953. An armistice was signed but no permanent peace treaty was agreed. The war caused great destruction and loss of life, with 1.6 million Communist troops killed, wounded or reported missing.

POLITICS

Between 1948 and his death in 1994, Kim Il Sung was a virtual dictator, ruling along similar lines to Stalin in the Soviet Union. After the war, North

Korea adopted a hostile policy towards South Korea in pursuit of its aim of reunification. The situation was at times so tense as to warrant international concern.

The end of the Cold War in the late 1980s eased relations between North and South and they both joined the UN in 1991. The two countries made several agreements, including one in which they agreed not to use force against each other. However, the collapse of Communism in the Soviet Union meant that North Korea remained isolated.

In 1993, North Korea triggered a new international crisis by announcing that it was withdrawing from the Nuclear Non-Proliferation Treaty, leading to suspicions that it, was developing its own nuclear weapons. Upon his death in 1994, Kim Il Sung was succeeded by his son, Kim Jong Il.

In the early 2000s, uncertainty surrounding North Korea's nuclear capabilities cast unease across the entire region. The United States accused North Korea of supporting international terrorism, while at the same time, talks between North and South Korea continued in an attempt to normalize relations between them. In 2003 North Korea's relations with the United States further deteriorated when the US accused the country of having a secret nuclear weapons programme. North Korea withdrew from international talks in early 2005 stating that it had already produced nuclear weapons. However in September North Korea agreed to give up all its nuclear activities and rejoin the nuclear Non-Proliferation Treaty. Despite reports of malnutrition North Korea formally requested an end to food aid in September 2005. It was thought that the government might be worried that taking more food aid might be perceived as a sign of weakness.

ECONOMY

North Korea's considerable resources include coal, copper, iron ore, lead, tin, tungsten and zinc. Under Communism, North Korea has concentrated on developing heavy, state-owned industries. Manufactures include chemicals, iron and steel, machinery, processed food and textiles. Agriculture employs about a third of the population and rice is the leading crop. Economic decline and mismanagement, aggravated by three successive crop failures caused by floods in 1995 and 1996, and a drought in 1997, led to famine on a large scale.

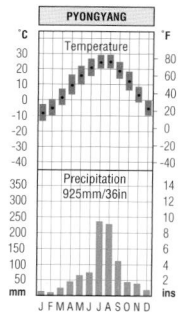

Music students from the Children's Palace in Pyongyang performing

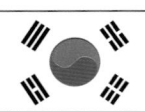

South Korea's flag, adopted in 1950, is white, the traditional symbol for peace. The central 'yin-yang' symbol signifies the opposing forces of nature. The four black symbols stand for the four seasons, the points of the compass, and the Sun, Moon, Earth and Heaven.

Area 99,268 sq km [38,327 sq mi]
Population 48,598,000
Capital (population) Seoul (9,888,000)
Government Multiparty republic
Ethnic groups Korean 99%
Languages Korean (official)
Religions No affiliation 46%, Christianity 26%, Buddhism 26%, Confucianism 1%
Currency South Korean won = 100 chon
Website www.kois.go.kr

The Republic of Korea, as South Korea is officially known, occupies the southern part of the Korean Peninsula. Mountains cover much of the country. The southern and western coasts are major farming regions. There are many islands along the west and south coasts, the largest of which is Cheju-do, with South Korea's highest peak, Halla-san (1,950 m [6,398 ft]).

CLIMATE

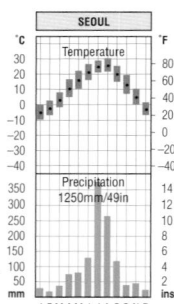

South Korea is chilled in winter by cold, dry winds blowing from central Asia. Snow often covers the mountains in the east. The summers are hot and wet, especially in July and August.

HISTORY

The Chinese conquered the north in 108 BC and ruled until they were thrown out in AD 313. Mongol armies attacked Korea in the 13th century, but in 1388, a general, Yi Songgye, founded a dynasty of rulers which lasted until 1910.

From the 17th century, Korea prevented foreigners from entering the country, earning it the name the 'Hermit Kingdom' until 1876, when Japan forced it to open some of its ports. Soon, the United States, Russia and some European countries were trading with Korea. In 1910, Korea became a Japanese colony.

After Japan's defeat in World War II, North Korea was occupied by Soviet troops, while South Korea was occupied by United States forces. Attempts at reunification failed and, in 1948, a National Assembly was elected in South Korea. This Assembly created the Republic of Korea, with North Korea becoming a Communist state. North Korean troops invaded the South in June 1950, sparking off the Korean War (1950–3).

POLITICS

The story of South Korea after the civil war differs greatly from that of the North. Land reform based on smallholdings worked to produce some of the world's highest rice yields and self-sufficiency in food grains.

SEOUL (KYONGSONG)

Capital of South Korea, on the River Han. The political, commercial, industrial and cultural centre of South Korea, it was founded in 1392 as the capital of the Yi dynasty. It developed rapidly under the Japanese (1910–45). Following the 1948 partition, it became capital of South Korea. Seoul's capture by North Korean troops precipitated the start of the Korean War (1950–3), and the following months witnessed the city's virtual destruction. In 1951, it became the headquarters of the UN command in Korea and a rebuilding programme commenced. By the 1970s, it was the hub of one of the most successful economies of South east Asia. In 1996, there were violent student demonstrations for reunification with North Korea. Seoul hosted the Summer Olympics in 1988 and the semi-final of the 2002 Fifa World Cup.

The real economic miracle came with industrial expansion started in the early 1960s. Initiated by a military government and based on limited natural resources, the country used its cheap, plentiful, well-educated labour force to transform the economy. The manufacturing base of textiles remained important, South Korea also became a world leader in footwear, shipbuilding, consumer electronics, toys and vehicles.

In 1988, a new constitution came into force, enabling presidential elections to be held every five years. Evidence of the new spirit of democracy came in 1997 when, in presidential elections, Kim Dae-jung, leader of past pro-democracy campaigns, narrowly defeated Hoi-chang, the governing party's candidate. In foreign affairs, a major breakthrough had occurred in 1991 when both North and South Korea were admitted as full members of the United Nations. The two countries signed several agreements, including one in which they agreed not to use force against each other, but tensions between them continued. In 2000, South Korea's President Dae-jung met with North Korea's Kim Jong Il in talks aimed at establishing better relations between the countries. But the prospect of reunification seemed as distant as ever.

ECONOMY

The World Bank classifies South Korea as an 'upper-middle-income' developing country. It is one of the world's fastest growing industrial economies. Resources include coal and tungsten. The main manufactures are processed food and textiles. The heavy industries are chemicals, fertilizers, iron, steel, and ships. Computers, cars and televisions are leading industrial products. Farming and fishing remain important activities. Rice is the chief food crop.

Ginseng is displayed for sale in jars, at a stall in Namdaemun Market, Seoul; the largest market in the country it has over 1,000 vendors from tiny street stalls to more established shops; it takes its name from the nearby Great South Gate and is situated close to the centre of the city

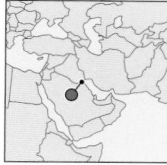

Kuwait 121

The colours of Kuwait's flag are pan-Arab. The green symbolizes Kuwaiti hospitality. The white represents the commitment to peace. The red symbolizes Kuwait's determination to resist aggression. The black signifies decisiveness.

The State of Kuwait is a small, oil-rich, Arab country at the head of the Persian Gulf. It consists of a mainland area and several offshore islands. The capital, Kuwait City, stands on a natural harbour called Kuwait Bay.

Most of the land is a flat or gently undulating plain. The highest point is about 250 m [820 ft]. There are no rivers or lakes and water supply is a problem. Water is imported, but drinking water is also produced by desalination plants. Desert scrub covers some areas, but much of Kuwait has no vegetation.

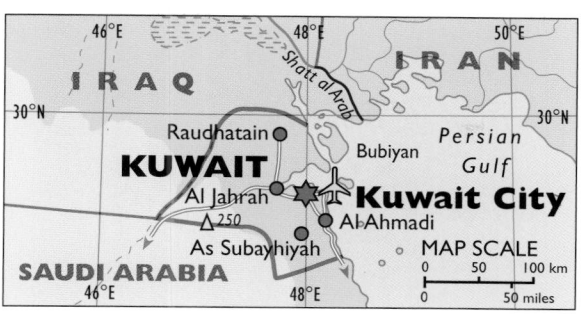

Area 17,818 sq km [6,880 sq mi]
Population 2,258,000
Capital (population) Kuwait City (29,000)
Government Constitutional monarchy
Ethnic groups Kuwaiti 45%, other Arab 35%, South Asian 9%, Iranian 4%, other 7%
Languages Arabic (official), English
Religions Islam 85%, Christianity, Hinduism
Currency Kuwaiti dinar = 1000 fils
Website www.kuwait-info.org

CLIMATE

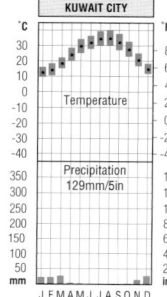

Kuwait has a hot desert climate. Annual rainfall is around 125 mm [5 in] and most rain occurs between November and March. Winters are mild and pleasant. But summers are hot, with average temperatures reaching 33°C to 35°C [91-95°F] between June and September. August to September are the most uncomfortable months, because the humidity is then at its highest. Periodically, conditions become most unpleasant in the interior when hot sandstorms or duststorms blow from central Arabia.

HISTORY

In the 17th century, the north-western part of the Arabian peninsula became part of the Turkish Ottoman empire. But the area was thinly populated until about 1710, when people from Arabia settled there and built the port that later became Kuwait City. They elected the head of the Al Sabah family as their ruler, and this family still rules Kuwait today.

British interest in the area began near the end of the 18th century when Kuwait's leader, Sheikh Mubarak, feared Turkish domination. In 1899, Britain became responsible for Kuwait's defence and, in 1914, the territory became a British protectorate. Britain provided naval protection, while taking control of Kuwait's external affairs.

Drilling for oil began in 1936 and large reserves were discovered by the US-British Kuwait Oil Company. Production was delayed by World War II (1939–45), but oil was produced commercially in 1946. Kuwait soon became a prosperous oil exporter. The country financed great improvements to the infrastructure, and Kuwaitis soon enjoyed a high standard of living.

KUWAIT CITY

Capital of Kuwait, it sits on the natural harbour Kuwait Bay in the Persian Gulf. It was first settled in the early 18th century and by the 19th century it was an important trading port. The city was invaded by Iraqi forces in the 1991 Gulf War and under Iraqi occupation renamed Saddam City, after Iraqi leader Saddam Hussein. It returned to its original name once Iraqi troops were expelled. Known as 'The City' to the people of Kuwait it includes the Majlis Al-Umma (Kuwait's parliament), most governmental offices, and the headquarters of most Kuwaiti businesses.

POLITICS

Kuwait became an independent state on 19 June 1961, and the Sheikh, the head of state, became an Amir (Emir). Kuwait joined the Arab League and Iraq renewed its claim that Kuwait was legally part of its territory. But British military intervention forced Iraq to back down. In 1963, elections were held for the National Assembly under a new constitution. However, the Amir suspended the National Assembly in 1976 saying that it was not acting in the interests of the nation. The National Assembly was restored in 1981 but dissolved again in 1986.

In the Iran-Iraq War, which began in 1980, Kuwait supported Iraq. But in August 1990, Iraq invaded Kuwait, after accusing it of taking oil from an Iraqi oilfield near the border. The Amir and his cabinet fled to Saudi Arabia. When Iraq refused to withdraw, a United States-led and UN-supported international force began an aerial bombing campaign, called 'Operation Desert Storm', in January 1991. They took Kuwait City in late February and expelled the Iraqis; however, prior to expulsion the Iraqis set fire to more than 500 oil wells, causing massive pollution, and destroying almost all the country's commercial and industrial installations. Kuwait's revenge was directed mainly at the huge contingent of Palestinian, Jordanian and Yemeni immigrant workers, who were seen as pro-Iraq. In 1994, Iraq, under pressure from the UN, officially recognized Kuwait's independence and boundaries, although the countries still have no recognized maritime boundaries in the Persian Gulf.

In 1992, elections were held for a new National Assembly. In 1999, the Amir, Jabir al-Ahmad al-Jabir Al Sabah, suspended the Assembly, but liberals and Islamists predominated in the new Assembly. But the liberals did badly in elections in 2003, though Islamists again did well. In 1999, the Assembly had narrowly rejected a proposal to give women full political rights, but parliament approved these rights in May 2005. Kuwait's first woman cabinet minister was appointed in June. In 2006, women were given the opportunity to exercise their right to vote in national elections for the first time. The Amir died in 2006 and was succeeded by his cousin Sheikh Sabah al-Sabah.

A recent problem faced by Kuwait is violent activity by Islamist militants, some of whom are alleged to be linked to al-Qaida. These groups have been accused of conspiring to attack Western targets.

ECONOMY

The economy is based on oil, and this accounts for more than 90% of the exports. Kuwait has about 10% of the world's known reserves. Agriculture is practically non-existent, though the country has a small fishing fleet. Kuwait has to import most of its food. The shortage of water has inhibited the development of industries. However, industrial products include petrochemicals, cement, food products and construction materials.

Opened in 1979, *Kuwait Towers in Kuwait City rise high above the city; a symbol of the city's vast oil wealth, two of the towers hold water, a less accessible, but equally vital commodity for the city*

Kyrgyzstan's flag was adopted in March 1992. The flag depicts a bird's-eye view of a 'yurt' (circular tent) within a radiant sun. The 'yurt' recalls the traditional nomadic way of life. The 40 rays of the sun stand for the 40 traditional tribes.

Area 199,900 sq km [77,181 sq mi]
Population 5,081,000
Capital (population) Bishkek (824,000)
Government Multiparty republic
Ethnic groups Kyrgyz 65%, Russian 13%,
Uzbek 13%, Ukranian 1%, others
Languages Kyrgyz and Russian
(both official)
Religions Islam 75%, Russian
Orthodox 20%
Currency Kyrgyzstani som = 100 tyiyn
Website www.gov.kg

TIAN SHAN (TIEN SHAN)

Mountain range in central Asia, 2,400 km [1,500 mi] long, forming the border between Kyrgyzstan and Xinjiang, north-west China. At their western edge, the Tian Shan ('Celestial Mountains') divide the Tarim and Junggar Basins. The range rises to 7,439 m [24,406 ft] at Pik Pobedy, on the Chinese border with Kazakhstan and Kyrgyzstan. The Issyk Kul in Kyrgyzstan is one of the world's largest mountain lakes.

The Kyrgyz Republic, is a land-locked country between China, Tajikistan, Uzbekistan and Kazakhstan. The country is mountainous, with spectacular scenery. The highest mountain, Pik Pobedy (Peak of Victory) in the Tian Shan Range, reaches 7,439 m [24,406 ft] above sea level in the east. Less than a sixth of the country is below 900 m [2,950 ft].

The largest of the country's many lakes is Lake Issyk Kul (Ysyk-Köl) in the north-east which is 182 km (113 mi) long and up to 61 km (38 mi) wide.

CLIMATE

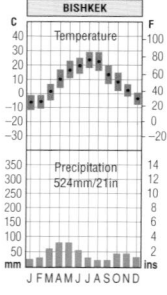

The lowlands of Kyrgyzstan have warm summers and cold winters. The altitude influences the climate in the mountains, where the January temperatures drop plummet to –28°C [18°F]. Far from any sea, Kyrgyzstan has a low annual rainfall.

HISTORY

The area that is now Kyrgyzstan was populated in ancient times by nomadic herders. Mongol armies conquered the region in the early 13th century. They set up areas called *khanates*, ruled by chieftains, or *khans*. Islam was introduced in the 17th century.

China gained control of the area in the mid-18th century, but, in 1876, Kyrgyzstan became a province of Russia, and Russian settlement in the area began. In 1916, Russia crushed a rebellion among the Kyrgyz, and many subsequently fled to China.

In 1922, the area became an autonomous *oblast* (self-governing region) of the newly formed Soviet Union and, in 1936, it became one of the Soviet Socialist Republics. Under Communist rule, nomads were forced to work on government-run farms, while local customs and religious worship were suppressed. However, education and health services were greatly improved.

POLITICS

In 1991, Kyrgyzstan became an independent country following the break-up of the Soviet Union. The Communist Party was dissolved, but the country retained ties with Russia through the Commonwealth of Independent States. Kyrgyzstan adopted a new constitution in 1994 and elections were held in 1995.

In the late 1990s, Askar Akayev, president since 1990, introduced constitutional changes and other measures which gave him greater powers and limited press freedom. In 2000, Akayev was elected to a third five-year term as president. Alleged government interference in the parliamentary elections of March 2005 sparked massive popular protest, with the people demanding a rerun of the vote and the resignation of Askar Akayev. Official buildings in the capital were seized and, with virtually no resistance from the security forces, Akayev fled to Russia. Kurmanbek Bakiev was appointed acting president and prime minister and he subsequently won a landslide victory in a presidential election in July 2005. The election was deemed to have shown clear progress in democratic standards, according to independent foreign observers. However, one year on civil unrest remained a problem for the government.

Kyrgyzstan has the potential to be an ethnic tinderbox, with its large Russian minority (who held positions of power in Soviet days), disenchanted Uzbeks, and an influx of Chinese Muslim immigrants. In the early 2000s, many people were alarmed when Islamic guerrillas staged border raids on Kyrgyzstan as they sought to set up an Islamic state in the Fergana valley, where Kyrgyzstan borders Uzbekistan and Tajikistan.

ECONOMY

The chief economic activity is agriculture, especially livestock rearing. The main products include cotton, eggs, fruits, grain, tobacco, vegetables and wool. Food is imported. Manufactures include machinery, processed food, metals and textiles.

BISHKEK

Capital of Kyrgyzstan, central Asia, on the River Chu. Founded in 1862 as Pishpek, it was the birthplace of a Soviet general, Mikhail Frunze, after whom it was renamed in 1926 when it became administrative centre of the Kyrghyz Soviet Republic. Its name changed to Bishkek in 1991, when Kyrgyzstan declared independence. The city has a university (1951). Industries include textiles, food processing, and agricultural machinery.

Kyrgyz villagers from Bash Chimghan return home after attending a Nazir, or funeral, ceremony in Tom Kurghan

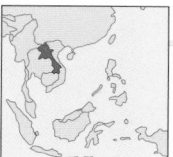

Since 1975, Laos has flown the flag of the Pathet Lao, the Communist movement which won control of the country after a long struggle. The blue stands for the River Mekong, the white disc for the Moon, and the red for the unity and purpose of the people.

The Lao People's Democratic Republic is a landlocked country in South-east Asia. Mountains and plateaus cover much of the country. The highest point is Mount Bia in central Laos, which reaches 2,817 m [9,242 ft].

Most people live on the plains bordering the River Mekong and its tributaries. This river, one of Asia's longest, forms much of the country's north-western and south-western borders. A range of mountains called the Annam Cordillera (Chaîne Annamatique) runs along the eastern border with Vietnam.

CLIMATE

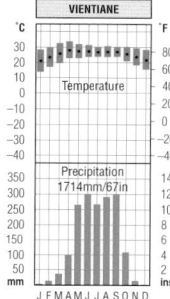

Laos has a tropical monsoon climate. Winters are dry and sunny, with winds blowing in from the north-east. The temperatures rise until April, when the wind directions are reversed and moist south-westerly winds reach Laos, heralding the start of the wet monsoon season.

HISTORY

From the 9th century AD, Lao and Tai peoples set up a number of small states ruled by princes. In 1353 the area that is now Laos was united in a kingdom called Lan Xang ('land of a million elephants'). Apart from a period of Burmese rule between 1574 and 1637, the Lan Xang ruled Laos until the early 18th century. The region was divided into three separate kingdoms, Champasak, Vientiane and Louangphrabang, which became vassals of Siam (now Thailand).

In the 19th century, Chao Anou, the king of Vientiane, united his kingdom with Vietnam in an attempt to break Siamese domination, but he was defeated and Vientiane became a Siamese province. In the late 19th century, France gradually gained control of all Siamese territory east of the River Mekong and made it a protectorate, ruling it as part of French Indo-China, a region which also included Cambodia and Vietnam. After France's surrender to Germany in 1945, Japanese forces moved into Indo-China. They allowed the French to continue as puppet rulers until 1945, when they interned all French authorities and military units. A Free Laos movement set up a government, but it collapsed when the French returned in 1946.

VIENTIANE (VIANGCHAN)

Capital and chief port of Laos, on the River Mekong, close to the Thai border, north central Laos. It was the capital of the Lao kingdom (1707–1828). It became part of French Indo-China in 1893, and in 1899 became the capital of the French Protectorate. It is a major source of opium for world markets. Industries include textiles, brewing, cigarettes, hides, wood products.

Area 236,800 sq km [91,428 sq mi]
Population 6,068,000
Capital (population) Vientiane (528,000)
Government Single-party republic
Ethnic groups Lao Loum 68%, Lao Theung 22%, Lao Soung 9%
Languages Lao (official), French, English
Religions Buddhism 60%, traditional beliefs and others 40%
Currency Kip = 100 at
Website www.un.int/lao

POLITICS

Under a new constitution, Laos became a monarchy in 1947 and, in 1949, the country became a self-governing state within the French Union. After full independence in 1954, Laos suffered from instability caused by a power struggle between royalist government forces and a pro-Communist group called the Pathet Lao. The Pathet Lao took power in 1975 after two decades of chaotic civil war in which the royalist forces were supported by American bombing and Thai mercenaries, while the Pathet Lao was assisted by North Vietnam. The king, Savang Vatthana, abdicated in 1975, and the People's Democratic Republic of Laos was proclaimed. Over 300,000 Laotians, including technicians and other experts, as well as farmers, and members of ethnic minorities, fled the country. Many opponents of the government who remained were sent to re-education camps.

Communist policies brought isolation and stagnation under the domination of the Vietnamese government in Hanoi, which had used Laos as a supply line in their war against the US. In 1986, the Laotian Politburo embarked upon its own *perestroika*, opening its doors to tourists and opening trade links with its neighbours, notably China and Japan. Laos became a member of the Association of South-east Asian Nations (ASEAN) in 1997.

The economy deteriorated from the 1980s and latterly opposition has appeared with sporadic bombings occurring in Vientiane. These have been attributed to rebels in the minority Hmong tribe. Any dissent is dealt with harshly by the authorities.

ECONOMY

Laos is one of the world's poorest countries. Agriculture employs about 76% of the workforce even though only 5% of the land is suitable for such cultivation. 7% of the people work in industry and 17% in services. Rice is the main crop, and timber and coffee are both exported. The most valuable export is electricity, which is produced at hydro-electric power stations on the River Mekong and exported to Thailand.

Laos also produces opium and in the early 1990s was thought to be the world's third biggest source of this illegal drug. Most enterprises are now outside state control. The government is working to develop alternative crops to opium.

Reclining Buddha Statue at Buddha Park in Vientiane

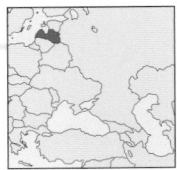

The burgundy and white Latvian flag, which dates back to at least 1280, was revived after Latvia achieved its independence in 1991. According to one legend, the flag was first made from a white sheet which had been stained with the blood of a Latvian hero.

Area 64,600 sq km [24,942 sq mi]
Population 2,306,000
Capital (population) Riga (793,000)
Government Multiparty republic
Ethnic groups Latvian 58%, Russian 30%,
Belarusian, Ukranian, Polish, Lithuanian
Languages Latvian (official), Lithuanian,
Russian
Religions Lutheran, Roman Catholic,
Russian Orthodox
Currency Latvian lat = 100 santimi
Website www.lv

The Republic of Latvia is one of three states on the south-eastern corner of the Baltic Sea, known as the Baltic States. Latvia consists mainly of flat plains separated by low hills, composed of moraine (ice-worn rocks)thatwas dumped there by ice sheets during the Ice Age. The country's highest point is only 311 m [1,020 ft] above sea level. Small lakes and peat bogs are common. The country's main river, the Daugava, is also known as the Western Dvina.

CLIMATE

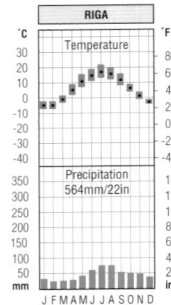

Air masses from the Atlantic influence the climate of Latvia, bringing warm and rainy conditions in summer. Winters are cold. The average temperature range is 16°C-18°C [61–64°F] in July, and –7°C - –3°C [19-27°F] in January.

HISTORY

Between the 9th and 11th centuries, the region was attacked by Vikings from the west and Russians from the east. In the 13th century, German invaders took over, naming the country Livland.

In 1561, Latvia was partitioned and most of the land came under Polish or Lithuanian rule. A Germany duchy was also established there. In 1621, the Swedish king Gustavus II Adolphus took over Riga. In 1629, the greater part of the country north of the Daugava River was ceded to Sweden, with the south-east remaining under Lithuanian rule. But, in 1710, Peter the Great took control of Riga and, by the end of the 18th century, all of Latvia was under Russian control, although the German landowners and merchants continued to exercise considerable power. The 19th century saw the rise of Latvian nationalism and calls for independence became increasingly frequent.

After the Russian Revolution of March 1917, the Latvian National Political Conference demanded independence, but Germany occupied Riga in September. However, after the October Revolution, the Latvian National Political Conference proclaimed the country's independence in November 1918. Russia and Germany, finally recognized Latvia's independence in 1920. In 1922, Latvia adopted a democratic constitution and the elected government introduced land reforms. However, a coup in May 1934 ended this period of democratic rule. In 1939, Germany and the Soviet Union agreed to divide up much of eastern Europe. Soviet troops invaded Latvia in June 1940 and Latvia was made a part of the Soviet Union. But German forces invaded the area in 1941 and held it until 1944, when Soviet troops reoccupied the country. Many Latvians opposed to Russian rule were killed or deported.

POLITICS

Under Soviet rule, many Russians settled in Latvia leading Latvians to fear that the Russians would become the dominant ethnic group. From the mid-1980s, when Mikhail Gorbachev was introducing reforms in the Soviet Union, Latvian nationalists campaigned against Soviet rule. In the late 1980s, the Latvian government ended absolute Communist rule and voted to restore the banned national flag and anthem. It also proclaimed Latvian the official language.

In 1990, Latvia established a multiparty political system. In elections in March, candidates in favour of separation from the Soviet Union won two-thirds of parliamentary seats. The parliament declared Latvia independent on 4 May 1990, though the Soviet Union declared this act illegal. However, the Soviet government recognized Latvia's independence in September 1991, shortly before the Soviet Union itself was dissolved.

Latvia held its first free elections to its parliament (the Saeima) in 1993. Voting was limited only to those who were citizens on 17 June 1940 and their descendants. This meant that about 34% of Latvian residents were unable to vote. In 1994, Latvia restricted the naturalization of non-Latvians, denying them the vote and land ownership. In 1998, the government agreed that all children born since independence should have automatic citizenship, regardless of their parents' status. There are tests in place that ethnic Russians must take in order to gain citizenship, however many have not taken them and so remain stateless.

Latvia became a member of NATO and the EU in 2004.

ECONOMY

The World Bank classifies Latvia as a 'lower-middle-income' country. The country's only natural resources are land and forests, so many raw materials have to be imported. Its industries include electronic goods, farm machinery, fertilizers, processed food, plastics, radios, washing machines and vehicles. Farm products include barley, dairy, beef, oats, potatoes and rye. Latvia produces only about a tenth of its electricity needs. The rest has to be imported from Belarus, Russia and Ukraine.

Statueof St Roland in Ratslaukums, Riga with the tower of St Peter's Church in the background; St Roland was said to represent freedom

RIGA

Capital of Latvia, on the River Daugava, Gulf of Riga. Founded at the beginning of the 13th century, it joined the Hanseatic League in 1282, growing into a major Baltic port. Tsar Peter the Great took the city in 1710. In 1918, it became capital of independent Latvia. In 1940, when Latvia was incorporated into the Soviet Union, thousands of its citizens were deported or executed. Under German occupation from 1941, the city reverted to Soviet rule in 1944 and subsequently suffered further deportations and an influx of Russian immigrants. In 1991, it reassumed its status as capital of an independent Latvia.

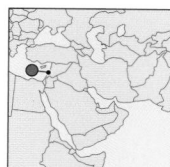

Lebanon 125

Lebanon's flag was adopted in 1943. It uses the colours of Lebanese nationalists in World War I (1914–18). The cedar tree on the white stripe has been a Lebanese symbol since Biblical times. Because of deforestation, only a few of Lebanon's giant cedars survive.

The Republic of Lebanon is a country on the eastern shores of the Mediterranean Sea. Behind the coastal plain are the rugged Lebanon Mountains (Jabal Lubnán), which rise to 3,088 m [10,131 ft]. Another range, the Anti-Lebanon Mountains (Al Jabal ash Sharqi), form the eastern border with Syria. Between the two ranges is the Bekaa (Beqaa) Valley, a fertile farming region.

CLIMATE

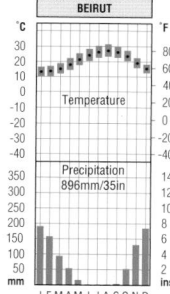

The Lebanese coast has hot, dry summers and mild, wet winters. Inland, onshore winds bring heavy rain to the western slopes of the mountains in the winter months, with snow on the western slopes of the mountains.

HISTORY

There were waves of invaders from 800 BC – Egyptians, Hittites, Assyrians, Babylonians and Persians. The armies of Alexander the Great seized the area in 332 BC and the Romans took control in 64 BC. Christianity was introduced in AD 325 and in 395, the area became part of the Byzantine Empire. Muslim Arabs occupied the area in the early 7th century, converting many people to Islam.

European Crusaders arrived in Lebanon in about 1100 and the area became a battlefield between Christian and Muslim armies. The Muslim Mamelukes of Egypt drove the last of the Crusaders out of the area around 1300. In 1516, Lebanon was taken over by the Turkish Ottoman Empire. Turkish rule continued until World War I, when British and French forces defeated the Ottoman Turks. France took over Lebanon's political affairs from 1923 until 1944 with Lebanon becoming independent in 1946.

POLITICS

The Muslims and Christians agreed to share power and Lebanon made rapid economic progress. But from the late 1950s, development was slowed by periodic conflict between Sunni and Shia Muslims, Druze and Christians. The situation was further complicated by the presence of Palestinian refugees who used bases in Lebanon to attack Israel.

In March 1975, fierce civil war broke out between Christians, Muslims and Druzes. Lebanon sank into a state of chaos. Assassinations, bombings and kidnappings became routine as numerous factions fought for control.

The situation was complicated by interventions by Palestinian refugees, the Syrian army, Western and then UN forces as the country became a patchwork of occupied zones and 'no-go areas'. The core religious confrontation has deep roots. In 1860, thousands of Maronites, who are

Area 10,400 sq km [4,015 sq mi]
Population 3,777,000
Capital (population) Beirut (1,148,000)
Government Multiparty republic
Ethnic groups Arab 95%, Armenian 4%, others
Languages Arabic (official),French, English
Religions Islam 70%, Christianity 30%
Currency Lebanese pound = 100 piastres
Website www.lebanon-tourism.gov.lb

aligned to the Roman Catholic Church, were murdered by Druzes, who are so tangential to other Islamic sects that they are not now regarded as Muslims.

Although not directly involved, Lebanon was destabilized by the Arab-Israel War of 1967 and by the exile of the PLO leadership to Beirut in 1970. By 1990, the Syrian army had crushed the two-year revolt of Christian rebels against the Lebanese government, peace proved fragile and a solution elusive. In 1996, Israeli forces launched a sustained attack on the pro-Iranian Hezbollah positions in southern Lebanon, with heavy civilian casualties. Sporadic fighting continued in southern Lebanon in 1997, flaring up again in early 2000. In 2005, former prime minister Rafik Hariri, a critic of Syria's military presence in Lebanon, was assassinated. Opposition groups accused Syria of involvement, a charge denied by the Damascus government. Following demonstrations, Syria withdrew its forces.

ECONOMY

Civil war almost destroyed valuable trade and financial services which, together with tourism, had been Lebanon's chief source of income. Manufactures also suffered, they now include chemicals, electrical goods, processed food and textiles. Fruits, vegetables and sugar beet are farmed.

The Church of Le Christ Roi *sits above a bay along the Mediterranean Sea near Beirut*

BEIRUT (BAYRUT)

Capital and chief port of Lebanon, on the Mediterranean. From AD 635 Beirut was under Arab rule. Christian crusaders made it part of the Latin Kingdom of Jerusalem from 1110–1291. In 1516, under Druze control, it became part of the Ottoman Empire and remained so until World War I. In 1920 it became capital of Lebanon under French mandate. With the creation of Israel, thousands of Arabs sought refuge there. The outbreak of civil war in 1976 saw Beirut rapidly fracture along religious lines. In 1982, Israel devastated West Beirut in the war against the PLO. Israel began a phased withdrawal in 1985. Syrian troops entered in 1987 as part of an Arab peace-keeping force and in 1990, they dismantled the 'Green Line' separating Muslim West from Christian East Beirut. All militias withdrew by 1991and restoration began. The infrastructure, economy, and culture of Beirut suffered terribly during the civil war.

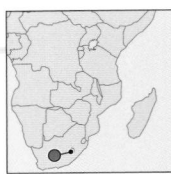

Based on the national motto: white for peace, blue for rain and green for prosperity. The brown animal-skin shield is supported by an assegai (stabbing spear), a plumed spine and a bludgeon, signifying the nation's traditional peace safeguards.

Area 30,355 sq km [11,720 sq mi]
Population 1,865,000
Capital (population) Maseru (109,000)
Government Constitutional monarchy
Ethnic groups Sotho 99%
Languages Sotho and English (both official)
Religions Christianity 80%, traditional beliefs 20%
Currency Loti = 100 lisente
Website www.lesotho.gov.ls

The Kingdom of Lesotho is a land-locked country, surrounded by South Africa on all sides. The scenic Drakensberg Range covers most of the country and forms Lesotho's north eastern border with KwaZulu Natal. It includes Lesotho's highest peak Thabana Ntlenyana, at 3,482 m [11,424 ft].

Most people live in the western lowlands, site of Maseru, or in the southern valley of the River Orange, which rises in north-east Lesotho and flows through South Africa to the Atlantic Ocean. Grassland covers much of Lesotho. The King holds all land in Lesotho, in trust for the Sotho nation.

CLIMATE

The climate is greatly affected by altitude, with 66% of the country lying above 1,500 m [4,921 ft]. Maseru has warm summers, but the temperatures fall below freezing in the winter and the mountains are colder. Rainfall varies, averaging around 700 mm [28 in].

HISTORY

The early 19th century tribal wars dispersed the Sotho. The Basotho nation was founded in the 1820s by King Moshoeshoe I, who united various groups fleeing from tribal wars in southern Africa. Moshoeshoe I was forced to yield to the British and Britain made the area a protectorate in 1868. In 1871, it became part of the British Cape Colony in South Africa. However, in 1884, Basutoland, as the area was called, was reconstituted as a British protectorate, where whites were not allowed to own land.

POLITICS

In 1966, Sotho opposition to incorporation into the Union of South Africa saw the creation of the independent Kingdom of Lesotho, with Moshoeshoe II, great-grandson of Moshoeshoe I, as its king.

In 1970, Leabua Jonathan suspended the constitution and banned opposition parties. Civil conflict between the government and Basuto Congress Party (BCP) forces characterized the next 16 years. In 1986, a military coup led to the reinstatement of Moshoeshoe II. In 1990, he was deposed and replaced by his son, Letsie III, as monarch. The BCP won the 1992 multiparty elections, and the military council dissolved. In 1994, Letsie III attempted to overthrow the government. In 1995, Moshoeshoe II returned to the throne. But after his death in a car crash in 1996, Letsie III again became king. In 1997, a majority of BCP politicians formed a new governing party, the Lesotho Congress for Democracy (LCD).

In 1998, an army revolt, following an election in which the ruling party won 79 out of the 80 seats, caused much damage to the economy, despite the intervention of a South African force intended to maintain order. In 2004, the government declared a state of emergency following three years of drought

ECONOMY

Lesotho is a 'low-income' developing country. It lacks natural resources except diamonds. Agriculture employs two-thirds of the workforce, but most farmers live at subsistence level. Livestock farming is important. Major crops include maize and sorghum. Tourism is developing. Other sources of income include the products of light manufacturing and remittances sent home by Basotho working abroad, mainly in the mines of South Africa.

MASERU

Capital of Lesotho, located on the River Caledon, near the western border with South Africa. It is the only large city in the whole country. Originally a small trading town, it was capital of British Basutoland protectorate (1869–71, 1884–1966). It remained the capital when the Kingdom of Lesotho achieved independence in 1966. It is a commercial, transport and administrative centre. Places of interest include the Catholic Cathedral of Our Lady of Victories and Lancer's Gap which has great views of the city and the Caledon Valley. The National University of Lesotho is in the town of Roma, some 35 km (21 mi) away; and the country's main international airport is also adjacent.

SOTHO

Major cultural and linguistic group of southern Africa. Includes the Northern Sotho of Transvaal, South Africa, the Western Sotho (better known as the Tswana) of Botswana, and the Southern Sotho (Basotho or Basuto) of Lesotho. Although dominating the rural territories they inhabit, the 4 million Sotho share the areas with people of other Bantu-speaking tribes. Many work and live in the urban areas and surrounding townships.

***Round stone huts** in verdant mountains*

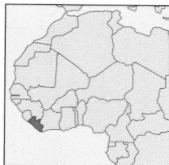

Liberia was founded in the early 19th century as an American colony for freed slaves who wanted to return to Africa. Its flag was adopted upon its independence in 1847. The 11 red and white stripes represent the 11 men who signed the Declaration of Independence.

The Republic of Liberia is located on the Atlantic coast of west Africa. Behind the coastline 500 km [311 mi] long, lies a narrow coastal plain. Beyond, the land rises to a plateau region, with the highest land along the border with Guinea. The most important rivers are the Cavally, which forms the border with Ivory Coast, and the St Paul.

Mangrove swamps and lagoons line the coast, while inland, forests cover nearly 40% of the land. Liberia also has areas of tropical savanna. Only 5% of the land is cultivated.

CLIMATE

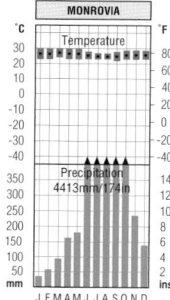

Liberia has a tropical climate. There are high temperatures and humidity throughout the year. Rainfall is abundant all year round, but there is a particularly wet period from June to November. The rainfall generally increases from east to west.

Area 111,369 sq km [43,000 sq mi]
Population 3,391,000
Capital (population) Monrovia (421,000)
Government Multiparty republic
Ethnic groups Indigenous African tribes 95% (including Kpelle, Bassa, Grebo, Gio, Kru, Mano)
Languages English (official), ethnic languages
Religions Christianity 40%, Islam 20%, traditional beliefs and others 40%
Currency Liberian dollar = 100 cents
Website www.un.org/Depts/dpko/missions/unmil/index.html

HISTORY

In the late 18th century, some white Americans in the United States wanted to help freed black slaves to return to Africa. They set up the American Colonization Society in 1816, which bought land in what is now Liberia.

In 1822, the Society landed former slaves at a settlement on the coast which they named Monrovia. In 1847, Liberia became a fully independent republic with a constitution much like that of the United States. For many years, the Americo-Liberians controlled the government. US influence remained strong and the American Firestone Company, which ran Liberia's rubber plantations covering more than 400,000 ha [1 million acres], was especially influential. Foreign countries were also involved in exploiting Liberia's mineral resources, including its huge iron-ore deposits.

MONROVIA

Capital and chief port of Liberia, west Africa, on the estuary of the River St Paul.
In 1822 freed US slaves settled Monrovia, on a site chosen by the American Colonization Society. The city is named after James Monroe, US president from 1817–25. Monrovia is Liberia's largest city and the administrative, commercial and financial centre of the country. It suffered extensive damage in the civil war with the city's infrastructure bearing the brunt. It exports latex and iron ore. Industries include bricks and cement.

POLITICS

Under the leadership (1944–71) of William Tubman, Liberia's economy grew and it adopted social reforms. In 1980, a military force composed of people from the local population killed the Americo-Liberian president William R. Tolbert, Tubman's successor. An army sergeant, Samuel K. Doe, became president. In 1985, Doe's brutal and corrupt regime won a fraudulent election.

Civil war broke out in 1989, and the Economic Community of West African States (ECOWAS) sent a five-nation peace-keeping force. Doe was assassinated and an interim government, led by Amos Sawyer, took office. Civil war raged on, claiming 150,000 lives and leaving hundreds of thousands of people homeless by 1994. In 1995, a cease-fire occurred and the former warring factions formed a council of state. Former warlord Charles Taylor of the National Patriotic Council secured a resounding victory in 1997 elections. In 2001, the UN imposed an arms embargo on Liberia for trading weapons for diamonds with rebels in Sierra Leone. In 2002, Taylor imposed a state of emergency as fighting intensified with rebels. In 2003, the fighting largely ended; Taylor went into exile. The UN helped to restore order and, in 2005, Ellen Johnson-Sirleaf was elected president. After a lengthy campaign Charles Taylor was extradited to the international court in The Hague to be tried for war crimes.

ECONOMY

Liberia's civil war devastated the economy. Agriculture employs 75% of the workforce, but many families live at subsistence level. Food crops include cassava, fruits, rice and sugar cane. Rubber is grown on plantations and cash crops include cocoa and coffee. Liberia's natural resources include its forests and iron ore, while gold and diamonds are also mined. Liberia has an oil refinery, but manufacturing is small-scale. Exports include rubber, timber, diamonds, gold and coffee. Revenue is also obtained from its 'flag of convenience', which is used by about one-sixth of the world's commercial shipping, exploiting low taxes.

Mud bricks *set out to dry at the edge of a street in Monrovia*

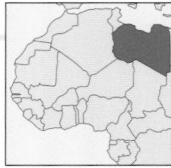

Libya's flag was adopted in 1977. It replaced the flag of the Federation of Arab Republics which Libya left in that year. Libya's flag is the simplest of all world flags. It represents the country's quest for a green revolution in agriculture.

Area 1,759,540 sq km [679,358 sq mi]
Population 5,632,000
Capital (population) Tripoli (1,500,000)
Government Single-party socialist state
Ethnic groups Libyan Arab and Berber 97%
Languages Arabic (official), Berber
Religions Islam (Sunni Muslim) 97%
Currency Libyan dinar = 1000 dirhams
Website www.libyana.org

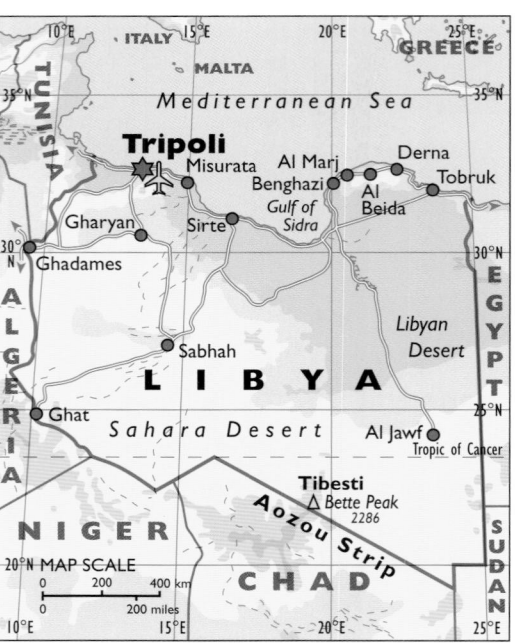

The Great Socialist People's Libyan Arab Jamahiriya (Libya's official name) is located in North Africa. The majority live on the Mediterranean coastal plains in the north-east and north-west. The Sahara, the world's largest desert, occupies 95% of Libya, reaching the Mediterranean coast along the Gulf of Sidra (Khalīj Surt). The Sahara is virtually uninhabited except around scattered oases.

The land rises towards the south, reaching 2,286 m [7,500 ft] at Bette Peak (Bikku Bitti) on the border with Chad. Shrubs and grasses grow on northern coasts, with some trees in wetter areas. Few plants grow in the desert, except at oases where date palms provide protection from the hot sun.

CLIMATE

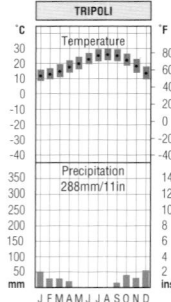

The coastal plains experience hot summers. Winters are mild with some rain. Inland, the average yearly rainfall drops to around 100 mm [4 in] or less. Daytime temperatures are high but nights are cool.

HISTORY

Libya's first known inhabitants were the Berbers. From the 7th century BC to the 5th century AD, Libya came under the Carthaginians, Greeks and Romans. The Romans left superb ruins, but the Arabs, who invaded the area in AD 642, imposed their culture, including their religion, Islam. From 1551, Libya was part of the Ottoman empire. Italy took control in 1911, but lost the territory in World War II. Britain and France then jointly ruled Libya until 1951, when it became an independent kingdom.

POLITICS

In 1969, a military group headed by Colonel Muammar Gaddafi deposed the king and set up a military government. Under Gaddafi, the government took control of the economy and used money from oil exports to finance welfare services and development projects. However, although Libya appears to be democratic, political parties are not permitted.

Gaddafi has attracted international criticism for his support for radical movements, such as the PLO (Palestine Liberation Organization) and various terrorist groups. In 1986, his policies led the United States to bomb installations in the capital and in Benghazi. In 1994, the International Court of Justice ruled against Libya's claim to an area in northern Chad.

In 1999, Gaddafi sought to restore good relations with the outside world by surrendering for trial two Libyans suspected of planting a bomb on a PanAm plane, which exploded over the Scottish town of Lockerbie in 1988. In addition Libya agreed to pay compensation to victims of the bombing. Gaddafi also accepted Libya's responsibility for the shooting of a British policewoman in London in 1984 and diplomatic relations with Britain were restored. In 2004 it was announced that Libya was abandoning programmes to produce weapons of mass destruction, an initiative that was rewarded by visits to Libya by many Western leaders.

ECONOMY

Libya is Africa's richest country, per capita, but remains a developing country because of its dependence on oil, which accounts for nearly all of its export revenues.

Agriculture is important, although Libya still imports food. Crops include barley, citrus fruits, dates, olives, potatoes and wheat. Cattle, sheep and poultry are raised. Libya has oil refineries and petrochemical plants. It also manufactures cement, processed food and steel.

The 'Great Man-Made River' is an ambitious project involving the tapping of subterranean water from rocks beneath the Sahara and piping it to the dry, populated areas in the north. But, the water in the aquifers is non-renewable and will eventually run dry.

Leptis Magna, *on the Mediterranean coast; originally founded by the Phoenicians in the 10th century BC it flourished under the Romans; granted UNESCO World Heritage Site status in 1982*

TRIPOLI (TARABULUS)

Capital and chief port of Libya, on the Mediterranean Sea. Founded as Oea in the 7th century BC by the Phoenicians and developed by the Romans. From the 7th century AD, the Arabs developed Tripoli as a market centre for the trans-Saharan caravans. In 1551, it was captured by the Ottoman Turks. It was made capital of the Italian colony of Libya in 1911, and was an important base for Axis forces during World War II. After intensive Allied bombing in 1941–2, Britain captured the city. In 1986, the US Air Force bombed Tripoli in retaliation for Libya's alleged support of worldwide terrorism. The city is the commercial, industrial, transport and communications centre of Libya. Its oases are the most fertile agricultural area in northern Africa.

Lithuania 129

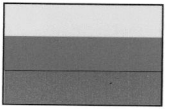

This flag was created in 1918 when Lithuania became an independent republic. After the Soviet Union annexed Lithuania in 1940, the flag was suppressed. It was revived in 1988 and again became the national flag when Lithuania became fully independent in 1991.

The Republic of Lithuania is the southernmost of the three Baltic states. The land is essentially flat with the highest point a hill, north-east of Vilnius (292 m [958 ft]). From the south-east, the land slopes down to the fertile central lowland. In the west is an area of forested sandy ridges, dotted with lakes. South of Klaipeda, sand dunes separate a large lagoon from the Baltic Sea.

Most of the land is covered by moraine deposited by ice sheets during the Ice Age. Hollows in the moraine contain about 3,000 lakes. The longest river is the Neman, which rises in Belarus and flows through Lithuania to the Baltic Sea.

Area 65,200 sq km [25,174 sq mi]
Population 3,608,000
Capital (population) Vilnius (578,000)
Government Multiparty republic
Ethnic groups Lithuanian 80%, Russian 9%, Polish 7%, Belarusian 2%
Languages Lithuanian (official), Russian, Polish
Religions Mainly Roman Catholic
Currency Litas
Website www.lietuva.lt

CLIMATE

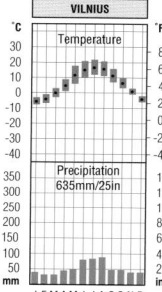

Winters are cold with temperatures averaging −3°C [27°F] in January. But summers are warm, with average temperatures in July of 17°C [63°F]. The average rainfall in the west is 630 mm [25 in]. Inland areas are drier.

VILNIUS

Capital of Lithuania, on the River Neris. Founded in 1323 as the capital of the Grand Duchy of Lithuania, the city declined after the union of Lithuania-Poland. Vilnius was captured by Russia in 1795.

After World War I, it was made capital of an independent Lithuania. In 1939, Soviet troops occupied the city and, in 1940, Lithuania became a Soviet republic. During World War II, the city was occupied by German troops, and its Jewish population was all but exterminated. In 1944, it reverted to its Soviet status. In 1990, Lithuania unilaterally declared independence, leading to clashes with Soviet troops and battles on the streets of Vilnius. In 1991, the Soviet Union recognized Lithuanian independence. The old city has many historic synagogues, churches, and civic buildings, and the ruins of a 14th-century castle.

HISTORY

The Lithuanian people were united into a single nation in the 12th century. The first great ruler was Mindaugas who became king in 1251. By the 14th century, Lithuania's territory extended nearly to Moscow in the east and the Black Sea in the south. Lithuania and Poland became a single state in 1569. This state collapsed in the 18th century and, by 1795, Lithuania was under Russian control. Despite rebellions, Lithuania failed to regain its independence.

In 1905, a conference of elected representatives called for self-government, Russia refused. German troops occupied Lithuania during World War I and, in February 1918, Lithuania declared its independence from Germany and Russia. Lithuania established a democratic form of government, and in 1920, Russia and Lithuania signed a peace treaty. Poland occupied Vilnius from 1920 until 1939, having incorporated it into Poland in 1923. In 1926, a coup overthrew Lithuania's democratic regime.

In 1939, Germany and the USSR agreed to divide up much of eastern Europe. Lithuania and Vilnius were ceded to the USSR in 1940 and a government was set up. German forces invaded in 1941 and held it until 1944, when Soviet troops reoccupied the country. Many Lithuanian guerrillas fought against Soviet rule between 1944 and 1952. Thousands of Lithuanians were killed and many sent to labour camps.

POLITICS

From 1988, Lithuania led the way among the Baltic states in the drive to shed Communism and regain nationhood. In 1989, the parliament in Lithuania declared Soviet laws invalid unless approved by the Lithuanian parliament and that Lithuanian should be the official language. Religious freedom and the freedom of the press were restored, abolishing the monopoly of power held by the Communist Party and establishing a multiparty system.

Following parliamentary elections in February 1990, in which pro-independence candidates won more than 90% of the seats, Lithuania declared itself independent in March 1990, a declaration that was rejected by the Soviet leaders. Most of the capital was then occupied by Soviet troops and a crippling economic blockade put in place. After negotiations to end the sanctions failed, Soviet troops moved into Lithuania and 14 people were killed when the troops fired on demonstrators. Finally, on 6 September 1991, the Soviet government recognized Lithuania's independence.

Parliamentary elections in 1992 were won by the Lithuanian Democratic Labour Party (former Communists). Russian troops withdrew from the country in 1993. In 1996, following new parliamentary elections, a coalition government was set up by the conservative Homeland Union and the Christian Democratic Party. In 1998, an independent, Valdas Adamkus, a Lithuanian-American who had fled in 1944, was elected president. Lithuania had better relations with Russia than the other two Baltic states, partly because ethnic Russians make up a lower proportion of the population than in Estonia and Latvia. Lithuania became a member of NATO and of the EU in 2004.

ECONOMY

The World Bank classifies Lithuania as a 'lower-middle-income' developing country. Manufacturing is the most valuable activity. Products include chemicals, electronic goods, processed food and machine tools. Dairy and meat farming are important, as also is fishing.

View of Vilnius, *from the Hill of Three Crosses*

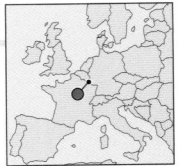

Luxembourg's tri-colour flag derives from its coat of arms which shows a red lion on front of blue and white horizontal stripes. The first recorded use of the coat of arms is on the banner of Earl Heinrich VI in 1228.

Area 2,586 sq km [998 sq mi]
Population 463,000
Capital (population) Luxembourg (77,000)
Government Constitutional monarchy (Grand Duchy)
Ethnic groups Luxembourger 71%, Portuguese, Italian, French, Belgian, Slav
Languages Luxembourgish (official), French, German
Religions Roman Catholic 87%, others 13%
Currency Euro = 100 cents
Website www.luxembourg.lu

The Grand Duchy of Luxembourg is one of the smallest and oldest countries in Europe. The north belongs to an upland region which includes the wooded plateau of the Ardennes in Belgium and Luxembourg, and the Eiffel Highlands in Germany. This scenic region contains the country's highest point, Buurgplaatz, in the north which reaches 565 m [1,854 ft] above sea level.

The southern two-thirds of Belgium, which is geographically part of French Lorraine, is a hilly or rolling plateau called the Bon Pays or Gut Land ('Good Land'). This region contains rich farmland, especially in the fertile Alzette, Moselle and Sûre (or Sauer) river valleys in the south and east.

Forests cover about a fifth of Luxembourg, mainly in the north, where deer and wild boar are found. Farms cover about 25% of the land and pasture another 20%.

CLIMATE

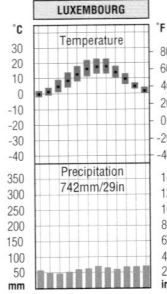

Luxembourg has a temperate climate. In the south of the country summers and autumns are warm. This is when grapes ripen in the sheltered south-eastern valleys. Winters are sometimes severe, particularly in the Ardennes region, where snow can cover the land for some weeks.

HISTORY

Luxembourg became an independent state in AD 963 and a duchy in 1354. In the 1440s, Luxembourg came under the House of Burgundy and, in the early 16th century, under the rule of the Habsburgs. From 1684, it came successively under France (between 1684 and 1697), Spain (from 1697 to 1714) and Austria until

LUXEMBOURG

Capital of the Grand Duchy of Luxembourg, at the confluence of the Alzette and Pétrusse rivers. Luxembourg was a Roman stronghold. The walled town developed around a 10th-century fortress. The Treaty of London (1867) dismantled the fortress and demilitarized the city. It is the seat of the European Court of Justice, the Secretariat of the Parliament of the European Union, the European Monetary Fund, the European Investment Bank, and the European Coal and Steel Union. Industries include iron and steel, chemicals, textiles and tourism.

1795, when it reverted to French rule. In 1815, following the defeat of France, Luxembourg became a Grand Duchy under the Netherlands. This was due to the Grand Duke also being the king of the Netherlands.

In 1890, when Wilhelmina became queen of the Netherlands, Luxembourg broke away as its laws did not permit a woman monarch. The Grand Duchy then passed to Adolphus, Duke of Nassau-Weilburg. But, in 1912, Luxembourg's laws were changed to allow Marie Adélaïde of Nassau to become the ruling grand duchess. Her sister Charlotte succeeded in 1919, but she abdicated in 1964 in favour of her son, Jean. In 2000, Grand Duke Jean handed over the role as head of state to his son, Prince Henri.

Germany occupied Luxembourg in both World Wars. In 1944–5, northern Luxembourg was the scene of the Battle of the Bulge. Following World War II, the economy recovered rapidly.

POLITICS

In 1948, Luxembourg joined Belgium and the Netherlands in a union by the name of Benelux and, in the 1950s, was one of the six founders of what is now the European Union. The country's capital, a major financial centre, contains the headquarters of several international agencies, including the European Coal and Steel Community and the European Court of Justice.

ECONOMY

Luxembourg has iron-ore reserves and is a major steel producer. It also has many high-technology industries, producing electronic goods and computers. Steel and other manufactures, including chemicals, glass and rubber products, are exported.

Other activities include tourism and financial services. Half the land area is farmed, but agriculture employs only 3% of the workforce. Crops include barley, fruits, oats, potatoes and wheat. Cattle, sheep, pigs and poultry are reared.

View over Luxembourg
with the Bisserbreck viaduct to the fore; constructed in 1861, the viaduct carries a railway line and crosses the river Pétrusse; it is 290 m (951 ft) in length and has 24 arches

Macedonia's flag was introduced in August 1992. The emblem in the centre of the flag was the device from the war-chest of Philip of Macedon; however, the Greeks claimed this symbol as their own. In 1995, Macedonia agreed to redesign their flag, as shown here.

The Republic of Macedonia is in south-eastern Europe. This land-locked country is largely mountainous or hilly, the highest point being Mount Korab (2,764 m [9,068 ft]) on the border with Albania. Most of the country is drained by the River Vardar and its many tributaries. In the south-west, Macedonia shares two large lakes – Ohrid and Prespa – with Albania and Greece. Forests of beech, oak and pine cover large areas, especially in the west.

The small church of Sv. Jovan Kaneo *in the town of Orid, overlooking Lake Ohrid; built in the 13th century in the plan of a Greek cross, it is constructed in layers of brick and stone*

Area 25,713 sq km [9,928 sq mi]
Population 2,071,000
Capital (population) Skopje (430,000)
Government Multiparty republic
Ethnic groups Macedonian 64%, Albanian 25%, Turkish 4%, Romanian 3%, Serb 2%
Languages Macedonian and Albanian (official)
Religions Macedonian Orthodox 70%, Islam 29%
Currency Macedonian denar = 100 paras
Website www.vlada.mk/english/index_en.htm

World War I, Serbian Macedonia became part of the Kingdom of the Serbs, Croats and Slovenes, which was renamed Yugoslavia in 1929. Yugoslavia was conquered by Germany during World War II, but when the war ended in 1945 the Communist partisan leader Josip Broz Tito set up a Communist government. Tito maintained unity among the diverse peoples of Yugoslavia but, after his death in 1980, the ethnic and religious differences began to reassert themselves. Yugoslavia broke apart into five sovereign republics with Macedonia declaring its independence on 18 September 1991 thereby avoiding the civil war that shattered other parts of the former Yugoslavia.

However, Macedonia ran into problems concerning recognition. Greece, worried by the consequences for its own Macedonian region, vetoed any acknowledgement of an independent Macedonia on its borders. It considered Macedonia to be a Greek name. It also objected to a symbol on Macedonia's flag, which was associated with Philip of Macedon, and a reference in the country's constitution to the desire to reunite the three parts of the old Macedonia.

Macedonia adopted a new clause in its constitution rejecting all claims on Greek territory and, in 1993, joined the United Nations under the name of The Former Yugoslav Republic of Macedonia (FYROM). In late 1993, all EU countries, except Greece, established diplomatic relations with the FYROM. Greece barred Macedonian trade in 1994, but this ban was subsequently lifted in 1995. Macedonia's stability was threatened in 1999 when Albanian-speaking refugees flooded into Macedonia from Kosovo. In 2001, Albanian-speaking Macedonians in northern Macedonia launched an armed struggle. The uprising ended when the government introduced changes that gave Albanian-speakers increased rights, including the recognition of Albanian as an official language. In 2004, the USA recognized the name Republic of Macedonia instead of FYROM, with other countries expected to follow this lead, despite objections from Greece.

CLIMATE

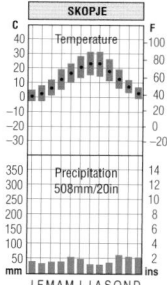

Summers are hot, though highland areas are cooler. Winters are cold and snowfall is often heavy. The climate is fairly continental with rainfall throughout the year. Average temperatures in Skopje range from 1°C [34°F] in January to 24°C [75°F] in July. The average annual rainfall in the city is 550 mm [21 in].

HISTORY

Until the 20th century, Macedonia's history was closely tied to that of a larger area, also called Macedonia, which covered of northern Greece and south-western Bulgaria. This region reached its peak in power at the time of Philip II (382–336 BC) and his son Alexander the Great (336–323 BC), who conquered an empire that stretched from Greece to India. The area became a Roman province in the 140s BC and part of the Byzantine Empire from AD 395. In the 6th century, Slavs from eastern Europe attacked and settled in the area, followed by Bulgars from central Asia in the late 9th century. The Byzantine Empire regained control in 1018. Serbia took Macedonia in the early 14th century.

The area was conquered by the Ottoman Turks in 1371 and was under their rule for more than 500 years. The Ottoman Empire began to collapse in the late 19th century and in 1913, at the end of the Balkan Wars, the area was divided between Bulgaria, Greece and Serbia.

POLITICS

As a result of the division of the area known as Macedonia, Serbia took the north and centre of the region, Bulgaria took a small area in the south-east, and Greece gained the south. At the end of

SKOPJE

Capital of Macedonia, on the River Vardar. Founded in Roman times, it became capital of the Serbian Empire in the 14th century, fell to the Ottoman Turks in 1392, and incorporated into Yugoslavia in 1918. In 1963 an earthquake destroyed most of the city. Industries include metals, textiles, chemicals, glassware.

ECONOMY

According to the World Bank, Macedonia ranks as a 'lower-middle-income' developing country. Macedonia mines coal, chromium, copper, iron ore, lead, manganese, uranium and zinc. Manufactures include cement, chemicals, cigarettes, cotton fabric, footwear, iron and steel, refrigerators, sulphuric acid, tobacco products and wool yarn.

Agriculture employs 9% of the workforce, as compared with 23% in manufacturing and mining. About a quarter of the land is farmed and major crops include cotton, fruits, maize, potatoes, tobacco, vegetables and wheat. Cattle, pigs, poultry and sheep are also raised. Forestry is another important activity in some areas.

The colours on this flag are those used on historic flags in South-east Asia. It was from this region that the ancestors of many Madagascans came around 2,000 years ago. This flag was adopted in 1958, when Madagascar became a self-governing republic under French rule.

Area 587,041 sq km [226,657 sq mi]
Population 17,502,000
Capital (population) Antananarivo (1,250,000)
Government Republic
Ethnic groups Merina, Betsimisaraka, Betsileo, Tsmihety, Sakalava and others
Languages Malagasy and French (both official)
Religions Traditional beliefs 52%, Christianity 41%, Islam 7%
Currency Malagasy franc = 100 centimes
Website www.madagascar.gov.mg

The Republic of Madagascar, lies 390 km [240 mi] off the south-east coast of Africa and is the world's fourth largest island. In the west, a wide coastal plain gives way to a central highland region, mostly between 600 m and 1,220 m [2,000ft to 4,000ft]. This is Madagascar's most densely populated region and home of the capital, Antananarivo. The land rises in the north to the volcanic peak of Tsaratanana, at 2,876 m [9,436 ft]. The land slopes off in the east to a narrow coastal strip.

Grass and scrub grow in the south. Forest and tropical savanna once covered much of Madagascar, but farming cleared large areas, destroying natural habitats and seriously threatening the island's unique and diverse wildlife.

CLIMATE

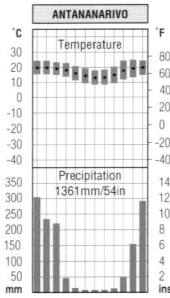

Altitude moderates temperatures in the highlands. Winters (April to September) are dry, but heavy rains occur in summer. Coastlands to the east are warm and humid. The west is drier, and the south and south-west are hot and dry.

HISTORY

People from South-east Asia began to settle on Madagascar around 2,000 years ago. Subsequent influxes from Africa and Arabia added to the island's diverse heritage, culture and language. The Malagasy language is of South-east Asian origin, though it included words from Arabic, Bantu languages and European languages.

The first Europeans to reach Madagascar were Portuguese missionaries who in the early 17th century vainly sought to convert the native population. The 17th century saw the creation of small kingdoms and later the French established trading posts along the east coast. The island became a haven for pirates from the late 18th to early 19th century. A major part of the island was was under

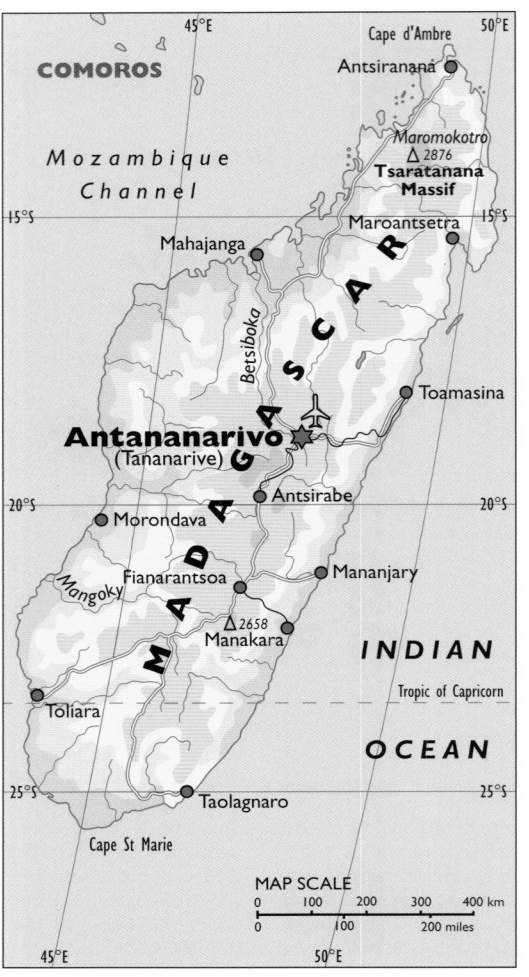

Merina rule from the late 18th century.

In 1817, the Merina ruler and the British governor of Mauritius agreed to the abolition of the slave trade. As a result of this, the island received British military and financial assistance. British influence remained strong for several decades. France made contacts with the island in the 1860s. Finally, French troops defeated a Malagasy army in 1895 and Madagascar became a French colony. In 1942, the British overthrew Vichy colonial rule and the Free French reasserted control. In 1946–8 France brutally crushed a rebellion against colonial rule, killing perhaps as many as 80,000 islanders.

POLITICS

In 1960, the country achieved full independence as the Malagasy Republic. In 1972, the military took control of government. Malagasy was renamed Madagascar in 1975, and Lieutenant Commander Didier Ratsiraka became president. He proclaimed martial law, banned opposition parties, and nationalized many industries.

In 1992 Ratsiraka bowed to political pressure and approved a new, democratic constitution. Multiparty elections in 1993 saw Albert Zafy become president. Zafy was impeached in 1996, and Ratsiraka regained the presidency in 1997 elections. In 2000, floods and tropical storms devastated Madagascar.

Madagascar came to the brink of civil war in 2002 when Ratsiraka and his opponent, Marc Ravalomanana, both claimed victory in presidential elections. Ravalomanana was eventually recognized as president and Ratsiraka went into exile.

ECONOMY

Madagascar is one of the world's poorest countries. The land has been eroded because of the cutting down of the forests and overgrazing of the grasslands. Farming, fishing and forestry employ about 80% of the people.

The country's food crops include bananas, cassava, rice and sweet potatoes. Coffee is the leading export. Other exports include cloves, sisal, sugar and vanilla. There are few manufacturing industries.

ANTANANARIVO (TANANARIVE)

Capital and largest city of Madagascar. Founded around 1625, the city became the residence for Imerina rulers in 1794 and the capital of Madagascar. Antananarivo was taken by the French in 1895, and became part of a French protectorate. It is the seat of the University of Madagascar (1961). A trade centre for a rice-producing region, it has textile, tobacco, and leather industries.

Seaweed farmers *harvest their crop*

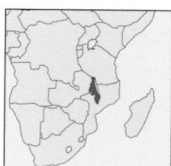

The colours in Malawi's flag come from the flag of the Malawi Congress Party, which was adopted in 1953. The symbol of the rising sun was added when Malawi became independent from Britain in 1964. It represents the beginning of a new era for Malawi and Africa.

The Republic of Malawi in southern Africa is a small, landlocked country, which is nowhere more than 160 km [100 mi] wide. Its dominant physical feature is Lake Malawi, which is drained in the south by the River Shire, a tributary of the Zambezi. The land is mostly mountainous, the highest point being Mulanje, in the south-east, which reaches 3,000 m [9,843 ft].

CLIMATE

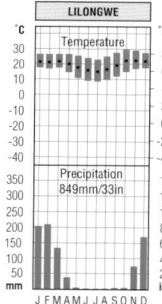

The low-lying regions of Malawi remain hot and humid all year long; the uplands have a pleasant climate. Lilongwe, at about 1,100 m [3,609 ft] above sea level, has a warm and sunny climate. Frosts can sometimes occur in July and August, the middle of the long dry season. The wet season extends from November to May.

Wooded savanna and tropical grasslands cover much of the country, with swampy vegetation in many river valleys.

LILONGWE

Capital of Malawi, south-east Africa, in the centre of the country, 80 km [50 mi] west of Lake Malawi. It replaced Zomba as the capital in 1975, and rapidly became Malawi's second-largest city.

HISTORY

The Bantu-speaking ancestors of the people of Malawi first reached the area around 2,000 years ago, introducing an iron age culture and developing kingdoms in the region. In the first half of the 19th century, two other Bantu-speaking groups, the Ngoni (or Angoni) and the Yao invaded the area. The Yao took slaves and sold them to Arabs who traded along the coast. In 1859, the British missionary-explorer David Livingstone reached the area and was horrified by the cruelty of the slave trade. The Free Church of Scotland established a mission in 1875, while Scottish businessmen worked to found businesses to replace the slave trade. The British made treaties with local chiefs on the western banks of what was then called Lake Nyasa and, in 1891, the area was made the British Protectorate of Nyasaland.

The Federation of Rhodesia and Nyasaland was established by Britain in 1953. This included Northern Rhodesia (Zambia) and Southern Rhodesia (Zimbabwe). The people of Nyasaland opposed the creation of the federation, fearing domination by the white minority community in

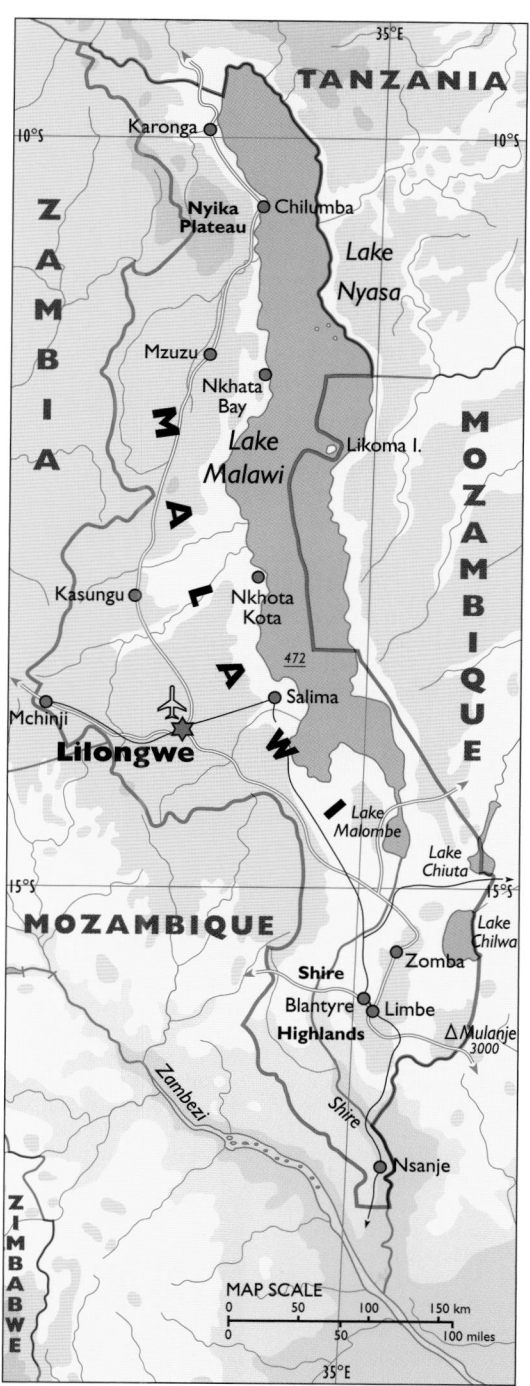

Area 118,484 sq km [45,747 sq mi]
Population 11,907,000
Capital (population) Lilongwe (440,000)
Government Multiparty republic
Ethnic groups Chewa, Nyanja, Tonga, Tumbuka, Lomwe, Yao, Ngoni and others
Languages Chichewa and English (both official)
Religions Protestant 55%, Roman Catholic 20%, Islam 20%
Currency Malawian kwacha = 100 tambala
Website www.malawi.gov.mw

Southern Rhodesia. In 1958, Dr Hastings Banda took over leadership of the opposition to the federation and also to the continuance of British rule. Faced with mounting protests, Britain dissolved the federation in 1963. During 1964, Nyasaland became fully independent as Malawi. Banda became the country's first prime minister and, in 1966, after the adoption of a new constitution, making the country a single-party republic, Banda became the first president.

POLITICS

Banda declared himself president for life in 1971. His autocratic regime differed from most of black Africa in being conservative and pragmatic, hostile to its socialist neighbours, but friendly with South Africa. His austerity programme and agricultural policies seemed to have wrought an economic miracle, but a swift decline in the 1980s, combined with the arrival of a million refugees from war-torn Mozambique, led to a return to poverty, despite massive aid packages. Another immediate and ongoing problem was the high incidence of AIDS putting pressure on the country's limited welfare services. Political dissent led to the restoration of a multiparty system in 1993. Banda and his party were defeated in the elections of 1994 with Bakili Muluzi becoming president. Banda was arrested and charged with murder, but he died in 1997.

ECONOMY

The overthrow of Banda led to a restoration of political freedoms. The abolition of school fees and school uniforms nearly doubled school enrolment. Malawi remains one of the world's poorest countries. Reforms in the 1990s included encouraging small farmers to diversify production, but free enterprise and privatization angered some farmers who have suffered from the ending of subsidies.

Although fertile farmland is limited, agriculture dominates the economy employing more than 80% of the workforce. Tobacco is the leading export, followed by tea, sugar and cotton. The main food crops include cassava, groundnuts, maize, rice and sorghum. Many farmers raise cattle, goats and other livestock.

This flag was adopted when the Federation of Malaysia was set up in 1963. The red and white bands date back to a revolt in the 13th century. The star and crescent are symbols of Islam. The blue represents Malaysia's role in the Commonwealth.

Malaysia consists of two main parts, Peninsular Malaysia (the Malay peninsula) and northern Borneo. Peninsular Malaysia is made up of 11 states and two of the three components of the federal territory (Kuala Lumpur and Putrajaya). Northern Borneo comprises two states and one component of the federal territory (Labuan)

Peninsular Malaysia is dominated by fold mountains with a north–south axis. The most important is the Main Range, which runs from the Thai border to the south-east of Kuala Lumpur, reaching 2,182 m [7,159 ft] at its highest point, Gunong Kerbau. South of the Main Range lie the flat, poorly drained lowlands of Johor. The short rivers have built up a margin of lowlands around the coast.

Northern Borneo has a mangrove-fringed coastal plain, backed by hill country, with east–west fold mountains in the interior. The most striking mountain, and Malaysia's highest point, is the granite peak of Mount Kinabalu, in Sabah, at 4,101 m [13,455 ft].

CLIMATE

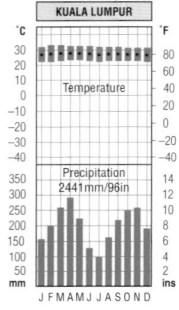

Malaysia has a hot equatorial climate. Temperatures are high all year, though the mountains are much cooler than lowland areas. Rainfall affects the whole country and is heavy throughout the year.

HISTORY

The Malay peninsula has long been a crossroads for sea traders from China and India. Hinduism and Buddhism were introduced from India in the 9th century AD. An early golden age of Malay political power came in the 15th century with the rise of the Kingdom of Malacca (now Melaka), on the south-western coast of the Malay peninsula. Malacca controlled the important sea routes and attracted traders from all parts of Asia. Arab traders introduced Islam and, in 1414, Malacca's ruler became a Muslim. Many of the people on the peninsula soon embraced Islam, which remains the official religion of Malaysia today.

The first Europeans to reach the area were the Portuguese and Malacca became a Portuguese possession in 1511. The Dutch, who had been trading in the area during the early 17th century, took Malacca in 1641, and many people from the Dutch-controlled Sulawesi and Sumatra settled in the peninsula, adding to the region's complex ethnic mix. The British, who had been seeking a suitable trading post in South-east Asia, took over Malacca in 1794 and though Malacca was returned to the Dutch in 1814, it reverted to British rule in 1824. Through the activities of Stamford Raffles, an agent for the British-owned East India Company, Singapore was occupied by the British in 1819 and made a British territory in 1824. The Straits Settlement, consisting of Penang (now Pinang), Malacca and Singapore, was founded by the British in 1826. In 1867, the Straits Settlement became a British colony. British rule was gradually extended, with Sabah and Sarawak becoming a British protectorate in 1888. In 1896, Negeri Sembilan, Penang, Perak and Selangor became the Federated Malay States. Under British rule, the economy developed and thousands of Chinese and Indian workers came to work on the rubber plantations.

Japan occupied the area that is now Malaysia and Singapore during World War II, but British rule was restored in 1945 following Japan's defeat. In the late 1940s and 1950s, inspired by the Chinese revolution, Communists fought the British, but guerrilla warfare ended with the independence of the Federation of Malaya in 1957. In 1963, Malaya joined with Singapore, and what is now Sabah and Sarawak, to form the nation of Malaysia, with Tunku Abdul Rahman of the Alliance Party as prime minister. Brunei was invited to join, but no agreement was achieved on entry terms. Arguments between Singapore and the Malaysian government occurred from the outset, causing Singapore to withdraw in 1965, and become an independent sovereign state.

One of the problems faced by the nation has been its great ethnic and religious diversity, with Malays of both Chinese and Indian origin, many brought in by the British to work the tin mines and rubber plantations. There are also a number of Eurasians, Europeans and aboriginal peo-

Area 329,758 sq km [127,320 sq mi]
Population 23,522,000
Capital (population) Kuala Lumpur (1,145,000), Putrajaya (administrative centre)
Government Constitutional monarchy
Ethnic groups Malay and other indigenous groups 58%, Chinese 24%, Indian 8%, others
Languages Malay (official), Chinese, English
Religions Islam, Buddhism, Daoism, Hinduism, Christianity, Sikhism
Currency Ringgit = 100 cents
Website www.tourism.gov.my

KUALA LUMPUR (MALAY, 'ESTUARY MUD')

Capital of Malaysia, southern Malay Peninsula. Founded in 1857, Kuala Lumpur became the capital of the Federated Malay States in 1895, capital of the Federation of Malaya in 1957, and capital of Malaysia in 1963. A commercial city, its striking modern architecture includes one of the world's tallest buildings, the twin Petronas Towers, at 452 m [1,483 ft]. Industries include tin and rubber.

Dragon Sculpture *at Buddhist Temple, Penang Island*

ples, notably in Sabah and Sarawak. This patchwork has caused tensions, especially between the Muslim Malays and the politically dominant, mainly Buddhist, Chinese. But while riots did break out in 1969, there was never any escalation into serious armed conflict, nor was economic development effected.

Malaysia faced attacks by Indonesia, which objected to Sabah and Sarawak joining Malaysia. Indonesia's policy of 'confrontation' forced Malaysia to increase its defence expenditure. Malaysia was also reluctant to have dealings with Communist countries, but at the same time was keen to remain independent of the Western bloc and aware of the need for South-east Asian nations to work together. From 1967, it was playing a major part in regional affairs, especially through its membership of ASEAN (Association of South-east Asian Nations), together with Indonesia, the Philippines, Singapore and Thailand. (Later members of ASEAN include Brunei in 1984, Vietnam in 1995, Laos and Burma (Myanmar) in 1997, and Cambodia in 1999.)

POLITICS

From the 1970s, Malaysia achieved rapid economic progress, especially under the leadership of Dr Mahathir Mohamad, who became prime minister in 1981. Mahathir encouraged the development of industry in order to diversify the economy and reduce the country's reliance on agriculture and mining. The first Malaysian car, the Proton Saga, went into production in 1985 and by the early 1990s, manufacturing accounted for about 20% of the gross domestic product. and by 1996 its share of the GDP had risen to nearly 35%. However, as with many of the economic 'tigers' in Asia's eastern rim, Malaysia was hit by a recession in 1997–8. In response to the crisis, the government ordered the repatriation of many temporary foreign workers and initiated a series of austerity measures aimed at restoring confidence and avoiding the chronic debt problems affecting some other Asian countries. In 1998, the economy shrank by about 5%.

During the economic crisis, differences developed between Mahathir Mohamad and his deputy prime minister and finance minister, Anwar Ibrahim. Anwar wanted Malaysia to work closely with the International Monetary Fund (IMF) to promote domestic reforms and strict monetary and fiscal policies. By the summer of 1998, he had gone further, attacking corruption and nepotism in government. Mahathir, who was suspicious of international 'plots' to undermine Malaysia's economy, put much of the blame for the crisis on foreign speculators. He sacked Anwar from the government and also from the ruling United Malays National Organization (UMNO). Anwar was later convicted of conspiracy and charged with sexual misconduct. He was jailed for six years.

In late 1999, Mahathir called a snap election to consolidate his power and strengthen his mandate to deal with the economy. With the economy appearing to be rebounding from recession, Mahathir's coalition retained its two-thirds majority in parliament. But many Malays voted for the conservative Muslim Parti Islam. This meant that Mahathir had to rely more on the Chinese and Indian parties in his coalition. The opposition also gained strength by forming a united front at the 1999 elections. In 2003, Mahathir was succeeded by Abdullah Ahmad Badawi, who won a landslide victory in 2004.

ECONOMY

The World Bank classifies Malaysia as an 'upper-middle-income' developing country. Manufacturing is the most important sector of the economy and accounts for a sizeable proportion of the exports. The manufacture of electronic equipment is now a major industry, and, by 1994, Malaysia ranked second in the world in producing radios and fifth in television receivers. Other electronic products include clocks, semiconductors for computers, stereo equipment, tape recorders and telephones. Other major industrial products include chemicals, petroleum products, plastics, processed food, textiles and clothing, rubber and wood products. Partly because of industrialization, Malaysia is becoming increasingly urbanized. By 2000, about 57% of the population lived in cities and towns.

Malaysia leads the world in the production of palm oil, and, in the mid-1990s, it ranked third in producing natural rubber. Malaysia also ranked fifth in the production of cocoa beans. Other important crops include

BRUNEI

Negara Brunei Darussalam (as Brunei is offically known), is a sultanate located in north Borneo, south-east Asia.

Bounded in the north-west by the South China Sea, the country consists of humid plains with forested mountains that run along its southern border with Malaysia.

Area 5,765 sq km [2,226 sq mi]
Population 358,000
Capital (population) Banda Seri Begawan (55,000)
Government Constitutional sultanate
Ethnic groups Malay 67%, Chinese 15%, others
Languages Malay (official), Chinese, English
Religions Islam (official) 67%, Buddhist 13%, Christian 10%, indigenous beliefs and others
Currency Bruneian dollar = 100 cents
Website www.brunei.gov.bn/index.htm

CLIMATE Brunei has an equatorial climate. Temperatures range from 23-32°C [73-90°F]. There is high humidity. Rainfall varies from 2,500 mm [98 in] on the coast to 7,500 mm [295 in] inland, but there is no defined rainy season.

HISTORY AND POLITICS During the 16th century, Brunei ruled over the whole of Borneo and parts of the Philippines. Brunei gradually lost its influence in the region. This was caused by problems regarding royal succession combined with European colonialism. It became a British protectorate in 1888.

In 1970 the capital, Brunei Town, was renamed Banda Seri Begawan. Brunei achieved independence in 1983. It has been ruled by the same family for over six centuries. The Sultan has executive authority.

ECONOMY Oil and gas are the main source of income, accounting for 70% of GDP. Recently, attempts have been made to increase agricultural production.

Lights illuminate *the Waqaf Mosque in Bandar Seri Begawan*

apples, bananas, coconuts, pepper, pineapples and many other tropical fruits, rice (Malaysia's chief food crop), sugar cane, tea and tobacco. Some farmers raise livestock, including cattle, pigs and poultry. The country's rainforests contain large reserves of timber, and wood and wood products, including plywood and furniture, play an important part in the economy.

The mining of tin is important with Malaysia the eighth largest producer of tin ore in the world. There is also bauxite, copper, gold, iron ore and ilmenite (an ore from which titanium is obtained). Since the 1970s, the production of oil and natural gas has steadily increased.

By the mid-1990s, the country's leading exports were machinery and transport equipment, accounting for about 55% of the value of the exports. Other exports included manufactures, mineral fuels, animal and vegetable oils, inedible raw materials and food.

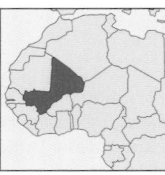

The colours on Mali's flag are those used on the flag of Ethiopia, Africa's oldest independent nation. They symbolize African unity. This flag was used by Mali's African Democratic Rally prior to the country becoming independent from France in 1960.

Area 1,240,192 sq km [478,838 sq mi]
Population 11,957,000
Capital (population) Bamako (1,016,000)
Government Multiparty republic
Ethnic groups Mande 50% (Bambara, Malinke, Soninke), Peul 17%, Voltaic 12%, Songhai 6%, Tuareg and Moor 10%, others
Languages French (official) and many African languages
Religions Islam 90%, Traditional beliefs 9%, Christianity 1%
Currency CFA franc = 100 centimes
Website www.officetourisme-mali.com

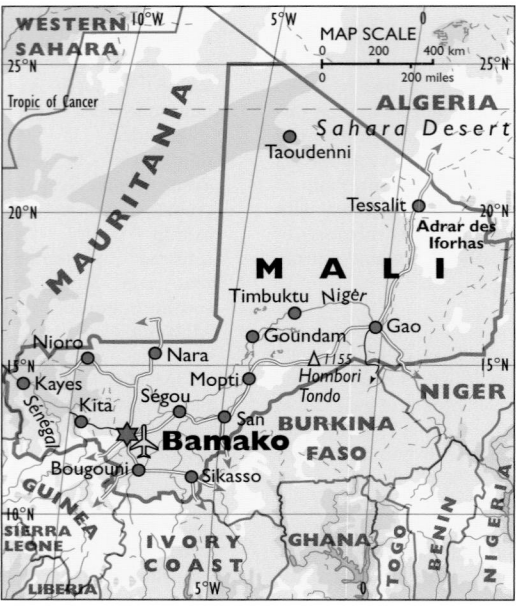

The Republic of Mali is the largest country in west Africa. It is mainly flat, with the highest land in the Adrar des Iforhas on the border with Algeria. Saharan Mali contains many wadis (dry river valleys). The old trading city of Timbuktu lies on the edge of the desert. The only permanent rivers are in the south, the main rivers being the Sénégal, which flows westwards to the Atlantic Ocean to the north of Kayes, and the Niger, which makes a large turn, called the Niger Bend, in south-central Mali.

More than 70% of Mali is desert or semi-desert with sparse vegetation. Central and south-eastern Mali is a dry grassland region known as the Sahel. In prolonged droughts, the northern Sahel dries up and becomes part of the Sahara. Fertile farmland and tropical savanna covers southern Mali, the most densely populated region.

CLIMATE

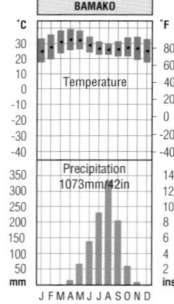

Northern Mali is part of the Sahara, with a hot, practically rainless climate. But the south has enough rain for farming. In the south-west of the country, unpleasant weather is experienced when dry and dusty harmattan winds blow from the Sahara Desert.

HISTORY

From the 4th to the 16th centuries, Mali was part of three major black African cultures – ancient Ghana, Mali and Songhai. Reports on these empires were made by Arab scholars who crossed the Sahara to visit them. One major centre was Timbuktu (Tombouctou), in central Mali. In the 14th century, this town was a great centre of learning in history, law and the Muslim religion. It was also a trading centre and stopping point for Arabs and their camel caravans. At its height, the Mali Empire was West Africa's richest and most powerful state. However, following the defeat of the Songhai empire by Morocco in 1591, the area was divided into small kingdoms.

In 1893, the region became known as French Sudan, and was incorporated into the Federation of West Africa in 1898. Nationalist movements grew more vocal in their opposition to colonialism. In 1958, French Sudan voted to join the French

BAMAKO

Capital of Mali, on the River Niger, 145 km [90 mi] north-east of the border with Guinea. Once a centre of Muslim learning (11th–15th centuries), it was occupied by the French in 1883 and became capital of the French Sudan (1908). Industries include shipping, groundnuts, meat, and metal products.

Community as an autonomous republic. In 1959, it joined with Senegal to form the Federation of Mali.

POLITICS

Shortly after gaining independence, Senegal seceded and, in 1960, Mali became a one-party republic. Its first president, Modibo Keita, committed Mali to nationalization and pan-Africanism. Mali adopted its own currency in 1962 and in 1963, it joined the Organization of African States (OAS). Economic crisis forced Keita to revert to the franc zone, and permit France greater economic influence. Opposition led to Keita's overthrow in a military coup in 1968. The military formed a National Liberation Committee and appointed Moussa Traoré as prime minister. During the 1970s, the Sahel suffered a series of droughts that contributed to a devastating famine in which thousands of people died.

In 1979, Mali adopted a new constitution, and Traoré was elected president. In 1991, a military coup overthrew Traoré, and a new constitution (1992) saw the establishment of a multiparty democracy. Alpha Oumar Konaré, leader of the Alliance for Democracy in Mali (ADEMA), won the ensuing presidential election. A political settlement provided a special administration for Tuaregs in northern Mali. Konaré was re-elected in 1997. In 1999, he commuted Traoré's death sentence for corruption to life imprisonment. General Amadou Toumani Toure succeeded Konaré as president in 2002 elections.

ECONOMY

Mali is one of the world's poorest countries and 70% of the land is desert or semi-desert. Only about 2% of the land is used for growing crops, while 25% is used for grazing animals. Despite this, agriculture employs nearly 85% of the workforce, many of whom still subsist by nomadic livestock rearing. Farming is hampered by water shortages, and the severe droughts in the 1970s and 1980s led to a great loss of animals and much human suffering. The farmers in the south grow millet, rice, sorghum and other food crops to feed their families.

The chief cash crops are cotton, groundnuts and sugar cane. Many of these crops are grown on land which is irrigated with river water. Only a few small areas in the south are worked without irrigation, while the barren deserts in the north are populated only by a few poor nomads. Fishing is an important economic activity. Mali has vital mineral deposits of gold and salt.

*A **Peul man** stands outside the village mosque in Djenne*

A red flag with a white cross was used by the Knights of Malta. In 1943 a George Cross was added after the award bestowed by King George VI of Britain. Upon independence, in 1964 a red edge was added to the cross.

VALLETTA

Port and capital of Malta, on the north-east coast of the island. Founded in the 16th century, it was named after Jean Parisot de la Valette, Grand Master of the Order of the Knights of St John, who organized the reconstruction of the city after repelling the Turks' Great Siege of 1565. Notable sights include the Royal University of Malta (1592) and the Cathedral of San Giovanni (1576).

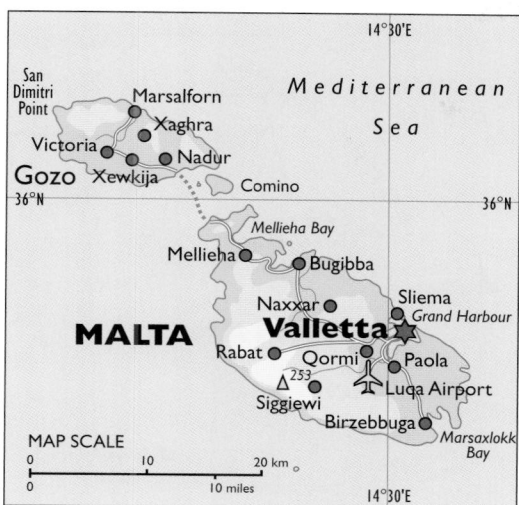

Area 316 sq km [122 sq mi]
Population 397,000
Capital (population) Valetta (9,000)
Government Multiparty republic
Ethnic groups Maltese 96%, British 2%
Languages Maltese and English (both official)
Religions Roman Catholic 98%
Currency Maltese lira = 100 cents
Website www.gov.mt

The Republic of Malta is an archipelago republic in the Mediterranean Sea, 100 km [60 mi] south of Sicily. Malta consists of two main islands, Malta (246 sq km [95 sq mi]) and Gozo (67 sq km [26 sq mi]), the small island of Comino, lies between the two large islands. There are also two tiny islets.

The islands are low-lying. Malta island is composed mostly of limestone. Gozo is largely covered by clay, and as a result its landscapes are less arid. Malta has no forests, and 38% of the land is arable.

CLIMATE

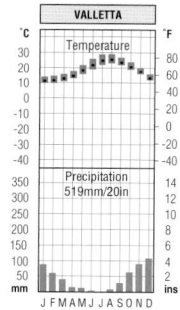

Malta is typically Mediterranean. Summers are hot and dry. Winters are mild and wet. The sirocco, a hot wind from North Africa, can raise temperatures considerably in the spring.

HISTORY

Malta has evidence of Stone Age settlement dating back 4,000 years. In 850 BC, the Phoenicians colonized Malta. The Carthaginians, Greeks, and Romans followed. In AD 395, Malta became part of the Eastern Roman (Byzantine) Empire. In 870, the Arab invasion brought Islam, but Roger I, Norman King of Sicily, restored Christian rule in 1091. In 1530, the Holy Roman Emperor gave Malta to the Knights Hospitallers. In 1565, the Knights, held Malta against a Turkish siege. In 1798, the French captured Malta but, with help from Britain, they were driven out in 1800. In 1814, Malta became a British colony and a strategic military base.

During World War I, Malta was an important naval base. In World War II, Italian and German aircraft bombed the islands. In recognition of the bravery of the Maltese resistance, the British King George VI awarded the George Cross to Malta in 1942. Malta became a base for NATO in 1953.

POLITICS

Malta became independent in 1964, and a republic in 1974. Britain's military agreement with Malta expired in 1979, with Malta then ceasing to be a military base. In the 1980s, the people declared Malta neutral. Malta applied to join the European Union in the 1990s, but the application was scrapped when the

Labour Party won the elections in 1996. But, following its election defeat in 1998, the bid for EU membership was renewed and Malta finally became a member in 2004.

ECONOMY

The World Bank classifies Malta as an 'upper-middle income' developing country, although it lacks natural resources. Most of the workforce is employed in commercial shipbuilding, manufacturing and the tourist industry. Machinery and transport equipment account for more than 50% of exports. Manufacturing industries include chemicals, electronic equipment and textiles. The rocky soil makes farming difficult, Malta produces only 20% of its food. It has a small fishing industry.

MALTESE (MALTI)

Maltese is a Semitic language, that is, one of a group of languages spoken by peoples native to North Africa and the Middle East and forming one of the five branches of the Afro-Asiatic language family. It is spoken by about 340,000 people in Malta and Gozo, and is the only Semitic tongue officially written in the Latin alphabet. The modern language is closely related to western Arabic dialects, but it also shows the strong influence of the Latin that was spoken in Malta. The language developed from the Arabic spoken by the Arabs who invaded Malta in 870. French-speaking Roger I, Norman King of Sicily, ruled from 1091. In 1530 the Knights Hospitallers, who spoke Italian and Latin, were given Malta by the Holy Roman Emperor and it remained under their rule until 1798. In 1814, Malta became a British colony and the British endeavoured to make English the local language. After independence in 1964 Maltese became the national language.

***Marsaxlokk Bay**, on the south-east coast*

The Islamic Republic of Mauritania adopted its flag in 1959, the year before it became fully independent from France. It features a yellow star and crescent. These are traditional symbols of the national religion, Islam, as also is the colour green.

Area 1,025,520 sq km [395,953 sq mi]
Population 2,999,000
Capital (population) Nouakchott (735,000)
Government Multiparty Islamic republic
Ethnic groups Mixed Moor/Black 40%, Moor 30%, Black 30%
Languages Arabic and Wolof (both official), French
Religions Islam
Currency Ouguiya = 100 5 khoums
Website www.mauritania.mr

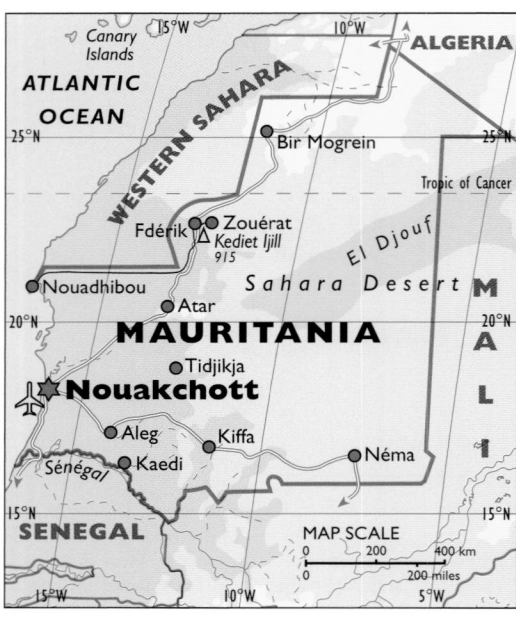

The Islamic Republic of Mauritania in north-western Africa is nearly twice the size of France, though France's population is more than 28 times that of Mauritania. Over two-thirds of the land is barren, most of it being part of the Sahara. Apart from a small nomadic population, most Mauritanians live in the south, either on the plains bordering the Senegal River in the south-west or on the tropical savanna in the south-east. The highest point is Kediet Ijill (915 m [3,002 ft]). It is an area rich in haematite (high-quality iron ore).

CLIMATE

The amount of rain and the length of the rainy season increases north to south. The desert is dry north-east and easterly winds throughout the year. South-westerly winds bring summer rain to the south.

HISTORY

From the 4th to the 16th centuries, parts of Mauritania belonged to two great African empires – ancient Ghana and Mali. Portuguese explorers arrived in the 1440s.

European contact did not begin in the area until the 17th century when trade in gum arabic, a substance obtained from an acacia tree, became important, with Britain, France and the Netherlands to the fore. France set up a protectorate in Mauritania in 1903, attempting to exploit the trade in gum arabic. In 1920 the country became a French colony and a territory of French West Africa (an area that included present-day Benin, Burkina Faso, Guinea, Ivory Coast, Mali, Niger and Senegal, as well as Mauritania). Mauritania became a self-governing territory in the French Union in 1958, achieving full independence in 1960.

BANC D'ARGUIN

Lying on the coast of Mauritania, the Banc d'Arguin is the most important area of intertidal flats on the coast of Africa. In winter it is home to over 2 million shorebirds, while some 40,000 waterbirds, including great white pelicans, greater flamingos, spoonbills, and several species of tern also breed here. The Banc d'Arguin is also an important fishing area and the Imraguen fishing community and their predecessors have lived from the local fishery for the past 500 years or more. The sight of their lanteen sailed boats working their way up the channels between the mudflats, backed by the dunes of the Sahara, is a unique spectacle in Africa.

Courtyard embellished *with a relief design of pigment-filled shapes, cut into a mud wall, Oualata in the south-east of the country*

POLITICS

In 1961, Mauritania's political parties were merged into one by the president, Mokhtar Ould Daddah, who made the country a one-party state. Upon the withdrawal by Spain from Spanish (now Western) Sahara, a territory bordering Mauritania to the north, in 1976,. Morocco occupied the northern two-thirds of the territory, while Mauritania took the rest. Saharan guerrillas belonging to POLISARIO (the Popular Front for the Liberation of Saharan Territories) then began an armed struggle for independence. In 1979, Mauritania withdrew from the southern part of Western Sahara, then occupied by Morocco.

From 1978, Mauritania was ruled by a series of military regimes. In 1991, the country adopted a new constitution when the people voted to create a multiparty democracy. In 1992, an army colonel, Maaouiya Ould Sidi Ahmed Taya, who had served as leader of a military administration since December 1984, was elected president. However, subsequent legislative elections in 1992 were boycotted by opposition parties. Taya was re-elected in 1997 and 2003.

ECONOMY

The World Bank classifies Mauritania as a 'low-income' developing country. Agriculture employs over half the workforce, with the majority living at subsistence level. Many are still cattle herders who drive their herds from the Senegal River through the Sahelian steppelands, coinciding with the seasonal rains. However, droughts in the 1980s greatly reduced the domestic animal populations, forcing many nomadic farmers to seek help in urban areas. Plagues of locusts in 2004 also caused severe damage. Farmers in the south-east grow such crops as beans, dates, millet, rice and sorghum. Rich fishing grounds lie off the coast. The country's chief natural resource is iron ore and the vast reserves around Fderik provide a major source of revenue.

NOUAKCHOTT

Capital of Mauritania, north west Africa, in the south-western part of the country, 8 km [5 mi] from the Atlantic Ocean. Originally a small fishing village, it was chosen as capital when Mauritania became independent in 1960. Nouakchott now has an international airport and is the site of modern storage facilities for petroleum. Light industries have been developed and handicrafts are important.

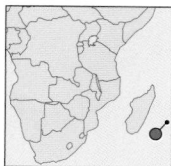

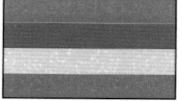

The flag is unique in having four equal horizontal bands. The colours derive from Mauritius' coat of arms. Red is for the blood shed in the liberation struggle, blue for the Indian Ocean, yellow for the bright future afforded by independence, and green for the islands' lush vegetation.

The Republic of Mauritius consists of the large island of Mauritius, which is situated 800 km [500 mi] east of Madagascar. This island makes up just over 90% of the country, which also includes the island of Rodrigues, about 560 km [348 mi] east of Mauritius, and several small islands. The main island is fringed by coral reefs, lagoons and sandy beaches. The land in the interior rises to a high lava plateau (828 m [2,717 ft]) enclosed by rocky peaks.

CLIMATE

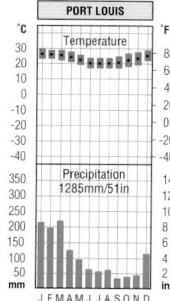

Mauritius has a tropical climate, with heavy rains in the winter. South-east winds bring rain to the interior plateau of the main island, which is also occasionally hit by destructive tropical cyclones in summer. Average annual rainfall on the interior plateau may reach 5,100 mm [200 in]. The south-west is much drier, with about 890 mm [35 in]. Temperatures range from 22°C [72°F] in the winter (June to October) to 26°C [79°F] in the summer (November to April).

HISTORY

In 1498, Vasco da Gama's fleet accidentally saw the island and, in 1510, a Portuguese navigator, Pedro Mascarenhas, arrived and named it Cimé. Later Portuguese navigators used the island as a port of call, but no permanent settlement was established. In 1598, the Dutch became the first nation to claim the island and they renamed it after Maurice, Prince of Orange and Count of Nassau. However, an attempt at settlement failed in the 1650s. A second attempt was abandoned in 1710, by which time the famous dodo, which was unique to Mauritius, had become extinct. Following the Dutch withdrawal, the island became a haven for pirates.

The French East India Company claimed Mauritius for France in 1715 and named it the Isle de France. The French developed the economy and imported African slaves. In 1767, control of the island passed to the French government, although the settlers revolted in 1796 when the French government tried to abolish slavery.

PORT LOUIS

Capital of Mauritius, a seaport in the northwest of the island. It was founded by the French in 1735. Taken by the British during the Napoleonic Wars, it grew in importance as a trading port after the opening of the Suez Canal. Industries include sugar, electrical equipment and textiles.

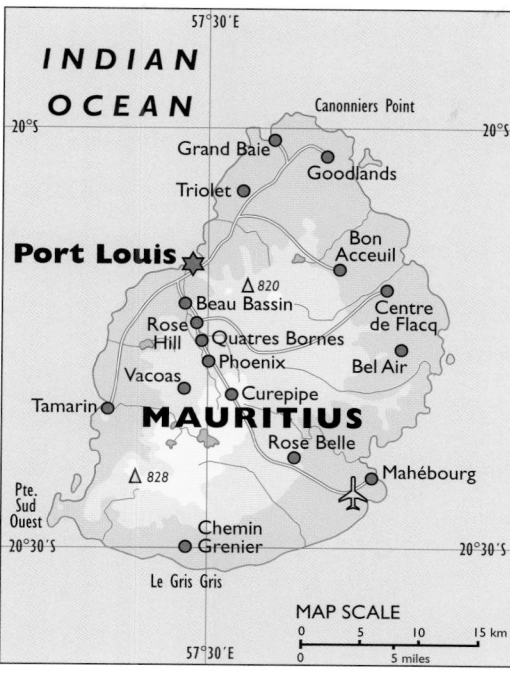

Women harvest peanuts *from the roots of a peanut plant*

British forces landed on Mauritius in 1810, starting a period of British rule. In 1834, Britain abolished slavery on the island which they renamed Mauritius. Most former slaves refused to work on the sugar plantations and so Britain introduced indentured labourers from India, recruiting around 450,000 workers between 1837 and 1910, when indentured labour was ended.

In 1926, the first Indo-Mauritians were elected to the government council while, in 1936, a Creole politician, Dr Maurice Cure, founded the Mauritian Labour Party (MLP). In 1942, representatives from all Mauritian communities were invited to serve on consultative committees and, in 1948, many Indian and Creole were given the vote in elections to a new, enlarged legislature. Internal self-government was introduced in 1957. Elections were held under universal adult suffrage following the introduction of a new constitution in 1958. The MLP, led by Dr Seewoosagur Ramgoolam, won a majority. However, ethnic riots between Indians and Creoles occurred in 1964.

POLITICS

Mauritius became independent in 1968. In 1969, Paul Berenger founded the socialist Mauritian Militant Movement (MMM). In 1971, the MMM supported strikers and organized opposition to the government. In response, the government declared a state of emergency which lasted until 1976. The MMM won the 1992 elections and Anerood Jugnauth became prime minister.

Mauritius became a republic in 1992 and Caseem Uteem of the MMM was elected president. In 1995, an alliance led by Navin Ramgoolam and Paul Berenger won the elections and Ramgoolam became prime minister. But Jugnauth was returned to power in 2000. He served as prime minister until 2003, when he handed over to Paul Berenger, who had been his deputy. Berenger was the first non-Hindu to become prime minister. Navin Ramgoolam again became prime minister after elections in July 2005.

Despite tensions between the Indian and Creole communities, Mauritius is a stable democracy with free elections and a good human rights record. As a result, it has attracted foreign investment.

ECONOMY

Mauritius has become one of Africa's success stories. It is now a middle-income country with a diversified economy. Arable land covers more than half of the country and sugar cane plantations cover about 90% of the cultivated land. Sugar remains a major export, tea and tobacco are also grown. Agriculture and fishing employ 14% of the workforce, compared with 36% in construction and industry. Textiles and clothing are the leading exports. Mauritius has growing industrial and financial sectors and is now a major tourist centre.

Area 2,040 sq km [788 sq mi]
Population 1,220,000
Capital (population) Port Louis (148,000)
Government Multiparty republic
Ethnic groups Indo-Mauritian 68%, Creole 27%, Sino-Mauritian 3%, Franco-Mauritian 2%
Languages English (official), Creole, French, Hindi, Urdu, Hakka, Bojpoori
Religions Hindu 50%, Roman Catholic 27%, Muslim (largely Sunni) 16%, Protestant 5%
Currency Mauritian rupee = 100 cents
Website www.gov.mu

Mexico's flag dates from 1821. The stripes were inspired by the French tricolour. The emblem in the centre contains an eagle, a snake and a cactus. It is based on an ancient Aztec legend about the founding of their capital, Tenochtitlán (now Mexico City).

Area 1,958,201 sq km [756,061 sq mi]
Population 104,960,000
Capital (population) Mexico City (4,000)
Government Federal republic
Ethnic groups Mestizo 60%, Amerindian 30%, White 9%
Languages Spanish (official)
Religions Roman Catholic 90%, Protestant 6%
Currency Mexican peso = 100 centavos
Website www.presidencia.gob.mx

The United Mexican States is the world's largest Spanish-speaking country. It is largely mountainous. The Sierra Madre Occidental begins in the north-west state of Chihuahua, and runs parallel to Mexico's west coast and the Sierra Madre Oriental. Monterrey lies in the foothills of the latter. Between the two ranges lies the Mexican Plateau. The southern part of the plateau contains a series of extinct volcanoes, rising to Orizaba, at 5,700 m [18,701 ft]. The southern highlands of the Sierra Madre del Sur include the archaeological sites in Oaxaca. Mexico contains two large peninsulas: the Baja California in the north-west; and the Yucatán peninsula in the south-east.

CLIMATE

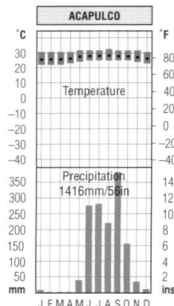

Mexico's climate is hugely varied according to altitude. Most rain occurs between June and September. More than 70% of Mexico experiences desert or semi-desert conditions.

Pyramid of Kukulcan, *Chichen-Itza*

MEXICO CITY

Capital of Mexico, at 2,380 m [7,800 ft], in a volcanic basin in the centre of the country. As the nation's political, economic and cultural centre, it suffers from overcrowding and pollution. Hernán Cortés destroyed the former Aztec capital (Tenochtitlán) in 1521. A new city was built, acting as the capital of Spain's New World colonies for 300 years. US troops occupied it in 1847, during the Mexican War. In 1863, French troops took the city, establishing Maximilian as Emperor. Benito Juárez's forces recaptured it in 1867. From 1914–15, Emiliano Zapata and Francisco Villa's revolutionary forces captured and lost the city three times.

HISTORY

Many Native American civilizations flourished in Mexico. The Olmec (800–400 BC), the Maya (AD 300–900), the Toltec Empire (900–1200). But it was the Aztec who dominated the central plateau from their capital at Tenochtitlán.

In 1519, Spanish conquistadors captured the capital and the Aztec emperor Montezuma. In 1535, the territory became the Viceroyalty of New Spain. Christianity was introduced. Spanish rule was harsh, divisive, and unpopular. Hidalgo y Costillo's revolt (1810) failed to win the support of creoles.

Mexico became independent in 1821 and a republic in 1824. War with Texas escalated into the Mexican War (1846–8) with the United States. Under the terms of the Treaty of Guadalupe-Hidalgo (1848), Mexico lost 50% of its territory. Liberal forces, led by Benito Juárez, triumphed in the War of Reform (1858–61), but conservatives with support from France installed Maximilian of Austria as Emperor in 1864. In 1867, republican rule was restored and Juárez became president. In 1876, an armed revolt gave Porfirio Díaz the presidency, his dictatorship lasted until 1910. Huerta's took power in 1913, his dictatorship prolonged the Mexican Revolution (1910–40) and led to US intervention. During the 1920s and 1930s, Mexico introduced land and social reforms. After World War II, Mexico's economy developed with the introduction of liberal reforms. Relations with the US improved but problems remain over Mexican economic migration and drug trafficking.

POLITICS

The Institutional Revolutionary Party (PRI) ruled Mexico continuously from 1929 to 2000. In 1994 the Zapatista National Liberation Army (ZNLA) staged an armed revolt in the southern state of Chiapas, calling for land reforms and recognition of Native American rights. Vicente Fox became the first non-PRI leader of Mexico in 2000. In 2001, after a nationwide march by the Zapatistas, the Mexican parliament passed a new rights' bill for indigenous peoples.

ECONOMY

The World Bank classifies Mexico as an 'upper-middle-income' developing country. Agriculture is important. Oil and oil products are the chief exports, while manufacturing is the most valuable activity. Many factories near the northern border assemble goods such as car parts and electrical products, for US companies, known as *maquiladoras*.

Adopted in 1990, using the same colours as the Romanian flag to emphasize their strong ties. Blue is for Transylvania, yellow for Wallachia, red for Moldavia. The eagle symbolizes the Byzantine Empire; the bison's head, star, rose and crescent, the medieval principality.

The Republic of Moldova is a small country sandwiched between Ukraine and Romania. It was formerly one of the 15 republics that made up the Soviet Union. Much of the land is hilly and the highest areas are near the centre of the country. The main river is the Dniester, which flows through eastern Moldova.

Forests of hornbeam and oak grow in northern and central Moldova. In the drier south, most of the region is now used for farming, with rich pasture along the rivers.

CLIMATE

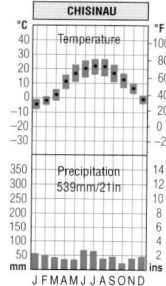

Moldova has a moderately continental climate, with warm summers and fairly cold winters when temperatures dip below freezing point. Most of the rain falls in the warmer months.

HISTORY

Moldavia was a historic Balkan region, between the Carpathian Mountains in Romania and the Dniester River.

Under Roman rule, it formed the major part of the province of Dacia, and today's population is Romanian-speaking. In the 14th century, it became an independent principality ruled by the Vlachs; its lands included Bessarabia and Bukovina. In 1504, the Turks conquered Moldavia, and it remained part of the Ottoman Empire until the 19th century.

In 1775, the Austrians gained Bukovina, and in 1815 Russia conquered Bessarabia. After the Russo-Turkish War (1828–9), Russia became the dominant power. In 1856, the twin principalities of Moldavia and Wallachia gained considerable autonomy. Three years later, they united under one crown to form Romania, but Russia reoccupied southern Bessarabia in 1878.

In 1920, Bessarabia and Bukovina were incorporated into the Romanian state. In 1924, the Soviet republic of Moldavia was formed, which in 1947 enlarged to include Bessarabia and northern Bukovina. In 1989, the Moldavians asserted their independence

CHISINAU (KISHINEV)

Capital of Moldova, in the centre of the country, on the River Byk. Founded in the early 15th century, it came under Turkish then Russian rule. Romania held the city from 1918 to 1940 when it was annexed by the Soviet Union. In 1991 it became capital of independent Moldova. It has a 19th-century cathedral and a university (1945). Industries include plastics, rubber, textiles, tobacco.

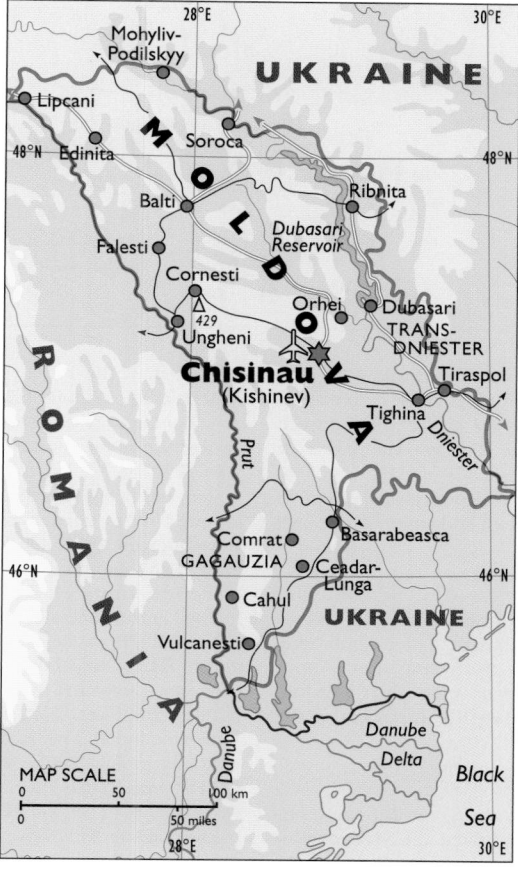

The Palace of Culture in Chisinau

Area 33,851 sq km [13,070 sq mi]
Population 4,446,000
Capital (population) Chisinau (658,000)
Government Multiparty republic
Ethnic groups Moldovan/Romanian 65%, Ukrainian 14%, Russian 13%, others
Languages Moldovan/Romanian, Russian (official)
Religions Eastern Orthodox 98%
Currency Moldovan leu = 100 bani
Website www.moldova.org/index/eng/

by making Romanian the official language, and in 1991, following the dissolution of the Soviet Union, Moldavia became the independent republic of Moldova.

POLITICS

Following independence in 1991, the majority Moldovan population wished to rejoin Romania, but this alienated the Ukrainian and Russian populations east of the Dniester, who declared their independence from Moldova as the Transdniester Republic. War raged between the two, with Transdniester supported by the Russian 14th Army. In August 1992, a cease-fire was declared.

The former Communists of the Agrarian Democratic Party won multiparty elections in 1994. A referendum rejected reunification with Romania. Parliament voted to join the Commonwealth of Independent States (CIS).

In 1994 a new constitution established a presidential parliamentary republic. In 1995, Transdniester voted in favour of independence in a referendum and in 1996, Russian troops began their withdrawal. On 1 January 1997, a former Communist, Petru Lucinschi, became president. In 1998 and 2001, the Party of the Moldovan Communists (PCRM) won the highest share of the votes. The constitution was changed in 2000, turning Moldova from a semi-presidential republic to a parliamentary republic. In 2001, the Communist leader Vladimir Voronin was elected president. The Communist party was re-elected in 2005, though it now advocates close ties with the West, a matter of some concern to Russia.

ECONOMY

According to the World Bank, Moldova is a lower-middle income developing country, and in terms of GNP per capita, Europe's poorest country. It is fertile and agriculture remains central to the economy. Major products include fruits, maize, tobacco and grapes for wine-making. Farmers also raise livestock, including dairy cattle and pigs.

There are few natural resources within Moldova, which means that the government is obliged to import materials and fuels for its industries. Light industries, such as food processing and the manufacturing of household appliances, are expanding.

Mongolia's flag contains blue, the national colour, together with red for Communism. The traditional Mongolian golden 'soyonbo' symbol represents freedom. Within this, the flame is seen as a promise of prosperity and progress.

Area 1,566,500 sq km [604,826 sq mi]
Population 2,751,000
Capital (population) Ulan Bator (760,000)
Government Multiparty republic
Ethnic groups Khalkha Mongol 85%, Kazakh 6%
Languages Khalkha Mongolian (official), Turkic, Russian
Religions Tibetan Buddhist Lamaism 96%
Currency Tugrik = 100 möngös
Website www.mongoliatourism.gov.mn

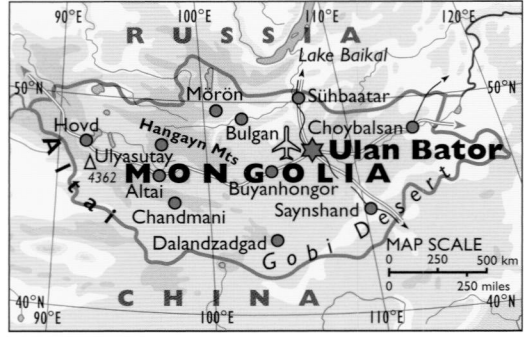

ULAN BATOR

Capital of Mongolia, on the River Tola. Ulan Bator dates back to the founding of the Lamaistic Temple of the Living Buddha in 1639. It grew as a stop for caravans between Russia and China and was later a focus for the Mongolian autonomy movement, becaming the capital in 1921. It is the political, cultural and economic centre of Mongolia. Industries include textiles, building materials, leather, paper, alcohol and carpets.

Mongolia, which is sandwiched between China and Russia, is the world's largest landlocked country. It consists mainly of high plateaux, the highest of which are in the west, between the Altai Mountains (or Aerhtai Shan) and the Hangayn Mountains (or Hangayn Nuruu).

The Altai Mountains contain the country's highest peaks (4,362 m [14,311 ft]). The land descends towards the east and south, where part of the Gobi Desert is situated.

CLIMATE

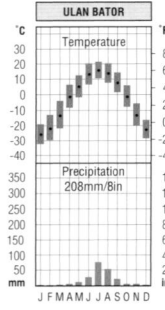

Due to its remote position, Mongolia has an extreme continental climate, with long, bitterly cold winters and short, warm summers. Annual rainfall ranges from no more than 500 mm [20 in] in the highlands to 125 mm [5 in] in the lowlands.

HISTORY

In the 13th century, the great Mongol conqueror Genghis Khan united the Mongol people, created a ruthless army, and founded the largest land empire in history. Under his grandson, Kublai Khan, the Mongol empire stretched from Korea and China, across Asia into what is now Iraq. In the north-west, Mongol rule extended beyond the Black Sea into eastern Europe. Learning flourished under Kublai Khan, but, after his death in 1294, the empire broke up into several parts. It was not until the late 16th century that Mongol princes reunited Mongolia. During their rule, they introduced Lamaism (a form of Buddhism).

In the early 17th century, the Manchu leaders of Manchuria took over Inner Mongolia. They conquered China in 1644 and Outer Mongolia some 40 years later. Present-day Mongolia then became a remote Chinese province scarcely in contact with the outside world.

Outer Mongolia broke away from China following the collapse of the Qing Dynasty in 1911, and the Mongols appointed a priest, the Living Buddha, as their king. Legally, Outer Mongolia remained Chinese territory, but China and Russia agreed to grant it control over its own affairs in 1913. Russian influence increased and, in 1921, Mongolian and Russian Communists took control of Outer Mongolia, proclaiming the Mongolian People's Republic in 1924.

POLITICS

Mongolia became an ally of the Soviet Union, its support being particularly significant from the 1950s, when the Soviet Union was in dispute with Mongolia's neighbour, China. The Soviet Union helped develop Mongolia's mineral reserves so by the late 1980s, minerals had overtaken agriculture as the country's main source of revenue.

In 1990, the people, influenced by reforms taking place in the Soviet Union, held demonstrations, demanding more freedom. Free elections in June 1990 resulted in victory for the Communist Mongolian People's Revolutionary Party (MPRP). The new government began to move away from Communist policies, launching into privatization and developing a free-market economy. The 'People's Democracy' was abolished in 1992 and democratic institutions were introduced.

The MPRP was defeated in elections in 1996 by the opposition Mongolian Democratic Union coalition. The Democratic Union ran into economic problems and, in the presidential elections of 1997, the MPRP candidate, Natasagiyn Babagandi, defeated the Democratic Union nominee. This achievement was followed by the parliamentary elections in July 2000, which resulted in a landslide victory for the MPRP, who gained 72 out of the 76 available seats in the Great Hural (parliament). The MPRP chairman, Nambaryn Enhbayar, became prime minister. Following disputed elections in 2004 a coalition government was set up.

ECONOMY

The World Bank classifies Mongolia as a 'lower-middle-income' developing country. Many Mongolians were once nomads, moving around with their livestock. Under Communist rule, most were moved into permanent homes on government-owned farms. Livestock and animal products remain important.

The Communists developed mining and manufacturing and by 1996, mineral products accounted for nearly 60% of the country's exports. Minerals produced in Mongolia include coal, copper, fluorspar, gold, molybdenum, tin and tungsten. The leading manufactures are textiles and metal products.

Taking a break during eagle training; it takes between four to six months to train an eagle for the hunt, after six or seven years, the eagle is released so it can breed in the wild and produce offspring for the next generation of Kazaks

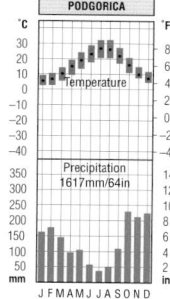

The flag of Montenegro has been in existence since 2004 when it was adopted by the Parliament of Montenegro. It is made up of a red background with the country's coat of arms which themselves derive from the coat of arms of King Nikola I who ruled 1910–1918.

The Republic of Montenegro, together with Serbia, was formerly part of Yugoslavia. In 2003, it became part of the Union of Serbia and Montenegro, but, in 2006, it became fully independent. Ethnic Montenegrins make up 62% of the population. There are Albanian, Croat, Muslim and Serb minorities.

CLIMATE

The coast has a Mediterranean climate, with hot, generally dry summers, with occasional thunderstorms, and mild, moist winters. Inland, the mountains have a more extreme climate, with heavy rainfall on the Dinaric Alps.

Area 14,026 sq km [5,415 sq mi]
Population 630,540
Capital (population) Podgorica (152,000)
Government Federal republic
Ethnic groups Montenegrin 43%, Serbian 32%, Bosniak 8%, Albanian 5%, others
Languages Serbian (Ijekavian dialect)
Religions Orthodox, Muslim, Roman Catholic
Currency Euro = 100 cents
Website www.montenegro.yu/english/naslovna

HISTORY

South Slavs began to move into the region around 1,500 years ago. Each group founded its own state. In the late 12th century, the province of Zeta (modern Montenegro) was incorporated into the Serbian empire. But it began to reassert its independence in the 14th century following the Turkish defeat of the Serbians in 1389. Between the 15th and 18th centuries, Serbia was part of the Turkish Ottoman Empire, while Montenegro was ruled by Christian dynasties headed by bishops who were elected by popular assemblies.

Montenegro's independence was recognized at the Congress of Berlin in 1878. Between 1860 and 1918, the country was ruled by Nicholas I, who declared himself king of Montenegro in 1910. In 1912-1913, Montenegro and Serbia joined in the fight against Turkey and, during World War I, Montenegro supported Serbia.

In 1918, Nicholas was dethroned and Montenegro was absorbed into Serbia. The South Slavs were united in the Kingdom of the Serbs, Croats and Slovenes. In 1929, King Alexander renamed the kingdom Yugoslavia. Italy occupied parts of Montenegro in 1941. But resistance continued until 1944, with Montenegrins prominent among the Communist-led partisans of Josip Broz Tito, who emerged victorious in 1945.

POLITICS

The new Federal People's Republic of Yugoslavia adopted a constitution in 1946, which recognized Montenegro as one of the six autonomous federal units in the republic. The capital of Montenegro was moved to Podgorica, then called Titograd. After Tito's death in 1980, the country was divided. In 1991-2, Yugoslavia broke up. Bosnia-Herzegovina, Croatia, Macedonia and Slovenia each proclaimed its independence, while the remaining republics of Serbia and Montenegro were jointly called Yugoslavia.

The break-up of the country was marked by ethnic conflict. In 1992, the United Nations withdrew recognition of Yugoslavia due to its failure to halt atrocities committed by Serbs living in Croatia and Bosnia-Herzegovina. However, in 1995, Yugoslavia took part in talks that led to the Dayton Peace Accord. In the 1990s, Yugoslavia was rocked by con-

PODGORICA

Capital of Montenegro at the confluence of the Ribnica and Moraca rivers. Podgorica has the mountains close by to the north, and to the south, the Adriatic Sea. The name Podgorica was first documented in the early 14th century, formerly Ribnica, after the river. It came under Turkish occupation from the late 15th to the late 19th century. After freedom from Turkish rule the city developed quickly as a financial and commercial centre. In 1946 it was renamed Titograd and became capital of Montenegro. The city flourished under Communist rule. The name Podgorica was reinstated in 1992.

flict in the autonomous province of Kosovo in southern Serbia. NATO forces intervened by launching attacks on administrative and industrial targets in Kosovo and Serbia.

Many people became increasingly opposed to Serbia's dominance in Yugoslavia and, in 2003, the country was reconstituted in a loose union called the Union of Serbia and Montenegro. Both republics became semi-independent, each with their own customs, currencies and laws. However, most ethnic Montenegrins and Albanians still favoured full independence. In 2006, by a narrow majority, Montenegrins voted to withdraw from the Union. Montenegro then became a fully independent republic led by its pro-independence prime minister, Milo Djukanovic.

ECONOMY

From the 1990s, the economy has been increasingly privatized. Manufacturing is the most valuable activity and steel and aluminium are major products. Farmers produce meat, dairy products and a variety of crops, including citrus fruits and olives. Forests cover about 54% of the country's surface area.

The Bay of Kotor, *on the Adriatic Sea in Montenegro is often regarded as one of the most beautiful in the world*

Morocco has flown a red flag since the 16th century. The green pentagram (five-pointed star), called the Seal of Solomon, was added in 1915. This design was retained when Morocco gained its independence from French and Spanish rule in 1956.

Area 446,550 sq km [172,413 sq mi]
Population 32,209,000
Capital (population) Rabat (1,220,000)
Government Constitutional monarchy
Ethnic groups Arab-Berber 99%
Languages Arabic (official), Berber dialects, French
Religions Islam 99%
Currency Moroccan dirham = 100 centimes
Website www.mincom.gov.ma

The Kingdom of Morocco lies in north-western Africa. Its name comes from the Arabic Maghreb-el-Aksa (the furthest west). Behind the western coastal plain the land rises to a broad plateau and the Atlas Mountains. The High (Haut) Atlas contains the highest peak, Djebel Toubkal, at 4,165 m [13,665 ft]. Other ranges include the Anti Atlas, the Middle (Moyen) Atlas and the Rif Atlas (or Er Rif). East of the mountains the land lies the arid Sahara.

CLIMATE

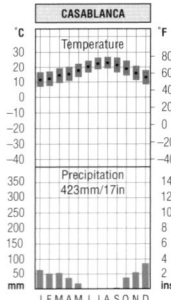

The Atlantic coast is cooled by the Canaries Current. Inland, summers are very hot and dry while winters are mild. From October to April south-westerly Atlantic winds bring rain; there is frequent snowfall in the High Atlas.

HISTORY

The original people of Morocco were the Berbers. In the 680s, Arab invaders introduced Islam and the Arabic language. By the early 20th century, France and Spain controlled Morocco.

It finally became an independent kingdom in 1956, becoming an independent monarchy in 1957 when Sidi Muhammad changed his title to King Muhammad V. In 1961, his son succeeded as King Hassan II.

POLITICS

King Hassan II ruled the country in an authoritarian way until his death in 1999. His successor, King Mohamed VI, faced a number of problems, including finding a solution to the future of Western Sahara. Relations with Spain became strained in 2002 over the disputed island of Leila (Perejil in Spanish), in the Strait of Gibraltar. Diplomatic relations were restored in 2003. Another problem faced by Morocco is activity by Islamic extremists. Its opposition to extremism led the United States to designate Morocco as a major non-NATO ally in 2004.

ECONOMY

Morocco is classified as a 'lower-middle-income' developing country. It is the world's third largest producer of phosphate rock. Farming employs 38% of Moroccans. Fishing and tourism are important.

WESTERN SAHARA

Desert territory on the Atlantic coast of north-west Africa, covering 266,769 sq km [102,680 sq mi]; the capital is El Aaiun. It comprises two districts: Saguia el Hamra in the north, and Río de Oro in the south. The population consists of Arabs, Berbers, and pastoral nomads, most of whom are Sunni Muslims.

The first European discovery was in 1434, but it remained unexploited until Spain took control of the coastal area in the 19th century. In 1957, a nationalist movement temporarily overthrew the Spanish but they regained control of the region in 1958, and merged the two districts to form the province of Spanish Sahara. Large phosphate deposits were discovered in 1963.

The Polisario Front began a guerrilla war in 1973, eventually forcing a Spanish withdrawal in 1976. Within a month, Morocco and Mau-

ritania partitioned the country. Polisario (backed by Algeria) continued to fight for independence, renaming the country the Saharawi Arab Democratic Republic. In 1979, Mauritania withdrew and Morocco assumed full control. In 1982, the Saharawi Republic became a member of the Organization of African Unity. By 1988 it controlled most of the desert up to the Moroccan defensive line. Fragile cease-fires were agreed in 1988 and 1991. About 200,000 Saharawis continue to live in refugee camps, mostly in Algeria. Talks between Morocco and Western Sahara began in 1997 and have been inconclusive.

Livestock-rearing dominates agriculture. The government hopes to diversify the economy and explore the prospects of offshore oil and gas fields. The islands benefit from a Danish subsidy which accounts for 15% of the GDP.

RABAT

Capital of Morocco, on the Atlantic coast, northern Morocco. Rabat dates from Phoenician times, but the fortified city was founded in the 12th century by the Almohad ruler, Abd al-Mumin. Under French rule, it was made the capital of the protectorate of Morocco.

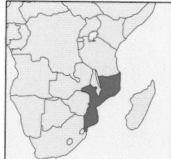

Mozambique's flag was adopted when the country became independent from Portugal in 1975. The green stripe represents fertile land, the black stands for Africa and the yellow for mineral wealth. The badge on the red triangle contains a rifle, a hoe, a cogwheel and a book.

The Republic of Mozambique borders the Indian Ocean in south-eastern Africa. The coastal plains are narrow in the north but broaden to the south making up nearly half of the country. Inland lie plateaux and hills, which make up another two-fifths of the country, with highlands along the borders with Zimbabwe, Zambia, Malawi and Tanzania.

CLIMATE

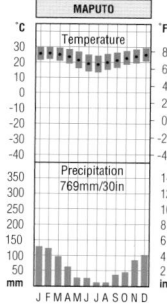

Most of Mozambique has a tropical maritime climate, with two main seasons. The hot, wet season runs from November to March, with a dry, milder season between April and October. Rainfall varies, being greatest on the north-western highlands and lowest on the south-eastern lowlands.

Temperatures in the lowlands vary from between 20°C and 30°C [79–86°F] in January, and between 11°C and 15°C [52–59°F] in January. The interior highlands are much cooler and generally less humid.

HISTORY

Arab traders began to operate in the area in the 9th century AD, with Portuguese explorers arriving in 1497. The Portuguese set up trading stations in the early 16th century and the area became a source of slaves. When the European powers divided Africa in 1885, Mozambique was recognized as a Portuguese colony. Black African opposition to European rule gradually increased and in 1961, the Front for the Liberation of Mozambique (FRELIMO) was founded to oppose Portuguese rule. FRELIMO launched a guerrilla war in 1964, which continued for ten years. Mozambique achieved independence in 1975, when the Marxist-Leninist FRELIMO, took over the government.

POLITICS

After independence, Mozambique became a one-party state. Its government aided African nationalists in Rhodesia (now Zimbabwe) and South Africa. However, the white governments of these countries helped an opposition group, the Mozambique National Resistance Movement (RENAMO), to lead an armed struggle against Mozambique's government. This civil war, combined with severe droughts, caused much human suffering in the 1980s.

In 1989, FRELIMO declared that it had dropped its Communist policies and ended one-party rule. The war officially ended in 1992 and multiparty elections in 1994 were won by FRELIMO, whose leader, Joaquim

Area 801,590 sq km [309,494 sq mi]
Population 18,812,000
Capital (population) Maputo (1,015,000)
Government Multiparty republic
Ethnic groups Indigenous tribal groups (Shangaan, Chokwe, Manyika, Sena, Makua, others) 99%
Languages Portuguese (official), many others
Religions Traditional beliefs 50%, Christianity 30%, Islam 20%
Currency Metical = 100 centavos
Website www.mozambique.mz

A. Chissano, became president. REN-AMO's leader, Afonso Dhlakama, accepted the election results and stated that the civil war would not be resumed. This led to a period of relative stability. In 1995, Mozambique became the 53rd member of the Commonwealth, joining its English-speaking allies in southern Africa.

MAPUTO (LOURENÇO MARQUES)

Capital and chief port of Mozambique, on Maputo Bay, southern Mozambique. It was visited by the Portuguese in 1502, and was made the capital of Portuguese East Africa in 1907, being known as Lourenço Marques until 1976. It is linked by rail to South Africa, Swaziland, and Zimbabwe, and is a popular resort area. Industries include footwear, textiles, rubber.

ECONOMY

By the early 1990s, Mozambique was one of the world's poorest countries. Battered by a civil war, which had killed around a million people and had driven 5 million from their homes, and combined with devastating droughts and floods, the economy collapsed.

By the end of the twentieth century, economists were praising Mozambique for its economic recovery. Although 80% of the people are poor, support from the World Bank and other international institutions, privatization and rescheduling of the country's foreign debts, led to an expansion of the economy and the bringing down of inflation to less than 10% by 1999.

Oxen pull a cart *filled with coconuts during the coconut harvest on a plantation, Quelimane*

Massive floods at the start of 2000 affected about a quarter of the population making thousands homeless and devastating the economy for many years to come.

Agriculture is important. Crops include cassava, cotton, cashew nuts, fruits, maize, rice, sugar cane and tea. Fishing is important and shrimps, cashew nuts, sugar and copra are exported. Despite its large hydroelectric plant at the Cahora Bassa Dam on the River Zambezi, manufacturing is at a small-scale. Electricity is exported to South Africa.

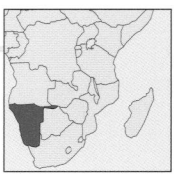

Namibia adopted this flag in 1990 when it gained its independence from South Africa. The red diagonal stripe and white borders are symbols of Namibia's human resources. The green and blue triangles and the gold sun represent the country's resources.

The Republic of Namibia lies on the Atlantic coast to the south of Angola and to the north of South Africa. The coastal region contains the arid Namib Desert, mostly between 900 m and 2,000 m [2,950–6,560 ft] above sea level, which is virtually uninhabited. Inland is a central plateau, bordered by a rugged spine of mountains stretching north–south.

Eastern Namibia contains part of the Kalahari, a semi-desert area which extends into Botswana. The Orange River forms Namibia's southern border, while the Cunene and Cubango rivers form parts of the northern borders.

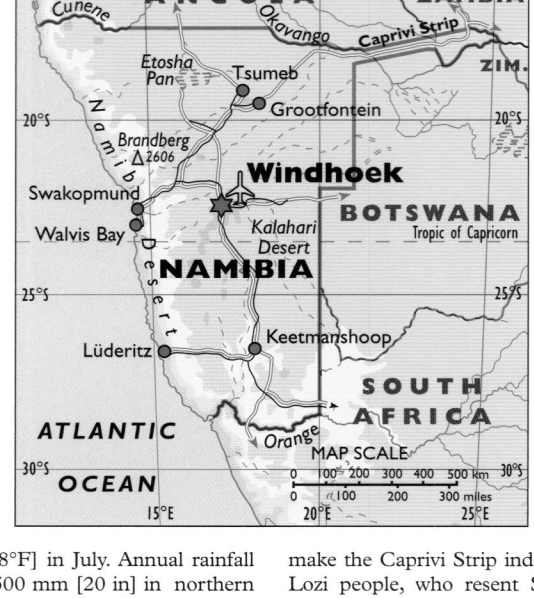

Area 824,292 sq km [318,259 sq mi]
Population 1,954,000
Capital (population) Windhoek (147,000)
Government Multiparty republic
Ethnic groups Ovambo 50%, Kavango 9%, Herero 7%, Damara 7%, White 6%, Nama 5%
Languages English (official), Afrikaans, German, indigenous dialects
Religions Christianity 90% (Lutheran 51%)
Currency Namibian dollar = 100 cents
Website www.grnnet.gov.na

CLIMATE

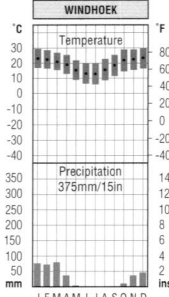

Namibia has a warm and largely arid climate. Daily temperatures range from about 24°C [75°F] in January to 20°C [68°F] in July. Annual rainfall ranges from about 500 mm [20 in] in northern areas to between 25 mm and 150 mm [1–6 in] in the south. Most of the rain falls in summer.

HISTORY

The earliest people in Namibia were the San (also called Bushmen) and the Damara (Hottentots). Later arrivals were people who spoke Bantu languages. They migrated into Namibia from the north and included the Ovambo, Kavango and Herero. From 1868, Germans began to operate along the coast and, in 1884, Germany annexed the entire territory which they called German South West Africa. In the 1890s, the Germans forcibly removed the Damara and Herero from the Windhoek area. About 65,000 Herero were killed when they revolted against their eviction.

South African troops took over the territory in 1915 and five years later the League of Nations gave South Africa a mandate to govern the country, however, South Africa chose to rule it as though it were a South African province.

After World War II, many people challenged South Africa's right to govern the territory. A civil war began during the 1960s between African guerrillas and South African troops, with a cease-fire as finally being agreed in 1989. The country became independent in 1990.

Namibia's Caprivi Strip is a geographical oddity. The Strip was given to Germany by European powers in the late 19th century in order that Germany would have access to the River Zambezi. It became the scene of a rebellion in 1999 when a small band of rebels tried, unsuccessfully, to seize the regional capital, Kutima Mulilo, as part of an attempt to make the Caprivi Strip independent. The Strip is populated mainly by Lozi people, who resent SWAPO rule. Lozi separatists also live in Botswana and Zambia.

ECONOMY

Namibia has important mineral reserves, including diamonds, zinc, uranium, copper, lead and tin. Mining is the most valuable economic activity and, by the mid-1990s, minerals accounted for as much as 90% of the exports, with diamonds making up over half the total revenue from minerals.

Farming employs around two out of every five Namibians, although many farmers live at subsistence level, contributing little to the economy. Because most of the land in Namibia has too little rainfall for arable farming, the principal agricultural activities are cattle and sheep raising. However, livestock raising has been hit in the last 20 years by extended droughts that have depleted the number of farm animals. The chief crops are maize, millet and vegetables.

Fishing in the Atlantic Ocean is also important, though overfishing has reduced the yields of Namibia's fishing fleet. The country has few manufacturing industries apart from jewellery-making, some metal smelting, the processing of farm products, such as karakul pelts (sheepskins that are used to make fur coats), and textiles. Tourism is developing, especially in the Etosha National Park in northern Namibia, which is rich in wildlife.

POLITICS

After achieving independence, the government pursued a policy of 'national reconciliation'. An enclave on Namibia's coast, called Walvis Bay (Walvisbaai), remained part of South Africa until 1994, when South Africa transferred it to Namibia. In 2004, Sam Nujoma of the South West African People's Organization (SWAPO), who had been president since independence, retired. His successor was Hifikepunye Pohama.

Himba settlement, *girl standing beside herd; the Himba are a semi-nomadic pastoralist Herero people who live in Kaokoland to the north-west of Namibia; they herd sheep, goats and cattle*

WINDHOEK

Capital and largest city of Namibia, situated some 300 km [190 mi] inland from the Atlantic at a height of 1,650 m [5,410 ft]. Originally serving as the headquarters of a Nama chief, in 1892 it was made the capital of the new German colony of South West Africa. It was taken by South African troops in World War I. In 1990, it became capital of independent Namibia. An important world trade market for karakul sheepskins, its industries include diamonds, copper and meat-packing. The German heritage is still very much in evidence with German restaurants selling traditional food and the German language still prevalent.

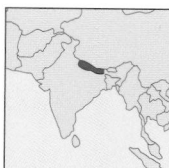

This Himalayan kingdom's uniquely shaped flag was adopted in 1962. It came about in the 19th century when two triangular pennants – the royal family's crescent moon symbol and the powerful Rana family's sun symbol – were joined together.

The Kingdom of Nepal in central Asia, lies between India to the south and China to the north. More than three-quarters of the country is in the Himalayan mountain heartland, culminating in the world's highest peak Mount Everest (or Chomolongma in Nepali), at 8,850 m [29,035 ft].

Nepal comprises three distinct regions. A southern lowland area (*terai*) of grassland and forests is the main location of Nepal's agriculture and timber industry. The central Siwalik mountains and valleys are divided between the basins of the Ghaghara, Gandak, and Kosi rivers. Between the Gandak and Kosi lies Katmandu valley, Nepal's most populous area. The last region is the main section of the Himalayas. Vegetation varies widely according to altitude.

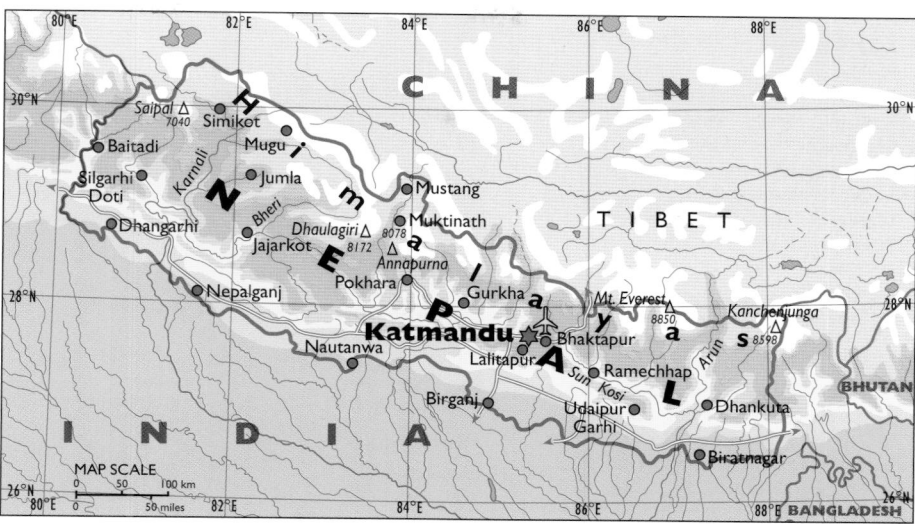

CLIMATE

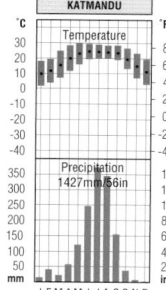

The huge differences in altitude give Nepal a wide variety of climatic regions.

HISTORY

In 1482 the kingdom of Nepal was divided into three, Bhadgaon, Kathmandu and Patan. It was nearly four hundred years later in 1768 when the three kingdoms finally resolved their differences and unified to form what is now known as Nepal. Between 1815 and 1816 the Anglo-Nepalese War took place as a result of rivalry between Nepal and the British East India Company over the annexation of minor states bordering Nepal. In exchange for autonomy the Nepalese signed The Treaty of Sugauli ceding parts of the Terrai and Sikkim to the British East India Company.

From 1846 to 1951, hereditary prime ministers from the Rana family ruled Nepal. In 1923, Britain recognized Nepal as a sovereign state. Gurkha soldiers fought in the British Army during both World Wars. In 1951, the Rana government was overthrown and the monarchy re-established. The first national constitution was adopted in 1959, and free elections were held. In 1960, King Mahendra dissolved parliament and introduced a political system based on village councils (*panchayat*). In 1972, Birendra succeeded his father as king.

POLITICS

In 1990, after mass protests, a new constitution limited the power of the monarchy. In 1991 the Nepali Congress Party (NCP), led by G.P. Koirala, won multi-party elections. The NCP dominated the unstable politics of the 1990s, and Koirala led nine governments in ten years. Since the 1990s, a Maoist revolt has claimed more than 3,500 lives. A brief cease-fire was agreed in 2003, but fighting continued.

In 2001, King Birendra, his queen and six other members of his family were shot dead by his heir, Crown Prince Dipendra, who then took his own life. Gyanendra, Birendra's brother, became king.

Increasing Maoist activity led the king to take direct control of the government and appoint a new cabinet early in 2005.

ECONOMY

Nepal is one of the world's poorest countries, with a per capita gross national product of US$220 in 1999. Agriculture employs over 80% of the workforce, accounting for two-fifths of the gross domestic product. Export crops include herbs, jute, rice, spices and wheat. Tourism, which is centred around the high Himalayas, has grown in importance since 1951, when the country first opened to foreigners. The government is highly dependent on aid to develop the infrastructure. There are also plans to exploit the hydroelectric potential offered by the Himalayan rivers.

Area 56,827 sq miles [147,181 sq km]
Population 27,071,000
Capital (population) Katmandu (695,000)
Government Constitutional monarchy
Ethnic groups Brahman, Chetri, Newar, Gurung, Magar, Tamang, Sherpa and others
Languages Nepali (official), local languages
Religions Hinduism 86%, Buddhism 8%, Islam 4%
Currency Nepalese rupee = 100 paisa
Website www.welcomenepal.com

Tengboche Monastery, *in the Everest region*

KATMANDU (KATHMANDU)

Capital of Nepal, situated 1,370 m [4,500 ft] above sea level in a Himalayan valley. Founded in ad 723, it was independent from the 15th century to 1768, when Gurkhas captured it. Katmandu is Nepal's administrative, commercial, and religious centre. Sights of interest include many beautiful temples including Kasthamandap from which the city derives its name, the Royal Palace (Narayanhity Durbar) and the neo-classical Singha Durbar, former private residence of Rana prime ministers.

HIMALAYAS

System of mountains in southern Asia, extending 2,400 km [1,500 mi] north–south in an arc between Tibet and India-Pakistan. The mountains are divided into three ranges: the Greater Himalayas (north), which include Mount Everest and K2; the Lesser Himalayas; and the Outer Himalayas (south)

The flag of the Netherlands, one of Europe's oldest, dates from 1630, during the long struggle for independence from Spain which began in 1568. The tricolour became a symbol of liberty which inspired many other revolutionary flags around the world.

Area 41,526 sq km [16,033 sq mi]
Population 16,318,000
Capital (population) Amsterdam (729,000);
The Hague (seat of government, 440,000)
Government Constitutional monarchy
Ethnic groups Dutch 83%, Indonesian,
Turkish, Moroccan and others
Languages Dutch (official), Frisian
Religions Roman Catholic 31%, Protestant
21%, Islam 4%, others
Currency Euro = 100 cents
Website www.holland.com

The Kingdom of the Netherlands lies at the western end of the North European Plain, which extends to the Ural Mountains in Russia. The country is largely flat, about 40% being below sea level at high tide. To prevent flooding, dykes have been built to hold back the waves. There are large areas called polders made up of land reclaimed from the sea.

CLIMATE

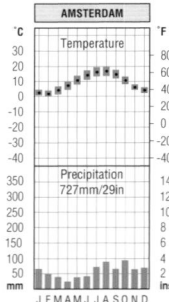

Because of its position on the North Sea, the Netherlands has a temperate climate. Winters are mild, with rain coming from the Atlantic depressions which pass over the country. North Sea storms often batter the coasts. Storm waves have periodically breached the dykes, causing flooding and sometimes loss of life.

HISTORY

Before the 16th century, the area that is now the Netherlands was under a succession of foreign rulers, including the Romans, the Germanic Franks, the French and the Spanish. The Dutch declared their independence from Spain in 1581 this status finally being recognized by Spain in 1648. In the 17th century the Dutch built up a great overseas empire, especially in South-east Asia.

France controlled the Netherlands from 1795 to 1813 and in 1815 the Netherlands, then containing both Belgium and Luxembourg, became an independent kingdom. Belgium broke away in 1830, Luxembourg followed in 1890.

The Netherlands was neutral in World War I, but occupied by German troops in World War II. Much of the Dutch fleet escaped and served with the Allies, but around three-quarters of the country's Jews were murdered, while many other people were forced to work in German factories. By the end of the war, about 270,000 Netherlanders had been killed or had died of starvation.

POLITICS

In 1948, the Netherlands formed an economic union called Benelux with Belgium and Luxembourg and, in 1949, it became a member of NATO. Economic

recovery was rapid and in 1957 it became a founder member of the EEC.

In 1949, after much fighting, the Dutch recognized the independence of its largest overseas possession, Indonesia. In 1954, Suriname and the Netherlands Antilles were granted self-government. In 1962, the Dutch handed over Netherlands New Guinea to the United Nations, which handed it over, as Irian Jaya, to Indonesia in 1963. Suriname became fully independent in 1975.

In 1953, waves penetrated the coastal defences in the south-western delta region, flooding about 4.3% of the country, destroying or damaging more than 30,000 houses and killing 1,800 people. Within three weeks, a commission of enquiry had recommended the Delta Plan, a huge project to protect the delta region. Completed in 1986, it involved the construction of massive dams and floodgates, which are closed during severe storms.

The Maastricht Treaty, which transformed the EEC into the European Union, was signed in the Dutch city of Maastricht in 1991. Since 1 January 2002, the euro has been its sole currency.

ECONOMY

The Netherlands has the world's 14th largest economy, it is a highly industrialized country. Manufacturing and commerce are the most valuable activities. Mineral resources include china clay, natural gas, oil and salt. It imports many of the materials needed by its industries. The products are wide-ranging, including aircraft, chemical products, electronic equipment, machinery, textiles and vehicles. In the area south of Rotterdam, the Dutch have constructed a vast port and industrial area, Europoort. Together with Rotterdam's own facilities, the complex is the largest and busiest in the world.

Agriculture employs only 5% of the workforce, but, through the use of scientific techniques, yields are high. The Dutch cut and sell more than 3 billion flowers a year. Dairy farming is the leading farming activity. In the areas above sea level, farming includes both cattle and crops. Major food crops include barley, potatoes, sugar beet and wheat.

Keizersgracht, Amsterdam; one of the canals that runs from the Amstel clockwise towards het IJ

AMSTERDAM

Capital and largest city in the Netherlands, on the River Amstel, linked to the North Sea by the North Sea Canal. Amsterdam was chartered in 1300 and joined the Hanseatic League in 1369. The Dutch East India Company (1602) brought great prosperity to the city. It became a notable centre of learning and book printing during the 17th century. It was captured by the French in 1795 and blockaded by the British during the Napoleonic Wars. Amsterdam was badly damaged during the German occupation during World War II. A major port and one of Europe's leading financial and cultural centres, it has an important stock exchange and diamond-cutting industry.

New Zealand's flag was designed in 1869 and adopted as the national flag in 1907 when New Zealand became an independent dominion. The flag includes the British Blue Ensign and four of the five stars in the Southern Cross constellation.

New Zealand lies about 1,600 km [994 mi] south-east of Australia. It consists of two main islands and several other small ones. New Zealand is mountainous and partly volcanic. The Southern Alps contain the country's highest peak, Aoraki Mount Cook, at 3,753 m [12,313 ft]. Minor earthquakes are common and there are several areas of volcanic and geothermal activity, especially on North Island.

About 75% of New Zealand lies above the 200 m [650 ft] contour. In the south east, broad, fertile valleys have been cut by rivers between the low ranges. The only extensive lowland area of New Zealand is the Canterbury Plains. As a result of its isolation, almost 90% of the indigenous plants are unique to the country.

Much of the original vegetation has been destroyed and only small areas of the kauri forests have survived. Mixed evergreen forest grows on the western side of South Island. Beech forests grow in the highlands and large plantations are grown for timber.

CLIMATE

Auckland in the north has a warm, humid climate throughout the year. Wellington has cooler summers, while in Dunedin, to the south-east, temperatures sometimes dip below freezing in winter. The rainfall is heaviest on the western highlands.

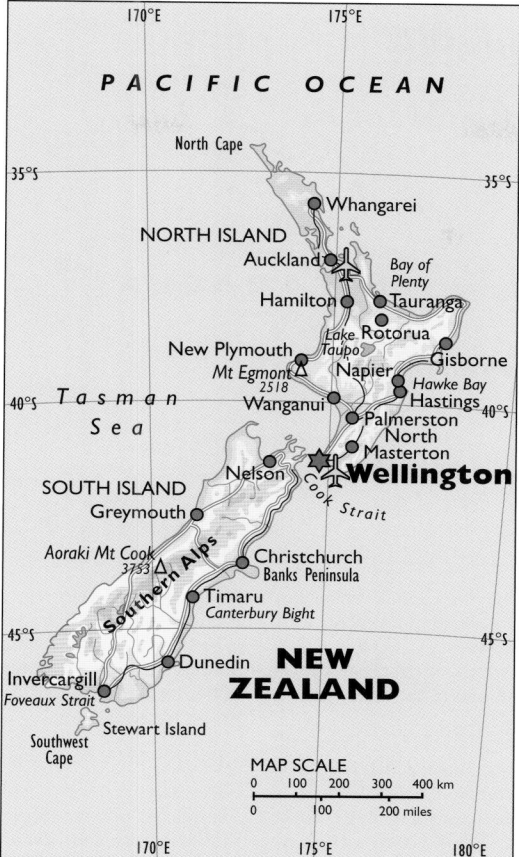

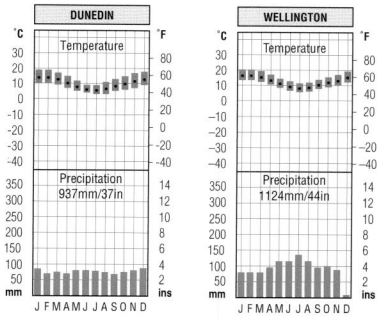

HISTORY

Early Maori settlers arrived in New Zealand more than 1,000 years ago. The Dutch navigator Abel Janszoon Tasman reached the area in 1642, but after several of his men were killed by Maoris, he made no further attempt to land. His discovery was not followed up until 1769, when the British Captain James Cook rediscovered the islands.

British settlers arrived in the early 19th century and in 1840, under the Treaty of Waitangi, Britain took possession of the islands. Clashes occurred with the Maoris in the 1860s, but from the 1870s the Maoris were gradually integrated into society. In 1893, New Zealand became the first country in the world to give women the vote and in 1907, it became a self-governing dominion in the British Empire.

New Zealanders fought alongside the Allies in both World Wars. In 1952, New Zealand signed the ANZUS treaty, a mutual defence pact

The peaceful waters of Milford Sound *reflect surrounding wooded mountains, South Island*

Area 104,453 sq miles [270,534 sq km]
Population 3,994,000
Capital (population) Wellington (167,000)
Government Constitutional monarchy
Ethnic groups New Zealand European 74%, New Zealand Maori 10%, Polynesian 4%
Languages English and Maori (both official)
Religions Anglican 24%, Presbyterian 18%, Roman Catholic 15%, others
Currency New Zealand dollar = 100 cents
Website www.govt.nz

with Australia and the United States. Troops from New Zealand served in the Korean War (1950–3) and a few units later served in the war in Vietnam.

POLITICS

After Britain joined the EEC (now the EU) in 1973, New Zealand's exports to Britain shrank from 70% to 10%. Along with its re-evaluation of its defence position through ANZUS, it also had to reassess its economic strategy. This has involved seeking new markets in Asia, cutting subsidies to farmers, privatization and cutting back on its extensive welfare programmes in the 1990s. The rights of Maoris and the preservation of their culture are other major political issues in New Zealand. In 1998, New Zealand completed a NZ$170 million settlement with the Ngai Tahu group on South Island in compensation for forced land purchases in the 19th century. The government expressed its profound regret for past suffering and for injustices that had impaired the development of the Ngai Tahu. Ties with Britain have been gradually reduced and in 2005 the prime minister, Helen Clark, stated that the country would eventually abolish the monarchy and become a republic.

ECONOMY

Manufacturing now employs twice as many people as agriculture. Meat and dairy products are the most valuable agricultural products. The country has more than 45 million sheep, 4.3 million dairy cattle, and 4.6 million beef cattle. Major crops include barley, fruits, potatoes and other vegetables, and wheat. Fishing is also important. The chief manufactures are processed food products, including butter, cheese, frozen meat and woollen products.

WELLINGTON

Capital and region of New Zealand, in the extreme south of North Island, on Port Nicholson, an inlet of Cook Strait. First visited by Europeans in 1826, it was founded in 1840. In 1865 it replaced Auckland as capital. Wellington's excellent harbour furthered its development as a transport and trading centre. It is the world's southernmost capital city.

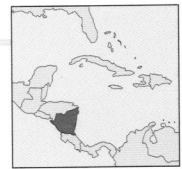

The colours of the flag are in homage to Argentina. Central America i s represented by the white stripe; the Atlantic and Pacific Oceans are the blue stripes. The coat of arms features five volcanoes, a rainbow for hope and red Liberty cap for freedom.

Area 130,000 sq km [50,193 sq mi]
Population 5,360,000
Capital (population) Managua (1,109,000)
Government Multiparty republic
Ethnic groups Mestizo 69%, White 17%, Black 9%, Amerindian 5%
Languages Spanish (official)
Religions Roman Catholic 85%, Protestant
Currency Córdoba oro (gold córdoba) = 100 centavos
Website www.intur.gob.ni/index_eng.html

MANAGUA

Capital of Nicaragua, on the southern shore of Lake Managua, west-central Nicaragua. It became the capital in 1855. Managua suffered damage from earthquakes in 1931 and 1962. It is the economic, industrial and commercial hub of Nicaragua. Industries include textiles, tobacco, and cement.

The Republic of Nicaragua is the largest country in Central America. The Central Highlands rise in the north west Cordillera Isabella to more than 1,800 m [6,000 ft] and are the source for many of the rivers that drain the eastern plain. The Caribbean coast forms part of the Mosquito Coast. Lakes Managua and Nicaragua lie on the edge of a narrow volcanic region, which contains Nicaragua's major urban areas, including the capital, Managua, and the second-largest city, León. This region is highly unstable, with many active volcanoes, and is prone to earthquakes.

Rainforests cover large areas in the east, with trees such as cedar, mahogany and walnut. Tropical savanna is common in the drier west.

CLIMATE

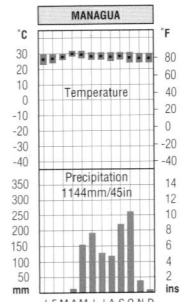

Nicaragua has a tropical climate, with a rainy season from June to October. Cooler weather is found in the Central Highlands. The wettest part is the Mosquito Coast, with 4,200 mm [165 in] of rain.

HISTORY

Spanish explorer Christopher Columbus reached Nicaragua in 1502, and claimed the land for Spain. Colonization claimed the lives of c. 100,000 Native Americans. By 1518 Nicaragua had become part of the Spanish Captaincy-General of Guatemala.

In 1821, Nicaragua gained independence, later forming part of the Central American Federation from 1825 to 1838. In the mid-19th century, civil war and US and British interference ravaged Nicaragua. The USA sought the construction of a trans-isthmian canal through Nicaragua. In 1855, William Walker invaded and briefly established himself as president. José Santos Zemalya's dictatorship from 1893 to 1909 gained control of Mosquito Coast and formed close links with the British. Following his downfall, civil war raged once more. In 1912, US marines landed to protect the pro-US regime, and in 1916 the USA gained exclusive rights to the canal. Opposition to US occupation resulted in guerrilla war, led by Augusto César Sandino. In 1933, the US marines withdrew but set up a National Guard to help defeat the rebels.

In 1934 Anastasio Somoza, director of the National Guard, assassinated Sandino. Somoza became president in 1937. His dictatorial regime led to political isolation. Somoza was succeeded by his sons Luis in 1956 and Anastasio in 1967. Anastasio's diversion of international relief aid following the devastating 1972 Managua earthquake cemented opposition.

POLITICS

In 1979, the Sandinista National Liberation Front (FSLN) overthrew the Somoza regime. The Sandinista government, led by Daniel Ortega, instigated wide-ranging socialist reforms. The USA, concerned about the Sandinistas' ties with communist regimes, sought to destabilize the government by supporting the Contra rebels. A ten-year civil war devastated the economy and led to political dissatisfaction. The conflict ended when the Sandinista agreed to free elections.

In the 1990 elections, the National Opposition Union coalition, led by Violeta Chamorro, defeated the Sandinistas. However, the Contra were disbanded and Chamorro's coalition partners and the Sandinista-controlled trade unions blocked many of her reforms. In 1996 elections, Liberal leader Arnoldo Aleman defeated Chamorro.

In 1998, Hurricane Mitch killed c. 4,000 people and caused extensive damage. Enrique Bolanos became president at elections in 2001. In 2003, former president Arnoldo Aleman was sentenced to 20 years in prison for corruption.

ECONOMY

Nicaragua faces problems in rebuilding its economy and introducing free-market reforms. Agriculture is the main activity, employing 50% of the workforce and accounting for 70% of exports. Major cash crops include coffee, cotton, sugar and bananas. Rice is the main food crop.

There is some copper, gold, and silver, but mining is underdeveloped. Most manufacturing is based around Managua.

Cotton picking; *cotton is one of the key crops of Nicaragua*

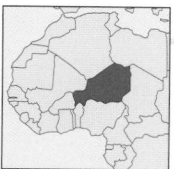

This flag was adopted shortly before Niger became independent from France in 1960. The orange stripe represents the Sahara in the north and the green represents the grasslands in the south. Between them, the white stripe represents the River Niger, with a circle for the sun.

The Republic of Niger is a land-locked nation in north-central Africa. The northern plateaux lie in the Sahara, while north-central Niger contains the rugged Aïr Mountains, which reach a height of 2,022 m [6,632 ft] above sea level near Agadez. The rainfall in the mountains – averaging around 175 mm [7 in] per year – is sufficient in places to permit the growth of thorny shrub. Severe droughts since the 1970s have crippled the traditional lifestyle of the nomads in northern and central Niger as the Sahara has slowly advanced south. The southern region has also been hit by droughts.

The south consists of broad plains. The Lake Chad Basin lies in south-eastern Niger on the borders with Chad and Nigeria. The only permanent rivers are the Niger and its tributaries in the southwest. The narrow Niger Valley is the country's most fertile and densely populated region and includes the capital Niamey. Yet Niger, a title which comes from a Tuareg word meaning 'flowing water', seems scarcely appropriate for a country which consists mainly of hot, arid, sandy, and stony basins.

Buffaloes, elephants, giraffes. and lions are found in the 'W' National Park, which Niger shares with Benin and Burkina Faso. Most of southern Niger lies in the Sahel region of dry grassland. The Aïr Mountains support grass and scrub. The northern deserts are generally barren.

Grand Marché, Niamey; *the largest of Niamey's markets and one of the best in west Africa, selling everything from beads to mosquito nets*

CLIMATE

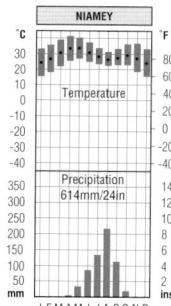

Niger is one of the world's hottest countries. The warmest months are March to May, when the harmattan wind blows from the Sahara. Niamey has a tropical climate, with a rainy season from June to September. Rainfall decreases from south to north. Northern Niger is practically rainless. The far south consists of tropical savanna.

HISTORY

Neolithic remains have been found in the northern desert. Nomadic Tuareg settled in the Aïr Mountains in the 11th century AD, and by the 13th century established a state centred around Agadez and the trans-Saharan trade. In the 14th century, the Hausa settled in southern Niger. In the early 16th century, the Songhai Empire controlled much of Niger, but the Moroccans supplanted the Songhai at the turn of the century.

NIAMEY
Capital of Niger, West Africa, in the south-western part of the country, on the River Niger. It became capital of the French colony of Niger in 1926. It grew rapidly after World War II and is now the country's largest city and its commercial and administrative centre. Manufactures include textiles, ceramics, plastics, and chemicals.

Area 1,267,000 sq km [489,189 sq mi]
Population 11,361,000
Capital (population) Niamey (732,000)
Government Multiparty republic
Ethnic groups Hausa 56%, Djerma 22%, Tuareg 8%, Fula 8%, others
Languages French (official), Hausa, Djerma
Religions Islam 80%, indigenous beliefs, Christianity
Currency CFA franc = 100 centimes
Website www.un.int/niger

Later on, the Hausa and then the Fulani set up kingdoms in the region. In the early 19th century, the Fulani gained control of much of southern Niger. The first French expedition arrived in 1891, but Tuareg resistance prevented full occupation until 1914.

POLITICS

In 1922, Niger became a colony within French West Africa. In 1958, Niger voted to remain an autonomous republic within the French Community. It gained full independence in 1960, and Hamani Diori became Niger's first president. He maintained close ties with France.

Drought in the Sahel began in 1968, and killed many livestock and destroyed crops. In 1974, a group of army officers, led by Lieutenant Colonel Seyni Kountché, overthrew Hamani Diori and suspended the constitution. Kountché died in 1987, and was succeeded by his cousin General Ali Saibou. In 1991, the Tuareg in northern Niger began an armed campaign for greater autonomy. A national conference removed Saibou and established a transitional government. In 1993 multiparty elections, Mahamane Ousmane of the Alliance of Forces for Change (AFC) coalition became president. The collapse of the coalition led to fresh elections in 1995, which were won by the National Movement for a Development Society (MNSD), but a military coup, led by Colonel Ibrahim Bare Mainassara, seized power. In 1995, the government and the Tuaregs signed a peace accord. Elections in 1996 confirmed Mainassara as president. In 1999, bodyguards assassinated Mainassara and he was replaced briefly by Major Daouda Malam Wanke. Parliamentary rule was restored and, later that year, Tandjou Mamadou was elected president. He was re-elected in 2004.

ECONOMY

Droughts have caused great hardship and food shortages in Niger, and have destroyed much of the traditional nomadic lifestyle. Niger's chief resource is uranium, and it is the world's second-largest producer. Uranium accounts for more than 80% of exports, most of which goes to France. Some tin and tungsten are also mined. Other mineral resources are largely unexploited.

Niger is one of the world's poorest countries, despite its resources. Farming employs 85% of the workforce, although only 3% of the land is arable and 7% is used for grazing. Food crops include beans, cassava, millet, rice, and sorghum. Cotton and groundnuts are leading cash crops.

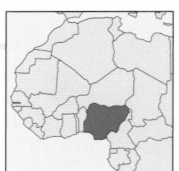

Nigeria's flag was adopted in 1960 when Nigeria became independent from Britain. It was selected after a competition to find a suitable design. The green represents Nigeria's forests. The white in the centre stands for peace.

The Federal Republic of Nigeria is the most populous nation in Africa. The country's main rivers are the Niger and Benue, which meet in central Nigeria. North of the two river valleys are high plains and plateaux. The Lake Chad Basin is in the north-east, with the Sokoto plains in the north-west. Southern Nigeria contains hilly uplands and broad coastal plains, including the swampy Niger Delta. Highlands form the border with Cameroon. Mangrove swamps line the coast, behind which are rainforests. The north contains large areas of savanna with forests along the rivers. Open grassland and semi-desert occur in drier areas.

CLIMATE

The south of the country has high temperatures and rain all year. Parts of the coast have an average annual rainfall of 3,800 mm [150 in]. The north has a marked dry season and higher temperatures than the south.

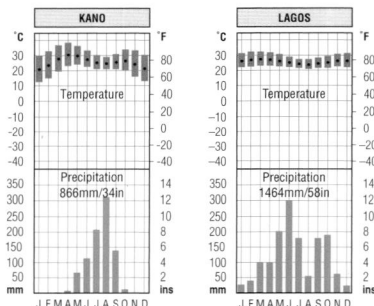

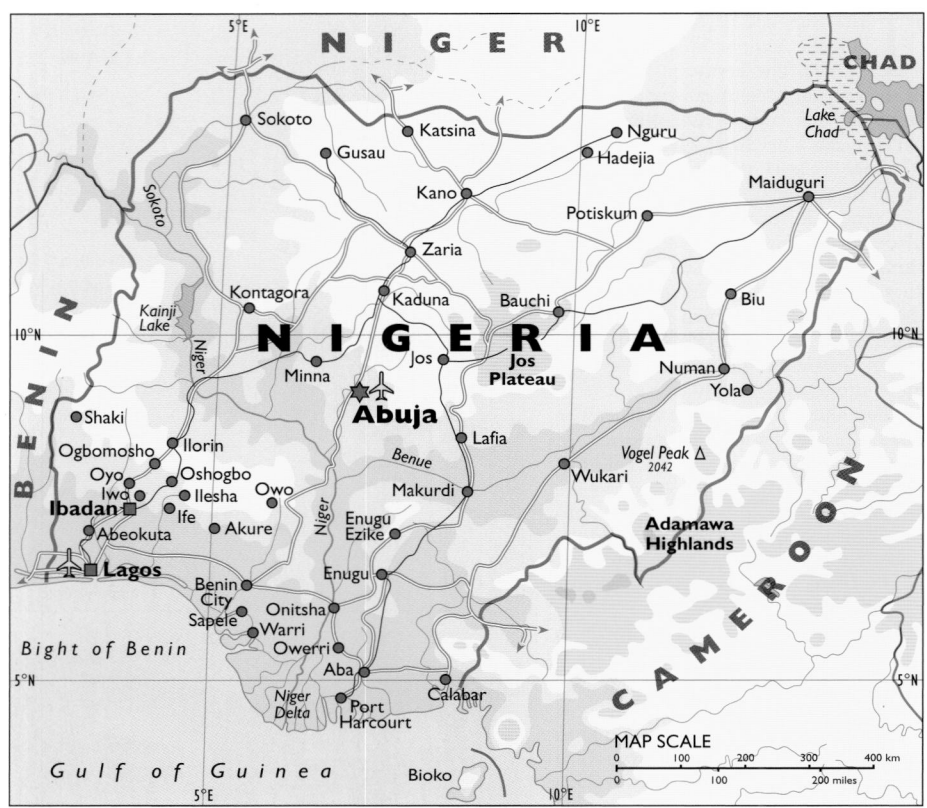

HISTORY

Nigeria has a long artistic tradition. Major cultures include the Nok (500 BC to AD 200), Ife, which developed about 1,000 years ago, and Benin, which flourished between the 15th and 17th centuries.

Britain outlawed slavery in 1807 and soon afterwards the British began to trade in agricultural products. In 1851, Britain made Lagos a base from which they could continue their efforts to stop the slave trade. During the second half of the 19th century, Britain gradually extended its influence over Nigeria. By 1914 it ruled the entire country.

POLITICS

Nigeria became independent in 1960 and a federal republic in 1963. A federal constitution dividing the country into regions was necessary because Nigeria contains more than 250 ethnic and linguistic groups, as well as several religious ones. Local rivalries have long been a threat to national unity. In 1967, in an attempt to meet the demands of more ethnic groups, the country's four regions were replaced by 12 states. The division of the Eastern Region provoked an uprising. In 1967, the governor of the Eastern Region, Colonel Odumegwu Ojukwu, proclaimed it an independent republic called Biafra. Civil war continued until Biafra's surrender in January 1970.

The country had only nine years of civilian government between independence in 1960 and 1998. In 1998-9 civilian rule was restored. A former military leader, Olusegun Obasanjo, was elected president and

ABUJA

Nigeria's administrative capital since 1991. The new city was designed by the Japanese architect Kenzo Tange, and work began in 1976. The change was decided upon because it was thought that the capital city should be in the centre of the country. The previous capital, Lagos, which lies on the coast close to the border of Benin is still the commercial capital. Although the government has moved to Abuja, much of the city remains under construction.

re-elected in 2003. Ethnic and religious differences are a threat to national unity. In the late 1990s and early 2000s, ethnic riots broke out between Yorubas and Hausas in the south-west, while the introduction of *sharia* (Islamic law) in northern states has caused friction between Muslims and Christians. The government declared in 2004 that it had put down an uprising in the north-east aimed at creating a Muslim state, while ethnic and religious conflict continued in other parts of the country. In 2006 parliament blocked an attempt by Obasanjo's supporters to amend the charter to allow the president to stand for a third term.

ECONOMY

Despite its many natural resources, including oil reserves, metals, forests and fertile farmland, Nigeria is a 'low-income' developing economy. Agriculture employs 43% of the workforce and Nigeria is one of the world's leading producers of cocoa beans, groundnuts, palm oil and kernels, and natural rubber. Leading food crops include beans, cassava, maize, millet, plantains, rice, sorghum and yams.

Area 923,768 sq km [356,667 sq mi]
Population 137,253,000
Capital (population) Abuja (339,000)
Government Federal multiparty republic
Ethnic groups Hausa and Fulani 29%, Yoruba 21%, Ibo (or Igbo) 18%, Ijaw 10%, Kanuri 4%
Languages English (official), Hausa, Yoruba, Ibo
Religions Islam 50%, Christianity 40%, traditional beliefs
Currency Naira = 100 kobo
Website www.nigeria.gov.ng

This flag became the national flag of Norway in 1898, although merchant ships had used it since 1821. The design is based on the Dannebrog, the flag of Denmark, the country which ruled Norway from the 14th century until the early 19th century.

The Kingdom of Norway forms the western part of the mountainous Scandinavian Peninsula. The landscape is dominated by rolling plateaus, the vidda, which are generally between 300 m and 900 m [1,000–3,000 ft] high, but some peaks rise from 1,500 m to 2,400 m [5,000–8,000 ft] in the area between Oslo, Bergen and Trondheim. The highest areas retain permanent ice-fields, as in the Jotunheimen Mountains above Sognefjord.

Norway's jagged coastline is the longest in Europe. The vidda are cut by long, narrow, steep-sided fjords on the west coast. The largest of the fjords, is Sognefjord, which is 203 km [127 mi] long and less than 5 km [3 mi] wide.

CLIMATE

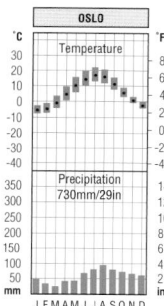

The warm North Atlantic Drift flows off the coast and moderates the country's climate, with milder winters and cooler summers. Most of Norway's ports remain ice-free all year. Inland, away from the moderating effects of the sea, the climate becomes more severe. Winters are bitterly cold with snow cover for at least three months of the year.

HISTORY

From about AD 800, Vikings from Norway roamed the northern seas, raiding and founding colonies around the coasts of Britain, Iceland and even North America. In about 900, Norway was united under Harold I, the country's first king. Viking power ended in the late 11th century. In 1380, Norway was united with Denmark and in 1397 Sweden joined the union. Sweden broke away in 1523 and, in 1526, Denmark, which had become increasingly powerful, made Norway a Danish province.

OSLO

Capital of Norway, in the south of the country. The city is located at the head of Oslo Fjord and is surrounded by forest. Founded in the 11th century it was largely destroyed by fire in 1624. Christian IV rebuilt the city, naming it Christiania. In 1905, it became the capital of independent Norway. It acquired the name Oslo in 1925. Home to the Vigeland Sculpture Park, the Viking Ship Museum, and the Munch Museum, it is an important tourist centre.

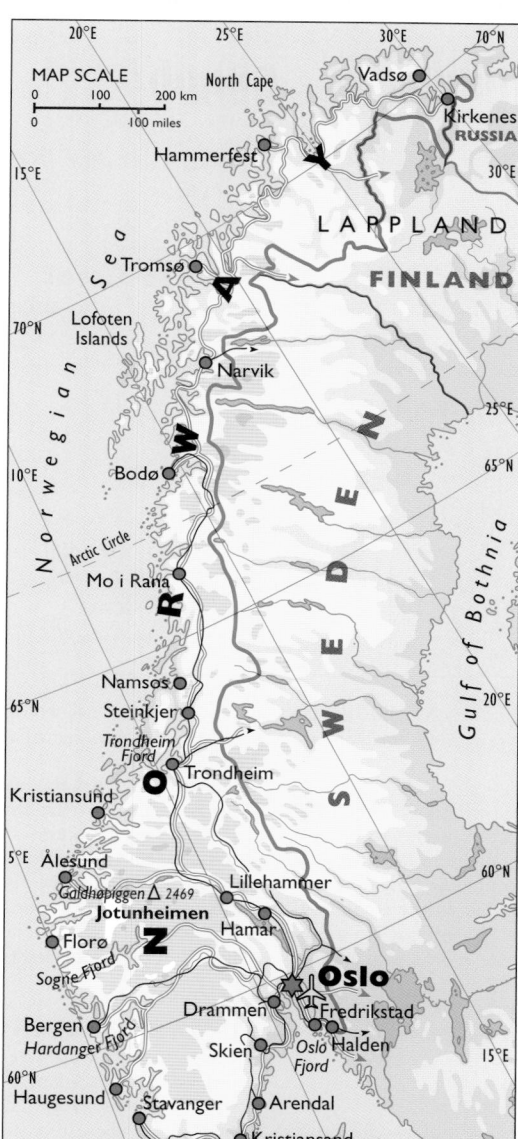

In 1814, Denmark ceded Norway to Sweden, but retained Norway's colonies of Greenland, Iceland and the Faeroe Islands. Norway finally ended its union with Sweden in 1905. The Norwegians chose as their king a Danish prince, who took the title Haakon VII.

Farmer with a reindeer herd, *Arrisovarre, Norwegian Lappland*

Area 323,877 sq km [125,049 sq mi]
Population 4,575,000
Capital (population) Oslo (513,000)
Government Constitutional monarchy
Ethnic groups Norwegian 97%
Languages Norwegian (official)
Religions Evangelical Lutheran 86%
Currency Norwegian krone = 100 øre
Website www.norge.no

Despite being neutral in World War I, and seeking to remain so in World War II, German troops invaded in 1940.

POLITICS

After World War II, Norwegians worked to rebuild their economy and their merchant fleet. The economy was boosted in the 1970s, when Norway began producing petroleum and natural gas from wells in the North Sea. Rapid economic growth has ensured that Norwegians are among the most prosperous in Europe.

In 1949, it became a member of NATO, though neither NATO bases nor nuclear weapons were permitted on its soil for fear of provoking its neighbour, the Soviet Union. In 1960, Norway and six other countries formed the European Free Trade Association while continuing to work with its Scandinavian neighbours through the Nordic Council. In 1994, Norwegians again voted against membership of the EU. The 1990s–2000s saw Norwegian diplomats seeking to broker peace deals in Sri Lanka and Palestine.

ECONOMY

Norway's chief resources and exports are oil and natural gas. Dairy farming and meat production are the chief farming activities, though Norway has to import food. Industries include petroleum products, chemicals, aluminium, wood products, machinery and clothing.

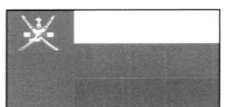

White symbolizes peace. Green is traditional Islamic colour, also standing for the fertility of the land. Red represents the blood shed in the struggle for liberation. The Sultanate's white coat of arms consists of two crossed swords, a khnajar (dagger), and belt.

Area 309,500 sq km [119,498 sq mi]
Population 2,903,000
Capital (population) Muscat (41,000)
Government Monarchy with consultative council
Ethnic groups Arab, Baluchi, Indian, Pakistani
Languages Arabic (official), Baluchi, English
Religions Islam (mainly Ibadhi), Hinduism
Currency Omani rial = 100 baizas
Website www.omanet.com/english/home.asp

The Sultanate of Oman is the oldest independent nation in the Arab world. It occupies the south-eastern corner of the Arabian peninsula and includes the tip of the Musandam Peninsula which is separated from the rest of Oman by UAE territory. This peninsula overlooks the strategic Strait of Hormuz.

The Al Halar al Gharbi range, rising to 3,019 m [9,904 ft] above sea level, borders the narrow coastal plain in the north. This fertile plain along the Gulf of Oman is called Al Battinah. Inland are deserts, including part of the Rub' al Khali (Empty Quarter). Much of the land along the Arabian Sea is barren, but the province of Zufar (or Dhofar) in the south-east is a hilly, fertile region.

CLIMATE

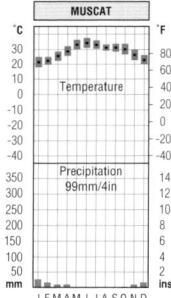

Temperatures in Oman can reach 54°C [129°F] in summer, but winters are mild to warm. Rainfall in the northern mountains can exceed 400 mm [16 in] per year, while in the south-east it can be up to 630 mm [25 in], but for most of Oman the desert climate means less than 150 mm [6 in] per year.

Sandstorms, duststorms and droughts feature and occasionally, tropical cyclones bring stormy weather.

HISTORY

Oman first became a major trading region 5,000 years ago. Islam was introduced into the area in the 7th century and today, 75% of the population follow the strict Ibadi Islam sect.

The Portuguese conquered its ports in the early 16th century, but local Arabs forced them out in 1650. The Al Bu Said family came to power in the 1740s and has ruled the country ever since. British influence dates back to the end of the 18th century, when the two countries entered into the first of several treaties.

In 1920, Britain brokered an agreement whereby the interior was ruled by imams, with coastal areas under the control of the Sultan. Clashes between the two groups continued into the 1950s, but Sultan Said bin Taimur regained control of the whole country in 1959.

New houses in Al Khuwair, *Muscat*

POLITICS

Under Sultan Said bin Taimur, Oman had been an isolated, feudal country. Its economy was backward compared to its oil-rich Gulf neighbours. However, after Sultan Said bin Taimur was deposed by his son, Sultan Qaboos ibn Said, in 1970, Oman made substantial strides. With the help of soldiers from Iran and Jordan, he saw an end to war against Yemen-backed separatist guerrillas in the province of Zufar (1965–1975). He also led the way in developing an expanding economy based on oil reserves far larger than expected when production began in 1967. Qaboos opened up Oman to the outside world, ending the isolation it had long endured. At home, he avoided the prestigious projects favoured by Arab leaders to concentrate on social programmes, including the education of girls. His leadership proved popular despite the lack of a democratic government.

In 1991, Oman took part in the military campaign to liberate Kuwait. In 1997, Oman held its first direct elections to a Consultative Council. Unusual for the Gulf region, two women were elected. In 1999, Oman and the United Arab Emirates signed an agreement, confirming most of the borders between them. In 2001, while a military campaign was being launched in Afghanistan, Britain held military exercises in the Omani desert. This was an example of the long-standing political and military relationship between the two countries. In 2003, elections were held to the Consultative Council. For the first time, all citizens over 21 were allowed to vote although no parties are allowed. In 2004, the Sultan appointed the first woman minister with portfolio. In 2005, nearly 100 suspected Islamists were arrested and 31 were convicted of trying to overthrow the government, but they were later pardoned.

ECONOMY

The World Bank classifies Oman as an 'upper-middle-income' developing country. It has sizeable oil and natural gas deposits, a large trade surplus and low inflation. Oil accounts for more than 90% of Oman's export revenues. Huge natural gas deposits, equal to all the finds of the previous 20 years, were discovered in 1991. Although only about 0.3% of the land is cultivated, agriculture and fishing are the traditional economic activities. Major crops include alfalfa, bananas, coconuts, dates, tobacco and wheat. Water supply is a major problem. Oman depends on water from underground aquifers, which will eventually run dry. and also from desalination plants. Industries include copper smelting, cement and chemicals, as well as food processing and import substitution. Tourism is a growing activity.

MUSCAT (MASQAT, MASKAT)
Capital of Oman, on the Gulf of Oman, in the south-east Arabian Peninsula. The Portuguese held Muscat from 1508 to 1650, when it passed to Persia. After 1741 it became capital of Oman. In the 20th century, Muscat's rulers developed treaty relations with Britain.

AMERICAN SAMOA

The Territory of American Samoa is an unincorporated territory of the United States and lies in the south-central Pacific Ocean. Two of its islands are coral islands, the other five are extinct volcanoes. The US took control of the islands between 1900 and 1904. The main industry is the canning of tuna; fish products dominate the economy.

Area 199 sq km [77 sq mi]
Population 58,000
Capital (population) Pago Pago (4,000)
Government Territory of the USA
Ethnic groups Native Pacific Islander 93%, Asian, White
Languages Samoan 91%, English 3%, Tongan 2%, other Pacific islander 2%
Religions Christian Congregationalist 50%, Protestant 30%, Roman Catholic 20%
Currency US dollar = 100 cents
Website www.asg-gov.net

COOK ISLANDS

A group of 15 islands in the south Pacific Ocean to the north-east of New Zealand consisting of the Northern (Manihiki) Cook Islands and the Southern (Lower) Cook Islands. A self-governing territory in free association with New Zealand. Discovered in 1773 by Captain James Cook, the islands became a British protectorate in 1888 and were annexed to New Zealand in 1901. They became self-governing in 1965. Products include copra and citrus fruits.

Area 293 sq km [113 sq mi]
Population 21,388
Capital (population) Avarua (12,188)
Government Self-governing parliamentary democracy
Ethnic groups Cook Island Maori (Polynesian) 88%
Languages English (official), Maori
Religions Cook Islands Christian Church 57%, Roman Catholic 17%, Seventh Day Saint 8%, Church of Latter Day Saints 4%, other Protestant 6%, others
Currency New Zealand dollar = 100 cents
Website www.ck

FRENCH POLYNESIA

French Polynesia consists of 130 islands, scattered over 2.5 million sq km [1 million sq mi] of the Pacific Ocean. The most densely populated island is Tahiti which is part of a group called the Society Islands. Tribal chiefs agreed to a French protectorate in 1843. They gained increased autonomy in 1984. Links with France ensure a high standard of living. Some favour independence. Following a struggle for power in 2004, the pro-independence Union for Democracy party, ousted the pro-French ruling party. The government is based in Papeete on Tahiti.

Area 4,000 sq km [1,544 sq mi]
Population 266,000
Capital (population) Papeete (24,000)
Government Overseas territory of France
Ethnic groups Polynesian 78%, Chinese 12%, local French 6%, metropolitan French 4%
Languages French 61%, Polynesian 31% (both official), Asian languages
Religions Protestant 54%, Roman Catholic 30%
Currency Comptoirs Francais du Pacifique franc = 100 centimes
Website www.presidence.pf

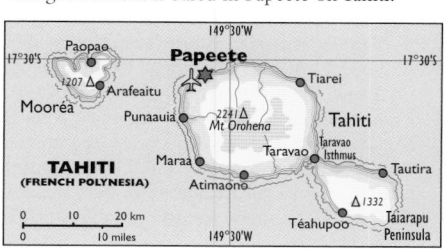

GUAM

The Territory of Guam is a strategically important 'unincorporated territory' of the USA and the largest of the Mariana Islands in the Pacific Ocean. It is composed of a coralline limestone plateau. Guam was ruled by Spain from 1668 until it was ceded to the US in 1899 after the Spanish-American War in an agreement whereby the US paid $20 million for Guam and other Spanish-held territorie. Temperatures range from 26–30°C (75–86°F).

Area 549 sq km [212 sq mi]
Population 166,000
Capital (population) Hagatna (Agana) (1,000)
Government Territory of the USA
Ethnic groups Chamorro 37%, Filipino 26%, other Pacific islander 11%, white 7%, other Asian 6%
Languages English 38%, Chamorro 22%, Philippine languages 22%, other Pacific island languages 7%, Asian languages 7%, others
Religions Roman Catholic 85%, others 15%
Currency US dollar = 100 cents
Website www.visitguam.org

KIRIBATI

The Republic of Kiribati is an independent nation in the west Pacific Ocean. It comprises about 33 islands, including the Gilbert, Phoenix, and Line Islands, and straddles the Equator over an area of 5 million sq km (2 million sq mi). The islands are threatened by global warming and consequent rising sea levels. Rainfall is abundant.

British navigators first visited the Gilbert and Ellice Islands during the late 18th century. They became a British protectorate in 1892 and a colony in 1915. In 1975 the Ellice Islands, following a referendum, officially severed links with the Gilbert Islands and became a separate territory called Tuvalu in 1978. The Gilbert Islands became fully independent within the Commonwealth of Nations in 1979 as the Republic of Kiribati. Agriculture is now the major economic activity.

Area 726 sq km [280 sq mi]
Population 101,000
Capital (population) Bairiki (on Tarawa) (32,000)
Government Multiparty republic
Ethnic groups Micronesian 99%
Languages I-Kiribati and English (both official)
Religions Roman Catholic 52%, Protestant (Congregational) 40%, others
Currency Australian dollar = 100 cents
Website www.janeresture.com/kirihome/index.htm

MARSHALL ISLANDS

The Republic of the Marshall Islands consists of 31 coral atolls, five single islands and more than 1,000 islets. It lies north of Kiribati in the region of Micronesia. The temperature averages 27°C [81°F]. The islands came under German rule in 1885 and became a Japan-

Area 181 sq km [70 sq mi]
Population 58,000
Capital (population) Majuro (20,000)
Government Constitutional government in free association with the US
Ethnic groups Micronesian
Languages Marshallese 98% and English (both official)
Religions Protestant 55%, Assembly of God 26%, Roman Catholic 9%, Bukot nan Jesus 3%, Mormon 2%
Currency US dollar = 100 cents
Website www.visitmarshallislands.com

ese mandate after World War I. US forces took the main islands in 1944 and they became a US Trust Territory in 1947. Independence was achieved in 1991, but the islands remain heavily dependent on US aid. The main activities are agriculture and tourism.

Woman cooking on outdoor grill, Laura Island, Marshall Islands

MICRONESIA

Area 702 sq km [271 sq mi]
Population 108,000
Capital (population) Palikir (on Pohnpei) (5,000)
Government Constitutional government in free association with the US
Ethnic groups Micronesian and Polynesian
Languages English (official), others
Religions Roman Catholic 50%, Protestant 47%
Currency US dollar = 100 at
Website www.visit-fsm.org

Federated States of Micronesia is a republic in the western Pacific Ocean, consisting of all the Caroline Islands except Belau. The 607 islands of the republic divide into four states: Chuuk, Pohnpei, Yap and Kosrae. The government is based in Palikir on Pohnpei. The temperature remains around 27°C [80°F] all year.

After 1874 the islands were under a succession of rulers from Spain to Germany in 1899, to Japan in 1920. They came under US administration in 1947. In 1979, the Federated States of Micronesia came into being, with Belau remaining a US trust territory. In 1986, a compact of free association with the USA was signed. In 1991 Micronesia became a full member of the UN. The economy depends heavily on US aid. Land use is limited to subsistence agriculture.

NAURU

Area 21 sq km [8 sq mi]
Population 13,000
Capital (population) Yaren (4,500)
Government Multiparty republic
Ethnic groups Nauruan 58%, other Pacific Islander 26%, Chinese 8%, European 8%
Languages Nauruan (official), English
Religions Protestant 66%, Roman Catholic 33%
Currency Australian dollar = 100 cents
Website www.un.int/nauru/

A former UN Trust Territory ruled by Australia, Nauru became independent in 1968. It has its government offices in the Yaren district though there is no official capital. Located in the western Pacific close to the Equator, it is the world's smallest republic. Nauru's prosperity is based on phosphate mining, but reserves are running out. It relies on Australia for support as well as for its day-to-day needs. Tourism and off-shore banking are being developed to off-set the lack on income when the phosphate runs out.

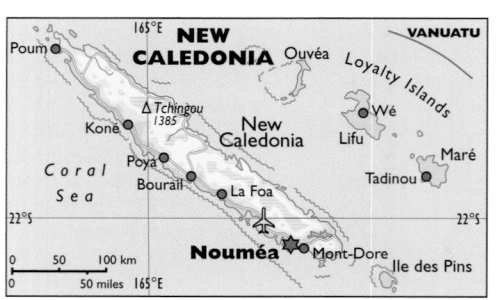

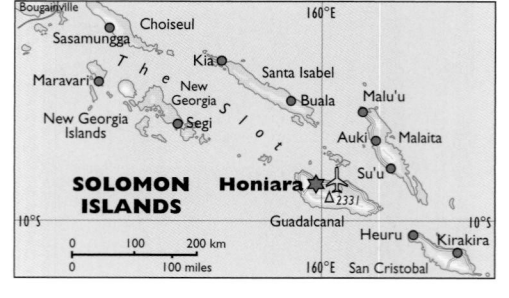

NEW CALEDONIA

Area 18,575 sq km [7,172 sq mi]
Population 214,000
Capital (population) Nouméa (76,000)
Government Overseas territory of France
Ethnic groups Melanesian 43%, European 37%, Wallisian 8%, Polynesian 4%, Indonesian 4%
Languages French (official), 33 Melanesian-Polynesian dialects
Religions Roman Catholic 60%, Protestant 30%
Currency Comptoirs Français du Pacifique franc = 100 centimes
Website www.newcaledoniatourism-south.com

New Caledonia is the most southerly of the Melanesian countries in the Pacific. A French possession since 1853 and an Overseas Territory since 1958. In 1998, France announced an agreement with local Melanesians that a vote on independence would be postponed until 2014. The country is rich in mineral resources. Experts claim that it has about a quarter of the world's nickel reserves.

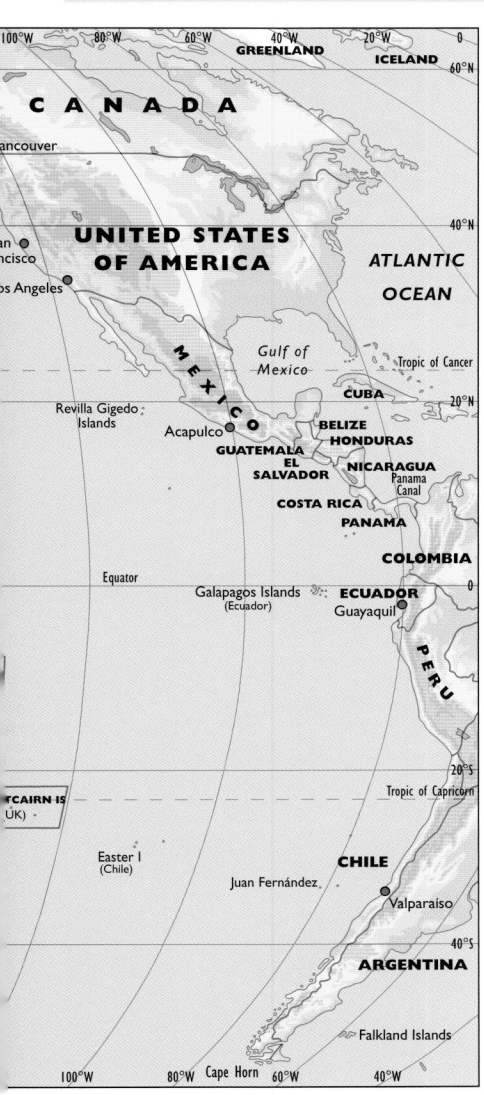

NORFOLK ISLAND

Area 34 sq km [13 sq mi]
Population 1,828
Capital (population) Kingston
Government Territory of Australia
Ethnic groups Descendants of the Bounty mutineers, Australian, New Zealander, Polynesians
Languages English, Norfolk
Religions Anglican 35%, Roman Catholic 12%, Uniting Church in Australia 11%, others
Currency Australian dollar = 100 cents
Website www.nf

The Territory of Norfolk Island lies in the south-west Pacific Ocean 1,450 km [900 mi] east of Australia. Visited in 1774 by Captain James Cook, it was a British penal colony. Many Pitcairn Islanders, descendents of the *Bounty* mutineers, resettled here in 1856. Agriculture and tourism are key earners.

NORTHERN MARIANA ISLANDS

Area 464 sq km [179 sq mi]
Population 78,000
Capital (population) Saipan (39,000)
Government Commonwealth in political union with the US
Ethnic groups Asian 56%, Pacific islander 36%
Languages Philippine languages 24%, Chinese 23%, Chamorro 22%, English 10%, others
Religions Christianity
Currency US dollar = 100 cents
Website www.cnmi.net

The Commonwealth of the Northern Mariana Islands contains 16 mountainous islands north of Guam in the western Pacific Ocean. In a 1975 plebescite, the islanders voted for Commonwealth status in union with the USA and in 1986 they were granted US citizenship. The economy is reliant upon tourism and the export of clothing.

PALAU

Area 459 sq km [177 sq mi]
Population 20,000
Capital (population) Koror (11,000)
Government Multiparty republic
Ethnic groups Palauan 70%, Filipino 15%, Chinese 5%, others
Languages Palauan (official except – Sonsoral:Sonsoralese and English; Tobi: Tobi and English; Anguar: Anguar, Japanese and English), Filipino, English Chinese
Religions Roman Catholic 42%, Protestant 23%, Modekngei 9% (indigenous)
Currency US dollar = 100 cents
Website www.visit-palau.com

The Republic of Palau became fully independent in 1994 after the US refused to accede to a 1979 referendum that declared Palau a nuclear-free zone. It relies on US aid, tourism, fishing and subsistence farming. Main crops include cassava, coconuts and copra.

NIUE

Area 260 sq km [100 sq mi]
Population 2,000
Capital (population) Alofi (404)
Government Self-governing parliamentary democracy
Ethnic groups Niuen 78%, Pacific islander 10%, European 4%, others
Languages Niuean, English
Religions Ekalesia Niue 61%, Latter-Day Saints 9%, Roman Catholic 7%, others
Currency New Zealand dollar = 100 cents
Website www.niueisland.com

Niue is an island territory in the southern Pacific Ocean, 2,160 km [1,340 mi] north-east of New Zealand. It has an average temperature of 25°C [27°F]. The largest coral island in the world, Niue was first visited by Europeans in 1774. In 1901 it was annexed to New Zealand. In 1974 it achieved self-government in free association with New Zealand. Its economy is mainly agricultural; the major export is coconut.

PITCAIRN ISLAND

Area 55 sq km [21 sq mi]
Population 46
Capital (population) Adamstown
Government Overseas territory of the UK
Ethnic groups Descendants of the Bounty mutineers and their Tahitian wives
Languages English (official), Pitcairnese
Religions Seventh-Day Adventist
Currency New Zealand dollar = 100 cents
Website www.government.pn/homepage.htm

Pitcairn Island is a British overseas territory in the Pacific Ocean. Its inhabitants are descendents of the original settlers – nine mutineers from HMS *Bounty* and 18 Tahitians who arrived on this formerly uninhabited island in 1790.

SAMOA

Area 2,831 sq km [1,093 sq mi]
Population 178,000
Capital (population) Apia (32,000)
Government Parliamentary democracy and constitutional monarchy
Ethnic groups Samoan 93%, Euronesians
Languages Samoan, English
Religions Congregationalist 35%, Roman Catholic 20%, Methodist 15%, Latter-Day Saints 13%
Currency Tala = 100 sene
Website www.visitsamoa.ws

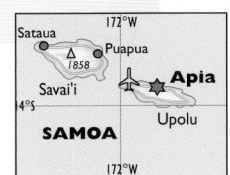

The Independent State of Samoa comprises two islands in the South Pacific Ocean. The ownership of these Polynesian islands was disputed by European powers, but Germany took control in 1900. Following Germany's defeat in World War I, New Zealand governed from 1920 until 1961. The country became independent in 1962. The economy is based on agriculture, plus coco-nut products, copra and fishing.

SOLOMON ISLANDS

Area 28,896 sq km [11,157 sq mi]
Population 524,000
Capital (population) Honiara (49,000)
Government Parliamentary democracy
Ethnic groups Melanesian 95%, others
Languages Melanesian pidgin
Religions Church of Melanesia 33%, Roman Catholic 19%, South Seas Evangelical 17%, Seventh-Day Adventist 11%, United Church 10%
Currency Solomon Islands dollar = 100 cents
Website www.solomons.com

The Solomon Islands, a chain of mainly volcanic islands in the Pacific Ocean, extending 2,250 km [1,400 mi]. A British territory between 1893 and 1978. In 2003 an Australian peace-keeping force was sent in the belief that the islands were threatened with anarchy. Fish, coconuts and cocoa are important.

TOKELAU

Tokelau was originally settled by Polynesian emigrants from surrounding islands. It was made a British protectorate in 1889 and transferred to New Zealand administration in 1925. It is made up of three villages, there is little economic development and agriculture is at subsistence level. The people produce copra, postage stamps, souvenir coins, and handicrafts, but rely heavily on aid from New Zealand.

Area 10 sq km [3.86 sq mi]
Population 1,405
Government Self-administering territory of New Zealand
Ethnic groups Polynesian
Languages Tokelauan, English
Religions Congregational Christian Church 70%, Roman Catholic 28%
Currency New Zealand dollar = 100 cents
Website www.tokelau.org.nz

TONGA

Originally called the Friendly Islands, the Kingdom of Tonga is an island kingdom in the South Pacific, 2,200 km [1,370 mi] north east of New Zealand. The archipelago consists of c. 170 islands in five administrative groups. Only 36 of the islands are inhabited. They are mainly coral atolls, but the western group are volcanic, with some active craters. The largest island is Tongatapu, the seat of the capital, Nukualofa, and home to 66% of the population.

Area 650 sq km [251 sq mi]
Population 110,000
Capital (population) Nuku'alofa 22,000)
Government Constitutional monarchy
Ethnic groups Polynesian
Languages Tongan, English
Religions Christian (Free Wesleyan Church)
Currency Pa'anga = 100 seniti
Website http://pmo.gov.to

The northern islands were discovered by Europeans in 1616, and the rest by Abel Tasman in 1643. During the 19th century, British missionaries converted the indigenous population to Christianity. In 1900, Tonga became a British Protectorate.

In 1970, the country achieved independence. The economy is dominated by agriculture, the chief crops are yams, tapioca and fish.

TUVALU

Tuvalu, formerly the Ellice Islands (see Kiribati), is an independent republic in western Pacific Ocean. None of the cluster of nine low-lying coral islands rises more than 4.6 m [15 ft] out of the Pacific, making them vulnerable to rising sea levels. There are no streams or rivers, so the collection of rainwater is vital.

The first European to discover the islands was the Spanish navigator Alvaro de

Area 26 sq km [10 sq mi]
Population 11,000
Capital (population) Fongafale (3,000)
Government Constitutional monarchy with a parliamentary democracy
Ethnic groups Polynesian 96%, Micronesian 4%
Languages Tuvaluan, English, Samoan, Kiribati
Religions Church of Tuvalu (Congregationalist) 97%, others
Currency Tuvaluan dollar and Australian dollar = 100 cents
Website www.tuvaluislands.com

Mendaña in 1568. Between 1850 and 1880, the population was reduced from around 20,000 to just 3,000 by Europeans abducting workers for other Pacific plantations. In 1892, the British assumed control, and Tuvalu was subsequently administered with the nearby Gilbert Islands (now Kiribati). In 1978, Tuvalu became a separate self-governing colony within the Commonwealth.

Poor soil restricts vegetation to coconut palms, breadfruit, and bush. The population survives by subsistence farming, raising pigs and poultry, and by fishing. Copra is the only significant export crop, but more foreign exchange is derived from the sale of elaborate postage stamps. In addition, it has sold its internet suffix – .tv – for several million dollars a year.

VANUATU

The Republic of Vanuatu, formerly the Anglo-French Condominium of the New Hebrides, became independent in 1980. The word Vanuatu means 'Our Land Forever'. The republic consists of a chain of 80 islands in the South Pacific Ocean. Espiritu Santo is the largest island, though Efate is home to the government and the republic's capital, Port Vila.

The oldest archaeological evidence dates back to 2000 bc. Efate and Espiritu Santo were used as allied bases in World War II. The economy of Vanuatu is based on agriculture and it exports copra, beef and veal, timber and cocoa. Fishing, offshore financial services, and tourism are also important. 113 languages are spoken across the islands.

Area 12,189 sq km [4,706 sq mi]
Population 203,000
Capital (population) Port Vila (19,000)
Government Multiparty republic
Ethnic groups Ni-Vanuatu 99%
Languages Local languages (more than 100) 73%, pidgin (known as Bislama or Bichelama) 23%, others
Religions Presbyterian 31%, Anglican 13%, Roman Catholic 13%, Seventh-Day Adventist 11%, indigenous beliefs 6% (including Jon Frum cargo cult), others
Currency Vatu
Website www.vanuatugovernment.gov.vu

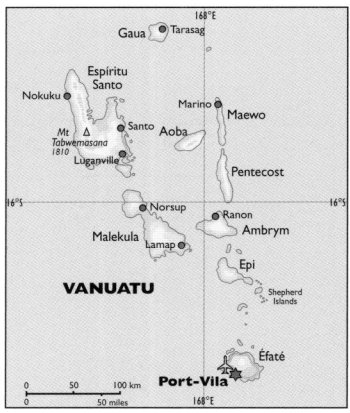

Yassur volcano throws smoke high into the air on Tanna Island, Vanuatu

WALLIS & FUTUNA

The Territory of the Wallis and Futuna Islands in the South Pacific Ocean form the smallest and the poorest of France's overseas territories, although they were in fact discovered by the Dutch and the British in the 17th and 18th centuries.

In 1959, the inhabitants of the islands voted to become a French overseas territory. A French dependency since

Area 200 sq km [77 sq mi]
Population 16,000
Capital (population) Mata-Utu (1,000)
Government Overseas territory of France
Ethnic groups Polynesian
Languages Wallisian 59%, Futunian 30%, French 11%
Religions Roman Catholic
Currency Comptoirs Français du Pacifique franc = 100 centimes
Website www.wallis.co.nc

1842, the territory comprises two groups of islands. The Isles de Hoorn, which includes Futuna is situated to the north east of the Fiji Islands. The other is the Wallis Archipelago.

The economy is based on subsistence agriculture, and 80% of the workforce makes their living from either coconuts and vegetables, livestock or fishing. Other revenue comes from the licensing of fishing rights to Japan and South Korea.

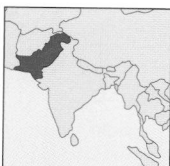

ASIA

Pakistan 159

Pakistan's flag was adopted in 1947, when the country gained independence. The colour green, the crescent Moon and the five-pointed star are all traditional symbols of Islam. The white stripe represents the other religions in Pakistan.

The Islamic Republic of Pakistan, a federal republic, contains high mountains, fertile plains and rocky deserts. The Karakoram range contains K2, the world's second highest peak at 8,611 m [28,251 ft] It lies in the northern part of Jammu and Kashmir.

The Punjab plains, which are drained by the Indus River and its tributaries, the Chenab, Jhelum, Ravi and Sutlej, and the Sind plains to the south contain fertile agricultural land, irrigated by river water. East of the Sind plains lies the Thar (or Great Indian) Desert, while the arid Baluchistan Plateau covers the south-west, bordering Iran and Afghanistan.

CLIMATE

Most of Pakistan has hot summers and cool winters. The country is generally arid, though occasional storms cause floods. The eastern part of the Punjab plains has the highest average annual rainfall with around 500 mm [20 in]. Winters in the mountains are cold and snowy. The coastal region has a generally mild, humid climate.

HISTORY

Around 4,500 years ago, what is now the Indus Valley in Pakistan became the home of one of the world's great early civilizations. At its

Shalimar Gardens, Lahore; the gardens date from the mid-17th century and were built during the reign of the Emperor Shah Jahan; they were inscribed as a UNESCO World Heritage Site in 1981

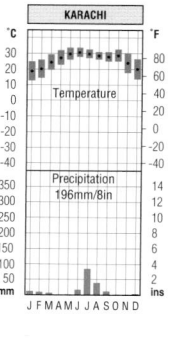

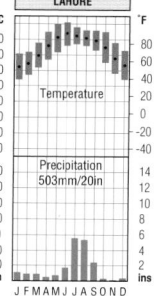

MAP SCALE

Area 796,095 sq km [307,372 sq mi]
Population 159,196,000
Capital (population) Islamabad (529,000)
Government Federal republic
Ethnic groups Punjabi, Sindhi, Pashtun
(Pathan), Baluchi, Muhajir
Languages Urdu (official), many others
Religions Islam 97%, Christianity, Hinduism
Currency Pakistani rupee = 100 paisa
Website www.infopak.gov.pk

KASHMIR

In 1947, British India was partitioned into India and Pakistan. The region known as Kashmir (officially Jammu and Kashmir) was claimed by both India and Pakistan. Muslims formed the majority, but there were also large numbers of Hindus and people of other faiths. In 1947, the region was ruled by a maharaja, who was a Hindu, and he made Kashmir part of India. But Pakistani Muslims invaded in an attempt to make Kashmir part of Pakistan. War ensued until 1949, when a truce line was established, leaving the north-western two-thirds of the territory under Pakistani control. This area was named Azad (or 'Free') Kashmir. In 1957, under a new constitution, India declared Jammu and Kashmir to be part of India. China seized part of Kashmir in 1959 and 1962 and, in 1965, fighting again broke out between India and Pakistan. Finally, in 1972, a new truce line was established and this line remains the boundary on the ground. In the 21st century, India and Pakistan have sought to improve relations between them and, in 2005, bus services began to operate across the cease-fire line. But no solution has been found to the problem of Kashmir, the most explosive issue dividing them.

Prayer flags lead to Tsemo Gompa, *Ladakh, Jammu-Kashmir State*

height, the Indus Valley civilization included most of what is now Pakistan and parts of Afghanistan and India. Ruins have been excavated at Harrappa and Mohenjodaro, revealing that these ancient people developed planned cities and had their own systems of writing and weights and measures. The break-up of this civilization into smaller cultures in around 1700 BC may have been caused by changes in the courses of the rivers.

The region was later conquered by waves of invaders from central and south-western Asia, including the Persians and, briefly by Alexander the Great. Islam was introducedby Arab Muslims in AD 711. In 1526, what is now Pakistan became part of the Mogul Empire, under which Sikhism emerged, combining elements of Hinduism and Islam, and Urdu became a dominant language. The Mogul Empire, included most of what is now Pakistan, India and Bangladesh, began to decline in the 18th century. In the 1840s, the British East India Company gained areas in Punjab and Sind. The British government took over this region, together with all of the company's other possessions. It became known as British India.

POLITICS

Independence movements began to develop in the early 20th century and, in 1947, British India was divided into Pakistan, led by Muhammed Ali Jinnah, who is regarded as 'father of the nation', who died in 1948. Slaughter ensued as Hindus and Sikhs fled Pakistan and Muslims fled India. In 1947, Pakistan consisted of two areas: West and East Pakistan. Following a bitter civil war, East Pakistan broke away in 1971 to become Bangladesh. In 1948-9, 1965 and 1971, Pakistan and India clashed over the disputed territory of Kashmir– the present cease-fire line was agreed in 1972 under the Simla peace agreement.

Pakistan has been ruled by a succession of civilian and military regimes. Following a period of military rule, elections were held in 1988 and Benazir Bhutto, daughter of a previous prime minister, became

ISLAMABAD

Capital of Pakistan, Islamabad lies north-east of Rawalpindi, which became the interim capital following the decision in 1959 to build a new capital replacing Karachi. Islamabad became the official capital in 1967 and most government offices had been relocated in the city by the end of the 1960s. This new city has been carefully planned and contains a blend of modern and traditional Islamic architectural styles. The city stands on the Potwar Plateau, at the heart of an agricultural region. The city is divided into administrative, diplomatic, business and residential zones. Most of the people work in administrative and governmental posts. Some people in non-government jobs have homes in nearby Rawalpindi. Islamabad lies in a region of seismic activity and suffered damage during the 2005 earthquake in north-western Pakistan and Kashmir. The city has hot summers, with monsoon rains in July-August and mild winters.

prime minister. She was removed from office in 1990 but returned as prime minister from 1993 to 1996. In 1997 Narwaz Sharif was elected prime minister but a military coup brought General Pervez Musharraf to power.

In 2001 Pakistan supported the Western assault on Taliban forces in Afghanistan. In 2002, voters agreed to extend Musharraf's term in office by five years. He then changed the constitution to increase his own powers. Pakistan1s declaration of support for the international coalition against terrorism provoked a backlash by Islamic fundamentalists. In 2004, Musharraf announced, despite much criticism, that he would remain army chief as well as head of state.

In 1998 Pakistan responded to a series of Indian nuclear weapon tests by conducting its own nuclear tests, provoking global controversy. In 21st century, Pakistan and India sought to normalize relations through a series of peace moves, raising hopes of a settlement in Kashmir, though activity by Kashmiri militants continued.

In October 2005 nearly 75,000 people were killed and 3 million left homeless in an earthquake centred on Pakistan-administered Kashmir. Among the worst hit areas was the city of Muzaffarabad.

ECONOMY

Pakistan is a 'low-income' developing country, whose economy has been damaged by internal political disputes, the ongoing confrontation with India and the low level of foreign investment. However, some economic progress has been made since 2001, especially because of generous foreign assistance, which has come partly because of the country's support for the war against international terrorism.

Agriculture employs 42% of the workforce, industry 20% and services 38%. Major crops are cotton, fruits, rice, sugar cane, vegetables and wheat. Livestock include goats and sheep. Manufactures include bicycles, car tyres, cement, industrial chemicals, and jute. Textiles, including cotton fabric, knitwear, bedding, garments and cotton yarn, are the leading exports. Other exports include rice, leather products and petroleum products.

The blue quarter stands for the Conservative Party. The red quarter represents the Liberal Party. The white quarters symbolize peace between the parties The blue star stands for purity and honesty. The red star denotes government and law.

The Republic of Panama forms an isthmus linking Central America to South America. The narrowest part of Panama is less than 60 km [37 mi] wide. The Panama Canal, which is 81.6 km [50.7 mi] long and cuts straight across the isthmus, has made the country a major transport centre. and most Panamanians live within 20 km [12 mi] of it. Most of the land between the Pacific and Caribbean coastal plains is mountainous, rising to 3,475 m [11,400 ft] at the volcano Barú.

Tropical forests cover approximately 50% of Panama. Mangrove swamps line the coast, though in recent years more than 400 sq km [150 sq mi] have been lost to agriculture, ranching and shrimp mariculture. Subtropical woodland grows on the mountains, while tropical savanna occurs along the Pacific coast.

Area 75,517 sq km [29,157 sq mi]
Population 3,000,000
Capital (population) Panamá (484,000)
Government Multiparty republic
Ethnic groups Mestizo 70%, Black and Mulatto 14%, White 10%, Amerindian 6%
Languages Spanish (official), English
Religions Roman Catholic 85%, Protestant 15%
Currency US dollar; Balboa = 100 centésimos
Website www.visitpanama.com

CLIMATE

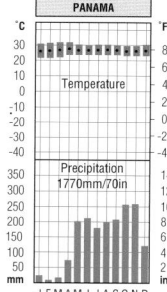

Panama has a tropical climate, though the mountains are much cooler than the coastal plains. The rainy season is between May and December. The Caribbean side of has about twice as much rain as the Pacific side.

HISTORY

Christopher Columbus landed in Panama in 1502. In 1510, Vasco Núñez de Balboa became the first European to cross Panama and see the Pacific Ocean. The indigenous population was soon wiped out and Spain established control. In 1821, Panama became a province of Colombia. The USA exerted great influence from the mid-19th century.

After a revolt in 1903, Panama declared independence from Colombia. In 1904, the USA began construction of the Panama Canal, and established the Panama Canal Zone. Since it opened in 1914, the status of the Canal has dominated Panamanian politics. The Panama Canal Zone, a strip of land along the canal, was then administered by the United States. US forces intervened in 1908, 1912 and 1918 to protect US interests.

POLITICS

Panama has been politically unstable throughout the 20th century, with a series of dictatorial regimes and military coups.

Civil strife during the 1950s and 1960s led to negotiations with the USA for the transfer of the Canal Zone. In 1977, a treaty confirmed Panama's sovereignty over the Canal, while providing for US bases in the Canal Zone. The USA agreed to hand over control of the Canal on 31 December 1999. In 1979, the Canal Zone disestablished.

In 1983, General Noriega took control of the National Guard and ruled Panama through a succession of puppet govern-

ments. In 1987, the USA withdrew its support for Noriega after he was accused of murder, electoral fraud, and aiding drug smuggling. In 1988, the USA imposed sanctions and in 1989, Noriega annulled elections, made himself president, and declared war on the USA. On 20 December 1989, 25,000 US troops invaded Panama. Noriega was quickly captured, and taken to the USA for trial.

Pérez Balladares became president in 1994 elections. In 1999, Mireya Moscoso, Panama's first woman president, succeeded Balladares. She was succeeded in 2004 by Martin Torrijos, son of a former military dictator.

Revenues from the Canal rose in the early 21st century, but, overall, the economy slowed, causing social discontent and problems for the government.

ECONOMY

The World Bank classifies Panama as a 'lower-middle-income' developing country. The Panama Canal is a major source of revenue, generating jobs in commerce, trade, manufacturing and transport.

After the Canal, the main activity is agriculture, which employs 27% of the workforce. Rice is the main food crop. Bananas, shrimps, sugar, and coffee are exported. Tourism is also important. Many ships are registered under Panama's flag, due to its low taxes.

PANAMA CITY

Capital of Panama, on the shore of the Gulf of Panama, near the Pacific end of the Panama Canal. It was founded by Pedro Arias de Avila in 1519, and was destroyed and rebuilt in the 17th century. It includes an area known as Casco Antiguo (Colonial Panama), which was constructed inland after the destruction of the first city. Casco Antiguo has been declared 'Patrimony of Humanity' by UNESCO. The city became the capital of Panama in 1903 and it developed rapidly after the construction of the Panama Canal in 1914. Industries include brewing, shoes, textiles, oil-refining,and plastics.

PANAMA CANAL

Waterway connecting the Atlantic and Pacific oceans across the Isthmus of Panama. A canal, begun in 1882 by Ferdinand de Lesseps, was subsequently abandoned because of bankruptcy. The US government decided to finance the project to provide a convenient route for its warships. The main construction took about ten years to complete, and the first ship passed through in 1914. The 82 km [51 mi] waterway reduces the sea voyage between San Francisco and New York by about 12,500 km [7,800 mi]. Control of the Canal passed from the USA to Panama at the end of 1999.

Papua New Guinea's flag was first adopted in 1971, four years before the country became independent from Australia. It includes a local bird of paradise, the 'kumul', in flight, together with the stars of the Southern Cross. The colours are those often used by local artists.

Area 462,840 sq km [178,703 sq mi]
Population 5,420,000
Capital (population) Port Moresby (193,000)
Government Constitutional monarchy
Ethnic groups Papuan, Melanesian, Micronesian
Languages English (official), Melanesian Pidgin, more than 700 other indigenous languages
Religions Traditional beliefs 34%, Roman Catholic 22%, Lutheran 16%, others
Currency Kina = 100 toea
Website www.pngonline.gov.pg

The Independent State of Papua New Guinea is part of a south-west Pacific island region called Melanesia 160 km [100 mi] north-east of Australia that includes the eastern part of New Guinea, Bismarck Archipelago, Solomon Islands, New Hebrides, the Trobriand and D'Entrecasteaux Islands, the Louisiade Archipelago and the Tonga group.

The land is largely mountainous, rising to Mount Wilhelm, at 4,508 m [14,790 ft], eastern New Guinea. In 1995, two volcanoes erupted in Eastern New Britain. East New Guinea also has extensive coastal lowlands.

Forests cover more than 70% of the land. The dominant vegetation is rainforest. Mangrove swamps line the coast. 'Cloud' forest and tussock grass are found on the higher peaks.

CLIMATE

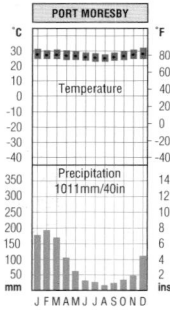

The climate is tropical. It is hot all year with most rain occurring during the monsoon from December to April, when winds blow from the north-east. Winds blow from the south-west during the dry season.

HISTORY

The Portuguese made the first European sighting of the island in 1526, although no settlements were established until the late 19th century. The Dutch took western New Guinea (now Papua part of Indonesia) in 1828, but it was not until 1884 that Germany took north-eastern New Guinea as German New Guinea and Britain formed the protectorate of British New Guinea in south-east New Guinea. In 1906, Britain handed the south-east over to Australia. It then became known as the Territory of Papua. When World War I broke out in 1914, Australia took German New Guinea. In 1921, the League of Nations gave Australia a mandate to rule the area, which was named the Territory of New Guinea.

Japan invaded New Guinea in 1942, but the Allies reconquered in 1944. In 1949, Papua and New Guinea were combined into the Territory of Papua and New Guinea. In 1973, the Territory achieved self-government as a prelude to full independence as Papua New Guinea in 1975.

POLITICS

Since independence, the government has worked to develop mineral reserves. One of the most valuable reserves was a copper mine at Panguna on Bougainville. Conflict developed when the people of Bougainville demanded a larger share in mining profits.

Following an insurrection, the Bougainville Revolutionary Army proclaimed independence in 1990. Bougainville's secession was not recognized internationally. In 1992 and 1996, Papua New Guinea launched offensives against the rebels. The use of highly paid mercenaries created unrest in the army. In 1997, troops and civilians surrounded Parliament, forcing the resignation of Prime Minister Sir Julius Chan. He was succeeded by Bill Skate. In April 1998, a cease-fire was declared on Bougainville.

In July 1998, a tidal wave hit northern Papua New Guinea, killing more than 1600 people. Local autonomy was granted to Bougainville in 2000. In 2004 Australia sent police to the country to help fight crime after a report had stated that the country was heading for social and economic collapse. In 2005 global warming lead to the proposed evacuation of all the residents of the Cartaret atolls due to rising sea levels.

ECONOMY

The World Bank classifies Papua New Guinea as a 'lower-middle-income' developing country. Agriculture employs 75% of the workforce, many at subsistence level. Minerals, notably copper and gold, are the most valuable exports. Papua New Guinea is the world's ninth-largest producer of gold.

House and boat *along Sepik River; the river is fundamental to the lives of those who live by it, depending on it as they do for transport, food and water*

PORT MORESBY

Capital of Papua New Guinea, on the south east coast of New Guinea, built around Fairfax Harbour, the island's largest harbour. Settled by the British in the 1880s and named after British explorer John Moresby, its sheltered harbour was the site of an important Allied base in World War II. It developed rapidly in the post-war period. In recent years it has experienced problems with a growing disparity in income which has lead to an increase in crime. Exports include gold, copper and rubber.

The front (obverse) side of Paraguay's tricolour flag, which evolved in the early 19th century, contains the state emblem, which displays the May Star, commemorating liberation from Spain in 1811. The reverse side shows the treasury seal – a lion and staff.

The Republic of Paraguay is a landlocked country in South America. Rivers, form most of its borders. They include the Paraná in the south and the east, the Pilcomayo (Brazo Sur) in the south-west, and the Paraguay in the north-east. West of the River Paraguay is a region known as the Gran Chaco, which extends into Bolivia and Argentina. The Gran Chaco is mostly flat, but the land rises to the north-west. East of the Paraguay is a region of plains, hills and, in the east, the Paraná Plateau region.

CLIMATE

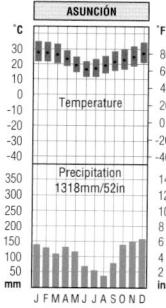

The northern half of Paraguay lies in the tropics, while the southern half is subtropical. Most of the country has a warm, humid climate. The Gran Chaco is the driest and hottest part of the country. Rainfall increases to the Paraná Plateau in the south-east.

HISTORY

The Guarani, an Amerindian people, were the indigenous people of what is now Paraguay. Spanish and Portuguese explorers reached the area in the early 16th century and, in 1537, a Spanish expedition built a fort at Asunción, which later became the capital of Spain's colonies in south-eastern South America. The Spaniards were attracted by the potential labour supply of the Guarani and the chance to find a short cut to the silver mines of Peru. From the late 16th century, Jesuit missionaries arrived to convert the Guarani to Christianity and to protect them against those who wanted to exploit them as cheap labour. Complaints against the Jesuits' power led to their expulsion in 1767.

From 1776, Paraguay formed part of the Rio de la Plata Viceroyalty, with its capital at Buenos Aires. However, this proved unpopular and Paraguay broke free in 1811, achieving its independence from Buenos Aires in 1813.

Between 1865 and 1870, war against Brazil, Argentina and Uruguay cost the country more than half of its 600,000 population, and much of its territory. Some territory was regained after the Chaco Wars against Bolivia between 1920 and 1935, and, in 1947, a period of civil war was followed by a spell of political and economic stability. While most other South American countries were attracting European settlers and foreign capital, Paraguay remained isolated and forbidding.

ASUNCIÓN

Capital, chief port, and largest city of Paraguay, located on the e bank of the Paraguay River near its junction with the River Pilcomayo. Founded by the Spanish 1536 as a trading post, Asunción was the scene of the Communeros rebellion against Spanish rule in 1721 and was later occupied by Brazil (1868–76). City sites include the Pantéon Nacional, Encarnación Church, National University (1889) and the Catholic University (1960). It is an administrative, industrial and cultural centre. Industries include vegetable oil and textiles.

Harvest of sugar cane in San Pedro; the capital of the department also called San Pedro, it is located in the centre of the country

Area 406,752 sq km [157,047 sq mi]
Population 6,191,000
Capital (population) Asunción (547,000)
Government Multiparty republic
Ethnic groups Mestizo 95%
Languages Spanish and Guarani (both official)
Religions Roman Catholic 90%, Protestant
Currency Guarani = 100 céntimos
Website www.paraguay.com

POLITICS

In 1954, General Alfredo Stroessner seized power and assumed the presidency. During his dictatorship, there was considerable economic growth, with an emphasis on developing hydroelectricity. By 1976, Paraguay was self-sufficient in electrical energy due to the completion of the Aracay complex. A second hydroelectric project, the world's largest, started production in 1984, at Itaipu. This was a joint US$20 billion venture with Brazil to harness the Paraná. Paraguay was then generating 99.9% of its electricity from water power. However, demand slackened and income declined, making it difficult for Paraguay to repay foreign debts incurred on the projects. High inflation and balance of payments problems followed.

Stroessner's regime was an unpleasant variety of nepotism. He ruled with an increasing disregard for human rights during nearly 35 years of fear and fraud until his supporters deposed him in 1989.

Three elections were held in the 1990s. The fragility of democracy was demonstrated in 1998, when the newly elected president, Raul Cubas Grau, was threatened with impeachment after issuing a decree freeing his former running mate, General Lino Oviedo, who had been imprisoned for attempting a coup against the previous president, Juan Carlos Wasmosy. In March 1999, Paraguay's vice-president, an opponent of Cubas, was assassinated and the Congress impeached Cubas, who resigned and fled to Argentina. In 2003, Nicanor Duarte Frutos was elected president.

ECONOMY

The World Bank classifies Paraguay as a 'lower-middle-income' developing country. Agriculture and forestry are the leading activities, employing 48% of the workforce. The country has very large cattle ranches, while crops are grown in the fertile soils of eastern Paraguay. Major exports include cotton, soya beans, timber, vegetable oils, sugar cane, coffee, tannin and meat products.

The country has abundant hydroelectricity and exports power to Argentina and Brazil. Its factories produce cement, processed food, leather goods and textiles.

Peru's flag was adopted in 1825. The colours are said to have been inspired by a flock of red and white flamingos which the Argentine patriot General José de San Martín saw flying over his marching army when he arrived in 1820 to liberate Peru from Spain.

Area 1,285,216 sq km [496,222 sq mi]
Population 27,544,000
Capital (population) Lima (5,681,000)
Government Constitutional republic
Ethnic groups Mestizo (Spanish-Indian) 44%, Creole (mainly African American) 30%, Mayan Indian 11%, Garifuna (Black-Carib Indian) 7%, others 8%
Languages English (official), Creole, Spanish
Religions Roman Catholic 62%, Protestant 30%
Currency Belize dollar = 100 cents
Website www.peru.info/perueng.asp

The Republic of Peru lies in the tropics in western South America. A narrow coastal plain borders the Pacific Ocean in the west. Inland are ranges of the Andes Mountains, which rise to 6,768 m [22,205 ft] at Mount Huascarán, an extinct volcano. The Andes also contain active volcanoes, windswept plateaux, broad valleys and, in the far south, part of Lake Titicaca, the world's highest navigable lake. To the east the Andes descend to a hilly region and a huge plain. Eastern Peru is part of the Amazon basin.

CLIMATE

Lima, on the coastal plain has an arid climate. The coastal region is chilled by the cold offshore Humboldt Current. In the Andes, temperatures are moderated by the altitude and many mountains are snow-capped. The eastern lowlands are hot and humid.

HISTORY

Amerindian people reached the area about 12,000 years ago. Several civilizations developed in the Andes region. By about AD 1200, the Inca were established in southern Peru. In 1500, their empire extended from Ecuador to Chile. The Spanish adventur-er Francisco Pizarro visited Peru in the 1520s. Hearing of Inca riches, he returned in 1532. By 1533, he had conquered most of Peru.

In 1820, the Argentinian José de San Martín led an army into Peru and declared the country to be independent. However, Spain still held large areas. In 1823, the Venezuelan Simón Bolívar led another army into Peru and, in 1824, one of his generals defeated the Spaniards at Ayacucho. The Spaniards surrendered in 1826. Peru suffered much instability throughout the 19th century.

POLITICS

Instability continued into the 20th century. When civilian rule was restored in 1980, a left-wing group called the Sendero Luminoso (Shining Path), began guerrilla warfare against the government. In 1990, Alberto Fujimori, son of Japanese immigrants, became president. In 1992, he suspended the constitution and dismissed the legislature. The guerrilla leader, Abimael Guzmán, was arrested in 1992, but instability continued.

A new constitution was introduced in 1993, giving increased power to President Albert Fujimori. In 1996, Tupac Amaru (MRTA) rebels seized the Japanese ambassador's residence, taking hostages and demanding the release of guerrilla prisoners. The stalemate ended in April 1997, when Peruvian troops attacked and freed the remaining 72 hostages.

Peru faced many problems in the 1990s, including a cholera outbreak, the worst El Niño in the 20th century, and a border dispute with Ecuador which was finally settled in 1998. Fujimori began his third term as president in 2000, but, in November, the Congress declared him 'morally unfit' to govern. He resigned and sought sanctuary in Japan. In his absence he was banned from holding office until 2011. In 2005 the government began its attempt to extradite him and try for financial corruption and sanctioning death squads. In 2001, Alejandro Toledo became the first Peruvian of Amerindian descent to hold the office of president. Toledo faced many problems including in 2003–4, a resurgence of activity by the 'Shining Path' guerillas.

ECONOMY

The World Bank classifies Peru as a 'lower-middle-income' developing country. Agriculture employs 35% of the workforce and major food crops include beans, maize, potatoes and rice. Coffee, cotton and sugar are the chief cash crops. Many farmers live at subsistence level. Other farms are co-operatives. Fishing is important.

Peru is one of the world's main producers of copper, silver and zinc. Iron ore, lead and oil are also produced, while gold is mined in the highlands. Most manufacturing is small-scale.

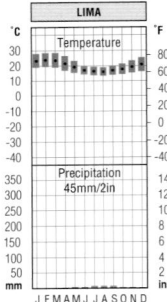

Machu Picchu ruins; created by the Inca empire and situated in the middle of tropical mountain forest the ruins are a World Heritage Site

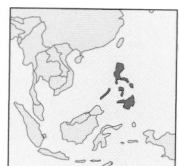

This flag was adopted in 1946, when the country won its independence from the United States. The eight rays of the large sun represent the eight provinces which led the revolt against Spanish rule in 1898. The three smaller stars stand for the three main island groups.

The Republic of the Philippines is an island country in south-eastern Asia. It includes about 7,100 islands, of which 2,770 are named and about 1,000 are inhabited. Luzon and Mindanao, the two largest islands, make up more than two-thirds of the country.

The land is mainly mountainous, it is also unstable and prone to earthquakes. The islands also have several active volcanoes, one of which is the highest peak, Mount Apo, at 2,954 m [9,692 ft].

CLIMATE

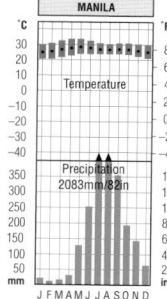

The climate is tropical with high temperatures all year. The dry season runs from December to April. The rest of the year is wet. Typhoons periodically strike the east coast bringing high rainfall.

HISTORY

The first European to reach the Philippines was Ferdinand Magellan in 1521. Spanish explorers claimed the region in 1565 when they established their first permanent settlement on Cebu. Manila was founded in 1571. The Spaniards regarded their new territory as a stepping stone to the Spice Islands to the south. But they also converted most people (except the Muslims on Mindanao and Sulu) to Roman Catholicism.

The economy grew from the late 18th century when the islands were opened up to foreign trade. In 1896 a secret revolutionary society called Katipunan launched a revolt against Spanish rule. The revolt was put down and the rebel leader Emilio Aguinaldo left the country. In 1898, the United States declared war on Spain and the first major engagement was the destruction of all the Spanish ships in Manila Bay. Aguinaldo returned to the Philippines and formed an army which fought alongside the Americans. He proclaimed the Philippines an independent nation and a peace treaty between Spain and the United States was signed with the US taking over the government of the Philippines. However, Aguinaldo still wanted independence and fighting continued between 1899 and 1901.

The Philippines became a self-governing US Commonwealth in 1935 and was guaranteed full independence after a ten-year transitional period. During World War II Japanese troops occupied the islands but the Philippines finally achieved independence on 4 July 1946.

POLITICS

From 1946 until 1971, the country was governed under a constitution similar to that of the United States. In 1971, constitutional changes were proposed, but before ratification, President Ferdinand Marcos declared martial law. In 1977, the main opposition leader, Benigno Aquino, Jr, was

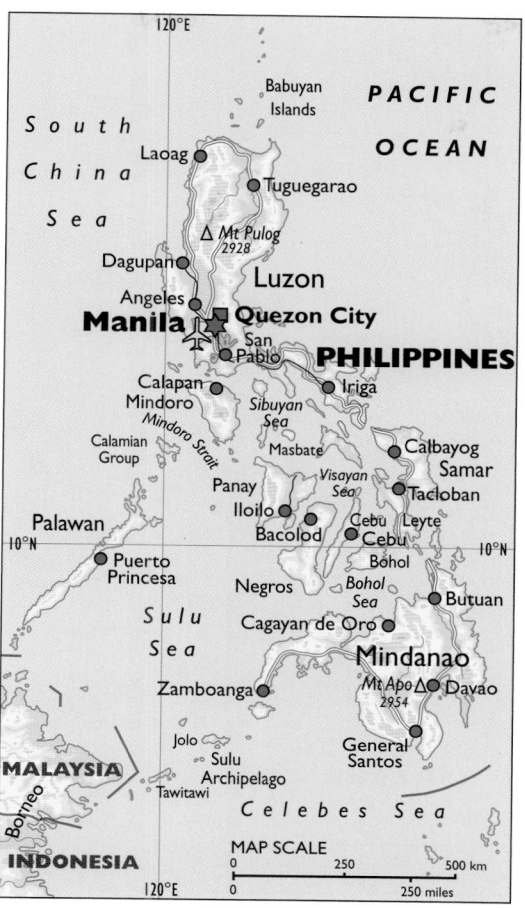

Data panel

Area 300,000 sq km [115,830 sq mi]
Population 86,242,000
Capital (population) Manila (1,581,000)
Government Multiparty republic
Ethnic groups Christian Malay 92%, Muslim Malay 4%, Chinese and others
Languages Filipino (Tagalog) and English (both official), Spanish and many others
Religions Roman Catholic 83%, Protestant 9%, Islam 5%
Currency Philippine peso = 100 centavos
Website www.gov.ph

sentenced to death. He was allowed a stay of execution and went to the United States for medical treatment. Martial law was lifted in 1981, but Aquino was shot dead on his return to the Philippines in 1983.

Following presidential elections in 1986, Marcos was proclaimed president, but the elections proved to be fraudulent and his opponent, Corazon Aquino, the widow of Benigno Aquino, became president. In 2001 Gloria Macapagal-Arroyo, became president and set out to try to find peace in the southern Philippines. In 2003, the government put down military rebellion. Gloria Arroyo was re-elected president in 2004 and a cease-fire was agreed in the south with the Moro Islamic Liberation Front. This cease-fire was broken in 2005.

ECONOMY

The Philippines is a 'lower-middle-income' developing country. Agriculture employs 40% of the workforce. Rice and maize are the main food crops, with bananas, cassava, coconuts, coffee, cocoa, fruits, sugar cane, sweet potatoes and tobacco. Water buffalo, goats and pigs are farmed. Forestry is valuable as nearly half the land is forested. Sea fishing is important, shellfish come from inshore waters.

MANILA

Capital of the Philippines, on Manila Bay, south-west Luzon island. Industrial, commercial, and administrative heart of the Philippines. The River Pasig bisects the city. On the south bank is the old walled city (Intramuros), built by the Spanish in the 16th century on the site of a Muslim settlement. It became a trading centre for the Pacific area. On the north bank lies Ermita, the administrative and tourist centre. Japan occupied the city in 1942 and in 1945 a battle between Japanese and Allied forces destroyed the old city.

Vintas, the traditional sailing outrigger of the Badjao, Zamboanga, Mindanao

Poland's flag was adopted when the country became a republic in 1919. Its colours were taken from the 13th-century coat of arms of a white eagle on a red field. This coat of arms still appears on Poland's merchant flag.

The Republic of Poland faces the Baltic Sea in north-central Europe. Behind the lagoon-fringed coast is a broad plain. The land rises to a plateau region in the south-east of the country. The Sudeten Highlands straddle the border with the Czech Republic. Part of the Carpathian Range lies on the south-eastern border with the Slovak Republic.

CLIMATE

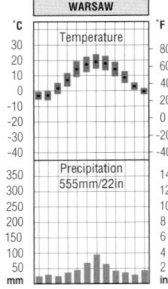

Poland's climate is influenced by its geographical position. Warm, moist air masses come from the west, while cold air masses come from the north and east. Summers are warm, winters cold and snowy.

HISTORY

Poland's boundaries have changed several times in the last 200 years. It disappeared from the map in the late 18th century, when a Polish state called the Grand Duchy of Warsaw was set up. In 1815, the country was partitioned, between Austria, Prussia and Russia. Poland became independent in 1918, but in 1939 it was divided between Germany and the USSR. The country again became independent in 1945, when it lost land (poor agricultural land), and around 6 million people, to the Soviet Union. In compensation, it gained parts of Germany as far as the River Oder, an important industrial region in the west. Other gains were, in the south-west, Silesia and Breslau (now Wroclaw), in the north-west the Baltic port of Stettin (now Szczecin), and in the north the port of Danzig (now Gda´nsk). Acquisition of a length of Baltic coastline gave Poland an opportunity to develop maritime interests.

POLITICS

Communists took power in 1948. Opposition mounted and focused through an organization called Solidarity, led by trade unionist, Lech Walesa. A coalition government was formed between Solidarity and the Communists in 1989. In 1990, the Communist Party was dissolved and Walesa became president. He faced many problems in turning Poland towards a market economy. Solidarity divided in 1990 over personality and the speed of reform. The adoption of its reforms was interrupted in 1993, when the former Communists won the parliamentary elections. In 1995, the ex-Communist Aleksander Krasniewski defeated

Area 323,250 sq km [124,807 sq mi]
Population 38,626,000
Capital (population) Warsaw (1,615,000)
Government Multiparty republic
Ethnic groups Polish 97%, Belarusian, Ukranian, German
Languages Polish (official)
Religions Roman Catholic 95%, Eastern Orthodox
Currency Zloty = 100 groszy
Website www.poland.pl

Walesa in presidential elections, but he continued to follow westward-looking policies. Poland became a member of NATO in 1999 and of the EU in 2004. Having lost elections in 1997, Krasniewski was re-elected president in 2000. In 2005, Lech Kaczynski of the right-wing Law and Justice party became president.

ECONOMY

Poland has large reserves of coal and deposits of minerals which are used in its factories. Manufactures include chemicals, processed food, machinery, ships, steel and textiles. Major crops include barley, potatoes, rye, sugar beet and wheat.

WARSAW

Capital city of Poland, on the River Vistula. Dating from the 11th century it became Poland's capital in 1596. Controlled by Russia from 1813 to 1915, German troops occupied it during World War I. The 1939 German invasion and occupation of Warsaw marked the beginning of World War II. In 1940, the Germans isolated the Jewish ghetto. In January 1945, the Red Army liberated Warsaw and found only 200 surviving Jews. The old town was painstakingly reconstructed. Warsaw became a major transport and industrial centre.

Portugal's colours, which were adopted in 1910 when the country became a republic, represent the soldiers who died in the war (red), and hope (green). The armillary sphere – an early navigational instrument – reflects Portugal's leading role in world exploration.

The Portuguese Republic shares the Iberian Peninsula with Spain. It is the most westerly of Europe's mainland countries. The land rises from the coastal plains on the Atlantic Ocean to the western edge of the huge plateau, or Meseta, which occupies most of the Iberian Peninsula. In central Portugal, the Sera da Estrela contains Portugal's highest point, at 1,993 m [6,537 ft]. Portugal also contains two autonomous regions, the Azores and Madeira islands.

CLIMATE

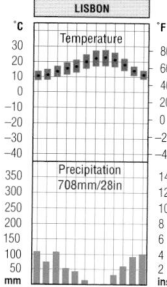

Winds blowing in from the Atlantic Ocean moderate the climate. Portugal experiences cooler summers and milder winters than in other lands on the Mediterranean. In the south, temperatures range from 15–28°C [59–82°F], temperatures in the north are only a few degrees lower year round.

HISTORY

The Romans completed their conquest of the Iberian Peninsula around 2,000 years ago and Christianity was introduced in the 4th century AD. The Romans called Portugal Lusitania. Following the collapse of the Roman Empire in the 5th century, Portugal was conquered by the Christian Visigoths, but in the early 8th century, the Iberian Peninsula was conquered by Muslim Moors. The Christians strove to drive out the Muslims and, by the mid-13th century, they had retaken Portugal and most of Spain.

In 1143, Portugal became a separate country, independent from Spain. In the 15th century, the Portuguese, who were skilled navigators, led the 'Age of Exploration', pioneering routes around Africa onwards to Asia.

Although Portugal set up colonies in Africa and Asia, the most valuable was Brazil. Portugal became wealthy through trade and the exploitation of its colonies. Its power began to decline in the 16th century, when it could no longer defend its far-flung empire. Spain ruled Portugal from 1580 until 1640, when Portugal's independence was restored by John, Duke of Braganza, who took the title of John IV. England supported Portuguese independence and several times defended it from invasion or threats by Spain and its allies. In 1822, Portugal lost Brazil.

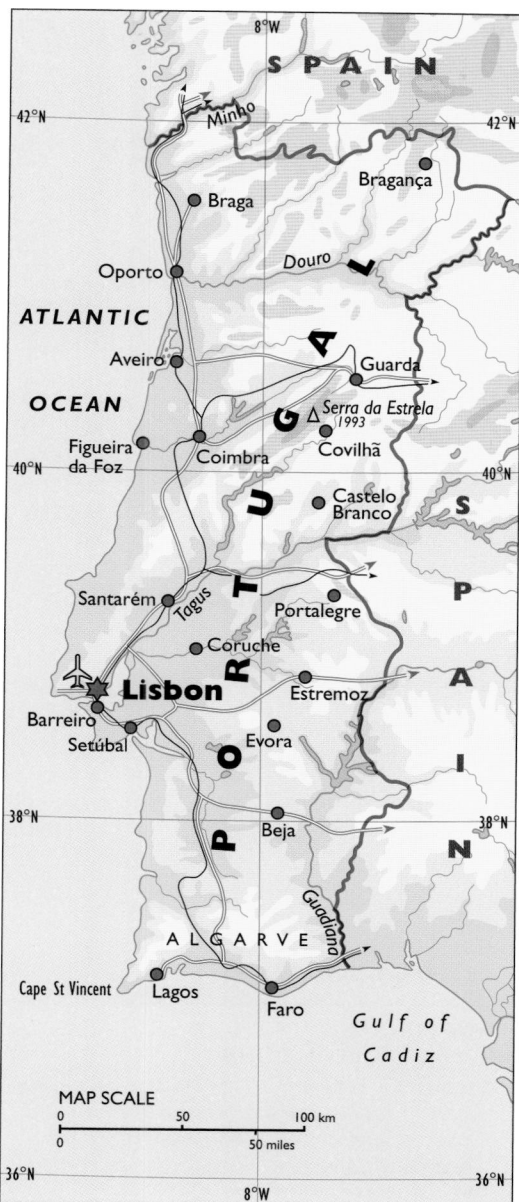

LISBON (LISBOA)

Capital, largest city and chief port of Portugal, at the mouth of the River Tagus, on the Atlantic Ocean. An ancient Phoenician settlement, the Romans conquered the city in 205 BC. After Teutonic invasions in the 5th century AD, it fell to the Moors in 716. In 1147, the Portuguese reclaimed Lisbon, and in 1260 it became the capital. It declined under Spanish occupation (1580–1640). In 1755, an earthquake devastated the city and Marques de Pombal oversaw its reconstruction. It is an international port and tourist centre. Baixa is the neoclassical heart of Lisbon with the Praça do Comércio and Rosso squares. São Jorge castle is surrounded by the medieval quarters. The Monastery of Jerónimos is exceptional.

Area 88,797 sq km [34,285 sq mi]
Population 10,524,000
Capital (population) Lisbon (663,000)
Government Multiparty republic
Ethnic groups Portuguese 99%
Languages Portuguese (official)
Religions Roman Catholic 94%, Protestant
Currency Euro = 100 cents
Website www.portugal.org

POLITICS

Portugal became a republic in 1910, but its first attempts at democracy led to great instability. Portugal fought alongside the Allies in World War I. A coup in 1926 brought an army group to power. They abolished the parliament and set up a dictatorial regime. In 1928, they selected António de Oliviera Salazar, an economist, as minister of finance. He became prime minister in 1932 and ruled as a dictator from 1933. After World War II, when other European powers began to grant independence to their colonies, Salazar was determined to maintain his country's empire. Colonial wars flared up and weakened Portugal's economy. Salazar suffered a stroke in 1968 and died two years later. His successor, Marcello Caetano, was overthrown by another military coup in 1974 and the new military leaders set about granting independence to Portugal's colonies. Free elections were held in 1978 and full democracy was restored in 1982, when a new constitution abolished the military Council of the Revolution and reduced the powers of the president.

Portugal joined the European Community (now the EU) in 1986, and in 1999 became one of the 12 EU countries to adopt the euro, the single currency of the EU. In 2005 the Socialists led by a moderate, José Socrates, won a decisive victory in parliamentary elections.

ECONOMY

Although its economy was growing strongly in the late 1990s, Portugal remains one of the EU's poorer members. Agriculture and fishing were the mainstays of the economy until the mid-20th century. But manufacturing is now the most valuable sector. Textiles, processed food, paper products and machinery are important manufactures. Major crops include grapes for winemaking, olives, potatoes, rice, maize and wheat. Cattle and other livestock are raised and fishing catches include cod, sardines and tuna.

Forest products including timber and cork are important, though forest fires often cause much damage.

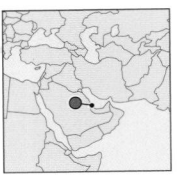

The white stripe, added at the request of the British, denotes friendly Arab states. The nine point serrated line indicates Qatar is the ninth member of the reconciled Emirates of the Arabian Gulf. The maroon area represents blood shed in the 19th century wars.

Area 11,437 sq km [4,415 sq mi]
Population 522,000
Capital (population) Doha (264,000)
Government Absolute monarchy
Ethnic groups Arab 40%, Pakistani 18%, Indian 18%, Iranian 10%
Languages Arabic (official), English
Religions Islam 95% (all native Qataris are Wahhabi Sunni)
Currency Rial = 100 dirham
Website http://english.mofa.gov.qa

The State of Qatar occupies a long, narrow peninsula jutting into the Persian Gulf. The peninsula is about 200 km [124 mi] long, with a greatest width of 90 km [56 mi]. The land is mostly flat desert covered by gravel and loose, wind-blown sand. Sand dunes occur in the south-east. There are also some barren salt flats. The highest point, on a central limestone plateau, is only 98 m [321 ft] above sea level. Qatar also includes several offshore islands and coral reefs. Fresh water is scarce and much of the water supply comes from desalination plants.

CLIMATE

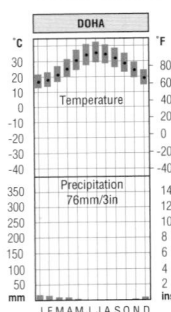

The weather from May to September is extremely hot and dry, with temperatures soaring to 49°C [120°F]. Sand and dust storms are common. Winters are mild to warm, with the weather generally sunny and pleasant. The total annual rainfall seldom exceeds 100 mm [4 in]. Most of the rain occurs in winter.

HISTORY

In the 18th century, migrants established trading settlements along the coast of the peninsula. Since the mid-19th century, members of the Al-Thani family have been the leaders of Qatar. Between 1871 and 1913, the Ottoman Turks, with Qatar's consent, occupied a garrison on the peninsula. In 1916, Qatar agreed that Britain would take responsibility for the country's foreign affairs. Oil was struck in 1939 but exploitation was delayed by World War II. Commercial exploitation began in 1949, leading to the rapid development and modernization of the country's infrastructure.

In 1968, Britain announced the withdrawal of its forces from the Gulf. Qatar negotiated with Bahrain and the United Arab Emirates concerning the formation of a federation, but this proposal was finally rejected.

DOHA

Capital of Qatar, on the east coast of the Qatar peninsula, in the Persian (Arabian) Gulf. Doha was a small fishing village until oil production began in 1949. It is now a modern city and trade centre. Industries include oil refining, shipping, engineering.

POLITICS

Qatar became fully independent on 3 September, 1971. In 1972, because of rivalries in the ruling family, the deputy ruler Khalifa bin Hamad Al Thani seized power, from his cousin, Emir Ahmad in Al-Thani, in a coup. In 1982, Qatar together with Bahrain, Kuwait, Oman, Saudi Arabia and the United Arab Emirates united to form the Gulf Co-operation Council, which is concerned with such matters as defence and economic development.

In 1990, following Iraq's invasion of Kuwait, Qatar agreed to allow foreign troops on its soil and, in 1991, Qatari troops were involved in the military campaign to free Kuwait. In 1995, Qatar signed a security pact with the United States. A bloodless coup occurred in 1995, when the heir apparent, Sheikh Hamad bin Khalifa Al-Thani, deposed his father, while Khalifa was abroad. An attempted counter-coup failed in 1996.

In 1996, the Al-Jazeera satellite television was launched in Qatar. It soon won a worldwide reputation for tackling controversial issues, especially those connected with the Arab world. In 2001, it became famous when it became the first station to air recorded statements by the al Qaida leader Osama bin Laden and, from 2003, it covered the conflict in Iraq graphically. Qatar is an emirate, ruled by the Emir and his appointed Council of Ministers. Municipal elections in 1999 heralded moves towards democracy.

A new constitution introduced in 2004 provided for a 45-member Consultative Council. This Council consisted of 45 members, two-thirds of whom would be elected by the public and one-third appointed by the Emir. The new constitution came into force in 2005 with elections expected by 2007. In foreign affairs, Qatar resolved long-standing boundary disputes with Bahrain and Saudi Arabia in 2001. In 2003, the US Central Command forward base on Qatar became the main centre for the US-led invasion of Iraq.

ECONOMY

The people of Qatar enjoy a high standard of living, which derives from oil revenues. The country has a comprehensive welfare system, and many of its services are free or highly subsidized. Oil production has given Qatar one of the world's highest per capita incomes and accounts for more than 80% of the country's export revenues. Qatar has about 5% of the world's proved oil reserves and more than 15% of the world's proven natural gas reserves.

Besides oil refining, they produce ammonia, cement, fertilizers, petrochemicals and steel bars. Wells have been dug to develop agriculture and products include beef, dairy products, fruits, poultry and vegetables.

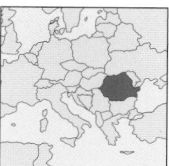
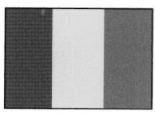

Romania's flag, adopted in 1948, uses colours from the arms of the provinces, which united in 1861 to form Romania. A central coat of arms, added in 1965, was deleted in 1990 after the fall of the Communist regime under the dictator Nicolae Ceaucescu.

Romania is on the Black Sea in eastern Europe. Eastern and southern Romania form part of the Danube River Basin. The delta region where the river flows into the Black Sea, is one of Europe's finest wetlands. The southern part of the coast contains several resorts.

The country is dominated by the Carpathian mountains which curve around the plateaux of Transylvania in central Romania. The southern arm of the mountains, including Mount Moldoveanu (2,543 m [8,341 ft]), is known as the Transylvanian Alps. On the border with Serbia and Montenegro, the River Danube (Dunav/Duna˜rea) has cut a gorge, the Iron Gate (Portile de Fier) whose rapids have been tamed by a huge dam. Forests cover large areas in Transylvania and the Carpathians, while farmland dominates in the Danubian lowlands and the plateaux.

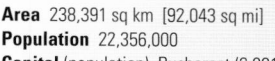

Area 238,391 sq km [92,043 sq mi]
Population 22,356,000
Capital (population) Bucharest (2,001,000)
Government Multiparty republic
Ethnic groups Romanian 89%, Hungarian 7%, Roma 2%, Ukranian
Languages Romanian (official), Hungarian, German
Religions Eastern Orthodox 87%, Protestant 7%, Roman Catholic 5%
Currency Leu = 100 bani
Website www.gov.ro/engleza/

CLIMATE

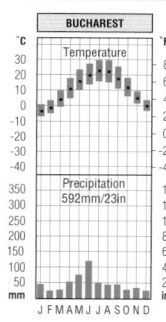

Romania has hot summers and cold winters. Rainfall is heaviest in spring and early summer, when thundery showers are common.

HISTORY

Around 2,300 years ago, Romania was called Dacia. After the Romans conquered the area in AD 106, the Dacians embraced Roman culture and language so completely that the region became known as Romania. The first step towards the creation of the modern state occurred in the 14th century when two principalities were formed: Walachia (or Valachi) in the south and Moldavia in the east. But they were conquered by the Ottoman Turks around 1500.

Museum of Peles, *Sinaia, Transylvania*

BUCHAREST (BUCURESTI)

Capital and largest city of Romania, on the River Dimbovita, southern Romania. Founded in the 14th century on an important trade route, it became capital in 1862. Occupied by Germany in both World Wars. An industrial, commercial and cultural centre. The seat of the patriarch of the Romanian Orthodox Church, it has notable churches, museums and galleries. The infamous 1980s Civic Centre is a symbol of dictatorial aggrandisement.

Walachia and Moldavia united in 1861 to form modern Romania. After World War I, Romania, which had fought with the Allies, gained much land, including Transylvania, almost doubling the country's size and population. In 1939 Romania lost territory to Bulgaria, Hungary and the Soviet Union. Romania fought alongside Germany in World War II, and was occupied by Soviet in 1944. Hungary returned northern Transylvania to Romania in 1945, but Bulgaria and the Soviet Union kept former Romanian territory when King Michael was forcibly removed from the throne.

In the 1960s, Romania's Communist Party, led by Gheorghe Gheorghiu-Dej, began to oppose Soviet control, a policy continued by Nicolae Ceaucescu, who became Communist Party chief in 1965.

Under Ceaucescu Romania developed industries based on its oil and natural gas reserves. His rule was corrupt and self-seeking, but he won plaudits from the West for his independent stance against Soviet control, including a knighthood from Queen Elizabeth II. However, he pursued a strict Stalinist approach and the remorseless industrialization and urbanization programmes of the 1970s caused severe debt. In the 1980s, he cut imports and diverted output to exports. Self-sufficiency turned to subsistence and shortages, with savage rationing of food and energy.

Ceaucescu's building schemes desecrated some of the country's finest architecture and demolished thousands of villages. In December 1989, mass anti-government demonstrations were held in Timisoara with protests across Romania. Security forces fired on crowds, causing many deaths. But after army units joined the protests, Nicolae Ceaucescu and his wife Elena fled from Bucharest on 22 December. Both were executed on Christmas Day on charges of genocide and corruption. A provisional government of the National Salvation Front (NSF), took control, much of the old administrative apparatus was dismantled, and the Communist Party was dissolved.

POLITICS

In May 1990, under Ion Iliescu, the NSF won Romania's first free elections since World War II, a result judged to be flawed but not fraudulent. A new constitution enshrining pluralist democracy, human rights and a market economy was passed by parliament in 1991. There were strikes and protests against the new authorities and also against the effects of the switch to a market economy, which caused food shortages, rampant inflation and increased unemployment. Foreign investment was sluggish, deterred by the political instability. Presidential elections in 1996 led to defeat for Iliescu and victory for the centre-right Emil Constantinescu. In 2000, Iliescu was re-elected president, though the government continued its privatization policies. He stood down in 2004. Romania became a member of NATO in 2004 and is expected to join the EU in 2007.

ECONOMY

According to the World Bank, Romania is a 'lower-middle-income' economy. Oil and natural gas are the chief mineral resources and the aluminium, copper, lead and zinc industries use domestic supplies. Manufactures include cement, processed food, petroleum products, textiles and wood. Agriculture employs nearly a third of the workforce. Crops include fruits, maize, potatoes, sugar beet and wheat. Sheep are the chief livestock.

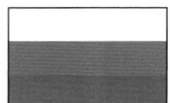

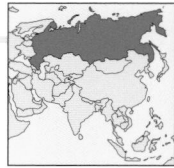

In August 1991, Russia's traditional flag, which had first been used in 1699, was restored as Russia's national flag. It uses colours from the flag of the Netherlands. This flag was suppressed when Russia was part of the Soviet Union.

The Russian Federation is the world's largest country. About 25% lies west of the Ural Mountains (Uralskie Gory) in European Russia, where 80% of the population lives. It is mostly flat or undulating, but the land rises to the Caucasus Mountains in the south, with Russia's highest peak, Elbrus (5,633 m [18,481 ft]). Siberia, contains vast plains and plateaux, with mountains in the east and south. The Kamchatka peninsula in the far east has many active volcanoes.

Russia contains many of the world's longest rivers, including Yenisey-Angara and the Ob-Irtysh. It also includes part of the world's largest inland body of water, the Caspian Sea, and Lake Baikal, the world's deepest lake.

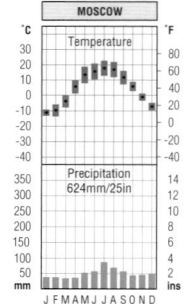

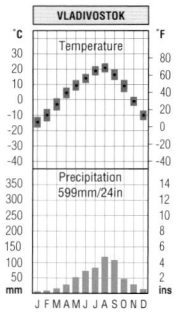

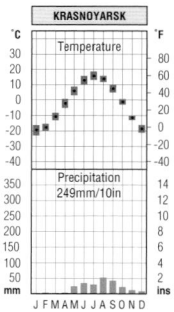

CLIMATE

The Moscow climate is continental with cold and snowy winters and warm summers. While Krasnoyarsk in south-central Siberia has a harsher, drier climate, but it is not as severe as parts of northern Siberia.

HISTORY

In the 9th century AD, a state called Kievan Rus was formed at the junction of the forest and the steppe in what is now Ukraine. Other states then formed further to the north and all were eventually united under the principality of Muscovy. In the 13th century, Mongol armies from the east penetrated the forests and held sway over the Slavic peoples there. It was only in the 16th century that the Mongol yoke was thrown off as the Slavs, under Ivan the Terrible (1530–84), began to advance across the steppes.

There began a period of expansion from the core area of Slavic settlement to the south, east and west. Expansion across Siberia was rapid and the first Russian settlement on the Pacific, Okhotsk, was established in 1649. By 1696, Azov, the key to the Black Sea, was secured. A series of struggles in the 17th and 18th centuries against the Swedes and the Poles resulted in the addition of the Gulf of Finland, the Baltic coast and part of Poland to the growing Russian Empire, while, in the 19th century, the Caucasus, Central Asia and new territories in the Far East were added.

The Russian Revolution took place in 1917, Tsar Nicholas II was forced to abdicate and a Bolshevik (Communist) government was established under Vladimir Ilyich Lenin (1870–1924). The Union of Soviet Socialist Republics (the USSR or the Soviet Union) was established in 1922.

POLITICS

From 1924 Joseph Stalin introduced a socialist economic programme, suppressing all opposition both within the Party and among the population. His authority was consolidated with the Great Purge, a period of widespread arrests and execu-

ST PETERSBURG

Second-largest city in Russia, and a major Gulf of Finland seaport, on the delta of the River Neva. Founded in 1703 by Peter I (the Great), the city was the capital of Russia from 1712 to 1918. It was the scene of the Decembrist revolt (1825), and the Bloody Sunday incident in the Russian Revolution of 1905. Renamed Petrograd in 1914, it was a centre of the political unrest that culminated in the Russian Revolution. Petrograd workers were the spearhead of the 1917 Revolution, and the city was renamed Leningrad in 1924. Damaged during World War II, it has since been rebuilt. Renamed St Petersburg (1991), following the break-up of the Soviet Union, it has federal status within the Russian Republic.

Area 17,075,400 sq km [6,592,812 sq mi]
Population 143,782,000
Capital (population) Moscow (8,297,000)
Government Federal multiparty republic
Ethnic groups Russian 82%, Tatar 4%, Ukrainian 3%, Chuvash 1%, more than 100 others
Languages Russian (official), plus many others
Religions Russian Orthodox, Islam, Judaism
Currency Russian rouble = 100 kopeks
Website www.kremlin.ru/eng

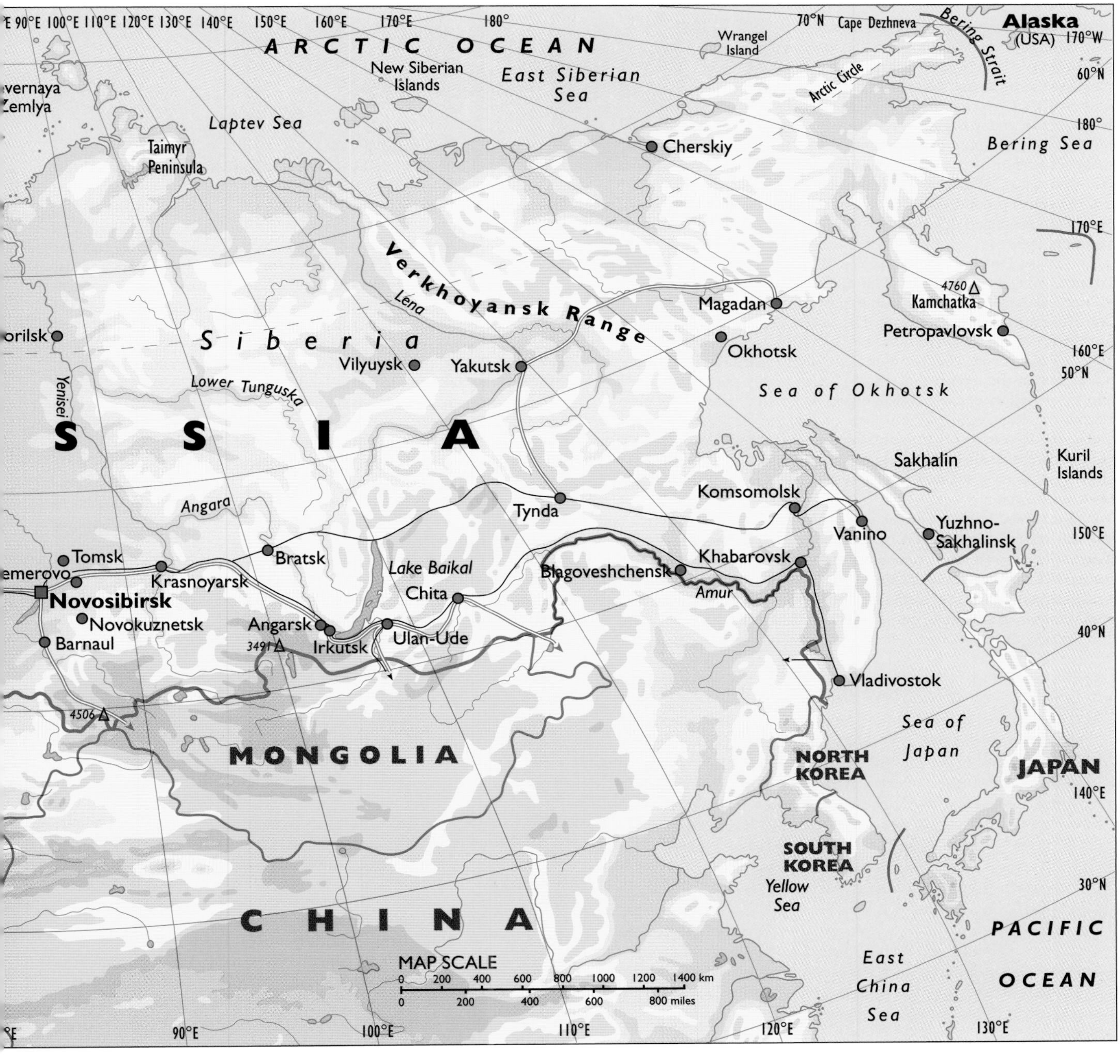

[Map of Russia]

LAKE BAIKAL

World's deepest lake in southern Siberia, Russia; the largest freshwater feature in Asia. Fed by numerous small rivers, its outlet is the River Angara. Framed by mountains, Baikal has rich fish stocks and the world's only freshwater seal species. Its ecology is threatened by pollutants from lakeside factories. Government schemes have been introduced to protect the environment. Irkutsk is on the north shore and the Trans-Siberian Railway runs along the south shore. Area: 31,494 sq km (12,160 sq mi),.maximum depth: 1,743 m (5,714 ft).

Russian fishermen net a catch of omul on Lake Baikal

tions which reached its peak in 1937. His introduction of five-year plans and collective farming transformed the Soviet Union from a largely peasant society to a major world industrial power by the end of the 1930s. Collectivization was violently resisted by many peasants, resulting in millions of casualties from famine and mass repression of peasants (*kulaks*) by the authorities. After Stalin's death, the Soviet leaders modified some policies, but remained true to the principles of Communism until Mikhail Gorbachev changed the face of Russia in the 1980s.

The Soviet Union joined World War II (known in Russia as the Great Patriotic War) in June 1941. The armed forces of the Soviet Union inflicted about 80% of losses suffered by German land forces in World War II (about 3 million soldiers). The Soviet Union, suffered enormous losses with 25 million dead.

Under Soviet rule, changes took place in the distribution of the population so that the former pattern of a small highly populated core and 'empty' periphery began to break down. As a result, a far higher proportion of the Russian population lives east of the Ural Mountains than before the Revolution. The redistribution was actively encouraged by a regime committed to developing the east. Migration to the towns and cities has also been marked and by 1997 73% of the population lived in cities and towns.

In the 1980s, Mikhail Gorbachev sought to introduce economic and political reforms necessitated by the failures of Communist economic policies. This was a time of *glasnost* (openness) and *perestroika* (restructuring). The Soviet Union broke up in December 1991. Russia maintained relations with 11 of the 15 former Soviet republics through a confederation called the Commonwealth of Independent States (CIS).

Despite Gorbachev's brave efforts at reform, his successor Boris Yeltsin

inherited an economy in crisis. The abolition of price controls sent the cost of basic commodities rocketing, there were food shortages and rising unemployment. Despite these difficulties, including rising corruption and crime, the government's programme of reforms was supported in a 1993 referendum and Yeltsin returned as president in July 1996.

Yeltsin resigned on 31 December 1999 due to poor health and appointed the prime minister Vladimir Putin as the acting president. Putin, was elected president by a landslide in March 2000.

Fighting began in the secessionist Chechnya during the 1990s and flared up into full-scale war in 1999. The conflict slowed in 2000, but Russia faced a new threat, namely bombings of its cities by Chechen terrorists. After the attacks on the United States on 11 September 2001, Putin and President George W. Bush found common cause in the campaign against international terrorism and the assault on the Taliban in Afghanistan, though relations soured when Russia opposed the attack on Iraq in 2003.

The conflict in Chechnya mounted and has lead to hundreds of deaths in Russia in a series of major terrorist attacks, such as the attack on a Moscow theatre in 2002, the bombing of two passenger flights in 2004, and the occupation of a school by Muslim extremists in 2004 which led to more than 300 deaths, caused international outrage.

ECONOMY

Under Soviet rule, Russia transformed from an agrarian economy into the world's second greatest industrial power. By the 1970s, concentration on the military-industrial complex and a bloated bureaucracy caused the economy to stagnate. Gorbachev's policy of perestroika was an attempt to correct this weakness. Yeltsin sped up the pace of reform. In 1993, the command economy was abolished, private ownership was re-introduced, and mass privatization began. In 1997 Russia was admitted to the Council of Europe, the same year Russia attended the G7 summit, suggesting that it was now counted among the world's leading economies. Industry employs 46% of the workforce and contributes 48% of GDP. Mining is the most valuable activity. Russia is the world's leading producer of natural gas and nickel, and the world's third-largest producer of crude oil, lignite, and brown coal. It is the world's second-largest manufacturer of aluminium and phosphates. Light industries are growing in importance. Most farmland is still government-owned or run as collectives. Russia is the largest producer of barley, oats, rye, and potatoes. It is the world's second-largest producer of beef and veal.

MOSCOW (MOSKVA)

Capital of Russia and largest city in Europe, on the River Moskva. The site has been inhabited since Neolithic times, but Russian records do not mention it until 1147. It had become a principality by the end of the 13th century, and in 1367 the first stone walls of the Kremlin were constructed. By the end of the 14th century, Moscow emerged as the focus of Russian opposition to the Mongols. Polish troops occupied the city in 1610, but were driven out two years later. Moscow was the capital of the Grand Duchy of Russia from 1547 to 1712, when the capital moved to St Petersburg. In 1812 Napoleon and his army occupied Moscow, but were forced to flee when the city burned to the ground. In 1918, following the Russian Revolution, it became the capital of the Soviet Union. The failure of the German army to seize the city in 1941 was the Nazis' first major setback in World War II. The Kremlin is the centre of the city, and the administrative heart of the country. Adjoining it are Red Square, the Lenin Mausoleum, and the 16th-century cathedral of Basil the Beatified. Industries include metalworking, oil-refining, motor vehicles, film-making, precision instruments, chemicals, publishing, wood and paper products, and tourism.

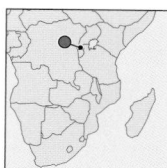

Rwanda's new flag was adopted in 2002. The blue is used to symbolize peace and tranquillity. Yellow represents wealth as the country works to achieve sustainable economic growth, while green denotes prosperity, work and productivity. The 24-ray golden sun symbolizes new hope.

The Republic of Rwanda is Africa's most densely populated country. It is a small state in the heart of Africa. The western border is formed by Lake Kivu and the River Ruzizi. Rwanda has a rugged landscape, dominated by high, volcanic mountains, rising to Mount Karisimbi, at 4,507 m [14,787 ft]. The capital, Kigali, stands on the central plateau. East Burundi consists of stepped plateaux, which descend to the lakes and marshland of the Kagera National Park on the Tanzania border.

The lush rainforests in the west are one of the last refuges for the mountain gorilla. Many of Rwanda's forests have been cleared and 35% of the land is now arable. The steep mountain slopes are intensively cultivated. Despite contour ploughing, heavy rains cause severe soil erosion.

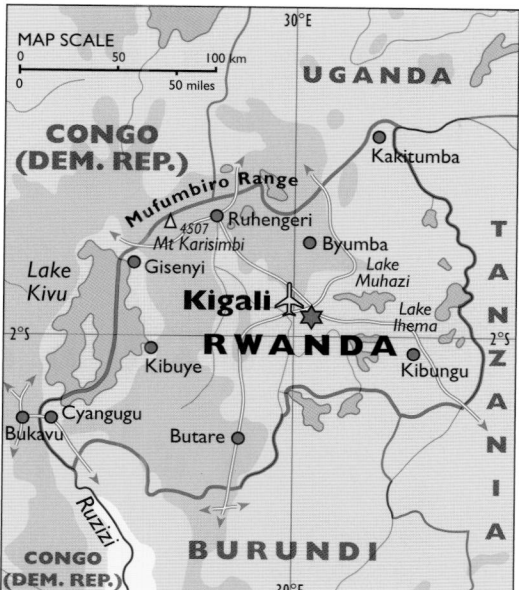

Area	26,338 sq km [10,169 sq mi]

Area 26,338 sq km [10,169 sq mi]
Population 7,954,000
Capital (population) Kigali (234,000)
Government Republic
Ethnic groups Hutu 84%, Tutsi 15%, Twa 1%
Languages French, English and Kinyarwanda (all official)
Religions Roman Catholic 57%, Protestant 26%, Adventist 11%, Islam 5%
Currency Rwandan franc = 100 centimes
Website www.gov.rw

CLIMATE

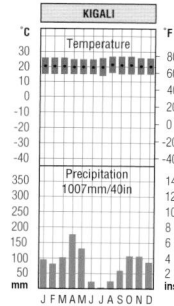

Temperatures in Kigali are moderated by the altitude. The rainfall is abundant, but much heavier rain falls on the western mountains. The dry season is June–August. The floor of the Great Rift Valley is warmer and drier than the rest of the country.

HISTORY

The Twa, a pygmy people, were the first known people to live in Rwanda. About 1,000 years ago, a farming people, the Hutu, settled in the area, gradually displacing the Twa.

From the 15th century, a cattle-owning people from the north, the Tutsi, began to dominate the Hutu, who had to serve the Tutsi overlords.

By the late 18th century, Rwanda and Burundi formed a single Tutsi-dominated state, ruled by a King (Mwami). In 1890, Germany conquered the area and subsumed it into German East Africa. During World War 1, Belgian forces occupied (1916) both Rwanda and Burundi. In 1919, it became part of the Belgian League of Nations mandate territory of Ruanda-Urundi (which in 1946 became a UN Trust Territory). The Hutu majority intensified their demands for political representation. In 1959, the Tutsi Mwami died. The ensuing civil war between Hutus and Tutsis claimed more than 150,000 lives. Hutu victory led to a mass exodus of Tutsis. The Hutu Emancipation Movement, led by Grégoire Kayibanda, won the 1960 elections. In 1961, Rwanda declared itself a republic. Belgium granted independence in 1962, and Kayibanda became president.

POLITICS

Rwanda was subject to continual Tutsi incursions from Burundi and Uganda. In 1973, Major General Habyarimana overthrew Kayibanda in a military coup. In 1978, Habyarimana became president. Drought devastated Rwanda in the 1980s. More than 50,000 refugees fled to Burundi. In 1990, the Tutsi-dominated Rwandan Patriotic Front (RPF) invaded Rwanda, forcing Habyari-

KIGALI

Capital city lying in the centre of Rwanda. It was a trade centre during the period of German and Belgian colonial administration, becoming the capital when Rwanda achieved independence in 1962. Industries include tin mining, cotton and coffee.

mana to adopt a multiparty constitution. In April 1994, Habyarimana and the president of Burundi died in a rocket attack. The Hutu army and militia launched an act of genocide against the Tutsi minority, massacring more than 800,000 Tutsis. In July 1994, an RPF offensive toppled the government, creating 2 million Hutu refugees. A government of national unity, comprising Tutsis and Hutus, emerged. More than 50,000 people died in refugee camps in eastern Zaïre (now DR Congo). Hutu militia controlled the camps, their leaders facing prosecution for genocide. The sheer number of refugees (1995, one million in Zaïre and 500,000 in Tanzania) destabilized the region. In 1997, Rwandan troops supported Laurent Kabila's successful overthrow of President Mobutu in Zaïre. Kabila failed to expel the Hutu militia from Congo, and Rwanda switched to supporting rebel forces. In 1998, the UN International Criminal Tribunal sentenced Rwanda's former prime minister Jean Kambanda to life imprisonment for genocide. Paul Kagame became president in 2000. He was re-elected in 2003.

In the early 21st century, prosecutions began in both Belgium and Tanzania of people accused of genocide. Rwanda finally withdrew from DR Congo in late 2002 after signing a peace deal with Kinshasa.

ECONOMY

According to the World Bank, Rwanda is a 'low-income' developing country. Agriculture employs 90% of the workforce, but many farmers live at subsistence level. Chief food crops include bananas, beans, cassava, plantains, potatoes, sorghum and sweet potatoes. Some farmers raise cattle and other livestock. The chief cash crop is coffee, also the leading export, followed by tea and hides and skins. Rwanda also produces pyrethrum, which is used to make insecticide. The country produces some cassiterite (tin ore) and wolframite (tungsten ore). Manufacturing is small-scale and include beverages, cement and sugar.

Kinigi farmland *extending to Virunga National Park*

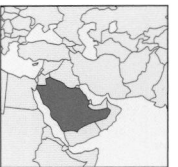

Area 2,149,690 sq km [829,995 sq mi]
Population 25,796,000
Capital (population) Riyadh (3,000,000)
Government Absolute monarchy
Ethnic groups Arab 90%, Afro-Asian 10%
Languages Arabic (official)
Religions Islam 100%
Currency Saudi riyal = 100 halalas
Website www.saudinf.com

The Kingdom of Saudi Arabia occupies about three-quarters of the Arabian Peninsula in southwest Asia. The land is mostly desert and includes the largest expanse of sand in the world, the Rub' al Khali (Empty Quarter), covering an area of 647,500 sq km [250,000 sq mi]. Mountains to the west border the Red Sea plains.

CLIMATE

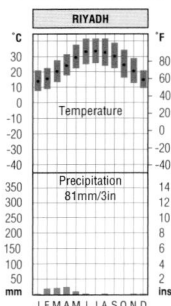

Saudi Arabia has a hot, dry climate. In the summer, the temperatures are extremely high and often exceed 40°C [104°F], though the nights are cool. Winter temperatures rarely go below 20°C [68°F].

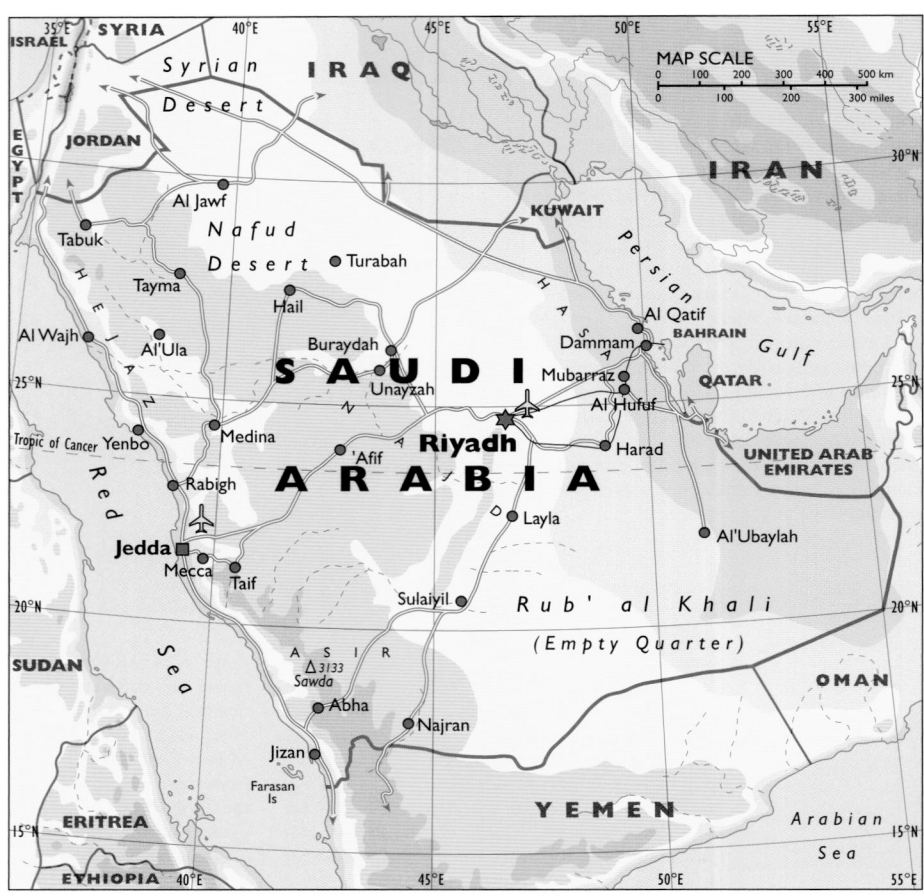

HISTORY

Saudi Arabia contains the two holiest places in Islam – Mecca, the birthplace of the Prophet Muhammad in 570, and Medina where Muhammad and his followers went in 622.

In the mid-15th century, the Saud Dynasty established control over a small area near present-day Riyadh. In the mid-18th century an alliance was established with a religious leader, Muhammad Ibn Abd al-Wahhab, who wanted to restore strict observance of Islam. The Wahhabi movement swept across Arabia and the Saud family took over areas converted to the Wahhabi beliefs. By the early 19th century, they had taken Mecca and Medina. The Ottoman governor of Egypt attacked to halt their expansion and by the late 19th century, most of the Arabian Peninsula was under the rule of Ottoman Turks.

In 1902 Abd al-Aziz Ibn Saud, led a force from Kuwait, where he had been living in exile, and captured Riyadh. From 1906, the Saud family gradually won control over the territory held by their ancestors and extended their land following the defeat of the Ottoman Empire in World War I. After further conquests in the 1920s, Ibn Saud proclaimed the country the Kingdom of Saudi Arabia in 1932.

POLITICS

The first major oil discovery was made in 1938, and full-scale production began after World War II. Saudi Arabia eventually became the world's leading oil exporter and highly influential in the Arab world where it played a major role in supplying development aid.

RIYADH

Capital of Saudi Arabia, in the east-central part of the country, 380 km [235 mi] inland from the Persian Gulf. In the early 19th century, it was the domain of the Saudi dynasty, becoming capital of Saudi Arabia in 1932. The chief industry is oil refining.

Saudi Arabia supported Egypt, Jordan and Syria in the Six-Day War against Israel, in 1967. It did not send troops, but gave aid to the Arab combatants.

King Fahd suffered a stroke in 1995 and appointed his half-brother, Crown Prince Abdullah Ibn Abdulaziz, to act on his behalf. Fahd died in 2005 and Abdullah succeeded him as king.

Although assisted by a Consultative Council, the monarch holds executive and legislative powers and is also the imam (supreme religious ruler). Saudi Arabia is an absolute monarchy with no formal constitution.

Despite its support of Iraq against Iran in the First Gulf War in the 1980s, Saudi Arabia asked for the protection of Western forces against possible Iraqi aggression following the invasion of Kuwait in 1990. In 1991, the country played a significant role in the quick victory over Iraq's Saddam Hussein.

Relations between Saudi Arabia and the United States became strained following the terrorist attacks on the US on 11 September 2001, in part because Osama bin Laden and many of his followers were Saudi-born. Saudi authorities denounced the attacks and severed relations with Afghanistan's Taliban regime. In 2003 and 2004, Saudi Arabia was hit by Islamic attacks. The government held nationwide municipal elections in 2005, its first exercise in democracy. However, political parties are banned and activists who publicly broach the subject of reform risk jail.

ECONOMY

Saudi Arabia has about 25% of the world's known oil reserves, and oil and oil products make up 85% of its exports.

This flag was adopted in 1960 when Senegal became independent from France. It uses the three colours that symbolize African unity. It is identical to the flag of Mali, except for the five-pointed green star. This star symbolizes the Muslim faith of most of the people.

The Republic of Senegal is situated on the north-west coast of Africa. The volcanic Cape Verde (Cap Vert), on which Dakar stands, is the most westerly point in Africa. The country entirely surrounds Gambia. The Atlantic coastline from St Louis to Dakar is sandy. Plains cover most of Senegal, though the land rises gently in the south-east. The north forms part of the Sahel. The main rivers are the Sénégal, which forms the north border, and the Casamance in the south. The River Gambia flows into the Gambia.

Desert and semi-desert cover north east Senegal. In central Senegal, dry grasslands and scrub predominate. Mangrove swamps border parts of the south coast. The far south is a region of tropical savanna, though large areas have been cleared for farming. Senegal has several protected parks, the largest is the Niokolo-Kobo Wildlife Park.

Area 196,722 sq km [75,954 sq mi]
Population 10,852,000
Capital (population) Dakar (880,000)
Government Multiparty republic
Ethnic groups Wolof 44%, Pular 24%, Serer 15%
Languages French (official), tribal languages
Religions Islam 94%, Christianity (mainly Roman Catholic) 5%, traditional beliefs 1%
Currency CFA franc = 100 centimes
Website www.senegalembassy.co.uk

century, battled for control of the interior. The French founded Dakar in 1857. In 1895, Senegal became a French colony within the Federation of French West Africa. In 1902, the capital of this huge empire transferred from St Louis to Dakar. Dakar became a major trading centre. In 1946, Senegal joined the French Union.

CLIMATE

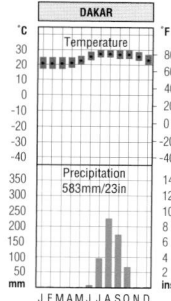

Dakar has a tropical climate, with a short rainy season between June and September when moist winds blow from the south-west. Temperatures are higher inland. Rainfall is greatest in the south.

HISTORY

From the 6th to the 10th century, Senegal formed part of the Empire of ancient Ghana. Between the 10th and 14th centuries, the Tukolor state of Tekrur dominated the Sénégal valley. The Almoravid dynasty of Zenega Berbers introduced Islam and it is from the Zenega that Senegal got its name. In the 14th century, the Wolof established the Jolof Empire. The Songhai Empire began to dominate the region.

In 1444, Portuguese sailors became the first Europeans to reach Cape Verde. Trading stations were rapidly established in the area. In the 17th century, France and the Netherlands replaced Portuguese influence. France gradually gained control of the valuable slave trade and founded St Louis in 1658. By 1763 Britain expelled the French from Senegal and in 1765, set up Senegambia, the first British colony in Africa. In 1783 France regained control and in the mid 19th

POLITICS

In 1959, Senegal joined French Sudan (now Mali) to form the Federation of Mali. Senegal withdrew in 1960 to become the separate Republic of Senegal, within the French community. Its first post-colonial president, Léopold Sédar Senghor, was a noted African poet.

Following an unsuccessful coup in 1962, Senghor gradually assumed wider powers. During the 1960s Senegal's economy deteriorated and a succession of droughts caused starvation and widespread civil unrest.

During the 1970s southern Senegal was a base for guerrilla movements in Guinea and Portuguese Guinea (modern Guinea-Bissau). In 1974, Senegal was a founding member of the West African Economic Community.

Senghor continued in office until 1981, when he was succeeded by the prime minister, Abdou Diouf. In that same year, Senegalese troops suppressed a coup in the Gambia. In 1982 the two countries joined to form the Confederation of Senegambia, but the union collapsed in 1989. From 1989 to 1992, Senegal was at war with Mauritania.

In 2000, Diouf was surprisingly beaten in presidential elections by veteran opposition leader Abdoulaye Wade of the Senegalese Democratic Party, ending 40 years of Socialist Party rule. In 2001, the government signed a peace treaty with the separatist rebels in the southern Casamance province.

ECONOMY

According to the World Bank, Senegal is a 'lower-middle-income' developing country. Agriculture still employs 65% of the population, though many farmers produce little more than they need to feed their families. Food crops include cassava, millet and rice. Senegal is the world's sixth largest producer of groundnuts. Phosphates are the chief resource, and Senegal also refines oil imported from Gabon and Nigeria. Fishing is important.

DAKAR

Capital and largest city of Senegal. Founded in 1857 as a French fort, the city grew rapidly with the arrival of a railway (1885). A major Atlantic port, it later became capital of French West Africa. There is a Roman Catholic cathedral and a presidential palace. Dakar has excellent educational and medical facilities, including the Pasteur Institute. Industries include textiles, oil refining, brewing.

A group of fishermen sit at the base of a large fig tree along the bank of the Casamance river in Kafountine, Senegal

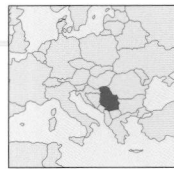

The tricolour flag uses the Pan-Slavic colours of blue, white and red. These colours derive from the 19th century flag of Russia.

Area 88,361 sq km [34, 116 sq mi]
Population 9,396,411
Capital (population) Belgrade (1,594,000)
Government Federal republic
Ethnic groups Serb 66%, Albanian 17%, Hungarian 3.5%, others
Languages Serbian (official), Romanian, Hungarian, Slovak, and Croatian (all official in Vojvodina); Albanian (official in Kosovo)
Religions Orthodox 65%, Islam 19%, others
Currency New dinar = 100 paras
Website
www.srbija.sr.gov.yu/?change_lang=en

BELGRADE (BEOGRAD)

Capital of Serbia, at the confluence of the Sava and Danube rivers. Belgrade became capital of Serbia in the 12th century, but fell to the Ottoman Turks in 1521. Freed from Ottoman rule in 1867, it became capital of the newly created Yugoslavia in 1929. The city suffered much damage under German occupation in World War II. In 1999 it was further damaged by Allied air strikes after Milossevic sent federal troops into Kosovo. In October 2000, more than 300,000 people marched through the streets of Belgrade, forcing Milossevic to step down as president.

The Republic of Serbia, with Montenegro, was formerly part of Yugoslavia, in the central part of the Balkan peninsula. From 2003, it was part of the Union of Serbia and Montenegro, but, in 2006, after the Montenegrins had voted for full independence, Serbia became a separate republic. Serbia includes the semi-independent Kosovo in the south. Serbia is a landlocked country. The south-east is mountainous, while the Pannonian Plains, drained by the River Danube, lie in the north.

CLIMATE

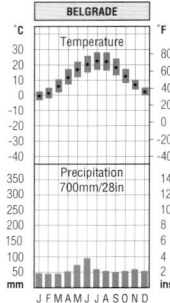

Central and northern Serbia has a continental climate, with hot, dry summers, with heavy rains in the spring and autumn, while the south-east has a more Mediterranean climate.

HISTORY

South Slavs began to move into the region around 1,500 years ago. Each group founded its own state, but by the 15th century Serbia was under the Turkish Ottoman Empire. In 1914, Austria-Hungary declared war on Serbia, blaming it for the assassination of Archduke Franz Ferdinand of Austria-Hungary. This led to World War I and the defeat of Austria-Hungary. In 1918, the South Slavs united in the Kingdom of the Serbs, Croats and Slovenes. In 1929, King Alexander abolished the constitution and renamed the country Yugoslavia. Ruling as a dictator, he sought to enforce the use of one language, Serbo-Croatian. His new political divisions failed to acknowledge the historic boundaries determined by the ethnic groups so the unity of the new state was under constant threat from nationalist and ethnic tensions. After the Germans invaded in 1941, Yugoslavs fought the Germans and themselves. The Communist-led partisans of Josip Broz Tito (a Croat) emerged victorious in 1945.

POLITICS

From 1945, the Communists ruled the country, then called the Federal People's Republic of Yugoslavia. But after Tito's death in 1980, the country was divided. In 1991-2, Yugoslavia split apart with Bosnia-Herzegovina, Croatia, Macedonia and Slovenia each proclaiming their inde-

pendence. The remaining two republics, Serbia and Montenegro, retained the name of Yugoslavia.

Fighting broke out in Croatia and Bosnia-Herzegovina as rival groups struggled for power. In 1992, the United Nations withdrew recognition of the rump Yugoslavia due to its failure to halt atrocities committed by Serbs living in Croatia and Bosnia-Herzegovina. However, in 1995, Yugoslavia took part in talks that led to the Dayton Peace Accord, but it had problems of its own as international sanctions struck the war-ravaged economy.

In 1998, the fragility of the region was again highlighted, in Kosovo, a former autonomous region in southern Serbia where most people are Albanian speaking Muslims. Serbians forced Muslim Albanians to leave their homes, but they were opposed by the Kosovo Liberation Army (KLA). The Serbs hit back and thousands of civilians fled for their lives.

In March 1999, after attempts to find an agreement had failed, NATO forces intervened by launching aerial attacks on administrative and industrial targets in Kosovo and Serbia. Serbian forces stepped up attacks on Albanian- speaking villages, forcibly expelling the people, who fled into Albania and Macedonia. The NATO offensive ended when Serbian forces withdrew from Kosovo and the KLA was disbanded. In 2000, the Yugoslav leader Slobodan Milosevic was defeated in presidential elections and, in February 2002, he faced charges at the UN War Crimes Tribunal in The Hague. Milosevic died in 2006.

In 2003, Yugoslavia became the Union of Serbia and Montenegro, making both republics semi-independent. But, in 2006, the people of Montenegro voted by a narrow majority for independence, and Serbia and Montenegro became separate republics. The Albanian-speakers in Kosovo also continue to press for full independence from Serbia.

ECONOMY

Serbia's resources include bauxite, coal, copper and other metals, together with oil and natural gas. Manufactures include aluminium, machinery, plastics, steel, textiles and vehicles. Agriculture remains important.

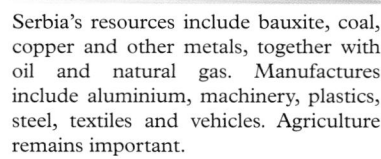

A quiet street in the city of Novi Sad, situated on a bend of the Danube River, in the region of Vojvodina

The green of the flag represents the nation's agriculture and its lush mountain slopes. Blue stands for the waters of the Atlantic that lap Sierra Leone's coast. White symbolizes the desire for peace, justice and unity

The Republic of Sierra Leone on the west coast of Africa is about the same size as the Republic of Ireland. The coast contains several deep estuaries in the north, with lagoons in the south. The most prominent feature is the mountainous Freetown (or Sierra Leone) peninsula. North of the peninsula is the River Rokel estuary, west Africa's best natural harbour. Behind the coastal plain, the land rises to mountains, with the highest peak, Loma Mansa, reaching 1,948 m [6,391 ft].

Swamps cover large areas near the coast. Inland, much of the rainforest has been destroyed. The north is largely covered by tropical savanna.

Area 71,740 sq km [27,699 sq mi]
Population 5,884,000
Capital (population) Freetown (470,000)
Government Single-party republic
Ethnic groups Native African tribes 90%
Languages English (official), Mende, Temne, Krio
Religions Islam 60%, traditional beliefs 30%, Christianity 10%
Currency Leone = 100 cents
Website www.visitsierraleone.org

CLIMATE

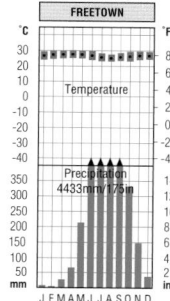

The climate is tropical, with heavy rainfall. In the north, it is dry between December and March. In the south, it is dry in January and February.

HISTORY

Portuguese sailors reached the coast in 1460. In the 16th century, the area became a source of slaves. Freetown was founded in 1787 as a home for freed slaves. In 1808, the settlement became a British Crown Colony. The interior was made a Protectorate in 1896 and in 1951, the Protectorate and Colony united.

Sierra Leone gained independence in 1961 and in 1971 became a republic.

POLITICS

A 1991 referendum voted for the restoration of multi-party democracy, but the military seized power in 1992. A civil war raged between government forces and the Revolutionary United Front (RUF). The RUF fought to end foreign interference and to nationalize the diamond mines. After 1996 elections, Ahmad Tejan Kabbah led a civilian government. In 1997,

Major Johnny Paul Koroma seized power in a military coup. The Economic Community of West African States (ECOWAS) imposed sanctions, and Nigeria led an intervention force that restored Kabbah as president in 1998.

A 1999 peace treaty and the arrival of UN peace-keeping forces seemed to signal an end to the civil war, but in 2000 RUF rebels, led by Foday Sankoh and backed by Liberia, abducted UN troops and renewed the war. British soldiers arrived to bolster the UN peace-keeping effort. Disarmament continued throughout 2001 through a UN-brokered peace plan. Sankoh was captured and, in 2002, the war, which had left about 50,000 people dead, appeared to be over. Rebel raids from Liberia in 2003 failed to disturb the country's fragile peace. Stability was gradually restored and, in late 2005, the last contingent of UN soldiers left the country.

ECONOMY

The World Bank classifies Sierra Leone among the 'low-income' economies. Agriculture provides a living for 70% of the workforce, though farming is mostly at subsistence level. Food crops include cassava, maize and rice, the staple food and export crops include cocoa and coffee. The most valuable exports include diamonds, bauxite and rutile (titanium ore).

FREETOWN

Capital and chief port of Sierra Leone, west Africa. First explored by the Portuguese in the 15th century and visited by Sir John Hawkins in 1562. Freetown was founded by the British in 1787 as a settlement for freed slaves from England, Nova Scotia and Jamaica. It was the capital of British West Africa (1808–74). West Africa's oldest university, Fourah Bay, was founded here in 1827. Freetown was made capital of independent Sierra Leone in 1961. Industries include platinum, gold, diamonds, oil refining, and palm oil.

DIAMOND

Crystalline form of carbon (C). The hardest natural substance known, it is found in kimberlite pipes and alluvial deposits. Appearance varies according to impurities. Bort, inferior in crystal and colour, carborondo, an opaque grey to black variety, and other non-gem varieties are used in industry. Industrial diamonds are used as abrasives, bearings in precision instruments such as watches, and in the cutting heads of drills for mining. Synthetic diamonds, made by subjecting graphite, with a catalyst, to high pressure and temperatures of 3,000°C [5,400°F] are fit only for industry. Diamonds are weighed in carats (0.2gm) and points (1/100 carat).

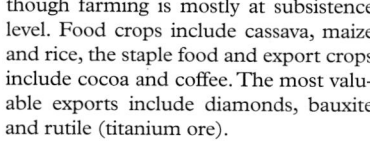

Sierra Leonian women walking in village near Freetown

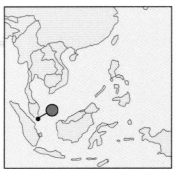

Singapore's flag was adopted in 1959 and it was retained when Singapore became part of the Federation of Malaysia in 1963. The crescent stands for the nation's ascent. The stars stand for Singapore's aims of democracy, peace, progress, justice and equality.

Area 683 sq km [264 sq mi]
Population 4,354,000
Capital (population) Singapore City (3,894,000)
Government Multiparty republic
Ethnic groups Chinese 77%, Malay 14%, Indian 8%
Languages Chinese, Malay, Tamil and English (all official)
Religions Buddhism, Islam, Hinduism, Christianity
Currency Singaporean dollar = 100 cents
Website www.gov.sg

The Republic of Singapore is an island country at the southern tip of the Malay Peninsula. It consists of the large Singapore Island and 59 small islands, 20 of which are inhabited.

Singapore Island is 42 km [26 mi] wide and 28 km [14 mi] across. It is linked to the peninsula by a 1,056 m [3,465 ft] long causeway. The land is mostly low-lying; the highest point, Bukit Timah, is only 176 m [577 ft] above sea level. Its strategic position, at the convergence of some of the world's most vital shipping lanes, ensured its growth.

Rainforest once covered Singapore, but forests now grow on only 5% of the land. Today, about 50% of Singapore is built-up. The distinction between island and city has all but disappeared. Most of the rest consists of open spaces, including parks, granite quarries and inland waters. Farmland covers 4% of the land and plantations of permanent crops make up 7%.

SINGAPORE CITY

The capital of Singapore, on Singapore Island, the largest island in the Republic of Singapore, at the mouth of the Singapore River. The city is home to an ethnic mix of Chinese, Malaysians and Indians with English the main language. It has a very high standard of living due to its very healthy export-based economy. Tourism is one of the largest industries with attractions including the Singapore Zoological Gardens and the Jurong Bird Park, not to mention the Orchard Road area which is the shopping and entertainment centre.

with Malaya, Sarawak, and Sabah to form the Federation of Malaysia. In 1965, Singapore broke away from the Federation to become an independent republic within the Commonwealth of Nations.

The People's Action Party (PAP) has ruled Singapore since 1959. Its leader, Lee Kuan Yew, served as prime minister from 1959 until 1990, when he resigned and was succeeded by Goh Chok Tong. Under the PAP, the economy has expanded rapidly, although some people consider that the PAP's rule has been dictatorial and oversensitive to criticism. In 2004, Lee Hsien Loong, eldest son of Lee Kuan Yew, succeeded Goh Chok Tong as prime minister and called for a more open society. He also called for more people to marry and have babies, a reflection of the country's falling birth rate.

ECONOMY

The World Bank classifies Singapore as a 'high-income' economy. It is one of the world's fastest growing (tiger) economies. Historically, Singapore's economy has been based on trans-shipment, and this remains a vital component. It is one of the world's busiest ports, annually handling more than 290 million tonnes of cargo. Post-1945 the economy diversified. Singapore has a highly skilled and productive workforce. The service sector employs 65% of the workforce; banking and insurance provide many jobs.

Manufacturing is the largest export sector. Industries include computers and electronics, telecommunications, chemicals, machinery, scientific instruments, ships, and textiles. It has a large oil refinery. Agriculture is relatively unimportant. Most farming is highly intensive, and farmers use the latest technology and scientific methods.

CLIMATE

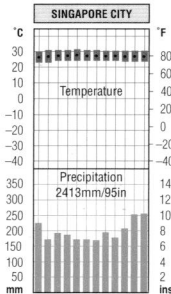

Singapore has a hot, humid equatorial climate, with temperatures averaging 30°C [86°F]. Total average annual rainfall is, 2,413 mm [95 in], with Rain occuring (on average) 180 days each year.

HISTORY

According to legend, Singapore was founded in 1299. It was first called Temasak ('sea town'), but was named Singapura ('city of the lion') when an Indian prince thought he saw a lion there. Singapore soon became a busy trading centre within the Sumatran Srivijaya kingdom. Javanese raiders destroyed it in 1377. Subsumed into Johor, Singapore became part of the powerful Malacca sultanate.

In 1819, Sir Thomas Stamford Raffles, agent of the British East India Company, made a treaty with the Sultan of Johor which allowed the British to build a settlement on Singapore Island. In 1826, Singapore, Pinang, and Malacca formed the Straits Settlement. Singapore soon became the most important British trading centre in Southeast Asia, and the Straits Settlement became a Crown Colony in 1867. Despite British defensive reinforcements in the early 20th century, Japanese forces seized the island in 1942.

POLITICS

British rule returned in 1945. In 1946, the Straits Settlement dissolved and Singapore became a separate colony. In 1959, Singapore achieved self-government. Following a referendum in 1963, Singapore merged

Skyline of Singapore City *from the water's edge*

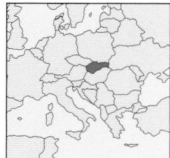

The flag uses the typical red, white and blue Slavic colours. The coat of arms is taken from part of the Hungarian arms and shows a double cross set on three hills to commemorate the arrival of Christianity in the Carpathian region in the 9th century.

The Slovak Republic (Slovakia), is a predominantly mountainous country, part of the Carpathian system that divides the Slovak Republic from Poland is found in the north. The highest peak (Gerlachovka, 2,655 m [8,711 ft]) is in the scenic Tatra (Tatry) Mountains on the Polish border.

Forests cover much of the mountain slopes and there is also extensive pasture. The south-western Danubian lowlands form a fertile lowland region. The Danube forms part of the southern border with Hungary.

Area 49,012 sq km [18,924 sq mi]
Population 5,424,000
Capital (population) Bratislava (449,000)
Government Multiparty republic
Ethnic groups Slovak 86%, Hungarian 11%
Languages Slovak (official), Hungarian
Religions Roman Catholic 60%, Protestant 8%, Orthodox 4%, others
Currency Slovak koruna = 100 halierov
Website www.government.gov.sk/english

A fine example of the traditional painted houses of the Slovak Republic

CLIMATE

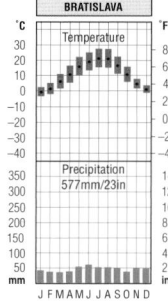

Slovakia has a transitional climate, in between the mild conditions of western Europe, and the continental conditions of Russia to the east. The conditions in Kosice, eastern Slovakia are fairly typical. Temperatures can range from –3°C [27°F] in January to 20°C [68°F] in July. Kosice has an average annual rainfall of 600 mm [24 in]. The mountains have a more extreme climate, with snow or rain throughout the year.

HISTORY

Slav peoples settled in the region in the 5th century AD. In the 9th century, the region, together with Bohemia and Moravia in what is now the Czech Republic, became part of the Greater Moravian Empire. Hungarians conquered this empire in 907 and ruled for nearly a thousand years. Religious wars in the 15th century led many Czech nobles to settle in what is now the Slovak Republic. Hungary was defeated by the Turkish Ottomans in 1526 and, soon afterwards, the Ottomans occupied much of eastern and central Hungary. As a result, the centre of Hungarian power shifted into Slovakia.

Slovak nationalism developed from the late 18th century, but it was kept in check by the Hungarians who enforced 'Magyarization'. In 1867, Hungary and Austria were united to form the dual monarchy of Austria-Hungary. At the end of World War I, Austria-Hungary collapsed and the Czechs and Slovaks united to form a new nation called Czechoslovakia. In 1938, Hungary forced Czechoslovakia to give up several areas with large Hungarian populations. These areas included Kosice in the east.

In 1939, fearing that it might be divided up between Germany, Poland and Hungary, Slovakia declared itself independent, but the country was then conquered by Germany. At the end of World War II, Slovakia again became part of Czechoslovakia. Communists seized control in 1948. In the late 1960s, many Czechs and Slovaks, led by Alexander Dubcek, tried to reform the Communist system. This movement, known as 'the Prague Spring', was put down in 1968 by Soviet troops. Demands for democracy re-emerged in the 1980s, when Soviet leader Mikhail Gorbachev launched a series of reforms in the USSR.

POLITICS

At the end of November 1989, Czechoslovakia's parliament abolished the Communist Party's sole right to govern. In December, the head of the Communist Gustáv Hável, resigned. Non-Communists led by the playwright and dissident Václav Havel formed a new government, they then won a majority in the elections of June 1990.

In the elections of 1992, the Movement for Democratic Slovakia, led by Vladimir Meciar, campaigned for Slovak independence and won a

BRATISLAVA

Capital of Slovakia, on the River Danube, western Slovakia. It became part of Hungary after the 13th century, and was the Hungarian capital from 1526–1784. Incorporated into Czechoslovakia in 1918, it became the capital of Slovakia in 1992. Industries include oil refining, textiles, chemicals, electrical goods.

majority in Slovakia's parliament. The Slovak National Council then approved a new constitution for the Slovak Republic, which came into existence on 1 January 1993.

The Slovak Republic became a member of the OECD in 1997 and maintained close contacts with its former partner. Slovak independence raised national aspirations among the Magyar-speaking community. Relations with Hungary were not helped in 1996, when the Slovak government initiated eight new administrative regions which the Hungarian minority claimed under-represented them politically. The government also made Slovak the only official language. The government's autocratic rule, human rights record and apparent tolerance of organized crime led to mounting international criticism. In 1998, Meciar's party was defeated in a general election by a four-party coalition and Mikulas Dzurinda, leader of the centre-right Slovak Democratic Coalition, became prime minister. Dzurinda narrowly won the parliamentary elections of 2002 and his government continued its policy of strengthening ties with the West. Slovakia became a member of both NATO and the EU in 2004.

ECONOMY

Communist governments developed manufacturing industries, producing chemicals, machinery, steel and weapons. Since the late 1980s, many state-run businesses have been handed over to private owners. Manufacturing employs around 33% of workers. Bratislava and Kosice are the chief industrial cities. Products include ceramics, machinery and steel. The armaments industry is based at Martin, in the north-west.

Farming employs about 12% of the workforce. Major crops include barley, grapes for wine-making, maize, sugar beet and wheat.

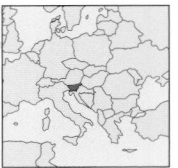

Slovenia's flag, based on the Russian flag, was originally adopted in 1848. A red star appeared at the centre under Communist rule. This flag, which was adopted in 1991 when Slovenia proclaimed independence, has a new emblem, the national coat of arms.

Area 20,256 sq km [7,821 sq mi]
Population 2,011,000
Capital (population) Ljubljana (264,000)
Government Multiparty republic
Ethnic groups Slovene 92%, Croat 1%, Serb, Hungarian, Bosniak
Languages Slovenian (official), Serbo-Croatian
Religions Mainly Roman Catholic
Currency Tolar = 100 stotin
Website www.slovenia-tourism.si

The Republic of Slovenia was one of the six republics which made up Yugoslavia. Much of the land is mountainous and forested. The highest peak is Mount Triglav (2,863 m [9,393 ft]) in the Julian Alps (Julijske Alpe), an extension of the main Alpine ranges in the north-west. Much of central and eastern Slovenia is hilly. The River Sava which flows through central Slovenia is a tributary of the Danube, as is the Drava in the north-east.

Central Slovenia contains the limestone Karst region, with numerous underground streams and cave networks. The Postojna Caves, south-west of Ljubljana, are among the largest in Europe. The country has a short coastline on the Adriatic Sea.

Forests cover about half of Slovenia. Mountain pines grow on higher slopes, with beech, oak and hornbeam at lower levels. The Karst region is largely bare of vegetation because of the lack of surface water. Farmland covers about a third of Slovenia.

CLIMATE

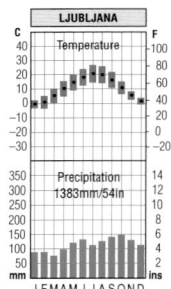

The Slovenian coast has a mild Mediterranean climate. The climate inland is more continental, with snow capping the mountains in winter. Eastern Slovenia has cold winters and hot summers. Rain occurs in every month in Ljubljana, late summer being the rainiest.

HISTORY

The ancestors of the Slovenes, the western branch of a group of people called the South Slavs, settled in the area around 1,400 years ago. An independent Slovene state was formed in AD 623, but the area came under Bavarian-Frankish rule in 748. Austrian royal family the Habsburgs took control of the region in 1278 and, apart from a short period of French rule between 1809 and 1815, it remained under Austrian control until 1918, when the dual monarchy of Austria-Hungary collapsed.

At the end of World War I, Slovenia became part of a new country called the Kingdom of the Serbs, Croats and Slovenes, renamed Yugoslavia in 1929. Slovenia was invaded by Germany and Italy in 1941 and was partitioned between them and Hungary. At the end of the war, Slovenia again became one of the six republics of Yugoslavia.

In the late 1960s and early 1970s, some Slovenes called for the secession of their federal republic from Yugoslavia, but the dissidents were removed from the Communist Party by President Josip Broz Tito, whose strong rule maintained the unity of his country.

POLITICS

After Tito's death in 1980, the federal government in Belgrade found it increasingly difficult to maintain the unity of the disparate elements of the population. It was also weakened by the fact that Communism was increasingly seen to have failed in Eastern Europe and the Soviet Union. In 1990, Slovenia held multiparty elections and a non-Communist coalition was formed to rule the country.

Slovenia and neighbouring Croatia proclaimed their independence in June 1991, but these acts were not accepted by the central government. After a few days of fighting between the Slovene militia and Yugoslav forces, Slovenia, the most ethnically homogenous of Yugoslavia's six component parts, found ready support from Italy and Austria (which had Slovene minorities of about 100,000 and 80,000, respectively), as well as Germany (an early supporter of Slovene independence). After a three-month moratorium, during which there was a negotiated, peaceful withdrawal, Slovenia became independent on 8 October 1991, thereby avoiding the conflict that was to plague other former Yugoslav states.

Slovenia's independence was recognized by the European Community in 1992. Multiparty elections were held and Milan Kucan (a former Communist) of the Party of Democratic Reform became president, while Janez Drnovsek, of the centre-left Liberal Democratic Party, became prime minister, heading a coalition government. The Liberal Democrat coalition government was returned again in 1996 and 2000. Slovenia became a member of NATO and the EU in 2004 and later that year, the centre-right Slovenian Democratic Party topped the polls in parliamentary elections and a centre-right coalition was formed.

ECONOMY

The reform of the formerly state-run economy, and the fighting in areas to the south caused problems for Slovenia. It remains one of the fastest growing economies in Europe.

Manufacturing is the principal activity and manufactures include chemicals, machinery and transport equipment, metal goods and textiles. Slovenia mines some iron ore, lead, lignite and mercury. The leading crops are maize, potatoes and wheat.

LJUBLJANA

Capital and largest city of Slovenia, at the confluence of the rivers Sava and Ljubljanica. In 34 BC Roman Emperor Augustus founded Ljubljana as Emona. From 1244 it was the capital of Carniola, an Austrian province of the Habsburg Empire. During the 19th century, it was the centre of the Slovene nationalist movement. The city remained under Austrian rule until 1918, when it became part of the Kingdom of Serbs, Croats, and Slovenes (later Yugoslavia). When Slovenia achieved independence in 1991, Ljubljana became the capital.

Lake Bled *in the north-west of Slovenia; the lake formed after the recession of the Bohinj glacier*

This flag was adopted in 1960, when Italian Somaliland in the south united with British Somaliland in the north to form Somalia. The colours are based on the United Nations flag and the points of the star represent the five regions of East Africa where Somalis live.

Somalia, is in a region known as the 'Horn of Africa'. A narrow, mostly barren, coastal plain borders the Indian Ocean and the Gulf of Aden. In the interior, the land rises to a plateau, of 1,000 m [3,300 ft]. In the north is a highland region. The south contains the only rivers, the Juba and the Scebeli.

Much of Somalia is dry grassland or semi-desert. There are areas of wooded grassland, with trees such as acacia and baobab. Plants are most abundant in the the lower Juba valley.

CLIMATE

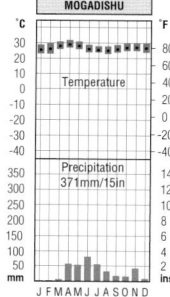

Rainfall is light throughout, the wettest regions being in the south and the northern mountains. The country is prone to droughts, with temperatures on the plateaux and the plains often reaching 32°C [90°F].

HISTORY

In the 7th century, Arab traders established coastal settlements and introduced Islam. Around 900, Mogadishu was founded as a trading centre. The interest of European imperial powers increased after the opening of the Suez Canal in 1869. In 1887, Britain established a Protectorate in what is now northern Somalia. In 1889, Italy formed a Protectorate in the central region, and extended its power to the south by 1905. The new boundaries divided the Somalis into five areas: the two Somalilands, Djibouti (taken by France in 1896), Ethiopia and Kenya. In 1936 Italian Somaliland united with the Somali regions of Ethiopia to form Italian East Africa. During World War II, Italy invaded British Somaliland. But, British forces conquered the region in 1941 and ruled both Somalilands until 1950, when Italian Somaliland returned to Italy as a UN Trust Territory. In 1960, both Somalilands gained independence and joined to form the United Republic of Somalia.

POLITICS

The new republic faced calls for the creation of a 'Greater Somalia' to include the Somali-majority areas in Ethiopia, Kenya, and Djibouti. In 1969, the army, led by Siad Barre, seized power and formed a socialist, Islamic republic. During the 1970s, Somalia and Ethiopia fought for control of the Ogaden Desert, inhabited mainly by Somali nomads. In

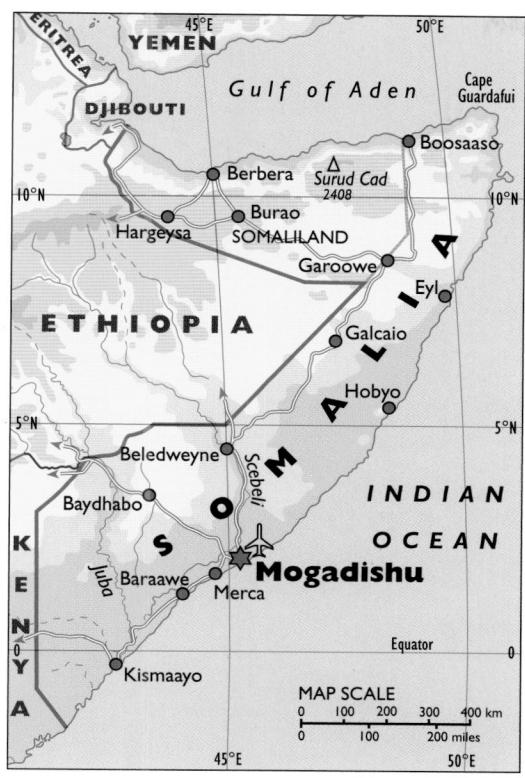

MOGADISHU

Capital and chief port of Somalia, on the Indian Ocean. It was founded by Arabs in the 10th century. In the 16th century, the Portuguese captured the city and it became a cornerstone of their trade with Africa. In 1871 the Sultan of Zanzibar took control. He first leased (1892) and then sold (1905) the port to the Italians. The city then became the capital of Italian Somaliland. It was occupied by the British during World War II. In 1960, Mogadishu became the capital of independent Somalia. The civil war of the 1980s/1990s devastated the city, its population swelled by refugees escaping famine and drought in the outlying regions. In 1992, UN troops flew in to control aid distribution but withdrew in 1995 after little success.

Area 637,657 sq km [246,199 sq mi]
Population 8,305,000
Capital (population) Mogadishu (900,000)
Government Transitional, parliamentary federal government
Ethnic groups Somali 85%, Bantu, Arab, others
Languages Somali (official), Arabic, English, Italian
Religions Islam (Sunni Muslim)
Currency CFA franc = 100 centimes
Website www.unsomalia.net

1978 Ethiopia forced Somalia to withdraw, but resistance continued, forcing one million refugees to flee to Somalia. In 1991, Barre was overthrown and the United Somali Congress (USC), led by Ali Mahdi Muhammad, gained power. Somalia disintegrated into civil war between rival clans. The Ethiopia-backed Somali National Movement (SNM) gained control of north west Somalia, and seceded as the Somaliland Republic in 1991. An attack from the Somali National Alliance (SNA), led by General Muhammad Aideed, shattered Mogadishu. War and drought resulted in a devastating famine. The UN was slow to provide relief and unable to secure distribution. US marines led a taskforce to aid food distribution, but became embroiled in conflict with Somali warlords.

In 1994, 30 US marines died in the fighting and US forces withdrew. Civil strife continued, and in 1996 Aideed was killed. The Cairo Declaration (1997), signed by 26 of the 28 warring factions, held out hope for an end to factional feuding. In 2000, clan leaders elected Abdulkassim Salat Hassan as president, but factional fighting continued. An interim parliament was set up in Kenya (for safety) in 2004, but attempts to move it to Somalia in 2005 saw limited success.

ECONOMY

Somalia is a developing country whose economy has been shattered by drought and war. Catastrophic flooding in late 1997 displaced tens of thousands of people, further damaging the country's infrastrucure, destroying hopes of economic recovery.

Many Somalis are nomads who raise livestock. Live animals, meat and hides are major exports, plus bananas grown in the wetter south. Other crops include citrus fruits, cotton, maize and sugar cane.

*A **Somali herdsman** watches over his mixed herd of cattle and a few camels in a dry riverbed Lugh Ganane, west of Mogadishu*

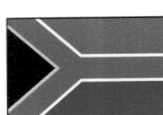

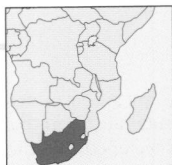

South Africa's flag was first flown in 1994 when the country adopted a new, non-racial constitution. It incorporates the red, white and blue of former colonial powers, Britain and the Netherlands, together with the green, black and gold of black organizations.

CAPE TOWN

City and seaport at the foot of Table Mountain, South Africa. It is South Africa's legislative capital and the capital of Western Cape province. Founded in 1652 by the Dutch East India Company, it came under British rule in 1795. Places of interest include the Union Parliament, a 17th-century castle, the National Historic Museum, and the University of Cape Town (founded 1829). It is an important industrial and commercial centre. Industries include clothing, engineering equipment, motor vehicles and wine.

The Republic of South Africa is geologically very ancient, with few deposits less than 600 million years old. The country can be divided into two main regions, the interior plateau, the southern part of the huge plateau that makes up most of southern Africa; and the coastal fringes.

The interior consists of two main parts. Most of Northern Cape Province and Free State are drained by the Orange River and its right-bank tributaries that flow over level plateaux, varying in height from 1,200 m to 2,000 m [4,000–6,000 ft]. The Northern Province is occupied by the Bushveld, an area of granites and igneous intrusions.

The Fringing Escarpment divides the interior from the coastal fringe. This escarpment makes communication within the country very difficult. In the east, the massive basalt-capped rock wall of the Drakensberg, at its most majestic near Mont-aux-Sources and rising to more than 3,000 m [10,000 ft], overlooks KwaZulu-Natal and Eastern Cape coastlands.

In the west there is a similar, though less well developed, divide between the interior plateau and the coastlands. The Fringing Escarpment also parallels the south coast, where it is fronted by a series of ranges, including the folded Cape Ranges.

CLIMATE

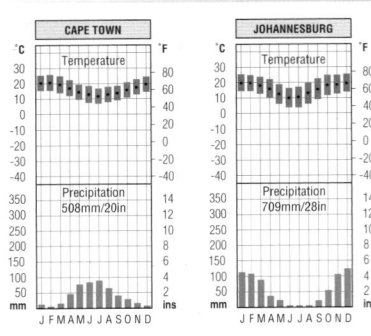

Most of South Africa is sub-tropical and has a mild, sunny climate. Much of the coastal strip, including the city of Cape Town, has warm, dry summers and mild, rainy winters, like the Mediterranean lands of northern Africa. Inland, large areas are arid and the Namib Desert is almost rainless.

Area 1,221,037 sq km [471,442 sq mi]
Population 42,719,000
Capital (population) Cape Town (legislative, 855,000); Tshwane/Pretoria (administrative, 2,200,000); Bloemfontein (judiciary, 350,000)
Government Multiparty republic
Ethnic groups Black 76%, White 13%, Coloured 9%, Asian 2%
Languages Afrikaans, English, Ndebele, Pedi, Sotho, Swazi, Tsonga, Tswana, Venda, Xhosa and Zulu (all official)
Religions Christianity 68%, Islam 2%, HInduism 1%
Currency CFA franc = 100 centimes
Website www.gov.za

HISTORY

Early inhabitants were the Khoisan (also called Hottentots and Bushmen). However, the majority of the people today are Bantu-speakers from the north who entered the country, introducing a cattle-keeping, grain-growing culture. Arriving via the plateaux of the north-east, they continued southwards into the well-watered zones below the Fringing Escarpment of KwaZulu-Natal and Eastern Cape. By the 18th century, these people had reached the south-east. They formed large groups, including the Zulu, Xhosa, Sotho and Tswana.

Also at this time, a group of Europeans was establishing a supply base for the Dutch East India Company on the site of present-day Cape Town. The first group was led by Jan van Riebeeck who founded the base in 1652. In 1657, some Company employees set up their own farms and were known as Boers (farmers). After Britain took over the Cape Town settlement in the early 19th century, many Boers, who resented British rule, began to move inland to develop their own Afrikaaner culture. Beginning in 1836, this migration was known as the Great Trek. Their advance was channelled in the south by parallel coastal ranges, and eventually black and white met near the Kei River. To the north, once the Fringing Escarpment had been overcome, the level plateau surfaces allowed a rapid spread northwards, with the Boers founding the Transvaal in 1852 and Orange Free State in 1854.

In 1870, diamonds were found near the site where Kimberley now stands. Both the British and the Boers claimed the area, but Britain annexed it in 1871. In 1880, the Boers rebelled and defeated the British in the First Boer War. In 1886, gold was discovered in the Witwatersrand in what is now Gauteng. Many immigrants, called *uitlanders*

(foreigners), flooded to the area. Most of them were British and, to maintain their control, the Boers restricted their freedom. Tension developed, culminating in the Second Boer War (1899–1902). The Boer republics of Orange Free State and Transvaal then surrendered and became British colonies. Meanwhile, British forces had overcome Zulu resistance to European settlement. By 1898, all opposition had been suppressed and the black people had lost their independence.

POLITICS

In 1906, Transvaal was granted self-rule, followed by Orange Free State in 1907. The other two parts of the country, Cape Colony and Natal, already had self-rule. In 1910, the entire country was united as the Union of South Africa, a self-governing country within the British Empire. During World War I, two Boer generals led South African forces against Germany. In German South West Africa (now Namibia), General Louis Botha conquered the Germans, while General Jan Christiaan Smuts led Allied forces in German East Africa (now Tanzania). In 1920, the League of Nations gave South Africa control over South West Africa, under a trusteeship agreement. In 1931, Britain granted South Africa full independence as a member of the Commonwealth of Nations.

The development of minerals and urban complexes in South Africa caused an even greater divergence between black and white. The African farmers gained little from the mineral boom. With taxes to pay, they had little alternative but to seek employment in the mines or on European-owned farms. Migrant labour became the normal way of life for many men, while agriculture in black areas stagnated. Groups of Africans took up urban life, living in communities set apart from the white settlements. These townships, with their rudimentary housing often supplemented by shanty dwellings and without any real services, mushroomed during World War II and left South Africa with a major housing problem in the late 1940s. Nowhere was this problem greater than in Johannesburg, where a vast complex of brick boxes called SOWETO (South-Western Townships) was built. The contrast between the living standards of blacks and whites increased rapidly.

At the start of World War II, opinion was divided as to whether South Africa should remain neutral or support Britain. The pro-British General Smuts triumphed. He became prime minister and South African forces served in Ethiopia, northern Africa and Europe. During the war, Daniel Malan, a supporter of Afrikaner nationalism, reorganized the National Party. The Nationalists came to power in 1948, with Malan as prime minister, and introduced the policy of apartheid. The African National Congress, which had been founded in 1912, became the leading black opposition group. Opposition to South Africa's segregationist policies mounted around the world. Stung by criticism from Britain and other Commonwealth members, South Africa became a republic and withdrew from the Commonwealth in 1961. In 1966, the United Nations voted to end South Africa's control over South West Africa, though it was not until 1990 that the territory finally became independent as Namibia.

In response to continuing opposition, South Africa repealed some apartheid laws and, in 1984, under a new constitution, a new three-house parliament was set up. The three houses were for whites, Coloureds and Asians, but there was still no provision for the black majority. In 1986, the European Community (now the European Union), the Commonwealth and the United States applied sanctions on South Africa, banning trade in certain areas. In 1989, F. W. de Klerk was elected president and in 1990 he released the banned ANC leader Nelson Mandela from prison.

In the early 1990s, more apartheid laws were repealed. The country began to prepare a new constitution giving all non-whites the right to vote, though progress towards majority rule was marred by fighting between the Zulu-dominated Inkatha Freedom Party and the ANC.

Elections held in 1994 resulted in victory for the ANC and Nelson Mandela became president. Mandela advocated reconciliation between whites and non-whites, and his government sought to alleviate the poverty of Africans in the townships. The slow rate of progress disappointed many as did other problems, including an increase in crime and the continuing massive gap in living standards between the whites and the blacks. However, in 1999, following the retirement of Nelson Mandela, his successor, Thabo Mbeki, led the African National Congress to an overwhelming electoral victory. Besides poverty, one of the biggest problems facing the country is the estimate given in a government study that one in five South Africans is infected with the HIV virus.

ECONOMY

South Africa is Africa's most developed country. However, most of the black people – rural and urban – are poor with low standards of living. Natural resources include diamonds and gold, which formed the basis of its economy from the late 19th century. Today, South Africa ranks first in the world in gold production and fifth in diamond production. South Africa also produces coal, chromite, copper, iron ore, manganese, platinum, phosphate rock, silver, uranium and vanadium. Mining and manufacturing are the most valuable economic activities and gold, metals and metal products, and gem diamonds are the chief exports.

Manufactures include chemicals, processed food, iron and steel, machinery, motor vehicles and textiles. The main industrial areas lie in and around the cities of Cape Town, Durban, Johannesburg, Port Elizabeth and Pretoria. Investment in South African mining and manufacturing declined in the 1980s, but foreign companies began to invest again following the abolition of apartheid.

Farmland is limited by the aridity of many areas, but the country produces most of the food it needs and food products make up around 7% of South Africa's exports. Major crops include apples, grapes (for wine-making), maize, oranges, pineapples, sugar cane, tobacco and wheat. Sheep-rearing is important on land which is unfit for arable farming. Other livestock products include beef, dairy products, eggs and milk.

TSHWANE (PRETORIA)

Administrative capital of South Africa, Gauteng province. Founded in 1855 and named after Andries Pretorius, a hero for the Afrikaaners who set up apartheid. It became the capital of the Transvaal in 1860, and of the South African Republic in 1881. The Peace of Vereeniging, which ended the South African Wars, was signed here in 1902. In 1910, it became the capital of the Union of South Africa. Early African people named the area Tshwane which means "We are the same". The city was renamed in 2005, Pretoria is still the name of the city centre.

The Outeniqua Choo-Tjoe steam train crossing a bridge at Dolphin Point near Wilderness on the Garden Route.

The Kingdom of Spain is the second largest country in Western Europe after France. It shares the Iberian Peninsula with Portugal. A plateau, called the Meseta, covers most of Spain. Much of it is flat, but crossed by several mountain ranges (*sierras*).

The northern highlands include the Cantabrian Mountains (Cordillera Cantabrica) and the high Pyrenees, which form Spain's border with France. Mulhacén, the highest peak on the Spanish mainland, is in the Sierra Nevada in the south-east. Spain also contains fertile coastal plains. Other lowlands are the Ebro River Basin in the north-east and the Guadalquivir River Basin in the south-west.

Spain also includes the Balearic Islands (Islas Baleares) in the Mediterranean Sea and the Canary Islands off the north-west coast of Africa. Tenerife in the Canary Islands contains Pico de Teide, Spain's highest peak (3,718 m [12,918 ft]).

Forests lie to the rainier north and north-west, with beech and deciduous oak being common. Towards the drier south and east, Mediterranean pines and evergreen oaks take over, and the forests resemble open parkland. Large areas are matorral, a Mediterranean scrub. Where soils are thin and drought is prevalent, matorral gives way to steppe.

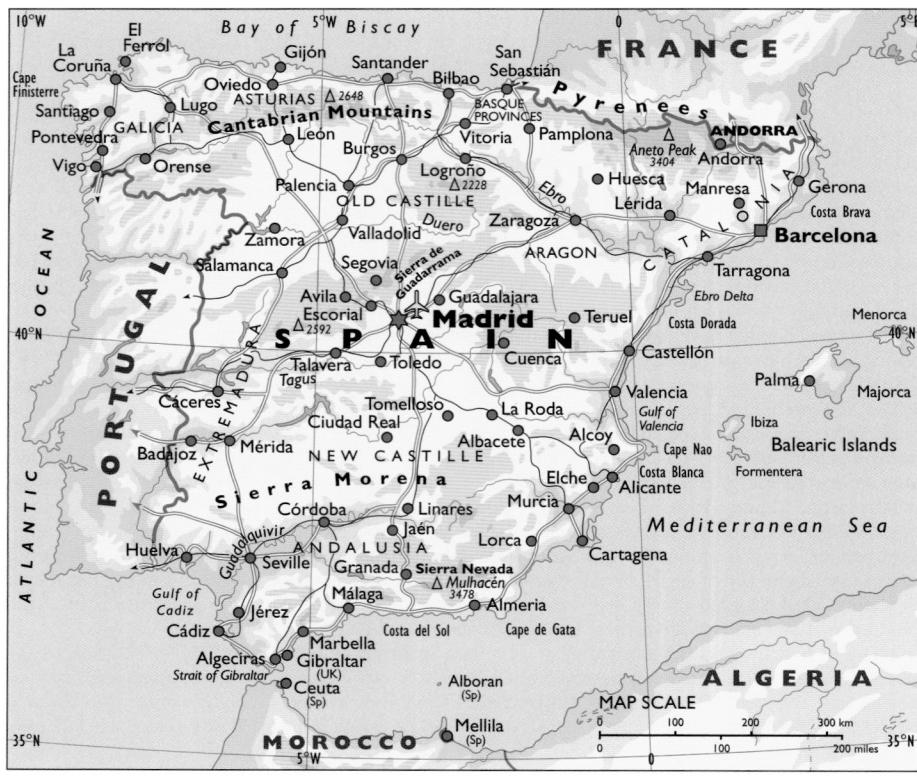

CLIMATE

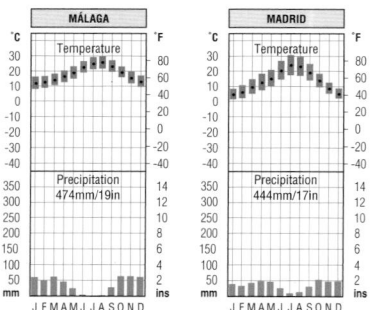

Spain has the widest range of climate in Western Europe. One of the most striking contrasts is between the humid north and north-west, where winds from the Atlantic bring mild, wet weather throughout the year, and the mainly arid remainder of the country. Droughts are common in much of Spain, though these are occasionally interrupted by thunderstorms.

The Meseta, removed from the influence of the sea, has a continental climate, with hot summers and cold winters, when frosts often occur and snow blankets the mountain ranges that rise above the plateau surface. By contrast, the Mediterranean coastlands and the

Wave-like balconies *and roof on the colourful Casa Ballto, Barcelona designed by the Catalan architect of the Art Nouveau Movement Antonio Gaudi y Cornet*

Area 497,548 sq km [192,103 sq mi]
Population 40,281,000
Capital (population) Madrid (2,939,000)
Government Constitutional monarchy
Ethnic groups Mediterranean and Nordic types
Languages Castillian Spanish (official) 74%, Catalan 17%, Galician 7%, Basque 2%
Religions Roman Catholic 94%, others
Currency Euro = 100 cents
Website www.spain.info

Balearic Islands have mild, moist winters. Summers along the Mediterranean coast are hot and dry. The Canary Islands have mild to warm weather throughout the year.

HISTORY

5,000 years ago, Spain was inhabited by farming people called Iberians. Some historians believe the Basques in northern Spain may be descendants of these people. Around 3,000 years ago, Phoenicians from the eastern Mediterranean reached the Iberian Peninsula and began to establish trading colonies, some on the sites of modern cities, such as Cádiz and Málaga. Celtic peoples arrived later from the north, while Greeks reached the east coast of Spain around 600 BC.

In the 5th century BC, Carthaginians conquered much of Spain, but after the Second Punic War (218–201 BC), the Iberian Peninsula gradually came under Roman rule. The Romans made Iberia a Roman province called Hispania.

By 573, the Visigoths had conquered the entire peninsula, including what is now Portugal, and they ruled until the early 8th century when the Muslim Moors invaded from North Africa. They introduced their culture and scholarship, far ahead of that of Europe, building superb mosques and palaces, some of which still stand. In the 11th century, the country began to divide into many small Moorish kingdoms, leaving them open to attack by the Christian kingdoms in the north. Portugal broke away from Spain in the 11th–12th centuries. By the late 13th century, Muslim power was confined to the southern Kingdom of Granada.

The rest of Spain was ruled by the Christian kingdoms of Aragon, Navarre and, the most powerful of all, Castile. In 1469, Prince Ferdinand of Aragon married Princess Isabella of Castile. Ferdinand and Isabella started the Spanish Inquisition which persecuted Jews, Muslims and other non-Roman Catholics. In 1492, Ferdinand's forces captured the last Muslim stronghold of Granada and, in 1512, the Kingdom of Navarre was taken by Ferdinand. This completed the union of Spain.

By the mid-16th century, Spain was a great world power controlling much of Central and South America, parts of Africa and the Philippines in Asia. A major disaster occurred in 1588, when King Philip II sent a fleet, the Armada, to conquer England, but the English navy and bad weather destroyed half of the Spanish ships. By the 20th century all that remained of Spain's empire were a few small African territories.

A military government was established in 1923 and King Alfonso III allowed General Miguel Primo de Rivera, the prime minister, to rule as a dictator. After Primo de Rivera was forced to resign in 1930, Alfonso called for city elections. Republican candidates scored such a major victory in these elections that he left the country, though he did not renounce his claim to the throne. The republicans took over the government.

In October 1936, rebel Nationalists chose General Francisco Franco (1892–1975) as their commander and, and in 1939 he became the dictator of Spain, though technically the country was a monarchy. During World War II, Spain was officially neutral.

POLITICS

The revival of Spain's shattered economy began in the 1950s through the growth of manufacturing industries and tourism. As standards of living rose, people began to demand more freedom. After Franco died in 1975, the monarchy was restored and Juan Carlos, grandson of Alfonso III, became king. The ban on political parties was lifted and, in 1977, elections were held. A new constitution making Spain a parliamentary democracy, with the king as head of state, came into effect in December 1978.

From the late 1970s, Spain began to tackle the problem of its regions.

In 1980, a regional parliament was set up in the Basque Country (Euskadi in Basque and Pais Vasco in Spanish). Similar parliaments were initiated in Catalonia (Cataluña) in the north-east and Galicia in the north-west. While regional devolution was welcomed in Catalonia and Galicia, it did not end the terrorist campaign of the Basque separatist movement, Euskadi Ta Askatasuna (ETA). ETA announced an indefinite cease-fire in September 1998, but the truce was ended in December 1999 and the conflict continued. The Supreme Court voted in 2003, to ban Batasuna, the Basque separatist party deemed to be the political wing of ETA.

In March 2004 terrorist bombs exploded in Madrid killing 191 people. This was seem as the work of Al Qaeda, though the govenerment were keen to persuade the people that it was the work of ETA. The country went to the polls three days later and voted out the rightwing Aznar. This was largely seen as a reaction to his support of the US in Iraq and the sending of troops which was to blame for the bombing some three days earlier. The new prime minister Zapatero immediately withdrew all troops from Iraq.

> ## MADRID
>
> Capital and largest city of Spain, lying on a high plain in the centre of Spain on the River Manzanares. It is Europe's highest capital city, at 655 m [2,149 ft]. Founded as a Moorish fortress in the 10th century, Alfonso VI of Castile captured Madrid in 1083. In 1561, Philip II moved the capital to Madrid. The French occupied the city during the Peninsular War (1808–14). Madrid expanded considerably in the 19th century. During the Spanish Civil War, it remained loyal to the Republican cause and was under siege for almost three years. Its capitulation in March 1939 brought the war to an end. Modern Madrid is a thriving centre of commerce and industry.

ECONOMY

Spain has the fifth largest economy in the EU. By the early 2000s, agriculture employed only 6% of the workforce as compared with industry at 17% and services including tourism who employ 77%. Farmland makes up two-thirds of the land, and forest most of the rest. Major crops include barley, citrus fruits, grapes for wine-making, olives, potatoes and wheat.

There is some high-grade iron ore in the north. Spain's many manufacturing industries include cars, chemicals, clothing, electronics, processed food, metal goods, steel and textiles.

ANDORRA

Andorra is a tiny state sandwiched between France and Spain. It lies in the Pyrenees Mountains. Most Andorrans live in the sheltered valleys.

The winters are cold and fairly dry. The summers are a little more wet, but pleasantly cool.

Tourism is Andorra's chief activity in both winter, for winter sports, and summer.

There is some farming in the valleys and tobacco is the main crop. Cattle and sheep are grazed on the mountain slopes.

Area 453 sq km [175 sq mi]
Population 68,000
Capital (population) Andorra La Vella (22,000)
Government Co-principality
Ethnic groups Spanish 43%, Andorran 33%, Portuguese 11%, French 7%
Languages Catalan (official)
Religions Mainly Roman Catholic
Currency Euro = 100 cents
Website www.turisme.ad

GIBRALTAR

Gibraltar is a tiny British dependency on the south coast of Spain, occupying a strategic position, overlooking the narrow Strait of Gibraltar which links the Mediterranean Sea with the Atlantic Ocean. The majority of the populous works for the government or in tourism.

Most of the land is a huge mass of limestone, known as the Rock of Gibraltar. Between AD 711 and 1309, and again between 1333 and 1462, Gibraltar was held by Moors from North Africa. Spaniards retook the area in 1462, but it became a British territory in 1713. Gibraltar became a vital British military base, but was still claimed by Spain.

In 1967 the Gibraltarians voted to remain British. Between 1969 and 1985 Spain closed its border with Gibraltar. Britain withdrew its military forces in 1991. In 2002, proposals that Gibraltar should come under joint Anglo-Spanish sovreignty were rejected by nearly all Gibraltarians.

Area 6.5 sq km [2.5 sq mi]
Population 28,000
Capital (population) Gibraltar Town (28,000)
Government British dependency
Ethnic groups English, Spanish, Maltese, Italian, Portuguese
Languages English (official), Spanish, Italian, Portuguese
Religions Mainly Roman Catholic
Currency Gibraltar pound = 100 pence
Website www.gibraltar.gov.uk

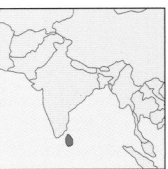

Sri Lanka's unusual flag was adopted in 1951, three years after the country, then called Ceylon, became independent from Britain. The lion banner represents the ancient Buddhist kingdom. The stripes symbolize the minorities – Muslims (green) and Hindus (orange).

Area 65,610 sq km [25,332 sq mi]
Population 19,905,000
Capital (population) Colombo (642,000)
Government Multiparty republic
Ethnic groups Sinhalese 74%, Tamil 18%, Moor 7%
Languages Sinhala and Tamil (both official)
Religions Buddhism 70%, Hinduism 15%, Christianity 8%, Islam 7%
Currency Sri Lankan rupee = 100 cents
Website www.gov.lk

The Democratic Socialist Republic of Sri Lanka is an island nation, often called the 'pearl of the Indian Ocean'. It lies on the same continental shelf as India, separated by the shallow Palk Strait. Most of the land is low-lying but, in the south-central part of Sri Lanka, the land rises to a mountain massif. The nation's highest peak is Pidurutalagala (2,524 m [8,281 ft]). The nearby Adam's Peak, at 2,243 m [7,359 ft], is a place of pilgrimage. The south-west is also mountainous, with long ridges.

Around the south-central highlands are broad plains, while the Jaffna Peninsula in the far north is made of limestone. Cliffs overlook the sea in the south-west, while elsewhere lagoons line the coast. Forests cover nearly two-fifths of the land, with open grasslands in the eastern highlands. Farmland, including pasture, covers another two-fifths of the country.

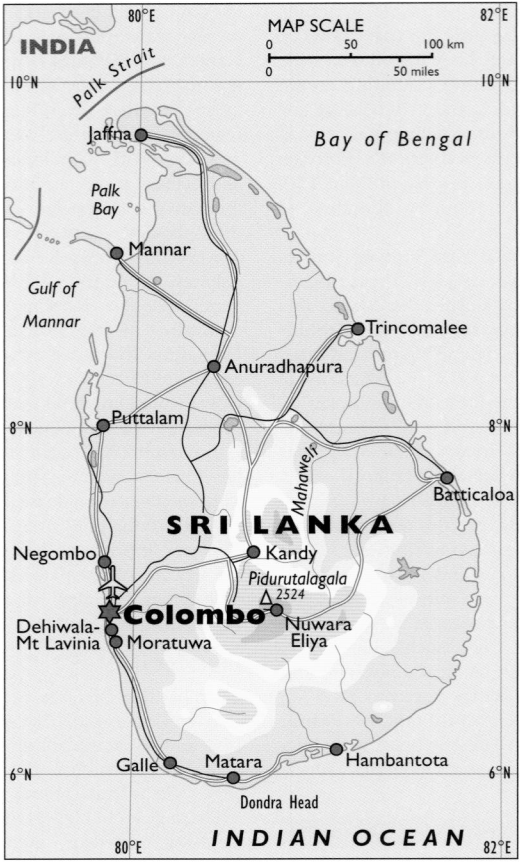

CLIMATE

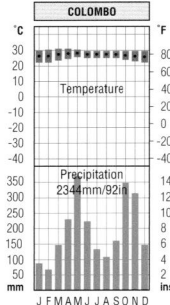

The western part of Sri Lanka has a wet equatorial climate. Temperatures are high and the rainfall is heavy. The wettest months are May and October as these months mark the advance and the retreat of the summer monsoon. Eastern Sri Lanka is drier.

HISTORY

The ancestors of the Sinhalese people settled on the island around 2,400 years ago pushing the Veddahs, descendants of the earliest inhabitants, into the interior. The Sinhalese founded the city of Anuradhapura, which was their centre from the 3rd century BC to the 10th century AD. Tamils arrived around 2,100 years ago and the early history of Ceylon, as the island was known, was concerned with a struggle between the Sinhalese and the Tamils. Victory for the Tamils led the Sinhalese to move south. From the 16th century, Ceylon was ruled successively by the Portuguese, Dutch and British.

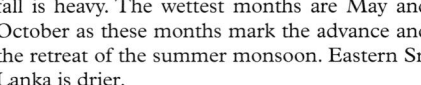

Tea leaf picking, Nuwara Eliya; tea plantation built during the 19th century in an English style

POLITICS

Independence was achieved in 1948 and the country was renamed Sri Lanka in 1972. After independence, rivalries between the two main ethnic groups, the Sinhalese and Tamils, marred progress. In the 1950s, the government made Sinhala the official language. Following protests, the prime minister made provisions for Tamil to be used in some areas. In 1959, the prime minister was assassinated by a Sinhalese extremist and he was succeeded by Sirimavo Bandanaraike, the world's first woman prime minister.

Conflict between Tamils and Sinhalese continued in the 1970s and 1980s. In 1987, India helped to engineer a cease-fire. Indian troops arrived to enforce the agreement. They withdrew in 1990 after failing to subdue the main guerrilla group, the Tamil Tigers, who wanted an independent Tamil homeland in northern Sri Lanka. In 1993, the country's president, Ranasinghe Premadasa, was assassinated by a suspected Tamil separatist. A cease-fire was signed in May 1993, but fighting soon broke out. In 1995, government forces captured Jaffna, the stronghold of the 'Liberation Tigers of the Tamil Eelam' (LTTE). But the 1998 bombing of the Temple of the Tooth in Kandy created great outrage among the Sinhalese Buddhists, who believe that the temple's treasured tooth belonged to Buddha.

The bombing led to rioting and provoked President Chandrika Kumaratunga to ban the LTTE. These events led to some of the fiercest fighting in the civil war, including several suicide bombings. The government lost most of the gains it had made in the mid-1990s. A long-term cease-fire agreement was signed in 2002. In December 2004, Sri Lanka was hit by a tsunami, which killed more than 30,000 people. In 2005 Mahinda Rajapakse was elected president. At the time of election he was in fact prime minister and it was hoped that under his leadership a long-sought-after resolution would be found to the conflict in the north.

ECONOMY

The World Bank classifies Sri Lanka as a 'low-income' developing country. Agriculture employs around a third of the workforce, coconuts, rubber and tea are the cash crops. Rice is the chief food crop. Cattle, water buffalo and goats are the chief farm animals, while fish provide another source of protein. Manufacturing is mainly the processing of agricultural products and textile production. The leading exports are clothing and accessories, gemstones, tea and rubber.

COLOMBO

Capital and chief seaport of Sri Lanka, on the south-west coast. Settled in the 6th century BC, it was taken by Portugal in the 16th century and later by the Dutch. Captured by the British in 1796, it gained independence in 1948. The town hall is of great interest.

Adopted in 1969, Sudan's flag uses colours associated with the Pan-Arab movement. The Islamic green triangle symbolizes prosperity and spiritual wealth. The flag is based on the one used in the Arab revolt against Turkish rule in World War I (1914–18).

The Republic of the Sudan is the largest country in Africa. It extends from the arid Sahara in the north to an equatorial swamp region (the Sudd) in the south.

Much of the land is flat, but there are mountains in the north east and south east; the highest point is Kinyeti, at 3,187 m [10,456 ft]. The River Nile (Bahr el Jebel) runs south to north, entering Sudan as the White Nile, converging with the Blue Nile at Khartoum, and flowing north to Egypt.

Khartoum is prone to summer dust storms (*haboobs*). From the bare deserts of the north, the land merges into dry grasslands and savanna. Dense rainforests grow in the south.

CLIMATE

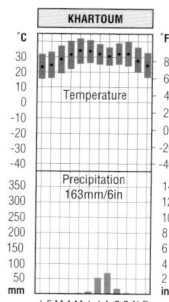

Northern Sudan is hot and arid. The centre has an average annual rainfall of 100 mm to 510 mm [4–32 in], while the tropical south has between 810 mm and 1,400 mm [32–55 in] of rain per year.

HISTORY

One of the earliest civilizations in the Nile region of northern Sudan was Nubia, which came under Ancient Egypt around 4,000 years ago. Another Nubian civilization, called Kush, developed from about 1000 BC, finally collapsing in AD 350. Christianity was introduced to northern Sudan in the 6th century. From the 13th to 15th centuries, northern Sudan came under Muslim control, and Islam became the dominant religion.

In 1821 Muhammad Ali's forces occupied Sudan. Anglo-Egyptian forces, led by General Gordon, attempted to extend Egypt's influence into the south. Muhammad Ahmad led a Mahdi uprising, which briefly freed Sudan from Anglo-Egyptian influence. In 1898, General Kitchener's forces defeated the Mahdists, and in 1899 Sudan became Anglo-Egyptian Sudan, governed jointly by Britain and Egypt.

POLITICS

After Sudan's independence in 1952, the southern Sudanese, who are mostly Christian or of traditional beliefs, revolted against the dominance of the Muslim north, and civil war broke out. In 1958, the military seized power. Civilian rule was re-established in 1964, but overthrown again in 1969, when Gaafar Muhammad Nimeri seized control. Southern Sudan received considerable autonomy in 1972, but unrest persisted.

In 1983, the imposition of strict Islamic law sparked off further conflict between the government and the Sudan People's Liberation Army (SPLA) in the south. In 1985, Nimeri was deposed and a civilian government installed. In 1989, the military, led by Omar Hassan Ahmed al-Bashir, established a Revolutionary Command Council. Civil war continued in the south. In 1996, Bashir was re-elected, virtually unopposed. The National Islamic Front (NIF) dominated the government

KHARTOUM

Capital of Sudan, at the junction of the Blue Nile and White Nile rivers. Khartoum was founded in the 1820s by Muhammad Ali and was besieged by the Mahdists in 1885, when General Gordon was killed. In 1898, it became the seat of government of the Anglo-Egyptian Sudan, and from 1956 the capital of independent Sudan. It was at the centre of controversy in 1998 when the US bombed a pharmaceuticals plant thinking it was producing chemical weapons. Industries include cement, gum arabic, chemicals, glass, cotton and textiles.

Area 2,505, 813 sq km [967,494 sq mi]
Population 39,148,000
Capital (population) Khartoum (947,000)
Government Military regime
Ethnic groups Black 52%, Arab 39%, Beja 6%, others
Languages Arabic (officia)l, Nubian, Ta Bedawie
Religions Islam 70%, traditional beliefs
Currency Sudanese dinar = 10 Sudanese pounds
Website www.sudan.net

Burial pyramids *at the Royal Necropolis of the ancient Kingdom of Kush, dated between 300 BC and 300 AD, at Meroe near Bejwaria*

and was believed to have strong links with Iranian terrorist groups.

In 1996, the UN imposed sanctions on Sudan. A South African peace initiative in 1997 led to the formation of a Southern States' Co-ordination Council. The US imposed sanctions on Bashir's regime and American Secretary of State Madeleine Albright met rebel leaders. In 1998, the USA bombed a pharmaceuticals factory in Khartoum in the mistaken belief that it produced chemical weapons. In 2003, conflict broke out in the Darfur region in the west, primarily involving rebels and government-backed militias. A severe humanitarian crisis developed, and the militias were accused of ethnic cleansing. In the south, government and rebels signed a comprehensive peace deal in 2005. The humanitarian crisis continued to worsen in 2006.

ECONOMY

The World Bank classifies Sudan as a 'low-income' economy. Food shortages and a refugee crisis worsened its economic plight Agriculture employs 60% of the population. The chief crop is cotton. Other crops include groundnuts, gum arabic, millet, sesame, sorghum and sugar cane, while many people raise livestock.

Minerals include chromium, gold, gypsum and oil. Manufacturing industries process foods, and produce such things as cement, fertilizers and textiles. The main exports are cotton, gum arabic and sesame seeds, but the most valuable exports are oil and oil products.

The star symbolizes national unity - each point being one of Suriname's five main ethnic groups. Yellow is for Suriname's golden future. Red stands for progress and the struggle for a better life. Green signifies hope and fertility. White symbolizes freedom and justice.

Area 163,265 sq km [63,037 sq mi]
Population 437,000
Capital (population) Paramaribo (216,000)
Government Multiparty republic
Ethnic groups Hindustani/East Indian 37%, Creole (mixed White and Black) 31%, Javanese 15%, Black 10%, Amerindian 2%, Chinese 2%, others
Languages Dutch (official), Sranang Tonga
Religions Hinduism 27%, Protestant 25%, Roman Catholic 23%, Islam 20%
Currency Surinamese dollar = 100 cents
Website www.parbo.com/tourism/

The Republic of Suriname is on the Atlantic Ocean in north-eastern South America bordered by Brazil to the south, French Guiana to the east and Guyana to the west.

Suriname is made up of the Guiana Highlands plateau, a flat coastal plain and a forested inland region. Its many rivers serve as a source of hydroelectric power. The narrow coastal plain was once swampy, but it has been drained and now consists mainly of farmland. Inland lie hills and low mountains which rise to 1,280 m [4,199 ft].

CLIMATE

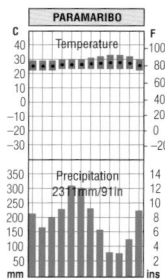

Suriname has a hot, wet and humid climate. Temperatures are high throughout the year.

HISTORY

Spanish explorer Alfonso de Ojeda discovered Suriname in 1499, but it was the British who founded the first colony in 1651. In 1667, Britain handed Suriname to the Dutch in return for New Amsterdam, an area that is now the state of New York. Slave revolts and Dutch neglect hampered development.

In the early 19th century Britain and the Netherlands disputed the ownership of the area. The British gave up their claims in 1813 and in 1815 the Congress of Vienna gave the Guyana region to Britain and reaffirmed Dutch control of 'Dutch Guiana'. Slavery was abolished in 1863 and soon afterwards Indian and Indonesian labourers were introduced to work on plantations. It gained autonomy in 1954.

POLITICS

Suriname became fully independent from the Netherlands in 1975 and gained membership of the United Nations, but the economy was weakened when thousands of skilled people emigrated to the Netherlands.

Following a coup in 1980, Suriname was ruled by a military dictator, Dési Bouterse who banned all political parties. Guerrilla warfare disrupted the economy. In 1987, a new constitution provided for a 51-member National Assembly, with powers to elect the president. Rameswak

PARAMARIBO

Capital of Suriname, a port on the River Suriname. It was founded in the early 17th century by the French and became a British colony in 1651. It was held intermittently by the British and the Dutch until 1816, when the latter finally took control until independence. Paramaribo is the administrative and economic centre. The name is derived from Paramurubo, meaning 'city of parwa blossoms' after an old Arrawak village. Places of interest include Fort Zeelandia/ Suriname Museum, the Palm Gardens and the Presidential Palace. Industries include bauxite, timber, sugar cane, rice, rum,coffee and cacao.

Shankar became president in 1988 elections, but he was overthrown by a military coup in 1990

In 1991, Ronald Venetiaan, leader of the New Front for Democracy and Development, became president. In 1992 the government negotiated a peace agreement with the *boschneger*, descendants of African slaves, who had launched a struggle against the government. That same year, the constitution was amended in order to limit the power of the military and a peace agreement was reached with the rebels. Elections were held in 1996 and again in 2000.

In 1999, Bouterse was convicted in absentia in the Netherlands of having led a cocaine-trafficking ring during and after his tenure in office. In 2004, the government announced that he and others would face trial over the killings of 15 people in 1982.

ECONOMY

The World Bank classifies Suriname as an 'upper-middle-income' developing country. Its economy is based on mining and metal processing. Suriname is a leading producer of bauxite, from which the metal aluminium is made.

The chief agricultural products are rice, bananas, sugar cane, coffee, coconuts, timber, and citrus fruits.

A woman trims a cassava cake with a leaf, as it cooks upon a griddle in Bigi Poika, a Carib Indian village in north-central Suriname

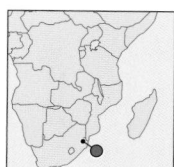

AFRICA

Swaziland 189

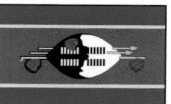

The oxhide shield with two spears and a fighting staff represent the defence of Swaziland, the tassels symbolise the Swazi monarchy. Black and white represent racial harmony, blue is for peace, yellow stands for the nation's mineral wealth; red signifies blood shed in past struggles.

The Kingdom of Swaziland is a small, landlocked country in southern Africa bounded by South Africa to the north, west and south and by Mozambique to the east. The country has four regions which run north–south.

In the west, the Highveld, with an average height of 1,200 m [3,937 ft], makes up 30% of Swaziland. The Middleveld, between 350 m and 1,000 m [1,148–3,281 ft], covers 28% of the country. The Lowveld, with an average height of 270 m [886 ft], covers another 33%. The Lebombo Mountains reach 800 m [2,600 ft] along the eastern border.

Meadows and pasture cover 65% of Swaziland. Arable land covers 8% of the land, and forests only 6%.

CLIMATE

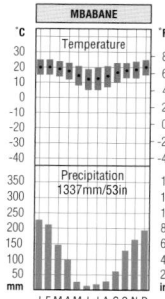

The Lowveld is almost tropical, with an average temperature of 22°C [72°F] and a low rainfall of 500 mm [20 in] a year. The altitude moderates the climate in the west of the country. Mbabane has a climate typical of the Highveld with warm summers and cool winters.

HISTORY

In the 18th century, according to tradition, a group of Bantu-speaking people, under the Swazi Chief Ngwane II, crossed the Lebombo range and united with local African groups to form the Swazi nation. In the 1840s, under attack from the Zulu, the Swazi sought British protection. Gold was discovered in the 1880s, and many Europeans sought land concessions from the King, who did not realize that in acceding to their demands he lost control of the land. In 1894, Britain and the Boers of South Africa agreed to put Swaziland under the control of the South African Republic (the

MBABANE

Capital of Swaziland, in the north-west of the country, at the northern end of the Ezulwini Valley in the Dlangeni Hills, which are part of the Highveld region of southern Africa. It is both an administrative and commercial centre, serving the surrounding agricultural region. Tin and iron ore are mined nearby.

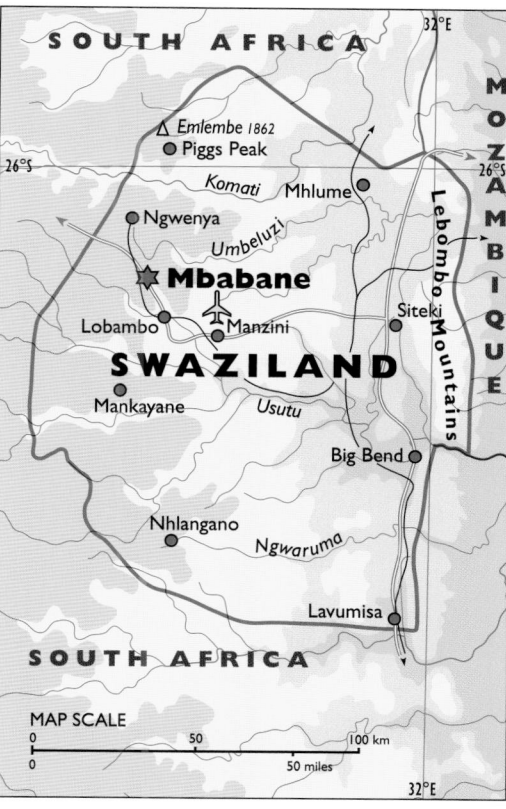

Man carving soapstone sculpture in Swaziland; soapstone is a soft stone that feels soapy to the touch, hence its name, it is commonly used in African sculpture

Area 17,364 sq km [6,704 sq mi]
Population 1,169,000
Capital (population) Mbabane (38,000)
Government Monarchy
Ethnic groups African 97%, European 3%
Languages Siswati and English (both official)
Religions Zionist (a mixture of Christianity and traditional beliefs) 40%, Roman Catholic 20%, Islam 10%
Currency Lilangeni = 100 cents
Website www.gov.sz

LOBAMBO

The traditional royal capital of Swaziland, lying in the Ezulwini Valley 16 km [10 mi] from Mbabane. It is the home of the Queen Mother. The National Assembly, National Museum and parliament are all based here.

Transvaal). Britain took control at the end of the second South African War (1899–1902).

POLITICS

In 1968, when Swaziland became fully independent as a constitutional monarchy, the head of state was King Sobhuza II. In 1973, Sobhuza suspended the constitution and assumed supreme power. In 1978, he banned all political parties. Sobhuza died in 1982 after a reign of 82 years.

In 1983, his son, Prince Makhosetive, was chosen as his heir. In 1986, he became King Mswati III. Elections in 1993 and 1998, in which political parties were banned, failed to satisfy protesters who opposed the absolute monarchy.

Mswati continued to rule by decree and in 2004 he announced plans to build palaces for each of his 11 wives. At the same time the government appealed for aid in the face of a national disaster caused by the spread of HIV/AIDS and a severe drought.

ECONOMY

The World Bank classifies Swaziland as a 'lower-middle-income' developing country. Agriculture employs 50% of the workforce, with many farmers living at subsistence level. Farm products and processed foods, including sugar, wood pulp, citrus fruits and canned fruit, are the leading exports. Swaziland exhausted its high-grade iron ore reserves in 1978, while the world demand for its asbestos fell. Swaziland is heavily dependent on South Africa and the two countries are linked through a customs union.

Sweden's flag was adopted in 1906, though it had been in use since the reign of Gustavus Vasa (r. 1523–60), a king who won many victories for Sweden and laid the foundations of the modern nation. The colours on the flag come from a coat of arms dating from 1364.

Area 449,964 sq km [173,731 sq mi]
Population 8,986,000
Capital (population) Stockholm (744,000)
Government Constitutional monarchy
Ethnic groups Swedish 91%, Finnish, Sami
Languages Swedish (official), Finnish, Sami
Religions Lutheran 87%, Roman Catholic, Orthodox
Currency Swedish krona = 100 öre
Website www.sweden.gov.se

The Kingdom of Sweden is the largest of the countries of Scandinavia both in terms of area and population. It shares the Scandinavian Peninsula with Norway. The western part of the country, along the border with Norway, is mountainous. The highest point is Kebnekaise, which reaches 2,117 m [6,946 ft] in the north-west. The southern lowlands contain two of Europe's largest lakes, Vänern and Vättern, and Sweden's largest cities: the capital, Stockholm, and Gothenburg.

CLIMATE

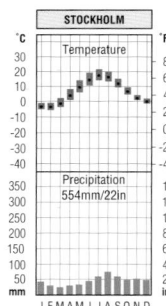

The northerly latitude and high mountains and plateaus of Norway cut Sweden off from the mild influences of the Atlantic in the west. The Gulf Stream warms the southern coastlands. The February temperature in the central lowlands is just below freezing, but in the north it is –15°C [5°F].

Precipitation is low throughout Sweden, but lies as snow for more than six months in the north. In summer there is little difference between the north and south. Most areas have an average temperature range between 15°C and 20°C [59–68°F].

HISTORY

People began to settle in Sweden around 8,000 years ago. Accounts were recorded in about AD 100.

By the seventh century, Teutonic peoples had occupied much of central Sweden. Between the 9th and 11th centuries the Swedish Vikings sailed to the east, across Russia and down to the Black and Caspian seas.

In the 11th century, Sweden, Norway and Denmark were separate kingdoms. However, in 1388, Sweden, fearing the growing influence of Germany on Swe-

den's affairs, turned to Queen Margaret of Denmark and Norway for help. The Germans were defeated in 1389 and, in 1397, Sweden, Denmark and Norway were united by a treaty called the Union of Kalmar. Sweden defeated the Danes in 1523 and under Gustavus Vasa, a Swedish noble, Sweden broke away from the union. Gustavus encouraged followers of Martin Luther to spread their ideas and by 1540, Lutheranism had become the official religion.

From the late 16th century, Sweden became involved in a series of wars, during which it gained territory around the Baltic Ocean. In 1658, Sweden forced Denmark to give up its provinces on the Swedish mainland. Following defeat at the hands of Tsar Peter the Great in 1709, a coalition of Russia, Poland and Denmark forced Sweden to give up most of its European possessions.

Sweden lost Finland to Russia in 1809, though it gained Norway from Denmark in 1814. By the late 19th century, Sweden was a major industrial nation. The Social Democratic Party was set up in 1889 to improve the conditions of workers. In 1905, Norway's parliament voted for independence from Sweden.

POLITICS

Sweden has a high standard of living, more than 70% of the national budget goes on one of the widest ranging welfare programmes in the world. In turn, the tax burden is the world's highest.

The elections of September 1991 saw the end of the Social Democratic government, which had been in power since 1932, with voters swinging towards parties advocating lower taxes. But the Social Democrats returned to power in 1994, advocating economic stringency.

A founder member of EFTA (European Free Trade Association), Sweden joined the European Union in 1985 following a referendum. However, it did not adopt the euro in 2001. In 2003, the government launched a referendum on replacing the krona with the euro. During the campaign Sweden's foreign minister, Anna Lindh, was murdered. Shortly afterwards Swedish voters rejected the adoption of the euro.

ECONOMY

Sweden is a highly developed industrial country. It has rich iron ore deposits, but imports other materials. Steel is a major product, and is used to manufacture aircraft, cars, machinery, and ships. Forestry and fishing are important. Farmland covers 10% of the land. Livestock and dairy farming are valuable; crops include barley and oats.

STOCKHOLM

Port and capital of Sweden, on Lake Mälaren's outlet to the Baltic Sea. Founded in the mid-13th century, it became a trade centre dominated by the Hanseatic League. Gustavus I made it the centre of his kingdom, and ended the privileges of Hanseatic merchants. Stockholm became the capital of Sweden in 1436, and developed as an intellectual centre in the 17th century. Industrial development dates from the mid-19th century. Industries include textiles, clothing, paper and printing, rubber, chemicals, shipbuilding, beer, and electronics.

Switzerland has used this square flag since 1848, though the white cross on the red shield has been Switzerland's emblem since the 14th century. The flag of the International Red Cross, which is based in Geneva, was derived from this flag.

The Swiss Confederation is a land-locked country in Western Europe. Much of the land is mountainous. The Jura Mountains lie along Switzerland's western border with France, while the Swiss Alps make up about 60% of the country in the south and east. Four-fifths of the people of Switzerland live on the fertile Swiss Plateau, which contains most of Switzerland's large cities.

CLIMATE

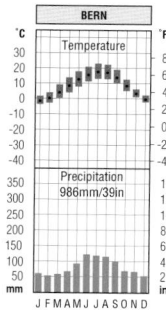

The climate varies greatly according to the height of the land. The plateau region has a central European climate with warm summers, but cold and snowy winters. Rain occurs throughout the year.

HISTORY

In 1291, three small cantons (states) united to defend their freedom against the Habsburg rulers of the Holy Roman Empire. They were Schwyz, Uri and Unterwalden, and they called the confederation 'Switzerland'. In the 14th century, Switzerland defeated Austria in three wars of independence. But after a defeat by the French in 1515, the Swiss adopted a policy of neutrality, which they still follow.

In 1815, the Congress of Vienna expanded Switzerland to 22 cantons and guaranteed its neutrality. Switzerland's 23rd canton, Jura, was created in 1979 from part of the capital Bern (Berne).

POLITICS

A referendum in 1986 rejected Swiss membership of the UN to avoid compromising its neutrality. In 1993 the Swiss voted against joining the EU. In 1999, Ruth Dreifuss became Switzerland's first woman president. However, in 2002, the

Area 41,284 sq km [15,940 sq mi]
Population 7,451,000
Capital (population) Bern (124,000)
Government Federal republic
Ethnic groups German 65%, French 18%, Italian 10%, Romansch 1%, others
Languages French, German, Italian and Romansch (all official)
Religions Roman Catholic 46%, Protestant 40%
Currency Swiss franc = 100 centimes
Website www.vlada.hr/default.asp?ru=2

Swiss voted by a narrow majority to end its centuries-old political isolationism and join the United Nations.

ECONOMY

Although lacking in natural resources, Switzerland is a wealthy, industrialized country with many highly skilled workers. Major products include chemicals, electrical equipment, machinery and machine tools, precision instruments, processed food, watches and textiles. Farmers produce about three-fifths of the country's food – the rest is imported. Livestock raising, especially dairy farming, is the chief agricultural activity. Crops include fruits, potatoes and wheat. Tourism and banking are important. Swiss banks attract investors from all over the world.

BERN (BERNE)

Capital of Switzerland, on the River Aare in Bern region. Founded in 1191 as a military post, it became part of the Swiss Confederation in 1353. Bern was occupied by France during the French Revolutionary Wars (1798). It has a Gothic cathedral, a 15th-century town hall, and is the headquarters of the Swiss National Library.

LIECHTENSTEIN

The Principality of Liechtenstein is sandwiched between Switzerland and Austria. The River Rhine flows along its western border, while Alpine peaks rise in the east and the south. The capital, Vaduz, is situated on the Oberland Plateau above the fields and meadows of the Rhine Valley. The climate is relatively mild and the average annual precipitation is about 890 mm [35 in].

Liechtenstein, whose people speak a German dialect, has been an independent principality since 1719. Switzerland has represented Liechtenstein abroad since 1918 and Swiss currency was adopted in 1921. It has been in customs union with Switzerland since 1924.

Liechtenstein is best known abroad for its postage stamps, but is a haven for international companies, attracted by the low taxation and the strictest banking codes in the world.

In 2003, the people voted to give the head of state, Prince Hans Adam III, sovereign powers. In 2004, he handed the running of the country to his son, Prince Alois, but remained titular head of state.

Area 160 sq km [62 sq mi]
Population 33,000
Capital (population) Vaduz (5,000)
Government Hereditary constitutional monarchy
Ethnic groups Alemannic 86%, Italian, Turkish
Languages German (official), Alemannic dialect
Religions Roman Catholic 76%, Protestant 7%
Currency Swiss franc = 100 centimes
Website www.liechtenstein.li

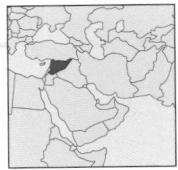

Syria has used this flag since 1980. The colours are those used by the Pan-Arab movement. This flag is the one that was used by the United Arab Republic between 1958 and 1961, when Syria was linked with Egypt and North Yemen.

Area 185,180 sq km [71,498 sq mi]
Population 18,017,000
Capital (population) Damascus (1,394,000)
Government Multiparty republic
Ethnic groups Arab 90%, Kurdish, Armenian, others
Languages Arabic (official), Kurdish, Armenian
Religions Sunni Muslim 74%, other Islam 16%
Currency Syrian pound = 100 piastres
Website www.syriatourism.org

The Syrian Arab Republic is in south-western Asia. The narrow coastal plain is overlooked by a low mountain range which runs north–south. Another range, the Jabal ash Sharqi, runs along the border with Lebanon. South of this range is a region called the Golan Heights. Israel has occupied this region since 1967. East of the mountains, the bulk of Syria consists of fertile valleys, grassy plains and large sandy deserts. This region contains the valley of the River Euphrates (Nahr al Furat).

CLIMATE

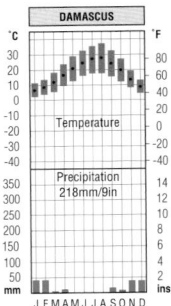

The coast has a Mediterranean climate, with dry, warm summers and wet, mild winters. The low mountains cut off Damascus from the sea. It has less rainfall than the coastal areas and becomes drier to the east.

The Central Bank of Syria *stands on the north side of Tajrida Al-Maghribiya Square in Damascus*

HISTORY

Syria is rich in historic sites from a wide range of periods. The earliest known settlers were Semites who arrived around 3,500 years ago. They set up city-states, such as Ebla, which existed between about 2700 and 2200 BC. The people of Ebla used clay tablets inscribed in cuneiform, an ancient system of writing developed by the Sumer people of Mesopotamia. Later conquerors of the area included the Akkadians, Canaanites, Phoenicians, Amorites, Aramaeans and the Hebrews, who introduced monotheism. The Assyrians occupied the area from 732 BC until 612 BC, when the Babylonians took over. The ancient Persians conquered the Babylonians in 539 BC, but the armies of Alexander the Great swept into the region in 331 BC, introducing Greek culture in their wake. The Romans took over in 64 BC, and Syria remained under Roman law for nearly 700 years.

Christianity became the state religion of Syria in the 4th century AD, but, in 636, Muslims from Arabia invaded the region. Islam gradually replaced Christianity as the main religion, and Arabic became the chief language. From 661, Damascus became the capital of a vast Muslim empire which was ruled by the Ummayad Dynasty. But the Abbasid Dynasty took over in 750 and the centre of power passed to Baghdad.

From the late 11th century, Crusaders sought to win the Holy Land

from the Muslims. But the Crusaders were unsuccessful in their aim because Saladin, a Muslim ruler of Egypt, defeated the Crusaders and ruled most of the area by the end of the 12th century. The Mameluke Dynasty of Egypt ruled Syria from 1260–1516, when the region became part of the huge Turkish Ottoman Empire. During World War I, Syrians and other Arabs fought alongside British forces and overthrew the Turks.

POLITICS

After the collapse of the Turkish Ottoman empire in World War I, Syria was ruled by France. Syria became fully independent from France in 1946. The partition of Palestine and the creation of Israel in 1947 led to the first Arab-Israeli war, when Syria and other Arab nations failed to defeat Israeli forces. In 1949, a military coup established a military regime, starting a long period of revolts and changes of government. In 1967, in the third Arab-Israeli war (known as the Six-Day War), Syria lost the strategically important Golan Heights to Israel.

In 1970, Lieutenant-General Hafez al Assad led a military revolt, becoming Syria's president in 1971. His repressive but stable regime attracted much Western criticism and was heavily reliant on Arab aid. But, Syria's anti-Iraq stance in the 1991 Gulf War, and the involvement of about 20,000 Syrian troops in the conflict, greatly improved its standing in the West. In the mid-1990s, Syria had talks with Israel over the future of the Golan Heights. Negotiations were suspended after the election of Binyamin Netanyahu's right-wing government in Israel in 1996. Assad died in 2000 and was succeeded by his son, Bashar al Assad, raising hopes of a more pliable policy on the Golan Heights.

Syria has been criticised for supporting Palestinian terrorist groups and keeping its troops in Lebanon. In 2005, following demonstrations against its continuing military presence in Lebanon, Syria announced the phased withdrawal of its troops.

ECONOMY

The World Bank classifies Syria as a 'lower-middle-income' developing country. Its main resources are oil, hydroelectricity and fertile land. Agriculture employs about 26% of the population. Oil is the chief mineral product, and phosphates are mined to make fertilizers.

DAMASCUS

Capital of Syria, on the River Barada, south-west Syria. Thought to be the oldest continuously occupied city in the world, in ancient times it belonged to the Egyptians, Persians and Greeks, and under Roman rule was a prosperous commercial centre. It was held by the Ottoman Turks for 400 years, and after World War I came under French administration. It became capital of an independent Syria in 1941. Sites include the Great Mosque and the Citadel. It is Syria's administrative and financial centre. Industries include damask fabric, metalware, leather goods, sugar.

In 1928, the Chinese Nationalists adopted this design as China's national flag and used it in the long struggle against Mao Zedong's Communist army. When the nationalists were forced to retreat to Taiwan in 1949, their flag went with them.

Taiwan (formerly Formosa), is an island about 140 km [87 mi] off the south coast of mainland China. The country administers a number of islands close to the mainland. They include Quemoy (Jinmen) and Matsu (Mazu).

High mountain ranges, extending the length of the island, occupy the central and eastern regions, and only a quarter of the island's surface is used for agriculture. The highest peak is Yü Shan (Morrison Mountain), 3,952 m [12,966 ft] above sea level. Several peaks in the central ranges rise to more than 3,000 m [10,000 ft], and carry dense forests of broadleaved evergreen trees, such as camphor and Chinese cork oak. Above 1,500 m [5,000 ft], conifers, such as pine, larch and cedar, dominate. In the east, where the mountains often drop steeply down to the sea, the short rivers have cut deep gorges. The western slopes are more gentle.

CLIMATE

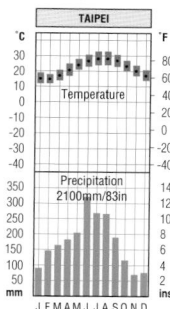

Taiwan has a tropical monsoon climate. The annual rainfall exceeds 2,000 mm [79 in] in almost all areas. From July to September, the island is often hit by typhoons. When humidity is high in the heat can be oppressive.

HISTORY

Chinese settlers arrived in Taiwan from the 7th century AD, displacing the Aboriginal people, but large settlements were not established until the 17th century. When the Portuguese first reached the island in 1590, they named the island Formosa (meaning 'beautiful island'), but chose not to settle there. The Dutch occupied a trading port in 1624, but they were driven out in 1661 by refugees from the deposed Ming Dynasty on the mainland. A Ming official tried to use the island as a base for attacking the Manchu Dynasty, but without success as the Manchus took the island in 1683 and incorporated it into what is now Fujian province.

The Manchus settled the island in the late 18th century and, by the mid 19th century, the population had increased to about 2,500,000. The island was a major producer of sugar and rice, which were exported to the mainland. In 1886, the island became a Chinese province and Taipei became its capital in 1894. However, in 1895, Taiwan was ceded to Japan following the Chinese-Japanese War. Japan used the island as a source of food crops and, from the 1930s, they developed manufacturing industries based on hydroelectricity.

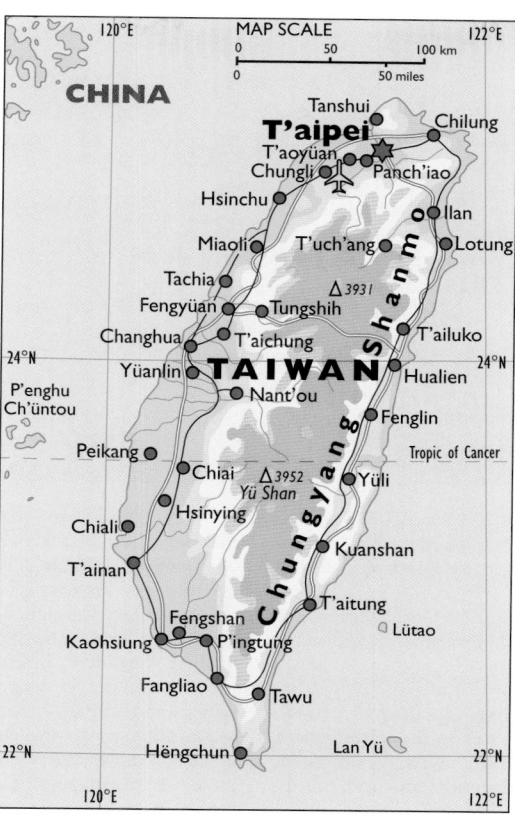

TAIPEI

Capital and largest city of Taiwan, at the northern end of the island. A major trade centre for tea in the 19th century, the city enlarged under Japanese rule (1895–1945), and became the seat of the Chinese Nationalist government in 1949. Industries include textiles, chemicals, fertilizers, metals, machinery. The city expanded from 335,000 people in 1945 to 2,619,022 in 2005.

Area 13,900 sq km [36,000 sq mi]
Population 22,750,000
Capital (population) Taipei (2,619,022)
Government Unitary multiparty republic
Ethnic groups Taiwanese 84%, mainland Chinese 14%
Languages Mandarin Chinese (official), Min, Hakka
Religions Buddhism, Taoism, Confucianism
Currency New Taiwan dollar = 100 cents
Website www.roc-taiwan.org.uk

POLITICS

In 1945, the Japanese army surrendered Taiwan to General Chiang Kai-shek's Nationalist Chinese government. Following victories by Mao Zedong's Communists, about 2 million Nationalists, together with their leader, fled the mainland to Taiwan in the two years before 1949, when the People's Republic of China was proclaimed. The influx was met with hostility by the 8 million Taiwanese, and the new regime, the 'Republic of China', was imposed with force. Boosted by help from the United States, Chiang's government set about ambitious programmes for land reform and industrial expansion and, by 1980, Taiwan had become one of the top 20 industrial nations. Economic development was accompanied by a marked rise in living standards.

Nevertheless, Taiwan remained politically isolated and it lost its seat in the United Nations to Communist China in 1971. It was then abandoned diplomatically by the United States in 1979, when the US switched its recognition to mainland China. However, in 1987 with continuing progress in the economy, martial law was lifted by the authoritarian regime in Taiwan. In 1988, a native Taiwanese became president and in 1991 the country's first general election was held.

China continued to regard Taiwan as a Chinese province and, in 1999, tension developed when the Taiwanese President Lee Teng-hui stated that relations between China and Taiwan should be on a 'special state-by-state' basis. This angered the Chinese President Jiang Zemin, whose 'one-nation' policy was based on the concept that China and Taiwan should be regarded as one country with two equal governments. Tension mounted in 2000, when Taiwan's opposition leader, Chen Shui-bian, was elected president, because Chen had adopted a pro-independence stance. However, after the elections, Chen adopted a more conciliatory approach to mainland China.

ECONOMY

The economy depends on manufacturing and trade. Manufactures include electronic goods, footwear and clothing, ships and television sets. The western coastal plains produce large rice crops. Other products include bananas, pineapples, sugar cane, sweet potatoes and tea.

Tajikistan's flag was adopted in 1993. It replaced the flag used during the Communist period which showed a hammer and sickle. The new flag shows an unusual gold crown under an arc of seven stars on the central white band.

Area 143,100 sq km [55,521 sq mi]
Population 7,012,000
Capital (population) Dushanbe (529,000)
Government Republic
Ethnic groups Tajik 65%,Uzbek 25%, Russian
Languages Tajik (official), Russian
Religions Islam (Sunni Muslim 85%)
Currency Somoni = 100 dirams
Website www.tajiktour.taknet.com

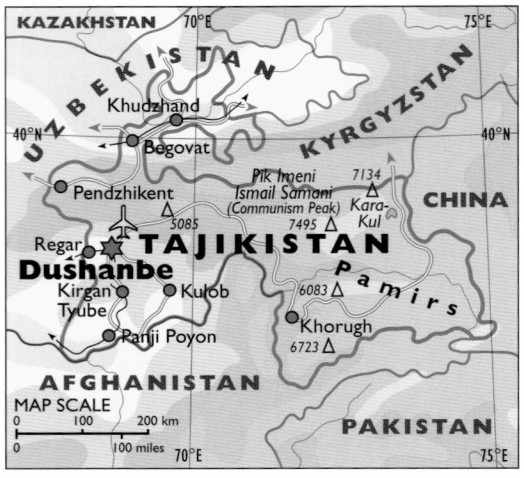

The Republic of Tajikistan is one of the five central Asian republics that formed part of the former Soviet Union. Only 7% of the land is below 1,000 m [3,280 ft], while almost all of eastern Tajikistan is above 3,000 m [9,840 ft]. The highest point is Communism Peak (Pik Kommunizma), which reaches 7,495 m [24,590 ft]. The main ranges are the westwards extension of the Tian Shan Range in the north and the snow-capped Pamirs (Pamir) in the south-east. Earthquakes are common throughout the country.

Vegetation varies greatly according to altitude. Much of Tajikistan consists of desert or rocky mountain landscapes capped by snow and ice.

CLIMATE

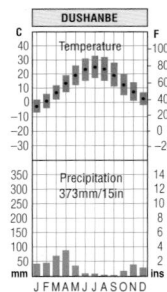

Tajikistan has an extreme continental climate. Summers are hot and dry in the lower valleys, and winters are long and bitterly cold in the mountains. Much of the country is arid, but the south east has heavy snowfalls.

HISTORY

Persians settled in the area about 2,500 years ago. The area was conquered many times with first the Persians in the 6th century BC, then the Macedonian Greeks led by Alexander the Great in 331 BC. From 323 BC, the area was split into several independent states. Arab armies conquered the area in the mid-7th century and introduced Islam, which remains the chief religion today. The region was later ruled by various Turkic tribes and later by the Mongols, led by Genghis Khan. Uzbeks, a Turkic people, ruled the area as the Khanate of Bukhara from the 16th to the 19th centuries.

The fragmentation of the region aided Russian conquest from 1868. Following the Russian Revolution (1917), Tajikistan rebelled against Russian rule. Although Soviet troops annexed northern Tajikistan into Turkistan in 1918, the Bukhara Emirate held out against the Red Army until 1921. In 1924 Tajikistan became an autonomous part of the Republic of Uzbekistan. In 1929 Tajikistan achieved full republic status, but Bukhara and Samarkand remained in the Republic of Uzbekistan. During the 1930s vast irrigation schemes greatly increased agricultural land. Many Russians and Uzbeks were settled in Tajikistan.

POLITICS

While the Soviet Union began to introduce reforms in the 1980s, many Tajiks demanded freedom. In 1989, the Tajik government made Tajik the official language in place of Russian and, in 1990, it stated that its local laws overruled Soviet laws. Tajikistan became fully independent in 1991, following the break-up of the Soviet Union. As the poorest of the ex-Soviet republics, Tajikistan faced many problems in trying to introduce a free-market system.

In 1992, civil war broke out between the government, which was run by former Communists, and an alliance of democrats and Islamic forces. The government maintained control, but it relied heavily on aid from the Commonwealth of Independent States, the organization through which most of the former Soviet republics kept in touch. Presidential elections in 1994 resulted in victory for Imomali Rakhmonov, though the Islamic opposition did not recognize the result.

A cease-fire was signed in December 1996. Further agreements in 1997 provided for the opposition to have 30% of the ministerial posts in the government. But many small groups excluded from the agreement continued to undermine the peace process through a series of killings and military actions. In 1999, Rakhmonov was re-elected president. Changes to the constitution in 2003 enabled Rakhmonov to serve two more seven-year terms after the elections in 2006. His party won parliamentary elections in 2005, though independent Western observers said that the vote did not meet international standards.

ECONOMY

The World Bank classifies Tajikistan as a 'low-income' developing country. Agriculture, mainly on irrigated land, is the main activity and cotton is the chief product. Other crops include fruits, grains and vegetables. The country has large hydroelectric power resources and it produces aluminium.

Cathedrals at sunset, *Dushanbe*

PAMIRS

A central Asian mountainous region, lying mostly in Tajikistan and partly in Pakistan, Afghanistan and China. The region forms a geological structural knot from which the Tian Shan, Karakoram, Kunlun and Hindu Kush mountain ranges radiate. The terrain includes grasslands and sparse trees. The highest peak is Pik Imeni Ismail Samani (Pik Kommunizma) at 7,495 m [24,590 ft].

DUSHANBE

Capital of Tajikistan, at the foot of the Gissar Mountains, central Asia. Founded in the 1920s, it was known as Stalinabad from 1929–61. An industrial, trade and transport centre, it is the site of Tajik University and Academy of Sciences. Industries include cotton milling, engineering, leather goods, and food processing.

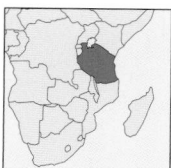

Tanzania's flag was adopted in 1964 when mainland Tanganyika joined with the island nation of Zanzibar to form the United Republic of Tanzania. The green represents agriculture and the yellow minerals. The black represents the people, while the blue symbolizes Zanzibar.

The United Republic of Tanzania consists of the former mainland country of Tanganyika and the island nation of Zanzibar, which also includes the island of Pemba.

Behind a narrow coastal plain, the majority of Tanzania is a plateau lying between 900 m and 1,500 m [2,950–4,920 ft] above sea level. The plateau is broken by arms of the Great African Rift Valley. The western arm contains lakes Nyasa (also called Malawi) and Tanganyika, while the eastern arm contains the strongly alkaline Lake Natron, together with lakes Eyasi and Manyara. Lake Victoria occupies a shallow depression in the plateau and it is not situated within the Rift Valley.

Kilimanjaro, the highest peak, is an extinct volcano. At 5,895 m [19,340 ft], it is also Africa's highest mountain. Zanzibar and Pemba are coral islands.

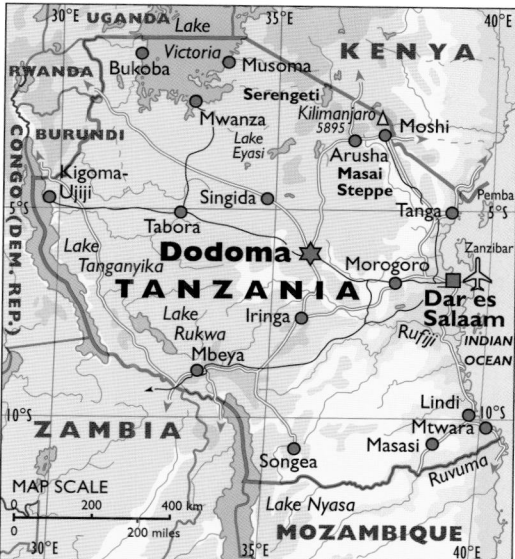

Area 945,090 sq km [364,899 sq mi]
Population 36,588,000
Capital (population) Dodoma (204,000)
Government Multiparty republic
Ethnic groups Native African 99% (Bantu 95%)
Languages Swahili (Kiswahili) and English (both official)
Religions Islam 35% (99% in Zanzibar), traditional beliefs 35%, Christianity 30%
Currency Tanzanian shilling = 100 cents
Website www.tanzania.go.tz/index2E.html

CLIMATE

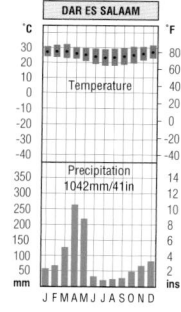

The coast has a hot, humid climate. The greatest rainfall is in April and May. Inland mountains and plateaux are cooler and less humid. The Rift Valley is hot.. Mount Kilimanjaro is permanently snow and ice covered.

HISTORY

Around 2,000 years ago, Arabs, Persians and Chinese traded along the Tanzanian coast. The old cities and ruins testify to its importance. Arab traders often intermarried with local people and the Arab-African people produced the distinctive Arab-Swahili culture. The Portuguese took control of coastal trade in the early 16th century, but the Arabs regained control in the 17th century.

In 1698, Arabs from Oman took control of Zanzibar. From this base, they developed inland trade, bringing gold, ivory and slaves from the interior. During the 19th century, European explorers and missionaries were active, mapping the country and striving to stop the slave trade.

POLITICS

Mainland Tanganyika became a German territory in the 1880s, while Zanzibar (including Pemba) became a British protectorate in 1890. The Germans introduced a system of forced labour to develop plantations. This led to a major rebellion in 1905, which was put down with great brutality.

Following Germany's defeat in World War I Britain gained control of Tanganyika and was granted a mandate to rule it by the League of Nations. Tanganyika remained a Briish territory until winning its independence in 1961, followed by Zanzibar in 1963. Tanganyika and Zanzibar united to form the United Republic of Tanzania in 1964.

The country's first president, Julius Nyerere, pursued socialist policies of self-help (called *ujamaa* in Swahili) and egalitarianism. While many of its social reforms were successful, the country failed to make economic progress.

DODOMA

Capital and third biggest city of Tanzania, it was chosen as the new capital due to its location in the centre of the country and replaced Dar es Salaam in 1974. It is in an agricultural region, crops include grain, seeds, and nuts.

Dhow *Sailing into the harbour, Zanzibar*

Nyerere resigned as president in 1985, though he remained influential until his death in 1999. His successors, Ali Hassan Mwinyi, who served from 1985 until 1995, and Benjamin Mkapa, who was re-elected in 2000, pursued more liberal economic policies. In 2005, Mkapa was succeeded by Jakaya Kikwete, another CCM (Chama Cha Mapinduzi) candidate.

ECONOMY

Tanzania is one of the world's poorest countries. Although crops are grown on only 5% of the land, agriculture employs 85% of the people. Most farmers grow only enough to feed their families. Food crops include bananas, cassava, maize, millet, rice and vegetables. Export crops include coffee, cotton, cashew nuts, tea and tobacco. Other crops grown for export include cloves, coconuts and sisal. Some farmers raise animals, but sleeping sickness and drought restrict the areas for livestock farming.

Diamonds and other gems are mined, together with some coal and gold. Industry is mostly small-scale. Manufactures include processed food, fertilizers, petroleum products and textiles.

Tourism is increasing. Tanzania has beautiful beaches, but its main attractions are its magnificent national parks and reserves, including the celebrated Serengeti and the Ngorongoro Crater. These are renowned for their wildlife and are among the world's finest.

Tanzania also contains a major archaeological site, Olduvai Gorge, west of the Serengeti. Here, in 1964, the British archaeologist and anthropologist, Louis Leakey, discovered the remains of ancient humanlike creatures.

Thailand's flag was adopted in 1917. In the late 19th century, it featured a white elephant on a plain red flag. In 1916, white stripes were introduced above and below the elephant, but in 1917 the elephant was dropped and a central blue band was added.

Area 513,115 sq km [198,114 sq mi]
Population 64,866,000
Capital (population) Bangkok (6,320,000)
Government Constitutional monarchy
Ethnic groups Thai 75%, Chinese 14%, others
Languages Thai (official), English, ethnic and regional dialects
Religions Buddhism 95%, Islam, Christianity
Currency Baht = 100 satang
Website www.thaigov.go.th

The Kingdom of Thailand is one of ten nations in South-east Asia. Central Thailand is a fertile plain drained mainly by the Chao Phraya. A densely populated region, it includes the capital, Bangkok. The highest land occurs in the north and includes the second largest city Chiang Mai and Doi Inthanon, the highest peak, which reaches 2,595 m [8,514 ft].

The Khorat Plateau, in the north-east, makes up about 30% of the country and extends to the River Mekong border with Laos. In the south, Thailand shares the finger-like Malay Peninsula with Burma and Malaysia.

The vegetation of Thailand includes many hardwood trees to the north. The south has rubber plantations. Grass, shrub and swamp make up 20% of land. 33% of the land is arable, mainly comprising rice fields.

CLIMATE

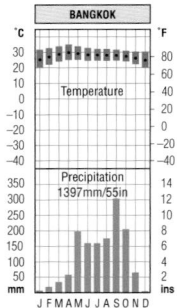

Thailand has a tropical climate. Monsoon winds from the south-west bring heavy rains May to October. Bangkok is drier than many parts of Southeast Asia because mountains shelter the central plains from the rain-bearing winds.

HISTORY

The Mongol capture in 1253 of a Thai kingdom in south-west China forced the Thai people to move south. A new kingdom was established around Sukothai. In the 14th century the kingdom expanded and the capital moved to Ayutthaya.

European contact began in the early 16th century. But, in the late 17th century, the Thais, fearing interference in their affairs, forced all Europeans to leave. This policy continued for 150 years. Thailand remained the only Southeast Asian nation to resist colonization.

In 1782, a Thai General, Chao Phraya Chakkri, became king, founding a dynasty which continues today. The country became known as Siam,

Traffic in Bangkok's Chinatown *surrounded by colourful signage*

and Bangkok became its capital. From the mid-19th century, contacts with the West were restored. In World War I, Siam supported the Allies against Germany and Austria-Hungary. In 1932, Thailand became a constitutional monarchy.

POLITICS

In 1938, Pibul Songkhram became premier and changed the country's name to Thailand. In 1941, Pibul, despite opposition, invited Japanese forces into Thailand. Pibul was overthrown in a military coup in 1957. The military governed Thailand until 1973.

Since 1967, when Thailand became a member of ASEAN (Association of South-east Asian Nations), its economy has grown, especially its manufacturing and service industries. However, in 1997, it suffered recession along with other eastern Asian countries and this persisted into the 21st century.

A military group seized power in 1991, but elections were held in 1992, 1995 and 2001. Then in 2004 Thailand was rocked by sectarian violence in the south where the majority of the population is Muslim, many of whom claim that they suffer discrimination by the central government.

ECONOMY

Despite its rapid progress, the World Bank classifies the country as a 'lower-middle-income' developing country. Manufactures, including commercial vehicles, food products, machinery, timber products and textiles, are exported.

Agriculture still employs two-thirds of the workforce. Rice is the chief crop, while other major crops include cassava, cotton, maize, pineapples, rubber, sugar cane and tobacco. Thailand also mines tin and other minerals.

Tourism is a major source of income, though the December 2004 tsunami, which killed over 5,000 people, cast a shadow over its future growth.

BANGKOK

Capital and chief port of Thailand, located on the east bank of the River Chao Phraya. Bangkok became the capital in 1782, when King Rama I built a royal palace here. It quickly became Thailand's largest city. The Grand Palace (including the sacred Emerald Buddha) and more than 400 Buddhist temples (wats) are notable examples of Thai culture. During World War II it was occupied by the Japanese. Bangkok is a busy market centre, much of the city's commerce taking place on the numerous canals (klongs) on the Thonburi (original site of the capital) side of the river that connect the city with the suburbs.

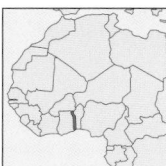

AFRICA

The five stripes represent action and the five regions of Togo, the alternation of colours is for unity in diversity. Red represents the blood shed in the struggle for independence, the star is for life, liberty and labour. Green is for hope and agriculture. Yellow is for Togo's mineral wealth.

The Republic of Togo is a long, narrow country in West Africa. From north to south, it extends about 500 km [311 mi]. Its coastline on the Gulf of Guinea is only 64 km [40 mi] long, and it is only 145 km [90 mi] at its widest point. The coastal plain is sandy. North of the coast is an area of fertile, clay soil. North again is the Mono Tableland which reaches an altitude of 450 m [1,500 ft], and is drained by the River Mono. The Atakora Mountains are the fourth region. The vegetation is mainly open grassland.

CLIMATE

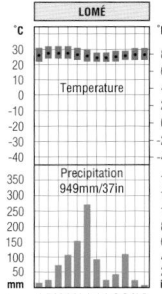

Togo has year-round high temperatures with a long dry season running from October to April. The main wet season runs from March to July, with a minor wet season in October and November. Rainfall is lower on the coast than even a short way inland.

HISTORY

The historic region of Togoland comprised what is now the Republic of Togo and West Ghana. From the 17th to the 19th century, the Ashanti raided Togoland and sold the indigenous inhabitants, the Ewe, to Europeans as slaves.

Togo became a German protectorate in 1884; it developed economically and Lomé was built. At the start of World War I, Britain and France captured Togoland from Germany. In 1922, it divided into two mandates, which in 1942 became UN Trust Territories. In 1956, the people of British Togoland voted to join Ghana, while French Togoland gained independent as the Republic of Togo in 1960.

In 1961 Sylvanus Olympio became Togo's first president. He was assassinated in 1963. Nicolas Grunitzky became president, but he was overthrown in the military coup of 1967, led by the head of the armed forces, General Gnassingbé Eyadéma who then became president. In 1969 a new constitution confirmed Togo as a single-party state, the sole legal party being the Rassemblement du Peuple Togolais (RPT).

Re-elected in 1972 and 1986, Eyadéma was forced to resign in 1991 after prodemocracy riots. Kokou Koffigoh led an interim government. Unrest contin-

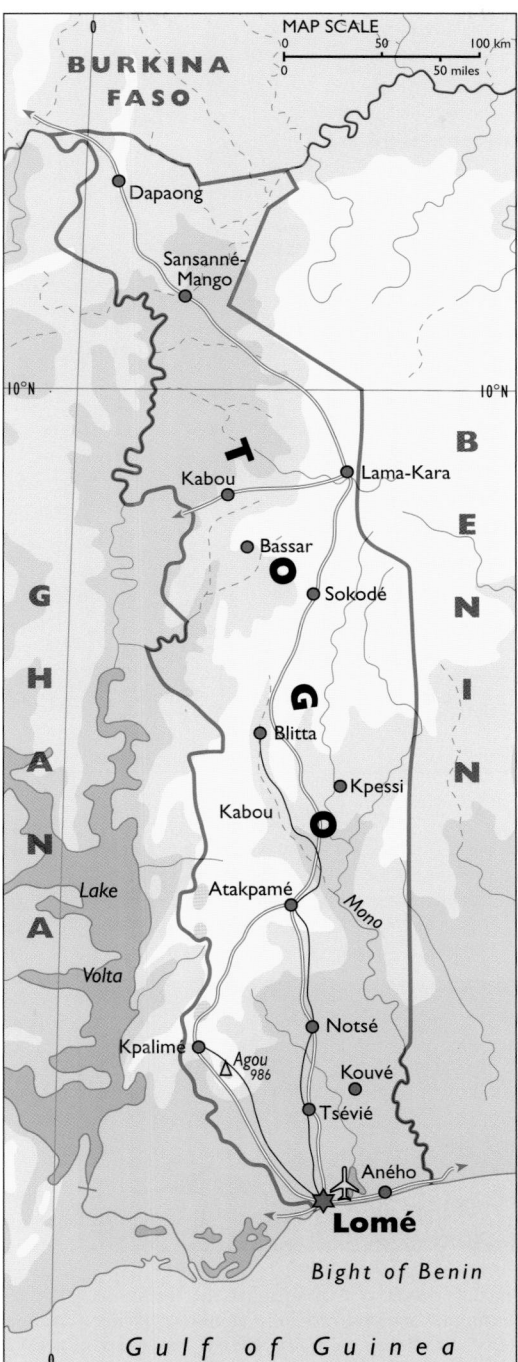

LOMÉ

Capital and largest city of Togo, on the Gulf of Guinea. Made capital of German Togoland in 1897, it later became an important commercial centre. It was the site of two conferences (1975, 1979) that produced a trade agreement (known as the Lomé Convention) between Europe and 46 African, Caribbean and Pacific states. Its main exports are coffee, cocoa, palm nuts, copra and phosphates.

Area 56,785 sq km [21,925 sq mi]
Population 5,557,000
Capital (population) Lomé (658,000)
Government Multiparty republic
Ethnic groups Native African 99% (largest tribes are Ewe, Mina and Kabre)
Languages French (official), African languages
Religions Traditional beliefs 51%, Christianity 29%, Islam 20%
Currency CFA franc = 100 centimes
Website www.republicoftogo.com

ued with troops loyal to Eyadéma attempting to overthrow Koffigoh.

POLITICS

A new constitution was adopted in 1992. In 1993 Eyadéma won rigged elections. Multiparty elections were held in 1994 and though these were won by an opposition alliance, Eyadéma formed a coalition government. In 1998, paramilitary police prevented the completion of the count in presidential elections when it became clear that Eyadéma had lost. Eyadéma continued in office and the main opposition parties boycotted the general elections in 1999. In late 2002 the constitution was changed to allow Eyadéma to stand for re-election. He won the subsequent 2003 elections.

Eyadéma died in 2005 and his son, Faure, became president. After international pressure he stepped down and called elections. Faure won these two months later amid claims by the opposition that the vote was rigged. In addition, the political violence surrounding the presidential poll was such that around 40,000 Togolese fled to neighbouring countries. These events called into question Togo's commitment to democracy which had been declared in 2004 when trying to normalise ties with the EU. The EU had cut off aid to Togo in 1993 over the country's human rights record.

In 2006 Togo played in the FIFA World Cup Finals for the first time in the country's history.

ECONOMY

Togo is a poor developing country. Farming employs 65% of the people, but most farmers grow little more than they need to feed their families. Major food crops include cassava, maize, millet and yams. The chief cash crops are cocoa, coffee and cotton. The leading exports are phosphate rock, which is used to make fertilizers, and palm oil.

Togo's small-scale manufacturing and mining industries employ about 6% of the people.

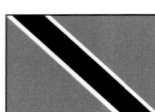

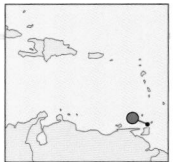

The colours represent earth, water and fire. The black stripe stands for the country's abundant oil and gas resources and the unity and determination of the people. The white stripes are for the Caribbean Sea, as well as purity and equality. The red field represents the Caribbean sun.

The Republic of Trinidad and Tobago consists of two main islands and is the most southerly in the Lesser Antilles. The largest island, Trinidad, is just 16 km [10 mi] off Venezuela's Orinoco delta. Tobago, a detached extension of Trinidad's hilly Northern Range, lies 34 km [21 mi] to the north. The country's highest point is Mount Aripo (940 m [3,085 ft]) in Trinidad's rugged and forested Northern Range. Fertile plains cover much of the country.

CLIMATE

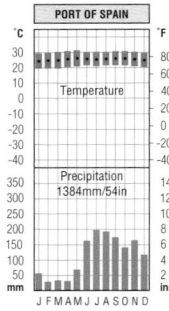

Temperatures are high throughout the year, ranging from 18°C to 33°C [64°F to 92°F]. Rainfall is heavy, with the wettest months from June to November. Annual rainfall ranges from 1,270 mm [50 in] on south-western Trinidad to more than 2,540 mm [100 in] on the highlands of Tobago.

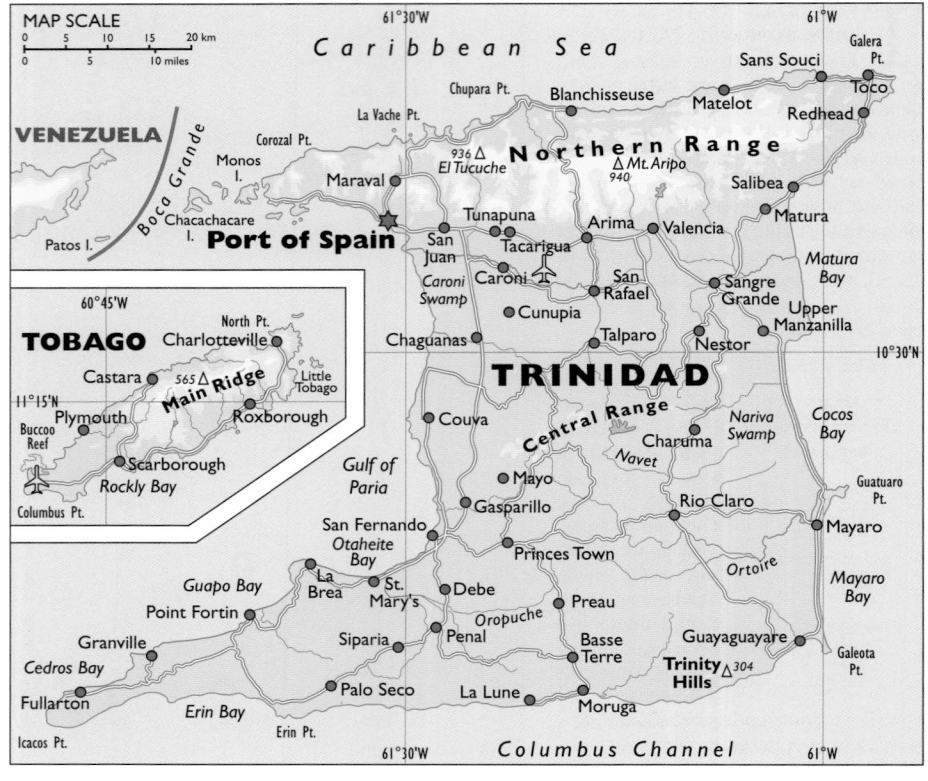

HISTORY

Christopher Columbus visited the islands, then populated by Arawak and Carib Amerindians in 1498. He named Trinidad after three peaks at its southern tip, and Tobago after a local tobacco pipe. Spain colonized Trinidad in 1532, while Dutch settlers planted sugar on plantations in Tobago in the 1630s. In 1781, France colonized Tobago and further developed its plantation economy. The British captured Trinidad from Spain in 1797 and, in 1802, Spain formally ceded the island to Britain. In 1814, France also ceded Tobago to Britain and, in 1869, the two islands were combined into one colony. Black slaves worked on the plantations until slavery was abolished in 1834. To meet the problem of labour shortages, the British recruited Indian and Chinese indentured labourers. The presence of people of African, Asian and European origin has resulted in a complex cultural mix in present-day Trinidad and Tobago.

POLITICS

Independence was achieved in 1962. Eric Williams, moderate leader of the People's National Movement (PNP), which he had founded in 1956, became prime minister. In 1970, the government declared a state of emergency following violence by black power supporters, who called for an end to foreign influence and unemployment. The emergency was lifted in 1972, but strikes caused problems in 1975. Trinidad and Tobago became a republic in 1976, with Williams continuing as prime minister. In 1986, after 30 years in office, the PNP was defeated in elections. The National Alliance for Reconstruction (NAR) coalition took office under

PORT OF SPAIN

Capital of Trinidad and Tobago, on the north-west coast of Trinidad. Founded by the Spanish in the late 16th century, it was seized by Britain in 1797. From 1958 to 1962 it was the capital of the Federation of the West Indies. It is a major tourist and shipping centre.

Area 5,130 sq km [1,981 sq mi]
Population 1,097,000
Capital (population) Port of Spain (51,000)
Government Multiparty republic
Ethnic groups Indian (South Asian) 40%, African 38%, mixed 21%, others
Languages English (official), Hindi, French, Spanish, Chinese
Religions Roman Catholic 26%, Hindu 23%, Anglican 8%, Baptist 7%, Pentecostal 7%, others
Currency Trinidad and Tobago dollar = 100 cents
Website www.visittnt.com

Arthur Robinson. In 1990, Islamists seized parliament and held Robinson and other officials hostage for several days. In 1991, Patrick Manning became prime minister following an election victory for the PNP, but, in 1994, Baseo Panday, leader of the Indian-based United National Congress (UNC), became prime minister, leading a coalition with the NAR. In the 2002 elections the PNP was victorious and Patrick Manning returned as prime minister.

Trinidad and Tobago is a major transshipment point for cocaine being moved from South America to North America and Europe. Cannabis is also produced in the country. The drug trade has fuelled gang violence and corruption. The death penalty was reintroduced in 1999, despite strong international pressure. In 2005, a Caribbean Court of Justice was set up in Trinidad as a final court of appeal to replace the British Privy Council.

ECONOMY

Oil is vital to the economy. Chief exports include refined and crude petroleum, anhydrous ammonia, and iron and steel.

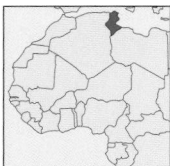

NORTH AFRICA

Tunisia 199

Tunisia's flag originated in about 1835 when the country was officially under Turkish rule. It became the national flag in 1956, when Tunisia became independent from France. The flag contains two traditional symbols of Islam, the crescent and the star.

The Republic of Tunisia is the smallest country in North Africa. The mountains in the north are an eastwards and comparatively low extension of the Atlas Mountains.

To the north and east of the mountains lie fertile plains, especially between Sfax, Tunis and Bizerte. South of the mountains lie broad plateaux which descend towards the south. This low-lying region contains a large salt pan, called the Chott Djerid, and part of the Sahara.

CLIMATE

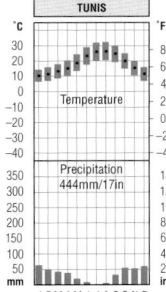

Northern Tunisia has a Mediterranean climate, with dry summers, and mild winters with a moderate rainfall. The average yearly rainfall decreases towards the south, which forms part of the Sahara.

HISTORY

Tunisia has come under the influence of a succession of cultures, each of which has left its mark on the country, giving Tunisia a distinct identity and a long tradition of urban life.

The Phoenicians began the Carthaginian Empire in Tunisia around 1100 BC and, according to legend, the colony of Carthage was established in 814 BC on a site near present-day Tunis. At its peak, Carthage controlled large areas in the eastern Mediterranean but, following the three Punic Wars with Rome, Carthage was destroyed in 146 BC. The Romans ruled the area for 600 years until the Vandals defeated the Romans in AD 439. The Vandals were finally conquered by the Byzantines. Arabs reached the area in the mid-7th century, introducing Islam and the Arabic language. In 1547, Tunisia came under the rule of the Turkish Ottoman Empire.

In 1881, France established a protectorate over Tunisia and ruled the country until 1956. Tunisian aspirations for independence were felt before World War I, but it was not until 1934 that Habib Bourguiba founded the first effective opposition group, the Neo-Destour (New Constitution) Party, which was renamed the Socialist Destour Party in 1964, and is now known as the Constitutional Assembly.

Tunisia supported the Allies during World War II and it was the scene of much fierce fighting. Following independence, the new parliament abolished the monarchy and declared Tunisia to be a republic in 1957. The nationalist leader, Habib Bourguiba, became president.

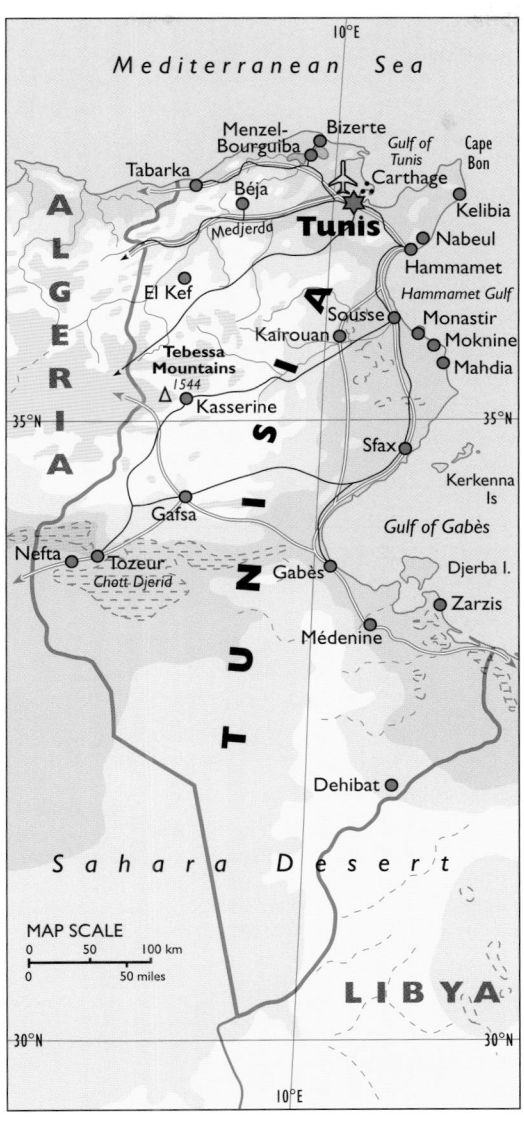

Area 163,610 sq km [63,170 sq mi]
Population 9,975,000
Capital (population) Tunis (702,000)
Government Multiparty republic
Ethnic groups Arab 98%, European 1%
Languages Arabic (official), French
Religions Islam 98%, Christianity 1%, others
Currency Tunisian dinar = 100 1,000 millimes
Website www.tourismtunisia.com

POLITICS

In 1975, Bourguiba was elected president for life. His government introduced many reforms, including votes for women. But problems arose from the government's successes. For example, the establishment of a national school system led to a very rapid increase in the number of educated people who were unable to find jobs that measured up to their qualifications. The growth of tourism, which provided a valuable source of foreign currency, also led to fears that Western influences might undermine traditional Muslim values.

Finally, the prime minister, Zine el Abidine Ben Ali, removed Bourguiba from office in 1987 and succeeded him as president. He was elected president in 1989, 1994, 1999 and 2004 with his party dominating the Chamber of Deputies, though some seats were reserved for opposition parties whatever their proportion of the popular vote. But he faced opposition from Islamic fundamentalists. Occasional violence and suppression of human rights, including the banning of al-Nahda, the main Islamic party, marred his presidency. However, Islamic fundamentalism in Tunisia did not prove to be anything like as effective as in Algeria.

ECONOMY

The World Bank classifies Tunisia as a 'middle-income' developing country. Its main natural resources are oil and phosphates. Agriculture employs 22% of the people. Chief crops are barley, citrus fruits, dates, grapes, olives, sugar beet, tomatoes and wheat. Sheep are the most important livestock, but goats and cattle are also raised. Tourism has grown considerably. Since independence, new industries and tourism have transformed a number of coastal towns. Major manufactures include cement, flour, phosphoric acid, processed food and steel. An important stimulus was the signing of a free-trade agreement with the EU in 1995. In doing so Tunisia became the first Arab country on the Mediterranean to sign such an agreement.

TUNIS

Capital and largest city of Tunisia it lies to the north of the country, adjacent to the Gulf of Tunis on the Mediterranean.

Tunis became the capital in the 13th century under the Hafsid dynasty. Seized by Barbarossa in 1534 and controlled by Turkey, it attained infamy as a haven for pirates. The French assumed control in 1881. During World War II it was held by the Axis forces from November 1942 to May 1943.

Tunis gained independence in 1956. The ruins of Carthage are nearby. The medina of Tunis is a UNESCO World Heritage Site and has been so since 1979 featuring as it does over 700 monuments, including fountains, palaces, mosques, mausoleums and madrasas (schools). Products include olive oil, carpets, textiles and handicrafts.

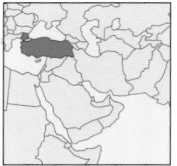

Turkey's flag was adopted when the Republic of Turkey was established in 1923. The crescent moon and the five-pointed star are traditional symbols of Islam. They were used on earlier Turkish flags used by the Turkish Ottoman Empire.

Area 774,815 sq km [299,156 sq mi]
Population 68,894,000
Capital (population) Ankara (2,984,000)
Government Multiparty republic
Ethnic groups Turkish 80%, Kurdish 20%
Languages Turkish (official), Kurdish, Arabic
Religions Islam (mainly Sunni Muslim) 99%
Currency New Turkish lira = 100 kurus
Website www.kultur.gov.tr/EN

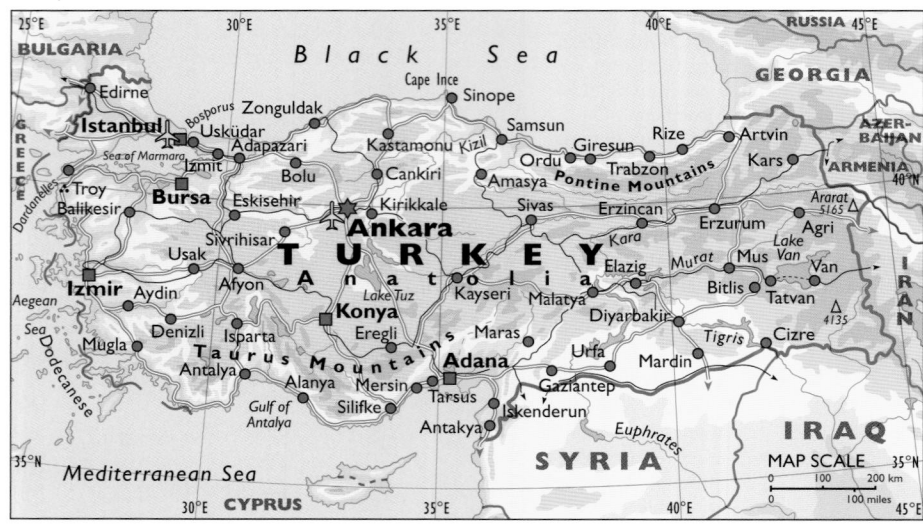

The Republic of Turkey lies in two continents. The European section (Thrace) lies west of a waterway between the Black and Mediterranean seas. This waterway consists of the Bosphorus, on which the city of Istanbul stands, the Sea of Marmara (Marmara Denizi) and a narrow strait called the Dardanelles.

Most of the Asian part of Turkey consists of plateaux and mountains, which rise to 5,165 m [16,945 ft] at Mount Ararat (Agri Dagi) near the border with Armenia. Earthquakes are common.

Deciduous forest grow inland with conifers on the mountains. The plateau is mainly dry steppe.

CLIMATE

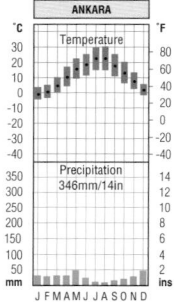

Central Turkey has a dry climate, with hot, sunny summers and cold winters. The driest part of the central plateau lies south of Ankara, around Lake Tuz. Western Turkey has a Mediterranean climate, while the Black Sea coast has cooler summers.

HISTORY

In AD 330, the Roman Empire moved its capital to Byzantium, renaming it Constantinople. Constantinople became the capital of the East Roman (or Byzantine) Empire in 395. Muslim Seljuk Turks from central Asia invaded Anatolia in the 11th century. In the 14th century, another group of Turks, the Ottomans, conquered the area. In 1453, the Ottoman Turks took Constantinople, which they called Istanbul. The Ottoman Turks built up a large empire which finally collapsed during World War I (1914–18). In 1923, Turkey became a republic. Its leader Mustafa Kemal, or Atatürk ('father of the Turks'), launched policies to modernize and secularize the country.

It joined NATO in 1951 and applied to join the European Economic Community in 1987. But Turkey's conflict with Greece, together with its invasion of northern Cyprus in 1974, have led many Europeans to treat Turkey's aspirations with caution. Political instability, military coups, conflict with Kurdish nationalists in eastern Turkey and concern about the country's record on human rights are other problems.

Pamukkale (Cotton Palace); *this landscape of mineral forests and petrified waterfalls is a designated UNESCO World Heritage Site*

ANKARA

Capital of Turkey, at the confluence of the Cubuk and Ankara rivers. In ancient times it was known as Ancyra, and was an important commercial centre as early as the 8th century BC. It flourished under Augustus as a Roman provincial capital. Tamerlane took the city in 1402. Kemal Atatürk set up a provisional government here in 1920. It replaced Istanbul as the capital in 1923, changing its name to Ankara in 1930. It is noted for its angora wool and mohair.

POLITICS

Turkey has enjoyed democracy since 1983, though, in 1998, the government banned the Islamist Welfare Party, accusing it of violating secular principles. In 1999, the largest numbers of parliamentary seats were won by the ruling Democratic Left Party and the far-right Nationalist Action Party. In 2001, the Turkish parliament adopted reforms to ease the country's entry into the European Union. One reform formally recognized men and women as equals – the former code designated the man as the head of the family.

In the elections of 2002 the moderate Islamic Justice and Development Party (AKP) won 362 of the 500 seats in parliament. None of the parties in the former ruling coalition won even 10%.

Turkey finally agreed to recognize Cyprus as an EU member and this led to EU membership talks being formally launched in October 2005 with negotiations expected to take about 10 years.

In the 1980s and 1990s civil war was a problem in the east and south-east of Turkey. Fighting took place between Turkish forces and those of the secessionist Kurdistan Workers' Party (PKK). Over 30,000 people died. The PKK seeks greater political and cultural rights for the Kurdish community. A five-year cease-fire was called off in 2004 by Kurdish secessionists after what they called annihilation operations against their fighters by the Turkish authorities. There have been subsequent clashes between Kurdish fighters and Turkish forces in the south-east causing many deaths.

ECONOMY

Turkey is a 'lower-middle-income' developing country. Agriculture employs 40% of the people, and barley, cotton, fruits, maize, tobacco and wheat are major crops. Livestock farming is important and wool is a leading product. Manufacturing is the chief activity, including processed farm products and textiles, cars, fertilizers, iron and steel, machinery, metal products and paper products. Turkey receives more than 9 million tourists a year.

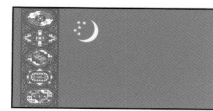

Turkmenistan's flag was adopted in 1992. It incorporates a typical Turkmen carpet design. The crescent is a symbol of Islam, while the five stars and the five elements in the carpet represent the traditional tribal groups of Turkmenistan.

The Republic of Turkmenistan is one of five central Asian republics which once formed part of the Soviet Union. Most of the land is low-lying, with mountains on the southern and south-western borders.

In the west lies the salty Caspian Sea. A depression called the Kara Bogaz Gol Bay contains the country's lowest point. Most of the country is arid and Asia's largest sand desert, the Garagum, covers 80% of the country, though parts of it are irrigated by the Garagum Canal.

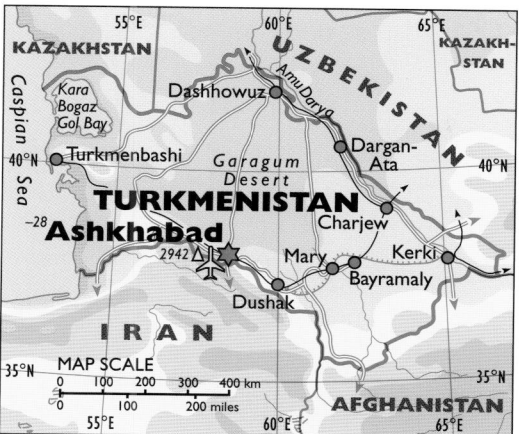

Area 488,100 sq km [188,455 sq mi]
Population 4,863,000
Capital (population) Ashkhabad (521,000)
Government Single-party republic
Ethnic groups Turkmen 85%, Uzbek 5%, Russian 4%, others
Languages Turkmen (official), Russian, Uzbek
Religions Islam 89%, Eastern Orthodox 9%
Currency Turkmen manat = 100 tenesi
Website www.turkmenistan.gov.tm/index_eng.html

CLIMATE

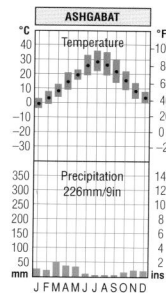

Turkmenistan has a continental climate, with average annual rainfall varying from 80 mm [3 in] in the desert to 300 mm [12 in] in the mountains. Summers are very hot, but temperatures during winter drop below freezing.

Islamic buildings; with a strong Islamic heritage Turkmenistan is rich in monuments to its past in the form of mosques and palaces

HISTORY

Just over 1,000 years ago, Turkic people settled in the lands east of the Caspian Sea and the name 'Turkmen' comes from this time. Genghis Khan and his Mongol armies conquered the area in the 13th century and it subsequently became part of Tamerlane's vast empire. With the break up of the Timurid dynasty, Turkmenistan came under Uzbek control. Islam was introduced in the 14th century.

Russia took over the region during the 1870s and 1880s. In 1899, despite resistance, Turkmenistan became part of Russian Turkistan. After the Russian Revolution of 1917, the area came under Communist rule and, in 1924, as part of the Turkistan Autonomous Soviet Socialist Republic, it joined the Soviet Union. The Communists strictly controlled all aspects of life and, in particular, they discouraged religious worship. But they also improved such services as education, health, housing and transport.

POLITICS

During the 1980s, the Soviet Union introduced reforms, and the Turkmen began to demand more freedom. In 1990, the Turkmen government stated that its laws overruled Soviet laws. In 1991, Turkmenistan became fully independent after the break-up of the Soviet Union, but kept ties with Russia through the Commonwealth of Independent States (CIS).

In 1992, Turkmenistan adopted a new constitution, allowing for political parties, providing that they were not ethnic or religious in character. But effectively Turkmenistan remained a one-party state and, in 1992, Saparmurad Niyazov, the former Communist and now Democratic leader, was the only candidate. In 1994 a referendum prolonged Niyazov's term of office to 2002, while in 1999 the parliament declared him president for life. In 2004, parliamentary elections were described as a 'sham' because all the candidates supported the president. In 2005 he surprised observers by calling for contested presidential elections to take place in 2009.

Niyazov seeks to influence every aspect of his people's lives. Turkmens are expected to take spiritual guidance from his book, Ruhnama, a collection of thoughts on Turkmen culture and history. After giving up smoking due to major heart surgery in 1997, he ordered all his ministers to give up and then banned smoking in public places. Subsequent bans include one on young men having beards and long hair, opera, ballet and the playing of recorded music on television, at public events and at weddings.

ECONOMY

Turkmenistan joined the Economic Co-operation Organization which was set up in 1985 by Iran, Pakistan and Turkey. In 1996, the completion of a rail link from Turkmenistan to the Iranian coast was seen as an important step in the development of Central Asia. The World Bank classifies Turkmenistan as a 'lower-middle-income' country. The chief resources are oil and natural gas, but agriculture is important. The chief crop, grown on irrigated land, is cotton. Grains and vegetables are also important. Manufactures include cement, glass, petrochemicals and textiles. Turkmenistan has extensive hydrocarbon and natural gas reserves that could be of major economic assistance.

ASHGABAT (ASHKHABAD)

Capital of Turkmenistan, located 40 km [25 mi] from the Iranian border. Founded in 1881 as a Russian fortress between the Garagum Desert and the Kopet Dagh Mountains, it was largely rebuilt after a severe earthquake in 1948. The city was known as Poltaratsk from 1919 to 1927. Its present name was adopted after the republic attained independence from the former Soviet Union in 1991.

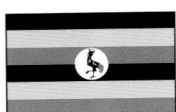

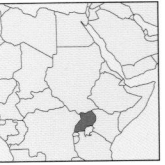

The flag used by the party that won the first national election was adopted as the national flag when Uganda became independent from Britain in 1962. The black represents the people, the yellow the sun, and the red brotherhood. The crested crane is the country's emblem.

Area 241,038 sq km [93,065 sq mi]
Population 26,405,000
Capital (population) Kampala (774,000)
Government Republic
Ethnic groups Baganda 17%, Ankole 8%, Basogo 8%, Iteso 8%, Bakiga 7%, Langi 6%, Rwanda 6%, Bagisu 5%, Acholi 4%, Lugbara 4% and others
Languages English and Swahili (both official), Ganda
Religions Roman Catholic 33%, Protestant 33%, traditional beliefs 18%, Islam 16%
Currency Ugandan shilling = 100 cents
Website www.statehouse.go.ug

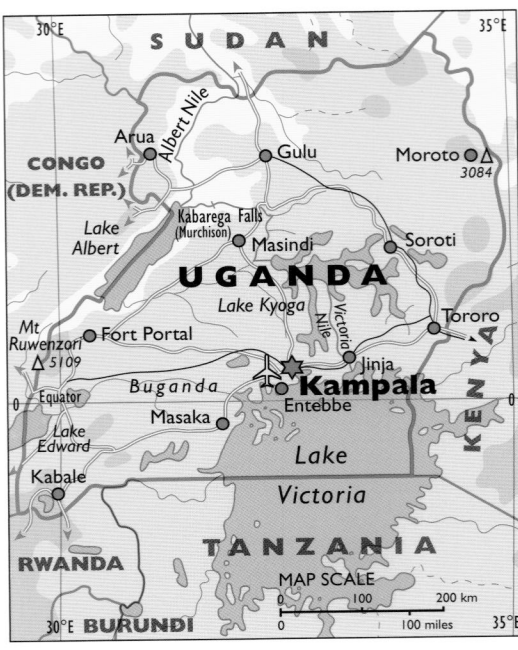

The Republic of Uganda is a land-locked country on the East African Plateau. It contains part of Lake Victoria, Africa's largest lake and a source of the River Nile, which occupies a shallow depression in the plateau.

The plateau varies in height from about 1,500 m [4,921 ft] in the south to 900 m [2,953 ft] in the north. The highest mountain is Margherita Peak, which reaches 5,109 m [16,762 ft] in the Ruwenzori Range in the south-west. Other mountains, including Mount Elgon at 4,321 m [14,177 ft], rise along Uganda's eastern border.

Part of the Great African Rift Valley, which contains lakes Edward and Albert, lies in western Uganda. The landscapes range from rainforests in the south, through savanna in the centre, to semi-desert in the north.

CLIMATE

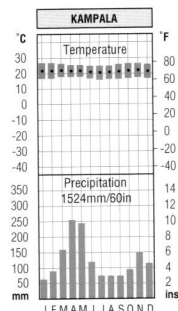

The Equator runs through Uganda and the country is warm throughout the year, though the high altitude moderates the temperature. The lands to the north of Lake Victoria, and the western mountains, especially the high Ruwenzori Range are the wettest regions. Much of Uganda has two rainy seasons from Apri to May and from October to December. In the centre and the north, these merge into one, with a distinct dry season.

Terraced fields of crops, *Kisoro*

HISTORY

In around 1500, the Nilotic-speaking Lwo people formced various kingdoms in south-western Uganda, including Buganda (kingdom of the Ganda) and Bunyoro. During the 18th century, the Buganda kingdom expanded and trade flourished. In 1862, a British explorer, John Speke, became the first European to reach Buganda. He was closely followed in 1875 by Sir Henry Stanley. The conversion activities of Christian missionaries led to conflict with Muslims. The Kabaka (king) came to depend on Christian support. In 1894, Uganda became a British Protectorate.

In 1962, Uganda gained independence with Buganda's Kabaka, Sir

Edward Mutesa II, as president and Milton Obote as prime minister. In 1966, Mutesa II was forced into exile. Obote also abolished the traditional kingdoms, including Buganda. Obote was overthrown in 1971 in a military coup led by General Idi Amin Dada. Amin quickly established a personal dictatorship and launched a war against foreign interference that resulted in the mass expulsion of Asians. Amin's regime was responsible for the murder of more than 250,000 Ugandans. Obote loyalists resisted the regime from neighbouring Tanzania. In 1976, Amin declared himself president for life and Israel launched a successful raid on Entebbe Airport to end the hijack of one of its passenger planes. In 1978 Uganda annexed the Kagera region of north-west Tanzania.

POLITICS

In 1979 Tanzanian troops helped the Uganda National Liberation Front (UNLF) to overthrow Amin and capture Kampala. In 1980, Apollo Milton Obote led his party to victory in the national elections. But after charges of fraud, Obote's opponents the National Resistance Movement (NRA) began guerrilla warfare. More than 200,000 Ugandans sought refuge in Rwanda and Zaïre. A military group overthrew Obote in 1985 and he lived in exile in Zambia for the last 20 years of his life. Upon his death in 2005 he was granted a state funeral, much to the surprise of his opponents.

Strife continued until 1986, when the NRA captured Kampala and Yoweri Museveni became president. Museveni began to rebuild the domestic economy and improve foreign relations. In 1993 the Kabaka of Uganda returned as monarch. Museveni won Uganda's first direct presidential elections in 1996 and was re-elected in 2001.

In 2005, the people voted in favour of restoring multi-party politics after years of non-party politics. Parliament also voted to remove presidential time limits, enabling Museveni to contest the elections in 2006 and beyond.

KAMPALA

Capital and largest city in Uganda, on the northern shore of Lake Victoria. Founded in the late 19th century on the remains of a royal palace of the Kings of Buganda, it replaced Entebbe as capital when Uganda attained independence in 1962. It is the trading centre for the agricultural goods and livestock produced in Uganda. Industries include textiles, food processing, tea blending, coffee and brewing.

ECONOMY

Stability was restored to the economy under President Museveni and it finally expanded. Agriculture dominates, employing 80% of the people. Food crops include bananas, cassava, maize, millet, sorghum and sweet potatoes, while the chief cash crops are coffee, cotton, sugar cane and tea. The only important metal is copper. The Owen Falls Dam at Jinja, on the outlet of Lake Victoria, produces cheap electricity.

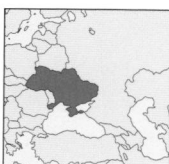

Ukraine's flag was first used between 1918 and 1922. It was readopted in September 1991. The colours were first used in 1848. They are heraldic in origin and were first used on the coat of arms of one of the Ukrainian kingdoms in the Middle Ages.

Ukraine is the second largest country in Europe after Russia. This mostly flat country faces the Black Sea in the south. The Crimean Peninsula includes a highland region overlooking Yalta. The highest point of the country is in the eastern Carpathian Mountains. The most extensive land region is the central plateau which descends in the north to the Dnipro-Pripet Lowlands. A low plateau occupies the north-east.

CLIMATE

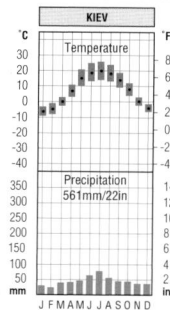

Ukraine has warm summers, but the winters are cold, becoming more severe from west to east. In the summer, the east of the country is often warmer than the west. The heaviest rainfall occurs in the summer.

HISTORY

In the 9th century AD, a civilization called Kievan Rus was founded, with its capital at Kiev. Russians took over the area in 980 and the region prospered. In the 13th century, Mongol armies ravaged the area. Later, the region was split into small kingdoms and large areas fell under foreign rule. In the 17th and 18th centuries, parts of Ukraine came under Polish and Russian rule. But Russia gained most of Ukraine in the late 18th century, although Austria held an area in the west, called Galicia. After the Bolshevik Revolution of 1917, the Ukrainians set up an independent, non-Communist republic. Austrian Ukraine declared itself a republic in 1918 and the two parts joined together, but in 1919, Ukrainian Communists set up a second government and proclaimed the country a Soviet Socialist Republic. The Communists ultimately triumphed and, during 1922, Ukraine became one of the four founding republics of the Soviet Union.

Millions of people died in the 1930s as the result of Soviet policies. Millions more died during the Nazi occupation between 1941 and 1944. In 1945, areas that were formerly in Czechoslovakia, Poland and Romania were added to Ukraine by the Soviet Union.

POLITICS

In the 1980s, the people demanded more say over their affairs. The country finally became independent when the Soviet Union broke up in 1991. Ukraine continued to work with Russia through the Commonwealth of Independent States. But Ukraine differed with Russia on some issues, including control over Crimea. In 1999, a treaty ratifying Ukraine's present boundaries failed to get the approval of Russia's upper house.

Area 603,700 sq km [233,089 sq mi]
Population 47,732,000
Capital (population) Kiev (2,590,000)
Government Multiparty republic
Ethnic groups Ukranian 78%, Russian 17%, Belarusian, Moldovan, Bulgarian, Hungarian, Polish
Languages Ukranian (official), Russian
Religions Mainly Ukranian Orthodox
Currency Hryvnia = 100 kopiykas
Website www.president.gov.ua/en

First day at elementary school in Crimea

KIEV (KYYIV)

Capital of Ukraine and a seaport on the Dnieper River. Founded in the 6th century AD, Kiev was the capital of Kievan Russia. It later came under Lithuanian, then Polish rule before being absorbed into Russia. It became the capital of the Ukrainian Soviet Socialist Republic in 1934, and of an independent Ukraine in 1991.

Leonid Kuchma, who became president in 1994, came under fire in the early 2000s for maladministration and for his alleged involvement in the murder of a journalist. In 2004, the prime minister, a supporter of Kuchma, was declared the winner in presidential elections, but after massive demonstrations, the election was declared invalid. The opposition and pro-Western leader Victor Yuschenko was elected president. This led to tensions with Russia. Russia feared that Ukraine might become aligned with the West. A dispute with Russia over the price of the gas it supplies to Ukraine in 2005-6 was said to be politically motivated.

ECONOMY

The World Bank classifies Ukraine as a 'lower-middle-income' economy. Agriculture is important, the major export crops are wheat and sugar beet. Livestock rearing and fishing are also important. Manufacturing is the chief economic activity and includes iron and steel, machinery and vehicles. The country has large coalfields and hydroelectric and nuclear power stations, but it imports oil and natural gas. In 1986, an accident at the Chernobyl nuclear power plant caused widespread nuclear radiation. The plant was finally closed in 2000.

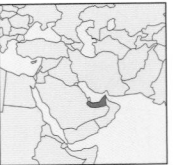

The flag was adopted on 2 December 1971, when the country was formed by a union of seven sheikdoms. Red, white, black and green are the Pan-Arab colours, historically linked to the Arab people and Islamic faith. They stand for Arab unity and independence.

Area 83,600 sq km [32,278 sq mi]
Population 2,524,000
Capital (population) Abu Dhabi (363,000)
Government Federation of Sheikdoms
Ethnic groups South Asian 50%, other Arab and Iranian 23%, Emirati 19%
Languages Arabic (official), Persian, English, Hindi, Urdu
Religions Muslim 96% (Shi'a 16%), others
Currency Emirati dirham = 100 fils
Website www.government.ae/gov/en/index.jsp

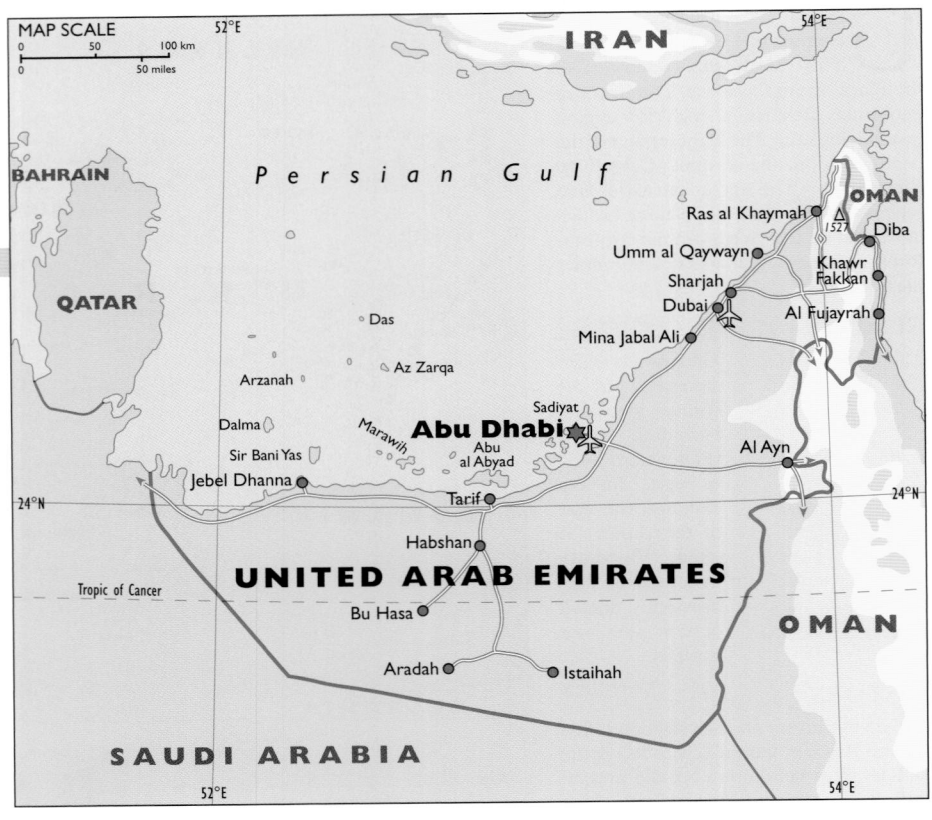

The United Arab Emirates (UAE) consists of a union of seven small Arab emirates (or sheikhdoms). Swamps and salt marshes border much of the coast in the north. The land is a flat, stony desert, with occasional oases. Sand dunes occur in the east. Highlands rise in the east, near the border with Oman. In the south, the land merges into the bleak Rub' al Khali (Empty Quarter) of Saudi Arabia.

CLIMATE

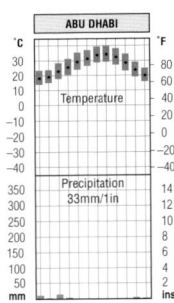

In most of the country, the average annual rainfall is less than 130 mm [5 in], most of it occurring between November and March. In summer (May to September), temperatures can soar to 49°C [120°F], with high humidity along the coast where conditions can become unpleasant. Winters are warm to mild. The eastern highlands are generally cooler and rainier than the rest of the country. Sandstorms and duststorms are common.

HISTORY

The area has its roots as a trading centre between the Mesopotamian and Indus Valley civilizations, later coming under Persian control and, in the 7th century AD, embracing Islam. In the 16th century various European nations set up coastal trading posts. The emirates of today began to develop in the 18th century. Their economies were based on pearl fishing and trading. In 1820, conflict between local rulers and piracy along the coast led Britain to force the states to sign a series of truces. Britain took control of the foreign affairs of the states, while promising protection from attack by outsiders. The states retained control over internal affairs. Because of these truces, the region became known as the Trucial States. In 1952, the emirates set up a Trucial Council to increase co-operation between them. Oil was discovered in 1958 and first exported in 1962. In 1968, Britain announced the withdrawal of its forces.

ABU DHABI (ABU ZABY)

Largest and wealthiest of the United Arab Emirates, lying on the south coast of the Persian Gulf. Also the name of its capital city, the federal capital of the UAE. Ruled since the 18th century by the Al-bu-Falah clan of the Bani Yas tribe. There are long-standing frontier disputes with Saudi Arabia and Oman. Abu Dhabi's economy is based almost entirely on crude oil production.

POLITICS

The country became independent in 1971, when six of its seven states, Abu Zaby (Abu Dhabi), Ajman, Dubayy (Dubai), Al Fujayrah, Ash Shariqah (Sharjah) and Umm-al-Qaywayn, agreed to form a single country, the United Arab Emirates. A seventh state, Ras al Khaymah, joined in 1972. Each of the seven Emirates has its own Emir, who controls internal affairs. The federal government controls foreign affairs and defence and plays a leading role in the social and economic development of the country. The seven Emirs form a Federal Supreme Council, which elects the federation's president and vice-president who serve five-year terms. The president appoints the prime minister. The country also has a Federal National Council with 40 members appointed by the rulers of the states. There are no elections and the role of the National Council is to review legislation; it cannot change or veto it. The country is one of the most liberal and tolerant of the Persian Gulf countries, but it is the only one without elected bodies. The UAE joined the allied force against Iraq in 1991 following the invasion of Kuwait, and the United States stationed forces there during the 2003 invasion of Iraq.

ECONOMY

The economy is based on oil production and the country is the world's sixth largest oil exporter.

The flag of the United Kingdom was officially adopted in 1801. The first Union flag, combining the cross of St George (England) and St Andrew (Scotland), dates back from 1603. In 1801, the cross of St Patrick, Ireland's emblem, was added to form the present flag.

The United Kingdom of Great Britain and Northern Ireland is a union of four countries. Three of them – England, Scotland and Wales – make up Great Britain. The Isle of Man and the Channel Islands, including Jersey and Guernsey, are not part of the UK, but are instead self-governing British dependencies.

Much of Scotland and Wales is mountainous, the highest peak is Scotland's Ben Nevis at 1,342 m [4,404 ft], with Snowdon in Wales reaching 1,085 m [3,560 ft]. England has some highland areas, including the Cumbrian Mountains (Lake District) and the Pennine range in the north. England also has large areas of fertile lowland. Northern Ireland is a mixture of lowlands and uplands and contains the United Kingdom's largest lake, Lough Neagh.

CLIMATE

The UK has a mild climate, influenced by the warm Gulf Stream flowing across the Atlantic from the Gulf of Mexico, then past the British Isles. Moist winds from the south-west bring rain, which diminishes west to east. Winds from the east and north bring cold conditions in winter. The weather is markedly changeable, because of the common occurrence of depressions with their associated fronts.

HISTORY

The isolation of the United Kingdom from mainland Europe has made a major impact on its history. Despite insularity, Britons are of mixed stock.

In ancient times, Britain was invaded by many peoples, including Iberians, celts, Romans, Angles, Saxons, Jutes, Norsemen, Danes and Normans, who arrived in 1066 and were the last people to successfully invade Britain. The Normans finally overcame Welsh resistance in 1282, when King Edward I annexed Wales and united it with England. Union with Scotland was achieved by the Act of Union of 1707. This created a country known as the United Kingdom of Great Britain.

Ireland came under Norman rule in the 11th century, and much of its later history was concerned with a struggle against English domination. In 1801, Ireland became part of the United Kingdom of Great Britain and Ireland, but in 1921 southern Ireland broke away to become

Area 241,857 sq k [93,381 sq mi]
Population 60,271,000
Capital (population) London (8,089,000)
Government Constitutional monarchy
Ethnic groups English 82%, Scottish 10%, Irish 2%, Welsh 2%, Ulster 2%, West Indian, Indian, Pakistani, others
Languages English (official), Welsh, Gaelic
Religions Christianity, Islam, Sikhism, Hinduism, Judaism
Currency Pound sterling = 100 pence
Website www.pm.gov.uk

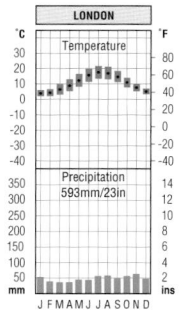
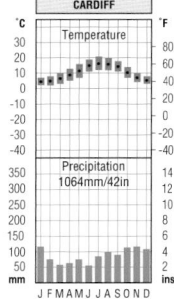
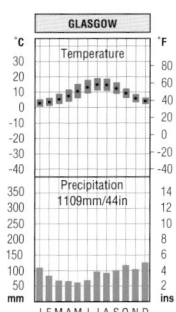

Irish Free State. Most of the people in Irish Free State were Roman Catholics. In Northern Ireland, where the majority were Protestants, most wanted to remain citizens of the United Kingdom, as a result the country's official name changed to the United Kingdom of Great Britain and Northern Ireland.

The British empire began to develop in the 18th century, despite the loss in 1783 of its North American colonies. In the late 18th century the UK was the first country to industrialise its economy.

The British Empire broke up after World War II (1939–45), though the UK still administers many small, territories around the world. The empire was transformed into the Commonwealth of Nations, a free association of independent countries, numbering 53 in 2005.

POLITICS

A welfare state was set up in 1945, with a social security system that provided welfare for people 'from the cradle to the grave'. In 1960, the UK helped to set up the European Free Trade Associationwith six other nations. In 1963, Britain's request to join the EEC was rejected, the UK finally joined the EEC in 1973, though a strong body of opinion still feared that the development of a federal Europe would jeopardize British sovereignty. Membership was endorsed by a referendum in 1975, but, at the turn of the century, Britons were still debating whether it was advisable for Britain to adopt the euro, the single European currency adopted by 12 of the 15 European Union members in 1999.

Since the 1960s, Northern Ireland has been the scene of conflict between the Protestant majority, who favour continuing union with the UK, and the Roman Catholic minority, many of whom are republicans who would like to see Ireland reunified. British troops were sent to the province in 1969 to control violence between the communities and, at various times, Britain has imposed direct rule. In 1998, the 'Good Friday' agreement held out hope for the future, when unionists and nationalists agreed that Northern Ireland would remain part of the United Kingdom, until a majority of its people voted in favour of a change. The agreement also allowed Ireland to play a part in the affairs of the north, while the republic amended its constitution to remove all claims to Northern Ireland. A Northern Ireland Assembly was set up to handle local affairs. In July 2005 the IRA issued a statement of full disarmament.

CHANNEL ISLANDS

Group of islands at the south west end of the English Channel, 16 km [10 mi] off the west coast of France. The main islands are Jersey, Guernsey, Alderney, and Sark; the chief towns are St. Helier (Jersey) and St. Peter Port (Guernsey). A dependency of the British crown since the Norman Conquest, they were under German occupation during World War II. They are divided into the administrative bailiwicks of Guernsey and Jersey, each with its own legislative assembly. The islands have a warm, sunny climate and fertile soil. The major industries are tourism and agriculture. They cover an area of 194 sq km (75 sq mi).

the UK, also focusing attention on the question of nationality.

The high cost of welfare services is a matter of political controversy. There is also concern about the changing economy, with a decline in traditional manufacturing and the growth of service industries, both of which affect employment. Another issue is immigration and the fear that economic migrants entering the UK will lessen the job opportunities of the indigenous workforce.

After the terrorist attacks on the United States on 11 September 2001, Britain was prominent in its support for the United States, helping to create the broad alliance that launched the attack on the Taliban government of Afghanistan. However, others are concerned at the cost and morality of British military operations especially the war with Iraq. In July 2005 four suicide bombers struck in central London, killing 52 and injuring hundreds.

LONDON

Capital of the United Kingdom, second-largest city in Europe, after Moscow. Located on the River Thames, 65km [40mi] from its mouth in the North Sea. Greater London, comprises the City of London 'square mile' plus 13 inner and 19 outer boroughs, covering a total of 1,580 sq km [610sq mi]. The Romans called it Londinium. In the 9th century, Alfred the Great made it the seat of government. Edward the Confessor built Westminster Abbey and made Westminster his capital in 1042. The Plague of 1665 killed 75,000 Londoners, and the following year the Fire of London destroyed many buildings. Sir Christopher Wren designed many churches, including St Paul's. The 19th century saw the population reach 4 million. and London become the world's biggest city. Further growth between the World Wars was accompanied by extensions to the transport system. Much of London was rebuilt after bomb damage during World War II, and the docklands were regenerated in the late 1980s. London is one of the world's most important administrative, financial and commercial cities.

Before 1999, Scotland and Wales were directly ruled by the British parliament in London. In 1997, following the landslide victory of the Labour Party under Tony Blair, 74% of voters in Scotland and 50.3% of voters in Wales opted for the setting up local assemblies.

The Scottish parliament is responsible for local affairs with limited powers to raise or reduce taxes. The Welsh Assembly, has no powers over taxation. Both met for the first time in 1999. Devolution has caused concern among those who fear that it might lead to the break-up of

ECONOMY

The UK is a major industrial and trading nation. Its natural resources are coal, iron ore, oil and natural gas, but it has to import most of the materials it needs for industry. It also has to import food. Service and high-technology industries are vital, financial and insurance services bring in much-needed foreign exchange. Historic and cultural attractions make tourism a vital industry while tourism is a major earner.

Agriculture employs only 2% of the workforce. Production is high. Major crops include barley, potatoes, sugar beet and wheat. Sheep are the leading livestock, beef and dairy cattle, pigs and poultry are also important as are cheese, milk and fishing.

Ullswater Lake *in the England's Lake District*

ISLE OF MAN

Island off the north-west coast of England, in the Irish Sea; the capital is Douglas. In the Middle Ages, it was a Norwegian dependency, subsequently coming under Scottish then English rule. It has been a British crown possession since 1828, but has its own government (the Tynwald). The basis of the economy is tourism although agriculture is important, the chief products being oats, fruit and vegetables. It covers an area of 572 sq km [221 sq mi].

United States

This flag, known as the 'Stars and Stripes', has had the same basic design since 1777, during the War of Independence. The 13 stripes represent the 13 original colonies in the eastern United States. The 50 stars represent the 50 states of the Union.

The United States of America is the world's fourth largest country in area and the third largest in population. It contains 50 states, 48 of which lie between Canada and Mexico, plus Alaska in north-western North America and Hawaii, a group of volcanic islands in the North Pacific Ocean.

Densely populated coastal plains lie toe the east and south of the Appalachian Mountains. The central lowlands drained by the Mississippi-Missouri rivers stretch from the Appalachians to the Rocky Mountains in the west. The Pacific region contains fertile valleys separated by mountain ranges.

CLIMATE

The climates of the United States vary greatly, ranging from the Arctic conditions in northern Alaska, where average temperatures plummet to −13°C [9°F], to the intense heat of Death Valley. which holds the record for the highest shade temperature ever recorded in the United States − 57°C [134°F].

The Midwest, New England and the Middle Atlantic States experience cold winters and warm summers. By contrast, the southern states have long, hot summers and mild, wet winters. In the central United States, a lack of topographical features bars the northwards movement of hot, moist air from the Gulf of Mexico, and in winter the southwards movement of dry, cold air from the Arctic. These air masses produce contrasts of climate, exacerbated by storms, blizzards and tornadoes. Parts of California have a pleasant Mediterranean-type climate, but the mountains of the west are much cooler and wetter. The central plains are arid, while deserts occur in parts of the west and south-west.

HISTORY

The first people in North America, the ancestors of the Native Americans arrived around 40,000 years ago from Asia. AlthoughVikings probably reached North America 1,000 years ago, European exploration proper did not begin until the late 15th century.

The first Europeans to settle in large numbers were the British, who founded settlements on the eastern coast in the early 17th century. British rule ended with the War of Independence (1775–83). The country expanded in 1803 when a vast territory in the south and west was acquired through the Louisiana Purchase, while the border with Mexico was fixed in the mid-19th century. The Civil War (1861–5) ended slavery and the serious threat that the nation might split into two parts. In the late 19th century the West was opened up, while immigrants flooded in from Europe and elsewhere.

__Manhattan,__ New York, New York State; New York's population of over 8 million is the largest for a city in the USA

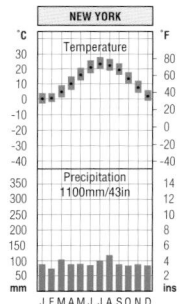
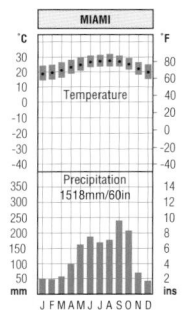
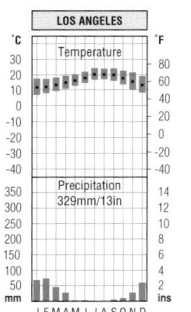
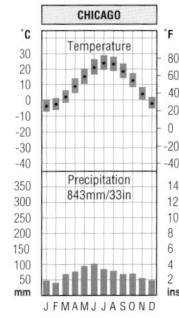

Area 9,629,091 sq km [3,717,792 sq mi]
Population 293,028,000
Capital (population) Washington, DC (572,000)
Government Federal republic
Ethnic groups White 77%, African American 13%, Asian 4%, Amerindian 2%, others
Languages English (official), Spanish, more than 30 others
Religions Protestant 56%, Roman Catholic 28%, Islam 2%, Judaism 2%
Currency US dollar = 100 cents
Website www.firstgov.gov

POLITICS

The United States has long played a leading role in industrial, economic, social and technological innovation. The majority of Americans continue to enjoy one of the world's highest material standards of living and the country continues to produce a highly skilled, literate and imaginative population. Yet at the same time, the country faces many problems. One concerns the maintenance of social cohesion as the composition of American society changes. Another is the issue of poverty and the low standards of living of a sizeable underclass of poor and inadequately educated people, many of whom are members of ethnic minorities. Other associated problems include crime, drug addiction and racial conflict.

Until about 1860, the population, with the exception of the Native Americans and the southern African Americans, was made up largely of immigrants of British and Irish origin, with small numbers of

WASHINGTON, DC

Capital of the USA, on the east bank of the Potomac River, covering the District of Columbia and extending into the neighbouring states of Maryland and Virginia. The site was chosen as the seat of government in 1790, and French engineer Pierre Charles L'Enfant planned the city. Construction of the White House began in 1793, and the building of the Capitol the following year. In 1800, Congress moved from Philadelphia to Washington. During the War of 1812, the British occupied the city and many public buildings were burned, including the White House and the Capitol. Washington is the legislative, judicial, and administrative centre of the USA. Despite its role, Washington has severe social problems; many of the large African-American population live in slum housing.

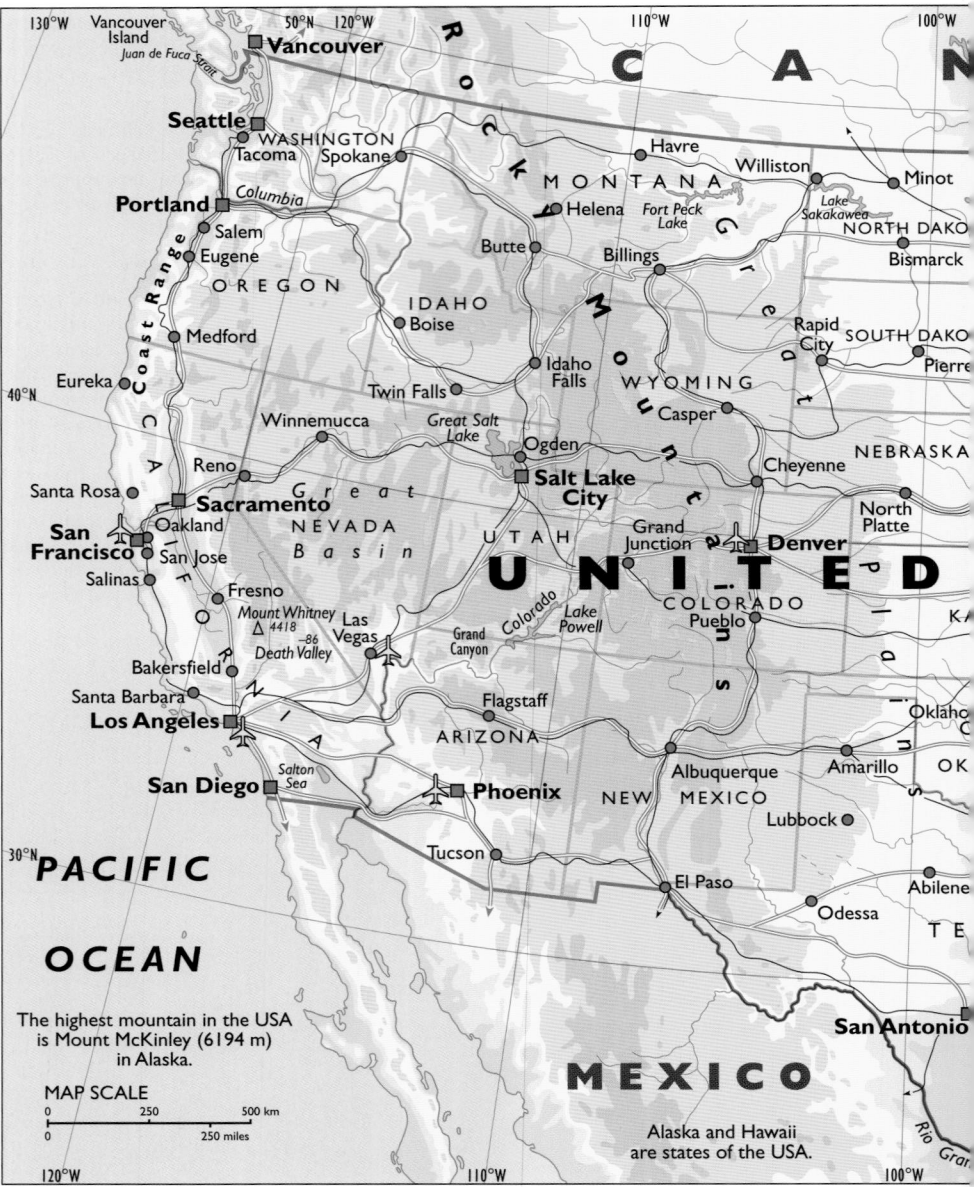

The highest mountain in the USA is Mount McKinley (6194 m) in Alaska.

MAP SCALE

Alaska and Hawaii are states of the USA.

Spaniards and French. However, after the Civil War, increasing numbers of immigrants arrived from the countries of central and south-eastern Europe, including Italy, the Balkans, Poland, Scandinavia and Russia. This vast influx of Europeans, numbering about 30 million between 1860 and 1920, was vastly different in culture and language from the established population. More recently, the country has received lesser influxes of Japanese, Chinese, Filipinos, Cubans, Puerto Ricans, and large numbers of Mexicans, many of them illegal immigrants. Although strong influences and pressures towards Americanization still exist, members of these groups have tended to maintain their own culture, establishing social and cultural enclaves within American society. Although the nation has never adopted an official language, English was readily adopted by most immigrants in the late 19th and early 20th century, because they sought acceptance in the 'melting pot' that makes up the United States. However, many of the recent Hispanic immigrants persist in speaking Spanish, which has become the country's second language. Many Americans are concerned about this trend towards 'cultural pluralism' rather than integration through the 'melting pot'. They argue that Hispanics who do not speak English are at a disadvantage in American society and believe that everyone should speak English, either as a first or second language. According to some population forecasts, today's white majority will be outnumbered by other ethnic groups in 2050. With a total projected population of 380 million, Hispanics are expected to number around 80 million by 2050, while African Americans will account for another 62 million. Such a rapid growth of these communities is seen by some as a threat to the majority.

From the 1890s, the United States developed into a world power, and played a leading role in international affairs throughout the 20th century. It played a key role in World Wars I and II, after which it was one of the world's two superpowers the other being the Soviet Union. After World War II, it assumed the leadership of the West during the Cold War. Since the end of the Cold War, the United States has faced new threats from terrorists and rogue states. Its vulnerability was demonstrated by the terrorist attacks on New York City and Washington, DC, on 11 September 2001. The United States responded vigorously, creating an international alliance to combat terrorism and the nations which shelter or aid terrorists. In 2001 it led a coalition force against the Taliban regime in Afghanistan which was protecting al Qaida terrorists. Then in 2003 the US led another coalition force to over throw the repressive regime of Saddam Hussein in Iraq. However, despite early military successes, the conflict continued. George W. Bush was re-elected in 2004.

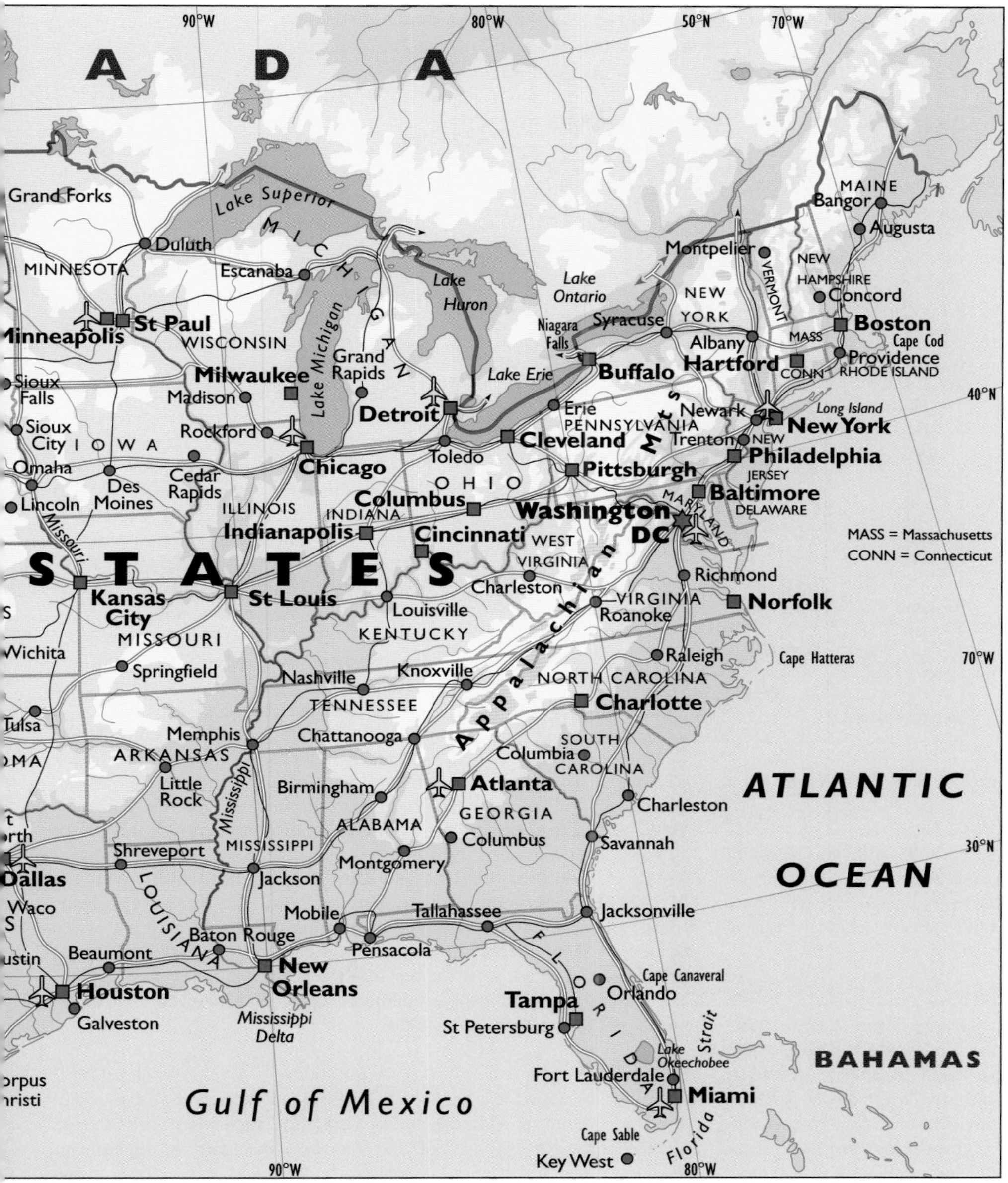

ECONOMY

Agriculture employs only 2.4% of the work force. The western plains are the main centres of production. Much of the land farmed by the Pilgrim Fathers and other settlers is now built over, or has reverted to forest. The US has become a leading producer of meat, dairy products, soya beans, maize, oats, wheat, barley, cotton, and sugar.

The spread of prosperity generated new consumer industries to satisfy the demands of a large middle class for ever-increasing standards of comfort. The US was a pioneer of large-scale industrial production. With almost every raw material available within its own boundaries, or readily gained through trading, its mining and extractive industries have been heavily exploited. Anthracite from eastern Pennsylvania, good bituminous and coking coals from the Appalachians, Indiana, Illinois, Colorado and Utah are still in demand, and vast reserves remain.

Oil, first drilled in Pennsylvania in 1859, was subsequently found in major fields underlying the Midwest, the eastern and central mountain states, the Gulf of Mexico, California and Alaska. Home consumption of petroleum products has grown steadily. Although the US is a major producer, it is also by far the world's greatest consumer and has long been a net importer of oil. In the Gulf Coast states, the exploitation of oil in Oklahoma, Texas and Louisiana has shifted the former dependence on agriculture to the refining and petrochemical industries. Dallas-Fort Worth has transformed into a major conurbation; Denver has changed from a small railhead town into a wealthy state capital. Natural gas is also found in abundance, usually associated with oil.

MASS = Massachusetts
CONN = Connecticut

ALASKA

State in north-west North America, separated from the rest of continental USA by the province of British Columbia, Canada, and from Russia by the Bering Strait. The capital is Juneau. The largest city is Anchorage on the southern coast. The USA purchased Alaska for US$7.2 million from Russia in 1867. Fishing drew settlers and, after the gold rush of the 1890s, the population doubled within a decade. It became the 49th state of the Union in 1959. About 25% lies inside the Arctic Circle. The main Alaska Range includes Mount McKinley, the highest peak in North America. The chief river is the Yukon. The Alaskan economy is based on fish, natural gas, timber, quartz and, primarily, oil. The national parks encourage tourism. Because of its strategic position and oil reserves, Alaska developed as a military area and is linked to the rest of the USA by the 2,450 km (1,500 mi) Alaska Highway. Although by far the largest US state, it has the third smallest population (after Wyoming and Vermont). Of the total state population, 98,043 are Native Americans (mainly Inuit-Aleut). It has an area of 1,530,700 sq km (591,004 sq mi) and a population of 626,932.

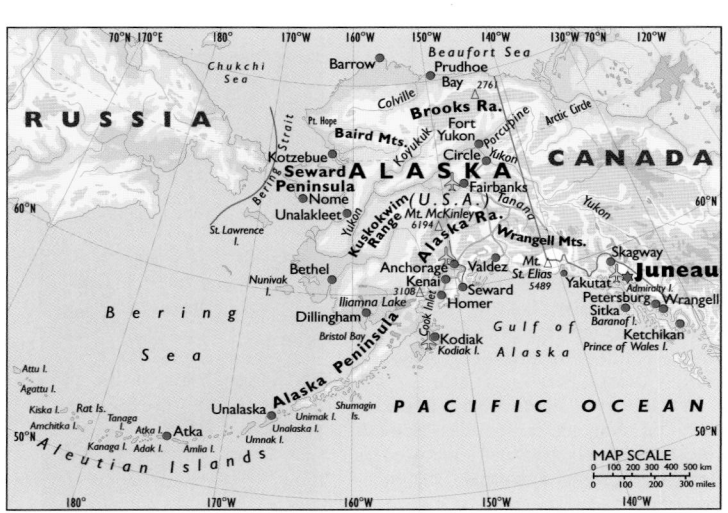

Uruguay has used this flag since 1830. The nine stripes represent the nine provinces which formed the country when it became an independent republic in 1828. The colours and the May Sun had originally been used by Argentina during its struggle against Spanish rule.

Area 175,016 sq km [67,574 sq mi]
Population 3,399,000
Capital (population) Montevideo (1,303,000)
Government Multiparty republic
Ethnic groups White 88%, Mestizo 8%, Mulatto or Black 4%
Languages Spanish (official)
Religions Roman Catholic 66%, Protestant 2%, Judaism 1%
Currency Uruguayan peso = 100 centésimos
Website www.turismo.gub.uy

The Oriental Republic of Uruguay, as Uruguay is officially known, is South America's second smallest independent nation after Suriname. The River Uruguay, which forms the country's western border, flows into the Río de la Plata (River Plate), a large estuary fringed with lagoons and sand dunes, which leads into the South Atlantic Ocean.

The land consists mainly of low-lying plains and hills. The highest point lies south of Minas and is only 501 m [1,644 ft] above sea level. The main river in the interior is the Rio Negro.

CLIMATE

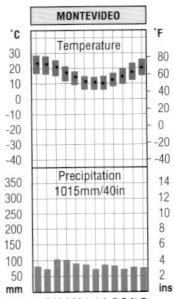

Uruguay has a mild climate, with rain throughout the year, though droughts sometimes occur. The summer is pleasantly warm, especially near the coast. The weather remains relatively mild in winter.

HISTORY

The first people of Uruguay were Amerindians. But the Amerindian population has largely disappeared. Many were killed by Europeans, some died of European diseases, while others fled into the interior. The majority of Uruguayans today are of European origin, though there are some mestizos (of mixed European and Amerindian descent). The first European to arrive in Uruguay was a Spanish navigator, Juan Diaz de Solis, in 1516. But he and part of his crew were killed by the local Charrúa Amerindians when they went ashore.

Few Europeans settled until the late 17th century. Spanish settlers founded Montevideo in order to prevent the Portuguese from gaining influence in the area. Uruguay was then little more than a buffer zone between the Portuguese territory to the north and Spanish territories to the west. By the late 18th century, Spaniards had settled in most of the country. Uruguay became part of a colony called the Viceroyalty of La Plata, which included Argentina, Paraguay, and parts of Bolivia, Brazil and Chile.

Uruguay was annexed by Brazil in 1820, bringing about an end to Spanish rule. In 1825, Uruguayans, supported by Argentina, began a struggle for independence.

POLITICS

Uruguay was recognized as an independent republic by Brazil and Argentina in 1828. Social and economic developments were slow in the 19th century, but, from 1903, governments made Uruguay a democratic and stable country. Since 1828, two political parties - the Colorados (Liberals) and the Blancos (Conservatives) - have dominated.

During World War II, Uruguay prospered because of its export trade, especially in meat and wool. However, from the 1950s, economic problems caused unrest. Terrorist groups, notably the Tupumaros (Marxist urban guerrillas), carried out murders and kidnappings in the 1960s and early 1970s. In 1972, President Juan Maria Bordaberry declared war on the Tupumaros and the army crushed them. In 1973, the military seized power, suspended the constitution and ruled with great severity, committing major human rights abuses.

Military rule continued until 1984, when elections were held. General Gregorio Alvarez, who had been president since 1981, resigned and Julio Maria Sanguinetti, leader of the Colorado Party, became president in February 1985, leading a government of National Unity. He ordered the release of all political prisoners. In the 1990s, Uruguay faced problems in trying to rebuild its weakened economy and shoring up its democratic traditions. In 1991, Uruguay joined with Argentina, Brazil and Paraguay to form Mercosur, which aimed to create a common market. Mercosur's secretariat is in Montevideo. The early 21st century brought economic problems, many of which were the result of the economic crisis in Argentina, and its imposition of banking controls. Uruguay elected its first leftist president, Tabare Vasquez, in 2004.

ECONOMY

Uruguay is classed by the World Bank as an 'upper-middle-income' developing country. Although 90% of the population live in urban areas and agriculture employs 3% of the population, the economy depends on the exports of hides and leather goods, beef and wool. Main crops include maize, potatoes, rice, sugar beet and wheat. Manufacturing concentrates on food processing and packing. The economy has diversified into cement, chemicals, leather goods, textiles and steel. Uruguay depends largely on hydroelectric power for energy and exports electricity to Argentina.

MONTEVIDEO

Capital of Uruguay, located in the south, on the River Plate. Originally a Portuguese fort (1717), it was captured by the Spanish in 1726 and became the capital in 1828. One of South America's major ports, Montevideo is the base of a large fishing fleet and handles most of the country's exports. Products include textiles, dairy goods, wine, and packaged meat.

Punta del Este, *known as the St Tropez of South America it lies on a peninsula that separates the Rio de la Plata and the Atlantic Ocean*

Uzbekistan 211

The white crescent moon is a traditional symbol of Islam and represents the rebirth of the nation. The white stars recall the 12 signs of the zodiac. Blue stands for water and the eternal sky. Red represents life. White symbolizes peace and green denotes nature.

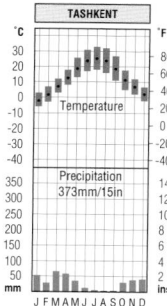

The Republic of Uzbekistan is one of five republics in Central Asia which were once part of the Soviet Union. Plains cover most of western Uzbekistan, with highlands in the east. The main rivers, the Amu (or Amu Darya) and Syr (or Syr Darya), drain into the Aral Sea. So much water has been taken from these rivers for irrigation that the Aral Sea is now only a quarter of its size in 1960. Much of the former sea is now desert.

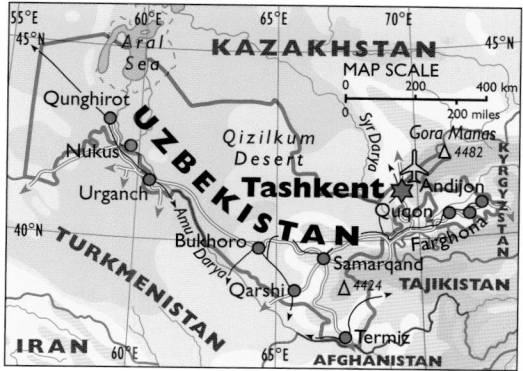

Area 447,400 sq km [172,741sq mi]
Population 26,410,000
Capital (population) Tashkent (2,143,000)
Government Socialist republic
Ethnic groups Uzbek 80%, Russian 5%, Tajik 5%, Kazakh 3%, Tatar 2%, Kara-Kalpak 2%
Languages Uzbek (official), Russian
Religions Islam 88%, Eastern Orthodox 9%
Currency Uzbekistani sum = 100 tyiyn
Website www.gov.uz

CLIMATE

Uzbekistan has a continental climate. Winters are cold, but temperatures soar in the summer. In the west conditions are extremely arid with an average annual rainfall of about 200 mm [8 in].

TASHKENT

Largest city and capital of Uzbekistan, in the Tashkent oasis in the foothills of the Tian Shan (Celestial Range) mountains (a 2,400 km [1,500 mi] long mountain range). Tashkent is watered by the River Chirchik. It was ruled by the Arabs from the 8th until the 11th century. The city was captured by Tamerlane in 1361, and by the Russians in 1865. The modern city is the transport and economic centre of the region. Industries include textiles, chemicals, food processing, mining machinery, paper, porcelain, clothing, leather, and furniture.

HISTORY

Uzbekistan lies on the ancient Silk Road between Europe and Asia. Great cities such as Samarkand and Bukhara, famed for their architectural opulence were important trade and cultural centres. Russia took the area in the 19th century. After the Russian Revolution of 1917, Communists took over, setting up the Uzbek Soviet Socialist Republic in 1924. Under Communism, all aspects of Uzbek life were controlled and religious worship was discouraged. The country did benefit though and health, housing, education and transport were all improved. In the late 1980s, people demanded more freedom and, in 1990, the government stated that its laws overruled those of the Soviet Union.

POLITICS

Uzbekistan became independent in 1991 with the break-up of the Soviet Union, but retained links with Russia through the Commonwealth of Independent States, but it subsequently pulled out due to the leader's opposition to closer integration on post-Soviet territory. Islam Karimov, leader of the People's Democratic Party (formerly the Communist Party), was elected president in December 1991. In 1992–3, many opposition leaders were arrested because the government said that they threatened national stability. In 1994-5, the PDP was victorious in national elections and in 1995 a referendum extended Karimov's term in office until 2000, when he was again re-elected.

In 2001, Karimov declared Uzbekistan's support for the United States in its campaign against the terrorist al Qaida bases in Afghanistan and indeed allowed the US forces to have a base on Uzbek territory.

Due to the country's poor record on human rights the European Bank for Reconstruction and Development announced in 2004 that it would cut aid to Uzbekistan.

Recent years have seen bombings and shootings for which the authorities have blamed Islamic extremists. In 2005 protests against the jailing of several people charged with Islamic extremism in the city of Andijan turned to violence with troops opening fire. Several hundred civilians were killed, though the government claimed a toll of 180.

Karimov blamed fundamentalists out to destabilise the country, his opponents blamed the determination of those in power to crush all dissent and maintain a repressive state. There were calls for an international enquiry which the government rejected, as a result of which the US threatened to withold aid. Uzbekistan's reaction to this was to order US forces to leave their base.

ECONOMY

The World Bank classifies Uzbekistan as a 'lower-middle-income' developing country. The government still controls most economic activity and economic reform has been very slow. Uzbekistan produces coal, copper, gold, oil and natual gas, while manufacturing industries include agricultural machinery, chemicals and textiles. Agriculture is important with cotton the main crop. Other crops include fruits, rice and vegetables; cattle, sheep and goats are raised.

Nomad Camp *in Pamir Mountains; the main activity is sheep herding, though some coal is mined; the terrain is largely grasslands and sparse trees*

SAMARKAND

City in the fertile Zeravshan Valley, south-east Uzbekistan. One of the oldest cities in Asia, it was conquered by Alexander the Great in 329 BC. A vital trading centre on the Silk Road, it flourished in the 8th century as part of the Umayyad Empire. Samarkand was destroyed in 1220 by Genghis Khan but became capital of the Mongol empire of Tamerlane in 1370. Ruled by the Uzbeks from the 16th century, it was captured by Russia in 1868, though it remained a centre of Muslim culture. It is now a major scientific research centre and has a population of 361,800.

Venezuela's flag, adopted in 1954, has the same basic tricolour as the flags of Colombia and Ecuador. The colours were used by the Venezuelan patriot Francisco de Miranda. The seven stars represent the provinces in the Venezuelan Federation in 1811.

Area 912,050 sq km [352,143 sq mi]
Population 25,017,000
Capital (population) Caracas (1,823,000)
Government Federal republic
Ethnic groups Spanish, Italian, Portuguese, Arab, German, African, indigenous people
Languages Spanish (official), indigenous dialects
Religions Roman Catholic 96%
Currency Bolivar = 100 céntimos
Website www.venezlon.co.uk

The Bolivarian Republic of Venezuela, in northern South America, contains the Maracaibo Lowlands in the west. The lowlands surround the oil-rich Lake Maracaibo (Lago de Maracaibo). Arms of the Andes Mountains enclose the lowlands and extend across most of northern Venezuela. Between the northern mountains and the scenic Guiana Highlands in the south-east, where the Angel Falls are found, lie the *llanos* (tropical grasslands), a low-lying region drained by the River Orinoco and its tributaries. The Orinoco is Venezuela's longest river.

CLIMATE

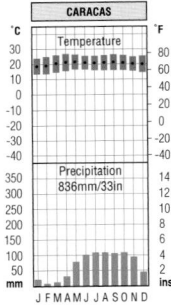

Venezuela has a tropical climate. Temperatures are high throughout the year on the lowlands, though far cooler in the mountains. There is a marked dry season in much of the country that falls between December and April. Most rainfall is in the mountains.

HISTORY

Arawak and Carib Amerindians were the main inhabitants of Venezuela before the arrival of Europeans. The first European to arrive was Christopher Columbus, who sighted the area in 1498. Spaniards began to settle in the early 16th century, but economic development was slow.

In the early 19th century, Spain's colonies in South America began their struggle for independence. The Venezuelan patriots Simón Bolívar and Francisco Miranda were prominent in the struggle. Venezuela was the first South American country to demand freedom and, in July 1811, it declared its independence, though Spaniards still held most of the country. In 1819, Venezuela became part of Gran Colombia, a republic led by Simón Bolívar that also included Colombia, Ecuador and Panama.

The country became fully independent in 1821, after the Venezuelans had defeated the Spanish in a battle at Carabobo, near Valencia. Venezuela broke away from Gran Colombia in 1829 and in 1830 a new constitution was drafted. The country's first president was General José Antonio Páez, one of the leaders of Venezuela's independence movement.

POLITICS

The development of Venezuela in the 19th century and the first half of the 20th century was marred by instability, violence and periods of harsh dictatorial rule. However, the country has had elected governments since 1958.

Venezuela has greatly benefited from its oil resources, which were first exploited in 1917. In 1960, Venezuela helped to form OPEC (the Organization of Petroleum Exporting Countries) and, in 1976, the government of Venezuela took control of the entire oil industry. Money from oil exports has helped Venezuela to raise living standards and diversify the economy.

Financial problems in the late 1990s led to the election of Hugo Chávez as president. Chávez, leader of the Patriotic Pole, a left-wing coalition, who had led an abortive military uprising in 1992, became president in February 1999. He announced that the country's official name would be changed to the Bolivarian Republic of Venezuela and held a referendum on a new constitution. This gave the president increased power over military and civilian institutions. Chávez argued that these powers were needed to counter corruption. In 2002, Chávez himself survived a coup and then in 2004 he won a majority in a referendum that had been intended by the opposition to remove him from office.

ECONOMY

The World Bank classifies Venezuela as an 'upper-middle-income' developing country. Oil accounts for 80% of the exports. Other exports include bauxite and aluminium, iron ore and farm products. Agriculture employs 9% of the people. Cattle ranching is important and dairy cattle and poultry are also raised. Major crops include bananas, cassava, citrus fruits, coffee, maize, plantains, rice and sorghum. Most commercial crops are grown on large farms, but many people in remote areas farm small plots and produce barely enough to feed their families.

Manufacturing industries now employ 21% of the population. The leading industry is petroleum refining, centred on Maracaibo. Other manufactures include aluminium, cement, processed food, steel and textiles.

CARACAS

Capital of Venezuela, on the River Guaire. Caracas was under Spanish rule until 1821. It was the birthplace of Venezuelan patriot Simón Bolívar. The city grew after 1930, encouraged by the exploitation of oil. It has the Central University of Venezuela (1725) and a cathedral (1614). Industries include motor vehicles, oil, brewing, chemicals, and rubber.

Angel Falls, the world's highest uninterrupted falls, descend through the clouds, dropping 980 metres from a high cliff in Venezuela's Canaima National Park

Vietnam's flag was first used by forces led by the Communist Ho Chi Minh during the liberation struggle against Japan in World War II (1939–45). It became the flag of North Vietnam in 1945 and it was retained when North and South Vietnam were reunited in 1975.

The Socialist Republic of Vietnam occupies an S-shaped strip of land facing the South China Sea in South-east Asia. The coastal plains include two densely populated, fertile river delta areas. The Red (Hong) Delta faces the Gulf of Tonkin in the north, while the Mekong Delta is in the south.

Inland are thinly populated highland regions, including the Annam Cordillera (Chaîne Annamitique), which forms much of the boundary with Cambodia. The highlands in the north-west extend into Laos and China.

CLIMATE

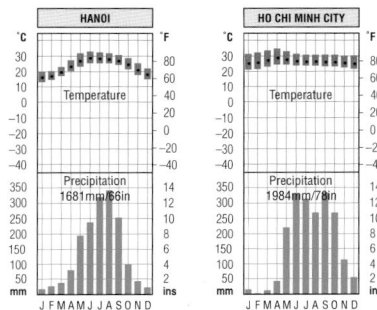

Vietnam has a tropical climate, though the drier months of January to March are cooler than the wet, hot summer months, when monsoon winds blow from the south-west. Typhoons sometimes hit the coast, causing much damage.

HISTORY

In 111 BC, China seized Vietnam, naming it Annam. In 939 AD, it became independent. In 1558, it split into two parts: Tonkin in the north, ruled from Hanoi; and Annam in the south, ruled from Hué. In 1802, with French support, Vietnam was united as the Empire of Vietnam, under Nguyen Anh. In 1859, the French seized Saigon, and by 1887 had formed Indo-China from the union of Tonkin, Annam, and Cochin China.

Japan conquered Vietnam during World War II, and established a Vietnamese state under Emperor Bao Dai. After the war, Bao Dai's government collapsed, and the nationalist Viet Minh, led by Ho Chi Minh, set up a Vietnamese republic. In 1946, the French tried to reassert control and war broke out. Despite aid from the USA, the Viet Minh defeated the French at Dien Bien Phu.

POLITICS

In 1954, Vietnam divided along the 17th Parallel – with North Vietnam under the communist government of Ho Chi Minh, and South Vietnam under the French-supported Bao Dai. In 1955, Bao Dai was deposed and Ngo Dinh Diem was elected president. Despite his authoritarian regime, many western countries recognized Diem as the legal ruler of Vietnam. North Vietnam, supported by China and the Soviet Union, extended its influence into South Vietnam, mainly through the Viet

HANOI

Capital of Vietnam and its second largest city, on the Red River. In the 7th century the Chinese ruled Vietnam from Hanoi; it later became capital of the Vietnamese empire. Taken by the French in 1883, the city became the capital of French Indo-China (1887–1945). In 1946–54, it was the scene of fierce fighting between the French and the Viet Minh. Hanoi was heavily bombed by the US during the Vietnam War.

Area 331,689 sq km [128,065 sq mi]
Population 82,690,000
Capital (population) Hanoi (1,074,000)
Government Socialist republic
Ethnic groups Vietnamese 87%, Chinese, Hmong, Thai, Khmer, Cham, mountain groups
Languages Vietnamese (official), English, French, Chinese, Khmer, mountain languages
Religions Buddhism, Christianity, indigenous beliefs
Currency Dong = 10 hao - 100 xu
Website www.vietnamtourism.com

Cong. The USA became increasingly involved in what they perceived to be a fight against communism. The conflict escalated into the Vietnam War (1954–75). In 1975, after the withdrawal of US troops, Ho Chi Minh's forces over-ran South Vietnam and it surrendered.

In 1976, the reunited Vietnam became a socialist republic. In 1979, Vietnam helped overthrow the Khmer Rouge government in Cambodia, only withdrawing in 1989. The United States opened an embassy in Hanoi in 1995 and in 2002 it implemented a trade agreement which normalized the trade status between the two countries.

The suppression of political dissent and religious belief has been noted along with the poor treatment of ethnic minorities.

ECONOMY

The World Bank classifies Vietnam as a 'low-income' developing country. Agriculture employs 67% of the workforce. The main food crop is rice. Other products include maize and sweet potatoes; commercial crops include bananas, coffee, groundnuts, rubber, soya beans and tea. Fishing is also important. Northern Vietnam has most of the country's natural resources, including coal. The country also produces chromium, oil, phosphates and tin. Manufactures include cement, fertilizers, processed food, machinery, steel and textiles.

The harvesting of tea leaves in a field near Bao Loc, to the south of the country

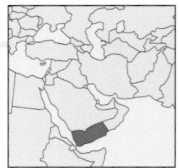

Yemen's flag was adopted in 1990 when the Yemen Arab Republic (or North Yemen) united with the People's Democratic Republic of Yemen (or South Yemen). This simple flag is a tricolour of red, white and black – colours associated with the Pan-Arab movement.

Area 527,968 sq km [203,848 sq mi]
Population 20,025,000
Capital (population) Sana'a (954,000)
Government Multiparty republic
Ethnic groups Predominantly Arab
Languages Arabic (official)
Religions Islam
Currency Yemeni rial = 100 fils
Website www.yemeninfo.gov.ye/ENGLISH/home.htm

The Republic of Yemen faces the Red Sea and the Gulf of Aden in the south-western corner of the Arabian Peninsula. Behind the narrow coastal plain along the Red Sea, the land rises to a mountain region called High Yemen. Beyond the mountains, the land slopes down towards the Rub' al Khali Desert. Other mountains rise behind the coastal plain along the Gulf of Aden. To the east lies a fertile valley called the Hadramaut and also the deserts of the Arabian Empty Quarter.

Palm trees grow along the coast. Plants such as acacia and eucalyptus flourish in the interior. Thorn shrubs and mountain pasture are found in the highlands.

SAN'A

Capital and largest city of Yemen, 65 km [40 mi] north-east of the Red Sea port of Hodeida. Situated on a high plateau at 2,286 m [7,500 ft], it claims to be the world's oldest city, founded by Shem, eldest son of Noah. During the 17th century and from 1872 to 1918, it was part of the Ottoman Empire. In 1918, it became capital of an independent Yemen Arab Republic, and in 1990 capital of the new, unified Yemen. It is noted for its handicrafts. Agriculture (grapes) and industry (iron) are also important.

was abolished.

Clashes occurred between the traditionalist Yemen Arab Republic in the north and the formerly British Marxist People's Democratic Republic of Yemen. But, in 1990, the two Yemens merged to form one country. The marrying of the needs of the two parts of Yemen has proved difficult. In May 1994, civil war erupted, with President Saleh, a northerner, attempting to remove the vice-president (a southerner). The war ended in July 1994, following the capture of Aden by government forces. In 1995, Yemen resolved border disputes with Oman and Saudi Arabia, but clashed with Eritrea over uninhabited islands in the Red Sea. In 1998 and 1999, militants in the Aden-Abyan Islamic Army sought to destabilize the country. In 2000, a suicide bomb attack on the USS Cole in Aden killed 17 US personnel. In 2001, President Salih offered support to the USA in its 'war on terrorism'.

President Saleh has said that although the constitution entitles him to run for president again in 2006, he has chosen not to.

Dar al-Hajar *(The Palace of the Rock) stands in the fertile valley of Wadi Dahr*

CLIMATE

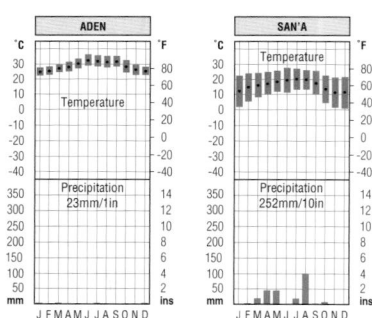

The climate in San'a is moderated by its altitude. Temperatures are much lower than in Aden (Al' Adan), which is at sea level. In summer, south-west monsoon winds bring thunderstorms. But most of Yemen is arid. The south coasts are particularly hot and humid, especially from June to September. There are two seasonal rainfalls, during March to May and from July to September. The average rainfall is about 50 mm [2 in] on most parts of the plateaux, but may rise to 1,000 mm [40 in] in the highlands, while the coastal lowlands may have no more than 12 mm [0.5 in].

HISTORY

From around 1400 BC, Yemen lay on an important trading route, with frankincense, pearls and spices being the major commodities. But its prosperity declined in the 4th century AD, when it became divided between warring groups.

Islam was introduced during the 7th century by the son-in-law of the Prophet Muhammad. From 897, the country was ruled by a Muslim leader. In 1517, the area was taken over by the Turkish Ottoman Empire and remained under Turkish rule for the next 400 years.

POLITICS

After World War I, northern Yemen, which had been ruled by Turkey, began to evolve into a separate state from the south, where Britain was in control. Britain withdrew in 1967 and a left-wing regime took power in the south. North Yemen became a republic in 1962 when the monarchy

ECONOMY

The World Bank classifies Yemen as a 'low-income' developing country. Agriculture employs up to 63% of the people. Herders raise sheep and other animals, while farmers grow such crops as barley, fruits, wheat and vegetables in highland valleys and around oases. Cash crops include coffee and cotton.

Imported oil is refined at Aden and petroleum extraction began in the north-west in the 1980s. Handicrafts, leather goods and textiles are manufactured.

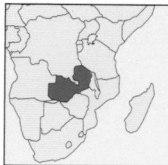

Zambia 215

Zambia's flag was adopted when the country became independent from Britain in 1964. The colours are those of the United Nationalist Independence Party, which led the struggle against Britain and ruled until 1991. The flying eagle represents freedom.

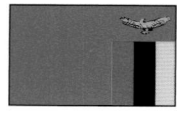

The Republic of Zambia is a land-locked country in southern Africa. The country lies on the plateau that makes up most of southern Africa. Much of the land is between 900 m and 1,500 m [2,950–4,920 ft] above sea level. The Muchinga Mountains in the north-east rise above this flat land.

Lakes include Bangweulu, which is entirely within Zambia, together with parts of lakes Mweru and Tanganyika in the north. Most of the land is drained by the Zambezi (from which the country takes its name) and its two main tributaries, the Kafue and Luangwa. Occupying part of the Zambezi Vally and stretching along the southern border Lake Kariba, which was dammed in 1961 is the largest artificial lake in Africa and the second largest in the world (280 km long and 40 km across at its widest point). Zambia shares Lake Kariba and the Victoria Falls with Zimbabwe.

Grassland and wooded savanna cover much of Zambia. There are also swamps. Evergreen forests exist in the drier south west.

CLIMATE

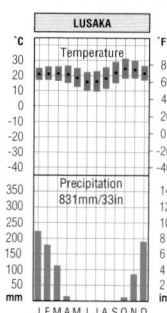

Zambia lies in the tropics, although temperatures are moderated by the altitude. The rainy season runs between November and March, when the rivers sometimes flood. Northern Zambia is the wettest region of the country. The average annual rainfall ranges from about 1,300 mm [51 in] in the north down to between 510 mm and 760 mm [20–30 in] in the south.

HISTORY

European contact with Zambia began in the 19th century, when the explorer David Livingstone crossed the River Zambezi. In the 1890s, the British South Africa Company, set up by Cecil Rhodes (1853–1902), the British financier and statesman, made treaties with local chiefs and grad-

LUSAKA

Capital and largest city of Zambia, in the south-central part of the country, at an altitude of 1,280 m [4,200 ft]. Founded by Europeans in 1905 to service the local lead-mining, it replaced Livingstone as the capital of Northern Rhodesia (later Zambia) in 1935. A vital road and rail junction, Lusaka is the centre of a fertile agricultural region, and is a major financial and commercial city.

ually took over the area. In 1911, the Company named the area Northern Rhodesia. In 1924, Britain took over the government of the country and the discovery of copper led to a large influx of Europeans in the late 1920s.

Following World War II, the majority of Europeans living in Zambia wanted greater control of their

Greater Kudus *nuzzling in open area, Kafue National Park; the park is located in southern Zambia to the west of Lusaka and covers over 22,400 sq km (8,649 sq mi)*

Area 752,618 sq km [290,586 sq mi]
Population 10,462,000
Capital (population) Lusaka (1,270,000)
Government Multiparty republic
Ethnic groups Native African (Bemba, Tonga, Maravi/Nyanja)
Languages English (official), Bemba, Kaonda
Religions Christianity 70%, Islam, IHinduism
Currency Zambian kwacha = 100 ngwee
Website www.zambiatourism.com

government and some favoured a merger with their southern neighbour, Southern Rhodesia (now Zimbabwe). In 1953, Britain set up a federation of Northern Rhodesia, Southern Rhodesia and Nyasaland (now Malawi). Local Africans opposed the setting up of the federation arguing that it concentrated power in the hands of the white minority in Southern Rhodesia. Their opposition proved effective and the federation was dissolved in 1963. In 1964, Northern Rhodesia became an independent nation called Zambia.

POLITICS

The leading opponent of British rule, Kenneth Kaunda, became president in 1964. His government enjoyed reasonable income until copper prices crashed in the mid-1970s, but his collectivist policies failed to diversify the economy and neglected agriculture. In 1972, he declared the United Nationalist Independence Party (UNIP) the only legal party, and it was nearly 20 years before the country returned to democracy.

Under a new constitution, adopted in 1990, elections were held in 1991 in which Kaunda was trounced by Frederick Chiluba of the Movement for Multiparty Democracy (MMD) – Kaunda's first challenger in the post-colonial period. Chiluba was re-elected in 1996, but he stood down in 2001 after an MMD proposal to amend the constitution to allow Chiluba to stand for a third term met with substantial popular and parliamentary opposition. In the 2001 elections, the MMD candidate, Levy Mwanawasa, was elected president. In 2005 the Supreme Court rejected a challenge to his election, but stated that the 2001 ballot had been flawed.

ECONOMY

Zambia holds 6% of the world's copper reserves and copper is the leading export, accounting for 49% of Zambia's total exports. Zambia also produces cobalt, lead, zinc and various gemstones, but the country's dependence on minerals has created problems, especially when prices fluctuate. Agriculture employs 69% of the workforce, compared with 4% in mining and manufacturing. Major food crops include cassava, fruits and vegetables, maize, millet and sorghum, while cash crops include coffee, sugar cane and tobacco.

The Copperbelt, centred on Kitwe, is the main urban region, while Lusaka, provides the other major growth pole. Rural to urban migration has increased since 1964, but work is scarce. The production of copper products is the leading industrial activity. Other manufactures include beverages, processed food, iron and steel, textiles and tobacco.

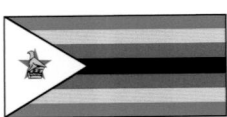

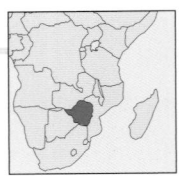

Zimbabwe's flag, adopted in 1980, is based on the colours used by the ruling Zimbabwe African National Union Patriotic Front. Within the white triangle is the Great Zimbabwe soapstone bird, the national emblem. The red star symbolizes the party's socialist policies.

Area 390,757 sq km [150,871 sq mi]
Population 12,672,000
Capital (population) Harare (1,189,000)
Government Multiparty republic
Ethnic groups Shona 82%, Ndebele 14%, other African groups 2%, mixed and Asian 1%
Languages English (official), Shona, Ndebele
Religions Christianity, traditional belief
Currency Zimbabwean dollar= 100 cents
Website www.zim.gov.zw

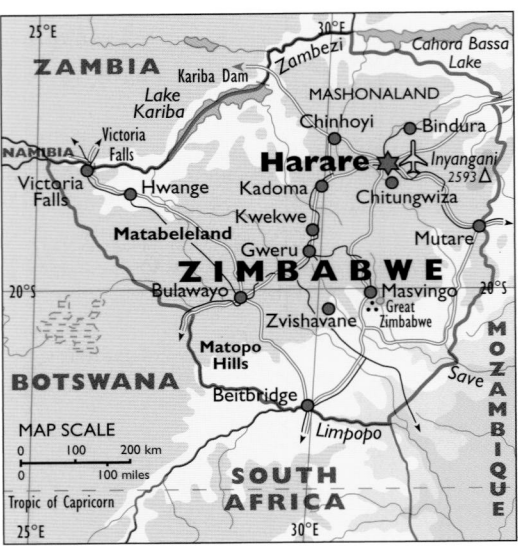

The Republic of Zimbabwe is a landlocked country in southern Africa. Most of the country lies on a high plateau between the Zambezi and Limpopo Rivers between 900 m and 1,500 m [2,950–4,920 ft] above sea level.

The principal land feature is the High Veld, a ridge that crosses Zimbabwe from north-east to south-west. Harare lies on the north east edge, Bulawayo on the south west edge. Bordering the High Veld is the Middle Veld, the country's largest region and the site of many large ranches. Below 900 m [2,950 ft] is the Low Veld.

The country's highest point is Mount Inyangani, which reaches 2,593 m [8,507 ft] near the Mozambique border. Zimbabwe's best-known physical feature, Victoria Falls, is in the north-east. The Falls are shared with Zambia, as too is the artificial Lake Kariba which is also on the River Zambezi.

Wooded savanna covers much of Zimbabwe. The Eastern Highlands and river valleys are forested. There are many tobacco plantations.

CLIMATE

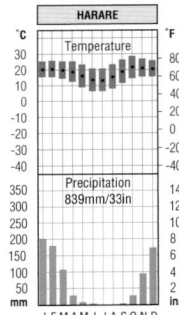

The subtropical climate varies greatly according to altitude. The Low Veld is much warmer and drier than the High Veld. November to March is mainly hot and wet. Winter in Harare is dry but cold. Frosts have been recorded between June and August.

HISTORY

The Shona people were dominant in the region about 1,000 years ago. They built the Great Zimbabwe, a city of stone buildings. Under the statesman Cecil Rhodes (1853–1902), the British South Africa Company occupied the area in the 1890s, after obtaining mineral rights from local chiefs. The area was named Rhodesia and later Southern Rhodesia. It became a self-governing British colony in 1923. Between 1953 and 1963, Southern and Northern Rhodesia (now Zambia) were joined to Nyasaland (Malawi) in the Central African Federation.

POLITICS

In 1965, the European government of Southern Rhodesia (then known as Rhodesia) declared their country independent. However, Britain refused to accept this declaration. Finally, after a civil war, the country became legally independent in 1980.

After independence, rivalries between the Shona and Ndebele people threatened its stability. But order was restored when the Shona prime minister, Robert Mugabe, brought his Ndebele rivals into his government. In 1987, Mugabe became the country's executive president and, in 1991, the government renounced its Marxist ideology. In 1990, the state of emergency that had lasted since 1965 was allowed to lapse - three months after Mugabe had secured a landslide election victory. Mugabe was re-elected in 1996. In the late 1990s, Mugabe threatened to seize white-owned farms without paying compensation to owners. His announcement caused much disquiet among white farmers. The situation worsened in the early 2000s, when landless 'war veterans' began to occupy white-owned farms, resulting in violence and deaths.

Food shortages have become a major problem with aid agencies blaming the land reform programme while the government blames drought.

In 2002, amid accusations of electoral irregularities, Mugabe was re-elected president. Mounting criticism of Mugabe led the Commonwealth to suspend Zimbabwe's membership. Later Zimbabwe confirmed that it had pulled out of the Commonwealth permanently. In 2004 the European Union renewed sanctions against the country. Zimbabwe was named by the United States, in 2005, as one of the world's six 'outposts of tyranny'. An accusation that was rejected by Zimbabwe.

ECONOMY

The World Bank classifies Zimbabwe as a 'low-income' economy. Its economy has become significantly more diverse since the 1960s, having evolved to virtual self-sufficiency during the days of international sanctions between 1965 and 1980. After independence, the economy underwent a surge in most sectors, with successful agrarian policies and the exploitation of the country's mineral resources. However, a fast-growing population continues to exert pressure both on land and resources.

Agriculture employs approximately 30% of the people. Maize is the chief food crop, while cash crops include cotton, sugar and tobacco. Cattle ranching is another important activity. Gold, asbestos, chromium and nickel are mined and the country also has some coal and iron ore. Manufactures include beverages, chemicals, iron and steel, metal products, processed food, textiles and tobacco. The principal exports include tobacco, gold, other metals, cotton and asbestos.

HARARE

Capital of Zimbabwe, in the north east of the country. Settled by Europeans in 1890 as Fort Salisbury, it became capital of Southern Rhodesia in 1902. The city served as capital of the Federation of Rhodesia and Nyasaland (1953–63) and of Rhodesia (1965–79). It has a university (1957) and two cathedrals. Industries include gold mining, textiles, steel, tobacco, chemicals and furniture.

Lake Kariba, *hippopotamus and waterbuck; the lake was formed as a result of the damming of the Zambezi River floodplain in the early 1960s, a process that caused the displacement of the Batonga tribe*

PICTURE ACKNOWLEDGEMENTS

17 Robert Harding World Imagery/Corbis; 19 Frans Lemmens/zefa/Corbis; 20 Paul Velasco Gallo Images/Corbis; 21 Dave G. Houser/Post-Houserstock/Corbis; 23 Charles & Josette Lenars/Corbis; 27 Theo Allofs/zefa/Corbis; 28 W. Geiersperger/Corbis; 29 Remi Benali/Corbis; 31 Karen Kasmauski/Corbis; 32 Nik Wheeler/Corbis; 33 Fridmar Damm/zefa/Corbis; 34 Kevin Schafer/Corbis; 36 Keren Su/Corbis; 37 Anders Ryman/Corbis; 38 Fehim Demir/epa/Corbis; 39 Theo Allofs/zefa/Corbis; 40 Richard T. Nowitz/Corbis; 42 Ladislav Janicek/zefa/Corbis; 43 Nicolas Cotto/Corbis; 45 Tom Craig/Corbis; 46 Jeremy Horner/Corbis; 47 Michael & Patricia Fogden/Corbis; 49 Rudy Sulgan/Corbis; 50 Paul C. Pet/zefa/Corbis; 51 Tom Bean/Corbis; 53 Owen Franken/Corbis; 54 Martin Harvey/Corbis; 55 Patrick Robert/Corbis; 57 Vittoriano Rastelli/Corbis; 58 Free Agents Limited/Corbis; 59t Jose Fuste Raga/Corbis; 59b Royalty-Free/Corbis; 60 Enzo & Paolo Ragazzini/Corbis; 61 Karl Ammann/Corbis; 63 Jose Fuste Raga/Corbis; 64 Robert Harding World Imagery/Corbis; 65 James Sparshatt/Corbis; 66 Chris Lisle/Corbis; 67 Jose Fuste Raga/Corbis; 68 José Fuste Raga/zefa/Corbis; 70 1996-98 AccuSoft Inc. All right/Robert Harding World Imagery/Corbis; 71 Danny Lehman/Corbis; 72 Robert Garvey/Corbis; 73 Pablo Corral V/Corbis; 74 Free Agents Limited/Corbis; 75 Galen Rowell/Corbis; 76 Robert van der Hilst/Corbis; 77 Chris Hellier/Corbis; 78 Jon Hicks/Corbis; 79 Caroline Penn/Corbis; 80 Larry Dale Gordon/zefa/Corbis; 81 Hans Strand/Corbis; 82 Owen Franken/Corbis; 83 Sergio Pitamitz/Corbis; 84 Nogues Alain/Corbis Sygma; 85 Le Segretain Pascal/Corbis Sygma; 86 Christine Osborne/Corbis; 87 Brooks Kraft/Corbis; 89 Bob Krist/Corbis; 90 Margaret Courtney-Clarke/Corbis; 91 Jose Fuste Raga/Corbis; 92 Royalty-Free/Corbis; 93 Pierre Holtz/epa/Corbis; 94 Dave G. Houser/Post-Houserstock/Corbis; 95 Louie Psihoyos/Corbis; 96 Gideon Mendel/Corbis; 97 Macduff Everton/Corbis; 98 Sandro Vannini/Corbis; 99 Mike McQueen/Corbis; 100 Charles & Josette Lenars/Corbis; 102 Robert van der Hilst/Corbis; 104 Jan Butchofsky-Houser/Corbis; 106 Michael S. Yamashita/Corbis; 107 Bo Zaunders/Corbis; 108 Sandro Vannini/Corbis; 109 Reinhard Krause/Reuters/Corbis; 110 Sandro Vannini/Corbis; 112 Charles & Josette Lenars/Corbis; 113 Denis Anthony Valentine/Corbis; 115 Jose Fuste Raga/Corbis; 116 Richard T. Nowitz/Corbis; 117 Buddy Mays/Corbis; 118 Wendy Stone/Corbis; 119 Jeremy Horner/Corbis; 120 Neil Beer/Corbis; 121 Royalty-Free/Corbis; 122 Nevada Wier/Corbis; 123 Michael Freeman/Corbis; 124 Jon Hicks/Corbis; 125 Roger Wood/Corbis; 126 Earl & Nazima Kowall/Corbis; 127 Eldad Rafaeli/Corbis; 128 Sergio Pitamitz/zefa/Corbis; 129 Keren Su/Corbis; 130 Fridmar Damm/zefa/Corbis; 131 Otto Lang/Corbis; 132 Chris Hellier/Corbis; 134 Bob Krist/Corbis; 135 Michael S. Yamashita/Corbis; 136 Nik Wheeler/Corbis; 137 Jose Fuste Raga/Corbis; 138 Margaret Courtney-Clarke/Corbis; 139 Wolfgang Kaehler/Corbis; 140 Free Agents Limited/Corbis; 141 Nik Wheeler/Corbis; 142 Hamid Sardar/Corbis; 143 Philippe Giraud/Goodlook/Corbis; 145 Jon Spaull/Corbis; 146 Frans Lemmens/zefa/Corbis; 147 Craig Lovell/Corbis; 148 Free Agents Limited/Corbis; 149 Robert Dowling/Corbis; 150 Bill Gentile/Corbis; 151 Nik Wheeler/Corbis; 153 Farrell Grehan/Corbis; 154 Arthur Thévenart/Corbis; 155 Douglas Peebles/Corbis; 158 Matthew McKee/Eye Ubiquitous/Corbis; 159 Chris Lisle/Corbis; 160 David Samuel Robbins/Corbis; 161 Danny Lehman/Corbis; 162 Robert Harding World Imagery/Corbis; 163 Pablo Corral Vega/Corbis; 164 Galen Rowell/Corbis; 165 Otto Lang/Corbis; 166 Yiorgos Nikiteas/Eye Ubiquitous/Corbis; 168 Jon Hicks/Corbis; 169 José Fuste Raga/zefa/Corbis; 171 David Ball/Corbis; 172 Dean Conger/Corbis; 173 Michael S. Lewis/Corbis; 175 Robert van der Hilst/Corbis; 176 Adam Woolfitt/Corbis; 177 Bill Gentile/Corbis; 178 Jose Fuste Raga/Corbis; 179 David Ball/Corbis; 180 Jose Fuste Raga/Corbis; 181 Kevin Fleming/Corbis; 183 Jon Hicks/Corbis; 184 Patrick Ward/Corbis; 186 Dallas and John Heaton/Free Agents Limited/Corbis; 187 Michael Freeman/Corbis; 188 Nicole Duplaix/Corbis; 189 Nik Wheeler/Corbis; 192 Eye Ubiquitous/Corbis; 193 Jose Fuste Raga/Corbis; 194 Jim Richardson/Corbis; 195 Nik Wheeler/Corbis; 196 William Manning/Corbis; 198 Bob Krist/Corbis; 200 Lawrence Manning/Corbis; 201 Gérard Degeorge/Corbis; 202 Michael S. Lewis/Corbis; 203 Ed Kashi/Corbis; 204 Jon Hicks/Corbis; 206 Richard Klune/Corbis; 207 Royalty-Free/Corbis; 210 Dave G. Houser/Post-Houserstock/Corbis; 211 Ludovic Maisant/Corbis; 212 James Marshall/Corbis; 213 Wolfgang Kaehler/Corbis; 214 Sergio Pitamitz/Corbis; 215 Peter Johnson/Corbis; 216 Frans Lemmens/zefa/Corbis.

WORLD
CITIES

CITY MAPS

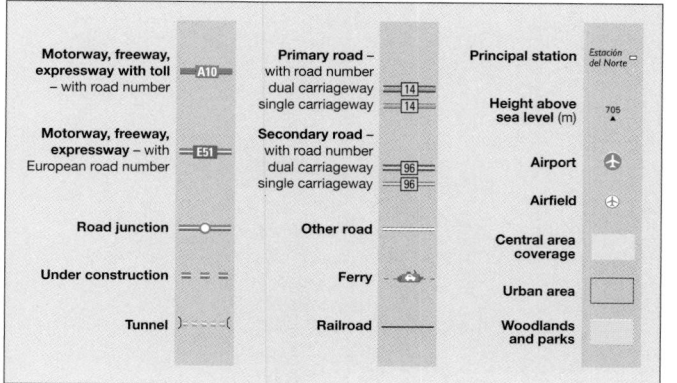

CENTRAL AREA MAPS

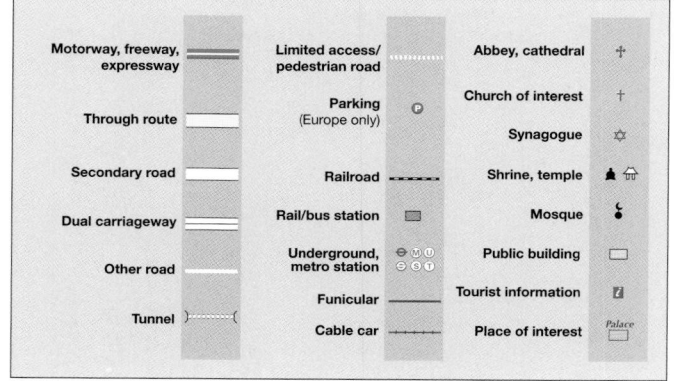

AMSTERDAM

CENTRAL AMSTERDAM

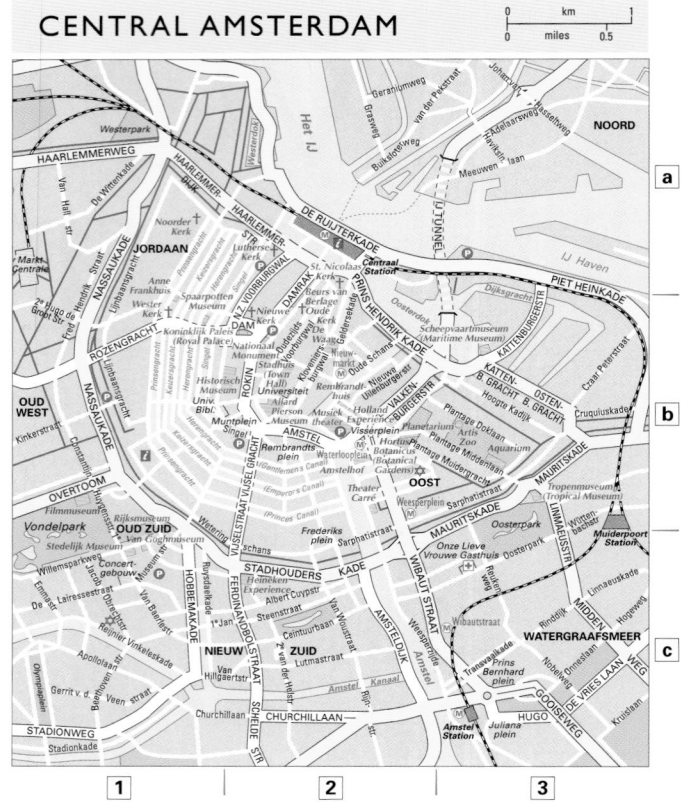

ATHENS

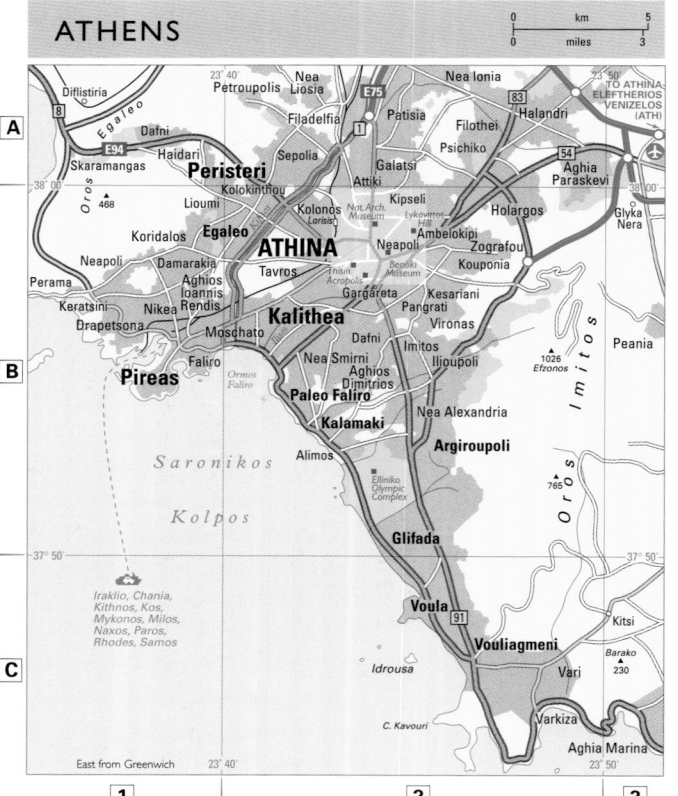

CENTRAL ATHENS

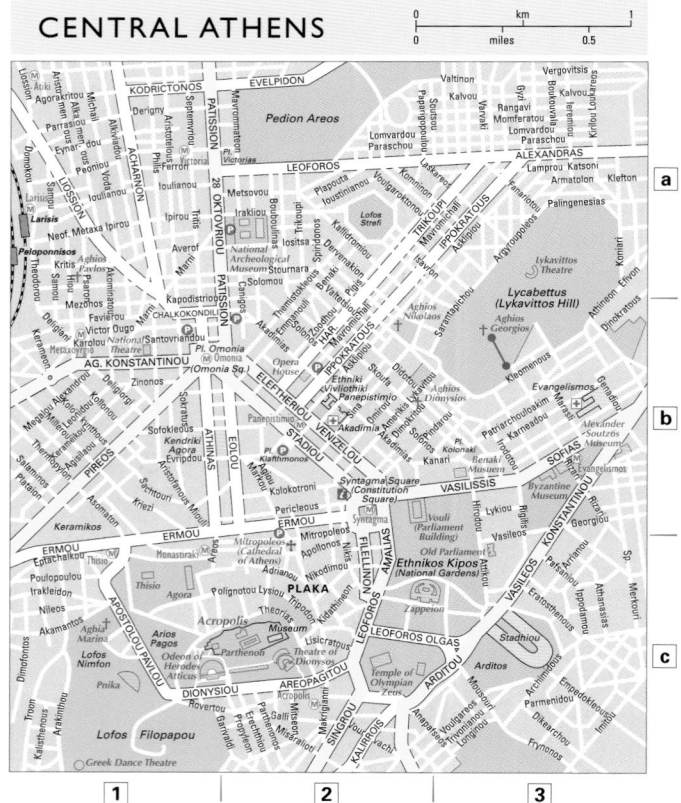

ATLANTA

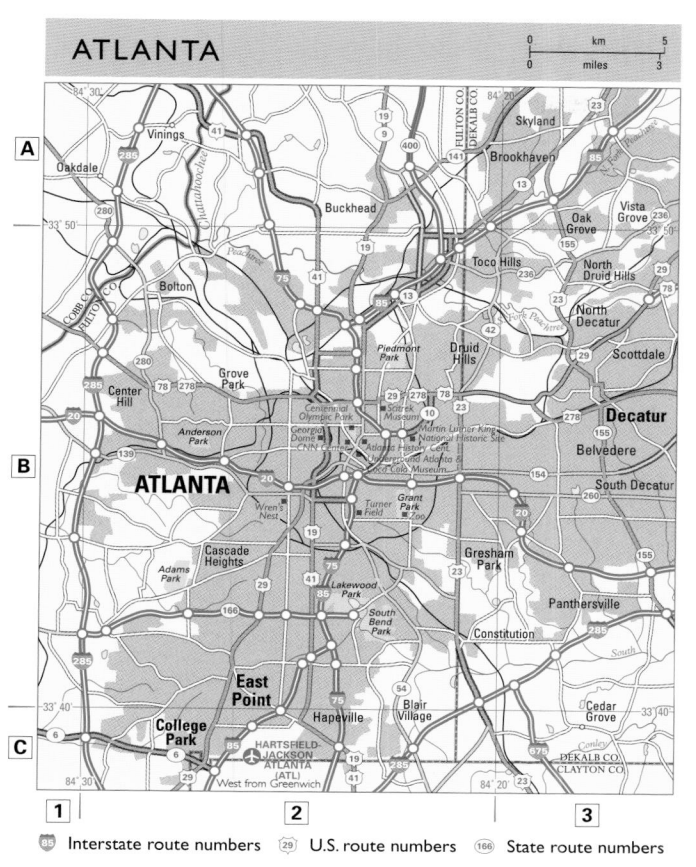

km 5
miles 3

A

Vinings 41
Oakdale
285
Skyland
Brookhaven 85
Buckhead 13
Oak Grove 155
Vista Grove 236
North Druid Hills 78
Toco Hills 236
North Decatur
Scottdale
Bolton
75 41
Grove Park
280
Center Hill 78 278
Piedmont Park 29 278
Druid Hills 42
Decatur 278
Belvedere 155

B

139
Anderson Park
Centennial Olympic Park
Georgia Dome CNN Center
Scitrek Museum
Martin Luther King National Historic Site
10
23
South Decatur 154
260
ATLANTA 20
Wren's Nest
Turner Field Zoo
Grant Park
Cascade Heights
Gresham Park
285
Adams Park 29
19
166 85
Lakewood Park
South Bend Park
Panthersville
285
Constitution

C

6
East Point
75
54
Blair Village
Cedar Grove
College Park
HARTSFIELD JACKSON ATLANTA (ATL)
Hapeville 41
6 29
West from Greenwich
85
285
Conley
DEKALB CO CLAYTON CO

1 **2** **3**

85 Interstate route numbers   29 U.S. route numbers   166 State route numbers

BAGHDAD

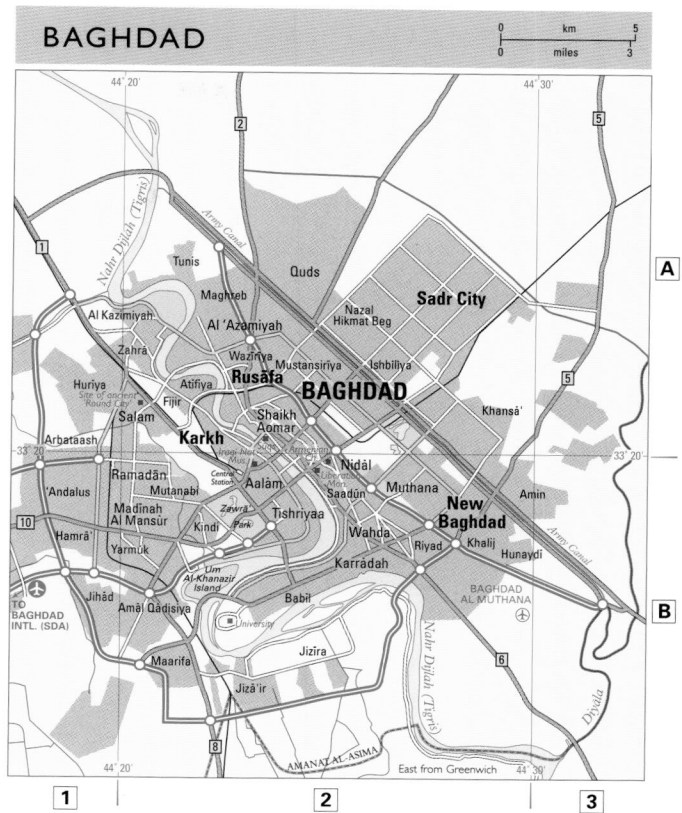

km 5
miles 3

A

Nahr Dijlah (Tigris)
2
5
Tunis
Quds
Maghteb
Sadr City
Al Kazimiyah
Nazal Hikmat Beg
Al 'Azamiyah
Zahrā
Waziriya
Mustansiriya
Ishbiliya
5
Huriya
Atifiya
Fijir
Site of ancient Round City
Rusafa
BAGHDAD
Khansá'
Salam
Shaikh Aomar
Karkh
Arbataash
Nidâl
Muthana
Amin

B

10
Ramadān
Central Station
Aâlám
Saadûn
Wahda
New Baghdad
Madinah Al Mansūr
Kindi
Zawra Park
Tishriyaa
'Andalus
Mutanabi
Hamrā
Yarmūk
Karrādah
Riyad
Khalij
Hunaydi
Jihâd
Amál Qâdisiya
Babil
University
Um Al-Khanazir Island
Jizira
Maarifa
Jizā'ir
6
BAGHDAD AL MUTHANA
Arrs Canal
Diyala
TO BAGHDAD INTL. (SDA)
8
AMANAT AL-ASIMA
East from Greenwich

1 **2** **3**

BANGKOK

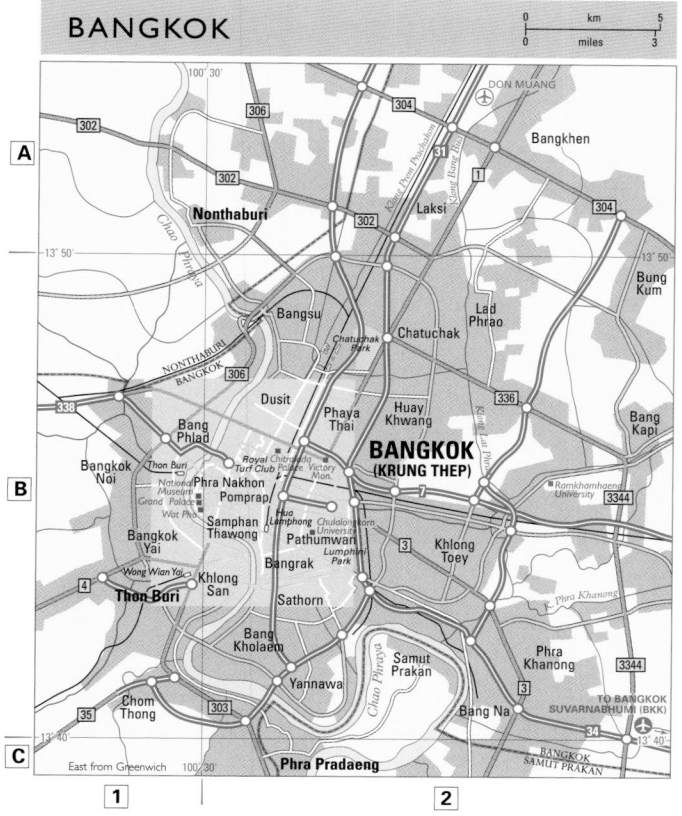

km 5
miles 3

A

302
306
DON MUANG
304
31
Bangkhen
Nonthaburi
302
Laksi
1
304
13° 50'
Chao Phraya
306
Bangsu
Chatuchak Park
Chatuchak
Lad Phrao
Bung Kum
NONTHABURI BANGKOK
338
Dusit
Phaya Thai
Huay Khwang
Bang Kapi

B

Bang Phlad
Royal Chitralada Turf Club Palace
Victory Mon.
336
Bangkok Noi
Thon Buri
Phra Nakhon
BANGKOK (KRUNG THEP)
Pomprap
Ramkhamhaeng University
3344
National Museum Grand Palace
Wat Pho
Hua Lamphong
Chulalongkorn University
Samphan Thawong
Pathumwan
Lumphini Park
Khlong Toey
Bang Kholaem
Bang Rak
Khlong San
Sathorn
4
Wong Wian Yai
Thon Buri
Phra Khanong
3344

C

35
Chom Thong
303
Yannawa
Bang Na
3
Phra Pradaeng
East from Greenwich 100° 30'
13° 40'
TO BANGKOK SUVARNABHUMI (BKK)
34
BANGKOK SAMUT PRAKAN

1 **2**

CENTRAL BANGKOK

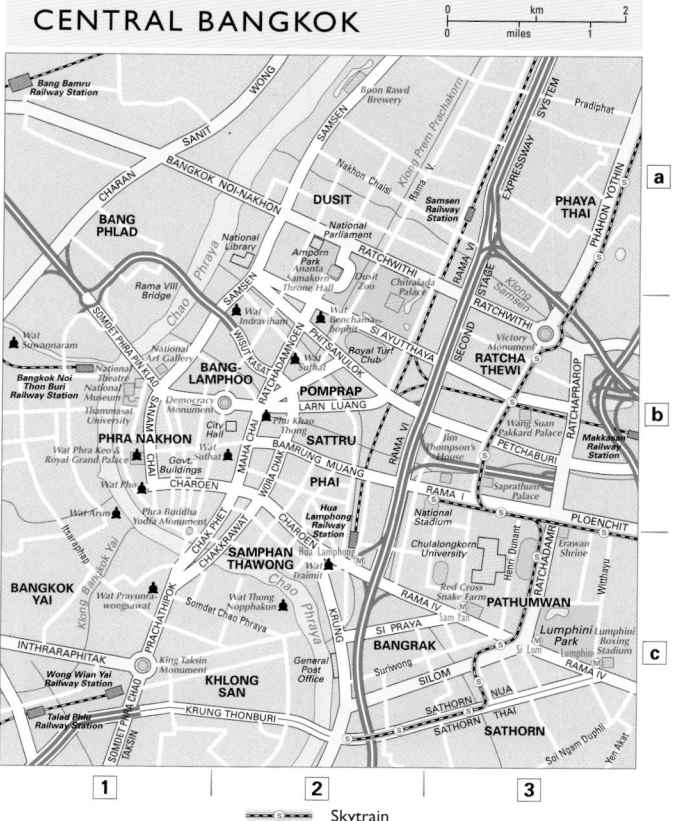

km 2
miles 1

Bang Bamru Railway Station
Boon Rawd Brewery
WONG
SANIT
SAMSEN
Khlong Prem Prachakorn
Pradiphat
a
CHARAN
Bangkok Noi-Nakhon
Nakhon Chaisi
EXPRESSWAY SYSTEM
PHAHON YOTHIN
BANG PHLAD
National Library
National Parliament
DUSIT
Samsen Railway Station
PHAYA THAI
Amporn Park Ananta Samakom Throne Hall
Dusit Zoo
RAMA VI
Rama VIII Bridge
Chitralada Palace
RATCHWITHI
SECOND STAGE
RATCHWITHI
Khlong Saen
Wat Suwannaram
Wat Indraviham
Wat Benchamabophit
Royal Turf Club
Victory Monument
RATCHA THEWI
Wat Samsen
National Art Gallery
SI AYUTTHAYA
Bangkok Noi Thon Buri Railway Station
National Museum
National Theatre
Thammasat University
BANG LAMPHOO
Wat Suthat
PHITSANULOK
Jim Thompson's House
Makkasan Railway Station
POMPRAP
b
Democracy Mon.
City Hall
LARN LUANG
Wat Suan Pakkard Palace
PETCHABURI
PHRA NAKHON
Wat Phra Keo & Royal Grand Palace
Govt. Buildings
SATTRU
BAMRUNG MUANG
RAMA I
Saprathum Palace
Wat Pho
CHAROEN
PHAI
National Stadium
PLOENCHIT
Wat Arum
Phra Buddha Yodfa Monument
Hua Lamphong Railway Station
Chulalongkorn University
Henri Dunant
Erawan Shrine
Witthayu
SAMPHAN THAWONG
Wat Traimit
PATHUMWAN
Red Cross Snake Farm
BANGKOK YAI
Wat Prayurn wongsawat
Somdet Chao Phraya
RAMA IV
Lumphini Park
Lumphini Boxing Stadium
BANGRAK
c
INTHRARAPHITAK
PRACHATHIPOK
King Taksin Monument
General Post Office
Si Praya
Suriwong
SILOM
SI PHRAYA
c
Wong Wian Yai Railway Station
KHLONG SAN
SATHORN
SATHORN
NUA
SATHORN THAI
RAMA IV
Talad Plu Railway Station
KRUNG THONBURI
Soi Ngam Duphli
Yen Akat
SATHORN

1 **2** **3**

▬▬▬ 9 ▬▬▬ Skytrain

BARCELONA

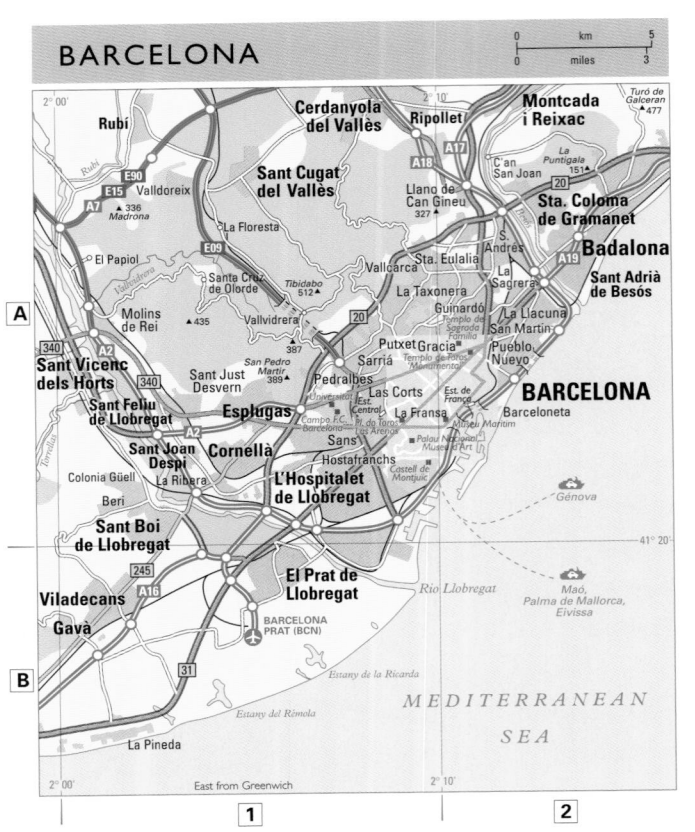

CENTRAL BARCELONA

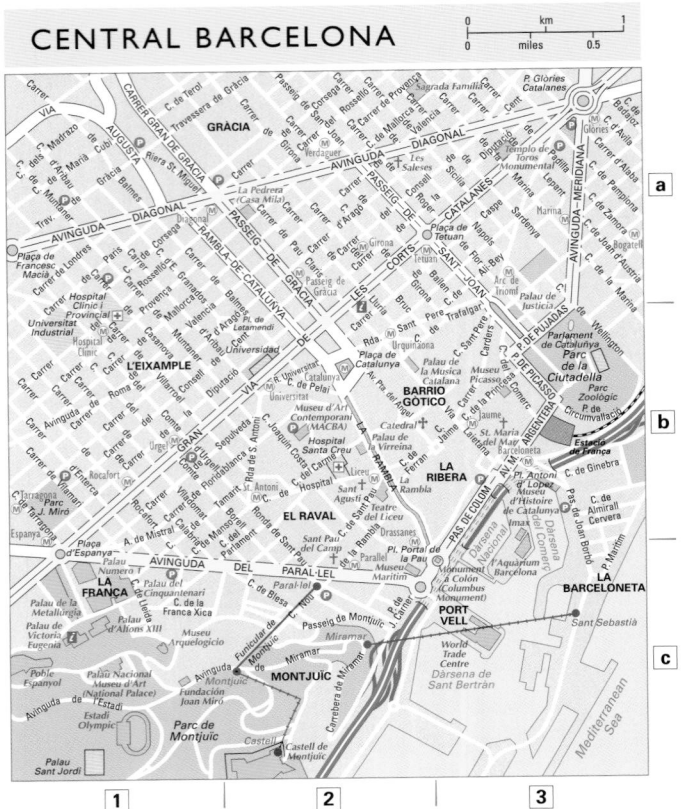

BEIJING

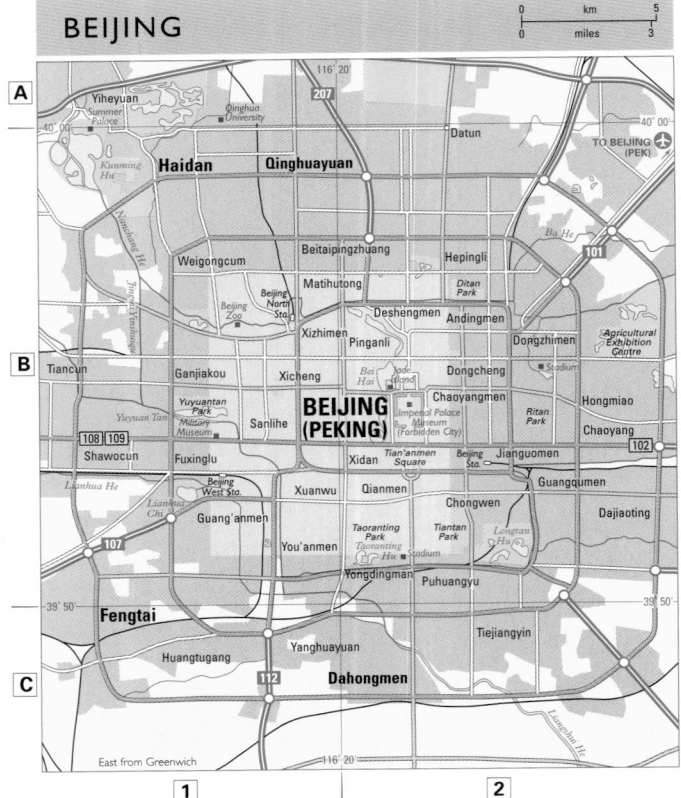

CENTRAL BEIJING

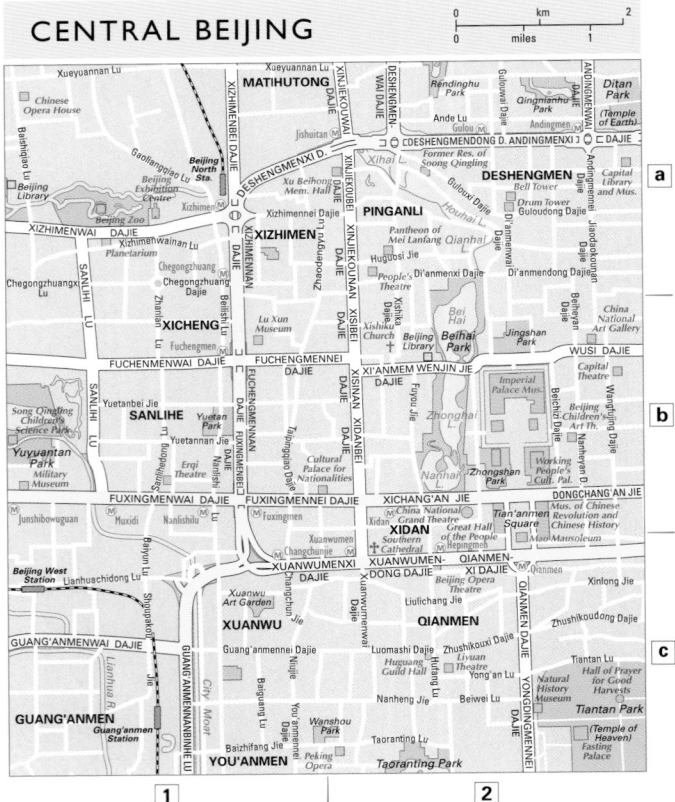

BERLIN

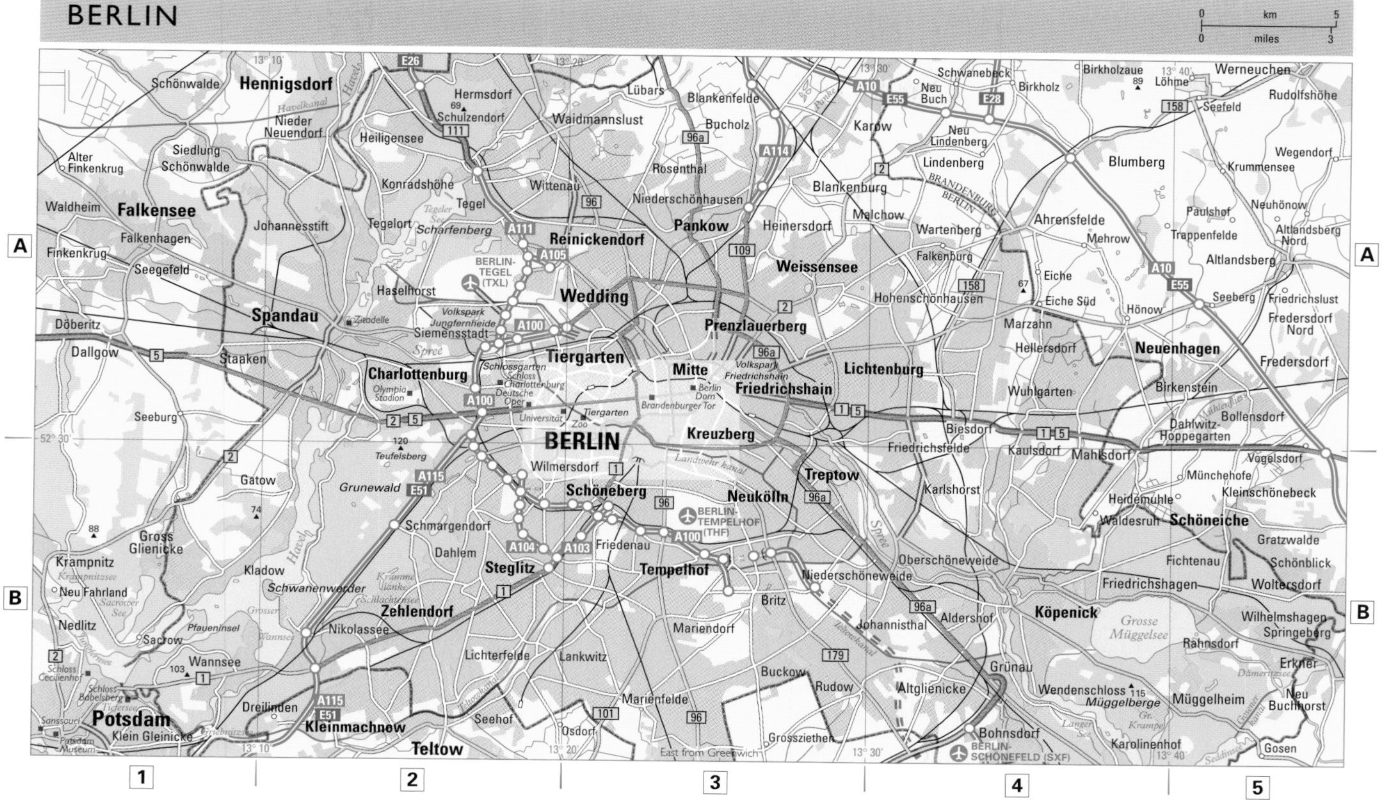

0 km 5
0 miles 3
Schönwalde
Hennigsdorf
Hermsdorf
Schulzendorf
Lübars
Waidmannslust
Blankenfelde
Bucholz
Schwanebeck
Neu Buch
Birkholz
Birkholzaue
Löhme
Werneuchen
Rudolfshöhe
Seefeld
Nieder Neuendorf
Heiligensee
Karow
Neu Lindenberg
Lindenberg
Blumberg
Wegendorf
Krummensee
Alter Finkenkrug
Siedlung Schönwalde
Konradshöhe
Tegel
Wittenau
Rosenthal
Niederschönhausen
Blankenburg
Malchow
Waldheim
Falkensee
Johannesstift
Tegelort
Scharfenberg
Reinickendorf
Pankow
Heinersdorf
Wartenberg
Ahrensfelde
Mehrow
Paulshof
Trappenfelde
Neuhönow
Altlandsberg Nord
Altlandsberg
Finkenkrug
Falkenhagen
Seegefeld
BERLIN-TEGEL (TXL)
Weissensee
Falkenburg
Hohenschönhausen
Eiche
Eiche Süd
Hönow
Seeberg
Friedrichslust
Fredersdorf Nord
Haselhorst
Wedding
Spandau
Zitadelle
Volkspark Jungfernheide
Siemensstadt
Prenzlauerberg
Marzahn
Hellersdorf
Neuenhagen
Döberitz
Dallgow
Staaken
Spree
Charlottenburg
Schlossgarten
Schloss Charlottenburg
Olympia Stadion
Deutsche Oper
Tiergarten
Mitte
Volkspark Friedrichshain
Friedrichshain
Lichtenberg
Wuhlgarten
Birkenstein
Fredersdorf
Berlin Dom
Brandenburger Tor
Universität
Zoo
Seeburg
BERLIN
Kreuzberg
Biesdorf
Bollensdorf
Dahlwitz-Hoppegarten
Teufelsberg
Wilmersdorf
Landwehr kanal
Friedrichsfelde
Kaulsdorf
Mahlsdorf
Vogelsdorf
Gatow
Grunewald
Treptow
Münchehofe
Schöneberg
Neukölln
Karlshorst
Heidemühle
Kleinschönebeck
BERLIN-TEMPELHOF (THF)
Waldesruh
Schöneiche
Schmargendorf
Gross Glienicke
Gratzwalde
Dahlem
Friedenau
Krampnitz
Kladow
Steglitz
Tempelhof
Oberschöneweide
Fichtenau
Schönblick
Niederschöneweide
Neu Fahrland
Schwanenwerder
Friedrichshagen
Woltersdorf
Britz
Zehlendorf
Köpenick
Nedlitz
Pfaueninsel
Johannisthal
Aldershof
Grosse Müggelsee
Wilhelmshagen
Springeberg
Sacrow
Nikolassee
Mariendorf
Rahnsdorf
Wannsee
Lichterfelde
Lankwitz
Buckow
Rudow
Grünau
Erkner
Schloss Cecilienhof
Schloss Babelsberg
Altglienicke
Wendenschloss
Müggelberge
Müggelheim
Neu Buchhorst
Dreilinden
Marienfelde
Sanssouci
Potsdam
Kleinmachnow
Seehof
Osdorf
Grossziethen
Bohnsdorf
Potsdam Museum
Klein Gleinicke
Teltow
East from Greenwich
BERLIN-SCHÖNEFELD (SXF)
Karolinenhof
Gosen
A
B
1
2
3
4
5

CENTRAL BERLIN

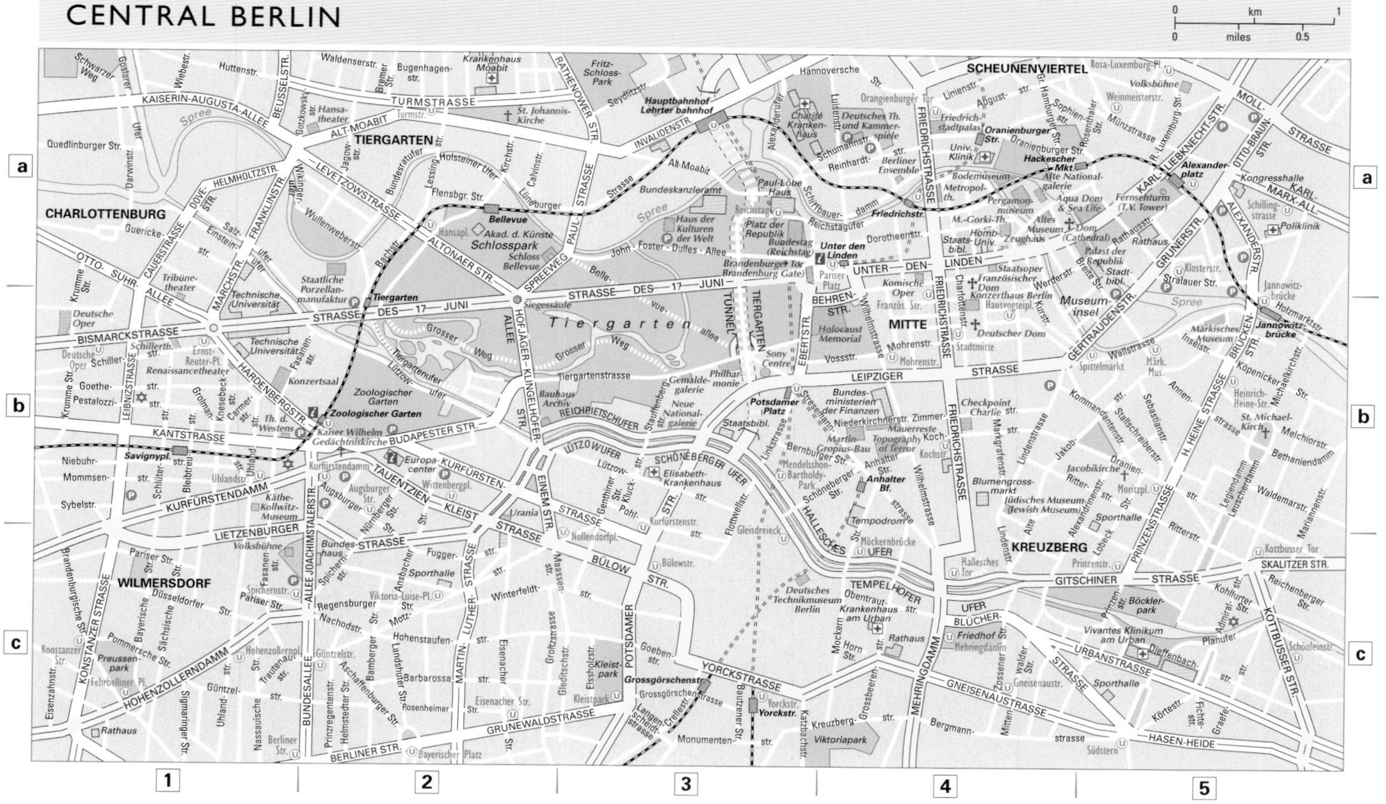

0 km 1
0 miles 0.5
Waldenserstr.
Huttenstr.
Bugenhagenstr.
Krankenhaus Moabit
Fritz-Schloss-Park
Hannoversche Str.
SCHEUNENVIERTEL
Rosa-Luxemburg-Pl.
KAISERIN-AUGUSTA-ALLEE
TURMSTRASSE
Hansatheater
St. Johannis-Kirche
Hauptbahnhof Lehrter bahnhof
Charité Krankenhaus
Deutsches Th. und Kammerspiele
Friedrichstadtpalast
Oranienburger Str.
Volksbühne
MOLL-STRASSE
ALT-MOABIT
TIERGARTEN
Quedlinburger Str.
INVALIDENSTR.
Berliner Ensemble
Hackescher Mkt.
Alexanderplatz
CHARLOTTENBURG
Bundeskanzleramt
Paul-Löbe Haus
Bodemuseum
Metropol-th.
Alte Nationalgalerie
Kongresshalle
KARL-MARX-ALL.
Bellevue
Akad. d. Künste
Schlosspark
Schloss Bellevue
Haus der Kulturen der Welt
Reichstag
Platz der Republik
Bundestag (Reichstag)
Friedrichstr.
Pergamonmuseum
Aqua Dom & Sea Life
Fernsehturm (T.V. Tower)
M.-Gorki-Th.
Altes Museum
Dom (Cathedral)
Zeughaus
Palast der Republik
Poliklinik
Staatl. Porzellanmanufaktur
Tiergarten
Technische Universität
Brandenburger Tor (Brandenburg Gate)
Unter den Linden
UNTER DEN LINDEN
Staatsoper
Französischer Dom
Konzerthaus Berlin
Stadtbibl.
Museumsinsel
Jannowitzbrücke
Deutsche Oper
Siegessäule
STRASSE DES 17. JUNI
Komische Oper
Deutscher Dom
Märkisches Museum
BISMARCKSTRASSE
Renaissancetheater
Holocaust Memorial
MITTE
Sony Centre
Philharmonie
Gemäldegalerie
Potsdamer Platz
LEIPZIGER STRASSE
Spittelmarkt
Konzertsaal
Zoologischer Garten
Bauhaus Archiv
Neue Nationalgalerie
Staatsbibl.
Bundesministerien der Finanzen
Checkpoint Charlie
Zoologischer Garten
Kaiser Wilhelm Gedächtniskirche
KANTSTRASSE
BUDAPESTER STR.
REICHPIETSCHUFER
Martin-Gropius-Bau
Topography of Terror
Savignypl.
Europa-center
LÜTZOWUFER
SCHÖNEBERGER UFER
Elisabeth-Krankenhaus
Anhalter Bf.
Jacobikirche
Blumengrossmarkt
Jüdisches Museum (Jewish Museum)
KURFÜRSTENDAMM
TAUENTZIEN
KLEIST STRASSE
Urania
Käthe-Kollwitz-Museum
Tempodrom
Sporthalle
KREUZBERG
LIETZENBURGER STRASSE
Volksbühne
BÜLOW STR.
Möckernbrücke
HALLESCHES UFER
Hallesches Tor
Kottbusser Tor
SKALITZER STR.
WILMERSDORF
Deutsches Technikmuseum Berlin
TEMPELHOFER UFER
GITSCHINER STRASSE
Böckler park
Krankenhaus am Urban
Rathaus
BLÜCHER UFER
Friedhof Mehringdamm
Vivantes Klinikum am Urban
Preussenpark
HOHENZOLLERNDAMM
Kleist-park
Grossgörschenstr.
YORCKSTRASSE
Yorckstr.
MEHRINGDAMM
URBANSTRASSE
GNEISENAUSTRASSE
GRUNEWALDSTRASSE
BUNDESALLEE
POTSDAMER STR.
Viktoriapark
Monumenten-str.
Bergmann-strasse
Südstern
HASEN-HEIDE
Rathaus
BERLINER STR.
Bayerischer Platz
a
b
c
1
2
3
4
5

BOSTON

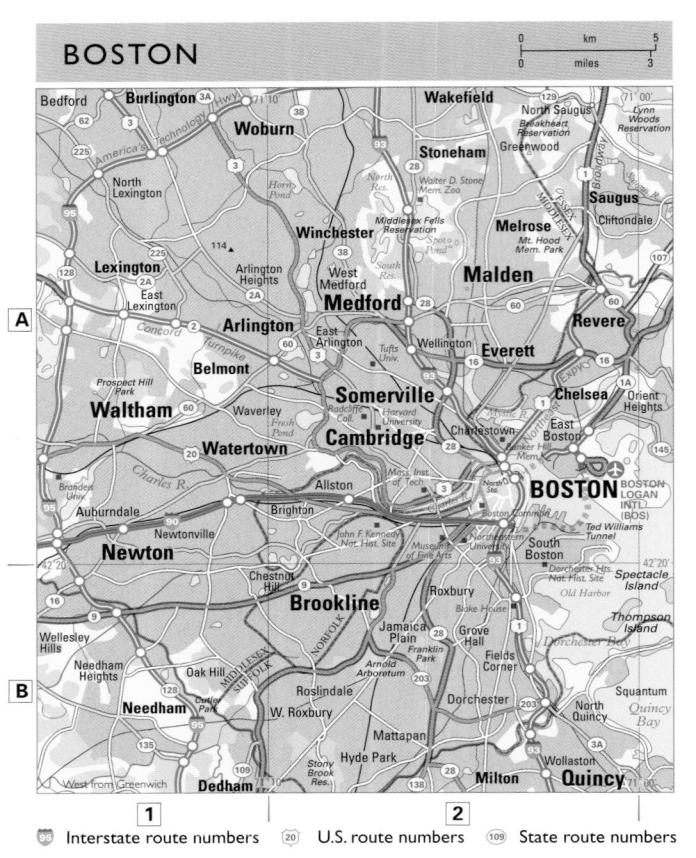

CENTRAL BOSTON

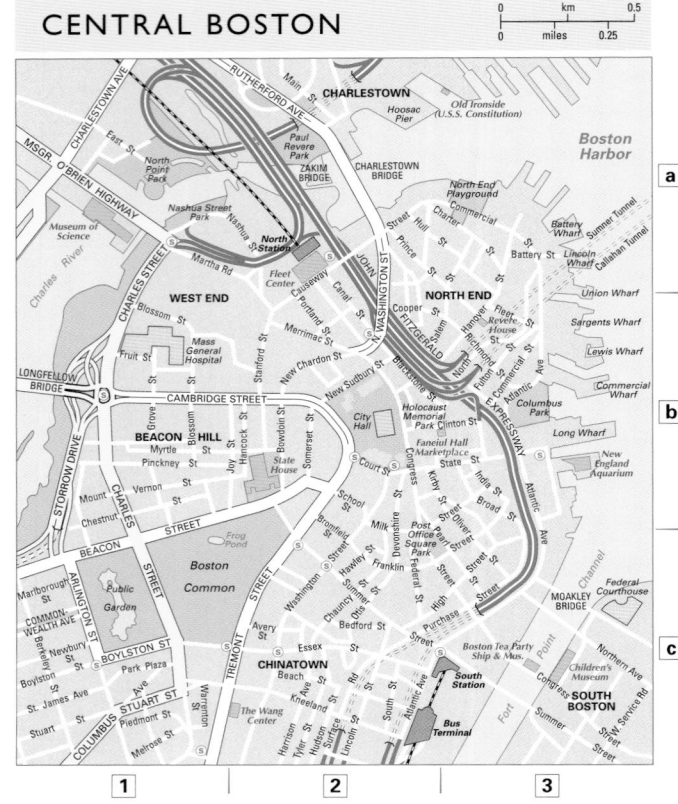

BRUSSELS

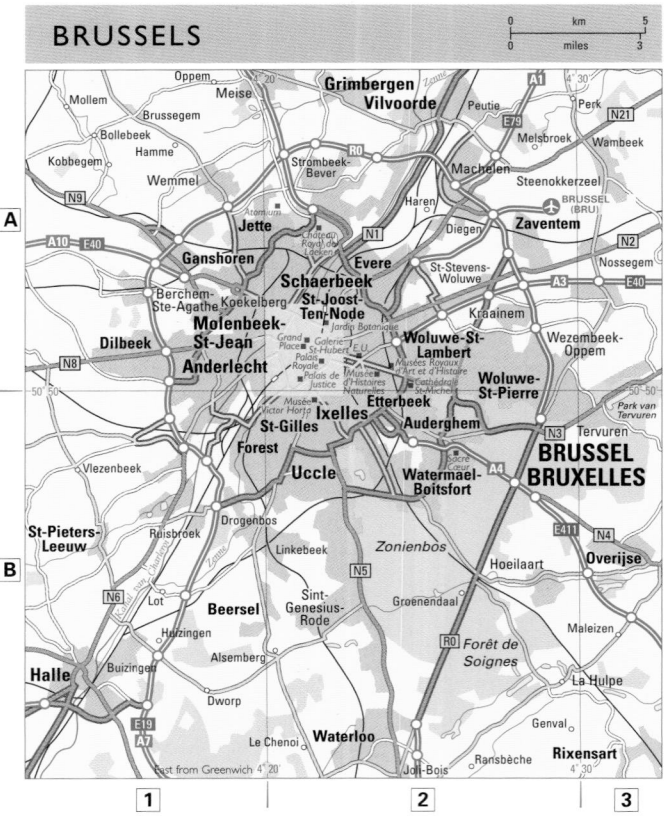

CENTRAL BRUSSELS

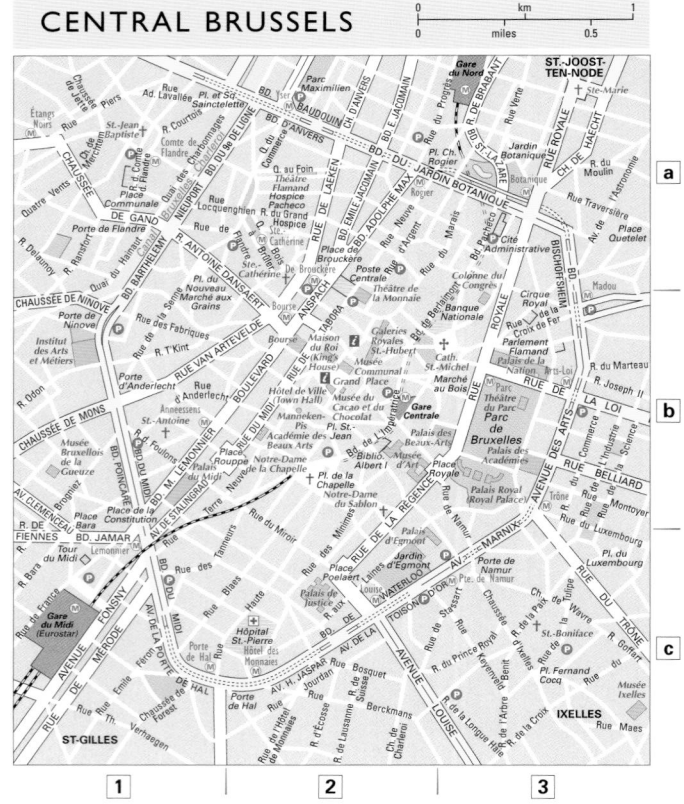

BUDAPEST

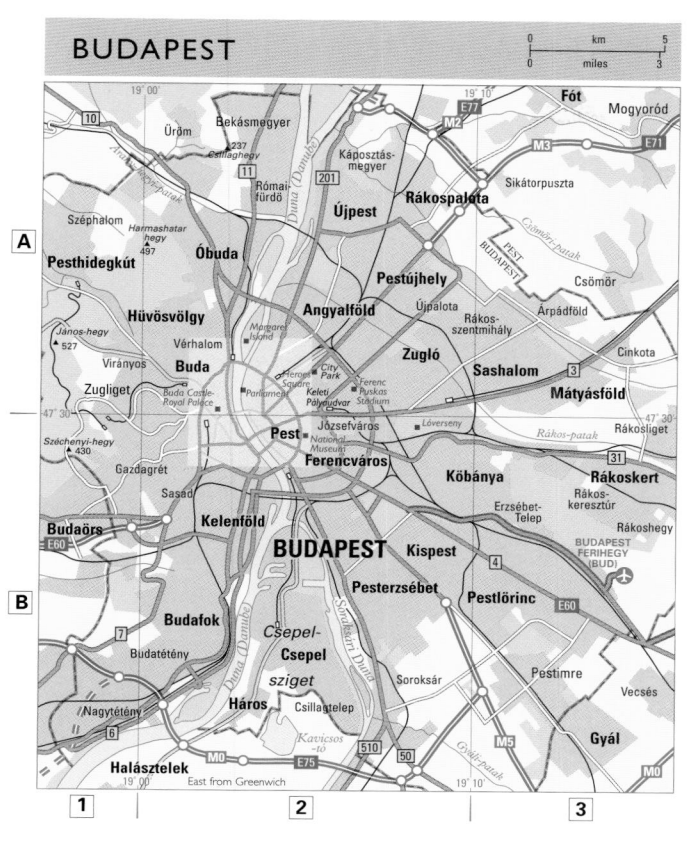

km
0   5
miles
0   3

10 Üröm Békásmegyer Fót Mogyoród
Kápolnás-
megyer Sikátorpuszta E71
Csillaghegy 237 11 Rákospalota
Római-
fürdő 201 Újpest
Széphalom 19°00' 19°10' M3 E77 Mz

A Pesthidegkút Óbuda Pestújhely
Harmashatár Újpalota
hegy Csömör
497 Angyalföld Rákos-
szentmihály
Hüvösvölgy Vérhalom Árpádföld
János-hegy Margaret Zugló Cinkota
527 Buda Island Sashalom Mátyásföld
Zugliget City Ferenc Puskás
Park Stadium Rákosliget
Széchenyi-hegy Keleti Rákos-patak
430 Pest Pályaudvar Rákoskert
Gazdagrét Józsefváros Rákos-
keresztúr
Sasad Ferencváros Köbánya Rákoshegy

B Budaörs Kelenföld **BUDAPEST** Kispest BUDAPEST
E60 FERIHEGY
Budafok Pesterzsébet Pestlörinc (BUD)
7 E60
Budatétény Csepel- 31
Csepel Pestimre
6 sziget Vecsés
Nagytétény Háros Csillagtelep
Kavicsos-
M0 tó Gyáli-patak
Halásztelek 510 50 M5 Gyál
E75 M0
East from Greenwich
1 19°00' **2** 19°10' **3**

CENTRAL BUDAPEST

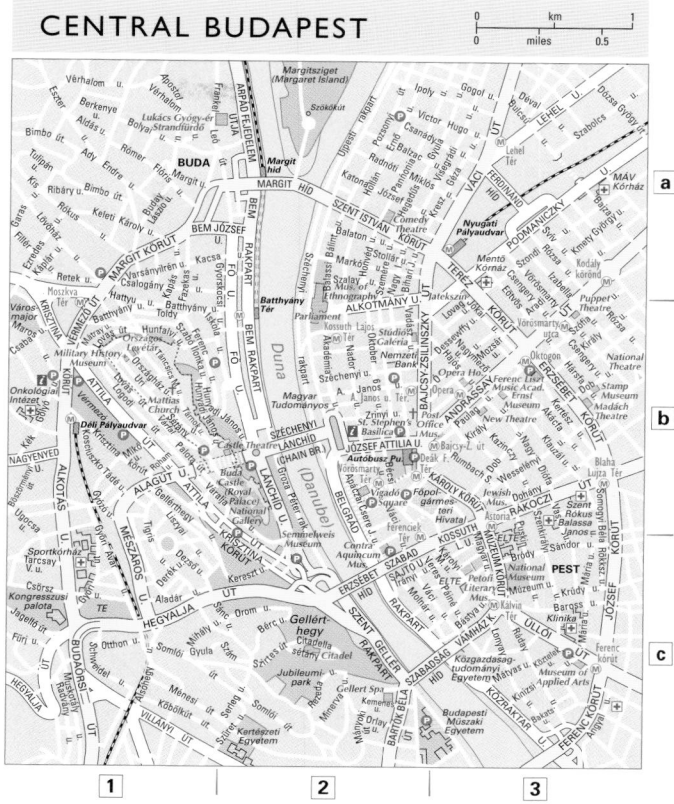

km
0   1
miles
0   0.5

BUENOS AIRES

km
0   5
miles
0   3

CAIRO

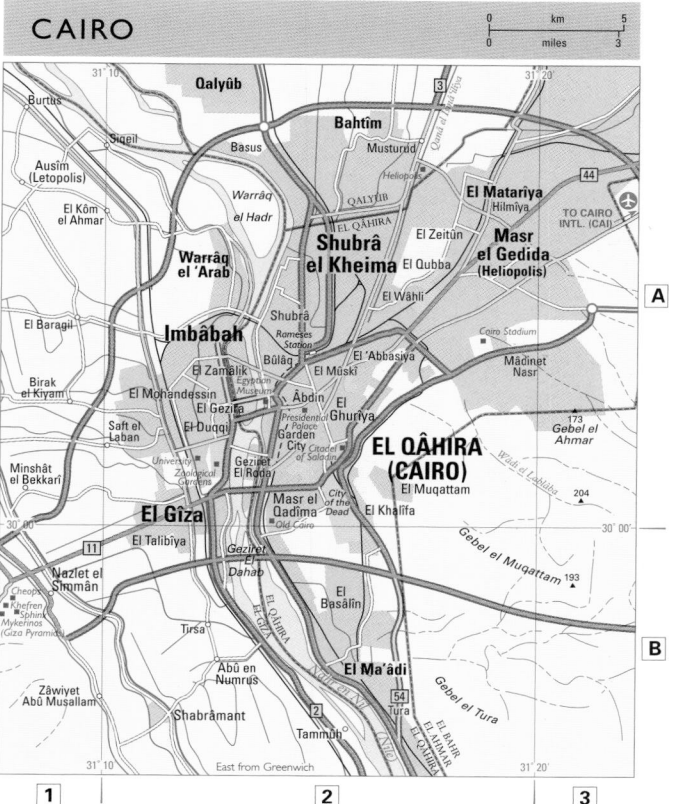

km
0   5
miles
0   3

COPYRIGHT PHILIP'S

CAPE TOWN

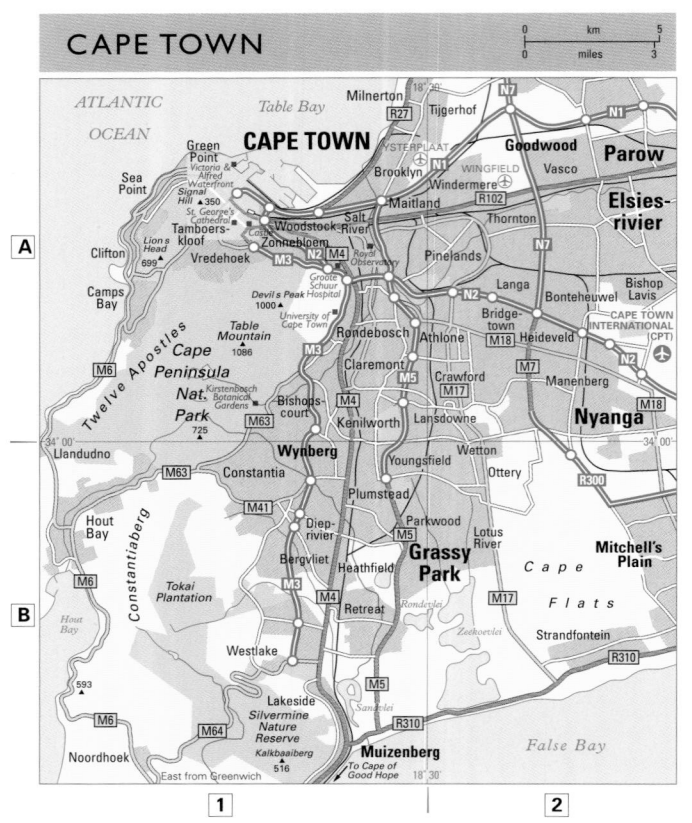

CENTRAL CAPE TOWN

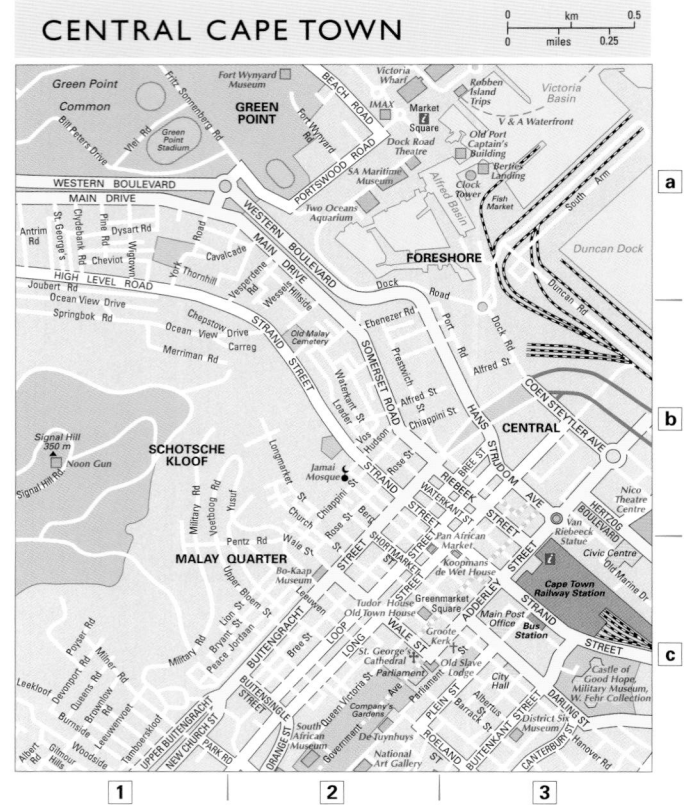

COPENHAGEN

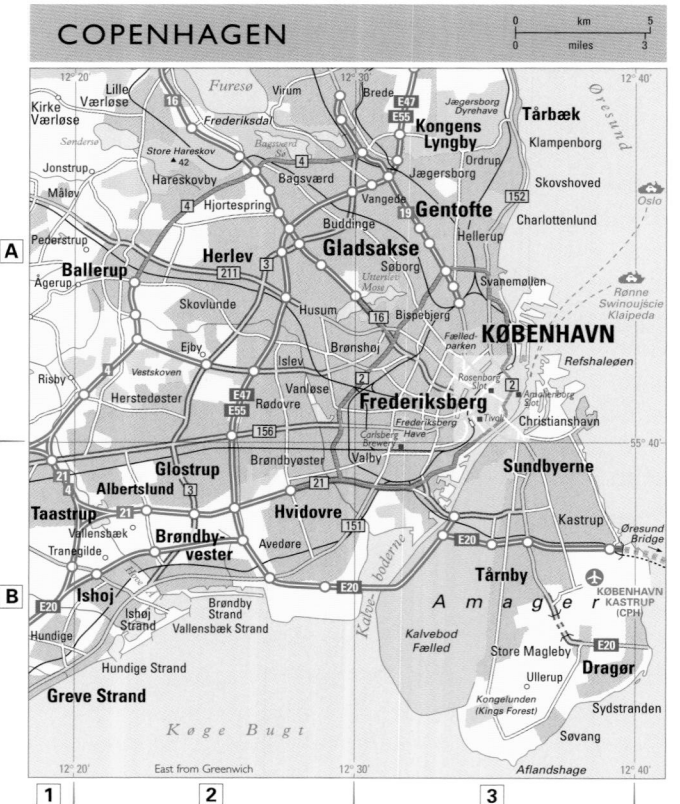

CENTRAL COPENHAGEN

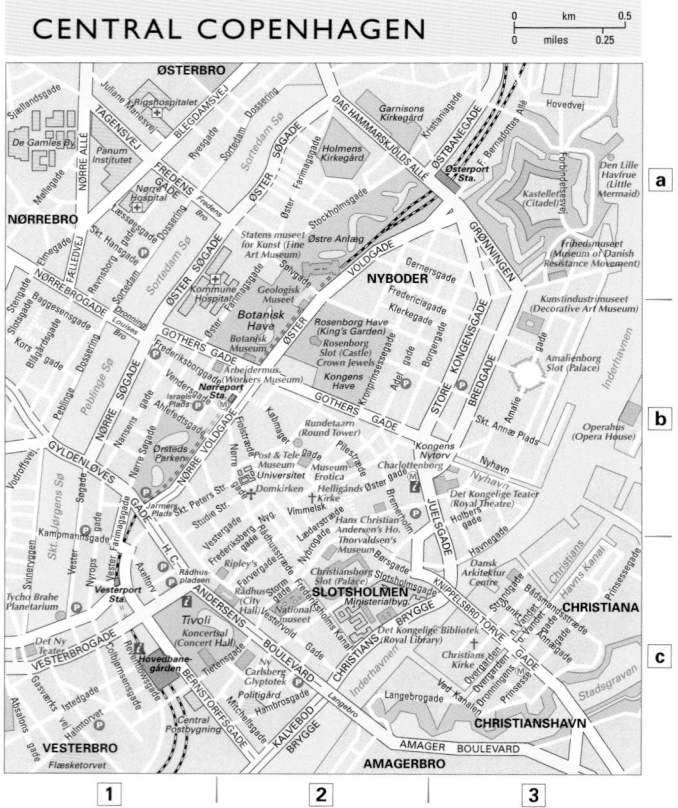

CHICAGO

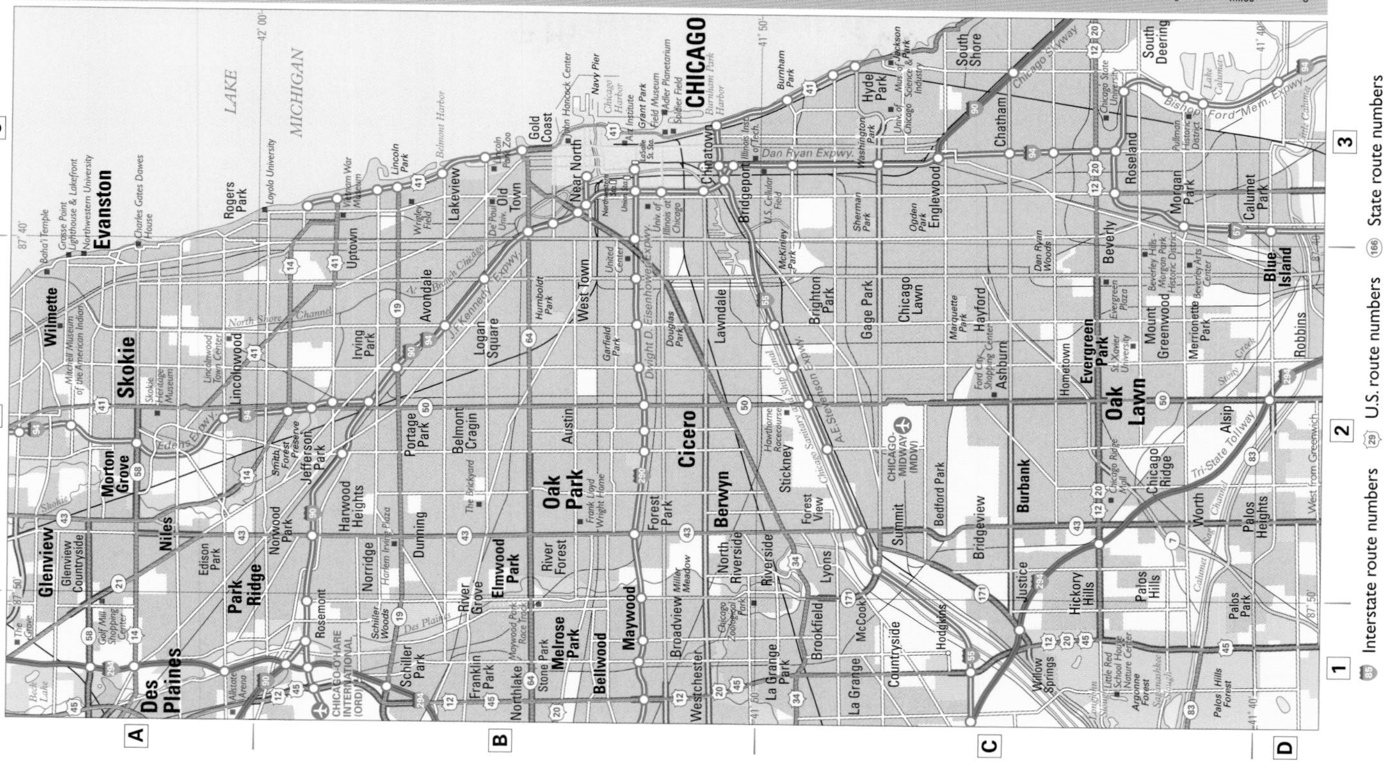

LAKE MICHIGAN

Des Plaines
Evanston
Wilmette
Skokie
Morton Grove
Glenview
Glenview Countryside
Niles
Park Ridge
Edison Park
Norwood Park
Harwood Heights
Norridge
Dunning
Schiller Park
Franklin Park
River Grove
Elmwood Park
Melrose Park
Bellwood
Maywood
Northlake
Westchester
La Grange Park
La Grange
Countryside
Hodgkins
Willow Springs
Summit
Bridgeview
Bedford Park
Justice
Hickory Hills
Palos Hills
Palos Heights
Palos Park
Worth
Chicago Ridge
Oak Lawn
Evergreen Park
Burbank
Alsip
Robbins
Blue Island
Calumet Park
Morgan Park
Beverly
Mount Greenwood
Merrionette Park
Roseland
South Deering
South Shore
Hyde Park
Chatham
Englewood
Washington Park
Woodlawn
Gage Park
Chicago Lawn
Ashburn
Hometown
Brighton Park
Sherman Park
McKinley Park
Bridgeport
Chinatown
Near North
Gold Coast
Lincoln Park
Uptown
Rogers Park
Lakeview
Avondale
Logan Square
Irving Park
Portage Park
Belmont Cragin
Austin
Oak Park
River Forest
Forest Park
Berwyn
Cicero
Lawndale
Lyons
Riverside
North Riverside
Brookfield
Broadview
Forest View
Stickney
West Town
Old Town
CHICAGO

CENTRAL CHICAGO

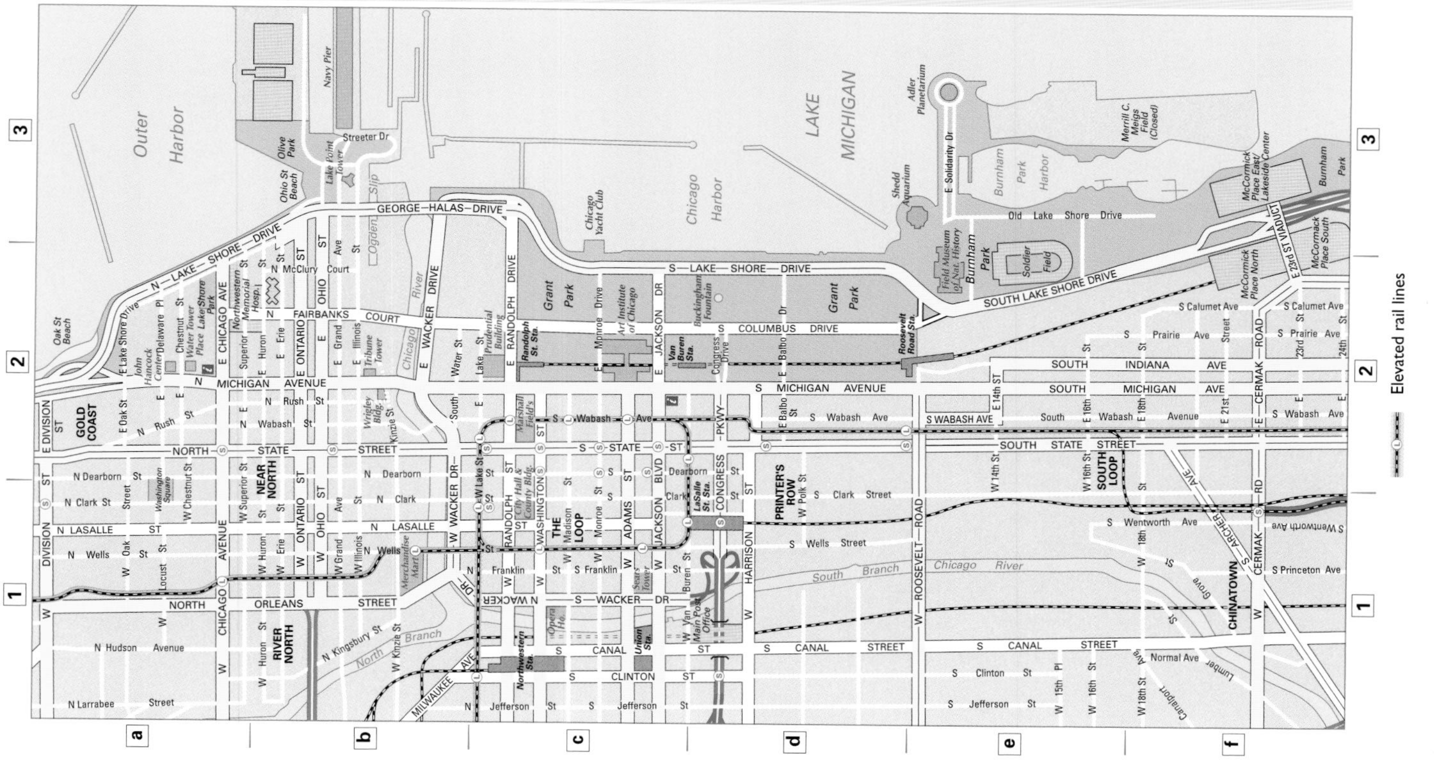

LAKE MICHIGAN

Outer Harbor
Navy Pier
Olive Park
Ohio St Beach
Streeter Dr
Lake Point
Chicago Harbor
Chicago Yacht Club
Grant Park
Adler Planetarium
Shedd Aquarium
Field Museum of Nat. History
Soldier Field
Burnham Park
Burnham Harbor
Meigs Field (Closed)
Merrill C. Meigs Field
McCormick Place
McCormick Place East
Lakeside Center
McCormick Place North
McCormick Place South
Gold Coast
Near North
River North
Chinatown
South Loop
Printer's Row
The Loop
GEORGE HALAS DRIVE
LAKE SHORE DRIVE
E SOLIDARITY DR
Old Lake Shore Drive
SOUTH LAKE SHORE DRIVE
COLUMBUS DRIVE
MICHIGAN AVENUE
SOUTH MICHIGAN AVENUE
STATE STREET
SOUTH STATE STREET
ROOSEVELT ROAD
CERMAK ROAD
CANAL STREET
Chicago River
South Branch
North Branch

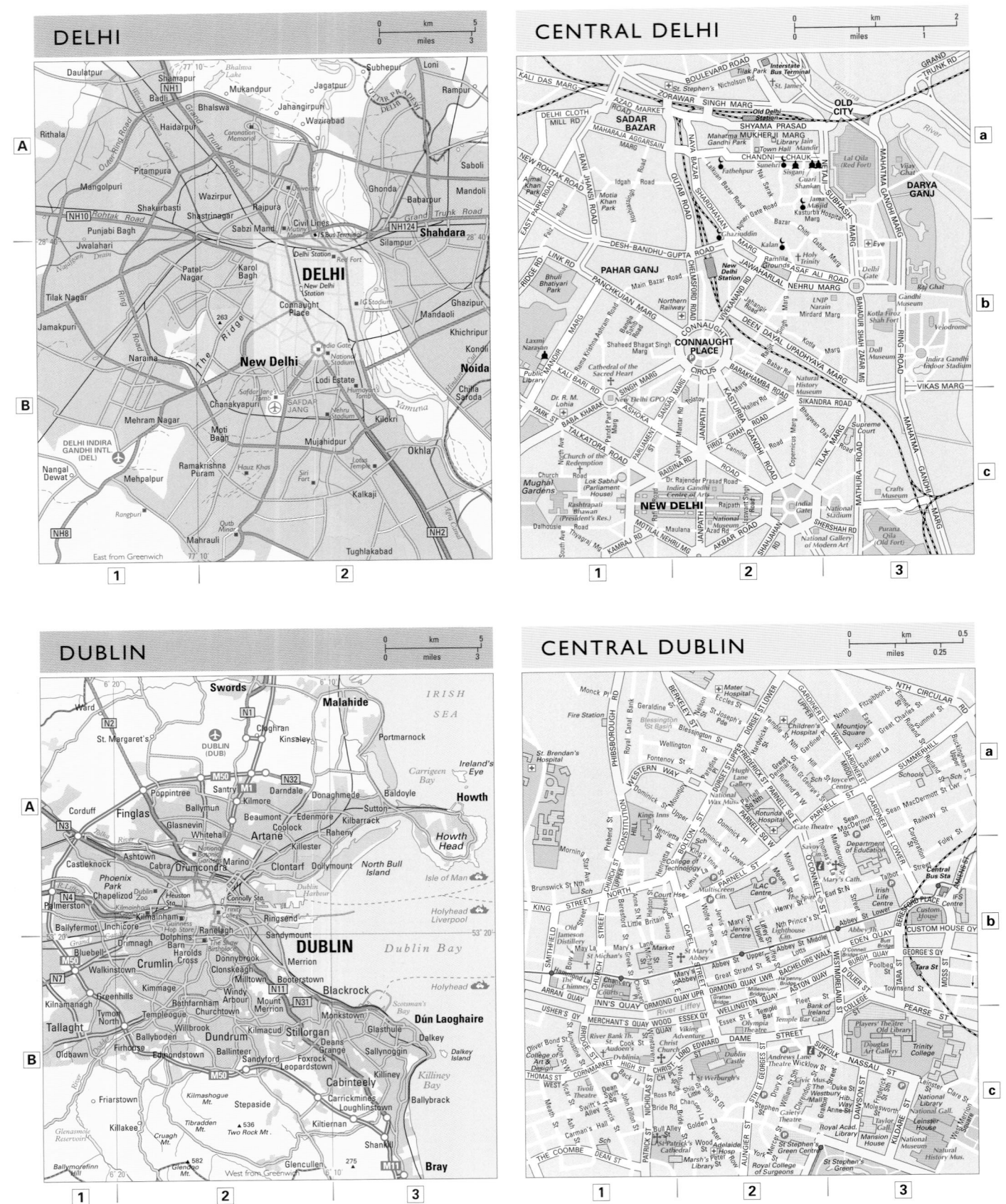

EDINBURGH

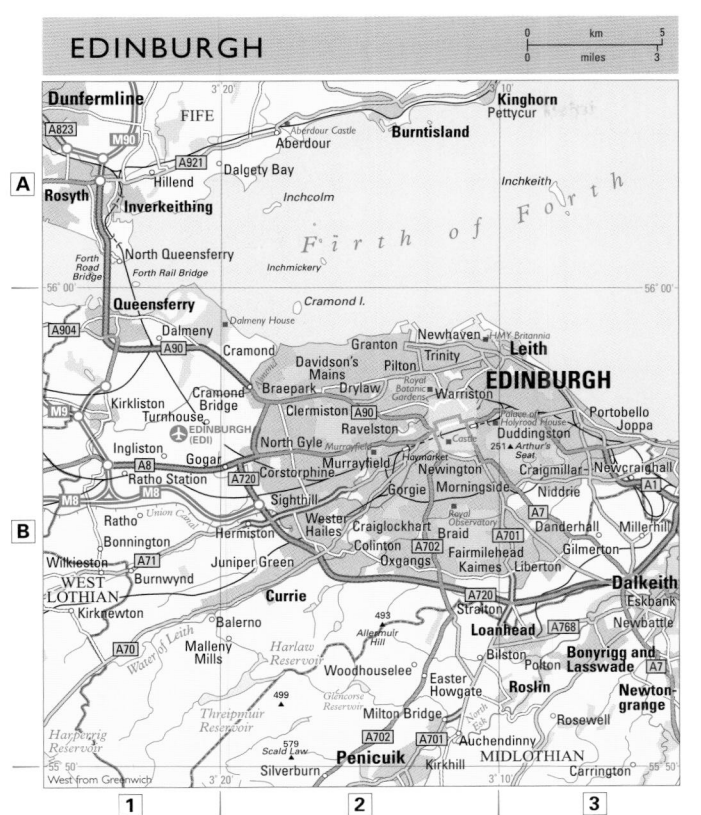

CENTRAL EDINBURGH

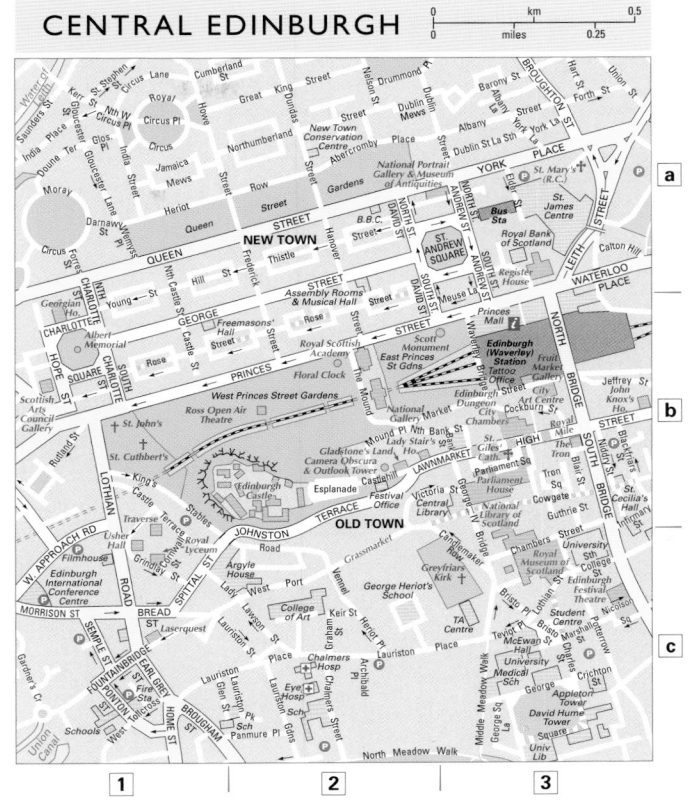

GUANGZHOU

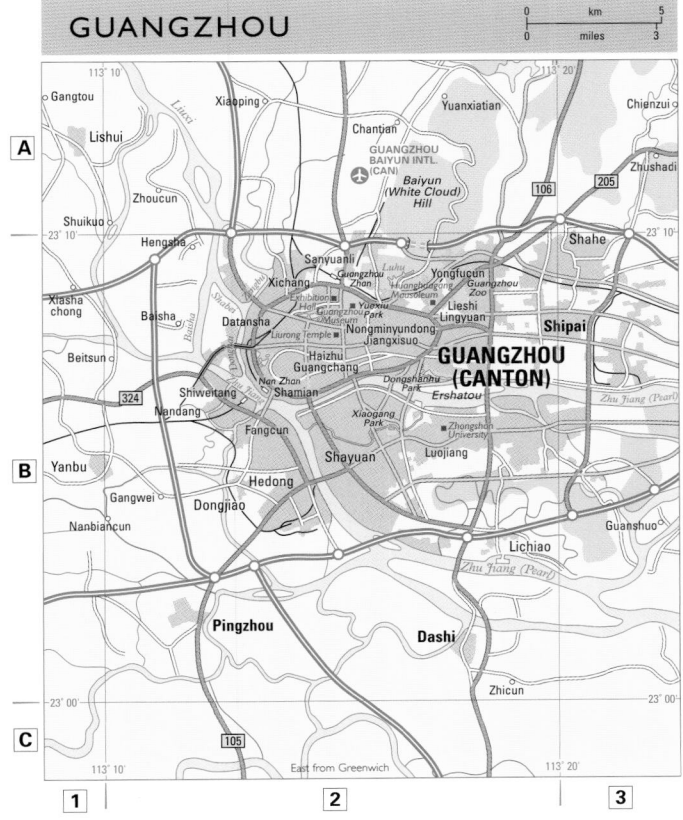

HELSINKI

HONG KONG

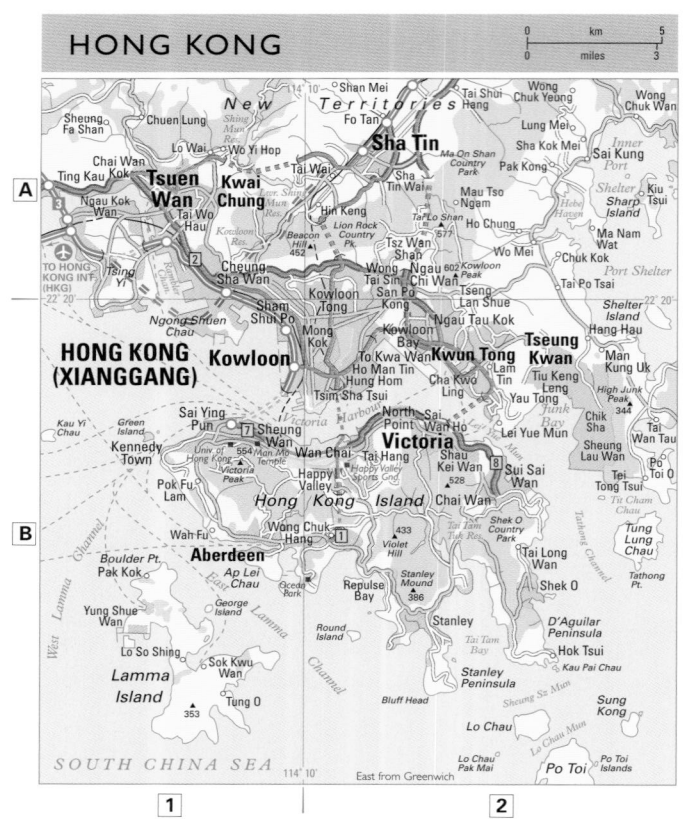

CENTRAL HONG KONG

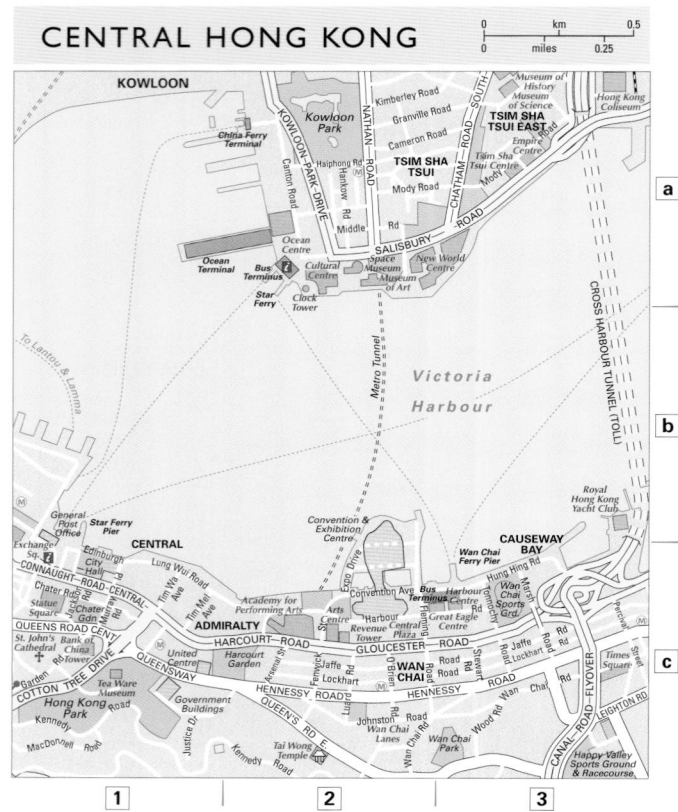

ISTANBUL

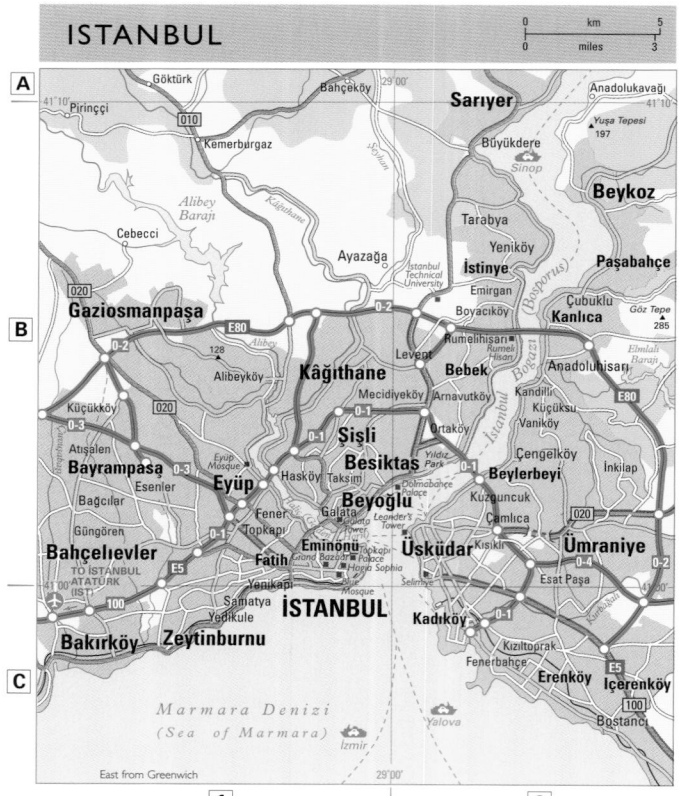

JAKARTA

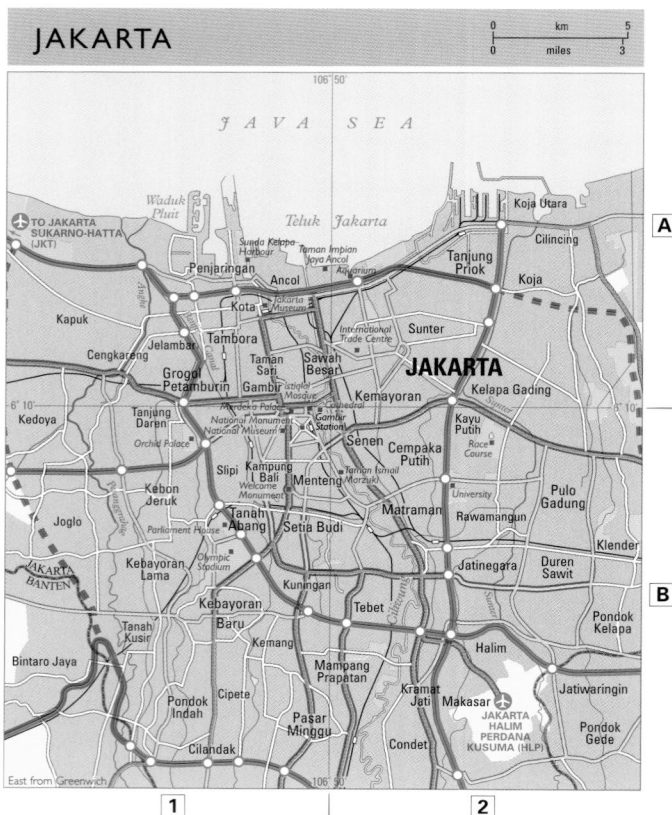

JERUSALEM

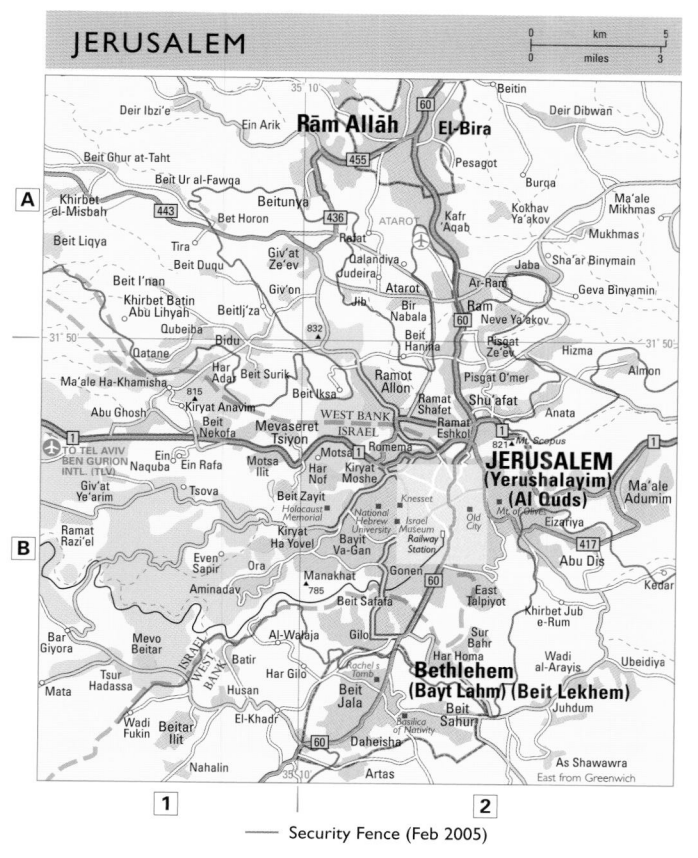

km 5

miles 3

Deir Ibzi'e
Ein Arik
Deir Dibwan
Beitin
Rām Allāh
El-Bira
Beit Ghur at-Taht
Pesagot
Khirbet
el-Misbah
Beitunya
Beit Ur al-Fawqa
Burqa
Ma'ale
Mikhmas
A
Beit Liqya
Beit Horon
Kafr
'Aqab
Kokhav
Ya'akov
Mukhmas
Tira
Giv'at
Ze'ev
Qalandiya
Judeira
Jaba
Sha'ar Binyamin
Geva Binyamin
Beit I'nan
Beit Duqu
Giv'on
Jib
Bir
Nabala
Ar-Ram
Almon
Khirbet Batin
Abu Lihyah
Beitlj'za
Neve Ya'akov
Qubeiba
Bidu
Beit
Hanina
Pisgat Ze'ev
31° 50'
Qatane
Ma'ale Ha-Khamisha
Beit Ada
Beit Surik
Ramot
Allon
Pisgat O'mer
Hizma
31° 50'
Abu Ghosh
Kiryat Anavim
Beit
Nekofa
Mevaseret
Tsiyon
Ramat
Shafet
Ramat
Eshkol
1
Mt. Scopus
Anata
WEST BANK
ISRAEL
Ein
Naquba
Ein Rafa
Motsa
Ilit
Har
Nof
Kiryat
Moshe
Shu'afat
Giv'at
Ye'arim
Tsova
Motsa
Romema
JERUSALEM
(Yerushalayim)
(Al Quds)
Mt. of Olive
Ma'ale
Adumim
Ramat
Razi'el
Even
Sapir
Ora
Kiryat
Ha Yovel
Bayit
Va-Gan
Israel
Museum
Railway
Station
Eizariya
B
Holocaust
Memorial
National
Hebrew
University
Old
City
Abu Dis
Aminadav
Manakhat
Gonen
East
Talpiyot
Kedar
Bar
Giyora
Mevo
Beitar
Beit Safafa
Khirbet Jub
e-Rum
Al-Walaja
Gilo
Sur
Bahir
Mata
Batir
Har Gilo
Har Homa
Wadi
al-Arayis
Ubeidiya
Tsur
Hadassa
Husan
Beit
Jala
Bethlehem
(Bayt Lahm) (Beit Lekhem)
Beit
Sahur
Juhdum
Wadi
Fukin
Beitar
Ilit
El-Khadr
Basilica
of Nativity
Nahalin
Daheisha
Artas
As Shawawra
East from Greenwich

1 **2**

— Security Fence (Feb 2005)

CENTRAL JERUSALEM

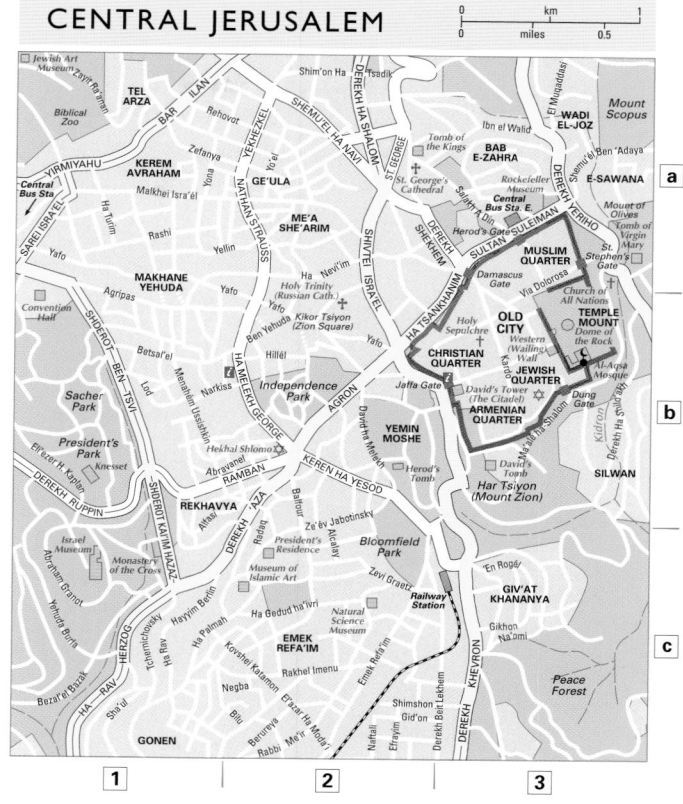

km 1

miles 0.5

Jewish Art
Museum
TEL
ARZA
a
Biblical
Zoo
KEREM
AVRAHAM
Central
Bus Sta
GE'ULA
Tomb of
the Kings
BAB
E-ZAHRA
WADI
EL-JOZ
Mount
Scopus
St. George's
Cathedral
Rockefeller
Museum
E-SAWANA
ME'A
SHE'ARIM
Herod's Gate
Mount of
Olives
Tomb of
Virgin
MAKHANE
YEHUDA
Holy Trinity
(Russian Cath.)
MUSLIM
QUARTER
St.
Stephen's
Gate
Church of
All Nations
Convention
Hall
Ben Yehuda
Kikar Tsiyon
(Zion Square)
Damascus
Gate
Via Dolorosa
TEMPLE
MOUNT
Dome of
the Rock
Holy
Sepulchre
OLD
CITY
Western
(Wailing)
Wall
Al-Aqsa
Mosque
Sacher
Park
Independence
Park
CHRISTIAN
QUARTER
JEWISH
QUARTER
b
President's
Park
Jaffa Gate
David's Tower
(The Citadel)
Dung
Gate
Knesset
YEMIN
MOSHE
ARMENIAN
QUARTER
SILWAN
Israel
Museum
Herod's
Tomb
David's
Tomb
REKHAVYA
Har Tsiyon
(Mount Zion)
Monastery
of the Cross
President's
Residence
Museum of
Islamic Art
Bloomfield
Park
En Rogel
GIV'AT
KHANANYA
Natural
Science
Museum
Railway
Station
Gikhon
Na'omi
c
EMEK
REFA'IM
Peace
Forest
GONEN
East from Greenwich

1 **2** **3**

JOHANNESBURG

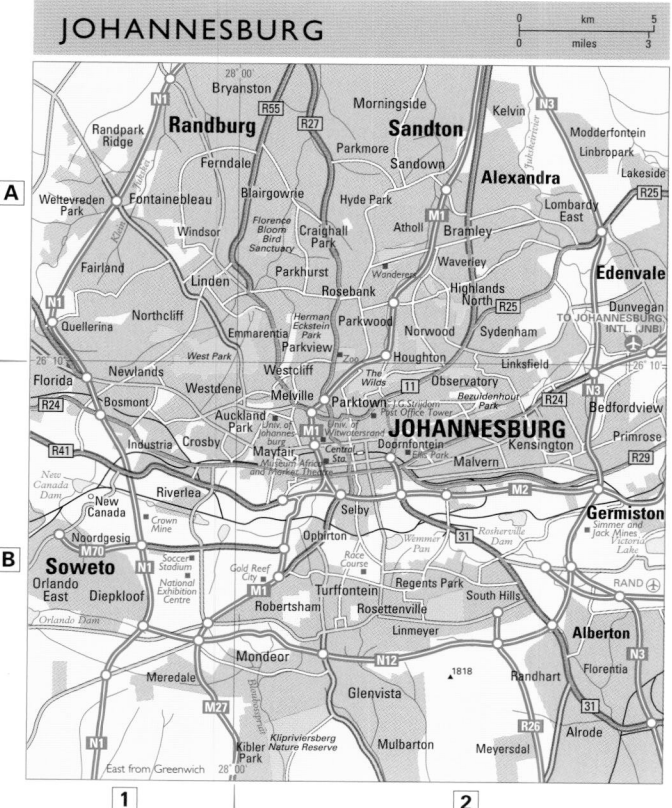

km 5

miles 3

28° 00'
Bryanston
Morningside
Kelvin
Randpark
Ridge
Randburg
Sandton
Modderfontein
Ferndale
Parkmore
Sandown
Linbropark
Lakeside
A
Welctevreden
Park
Fontainebleau
Blairgowrie
Hyde Park
Alexandra
Florence
Bloom
Bird
Sanctuary
Craighall
Park
Atholl
Bramley
Lombardy
East
Windsor
Parkhurst
Waverley
Highlands
North
Edenvale
Fairland
Linden
Rosebank
Norwood
Sydenham
Dunvegan
TO JOHANNESBURG
INTL. (JNB)
Northcliff
Quellerina
Emmarentia
Parkview
Zoo
Houghton
Linksfield
26° 10'
West Park
Westcliff
The
Wilds
Observatory
Bezuidenhout
Park
Bedfordview
Florida
Newlands
Bosmont
Westdene
Melville
Parktown
Univ. of
Witwatersrand
Kensington
Primrose
Riverlea
Auckland
Park
Mayfair
JOHANNESBURG
Doornfontein
Malvern
Industria
Crosby
Central
Sta.
Museum Africana
and Market Theatre
Selby
New
Canada
Dam
New
Canada
Ophirton
Germiston
Noordgesig
Crown
Mine
Wemmer
Pan
Race
Course
Roodekille
Dam
Simmer and
Jack Mines
Victoria
Lakes
B
Soweto
Soccer
City
Gold Reef
City
Turffontein
RAND
Orlando
East
Diepkloof
National
Exhibition
Centre
Robertsham
Regents Park
South Hills
Alberton
Orlando Dam
Rosettenville
Linmeyer
Meredale
Mondeor
Glenvista
Randhart
Florentia
Alrode
Kliprivensberg
Nature Reserve
Mulbarton
Meyersdal
28° 00'
East from Greenwich

1 **2**

KARACHI

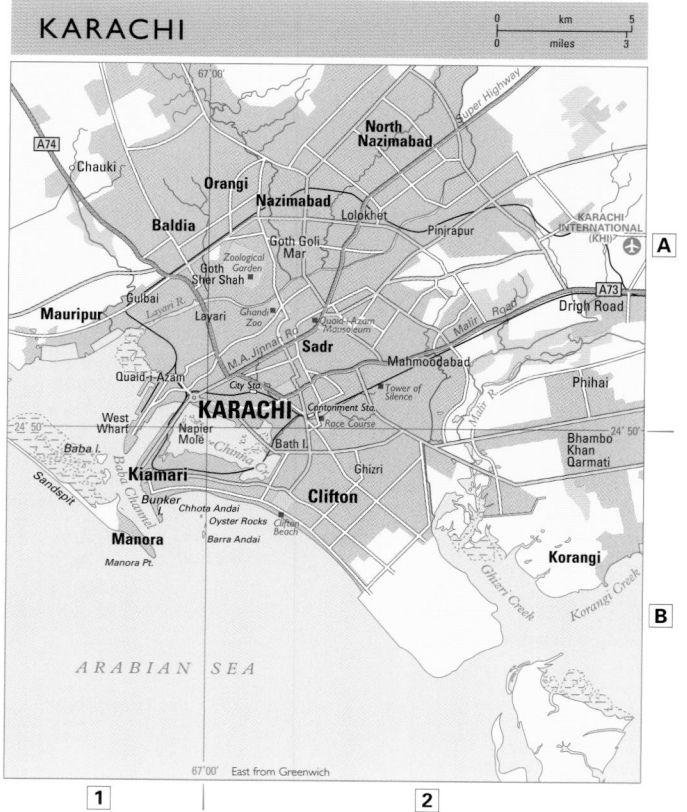

km 5

miles 3

67° 00'
Super Highway
Chauki
North
Nazimabad
A74
Orangi
Nazimabad
KARACHI
INTERNATIONAL (KHI)
Baldia
Lolokhet
Pinjrapur
Goth Goli
Mar
Zoological
Garden
Goth
Sher Shah
Gulbai
Ghandi
A
Layari
Zoo
A73
Mauripur
Lavari R.
Quaid-i-Azam
City Sta
M.A. Jinnah Rd.
Sadr
Mahmoodabad
Dright Road
Tower of
Silence
Phihai
West
Wharf
Centorment Sta
Race
Course
KARACHI
Napier
Mole
Bhambo
Khan
Qarmati
24° 50'
Baba I.
Bath I.
Ghizri
24° 50'
Kiamari
Quaid-i-Azam
Museum
Sandspit
Bunker
Chhota Andai
Oyster Rocks
Clifton
Beach
Clifton
Manora
Barra Andai
Korangi
Manora Pt.
B
Korangi Creek
Ghizri Creek
ARABIAN SEA
67° 00' East from Greenwich

1 **2**

COPYRIGHT PHILIP'S

KOLKATA

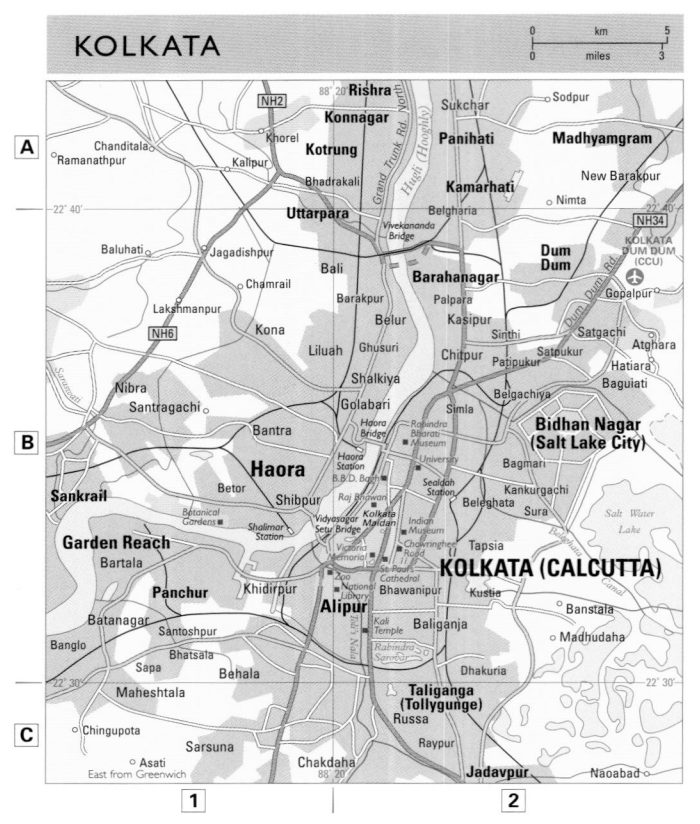

LAGOS

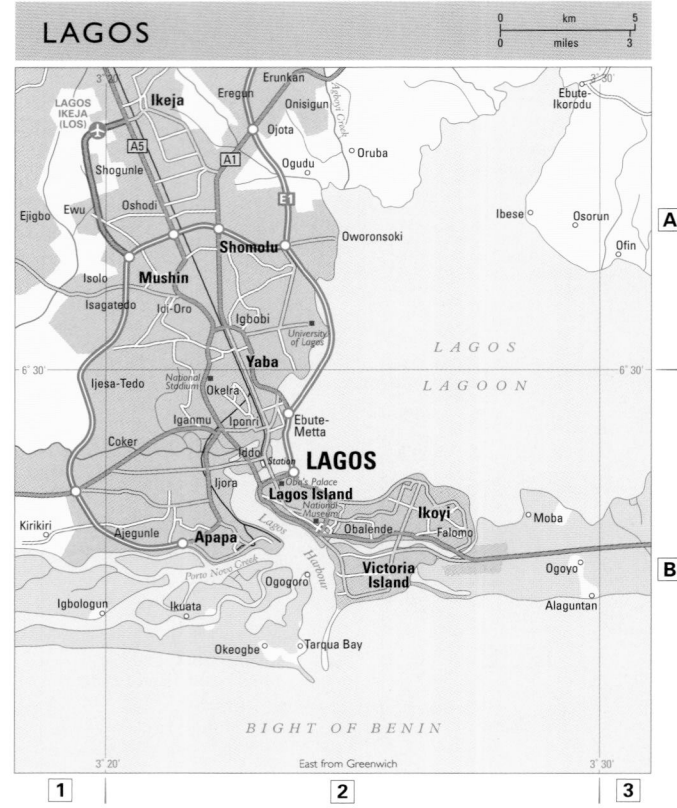

LAS VEGAS

LIMA

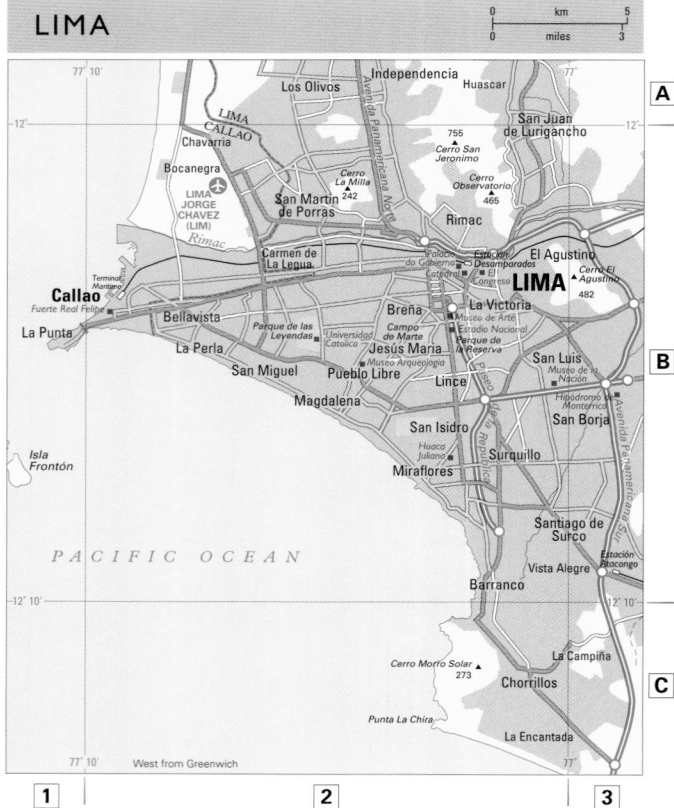

🛡 Interstate route numbers   95 U.S. route numbers   147 State route numbers

LONDON

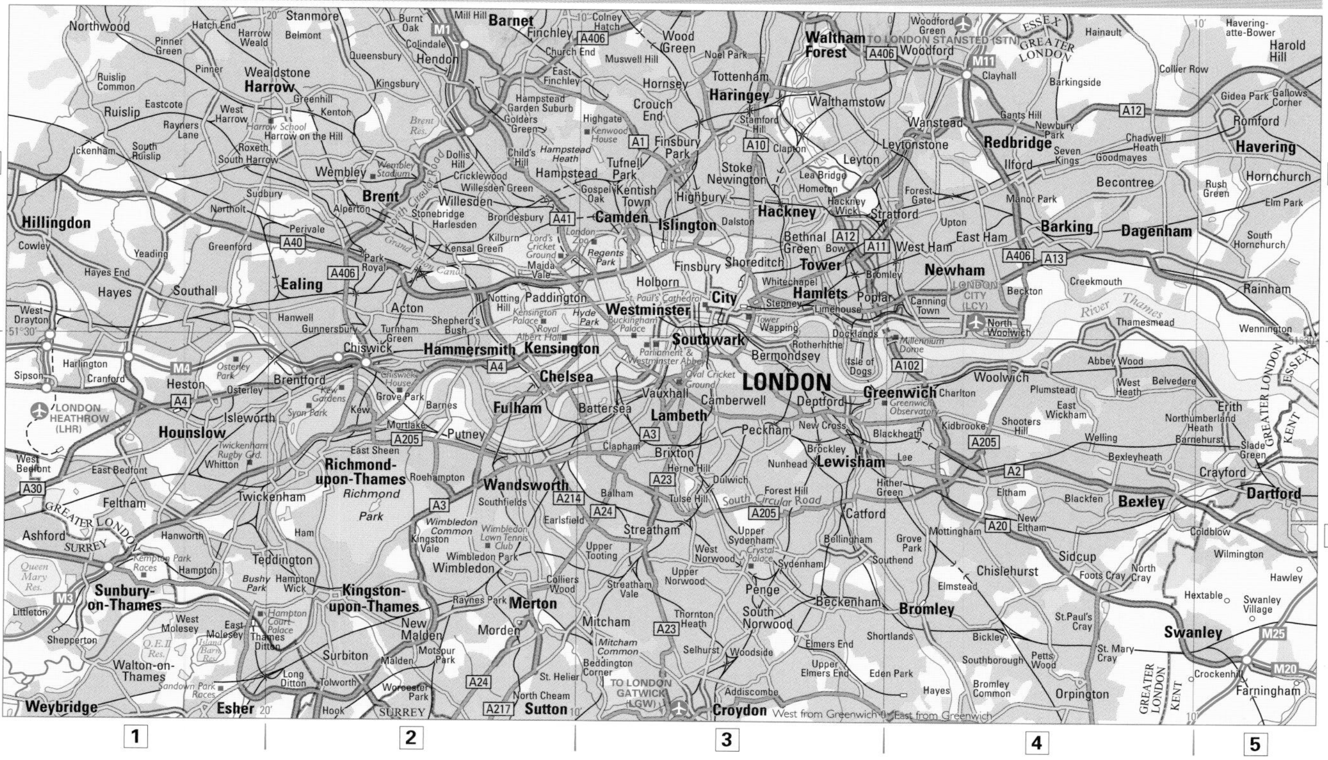

km 0 — 5
miles 0 — 3

Northwood · Hatch End · Stanmore · Mill Hill · Barnet · Finchley · Colney Hatch · Wood Green · Waltham Forest · Woodford · Hainault · Havering-atte-Bower · Harold Hill

Pinner Green · Belmont · Queensbury · Hendon · Church End · East Finchley · Muswell Hill · Noel Park · Woodford Green · ESSEX · GREATER LONDON · Collier Row · Gidea Park · Gallows Corner

Ruislip Common · Eastcote · West Harrow · Greenhill · Kenton · Kingsbury · Hampstead Garden Suburb · Golders Green · Highgate · Hornsey · Crouch End · Walthamstow · Wanstead · Leytonstone · Newbury Park · Chadwell Heath · Romford

Harrow · Wealdstone · Harrow on the Hill · Cricklewood · Willesden Green · Hampstead Heath · Tufnell Park · Kentish Town · Finsbury Park · Highbury · Stoke Newington · Clapton · Leyton · Wanstead · Ilford · Seven Kings · Goodmayes · **Havering**

Hillingdon · **Brent** · **Camden** · **Islington** · **Hackney** · Stratford · West Ham · **Barking** · Becontree · **Dagenham**

Cowley · Northolt · Perivale · Alperton · Stonebridge · Harlesden · Kilburn · Maida Vale · Regents Park · Holborn · Finsbury · Shoreditch · Bethnal Green · Bow · East Ham · Upton · Manor Park · Elm Park

Ealing · Acton · Shepherd's Bush · Notting Hill · Paddington · **Westminster** · **City** · **Tower Hamlets** · Poplar · Canning Town · **Newham** · Beckton · Creekmouth · Rainham

West Drayton · Hanwell · Gunnersbury · Turnham Green · Chiswick · **Hammersmith** · **Kensington** · **Chelsea** · Pimlico · **Southwark** · Bermondsey · Rotherhithe · Isle of Dogs · North Woolwich · Thamesmead

Hounslow · Brentford · Syon Park · Barnes · **Fulham** · Battersea · **Lambeth** · Camberwell · **LONDON** · Deptford · **Greenwich** · Charlton · Woolwich · Plumstead · Abbey Wood · Belvedere · Erith

Heston · Isleworth · Osterley · Grove Park · Putney · Clapham · Brixton · Peckham · New Cross · Blackheath · Kidbrooke · Shooters Hill · Welling · East Wickham · Bexleyheath · Barnehurst · Crayford

LONDON HEATHROW (LHR) · Twickenham · **Richmond-upon-Thames** · Richmond Park · Wandsworth · Earlsfield · Balham · Tooting · Herne Hill · Dulwich · Brockley · **Lewisham** · Hither Green · Eltham · New Eltham · Blackfen · **Bexley** · **Dartford**

Feltham · Hanworth · Teddington · Ham · Roehampton · Southfields · Wimbledon Common · Kingston Vale · Streatham · West Norwood · Sydenham · Catford · Mottingham · Sidcup · North Cray · Wilmington · Coldblow · Hawley

Ashford · SURREY · Hampton · Bushy Park · Kingston-upon-Thames · Wimbledon Park · **Wimbledon** · Colliers Wood · Streatham Vale · Upper Norwood · Penge · Bellingham · Grove Park · Elmstead · Chislehurst · Foots Cray · St Paul's Cray · **Swanley**

Sunbury-on-Thames · West Molesey · East Molesey · Thames Ditton · **Merton** · Morden · Mitcham · Mitcham Common · Thornton Heath · South Norwood · **Bromley** · Southborough · Bickley · Petts Wood · St Mary Cray · Swanley Village

Weybridge · Shepperton · Walton-on-Thames · **Esher** · Surbiton · Malden · Motspur Park · New Malden · Raynes Park · Beddington Corner · Woodside · Elmers End · Shortlands · **Orpington** · Crockenhill · **Farningham**

Littleton · Hook · Worcester Park · North Cheam · **Sutton** · **Croydon** · Addiscombe · Bromley Common · Hayes · Eden Park · Upper Elmers End · Hextable · GREATER LONDON · KENT

CENTRAL LONDON

km 0 — 2
miles 0 — 1

QUEEN'S PARK · ST. JOHN'S WOOD · King's Cross · HOXTON · SHOREDITCH

WEST KILBURN · MAIDA VALE · WESTBOURNE GREEN · PADDINGTON · MARYLEBONE · BLOOMSBURY · HOLBORN · CLERKENWELL · Farringdon · CITY

Regent's Park · Queen Mary's Gardens · Euston · St Pancras · British Library · Barbican · Moorgate · Liverpool St.

NOTTING HILL · BAYSWATER · Hyde Park · MAYFAIR · SOHO · Covent Garden · St Paul's · Bank · Aldgate

Kensington Gardens · Serpentine · Charing Cross · STRAND · Blackfriars · Cannon St. · Tower of London · Tower Bridge

KENSINGTON · KNIGHTSBRIDGE · Hyde Pk. Corner · Buckingham Palace · ST. JAMES'S · WESTMINSTER · SOUTHWARK · Tower Gateway (DLR) · BERMONDSEY

BROMPTON · BELGRAVIA · Houses of Parliament · Westminster Abbey · Lambeth Palace · London Bridge · Guy's Hosp. · The Design Museum

WEST KENSINGTON · SOUTH KENSINGTON · CHELSEA · PIMLICO · Victoria · Tate Britain · LAMBETH · NEWINGTON · Elephant & Castle · NEW KENT RD · WALWORTH

Olympia · CHELSEA EMBANKMENT · River Thames · Vauxhall · KENNINGTON · The Oval · Burgess Park

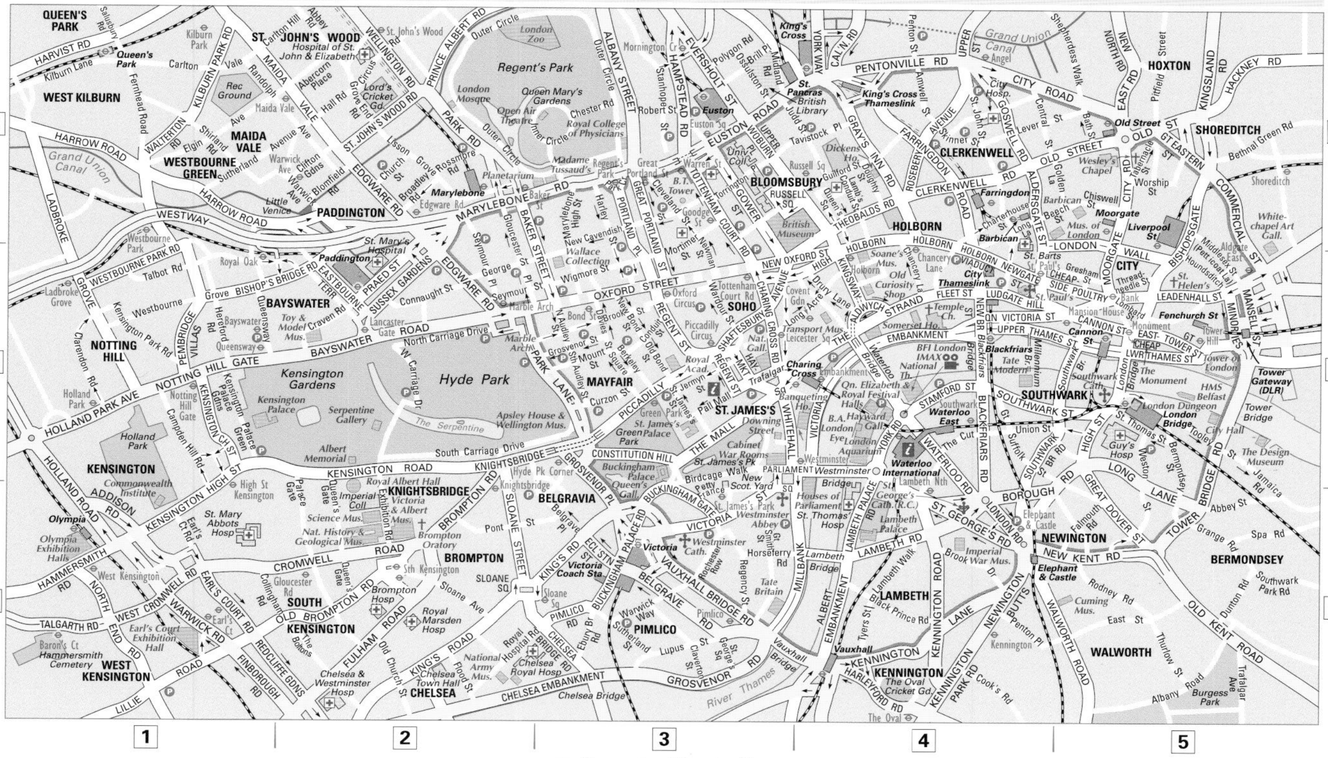

— Congestion Charging Zone

COPYRIGHT PHILIP'S

LISBON

0 km 5
0 miles 3

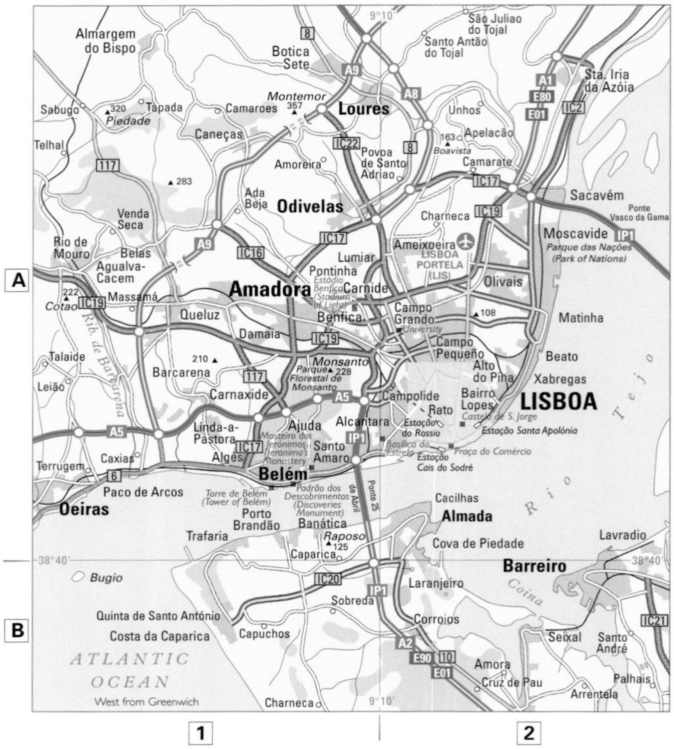

CENTRAL LISBON

0 km 1
0 miles 0.5

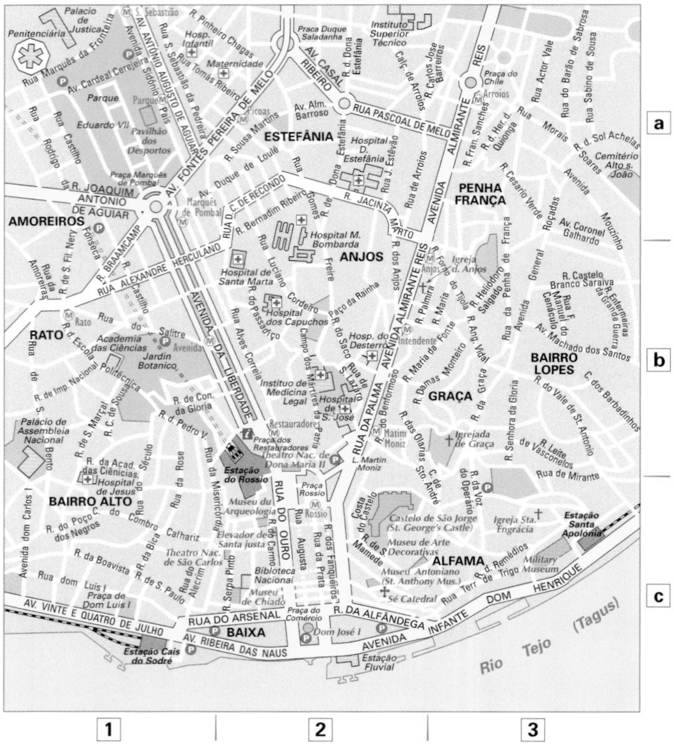

LOS ANGELES

0 km 5
0 miles 3

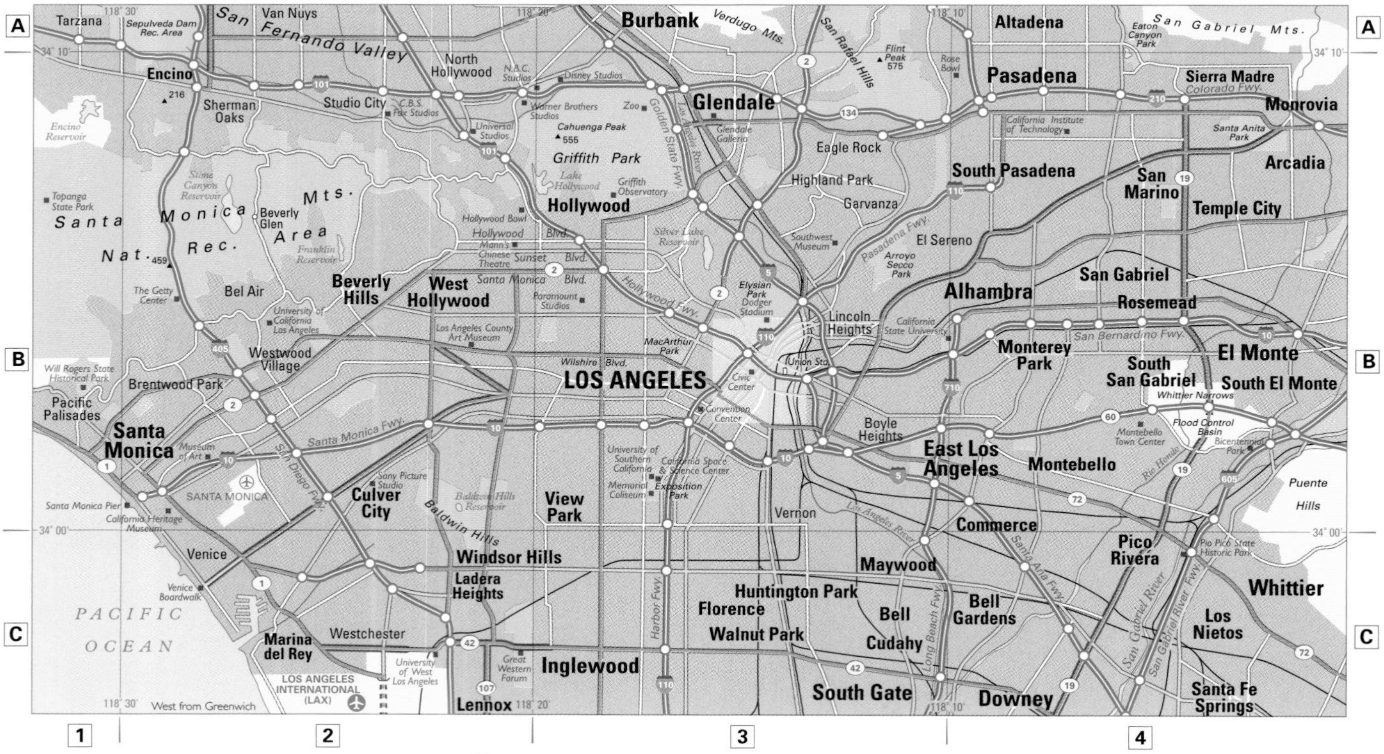

Interstate route numbers   State route numbers

MADRID

CENTRAL MADRID

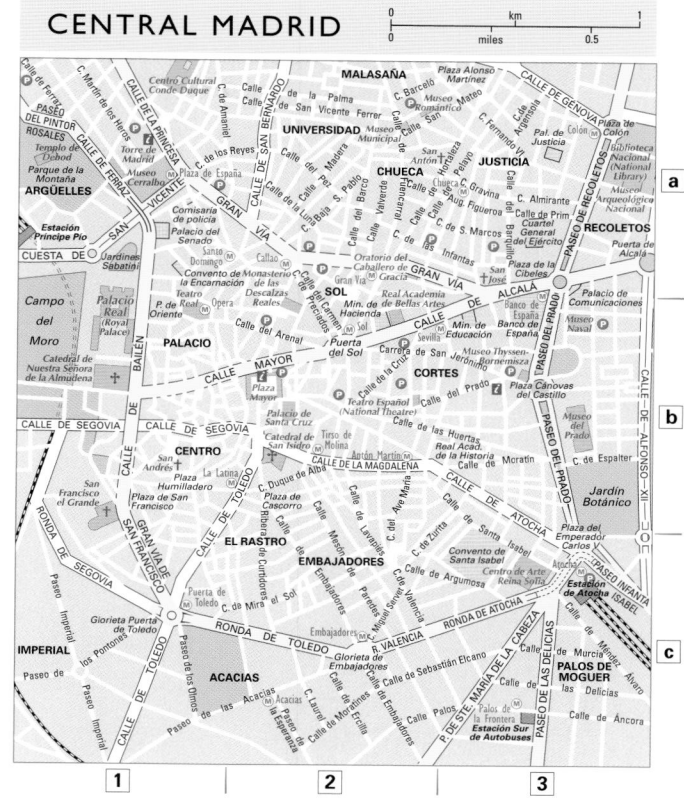

CENTRAL LOS ANGELES

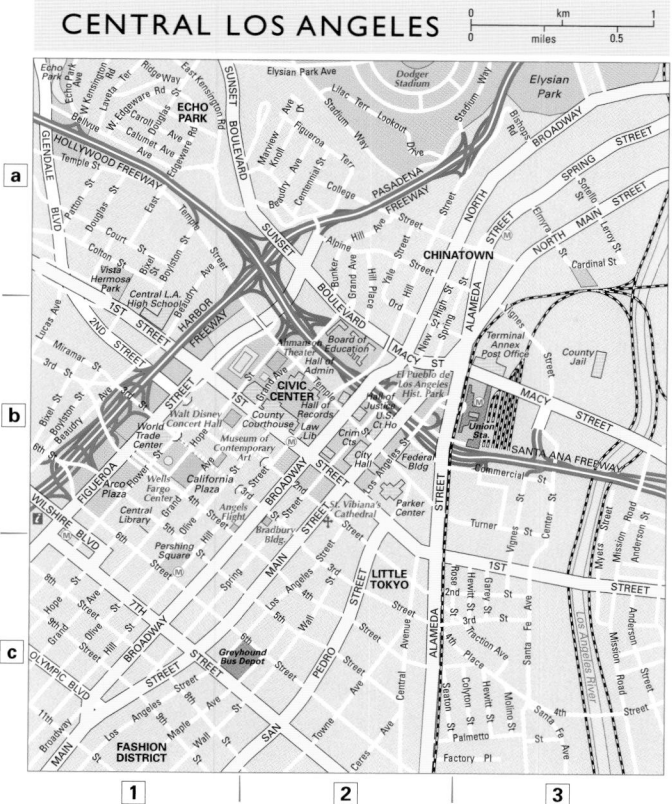

MANILA

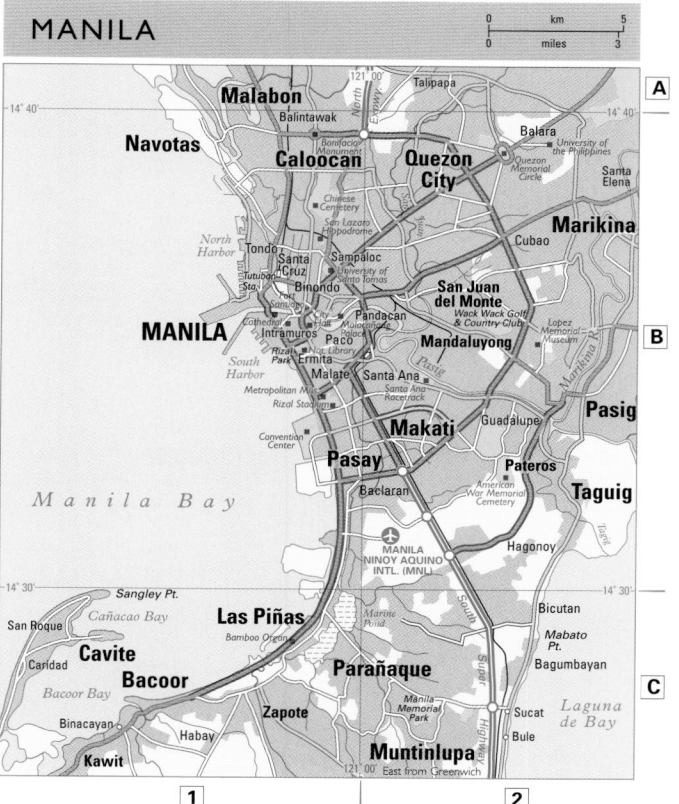

COPYRIGHT PHILIP'S

MEXICO CITY

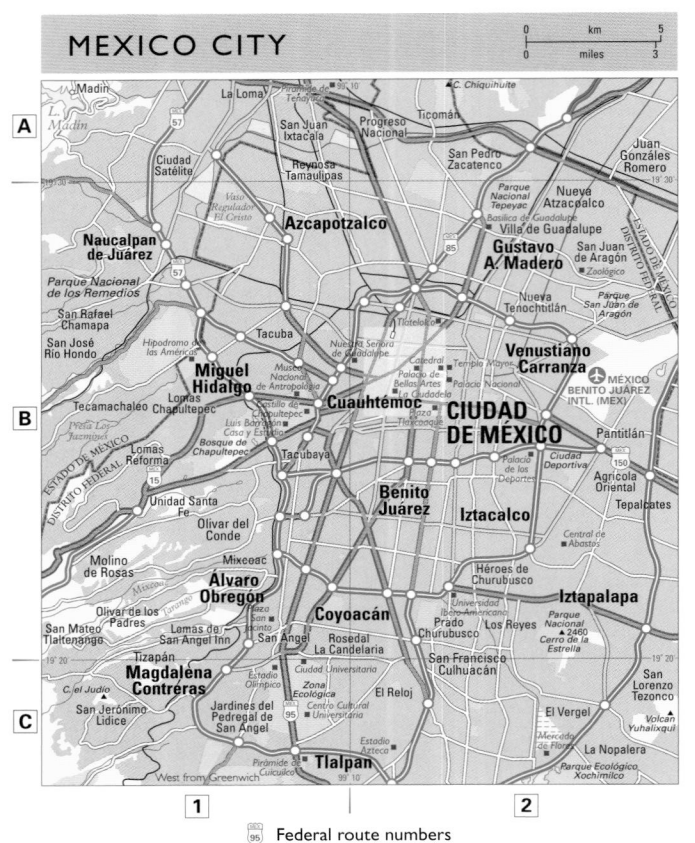

CENTRAL MEXICO CITY

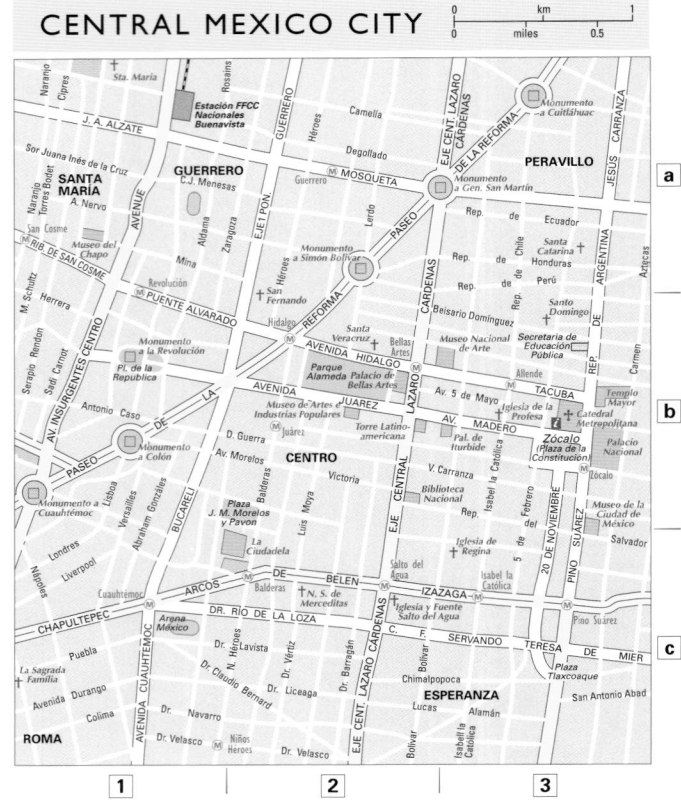

95 Federal route numbers

MELBOURNE

MIAMI

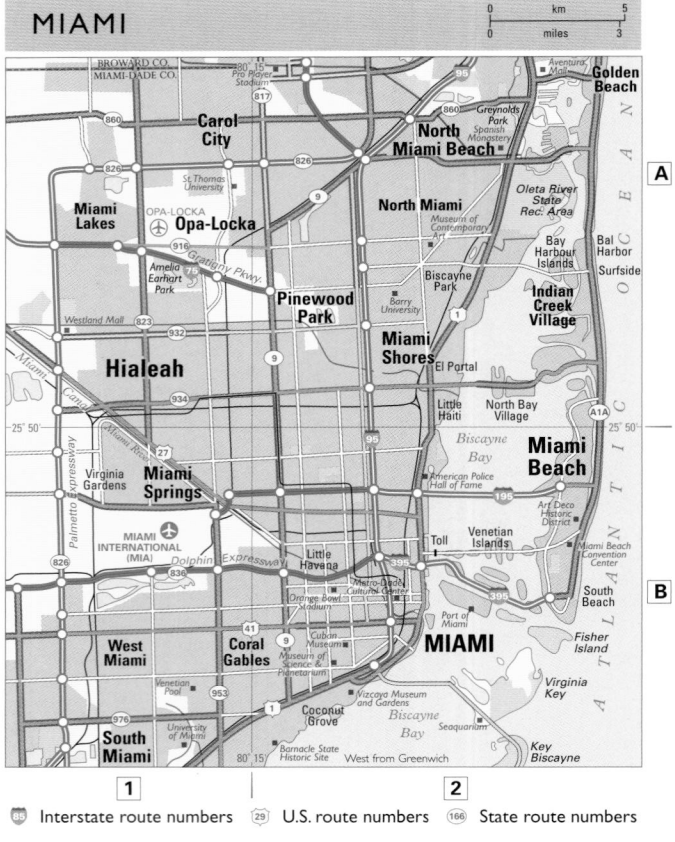

85 Interstate route numbers   29 U.S. route numbers   166 State route numbers

MILAN

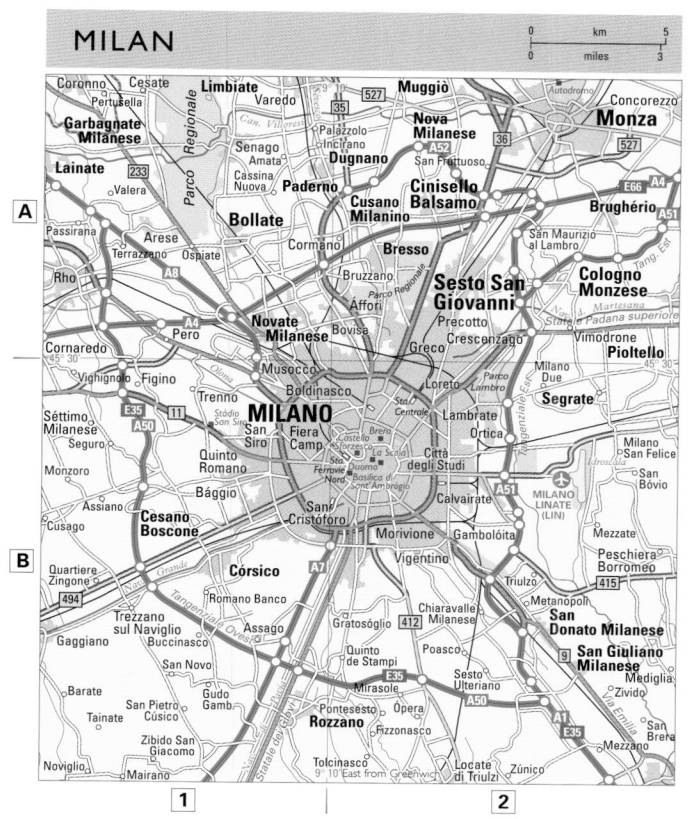

CENTRAL MOSCOW

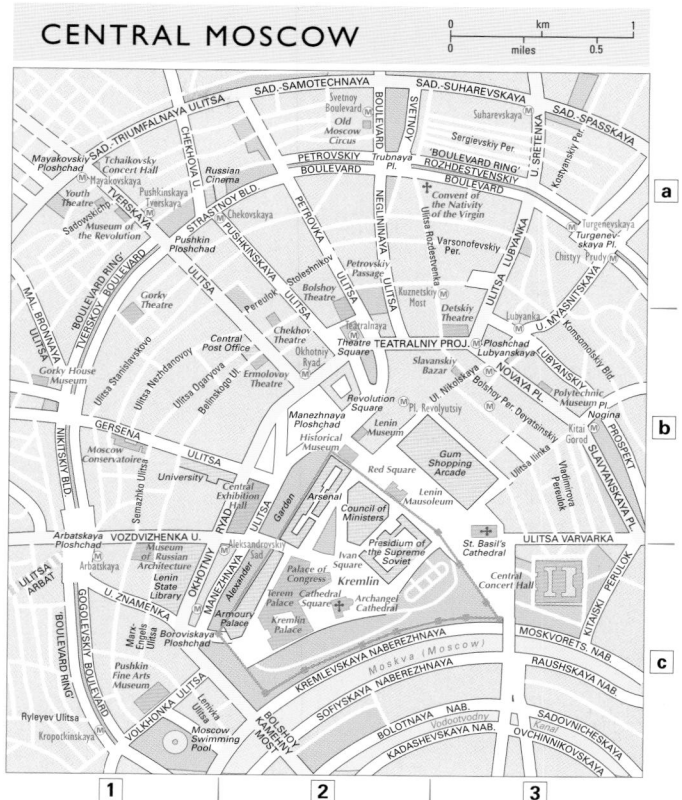

MOSCOW

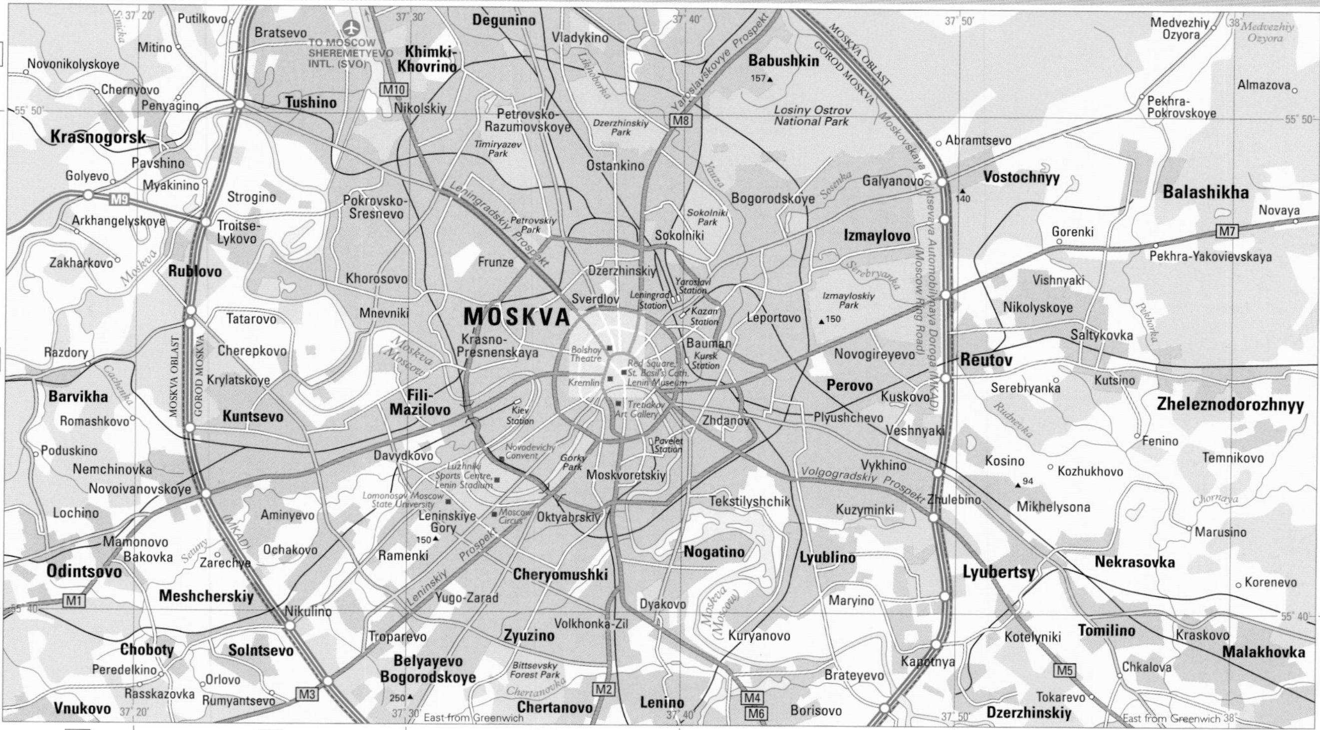

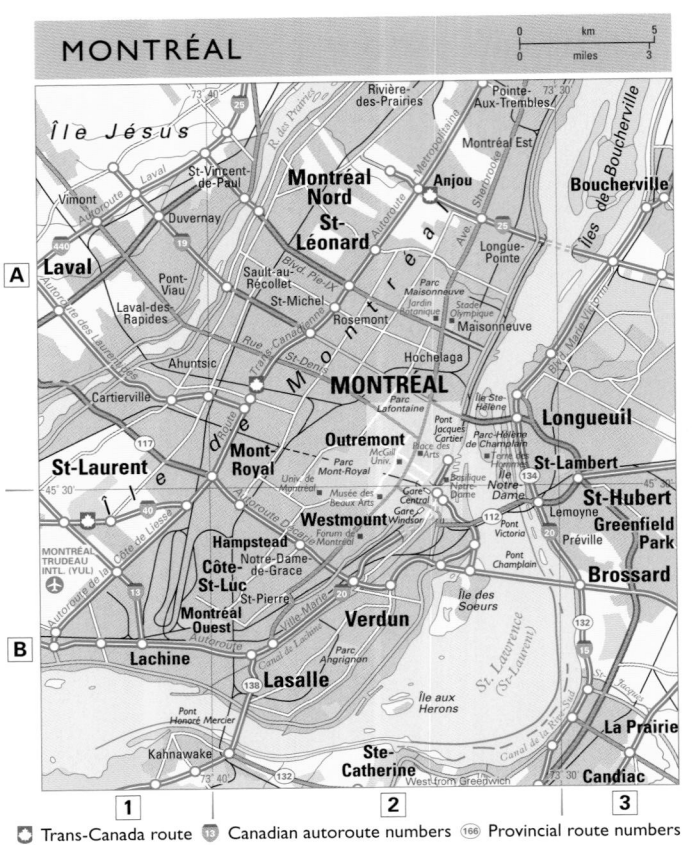

MONTRÉAL

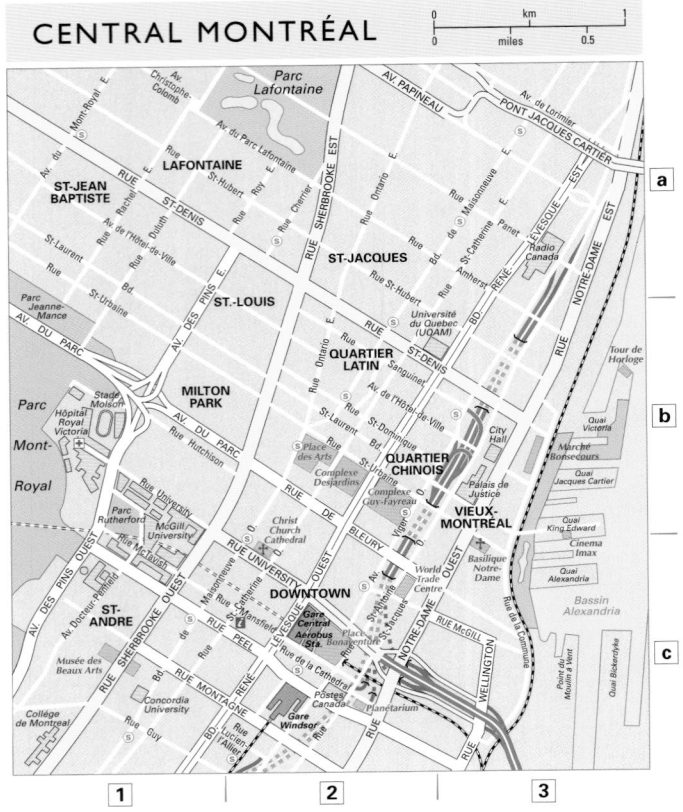

CENTRAL MONTRÉAL

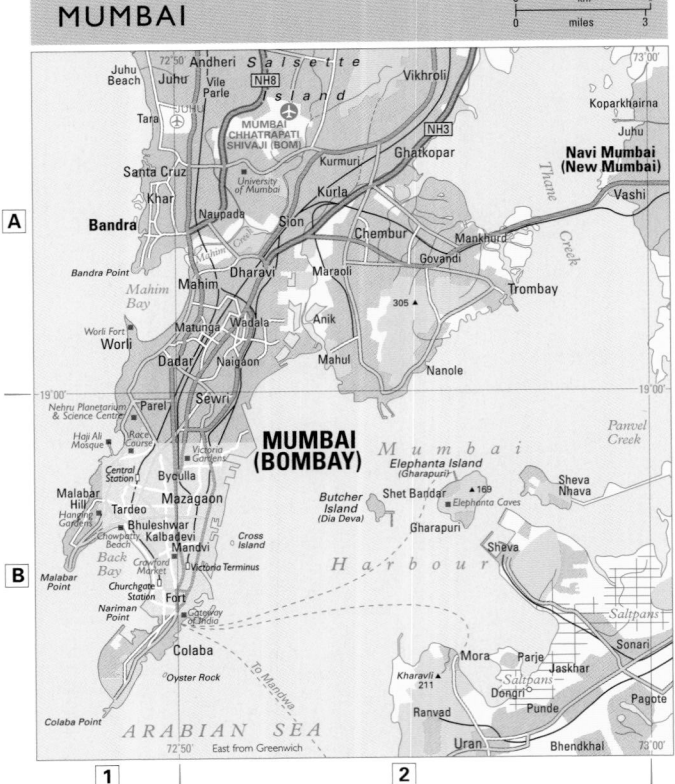

MUMBAI

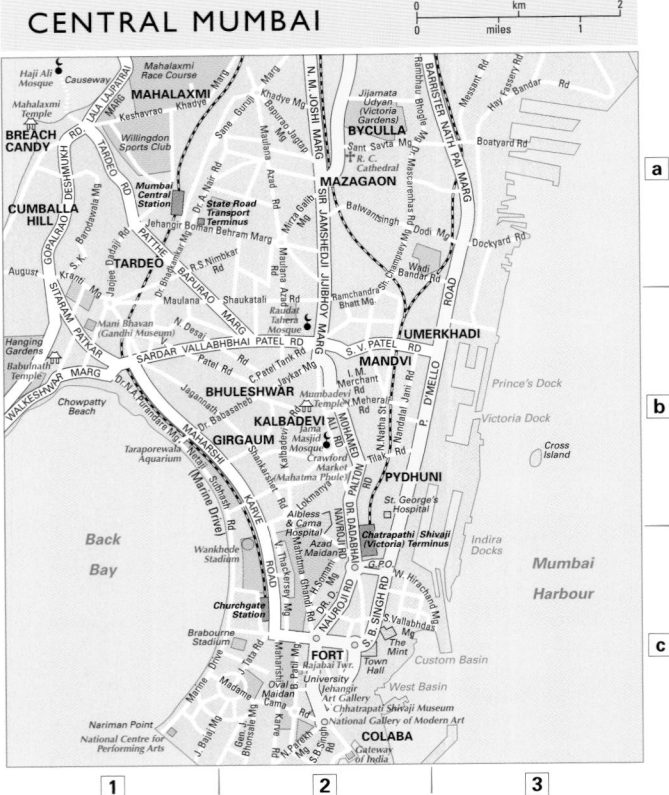

CENTRAL MUMBAI

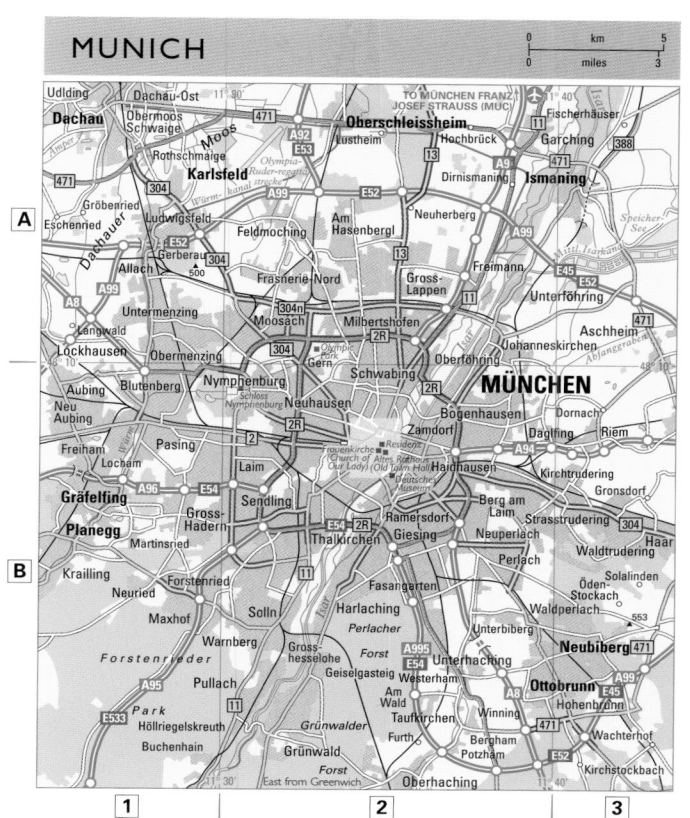

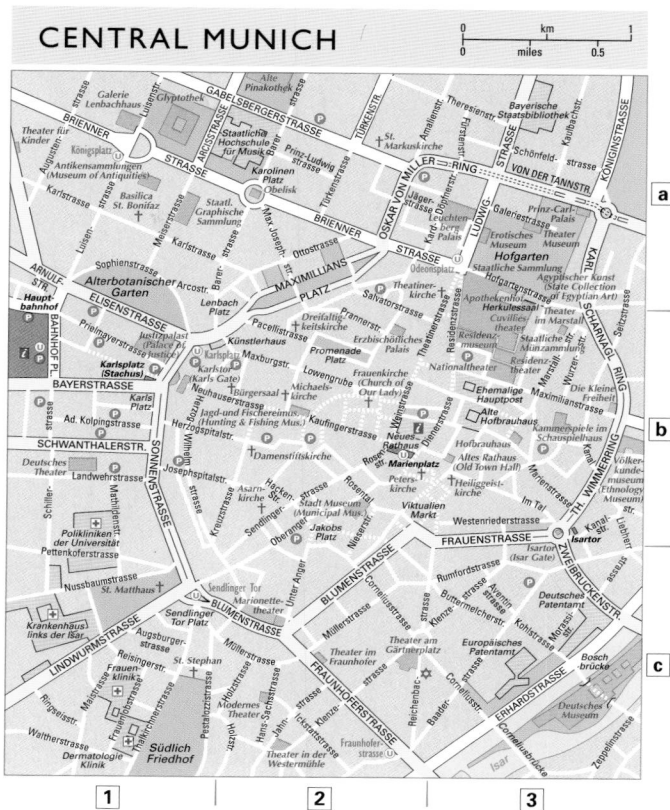

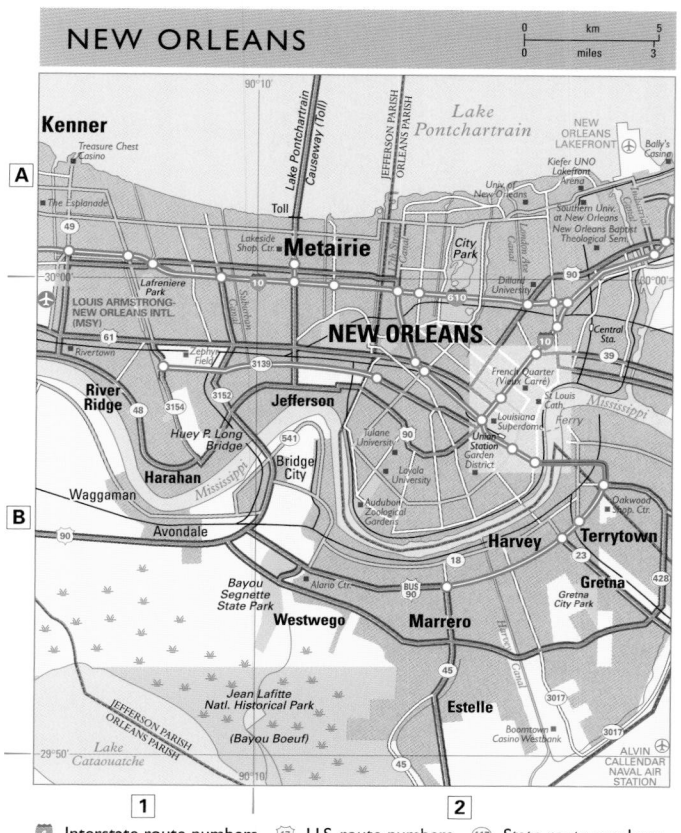

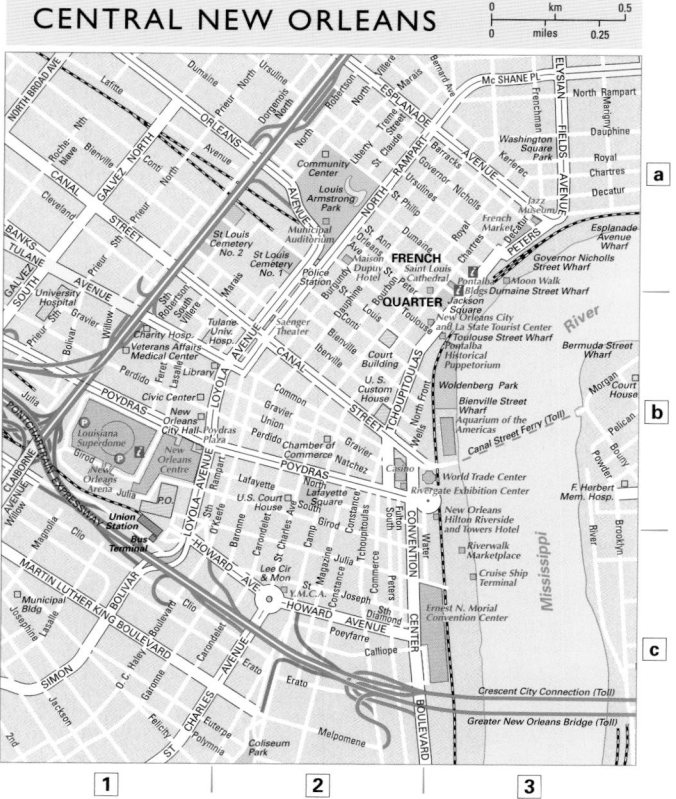

Interstate route numbers   U.S. route numbers   State route numbers

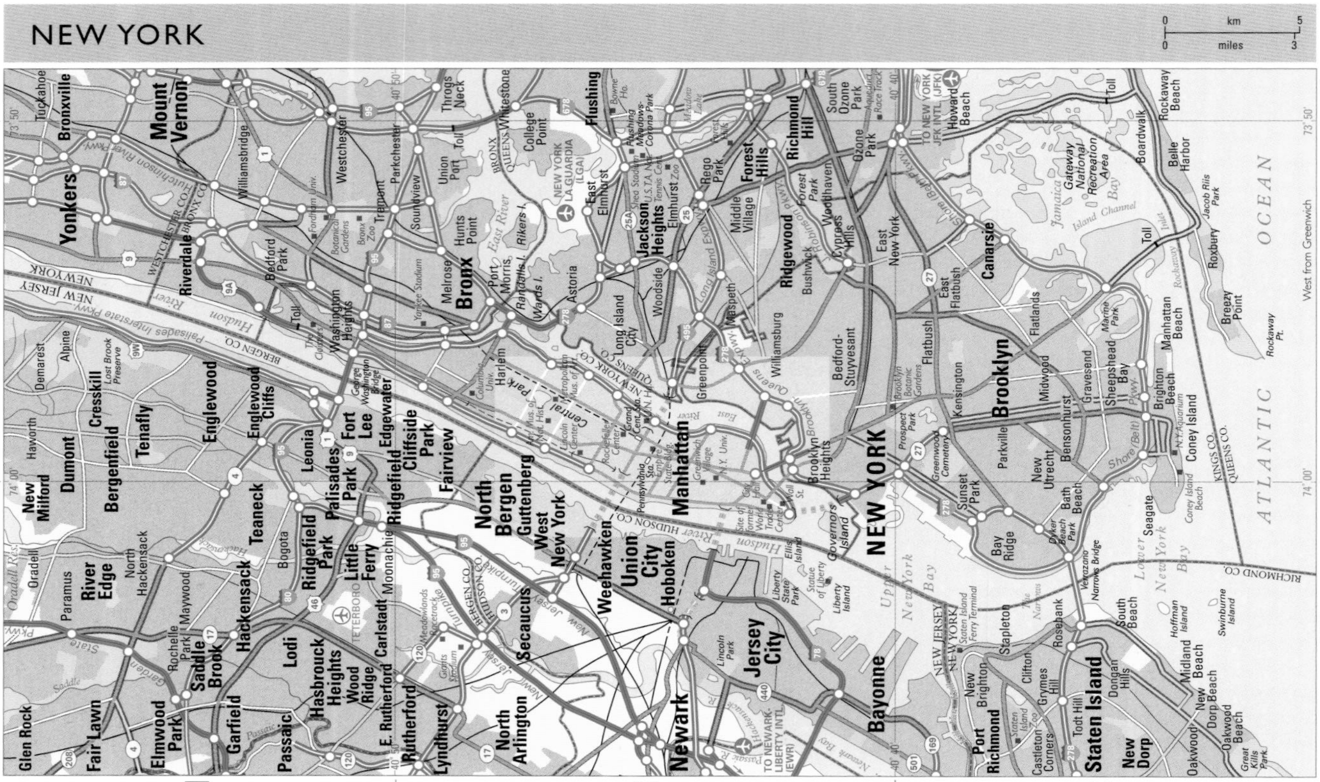

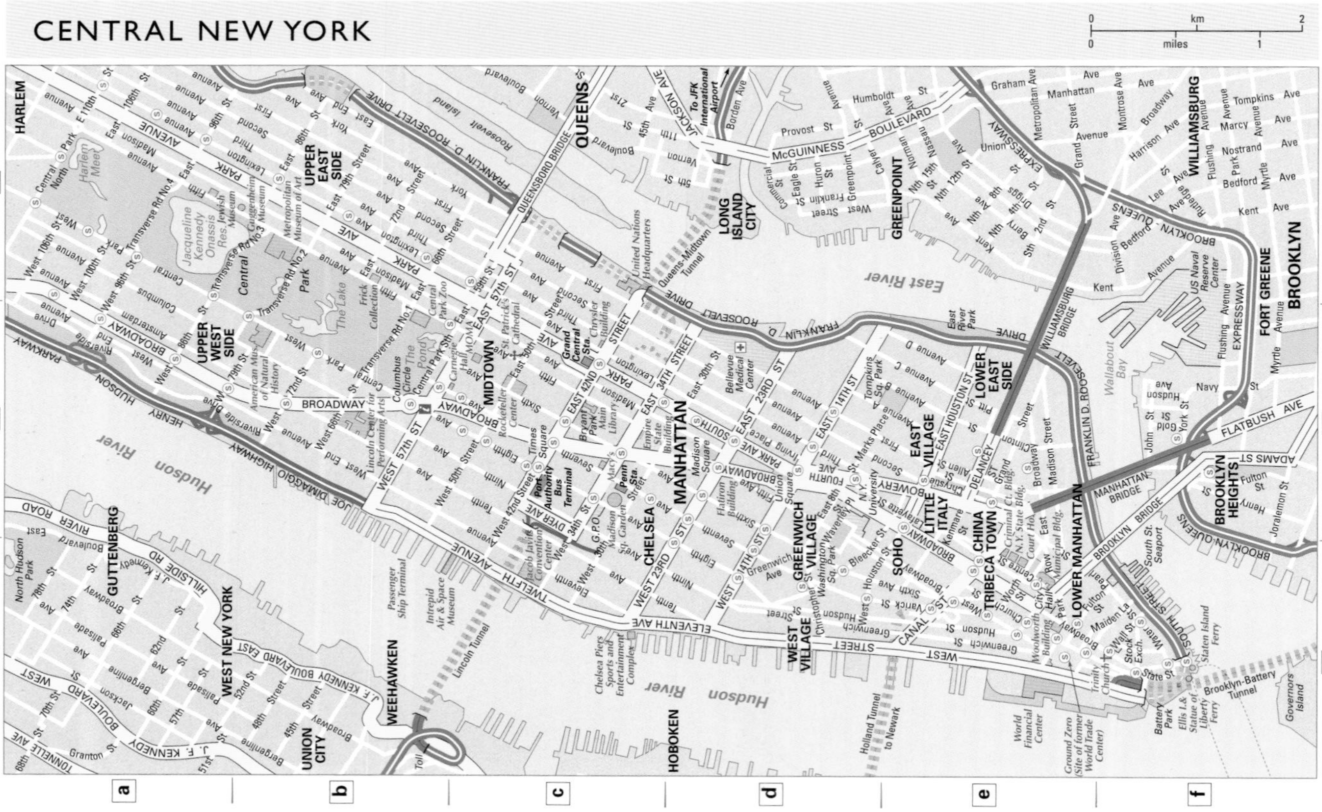

NEW YORK

km 5
miles 3

COPYRIGHT PHILIP'S

Interstate route numbers   U.S. route numbers   State route numbers

Yonkers · Mount Vernon · Bronxville · Tuckahoe · Westchester · Williamsbridge · Throgs Neck · Flushing · College Point · Richmond Hill · Ozone Park · Howard Beach · Rockaway Beach · Belle Harbor · Boardwalk · OCEAN

Riverdale · Bedford Park · Hunts Point · Bronx · Melrose · Astoria · Jackson Heights · Woodside · Elmhurst · Rego Park · Forest Hills · Woodhaven · East New York · Ridgewood · Bushwick · Canarsie · East Flatbush

Englewood · Englewood Cliffs · Tenafly · Cresskill · Demarest · Alpine · Fort Lee · Edgewater · Cliffside Park · Fairview · Washington Heights · Harlem · Central Park · Manhattan · Greenpoint · Williamsburg · Bedford-Stuyvesant · Brooklyn · Flatbush · Kensington · Midwood · Gravesend · Sheepshead Bay · Brighton Beach · Coney Island · Manhattan Beach

New Milford · Dumont · Bergenfield · Teaneck · Haworth · Leonia · Ridgefield · North Bergen · Guttenberg · West New York · Weehawken · Union City · Hoboken · NEW YORK · Sunset Park · Bay Ridge · Bath Beach · Bensonhurst · New Utrecht · ATLANTIC

River Edge · Paramus · Oradell · Maywood · Rochelle Park · Hackensack · Bogota · Little Ferry · Moonachie · Secaucus · Jersey City · Liberty State Park · Ellis Island · Governors Island · Upper New York Bay · Staten Island · South Beach · Midland Beach

Glen Rock · Fair Lawn · Elmwood Park · Garfield · Passaic · Lodi · Hasbrouck Heights · Wood Ridge · E. Rutherford · Carlstadt · Rutherford · Lyndhurst · North Arlington · Newark · Bayonne · Port Richmond · Castleton Corners · Todt Hill · New Dorp · Oakwood · Great Kills Park

CENTRAL NEW YORK

km 2
miles 1

HARLEM · UPPER WEST SIDE · UPPER EAST SIDE · QUEENS · LONG ISLAND CITY · GREENPOINT · WILLIAMSBURG · BROOKLYN · MIDTOWN · MANHATTAN · CHELSEA · GREENWICH VILLAGE · EAST VILLAGE · LITTLE ITALY · SOHO · CHINATOWN · TRIBECA · LOWER EAST SIDE · LOWER MANHATTAN · FORT GREENE · BROOKLYN HEIGHTS · WEST VILLAGE · WEEHAWKEN · UNION CITY · WEST NEW YORK · GUTTENBERG · Hudson River · East River

Central Park · Metropolitan Museum of Art · American Museum of Natural History · Lincoln Center · Times Square · Penn Station · Empire State Building · Grand Central Station · United Nations Headquarters · Chrysler Building · World Trade Center Site · Battery Park · Statue of Liberty

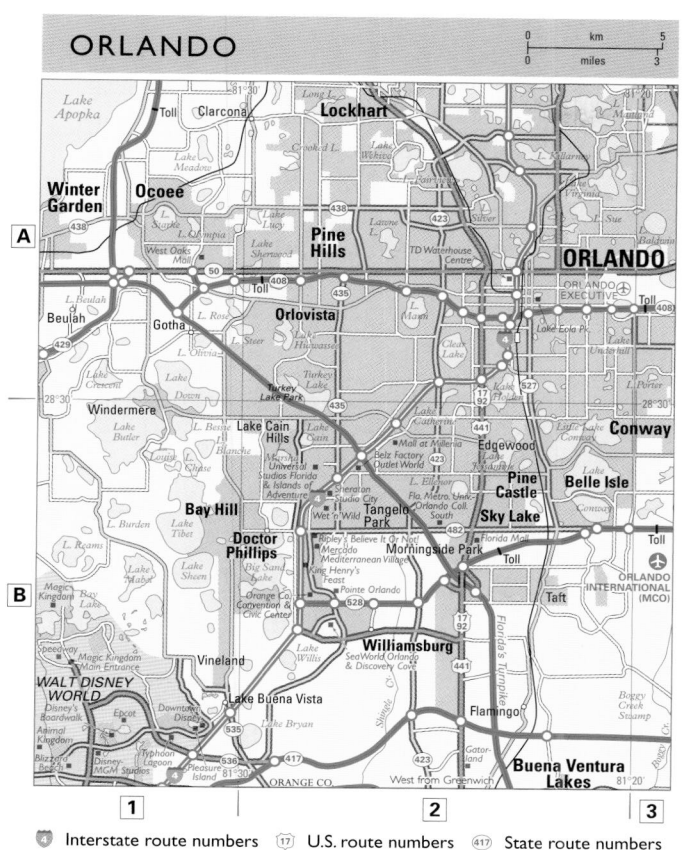

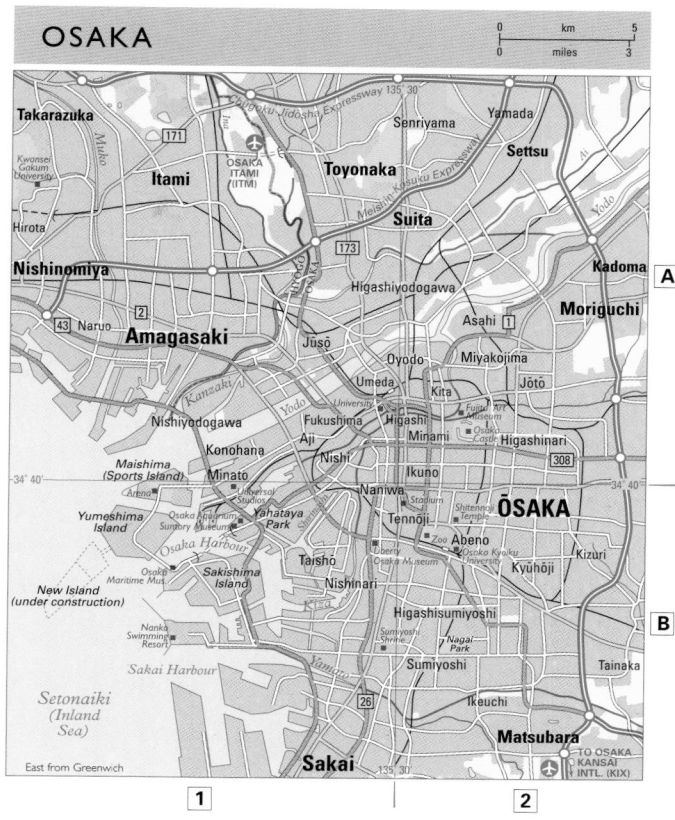

Interstate route numbers   U.S. route numbers   State route numbers

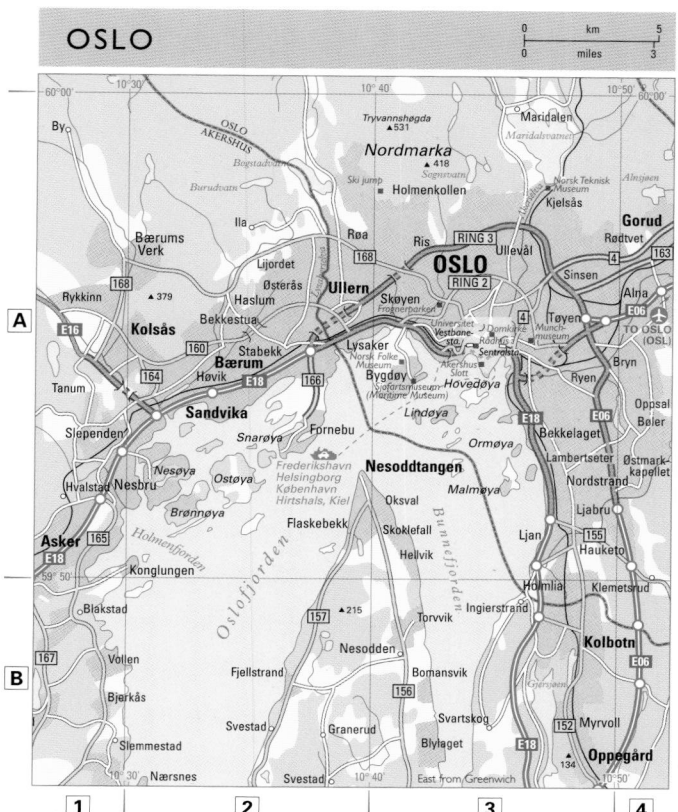

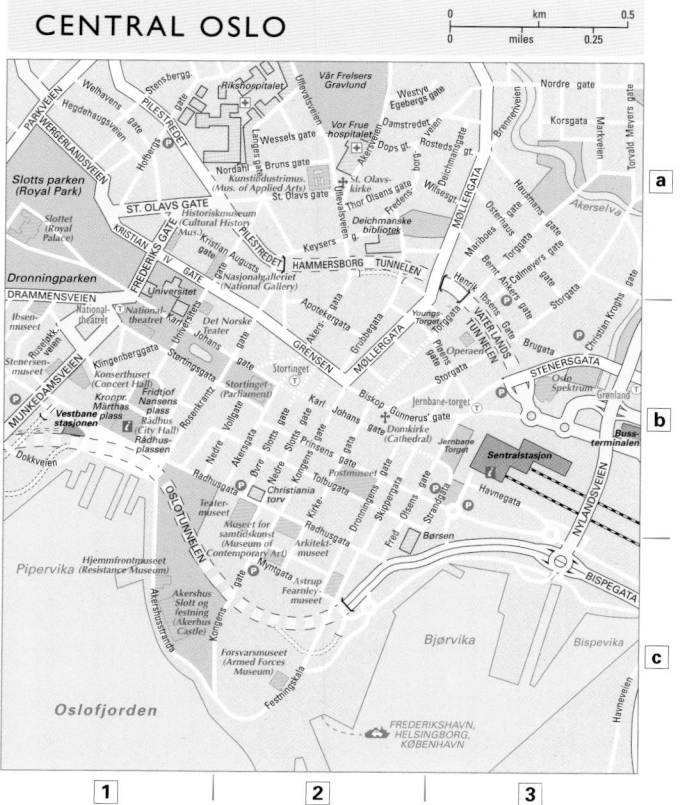

COPYRIGHT PHILIP'S

PARIS

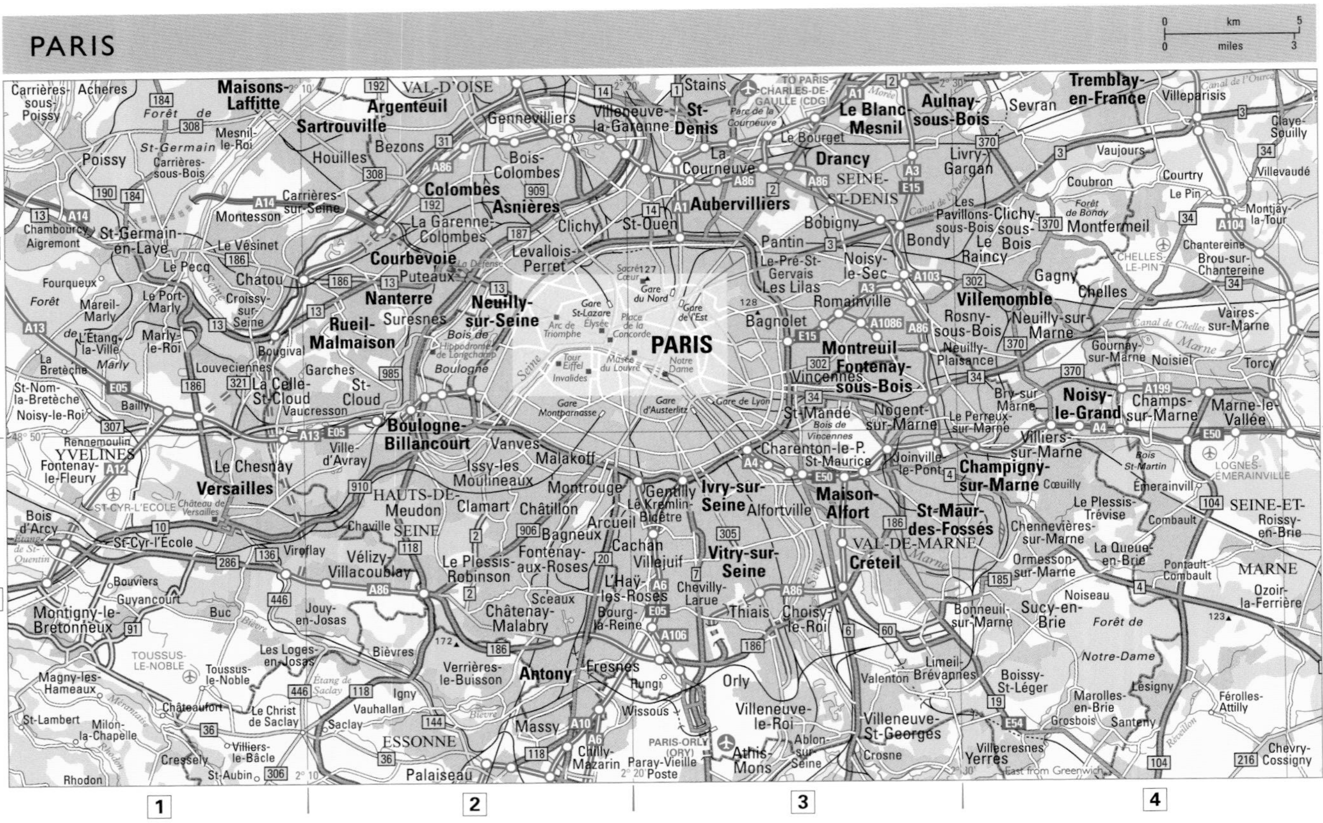

Carrières-sous-Poissy · Achères · **Maisons-Laffitte** · VAL-D'OISE · **Argenteuil** · Gennevilliers · Villeneuve-la-Garenne · **St-Denis** · Stains · TO PARIS CHARLES-DE-GAULLE (CDG) · Sevran · **Tremblay-en-France** · Villeparisis · Claye-Souilly

Poissy · Mesnil-le-Roi · Bezons · Houilles · Bois-Colombes · La Courneuve · Le Bourget · **Le Blanc-Mesnil** · **Drancy** · **Aulnay-sous-Bois** · Livry-Gargan · Vaujours · Coubron · Courtry · Villevaudé · Montjay-la-Tour

St-Germain-sous-Bois · Montesson · Carrières-sur-Seine · **Colombes** · La Garenne-Colombes · **Asnières** · Clichy · **Aubervilliers** · St-Ouen · SEINE-ST-DENIS · Bobigny · Les Pavillons-sous-Bois · Clichy-sous-Bois · Montfermeil · Chanterine · Brou-sur-Chantereine

A St-Germain-en-Laye · Le Vésinet · **Courbevoie** · Puteaux · Levallois-Perret · Pantin · Le Pré-St-Gervais · Les Lilas · Noisy-le-Sec · Bondy · Le Bois-Raincy · Gagny · Chelles **A**

Fourqueux · Le Pecq · Chatou · Croissy-sur-Seine · **Nanterre** · Suresnes · **Neuilly-sur-Seine** · **PARIS** · Bagnolet · Romainville · **Villemomble** · Rosny-sous-Bois · Neuilly-sur-Marne · Gournay-sur-Marne · Noisiel · Vaires-sur-Marne · Torcy

Mareil-Marly · L'Étang-la-Ville · Marly-le-Roi · Louveciennes · Bougival · **Rueil-Malmaison** · Garches · St-Cloud · Boulogne · **Montreuil** · **Fontenay-sous-Bois** · Vincennes · Bry-sur-Marne · Le Perreux-sur-Marne · **Noisy-le-Grand** · Champs-sur-Marne · Marne-la-Vallée

St-Nom-la-Bretèche · Noisy-le-Roi · La Celle-St-Cloud · Vaucresson · Sèvres · Vanves · St-Mandé · Nogent-sur-Marne · Villiers-sur-Marne · **Champigny-sur-Marne** · Chennevières-sur-Marne · Émerainville · SEINE-ET-MARNE

YVELINES · Fontenay-le-Fleury · **Versailles** · Le Chesnay · Ville-d'Avray · **Boulogne-Billancourt** · Malakoff · Montrouge · Gentilly · **Ivry-sur-Seine** · Charenton-le-P. · St-Maurice · Joinville-le-Pont · **Maisons-Alfort** · Le Plessis-Trévise · La Queue-en-Brie · Combault · MARNE

HAUTS-DE-SEINE · Meudon · Clamart · Châtillon · Issy-les-Moulineaux · Le Kremlin-Bicêtre · Alfortville · **St-Maur-des-Fossés** · Ormesson-sur-Marne · Roissy-en-Brie

B St-Cyr-l'École · Viroflay · SEINE · Chaville · Bagneux · Arcueil · Cachan · Villejuif · **Créteil** · VAL-DE-MARNE · Bonneuil-sur-Marne · Sucy-en-Brie · Noiseau · Ozoir-la-Ferrière **B**

Bois d'Arcy · Guyancourt · Buc · Jouy-en-Josas · Le Plessis-Robinson · Sceaux · Fontenay-aux-Roses · Châtenay-Malabry · Bourg-la-Reine · L'Haÿ-les-Roses · Chevilly-Larue · Thiais · Choisy-le-Roi · Forêt de Notre-Dame

Montigny-le-Bretonneux · Bièvres · Verrières-le-Buisson · **Antony** · Fresnes · Rungis · Orly · Valenton · Brévannes · Limeil · Boissy-St-Léger

Magny-les-Hameaux · Toussus-le-Noble · Les Loges-en-Josas · Igny · Vauhallan · Saclay · Massy · Wissous · Villeneuve-le-Roi · Crosne · Yerres · Villecresnes · Marolles-en-Brie · Grosbois · Santeny · Férolles-Attilly

St-Lambert · Châteaufort · Le Christ de Saclay · ESSONNE · PARIS-ORLY (ORY) · Paray-Vieille-Poste · Athis-Mons · Ablon-sur-Seine · Boissy-St-Léger · Chevry-Cossigny

Rhodon · St-Aubin · Palaiseau · Choisy-Mazarin · East from Greenwich

1 · **2** · **3** · **4**

CENTRAL PARIS

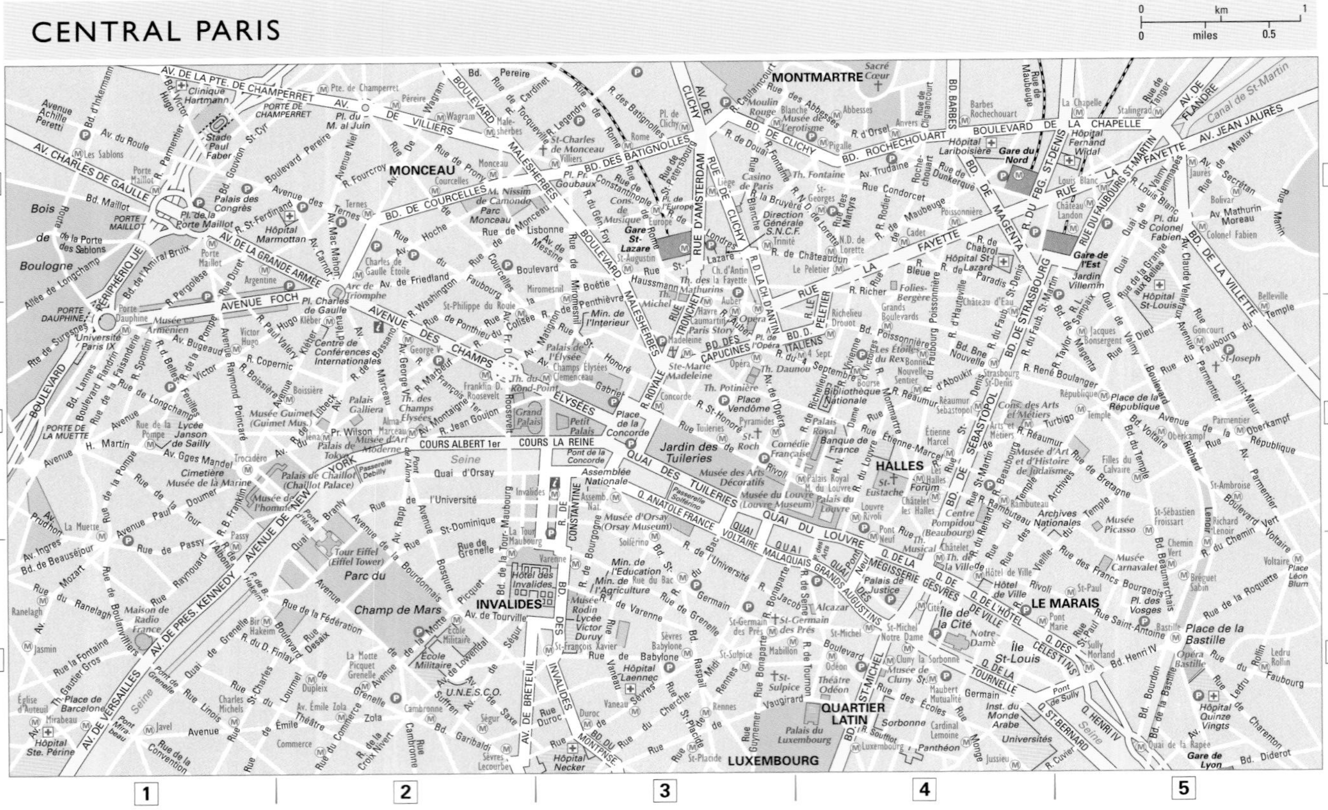

MONTMARTRE · Sacré Cœur · PORTE DE CHAMPERRET · Clinique Hartmann · Stade Paul Faber · BD. DE LA CHAPELLE · Canal St-Martin

a AV. CHARLES DE GAULLE · Bois de Boulogne · PORTE MAILLOT · **MONCEAU** · Parc Monceau · Gare St-Lazare · Gare du Nord · Gare de l'Est **a**

PORTE DAUPHINE · Arc de Triomphe · AVENUE FOCH · Pl. Charles de Gaulle Étoile · AVENUE DES CHAMPS-ÉLYSÉES · LA FAYETTE · Jardin Villemin · Hôpital St-Louis

b PORTE DE LA MUETTE · Palais de Chaillot (Chaillot Palace) · Musée Guimet · Grand Palais · Petit Palais · Place de la Concorde · Jardin des Tuileries · Comédie Française · **HALLES** · Musée Picasso · Place de la République **b**

Tour Eiffel (Eiffel Tower) · Parc du Champ de Mars · **INVALIDES** · Musée d'Orsay (Orsay Museum) · Musée du Louvre (Louvre Museum) · Centre Pompidou · Hôtel de Ville · **LE MARAIS** · Place des Vosges

c Maison de Radio France · École Militaire · U.N.E.S.C.O. · Hôtel des Invalides · Île de la Cité · Notre-Dame · Île St-Louis · Place de la Bastille **c**

Hôpital Ste-Périne · **QUARTIER LATIN** · Palais du Luxembourg · **LUXEMBOURG** · Panthéon · Sorbonne · Gare de Lyon

1 · **2** · **3** · **4** · **5**

PRAGUE

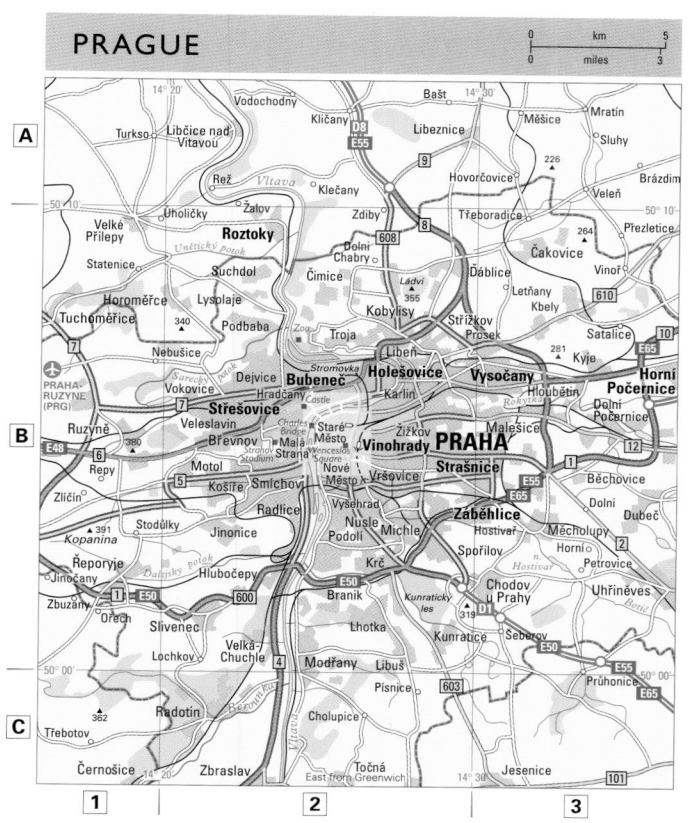

CENTRAL PRAGUE

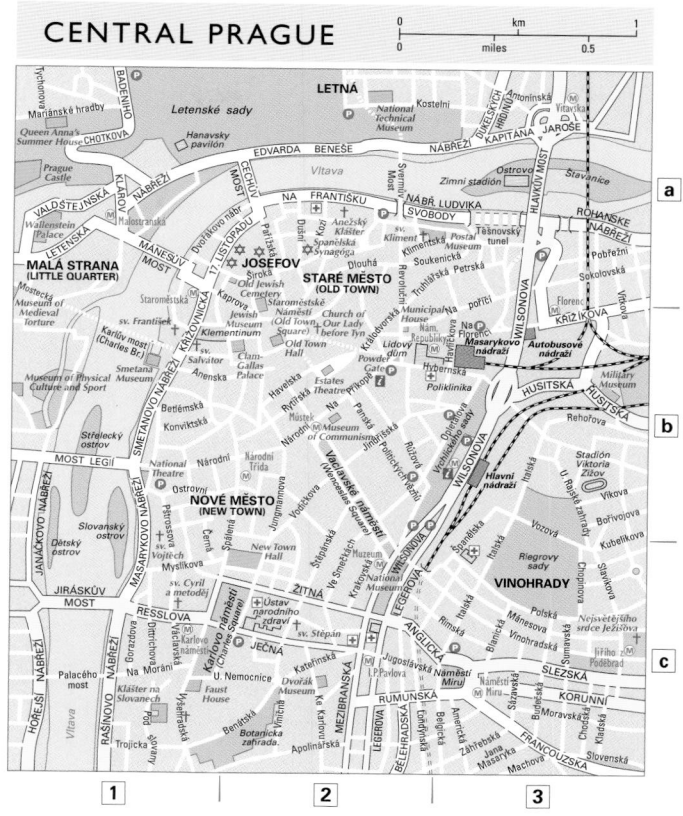

RIO DE JANEIRO

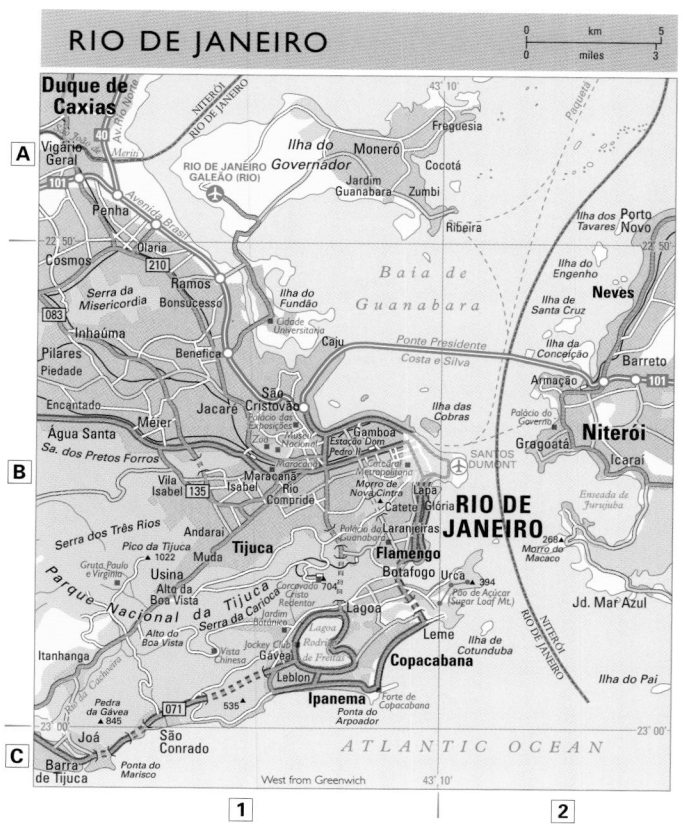

CENTRAL RIO DE JANEIRO

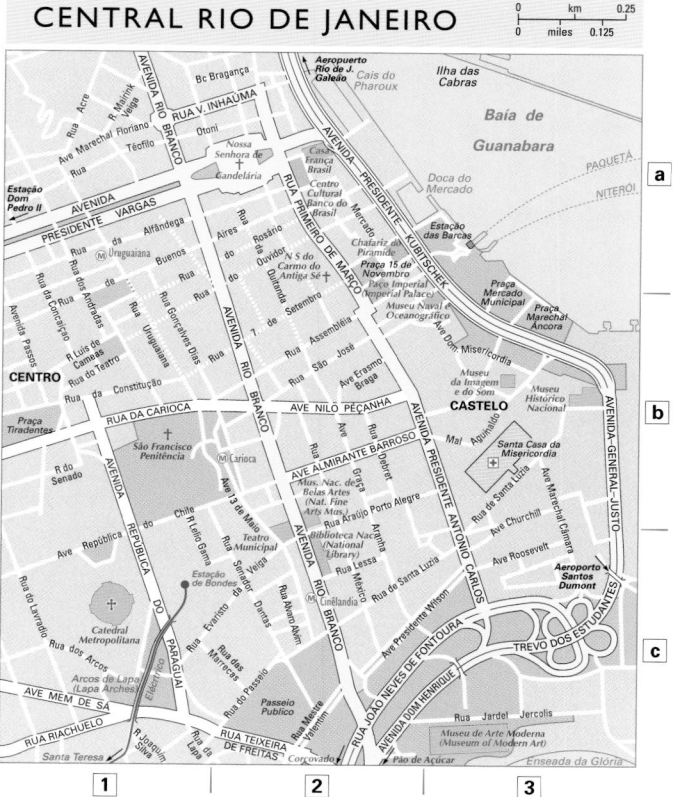

ROME

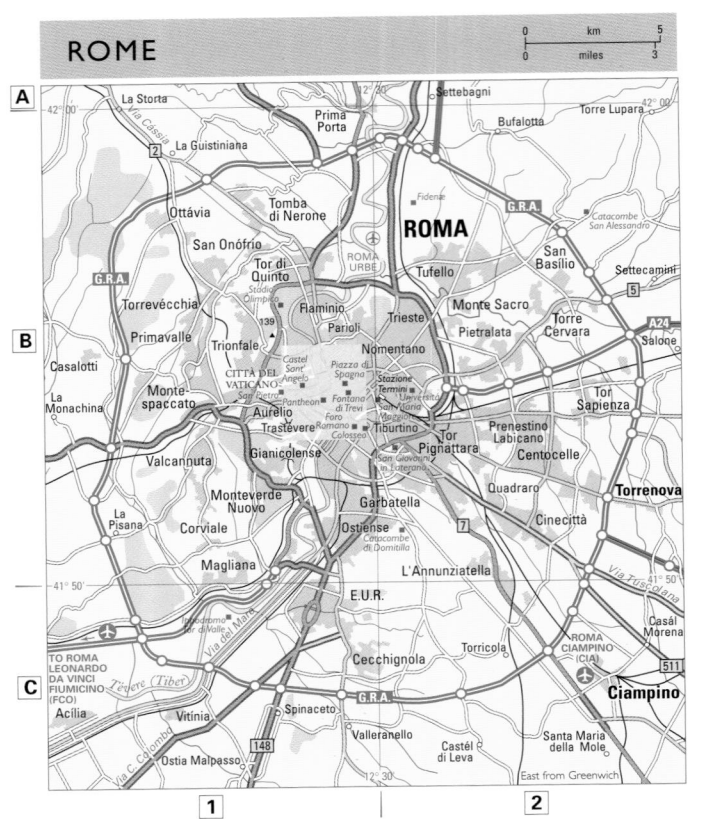

CENTRAL ROME

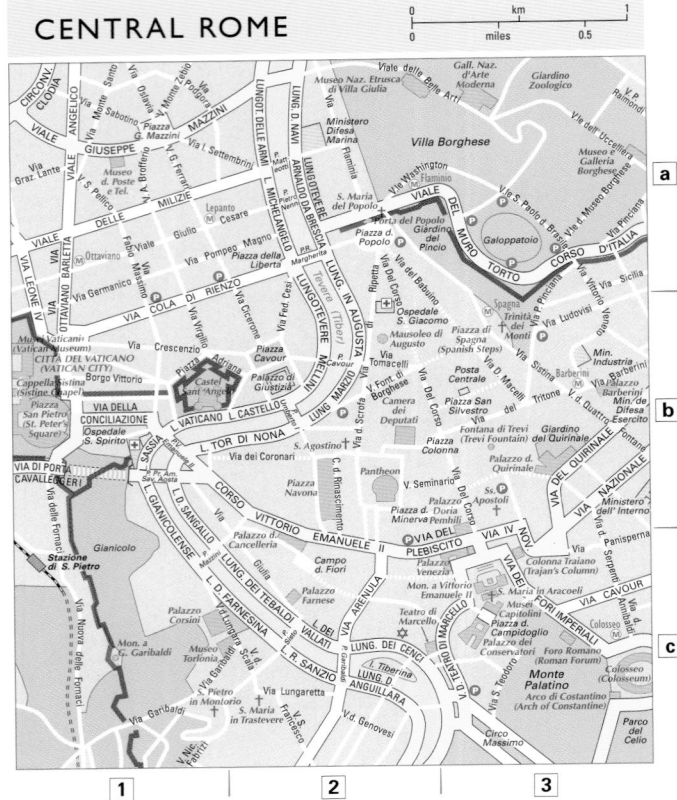

SAN FRANCISCO

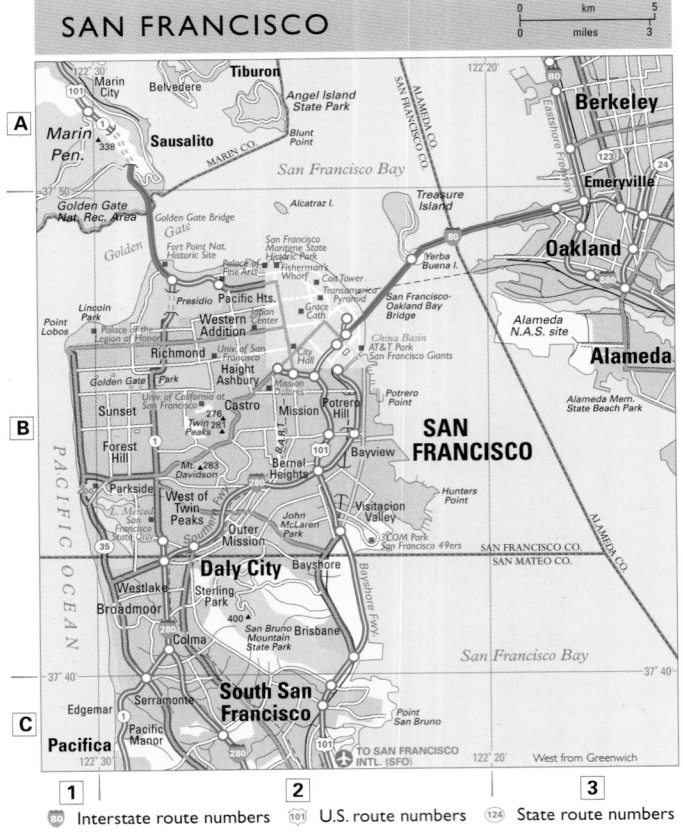

CENTRAL SAN FRANCISCO

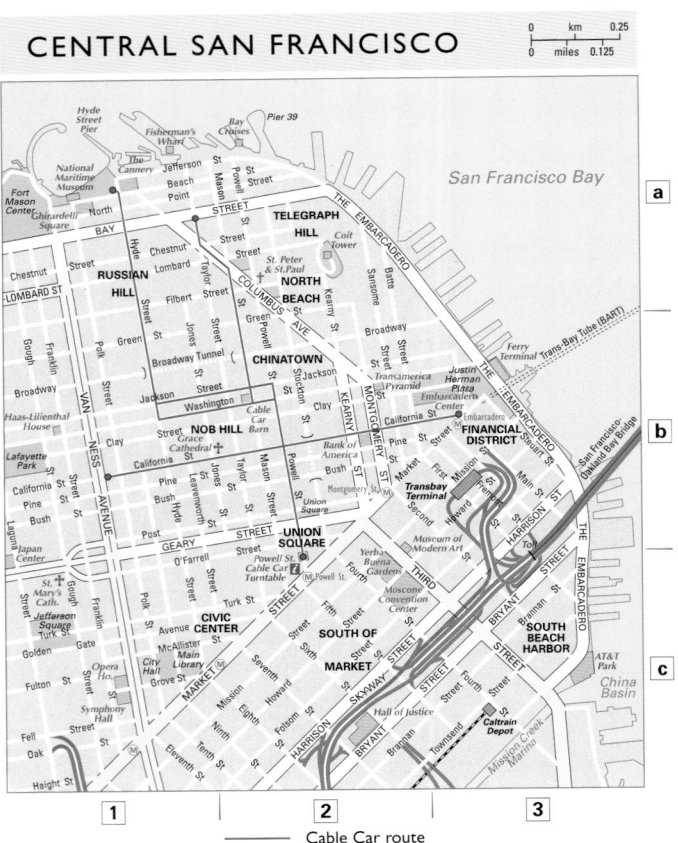

🛣 Interstate route numbers   🛡 U.S. route numbers   ⬡ State route numbers

— Cable Car route

ST PETERSBURG

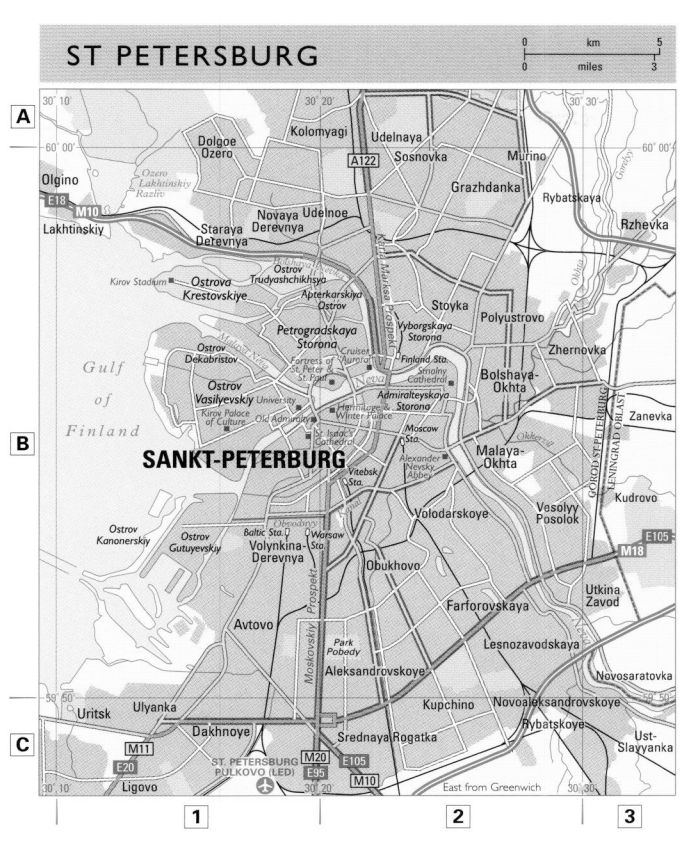

SANTIAGO

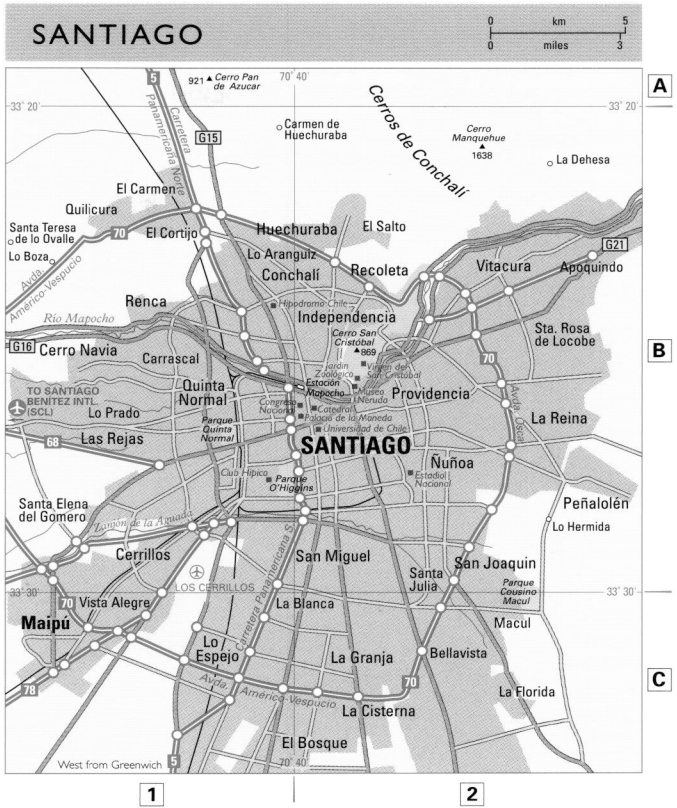

SÃO PAULO

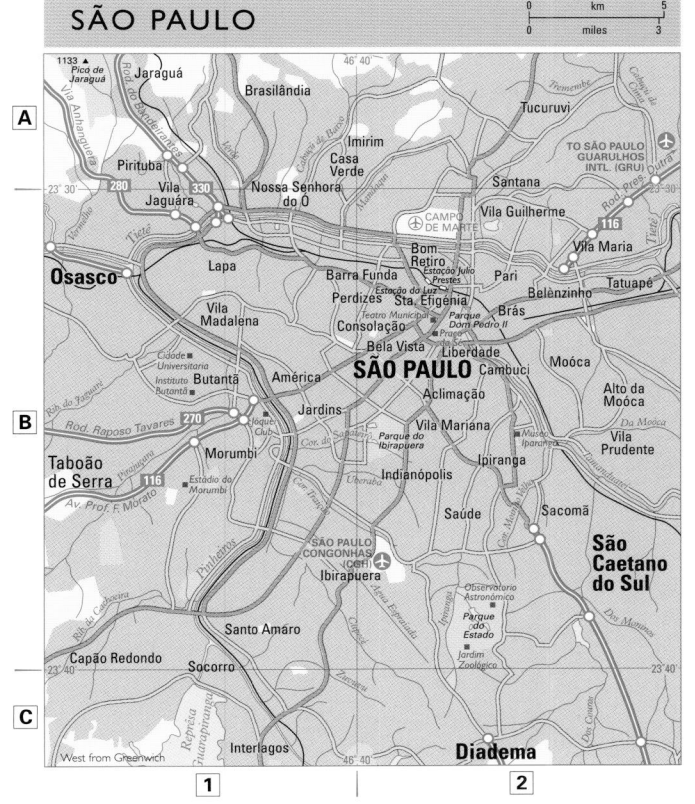

SEOUL

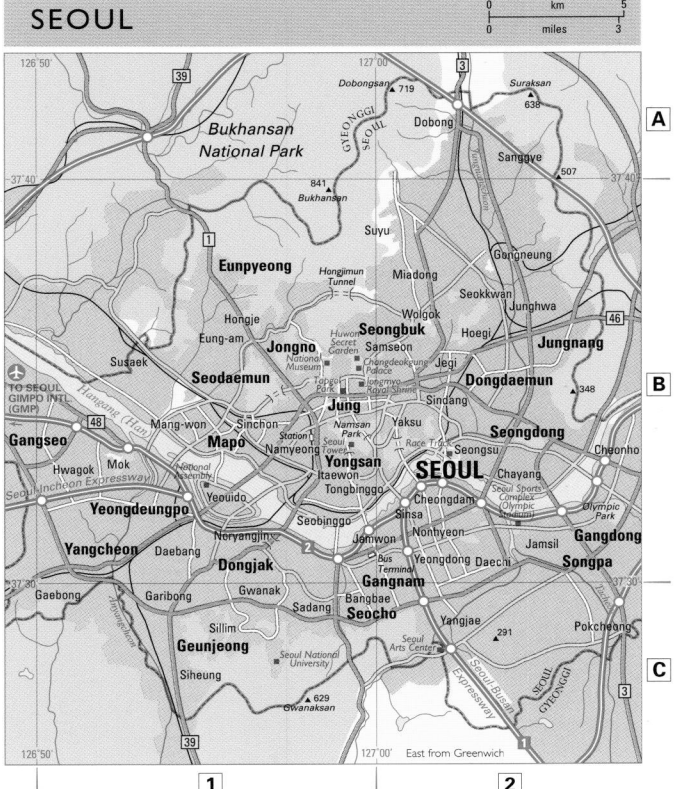

SHANGHAI

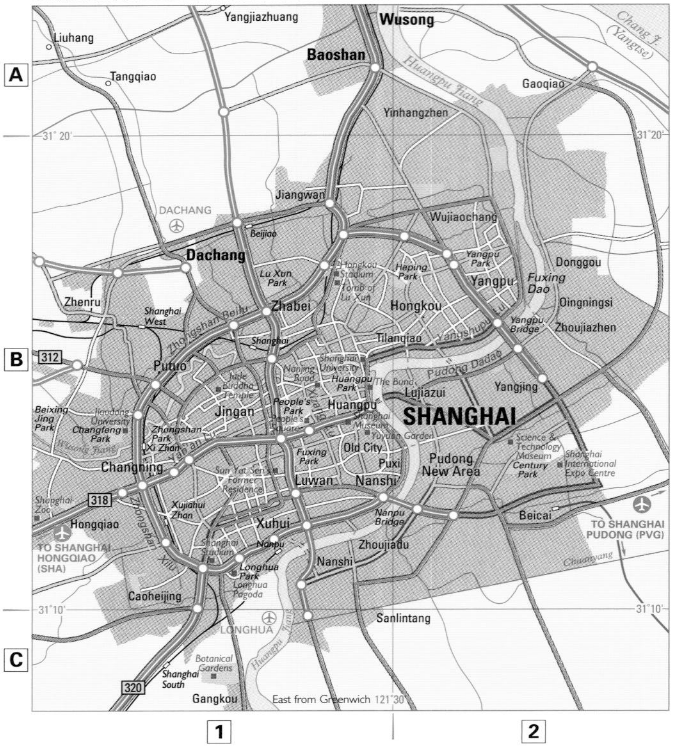

km 5
miles 3

A

Liuhang
Tanggiao
Yangjiazhuang
Wusong
Baoshan
Gaoqiao
Yinhangzhen

31°20'

Jiangwan
Wujiaochang
Dachang
DACHANG
Beijiao
Donggou

31°20'

Zhenru
Lu Xun Park
Tomb of Lu Xun
Heping Park
Yangpu
Fuxing Dao
Qingningsi
Zhabei
Hongkou
Yangpu Bridge
Zhoujiazhen

B

Putuo
312
Shanghai West
Zhongshan Belt
Shanghai
Nanjing University
The Bund
Pudong Dadao
Yangjing

Beixing Jing Park
Changfeng Park
Jingan
Jade Buddha Temple
People's Park
Huangpu
SHANGHAI
Lujiazui

Changning
Zhongshan Park
Xi Zhan
Sun Yat-Sen's Former Residence
Fuxing Park
Puxi
Old City
Pudong New Area
Science & Technology Museum
Century Park
Shanghai International Expo Centre

318
Hongqiao
TO SHANGHAI HONGQIAO (SHA)
Xujiahui
Xujiahui Zhan
Luwan
Nanshi
Nanpu Bridge
Beicai

Shanghai Zoo
Shanghai Stadium
Longhua Park
Longhua Pagoda
Longhua
Xuhui
Nanshi
Zhoujiadu
TO SHANGHAI PUDONG (PVG)

C

Caoheijing
LONGHUA
Sanlintang

31°10'
31°10'

Botanical Gardens
Shanghai South
320
Gangkou
East from Greenwich 121°30'

1   2

— Magnetic Levitation (Maglev) Railway

CENTRAL SINGAPORE

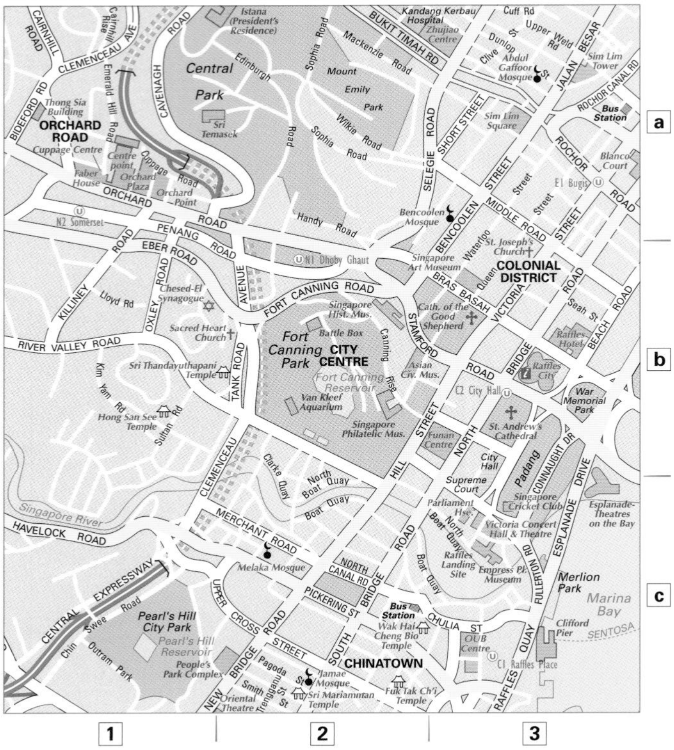

km 1
miles 0.5

CARNHILL ROAD
Istana (President's Residence)
Central Park
CLEMENCEAU AVE
CAVENAGH ROAD
Edinburgh
BUKIT TIMAH RD
Kandang Kerbau
Dhoby Ghaut
Upper Weld
Cuff Rd

a

Thong Sia Building
ORCHARD ROAD
Cuppage Centre
Centre point, Orchard Plaza
Orchard Point
Emerald Hill
Sri Temasek
Mount Emily Park
Sophia Road
White Park
Sim Lim Square
Sophia Road
Selegie Road
Short Street
Rochor
E1 Bugis
Sim Lim Tower
Jalan Besar
Blanco Court
Rochor Canal Rd
Bus Station

N2 Somerset
PENANG ROAD
EBER ROAD
Chesed-El Synagogue
Killiney
Lloyd Rd
OXLEY
Sacred Heart Church
FORT CANNING ROAD
Bencoolen Mosque
Bencoolen
Singapore Art Museum
BRAS BASAH
St Joseph's Church
VICTORIA
Seah St
COLONIAL DISTRICT
Cath. of the Good Shepherd
Raffles Hotel
BEACH

b

RIVER VALLEY ROAD
Sri Thandayuthapani Temple
Kim
TANK ROAD
Fort Canning Park
Fort Canning Reservoir
CITY CENTRE
Singapore Hist. Mus.
Asian Civ. Mus.
STAMFORD
CANNING
HILL
Funan Centre
NORTH BRIDGE ROAD
Raffles City
C2 City Hall
St. Andrew's Cathedral
War Memorial Park

Hong San See Temple
Sultan Rd
Van Kleef Aquarium
Singapore Philatelic Mus.
Supreme Court
Parliament Hse
City Hall
PADANG
Singapore Cricket Club
Esplanade–Theatres on the Bay

c

CLEMENCEAU
Clarke Quay
Boat Quay
MERCHANT ROAD
Boat Quay
Singapore River
HAVELOCK ROAD
Melaka Mosque
Raffles Landing Site
Empress Pl Museum
FULLERTON RD
Victoria Concert Hall & Theatre
ESPLANADE DRIVE
Merlion Park
Marina Bay

CENTRAL EXPRESSWAY
Pearl's Hill City Park
Pearl's Hill Reservoir
People's Park Complex
NEW BRIDGE
UPPER CROSS
NORTH CANAL ROAD
SOUTH
PICKERING ST
CHULIA ST
Wak Hai Cheng Bio Temple
OUB Centre
Clifford Pier
Raffles Place
SENTOSA

Chin Swee Rd
Chin
Outram Park
CHINATOWN
Smith St
Pagoda St
Jamae Mosque
Sri Mariamman Temple
Fuk Tak Ch'i Temple
RAFFLES QUAY
New Oriental Theatre
Bus Station

1   2   3

SINGAPORE

km 5
miles 3

103°40'E
103°50'E
104°00'E

Malaya
Sungei Buloh Nature Park
Johor Bahru
Senoko Ind. Est.
Sembawang
Selat Johor

A

Sarimbun Res.
Lim Chu Kang
Kranji Ind. Est.
Woodlands
Chong Pang
Yishun
Pulau Seletar
Punggol Point
Pulau Ubin
Pulau Tekong Kechil
Pulau Tekong
Tg. Ladang

MALAYSIA
SINGAPORE

Sarimbun
85
Ama Keng
Sungai Kadut Ind. Est.
Singapore Turf Club
Seletar Expy.
Zoological Gardens
Seletar Reservoir
Nee Soon
Seletar Golf Course
Jalan Kayu
Punggol
Pulau Serangoon
Pulau Ketam
Serangoon Harbour
Changi
Loyang Ind. Est.
SINGAPORE CHANGI (SIN)
Reclaimed Land

Munai Res.
Choa Chu Kang
Choa Chu Kang
Bukit Panjang
132
Bukit Timah Nature Reserve
162
Central Catchment Nature Reserve
Upper Peirce Res.
Pan Island Expy.
Ang Mo Kio
Yio Chu Kang
Hougang
Serangoon
Chia Keng
Pasir Ris Park
Pasir Ris
Yan Kit
Changi Prison Museum

Tengah Res.
Choa Chu Kang 88
Nanyang University
Raffles Golf Course & Country Club
Jurong West
Boon Lay
Chinese & Japanese Gardens
Jurong East
Air View Park
Bukit Batok Nature Park
Raffles Park
MacRitchie Reservoir
Bishan
Toa Payoh
Paya Lebar
Tai Seng
Bedok Reservoir
Tampines
Simei
Singapore Expo
Tanah Merah Golf Course

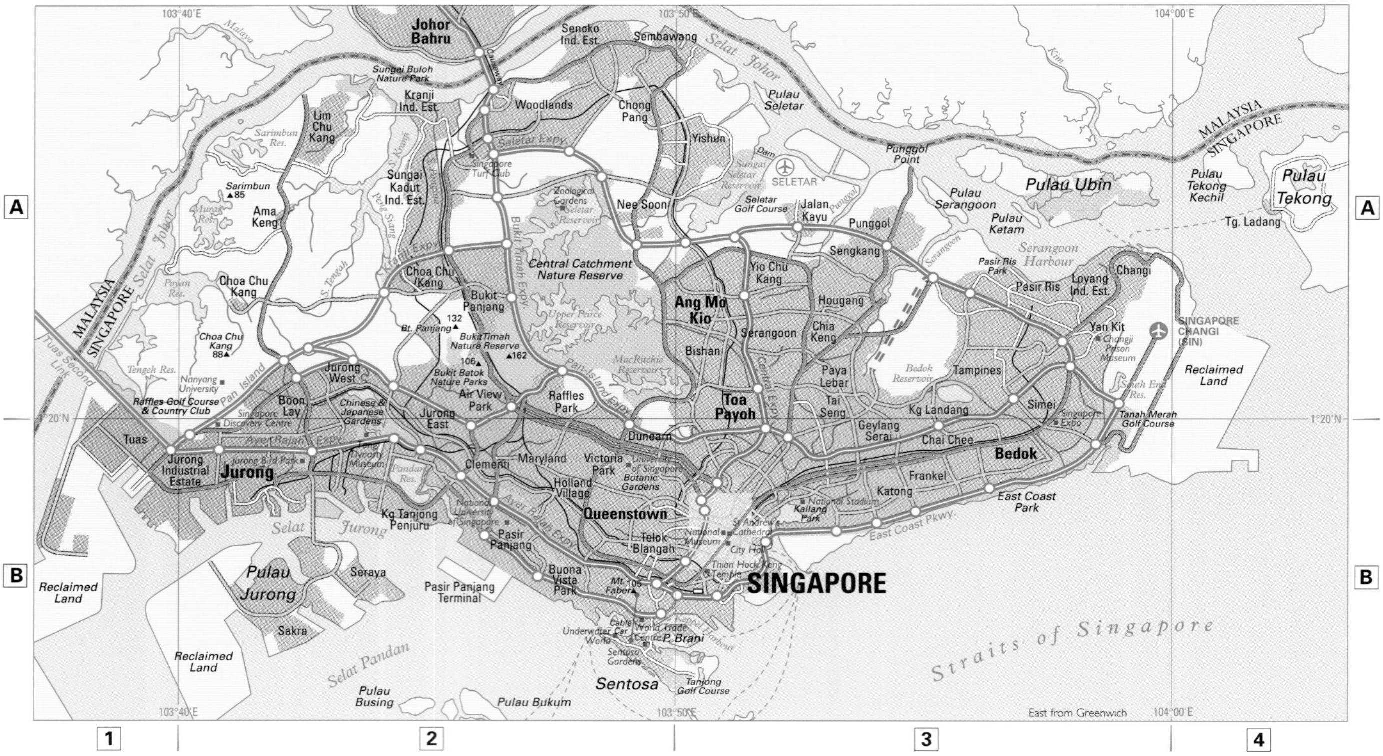

1°20'N
1°20'N

Reclaimed Land
Tuas
Jurong Bird Park
Jurong Industrial Estate
JURONG
Ayer Rajah Expy.
Singapore Discovery Centre
Pan Island Expy.
Jurong
Science Centre
Clementi
Pandan Res.
Maryland
National University of Singapore
Holland Village
Victoria Park
Botanic Gardens
Dunearn
Queenstown
National Museum
City Hall
St Andrew's Cathedral
Geylang Serai
Chai Chee
Katong
Kallang Stadium
Bedok
Frankel
East Coast Park

B

Pulau Jurong
Seraya
Sakra
Pasir Panjang
Kg Tanjong Penjuru
Pasir Panjang Terminal
Buona Vista Park
Mt 105 Faber
World Trade Centre
Telok Blangah
Thian Hock Keng Temple
SINGAPORE
East Coast Pkwy.

Reclaimed Land
Selat
Jurong
Selat Pandan
Pulau Busing
Pulau Bukum
Cable Car
Underwater World
P. Brani
Sentosa
Sentosa Gardens
Tanjong Golf Course
Straits of Singapore

East from Greenwich
104°00'E

1   2   3   4

STOCKHOLM

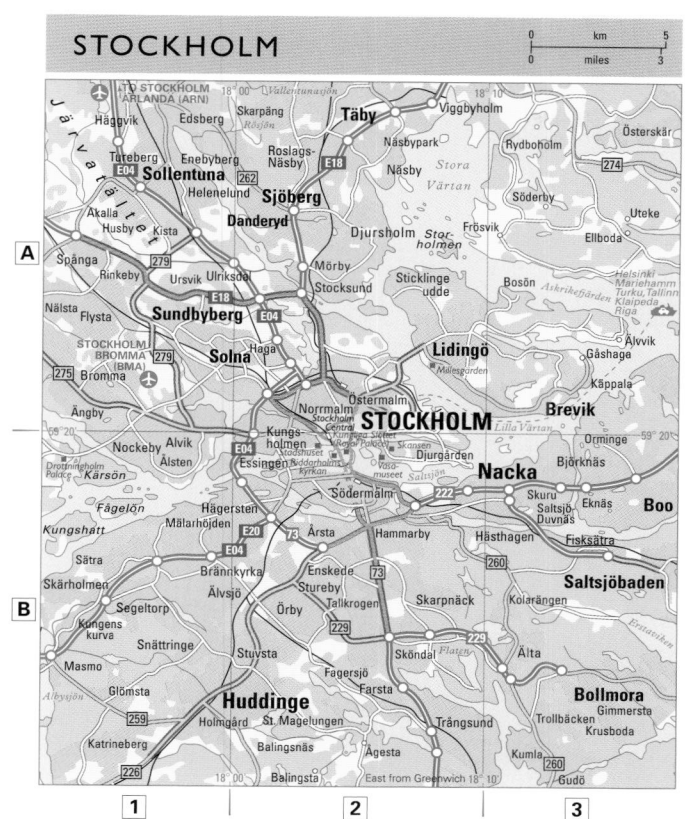

CENTRAL STOCKHOLM

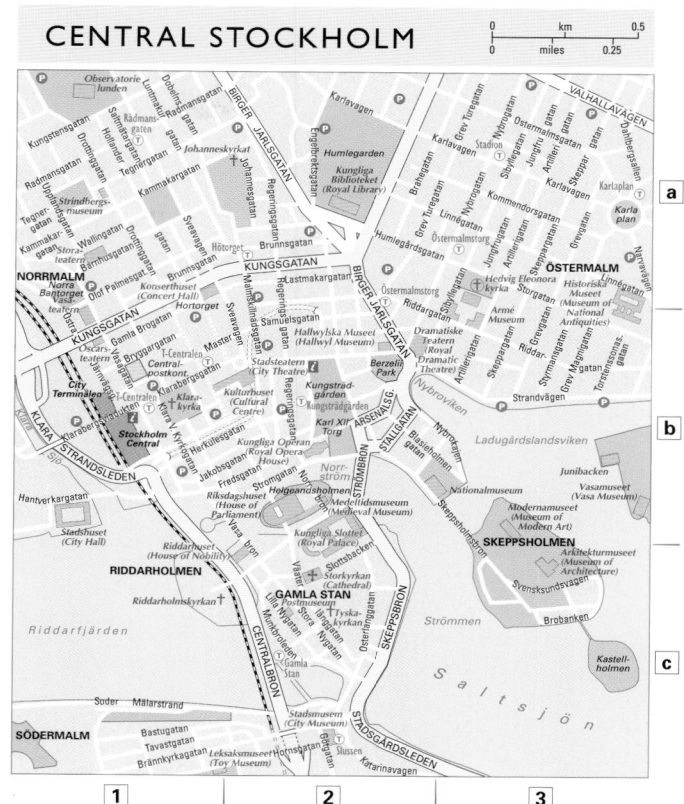

SYDNEY

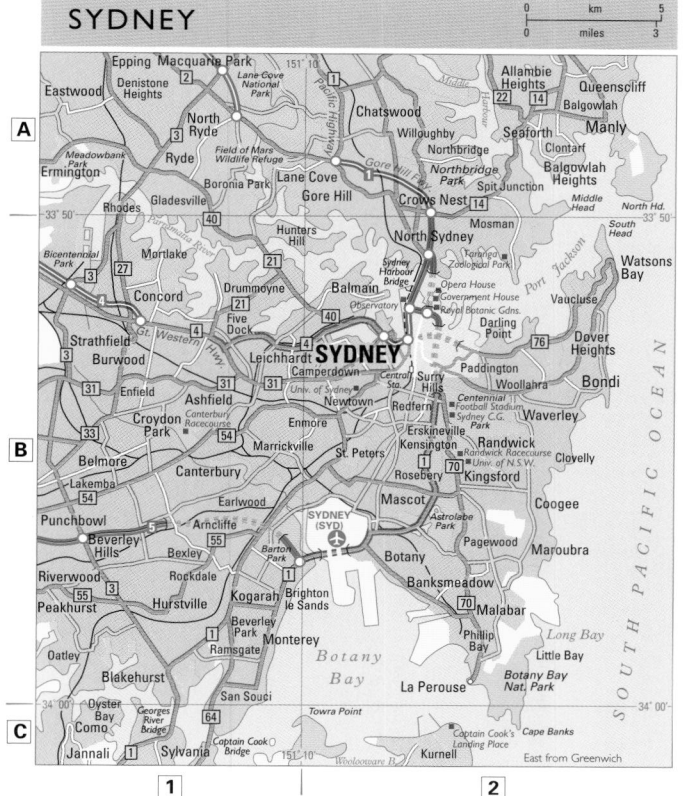

CENTRAL SYDNEY

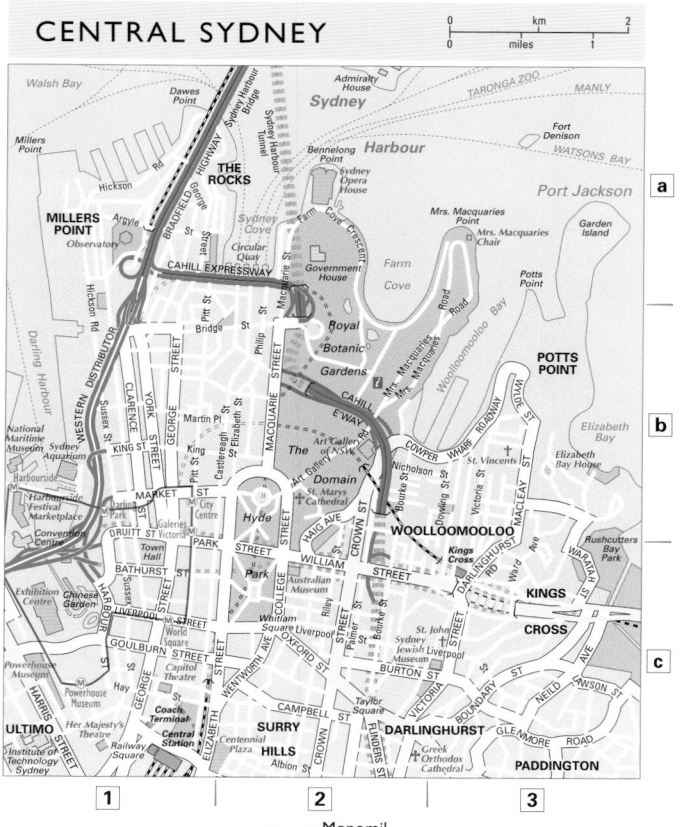

—— Monorail

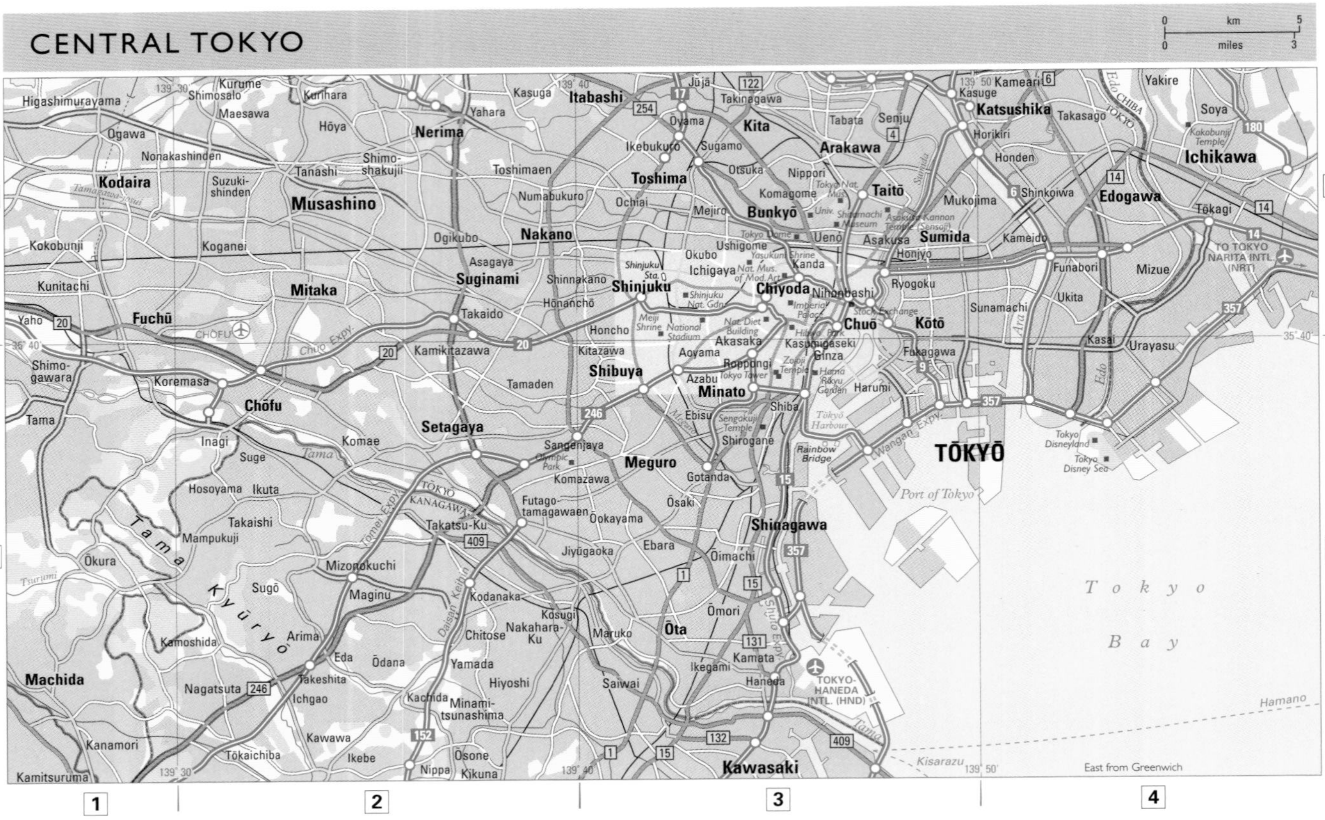

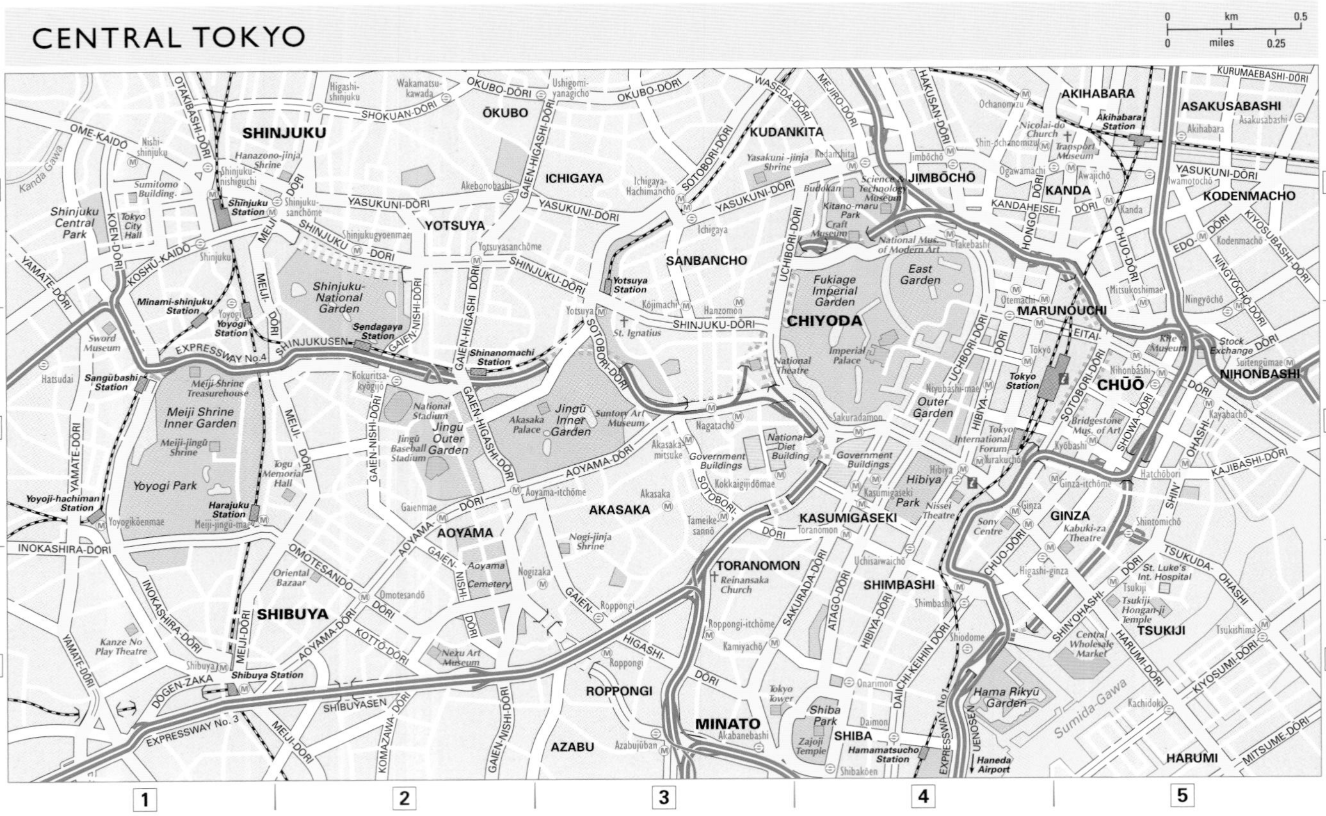

CENTRAL TOKYO

km 0 5
miles 0 3

Higashimurayama · Kurume · Kurihara · Kasuga · Itabashi · Takinegawa · Jūjō · Kameari · Yakire
Shimosato · Maesawa · Yahara · Ōyama · Kita · Tabata · Senju · Kasuge · Soya
Ogawa · Nonakashinden · Kuriha · Nerima · 254 · 122 · Sugamo · Arakawa · Horikiri · Honden · Katsushika · Takasago · Kokubunji Temple · Ichikawa
Kodaira · Suzuki-shinden · Shimo-shakuji · Toshimaen · Toshima · Otsuka · Nippori · Honjo · Shinkoiwa · Edogawa · 14
Musashino · Tanashi · Numabukuro · Ochiai · Mejiro · Komagome · Taitō · Mukojima · Sumida · Kameido · 14 · Tōkagi
Kokubunji · Koganei · Ogikubo · Asagaya · Shinnakano · Shinjuku · Bunkyō · Ueno · Asakusa · Honjo · 357
Mitaka · Koremasa · Kamikitazawa · Honchō · Chiyoda · Nihonbashi · Ryogoku · Kōtō · Sunamachi · Mizue
Fuchū · Takaido · 20 · Kitazawa · Akasaka · Kasumigaseki · Ginza · Fukagawa · Kasai · Urayasu
Shimo-gawara · Yaho · 20 · Tamaden · Shibuya · Aoyama · Roppongi · Harumi · 35 40
Tama · Chōfu · Komae · Setagaya · Sangenjaya · Meguro · Minato · Ebisu · Shibaura · 357 · TŌKYŌ · Tokyo Disneyland · Tokyo Disney Sea
Inagi · Suge · Komazawa · Shirogane · Rainbow Bridge · Port of Tokyo
Hosoyama · Ikuta · Futago-tamagawaen · Takatsu-Ku · Ōokayama · Gotanda · 15 · Shinagawa
Takaishi · Mizonokuchi · Maginu · Kodanaka · Ebara · Ōimachi · 357
Ōkura · Sugō · Arima · Chitose · Nakahara-Ku · Kosugi · Maruko · Ōmori · 1 · 15
Machida · Eda · Ōdana · Yamada · Hiyoshi · Saiwai · Ōta · 131 · Ikegami · Haneda · TOKYO-HANEDA INTL. (HND)
Kanamori · Nagatsuta · 246 · Takeshita · Ichigao · Kawawa · Minami-tsunashima · 132 · 15 · Kamata · 409
Kamitsuruma · Tōkaichiba · Nippa · Ōsone · Kikuna · Kawasaki · Kisarazu · 139 50 · East from Greenwich

Tokyo Bay · Hamano

CENTRAL TOKYO

km 0 0.5
miles 0 0.25

(Detailed inset map with labels including: SHINJUKU, ŌKUBO, AKIHABARA, ASAKUSABASHI, KUDANKITA, ICHIGAYA, JIMBŌCHŌ, KANDA, KODENMACHO, YOTSUYA, SANBANCHO, MARUNŌUCHI, CHIYODA, CHŪŌ, NIHONBASHI, Imperial Palace, AKASAKA, AOYAMA, KASUMIGASEKI, HIBIYA, GINZA, TSUKIJI, SHIBUYA, TORANOMON, SHIMBASHI, ROPPONGI, MINATO, AZABU, SHIBA, HARUMI)

⊖ Toei Subway   Ⓜ Tokyo Metro

TEHRAN

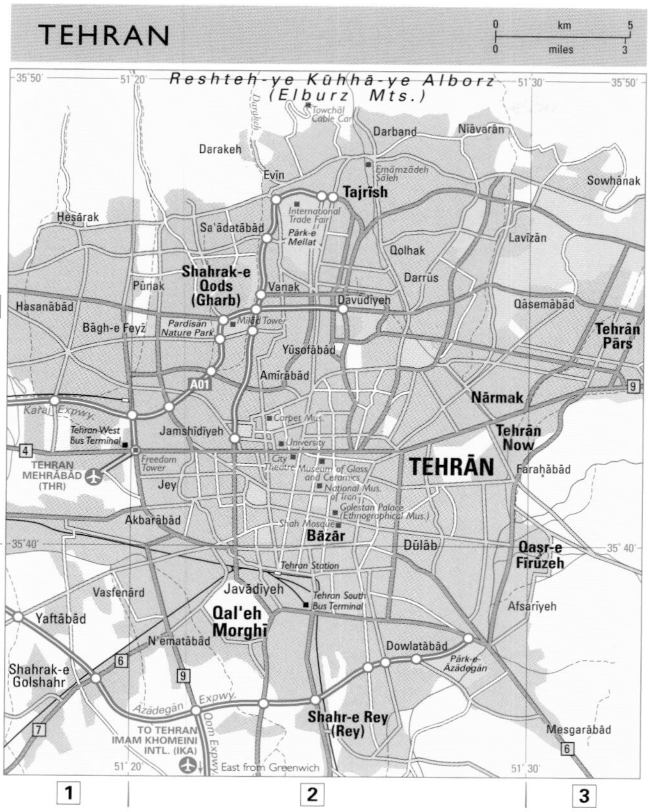

0 km 5
0 miles 3

Reshteh-ye Kūhhā-ye Alborz (Elburz Mts.)

35°50' 51°20' 51°30' 35°50'

Towchal Cable Car
Darakeh
Darband
Niāvarān
Evin
Emāmzādeh Sāleh
Sowhānak

Tajrīsh
International Trade Fair
Sa'ādatābād
Pārk-e Mellat
Lavīzān
Qolhak

Shahrak-e Qods (Gharb)
Vanak
Darrūs
Qāsemābād
Tehrān Pārs
Pūnak
Davūdīyeh

A Hasanābād
Bāgh-e Feyż
Pardisān Nature Park
Milad Tower
Yūsofābād
Amīrābād
Nārmak

A01
Jamshīdīyeh
Tehrān West Bus Terminal
Freedom Tower
Tehrān Now
Farahābād

4 TEHRAN MEHRĀBĀD (THR)
Jey
City Theatre
Museum of Glass and Ceramics
National Mus.
Carpet Mus.
University
TEHRĀN

Akbarābād
Shah Mosque
Golestan Palace (Ethnographical Mus.)
Iran (Ethnographical Mus.)
Bāzār
Dūlāb
Qasr-e Fīrūzeh

35°40' Tehrān Station 35°40'

Vasfenārd
Tehrān South Bus Terminal
Javādīyeh
Afsarīyeh
Qal'eh Morghi

B Yaftābād
6
N'ematābād
Dowlatābād
Pārk-e Āzādegān
Mesgarābād

Shahrak-e Golshahr
9
Āzādegān Expwy
Dom Expwy
Shahr-e Rey (Rey)
6

7 TO TEHRAN IMAM KHOMEINI INTL. (IKA)
East from Greenwich
51°20' 51°30'

1 2 3

CENTRAL TORONTO

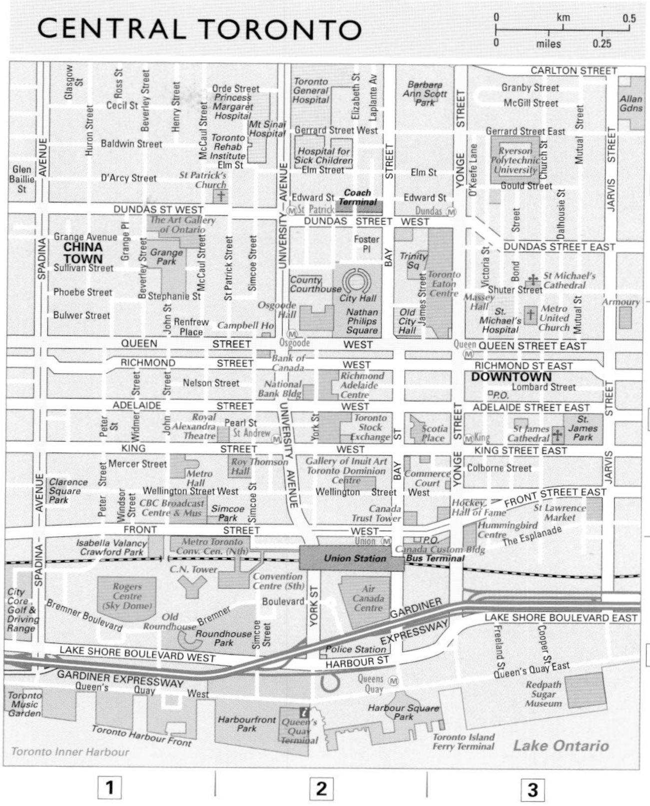

0 km 0.5
0 miles 0.25

(street grid labels — Toronto downtown)

TORONTO

0 km 5
0 miles 3

Vaughan **Markham** Brown
Woodbridge Pine Grove Edgeley Thornhill Concord Newtonbrook Agincourt Malvern Highland Creek Port Union Fairport
...
TORONTO

Mississauga Cooksville Long Branch

LAKE ONTARIO

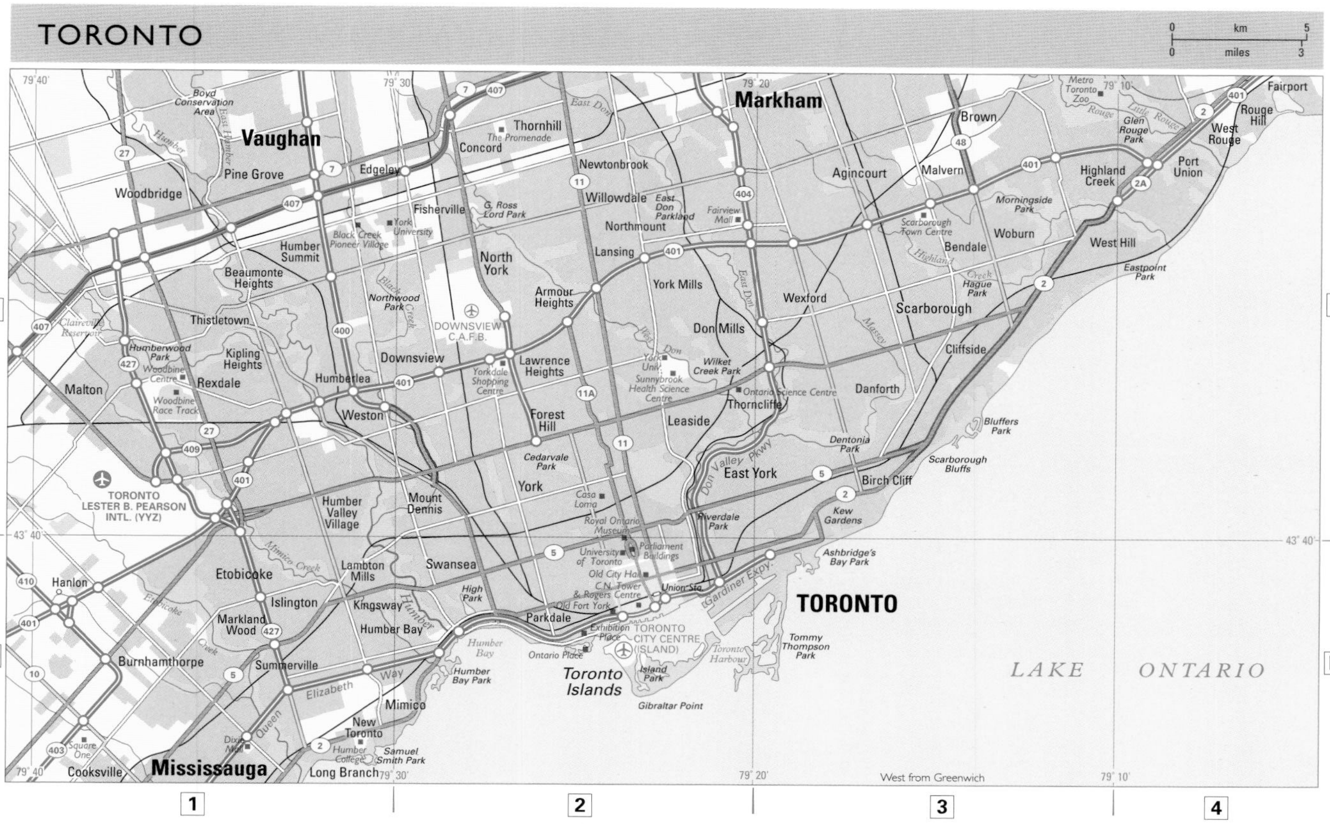

427 Provincial route numbers

COPYRIGHT PHILIP'S

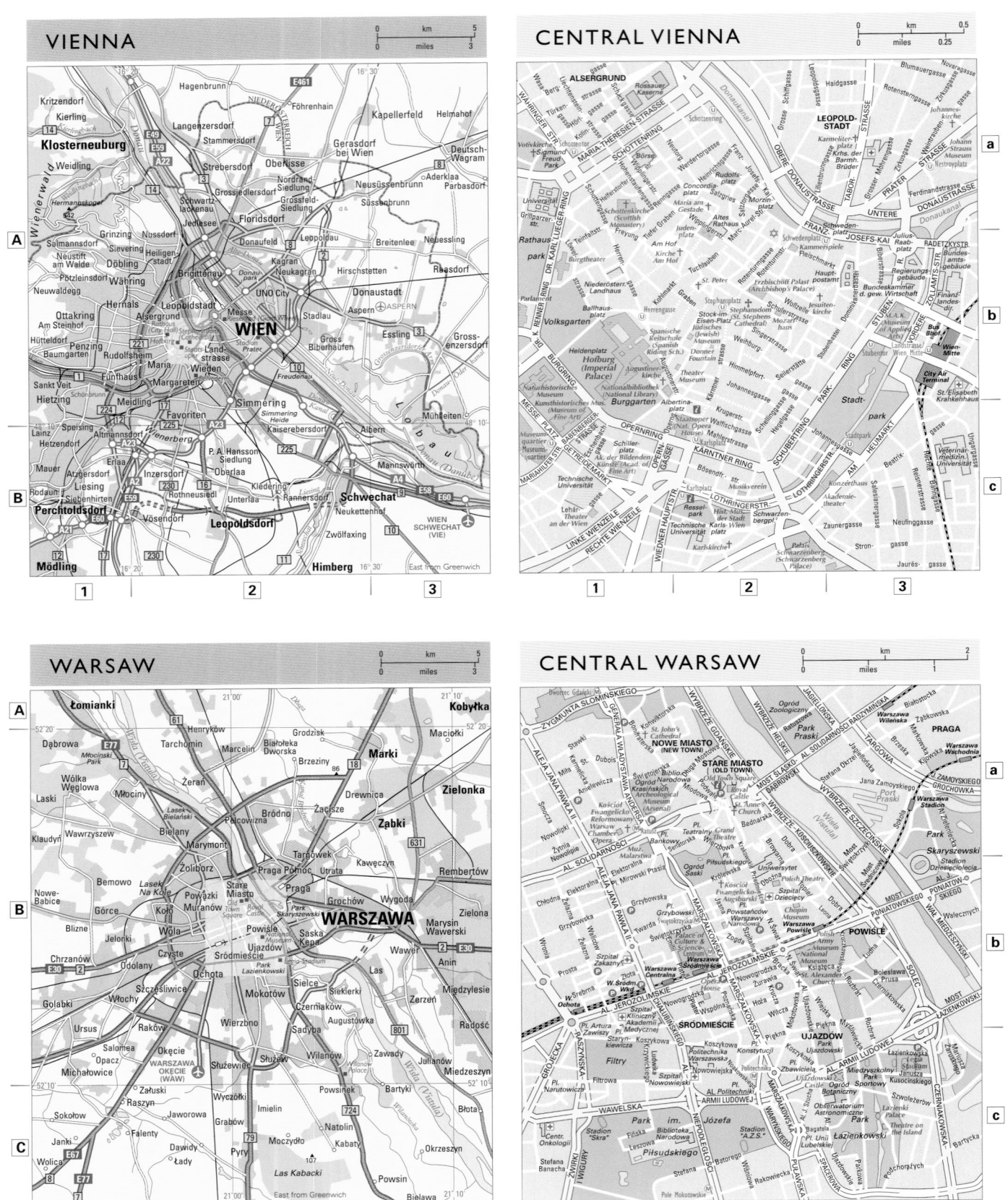

VIENNA

km 5
miles 3

Kritzendorf
Kierling
Klosterneuburg
Weidling
Hagenbrunn
Föhrenhain
Kapellerfeld
Helmahof
Langenzersdorf
Stammersdorf
Gerasdorf
bei Wien
Deutsch-
Wagram
Hermannskogel
Grossjedlersdorf
Streberdorf
Oberlisse
Nordrand-
Siedlung
Grossfeld-
Siedlung
Neusüssenbrunn
Süssenbrunn
Aderklaa
Parbasdorf
Neuwaldegg
Neustift
am Walde
Pötzleinsdorf
Grinzing
Nussdorf
Sievering
Heiligen-
stadt
Döbling
Währing
Schwartz-
lackenau
Jedlesee
Brigittenau
Floridsdorf
Donaufeld
Leopoldau
Breitenlee
Nebessling
Hernals
Alsergrund
Leopoldstadt
UNO City
Donaustadt
Hirschstetten
Raasdorf
Ottakring
Am Steinhof
Hütteldorf
Baumgarten
Penzing
Rudolfsheim
Fünfhaus
WIEN
Land-
strasse
Wieden
Essling
Gross
Biberhaufen
Gross-
enzersdorf
Sankt Veit
Hietzing
Margareten
Maria
Freudenau
Simmering
Simmering
Heide
Mühleiten
Lobau
Meidling
Favoriten
Kaiserebersdorf
Albern
Mannswörth
Speising
Lainz
Hetzendorf
Altmannsdorf
Atzgersdorf
Erlaa
P. A. Hansson
Siedlung
Oberlaa
Kledering
Unterlaa
Rothneusiedl
Rannersdorf
Schwechat
Neukettenhof
Mauer
Liesing
Siebenhirten
Vösendorf
Leopoldsdorf
WIEN
SCHWECHAT
(VIE)
Perchtoldsdorf
Rodaun
Zwölfaxing
Mödling
Himberg
East from Greenwich

1   2   3

CENTRAL VIENNA

km 0.5
miles 0.25

(Detailed central Vienna street map with labels including ALSERGRUND, LEOPOLDSTADT, Votivkirche, Sigmund Freud Park, Börse, Rathaus, Parlament, Volksgarten, Burgtheater, Hofburg (Imperial Palace), Stephansdom, St Stephens Cathedral, Stadtpark, Staatsoper, Karlskirche, etc.)

1   2   3

WARSAW

km 5
miles 3

Łomianki
Kobyłka
Dąbrowa
Henryków
Tarchomin
Grodzisk
Maciołki
Marki
Wólka
Węglowa
Młociny
Białołeka
Dworska
Brzeziny
Zielonka
Laski
Wawrzyszew
Bielany
Drewnica
Żabki
Klaudyń
Żoliborz
Marymont
Pelcowizna
Bródno
Targówek
Kawęczyn
Rembertów
Nowe-
Babice
Bemowo
Lasek
Na Kole
Powązki
Muranów
Stare
Miasto
Praga Północ
Praga
Utrata
Wygoda
Zielona
Górce
Koło
Wola
Park
Skaryszewski
Grochów
Marysin
Wawerski
Blizne
Jelonki
Powiśle
WARSZAWA
Saska
Kępa
Wawer
Anin
Chrzanów
Odolany
Czyste
Ujazdów
Śródmieście
Sielce
Siekierki
Zerzeń
Międzylesie
Ursus
Szczęśliwice
Włochy
Ochota
Mokotów
Czerniaków
Radość
Gołąbki
Raków
Sadyba
Augustówka
Zawady
Julianów
Michałowice
Salomea
Opacz
Okęcie
WARSZAWA
OKĘCIE
(WAW)
Służewiec
Służew
Wilanów
Miedzeszyn
Sokołów
Załuski
Raszyn
Wyczółki
Imielin
Powsinek
Bartyki
Błota
Janki
Jaworowa
Grabów
Natolin
Kabaty
Okrzeszyn
Wolica
Falenty
Dawidy
Łady
Pyry
Moczydło
Las Kabacki
Powsin
Bielawa
East from Greenwich

1   2   3

CENTRAL WARSAW

km 2
miles 1

(Detailed central Warsaw street map with labels including NOWE MIASTO (NEW TOWN), STARE MIASTO (OLD TOWN), PRAGA, St John's Cathedral, Royal Castle, Park Praski, POWIŚLE, ŚRÓDMIEŚCIE, UJAZDÓW, Łazienkowski Park, Warszawa Centralna, etc.)

1   2   3

WASHINGTON

km 5
miles 3

A Dranesville · Great Falls · Potomac · Silver Spring · Adelphi · Oak View · Greenbelt A
Cabin John Regional Park · Woodmont · Langley Park · College Park · Lanham-Seabrook
Bethesda · Chevy Chase · Takoma Park · East Pines · New Carrollton
Reston · L. Fairfax Park · Glen Echo · Glen Mar Park · Westgate · Brookmont · Chillum · Hyattsville · Riverdale
MARYLAND VIRGINIA · Belle View · Langley · Somerset · Brightwood · Mount Rainier · Edmonston · Landover Hills

B Tysons Corner · McLean · Franklin Park · WASHINGTON · Georgetown · Bladensburg · Kent Village · Glenarden · Palmer Park B
Pimmit Hills · Hunters Valley · Vienna · Dunn Loring · Oakton · Vale · Falls Church · Arlington · Rosslyn · Trinidad · Cheverly · Fairmount Heights · Seat Pleasant
Broyhill Park · Seven Corners · Arlington Nat. Cemetery · Pentagon · Fort Dupont Park · Capitol Heights · Kettering
Fairfax · Holmes Run Acres · Annalee Heights · Culmore · Baileys Crossroads · Parklawn · East Arlington · Anacostia · Oakland · Millwood · Ritchie · District Heights · Forestville

C Fairfax Station · Kings Park West · Annandale · Alexandria · Hillcrest Heights · Morningside · Coral Hills · Suitland C
Butts Corner · Kings Park · North Springfield · Huntington · Glassmanor · Forest Heights · Temple Hills · Silver Hill · Camp Springs
West Springfield · Springfield · Franconia · Rose Hill · Groveton · Woodrow Wilson Memorial Bridge · Fort Foote Village · South Lawn · Oxon Hill · Oaklawn · Andrews Air Force Base

1   2   3   4   5

🛡 85 Interstate route numbers   ◯ 29 U.S. route numbers   ◯ 166 State route numbers

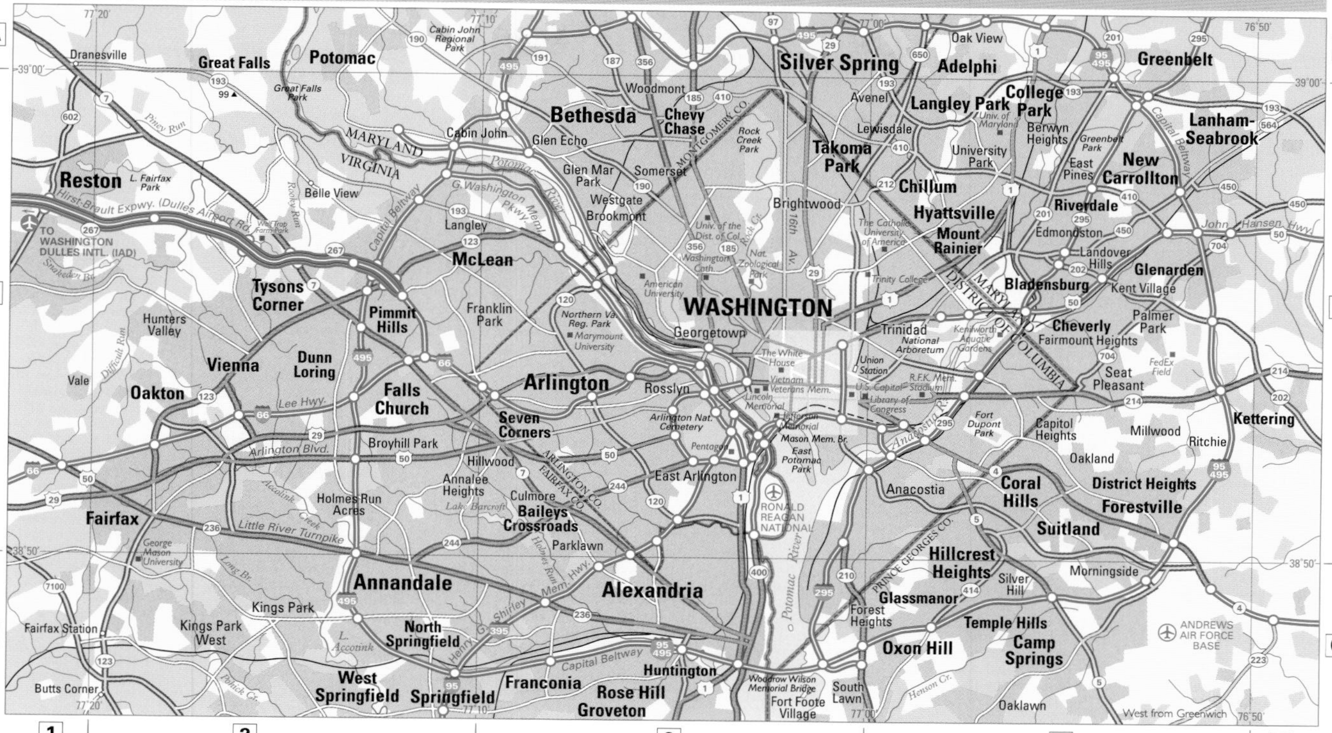

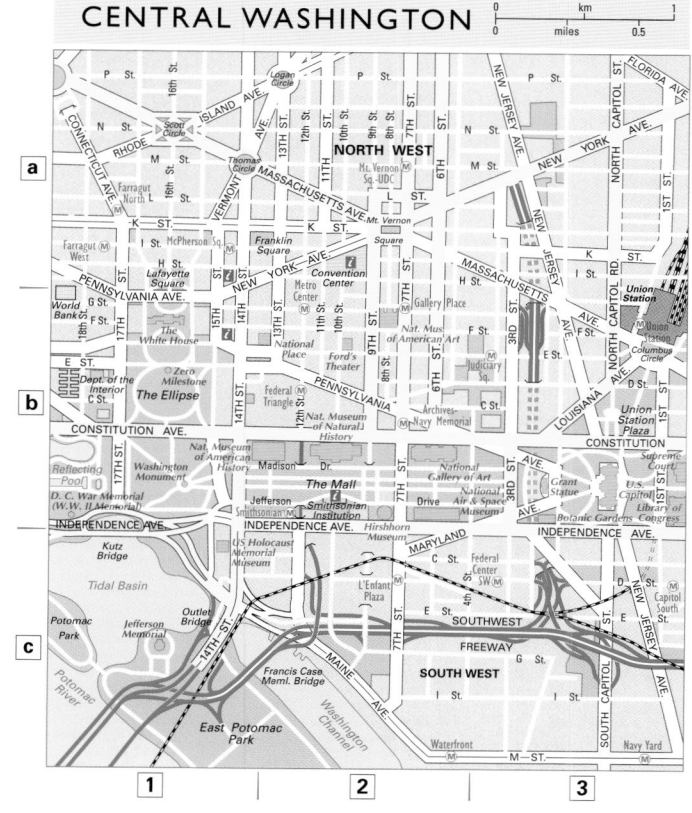

CENTRAL WASHINGTON

km 1
miles 0.5

a NORTH WEST · Logan Circle · Scott Circle · Thomas Circle · Mt. Vernon Sq.-UDC a
Farragut North · McPherson Sq. · Franklin Square · Mt. Vernon Square · Convention Center · Metro Center · Gallery Place · Union Station

b Farragut West · Lafayette Square · The White House · National Place · Ford's Theater · Nat. Mus. of American Art · Judiciary Sq. · Archives · Navy Memorial · Union Station Plaza b
World Bank · Dept. of the Interior · The Ellipse · Federal Triangle · Nat. Museum of Natural History · Columbus Circle · Union Station
CONSTITUTION AVE. · Washington Monument · Madison Dr. · National Gallery of Art · Supreme Court · U.S. Capitol · Library of Congress

c Reflecting Pool · D.C. War Memorial (W.W. II Memorial) · Nat. Museum of American History · The Mall · National Air & Space Museum · Botanic Gardens c
Tidal Basin · Kutz Bridge · Jefferson Memorial · US Holocaust Memorial Museum · L'Enfant Plaza · Federal Center SW · INDEPENDENCE AVE.
Potomac Park · Outlet Bridge · Francis Case Meml. Bridge · SOUTHWEST FREEWAY · SOUTH WEST · Navy Yard
East Potomac Park · Washington Channel · Waterfront

1   2   3

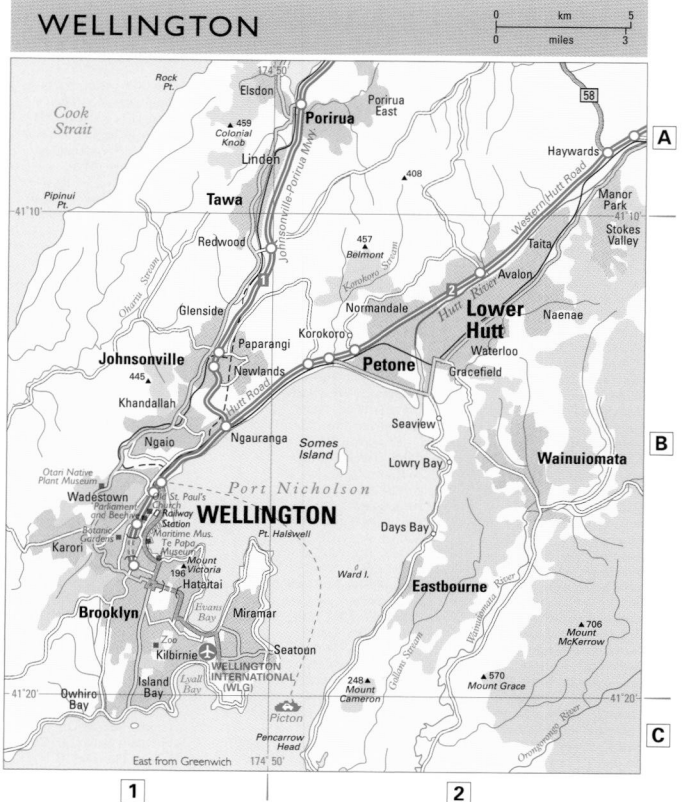

WELLINGTON

km 5
miles 3

A Cook Strait · Rock Pt. · Elsdon · Porirua · Porirua East · Haywards · 58 A
Colonial Knob · Linden · Tawa · Belmont · Manor Park · Stokes Valley
Pipinui Pt. · Redwood · Taita · Avalon

B Glenside · Johnsonville · Normandale · Lower Hutt · Naenae B
Paparangi · Newlands · Korokoro · Petone · Waterloo · Gracefield
Ngaio · Ngauranga · Somes Island · Seaview · Wainuiomata
Otari Native Plant Plant Reserve · Wadestown · Port Nicholson · Lowry Bay
Karori · WELLINGTON · Days Bay · Eastbourne

C Brooklyn · Mount Victoria · Hataitai · Miramar · Evans Bay · Ward I. · Mount McKerrow C
Kilbirnie · Seatoun · Island Bay · Owhiro Bay · WELLINGTON INTERNATIONAL (WLG) · Mount Cameron · Mount Grace · Picton · Pencarrow Head

1   2

East from Greenwich 174° 50'

COPYRIGHT PHILIP'S

INDEX TO CITY MAPS

The index contains the names of all the principal places and features shown on the City Maps. Each name is followed by an additional entry in italics giving the name of the City Map within which it is located.

The number in bold type which follows each name refers to the number of the City Map page where that feature or place will be found.

The letter and figure which are immediately after the page number give the grid square on the map within which the feature or place is situated.

The letter represents the latitude and the figure the longitude. The full geographic reference is provided in the border of the City Maps.

The location given is the centre of the city, suburb or feature and is not necessarily the name. Rivers, canals and roads are indexed to their name. Rivers carry the symbol → after their name.

An explanation of the alphabetical order rules and a list of the abbreviations used are to be found at the beginning of the World Map Index.

A

Aalām *Baghdad* **223** B2
Abbey Wood *London* **235** B4
Abcoude *Amsterdam* **222** B2
Ābdīn *Cairo* **227** A2
Abeno *Osaka* **243** B2
Aberdeen *Hong Kong* **232** B1
Aberdour *Edinburgh* **231** A2
Aberdour Castle *Edinburgh* **231** A2
Abfanggraben → *Munich* **241** A3
Ablon-sur-Seine *Paris* **244** B3
Abramtsevo *Moscow* **239** B3
Abu Dis *Jerusalem* **233** B2
Abû en Numrus *Cairo* **227** B2
Abu Ghosh *Jerusalem* **233** B1
Acassuso *Buenos Aires* **227** A1
Accotink, L. *Washington* **253** C2
Accotink Cr. → *Washington* **253** B2
Achères *Paris* **244** A1
Acília *Rome* **246** C1
Aclimação *São Paulo* **247** B2
Acropolis *Athens* **222** B2
Acton *London* **235** A2
Açúcar, Pão de *Rio de Janeiro* **245** B2
Ada Beja *Lisbon* **236** A1
Adams Park *Atlanta* **223** B2
Addiscombe *London* **235** B3
Adelphi *Washington* **253** A4
Aderklaa *Vienna* **252** A3
Adler Planetarium *Chicago* **229** B3
Admiralteyskaya Storona *St. Petersburg* **247** B2
Affori *Milan* **239** A2
Aflandshage *Copenhagen* **228** B3
Afsarīyeh *Tehran* **251** B2
Agboyi Cr. → *Lagos* **234** A2
Agerup *Copenhagen* **228** A1
Ågesta *Stockholm* **249** B2
Aghia Marina *Athens* **222** C3
Aghia Paraskevi *Athens* **222** A2
Aghios Dimitrios *Athens* **222** B2
Aghios Ioannis Rendis *Athens* **222** B1
Agincourt *Toronto* **251** A3
Agra Canal *Delhi* **230** B2
Agricola Oriental *Mexico City* **238** B2
Agua Espraiada → *São Paulo* **247** B2
Agualva-Cacem *Lisbon* **236** A1
Agustino, Cerro El *Lima* **234** B3
Ahrensfelde *Berlin* **225** A4
Ahuntsic *Montreal* **240** A1
Ai → *Osaka* **243** A2
Aigremont *Paris* **244** A1
Air View Park *Singapore* **248** A2
Airport West *Melbourne* **238** A1
Ajegunle *Lagos* **234** B2
Aji *Osaka* **243** A1
Ajuda *Lisbon* **236** A1
Akalla *Stockholm* **249** A1
Akasaka *Tokyo* **250** A3
Akbarābād *Tehran* **251** A2
Akershus Castle = Akershus Slott *Oslo* **243** A3
Akershus Slott *Oslo* **243** A3
Al 'Aẓamīyah *Baghdad* **223** A2
Al Quds = Jerusalem *Jerusalem* **233** B2
Al-Walaja *Jerusalem* **233** B1
Alaguntan *Lagos* **234** B2
Alameda *San Francisco* **246** B3
Alameda Memorial State Beach Park *San Francisco* **246** B3
Albern *Vienna* **252** B2
Albert Park *Melbourne* **238** B1
Alberton *Johannesburg* **233** B2
Albertslund *Copenhagen* **228** B2
Albysjön *Stockholm* **249** B1
Alcantara *Lisbon* **236** A1
Alcatraz I. *San Francisco* **246** B2
Alcobendas *Madrid* **237** A2
Alcorcón *Madrid* **237** B1
Aldershof *Berlin* **225** B4
Aldo Bonzi *Buenos Aires* **227** C1
Aleksandrovskoye *St. Petersburg* **247** B2
Alexander Nevsky Abbey *St. Petersburg* **247** B2
Alexandra *Johannesburg* **233** A2
Alexandra *Singapore* **248** B2
Alexandria *Washington* **253** C3
Alfortville *Paris* **244** B3
Algés *Lisbon* **236** A1
Alhambra *Los Angeles* **236** B4
Alibey → *Istanbul* **232** B1
Alibey Barajı *Istanbul* **232** B1
Alibeyköy *Istanbul* **232** B1
Alimos *Athens* **222** B2
Alipur *Kolkata* **234** B1
Allach *Munich* **241** A1
Allambie Heights *Sydney* **249** A2
Allermuir Hill *Edinburgh* **231** B2
Allstate Arena *Chicago* **229** A1
Allston *Boston* **226** A2
Almada *Lisbon* **236** A2
Almagro *Buenos Aires* **227** B2
Almargem do Bispo *Lisbon* **236** A1
Almirante G. Brown, Parque *Buenos Aires* **227** C2
Almon *Jerusalem* **233** B2
Almond → *Edinburgh* **231** B2
Alna *Oslo* **243** A4
Alnsjøen *Oslo* **243** A4
Alperton *London* **235** A2
Alpine *New York* **242** A2
Alrode *Johannesburg* **233** B2
Alsemberg *Brussels* **226** B1
Alsergrund *Vienna* **252** A2
Alsip *Chicago* **229** C2
Ålsten *Stockholm* **249** B1
Älta *Stockholm* **249** B3
Altadena *Los Angeles* **236** A4
Alte-Donau → *Vienna* **252** A2
Alter Finkenkrug *Berlin* **225** A1
Altes Rathaus *Munich* **241** B2
Altglienicke *Berlin* **225** B4
Altlandsberg *Berlin* **225** A5
Altlandsberg Nord *Berlin* **225** A5
Altmannsdorf *Vienna* **252** B1
Alto da Boa Vista *Rio de Janeiro* **245** B1
Alto da Moóca *São Paulo* **247** B2
Alto do Pina *Lisbon* **236** A2
Altona *Melbourne* **238** B1
Alvik *Stockholm* **249** B1
Älvsjo *Stockholm* **249** B2
Älvvik *Stockholm* **249** A3
Am Hasenbergl *Munich* **241** A2
Am Steinhof *Vienna* **252** A1
Am Wald *Munich* **241** B2
Ama Keng *Singapore* **248** A2
Amadora *Lisbon* **236** A1
Amagasaki *Osaka* **243** A1
Amager *Copenhagen* **228** B3
Amāl Qādisiya *Baghdad* **223** B2
Amalienborg Slot *Copenhagen* **228** A3
Amata *Milan* **239** A1
Ambelokipi *Athens* **222** B2
Ameixoeira *Lisbon* **236** A2
América *São Paulo* **247** B1
American Police Hall of Fame *Miami* **238** B2
American University *Washington* **253** B3
Amin *Baghdad* **223** B2
Aminadav *Jerusalem* **233** B1
Amīrābād *Tehran* **251** A2
Amora *Lisbon* **236** B2
Amoreira *Lisbon* **236** A1
Amper → *Munich* **241** A1
Amstel-Drecht-Kanaal *Amsterdam* **222** B2
Amstelveen *Amsterdam* **222** B2
Amsterdam *Amsterdam* **222** A2
Amsterdam ✕ (AMS) *Amsterdam* **222** B1
Amsterdam-Rijnkanaal *Amsterdam* **222** B3
Amsterdam Zuidoost *Amsterdam* **222** B2
Amsterdamse Bos *Amsterdam* **222** B2
Anacosta → *Washington* **253** B4
Anacostia *Washington* **253** B4
Anadoluhisarı *Istanbul* **232** B2
Anadolukavağı *Istanbul* **232** A2
Anata *Jerusalem* **233** B2
Ancol *Jakarta* **232** A1
'Andalus *Baghdad* **223** B1
Andaraí *Rio de Janeiro* **245** B1
Anderlecht *Brussels* **226** A1
Anderson Park *Atlanta* **223** B2
Andingmen *Beijing* **224** B2
Ang Mo Kio *Singapore* **248** A3
Ängby *Stockholm* **249** A1
Angel I. *San Francisco* **246** A2
Angel Island State Park ⌂ *San Francisco* **246** A2
Angke, Kali → *Jakarta* **232** A1
Angyalföld *Budapest* **227** A2
Anik *Mumbai* **240** A2
Anin *Warsaw* **252** B2
Anjou *Montreal* **240** A2
Annalee Heights *Washington* **253** B2
Annandale *Washington* **253** C2
Anne Frankhuis *Amsterdam* **222** A2
Antony *Paris* **244** B2
Aoyama *Tokyo* **250** B3
Ap Lei Chau *Hong Kong* **232** B1
Apapa *Lagos* **234** B2
Apelacão *Lisbon* **236** A2
Apopka, L. *Orlando* **243** A1
Apoquindo *Santiago* **247** B2
Apterkarskiy Ostrov *St. Petersburg* **247** B2
Ar Kazimiyah *Baghdad* **223** B1
Ar Ram *Jerusalem* **233** A2
Ara → *Tokyo* **250** A4
Arakawa *Tokyo* **250** A3
Arany-hegyi-patak → *Budapest* **227** A2
Aravaca *Madrid* **237** B1
Arbataash *Baghdad* **223** A1
Arc de Triomphe *Paris* **244** A2
Arcadia *Los Angeles* **236** B4
Arcueil *Paris* **244** B2
Arese *Milan* **239** A1
Arganzuela *Madrid* **237** B1
Argenteuil *Paris* **244** A2
Argiroupoli *Athens* **222** B2
Argonne Forest *Chicago* **229** C1
Arima *Tokyo* **250** B2
Arlanda ✕ (ARN) *Stockholm* **249** A1
Arlington *Boston* **226** A1
Arlington *Washington* **253** B3
Arlington Heights *Boston* **226** A1
Arlington Nat. Cemetery *Washington* **253** B3
Armação *Rio de Janeiro* **245** B2
Armadale *Melbourne* **238** B2
Armour Heights *Toronto* **251** A2
Arncliffe *Sydney* **249** B1
Arnold Arboretum *Boston* **226** B2
Árpádföld *Budapest* **227** A3
Arrentela *Lisbon* **236** B2
Arroyo Seco Park *Los Angeles* **236** B3
Ārsta *Stockholm* **249** B2
Art Institute *Chicago* **229** B3
Artane *Dublin* **230** A2
Artas *Jerusalem* **233** B2
Arthur's Seat *Edinburgh* **231** B3
Arts, Place des *Montreal* **240** A2
As Shawawra *Jerusalem* **233** B2
Asagaya *Tokyo* **250** A2
Asahi *Osaka* **243** A2
Asakusa *Tokyo* **250** A3
Asati *Kolkata* **234** C1
Aschheim *Munich* **241** A3
Ascot Vale *Melbourne* **238** A1
Ashbridge's Bay Park *Toronto* **251** B3
Ashburn *Chicago* **229** C2
Ashburton *Melbourne* **238** B2
Ashfield *Sydney* **249** B1
Ashford *London* **235** B1
Ashtown *Dublin* **230** A2
Askisto *Helsinki* **231** B1
Askrikefjärden *Stockholm* **249** A3
Asnières *Paris* **244** A2
Aspern *Vienna* **252** A2
Aspern ✕ *Vienna* **252** A3
Assago *Milan* **239** B1
Assendelft *Amsterdam* **222** A1
Assiano *Milan* **239** B1
Astoria *New York* **242** B2
Astrolabe Park *Sydney* **249** B2
Atarot *Jerusalem* **233** A2
Atarot ✕ *Jerusalem* **233** A2
Atghara *Kolkata* **234** B2
Athens = Athina *Athens* **222** B2
Athina *Athens* **222** B2
Athina ✕ (ATH) *Athens* **222** A3
Athínai = Athina *Athens* **222** B2
Athis-Mons *Paris* **244** B3
Athlone *Cape Town* **228** A2
Atholl *Johannesburg* **233** A2
Atīfiya *Baghdad* **223** A2
Atişalen *Istanbul* **232** B1
Atlanta *Atlanta* **223** B2
Atlanta Hartsfield Int. ✕ (ATL) *Atlanta* **223** C2
Atlanta Zoo *Atlanta* **223** B2
Atomium *Brussels* **226** A2
Attiki *Athens* **222** A2
Atzgersdorf *Vienna* **252** B1
Aubervilliers *Paris* **244** A3
Aubing *Munich* **241** B1
Auburndale *Boston* **226** A1
Auchendinny *Edinburgh* **231** B2
Auckland Park *Johannesburg* **233** B2
Auderghem *Brussels* **226** B2
Augustówka *Warsaw* **252** B2
Aulnay-sous-Bois *Paris* **244** A3
Aurelio *Rome* **246** B1
Ausîm *Cairo* **227** A1
Austerlitz, Gare d' *Paris* **244** A3
Austin *Chicago* **229** B2
Avalon *Wellington* **253** B2
Avedøre *Copenhagen* **228** B2
Avellaneda *Buenos Aires* **227** C2
Avenel *Washington* **253** B4
Avondale *Chicago* **229** B2
Avondale Heights *Melbourne* **238** A1
Avtovo *St. Petersburg* **247** B1
Ayazağa *Istanbul* **232** B1
Ayer Chawan, Pulau *Singapore* **248** B2
Ayer Merbau, Pulau *Singapore* **248** B2
Azabu *Tokyo* **250** B3
Azcapotzalco *Mexico City* **238** B1
Azteca, Estadia *Mexico City* **238** C2
Azucar, Cerro Pan de *Santiago* **247** A1

B

Baambrugge *Amsterdam* **222** B2
Baba Ch. *Karachi* **233** B1
Baba I. *Karachi* **233** B1
Babarpur *Delhi* **230** A2
Babushkin *Moscow* **239** A3
Back B. *Mumbai* **240** B1
Baclaran *Manila* **237** B2
Bacoor *Manila* **237** C1
Bacoor B. *Manila* **237** C1
Badalona *Barcelona* **224** A2
Badhoevedorp *Amsterdam* **222** A1
Badli *Delhi* **230** A1
Bærum *Oslo* **243** A2
Bağcılar *Istanbul* **232** B1
Bággio *Milan* **239** B1
Bāgh-e-Feyz *Tehran* **251** A1
Baghdād *Baghdad* **223** A2
Baghdad al Muthana ✕ *Baghdad* **223** B2
Baghdad Int. ✕ (SDA) *Baghdad* **223** B1
Bagmari *Kolkata* **234** B2
Bagneux *Paris* **244** B2
Bagnolet *Paris* **244** A3
Bagsværd *Copenhagen* **228** A2
Bagsværd Sø *Copenhagen* **228** A2
Baguiati *Kolkata* **234** B2
Bagumbayan *Manila* **237** C2
Baha'i Temple *Chicago* **229** A2
Bahçeköy *Istanbul* **232** A1
Bahçelıevler *Istanbul* **232** B1
Bahtîm *Cairo* **227** A2
Baile Atha Cliath = Dublin *Dublin* **230** A2
Baileys Crossroads *Washington* **253** B3
Bailly *Paris* **244** A1
Bairro Lopes *Lisbon* **236** A2
Baisha *Guangzhou* **231** B2
Baiyun Hill *Guangzhou* **231** B2
Baiyun Int. ✕ (CAN) *Guangzhou* **231** A2
Bakırköy *Istanbul* **232** C1
Bal Harbor *Miami* **238** A2
Balara *Manila* **237** B2
Baldia *Karachi* **233** A1
Baldoyle *Dublin* **230** A3
Baldwin, L. *Orlando* **243** A3
Baldwin Hills *Los Angeles* **236** B2
Baldwin Hills Res. *Los Angeles* **236** B2
Balgowlah *Sydney* **249** A2
Balgowlah Heights *Sydney* **249** A2
Balham *London* **235** B3
Bali *Kolkata* **234** B1
Baliganja *Kolkata* **234** B2
Balingsnäs *Stockholm* **249** B2
Balingsta *Stockholm* **249** B2
Balintawak *Manila* **237** B1
Ballerup *Copenhagen* **228** A2
Ballinteer *Dublin* **230** B2
Ballyboden *Dublin* **230** B2
Ballybrack *Dublin* **230** B3
Ballyfermot *Dublin* **230** A1
Ballymorefinn Hill *Dublin* **230** B1
Ballymun *Dublin* **230** A2
Balmain *Sydney* **249** B2
Baluhati *Kolkata* **234** B1
Balvanera *Buenos Aires* **227** B2
Balwyn *Melbourne* **238** A2
Balwyn North *Melbourne* **238** A2
Banática *Lisbon* **236** A1
Bandra *Mumbai* **240** A1
Bandra Pt. *Mumbai* **240** A1
Bang Kapi *Bangkok* **223** B2
Bang Na *Bangkok* **223** B2
Bangbae *Seoul* **247** C1
Bangkhen *Bangkok* **223** A2
Bangkok *Bangkok* **223** B2
Bangkok Noi *Bangkok* **223** B1
Bangkok Yai *Bangkok* **223** B1
Banglo *Kolkata* **234** B1
Bangrak *Bangkok* **223** B2
Bangsu *Bangkok* **223** B2
Banks, C. *Sydney* **249** C2
Banksmeadow *Sydney* **249** B2
Banstala *Kolkata* **234** B2
Bantra *Kolkata* **234** B1
Baoshan *Shanghai* **248** A1
Bar Giyora *Jerusalem* **233** B1
Barahanagar *Kolkata* **234** B2
Barajas *Madrid* **237** B2
Barajas, Madrid ✕ (MAD) *Madrid* **237** B2
Barakpur *Kolkata* **234** A2
Barcarena *Lisbon* **236** A1
Barcarena, Rib. de → *Lisbon* **236** A1
Barcelona *Barcelona* **224** A2
Barcelona-Prat ✕ (BCN) *Barcelona* **224** B1
Barceloneta *Barcelona* **224** A2
Barcroft, L. *Washington* **253** B3
Barking *London* **235** A4
Barkingside *London* **235** A4
Barnes *London* **235** B2
Barnet *London* **235** A2
Barra Andai *Karachi* **233** B2
Barra Funda *São Paulo* **247** B2
Barracas *Buenos Aires* **227** B2
Barrackpur = Barakpur *Kolkata* **234** A2
Barranco *Lima* **234** B2
Barreiro *Lisbon* **236** B2
Barreto *Rio de Janeiro* **245** B2
Bartala *Kolkata* **234** B1
Barton Park *Sydney* **249** B1
Bartyki *Warsaw* **252** C2
Basus *Cairo* **227** A2
Batanagar *Kolkata* **234** B1
Bath Beach *New York* **242** C1
Bath I. *Karachi* **233** B2
Batir *Jerusalem* **233** B1
Batok, Bukit *Singapore* **248** A2
Battersea *London* **235** B3
Bauman *Moscow* **239** B3
Baumgarten *Vienna* **252** A1
Bay, L. *Orlando* **243** A2
Bay Harbour Islands *Miami* **238** A2
Bay Hill *Orlando* **243** B1
Bay Ridge *New York* **242** C1
Bayit Va-Gan *Jerusalem* **233** B2
Bayonne *New York* **242** B1
Bayrampaşa *Istanbul* **232** B1
Bayshore *San Francisco* **246** B2
Bayt Lahm *Jerusalem* **233** B2
Bayview *San Francisco* **246** B2
Bāzār *Tehran* **251** A2
Beacon Hill *Hong Kong* **232** A2
Beato *Lisbon* **236** A2
Beaumont *Dublin* **230** A2
Beaumonte Heights *Toronto* **251** A1
Bebek *Istanbul* **232** B2
Běchovice *Prague* **245** B3
Beck L. *Chicago* **229** A1
Beckenham *London* **235** B3
Beckton *London* **235** A4
Becontree *London* **235** A4
Beddington Corner *London* **235** B3
Bedford *Boston* **226** A1
Bedford Park *Chicago* **229** C2
Bedford Park *New York* **242** A2
Bedford Stuyvesant *New York* **242** B2
Bedford View *Johannesburg* **233** B2
Bedok *Singapore* **248** B3
Bedok, Res. *Singapore* **248** A3
Beersel *Brussels* **226** B1
Behala *Kolkata* **234** B1
Bei Hai *Beijing* **224** B2
Beicai *Shanghai* **248** B2
Beijing *Beijing* **224** B1
Beit Duqu *Jerusalem* **233** A1
Beit Ghur at-Taht *Jerusalem* **233** A1
Beit Ghur el-Fawqa *Jerusalem* **233** A1
Beit Hanina *Jerusalem* **233** B2
Beit Ij'za *Jerusalem* **233** A1
Beit Iksa *Jerusalem* **233** B2
Beit I'nan *Jerusalem* **233** A1
Beit Jala *Jerusalem* **233** B2
Beit Lekhem = Bayt Lahm *Jerusalem* **233** B2
Beit Liqya *Jerusalem* **233** A1
Beit Nekofa *Jerusalem* **233** B1
Beit Sahur *Jerusalem* **233** B2
Beit Sofafa *Jerusalem* **233** B2
Beit Surik *Jerusalem* **233** B1
Beit Ur al-Fawqa *Jerusalem* **233** A1
Beit Zayit *Jerusalem* **233** B1
Beitaipingzhuan *Beijing* **224** B1
Beitar Illit *Jerusalem* **233** B1
Beitin *Jerusalem* **233** A2
Beitsun *Guangzhou* **231** B2
Beitunya *Jerusalem* **233** A2
Beixing Jing Park *Shanghai* **248** B1
Békásmegyer *Budapest* **227** A2
Bekkelaget *Oslo* **243** A3
Bekkestua *Oslo* **243** A2
Bel Air *Los Angeles* **236** B2
Bela Vista *São Paulo* **247** B2
Bélanger *Montreal* **240** A1
Belas *Lisbon* **236** A1
Beleghata *Kolkata* **234** B2
Belém *Lisbon* **236** A1
Belém, Torre de *Lisbon* **236** A1
Belènzinho *São Paulo* **247** B2
Belgachiya *Kolkata* **234** B2
Belgharia *Kolkata* **234** B2
Belgrano *Buenos Aires* **227** B2
Bell *Los Angeles* **236** C3
Bell Gardens *Los Angeles* **236** C4
Bellavista *Lima* **234** B2
Bellavista *Santiago* **247** C2
Belle Harbor *New York* **242** C2
Belle Isle *Orlando* **243** B2
Belle View *Washington* **253** B2
Bellingham *London* **235** B3
Bellwood *Chicago* **229** B1
Belmont *Boston* **226** A1
Belmont *London* **235** A2
Belmont, Mt. *Wellington* **253** B2
Belmont Cragin *Chicago* **229** B2
Belmont Harbor *Chicago* **229** B3
Belmore *Sydney* **249** B1
Belur *Kolkata* **234** B2
Belvedere *Atlanta* **223** B3
Belvedere *London* **235** B4
Belvedere *San Francisco* **246** A2
Belyayevo Bogorodskoye *Moscow* **239** C2
Bemowo *Warsaw* **252** B1
Benaki Museum *Athens* **222** B2
Bendale *Toronto* **251** A3
Benefica *Rio de Janeiro* **245** B1
Benfica *Lisbon* **236** A1
Benito Juárez *Mexico City* **238** B2

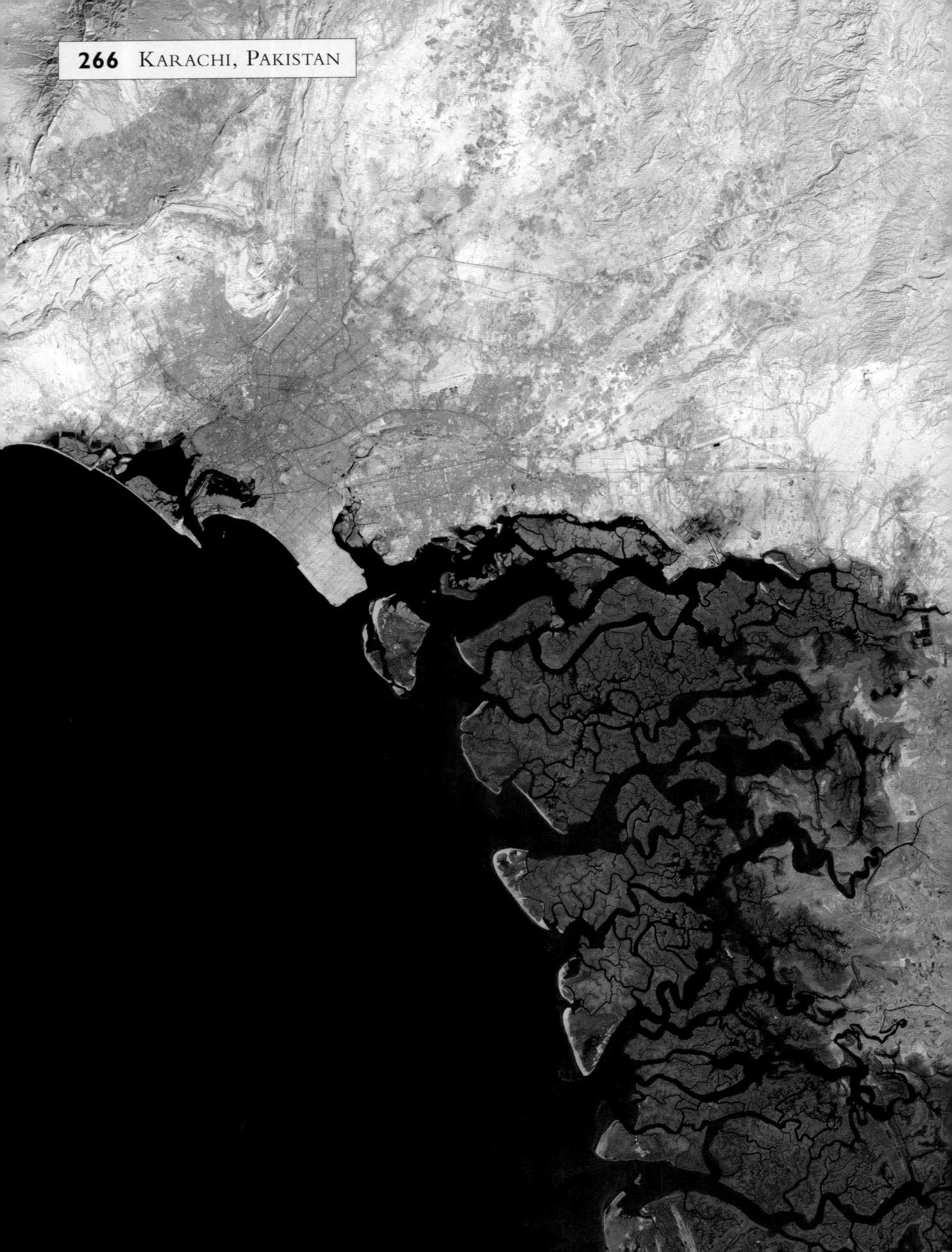

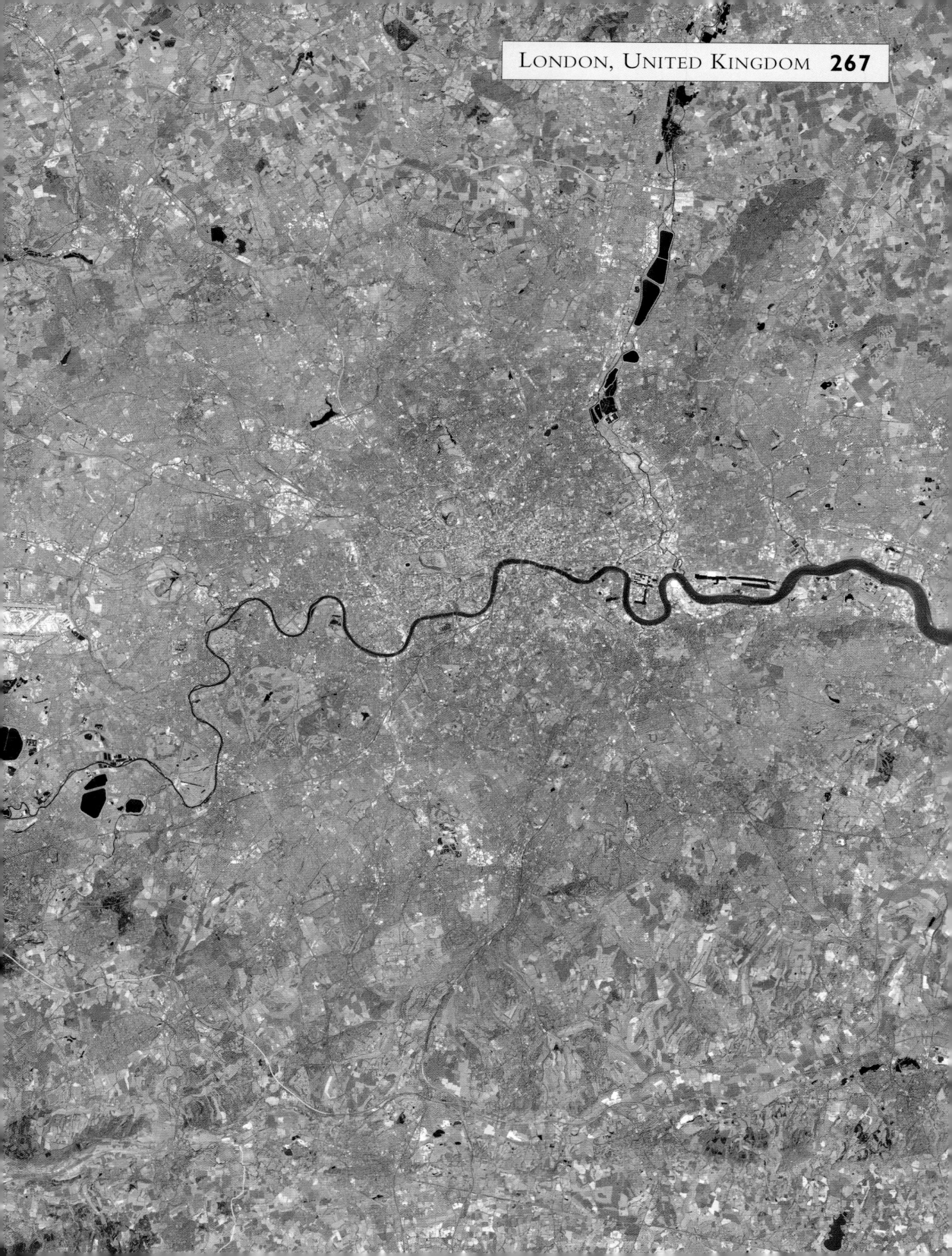

WORLD MAPS

SETTLEMENTS

■ **PARIS**　◉ **Rotterdam**　◉ **Livorno**　◉ Brugge　◎ Exeter　○ Torremolinos　○ Oberammergau　○ Thira

Settlement symbols and type styles vary according to the scale of each map and indicate the importance
of towns on the map rather than specific population figures

• Vaduz　Capital cities have red infills

⬠　Urban agglomerations

∴　Ruins or archaeological sites

⌣　Wells in desert

ADMINISTRATION

───── International boundaries

─ ─ ─ ─ International boundaries
(undefined or disputed)

········· Internal boundaries

⬡ National parks

PERU Country names

KENT Administrative
area names

International boundaries show the *de facto* situation where there are rival claims to territory

COMMUNICATIONS

═══ Motorways, freeways
and expressways

──── Principal roads

──── Other roads

─⊣- - -⊢─ Road tunnels

──── Principal railways

─ ─ ─ Railways
under construction

──── Other railways

─⊣- - -⊢─ Railway tunnels

LHR ⊕ Principal airports

⊕ Other airports

············· Principal canals

⌣ Passes

PHYSICAL FEATURES

∼∼∼ Perennial streams

─ ─ ─ Intermittent streams

⬭ Perennial lakes

◯ Intermittent lakes

◌ Swamps and marshes

▨ Permanent ice
and glaciers

▲ 8850 Elevations in metres

▼ 8500 Sea depths in metres

1134 Height of lake surface
above sea level in metres

ELEVATION AND DEPTH TINTS

Height of land above sea level

in metres	6000	4000	3000	2000	1500	1000	400	200	0
in feet	18 000	12 000	9000	6000	4500	3000	1200	600	

Land below sea level

Depth of sea

	6000	12 000	15 000	18 000	24 000	in feet
0	200	2000	4000	5000	6000	8000	in metres

Some of the maps have different contours to highlight and clarify the principal relief features

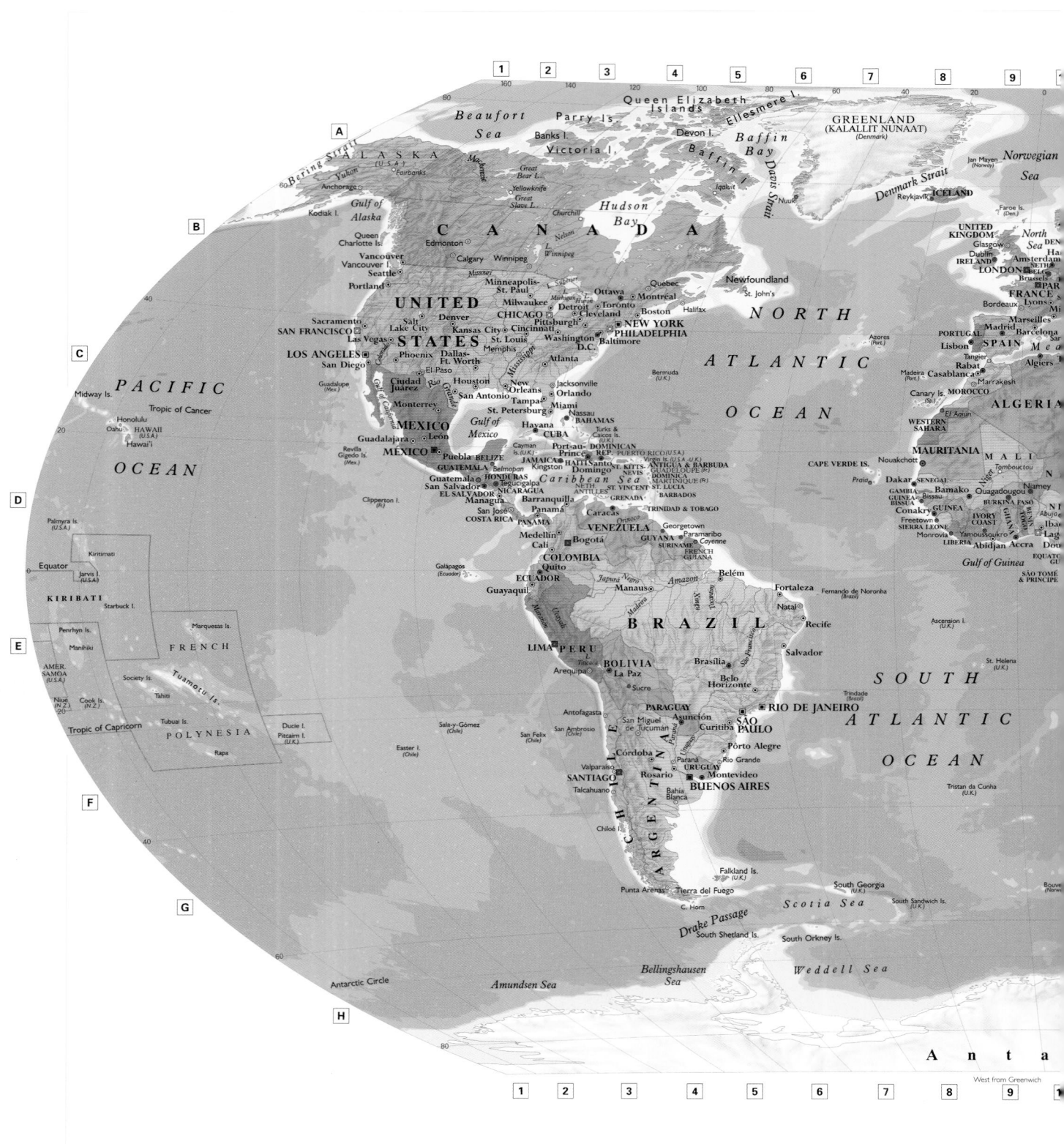

Projection: Winkel III

West from Greenwich

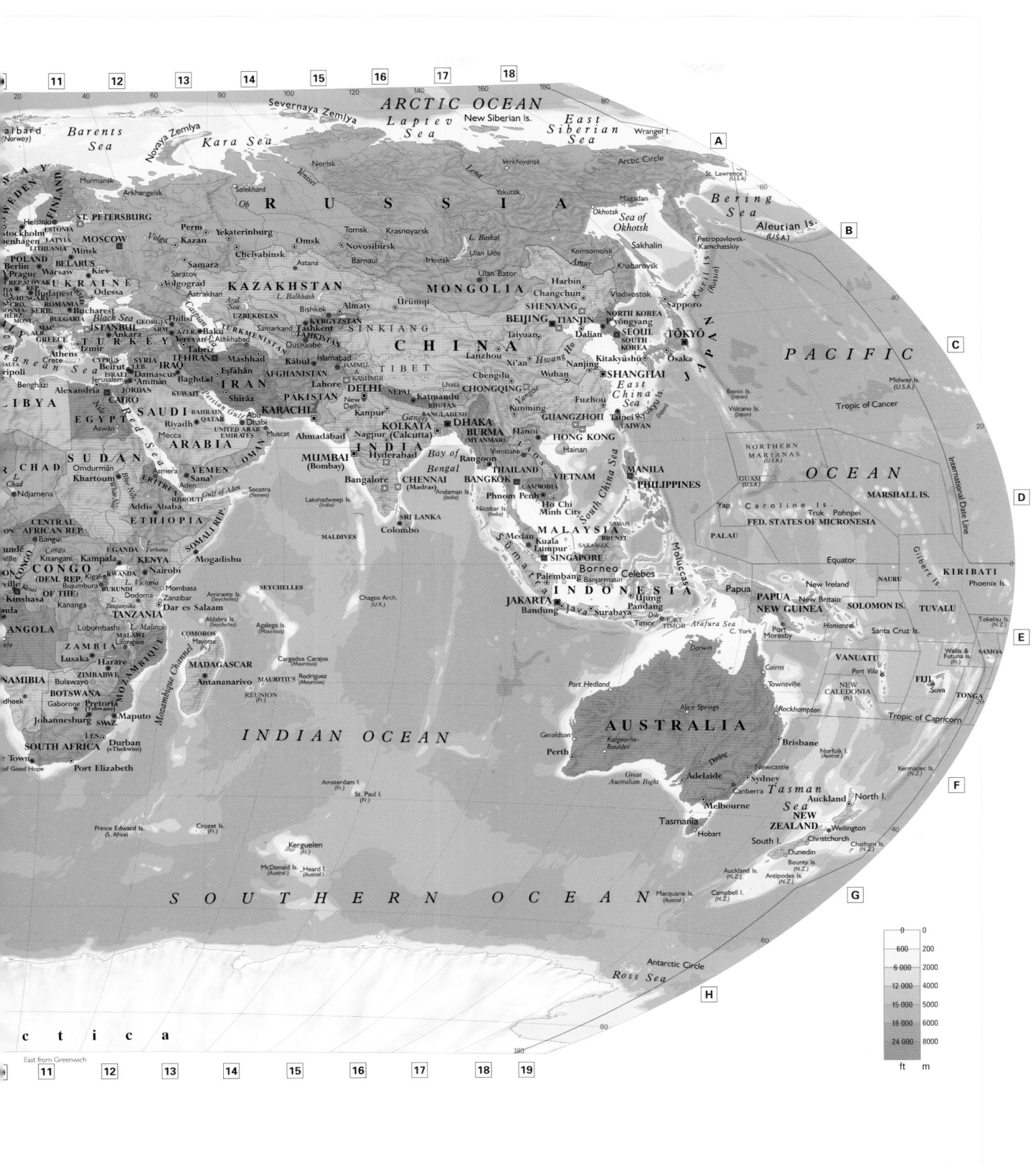

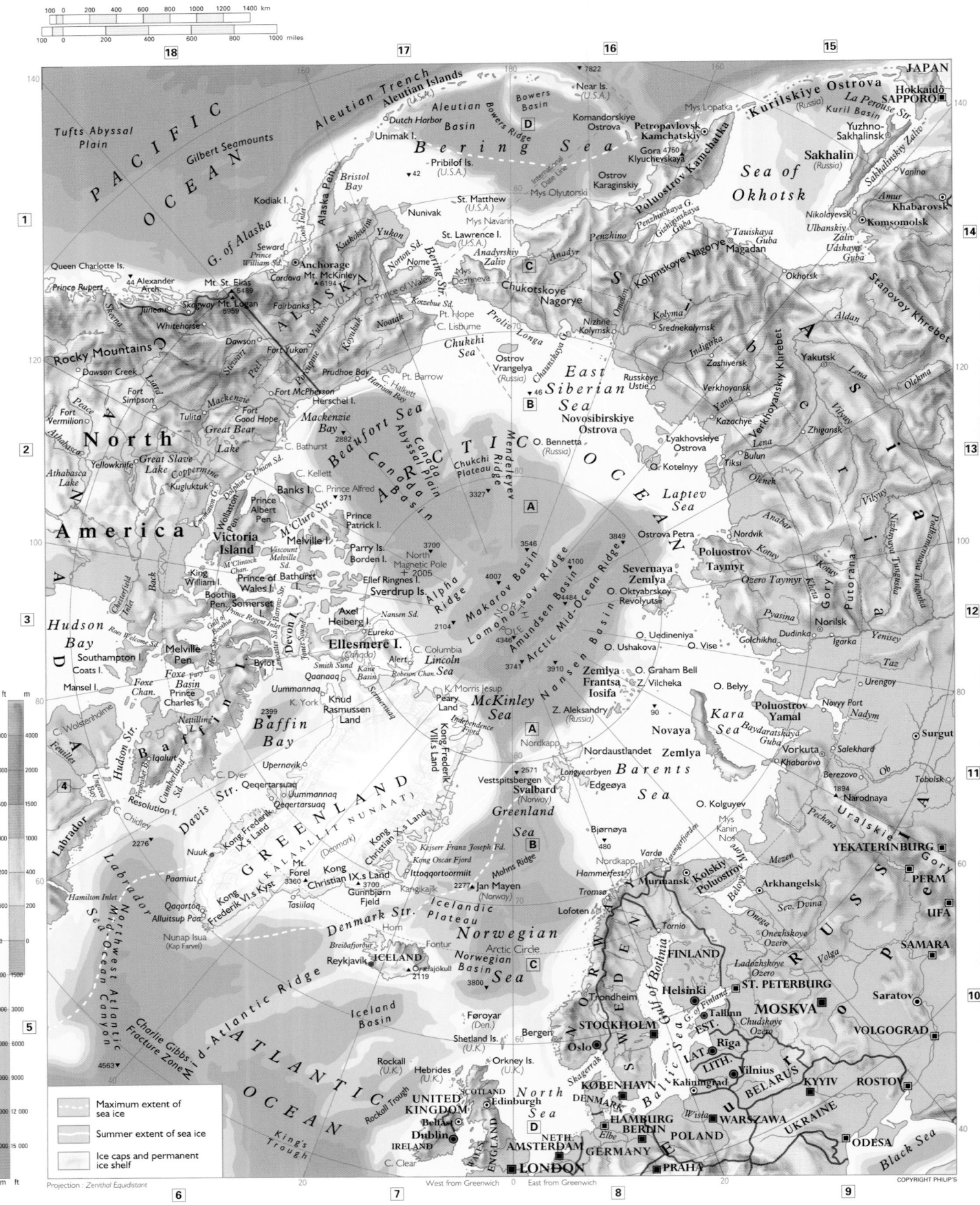

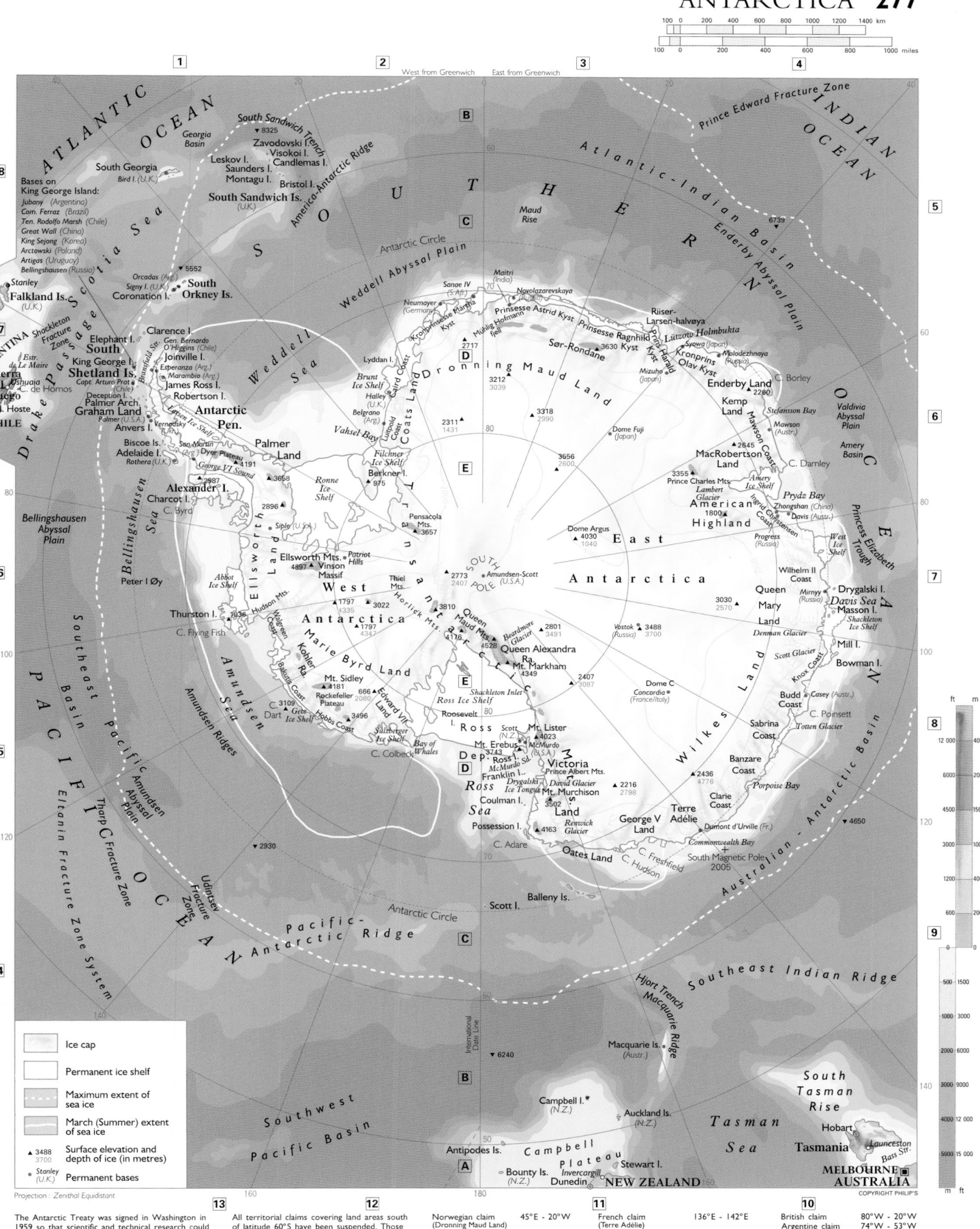

100 0   200   400   600   800   1000 1200 1400 km
100 0   200   400   600   800   1000 miles

ATLANTIC OCEAN

Georgia Basin

Bases on King George Island:
Jubany (Argentina)
Com. Ferraz (Brazil)
Ten. Rodolfo Marsh (Chile)
Great Wall (China)
King Sejong (Korea)
Arctowski (Poland)
Artigas (Uruguay)
Bellingshausen (Russia)

South Georgia
Bird I. (U.K.)

South Sandwich Trench
▼ 8325
Zavodovski I.
Leskov I.   Visokoi I.   Candlemas I.
Saunders I.
Montagu I.
Bristol I.
South Sandwich Is.
(U.K.)

Stanley
Falkland Is.
(U.K.)

Scotia Sea

▼ 5552
Orcadas (Arg.)
Signy I. (U.K.)   South
Coronation I.   Orkney Is.

Shackleton Fracture Zone
South Shetland Is.
Elephant I.
King George I.
Clarence I.
Gen. Bernardo O'Higgins (Chile)
Joinville I.
Esperanza (Arg.)
Capt. Arturo Prat (Chile)
Marambio (Arg.)
Deception I.
James Ross I.
Robertson I.
Palmer (U.S.A.)
Graham Land
Anvers I.
Vernadsky (Ukr.)
San Martín (Arg.)
Palmer Arch.
Biscoe Is.
Adelaide I.
Rothera (U.K.)
▲ 2987
Charcot I.

ATLANTIC-INDIAN BASIN

Prince Edward Fracture Zone

INDIAN OCEAN

Enderby Abyssal Plain

SOUTHERN OCEAN

Maud Rise
▲ 6739

Antarctic Circle

Weddell Abyssal Plain

Sanae IV (S. Afr.)
Neumayer (Germany)
Maitri (India)
Novolazarevskaya
Kronprinsesse Martha Kyst
Prinsesse Astrid Kyst
Prinsesse Ragnhild Kyst
Sør-Rondane
▲ 3630 Kyst
Riiser-Larsen-halvøya
Lützow Holmbukta
Syowa (Japan)
Kronprins Olav Kyst
Molodezhnaya (Russia)
Mizuho (Japan)
C. Borley
Enderby Land ▲ 2260

Weddell Sea

Lyddan I.
▲ 2717
Brunt Ice Shelf
Halley (U.K.)
Belgrano (Arg.)
Coats Land
Vahsel Bay
Filchner Ice Shelf
Ronne Ice Shelf
Berkner I.
▲ 975
Pensacola Mts.
▲ 3657

Dronning Maud Land
▲ 3212   3039
▲ 2311   1431
▲ 3318   2990
Dome Fuji (Japan)
▲ 3656   2600
Kemp Land
Stefansson Bay
Mawson (Austr.)
▲ 2645
MacRobertson Land
Prince Charles Mts. ▲ 3355
1800
Amery Ice Shelf
Lambert Glacier
Zhongshan (China)
Davis (Austr.)
Prydz Bay
Valdivia Abyssal Plain
Amery Basin
C. Darnley

East Antarctica

American Highland
Dome Argus ▲ 4030   1040

Progress (Russia)
Ingrid Christensen Coast
West Ice Shelf
Princess Elizabeth Trough
Wilhelm II Coast
Drygalski I.
Davis Sea
Masson I.
Shackleton Ice Shelf

South Pole ▲ 2773   2407
Amundsen-Scott (U.S.A.)

Queen Mary Land
▲ 3030   2570
Mirnyy (Russia)
Vostok (Russia) ▲ 3488   3700
Denman Glacier
Mill I.
Bowman I.

C. Byrd
Siple (U.S.A.)
Ellsworth Mts. ▲ 4897
Vinson Massif
Patriot Hills
Thiel Mts.
▲ 2407
Horlick Mts.
Queen Maud Mts. ▲ 4416
▲ 3810
Queen Alexandra Ra. ▲ 4528
Mt. Markham ▲ 4349

Dome C
Concordia (France/Italy)
▲ 2407   3087

Scott Glacier
Knox Coast
Budd Coast
Casey (Austr.)
C. Poinsett
Totten Glacier
Sabrina Coast

West Antarctica
Ellsworth Land
▲ 1797   4335
▲ 3022
Marie Byrd Land
Mt. Sidley ▲ 4181
Rockefeller Plateau
▲ 2080
Kohler Ra.
Executive Committee Ra.
Edward VII Land
▲ 3496
Shackleton Inlet
Ross Ice Shelf
Roosevelt I.
Beardmore Glacier
▲ 2801   3491

Wilkes Land

Banzare Coast
Sabrina Coast
Porpoise Bay
▲ 2436   4776
Clarie Coast
Commonwealth Bay
South Magnetic Pole 2005
Terre Adélie
Dumont d'Urville (Fr.)
▲ 4650
George V Land
▲ 2216   2798

Thurston I.
C. Flying Fish
Abbot Ice Shelf
Hudson Mts.
Walgreen Coast
▲ 1938
Amundsen Sea
Amundsen Ridges
Dart I.
▲ 3109
Gets Ice Shelf
Cobbs Coast
Sulzberger Ice Shelf
C. Colbeck
Bay of Whales
Ross Sea
Ross Dep.
Mt. Lister ▲ 4023
Scott (N.Z.)
Mt. Erebus ▲ 3743
Ross I.
McMurdo (U.S.A.)
McMurdo Sd.
Franklin I.
Victoria Land
Prince Albert Mts.
David Glacier ▲ 3502
Drygalski Ice Tongue
Mt. Murchison
Coulman I.
Renwick Glacier
▲ 4163
Possession I.
C. Adare
Oates Land
C. Freshfield
C. Hudson

Bellingshausen Sea
Bellingshausen Abyssal Plain
Peter I Øy

Southeast Pacific Basin
Eltanin Fracture Zone System
Amundsen Abyssal Plain
Tharp Fracture Zone
Udintsev Fracture Zone
▲ 2930
▼ 6240

PACIFIC OCEAN

Pacific-Antarctic Ridge
Antarctic Circle

Macquarie Ridge
Hjort Trench
Southeast Indian Ridge
Australian-Antarctic Basin

International Date Line

Campbell I. (N.Z.)
Auckland Is. (N.Z.)

Macquarie Is. (Austr.)

South Tasman Rise
Tasman Sea
Hobart
Launceston
Tasmania
Bass Str.
MELBOURNE AUSTRALIA
COPYRIGHT PHILIP'S

Southwest Pacific Basin

Antipodes Is.
Bounty Is. (N.Z.)
Campbell Plateau
Invercargill
Dunedin
Stewart I.
NEW ZEALAND

Legend

Ice cap
Permanent ice shelf
Maximum extent of sea ice
March (Summer) extent of sea ice
▲ 3488 / 3700   Surface elevation and depth of ice (in metres)
● Stanley (U.K.)   Permanent bases

Projection: Zenithal Equidistant

The Antarctic Treaty was signed in Washington in 1959 so that scientific and technical research could continue unhampered by international politics.

All territorial claims covering land areas south of latitude 60°S have been suspended. Those claims were:

Norwegian claim (Dronning Maud Land)	45°E – 20°W
Australian claims	45°E – 136°E 142°E – 160°E
French claim (Terre Adélie)	136°E – 142°E
New Zealand claim (Ross Dependency)	160°E – 150°W
British claim	80°W – 20°W
Argentine claim	74°W – 53°W
Chilean claim	90°W – 53°W

Elevation scale

ft	m
12 000	4000
6000	2000
4500	1500
3000	1000
1200	400
600	200
0	0
500	1500
1000	3000
3000	9000
4000	12 000
5000	15 000
m	ft

100 0 100 200 300 400 500 600 700 800 km
100 0 100 200 300 400 500 miles

COPYRIGHT PHILIP'S

Labels (seas and oceans):
ATLANTIC OCEAN
Norwegian Sea
North Sea
Baltic Sea
White Sea
Caspian Sea
Caspian Depression
Black Sea
Sea of Azov
Sea of Marmara
Adriatic Sea
Tyrrhenian Sea
Ligurian Sea
Ionian Sea
Aegean Sea
Mediterranean Sea
Sea of Crete
Irish Sea
Celtic Sea
North Sea
Kattegat
Skagerrak
Gulf of Bothnia
Gulf of Finland
Bay of Biscay

Physical regions and ranges:
West Siberian Lowlands
Ural Mountains
Timan Ridge
Northern Urals
Kirgiz Steppe
Obshchi Syrt
Volga Hts.
Central Russian Uplands
Donets Basin
East European Plain
Finland
Lapland
Scandinavia
Caucasus
Transcaucasia
Armenia
Kurdistan
Anatolia (Asia Minor)
Mesopotamia
Pontine Mts.
Taurus Mts.
Balkans
Carpathians
Transylvanian Alps
Wallachia
Plain of Hungary
Dinaric Alps
Apennines
Pindus
Peloponnese
Alps
Pyrenees
Cantabrian Mts.
Massif Central
Iberian Peninsula
Old Castile
New Castile
Sierra Morena
Sierra Nevada
Andalusia
Africa
Plateau of the Shotts
Great Britain
British Isles
Ireland
Pennines
Grampian Mts.
Hebrides
Iceland
Faeroe Is.
Shetland
Orkney Is.
Rockall
Jutland
Zealand
Gotland
Öland
Bornholm
Corsica
Sardinia
Sicily
Malta
Balearic Is.
Majorca
Minorca
Ibiza
Crete
Rhodes
Cyprus
Sardinia
Elba

Rivers and lakes:
Ob
Volga
Kama
Pechora
Don
Dnieper
Dniester
Danube
Rhine
Elbe
Oder
Seine
Loire
Garonne
Rhône
Ebro
Tagus
Douro
Po
Tiber
Tigris
Euphrates
L. Ladoga
L. Onega
L. Vänern
L. Vättern
L. Constance
L. Geneva

Weather forecast sea areas (left margin):
ROCKALL Sea areas named in weather forecasts
SOUTH EAST ICELAND
BAILEY
FAEROES
FAIR ISLE
CROMARTY
FORTH
TYNE
DOGGER
FISHER
GERMAN BIGHT
HUMBER
THAMES
FORTIES
VIKING
FORTH
PLYMOUTH
PORTLAND
WIGHT
BISCAY
FINISTERRE
SOLE
FASTNET
LUNDY
SHANNON
FITZROY
TRAFALGAR

Projection: Bonne

m ft
5000 15 000
4000 12 000
3000 9000
2000 6000
1000 3000
600 1800
400 1200
200 600
0
200 600
2000
4000 12 000

100 0 100 200 300 400 500 600 700 800 km

100 0 100 200 300 400 500 miles

Projection: Bonne

East from Greenwich

West from Greenwich

■ LONDON Capital Cities

Seas and Oceans:
Norwegian Sea · North Sea · ATLANTIC OCEAN · White Sea · Baltic Sea · Gulf of Bothnia · Kattegat · Skagerrak · English Channel · Bay of Biscay · Mediterranean Sea · Tyrrhenian Sea · Adriatic Sea · Ionian Sea · Ægean Sea · Black Sea · Caspian Sea

Countries and regions:
ICELAND · NORWAY · SWEDEN · FINLAND · DENMARK · UNITED KINGDOM · IRELAND · SCOTLAND · ENGLAND · WALES · NETHERLANDS · BELGIUM · LUXEMBOURG · FRANCE · SPAIN · PORTUGAL · GERMANY · SWITZERLAND · AUSTRIA · ITALY · MALTA · POLAND · CZECH REP. · SLOVAK REP. · HUNGARY · SLOVENIA · CROATIA · BOSNIA-HERZ. · SERBIA · MONTENEGRO · MACEDONIA · ALBANIA · GREECE · ROMANIA · BULGARIA · MOLDOVA · UKRAINE · BELARUS · LITHUANIA · LATVIA · ESTONIA · RUSSIA · KARELIA · KOMI · MORDVINIA · TATARSTAN · UDMURTIA · KAZAKHSTAN · TURKEY · CYPRUS · SYRIA · IRAQ · IRAN · GEORGIA · ARMENIA · AZERBAIJAN · DAGESTAN · CHECHENIA · NORTH OSSETIA · INGUSHETIA · KABARDINO-BALKARIA · KARACHAY-CHERKESSIA · ADYGEA · KALMYKIA · MOROCCO · ALGERIA · TUNISIA · Africa · Asia

Selected cities: Reykjavik · Tromsø · Narvik · Bodø · Trondheim · Bergen · Stavanger · Oslo · Luleå · Umeå · Sundsvall · Uppsala · Stockholm · Göteborg · Jönköping · Malmö · Aalborg · Århus · Copenhagen · Helsinki · Turku · Tampere · Murmansk · Arkhangelsk · ST. PETERSBURG · MOSCOW · Yaroslavl · Kostroma · Vologda · Kazan · Samara · Ufa · Orenburg · Saratov · Volgograd · Voronezh · Kursk · Tula · Orel · Smolensk · Rostov · Krasnodar · Stavropol · Astrakhan · Makhachkala · Baku · Tbilisi · Yerevan · Tabriz · Baghdad · Aleppo · Nicosia · Antalya · Konya · Ankara · Izmir · Istanbul · Athens · Thessaloníki · Sofia · Bucharest · Belgrade · Sarajevo · Zagreb · Ljubljana · Vienna · Budapest · Warsaw · Kraków · Prague · Berlin · Hamburg · Hannover · Cologne · Frankfurt · Munich · Stuttgart · Zürich · Bern · Milan · Turin · Genoa · Rome · Naples · Palermo · Catania · Valletta · Barcelona · Madrid · Lisbon · Porto · Seville · Cádiz · Valencia · Zaragoza · Bilbao · Toulouse · Bordeaux · Lyons · Marseilles · PARIS · LONDON · Dublin · Belfast · Edinburgh · Glasgow · Manchester · Liverpool · Birmingham · Bristol · Cardiff · Amsterdam · The Hague · Rotterdam · Antwerp · Brussels · Kiev · Minsk · Vilnius · Riga · Tallinn · Kaliningrad

Rivers: Ob · Ural · Volga · N. Dvina · L. Onega · L. Ladoga · W. Dvina · Dnieper · Dniester · Don · Danube · Vistula · Oder · Elbe · Rhine · Loire · Seine · Tagus · Duero · Ebro · Garonne · Po · Tigris · Euphrates

ICELAND
on same scale

FAEROE
ISLANDS
on same scale

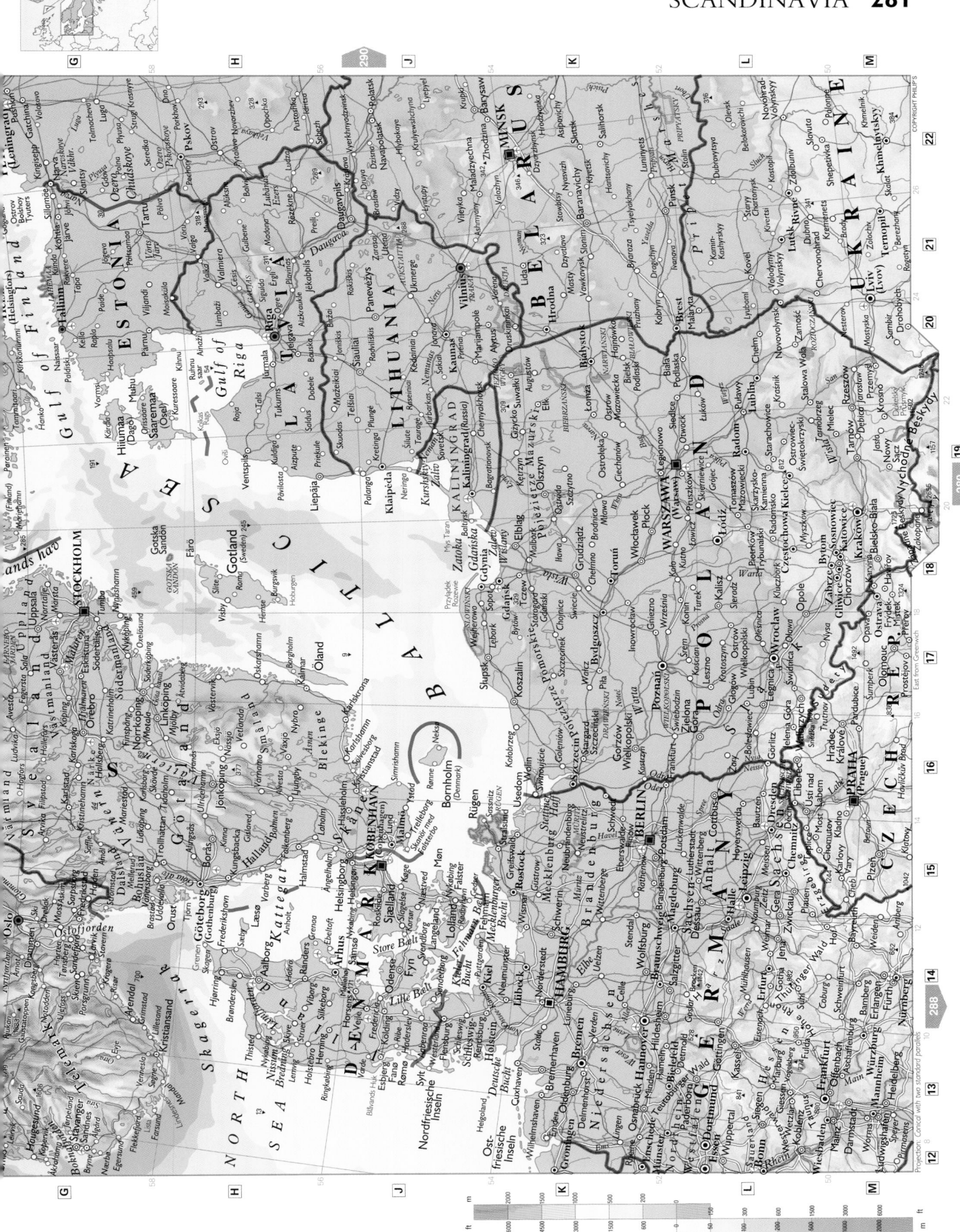

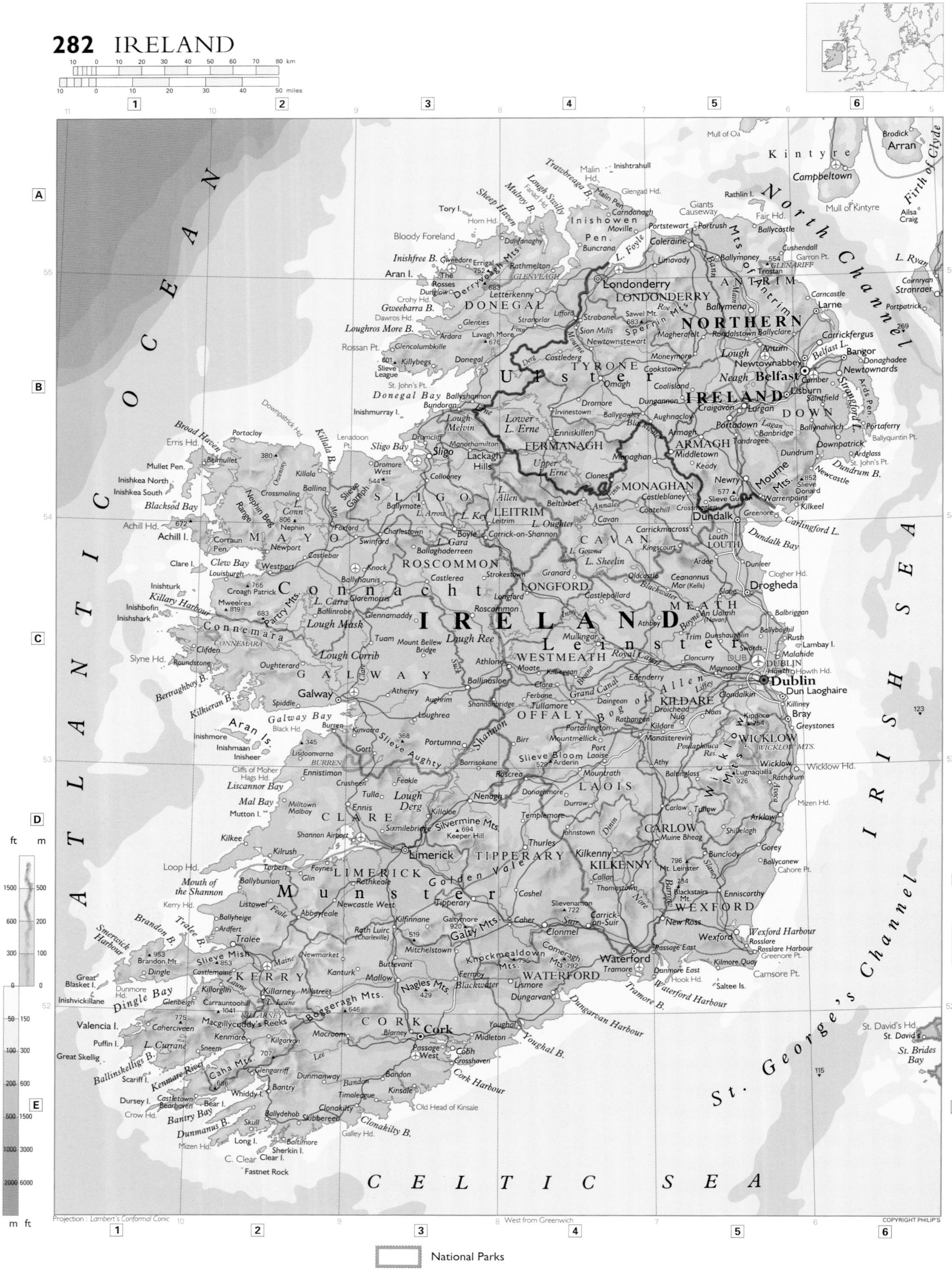

10 0 10 20 30 40 50 60 70 80 km
10 0 10 20 30 40 50 miles

ATLANTIC OCEAN

CELTIC SEA

IRISH SEA

St. George's Channel

North Channel

Firth of Clyde

NORTHERN IRELAND

IRELAND

Ulster

Connacht

Leinster

Munster

Provinces & Counties
DONEGAL, LONDONDERRY, ANTRIM, TYRONE, FERMANAGH, MONAGHAN, ARMAGH, DOWN, CAVAN, LEITRIM, SLIGO, MAYO, ROSCOMMON, LONGFORD, WESTMEATH, MEATH, LOUTH, GALWAY, OFFALY, KILDARE, DUBLIN, WICKLOW, CLARE, TIPPERARY, LAOIS, CARLOW, KILKENNY, WEXFORD, LIMERICK, KERRY, CORK, WATERFORD

Cities & Towns
Londonderry, Belfast, Bangor, Newtownards, Coleraine, Ballymoney, Larne, Carrickfergus, Antrim, Ballymena, Lisburn, Lurgan, Craigavon, Portadown, Banbridge, Newry, Armagh, Monaghan, Enniskillen, Omagh, Strabane, Letterkenny, Buncrana, Sligo, Ballina, Westport, Castlebar, Knock, Boyle, Carrick-on-Shannon, Longford, Mullingar, Athlone, Tullamore, Roscommon, Galway, Tuam, Ballinasloe, Ennis, Limerick, Tralee, Killarney, Kenmare, Bantry, Skibbereen, Clonakilty, Kinsale, Bandon, Macroom, Cork, Midleton, Cobh, Youghal, Dungarvan, Waterford, Tramore, New Ross, Wexford, Rosslare, Enniscorthy, Gorey, Arklow, Wicklow, Bray, Greystones, Dun Laoghaire, Dublin, Drogheda, Dundalk, Navan, Trim, Kells, Cavan, Carrickmacross, Kingscourt, Kilkenny, Carlow, Athy, Portlaoise, Tipperary, Cashel, Clonmel, Carrick-on-Suir, Thurles, Nenagh, Mallow, Fermoy, Listowel, Dingle

Physical Features
Lough Neagh, Lough Erne, Upper L. Erne, Lower L. Erne, Lough Allen, Lough Ree, Lough Corrib, Lough Mask, Lough Derg, Lough Gill, Shannon, Blackwater, Barrow, Nore, Suir, Boyne, Liffey, Slaney, Donegal Bay, Clew Bay, Galway Bay, Dingle Bay, Bantry Bay, Dundalk Bay, Carlingford L., Strangford L., Belfast Lough, Errigal 752, Croagh Patrick 765, Mweelrea 819, Nephin 806, Carrauntoohil 1041, Macgillycuddy's Reeks, Brandon Mt. 953, Galty Mts., Knockmealdown Mts., Comeragh Mts., Wicklow Mts., Lugnaquilla 926, Slieve Donard 852, Mourne Mts., Sperrin Mts., Mts. of Antrim, Ox Mts., Nephin Beg Range, Connemara, The Burren, Cliffs of Moher, Golden Vale, Bog of Allen

Achill I., Aran Is., Inishmore, Inishmaan, Inisheer, Clare I., Tory I., Rathlin I., Valencia, Great Blasket I., Fastnet Rock, Cape Clear

Mizen Hd., Loop Hd., Slyne Hd., Erris Hd., Malin Hd., Fair Hd., Howth Hd., Carnsore Pt., Old Head of Kinsale

Projection: Lambert's Conformal Conic

West from Greenwich

COPYRIGHT PHILIP'S

National Parks

ft m
1500 500
600 200
300 100
0 0
150 50
300 100
600 200
1500 500
3000 1000
6000 2000
m ft

Key to Scottish unitary
authorities on map
1 CITY OF ABERDEEN   8 EAST RENFREWSHIRE
2 DUNDEE CITY   9 NORTH LANARKSHIRE
3 WEST DUNBARTONSHIRE   10 FALKIRK
4 EAST DUNBARTONSHIRE   11 CLACKMANNANSHIRE
5 CITY OF GLASGOW   12 WEST LOTHIAN
6 INVERCLYDE   13 CITY OF EDINBURGH
7 RENFREWSHIRE   14 MIDLOTHIAN

ORKNEY IS.
on same scale

ORKNEY

SHETLAND IS.
on same scale

SHETLAND

ATLANTIC

OCEAN

WESTERN
ISLES

Outer Hebrides

Lewis

Harris

North
Uist

South
Uist

Barra

Sea of the Hebrides

Inner Hebrides

Skye

Cuillin Hills

Rhum
(Rùm)

Eigg

Muck

Coll

Tiree

Mull

Iona

Colonsay

Oronsay

Islay

Jura

Arran

HIGHLAND

Sutherland

Caithness

Thurso
Wick

Reay
Forest

Ben Hope
927

Ben More
Assynt
998

L. Shin

Lairg

Brora

Golspie

Helmsdale

Ullapool

Ben Wyvis
1045

Inverness

MORAY

Elgin

Buckie

Fraserburgh

Peterhead

Buchan

ABERDEENSHIRE

Aberdeen

Grampian Mountains

Cairngorm Mts.

Fort William

Ben Nevis
1344

Glen Coe

Rannoch Moor

Ben Lawers
1214

PERTH AND
KINROSS

ANGUS

Montrose

Arbroath

Forfar

Brechin

Oban

ARGYLL
AND BUTE

Loch Lomond

STIRLING

Perth

Dundee

FIFE

St. Andrews

SCOTLAND

Glasgow

Edinburgh

Paisley

Hamilton

Motherwell

SOUTH
LANARKSHIRE

EAST
AYRSHIRE

NORTH
AYRSHIRE

SOUTH
AYRSHIRE

Ayr

Prestwick

Kilmarnock

Irvine
Troon

SCOTTISH
BORDERS

Galashiels

Hawick

Peebles

DUMFRIES &
GALLOWAY

Dumfries

Stranraer

NORTH
SEA

ENGLAND

Newcastle-upon-Tyne

NORTHUMBERLAND

CUMBRIA

Carlisle

DURHAM

NORTHERN
IRELAND

Belfast

NORTH
CHANNEL

Projection : Lambert's Conformal Conic

West from Greenwich

COPYRIGHT PHILIP'S

National Parks and Forest Parks in Scotland

10 0 10 20 30 40 50 60 70 80 km
10 0 10 20 30 40 50 miles

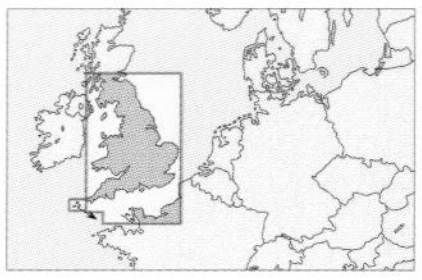

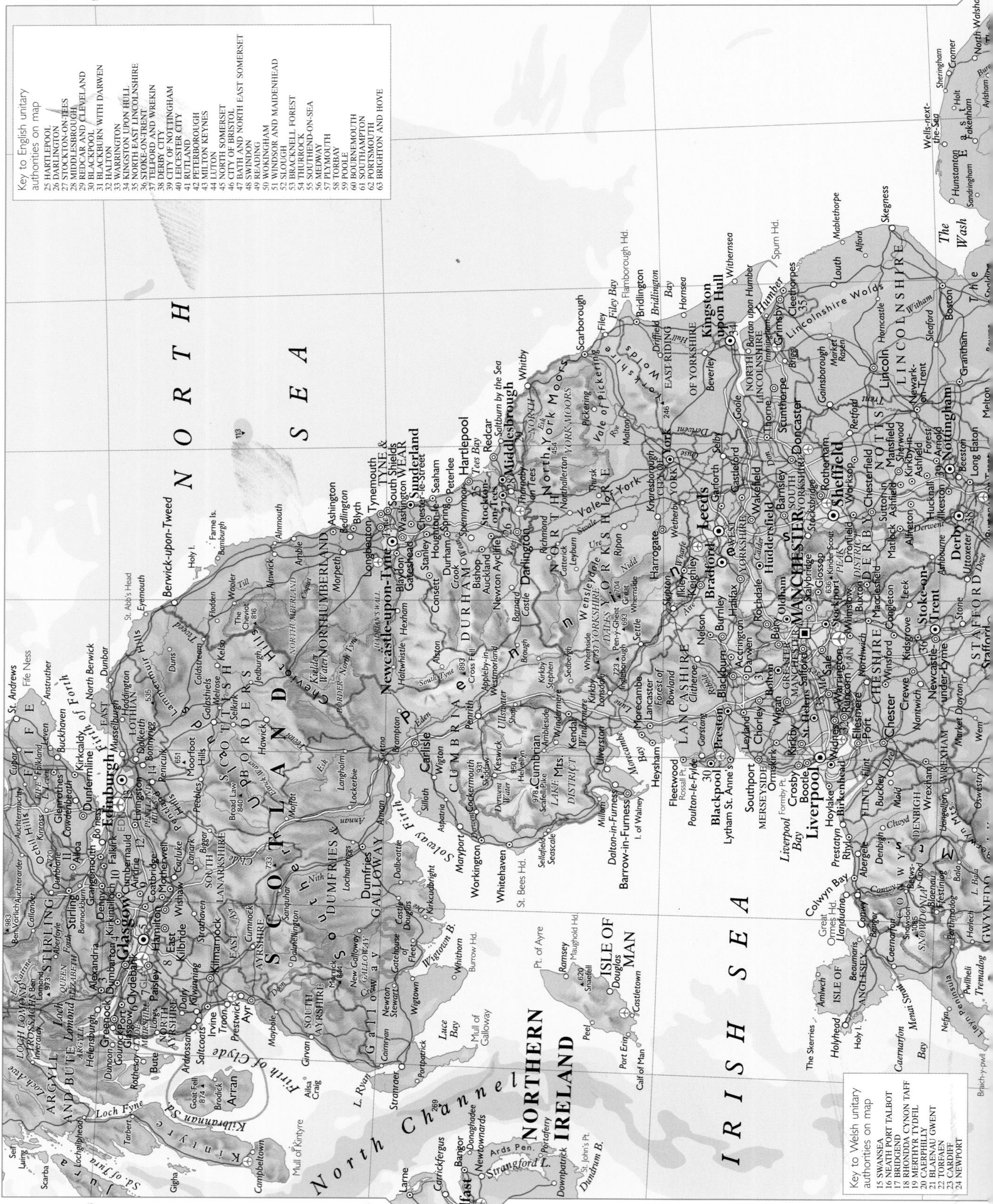

Key to English unitary authorities on map

25 HARTLEPOOL
26 DARLINGTON
27 STOCKTON-ON-TEES
28 MIDDLESBROUGH
29 REDCAR AND CLEVELAND
30 BLACKPOOL
31 BLACKBURN WITH DARWEN
32 HALTON
33 WARRINGTON
34 KINGSTON UPON HULL
35 NORTH EAST LINCOLNSHIRE
36 STOKE-ON-TRENT
37 TELFORD AND WREKIN
38 DERBY CITY
39 CITY OF NOTTINGHAM
40 LEICESTER CITY
41 RUTLAND
42 PETERBOROUGH
43 MILTON KEYNES
44 LUTON
45 NORTH SOMERSET
46 CITY OF BRISTOL
47 BATH AND NORTH EAST SOMERSET
48 SWINDON
49 READING
50 WOKINGHAM
51 WINDSOR AND MAIDENHEAD
52 SLOUGH
53 BRACKNELL FOREST
54 THURROCK
55 SOUTHEND-ON-SEA
56 MEDWAY
57 TORBAY
58 PLYMOUTH
59 POOLE
60 BOURNEMOUTH
61 SOUTHAMPTON
62 PORTSMOUTH
63 BRIGHTON AND HOVE

Key to Welsh unitary authorities on map

15 SWANSEA
16 NEATH PORT TALBOT
17 BRIDGEND
18 RHONDDA CYNON TAFF
19 MERTHYR TYDFIL
20 CAERPHILLY
21 BLAENAU GWENT
22 TORFAEN
23 CARDIFF
24 NEWPORT

NORTH SEA

IRISH SEA

North Channel

NORTHERN IRELAND

SCOTLAND

ENGLAND

WALES

ATLANTIC OCEAN

Shetland Is.
Yell
Unst
Fetlar
Foula
Mainland
Lerwick

Fair Isle

NORWAY
Askøyna
Bergen
Osøyro
Stord
Haugesund
Kopervik
Åkrahamn
Bokn
Stavanger
Sandne
Bryn
Nærb

Orkney Is.
Westray
Sanday
Stronsay
Mainland
Kirkwall
Hoy
South
Ronaldsay

C. Wrath
Pentland Firth
Thurso
Wick
Helmsdale

Lewis
Stornoway
North Minch
Golspie
Laird
Ullapool
Tain
Moray Firth
Buckie
Banff
Fraserburgh

Outer Hebrides
Harris
North Uist
Benbecula
Portree
Skye
Invergordon
Dingwall
Nairn
Elgin
Peterhead
Inverness
CAIRNGORMS
Huntly
Inverurie
Aberdeen

St. Kilda
South Uist
Barra
Rhum
Eigg
Coll
Tobermory
Mull
Tiree
Oban
Fort William
SCOTLAND
Glen More
L. Ness
Aviemore
Don
Ballater
Stonehaven
Grampian Mts.
Forfar
Montrose
Arbroath
Dundee
St. Andrews

Sea of the Hebrides
Inner Hebrides

NORTH SEA

Colonsay
Islay
Jura
L. Fyne
L. Awe
L. Lomond
Perth
Glenrothes
Kirkcaldy
Dunbar
Stirling
Dunfermline
Campbeltown
Dumbarton
Greenock
Paisley
GLASGOW
Motherwell
Hamilton
East Kilbride
Irvine
Kilmarnock
EDINBURGH
Galashiels
Berwick-upon-Tweed
Arran
Ayr
Southern Uplands
Jedburgh
Cheviot Hills
Alnwick
Campbeltown
Hawick
NORTHUMBERLAND
Newcastle-upon-Tyne
Girvan
Dumfries
South Shields
Annan
Hexham
Sunderland
Stranraer
Carlisle
Gateshead
Durham
Hartlepool
Kirkcudbright
Workington
Darlington
Redcar
Mull of Galloway
Whitehaven
Cumbrian Mts.
Middlesbrough
Stockton-on-Tees
N. YORK MOORS
Scarborough
Douglas
I. of Man
LAKE DISTRICT
Barrow-in-Furness
Lancaster
YORKSHIRE DALES
Bridlington

238

Bancrana
Letterkenny
Coleraine
Ballymena
Larne
Lifford
Londonderry
Ballymena
Donegal
ULSTER
Omagh
NORTHERN IRELAND
Bangor
Lough Neagh
Belfast
Bundoran
Lower L. Erne
Enniskillen
Lisburn
Lurgan
Portadown
Armagh
Sligo
Leitrim
Cavan
Newry
Castleblaney
Dundalk
Ballina
L. Conn
Castlebar
UNITED KINGDOM
Harrogate
Keighley
York
Beverley
Kingston upon Hull
Leeds
Bradford
Blackpool
Preston
Burnley
Huddersfield
Barnsley
Scunthorpe
Grimsby
Blackburn
Bolton
Halifax
Doncaster
Rotherham
Humber
Louth
Boston
Skegness
IRISH SEA
Anglesey
MANCHESTER
Liverpool
Warrington
Oldham
Sheffield
PEAK DISTRICT
Lincoln
Holyhead
Chester
Chesterfield
Mansfield
Crewe
Derby
Nottingham
The Wash
Cromer
Bangor
Colwyn Bay
Stoke on Trent
Stafford
Nottingham
Grantham
THE BROADS
Wrexham
Pwllheli
Snowdon
SNOWDONIA
Shrewsbury
Telford
ENGLAND
Leicester
Peterborough
King's Lynn
Norwich
Great Yarmouth
Lowestoft
Cardigan Bay
Welshpool
Cambrian Mts.
Wolverhampton
BIRMINGHAM
Coventry
Rugby
Corby
Northampton
Ely
Thetford
Bury St. Edmunds
Ipswich
Aberystwyth
Redditch
Worcester
Royal Leamington Spa
Bedford
Cambridge
NETHERLAN
's-Gravenhage (Den Haag)
Hereford
Cheltenham
Milton Keynes
Luton
Harlow
Colchester
Felixstowe
Harwich
ROTTERDA
Dordre
WALES
Brecon
Gloucester
Oxford
High Wycombe
Stevenage
Chelmsford
Carmarthen
BRECON BEACONS
Hemel Hempstead
Haverfordwest
Milford Haven
Pembroke
Llanelli
Neath
Cwmbran
Newport
Cardiff
Bristol
Bath
Swindon
Newbury
Reading
Slough
LONDON
Basildon
Southend-on-Sea
Vlissingen
Zeebrugge
BELGIU
BRUSSE
(Bruxelle)
PEMBROKESHIRE COAST
Swansea
Port Talbot
Barry
Weston-super-Mare
Chatham
Margate
Oostende
Brugge
Gent
Bristol Channel
EXMOOR
Exmoor
Salisbury
Guildford
Maidstone
Canterbury
Dover
Folkestone
Antwerp
Barnstaple
Taunton
Yeovil
Winchester
Fareham
Crawley
Ashford
Hastings
Str. of Dover
Dunkerque
Lille
Tournai
Bude
Bournemouth
Poole
NEW FOREST
Southampton
Havant
Brighton
Eastbourne
Worthing
Gris-Nez
Boulogne-sur-Mer
Calais
St-Omer
Béthune
Bruay-la-Buissière
DARTMOOR
Exeter
Newport
Weymouth
Isle of Wight
Portsmouth
Le Touquet-Paris-Plage
33
Exmouth
Torbay
ENGLISH CHANNEL
Newquay
Truro
St. Austell
Plymouth
Penzance
Falmouth
Land's End
Isles of Scilly
618
Le Tréport
Dieppe
Abbeville
PICARDIE
Amiens
Fécamp
Pays de Caux
FRANCE
Rouen
292
East from Greenwich
COPYRIGHT PHILIP'S

CELTIC SEA

C. de la Hague
Pte. de Barfleur
Alderney
Guernsey
St. Peter Port
Sark
Cotentin
Cherbourg
Valognes
Le Havre
Honfleur
Seine
Channel Is. (U.K.)
St. Helier
Jersey
Bayeux
Trouville-sur-Mer
Caen
Lisieux
Elbeuf
West from Greenwich

IRELAND
Westport
Roscommon
Longford
Lough Mask
Connemara
Lough Corrib
Athlone
Lough Ree
Mullingar
Boyne
Galway B.
Galway
Ballinasloe
Tullamore
Laois
Aran Is.
Ennis
Lough Derg
Port Laoise
Athy
Carlow
Arklow
Kilrush
Limerick
Thurles
Kilkenny
Tipperary
Dublin
Dun Laoghaire
Bray
Ceanannus Mor
Cavan
Drogheda
Wicklow Mts.
Listowel
Dingle
Tralee
Mallow
Clonmel
Carrick-on-Suir
Wexford
Rosslare
Killarney
Shannon
Blackwater
Waterford
Dungarvan
Valencia I.
Macgillycuddy's Reeks
1041
Bandon
Cobh
Youghal
953
Carrauntoohil
Cork
Kinsale
Bantry
C. Clear
99

Projection: Conical with two standard parallels

ft m
3000 1000
1500 500
600 200
0 0
150 50
300 100
600 200
1500 500
3000 1000
6000 2000
m ft

50 0 25 50 75 100 125 150 175 km
50 0 25 50 75 100 125 miles

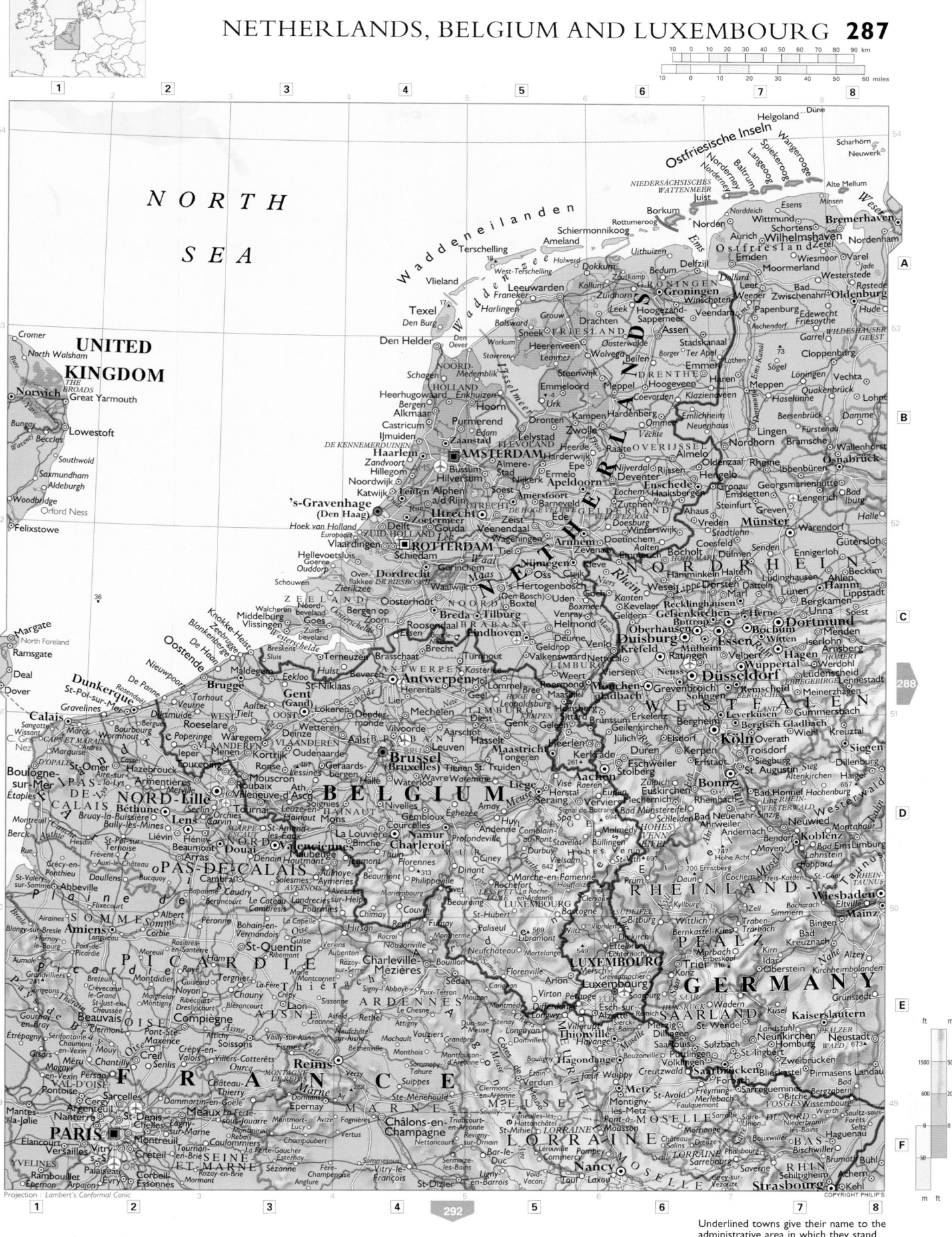

Projection : Lambert's Conformal Conic

COPYRIGHT PHILIP'S

Underlined towns give their name to the
administrative area in which they stand.

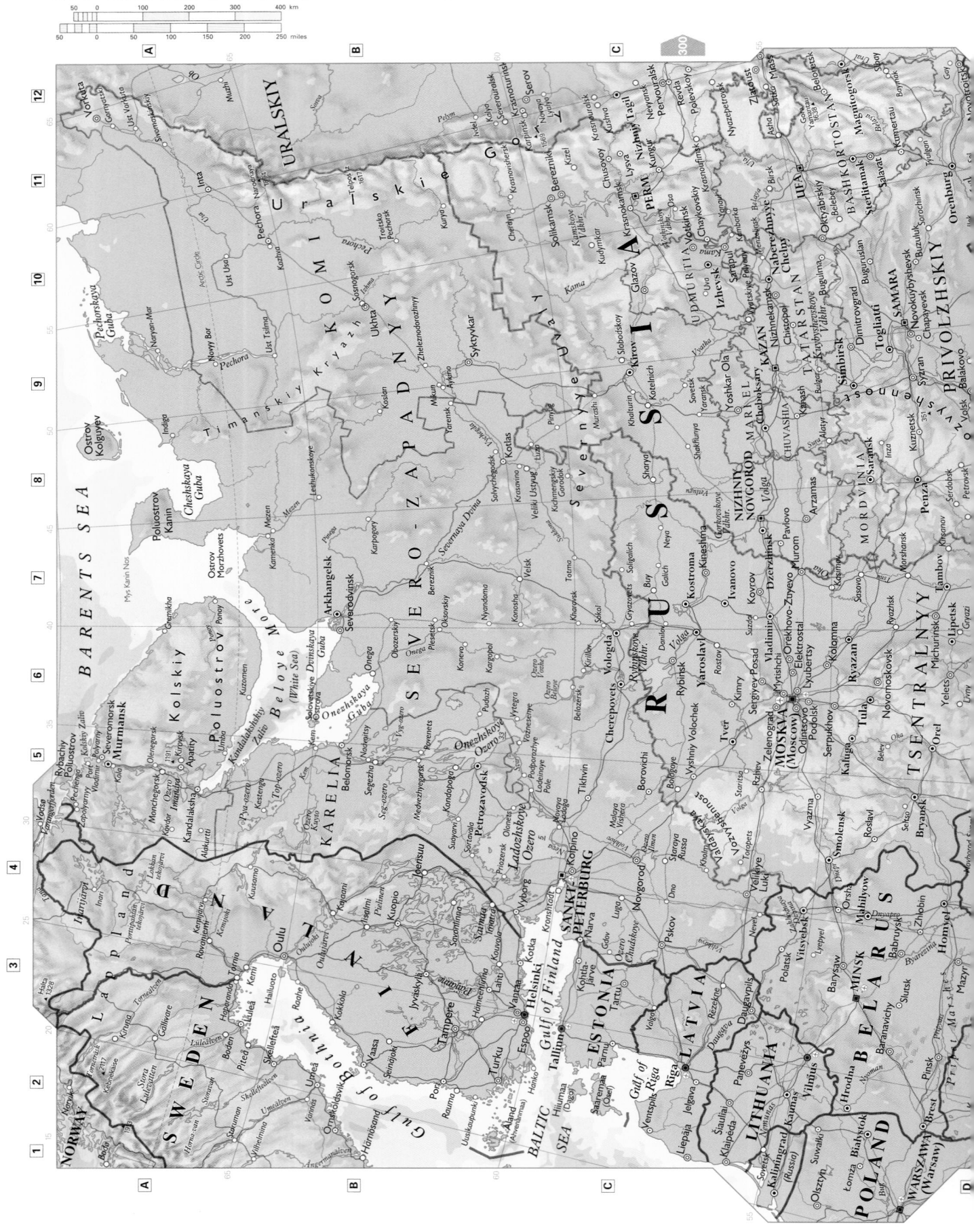

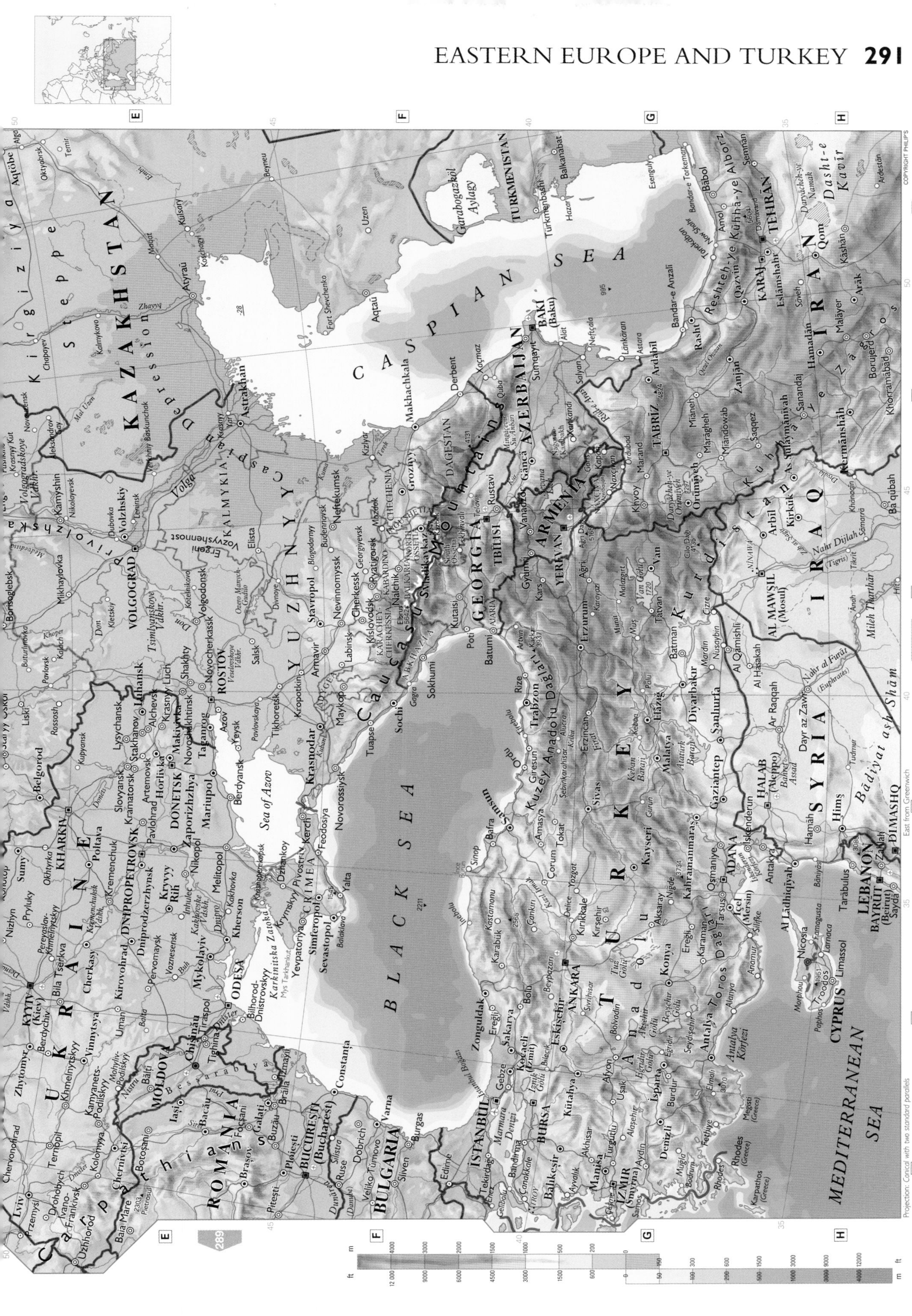

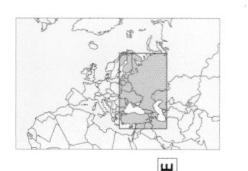

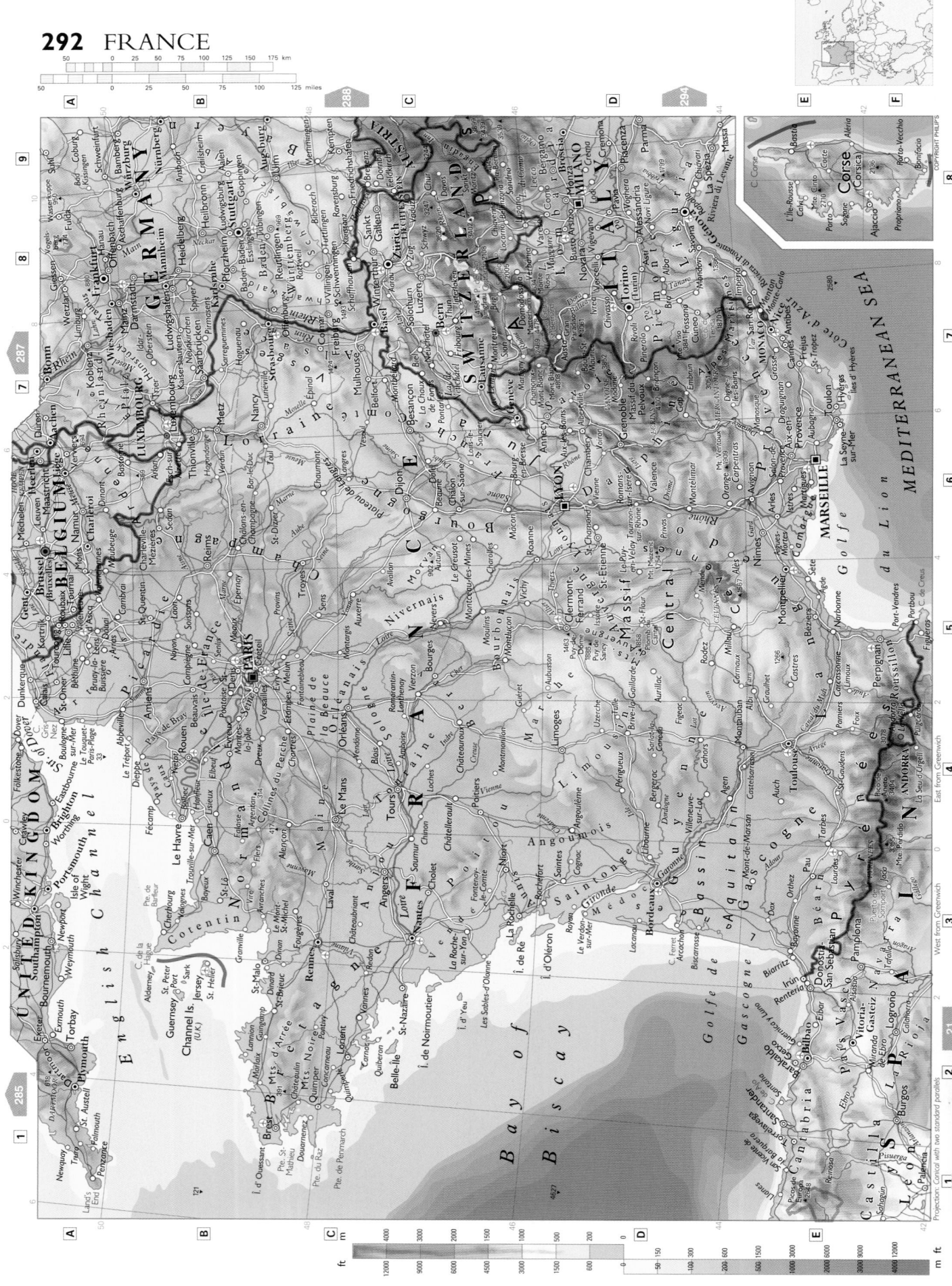

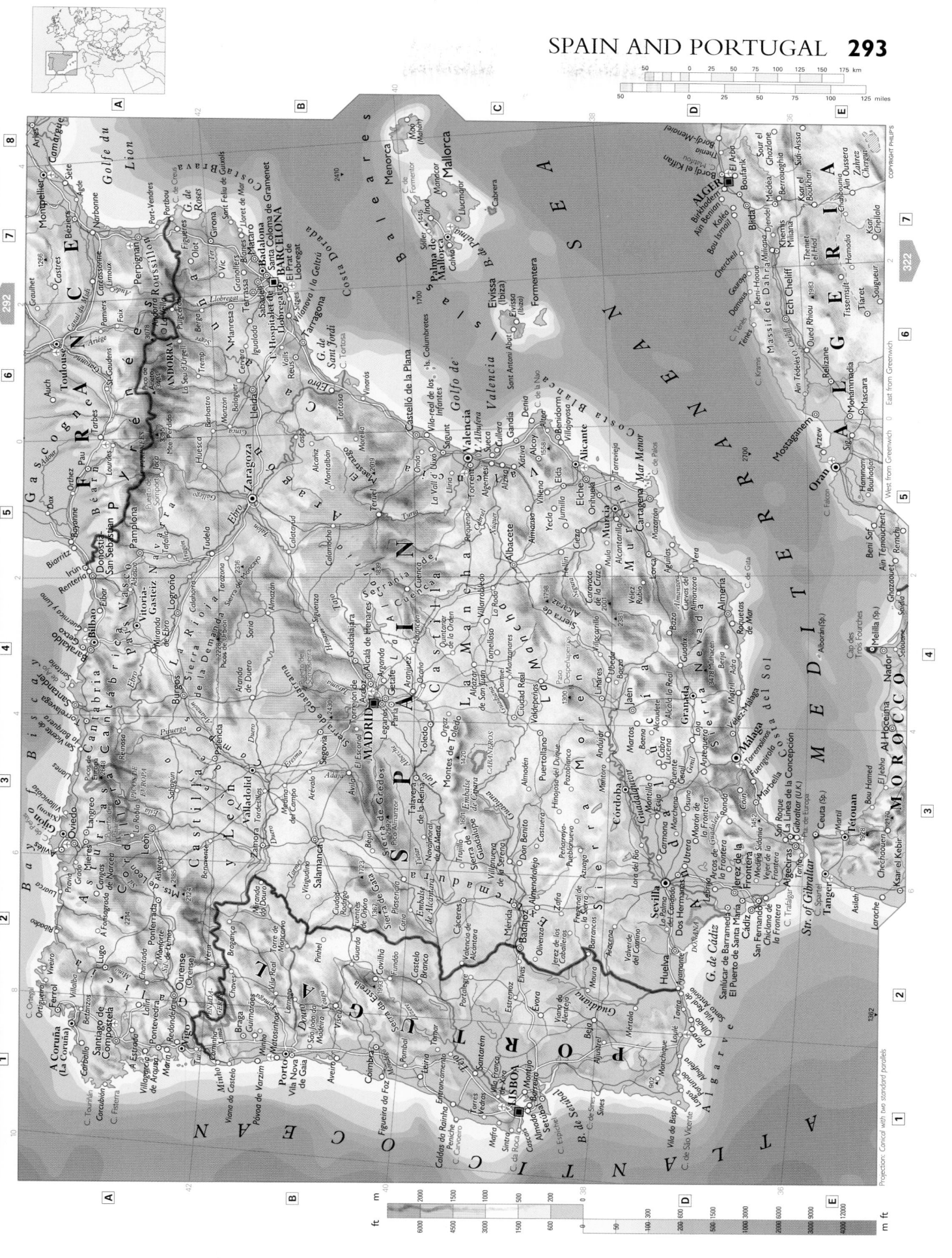

288

292

322

Projection: Conical with two standard parallels

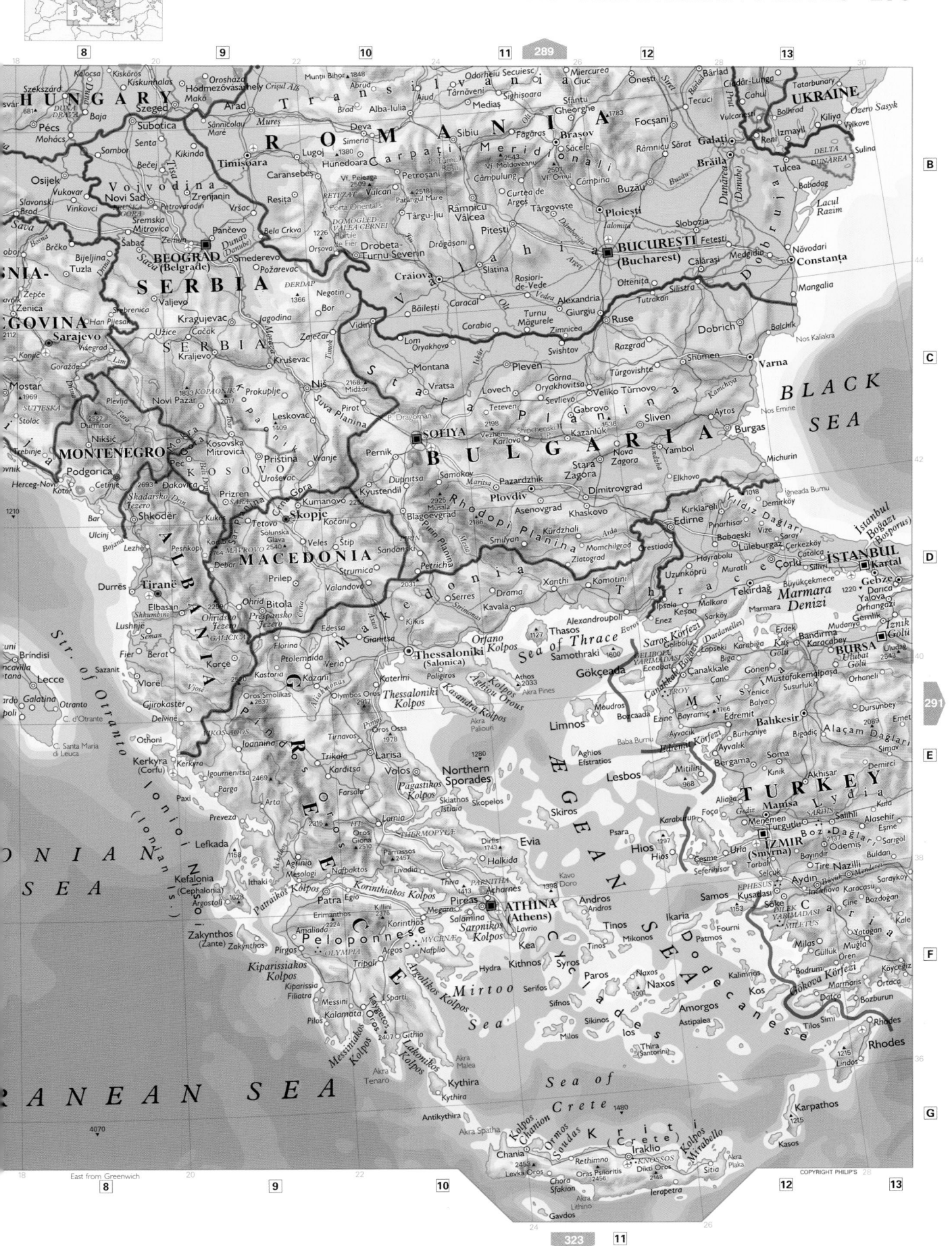

HUNGARY

Szekszárd Kalocsa Kiskőrös
Kiskunhalas Oroshaza Hódmezővásárhely Crisul Alb Muntii Bihor 1848 Odorheiu Secuiesc Miercurea Onesti Siret Radauti Barlad Ciddr-Lunga Tatarbunary
Makó Arad Abrud Aiud Tárnáveni Medias Sighisoara a Ciuc Onesti Tecuci Cahul Balhrad Kiliya Ozero Sasyk
UKRAINE
681 Baja Szeged Sánnicolau Brad Deva Alba-Iulia Sibiu Fágáras Brasov Sfántu Gheorghe 1783 Focsani Vulcanesti Renii Izmayil Vylkove
Pécs Mare Simeria Sácele Tulcea
Mohács Senta Kikinda Timisoara Lugoj 1380 Hunedoara Petrosani Cámpulung 2543 Vf. Omul 2507 Buzau Braila DELTA Sulina
Osijek Vojvodina Zrenjanin Reschita Caransebes VI. Peleaga 2509 Parângul Mare 2518 Curtea de Cómpina DUNAREA Babadag
Vukovar Novi Sad Petrovaradin Vršac RETEZAT Vulcan Arges Targoviste Ploiesti Slobozia Lacul
Slavonski Bela Crkva 1226 DOMOGLED-VALEA CERNEI Rámnicu Razim
Brod Sremska Pancevo Orsova Drobeta- Válcea Pitesti BUCURESTI Fetesti Návodari
Sava Mitrovica Danube Turnu Severin Drágásani (Bucharest) Cálárasi Constanta
Brčko Sabac SERBIA Craiova Slatina Olt Oltenita Silistra
Bijeljina Valjevo Báilesti Caracal Turnu Tutrakan Dobrich
Tuzla Kragujevac Jagodina Bor Vidin Magurele Giurgiu Ruse Razgrad
Srebrenica Han Pijesak Zaječar Lom Oryakhovo Corabia Zimnicea Svishtov Shumen Varna
Zepče Užice Čačak Timok Montana Pleven Gorna Veliko Tŭrnovo
Zenica Kralevo Kruševac Niš 2168 Vratsa Oryakhovitsa Sevlievo Gabrovo Sliven Nos Emine
Sarajevo Višegrad SERBIA Midžor Lovech Teteven Shipchenski Sliven Aytos Burgas
Goražde KOPAONIK 2017 Prokuplje Pirot 1409 Suva Planina P. Dragoman SOFIYA Karlovo 2198 Kazanlŭk 636 Yambol
Konjic 1833 Leskovac Vezhen BULGARIA Stara Nova Zagora Elkhovo
Mostar 1969 Novi Pazar Kosovska Vanje Pernik Musala 2925 Plovdiv Dimitrovgrad
Trebinje Plevlja Mitrovica Pristina Kyustendil Blagoevgrad 2186 Asenovgrad Haskovo
MONTENEGRO Niksić Durmitor 2522 Uroševac Kumanovo Kočani Smilyan Rhodopi Planina Kŭrdzhali Arda Crestlada
Podgorica Kolašin Skopje Veles Štip Momchilgrad Edirne Kirklareli Yildiz Daglari Istanbul
Herceg-Novi Cetinje Skadarsko Djakovica Prizren Tetovo Sandanski Strumica Zlatograd Uzunköprü Pinarhisar Vize Bogazi Bosporus
Kotor Jezero Shkodēr Kukës MACEDONIA Petrich Xanthi Komotini Hayrabolu Babaeski Lüleburgaz Çerkezköy ISTANBUL
Bar Peshkopi Debar Prilep Valandovo 2031 Drama Uzunköprü Muratli Çorlu Silivri Kartal
Ulcinj Lezhë ALBANIA Ohrid Bitola Edessa Serres Kavala Enez Ipsola Kesan Tekirdag Marmara Denizi Gebze Darica
Durrës Tiranē Elbasan Presbansko Jezero Florina Giannitsa Kilkis Alexandroupoli Saros Körfezi Malkara Sarköy Marmara Erdek Bandirma Yalova Iznik Gölü
Lushnje Ohridsko Jezero GALICICA Veria Thessaloniki Evros Samothraki Gelibolu Lapseki Karabiga Kus Gölü Gemlik BURSA
Berat Fier Seman Ptolemaida (Salonica) Poligiros Thasos Enez Eceabat Biga Gönen Mustafakemalpasa Uludag 2543 Orhaneli
Vlorë Kastoria Kazani Kasandra Kolpos 1600 Canakkale Çan Yenice Balya Susurluk Dursunbey
Gjirokastër Konitsa 2637 Olympos Athos 2033 TROY Lapseki Edremit Bergama Manisa Demirci
Delvinë Ioannina 2917 Oros Ossa Akra Pines MY Bozcaada Ezine Bayrami Edremit Ayvalik Soma Akhisar
Othoni 1978 Tirnavos Thessaliki Kolpos Limnos Baba Burnu Edremit Körfezi Mitilini TURKEY
Kerkyra Tinos Trikala Larisa Sea of Thrace Ayvacik 968 Izmir

BLACK SEA

MONTENEGRO

MACEDONIA

ALBANIA

BULGARIA

ROMANIA

SERBIA

UKRAINE

TURKEY

GREECE

Paxi Preveza Parga Arta Ágios Efstratios Lesbos Karaburun Foça Menemen Manisa Lydia
Lefkada Agrinio 1158 Mesologi Volos Northern Sporades Psara Turgutlu Salihli Alasehir Esme
Kefalonia Ithaki Farsala Skiathos Skopelos Skiros Çesme Urla Boz Daglar 2137 Sargol
(Cephalonia) 2469 Karditsa Istiaia Chios Seferihisar (Smyrna) Ödemis Buldan
Argostoli 1628 Nafpaktos Livadia Chios Selçuk Tire Nazilli
Patra Egio Korinthiakos Kolpos 2457 Parnassos THERMOPYLE Dirfis 1743 Evia Kavo Doro Andros Samos Kusadasi Aydin Inciralova Karacasu Saraiköy
Zakynthos Erimanthos 2224 Killini Corinthos Megara Thiva Parnitha 1413 Psari EPHESUS Kusadasi 1153 Söke PILEK YARIMADASI MILETUS Yatagan Bozdogan
(Zante) Amaliada 2376 Pireas ATHINA Ikaria Milas Gulluk Mugla
Pirgos Peloponnese Argos Nafplio Salamina Saronikos Kolpos Kea Tinos Mikonos Patmos Fourni Gulluk Körfezi Köycegiz
Kiparissiakos OLYMPIA MYCENAE Hydra Kithnos Naxos Kalimnos Bodrum Datça Ortaca
Kolpos Kiparissia Tripoli Argolikos Kolpos Syros Paros 1001 Amorgos Gökova Körfezi Marmaris Bozburun
Filiatra Messini Sparti Taygetos 2407 Mirtoo Serifos Sifnos Naxos Astipalea Kos Tilos Simi Rhodes
Pilos Kalamata Githio Sea Sikinos Ios Milos Thira (Santorini) Amorgos Rhodes Lindos
Koroni Messiniakos Kolpos Lakonikos Kolpos Akra Tenaro Kythira Karpathos
Kythira Antikythira Sea of Crete 1480 1215 Kasos

IONIAN SEA

AEGEAN SEA

Dodecanese

MEDITERRANEAN SEA

4070

Akra Spatha Chania Kolpos Chanion Ormos Soudas Rethimno Kriti (Crete) Iraklio Akra Plaka Sitia
Levka Oros 2453 KNOSSOS Oras Psiloritis 2456 Dikti Oros 2148 Kolpos Mirabello
Chora Sfakion Akra Lithino Ierapetra
Gavdos

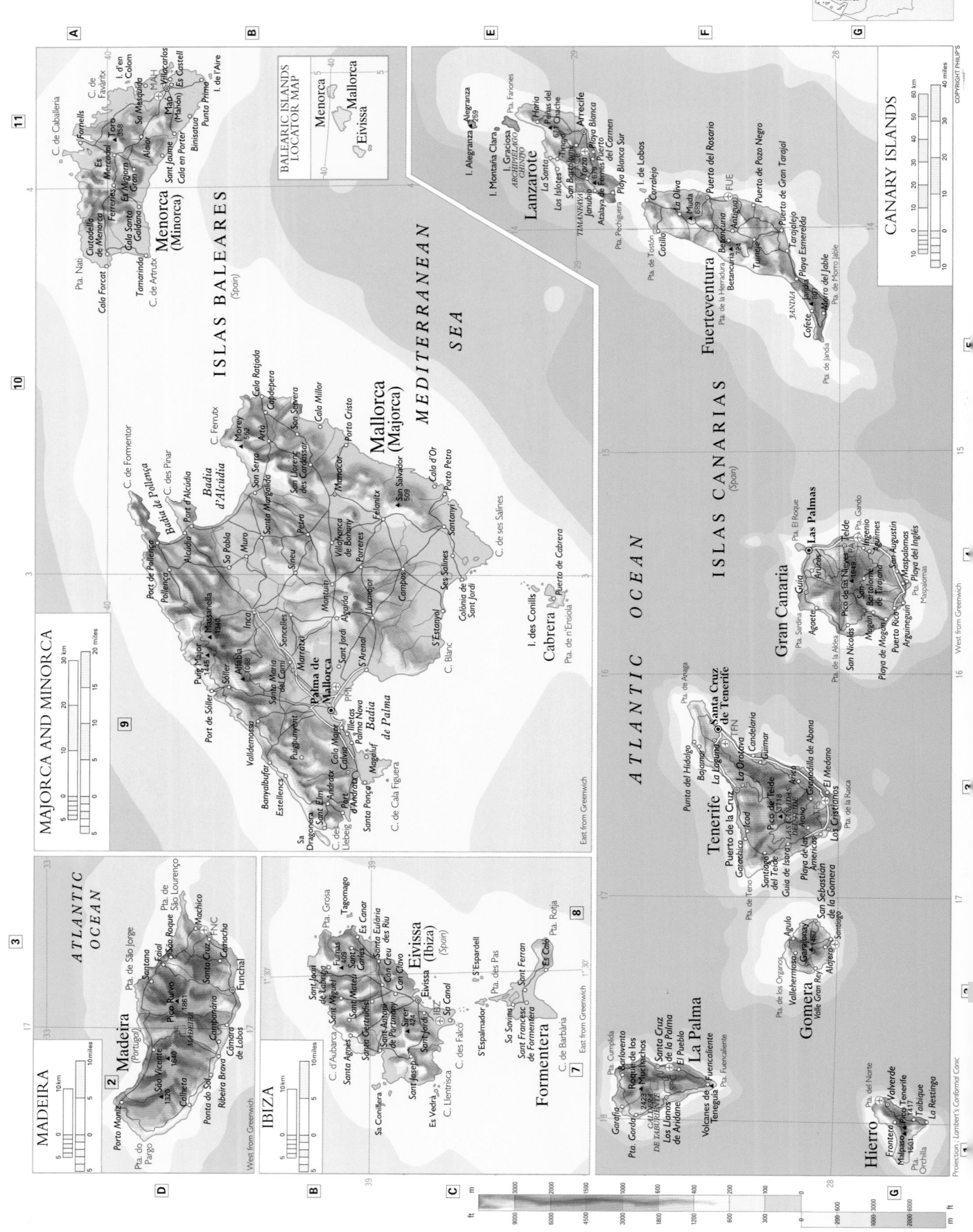

BALEARIC ISLANDS LOCATOR MAP

Menorca

Mallorca

Eivissa

CANARY ISLANDS

MAJORCA AND MINORCA

MADEIRA

IBIZA

ISLAS BALEARES
(Spain)

Menorca
(Minorca)

Mallorca
(Majorca)

MEDITERRANEAN SEA

Cabrera

ISLAS CANARIAS
(Spain)

Lanzarote

Fuerteventura

Gran Canaria

Tenerife

Gomera

La Palma

Hierro

ATLANTIC OCEAN

Madeira
(Portugal)

Eivissa
(Ibiza)
(Spain)

Formentera

ATLANTIC OCEAN

Projection: Lambert's Conformal Conic

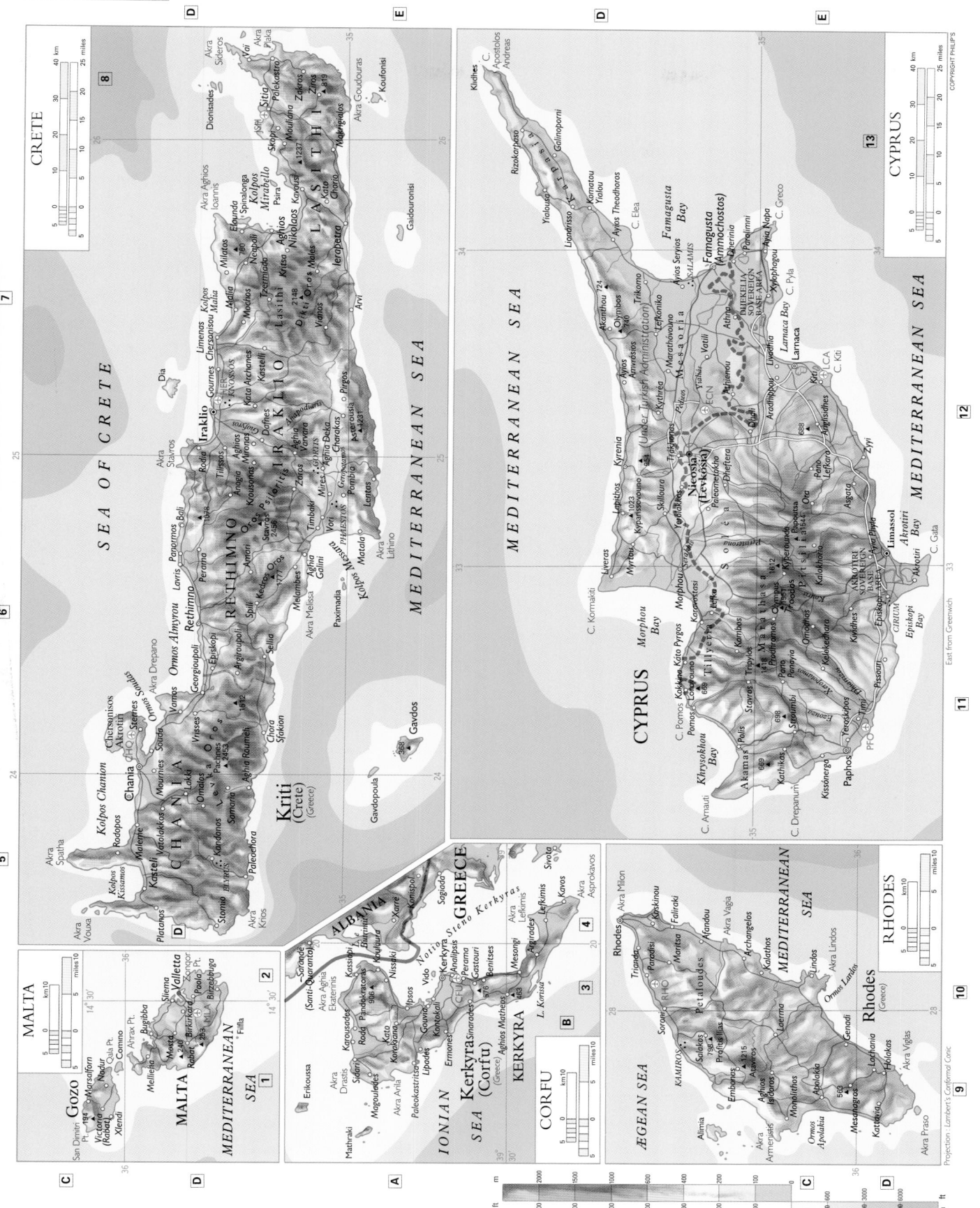

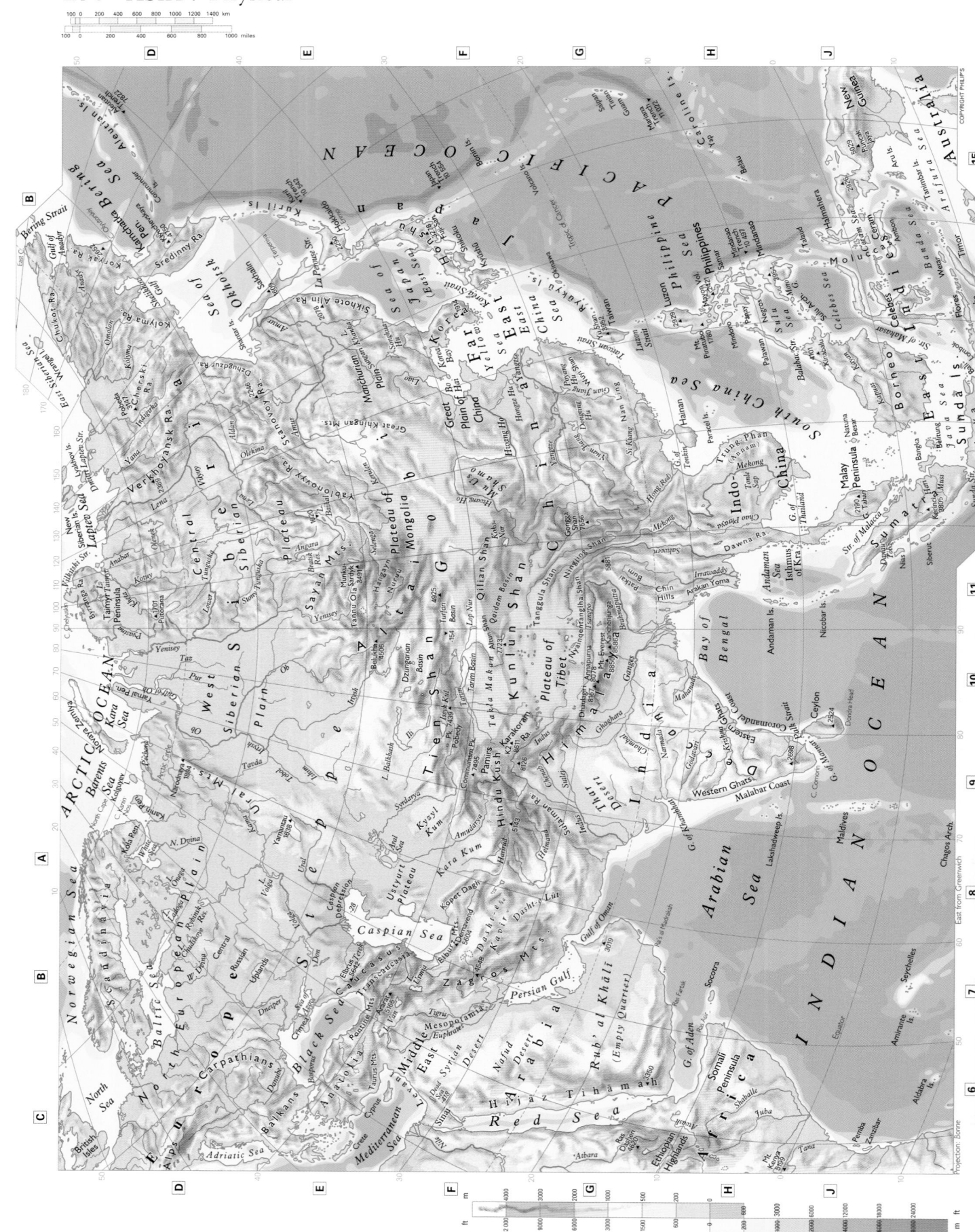

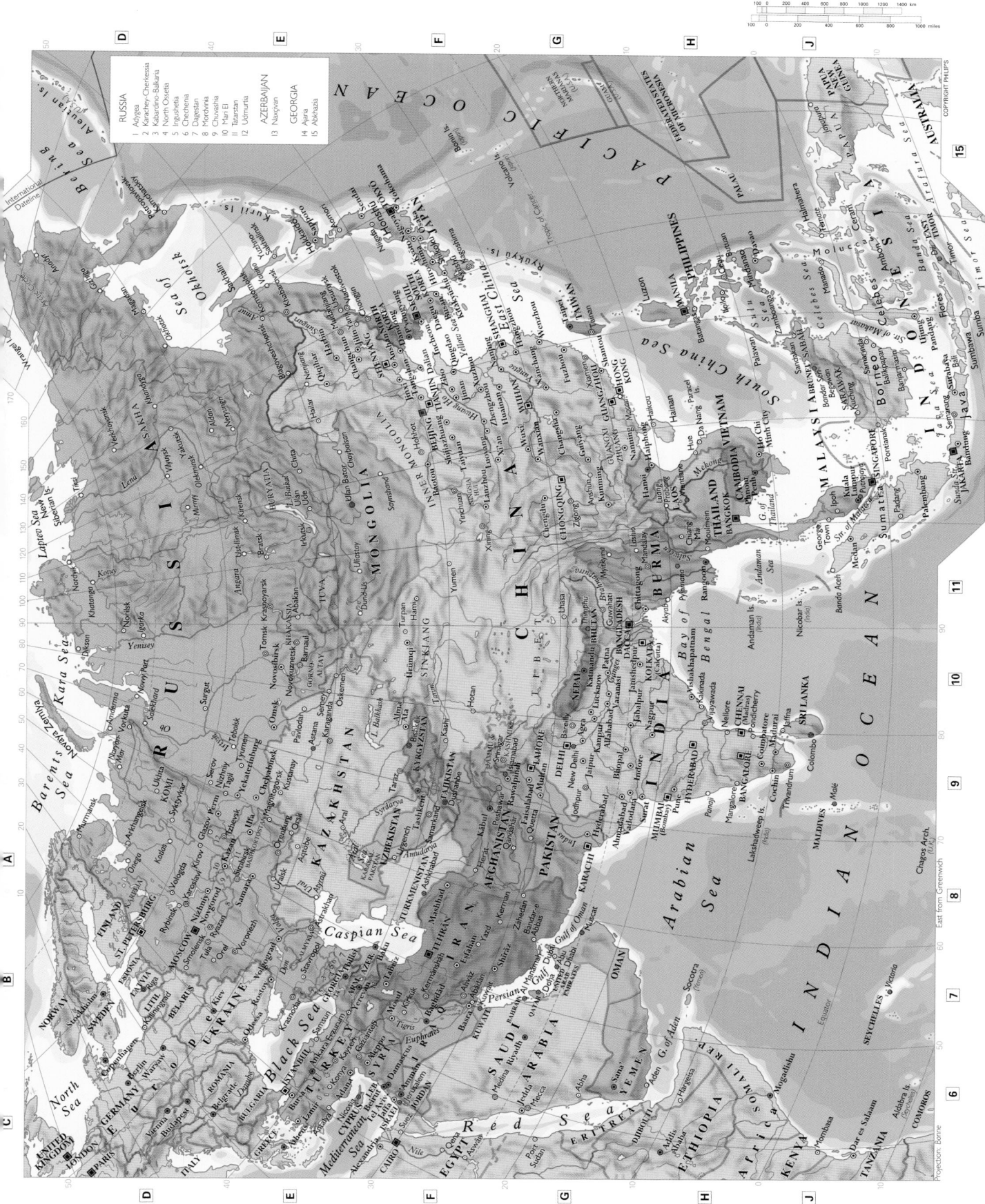

COPYRIGHT PHILIP'S

PACIFIC OCEAN

FEDERATED STATES OF MICRONESIA

PALAU

PAPUA NEW GUINEA

AUSTRALIA

Arafura Sea

EAST TIMOR

Timor Sea

INDONESIA

Banda Sea

Ceram

Ambon

Halmahera

Molucca Sea

Celebes Sea

Sulu Sea

PHILIPPINES

MANILA

Luzon

Mindanao

Davao

South China Sea

Hainan

TAIWAN

HONG KONG

GUANGZHOU

CHINA

SHANGHAI

BEIJING

Yellow Sea

SOUTH KOREA

NORTH KOREA

SEOUL

TOKYO

JAPAN

East China Sea

Sea of Japan

Hokkaido

Honshu

Sakhalin

Kuril Is.

Sea of Okhotsk

RUSSIA

ASIA

International Dateline

Bering Sea

Aleutian Is.

Wrangel I.

Laptev Sea

New Siberian Is.

Kara Sea

Barents Sea

Novaya Zemlya

North Sea

Baltic Sea

UNITED KINGDOM

LONDON

PARIS

NORWAY

SWEDEN

FINLAND

ST. PETERSBURG

MOSCOW

GERMANY

Berlin

ITALY

ROMANIA

BULGARIA

GREECE

UKRAINE

Black Sea

TURKEY

CYPRUS

Mediterranean Sea

SYRIA

IRAQ

IRAN

TEHRAN

Caspian Sea

KAZAKHSTAN

UZBEKISTAN

TURKMENISTAN

KYRGYZSTAN

TAJIKISTAN

AFGHANISTAN

KABUL

PAKISTAN

KARACHI

MONGOLIA

Ulan Bator

INNER MONGOLIA

SINKIANG

TIBET

NEPAL

BHUTAN

BANGLADESH

DHAKA

INDIA

DELHI

New Delhi

LAHORE

MUMBAI (Bombay)

HYDERABAD

BANGALORE

CHENNAI (Madras)

KOLKATA (Calcutta)

BURMA

Bay of Bengal

SRI LANKA

Colombo

MALDIVES

Chagos Arch. (U.K.)

INDIAN OCEAN

Arabian Sea

OMAN

Gulf of Oman

Persian Gulf

UNITED ARAB EMIRATES

QATAR

KUWAIT

SAUDI ARABIA

Riyadh

Mecca

Medina

Red Sea

EGYPT

CAIRO

Nile

Gulf of Aden

YEMEN

Socotra (Yemen)

ERITREA

DJIBOUTI

ETHIOPIA

SOMALIA

Mogadishu

KENYA

TANZANIA

Dar es Salaam

Mombasa

COMOROS

SEYCHELLES

Equator

Aldabra Is.

MALE

THAILAND

BANGKOK

CAMBODIA

Phnom Penh

VIETNAM

Ho Chi Minh City

Hanoi

LAOS

Gulf of Thailand

MALAYSIA

Kuala Lumpur

SINGAPORE

BRUNEI

SABAH

SARAWAK

Borneo

JAVA

JAKARTA

Sumatra

Sulawesi

Java Sea

East from Greenwich

Projection: Bonne

RUSSIA
1 Adygea
2 Karachey-Cherkessia
3 Kabardino-Balkaria
4 North Ossetia
5 Ingushetia
6 Chechenia
7 Dagestan
8 Mordvinia
9 Chuvashia
10 Mari El
11 Tatarstan
12 Udmurtia

AZERBAIJAN
13 Naxçıvan

GEORGIA
14 Ajaria
15 Abkhazia

RUSSIA
1 Adygea
2 Karachey-Cherkessia
3 Kabardino-Balkaria
4 North Osseta
5 Ingushetia
6 Chechenia
7 Dagestan
8 Mordvinia
9 Chuvashia
10 Mari El
11 Tatarstan
12 Udmurtia
13 Khakassia

AZERBAIJAN
14 Naxçivan

GEORGIA   UKRAINE
15 Ajaria   17 Crimea
16 Abkhazia

Projection: Conical Orthomorphic with two standard parallels

East from Greenwich

D

E

F

Mys Dezhneva
(East C.)

O C E A N

Severnaya
Zemlya

Poluostrov
Byrranga
Gory
Taymyr

L a p t e v
S e a

East Siberian Sea

Chukchi
Sea

St. Lawrence I.
(U.S.A.)

Providenya
Anadyrsky Zaliv

B e r i n g
S e a

Koryakskoye Nagorye

Sredinnyy Khrebet

Poluostrov
Kamchatka

Petropavlovsk-
Kamchatskiy

Kolymskoye Nagorye

Khrebet Cherskogo

D A L N E V O S T O C H N Y Y

Verkhoyanskiy Khrebet

S e a
o f
O k h o t s k

Sakhalin

S A K H A

Kurilskiye Ostrova

Yuzhno-Sakhalinsk

Khrebet Sikhote Alin

R U S S I A

Krasnoyarsk

Vostochnyy Sayan

Yablonovyy Khrebet

Stanovoy Khrebet

Da Hinggan Ling

Bratsk

Irkutsk

Ulan Ude

Khabarovsk

HOKKAIDO

SAPPORO

Hakodate

Aomori

Vladivostok

Nakhodka

Ulaanbaatar

Hangayn
Nuruu

Hentiyn
Nuruu

M O N G O L I A

QIQIHAR

DAQING

HARBIN

Dongbei
(Manchuria)

JILIN

CHANGCHUN

Ch'ŏngjin

S e a
o f
J a p a n
(East Sea)

Honshū

Niigata

J A P A N

KYOTO

OSAKA

KOBE

CHIFENG

SHENYANG

FUSHUN

ANSHAN

NORTH
KOREA

PYONGYANG

Nampo

INCHEON

SEOUL

SOUTH KOREA

DAEJEON

DAEGU

BUSAN

GWANGJU

C H I N A

BEIJING

BAOTOU

Hohhot

Zhangjiakou

DALIAN

Dandong

Wŏnsan

G o b i

COPYRIGHT PHILIP'S

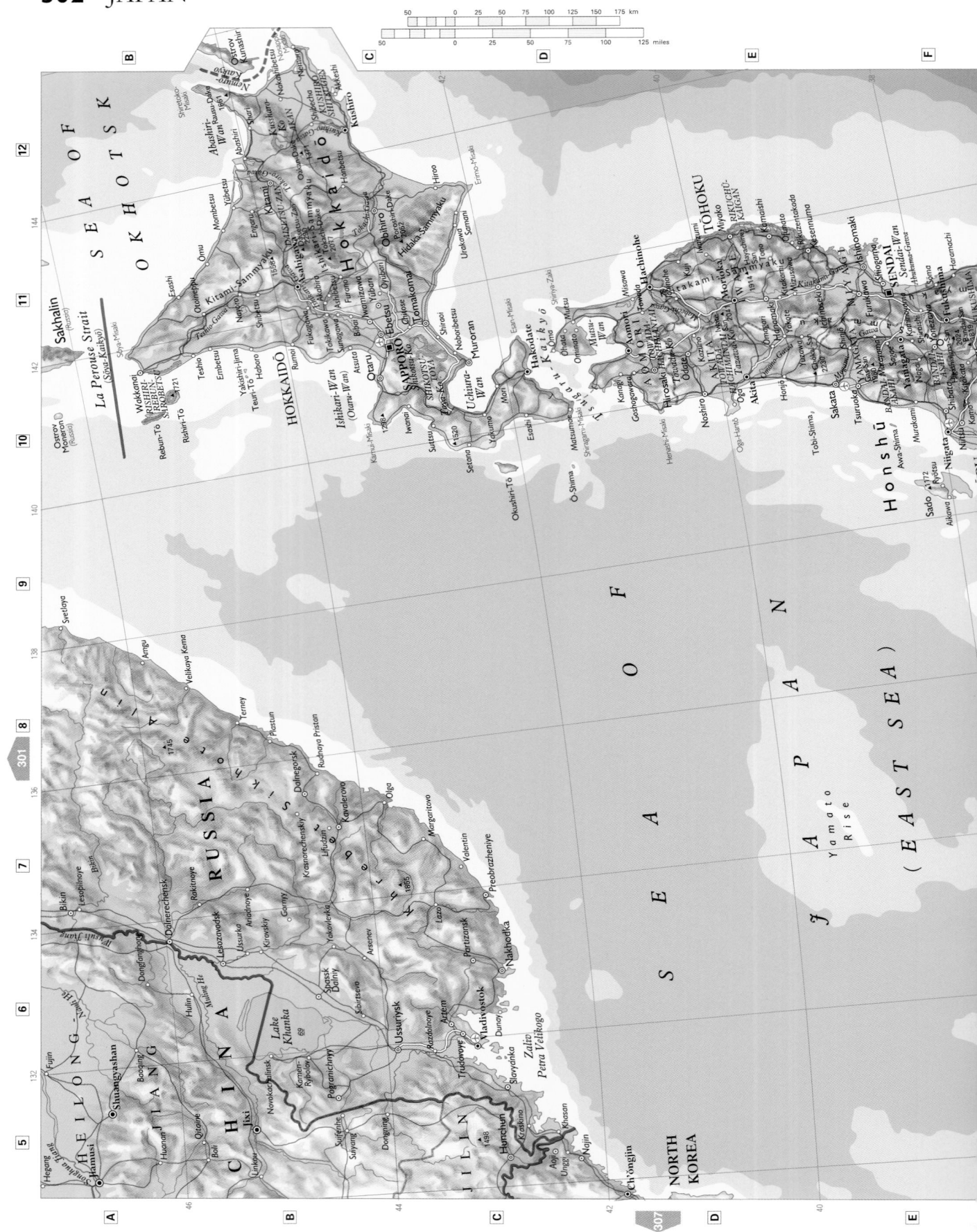

50   0   25   50   75   100   125   150   175 km

50   0   25   50   75   100   125 miles

12

11

SEA   OF   OKHOTSK

Sakhalin
(Russia)

La Perouse Strait
(Sōya-Kaikyō)

Ostrov
Moneron
(Russia)

Wakkanai
RISHIRI-
REBUN
SAROBETSU
Rebun-Tō
Rishiri-Tō

Shiretoko-
Misaki

Nemuro-
Kaikyō
Ostrov
Kunashir

Ostrov
Shikotan

Nosappu-Misaki

Nemuro
Nakashibetsu
Shibetsu
Rausu-Dake
1661
Shari
Shibecha
Akkeshi

Abashiri-
Wan

Abashiri
KUSHIRO
SHITSUGEN

Kushiro

Monbetsu
Ōmu
Yūbetsu
Kitami
Engaru
Esashi
Otoineppu

KITAMI-SAMMYAKU

Teshio
Embetsu
Yakishiri-Jima
Teuri-Tō

Nayoro
Shibetsu
Asahikawa
Asahi-
Dake
2290
DAISETSU-ZAN
ISHIKARI-
SAMMYAKU

Kamikawa

TOKACHI-
SAMMYAKU
Tokachi-Dake
2077
HIDAKA-SAMMYAKU
Obihiro
Hiroo
Erimo-Misaki

Rumoi
Fukagawa
Takikawa
Bibai
Sunagawa
Ashibetsu
Furano
Yūbari
Oyubari

HOKKAIDŌ

Ishikari-
Wan

HOKKAIDŌ

Otaru
SAPPORO
Ebetsu
Chitose
Tomakomai
Shiraoi
Noboribetsu
Muroran

Iwanai
1898
Suttsu
Setana

Okushiri-Tō

Esashi

Matsumae

Shiriuchi-
Misaki

Hakodate

Yokuran
Uchiura-
Wan

Mori

Ō-Shima

Tsugaru-
Kaikyō

Esan-Misaki

Shiriya-Zaki

Ōma

Tappi-
Zaki

HONSHŪ

10

SEA   OF

JAPAN

(EAST SEA)

Yamato
Rise

9

Svetlaya

Angu

Velikaya Kema

Terney

Plastun

SIKHOTE
ALIN'
1745

RUSSIA

Dalnegorsk
Kavalerovo
Krasnorechenskiy
Rudnaya Pristan'

Olga

Margaritovo

Valentin

Preobrazheniye

Nakhodka

Partizansk
Lazo

8

301

7

Bikin
Lesozovodsk

Bikin

Dalnerechensk

Rakitnoye
Gorny
Arsenev
Anuchino

Lifudzin
1855

Yakovlevka

Sibirtsevo
Razdolnoye

Spassk
Dalniy

Lake
Khanka
69

Kamen-
Rybolov
Novokachalinsk
Kirovskiy

Chernigovka

Ussuriysk

Dunoy

Razdolnoye
Artem
Trudovoye

Vladivostok

Zaliv
Petra Velikogo

6

CHINA

Fujin
Huanan

Songhua Jiang

Hegang

HEILONG-

JIANG

Jiamusi
Shuangyashan

Baoqing

Qitaihe
Boli

Linkou

Hulin
Mishan

Mudan He

Muling He

Dongningzhen

Suifenhe

JILIN

Dongning

Suiyang

Kamen-
Rybolov

Pogranichny

Slavyanka

Kraskino
Khasan

Zarubino

Unggi

Najin

Ch'ŏngjin

NORTH
KOREA

Hunchun
1498

Aoji

5

TŌHOKU

Hachinohe
Misawa
Towada
Noheji

Mutsu-
Wan
Aomori
Hirosaki

AOMORI

Ōminato
Tanabe
Ōhata

Shimokita-
Hantō

Kanagi
Goshogawara
Ōdate

Kazuno
Kosaka

AKITA

Kamaishi
Ōfunato

RIKUCHŪ-
KAIGAN

Morioka

KITAKAMI-
SAMMYAKU

Miyako

Rikuzentakada

Kesennuma

Ishinomaki

Sendai-
Wan

SENDAI

Soma

Noshiro

Oga-Hantō

Akita

Honjō

Ugo

Yamagata

Furukawa

YAMAGATA

BANDAI-
ASAHI

Shinjō
Yonezawa

Wakamatsu

FUKUSHIMA

Fukushima

Tobi-Shima

Sakata

Tsuruoka

Murakami

Ryōtsu

Sado

Niigata

Nii-tsu

Honshū

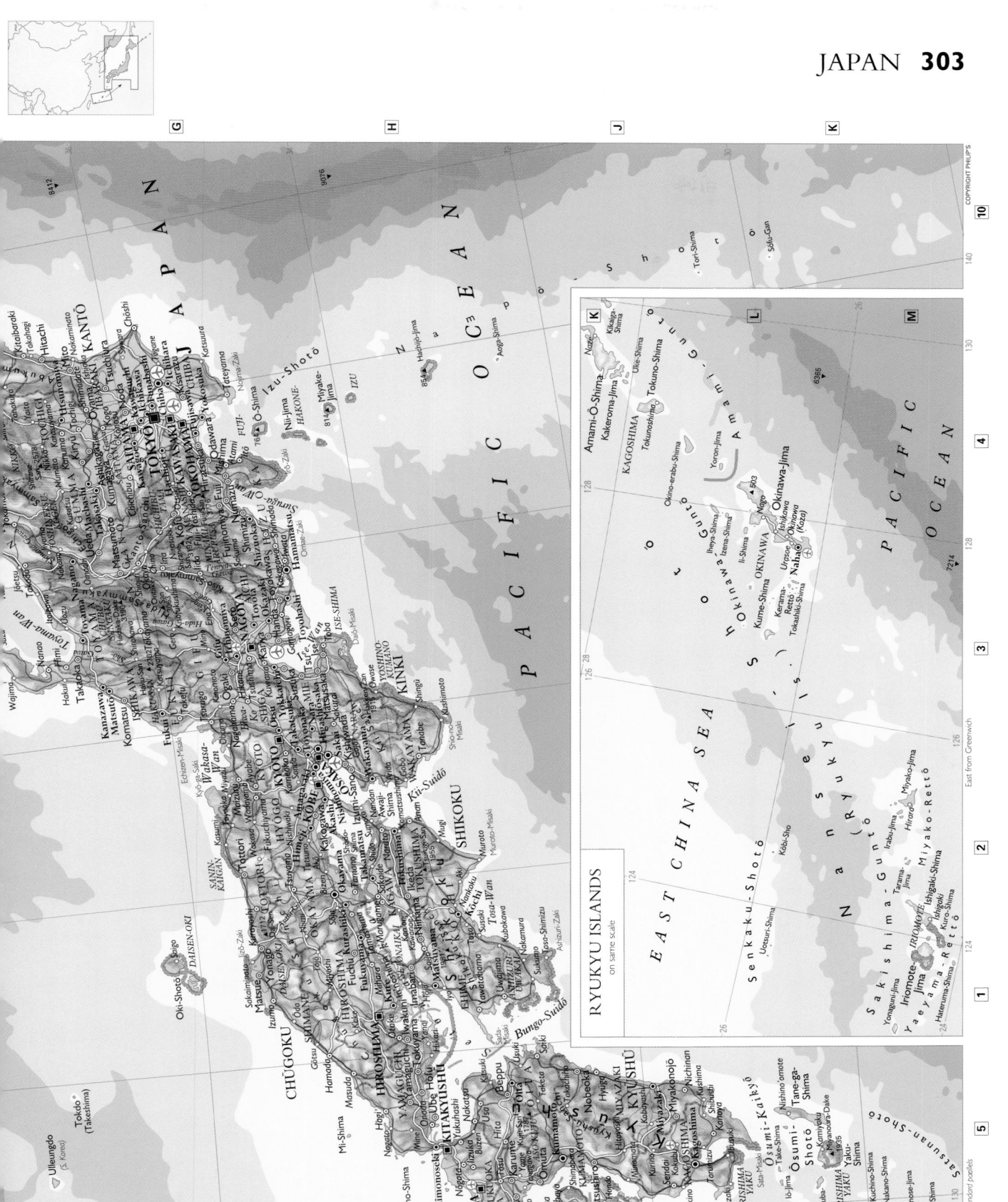

100   0   100   200   300   400   500   600 km
100   0   100   200   300   400 miles

| 1 | 2 | 3 | 4 | 5 |

B

K A Z A K H S T A N

Astana
Temirtau
Qaraghandy
Qaraqaraly
Karsakpay
Zhezqazghan
Moyynty
Betpaqdala
Balqash
Taldyqorghan
Moynqum
Taraz
Bishkek
KYRGYZSTAN
Kirghiz Ra.
ALMATY
Yssyk-Köl
Balqash Köl

Rubtsovsk
Semey
Öskemen
Leninogorsk
Zyryan
Belukha
Khrebet Tarbagatay
Zaysan
Tacheng
Karamay
Junggar Pendi
Shamo
Bole
Borohoro Shan
Yining
ÜRÜMQI
Changji
Shihezi
Manas
Turpan
Turpan Pendi

312

C

TAJIK.
Kongur Shan
Muztagh-Ata
Kashi
Artux
Shache
Yecheng
Pishan
Taklamakan Shamo
Hotan
Qira
Yutian
Minfeng

XINJIANG UYGUR ZIZHIQU
(SINKIANG)
Tarim Pendi
Lop Nur
Kuruktag
Korla
Aksu
Kuqa

JAMMU & KASHMIR
Srinagar
Leh
Aksai Chin
Karatax Shan
Muz Tag
Hoh Xil Shan
Kunlun Shan

Altun Shan
Dunhuang
Anxi
Kumtag Shamo
Ruoqiang
Qarqan He
Qiemo

D

HIMACHAL PRADESH
Shimla
Chandigarh
MEERUT
DELHI
New Delhi
AGRA
KANPUR
LUCKNOW
Gwalior
UTTAR PRADESH
JHANSI
ALLAHABAD
VARANASI
JABALPUR
MADHYA PRADESH
BHILAINAGAR-DURG
NAGPUR

I N D I A

XIZANG ZIZHIQU
(TIBET)
Gangdise Shan
Tanggula (Dangla) Shan
Nyainqentanglha Shan
Lhasa
Xigaze
KATMANDU
NEPAL
Mt. Everest
BHUTAN
Thimphu
Punakha
BANGLADESH
DHAKA
KOLKATA
(Calcutta)
KHULNA
CHITTAGONG

E

VISHAKHAPATNAM
Warangal
Vizianagaram
Brahmapur
ORISSA
Cuttack
BAY OF BENGAL

Sittwe (Akyab)
BURMA
(MYANMAR)
Mandalay
Arakan Yoma
Pegu Yoma
THAILAND (SIAM)
Toungoo

R U S S I A
Irkutsk
Angarsk
Cheremkhovo
Zapadnyy Sayan
Tannu Ola
Kyzyl
Munku-Sardyk
Hövsgöl Nuur
MONGOLIA
Aerhtai Shan (Altai)
Ulaangom
Hyargas Nuur
Ulaanbaatar

Qilian Shan
Zhangye
Yumen
Jiuquan
Bei Shan
Badain Jaran Shamo
Tengger Shamo
Yinchuan
NINGXIA HUIZU ZIZHIQU
Wuwei
Xining
QINGHAI
Qinghai Hu
Golmud
Bayan Har Shan
Qamdo

LANZHOU
Lanzhou
Linxia
TIANSHUI
Wudu
SICHUAN
CHENGDU
MIANYANG
CHONGQING
LESHAN
ZIGONG
NEIJIANG
GUIZHOU
GUIYANG
LIUPANSHUI
Anshun
KUNMING
YUNNAN
VIETNAM
HANOI
HAIPHONG
LAOS
Luang Prabang
Mekong

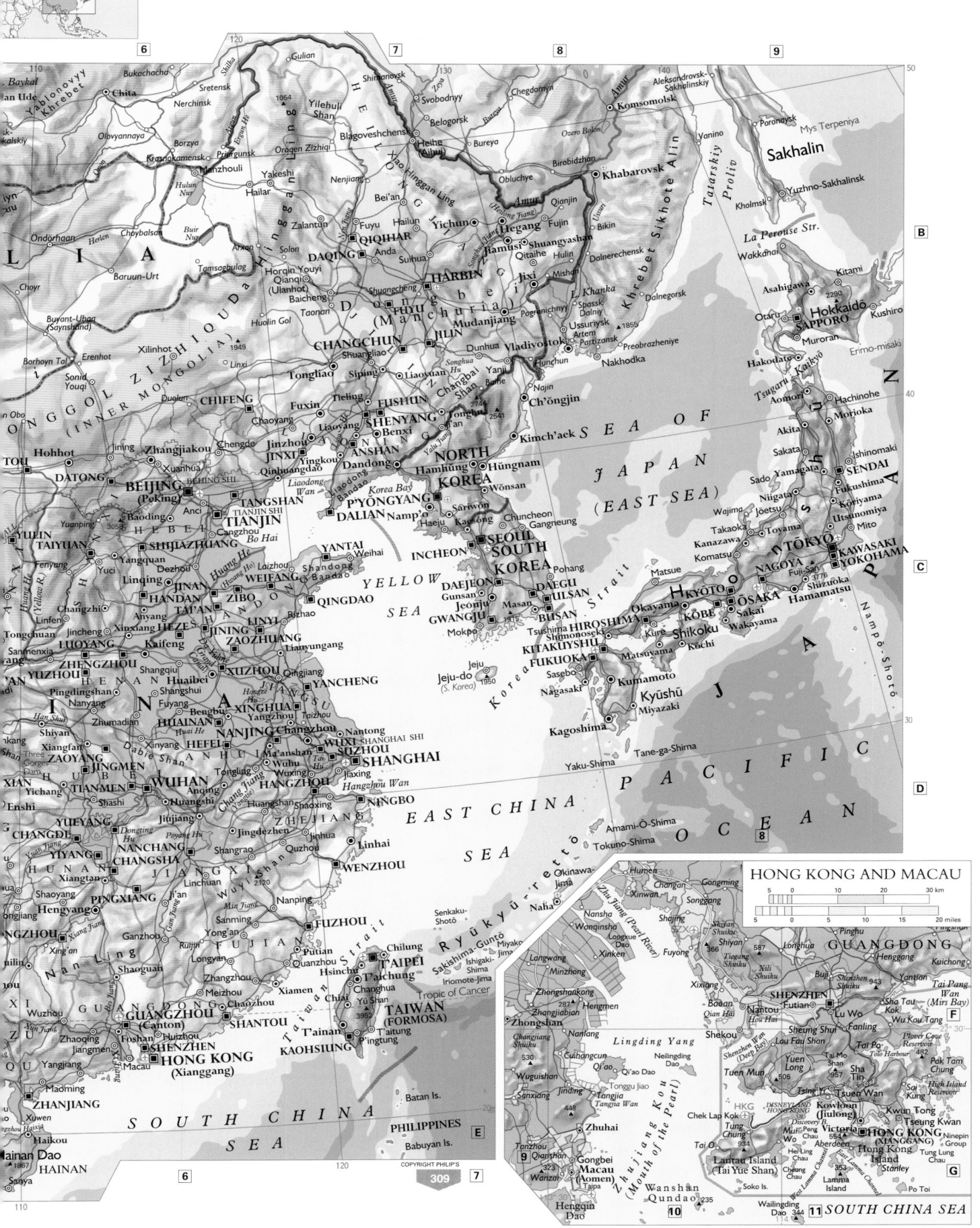

HONG KONG AND MACAU

COPYRIGHT PHILIP'S

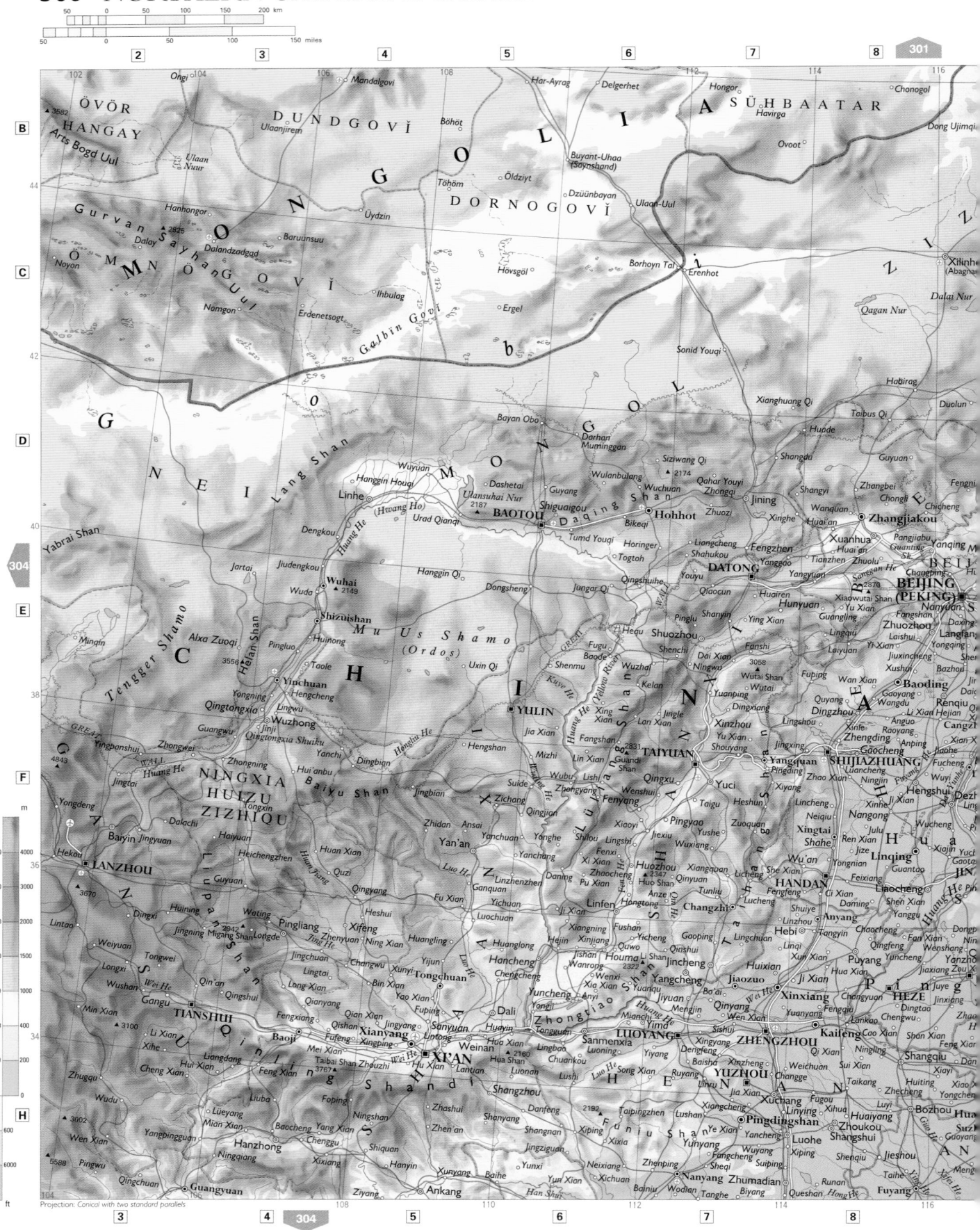

| 2 | 3 | 4 | 5 | 6 | 7 | 8 |

ÖVÖR HANGAY

Arts Bogd Uul
▲3582

DUNDGOVĬ

Mandalgovĭ

Ongi Ohgi

Ulaanjirem
Böhöt

Delgerhet
Har-Ayrag
Hongor
Chonogol

M O N G O L I A

SÜHBAATAR

Buyant-Uhaa (Saynshand)

Havirga
Ovoot
Dong Ujimqi

Hanhongor
Baruunsuu
Üydzin
Töhöm
Öldziyt
Ulaan-Uul

DORNOGOVĬ

Dzüünbayan

Gurvan Sayhan Uul
Dalay
▲2825
Dalandzadgad
Noyon
Ihbulag
Nomgon
Erdenetsogt
Hövsgöl
Ergel

Borhoyn Tal
Erenhot

Xilinhe (Abagnar)

Qagan Nur
Dalai Nur

Galbin Govi
b
Sonid Youqi

Xianghuang Qi
Taibus Qi
Duolun

Bayan Obo
Darhan Muminggan
Siziwang Qi
▲2174
Huade
Shangdu
Guyuan

N E I M O N G O L

Wuyuan
Hanggin Houqi
Dashetai
Guyang
Wulanbulang
Wuchuan
Qahar Youyi Zhongqi
Shangyi
Zhangbei
Chongli
Fengni

Lang Shan
Linhe
Ulansuhai Nur
Shiguaigou
▲2187
BAOTOU
Urad Qianqi
Daqing Shan
Bikeqi
Hohhot
Horinger
Liangcheng
Fengzhen
Yanggao
Tianzhen
Zhuolu
Xuanhua
Huai'an
Pangjiabu
Qianhe Sk
Yanqing

BEIJING (PEKING)

Dengkou
Jiudengkou
Hanggin Qi
Dongsheng
Jungar Qi
Qingshuihe
Youyu
Qiaocun
Huairen
Xiaowutai Shan
Yu Xian
Guangling
▲2870
Changping
Nanyuan
Daxing

Yabrai Shan
Jartai
Wuhai
▲2149
Wuda
M u U s S h a m o (Ordos)
Uxin Qi
Fugu
Baode
Wuzhai
Shenchi
Hequ
Shenmu
Kelan
Ningwu
Dai Xian
Dingxiang
▲3058
Wutai
Yuanping
Fuping
Wan Xian
Quyang
Baoding
Gaoyang
Wangdu
Li Xian
Renqiu
Cangzhou

Shizuishan
Huinong
Pingluo
Taole
Helan Shan
▲3556
Yinchuan
Hengcheng
Lingwu
Wuzhong
Yanchi
Dingbian
Hengshan
Mizhi
Jia Xian
Lin Xian
Fangshan
Lishi
Guandi Shan
▲2831
Xinzhou
Yu Xian
Lingshi
Shouyang
Pingding
Zhao Xian
Lincheng
Neiqiu
Nangong
Wuyi
Dezhou

YULIN

TAIYUAN
Yuci
Heshun
Linxiang
Xingtai
Shahe
Ren Xian
Linqing

Yangquan
SHIJIAZHUANG
Zhengding

Minqin
Alxa Zuoqi
C H I N A
Qingtongxia
Guangwu
Zhongwei
Zhongning
Hui'anbu
Jingbian
Zichang
Ansai
Yan'an
Yanchuan
Yonghe
Shilou
Lan Xian
Fenyang
Xiaoyi
Jiexiu
Wuxiang
Zuoquan

Tengger Shamo
▲4843
Huang He
Jingtai
Baiyu Shan
Huan Xian
Quzi
Qingyang
Yanchang
Xi Xian
Pu Xian
Anze
Tunliu
Lucheng
Changzhi
Fengfeng
Ci Xian
Daming
Shen Xian
Guantao

NINGXIA HUIZU ZIZHIQU
Tongxin
Haiyuan

Lanzhou
Yongdeng
Hekou
Baiyin Jingyuan
Dalachi
Huining
Guyuan
Pingliang
Huang Ling
Yijun
Chengcheng
Heshui
Ningxian
Linzhenzhen
Ganquan
Yichuan
Luochuan
Xiangning
Fushan
Yicheng
Gaoping
Jincheng
Linchuan
Hebi
Tangyin
Anyang
Huixian
Linqi

Lintao
Dingxi
Weiyuan
Tongwei
Jingning
Migang Shan
▲2942
Longde
Jing He
Zhenyuan
Ning Xian
Huangling
Hancheng
Houma
Li Shan
▲2322
Wanrong
Wenxi
Xia Xian
Yuanqu
Jiyuan
Ba'ai
Wen Xian
Jiaozuo
Ji Xian
Xinxiang
Puyang

Longxi
Wushan
Qin'an
Qingshui
Qianyang
Long Xian
Qianxian
Yao Xian
Bin Xian
Chengcheng
Jishan
Xinjiang
Quwo
Yuncheng
Anyi
Qinyang
Yuanyang
Changyuan
Kaifeng
Dingtao

TIANSHUI
Gangu
Min Xian
▲3100
Li Xian
Liangdang
Hui Xian
Fengxiang
Qian Xian
Jingyang
Sanyuan
Lintong
Huayin
Zhongtiao Shan
Tongguan
Sanmenxia
LUOYANG
Xingyang
Mianchi
Luoning
ZHENGZHOU
Xuchang
Qi Xian
Lankao
HEZE
Jinxiang

Zhouzhi
XI'AN
Weinan
Hua Xian
▲2160
Lingbao
Chuankou
Yiyang
Dengfeng
Yuzhou
Weichuan
Sui Xian
Shangqiu

Baoji
Mei Xian
Taibai Shan
▲3767
Hu Xian
Lantian
Huayin
Luonan
Lushi
Song Xian
Ruyang
YUZHOU
Changge
Linru
Jia Xian

Zhuqu
Wudu
Lüeyang
Liuba
Foping
Ningshan
Shanyang
Danfeng
Shangnan
▲2192
Taipingzhen
Lushan
Xiangcheng
Linying
Xihua

Wen Xian
▲3002
Yangpingguan
Mian Xian
Chenggu
Baocheng
Yang Xian
Zhashui
Zhen'an
Xixia
Xiping
Yunyang
Fangcheng
Wuyang
Xiping
Pingdingshan
Zhoukou
Shangshui

▲5588
Pingwu
Qingchuan
Hanzhong
Ningqiang
Xixiang
Hanyin
Xunyang
Yunxi
Zhenping
Neixiang
Sheqi
Suiping
Luohe
Shangshui

Guangyuan
Ankang
Ziyang
Baihe
Yun Xian
Baisha
Wodian
Nanyang
Zhumadian
Biyang
Queshan
Fuyang

| 3 | 4 | 5 | 6 | 7 | 8 |

ft m
12 000 4000
9000 3000
6000 2000
4500 1500
3000 1000
1200 400
600 200
0 0
200 600
2000 6000
m ft

Projection: Mercator

East from Greenwich

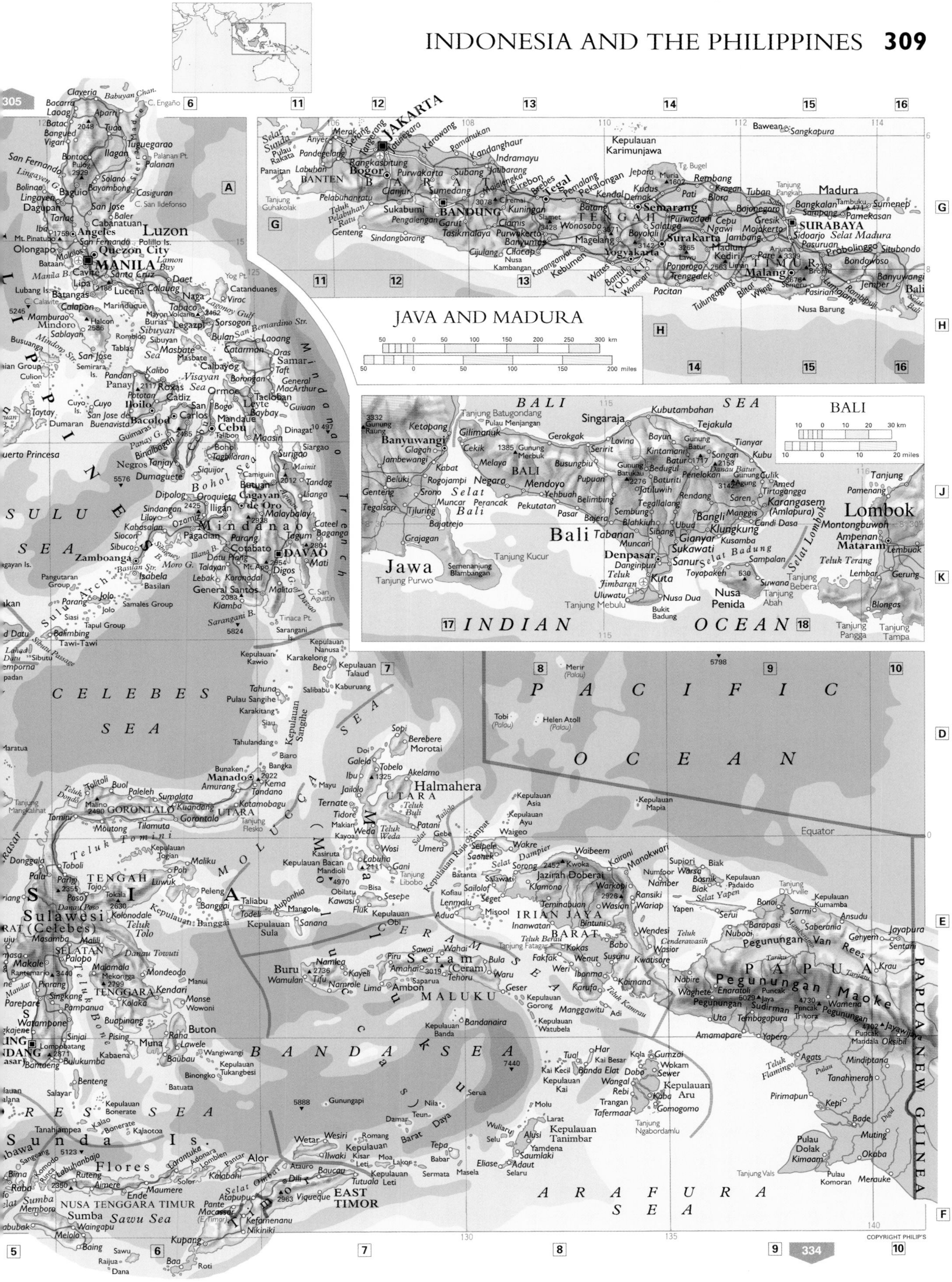

305

JAVA AND MADURA

50	0	50	100	150	200	250	300 km
50	0	50		100		150	200 miles

BALI

| 10 | 0 | 10 | 20 | 30 km |
| 10 | 0 | | 10 | 20 miles |

JAKARTA
BANTEN
Bogor
Bandung
Semarang
Surakarta
Yogyakarta
SURABAYA
Madura
Sumenep
Malang
Jember
Bali

BALI SEA
Singaraja
Banyuwangi
Bali
Jawa
Denpasar
Kuta
Lombok
Mataram
Ampenan
Nusa Penida
Selat Lombok

INDIAN OCEAN

PACIFIC OCEAN

Luzon
MANILA
QUEZON CITY
Batangas
Naga
Legazpi
Calbayog
Roxas
Iloilo
Bacolod
Cebu
Tacloban
Puerto Princesa
Zamboanga
DAVAO
General Santos
Mindanao
Cagayan de Oro
Cotabato
Jolo

SULU SEA

CELEBES SEA

MOLUCCA SEA

Manado
GORONTALO
Halmahera
UTARA
Ternate
Tidore

Equator

SULAWESI
Sulawesi (Celebes)
TENGAH
SELATAN
TENGGARA
Kendari
Buton
Makale
Palopo

BANDA SEA

FLORES SEA

Buru
Seram (Ceram)
Ambon
MALUKU

IRIAN JAYA
BARAT
Manokwari
Biak
Yapen

PAPUA
Pegunungan Maoke
Jayapura
Wamena

PAPUA NEW GUINEA

Flores
Sumba
NUSA TENGGARA TIMUR
Kupang
EAST TIMOR
Dili

Sawu Sea

Kepulauan Tanimbar
Kepulauan Aru
Merauke

ARAFURA SEA

COPYRIGHT PHILIP'S

334

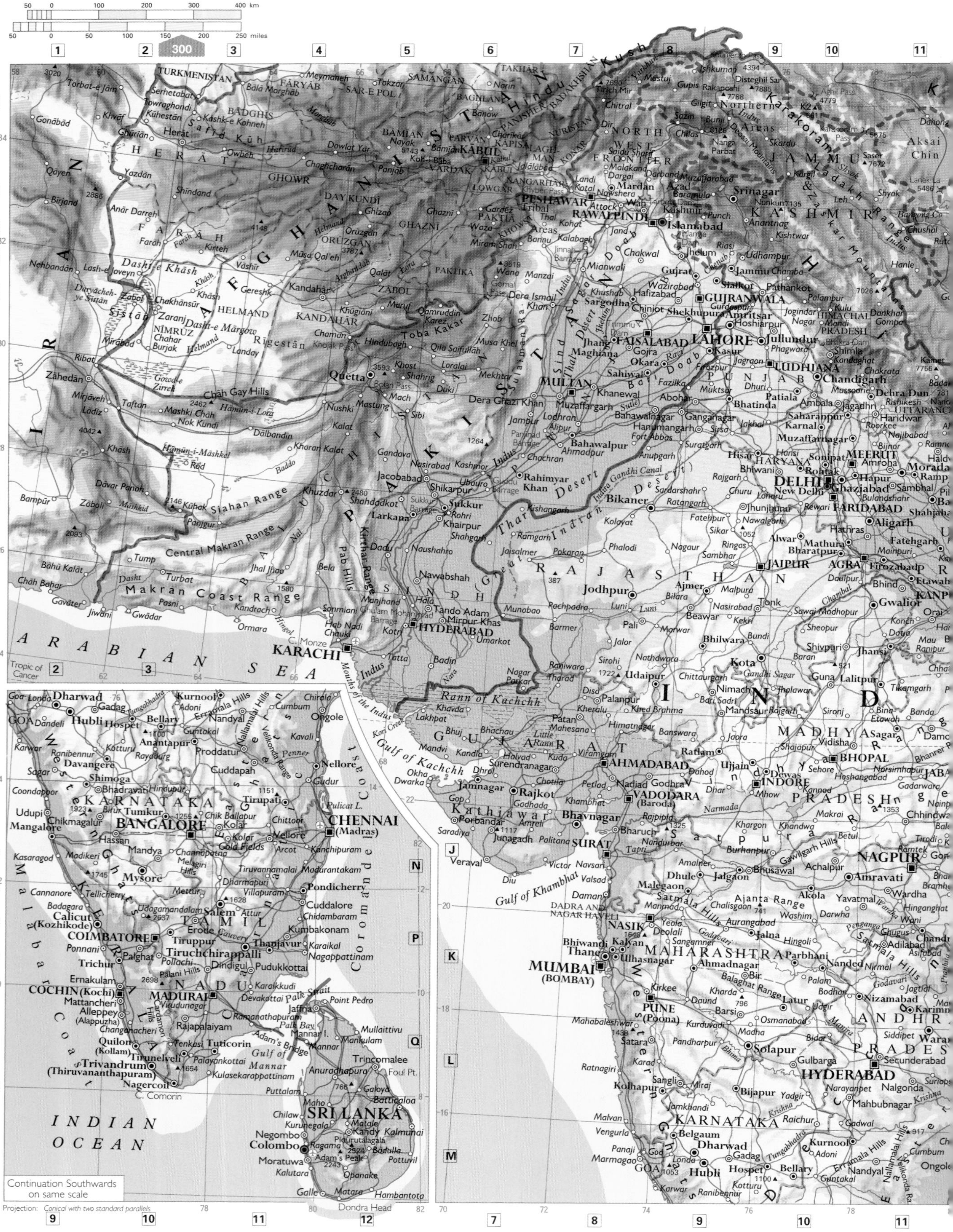

50 0   100   200   300   400 km
50 0   50   100   150   200   250 miles

| 1 | 2 | 300 | 3 | 4 | 5 | 6 | 7 | 8 | 9 | 10 | 11 |

TURKMENISTAN

TAKHAR Hindu Kush Karakoram Northern Areas K2 Aksai Chin JAMMU

AFGHANISTAN

HERAT GHOWR DAY KUNDI BADGHIS FARYAB SAR-E POL SAMANGAN BAGHLAN PANJSHER PARVAN NURISTAN NORTH WEST FRONTIER

KABUL WARDAK LOWGAR PAKTIA NANGARHAR PESHAWAR RAWALPINDI Islamabad KASHMIR Srinagar Leh

GHAZNI PAKTIKA ZABOL KANDAHAR ORUZGAN HELMAND NIMRUZ FARAH

IRAN

Herat Qayen Birjand Gonabad Torbat-e Jam Yazdan

PAKISTAN BALOCHISTAN Quetta Kalat Makran Coast Range Central Makran Range Siahan Range Kharan

SIND SINDH Sukkur Larkana Hyderabad **KARACHI**

PUNJAB MULTAN FAISALABAD **LAHORE** GUJRANWALA Amritsar **LUDHIANA** Chandigarh

HIMACHAL PRADESH UTTARANCHAL PUNJAB HARYANA **DELHI** New Delhi FARIDABAD

RAJASTHAN Bikaner Jodhpur **JAIPUR** **AGRA** Gwalior **KANPUR**

Thar Desert Indira Gandhi Canal

GUJARAT **AHMADABAD** VADODARA (Baroda) **SURAT** Rajkot Bhavnagar Jamnagar Junagadh Kathiawar

Rann of Kachchh Gulf of Kachchh Gulf of Khambhat

MADHYA PRADESH **BHOPAL** **INDORE** **NAGPUR** Ujjain

I N D I A

MAHARASHTRA **MUMBAI (BOMBAY)** **PUNE (Poona)** NASIK Thane Kalyan Ulhasnagar Solapur Aurangabad Amravati Akola Wardha

ANDHRA PRADESH **HYDERABAD** Nizamabad Nalgonda Gulbarga Bidar Secunderabad

KARNATAKA **BANGALORE** Hubli Dharwad Belgaum Bijapur Raichur Bellary Gadag Panaji GOA

Dharwad Gadag Hubli Hospet Bellary Kurnool Adoni Anantapur Cuddapah Nellore

Mangalore Udupi Chikmagalur Hassan Mysore Shimoga Davangere

KERALA **COCHIN (Kochi)** Calicut (Kozhikode) **COIMBATORE** Trichur Ernakulam Alleppey (Alappuzha) Quilon (Kollam) **Trivandrum (Thiruvananthapuram)** Nagercoil C. Comorin

TAMIL NADU **CHENNAI (Madras)** **MADURAI** Salem Tiruppur Erode Tiruchchirappalli Thanjavur Vellore Pondicherry Cuddalore Tirunelveli Tuticorin

Coromandel Coast Palk Strait Gulf of Mannar Adam's Bridge Point Pedro Jaffna

SRI LANKA **Colombo** Kandy Negombo Moratuwa Galle Matara Trincomalee Batticaloa Anuradhapura Dondra Head

A R A B I A N S E A

I N D I A N O C E A N

Mouths of the Indus Gulf of Kachchh Tropic of Cancer

Continuation Southwards on same scale

Projection: Conical with two standard parallels

| 9 | 10 | 11 | 12 |
| 7 | 8 | 9 | 10 | 11 |

304

13	14	15	16	17	18	19	20	21	22	

B

XIANG UYGUR ZIZHIQU (SINKIANG)
Muz Tag 7723

lun Shan

Pulu

Hoh Xil Shan

QINGHAI
Gyaring Hu 4287 Ngoring Hu
Huang He

6094
Huang He

34

C

Tanggula (Dangla) Shan

XIZANG

CHINA

Yushu

Dainkog

ZIZHIQU

5180 Tanggula
Shankou

Nangqén

SICHUAN

Garzè

32

long
ri 6596

(Tibet)

(Tong Kangri

Amdo

Baqèn

Dènggèn

Baiyù

D

N gangtong shan

Dongco

4495 Siling Co

Nagqu

Qamdo

Xinlong

Mapam
Yumco Shan

Tangra
Yumco

Ombu

Nu Jiang

Lhorong

Ningjing

Yidun Litang Yajiang

30

disè Shan

Coqèn

Gyaring Co

Xainza

Nam Co
4627

Nyainqentanglha Shan

Lhari

Zhaxizê

Gongbo'gyamda

Muli Zangzu
Zizhixian

Zhongdian

E

Simikot Namse
Shankou 7059
Mugu 4944

Zhongba

Saga

7088

Lhünzub

Namcha
Barwa 7756 Riga

Mainkung

Gogèn

Weixi

5890

Jido

28

Jumla Silgarhi Doti

Maquan He (Tsangpo)

Lhazê

Xigazê

Gyangzê

Yarlung Zangbo Jiang

Nang Xian

ARUNACHAL PRADESH

Nizamghat

Hkakabo Razi
5881 (Thala La)

Zizhixian

Zhongdian

ngarhi

NEPAL

Dhaulagiri 8167

Annapurna
8072 Feng 8012

Muktinath Gyala Shankou

Nepalganj

Pokhara

Dingyè

7554

Thunkar

7090

Cona

Kangto

Ruba

North

Subansiri

Murkongselek

Saikhoa
Ghat

Dum Duma

Dibrugarh Tinsukia

Hpunan Pass
3072 Putao
2432

Konglu

Lijiang

YUNNAN

Jianchuan

26

Nuwakot

Gurkha

Nawakot

Mt. Everest
8850

Kanchenjunga
8598

Tamchhap

SIKKIM

Punakha

Tongsa

Dzong

Tage Dzong

ASSAM

Rangia Tezpur

Lakhimpur

Jorhat

Sibsagar

Patkai Bum

Bumhpa Bum
3411

Hukawng
Valley

Maingkwan

2424 Kumon Burn

Singkaling
Hkamti

KACHIN

Mogaung
Myitkyina

Bhamo

Tengchong

Longling

Changning

G

KATMANDU
Bhaktapur

Ramechhap

Dhankuta

Darjiling

Gangtok

BHUTAN

Jayanti

Alipur Duar

Barpeta
Mangaldai

Nowgong

Shillong

Silghat

Mokokchung

NAGALAND

Kohima

Singkaling
Hkamti

Mong Yai
Lashio

Mong Pawk

24

Bhairawa

Nautanwa

Birganj

Raxaul Motihari

Bettiah

Sunsari

Udaipur
Garhi

Jaynagar

Kishanganj

Jalpaiguri

Shiligurii

Dinajpur

Purnia

Katihar

Koch Bihar

Dhuburi

Goalpara

Brahmaputra

Guwahati

1412

Tura

MEGHALAYA
Cherrapunji
1961

Mohanganj

Jamalpur

Sylhet

Silchar

Haflong

Barail Range

Ukhrul

Tamenglong

MANIPUR

Imphal

Churachandpur

Homalin

Thaungdut

Indaw Katha

Tigyaing

Shwegu

Mong Kung

Keng Tung

H

VARANASI

Ghazipur

PATNA

Mokama

Jahanabad

Ara

Munger

Bhagalpur

Tinpahar

Ganga

Ingraj
Bazar

Bogra

Jamalpur

Mymensingh

BANGLADESH

Brahmanbaria

Agartala

TRIPURA

Sairang

Aizawl

MIZORAM

Tiddim

Falam

Mingin

Gangaw

Alon Monywa

Sagaing

Kalewa

Budalin

Ye-U

Shwebo

Yinmabin

Kyukse

Mandalay

Gokteik

Maymyo

Madaya

Pang-Yang

Mong Hsu

Mong Pan

2698

22

RAJSHAHI

DHAKA

Narayanganj

Chandpur

KHULNA

Comilla

Belonia

Lunglei

Mt. Kennedy

Chin Hills

3053 Kanpetlet

BURMA
(MYANMAR)

Pakokku

Myingyan

Meiktila

J

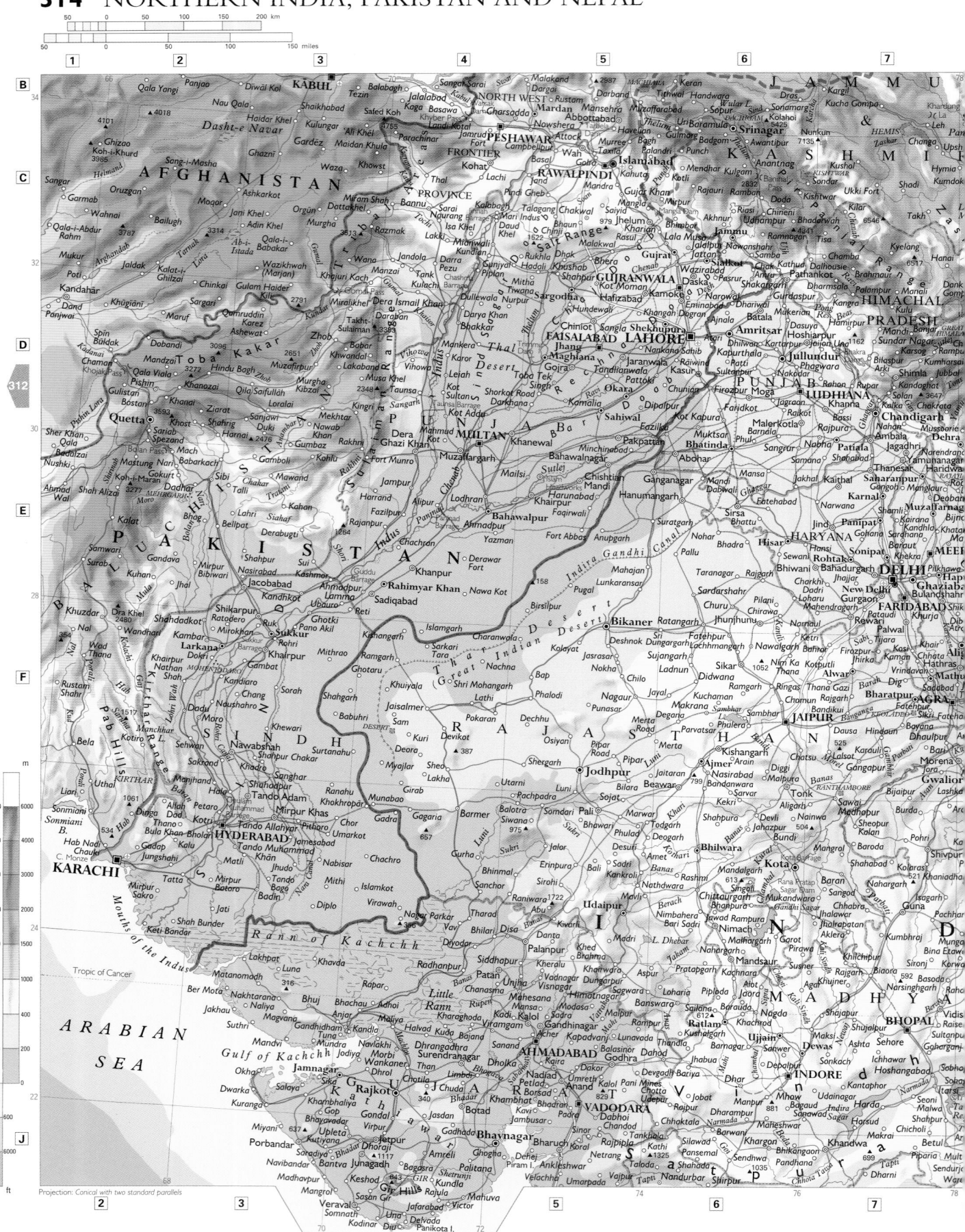

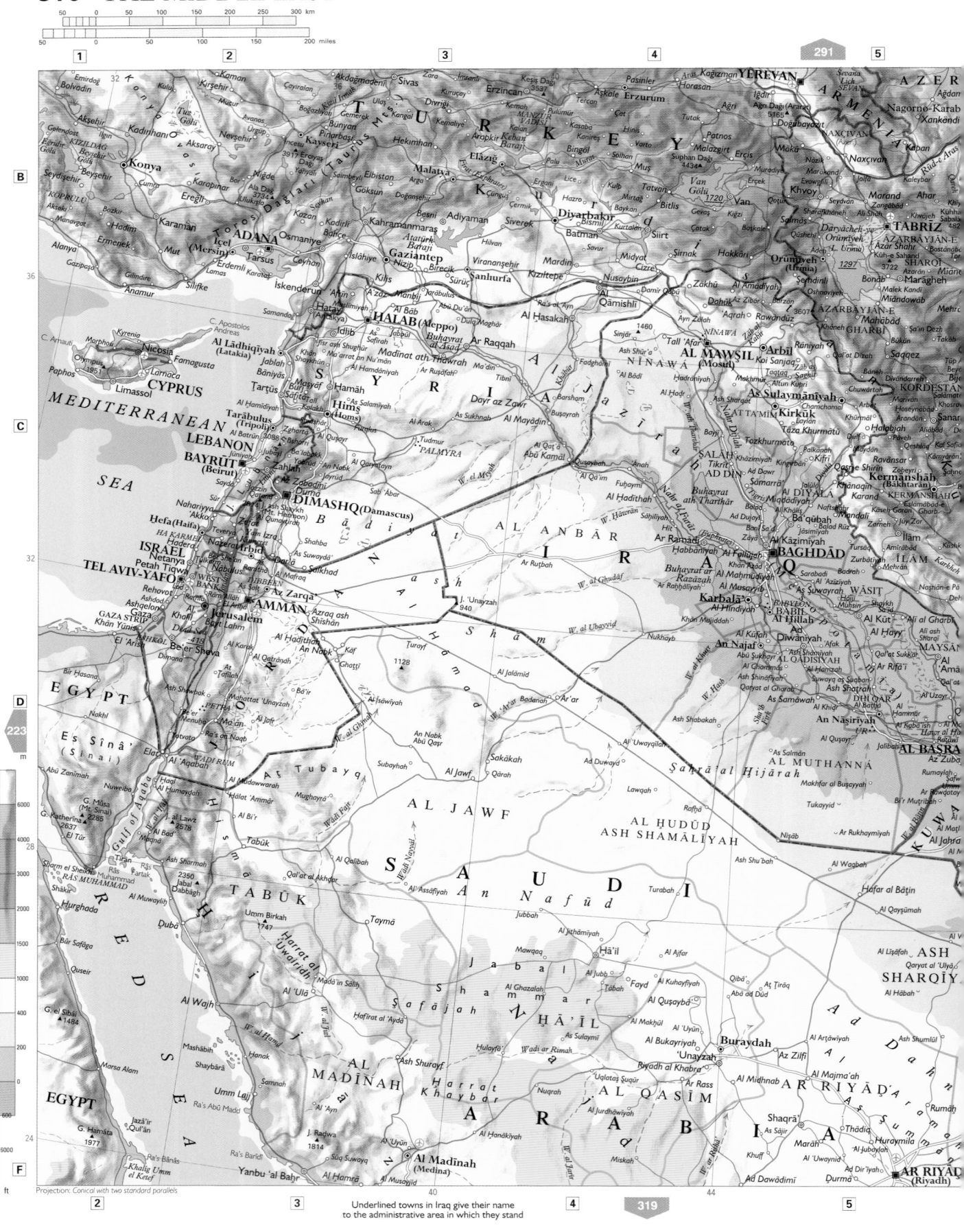

Underlined towns in Iraq give their name
to the administrative area in which they stand

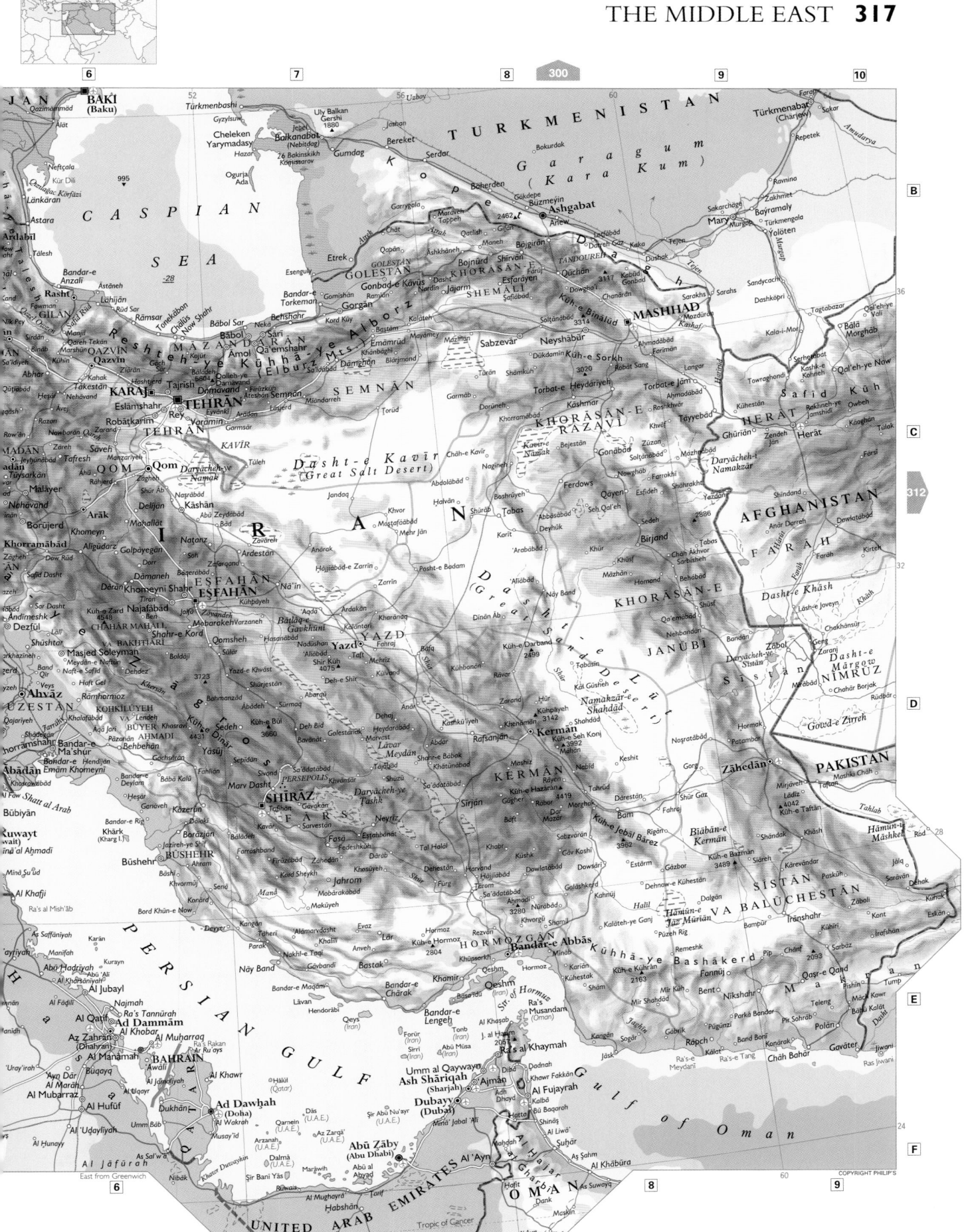

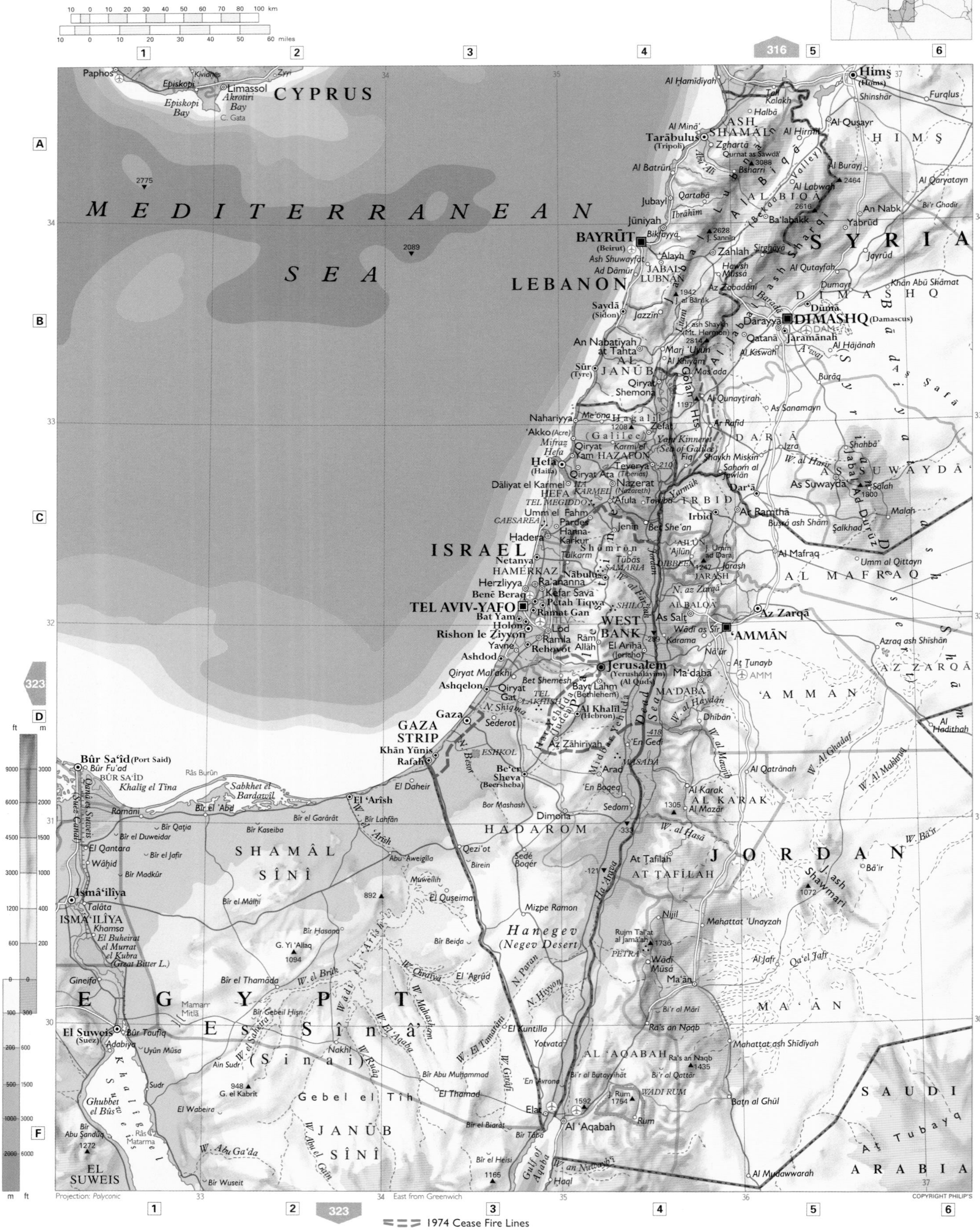

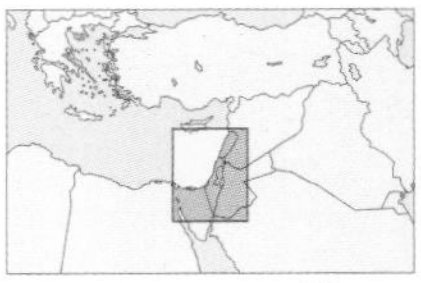

10 0 10 20 30 40 50 60 70 80 100 km
10 0 10 20 30 40 50 60 miles

316

A B C D F

CYPRUS

Paphos Kivides Zyri
Episkopi Limassol Akrotiri Bay
Episkopi Bay C. Gata

2775

M E D I T E R R A N E A N

2089

S E A

Al Hamidiyah Hims (Homs)
Tall Kalakh Shinshar Furqlus
ASH SHAMAL Al Hirmil Al Qusayr
Tarābulus (Tripoli) Zgharta Qurnat as Sawdā 3088 H I M S
Al Batrūn Bsharri Al Buqayʿ Al Qaryatayn
Jubayl Qartabā 2616 Ba'labakk Al Labwah 2464 Bi'r Ghadir
Ibrāhīm An Nabk
BAYRŪT (Beirut) Bikfayya J. Sannin 2628
Junīyah 'Alayh Zahlah Sirghāya SYRIA
Ash Shuwayfāt JABAL Hawsh Mūsā Al Qutayfah
Ad Dāmūr LUBNĀN 1942 Az Zabadānī Khān Abū Shāmat
J. al Bāriik DIMASHQ
Saydā (Sidon) Jazzīn Jdaydat Dūmā DIMASHQ (Damascus)
Darayyā Jaramānah
An Nabatīyah Ash Shayn (Mt. Hermon) 2814 Qatanā Al Hājānah
at Tahta Al Khiyām Al Kiswah
Sūr (Tyre) Mari 'Uyūn Q. Mas'ada Burāq
AL JANŪB Qiryat Majdal Shams
Shemona As Sanamayn
Naharīyya HA-GALIL 1208 Zefat Al Qunaytirah Ar Rafid DAR'A As Suwayda
'Akko (Acre) (Galilee) Yam Kinneret Shaykh Miskin Izra Shahbā
Mifraz Hefa Qiryat Karmi'el (Sea of Galilee) Fiq 1197 Sahem Dar'ā As Suwayda 1800
Hefa (Haifa) Yam HAZAFON Teverya (Tibering) 210 el Jawlan AL JARASH
HEFA Qiryat Ata Nazerat (Nazareth) Yarmuk At Ramthā
Dāliyat el Karmel KARMEL Afula Tayiba IRBID Busrá ash Shām Salkhad
Umm el Fahm TEL MEGIDDO Jenin Bet She'an
CAESAREA Pardes Hanna- Shömrön AJLŪN Umm al Qittayn
Hadera Karkur SAMARIA 'Ajlūn 'Ammān Al Mafraq
ISRAEL Tulkarm Tūbās 1247 Jorash Umm al Qittayn AL MAFRAQ
Netanya HA-MERKAZ Nābulus JARASH
Herzliyya Ra'anana SHILO Az Zarqā
Benē Beraq Kefar Sava AL BALQA
TEL AVIV-YAFO Petah Tiqwa WEST As Salt AMMAN
Ramat Gan BANK Wādī as Sīr Az Zarqā
Bat Yam Lod Ramla Rām Karama AZ ZARQA
Holon Yavne Allāh El Arīhā (Jericho) Nā'ūr
Rishon le Ziyyon Rehovot AMM
Ashdod Jerusalem (Yerushalayim) Ma'daba 'AMMAN
Qiryat Mal'akhi Bet Shemesh (Al Quds) Tunayb
Ashqelon Bayt Lahm (Bethlehem) MA'DABA
Qiryat Gat TEL Al Khalīl (Hebron) Dhībān
GAZA Sederot LAKHISH -418 Al Hadithah
STRIP Az Zāhirīya 'En Gedi W. al Mawjib
Khān Yūnis ESHKOL MASADA Al Karak
Rafah Be'er MA'AN Arad Sedom ALKARAK
Sheva (Beersheba) 'En Boqeq 1305 Al Mazar
Bor Mashash -333 W. al Hasa W. Bā'ir
Bûr Sa'îd (Port Said) Dimona JORDAN
Bûr Fu'ad Rās Burūn HADAROM At Tafīlah Bā'ir
BÛR SA'ÎD Sabkhet el Bardawīl W. al Ghadaf Al Qatrānah
Khalig el Tīna El Daheir -121 AT TAFILAH
Ramāni Bīr el 'Abd El 'Arīsh Qezi'ot Sedé 1072 J. ash Shawmari
El Qantara Bīr el Garārāt Birein Boqer Nijil MA'ĀN
Wāhid Bīr el Duweidar Bīr Kaseiba Abu 'Aweigila 'Arīsh Mahattat 'Unayzah
El Jafir Bīr el Māfhi El Quseima 892 Mizpe Ramon Rujm Tal'at al Jamā'ah 1736
Ismâ'ilîya Bīr Madkūr SHAMĀL Muweilih Hanegev PETRA
Talāta SÎNÎ (Negev Desert) Wādī Mūsā Ma'ān
ISMÂ'ÎLÎYA Khamsa G. Yi 'Allaq 1094 Bīr Hasana Al Jafr Qa'el Jafr
El Buheirat el Murrat el Kubra (Great Bitter L.) Bīr el Thamāda W. el Brūk W. Ghatiya El 'Agrūd N. Hiyyon Bī'r al Mārī
Gineifa Mamarr Mitlā Bīr Gebel Hisn EGYPT ES SÎNÂ' (Sinai) Bī'r al Butayyihāt Bī'r al Qattār SAUDI
El Suweis (Suez) Adabiya 'Uyūn Mūsa Ain Sudr Nakhl W. el Tamarāni El Kuntilla Yotvata Ra's an Naqb 1435 Mahattat ash Shidīyah ARABIA
Bûr Taufîq Sudr W. el 'Aqaba Bīr Abu Muhammad WADI RUM
948 G. el Kabrît El Thamad 'En 'Avrona Rum 1754 Batn al Ghūl
El Wabeira Gebel el Tîh JANŪB El Agrūd Elat 1592 Rum At Tubayq
Ghubbet el Bûs SÎNÎ Bīr el Biarāt Al 'Aqabah Haql Al Mudawwarah
Bīr Abu Sandûg 1272 Rās Matarma W. Abu Ga'da W. Abul Caîn Bīr el Heisi 1165 Gulf of Aqaba A R A B I A
EL SUWEIS

ft m
9000 3000
6000 2000
4500 1500
3000 1000
1200 400
600 200
0
100 300
200 600
500 1500
1000 3000
2000 6000
m ft

Projection: Polyconic

East from Greenwich

COPYRIGHT PHILIP'S

323

1974 Cease Fire Lines

100 0 100 200 300 400 500 600 km
100 0 100 200 300 400 miles

1 | 35 | 2 | 316 | 40 | 3 | 317 | 45 | 4 | 50 | 5 | 55 | 6 | 60 | 7

312

A

LEBANON
BAYRŪT (Beirut)
Ṣūr
DIMASHQ (Damascus)
SYRIA
Jabal ad Durūz 1801
ISRAEL
TEL AVIV-YAFO
Ḥefa
'AMMAN
JERUSALEM
WEST BANK
Ashdod
Bûr Sa'îd (Port Said) GAZA STRIP
Ismâ'ilîya
El Suweis (Suez)
JORDAN
Ma'ān
Ar Ramādī
Ar Ruṭbah
BAGHDĀD
Al Kūt
Karbalā'
Al Ḥillah
An Najaf
Khorramābād
Dezfūl
Al 'Amārah
IRAQ
Baādiyat ash Shām
Al Jawf
'Ar'ar
An Nāṣirīyah
Rafḥā'
Hafar al Bāṭin
Aḥvāz
Khorramshahr
Ābādān
ESFAHĀN
4548
Yazd
IRAN
Dasht-e Lut
Khvor
Birjand
Farāḥ
AFGHANISTAN
Zābol
Daryācheh-ye Sīstan

B

Qan es Suweis
Khalīg el Suweis
Es Sina'
G. Mûsa 2285
Eilat
Al 'Aqabah
Sharm el Sheikh 2187
Bûr Safâga
Duba
Al Muwayliḥ
Tabūk
Tamyā'
An Nafūd
Ḥā'il
Hurghada
Khalīj al 'Aqabah
2578
Qena
KARNAK
THEBES
El Qarn
El Uqsur (Luxor)
Esna
Quseir
Al Wajh
Yanbu 'al Baḥr
Buraydah
Unayzah
Shaqrā'
SAUDI
Al Başrah (Basra)
Al Kuwayt
KUWAIT
Shaṭṭ al 'Arab
Būbiyān
J. Khārk
Kāzerūn
Būshehr
Deyyer
Al Jubayl
Al Qaṭīf
Az Zahrān (Dhahran)
Ad Dammām
BAHRAIN
Al Manāmah
QATAR
Al Mubarraz
Al Ḥufūf
Ad Dawḥah (Doha)
Neyrīz
Sīrjān
Jahrom
4431
PERSEPOLIS
SHĪRĀZ
Kermān
Zāhedān
Bam
Khamīr
Qeshm
Bandar-e Abbās
Bāmpūr
Gābrīk
Jāsk
Ra's al-Khaymah
Str. of Hormuz
Ra's Musandam (Oman)
Ash Shāriqah (Sharjah)
Suḥār
Gulf of Oman

C

Idfū
Kôm Ombo
Aswân
Sadd el 'Ali
Buḥeirat en Naser (L. Nasser)
Halaib Triangle
Bîr Shalatein
Wadi Halfa
Ras Bânâs 1977
Muhammad Qol
2259
Halaib
RED SEA
Rābigh
Al Līth
Al Madīnah (Medina)
JIDDAH (Jedda)
MAKKAH (Mecca)
Aṭ Ṭā'if 2565
Turabah
Tropic of Cancer
As Sulaymānīyah
AR RIYĀḌ (Riyadh)
ARABIA
Ḥaraḍ
Layla
As Sulayyil
Al 'Ubaylah
UNITED ARAB EMIRATES
Ruwais
Abū Ẓaby (Abu Dhabi)
Al 'Ayn
Ibrī
Nizwā 3019
Izki
As Suwayq
Maṣqaṭ (Muscat)
Ṣūr
Ra's al Ḥadd
Khalūf
Maṣīrah
Khalīj Maṣīrah

D

ABU SIMBEL
Es Saḥrâ en Nûbîya
Delgo
4th Cataract
Dongola
Kareima
5th Cataract
Abu Hamed
Bûr Sûdân
Suakin
Sinkat
Haiya
Trinkitat
Karora
Al Qunfudhah
'Asīr
Abhā
Khamis Mushayt
Najrān
Ash Sharawrah
Rub' al Khālī (Empty Quarter)
Ẓufār
Salālah
Mirbāṭ
J. al Hallānīyat
Ras al Madrakah
Ḥaḍramawt
Rās Fartak
Shibām
Sayḥūt
Ḥaymā

E

Ed Debba
Berber
Atbara
Adarama
2480
Nakfa
Akordat
Mitsiwa
Zula
ERITREA
Asmera 3018
Dahlak Kebir
Farasān
Jīzān
Kamaran
Al Luḥayyah
Ḥanīsh
Ḥajjah
Khamir
Niṣāb
2469
Shibām
Omdurmân
EL KHARTÛM (Khartoum)
Kassalā
Khashm el Girba
Gedaref
Wâd Medanî
Adigrat
Aksum
Adwa
Mekele
Ras Dashen 4533
Lalibela 4190
Gonder 1830
L. Tana
Bahir Dar
Debre Tabor
Dese
Debre Markos
Abay (Blue Nile)
Bure
SAN'Ā'
Dhamar
Djebel Manar 3200
Ibb
Ta'izz
Al Mukhā
Madīnat ash Sha'b
Shaqrā'
Aḥwar
YEMEN
Al Ḥudaydah
'Abd al Kūrī (Yemen)
Hadiboh
Socotra (Yemen)
Bereda
Ras Asir
Xaafuun
Ras Xaafuun
El Gal
Bosaso
GULF OF ADEN
Al Mukallā

F

El Dueim
Umm Ruwaba
Singa
Sennar (Blue Nile)
Ed Damazin
Roseires Res.
Kôstî
Gezira
Jibalan
Nubah
SUDAN
Nekemte
Metu
Dembidolo 3302
Gore
Jima 3886
ADDIS ABEBA
ETHIOPIA
Ethiopian Highlands
Debre Zeyit
Awash
Nazret
Asela
Shashemene
Ginir
Kebri Dehar
Awasa
Yirga Alem
Mt. Batu 4307
Goba
L. Zeway
3381
Harer
Dire Dawa
Jijiga
Hargeisa
Burao
Ogaden
Galcaio
2408
Erigavo
Gardo
Bender Beila
Eil
SOMALILAND
Berbera
Karin
SOMALI REP.
INDIAN
DJIBOUTI
Djibouti
Tadjoura
Dikhil
L. Assal
L. Abbé
Zeila
Bāb el Mandeb
Aseb
Danakil Desert
Al 'Adan (Aden)
Tendaho

G

Bôr
Tali Post
Pibor Post
Juba
Yei
Kajo Kaji 3187
Mongalla
Kapoeta
Elemi Triangle
Lokitaung 1794
Lodwar
Arba Minch
L. Abaya
Dila
Kibre Mengist
Negele
Dolo
Imi
Scebeli
Ferfer
Belet Uen
El Dere
Sinadogo
Obbia
Mega
Chew Bahir
L. Turkana 375
Moyale
El Wak
Marsabit
Wajir
Lugh Ganana
Baidoa
Bur Acaba
Uanle Uen
Giohar
MUQDISHO (Mogadishu)
Merca
Bardera
KENYA
UGANDA
Gulu
Lira
Moroto 3084
Soroti 3206
Mbale
L. Kyoga
Mt. Elgon 4321
2344
Kitale
Atua
Pakwach
L. Albert
Masindi
Murchison Falls
Dif
Gelib
Genale
Giuba
Wabi Scebeli
Giamama
Equator
Kismayu
East from Greenwich

COPYRIGHT PHILIP'S

ft m
12 000 — 4000
9000 — 3000
6000 — 2000
4500 — 1500
3000 — 1200
— 600
— 400
— 200
0 — 0
— 200 600
1000 — 3000
2000 — 6000
4000 — 12 000
m ft

Projection: Sanson-Flamsteed's Sinusoidal

1 | 35 | 2 | 326 | 40 | 3 | 45 | 4 | 50 | 5 | 6

A B C D E F G

200 0 200 400 600 800 1000 1200 1400 1600 1800 km
200 0   200   400   600   800   1000   1200 miles

B NORTH
ATLANTIC
OCEAN

Europe

British
Isles

B. of Biscay

Carpathians

Black Sea

Caucasus

Elbrus
5633

Caspian Sea

Aral
Sea

Mont Blanc
4808

Alps
Dinaric Alps

Pyrénées

Adriatic Sea

Apennines

C

Azores

6578

Iberian
Peninsula

Corsica

Sardinia

Balearic Is.

Malta

Mediterranean Sea

Sicily

Bon

5121

Crete

Cyprus

Asia

Mesopotamia

Tigris

Madeira

Str. of Gibraltar

High Plateaux

Saharan Atlas

Chott Melrhir

Levant

Syrian Desert Euphrates

4165 Middle Atlas
High Atlas

Maghreb

Chott Djerid

G. of Gabès
Djerba

G. of Sidra

Cyrenaica

Nile Delta

Suez
Canal

Dead Sea

D

Canary Is.
Tenerife 3718

C. Juby

Oued Saoura

Erg Iguidi

Erg Chech Great Western Erg

Great Eastern Erg

Tripolitania

Libyan Desert

Egypt

Siwa Oasis

Sinai
2285

Arabian Desert

Hejaz

Arabia

Persian Gulf

C. Bojador

Tropic of Cancer

Tasili Plateau

Al Kufrah

El Khârga

Nile

Red Sea

D

Ras
Nouâdhibou

C. Timiris

Adrar

El Djouf

Sahara

Hoggar
2918

Tibesti
3415

Nubian Desert

Nubia

L. Nasser

Ras Bânâs

Cape
Verde Is.
2829

C. Vert

Senegambia

Senegal

Gambia

El Mreyye

Adrar
des Iforas

L. Faguibine

L. Débo

Niger

Aïr

Ténéré

Bilma

Bahr el Ghazal

Darfûr

Kordofan

White Nile

Dahlak
Is.

Blue Nile

L. Tana

−116

Barim Bab el Mandeb

G. of Aden

Ras Asir

Soco

F

Bijagos
Is.

Sahel

Fouta
Djallon

Guinea

Bani

White Volta

Black Volta

Niger

Kainji Res.

Hadejia

L. Chad

Chari

Wadai

Sahel

Dashen
4533

Ethiopian
Highlands

L. Abbé

Ras Hafun

Sherbro I.

Grain Coast

C. Palmas

Ivory Coast

L. de Kossou

L. Volta

Gold
Coast

C. Three
Points

Slave Coast

Bight of Benin

Niger
Delta

Mt.
Cameroon
4070

Bioko 3008

Benue

Adamawa
Highlands

Sanaga

Ubangi

Bahr Aouk

Oubangi

Dar Banda

Bahr el Arab

Jur

Bahr el Ghazâl

Sudd

Bahr el Jebel

Sobat

4307
L. Abaya

Somali
Peninsula

Ogaden

Shabelle

Juba

Lach Dera

F

Bight of Bonny

I. de Principe

São Tomé

Gulf of Guinea

Equator

C. Lopez

Annobón

Ogooué

Congo

L. Mai-
Ndombe

Kasai

Congo
Basin

Sankuru

Lomani

Lualaba

Uele

Bomu

Congo

Chutes
Boyoma

L. Albert

Ruwenzori
5109

L. Edward

1134

L. Kyoga
2321

Mt. Elgon
4321

Victoria

5199

Mt. Kenya
5895
Kilimanjaro

L. Turkana

Meru
4564

L. Kivu

Pangani

Pemba I.

Zanzibar I.

INDIAN
OCEAN

Seychelles

G

ft m

Ascension I.

Palmeirinhas Pt.

Cuanza

Kwango

Kasai

Lualaba

L. Tanganyika

L. Rukwa

Rungwe
2961

Great Ruaha

H

12000 4000

9000 3000

6000 2000

3000 1000

1500 500

South
ATLANTIC
OCEAN

St. Helena

Bié
Plateau

Cuango

Cunene

Kafue

Luapula

Luangwa

Zambezi

Cabora
Bassa

L. Mweru

L. Bangweulu

Katanga

L. Malawi
(L. Nyasa)

Shire

Ruvuma

Lurio

Aldabra
Is.

Comoros

Mayotte

C. Delgado

C. d'Ambre

Mozambique Channel

Madagascar

J

1500 500

200 600

C. Fria

Etosha Pan

Okavango
Delta

Victoria
Falls

Cuando

Okwa

L. Kariba

Zambezi

Limpopo

Makgadikgadi
Salt Pans

2643

Mauriti

Réunion

K

1000 3000

2000 6000

4000 12000

Tropic of Capricorn

Walvis Bay

Skeleton Coast

Namib Desert

Kalahari

Orange

Vaal

High Veld

Nossob

Thabana
Ntlenyana
3482

Maputo Bay

C. Ste. Marie

m ft

St. Helena Bay

C. of Good Hope

C. Agulhas

Great
Nieuwveldberge

Karoo

Swartberge

Orange

Compass Mt.
2502

Drakensberg

Algoa B.

Tristan de Cunha

200 0 200 400 600 800 1000 1200 1400 1600 1800 km

200 0 200 400 600 800 1000 1200 miles

1 **2** **3** **4** **5** **6** **7** **8** **9** **10**

B

NORTH

ATLANTIC

OCEAN

UNITED KINGDOM NETH.
LONDON
BELG.
PARIS
FRANCE
SWITZ.
B. of Biscay
GERMANY POLAND
Warsaw
CZECH REP.
Prague
Vienna
AUSTRIA
HUNGARY
SLOVAK REP.
CROATIA
BOS.-HERZ.
SERBIA
MONT.
N.MAC.
ROMANIA
BULGARIA
Kiev
UKRAINE
Odessa
RUSSIA
Volgograd
KAZAKHSTAN
Aral Sea
GEORGIA
ARM. AZER.
Baku
Caspian Sea
TURKMEN.

Black Sea

Azores
(Port.)
Ponta
Delgada

Corsica
Rome
Sardinia
ITALY
Adriatic Sea
GREECE
Athens
Crete
CYPRUS
Ankara
TURKEY
Aleppo
SYRIA
Mosul
Tigris
Baghdad
Tehrān
Esfahān
IRAN

Madrid
SPAIN
Lisbon
PORTUGAL

Mediterranean Sea

Madeira
(Port.)
Funchal

Santa Cruz
de Tenerife
Canary Is.
(Sp.)
Las Palmas

Algiers
Oran
Annaba
Constantine
Tunis
TUNISIA
Sfax
MALTA
Tripoli
Miṣrātah
Benghazi
Alexandria
Port Said
CAIRO
Suez
El Faiyûm
Nile
LEB.
Tel Aviv-Jaffa
Damascus
Jerusalem
ISRAEL
JORDAN
Basra
KUWAIT
Euphrates
Persian Gulf
BAHRAIN
QATAR
SAUDI
Riyadh

Rabat
Tetouán
Casablanca
Fes
MOROCCO
Marrakesh
Chott Djerid
Ghadâmes

El Aaiún
WESTERN SAHARA
In Salah
ALGERIA
LIBYA
Sabhā
Marzūq
Al Jawf
EGYPT
Asyût
Aswân
Red Sea
Medina
ARABIA
Mecca
Jedda

Dakhla
Tropic of Cancer
Fdérik
Ras Nouâdhibou

Sahara

Wâdi Halfa
Port Sudan

C. VERDE IS.
Praia
C. Vert
Dakar
St-Louis
SENEGAL
GAMBIA
Banjul
GUINEA-BISSAU
Bissau
Senegal
Nouakchott
MAURITANIA
Tombouctou
Agades
NIGER
CHAD
Abéché
L. Chad
Ndjamena
SUDAN
El Fasher
El Obeid
Atbara
Omdurman
Khartoum
Wâd Medani
White Nile
Blue Nile
L. Tana
ERITREA
Asmera
Massawa
YEMEN
G. of Aden
Socotra
(Yemen)
Ras Asir

GUINEA
Conakry
Freetown
SIERRA LEONE
LIBERIA
Monrovia
MALI
Bamako
BURKINA FASO
Ouagadougou
Bobo-Dioulasso
IVORY COAST
Yamoussoukro
Bouaké
GHANA
Kumasi
Niamey
Kano
Maiduguri
NIGERIA
Abuja
BENIN
TOGO
Enugu
Ibadan
LAGOS
Porto Novo
Lomé
Accra
Sekondi-Takoradi
Abidjan
Niger
Bight of Benin
Port Harcourt
Douala
CAMEROON
Yaoundé
Rey Malabo
EQUATORIAL GUINEA
Benue
Chari
CENTRAL AFRICAN REP.
Bangui
Wâw
Malakâl
Bahr el Jebel
Addis Ababa
Harer
ETHIOPIA
Berbera
Shabelle
DJIBOUTI
Djibouti
SOMALI REP.

Gulf of Guinea
SÃO TOMÉ & PRÍNCIPE
Libreville
C. Lopez
Annobón
GABON
CONGO
Brazzaville
Pointe Noire
CABINDA (Angola)
KINSHASA
Matadi
Kananga
Mbuji-Mayi
CONGO (DEM. REP. OF THE)
Kisangani
Mbandaka
Congo
Kasai
Ubangi
L. Albert
L. Edward
L. Kivu
UGANDA
Kampala
RWANDA
Kigali
BURUNDI
Bujumbura
L. Victoria
Kisumu
Nairobi
KENYA
Kismayu
Mombasa
Mogadishu
Tana
Juba
L. Turkana
Equator

INDIAN

OCEAN

SEYCHELLES
Victoria

Ascension I.
(U.K.)

SOUTH

ATLANTIC

OCEAN

St. Helena
(U.K.)

Tristan da Cunha
(U.K.)

Luanda
ANGOLA
Huambo
Namibe
Lobito
Cunene
C. Fria
TANZANIA
Dodoma
Zanzibar
Dar es Salaam
L. Tanganyika
L. Mweru
Likasi
Lubumbashi
ZAMBIA
Ndola
Lusaka
Lilongwe
L. Malawi
MALAWI
Blantyre
Zambezi
Kafue
C. Delgado
Aldabra Is.
COMOROS
Moroni
Mamoudzou
Mayotte
(Fr.)
Antsiranana
Mahajanga

Livingstone
ZIMBABWE
Harare
Bulawayo
Beira
MOZAMBIQUE
Moçambique
Mozambique Channel
Toamasina
MADAGASCAR
Antananarivo
Fianarantsoa
MAURITIUS
Port Louis
Réunion
(Fr.)
St Denis

NAMIBIA
Windhoek
BOTSWANA
Gaborone
Tropic of Capricorn
Limpopo
Orange
Vaal
Kimberley
Pretoria (Tshwane)
Johannesburg
Maputo
Mbabane
SWAZ.
Maseru
LESOTHO
Durban (eThekwini)
SOUTH AFRICA
Cape Town
C. of Good Hope
Port Elizabeth
East London
C. Agulhas

Projection: Azimuthal Equidistant

West from Greenwich   East from Greenwich

COPYRIGHT PHILIP'S

● Dakar Capital Cities

100 0 100 200 300 400 500 600 km

100 0 100 200 300 400 miles

Projection: Sanson-Flamsteed's Sinusoidal

West from Greenwich · East from Greenwich

AZORES
Inset (a)
on same scale as main map

ATLANTIC OCEAN

Corvo · Flores · Graciosa · Terceira · Faial · Horta 2351 · Pico · São Jorge 1103 · Angra do Heroismo · São Miguel · Ponta Delgada · Santa Maria

Açores (Azores) (Portugal)

CAPE VERDE IS.
Inset (b)

Barlavento

Santo Antão 1979 · Ribeira Grande · Mindelo · Santa Luzia · São Vicente 79 · Sal · Pedra Lume · São Nicolau · Vila da Ribeira Brava · Santa Maria · Sal Rei · Boa Vista · Curral Velho

CAPE VERDE IS.

4270

Fogo · São Tiago · Tarrafal · Maio · Brava 2829 1392 · São Filipe · Praia · Porto Inglês

Sotavento

ATLANTIC OCEAN

Main map

ATLANTIC OCEAN

SPAIN · Málaga · Almería · Cádiz · Cabo de São Vicente · Gibraltar (U.K.) · Str. of Gibraltar · Ceuta · Tanger · Tétouan · Al Hoceima · Melilla (Sp.) · Nador

Madeira (Port.) · Funchal · Porto Santo

La Palma · Gomera · Hierro · Tenerife 3718 · Gran Canaria · Santa Cruz de Tenerife · Las Palmas · Lanzarote · Arrecife · Fuerteventura

Islas Canarias (Sp.)

MOROCCO · Rabat · Salé · Kenitra · Meknès · Fès · Taza · Oujda · Casablanca · Mohammedia · El Jadida · Settat · Khouribga · Safi · Ras Beddouza · Beni Mellal · Marrakech · Chichaoua · Dj. Toubkal 4165 · Essaouira · Agadir · C. Rhir · Taroudannt · Tiznit · Sidi Ifni · Tata · Goulimine · Tan-Tan · Tarfaya · C. Drâa · Oued Drâa · Er Rachidia · Ouarzazate · Figuig · Boudfa · Béchar · Abadla · El Goléa

Moyen Atlas · Haut Atlas · Anti Atlas · Hauts Plateaux

ALGERIA · Alger (Algiers) · Oran · Mostaganem · Ech Chéliff · Médéa · Blida · Blida · Setif · Constantine · Bejaia · Tizi-Ouzou · Skikda · Batna · Tébessa · Biskra · El Oued · Touggourt · Ouargla · Ghardaïa · Berriane · Laghouat · Hassi Messaoud · El Bayadh · Aflou · Messaad · Djelfa · Tiaret · Saïda · Mascara · Sidi-bel-Abbès · Tlemcen · Mecheria · Aïn-Sefra · Kerzaz · Timimoun · Adrar · Reggane · Zaouiet Reggane · In Salah · Arak · Bordj Omar Driss · Illizi · Ohanet · Bordj Fly Ste. Marie · Bordj-in-Eker · Tamanrasset · Tahat 2918 · Adrar Edekel 2306

Grand Erg Occidental · Grand Erg Oriental · Plateau du Tademaït · Erg Iguidi · Erg Chech · Tanezrouft · Ahaggar · Tassili n'Ajjer · Tassili Oua-n-Ahaggar

WESTERN SAHARA · Dakhla · C. Bojador · C. Barbas · Bu Craa · Smara · El Aaiún · Ain Ben Tili · Chegga · Pta. Negra

Ghallamane · El Djouf · Tropic of Cancer · Taoudenni

MAURITANIA · Nouâdhibou · Râs Nouâdhibou · Atâr · Chinguetti · Akjoujt · Rachid · Tidjikja · Nouakchott · Râs Timiris · Rosso · Aleg · Bogué · Kaédi · Kiffa · 'Ayoûn el 'Atroûs · Néma · Séléibabi

Adrar · Ijâfene · Aoukâr · Azaouad · Adrar des Iforas · Tessalit · Kidal

MALI · Tombouctou · Goundam · Bourem · Gao · Ansongo · Ménaka · Hombori · Nioro du Sahel · Nara · Diafarabé · Mopti · Ségou · Bamako · San · Koutiala · Sikasso · Bougouni · Kayes · Bafoulabé · Kita · Satadougou · Didiéni

SENEGAL · Dakar · St. Louis · Louga · Mboro · C. Thiès · C. Vert · Thiès · Diourbel · Mbour · Kaolack · Linguère · Matam · Bakel · Tambacounda · Kolda · Ziguinchor · Vélingara · Kédougou · Bafatá

GAMBIA · Banjul

GUINEA-BISSAU · Bissau · Arq. dos Bijagós

GUINEA · Conakry · Boké · Fria · Kindia · Dubréka · Kankan · Kissidougou · Siguiri · Kouroussa · Dabola · Faranah · Mamou · Dalaba · Labé · Gaoual · Koundara

Fouta Djallon · Vallée du Ferlo

SIERRA LEONE · Freetown · Makeni · Bo · Kenema · Port Loko · 1948 · Yonibana

LIBERIA · Monrovia · Buchanan · River Cess · Greenville · Harper · San Pédro · C. Palmas · Tabou · 914

BURKINA FASO · Ouagadougou · Bobo Dioulasso · Koudougou · Ouahigouya · Dori · Kaya · Tougan · Banfora · Gaoua · Tenkodogo

NIGER · Niamey · Tahoua · Tanout · Agadez · Arlit · In-Gall · Birni Nkonni · Maradi · Zinder · Tessaoua · Gouré · Dosso · Tillabéri · Filingué · Gaya · Baleyara

Aïr (Azbine) 1922 · Iférouâne 4070 · Ténéré

IVORY COAST · Abidjan · Yamoussoukro · Bouaké · Daloa · Gagnoa · Man · Korhogo · Bondoukou · Divo · Abengourou · Ferkessédougou · Odienné · Séguéla · Katiola · Bouna · Boundiali · Grand Bassam · Sassandra · San Pédro

GHANA · Accra · Kumasi · Tamale · Obuasi · Tema · Winneba · Cape Coast · Sekondi-Takoradi · Sunyani · Wa · Bolgatanga · Ho · Salaga · Savalugu · C. Three Points · Gold Coast

TOGO · Lomé · Atakpamé · Kpalimé · Tsévié

BENIN · Porto-Novo · Cotonou · Abomey · Parakou · Natitingou · Djougou · Kandi · Savalou · Dassa · Save · Bembéréké

NIGERIA · Lagos · Ibadan · Abeokuta · Ijebu-Ode · Ogbomosho · Oyo · Ife · Ilesha · Oshogbo · Iwo · Offa · Ilorin · Kaduna · Kano · Zaria · Katsina · Sokoto · Gusau · Birnin Kebbi · Minna · Abuja · Keffi · Lafia · Makurdi · Jos · Enugu · Benin City · Warri · Sapele · Onitsha · Aba · Calabar · Port Harcourt · Owerri · Umuahia · Bioko 3008 · Rey Malabo · Limbe · Mt. Cameroun

L. de Kossou · Lac Volta · Black Volta · White Volta · Kainji Res. · Niger · Benue · Bight of Benin · Slave Coast · Ivory Coast · Grain Coast · Gold Coast

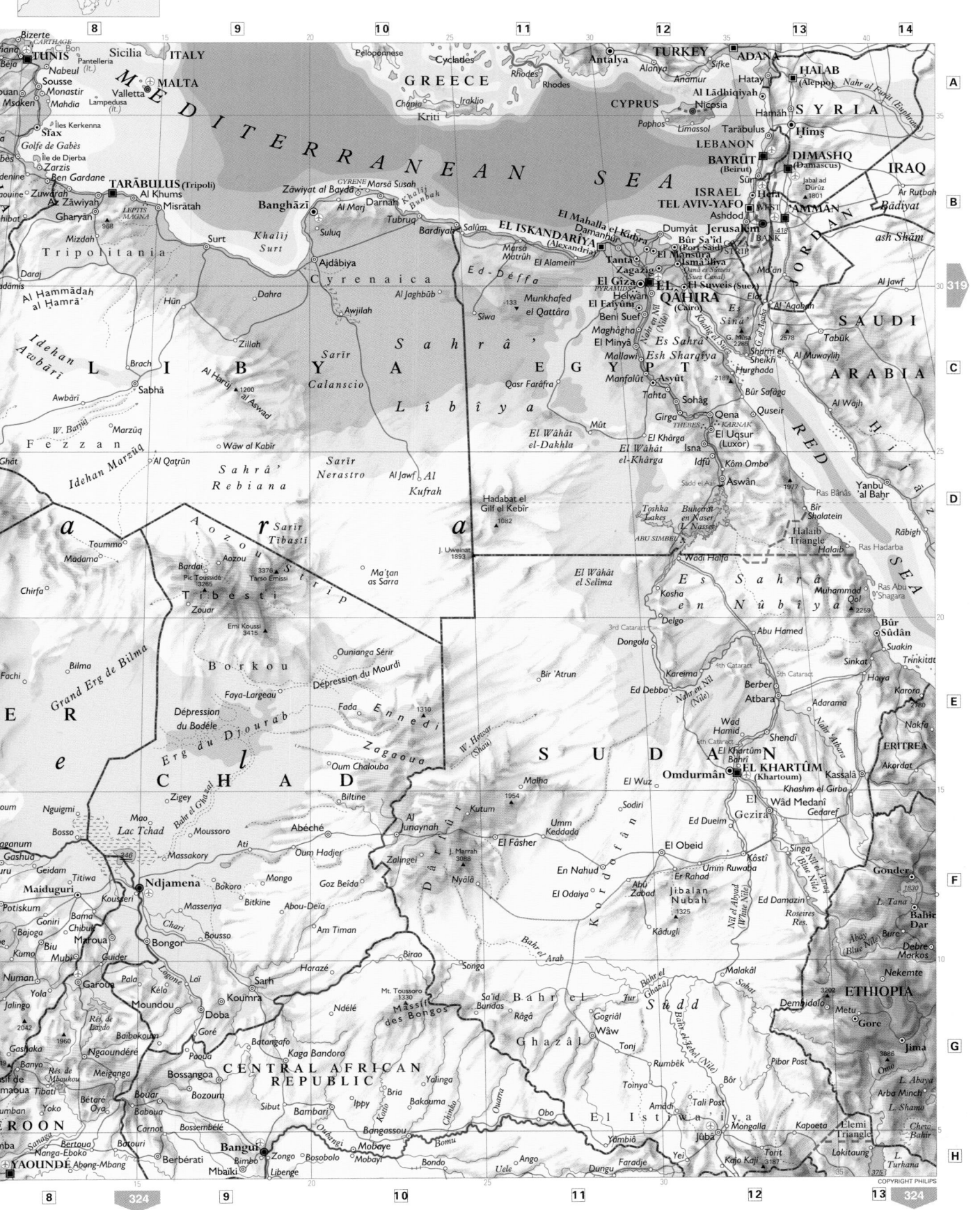

Bizerte
CARTHAGE
Bon
Beja
TUNIS
Nabeul
Pantelleria (It.)
Sousse
Monastir
Sicilia
ITALY
Msaken
Mahdia
Valletta
MALTA
Sfax
Golfe de Gabès
Îles Kerkenna
Lampedusa (It.)
bès
Zarzis
Île de Djerba
GREECE
Peloponnese
Cyclades
Rhodes
Antalya
Alanya
Anamur
TURKEY
Sifke
Hatay
ADANA
HALAB (Aleppo)
SYRIA
dinine
Ben Gardane
Chania
Kriti
Iraklio
Rhodes
CYPRUS
Nicosia
Al Lādhiqiyah
Hamāh
Nahr al Furāt (Euphrates)

M E D I T E R R A N E A N   S E A

Paphos
Limassol
Tarābulus
Hims
Ar Rutbah
Bādiyat
Zuwārah
TARĀBULUS (Tripoli)
Al Khums
Misrātah
LEPTIS MAGNA
968
CYRENE
Zāwiyat al Bayda
Marsā Susah
Banghāzī
Al Marj
Darnah
Khalīj Bunbah
Tubruq
Salūm
Mersa Matrûh
El Alamein
LEBANON
BAYRŪT (Beirut)
ISRAEL
TEL AVIV-YAFO
Ashdod
DIMASHQ (Damascus)
Jabal ad Durūz 1801
'AMMĀN
ash Shām

Gharyān
Mizdah
Surt
Khalīj Surt
Ajdābiya
Dahra
Awjilah
El Mahalla el Kubra
Damanhûr
Dumyāt
EL ISKANDARÎYA (Alexandria)
Tanta
Zagazig
El Mansûra
Ismâ'ilîya
Bûr Sa'îd (Port Said)
JORDAN
Al Jawf

Tripolitania
Daraj
Al Hammādah al Hamrā'
Hün
Siwa
-133
Munkhafed el Qattâra
El Gîza PYRAMIDS
EL QÂHIRA (Cairo)
Helwân
El Faiyûm
Beni Suef
Maghâgha
El Minyâ
Mallawi
Es Suweis (Suez)
Qanâ es Suweis Suez Canal
Khalîg el Suweis
El 'Arîsh
G. Mûsa 2665
Sharm el Sheikh
Al 'Aqabah
Al Muwayliḥ
Tabūk
SAUDI ARABIA

319

Idehan Awbāri
Brach
Zillah
Sahrâ' Lîbîya
Sarîr Calanscio
Qasr Farâfra
Es Sahrâ
Esh Sharqîya
Manfalût
Asyût
Tahta
Sohâg
2578
Bûr Safâga
Hurghada
Al Wejh
Al Harūj al Aswad 1200

Awbārī
Sabhā
Waw al Kabîr
Sarîr Rebiana
Sarîr Nerastro
El Wâhât el-Dakhla
Mût
Girga
KARNAK
THEBES
Qena
El Khârga
Isna
El Uqsur (Luxor)
Quseir
W. Bartāi
Marzūq
2187
RED
HIJĀZ

Fezzan
Ghāt
Idehan Marzūq
Al Qatrūn
Al Jawf
Al Kufrah
El Wâhât el-Khârga
Idfû
Kôm Ombo
Sâdd el 'Ali
Aswân
1977
Ras Bânâs
Bîr Shalatein
Yanbu' al Bahr
Rābigh

a
Toummo
Madama
Aozou Strip
Sarîr Tibastî
Hadabat el Gilf el Kebîr 1082
a
Toshka Lakes
Buheirat en Naser (L. Nasser)
ABU SIMBEL
Wadi Halfa
Halaib Triangle
Halaib
Ras Hadarba
SEA
Ras Abu Shagara

Chirfa
Bardai
Pic Toussidé 3265
Tarso Emissi 3376
Aozou
Ma'tan as Sarra
El Wâhât el Selima
Kosha
Es Sahrâ
en Nûbîya
Muhammad Qol
2259
Bûr Sûdân

Fachi
Bilma
Tibesti
Emi Koussi 3415
Zouar
Ouanianga Sérir
Bir 'Atrun
Delgo
Abu Hamed
Dongola
3rd Cataract
Suakin
Trinkitat
Grand Erg de Bilma
ER

E
Borkou
Faya-Largeau
Dépression du Mourdi
Fada
Ennedi 1310
Kareima
Ed Debba
4th Cataract
Berber
Atbara
5th Cataract
Adarama
2760
Karora
Nakfa
ERITREA
Akordat

e
CHAD
Zigey
Mao
Dépression du Bodélé
Erg du Djourab
Zagaoua
Oum Chalouba
Biltine
1954
Kutum
Malha
El Wuz
Sodiri
Wad Hamid
6th Cataract
Shendî
OMDURMÂN
EL KHARTÛM (Khartoum)
Kassalâ
Wâd Medanî
Gedaref
L. Tana
1830
Gonder
Bahir Dar

Nguigmi
Bosso
Lac Tchad
Moussoro
Ati
Abéché
Oum Hadjer
Al Junaynah
Zalingei
Nyâlâ
Jebel Marrah 3088
En Nahud
El Fâsher
Umm Keddada
Er Rahad
El Obeid
Kôstî
Umm Ruwaba
Nil el Azraq (Blue Nile)
Ed Damazin
Roseires Res.

Gashua
Geidam
Titiwa
246
Massakory
Mongo
Goz Beïda
Am Timan
Abou-Deïa
El Odaiya
Abu Zabad
Jibalan Nubah 1325
Kâdugli
Malakâl
Debre Markos
Nekemte

Maiduguri
Kouseri
Ndjamena
Bokoro
Bitkine
Massenya
Chari
Bousso
Bongor
Birao
Harazé
Mt. Toussoro 1330
Massif des Bongos
Ndélé
Sa'id Bundas
Râga
Bahr el Ghazâl
Wâw
Tonj
Rumbêk
Bôr
Pibor Post
Toinya
3202
Dembidolo
Metu
Gore
ETHIOPIA
Jima
3886
L. Abaya

Garoua
Moundou
Doba
Goré
Batangafo
Kaga Bandoro
Bria
Yalinga
Bakouma
El Istiwa'iya
Amadi
Tali Post
Mongalla
Jûba
Kapoeta
Elemi Triangle
Chew Bahir
L. Turkana
375

CENTRAL AFRICAN REPUBLIC
Bossangoa
Bozoum
Bossembélé
Sibut
Bambari
Ippy
Kotto
Chinko
Obo
Yambio
Yei
Kajo Kaji
2187
Lokitaung

YAOUNDÉ
Bangui
Zongo
Mbaïki
Libenge
Bosobolo
Mobayi
Bondo
Uele
Ango
Dungu
Faradje

324

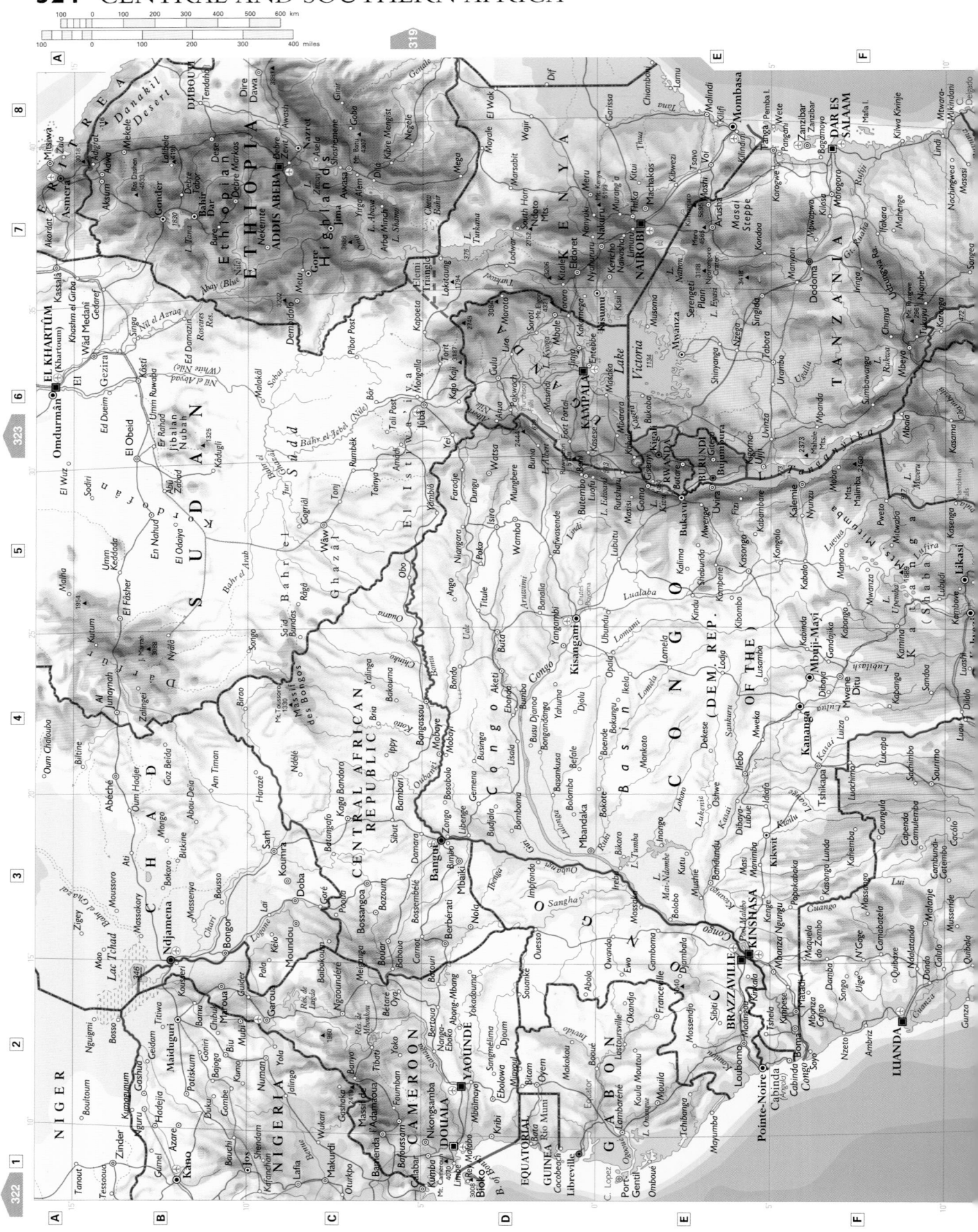

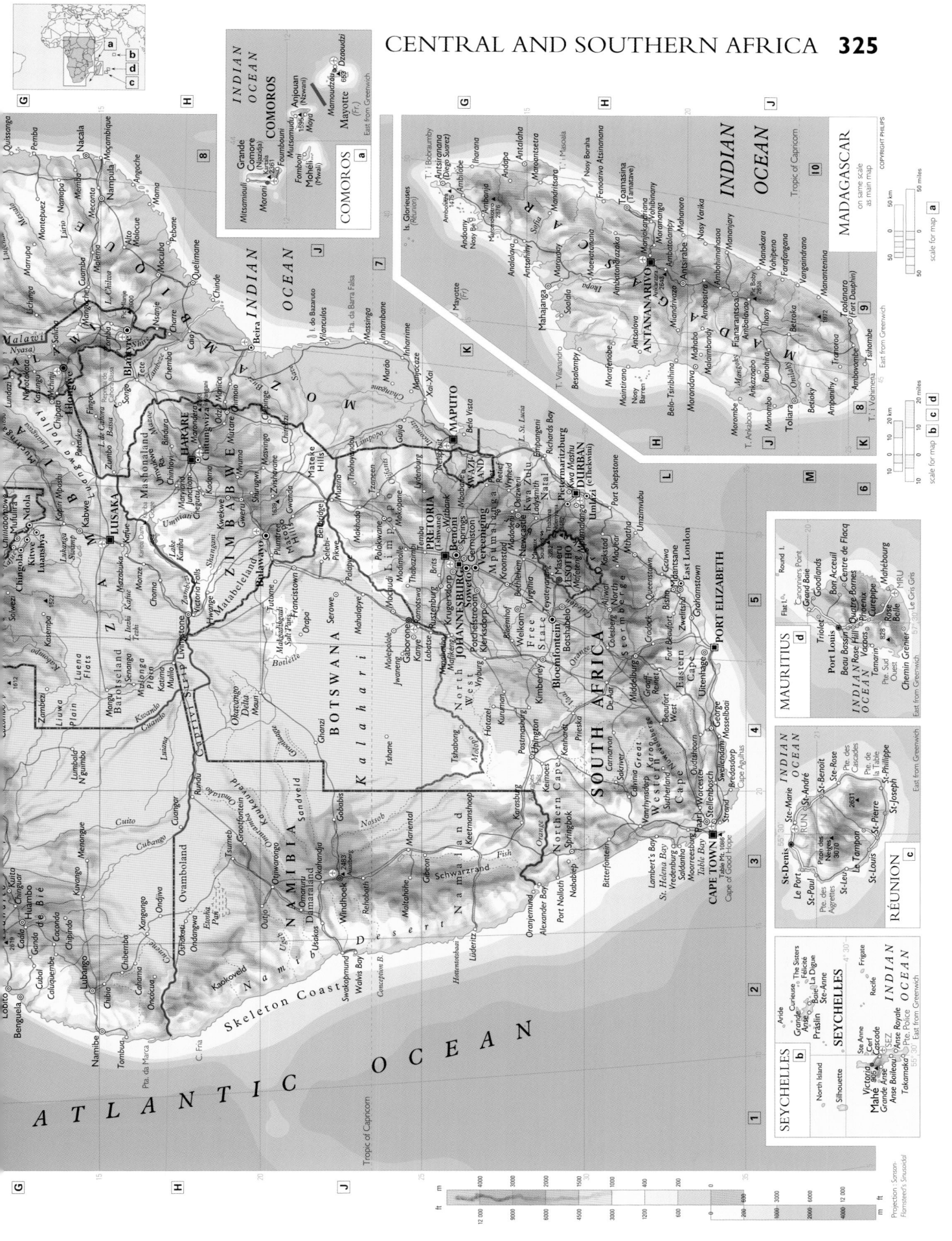

INDIAN OCEAN

COMOROS

Grande Comore (Njazidja)
Moroni
Fomboni
Mohéli (Mwali)
Mutsamudu
Anjouan (Nzwani)
Foumbouni
Mamoudzou
Dzaoudzi
Mayotte (Fr.)

MADAGASCAR
on same scale as main map

ANTANANARIVO

INDIAN OCEAN

COMOROS

MADAGASCAR

MAPUTO

HARARE

LUSAKA

BULAWAYO

ZIMBABWE

BOTSWANA

NAMIBIA

Kalahari

SOUTH AFRICA

JOHANNESBURG

PRETORIA

DURBAN

CAPE TOWN

PORT ELIZABETH

Cape of Good Hope

ATLANTIC OCEAN

INDIAN OCEAN

Skeleton Coast

MAURITIUS

RÉUNION

SEYCHELLES

MAHÉ

Victoria

SEYCHELLES

Tropic of Capricorn

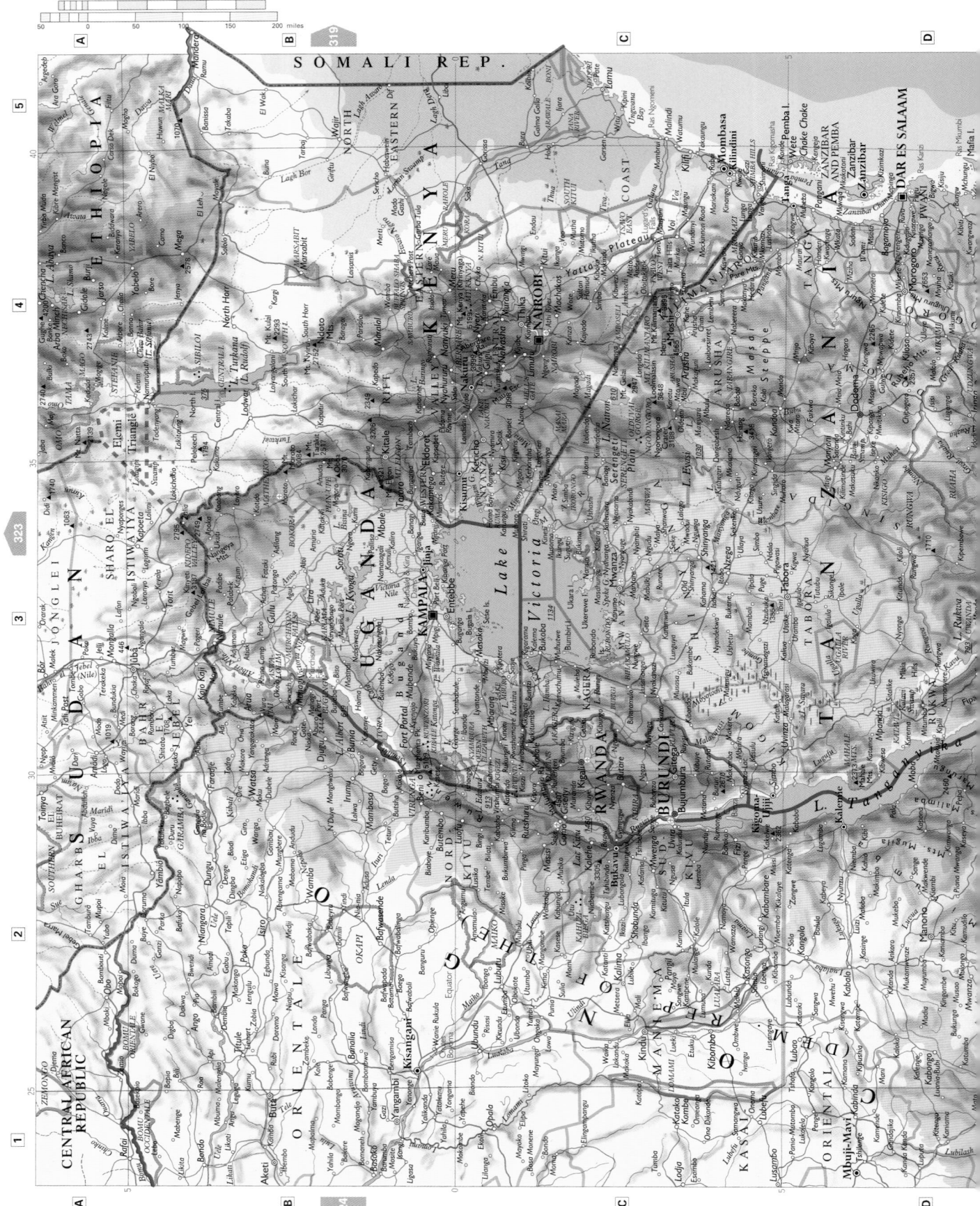

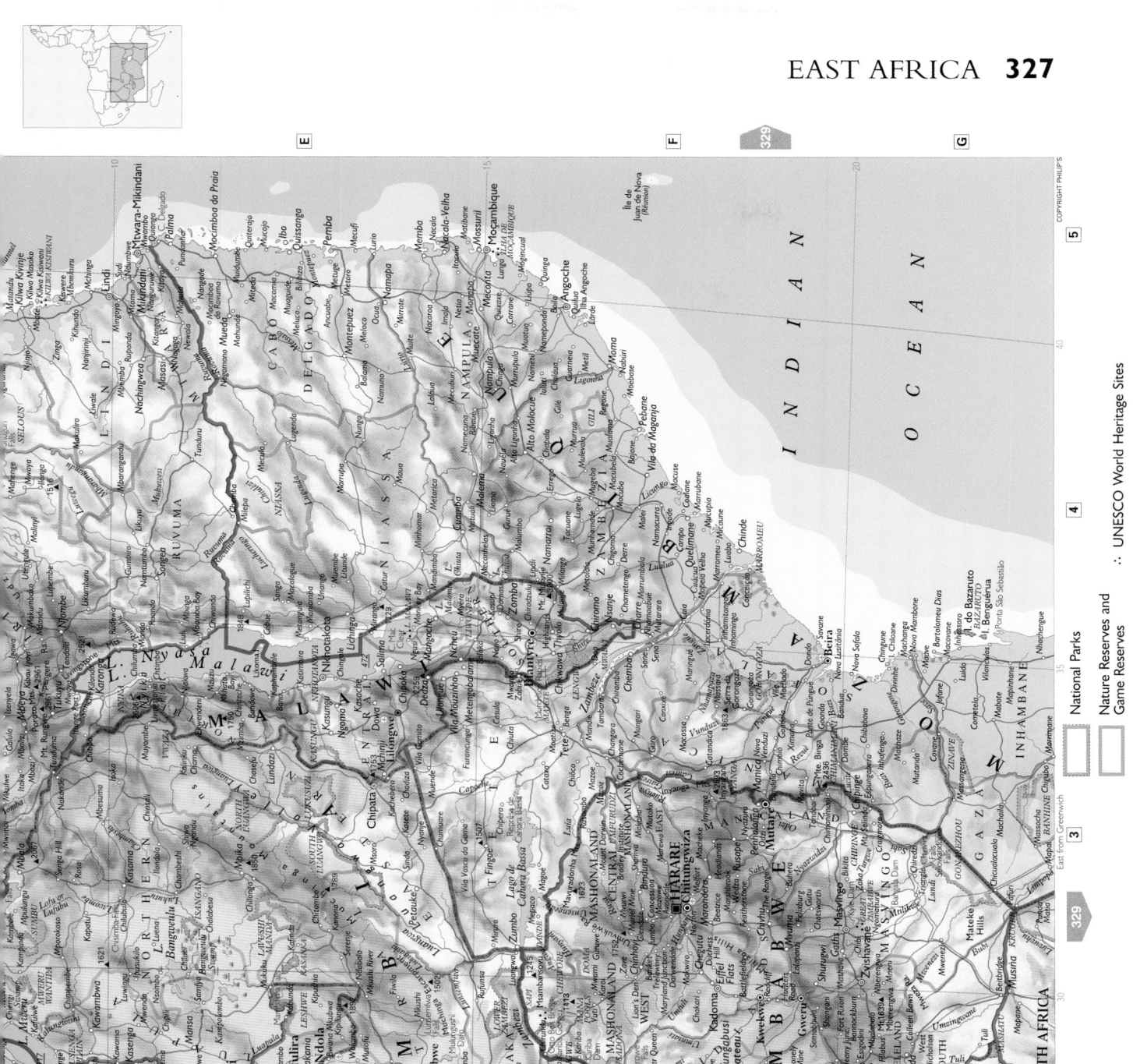

National Parks

:: UNESCO World Heritage Sites

Nature Reserves and
Game Reserves

Projection: Lambert's Equivalent Azimuthal

Projection: Lambert's Equivalent Azimuthal

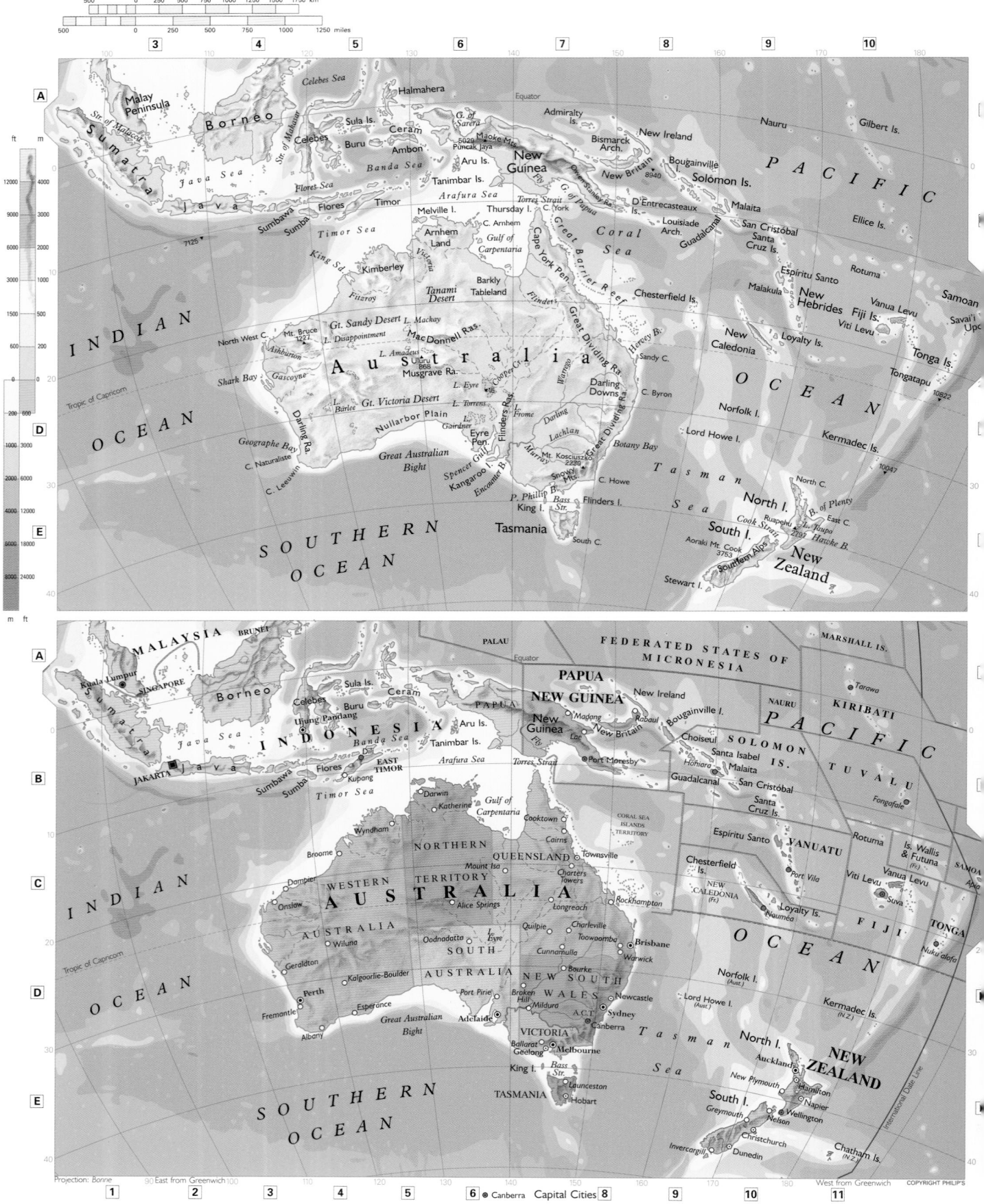

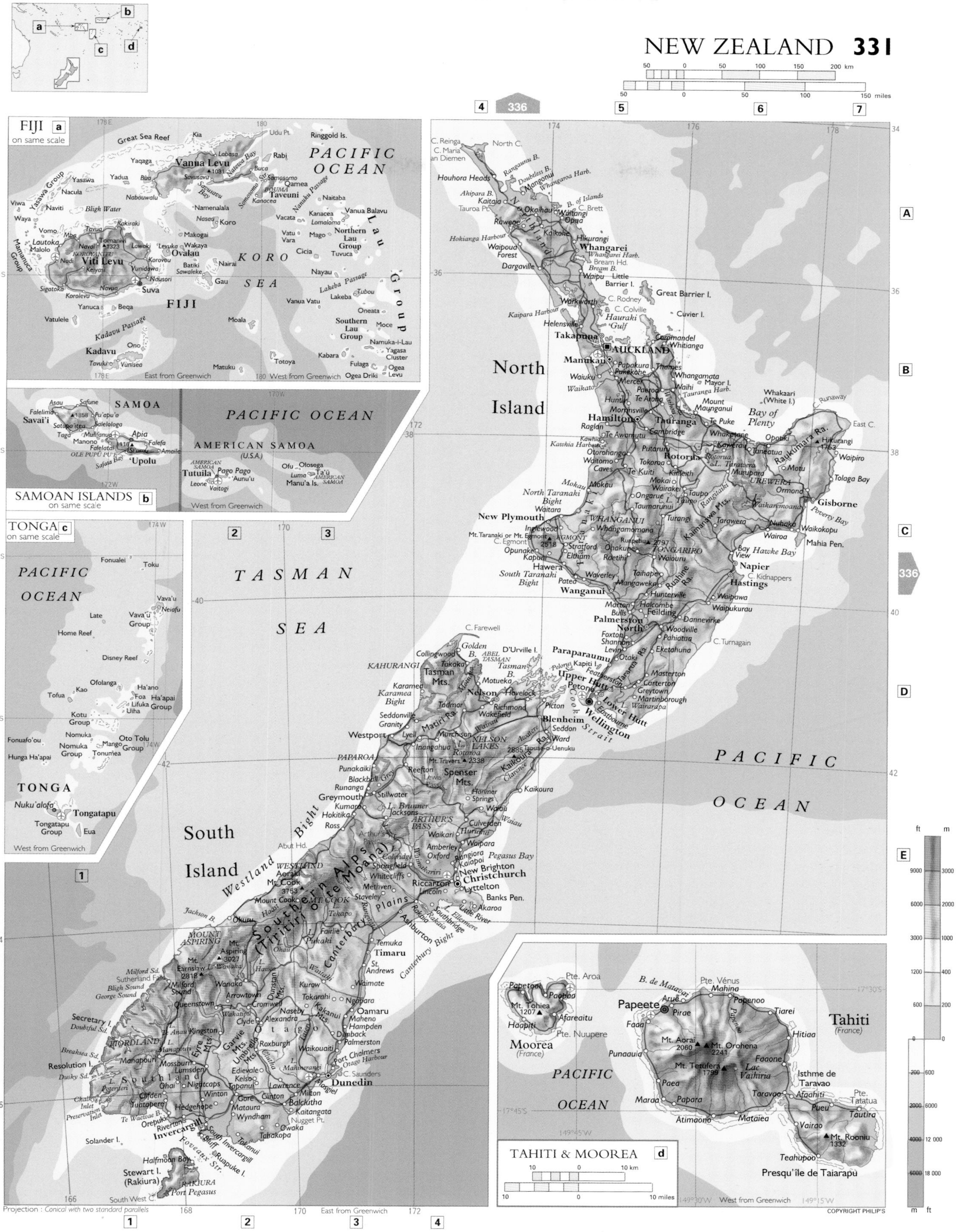

FIJI a
on same scale
PACIFIC OCEAN
KORO SEA
Vanua Levu
Viti Levu
Taveuni
Suva
Lautoka
Kadavu
Ovalau
Koro
Lau Group
Northern Lau Group
Southern Lau Group
Yasawa Group
Bligh Water
Kadavu Passage
Lakeba Passage
East from Greenwich
West from Greenwich
SAMOAN ISLANDS b
on same scale
SAMOA
Savai'i
Upolu
Apia
PACIFIC OCEAN
AMERICAN SAMOA
(U.S.A.)
Tutuila
Pago Pago
Manu'a Is.
West from Greenwich
TONGA c
on same scale
PACIFIC OCEAN
Vava'u Group
Ha'apai Group
Nomuka Group
Kotu Group
TONGA
Nuku'alofa
Tongatapu
Tongatapu Group
Eua
West from Greenwich
North Island
South Island
TASMAN SEA
PACIFIC OCEAN
AUCKLAND
Wellington
Hamilton
Tauranga
Rotorua
Gisborne
Napier
Hastings
New Plymouth
Wanganui
Palmerston North
Nelson
Blenheim
Westport
Greymouth
Christchurch
Timaru
Oamaru
Dunedin
Invercargill
Queenstown
Whangarei
Bay of Plenty
Hawke Bay
Cook Strait
Southern Alps (Tiritiri o te Moana)
Canterbury Plains
Canterbury Bight
Pegasus Bay
Westland Bight
Foveaux Str.
Stewart I. (Rakiura)
Mt. Cook 3753
Mt. Ruapehu 2797
Mt. Taranaki or Mt. Egmont 2518
TAHITI & MOOREA d
Tahiti (France)
Moorea (France)
Papeete
PACIFIC OCEAN
Presqu'île de Taiarapu
Mt. Orohena 2241
Projection : Conical with two standard parallels
COPYRIGHT PHILIP'S

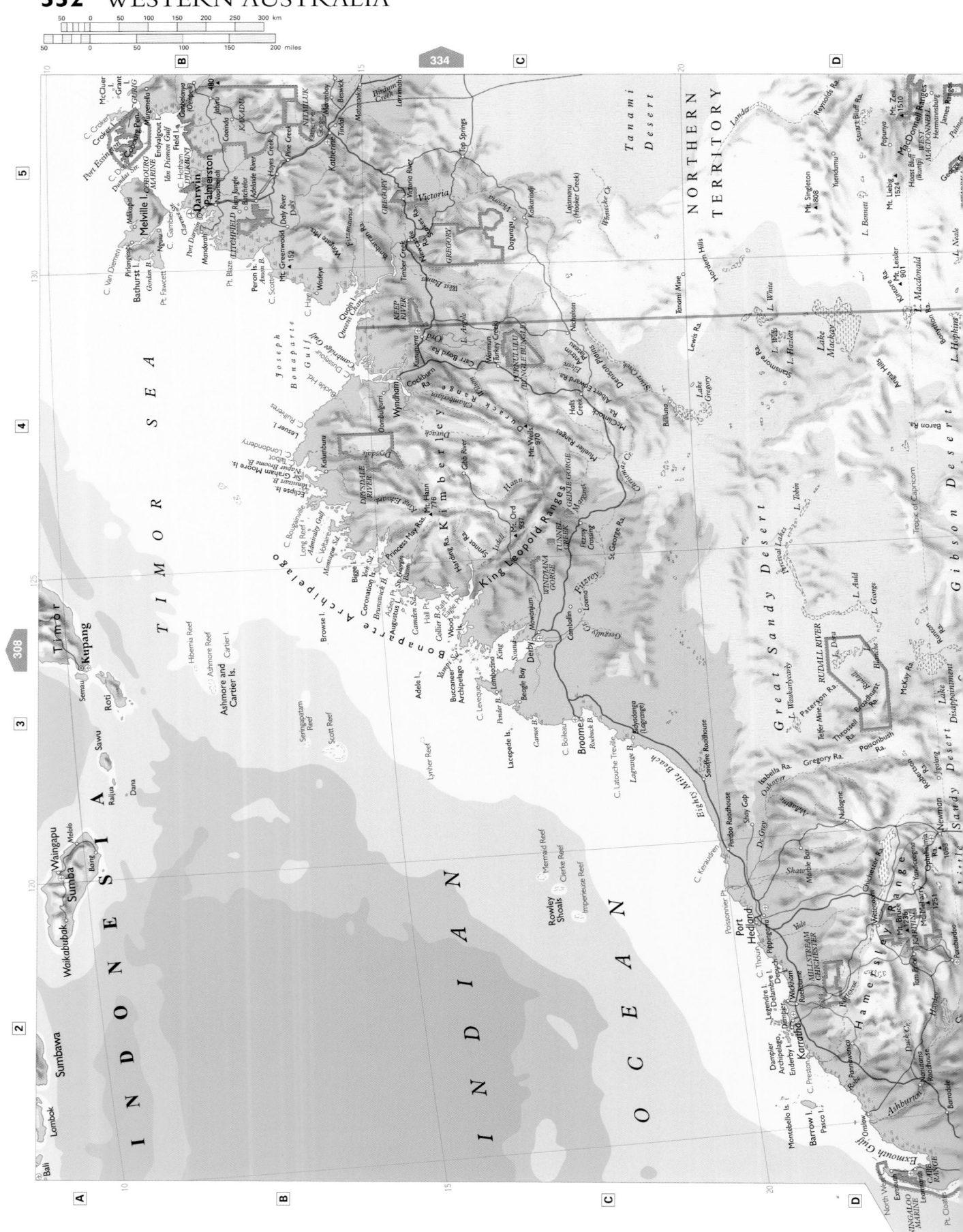

50 50 100 150 200 250 300 km
50 0 50 100 150 200 miles

INDONESIA

Lombok
Bali
Sumbawa
Waikabubak
Sumba
Waingapu
Melolo
Boing
Dana
Rajua
Savu
Roti
Semau
Kupang
Timor

TIMOR SEA

Hibernia Reef
Ashmore Reef
Ashmore and
Cartier Is.
Cartier I.
Seringgapatam Reef
Scott Reef

INDIAN

Rowley
Shoals
Mermaid Reef
Clerke Reef
Imperieuse Reef

OCEAN

INDIAN

Montebello Is.
Barrow I.
Pasco I.
North West C.
Exmouth Gulf
NINGALOO MARINE
Learmonth
Exmouth
CAPE RANGE
Pt. Cloates

C. McCluer
C. Croker
Croker I.
Cobourg Pen.
COBOURG MARINE
Port Essington
C. Don
Dundas Str.
Pirlangimpi
C. Van Diemen
Melville I.
Bathurst I.
Gordan I.
C. Gambier
Ngaui
Pt. Fawcett
Mullaquli
Milikapiti
Port Darwin
Mandorah
Darwin
Palmerston
LITCHFIELD
Peron Is.
C. Scott
Anson B.
Pt. Blaze
C. Hay
Wadeye
Mt. Greenwood
152
LOBOURG MARINE
Endyalgout
Van Diemen Gulf
Iaru
Hotham
Adelaide River
Batchelor
Rum Jungle
Field I.
Goomba
Hayes Creek
480
Grant
NITMILUK
KAKADU
Pine Creek
Katherine
Timber Creek

NORTHERN

TERRITORY

Tanami
Desert
Tanami Mine

Reynolds Ra.
Mt. Zeil
1510
MacDonnell Ranges
Hermannsburg
Mt. Liebig
1524
Mt. Leisler
901
L. Mackay

Great Sandy Desert

Port
Hedland
Poissonier Pt.
Eighty Mile Beach
Broome
C. Bossut
C. Boileau
Lagrange B.
Roebuck B.
Derby
Mowanjum
Camel B.
Lacepede Is.
Pender B.
Beagle Bay
Lombadina
C. Leveque
King
Sound
Buccaneer
Archipelago
Adele I.
Sunday I.
Cockatoo I.
Cygnet B.
Yampi
Koolan I.

King Leopold Ranges
Kimberley
WINDJANA
GORGE
TUNNEL
CREEK
GEIKIE GORGE
Fitzroy
Crossing
Fitzroy
Looma
Noonkanbah
Camballin
St. George Ra.
Mt. Ord
Iddall I.
Liddell I.
Hann
Mt. Hann
776
Mt. Wells
970
Gibb River
Durack
Mueller Ranges
Halls Creek
Mt. Elizabeth
Mt. Barnett
Kalumburu
Drysdale
DRYSDALE RIVER
Kune Edward
Theda
Mitchell
Plateau

Joseph
Bonaparte
Gulf
Wyndham
Cambridge Gulf
Rutherns
Buckle Hd.
Kununurra
Cockburn
Carr Boyd Ra.
ORD
Lake
Argyle
PURNULULU
(BUNGLE BUNGLE)
Turkey Creek
Warmun
Nicholson

Hooker Creek
(Lajamanu)
Top Springs
Victoria
GREGORY
GREGORY
Victoria River
Fitzmaurice
Keep River
KEEP RIVER
Queens Channel
Ord
Osborn
Koolan
Dussejour
Lesueur I.
L. Rutherns
Napier Broome B.
Talbot
Londonderry
C. Londonderry
Eclipse Is.
Sir Graham Moore Is.
Mianar I.
C. Bougainville
Long Reef
Admiralty Gulf
Montague Sd.
Bigge I.
York Sd.
Prince Frederick Hbr.
Brunswick B.
Coronation Is.
C. Voltaire
C. Pond
Augustus I.
Camden Sd.
Collier B.
Hall Pt.
Wood Weel Pt.
Walcott Inlet
Secure B.

Bonaparte
Archipelago

L. Auld
L. Gregory
Lake
Gregory
Billiluna
L. Dora
RUDALL RIVER
Telfer Mine
L. Blanche
L. Percival
McKay Ra.
Broadhurst
Ra.
Throssell
Ra.
Poisonbush
Ra.

Little Sandy Desert
Lake
Disappointment
Newman
1055
Ophthalmia
Ra.
Nullagine

Pilbara
Port
Hedland
Shay Gap
De Grey
Marble Bar
Shasha Bar
Roebourne
Karratha
Dampier
Dampier
Archipelago
Legendre I.
Enderby I.
C. Preston
C. Thouin
Delambre I.
Depuch I.
Wedham
Roebuck
Cossack
Whim Creek
Pannawonica
Mardie
Fortescue R.
Yale
Pippingarra
Mundabullangana
Nanutarra Roadhouse
Ashburton
Barrodale
Onslow

Hamersley Range
Mt. Bruck
Mt. Meharry
1251
Mt. Newman
Mt. Tom Price
1105
Yandicoogina
Paraburdoo
Channar
Tom Price
Wittenoom

Gregory Ra.
Isabella Ra.
Oakover
Gregory Ra.
Nullagine
Jigalong

Gibson Desert
Baron Ra.
Tropic of Capricorn
L. Hopkins
L. Macdonald
Mt. Macdonald

335

E

F

G

WESTERN AUSTRALIA

SOUTH AUSTRALIA

Great Victoria Desert

Nullarbor Plain

Hampton Tableland

Great Australian Bight

SOUTHERN OCEAN

INDIAN OCEAN

PERTH

Kalgoorlie-Boulder

Albany

Geraldton

Bunbury

Mandurah

Rockingham

Fremantle

Esperance

Norseman

Uluru KATA TJUTA (Ayers Rock)

Kata Tjuta (The Olgas)

Petermann Ranges

Everard Ranges

Mt Musgrave Ranges

Projection: Bonne

East from Greenwich

m ft
3000
1000
1200
400
600
200
0
0
200 600
2000 6000
4000 12000
m ft

25

30

35

115

120

125

130

35

5

4

3

2

1

50 0 50 100 150 200 250 300 km
50 0 50 100 150 200 miles

H   J   K   B   C

WHITSUNDAY ISLANDS

CORAL SEA

Cumberland

Whitsunday
Whitsunday I.
ISLANDS
Hayman I.
Hook I.
Long I.
Hamilton I.
Lindeman I.
Shaw I.

Carlisle I.
Islands
Brampton I.
St. Bees I.
Hillsborough Channel
Slade Pt.
Mackay

SOUTH
CUMBERLAND IS.

Gloucester I.
Gloucester Pt.
George Pt.
Bowen

Whitsunday
Airlie Beach
Cannonvale
PROSERPINE
Shute Harbour
Whitsunday Pass.
C. Conway
Repulse Bay
Midge Point

Mt. McGuire
820
Kelsey Creek
Mt. Dalrymple
1259
EUNGELLA
Broken River
Ra.
Nebo

QUEENSLAND

Foxdale
Mt. Charlton
Bloomsbury
Yalboroo
Kuttabul
Kinchant
Mirani
Fairlie

0 10 20 30 40 50 60 km
10 20 30 40 50 miles

CORAL SEA

Magdelaine Cays
Coringa Is.
Lihou Reefs and Cays
Diamond Is.
Tregrosse Is.
Abington Reef
Herald Cays
Holmes Reefs
Flinders Reefs

Osprey Reef
Bougainville Reef

Great Barrier Reef

GREAT BARRIER REEF
(FAR NORTH)

GREAT BARRIER REEF
(NORTH)

GREAT BARRIER REEF
(CENTRAL)

GREAT BARRIER REEF
(CAPRICORN)

Swain Reefs

Capricorn Channel

Capricorn Group
Curtis I.
Gladstone
Rockhampton

Thursday I.
Horn I.
Prince of Wales I.
Turtle Head I.
Sharp Pt.
Bamaga
Jardine River
IRON RANGE
C. Melville
Cooktown
Cape Tribulation
Port Douglas
CAIRNS
Gordonvale
Innisfail
Tully
Cardwell
HINCHINBROOK
Hinchinbrook I.
Ingham
Halifax Bay
Palm Is.
Rollingstone
TOWNSVILLE
Magnetic I.
Cape Cleveland
Bowling Green Bay
Cape Bowling Green
Ayr
Home Hill

Hook I.
Whitsunday I.
CUMBERLAND
Islands
MACKAY
Northumberland Islands
Percy Is.

QUEENSLAND

Cape York Peninsula
Great Dividing Range

Great Barrier Reef
Cape Weymouth
Lloyd B.
Lockhart River
Cape Direction
Princess Charlotte Bay
Cape Melville

CORAL SEA

NORTHERN TERRITORY

Gulf of Carpentaria

Arnhem Land

Wessel Is.
C. Wessel
Goulburn Is.
Warruwi
Milingimbi
Ramingining
Elcho I.
Galiwinku
Nhulunbuy
Yirrkala
Port Bradshaw
Blue Mud Bay
C. Shield
Groote Eylandt
Angurugu
Numbulwar
Roper Bar
Mataranka
Larrimah
Daly Waters
Dunmarra
Newcastle Waters
Elliott
Renner Springs
Tennant Creek
Barrow Creek
Ti-Tree

Sir Edward Pellew Group
Borroloola

Barkly Tableland

Mount Isa
Cloncurry
Julia Creek
Richmond
Hughenden
Winton
Longreach
Blackall
Barcaldine
Emerald
Blackwater
Clermont
Mackenzie R.
Dawson Range

Simpson Desert
SIMPSON DESERT
Channel Country
DIAMANTINA
Birdsville
Bedourie
Boulia

Alice Springs
1168
MacDonnell Ranges
Tropic of Capricorn

330   332

GREAT ARTESIAN BASIN

GREAT DIVIDING RANGE

COPYRIGHT GEORGE PHILIP LTD.

T A S M A N   S E A

BRISBANE
Sunshine Coast
Gold Coast
Southport
Coffs Harbour
Port Macquarie
Newcastle
Gosford
SYDNEY
Blacktown
Campbelltown
Wollongong
Shellharbour
Nowra

Toowoomba
Darling Downs
Warwick
Tamworth
Armidale

N E W   S O U T H   W A L E S

Dubbo
Bathurst
Orange
Parkes
Forbes
Penrith
Katoomba
Lithgow
Goulburn
Canberra
Queanbeyan

Darling Range
Broken Hill

S O U T H   A U S T R A L I A

Sturt Stony Desert
Strzelecki Desert
Simpson Desert

L. Eyre
Lake Eyre (North)
Lake Torrens
Lake Gairdner
Lake Frome
Lake Blanche
Lake Gregory

FLINDERS RANGES
GAMMON RANGES

Port Augusta
Port Pirie
Whyalla
ADELAIDE
Elizabeth
Salisbury
Kangaroo Island
Spencer Gulf
Gulf St Vincent
Eyre Peninsula
Yorke Peninsula
Port Lincoln

Murray Bridge
Mount Gambier
Warrnambool
Portland
Hamilton
Horsham
Ballarat
Bendigo
MELBOURNE
Geelong
Dandenong
Frankston
Mornington
Morwell
Traralgon
Sale
Bairnsdale
Wangaratta
Wodonga
Albury
Wagga Wagga
Griffith
Mildura
Shepparton
Echuca

V I C T O R I A

G R E A T   D I V I D I N G   R A N G E

Bass Strait
King Island
Flinders Island
Furneaux Group
Cape Barren I.
Banks Strait

T A S M A N I A

Launceston
Devonport
Burnie
Hobart

on same scale

Projection: Bonne

East from Greenwich

ft   m   1500   1000   400   200   0
m   ft   9000   6000   4000   12 000

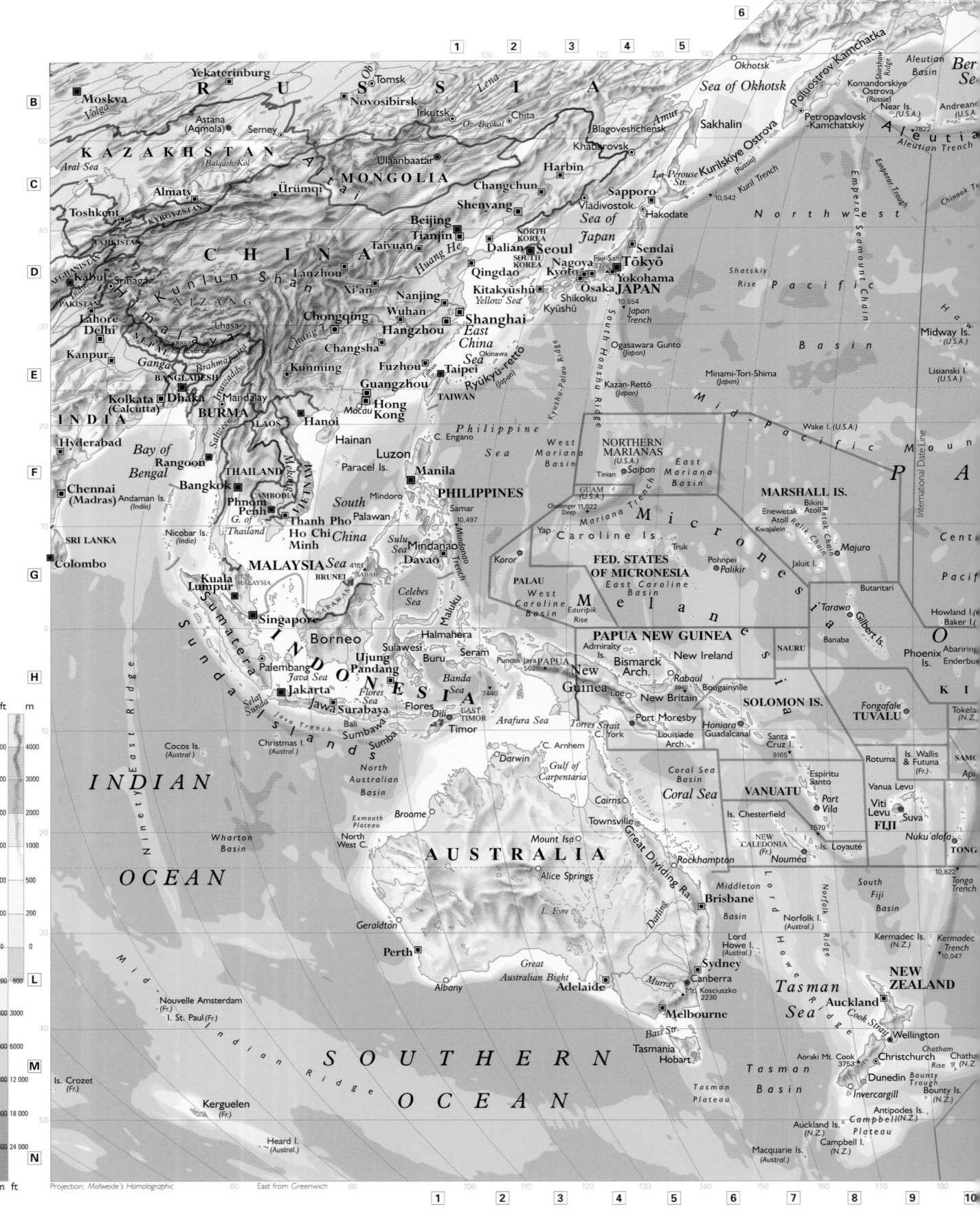

Arctic Circle

ALASKA (U.S.A.)
Anchorage
Bristol Bay

Gulf of Alaska

Prince of Wales I. (U.S.A.) Prince Rupert
Queen Charlotte Is. (Canada)

5959

C A N A D A

Edmonton

Calgary

Regina

Winnipeg

L. Winnipeg

Newfoundland

N O R T H

Vancouver
Vancouver I. Victoria
Seattle
Portland
Boise

L. Superior

Québec
Montréal
Ottawa

St. Lawrence

St. John's

B

Minneapolis
Missouri

L. Huron
L. Michigan Toronto
Ontario Detroit
L. Erie Buffalo

Boston
New York
Philadelphia
Baltimore
Washington D.C.

C

N o r t h e a s t

Mendocino Fracture Zone C. Mendocino

Salt Lake City
Denver
Kansas City
St. Louis

Chicago

Cincinnati
Pittsburgh

Appalachian Mts.

A T L A N T I C

D

Sacramento
San Francisco

6741

4418

Colorado

U N I T E D   S T A T E S

Oklahoma City
Memphis

Atlanta

C. Hatteras

Bermuda (U.K.)

Murray Fracture Zone

Los Angeles
San Diego

Phoenix

Dallas

Mississippi

Jacksonville

D

P a c i f i c

Guadalupe (Mex.)

Baja California

Ciudad Juárez

Houston

San Antonio

New Orleans

Monterrey

Gulf of Mexico

Miami

Tampa

Sargasso Sea

O C E A N

E

Molokai Fracture Zone

Tropic of Cancer

B a s i n

Golfo de California

C. San Lucas

La Habana

Florida Str.

BAHAMAS

West Indies

E

Honolulu
Oahu Maui HAWAIIAN IS. (U.S.A.)
Kauai Hilo Hawaii

4205

Clarion Fracture Zone Is. Revilla Gigedo (Mex.)

Guadalajara

Mexico
Puebla

6610

Mérida

7680

9200

CUBA

Canal de Yucatán

HAITI DOMINICAN REP.

JAMAICA Kingston

PUERTO RICO (U.S.A.)

Leeward Is.

F

C I F I C

Acapulco

M É X I C O

GUATEMALA
Guatemala

BELIZE

Caribbean Sea

BARBADOS

Windward Is.

F

F I C

Middle America Trench

6662

HONDURAS

San Salvador
EL SALVADOR

NICARAGUA

Managua

Guatemala Basin

Barranquilla

Maracaibo

Caracas

West Christmas Ridge

Palmyra Is. (U.S.A.)

Clipperton Fracture Zone

I. Clipperton (Fr.)

San José

COSTA RICA

Colón
Panamá
PANAMÁ

Coco Ridge

Orinoco

VENEZUELA

G

Teraina
Tabuaeran
Kiritimati

I. del Coco (Costa Rica)

Medellín

I. de Malpelo (Colombia)

Bogotá

Cali

COLOMBIA

G

E Jarvis I. (U.S.A.) **A** **N**

Equator

Galápagos Fracture Zone

Galápagos (Ecuador)

Carnegie Ridge

Quito

ECUADOR

H

B A T I
Malden I.
Starbuck I.

Guayaquil

C. Paliñas

Iquitos

Amazonas

BRAZIL

H

Penrhyn (Tongareva)
Manihiki
Pukapuka Manihiki
Plateau
Suwarrow Is.

Vostok I.
Caroline I. (Millennium I.)
Flint I.

Nuku Hiva
Is. Marquises
Hiva Oa

Marquesas Fracture Zone

Trujillo

6369

Lima

PERU

Cuzco

East Pacific Ridge

Galápagos Rise

J

Is. de la Société
Bora Bora Huahine
Rarotonga Raiatea Tahiti
Cook Is. (N.Z.) Papeete
Atiu
Rarotonga
Mangaia

Rangiroa

Is. Tuamotu

L. Titicaca
Arequipa

Nevada Ancohuma 6550

6866

Peru-Chile Trench

Peru Basin

La Paz
BOLIVIA

J

Australes Seamount Chain

Gambier Is.

Mururoa

Is. Tubuai

Tropic of Capricorn

Sala y Gómez Ridge

Arica
Iquique

Antofagasta

Nazca Ridge

PARAGUAY

Asunción

K

Oeno I.
Henderson I.
Pitcairn I. Ducie I. (U.K.)

Rapa

Easter Fracture Zone

Sala-y-Gómez
I. de Pascua (Chile)

San Felix (Chile)

San Ambrosio (Chile)

8050

Chile Trench

San Miguel de Tucumán

Pôrto Alegre

K

S o u t h w e s t

Arch. de Juan Fernández (Chile)

Córdoba
Aconcagua 6960

Valparaíso
Santiago

URUGUAY

Rosario
Buenos Aires

Montevideo

Río de la Plata

L

Challenger Fracture Zone

Chile Rise

Concepción

ARGENTINA

SOUTH

ATLANTIC

M

P a c i f i c

Ménard Fracture Zone

OCEAN

6212

M

B a s i n

Pacific-Antarctic Ridge

Punta Arenas

Est. de Magallanes
Tierra del Fuego
C. de Hornos

Drake Passage

Falkland Is. (U.K.)

South Georgia (U.K.)

N

S o u t h e a s t
Pacific Basin

West from Greenwich

7 ■ MÉXICO Capital Cities **8**   **9**   **10**   **11**   **12**

COPYRIGHT PHILIP'S

100   0   100   200   300   400   500   600 km
100   0   100   200   300   400 miles

| 4 | 5 | 346 | 6 | 7 | 8 | 9 | 276 | 10 |

Projection : Bonne

| 7 | 8 | 346 | 9 | 10 |

NORTHERN CANADA
continuation northwards on same
scale as main map

ARCTIC
OCEAN

A

276

B

Devon I.
Lancaster Sound
Arctic Bay
Nanisivik
Bylot I.
Borden
Pen.
Pond Inlet
2136
Baffin Bay
C. Adair
Clyde River
C. Raper
Home B.

Fury and Hecla Str.
Igloolik
Hall Beach
Prince
Charles
Air
Force I.
Melville
Peninsula

Meighen
Borden I.
Prince Patrick I.
Eglinton
M'Clure Strait
Brock I.
Mackenzie
King I.
Loug-
heed
Amund
Ringnes I.
Cornwall
Eller
Ringnes I.
Axel
Heiberg
Sverdrup
Islands
Greely
Eureka
Grise
Fiord
Ellesmere Island
GREENLAND
(Denmark)
Hans I.
Alert
C. Columbia
2616
Smith Sound

Southampton
Coral Harbour
Bell
Pen.
Rae Isthmus
Repulse
Bay
Coats
I.
Mansel I.
Nottingham
Salisbury
Cape Dorset
Foxe
Pen.
Amadjuak
Meta
Incognita
Pen.
Kimmirut
Iqaluit
Hall
Peninsula
Frobisher Bay
Resolution I.

Baffin Island

NUNAVUT
Foxe
Basin
Foxe Channel
Hudson Strait
Cumberland
Peninsula
Pangnirtung
Hoare B.
C. Mercy
Cumberland Sd.
Qikiqtarjuaq
Dyer
Netilling L.
C. Dorchester

Banks
Island
C. Prince Alfred
Victoria Island
Holman
Prince Albert
Pen.
747
M'Clintock
Channel
NORTHWEST
TERRITORIES
Viscount Melville
Sound
Bathurst
Corn-
wallis
Resolute
Wellington Chan.
Devon Island
Lancaster Sound
Jones Sound
Belcher Chan.
North
Magnetic
Pole
Prince
of
Wales Island
Prince
Somerset
Island
NUNAVUT
Brodeur
Peninsula
Arctic
Bay
Nanisivik
Bylot I.
1951
Pond
Inlet
Queen
Elizabeth
Is.
Parry Islands
Penny Str.
Grant
Land
Norwegian
Bay
Penny Str.

Hudson
Bay
Ottawa Is.
257
Sleeper Is.
King George Is.
Bakers
Dozen
Is.
Sanikiluaq
Belcher Is.
C. Henrietta
Maria
Pte. Louis
XIV

D

Labrador
Sea
3809
Hudson
Bay
C. Chidley
Akpatok I.
Ungava Bay
Kangirsuk
Kangiqsualujjuaq
Hebron
Nain
Hopedale
Rigolet
Cartwright
Hamilton
Port Hope Simpson
Harrison

ATLANTIC

50

D

Kuujjuaq
Péninsule
d'Ungava
Puvirnituq
Ivujivik
Salluit
Quaqtaq
Kangiqsujuaq
Arnaud
Feuilles
Kovitik
Baleine
George
1652
L. Payne
L. Minto
Inukjuak
Kuujjuarapik
Mélèzes
Caniapiscau

Smallwood
Res.
North West River
Happy Valley-
Goose Bay
Churchill
Falls
Churchill
L A B R A D O R
St-Augustin
Baie
Verte
Deer
Lake
Grand
Falls
Windsor
Grand Falls
Bonavista
Gander
Carbonear
St. John's

Chisasibi
Kanaaupscow
La Grande
Caniapiscau
Labrador
City
Fermont
Ashuanipi
L.
Gagnon
1135
Manicouagan
Moisie
Romaine
Natashquan
Havre-
St-Pierre
I. d'Anticosti
814
Corner Brook
Stephenville
Newfoundland
Notre Dame B.
Placentia B.
Marystown
Trinity B.
Placentia
C. Race

Big
Trout L.
Peawanuck
Winisk
James Bay
Akimiski I.
Wemindji
Eastmain
Waskaganish
Fort Albany
Charlton
Moosonee
Albany
Missinaibi
Attawapiskat
Attawapiskat

L à l'Eau
Claire
L. Bienville
Petitsikapau L.
Esker
Mistassini
L.
Albanel
Chibougamau
Rés.
Gouin
Baie-
Comeau
Sept-Îles
Port-Cartier
Gulf of
St. Lawrence
Cabot Str.
Îs. de la Madeleine
C. North
Channel-Port
aux Basques
Ray
St-PIERRE
et MIQUELON
(Fr.)

E

40

6309

F

Thunder Bay
Greenstone
Marathon
Nakina
Kenogami
Hearst
Kapuskasing
Oba
Cochrane
Timmins
Kirkland
Lake
New
Liskeard
Rouyn-
Noranda
Val-d'Or
Amos
L. Abitibi
Matagami
Lac St-Jean
Dolbeau-
Mistassini
Roberval
Jonquière
Chicoutimi
La Tuque
Québec
1190
Grand Falls
Woodstock
NEW
BRUNSWICK
Miramichi
Bathurst
Campbellton
Edmundston
Rimouski
Rivière-du-Loup
Matane
Pen. de la
Gaspésie
Gaspé
St. Lawrence

PR. EDWARD I.
Summerside
Charlottetown
Moncton
Amherst
Truro
New
Glasgow
Sydney
Glace Bay
Port Hawkesbury
Cape Breton I.
Antigonish
NOVA
SCOTIA
Dartmouth
Halifax
Sable I.
(Nova Scotia)

Houghton
183
Sault Ste.
Marie
Elliot
Lake
Sudbury
North
Bay
Pembroke
Mont-
Laurier
Shawinigan
Trois-Rivières
Rés.
Cabonga
Joliette
Hull
OTTAWA
St-Jérôme
St-Hyacinthe
MONTREAL
Sherbrooke
Granby
Thetford
Mines
Lévis
MAINE
Fredericton
Saint
John
B. of Fundy
Digby
Kentville
Bridgewater
Liverpool
Yarmouth
C. Sable

Wawa
Chapleau
Marquette
Sault Ste.
Marie
Manistique
Escanaba
Menominee
Green
Bay
Wausau
Petoskey
Traverse
City
Cadillac
Manitoulin
I.
Georgian
Bay
Parry
Sound
Huntsville
Lake
Huron
Barrie
Owen Sound
Peterborough
Kingston
Belleville
Oshawa
Cornwall
Burlington
Montpelier
VERMONT
NEW
HAMPSHIRE
Concord
Lewiston
Portland
Augusta
Bangor
L. Champlain

WI
SCON
SIN
MILWAUKEE
Grand
Rapids
Racine
Kenosha
Lansing
Flint
Saginaw
L. Michigan
Petoskey
TORONTO
Kitchener
Hamilton
London
Sarnia
Niagara
Falls
Buffalo
Rochester
Syracuse
Elmira
Binghamton
L. Ontario
15
Albany
NEW YORK
Springfield
Hartford
CONN.
New Haven
Bridgeport
Newark
NEW YORK
Trenton
Allentown
Scranton
MASS.
BOSTON
PROVIDENCE
R.I.
C. Cod
N.J.

CHICAGO
DETROIT
Windsor
South Bend
Gary
Toledo
CLEVELAND
INDIANA
OHIO
PENNSYLVANIA
Jamestown
Erie
L. Erie
174
INOIS

West from Greenwich

COPYRIGHT PHILIP'S

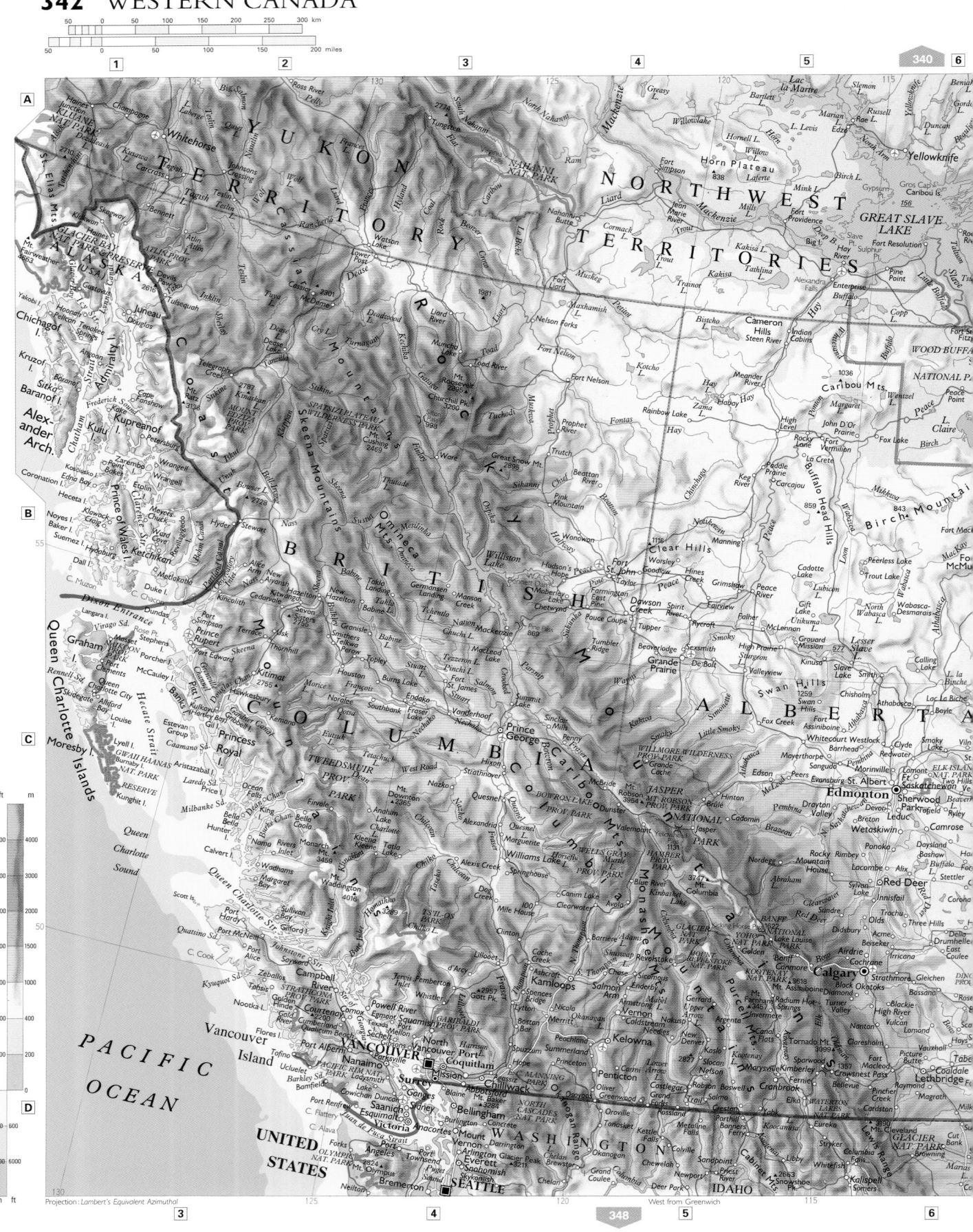

COPYRIGHT PHILIP'S

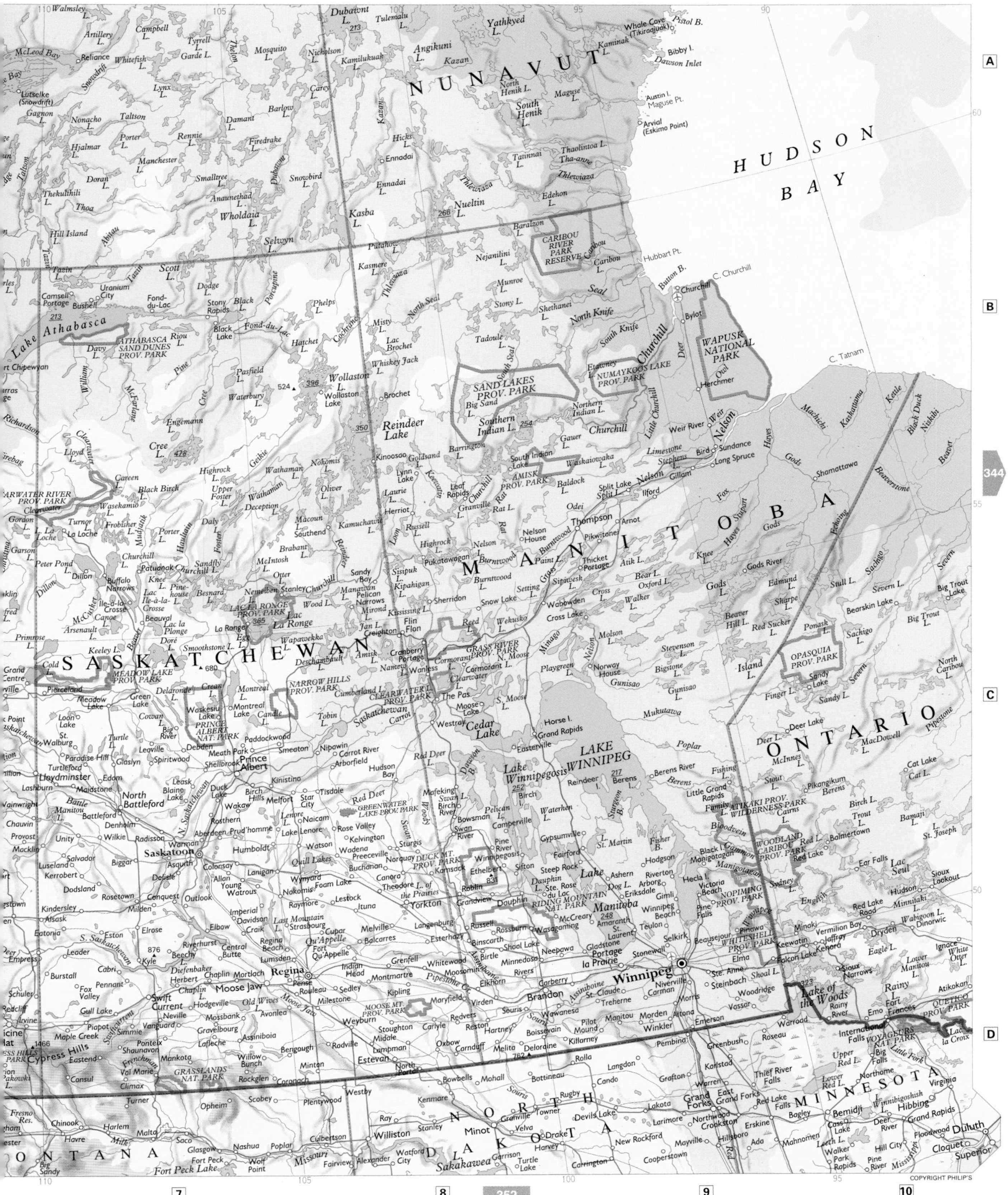

Projection: Lambert's Equivalent Azimuthal

6   7   8   9

A

B

C

D

LABRADOR SEA

L A B R A D O R

NEWFOUNDLAND &

Labrador Plateau

Q U É B E C

LABRADOR

Newfoundland

Smallwood Reservoir

Churchill Falls

Happy Valley-Goose Bay

Long Range Mts.

Str. of Belle Isle

L'Anse aux Meadows

St. Anthony

GROS MORNE NAT. PARK

Corner Brook

TERRA NOVA NAT. PARK

Gander

Grand Falls-Windsor

St. John's

Mt. Pearl

Labrador City

Wabush

Sept-Îles

Î. d'Anticosti

Dét. de Jacques-Cartier

GULF OF

ST. LAWRENCE

Baie-Comeau

Chicoutimi

Jonquière

Pén. de la Gaspésie

Mts. Chic-Chocs

Gaspé

Îs. de la Madeleine
(Québec)

Cabot Strait

ST-PIERRE et MIQUELON
(France)

Rimouski

Edmundston

NEW

BRUNSWICK

PRINCE EDWARD

ISLAND

Charlottetown

CAPE BRETON HIGHLAND NAT. PARK

Sydney

Cape Breton

Island

MAINE

Fredericton

Moncton

Summerside

FUNDY NAT. PARK

Saint John

N O V A S C O T I A

Truro

A T L A N T I C

Saint John

Bay of Fundy

KEJIMKUJIK NAT. PARK

Halifax

Dartmouth

Sable I.
(Nova Scotia)

Bangor

Augusta

Bar Harbor

Yarmouth

Portland

C. Sable

O C E A N

UNITED

STATES

BOSTON

West from Greenwich

70   65   60

COPYRIGHT PHILIP'S

100 0 100 200 300 400 500 km
100 0 50 100 150 200 250 300 350 miles

1   2   3   340   5   6

A
B
C
D

ft   m
12 000   4000
9000   3000
6000   2000
4500   1500
3000   1000
1200   600
600   200
0   0
200   600
1000   3000
2000   6000
4000   12 000
m   ft

Projection: Albers' Equal Area with two standard parallels

ALASKA a

100 0 100 200 300 400 500 600 km
100 0 100 200 300 400 miles

CHUKCHI SEA
RUSSIA
BERING SEA
ALASKA
Brooks Range
Point Hope
Kotzebue
Seward Pen.
Nome
Fairbanks
Anchorage
Valdez
Juneau
Mt. McKinley 6194
GULF OF ALASKA
Aleutian Is.
PACIFIC OCEAN
Alexander Archipelago
Kodiak I.
Alaska Peninsula

HAWAI'I b

Kaua'i
Ni'ihau
O'ahu
Honolulu
Pearl Harbor
Moloka'i
Lāna'i
Maui
Kaho'olawe
Hawai'i
Mauna Kea 4205
Mauna Loa 4169
Hilo
Kailua
PACIFIC OCEAN
Hawaiian Islands

50 0 100 km
50 0 50 miles

West from Greenwich

CANADA — BRITISH COLUMBIA, ALBERTA, SASKATCHEWAN, MANITOBA

Vancouver, Victoria, Calgary, Saskatoon, Regina, Winnipeg

Seattle, Portland, Salem, Spokane, Tacoma, Olympia
WASHINGTON, OREGON, IDAHO, MONTANA, WYOMING, NORTH DAKOTA, SOUTH DAKOTA, NEBRASKA

San Francisco, Sacramento, San Jose, Oakland, Fresno, Los Angeles, San Diego, Long Beach
CALIFORNIA, NEVADA, UTAH, COLORADO, ARIZONA, NEW MEXICO

Las Vegas, Salt Lake City, Denver, Colorado Springs, Phoenix, Tucson, Albuquerque, El Paso

MEXICO — SONORA, CHIHUAHUA, COAHUILA
Tijuana, Mexicali, Ciudad Juárez, Monterrey, Nuevo Laredo

PACIFIC OCEAN

340
358

Tallahassee ✶   State capitals

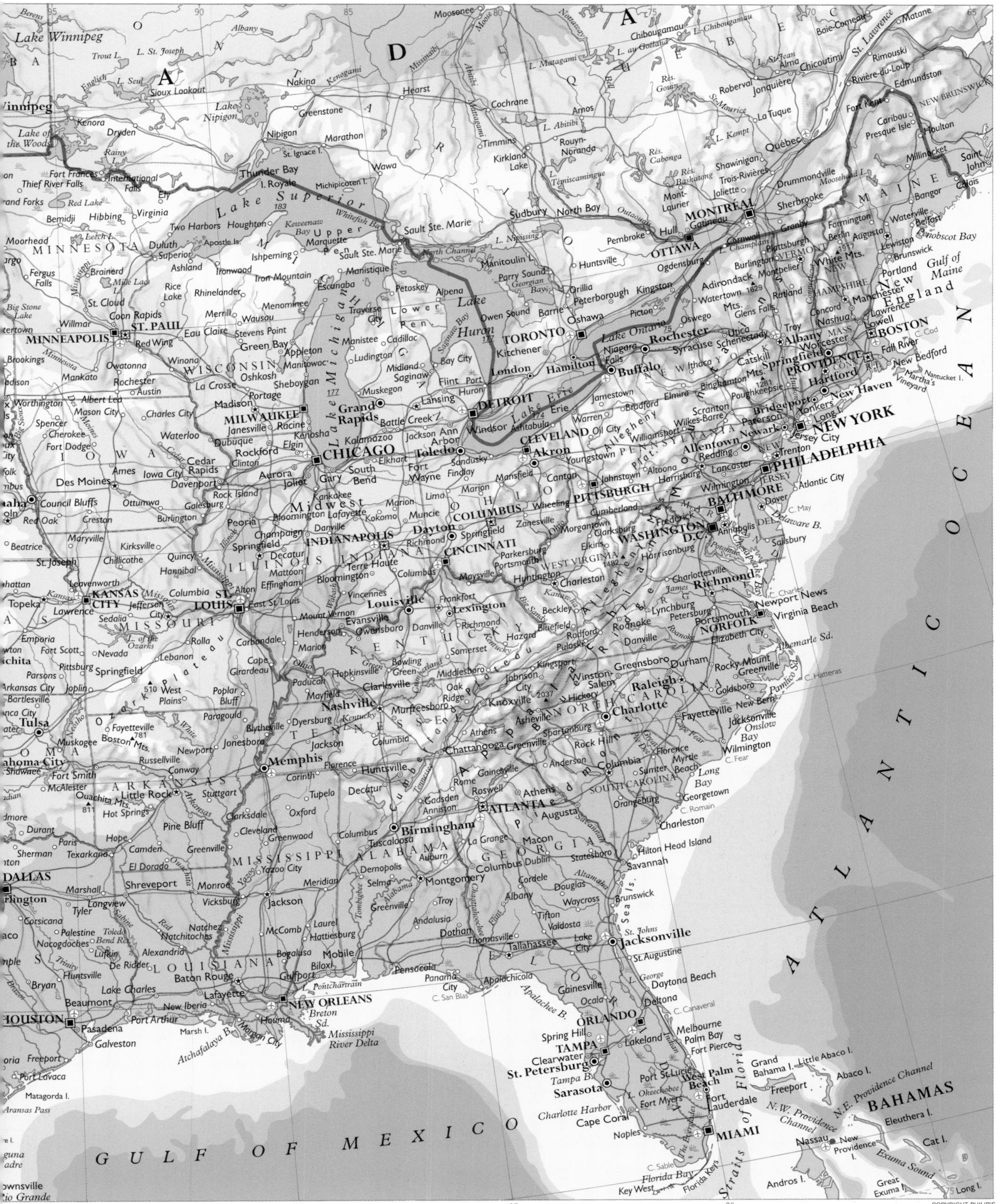

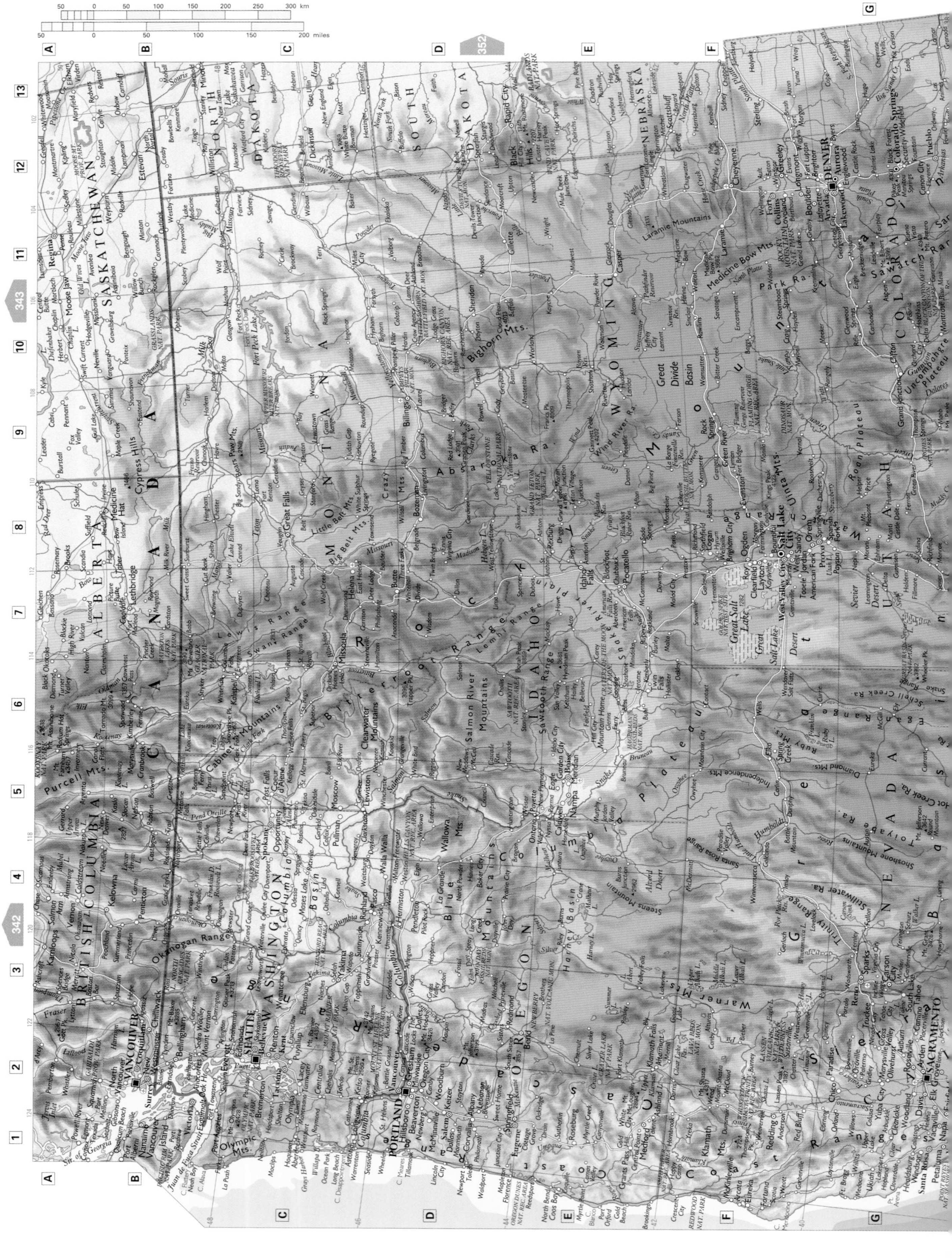

50 0 50 100 150 200 250 300 km
50 0 50 100 150 200 miles

CANADA

SASKATCHEWAN

ALBERTA

BRITISH COLUMBIA

NORTH DAKOTA

SOUTH DAKOTA

NEBRASKA

MONTANA

WYOMING

COLORADO

IDAHO

UTAH

NEVADA

WASHINGTON

OREGON

CALIFORNIA

Regina

Moose Jaw

Medicine Hat

Lethbridge

Great Falls

Helena

Butte

Missoula

Billings

Bozeman

Rapid City

Cheyenne

DENVER

Aurora

Boulder

Longmont

Fort Collins

Casper

Laramie

Rock Springs

Green River

Salt Lake City

Ogden

Provo

Pocatello

Idaho Falls

Twin Falls

Boise

Nampa

Caldwell

Reno

Sparks

Carson City

SACRAMENTO

VANCOUVER

SEATTLE

Tacoma

Bellevue

Renton

Everett

Spokane

Yakima

PORTLAND

Salem

Eugene

Bend

Medford

Klamath Falls

Bighorn Mts

Absaroka Ra

Wind River Ra

Uinta Mts

Sawtooth Range

Salmon River Mountains

Bitterroot Range

Clearwater Mountains

Cascade Range

Blue Mountains

Coast Ranges

Sierra Nevada

Great Divide Basin

Great Salt Lake

Great Salt Lake Desert

Snake River

Columbia R

Missouri R

Yellowstone

Olympic Mts

Wasatch Range

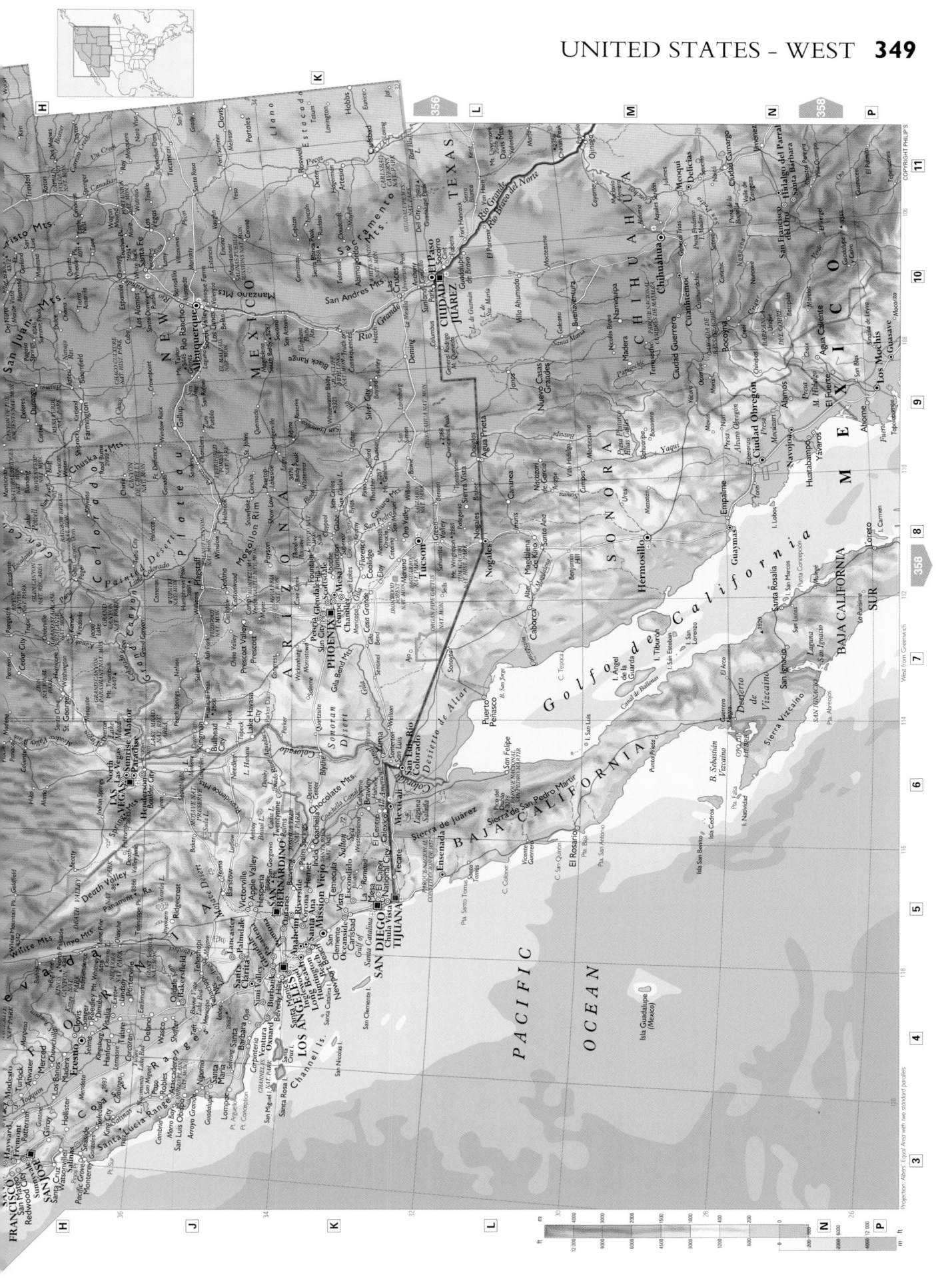

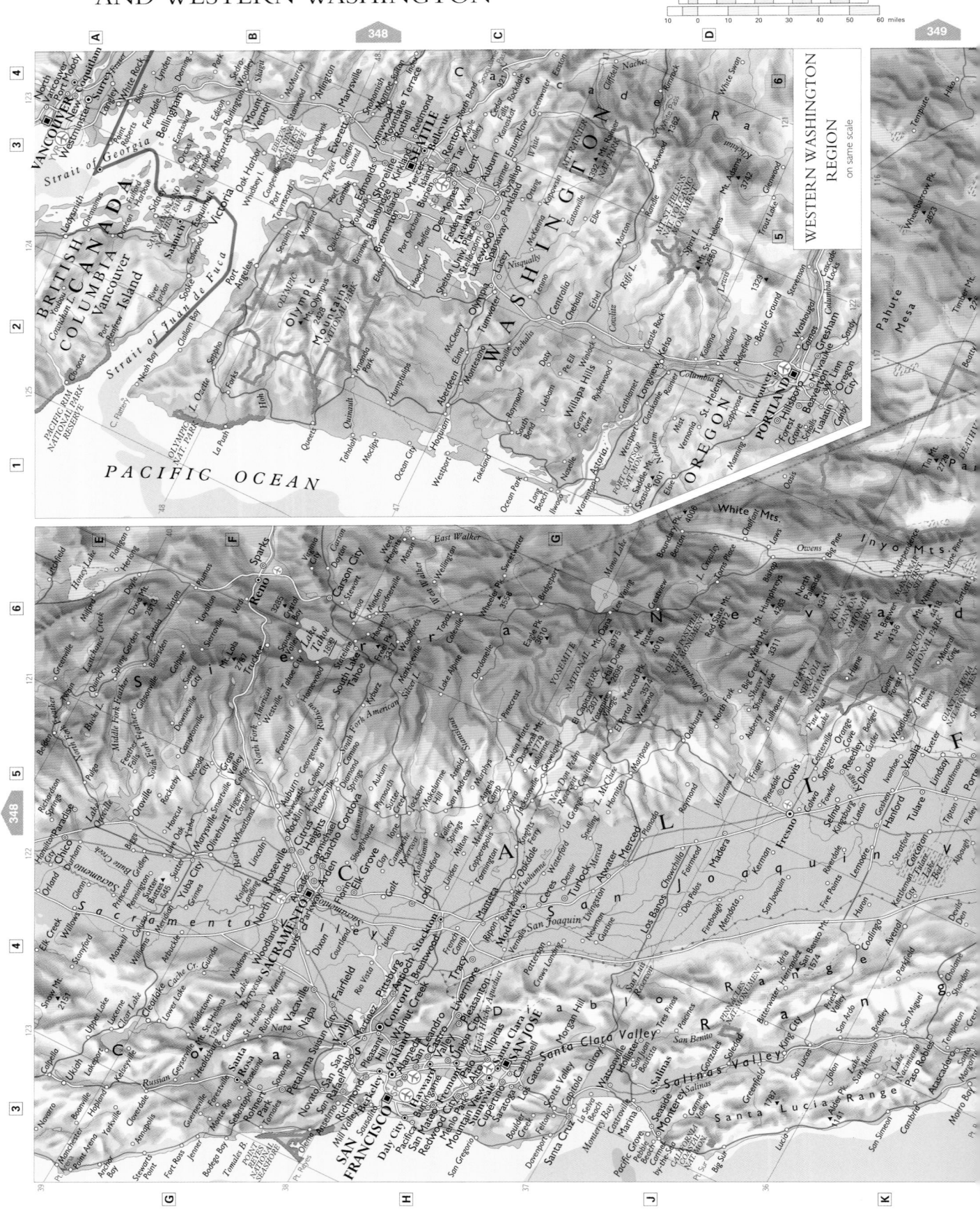

WESTERN WASHINGTON
REGION
on same scale

West from Greenwich

Projection: Bonne

COPYRIGHT PHILIP'S

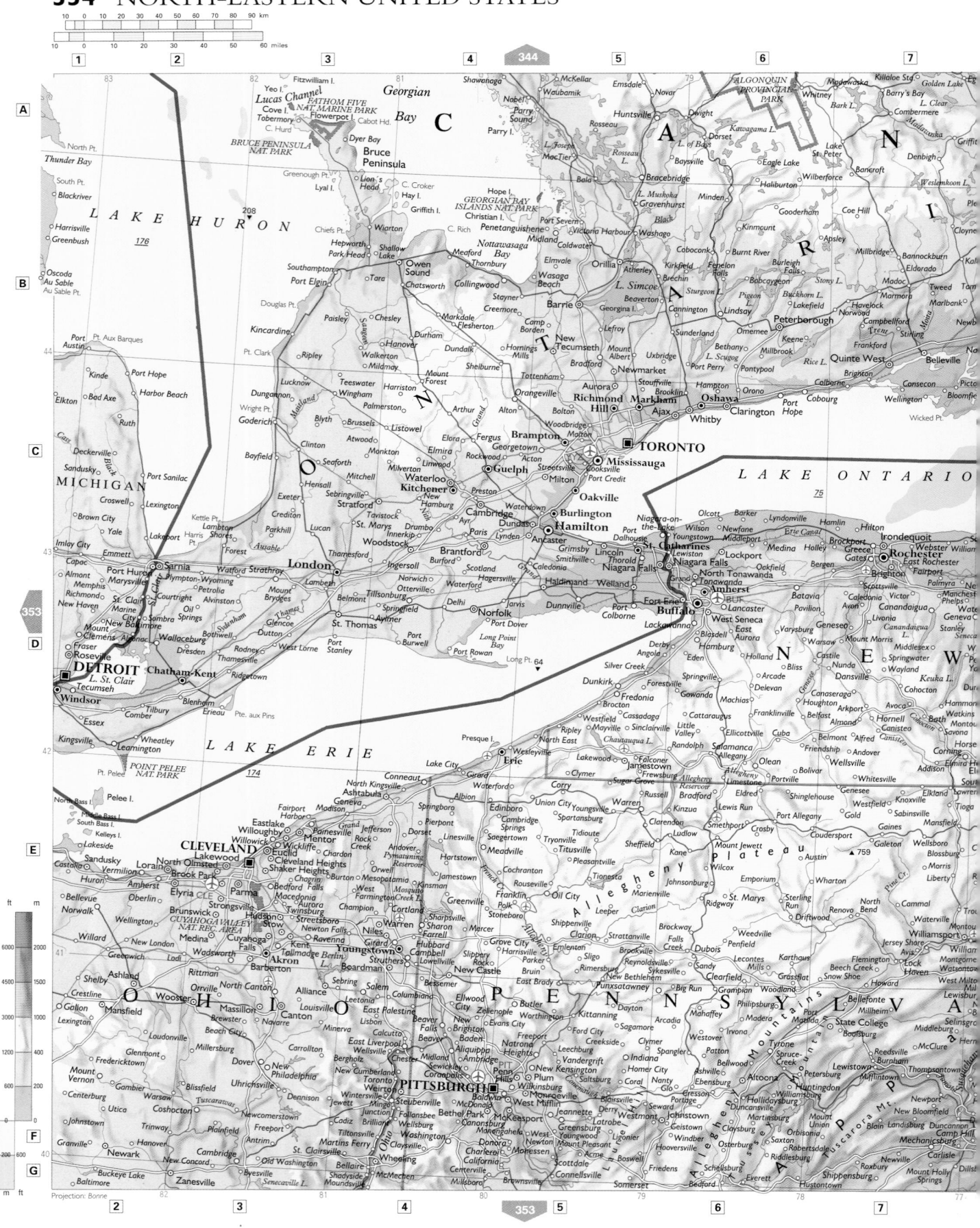

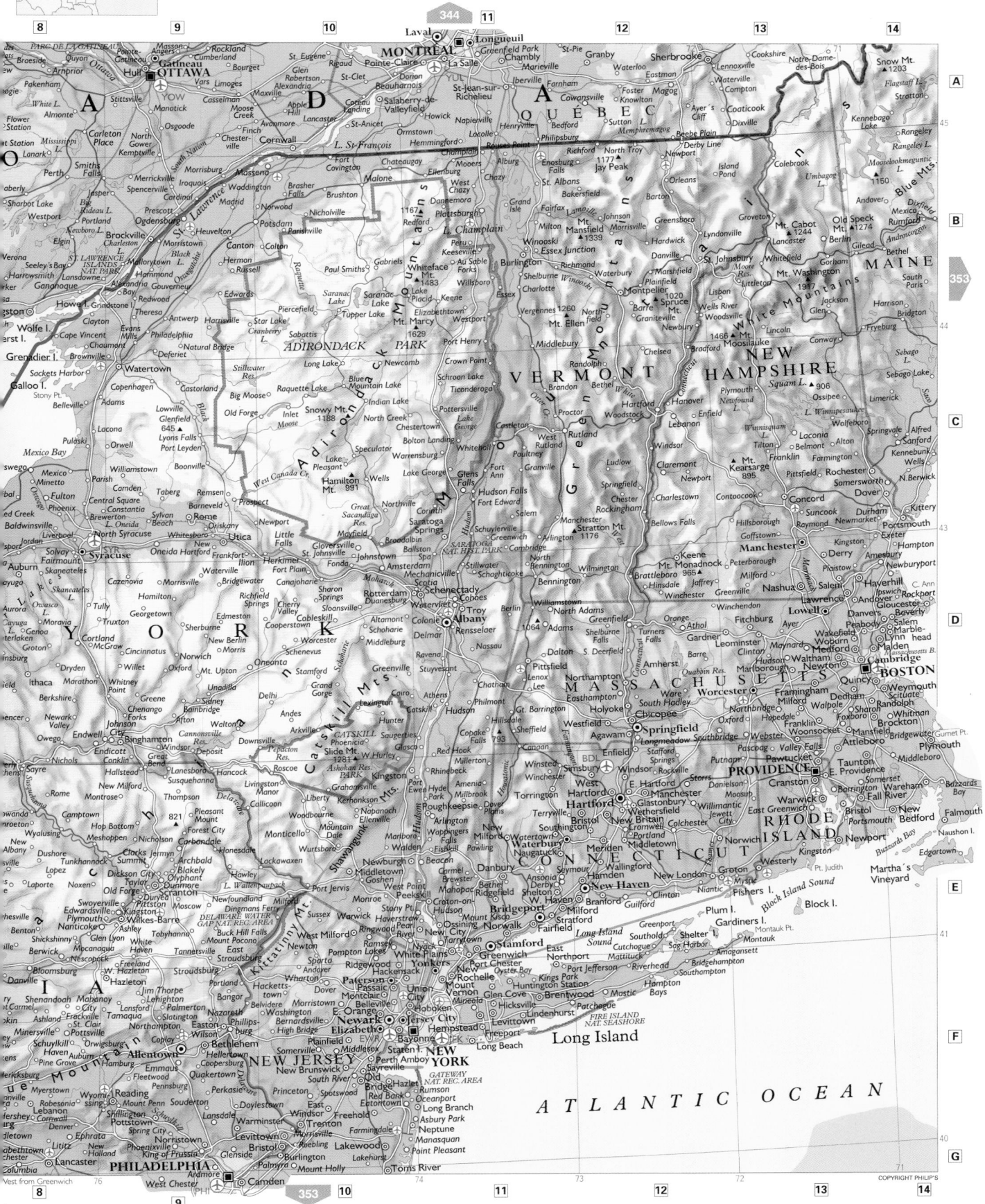

349

359

Projection: Albers' Equal Area with two standard parallels

West from Greenwich

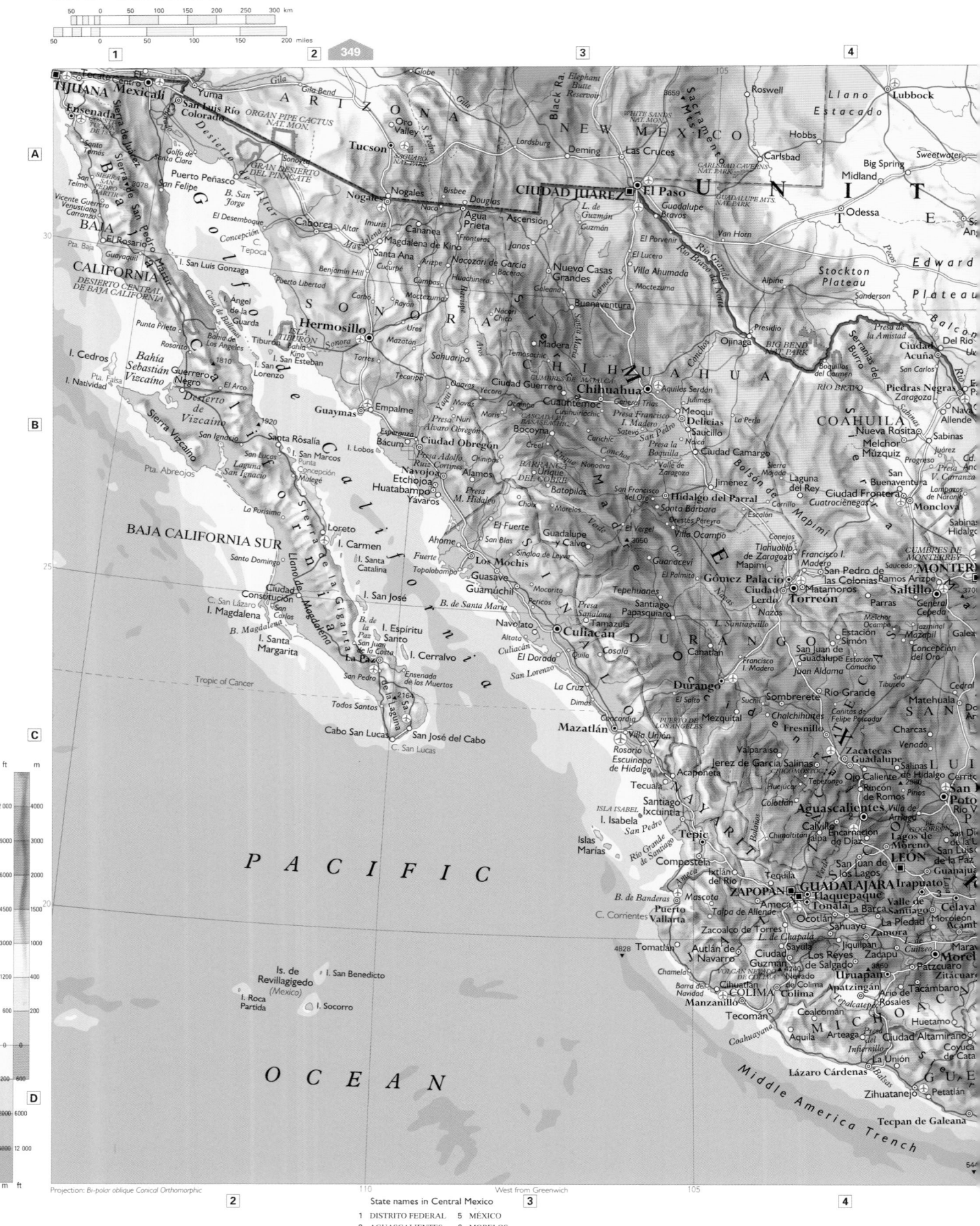

50   0   50   100   150   200   250   300 km
50   0   50   100   150   200 miles

1   **2**   **3**   **4**

A

B

C

D

ft   m

12 000   4000

9000   3000

6000

4500   1500

3000   1000

1200   400

600   200

0   0

200   600

2000   6000

4000   12 000

m   ft

Projection: Bi-polar oblique Conical Orthomorphic

P A C I F I C

O C E A N

Middle America Trench

State names in Central Mexico

1 DISTRITO FEDERAL   5 MÉXICO
2 AGUASCALIENTES   6 MORELOS
3 GUANAJUATO   7 QUERÉTARO
4 HIDALGO   8 TLAXCALA

2   **3**   **4**

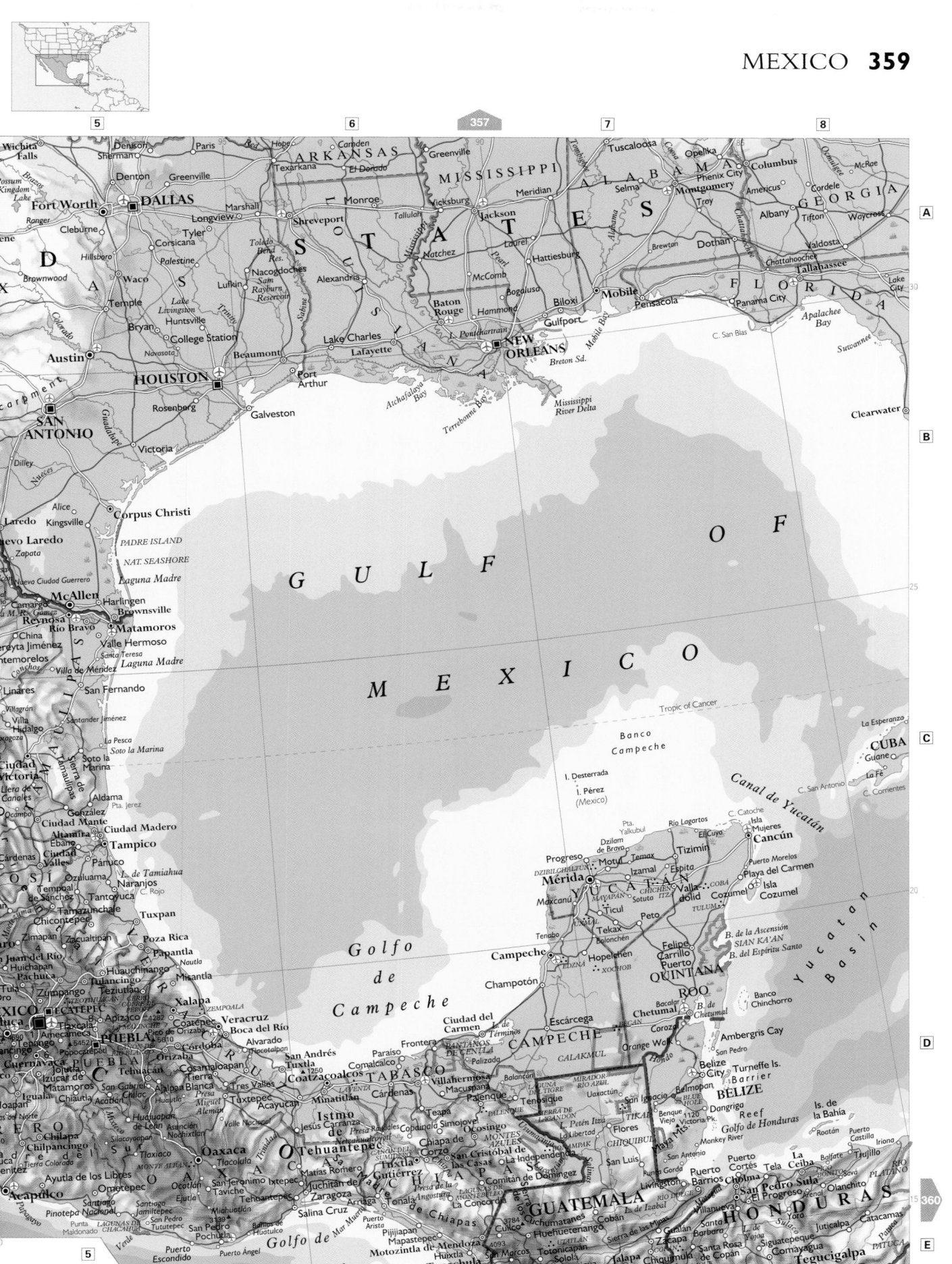

A

B

C

D

E

5

6

7

8

Wichita
Falls
Denison
Sherman
Paris
Red
Hope
Camden
ARKANSAS
Greenville
90
Tuscaloosa
Opelika
McRae
Columbus
Denton
Greenville
Texarkana
El Dorado
MISSISSIPPI
Meridian
Phenix City
Montgomery
Cordele
Fort Worth
DALLAS
Marshall
Monroe
Vicksburg
Jackson
Selma
Troy
Americus
Tifton
GEORGIA
Waycross

Cleburne
Longview
Shreveport
Tallulah
Laurel
Hattiesburg
Brewton
Dothan
Valdosta
Lake
City

Tyler
Corsicana
Palestine
Nacogdoches
Alexandria
McComb
Bogalusa
Biloxi
Mobile
Panama City
FLORIDA
30

Waco
Lufkin
Baton
Rouge
Gulfport
Pensacola
Apalachee
Bay
Suwannee
Tallahassee

Temple
Bryan
College Station
Lake
Charles
Lafayette
NEW
ORLEANS
Gulfport
C. San Blas

AUSTIN
Beaumont
Port
Arthur
Atchafalaya
Bay
Breton Sd.
Mississippi
River Delta
Clearwater

SAN
ANTONIO
Rosenberg
Galveston
Terrebonne Bay

HOUSTON

Victoria
Dilley
Corpus Christi
PADRE ISLAND
NAT. SEASHORE
Laguna Madre
G U L F   O F

Alice
Kingsville

Laredo
Nuevo Laredo
Zapata
Laguna Madre
M E X I C O

McAllen
Harlingen
Brownsville
25

Reynosa
Rio Bravo
Valle Hermoso
Matamoros
Santa Teresa
Laguna Madre

China
Villa de Méndez
Banco
Campeche
CUBA
Guane

Linares
San Fernando
Tropic of Cancer
La Esperanza
La Fé
C. Corrientes

Villagrán
Villa
Hidalgo
La Pesca
Soto la Marina
I. Desterrada
I. Pérez
(Mexico)
Canal de Yucatán
C. San Antonio

Ciudad
Victoria
Sierra de
Tamaulipas
Pta. Jerez
Pta.
Yalkubul
Río Lagartos
El Cuyo
C. Catoche
Isla
Mujeres
Cancún

Aldama
Dzilam
de Bravo
Temax
Tizimín
Espita
Puerto Morelos
Playa del Carmen

Ciudad Mante
Ciudad Madero
Altamira
Tampico
Ciudad Madero
Progreso
Motul
Izamal
YUCATÁN
Valla-
dolid
COBÁ
Cozumel
Isla
Cozumel

Ebano
Cárdenas
Valles
Pánuco
DZIBILCHALTÚN
MÉRIDA
CHICHÉN
ITZA
Sotuta
TULUM
Puerto

Ozuluama
Naranjos
Tantoyuca
L. de Tamiahua
Maxcanú
MAYAPÁN
Ticul
Peto
B. de la Ascensión

Tempoal
de Sánchez
Tamazunchale
C. Rojo
UXMAL
Tekax
Bolonchén
SIAN KA'AN
B. del Espíritu Santo
Yucatan Basin

Chicontepec
Tuxpan
Tenabo
Felipe
Carrillo
Puerto

Zimapán
Zacualtipán
Poza Rica
Papantla
Campeche
EDZNÁ
Hopelchén
QUINTANA
ROO
Banco
Chinchorro

Juan del Río
Huichapan
Pachuca
Huauchinango
Misantla
Nautla
Golfo
de
Campeche
Champotón
XOCHOB
Bacalar
Chetumal
B. de
Chetumal

Tula
Zumpango
Tulancingo
Teziutlán
Escárcega
CALAKMUL
BECÁN
Corozal
Orange Walk
Ambergris Cay
San Pedro
Turneffe Is.

MÉXICO
ECATEPEC
TEOTIHUACAN
CERRO
GORDO
4262
Apizaco
Xalapa
ZEMPOALA
Veracruz
Boca del Río
Ciudad del
Carmen
L. de
Términos
Frontera
CAMPECHE
BELIZE
Belize
City

TLAXCALA
PUEBLA
5452
Pico de Orizaba
Córdoba
Orizaba
Alvarado
Tlacotalpan
San Andrés
Tuxtla
1250
Paraíso
Palizada
BANTANOS
DE CENTLA
Reef
Barrier

PUEBLA
5610
Popocatépetl
RÍO BLANCO
Tehuacán
Cosamaloapan
Tierra
Blanca
Coatzacoalcos
Minatitlán
Comalcalco
Villahermosa
Balancán
Uaxactún
Dangriga

Cuernavaca
Jojutla
Izúcar de
Matamoros
San Gabriel
Chilac
Acatlán
Tres Vallés
Tuxtepec
Acayucan
LA VENTA
Cárdenas
Macuspana
Palenque
LAGUNA
DEL TIGRE
MIRADOR
RÍO AZUL
SIERRA DE
LACANDON
TIKAL
Benque
Viejo
Belmopan
Golfo de Honduras
Is. de
la Bahía

Iguala
Chiautla
Chiapa de
Corzo
Presa
Miguel
Alemán
Valle Nacional
Teapa
Tenosique
El Petén Itzá
CHIQUIBUL
Victoria Pk.
120
Roatán

Chilapa
Chilpancingo
Tlaxiaco
Oaxaca
OAXACA
Tlacolula
Matías Romero
Juchitán de
Zaragoza
Jesús Carranza
Copainala Simojovel
Ocosingo
San Cristóbal de
las Casas
Comitán de Domínguez
La Independencia
San Ignacio
San Luis
MAYA
San Antonio
Punta Gorda
Monkey River
La
Ceiba

Ayutla de los Libres
Ometepec
MONTE ALBÁN
Ocotlán
Ejutla
Tehuantepec
Istmo
de
Tehuantepec
Tuxtla
Gutiérrez
MONTES
AZULES
LAGUNAS DE
MONTEBELLO
RÍO DULCE
La
Libertad
Flores
Livingston
Puerto
Barrios
Cholma
San Pedro Sula
Olanchito
PLATAÑO

Acapulco
Santiago
Pinotepa Nacional
San Pedro
San Pedro
Pochutla
Salina Cruz
Tonalá
Sierra Madre de Chiapas
Presa de la
Angostura
La Concordia
San Marcos
Totonicapán
SIERRA DE LAS MINAS
Zacapa
Santa Rosa
de Copán
Santa
Barbara
Yojoa
Siguatepeque
Comayagua
Juticalpa
Catacamas

Punta
Maldonado
LAGUNAS DE
CHACAHUA
Santiago
Tututepec
Bahías de
Huatulco
Pijijiapan
Mapastepec
Motozintla de Mendoza
Tapachula
Huixtla
4093
Huehuetenango
Cuilco
Cuchumatanes
Sololá
ATITLÁN
3784
Antigua
Jalapa
Chiquimula
El Progreso
TEGUCIGALPA
PATUCA

Puerto
Escondido
Puerto
Ángel
Golfo de
Tehuantepec
Puerto
Arista
Puerto Madero
Retalhuleu
Mazate-
nango
GUATEMALA
GUATEMALA
Amatitlán
La Esperanza
La Paz
Danlí
360

15

20

25

30

95

90

COPYRIGHT PHILIP'S

JAMAICA
a

CARIBBEAN SEA

Montego Bay
Lucea
Negril
South Negril Pt.
Savanna-la-Mar
Black River
Great Pedro Bluff
Maggotty
Santa Cruz Mts.
Mandeville
May Pen
Cambridge
Wakefield
The Cockpit Country
Mount Denham 985▲
Don Figuero Mts.
Alligator Pond
Portland Bight
Portland Point
Falmouth
Runaway Bay
Ocho Rios
Dry Harbour Mountains
Linstead
Spanish Town
Portmore
St. Ann's Bay
Galina Point
Port Maria
Moneague
Annotto Bay
The Blue Mountains 2256 Blue Mountain Peak
John Crow Mts.
KINGSTON
Morant Point
Morant Bay
Port Antonio
Port Morant

B

GULF OF MEXICO

I. Desterrada
I. Pérez (Mexico)
Canal de Yucatán
C. Catoche
C. San Antonio
Punta Yalkubul
Progreso
Dzilam de Bravo
Río Lagartos
El Cuyo
Tizimín
Isla Mujeres
Cancún
Mérida
Motul
Temax
Espita
Puerto Morelos
Maxcanú
Izamal
Valladolid
Playa del Carmen
Calkiní
Ticul
Cozumel
Isla Cozumel
Tenabo
Peto
Campeche
Hopelchén
Felipe Carrillo Puerto
B. de la Ascensión
SIAN KA'AN
Champotón
San José Carpizo
Balcanchén
B. del Espíritu Santo

YUCATAN
QUINTANA ROO
CAMPECHE
MEXICO

Ciudad del Carmen
I. de Términos
PANTANOS DE CENTLA
Palizada
Balancán
Bacalar
Chetumal
Corozal
B. de Chetumal
Banco Chinchorro

Tenosique
Ocosingo
Palenque
SIERRA DE LACANDON
MIRADOR-RIO AZUL
Uaxactún
Orange Walk
Ambergris Cay
San Pedro
Belize City
Turneffe Is.

Comitán de Domínguez
MONTES AZULES
L. Petén Itzá
Flores
Belmopan
San Ignacio
Benque Viejo
Middlesex
Dangriga
Reef
BLUE HOLE
T120
Maya Mts.
CARACOL
CHIQUIBUL
Barrier

GUATEMALA
BELIZE

La Libertad
San Luis
Sebol
Livingston
Punta Gorda
Puerto Barrios
Golfo de Honduras
Monkey River
San Antonio

Cuilco
Huehuetenango
Cobán
L. de Izabal
Puerto Cortés
Tela
Roatán
Puerto Castilla

Cayman Islands (U.K.)
George Town
Grand Cayman
Cayman Brac
Little Cayman
7680

Is. Santanilla (Swan Islands) (Honduras)
Bajo Nuevo (Colombia)

D

San Marcos
Totonicapán
Antigua
Quezaltenango
Mazatenango
Retalhuleu
Escuintla
GUATEMALA
Amatitlán
Jalapa
Chiquimula de Copán
Santa Rosa
Zacapa
El Progreso
Yoro
El Jaral
Santa Bárbara
Olanchito
Trujillo
Balfate
PICO BONITO
La Ceiba
La Esperanza
Tegucigalpa
Yuscarán
Juticalpa
Catacamas
Comayagua
Siguatepeque
Nacaome
Comayagua
Danlí
El Paraíso
Estelí
Jinotega
El Sauce
RIO PLATANO
Mosquitia
C. Falso
C. Gracias á Dios
Puerto Cabo Gracias á Dios
Kisalaya
Cayos Miskitos (Nicaragua)
Puerto Cabezas

HONDURAS

San Pedro Sula
Sula
Sulaco
Arenal
Olancho
PATUCA
Bonanza
Siuna
SASLAYA
Tungla
Prinzapolca

El Salvador
San Salvador
Santa Ana
Sonsonate
Ahuachapán
Acajutla
Nueva San Salvador
Usulután
San Miguel
La Unión
G. de Fonseca
Choluteca
Somoto
Cord. Isabella
1963
Tuma
Matagalpa
Muy Muy
Río Grande del Norte
Río Grande
Punta de Perlas
I. de Providencia (Colombia)
Cayos Roncador (Colombia)

SAN SALVADOR
EL SALVADOR

1
2

NICARAGUA

León
Boaco
Siguia
Chinandega
Corinto
La Paz Centro
L. de Managua
Masaya
Granada
Juigalpa
Santo Domingo
Rama
Bluefields
El Bluff
MANAGUA
Diriamba
Jinotepe
Lago de Nicaragua
Cord. de Yolaina
Pta. Mico
B. de San Juan del Norte
Rivas
I. de Ometepe
San Carlos
San Juan del Norte
B. de Salinas
San Juan del Sur
Is. del Maíz (Nicaragua)
Cayos de Albuquerque (Colombia)
I. de San Andrés (Colombia)

E

PACIFIC
OCEAN

Liberia
La Cruz
Los Chiles
GUANACASTE
SANTA ROSA
G. de Papagayo
Santa Cruz
Nicoya
Carmona
Puntarenas
Pen. de Nicoya
C. Velas
G. de Nicoya
C. Blanco
Pen. de Osa
B. de Coronado
Puerto Quepos
Esparta
Alajuela
San José
Cartago
Central
COSTA RICA
Guápiles
Siquirres
Limón
Pandora
Bribri
Buenos Aires
Volcán Barú 3475
CORCOVADO
San Vito
Golfito
G. Dulce
Pta. Burica
Puerto Armuelles
Boquete
Concepción
David
Remedios
Santiago
Sona
Bocas del Toro
Almirante
Chiriquí
G. de los Mosquitos
Pen. de Azuero
Las Tablas
Pocrí
Chitré
Pta. Mala
CERRO HOYA

Panama Canal
Colón
Portobelo
Nombre de Dios
Archipiélago de San Blas
Serranía del Darién
Golfo del Darién
PANAMA
Chepo
La Chorrea
Balboa
Penonomé
Aguadulce
Anton
Chimán
San Miguel
Arch. de las Perlas
El Real
La Palma
Garachiné
Jaqué
Golfo de Panamá
Golfo de San Miguel
DARIEN
I. de San Bernardo

G. de Chiriquí
I. de Coiba
COIBA
I. de Cebaco
I. Jicarón
Punta Mariato
Tonosí

GUADELOUPE
b

Port-Louis
Petit-Canal
Pte. de la Grande Vigie
Grande-Terre
Ste-Rose
Le Moule
La Désirade
Pointe Allègre
Pointe-Noire
Pointe-à-Pitre
Ste-Anne
Pointe des Châteaux
Basse-Terre
Le Gosier
Îles de la Petite Terre
GUADELOUPE (Fr.)
Soufrière 1467
Capesterre-Belle-Eau
St-Louis
Marie-Galante
Basse-Terre
Trois-Rivières
204▲
Grand-Bourg
Capesterre
Îles des Saintes
Pte. des Basses

MARTINIQUE
c

Cap St-Martin
Basse-Pointe
Le Prêcheur
Montagne Pelée 1463
Ste-Marie
St-Pierre
La Trinité
St-Joseph
Le Robert
Schœlcher
Le François
Fort-de-France
Le Lamentin
Rivière-Salée
Le St-Esprit
MARTINIQUE (Fr.)
Rivière-Pilote
Le Marin
Pte. d'Enfer

GUADELOUPE AND MARTINIQUE

A

U.S.A.
Cape Coral
Fort Myers
Naples
C. Romano
West Palm Beach
Boca Raton
Fort Lauderdale
West End
Freeport
Grand Bahama
Little Abaco I.
Hope Town
Abaco I.
EVERGLADES NAT. PARK
MIAMI
Hialeah
Everglades
C. Sable
Florida Bay
Dry Tortugas (U.S.A.)
Key West
Florida Keys
Straits of Florida
Bimini Is.
Berry Is.
Nicolls Town
Nassau
New Providence
Adelaide
Andros Town
Andros Island
Northwest Providence Channel
Northeast Providence Channel
Eleuthera I.
Dunmore
Great Exuma
Great Guana Cay
Great Abaco

LA HABANA (Havana)
Marianao
Guanabacoa
Bahía Honda
La Esperanza
Los Palacios
San Antonio de los Baños
Pinar del Río
Guane
San Luis
La Fé
Corrientes
I. de la Juventud
Güines
Santa Cruz del Norte
Matanzas
Cárdenas
Jovellanos
Colón
Sagua la Grande
Jagüey Grande
Santa Clara
Placetas
Cienfuegos
Trinidad
Sancti Spíritus
Morón
Ciego de Ávila
Cayo Romano
Caibarién
Canal Viejo de Bahama
Júcaro
Tunas de Zaza
Florida
Camagüey
Santa Cruz del Sur
Arch. de los Canarreos
Arch. de Jardines de la Reina
Nuevitas
Puerto Padre
Gibara
Holguín
Victoria de las Tunas
Bayamo
Manzanillo
Golfo de Guacanayabo
Sierra Maestra 1972
Santiago de Cuba
C. Cruz

CUBA

Cay Sal Bank
Canal Nicholas
Samana Channel
Great Bahama Bank
Jumei
Cay
Duncan
Canal de Yucatán

3

JAMAICA
Montego Bay
Lucea
Negril
South Negril Pt.
Savanna-la-Mar
Black River
Mandeville
May Pen
Cambridge
Spanish Town
Falmouth
St. Ann's Bay
Port Maria
Annotto Bay
Kingston
Pedro Cays (Jamaica)

CARIBBEAN SEA

Is. de la Bahía

4

COPYRIGHT PHILIP'S

PUERTO RICO **d**

10 0 10 20 30 40 50 km
10 0 10 20 30 miles

VIRGIN ISLANDS **e**

10 0 10 20 30 km
10 0 10 20 miles

ATLANTIC OCEAN

PUERTO RICO
(U.S.A.)

Pta. Aguijereada
Isabela
Aguadilla
Barceloneta
Arecibo
Manati
Vega
Baja Bayamón
Carolina
SAN JUAN
Rio Grande
Fajardo
Dewey
Puerca
Culebra
Sierra de
Luquillo
Naguabo
Vieques
Esperanza
Mayagüez
San
Sebastian
Utuado
Caguas
Humacao
Adjuntas
Cordillera Central
Cerro
1338 de Punta
Yauco
Cayey
Coamo
Yabucoa
San German
Ponce
Guayama
Pta. Aguila
Guanica
Guayanilla
I. Caja de Muertos

VIRGIN ISLANDS
(U.K.)
Virgin Islands

Rufling Pt.
The Settlement
Anegada
East Pt.
Great Camanoe
Jost Van Dyke I.
Guana I.
Virgin Gorda
Tortola
521
Road Town
Beef
Spanish Town
Virgin Is.
(U.S.A.)
Lollik I.
Cruz Bay
VIRGIN IS.
Peter I.
Charlotte Amalie
St. John I.
St. Thomas I.

ST. LUCIA **f**

5 0 10 km
5 0 10 miles

Cap Point
Pte. Hardy
Gros Islet
Esperance Bay
Castries
Marquis
L'Anse la Raye
Canaries
Dennery
Soufrière
Millet
Mt. Gimie
Trou Gras Pt.
1950
Soufrière Bay
750
Petit Piton
Micoud
Gros Piton Pt.
796
Vierge Pt.
Grds Piton
Choiseul
ST. LUCIA
Laborie
Vieux Fort
C. Moule à Chique

BARBADOS **g**

5 0 10 km
5 0 10 miles

ATLANTIC OCEAN
Crabhill
North Point
Spring Hall
Boscobelle
Fustic
Portland
245
Belleplaine
Speightstown
Bathsheba
BARBADOS
Westmoreland
Hillcrest
Alleynes Bay
Mt. Hillaby
Martin's Bay
Holetown
340
Massiah
Jackson
Bridgefield
Street
Black Rock
Ellerton
Six Cross Roads
Bridgetown
Ivy
Edey
The Crane
Carlisle Bay
BGI
St. Martins
Worthing
Oistins
Chancery Lane
Bay
South Point

ATLANTIC OCEAN

MAS

Nur's Town
The Bight
Cat I.
Conception I.
Rum Cay
Long I.
Clarence Town
Samana Cay
Crooked I.
Albert Town
Snug Corner
Plana Cays
Mayaguana I.
Acklins I.
Mira por vos Cay
Cay Verde
Hogsty Reef
Turks & Caicos
(U.K.)
Caicos Is.
Cockburn Town
Little Inagua I.
Turks Is.
INAGUA
Santa
mingo
Lake Rose
Great Inagua I.
Matthew Town
Moa
Baracoa
Pta. de Maisi
Maisi
Monte Cristi
LA ISABELA
uantanamo
GUANTANAMO
(U.S.A.)
Î. de la Tortue
Cap-Haïtien
Santiago de los Caballeros
San Francisco de Macorís
Milwaukee Deep
9200
Puerto Rico Trench
Jean Rabel Port-de-Paix
Puerto Plata
La Vega
Nagua
Samana
Fort Liberté
Cap-à-Foux
G. de la Gonâve
Gonaïves
Cord.
3175
Sabana de la Mar
St-Marc
Central
ARMANDO
BERMÚDEZ
Pico Duarte
3175
Sánchez
HAITI
HAÏTISES
Hinche
DOMINICAN
Hato Mayor
Jérémie
Î. de la Gonâve
PORT-AU-PRINCE
San Juan
REP.
San Pedro
de Macorís
Higüey
C. Engaño
Dame
Marie
Petit
2680
L. Enriquillo
SANTO
DOMINGO
Esta
B. de Yuma
Les Cayes
Godve
Jacmel
SIERRA DE
BAHORUCO
Barahona
Bani
San Cristóbal
Compostela
I. Saona
Aquin
Pedernales
Isla Mona
(U.S.A.)
Pointe-à-Gravois
Hispaniola
I. Beata
C. Beata
PUERTO RICO
(U.S.A.)

ATLANTIC OCEAN

Bayamón SAN JUAN
Arecibo
Virgin Is.
Anegada
Sombrero (U.K.)
Carolina
St. Thomas
Virgin Gorda
Virgin Is.
Anguilla (U.K.)
Aguadilla
1338
Fajardo
Tortola
Road Town
St-Martin (Fr.)
Mayagüez
Ponce
Caguas
Charlotte Amalie
Virgin Is.
(U.S.A.)
St. Maarten
St-Barthélemy (Fr.)
Guayama
Christiansted
St. Eustatius
Saba (Neth.)
Barbuda
Frederiksted
St. Croix
(Neth.)
ST. KITTS
& NEVIS
ANTIGUA
& BARBUDA
Basseterre
St. John's
Nevis
Antigua
Redonda
Montserrat
Guadeloupe Passage
Ste-Rose
Le Moule
La Désirade
GUADELOUPE
1467
Pointe-à-Pitre
(Fr.)
Marie-Galante (Fr.)
Basse-Terre
Grand-Bourg
I. des Saintes
(Fr.)
Dominica Passage
I. de Aves
(Venezuela)
Portsmouth
1447
DOMINICA
Roseau
MORNE
TROIS PITONS
Martinique Passage
Mt. Pelée
Ste-Marie
1397
Le François
Fort-de-France
Rivière-Pilote
MARTINIQUE
St. Lucia Channel (Fr.)
Castries
ST. LUCIA
Soufrière
St. Vincent Passage
Soufrière 1234
St. Vincent
Speightstown
Kingstown
Bridgetown
BARBADOS
Grenadines
ST. VINCENT
& THE
GRENADINES
Hillsborough
GRENADA
St. George's

Antilles
Lesser Antilles
Leeward Islands
Windward Islands

BEAN
SEA
CARIBBEAN SEA

Lesser
Antilles

Oranjestad
Aruba
(Neth.)
Curaçao
Bonaire
NETH.
ANTILLES
Willemstad
ARC. LOS
ROQUES
I. Blanquilla (Ven.)
Is. Los Hermanos
(Ven.)
Tobago
C. San Román
Pen. de
Paraguaná
Is. Las Aves
(Ven.)
I. Orchila
(Ven.)
Is. Los Roques
(Ven.)
I. Los Testigos
(Ven.)
NUEVA
ESPARTA
I. de Margarita
Scarborough
Port of Spain
Galera Pt.
COLOMBIA
Pta. Gallinas
MACUIRA
Pta. Espada
Punto Fijo
MÉDANOS DE CORO
La Asunción
Porlamar
TRINIDAD
Toco
Santa Marta
Ríohacha
Uribia
Golfo de
Venezuela
Coro
La Vela de Coro
I. La Tortuga
(Ven.)
LAGUNA
DE
LA RESTINGA
Rio Caribe
Güiria
Pen. de Paria
Trinidad
TAYRONA
GUAJIRA
Punta
Cardón
QUEBRADA
DEL TORO
Tucacas
Cumaná
Carúpano
Río Claro
RRAN-
QUILLA
Cienaga
S. NEVADA DE
STA. MARTA
San Rafael
Altagracia
FALCÓN
Puerto Cabello
Higuerote
Cariaco
SUCRE
San Fernando
TRINIDAD
& TOBAGO
Soledad
Mene de Mauroa
CERRO
SARACHAGUE
Maiquetía
La Guaira
VARGAS
Río Chico
La Cruz
Barcelona
Carúpano
Serpent's Mouth
Fundación
La Concepción
Santa Rita
Cabimas
Baragua
San Felipe
ARAGAY
CARACAS
Ocumare del Tuy
Caripito
MONAGAS
Maturín
MARIUSA
DELTA
Valledupar
Villa del Rosario
Ciudad Ojeda
Lago de
Maracaibo
Carora
Barquisimeto
Villa de Cura
San Juan de los Morros
Altagracia de Orituco
Caicara
Anaco
Cantaura
Calamar
MARACAIBO
Machiques
LARA
Villa
TEREBINA
VALENCIA
Aragua de
Barcelona
ZULIA
Mene Grande
Acarigua
COJEDES
El Sombrero
El Tigre
Magangué
TRUJILLO
Betijoque
GUACHE
GUARICO
Valle de
la Pascua
Tucupita
Mompos
PERITA
San Carlos
del Zulia
Valera
PORTUGUESA
El Baúl
Calabozo
Santa María
de Ipire
AMACURO
El Banco
CIÉNAGAS DEL
CATATUMBO
El Tocuyo
Guanare
Portuguesa
El Pao
Ciudad Guayana
Encontrados
Barinas
AGUARO-
GUARIQUITO
Soledad
Upata
Sierra Imataca
SANTANDER
NORTE
DE OCAÑA
San Carlos
Mérida
Ciudad Bolivia
BARINAS
Libertad
San Fernando
de Apure
Embalse de Guri
Ciudad Bolívar
San Cristóbal
TÁCHIRA
VENEZUELA
Pagos de Nutrias
Achaguas
Apure
Caicara
Orinoco
Mapire
Guasipati
Tumeremo
El Callao

West from Greenwich

75   70   65   60

A
B
C
D
E

5 6 7

4000 3000 2000 1500 1000 600 400 200
ft
m

364
5   6   7

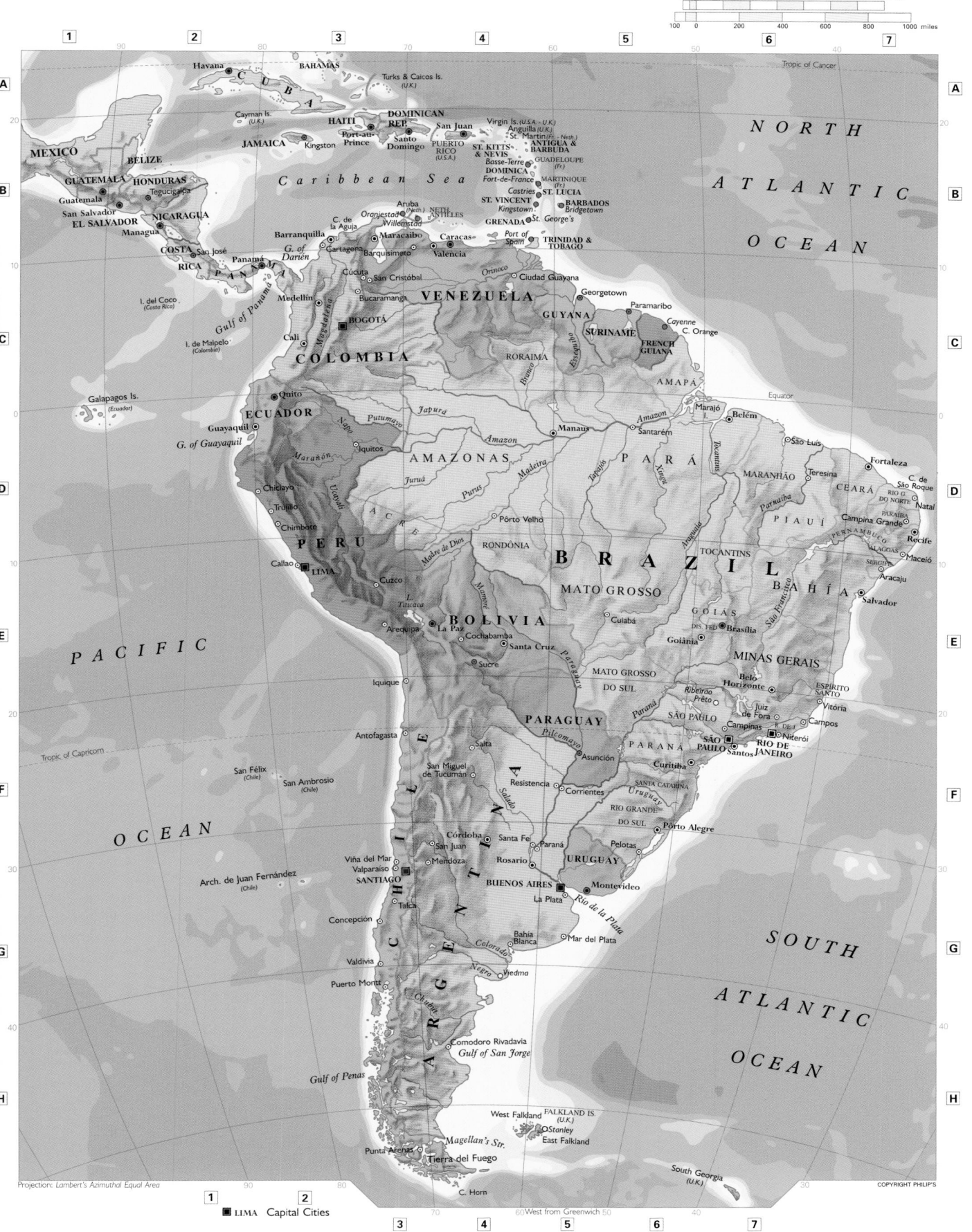

100 0 200 400 600 800 1000 1200 1400 km
100 0 200 400 600 800 1000 miles

1 90 **2** 80 **3** 70 **4** 60 **5** 50 **6** **7** 40

A
Havana
BAHAMAS
Turks & Caicos Is.
(U.K.)
CUBA
Tropic of Cancer
Cayman Is.
(U.K.)
HAITI
DOMINICAN
REP.
Virgin Is. (U.S.A. – U.K.)
Anguilla (U.K.)
St. Martin (Fr. – Neth.)
NORTH
B
MEXICO
JAMAICA
Kingston
Port-au-
Prince
San Juan
PUERTO
RICO
(U.S.A.)
Santo
Domingo
ST. KITTS
& NEVIS
Basse-Terre
DOMINICA
Fort-de-France
ANTIGUA &
BARBUDA
GUADELOUPE
(Fr.)
MARTINIQUE
(Fr.)
ATLANTIC
BELIZE
GUATEMALA
HONDURAS
Guatemala
Tegucigalpa
Caribbean Sea
Castries
ST. LUCIA
ST. VINCENT
BARBADOS
Bridgetown
OCEAN
San Salvador
EL SALVADOR
NICARAGUA
Managua
Aruba
(Neth.)
Oranjestad
Willemstad
NETH.
ANTILLES
Kingstown
GRENADA
St. George's
COSTA
RICA
San José
C. de
la Aguja
Barranquilla
Maracaibo
Caracas
Port of
Spain
TRINIDAD &
TOBAGO
Panamá
Cartagena
Barquisimeto
Valencia
G. of
Darién
Cúcuta
San Cristóbal
Orinoco
Ciudad Guayana
I. del Coco
(Costa Rica)
Gulf of Panama
PANAMA
Medellín
Bucaramanga
VENEZUELA
Georgetown
Paramaribo
C
I. de Malpelo
(Colombia)
BOGOTÁ
GUYANA
SURINAME
Cayenne
FRENCH
GUIANA
C. Orange
Cali
COLOMBIA
RORAIMA
Branco
AMAPÁ
Galapagos Is.
(Ecuador)
Quito
ECUADOR
Equator
Marajó
Belém
São Luís
Fortaleza
C. de
São Roque
Guayaquil
Putumayo
Japurá
Amazon
Santarém
G. of Guayaquil
Napo
Marañón
Iquitos
AMAZONAS
Amazon
Manaus
PARÁ
MARANHÃO
Teresina
CEARÁ
RIO G.
DO NORTE
Natal
D
Chiclayo
Juruá
Purus
Madeira
Tapajós
Xingu
Tocantins
PIAUÍ
PARAÍBA
Campina Grande
Trujillo
ACRE
Pôrto Velho
Parnaíba
PERNAMBUCO
Recife
Chimbote
Madre de Dios
RONDÔNIA
B R A Z I L
ALAGOAS
Maceió
PERU
Callao LIMA
Cuzco
Mamoré
Araguaia
São Francisco
MATO GROSSO
Cuiabá
TOCANTINS
GOIÁS
DIS. FED.
Brasília
BAHIA
SERGIPE
Aracaju
Salvador
E
L.
Titicaca
BOLIVIA
La Paz
Cochabamba
Santa Cruz
Paraguay
Goiânia
MINAS GERAIS
Arequipa
Sucre
MATO GROSSO
DO SUL
Belo
Horizonte
ESPÍRITO
SANTO
Iquique
Paraná
Ribeirão
Prêto
Juiz
de Fora
Vitória
Campos
PACIFIC
PARAGUAY
SÃO PAULO
Campinas
R. DE J.
Antofagasta
Salta
Pilcomayo
Asunción
PARANÁ
SÃO
PAULO
Niterói
RIO DE
JANEIRO
F
San Félix
(Chile)
San Ambrosio
(Chile)
San Miguel
de Tucumán
Resistencia
Corrientes
Uruguay
SANTA CATARINA
Curitiba
Santos
RIO GRANDE
DO SUL
Tropic of Capricorn
OCEAN
Salado
Paraná
Pôrto Alegre
Arch. de Juan Fernández
(Chile)
Córdoba
San Juan
Santa Fe
Paraná
Pelotas
G
Viña del Mar
Valparaíso
SANTIAGO
Mendoza
Rosario
URUGUAY
Montevideo
ARGENTINA
CHILE
Talca
BUENOS AIRES
La Plata
Río de la Plata
Concepción
Bahía
Blanca
Mar del Plata
SOUTH
Valdivia
Colorado
ATLANTIC
Puerto Montt
Negro
Viedma
Chubut
Comodoro Rivadavia
Gulf of San Jorge
OCEAN
H
Gulf of Penas
West Falkland
FALKLAND IS.
(U.K.)
Stanley
East Falkland
Magellan's Str.
Punta Arenas
Tierra del Fuego
South Georgia
(U.K.)
C. Horn

Projection: Lambert's Azimuthal Equal Area

West from Greenwich

COPYRIGHT PHILIP'S

1 90 **2** 80 **3** 70 **4** 60 West from Greenwich 50 **5** **6** **7** 30

■ LIMA   Capital Cities

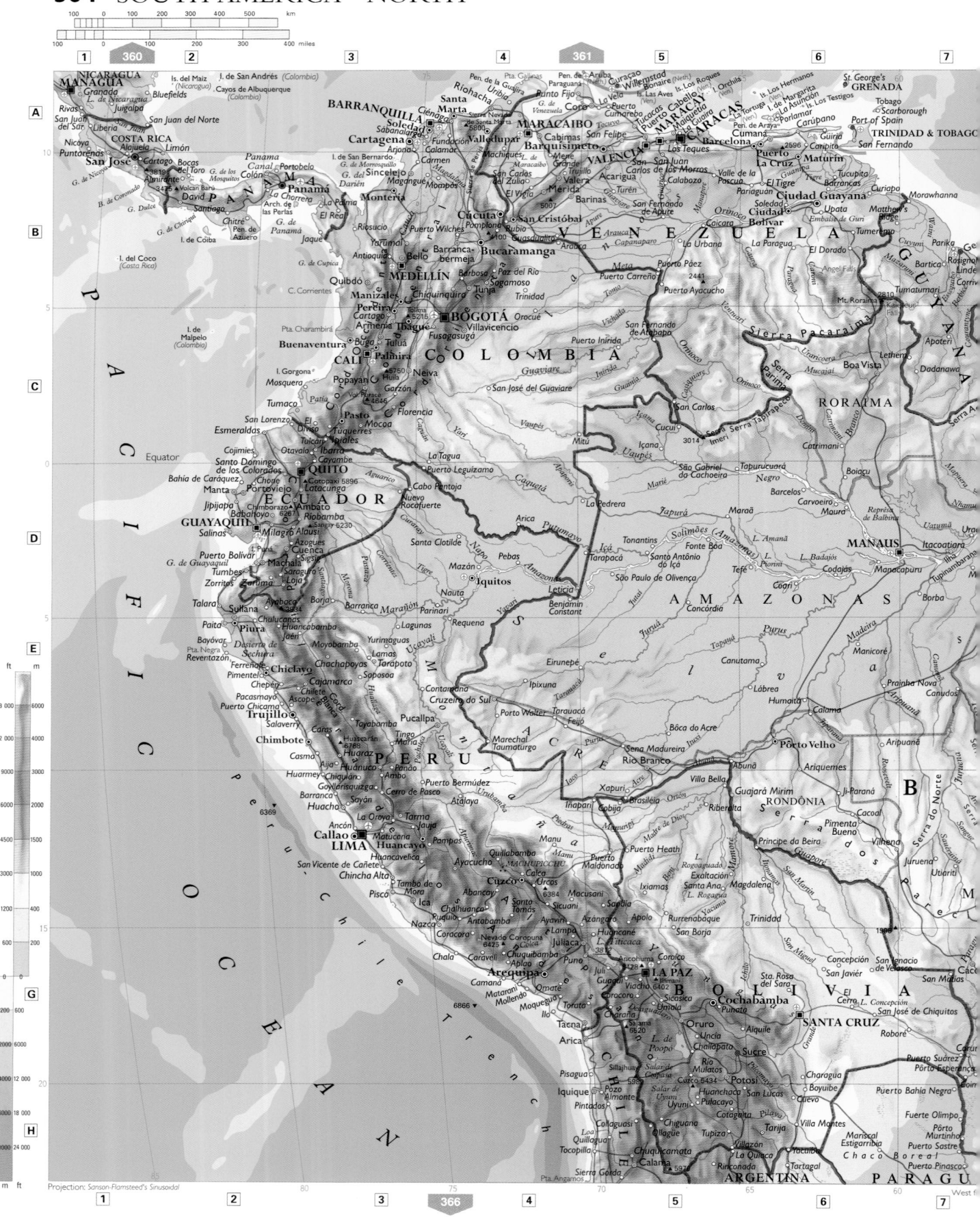

ATLANTIC

OCEAN

TRINIDAD AND TOBAGO

10   0   10   20   30   40   50 km
10   0   10   20   30 miles

Charlotteville
Castara   565   Little
Tobago   Main Ridge   Tobago
Plymouth   Roxborough
Buccoo Reef   Scarborough
Crown Pt.   Rocky Bay

Tobago

North Pt.

J

ATLANTIC
OCEAN

VENEZUELA
Pen. de
Paria   Macuro
Güiria   Corozal
Pt.   Monos I.   Maraval
Dragon's Mouths

Toco
Galera Pt.
Redhead
Salybia

Trinidad

Northern Range
936   940   Mt. Aripo
Tunapuna   Valencia   Guaico
Port
of
Spain   San
Juan   Arima   Matura
Bay

**Port
of
Spain**

San   Caroni   Talparo   Upper Manzanilla
Chaguanas   Couva   Sangre Grande   Narica
Swamp   Cocos
Point Lisas   Gasparillo   Bay
Otaheite Bay   Rio Claro   Guatuaro Pt.
San Fernando   Pierreville
Brighton   La Brea   Mayaro Bay
Point Fortin   Guapo Bay   Pitch   Princes Town   Guayaguayare
Lake   Penal   Galeota Pt.
Cedros Bay   Palo Seco   Siparia   Basse Terre
Bonasse   304
Icacos Pt.   La Lune   Moruga   Trinity
Erin Pt.   Hills

Golfo de Paria

K

Serpent's Mouth

VENEZUELA   Pta. Bombedor   West from Greenwich

L

São Pedro &
São Paulo
(*Braz.*)

Equator

D

FRENCH
GUIANA

RINAME

Amsterdam
Nickerie
Totness   Nieuw Amsterdam
wakoegron   Albina   St-Laurent   Iracoubo
Kourou
Sinnamary
Cayenne
Van Blommestein-
meer   Kaw   C. Orange
atop   Mana   Oiapoque
1230

C. Georges
Camopi

Serra Tumucumaque   Amapá   I. de Maracá

AMAPÁ   Araguari
Meriumá   Serra do
Navio
Macapá
Mazagão   I. Caviana
Afuá   I. Mexiana
Chaves   C. Maguarinho
I. Grande   Soure   Curuçá   Salinópolis
de Gurupá   Vigia   Bragança
Breves   **BELÉM**   Viseu
Almeirim   Marajó   Castanhal   Gururupu
PARÁ   Cametá   Abaetetuba   Turiaçu   B. de São Marcos
Gurupá   Baião   Tucuruí   **São Luís**   Barreirinhas
Pôrto de Maz   Alcântara   Tutóia   Luís Correia
Pinheiro   Rosário   Parnaíba   Camocim
Itapecuru-   Granja   Itapipoca
Viana   Mirim   Caucaia
Santa Inês   **FORTALEZA**
Brejo   Piracuruca   Sobral   Cascavel
Codó   Caxias   Marangupe   Baturité   Aracati
Coroatá   Campo   Oiticica   Russos   Macau   Ceará Mirim
Piripiri   Maior   Ipu   Quixadá   C. de São Roque
Teresina   Crateús   Quixeramobim   Mossoró   **Natal**
Imperatriz   Grajaú   Barra   Amarante   Senador Pompeu   Caraúbas   Currais   RIO GRANDE
do Corda   Colinas   do Piauí   Iguatu   Caicó   Novos   DO NORTE
Floriano   Valença   Cedro   Caicó   Canguaretama
Nova Iorque   Oeiras   do Piauí   Cajazeiras   Sousa   Alagoa   Mamanguape
Picos   Crato   Patos   Grande   Cabedelo
Caicó   Ouricuri   Juàzeiro   **João Pessoa**
Santa   do Norte   PARAÍBA   **Olinda**
Filomena   Paulistana   Chapada do Araripe   Campina   **RECIFE**
São João   Salgueiro   Grande   Jaboatão
do Piauí   Caruaru
PERNAMBUCO   Vitória de Santo Antão
Caracol   Novo Remanso   Petrolina   Garanhuns   Palmares
Novo Remanso   Nova   Casa   Petrolândia   Palmeira
Represa de   Juàzeiro   Paulo Afonso   Rio Largo
Sobradinho   Indios   Propriá   **Maceió**
Senhor do   Capela   Penedo   LAGOAS
Bonfim   SERGIPE
Jacobina   Itaporanga   **Aracaju**
Xique-Xique   Queimadas   Serrinha   São Cristóvão
Barra   Estância
Mundo   Feira de   Alagoinhas
Novo   Santa   Santo Amaro
Ibotirama   Cachoeira   Santo Amaro
BAHIA   Itaberaba   Nazaré   **SALVADOR**
Barreiras   Castro   Valença   B. de Todos os Santos
Alves
Santa Maria   Bom Jesus   Ubaitaba   Itaparica
da Vitória   da Lapa Serra do Sincorá
Caetité   Contas   Jequié   Ilhéus
Brumado   Canavieiras
Carinhanha   Condeúba   Vitória da   Itabuna
Januária   Monte Azul   Conquista   Belmonte
Formosa   São Francisco   Pedra Azul   Pôrto Seguro
Luziânia   Januba   Salinas   Itamaraju
Montes   Araçuaí   Prado
Unaí   Claros   Jequitinhonha   Caravelas
Paracatu   Pirapora   Teófilo Otoni   Nanuque   Banco
Ipamen   Patos de   Diamantina   Mucuri   Conceição da Barra
Catalão   Minas   Governador   Nova
Araguari   Corinto   Valadares   Venécia   São Mateus
Ituiutaba   Curvelo   Ipatinga   Colatina   Abrolhos
MINAS GERAIS   Caratinga   Linhares
Uberlândia   Ibiá   Itabira   Cariacica   Trindade
Uberaba   Prata   Araxá   **BELO HORIZONTE**   Ponte Nova   **Vitória**   (*Braz.*)
Patrocínio   Sabará   Vila Velha
Igarapava   Divinópolis   Nova   Cachoeiro de Itapemirim
Franca   Lima   Oura   Prêto
Ribeirão   Passos   Conselheiro   Ponte Nova   Itaperuna
Prêto   Lafaiete   Barbacena   Cabo Frio
São Carlos   Poços   São João   Campos
Bauru   de Caldas   del Rei   Três Rios
Jaú   Mogi-Mirim   São   Nova Friburgo
Piracicaba   Limeira   Lourenço   Petrópolis
CAMPINAS   Volta   Niterói
Redonda   **RIO DE JANEIRO**

E

6059

F

G

15

H

20

ATLANTIC
OCEAN

Rocas

Fernando de Noronha
(*Braz.*)

BRAZIL

O GROSSO
Planalto do

TOCANTINS
Palmas
Pôrto Nacional
Gurupi
Peixe
Paranã
Campos Belos
São Domingos
Niquelândia   1678
Uruaçu
Barragem de
Serra da Mesa
Aruanã
Alto Araguaia
GOIÁS
Vianópolis
Morrinhos
Itumbiara
Catalão
Quirinópolis
Rio Verde
Jataí

MATO GROSSO
Barra do Garças
Rondonópolis
DO SUL
Santo Antonio

GOIÂNIA
BRASÍLIA
Anápolis
Taguatinga   DIST.
FED.

Formosa

Serra Formosa
Serra do Roncador

Serra do Cachimbo

Campo
Grande
Dourados
Ponta Porã
nwich   55

Três Lagoas
Ribas
do Rio
Pardo
Presidente Epitácio
Presidente
Prudente   Panorama
Marília
Assis   Botucatu
Araçatuba
Penápolis
Birigui   Lins   São
Carlos
Bauru   SÃO
PAULO

Santa Fé do Sul
Água Clara
Andradina
São José do Rio Prêto
Araraquara

Aquidauana
Miranda
Lourenço
Coxim
Aporé

50   367   9   45   10   RIO DE JANEIRO   11   40   35   12   30   13

COPYRIGHT PHILIP'S

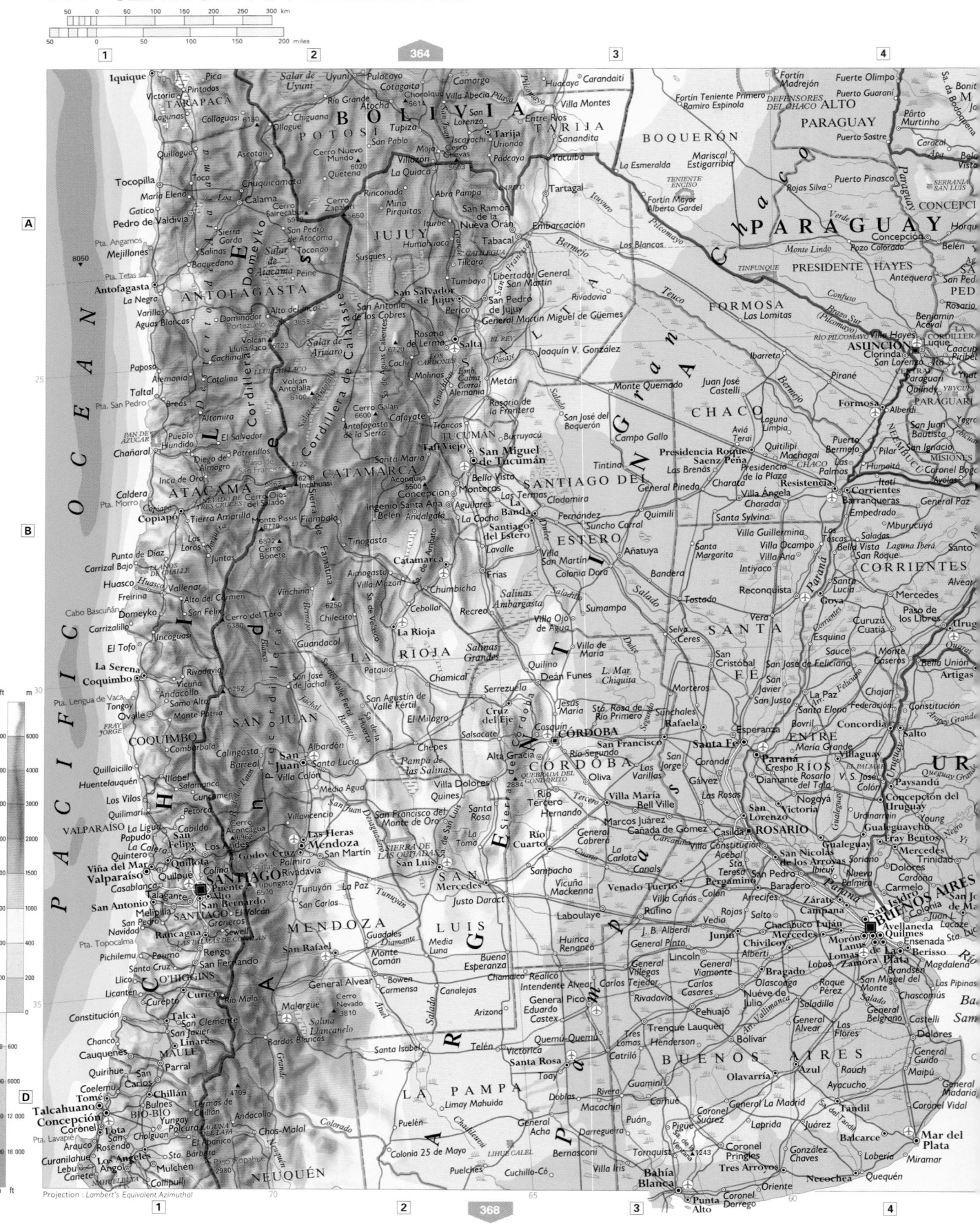

50 0 50 100 150 200 250 300 km

50 0 50 100 150 200 miles

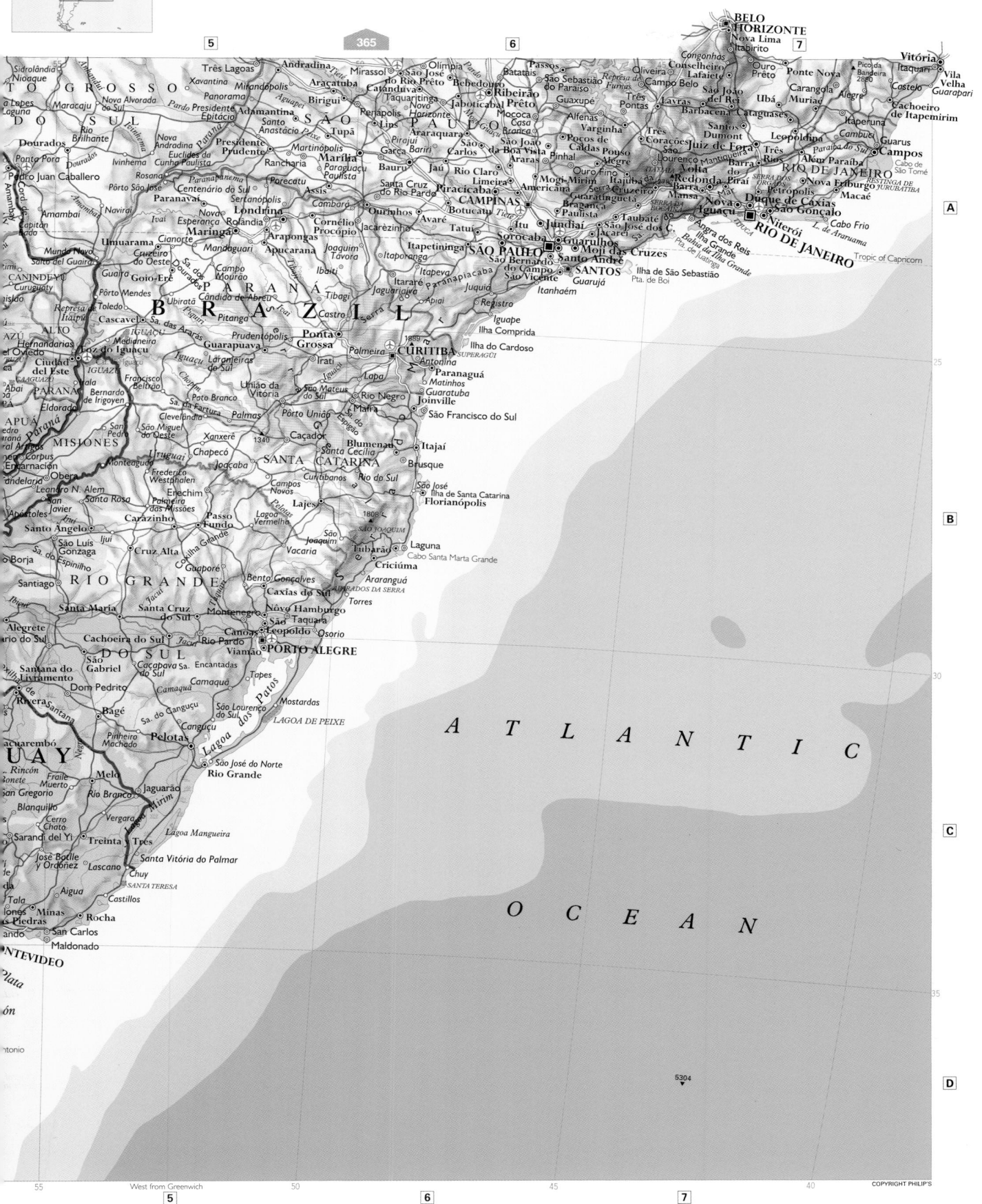

BELO
HORIZONTE
Nova Lima
Itabirito
Congonhas
Conselheiro
Oliveira   Lafaiete   Ouro
Ponte Nova   VITÓRIA
Itaquari   Vila
Pico da   Velha
Bandeira   Guarapari
2890   Castelo
Passos   Campo Belo   Carangola
Batatais   São Sebastião   Barbacena   Cataguases   Muriaé   Alegre
Mococa   do Paraíso   Campo Belo   Ubá   Cachoeiro
de Itapemirim
Guaxupé   Alfenas   Varginha   Coracões   Juiz de Fora   Leopoldina   Cambuci
Poços de   Barra   Santos   Três   Paraíba do Sul   Guarus
Caldas   Ponso   Dumont   Rios   Campos
Ouro Fino   Alegre   Volta   Três   Cabo de
São Tomé
Serra   Cruzeiro   RIO DE JANEIRO
Limeira   Redonda   Barra   Nova Friburgo   Macaé
Cruzeiro   Petrópolis   RESTINGA DE
JURUBATIBA
Mogi-Mirim   Guaratinguetá   Duque de Caxias
Campinas   Bragança   São Gonçalo
Paulista   Niterói   L. de Araruama
Itu   Jundiaí   São José dos C.   Angra dos Reis   Cabo Frio
SÃO PAULO   Guarulhos   Mogi das Cruzes   Baía de Ilha Grande   Tropic of Capricorn
São Bernardo   Santo André   Pta. de Juatinga
do Campo   SANTOS
São Vicente   Ilha de São Sebastião
Guarujá   Pta. de Boi
Itanhaém

ATLANTIC

OCEAN

5304

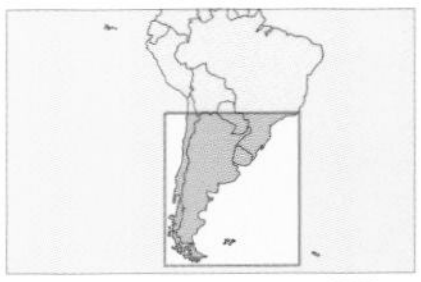

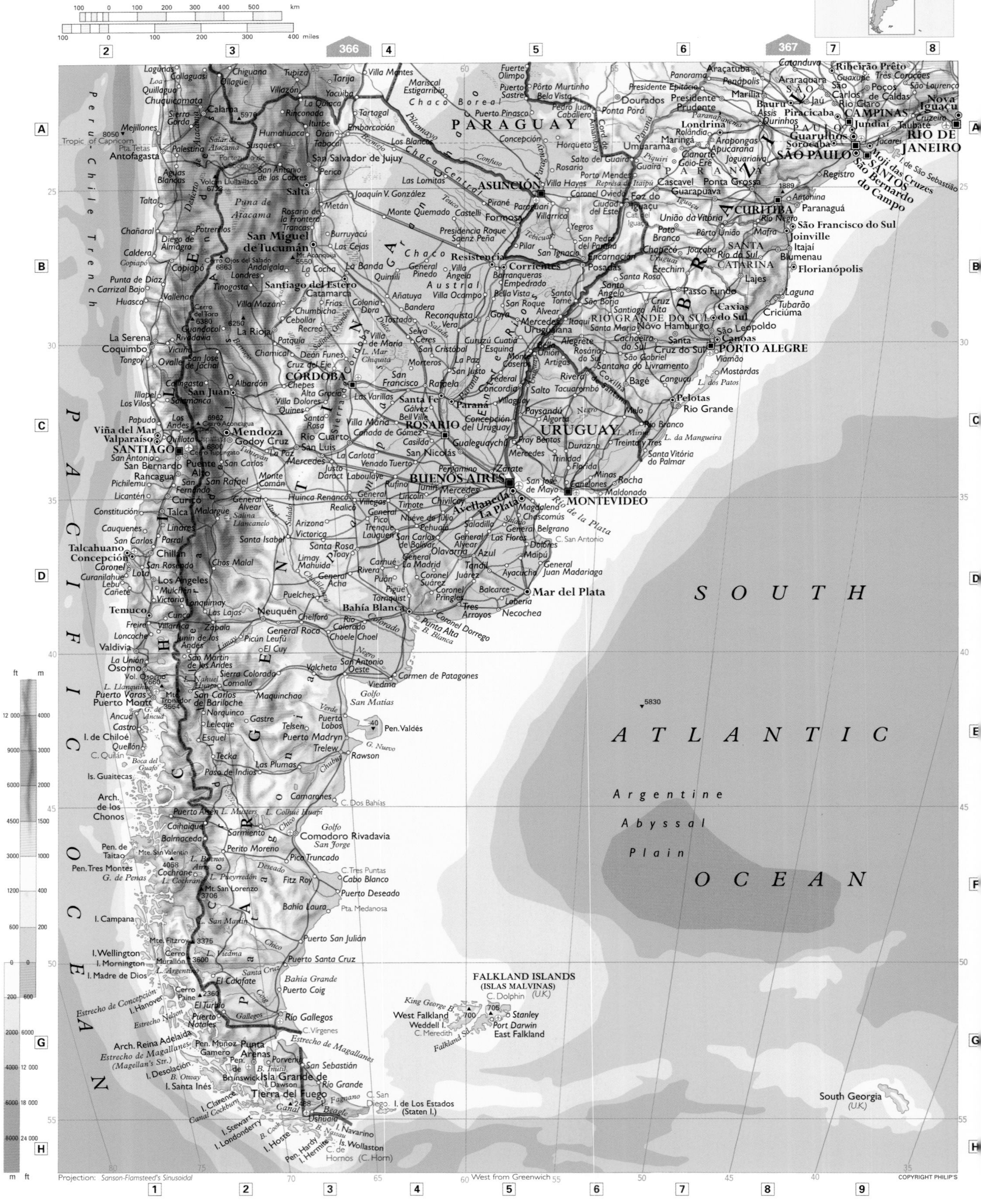
100 0 100 200 300 400 500 km
100 0 100 200 300 400 miles
366
367
2 3 4 5 6 7 8
A B C D E F G H
Peru-Chile Trench
Tropic of Capricorn
PARAGUAY
URUGUAY
BRAZIL
ARGENTINA
CHILE
PACIFIC OCEAN
SOUTH ATLANTIC OCEAN
Argentine Abyssal Plain
5830
Chaco Boreal
Chaco Central
Chaco Austral
Gran Chaco
Puna de Atacama
Desierto de Atacama
Pampas
Patagonia
Sierras de Córdoba
Cordillera de los Andes
Lagunas
Collaguasi
Quillagua
Chuquicamata
Sierra Gorda
Calama
Mejillones
Antofagasta
Pta. Tetas
Palestina
Salar de Atacama
Aguas Blancas
Volcán Llullaillaco 6723
Taltal
Chañaral
Diego de Almagro
Potrerillos
Caldera
Copiapó
Cerro Ojos del Salado 6863
Punta de Díaz
Carrizal Bajo
Huasco
Vallenar
Cerro del Toro 6380
La Serena
Coquimbo
Tongoy
Ovalle
Vicuña
Illapel
Los Vilos
Papudo
Los Andes
Cerro Aconcagua 6962
Viña del Mar
Valparaíso
Quillota
SANTIAGO
San Antonio
San Bernardo
Rancagua
Pichilemu
Licantén
Curicó
Constitución
Talca
Cauquenes
Linares
San Carlos
Parral
Talcahuano
Concepción
Chillán
Coronel
Lota
San Rosendo
Curanilahue
Lebu
Cañete
Los Ángeles
Mulchén
Victoria
Temuco
Freire
Villarrica
Loncoche
Valdivia
La Unión
Osorno
Vol. Osorno 2660
L. Llanquihue
Puerto Varas
Puerto Montt
Mte. Tronador 3554
Ancud
Castro
I. de Chiloé
Quellón
C. Quilán
Boca del Guafo
Is. Guaitecas
Arch. de los Chonos
Puerto Aisén
L. Musters
L. Colhué Huapi
Coihaique
Balmaceda
Pen. de Taitao
Mte. San Valentín 4058
L. Buenos Aires
Pen. Tres Montes
G. de Penas
Cochrane
L. Cochrane
L. Pueyrredón
Mt. San Lorenzo 3706
I. Campana
L. San Martín
Mte. Fitzroy 3375
I. Wellington
I. Mornington
I. Madre de Dios
Cerro Murallón 3600
L. Viedma
L. Argentino
El Calafate
Cerro Paine 2360
El Turbio
Estrecho de Concepción
I. Hanover
Estrecho Nelson
Puerto Natales
Arch. Reina Adelaida
Estrecho de Magallanes (Magellan's Str.)
I. Desolación
B. Otway
I. Santa Inés
Pen. Muñoz Gamero
Punta Arenas
Pen. de Brunswick
Porvenir
B. Inútil
I. Dawson
Isla Grande de Tierra del Fuego
Canal Beagle
Ushuaia
2488
I. Clarence
Canal Cockburn
I. Stewart
I. Londonderry
I. Hoste
I. Navarino
Is. Wollaston
Pen. Hardy
I. Hermite
C. de Hornos (C. Horn)
Chiguana
Ollagüe
Tupiza
Tarija
Villa Montes
Villazón
La Quiaca
Yacuiba
Rinconada
Iturbe
Tartagal
Humahuaca
Orán
Embarcación
Tabacal
Susques
San Salvador de Jujuy
San Antonio de los Cobres
Perico
Salta
Las Lomitas
Joaquín V. González
Metán
Monte Quemado
Rosario de la Frontera
Trancas
San Miguel de Tucumán
Burruyacú
Las Cejas
Mt. Aconquija 5550
Andalgalá
La Cocha
La Banda
Londres
Tinogasta
Santiago del Estero
Quimili
Catamarca
Villa Mazán
Frías
Chumbicha
Colonia Dora
Añatuya
Cebollar
Recreo
Tostado
La Rioja
6250
Guandacol
Patquia
Chamical
Dean Funes
Cruz del Eje
Chepes
San José de Jáchal
Calingasta
San Juan
Albardón
Córdoba
Alta Gracia
Villa Dolores
Quines
Las Varillas
Villa María
Santa Rosa
Río Cuarto
San Luis
Mendoza
Godoy Cruz
Cerro Tupungato
Puente Alto
San Carlos
San Rafael
Mercedes
Justo Daract
La Carlota
Venado Tuerto
La Paz
Monte Comán
General Alvear
Salina Llancanelo
Malargüe
Santa Isabel
Arizona
Victorica
Chos Malal
Santa Rosa
Toay
Limay Mahuida
General Acha
Puelches
Neuquén
Las Lajas
Zapala
Junín de los Andes
San Martín de los Andes
Picún Leufú
El Cuy
Chelforó
General Roca
Choele Choel
Río Colorado
Bahía Blanca
Punta Alta
B. Blanca
Coronel Dorrego
San Carlos de Bariloche
L. Nahuel Huapi
Sierra Colorada
Comallo
Valcheta
San Antonio Oeste
Golfo San Matías
Carmen de Patagones
Viedma
Maquinchao
Norquinco
Gastre
Leleque
Esquel
Telsen
Puerto Lobos
Puerto Madryn
Pen. Valdés
G. Nuevo
Trelew
Rawson
Tecka
Las Plumas
Paso de Indios
Camarones
C. Dos Bahías
Sarmiento
Golfo San Jorge
Comodoro Rivadavia
Perito Moreno
Pico Truncado
Fitz Roy
C. Tres Puntas
Cabo Blanco
Puerto Deseado
Bahía Laura
Pta. Medanosa
Puerto San Julián
Puerto Santa Cruz
Bahía Grande
Puerto Coig
Río Gallegos
C. Vírgenes
San Sebastián
Río Grande
C. San Diego
I. de Los Estados (Staten I.)
FALKLAND ISLANDS (ISLAS MALVINAS) (U.K.)
C. Dolphin
King George B.
West Falkland
Weddell I.
C. Meredith
Falkland Sd.
700
705
Stanley
Port Darwin
East Falkland
South Georgia (U.K.)
Fuerte Olimpo
Puerto Sastre
Pôrto Murtinho
Bela Vista
Mariscal Estigarribia
Puerto Pinasco
Pedro Juan Caballero
Concepción
Horqueta
Rosario
ASUNCIÓN
Villa Hayes
Pirané
Paraguarí
Formosa
Villarrica
Castelli
Presidencia Roque Sáenz Peña
Resistencia
Corrientes
Pilar
San Ignacio
Encarnación
Posadas
General Pinedo
Villa Ángela
Barranqueras
Empedrado
Bella Vista
Santo Tomé
San Roque
Villa Ocampo
Reconquista
Goya
Alvear
Mercedes
Uruguaiana
Vera
Curuzú Cuatiá
Esquina
Ceres
San Cristóbal
Morteros
La Paz
San Justo
San Francisco
Rafaela
Federal
Concordia
Paraná
Santa Fe
Gálvez
Bell Ville
ROSARIO
Cañada de Gómez
Casilda
San Nicolás
Concepción del Uruguay
Gualeguaychú
Pergamino
Zárate
BUENOS AIRES
Junín
Chivilcoy
Rufino
Laboulaye
Huinca Renancó
General Villegas
Lincoln
Timote
Realicó
General Pico
Trenque Lauquen
Nueve de Julio
Pehuajó
Saladillo
Avellaneda
La Plata
Magdalena
Chascomús
Carlos Tejedor
San Carlos de Bolívar
General Alvear
Las Flores
General Belgrano
Dolores
Olavarría
Azul
Maipú
Tandil
General Juan Madariaga
Ayacucho
Coronel Suárez
Juárez
Balcarce
Mar del Plata
Lobería
Necochea
Tres Arroyos
Coronel Pringles
Tornquist
Pigüé
Carhué
Rivera
Puán
C. San Antonio
Río de la Plata
San José de Mayo
Canelones
MONTEVIDEO
Maldonado
Rocha
Florida
Minas
Trinidad
Durazno
Mercedes
Fray Bentos
Paysandú
Salto
Artigas
Rivera
Tacuarembó
Melo
Treinta y Tres
L. Mirim
L. da Mangueira
Santa Vitória do Palmar
Rio Branco
Bagé
Dom Pedrito
Rosário do Sul
Alegrete
Itaqui
São Borja
Santiago
Santo Ângelo
Cruz Alta
Santa Maria
Cachoeira do Sul
São Gabriel
Santana do Livramento
RIO GRANDE DO SUL
Santa Cruz do Sul
PÔRTO ALEGRE
Canoas
São Leopoldo
Nôvo Hamburgo
Caxias do Sul
Passo Fundo
Erechim
Santa Rosa
Chapecó
Joaçaba
Lajes
Viamão
Mostardas
L. dos Patos
Camaquã
Pelotas
Rio Grande
Laguna
Tubarão
Criciúma
Florianópolis
SANTA CATARINA
Blumenau
Itajaí
Joinville
São Francisco do Sul
Mafra
Rio Negro
Pôrto União
União da Vitória
Pato Branco
Rio do Sul
CURITIBA
Paranaguá
Antonina
1889
Registro
PARANÁ
Guarapuava
Cascavel
Ponta Grossa
Foz do Iguaçu
Cataratas do Iguaçu
Guaíra
Umuarama
Maringá
Cianorte
Apucarana
Arapongas
Londrina
Rolândia
Goio-Erê
Piquiri
Jaguariaíva
Represa de Itaipú
Ciudad del Este
Coronel Oviedo
Yegros
San Pedro del Paraná
Salto del Guairá
Porto Mendes
Dourados
Ponta Porã
Presidente Epitácio
Presidente Prudente
Panorama
Araçatuba
Penápolis
Marília
Bauru
Assis
Ourinhos
Jaú
São Carlos
Araraquara
Catanduva
Ribeirão Prêto
Guaxupé
Três Corações
Poços de Caldas
São Lourenço
Rio Claro
Piracicaba
CAMPINAS
Jundiaí
Sorocaba
Guarulhos
SÃO PAULO
Taubaté
Jacareí
Cruzeiro
Nova Iguaçu
RIO DE JANEIRO
Moji das Cruzes
SANTOS
São Bernardo do Campo
I. de São Sebastião
SÃO PAULO
Pilcomayo
Bermejo
Paraná
Paraguay
Uruguay
Iguaçu
Salado
Dulce
Colorado
Negro
Chubut
Chico
Deseado
Santa Cruz
Gallegos
Limay
Tebicuary
Confuso
Teuco
Jacuí
Coxilha de Santana
Projection: Sanson-Flamsteed's Sinusoidal
West from Greenwich
COPYRIGHT PHILIP'S
25 30 35 40 45 50 55
80 75 70 65 60 55 50 45 40 35
1 2 3 4 5 6 7 8 9
ft m
12 000 4000
9000 3000
6000 2000
4500 1500
3000 1000
1200 400
600 200
0 0
200 600
2000 6000
4000 12 000
6000 18 000
8000 24 000
m ft

INDEX TO WORLD MAPS

The index contains the names of all the principal places and features shown on the World Maps. Each name is followed by an additional entry in italics giving the country or region within which it is located. The alphabetical order of names composed of two or more words is governed primarily by the first word, then by the second, and then by the country or region name that follows. This is an example of the rule:

Mīr Kūh *Iran*	26°22N 58°55E	**317** E8
Mīr Shahdād *Iran*	26°15N 58°29E	**317** E8
Mira *Italy*	45°26N 12°8E	**294** B5
Mira por vos Cay *Bahamas*	22°9N 74°30W	**361** B5

Physical features composed of a proper name (Erie) and a description (Lake) are positioned alphabetically by the proper name. The description is positioned after the proper name and is usually abbreviated:

Erie, L. *N. Amer.*	42°15N 81°0W	**354** D4

Where a description forms part of a settlement or administrative name, however, it is always written in full and put in its true alphabetical position:

Mount Morris *U.S.A.*	42°44N 77°52W	**354** D7

Names beginning with M' and Mc are indexed as if they were spelled Mac. Names beginning St. are alphabetized under Saint, but Sankt, Sint, Sant', Santa and San are all spelt in full and are alphabetized accordingly. If the same place name occurs two or more times in the index and all are in the same country, each is followed by the name of the administrative subdivision in which it is located.

The geographical co-ordinates which follow each name in the index give the latitude and longitude of each place. The first co-ordinate indicates latitude – the distance north or south of the Equator. The second co-ordinate indicates longitude – the distance east or west of the Greenwich Meridian. Both latitude and longitude are measured in degrees and minutes (there are 60 minutes in a degree).

The latitude is followed by N(orth) or S(outh) and the longitude by E(ast) or W(est).

The number in bold type which follows the geographical co-ordinates refers to the number of the map page where that feature or place will be found. This is usually the largest scale at which the place or feature appears.

The letter and figure that are immediately after the page number give the grid square on the map page, within which the feature is situated. The letter represents the latitude and the figure the longitude. A lower-case letter immediately after the page number refers to an inset map on that page.

In some cases the feature itself may fall within the specified square, while the name is outside. This is usually the case only with features that are larger than a grid square.

Rivers are indexed to their mouths or confluences, and carry the symbol ➤ after their names. The following symbols are also used in the index: ■ country, ☑ overseas territory or dependency, ☐ first-order administrative area, △ national park, ⌂ other park (provincial park, nature reserve or game reserve), ✈ (LHR) principal airport (and location identifier).

Abbreviations used in the index

A.C.T. – Australian Capital Territory
A.R. – Autonomous Region
Afghan. – Afghanistan
Afr. – Africa
Ala. – Alabama
Alta. – Alberta
Amer. – America(n)
Ant. – Antilles
Arch. – Archipelago
Ariz. – Arizona
Ark. – Arkansas
Atl. Oc. – Atlantic Ocean
B. – Baie, Bahía, Bay, Bucht, Bugt
B.C. – British Columbia
Bangla. – Bangladesh
Barr. – Barrage
Bos.-H. – Bosnia-Herzegovina
C. – Cabo, Cap, Cape, Coast
C.A.R. – Central African Republic
C. Prov. – Cape Province
Calif. – California
Cat. – Catarata
Cent. – Central
Chan. – Channel
Colo. – Colorado
Conn. – Connecticut
Cord. – Cordillera
Cr. – Creek
Czech. – Czech Republic
D.C. – District of Columbia
Del. – Delaware
Dem. – Democratic
Dep. – Dependency
Des. – Desert
Dét. – Détroit
Dist. – District
Dj. – Djebel
Dom. Rep. – Dominican Republic

E. – East
El Salv. – El Salvador
Eq. Guin. – Equatorial Guinea
Est. – Estrecho
Falk. Is. – Falkland Is.
Fd. – Fjord
Fla. – Florida
Fr. – French
G. – Golfe, Golfo, Gulf, Guba, Gebel
Ga. – Georgia
Gt. – Great, Greater
Guinea-Biss. – Guinea-Bissau
H.K. – Hong Kong
H.P. – Himachal Pradesh
Hants. – Hampshire
Harb. – Harbor, Harbour
Hd. – Head
Hts. – Heights
I.(s). – Île, Ilha, Insel, Isla, Island, Isle
Ill. – Illinois
Ind. – Indiana
Ind. Oc. – Indian Ocean
Ivory C. – Ivory Coast
J. – Jabal, Jebel
Jaz. – Jazīrah
Junc. – Junction
K. – Kap, Kapp
Kans. – Kansas
Kep. – Kepulauan
Ky. – Kentucky
L. – Lac, Lacul, Lago, Lagoa, Lake, Limni, Loch, Lough
La. – Louisiana
Ld. – Land
Liech. – Liechtenstein
Lux. – Luxembourg
Mad. P. – Madhya Pradesh
Madag. – Madagascar
Man. – Manitoba
Mass. – Massachusetts

Md. – Maryland
Me. – Maine
Medit. S. – Mediterranean Sea
Mich. – Michigan
Minn. – Minnesota
Miss. – Mississippi
Mo. – Missouri
Mont. – Montana
Mozam. – Mozambique
Mt.(s) – Mont, Montaña, Mountain
Mte. – Monte
Mti. – Monti
N. – Nord, Norte, North, Northern, Nouveau, Nahal, Nahr
N.B. – New Brunswick
N.C. – North Carolina
N. Cal. – New Caledonia
N. Dak. – North Dakota
N.H. – New Hampshire
N.I. – North Island
N.J. – New Jersey
N. Mex. – New Mexico
N.S. – Nova Scotia
N.S.W. – New South Wales
N.W.T. – North West Territory
N.Y. – New York
N.Z. – New Zealand
Nac. – Nacional
Nat. – National
Nebr. – Nebraska
Neths. – Netherlands
Nev. – Nevada
Nfld & L. – Newfoundland and Labrador
Nic. – Nicaragua
O. – Oued, Ouadi
Occ. – Occidentale
Okla. – Oklahoma
Ont. – Ontario
Or. – Orientale

Oreg. – Oregon
Os. – Ostrov
Oz. – Ozero
P. – Pass, Passo, Pasul, Pulau
P.E.I. – Prince Edward Island
Pa. – Pennsylvania
Pac. Oc. – Pacific Ocean
Papua N.G. – Papua New Guinea
Pass. – Passage
Peg. – Pegunungan
Pen. – Peninsula, Péninsule
Phil. – Philippines
Pk. – Peak
Plat. – Plateau
Prov. – Province, Provincial
Pt. – Point
Pta. – Ponta, Punta
Pte. – Pointe
Qué. – Québec
Queens. – Queensland
R. – Rio, River
R.I. – Rhode Island
Ra. – Range
Raj. – Rajasthan
Recr. – Recreational, Récréatif
Reg. – Region
Rep. – Republic
Res. – Reserve, Reservoir
Rhld-Pfz. – Rheinland-Pfalz
S. – South, Southern, Sur
Si. Arabia – Saudi Arabia
S.C. – South Carolina
S. Dak. – South Dakota
S.I. – South Island
S. Leone – Sierra Leone
Sa. – Serra, Sierra
Sask. – Saskatchewan
Scot. – Scotland
Sd. – Sound
Sev. – Severnaya
Sib. – Siberia

Sprs. – Springs
St. – Saint
Sta. – Santa
Ste. – Sainte
Sto. – Santo
Str. – Strait, Stretto
Switz. – Switzerland
Tas. – Tasmania
Tenn. – Tennessee
Terr. – Territory, Territoire
Tex. – Texas
Tg. – Tanjung
Trin. & Tob. – Trinidad & Tobago
U.A.E. – United Arab Emirates
U.K. – United Kingdom
U.S.A. – United States of America
Ut. P. – Uttar Pradesh
Va. – Virginia
Vdkhr. – Vodokhranilishche
Vdskh. – Vodoskhovyshche
Vf. – Vîrful
Vic. – Victoria
Vol. – Volcano
Vt. – Vermont
W. – Wadi, West
W. Va. – West Virginia
Wall. & F. Is. – Wallis and Futuna Is.
Wash. – Washington
Wis. – Wisconsin
Wlkp. – Wielkopolski
Wyo. – Wyoming
Yorks. – Yorkshire

A

A Coruña Spain 43°20N 8°25W 293 A1
A Estrada Spain 42°43N 8°27W 293 A1
A Fonsagrada Spain 43°8N 7°4W 293 A2
Aabenraa Denmark 55°3N 9°25E 281 J13
Aachen Germany 50°45N 6°6E 288 C4
Aalborg Denmark 57°2N 9°54E 281 H13
Aalen Germany 48°51N 10°6E 288 D6
Aalst Belgium 50°56N 4°2E 287 D4
Aalten Neths. 51°56N 6°35E 287 C6
Aalter Belgium 51°5N 3°28E 287 C3
Äänekoski Finland 62°36N 25°44E 280 E21
Aarau Switz. 47°23N 8°4E 292 C8
Aare → Switz. 47°33N 8°14E 292 C8
Aarhus = Århus Denmark 56°8N 10°11E 281 H14
Aarschot Belgium 50°59N 4°49E 287 D4
Aba Dem. Rep. of the Congo 3°58N 30°17E 326 B3
Aba Nigeria 5°10N 7°19E 322 G7
Abaco I. Bahamas 26°25N 77°10W 360 A4
Ābādān Iran 30°22N 48°20E 317 D6
Ābādeh Iran 31°8N 52°40E 317 D7
Abadla Algeria 31°2N 2°45W 322 B5
Abaetetuba Brazil 1°40S 48°50W 365 D9
Abagnar Qi China 43°52N 116°2E 306 C9
Abah, Tanjung Indonesia 8°46S 115°38E 309 K18
Abai Paraguay 25°58S 55°54W 367 B4
Abakan Russia 53°40N 91°10E 301 D10
Abancay Peru 13°35S 72°55W 364 F4
Abariringa Kiribati 2°50S 171°40W 336 H10
Abarqū Iran 31°10N 53°20E 317 D7
Abashiri Japan 44°0N 144°15E 302 B12
Abashiri-Wan Japan 44°0N 144°30E 302 C12
Ābay = Nîl el Azraq → Sudan 15°38N 32°31E 323 E12
Abay Kazakhstan 49°38N 72°53E 300 E8
Abaya, L. Ethiopia 6°30N 37°50E 319 F2
Abaza Russia 52°39N 90°6E 300 D9
'Abbāsābād Iran 33°34N 58°23E 317 C8
Abbay = Nîl el Azraq → Sudan 15°38N 32°31E 323 E12
Abbaye, Pt. U.S.A. 46°58N 88°8W 352 B9
Abbé, L. Ethiopia 11°8N 41°47E 319 E3
Abbeville France 50°6N 1°49E 292 A4
Abbeville Ala., U.S.A. 31°34N 85°15W 357 F12
Abbeville La., U.S.A. 29°58N 92°8W 356 G8
Abbeville S.C., U.S.A. 34°11N 82°23W 357 D13
Abbeyfeale Ireland 52°23N 9°18W 282 D2
Abbot Ice Shelf Antarctica 73°0S 92°0W 277 D16
Abbotsford Canada 49°5N 122°20W 342 D4
Abbottabad Pakistan 34°10N 73°15E 314 B5
ABC Islands = Netherlands Antilles ☒ W. Indies 12°15N 69°0W 364 A5
Abd al Kūrī Yemen 12°5N 52°20E 319 E5
Ābdar Iran 30°16N 55°19E 317 D7
'Abdolābād Iran 34°12N 56°30E 317 C8
Abdulpur Bangla. 24°15N 88°59E 315 G13
Abéché Chad 13°50N 20°35E 323 F10
Abel Tasman △ N.Z. 40°59S 173°3E 331 D4
Abengourou Ivory C. 6°42N 3°27W 322 G5
Åbenrå = Aabenraa Denmark 55°3N 9°25E 281 J13
Abeokuta Nigeria 7°3N 3°19E 322 G6
Aber Uganda 2°12N 32°25E 326 B3
Aberaeron U.K. 52°15N 4°15W 285 E3
Aberayron = Aberaeron U.K. 52°15N 4°15W 285 E3
Aberchirder U.K. 57°34N 2°37W 283 D6
Abercorn Australia 25°12S 151°5E 335 D5
Aberdare U.K. 51°43N 3°27W 285 F4
Aberdare △ Kenya 0°22S 36°44E 326 C4
Aberdare Ra. Kenya 0°15S 36°50E 326 C4
Aberdeen Australia 32°9S 150°56E 335 E5
Aberdeen Canada 52°20N 106°8W 343 C7
Aberdeen China 22°14N 114°8E 305 G11
Aberdeen S. Africa 32°28S 24°2E 328 E3
Aberdeen U.K. 57°9N 2°5W 283 D6
Aberdeen Ala., U.S.A. 33°49N 88°33W 357 E10
Aberdeen Idaho, U.S.A. 42°57N 112°50W 348 E7
Aberdeen Md., U.S.A. 39°31N 76°10W 353 F15
Aberdeen S. Dak., U.S.A. 45°28N 98°29W 352 C4
Aberdeen Wash., U.S.A. 46°59N 123°50W 350 D3
Aberdeen, City of ☐ U.K. 57°10N 2°10W 283 D6
Aberdeenshire ☐ U.K. 57°17N 2°36W 283 D6
Aberdovey = Aberdyfi U.K. 52°33N 4°3W 285 E3
Aberdyfi U.K. 52°33N 4°3W 285 E3
Aberfeldy U.K. 56°37N 3°51W 283 E5
Aberfoyle U.K. 56°11N 4°23W 283 E4
Abergavenny U.K. 51°49N 3°1W 285 F4
Abergele U.K. 53°17N 3°35W 284 D4
Abernathy U.S.A. 33°50N 101°51W 356 E4
Abert, L. U.S.A. 42°38N 120°14W 348 E3
Aberystwyth U.K. 52°25N 4°5W 285 E3
Abhā Si. Arabia 18°0N 42°34E 319 D3
Abhar Iran 36°9N 49°13E 317 B6
Abhayapuri India 26°24N 90°38E 315 F14
Abidjan Ivory C. 5°26N 3°58W 322 G5
Abilene Kans., U.S.A. 38°55N 97°13W 352 F5
Abilene Tex., U.S.A. 32°28N 99°43W 356 E5
Abingdon U.K. 51°40N 1°17W 285 F6
Abingdon U.S.A. 36°43N 81°59W 353 G13
Abington Reef Australia 18°0S 149°35E 334 B4
Abitau → Canada 59°53N 109°3W 343 B7
Abitibi → Canada 51°3N 80°55W 344 B3
Abitibi, L. Canada 48°40N 79°40W 344 C4
Abkhaz Republic = Abkhazia ☐ Georgia 43°12N 41°5E 291 F7
Abkhazia ☐ Georgia 43°12N 41°5E 291 F7
Abminga Australia 26°8S 134°51E 335 D1
Åbo = Turku Finland 60°30N 22°19E 281 F20
Abohar India 30°10N 74°10E 314 D6
Abomey Benin 7°10N 2°5E 322 G6
Abong-Mbang Cameroon 4°0N 13°8E 324 D2
Abou-Deïa Chad 11°20N 19°20E 323 F9
Aboyne U.K. 57°4N 2°47W 283 D6
Abra Pampa Argentina 22°43S 65°42W 366 A2
Abraham L. Canada 52°15N 116°35W 342 C5
Abreojos, Pta. Mexico 26°50N 113°40W 358 B2
Abrolhos, Banco Brazil 18°0S 38°0W 365 F11
Abrud Romania 46°19N 23°5E 289 E12
Absaroka Range U.S.A. 44°45N 109°50W 348 D9
Abu India 24°41N 72°50E 314 G5
Abū al Abyad U.A.E. 24°11N 53°50E 317 E7
Abū al Khaṣīb Iraq 30°25N 48°0E 317 D6
Abū 'Alī Si. Arabia 27°20N 49°27E 317 E6
Abū 'Alī → Lebanon 34°25N 35°50E 318 A4
Abu Dhabi = Abū Ẓāby U.A.E. 24°28N 54°22E 317 E7
Abū Du'ān Syria 36°25N 38°15E 316 B3
Abu el Gaīn, W. → Egypt 29°35N 33°30E 318 F2
Abu Ga'da, W. → Egypt 29°15N 32°53E 318 F1
Abū Ḥadrīyah Si. Arabia 27°20N 48°58E 317 E6
Abu Hamed Sudan 19°32N 33°13E 323 E12
Abū Kamāl Syria 34°30N 41°0E 316 C4
Abū Madd, Ra's Si. Arabia 24°50N 37°7E 316 E3
Abū Mūsā U.A.E. 25°52N 55°3E 317 E7
Abū Qaṣr Si. Arabia 30°21N 38°34E 316 D3
Abu Shagara, Ras Sudan 21°4N 37°19E 323 D13
Abu Simbel Egypt 22°18N 31°40E 323 D12
Abū Ṣukhayr Iraq 31°54N 44°30E 316 D5
Abu Zabad Sudan 12°25N 29°10E 323 F11
Abū Ẓāby U.A.E. 24°28N 54°22E 317 E7
Abū Zeydābād Iran 33°54N 51°45E 317 C6
Abuja Nigeria 9°5N 7°32E 322 G7
Abukuma-Gawa → Japan 38°6N 140°52E 302 E10
Abukuma-Sammyaku Japan 37°30N 140°45E 302 F10
Abunã Brazil 9°40S 65°20W 364 E5
Abunã → Brazil 9°41S 65°20W 364 E5
Aburo Dem. Rep. of the Congo 2°4N 30°53E 326 B3
Abut Hd. N.Z. 43°7S 170°15E 331 E3
Acadia △ U.S.A. 44°20N 68°13W 353 C19
Açailândia Brazil 4°57S 47°0W 365 D9
Acajutla El Salv. 13°36N 89°50W 360 D2
Acámbaro Mexico 20°2N 100°44W 358 D4
Acaponeta Mexico 22°30N 105°22W 358 C3
Acapulco Mexico 16°51N 99°55W 359 D5
Acarai, Serra Brazil 1°50N 57°50W 364 C7
Acarigua Venezuela 9°33N 69°12W 364 B5
Acatlán Mexico 18°12N 98°3W 359 D5
Acayucán Mexico 17°57N 94°55W 359 D6
Accomac U.S.A. 37°43N 75°40W 353 G16
Accra Ghana 5°35N 0°6W 322 G5
Accrington U.K. 53°45N 2°22W 284 D5
Acebal Argentina 33°20S 60°50W 366 C3
Aceh ☐ Indonesia 4°15N 97°30E 308 D1
Achalpur India 21°22N 77°32E 312 J10
Acharnes Greece 38°5N 23°44E 295 E10
Acheloos → Greece 38°19N 21°7E 295 E9
Acheng China 45°30N 126°58E 307 B14
Acher India 23°10N 72°32E 314 H5
Achill Hd. Ireland 53°58N 10°15W 282 C1
Achill I. Ireland 53°58N 10°1W 282 C1
Achinsk Russia 56°20N 90°20E 301 D10
Acireale Italy 37°37N 15°10E 294 F6
Ackerman U.S.A. 33°19N 89°11W 357 E10
Acklins I. Bahamas 22°30N 74°0W 361 B5
Acme Canada 51°33N 113°30W 342 C6
Acme U.S.A. 40°8N 79°26W 354 F5
Aconcagua, Cerro Argentina 32°39S 70°0W 366 C2
Aconquija, Mt. Argentina 27°0S 66°0W 366 B2
Açores, Is. dos Atl. Oc. 38°0N 27°0W 322 a
Acornhoek S. Africa 24°37S 31°2E 329 C5
Acraman, L. Australia 32°2S 135°23E 335 E2
Acre = 'Akko Israel 32°55N 35°4E 318 C4
Acre ☐ Brazil 9°1S 71°0W 364 E4
Acre → Brazil 8°45S 67°22W 364 E5
Acton Canada 43°38N 80°3W 354 C4
Ad Dammām Si. Arabia 26°20N 50°5E 317 E6
Ad Dāmūr Lebanon 33°43N 35°27E 318 B4
Ad Dawādimī Si. Arabia 24°35N 44°15E 316 E5
Ad Dawḥah Qatar 25°15N 51°35E 317 E6
Ad Dawr Iraq 34°27N 43°47E 316 C4
Ad Dir'īyah Si. Arabia 24°44N 46°35E 316 E5
Ad Dīwānīyah Iraq 32°0N 45°0E 316 D5
Ad Dujayl Iraq 33°51N 44°14E 316 C5
Ad Duwayd Si. Arabia 30°15N 42°17E 316 D4
Ada Minn., U.S.A. 47°18N 96°31W 352 B5
Ada Okla., U.S.A. 34°46N 96°41W 356 D6
Adabiya Egypt 29°53N 32°28E 318 F1
Adair, C. Canada 71°30N 71°34W 341 B12
Adaja → Spain 41°32N 4°52W 293 B3
Adak I. U.S.A. 51°45N 176°45W 346 a
Adamaoua, Massif de l' Cameroon 7°20N 12°20E 323 G8
Adamawa Highlands = Adamaoua, Massif de l' Cameroon 7°20N 12°20E 323 G8
Adamello, Mte. Italy 46°9N 10°30E 292 C9
Adaminaby Australia 36°0S 148°45E 335 F4
Adams Mass., U.S.A. 42°38N 73°7W 355 D11
Adams N.Y., U.S.A. 43°49N 76°1W 355 C8
Adams Wis., U.S.A. 43°57N 89°49W 352 D9
Adams, Mt. U.S.A. 46°12N 121°30W 350 D5
Adam's Bridge Sri Lanka 9°15N 79°40E 312 Q11
Adams L. Canada 51°10N 119°40W 342 C5
Adam's Peak Sri Lanka 6°48N 80°30E 312 R12
Adana Turkey 37°0N 35°16E 316 B2
Adapazarı = Sakarya Turkey 40°48N 30°25E 291 F5
Adarama Sudan 17°10N 34°52E 323 E12
Adare, C. Antarctica 71°0S 171°0E 277 D11
Adaut Indonesia 8°8S 131°7E 309 F8
Adavale Australia 25°52S 144°32E 335 D3
Adda → Italy 45°8N 9°53E 292 D8
Addis Ababa = Addis Abeba Ethiopia 9°2N 38°42E 319 F2
Addis Abeba Ethiopia 9°2N 38°42E 319 F2
Addison U.S.A. 42°1N 77°14W 354 D7
Addo S. Africa 33°32S 25°45E 328 E4
Addo △ S. Africa 33°30S 25°50E 328 E4
Ādeh Iran 37°42N 45°11E 316 B5
Adel U.S.A. 31°8N 83°25W 357 F13
Adelaide Australia 34°52S 138°30E 335 E2
Adelaide S. Africa 32°42S 26°20E 328 E4
Adelaide I. Antarctica 67°15S 68°30W 277 C17
Adelaide Pen. Canada 68°15N 97°30W 340 C10
Adelaide River Australia 13°15S 131°7E 332 B5
Adelaide Village Bahamas 25°0N 77°31W 360 A4
Adelanto U.S.A. 34°35N 117°22W 351 L9
Adele I. Australia 15°32S 123°9E 332 C3
Adélie, Terre Antarctica 68°0S 140°0E 277 C10
Adelie Land = Adélie, Terre Antarctica 68°0S 140°0E 277 C10
Aden = Al 'Adan Yemen 12°45N 45°0E 319 E4
Aden, G. of Asia 12°30N 47°30E 319 E4
Adendorp S. Africa 32°15S 24°30E 328 E3
Adh Dhayd U.A.E. 25°17N 55°53E 317 E7
Adhoi India 23°26N 70°32E 314 H4
Adi Indonesia 4°15S 133°30E 309 E8
Adieu, C. Australia 32°0S 132°10E 333 F5
Adieu Pt. Australia 15°14S 124°35E 332 C3
Adige → Italy 45°9N 12°20E 294 B5
Adigrat Ethiopia 14°20N 39°26E 319 E2
Adilabad India 19°33N 78°20E 312 K11
Adirondack ⌂ U.S.A. 44°0N 74°20W 355 C10
Adirondack Mts. U.S.A. 44°0N 74°0W 355 C10
Adis Abeba = Addis Abeba Ethiopia 9°2N 38°42E 319 F2
Adjumani Uganda 3°20N 31°50E 326 B3
Adjuntas Puerto Rico 18°10N 66°43W 361 d
Adlavik Is. Canada 55°0N 58°40W 345 B8
Admiralty G. Australia 14°20S 125°55E 332 B4
Admiralty I. U.S.A. 57°30N 134°30W 342 B2
Admiralty Is. Papua N. G. 2°0S 147°0E 330 B7
Adolfo Ruiz Cortines, Presa Mexico 27°15N 109°6W 358 B3
Adonara Indonesia 8°15S 123°5E 309 F6
Adoni India 15°33N 77°18E 312 M10
Adour → France 43°32N 1°32W 292 E3
Adra India 23°30N 86°42E 315 H12
Adra Spain 36°43N 3°3W 293 D4
Adrano Italy 37°40N 14°50E 294 F6
Adrar Algeria 27°51N 0°11E 322 C6
Adrar Mauritania 20°30N 7°30W 322 D3
Adrar des Iforas Africa 19°40N 1°40E 322 E6
Adrian Mich., U.S.A. 41°54N 84°2W 353 E11
Adrian Tex., U.S.A. 35°16N 102°40W 356 D3
Adriatic Sea Medit. S. 43°0N 16°0E 294 C6
Adua Indonesia 1°45S 129°50E 309 E7
Adwa Ethiopia 14°15N 38°52E 319 E2
Adygea ☐ Russia 45°0N 40°0E 291 F7
Adzhar Republic = Ajaria ☐ Georgia 41°30N 42°0E 291 F7
Adzopé Ivory C. 6°7N 3°49W 322 G5
Ægean Sea Medit. S. 38°30N 25°0E 295 E11
Aerhtai Shan Mongolia 46°40N 92°45E 304 B4
Afaahiti Tahiti 17°45S 149°17W 331 d
'Afak Iraq 32°4N 45°15E 316 C5
Afandou Greece 36°18N 28°12E 297 C10
Afareaitu Moorea 17°33S 149°47W 331 d
Afghanistan ■ Asia 33°0N 65°0E 312 C4
Aflou Algeria 34°7N 2°3E 322 B6
Africa 10°0N 20°0E 320 E6
'Afrīn Syria 36°32N 36°50E 316 B3
Afton N.Y., U.S.A. 42°14N 75°32W 355 D9
Afton Wyo., U.S.A. 42°44N 110°56W 348 E8
Afuá Brazil 0°15S 50°20W 365 D8
'Afula Israel 32°37N 35°17E 318 C4
Afyon Turkey 38°45N 30°33E 291 G5
Afyonkarahisar = Afyon Turkey 38°45N 30°33E 291 G5
Agadès = Agadez Niger 16°58N 7°59E 322 E7
Agadez Niger 16°58N 7°59E 322 E7
Agadir Morocco 30°28N 9°55W 322 B4
Agaete Canary Is. 28°6N 15°43W 296 F4
Agalega Is. Mauritius 11°0S 57°0E 275 E12
Agar India 23°40N 76°2E 314 H7
Agartala India 23°50N 91°23E 313 H17
Agassiz Canada 49°14N 121°46W 342 D4
Agats Indonesia 5°33S 138°0E 309 F9
Agawam U.S.A. 42°5N 72°37W 355 D12
Agboville Ivory C. 5°55N 4°15W 322 G5
Ağdam Azerbaijan 40°0N 46°58E 316 B5
Agde France 43°19N 3°28E 292 E5
Agen France 44°12N 0°38E 292 D4
Āgh Kand Iran 37°15N 48°4E 317 B6
Aghia Deka Greece 35°3N 24°58E 297 D6
Aghia Ekaterinis, Akra Greece 39°50N 19°50E 297 A3
Aghia Galini Greece 35°6N 24°41E 297 D6
Aghia Varvara Greece 35°8N 25°1E 297 D7
Aghios Efstratios Greece 39°34N 24°58E 295 E11
Aghios Ioannis, Akra Greece 35°20N 25°40E 297 D7
Aghios Isidoros Greece 36°9N 27°51E 297 C9
Aghios Matheos Greece 39°30N 19°47E 297 B3
Aghios Nikolaos Greece 35°11N 25°41E 297 D7
Aghiou Orous, Kolpos Greece 40°6N 24°0E 295 D11
Aginskoye Russia 51°6N 114°32E 301 D12
Agnew Australia 28°1S 120°31E 333 E3
Agori India 24°33N 82°57E 315 G10
Agra India 27°17N 77°58E 314 F7
Ağri Turkey 39°44N 43°3E 291 G7
Agri → Italy 40°13N 16°44E 294 D7
Ağrı Dağı Turkey 39°50N 44°15E 316 B5
Ağri Karakose = Ağri Turkey 39°44N 43°3E 291 G7
Agrigento Italy 37°19N 13°34E 294 F5
Agrinio Greece 38°37N 21°27E 295 E9
Agua Caliente Mexico 32°29N 116°59W 351 N10
Agua Caliente Springs U.S.A. 32°56N 116°19W 351 N10
Água Clara Brazil 20°25S 52°45W 365 H8
Agua Fria ⌂ U.S.A. 34°14N 112°0W 349 J8
Agua Hechicera Mexico 32°28N 116°15W 351 N10
Agua Prieta Mexico 31°18N 109°34W 358 A3
Aguadilla Puerto Rico 18°26N 67°10W 361 d
Aguadulce Panama 8°15N 80°32W 360 E3
Aguanga U.S.A. 33°27N 116°51W 351 M10
Aguanish Canada 50°14N 62°2W 345 B7
Aguanus → Canada 50°13N 62°5W 345 B7
Aguapey → Argentina 29°7S 56°36W 366 B4
Aguaray Guazú → Paraguay 24°47S 57°19W 366 A4
Aguarico → Ecuador 0°59S 75°11W 364 D3
Aguaro-Guariquito △ Venezuela 8°20N 66°35W 361 E6
Aguas Blancas Chile 24°15S 69°55W 366 A2
Aguas Calientes, Sierra de Argentina 25°26S 66°40W 366 B2
Aguascalientes Mexico 21°53N 102°18W 358 C4
Aguascalientes ☐ Mexico 22°0N 102°20W 358 C4
Aguila, Punta Puerto Rico 17°57N 67°13W 361 d
Aguilares Argentina 27°26S 65°35W 366 B2
Aguilas Spain 37°23N 1°35W 293 D5
Agüimes Canary Is. 27°58N 15°27W 296 G4
Aguja, C. de la Colombia 11°18N 74°12W 362 B3
Agujereada, Pta. Puerto Rico 18°30N 67°8W 361 d
Agulhas, C. S. Africa 34°52S 20°0E 328 E3
Agulo Canary Is. 28°11N 17°12W 296 F2
Agung, Gunung Indonesia 8°20S 115°28E 308 F5
Agur Uganda 2°28N 32°55E 326 B3
Agusan → Phil. 9°0N 125°30E 309 C7
Aha Mts. Botswana 19°45S 21°0E 328 B3
Ahaggar Algeria 23°0N 6°30E 322 D7
Ahar Iran 38°35N 47°0E 316 B5
Ahipara B. N.Z. 35°5S 173°5E 331 A4
Ahiri India 19°30N 80°0E 312 K12
Ahmad Wal Pakistan 29°18N 65°58E 314 E1
Ahmadabad India 23°0N 72°40E 314 H5
Aḥmadābād Khorāsān, Iran 35°3N 60°50E 317 C9
Aḥmadābād Khorāsān, Iran 35°49N 59°42E 317 C8
Aḥmadī Iran 27°56N 56°42E 317 E8
Ahmadnagar India 19°7N 74°46E 312 K9
Ahmadpur Pakistan 29°12N 71°10E 314 E4
Ahmadpur Lamma Pakistan 28°19N 70°3E 314 E4
Ahmedabad = Ahmadabad India 23°0N 72°40E 314 H5
Ahmednagar = Ahmadnagar India 19°7N 74°46E 312 K9
Ahome Mexico 25°55N 109°11W 358 B3
Ahoskie U.S.A. 36°17N 76°59W 357 C16
Ahram Iran 28°52N 51°16E 317 D6
Ahrax Pt. Malta 36°0N 14°22E 297 D1
Āhū Iran 34°33N 50°2E 317 C6
Ahuachapán El Salv. 13°54N 89°52W 360 D2
Ahvāz Iran 31°20N 48°40E 317 D6
Ahvenanmaa = Åland Finland 60°15N 20°0E 281 F19
Aḥwar Yemen 13°30N 46°40E 319 E4
Ai → India 26°26N 90°44E 315 F14
Ai-Ais Namibia 27°54S 17°59E 328 D2
Ai-Ais and Fish River Canyon △ Namibia 24°45S 17°15E 328 C2
Aichi ☐ Japan 35°0N 137°15E 303 G8
Aigrettes, Pte. des Réunion 21°3S 55°13E 325 c
Aigua Uruguay 34°13S 54°46W 367 C5
Aigues-Mortes France 43°35N 4°12E 292 E6
Aihui China 50°10N 127°30E 305 A7
Aija Peru 9°50S 77°45W 364 E3
Aikawa Japan 38°2N 138°15E 302 E9
Aiken U.S.A. 33°34N 81°43W 357 E14
Aileron Australia 22°39S 133°20E 334 C1
Aillik Canada 55°11N 59°18W 345 A8
Ailsa Craig U.K. 55°15N 5°6W 283 F3
Aim Russia 59°0N 133°55E 301 D14
Aimere Indonesia 8°45S 121°3E 309 F6
Aimogasta Argentina 28°33S 66°50W 366 B2
Aïn Ben Tili Mauritania 25°59N 9°27W 322 C4
Aïn Sefra Algeria 32°47N 0°37W 322 B5
Ain Sudr Egypt 29°50N 33°6E 318 F2
Aïn Témouchent Algeria 35°16N 1°8W 322 A5
Ainaži Latvia 57°50N 24°24E 281 H21
Ainsworth U.S.A. 42°33N 99°52W 352 D4
Aiquile Bolivia 18°10S 65°10W 364 G5
Aïr Niger 18°30N 8°0E 322 E7
Air Force I. Canada 67°58N 74°5W 341 C12
Air Hitam Malaysia 1°55N 103°11E 311 M4
Airdrie Canada 51°18N 114°2W 342 C6
Airdrie U.K. 55°52N 3°57W 283 F5
Aire → U.K. 53°43N 0°55W 284 D7
Aire, I. de l' Spain 39°48N 4°16E 296 B11
Airlie Beach Australia 20°16S 148°43E 334 J6
Aisne → France 49°26N 2°50E 292 B5
Ait India 25°54N 79°14E 315 G8
Aitkin U.S.A. 46°32N 93°42W 352 B7
Aitutaki Cook Is. 18°52S 159°45W 337 J12
Aiud Romania 46°19N 23°44E 289 E12
Aix-en-Provence France 43°32N 5°27E 292 E6
Aix-la-Chapelle = Aachen Germany 50°45N 6°6E 288 C4
Aix-les-Bains France 45°41N 5°53E 292 D6
Aizawl India 23°40N 92°44E 313 H18
Aizkraukle Latvia 56°36N 25°11E 281 H21
Aizpute Latvia 56°43N 21°40E 281 H19
Aizuwakamatsu Japan 37°30N 139°56E 302 F9
Ajaccio France 41°55N 8°40E 292 F8
Ajai ⌂ Uganda 2°52N 31°16E 326 B3
Ajaigarh India 24°52N 80°16E 315 G9
Ajalpan Mexico 18°22N 97°15W 359 D5
Ajanta Ra. India 20°28N 75°50E 312 J9
Ajari Rep. = Ajaria ☐ Georgia 41°30N 42°0E 291 F7
Ajaria ☐ Georgia 41°30N 42°0E 291 F7
Ajax Canada 43°50N 79°1W 354 C5
Ajdābiyā Libya 30°54N 20°4E 323 B10
Ajka Hungary 47°4N 17°31E 289 E9
'Ajlūn Jordan 32°18N 35°47E 318 C4
'Ajlūn ☐ Jordan 32°18N 35°47E 318 C4
'Ajmān U.A.E. 25°25N 55°30E 317 E7
Ajmer India 26°28N 74°37E 314 F6
Ajnala India 31°50N 74°48E 314 D6
Ajo U.S.A. 32°22N 112°52W 349 K7
Ajo, C. de Spain 43°31N 3°35W 293 A4
Akabira Japan 43°33N 142°5E 302 C11
Akagera △ Rwanda 1°31S 30°33E 326 C3
Akamas Cyprus 35°3N 32°18E 297 D11
Akan △ Japan 43°20N 144°20E 302 C12
Akanthou Cyprus 35°22N 33°45E 297 D12
Akaroa N.Z. 43°49S 172°59E 331 E4
Akashi Japan 34°45N 134°58E 303 G7
Akbarpur Bihar, India 24°39N 83°58E 315 G10
Akbarpur Ut. P., India 26°25N 82°32E 315 F10
Akelamo Indonesia 1°35N 129°40E 309 D7
Aketi Dem. Rep. of the Congo 2°38N 23°47E 324 D4
Akhisar Turkey 38°56N 27°48E 295 E12
Akhnur India 32°52N 74°45E 315 C6
Akhtyrka = Okhtyrka Ukraine 50°25N 35°0E 291 D5
Aki Japan 33°30N 133°54E 303 H6
Akimiski I. Canada 52°50N 81°30W 344 B3
Akita Japan 39°45N 140°7E 302 E10
Akita ☐ Japan 39°40N 140°30E 302 E10
Akjoujt Mauritania 19°45N 14°15W 322 E3
Akkeshi Japan 43°2N 144°51E 302 C12
'Akko Israel 32°55N 35°4E 318 C4
Aklavik Canada 68°12N 135°0W 340 C6
Aklera India 24°26N 76°32E 314 G7
Akō Japan 34°45N 134°24E 303 G7
Akola India 20°42N 77°2E 312 J10
Akordat Eritrea 15°30N 37°40E 319 D2
Akpatok I. Canada 60°25N 68°8W 341 C13
Åkrahamn Norway 59°15N 5°10E 281 G11
Akranes Iceland 64°19N 22°5W 280 D2
Akron Colo., U.S.A. 40°10N 103°13W 348 F12
Akron Ohio, U.S.A. 41°5N 81°31W 354 E3
Akrotiri Cyprus 34°36N 32°57E 297 E11
Akrotiri Bay Cyprus 34°35N 33°10E 297 E12
Aksai Chin China 35°15N 79°55E 315 B8
Aksaray Turkey 38°25N 34°2E 316 B2
Aksay = Aqsay Kazakhstan 51°11N 53°0E 291 D9
Akşehir Turkey 38°18N 31°30E 316 B1
Akşehir Gölü Turkey 38°30N 31°25E 291 G5
Aksu China 41°5N 80°10E 304 B3
Aksum Ethiopia 14°5N 38°40E 319 E2
Aktsyabrski Belarus 52°38N 28°53E 289 B15
Aktyubinsk = Aqtöbe Kazakhstan 50°17N 57°10E 291 D10
Akure Nigeria 7°15N 5°22E 322 G7
Akureyri Iceland 65°40N 18°6W 280 D4
Akuseki-Shima Japan 29°27N 129°37E 303 K4
Akyab = Sittwe Burma 20°18N 92°45E 313 J18
Al 'Adan Yemen 12°45N 45°0E 319 E4
Al Aḥsā = Hasa Si. Arabia 25°50N 49°0E 317 E6
Al Ajfar Si. Arabia 27°26N 43°0E 316 E4
Al Amādīyah Iraq 37°5N 43°30E 316 B4
Al 'Amārah Iraq 31°55N 47°15E 316 D5
Al Anbār ☐ Iraq 33°25N 42°0E 316 C4
Al 'Aqabah Jordan 29°31N 35°0E 318 F4
Al 'Aqabah ☐ Jordan 29°30N 35°0E 318 F4
Al Arak Syria 34°38N 38°35E 316 C3
Al 'Aramah Si. Arabia 25°30N 46°0E 316 E5
Al 'Arṭāwīyah Si. Arabia 26°31N 45°20E 316 E5
Al 'Āṣimah = 'Ammān ☐ Jordan 31°40N 36°30E 318 D5
Al 'Assāfīyah Si. Arabia 28°17N 38°59E 316 D3
Al 'Ayn Si. Arabia 25°4N 38°6E 316 E3
Al 'Ayn U.A.E. 24°15N 55°45E 317 E7
Al 'Azīzīyah Iraq 32°54N 45°4E 316 C5
Al Bāb Syria 36°23N 37°29E 316 B3
Al Bad' Si. Arabia 28°28N 35°1E 316 D2
Al Bādī Iraq 35°56N 41°32E 316 C4
Al Baḥrah Kuwait 29°40N 47°52E 316 D5
Al Baḥral Mayyit = Dead Sea Asia 31°30N 35°30E 318 D4
Al Balqā' ☐ Jordan 32°5N 35°45E 318 C4
Al Bārūk, J. Lebanon 33°39N 35°40E 318 B4
Al Baṣrah Iraq 30°30N 47°50E 316 D5
Al Baṭḥā Iraq 31°6N 45°53E 316 D5
Al Batrūn Lebanon 34°15N 35°40E 318 A4
Al Bayḍā Libya 32°50N 21°44E 323 B10
Al Biqā Lebanon 34°10N 36°10E 318 A5
Al Bi'r Si. Arabia 28°51N 36°16E 316 D3
Al Bukayrīyah Si. Arabia 26°9N 43°40E 316 E4
Al Burayj Syria 34°15N 36°46E 318 A5
Al Faḍilī Si. Arabia 26°58N 49°10E 317 E6
Al Fallūjah Iraq 33°20N 43°55E 316 C4
Al Fāw Iraq 30°0N 48°30E 317 D6
Al Fujayrah U.A.E. 25°7N 56°18E 317 E8
Al Ghadaf, W. → Jordan 31°26N 36°43E 318 D5
Al Ghammās Iraq 31°45N 44°37E 316 D5
Al Ghazālah Si. Arabia 26°48N 41°19E 316 E4
Al Ḥadīthah Iraq 34°0N 41°13E 316 C4
Al Ḥadīthah Si. Arabia 31°28N 37°8E 318 D6
Al Ḥaḍr Iraq 35°35N 42°44E 316 C4

Askim Norway 59°35N 11°10E 281 G14
Askja Iceland 65°3N 16°48W 280 D5
Askøyna Norway 60°29N 5°10E 280 F11
Asmara = Asmera Eritrea 15°19N 38°55E 319 D2
Asmera Eritrea 15°19N 38°55E 319 D2
Åsnen Sweden 56°37N 14°45E 281 H16
Aso Kuju △ Japan 32°53N 131°6E 303 H5
Aspatria U.K. 54°47N 3°19W 284 C4
Aspen U.S.A. 39°11N 106°49W 348 G10
Aspermont U.S.A. 33°8N 100°14W 356 E4
Aspiring, Mt. N.Z. 44°23S 168°46E 331 F2
Asprokavos, Akra Greece 39°21N 20°6E 297 B4
Aspur India 23°58N 74°7E 314 H6
Asquith Canada 52°8N 107°13W 343 C7
Assab = Aseb Eritrea 13°0N 42°40E 319 E3
Assal, L. Djibouti 11°40N 42°26E 319 E3
Assam □ India 26°0N 93°0E 313 G18
Assateague Island ⌓ U.S.A. 38°15N 75°10W 353 F16
Asse Belgium 50°24N 4°10E 287 D4
Assen Neths. 53°0N 6°35E 287 A6
Assiniboia Canada 49°40N 105°59W 343 D7
Assiniboine → Canada 49°53N 97°8W 343 D9
Assiniboine, Mt. Canada 50°52N 115°39W 342 C5
Assis Brazil 22°40S 50°20W 367 A5
Assisi Italy 43°4N 12°37E 294 C5
Assynt, L. U.K. 58°10N 5°3W 283 C3
Astana Kazakhstan 51°10N 71°30E 300 D8
Āstāneh Iran 37°17N 49°59E 317 B6
Astara Azerbaijan 38°30N 48°50E 317 B6
Asterousia Greece 34°59N 25°3E 297 E7
Asti Italy 44°54N 8°12E 292 D8
Astipalea Greece 36°32N 26°22E 295 F12
Astorga Spain 42°29N 6°8W 293 A2
Astoria U.S.A. 46°11N 123°50W 350 D3
Astrakhan Russia 46°25N 48°5E 291 E8
Asturias □ Spain 43°15N 6°0W 293 A3
Asunción Paraguay 25°10S 57°30W 366 B4
Asunción Nochixtlán Mexico 17°28N 97°14W 359 D5
Aswa → Uganda 3°43N 31°55E 326 B3
Aswa-Lolim ⌓ Uganda 2°43N 31°35E 326 B3
Aswân Egypt 24°4N 32°57E 323 D12
Aswan Dam = Sadd el Aali Egypt 23°54N 32°54E 323 D12
Asyût Egypt 27°11N 31°4E 323 C12
At Ṭafīlah Jordan 30°45N 35°30E 318 E4
At Ṭafīlah □ Jordan 30°45N 35°30E 318 E4
At Ṭā'if Si. Arabia 21°5N 40°27E 319 C3
At Ta'mīm □ Iraq 35°30N 44°20E 316 C5
Aṭ Ṭirāq Si. Arabia 27°19N 44°33E 316 E5
Aṭ Tubayq Si. Arabia 29°30N 37°0E 316 D3
Aṭ Ṭunayb Jordan 31°48N 35°57E 318 D4
Atacama □ Chile 27°30S 70°0W 366 B2
Atacama, Desierto de Chile 24°0S 69°20W 366 A2
Atacama, Salar de Chile 23°30S 68°20W 366 A2
Atakpamé Togo 7°31N 1°13E 322 G6
Atalaya Peru 10°45S 73°50W 364 F4
Atalaya de Femes Canary Is. 28°56N 13°47W 296 F6
Atami Japan 35°5N 139°4E 303 G9
Atamyrat Turkmenistan 37°50N 65°12E 300 F7
Atapupu Indonesia 9°0S 124°51E 309 F6
Atâr Mauritania 20°30N 13°5W 322 D3
Atari Pakistan 30°56N 74°2E 314 D6
Atascadero U.S.A. 35°29N 120°40W 350 K6
Atasū Kazakhstan 48°30N 71°0E 300 E8
Atatürk Barajı Turkey 37°28N 38°30E 291 G6
Atauro E. Timor 8°10S 125°30E 309 F7
Ataviros Greece 36°12N 27°50E 297 C9
Atbara Sudan 17°42N 33°59E 323 E12
'Atbara, Nahr → Sudan 17°40N 33°56E 323 E12
Atbasar Kazakhstan 51°48N 68°20E 300 D7
Atchafalaya B. U.S.A. 29°25N 91°25W 356 G9
Atchison U.S.A. 39°34N 95°7W 352 F6
Āteshān Iran 35°35N 52°37E 317 C7
Ath Belgium 50°38N 3°47E 287 D3
Athabasca Canada 54°45N 113°20W 342 C6
Athabasca → Canada 58°40N 110°50W 343 B6
Athabasca, L. Canada 59°15N 109°15W 343 B7
Athabasca Sand Dunes ⌓ Canada 59°4N 108°43W 343 B7
Athboy Ireland 53°37N 6°56W 282 C5
Athenry Ireland 53°18N 8°44W 282 C3
Athens = Athina Greece 37°58N 23°43E 295 F10
Athens Ala., U.S.A. 34°48N 86°58W 357 D11
Athens Ga., U.S.A. 33°57N 83°23W 357 E13
Athens N.Y., U.S.A. 42°16N 73°49W 355 D11
Athens Ohio, U.S.A. 39°20N 82°6W 353 F12
Athens Pa., U.S.A. 41°57N 76°31W 355 E8
Athens Tenn., U.S.A. 35°27N 84°36W 357 D12
Athens Tex., U.S.A. 32°12N 95°51W 356 E7
Atherley Canada 44°37N 79°20W 354 B5
Atherton Australia 17°17S 145°30E 334 B4
Athi River Kenya 1°28S 36°58E 326 C4
Athienou Cyprus 35°3N 33°32E 297 D12
Athina Greece 37°58N 23°43E 295 F10
Athínai = Athina Greece 37°58N 23°43E 295 F10
Athlone Ireland 53°25N 7°56W 282 C4
Athna Cyprus 35°3N 33°47E 297 D12
Athol U.S.A. 42°36N 72°14W 355 D12
Atholl, Forest of U.K. 56°51N 3°50W 283 E5
Atholville Canada 47°59N 66°43W 345 C6
Athos Greece 40°9N 24°22E 295 D11
Athy Ireland 53°0N 7°0W 282 C5
Ati Chad 13°13N 18°20E 323 F9
Atiak Uganda 3°12N 32°2E 326 B3
Atik L. Canada 55°15N 96°0W 343 B9
Atikaki ⌓ Canada 51°30N 95°31W 343 C9
Atikameg → Canada 52°30N 82°46W 344 B3
Atikokan Canada 48°45N 91°37W 344 C1
Atikonak L. Canada 52°40N 64°32W 345 B7
Atimaono Tahiti 17°46S 149°28W 331 d
Atitlán △ Cent. Amer. 14°38N 91°10W 359 E6
Atiu Cook Is. 20°0S 158°10W 337 J12
Atka Russia 60°50N 151°48E 301 C16
Atka I. U.S.A. 52°7N 174°30W 346 a
Atkinson U.S.A. 42°32N 98°59W 352 D4
Atlanta Ga., U.S.A. 33°45N 84°23W 357 E12
Atlanta Tex., U.S.A. 33°7N 94°10W 356 E7
Atlantic U.S.A. 41°24N 95°1W 352 E6
Atlantic City U.S.A. 39°21N 74°27W 353 F16
Atlantic-Indian Basin Antarctica 60°0S 30°0E 277 B4
Atlantic Ocean 0°0 20°0W 274 D8
Atlas Mts. = Haut Atlas Morocco 32°30N 5°0W 322 B4
Atlin Canada 59°31N 133°41W 342 B2
Atlin, L. Canada 59°26N 133°45W 342 B2
Atlin ⌓ Canada 59°10N 134°30W 342 B2
Atmore U.S.A. 31°2N 87°29W 357 F11
Atoka U.S.A. 34°23N 96°8W 356 D6
Atolia U.S.A. 35°19N 117°37W 351 K9
Atrai → Bangla. 24°7N 89°22E 315 G13
Atrak = Atrek → Turkmenistan 37°35N 53°58E 317 B8
Atrauli India 28°2N 78°20E 314 E8
Atrek → Turkmenistan 37°35N 53°58E 317 B8
Atsuta Japan 43°24N 141°26E 302 C10
Attalla U.S.A. 34°1N 86°6W 357 D11
Attapu Laos 14°48N 106°50E 310 E6
Attawapiskat Canada 52°56N 82°24W 344 B3
Attawapiskat → Canada 52°57N 82°18W 344 B3
Attawapiskat L. Canada 52°18N 87°54W 344 B2
Attica Ind., U.S.A. 40°18N 87°15W 352 E10
Attica Ohio, U.S.A. 41°4N 82°53W 354 E2
Attikamagen L. Canada 55°0N 66°30W 345 B6
Attleboro U.S.A. 41°57N 71°17W 355 E13
Attock Pakistan 33°52N 72°20E 314 C5
Attopeu = Attapu Laos 14°48N 106°50E 310 E6
Attu I. U.S.A. 52°55N 172°55E 346 a
Attur India 11°35N 78°30E 312 P11
Atuel → Argentina 36°17S 66°50W 366 D2
Åtvidaberg Sweden 58°12N 16°0E 281 G17
Atwater U.S.A. 37°21N 120°37W 350 H6
Atwood Canada 43°40N 81°1W 354 C3
Atwood U.S.A. 39°48N 101°3W 352 F3
Atyraū Kazakhstan 47°5N 52°0E 291 E9
Au Sable U.S.A. 44°25N 83°20W 354 B1
Au Sable → U.S.A. 44°25N 83°20W 353 C12
Au Sable Forks U.S.A. 44°27N 73°41W 355 B11
Au Sable Pt. U.S.A. 44°20N 83°20W 354 B1
Auasberg Namibia 22°37S 17°13E 328 C2
Aubagne France 43°17N 5°37E 292 E6
Aubarca, C. d' Spain 39°4N 1°22E 296 B7
Aube → France 48°34N 3°43E 292 B5
Auberry U.S.A. 37°7N 119°29W 350 H7
Auburn Ala., U.S.A. 32°36N 85°29W 357 E12
Auburn Calif., U.S.A. 38°54N 121°4W 350 G5
Auburn Ind., U.S.A. 41°22N 85°4W 353 E11
Auburn Maine, U.S.A. 44°6N 70°14W 353 C18
Auburn N.Y., U.S.A. 42°56N 76°34W 355 D8
Auburn Nebr., U.S.A. 40°23N 95°51W 352 E6
Auburn Pa., U.S.A. 40°36N 76°6W 355 F8
Auburn Wash., U.S.A. 47°18N 122°14W 350 C4
Auburn Ra. Australia 25°15S 150°30E 335 D5
Auburndale U.S.A. 28°4N 81°48W 357 G14
Aubusson France 45°57N 2°11E 292 D5
Auch France 43°39N 0°36E 292 E4
Auchterarder U.K. 56°18N 3°41W 283 E5
Auchtermuchty U.K. 56°18N 3°13W 283 E5
Auckland N.Z. 36°52S 174°46E 331 B5
Auckland Is. Pac. Oc. 50°40S 166°5E 336 N8
Aude → France 43°13N 3°14E 292 E5
Auden Canada 50°14N 87°53W 344 B2
Audubon U.S.A. 41°43N 94°56W 352 E6
Augathella Australia 25°48S 146°35E 335 D4
Aughnacloy U.K. 54°25N 6°59W 282 B5
Aughrim Ireland 53°18N 8°19W 282 C3
Augrabies Falls S. Africa 28°35S 20°20E 328 D3
Augrabies Falls △ S. Africa 28°40S 20°22E 328 D3
Augsburg Germany 48°25N 10°52E 288 D6
Augusta Australia 34°19S 115°9E 333 F2
Augusta Italy 37°13N 15°13E 294 F6
Augusta Ark., U.S.A. 35°17N 91°22W 356 D9
Augusta Ga., U.S.A. 33°28N 81°58W 357 E14
Augusta Kans., U.S.A. 37°41N 96°59W 352 G5
Augusta Maine, U.S.A. 44°19N 69°47W 353 C19
Augusta Mont., U.S.A. 47°30N 112°24W 348 C7
Augustów Poland 53°51N 23°0E 289 B12
Augustus, Mt. Australia 24°20S 116°50E 333 D2
Augustus I. Australia 15°20S 124°30E 332 C3
Aujuittuq = Grise Fiord Canada 76°25N 82°57W 341 B11
Aukštaitija △ Lithuania 55°15N 26°0E 281 J22
Aukum U.S.A. 38°34N 120°43W 350 G6
Auld, L. Australia 22°25S 123°50E 332 D3
Ault U.S.A. 40°35N 104°44W 348 F11
Aunis France 46°5N 0°50W 292 C3
Aunu'u Amer. Samoa 14°20S 170°31W 331 b
Auponhia Indonesia 1°58S 125°27E 309 E7
Aur, Pulau Malaysia 2°35N 104°10E 311 L5
Auraiya India 26°28N 79°33E 315 F8
Aurangabad Bihar, India 24°45N 84°18E 315 G11
Aurangabad Maharashtra, India 19°50N 75°23E 312 K9
Aurich Germany 53°28N 7°28E 288 B4
Aurillac France 44°55N 2°26E 292 D5
Aurora Canada 44°0N 79°28W 354 C5
Aurora S. Africa 32°40S 18°29E 328 E2
Aurora Colo., U.S.A. 39°43N 104°49W 348 G11
Aurora Ill., U.S.A. 41°45N 88°19W 352 E9
Aurora Mo., U.S.A. 36°58N 93°43W 352 G7
Aurora N.Y., U.S.A. 42°45N 76°42W 355 D8
Aurora Nebr., U.S.A. 40°52N 98°0W 352 E5
Aurora Ohio, U.S.A. 41°21N 81°20W 354 E3
Aurukun Australia 13°20S 141°45E 334 A3
Aus Namibia 26°35S 16°12E 328 D2
Ausable → Canada 43°19N 81°46W 354 C3
Auschwitz = Oświęcim Poland 50°2N 19°11E 289 C10
Austin Minn., U.S.A. 43°40N 92°58W 352 D7
Austin Nev., U.S.A. 39°30N 117°4W 348 G5
Austin Pa., U.S.A. 41°38N 78°6W 354 E6
Austin Tex., U.S.A. 30°17N 97°45W 356 F6
Austin, L. Australia 27°40S 118°0E 333 E2
Austin I. Canada 61°10N 94°0W 343 A10
Austra Norway 65°8N 11°55E 280 D14
Austral Is. = Tubuaï, Îs. French Polynesia 25°0S 150°0W 337 K13
Austral Seamount Chain Pac. Oc. 24°0S 150°0W 337 K13
Australia ■ Oceania 23°0S 135°0E 330 D6
Australian-Antarctic Basin S. Ocean 60°0S 120°0E 277 C9
Australian Capital Territory □ Australia 35°30S 149°0E 335 F4
Australind Australia 33°17S 115°42E 333 F2
Austria ■ Europe 47°0N 14°0E 288 E8
Austvågøya Norway 68°20N 14°40E 280 B16
Autlán de Navarro Mexico 19°46N 104°22W 358 D4
Autun France 46°58N 4°17E 292 C6
Auvergne □ France 45°20N 3°15E 292 D5
Auvergne, Mts. d' France 45°20N 2°55E 292 D5
Auxerre France 47°48N 3°32E 292 C5
Ava U.S.A. 36°57N 92°40W 352 G7
Avallon France 47°30N 3°53E 292 C5
Avalon U.S.A. 33°21N 118°20W 351 M8
Avalon Pen. Canada 47°30N 53°20W 345 C9
Avanos Turkey 38°43N 34°51E 316 B2
Avaré Brazil 23°4S 48°58W 367 A6
Avawatz Mts. U.S.A. 35°40N 116°30W 351 K10
Aveiro Brazil 3°10S 55°5W 365 D7
Aveiro Portugal 40°37N 8°38W 293 B1
Āvej Iran 35°40N 49°15E 317 C6
Avellaneda Argentina 34°40S 58°22W 366 C4
Avellino Italy 40°54N 14°47E 294 D6
Avenal U.S.A. 36°0N 120°8W 350 K6
Aversa Italy 40°58N 14°12E 294 D6
Avery U.S.A. 47°15N 115°49W 348 C6
Aves, I. de W. Indies 15°45N 63°55W 361 C7
Aves, Is. las Venezuela 12°0N 67°30W 361 D6
Avesta Sweden 60°9N 16°10E 281 F17
Aveyron → France 44°5N 1°16E 292 D4
Avezzano Italy 42°2N 13°25E 294 C5
Aviá Terai Argentina 26°45S 60°50W 366 B3
Aviemore U.K. 57°12N 3°50W 283 D5
Avignon France 43°57N 4°50E 292 E6
Ávila Spain 40°39N 4°43W 293 B3
Avila Beach U.S.A. 35°11N 120°44W 351 K6
Avilés Spain 43°35N 5°57W 293 A3
Avis U.S.A. 41°11N 77°19W 354 E7
Avoca U.S.A. 42°25N 77°25W 354 D7
Avoca → Australia 35°40S 143°43E 335 F3
Avoca → Ireland 52°48N 6°10W 282 D5
Avola Canada 51°45N 119°19W 342 C5
Avola Italy 36°56N 15°7E 294 F6
Avon U.S.A. 42°55N 77°45W 354 D7
Avon → Australia 31°40S 116°7E 333 F2
Avon → Bristol, U.K. 51°29N 2°41W 285 F5
Avon → Dorset, U.K. 50°44N 1°46W 285 G6
Avon → Warks., U.K. 52°0N 2°8W 285 E5
Avon Park U.S.A. 27°36N 81°31W 357 H14
Avondale Zimbabwe 17°43S 30°58E 327 F3
Avonlea Canada 50°0N 105°0W 343 D8
Avonmore Canada 45°10N 74°58W 355 A10
Avonmouth U.K. 51°30N 2°42W 285 F5
Avranches France 48°40N 1°20W 292 B3
Awa-Shima Japan 38°27N 139°14E 302 E9
A'waj → Syria 33°23N 36°20E 318 B5
Awaji-Shima Japan 34°30N 134°50E 303 G7
'Awālī Bahrain 26°0N 50°30E 317 E6
Awantipur India 33°55N 75°3E 315 C6
Awasa Ethiopia 7°2N 38°28E 319 F2
Awash Ethiopia 9°1N 40°10E 319 F3
Awatere → N.Z. 41°37S 174°10E 331 D5
Awbārī Libya 26°46N 12°57E 323 C8
Awbārī, Idehan Libya 27°10N 11°30E 323 C8
Awe, L. U.K. 56°17N 5°16W 283 E3
Awjilah Libya 29°8N 21°7E 323 C10
Axe → U.K. 50°42N 3°4W 285 F5
Axel Heiberg I. Canada 80°0N 90°0W 341 B11
Axim Ghana 4°51N 2°15W 322 H5
Axios → Greece 40°57N 22°35E 295 D10
Axminster U.K. 50°46N 3°0W 285 G4
Ayabaca Peru 4°40S 79°53W 364 D3
Ayabe Japan 35°20N 135°20E 303 G7
Ayacucho Argentina 37°5S 58°20W 366 D4
Ayacucho Peru 13°0S 74°0W 364 F4
Ayaguz = Ayaköz Kazakhstan 48°10N 80°10E 300 E9
Ayaköz Kazakhstan 48°10N 80°10E 300 E9
Ayamonte Spain 37°12N 7°24W 293 D2
Ayan Russia 56°30N 138°16E 301 D14
Ayaviri Peru 14°50S 70°35W 364 F4
Aydın Turkey 37°51N 27°51E 295 F12
Aydingkol Hu China 42°40N 89°15E 304 B3
Ayer U.S.A. 42°34N 71°35W 355 D13
Ayer Hitam Malaysia 5°24N 100°16E 311 c
Ayer's Cliff Canada 45°10N 72°3W 355 A12
Ayers Rock = Uluru Australia 25°23S 131°5E 333 E5
Áyia Napa Cyprus 34°59N 34°0E 297 E13
Áyia Phyla Cyprus 34°43N 33°1E 297 E12
Áyios Amvrósios Cyprus 35°20N 33°35E 297 D12
Áyios Seryios Cyprus 35°12N 33°53E 297 D12
Áyios Theodhoros Cyprus 35°22N 34°1E 297 D13
Aykino Russia 62°15N 49°56E 290 B8
Aylesbury U.K. 51°49N 0°49W 285 F7
Aylmer Canada 42°46N 80°59W 354 D4
Aylmer, L. Canada 64°5N 108°30W 340 C9
'Ayn, Wādī al Oman 22°15N 55°28E 317 F7
Ayn Dār Si. Arabia 25°55N 49°10E 317 E7
Ayn Zālah Iraq 36°45N 42°35E 316 B4
Ayolas Paraguay 27°10S 56°59W 366 B4
Ayon, Ostrov Russia 69°50N 169°0E 301 C17
'Ayoûn el 'Atroûs Mauritania 16°38N 9°37W 322 E4
Ayr Australia 19°35S 147°25E 334 B4
Ayr Canada 43°17N 80°27W 354 C4
Ayr U.K. 55°28N 4°38W 283 F4
Ayr → U.K. 55°28N 4°38W 283 F4
Ayre, Pt. of I. of Man 54°25N 4°21W 284 C3
Ayton Australia 15°56S 145°22E 334 B4
Aytos Bulgaria 42°42N 27°16E 295 C12
Ayu, Kepulauan Indonesia 0°35N 131°5E 309 D8
Ayutla Guatemala 14°40N 92°10W 360 D1
Ayutla de los Libres Mexico 16°54N 99°13W 359 D5
Ayvacık Turkey 39°36N 26°24E 295 E12
Ayvalık Turkey 39°20N 26°46E 295 E12
Az Zabadānī Syria 33°43N 36°5E 318 B5
Aẓ Ẓāhirīyah West Bank 31°25N 34°58E 318 D3
Aẓ Ẓahrān Si. Arabia 26°10N 50°7E 317 E6
Az Zarqā Jordan 32°5N 36°4E 318 C5
Az Zarqā' U.A.E. 24°53N 53°4E 317 E7
Az Zarqā □ Jordan 32°5N 36°4E 318 C5
Az Zāwiyah Libya 32°52N 12°56E 323 B8
Az Zībār Iraq 36°52N 44°4E 316 B5
Az Zilfī Si. Arabia 26°12N 44°52E 316 E5
Az Zubayr Iraq 30°26N 47°40E 316 D5
Azad Kashmir □ Pakistan 33°50N 73°50E 315 C5
Azamgarh India 26°5N 83°13E 315 F10
Azangaro Peru 14°55S 70°13W 364 F4
Azaouad Mali 19°0N 3°0W 322 E5
Āzār Shahr Iran 37°45N 45°59E 316 B5
Azarān Iran 37°25N 47°16E 316 B5
Azărbayjan = Azerbaijan ■ Asia 40°20N 48°0E 291 F8
Āzarbāyjān-e Gharbī □ Iran 37°0N 44°30E 316 B5
Āzarbāyjān-e Sharqī □ Iran 37°20N 47°0E 316 B5
Azare Nigeria 11°55N 10°10E 322 F8
A'zāz Syria 36°36N 37°4E 316 B3
Azbine = Aïr Niger 18°30N 8°0E 322 E7
Azerbaijan ■ Asia 40°20N 48°0E 291 F8
Azerbaijchan = Azerbaijan ■ Asia 40°20N 48°0E 291 F8
Azimganj India 24°14N 88°16E 315 G13
Azogues Ecuador 2°35S 78°0W 364 D3
Azores = Açores, Is. dos Atl. Oc. 38°0N 27°0W 322 a
Azov Russia 47°3N 39°25E 291 E6
Azov, Sea of Europe 46°0N 36°30E 291 E6
Azovskoye More = Azov, Sea of Europe 46°0N 36°30E 291 E6
Azraq ash Shīshān Jordan 31°50N 36°49E 318 D5
Aztec U.S.A. 36°49N 107°59W 349 H10
Azúa de Compostela Dom. Rep. 18°25N 70°44W 361 C5
Azuaga Spain 38°16N 5°39W 293 C3
Azuero, Pen. de Panama 7°30N 80°30W 360 E3
Azul Argentina 36°42S 59°43W 366 D4
Azusa U.S.A. 34°8N 117°52W 351 L9
Azzel Matti, Sebkra Algeria 26°10N 0°43E 322 C6

B

Ba Be △ Vietnam 22°25N 105°37E 310 A5
Ba Don Vietnam 17°45N 106°26E 310 D6
Ba Dong Vietnam 9°40N 106°33E 311 H6
Ba Ngoi = Cam Lam Vietnam 11°54N 109°10E 311 G7
Ba Tri Vietnam 10°2N 106°36E 311 G6
Ba Vi △ Vietnam 21°1N 105°22E 310 B5
Ba Xian = Bazhou China 39°8N 116°22E 306 E9
Baa Indonesia 10°50S 123°0E 309 F6
Baardeere = Bardera Somali Rep. 2°20N 42°27E 319 G3
Baarle-Nassau Belgium 51°27N 4°56E 287 C4
Bab el Mandeb Red Sea 12°35N 43°25E 319 E3
Bābā, Koh-i- Afghan. 34°30N 67°0E 312 B5
Baba Burnu Turkey 39°29N 26°2E 295 E12
Bābā Kalū Iran 30°7N 50°49E 317 D6
Babadag Romania 44°53N 28°44E 289 F15
Babaeski Turkey 41°26N 27°6E 295 D12
Babahoyo Ecuador 1°40S 79°30W 364 D3
Babai = Sarju → India 27°21N 81°23E 315 F9
Babar Indonesia 8°0S 129°30E 309 F7
Babar Pakistan 31°7N 69°32E 314 D3
Babarkach Pakistan 29°45N 68°0E 314 E3
Babb U.S.A. 48°51N 113°27W 348 B7
Baberu India 25°33N 80°43E 315 G9
Babi Besar, Pulau Malaysia 2°25N 103°59E 311 L4
Bābil □ Iraq 32°30N 44°30E 316 C5
Babinda Australia 17°20S 145°56E 334 B4
Babine Canada 55°22N 126°37W 342 B3
Babine → Canada 55°45N 127°44W 342 B3
Babine L. Canada 54°48N 126°0W 342 C3
Babo Indonesia 2°30S 133°30E 309 E8
Bābol Iran 36°40N 52°50E 317 B7
Bābol Sar Iran 36°45N 52°45E 317 B7
Baboua C.A.R. 5°49N 14°58E 324 C2
Babruysk Belarus 53°10N 29°15E 289 B15
Babuhri India 26°49N 69°43E 314 F3
Babusar Pass Pakistan 35°12N 73°59E 315 B5
Babuyan Chan. Phil. 18°40N 121°30E 309 A6
Babylon Iraq 32°34N 44°22E 316 C5
Bac Can Vietnam 22°8N 105°49E 310 A5
Bac Giang Vietnam 21°16N 106°11E 310 B6
Bac Lieu Vietnam 9°17N 105°43E 311 H5
Bac Ninh Vietnam 21°13N 106°4E 310 B6
Bac Phan Vietnam 22°0N 105°0E 310 B5
Bac Quang Vietnam 22°30N 104°48E 310 A5
Bacabal Brazil 4°15S 44°45W 365 D10
Bacalar Mexico 18°43N 88°27W 359 D7
Bacan, Kepulauan Indonesia 0°35S 127°30E 309 E7
Bacarra Phil. 18°15N 120°37E 309 A6
Bacău Romania 46°35N 26°55E 289 E14
Bacerac Mexico 30°18N 108°50W 358 A3
Bach Long Vi, Dao Vietnam 20°10N 107°40E 310 B6
Bach Ma △ Vietnam 16°11N 107°49E 310 D6
Bachhwara India 25°35N 85°54E 315 G11
Back → Canada 65°10N 104°0W 340 C9
Bacolod Phil. 10°40N 122°57E 309 B6
Bacuk Malaysia 6°4N 102°25E 311 J4
Bácum Mexico 27°33N 110°5W 358 B2
Bād Iran 33°41N 52°1E 317 C7
Bad → U.S.A. 44°21N 100°22W 352 C3
Bad Axe U.S.A. 43°48N 83°0W 354 C2
Bad Ischl Austria 47°44N 13°38E 288 E7
Bad Kissingen Germany 50°11N 10°4E 288 C6
Bada Barabil India 22°7N 85°24E 315 H11
Badagara India 11°35N 75°40E 312 P9
Badajós, L. Brazil 3°15S 62°50W 364 D6
Badajoz Spain 38°50N 6°59W 293 C2
Badakhshān □ Afghan. 36°30N 71°0E 312 A7
Badalona Spain 41°26N 2°15E 293 B7
Badalzai Afghan. 29°50N 65°35E 314 E1
Badampahar India 22°10N 86°10E 313 H15
Badanah Si. Arabia 30°58N 41°30E 316 D4
Badarinath India 30°45N 79°30E 315 D8
Badas, Kepulauan Indonesia 0°45N 107°5E 308 D3
Baddo → Pakistan 28°0N 64°20E 312 F4
Bade Indonesia 7°10S 139°35E 309 F9
Baden Austria 48°1N 16°13E 288 D9
Baden U.S.A. 40°38N 80°14W 354 F4
Baden-Baden Germany 48°44N 8°13E 288 D5
Baden-Württemberg □ Germany 48°20N 8°40E 288 D5
Badgastein Austria 47°7N 13°9E 288 E7
Badger Canada 49°0N 56°4W 345 C8
Badger U.S.A. 36°38N 119°1W 350 J7
Bādghīs □ Afghan. 35°0N 63°0E 312 B3
Badgingarra △ Australia 30°23S 115°22E 333 F2
Badgom India 34°1N 74°45E 315 B6
Badin Pakistan 24°38N 68°54E 314 G3
Badlands U.S.A. 43°55N 102°30W 352 D2
Badlands △ U.S.A. 43°38N 102°56W 352 D2
Badrah Iraq 33°6N 45°58E 316 C5
Badrinath India 30°44N 79°29E 315 D8
Badulla Sri Lanka 7°1N 81°7E 312 R12
Badung, Selat Indonesia 8°40S 115°22E 309 K18
Baena Spain 37°37N 4°20W 293 D3
Baengnyeongdo S. Korea 37°57N 124°40E 307 F13
Baeza Spain 37°57N 3°25W 293 D4
Bafatá Guinea-Biss. 12°8N 14°40W 322 F3
Baffin B. N. Amer. 72°0N 64°0W 341 B13
Baffin I. Canada 68°0N 75°0W 341 C12
Bafing → Mali 13°49N 10°50W 322 F3
Bafliyūn Syria 36°37N 36°59E 316 B3
Bafoulabé Mali 13°50N 10°55W 322 F3
Bafoussam Cameroon 5°28N 10°25E 324 C2
Bāfq Iran 31°40N 55°25E 317 D7
Bafra Turkey 41°34N 35°54E 291 F6
Bāft Iran 29°15N 56°38E 317 D8
Bafwasende Dem. Rep. of the Congo 1°3N 27°5E 326 B2
Bagamoyo Tanzania 6°28S 38°55E 326 D4
Bagan Datoh Malaysia 3°59N 100°47E 311 L3
Bagan Serai Malaysia 5°1N 100°32E 311 K3
Baganga Phil. 7°34N 126°33E 309 C7
Bagani Namibia 18°7S 21°41E 328 B3
Bagansiapiapi Indonesia 2°12N 100°50E 308 D2
Bagasra India 21°30N 71°0E 314 J4
Bagaud India 22°19N 75°53E 314 H6
Bagdad U.S.A. 34°35N 115°53W 351 L11
Bagdarin Russia 54°26N 113°36E 301 D12
Bagé Brazil 31°20S 54°15W 367 C5
Bagenalstown = Muine Bheag Ireland 52°42N 6°58W 282 D5
Baggs U.S.A. 41°2N 107°39W 348 F10
Bagh Pakistan 33°59N 73°45E 315 C5
Baghain → India 25°32N 81°1E 315 G9
Baghdād Iraq 33°20N 44°23E 316 C5
Bagheria Italy 38°5N 13°30E 294 E5
Baghlān Afghan. 32°12N 68°46E 312 A6
Baghlān □ Afghan. 36°0N 68°30E 312 B6
Bagley U.S.A. 47°32N 95°24W 352 B6
Bago = Pegu Burma 17°20N 96°29E 313 L20
Bagodar India 24°5N 85°52E 315 G11
Bagrationovsk Russia 54°23N 20°39E 281 J19
Baguio Phil. 16°26N 120°34E 309 A6
Bah India 26°53N 78°36E 315 F8
Bahadurganj India 26°16N 87°49E 315 F12
Bahadurgarh India 28°40N 76°57E 314 E7
Bahama, Canal Viejo de W. Indies 22°10N 77°30W 360 B4
Bahamas ■ N. Amer. 24°0N 75°0W 361 B5
Baharampur India 24°2N 88°27E 315 G13
Baharu Pandan = Pandan Malaysia 1°32N 103°46E 311 d
Bahawalnagar Pakistan 30°0N 73°15E 314 E5
Bahawalpur Pakistan 29°24N 71°40E 314 E4
Bäherden Turkmenistan 38°25N 57°26E 317 B8
Baheri India 28°45N 79°34E 315 E8
Bahgul → India 27°45N 79°36E 315 F8
Bahi Tanzania 5°58S 35°21E 326 D4
Bahi Swamp Tanzania 6°10S 35°0E 326 D4
Bahia = Salvador Brazil 13°0S 38°30W 365 F11

Belan → *India* 24°2N 81°45E **315** G9
Belarus ■ *Europe* 53°30N 27°0E **289** B14
Belau = Palau ■ *Palau* 7°30N 134°30E **330** A6
Belavenona *Madag.* 24°50S 47°4E **329** C8
Belawan *Indonesia* 3°33N 98°32E **308** D1
Belaya → *Russia* 54°40N 56°0E **290** C9
Belaya Tserkov = Bila Tserkva *Ukraine* 49°45N 30°10E **289** D16
Belcher Chan. *Canada* 77°15N 95°0W **341** B10
Belcher Is. *Canada* 56°15N 78°45W **344** A3
Belden *U.S.A.* 40°2N 121°17W **350** E5
Belebey *Russia* 54°7N 54°7E **290** D9
Beled Weyne = Belet Uen *Somali Rep.* 4°30N 45°5E **319** G4
Belém *Brazil* 1°20S 48°30W **365** D9
Belén *Argentina* 27°40S 67°5W **366** B2
Belén *Paraguay* 23°30S 57°6W **366** A4
Belen *U.S.A.* 34°40N 106°46W **349** J10
Belet Uen *Somali Rep.* 4°30N 45°5E **319** G4
Belev *Russia* 53°50N 36°5E **290** D6
Belfair *U.S.A.* 47°27N 122°50W **350** C4
Belfast *S. Africa* 25°42S 30°2E **329** D5
Belfast *U.K.* 54°37N 5°56W **282** B6
Belfast *Maine, U.S.A.* 44°26N 69°1W **353** C19
Belfast *N.Y., U.S.A.* 42°21N 78°7W **354** D6
Belfast L. *U.K.* 54°40N 5°50W **282** B6
Belfield *U.S.A.* 46°53N 103°12W **352** B2
Belfort *France* 47°38N 6°50E **292** C7
Belfry *U.S.A.* 45°9N 109°1W **348** D9
Belgaum *India* 15°55N 74°35E **312** M9
Belgium ■ *Europe* 50°30N 5°0E **287** D4
Belgorod *Russia* 50°35N 36°35E **291** D6
Belgorod-Dnestrovskiy = Bilhorod-Dnistrovskyy *Ukraine* 46°11N 30°23E **291** E5
Belgrade = Beograd *Serbia* 44°50N 20°37E **295** B9
Belgrade *U.S.A.* 45°47N 111°11W **348** D8
Belgrano *Antarctica* 77°52S 34°37W **277** D1
Belhaven *U.S.A.* 35°33N 76°37W **357** D16
Beli Drim → *Europe* 42°6N 20°25E **295** C9
Belimbing *Indonesia* 8°24S 115°2E **309** J18
Belinyu *Indonesia* 1°35S 105°50E **308** E3
Beliton Is. = Belitung *Indonesia* 3°10S 107°50E **308** E3
Belitung *Indonesia* 3°10S 107°50E **308** E3
Belize ■ *Cent. Amer.* 17°0N 88°30W **359** D7
Belize City *Belize* 17°25N 88°10W **359** D7
Belkovskiy, Ostrov *Russia* 75°32N 135°44E **301** B14
Bell → *Canada* 49°48N 77°38W **344** C4
Bell I. *Canada* 50°46N 55°35W **345** B8
Bell-Irving → *Canada* 56°12N 129°5W **342** B3
Bell Peninsula *Canada* 63°50N 82°0W **341** C11
Bell Ville *Argentina* 32°40S 62°40W **366** C3
Bella Bella *Canada* 52°10N 128°10W **342** C3
Bella Coola *Canada* 52°25N 126°40W **342** C3
Bella Unión *Uruguay* 30°15S 57°40W **366** C4
Bella Vista *Corrientes, Argentina* 28°33S 59°0W **366** B4
Bella Vista *Tucuman, Argentina* 27°10S 65°25W **366** B2
Bellaire *U.S.A.* 40°1N 80°45W **354** F4
Bellary *India* 15°10N 76°56E **312** M10
Bellata *Australia* 29°53S 149°46E **335** D4
Belle Fourche *U.S.A.* 44°40N 103°51W **352** C2
Belle Fourche → *U.S.A.* 44°26N 102°18W **346** B6
Belle Glade *U.S.A.* 26°41N 80°40W **357** H14
Belle-Île *France* 47°20N 3°10W **292** C2
Belle Isle *Canada* 51°57N 55°25W **345** B8
Belle Isle, Str. of *Canada* 51°30N 56°30W **345** B8
Belle Plaine *U.S.A.* 41°54N 92°17W **352** E7
Bellefontaine *U.S.A.* 40°22N 83°46W **353** E12
Bellefonte *U.S.A.* 40°55N 77°47W **354** F7
Belleoram *Canada* 47°31N 55°25W **345** C8
Belleplaine *Barbados* 13°15N 59°34W **361** g
Belleville *Canada* 44°10N 77°23W **354** B7
Belleville *Ill., U.S.A.* 38°31N 89°59W **352** F9
Belleville *Kans., U.S.A.* 39°50N 97°38W **352** F5
Belleville *N.J., U.S.A.* 40°47N 74°9W **355** F10
Belleville *N.Y., U.S.A.* 43°46N 76°10W **355** C8
Bellevue *Canada* 49°35N 114°22W **342** D6
Bellevue *Idaho, U.S.A.* 43°28N 114°16W **348** E6
Bellevue *Nebr., U.S.A.* 41°9N 95°54W **352** E6
Bellevue *Ohio, U.S.A.* 41°17N 82°51W **354** E2
Bellevue *Wash., U.S.A.* 47°37N 122°12W **350** C4
Bellin = Kangirsuk *Canada* 60°0N 70°0W **341** D13
Bellingen *Australia* 30°25S 152°50E **335** E5
Bellingham *U.S.A.* 48°46N 122°29W **350** B4
Bellingshausen Abyssal Plain *S. Ocean* 64°0S 90°0W **277** C16
Bellingshausen Sea *Antarctica* 66°0S 80°0W **277** C17
Bellinzona *Switz.* 46°11N 9°1E **292** C8
Bello *Colombia* 6°20N 75°33W **364** B3
Bellows Falls *U.S.A.* 43°8N 72°27W **355** C12
Bellpat *Pakistan* 29°0N 68°5E **314** E3
Belluno *Italy* 46°9N 12°13E **294** A5
Bellwood *U.S.A.* 40°36N 78°20W **354** F6
Belmont *Canada* 42°53N 81°5W **354** D3
Belmont *S. Africa* 29°28S 24°22E **328** D3
Belmont *U.S.A.* 42°14N 78°2W **354** D6
Belmonte *Brazil* 16°0S 39°0W **365** G11
Belmopan *Belize* 17°18N 88°30W **359** D7
Belmullet *Ireland* 54°14N 9°58W **282** B2
Belo Horizonte *Brazil* 19°55S 43°56W **365** G10
Belo-sur-Mer *Madag.* 20°42S 44°0E **329** C7
Belo-Tsiribihina *Madag.* 19°40S 44°30E **329** B7
Belogorsk *Russia* 51°0N 128°20E **301** D13
Beloha *Madag.* 25°10S 45°3E **329** D8
Beloit *Kans., U.S.A.* 39°28N 98°6W **352** F4
Beloit *Wis., U.S.A.* 42°31N 89°2W **352** D9
Belokorovichi *Ukraine* 51°7N 28°2E **289** C15
Belomorsk *Russia* 64°35N 34°54E **290** B5
Belonia *India* 23°15N 91°30E **313** H17
Beloretsk *Russia* 53°58N 58°24E **290** D10
Belorussia = Belarus ■ *Europe* 53°30N 27°0E **289** B14
Belovo *Russia* 54°30N 86°0E **300** D9
Beloye, Ozero *Russia* 60°10N 37°35E **290** B6
Beloye More *Russia* 66°30N 38°0E **280** C25
Belozersk *Russia* 60°1N 37°45E **290** B6
Belpre *U.S.A.* 39°17N 81°34W **353** F13
Belrain *India* 28°23N 80°55E **315** E9
Belt *U.S.A.* 47°23N 110°55W **348** C8
Beltana *Australia* 30°48S 138°25E **335** E2
Belterra *Brazil* 2°45S 55°0W **365** D8
Belton *U.S.A.* 31°3N 97°28W **356** F6
Belton L. *U.S.A.* 31°6N 97°28W **356** F6
Beltsy = Bălţi *Moldova* 47°48N 27°58E **289** E14
Belturbet *Ireland* 54°6N 7°26W **282** B4
Belukha *Russia* 49°50N 86°50E **300** E9
Beluran *Malaysia* 5°48N 117°35E **308** C5
Belvidere *Ill., U.S.A.* 42°15N 88°50W **352** D9
Belvidere *N.J., U.S.A.* 40°50N 75°5W **355** F9
Belyando → *Australia* 21°38S 146°50E **334** C4
Belyy, Ostrov *Russia* 73°30N 71°0E **300** B8
Belyy Yar *Russia* 58°26N 84°39E **300** D9
Belzoni *U.S.A.* 33°11N 90°29W **357** E9
Bemaraha, Lembalemban' i *Madag.* 18°40S 44°45E **329** B7
Bemarivo *Madag.* 21°45S 44°45E **329** C7
Bemarivo → *Antsiranana, Madag.* 14°9S 50°9E **329** A9
Bemarivo → *Mahajanga, Madag.* 15°27S 47°40E **329** B8
Bemavo *Madag.* 21°33S 45°25E **329** C8
Bembéréke *Benin* 10°11N 2°43E **322** F6
Bembesi *Zimbabwe* 20°0S 28°58E **327** G2
Bembesi → *Zimbabwe* 18°57S 27°47E **327** F2
Bemetara *India* 21°42N 81°32E **315** J9
Bemidji *U.S.A.* 47°28N 94°53W **352** B6
Bemolanga *Madag.* 17°44S 45°6E **329** B8
Ben *Iran* 32°32N 50°45E **317** C6
Ben Cruachan *U.K.* 56°26N 5°8W **283** E3
Ben Dearg *U.K.* 57°47N 4°56W **283** D4
Ben En △ *Vietnam* 19°37N 105°30E **310** C5
Ben Gardane *Tunisia* 33°11N 11°11E **323** B8
Ben Hope *U.K.* 58°25N 4°36W **283** C4
Ben Lawers *U.K.* 56°32N 4°14W **283** E4
Ben Lomond *N.S.W., Australia* 30°1S 151°43E **335** E5
Ben Lomond *Tas., Australia* 41°38S 147°42E **335** G4
Ben Lomond *U.K.* 56°11N 4°38W **283** E4
Ben Lomond △ *Australia* 41°33S 147°39E **335** G4
Ben Luc *Vietnam* 10°39N 106°29E **311** G6
Ben Macdhui *U.K.* 57°4N 3°40W **283** D5
Ben Mhor *U.K.* 57°15N 7°18W **283** D1
Ben More *Argyll & Bute, U.K.* 56°26N 6°1W **283** E2
Ben More *Stirling, U.K.* 56°23N 4°32W **283** E4
Ben More Assynt *U.K.* 58°8N 4°52W **283** C4
Ben Nevis *U.K.* 56°48N 5°1W **283** E3
Ben Quang *Vietnam* 17°3N 106°55E **310** D6
Ben Vorlich *U.K.* 56°21N 4°14W **283** E4
Ben Wyvis *U.K.* 57°40N 4°35W **283** D4
Bena *Nigeria* 11°20N 5°50E **322** F7
Benalla *Australia* 36°30S 146°0E **335** F4
Benares = Varanasi *India* 25°22N 83°0E **315** G10
Benavente *Spain* 42°2N 5°43W **293** A3
Benavides *U.S.A.* 27°36N 98°25W **356** H5
Benbecula *U.K.* 57°26N 7°21W **283** D1
Benbonyathe Hill *Australia* 30°25S 139°11E **335** E2
Bend *U.S.A.* 44°4N 121°19W **348** D3
Bender Beila *Somali Rep.* 9°30N 50°48E **319** F5
Bendery = Tighina *Moldova* 46°50N 29°30E **289** E15
Bendigo *Australia* 36°40S 144°15E **335** F3
Benē Beraq *Israel* 32°6N 34°51E **318** C3
Benenitra *Madag.* 23°27S 45°5E **329** C8
Benevento *Italy* 41°8N 14°45E **294** D6
Benga *Mozam.* 16°11S 33°40E **327** F3
Bengal, Bay of *Ind. Oc.* 15°0N 90°0E **313** M17
Bengalûru = Bangalore *India* 12°59N 77°40E **312** N10
Bengbu *China* 32°58N 117°20E **307** H9
Benghazi = Banghāzī *Libya* 32°11N 20°3E **323** B10
Bengkalis *Indonesia* 1°30N 102°10E **308** D2
Bengkulu *Indonesia* 3°50S 102°12E **308** E2
Bengkulu □ *Indonesia* 3°48S 102°16E **308** E2
Bengough *Canada* 49°25N 105°10W **343** D7
Benguela *Angola* 12°37S 13°25E **325** G2
Benguérua, I. *Mozam.* 21°58S 35°28E **329** C6
Beni *Dem. Rep. of the Congo* 0°30N 29°27E **326** B2
Beni → *Bolivia* 10°23S 65°24W **364** F5
Beni Mellal *Morocco* 32°21N 6°21W **322** B4
Beni Suef *Egypt* 29°5N 31°6E **323** C12
Beniah L. *Canada* 63°23N 112°17W **342** A6
Benidorm *Spain* 38°33N 0°9W **293** C5
Benin ■ *Africa* 10°0N 2°0E **322** G6
Benin, Bight of *W. Afr.* 5°0N 3°0E **322** H6
Benin City *Nigeria* 6°20N 5°31E **322** G7
Benitses *Greece* 39°32N 19°55E **297** A3
Benjamin Aceval *Paraguay* 24°58S 57°34W **366** A4
Benjamin Constant *Brazil* 4°40S 70°15W **364** D4
Benjamín Hill *Mexico* 30°9N 111°7W **358** A2
Benkelman *U.S.A.* 40°3N 101°32W **352** E3
Bennett *Canada* 59°51N 135°0W **342** B2
Bennett, L. *Australia* 22°50S 131°2E **332** D5
Bennetta, Ostrov *Russia* 76°21N 148°56E **301** B15
Bennettsville *U.S.A.* 34°37N 79°41W **357** D15
Bennington *N.H., U.S.A.* 43°0N 71°55W **355** D11
Bennington *Vt., U.S.A.* 42°53N 73°12W **355** D11
Benoni *S. Africa* 26°11S 28°18E **329** D4
Benque Viejo *Belize* 17°5N 89°8W **359** D7
Benson *Ariz., U.S.A.* 31°58N 110°18W **349** L8
Benson *Minn., U.S.A.* 45°19N 95°36W **352** C6
Bent *Iran* 26°20N 59°31E **317** E8
Benteng *Indonesia* 6°10S 120°30E **309** F6
Bentinck I. *Australia* 17°3S 139°35E **334** B2
Bento Gonçalves *Brazil* 29°10S 51°31W **367** B5
Benton *Ark., U.S.A.* 34°34N 92°35W **356** D8
Benton *Calif., U.S.A.* 37°48N 118°32W **350** H8
Benton *Ill., U.S.A.* 38°0N 88°55W **352** F9
Benton *Pa., U.S.A.* 41°12N 76°23W **355** E8
Benton Harbor *U.S.A.* 42°6N 86°27W **352** D10
Bentong *Malaysia* 3°31N 101°55E **311** L3
Bentonville *U.S.A.* 36°22N 94°13W **356** C7
Benue → *Nigeria* 7°48N 6°46E **322** G7
Benxi *China* 41°20N 123°48E **307** D12
Beo *Indonesia* 4°25N 126°50E **309** D7
Beograd *Serbia* 44°50N 20°37E **295** B9
Beolgyo *S. Korea* 34°51N 127°21E **307** G14
Beppu *Japan* 33°15N 131°30E **303** H5
Beqa *Fiji* 18°23S 178°8E **331** a
Beqaa Valley = Al Biqā *Lebanon* 34°10N 36°10E **318** A5
Ber Mota *India* 23°27N 68°34E **314** H3
Berach → *India* 25°15N 75°2E **314** G6
Beraketa *Madag.* 23°7S 44°25E **329** C7
Berat *Albania* 40°43N 19°59E **295** D8
Berau, Teluk *Indonesia* 2°30S 132°30E **309** E8
Beravina *Madag.* 18°10S 45°14E **329** B8
Berber *Sudan* 18°0N 34°0E **323** E12
Berbera *Somali Rep.* 10°30N 45°2E **319** E4
Berbérati *C.A.R.* 4°15N 15°40E **324** D3
Berbice → *Guyana* 6°20N 57°32W **364** B7
Berdichev = Berdychiv *Ukraine* 49°57N 28°30E **289** D15
Berdsk *Russia* 54°47N 83°2E **300** D9
Berdyansk *Ukraine* 46°45N 36°50E **291** E6
Berdychiv *Ukraine* 49°57N 28°30E **289** D15
Berea *U.S.A.* 37°34N 84°17W **353** G11
Berebere *Indonesia* 2°25N 128°45E **309** D7
Bereda *Somali Rep.* 11°45N 51°0E **319** E5
Berehove *Ukraine* 48°15N 22°35E **289** D12
Bereket *Turkmenistan* 39°16N 55°32E **317** B7
Berekum *Ghana* 7°29N 2°34W **322** G5
Berens → *Canada* 52°25N 97°2W **343** C9
Berens I. *Canada* 52°18N 97°18W **343** C9
Berens River *Canada* 52°25N 97°0W **343** C9
Beresford *U.S.A.* 43°5N 96°47W **352** D5
Berestechko *Ukraine* 50°22N 25°5E **289** C13
Berevo *Mahajanga, Madag.* 17°14S 44°17E **329** B7
Berevo *Toliara, Madag.* 19°44S 44°58E **329** B7
Berezhany *Ukraine* 49°26N 24°58E **289** D13
Berezina = Byarezina → *Belarus* 52°33N 30°14E **289** B16
Bereznik *Russia* 62°51N 42°40E **290** B7
Berezniki *Russia* 59°24N 56°46E **290** C10
Berezovo *Russia* 64°0N 65°0E **300** C7
Berga *Spain* 42°6N 1°48E **293** A6
Bergama *Turkey* 39°8N 27°11E **295** E12
Bérgamo *Italy* 45°41N 9°43E **292** D8
Bergen *Neths.* 52°40N 4°43E **287** B4
Bergen *Norway* 60°20N 5°20E **280** F11
Bergen *U.S.A.* 43°5N 77°57W **354** C7
Bergen op Zoom *Neths.* 51°28N 4°18E **287** C4
Bergerac *France* 44°51N 0°30E **292** D4
Bergholz *U.S.A.* 40°31N 80°53W **354** F4
Bergisch Gladbach *Germany* 50°59N 7°8E **287** D7
Bergville *S. Africa* 28°52S 29°18E **329** D4
Berhala, Selat *Indonesia* 1°0S 104°15E **308** E2
Berhampore = Baharampur *India* 24°2N 88°27E **315** G13
Berhampur = Brahmapur *India* 19°15N 84°54E **313** K14
Bering Sea *Pac. Oc.* 58°0N 171°0W **346** a
Bering Strait *Pac. Oc.* 65°30N 169°0W **346** a
Beringovskiy *Russia* 63°3N 179°19E **301** C18
Berisso *Argentina* 34°56S 57°50W **366** C4
Berja *Spain* 36°50N 2°56W **293** D4
Berkeley *U.S.A.* 37°51N 122°16W **350** H4
Berkner I. *Antarctica* 79°30S 50°0W **277** D18
Berkshire *U.S.A.* 42°19N 76°11W **355** D8
Berkshire Downs *U.K.* 51°33N 1°29W **285** F6
Berlin *Germany* 52°31N 13°23E **288** B7
Berlin *Md., U.S.A.* 38°20N 75°13W **353** F16
Berlin *N.H., U.S.A.* 44°28N 71°11W **355** B13
Berlin *N.Y., U.S.A.* 42°42N 73°23W **355** D11
Berlin *Wis., U.S.A.* 43°58N 88°57W **352** D9
Berlin L. *U.S.A.* 41°3N 81°0W **354** E4
Bermejo → *Formosa, Argentina* 26°51S 58°23W **366** B4
Bermejo → *San Juan, Argentina* 32°30S 67°30W **366** C2
Bermen, L. *Canada* 53°35N 68°55W **345** B6
Bermuda ☒ *Atl. Oc.* 32°45N 65°0W **339** F13
Bern *Switz.* 46°57N 7°28E **292** C7
Bernalillo *U.S.A.* 35°18N 106°33W **349** J10
Bernardo de Irigoyen *Argentina* 26°15S 53°40W **367** B5
Bernardo O'Higgins □ *Chile* 34°15S 70°45W **366** C1
Bernardsville *U.S.A.* 40°43N 74°34W **355** F10
Bernasconi *Argentina* 37°55S 63°44W **366** D3
Bernburg *Germany* 51°47N 11°44E **288** C6
Berne = Bern *Switz.* 46°57N 7°28E **292** C7
Berneray *U.K.* 57°43N 7°11W **283** D1
Bernier I. *Australia* 24°50S 113°12E **333** D1
Bernina, Piz *Switz.* 46°20N 9°54E **292** C8
Beroroha *Madag.* 21°40S 45°10E **329** C8
Beroun *Czech Rep.* 49°57N 14°5E **288** D8
Berri *Australia* 34°14S 140°35E **335** E3
Berriane *Algeria* 32°50N 3°46E **322** B6
Berry *Australia* 34°46S 150°43E **335** E5
Berry *France* 46°50N 2°0E **292** C5
Berry Is. *Bahamas* 25°40N 77°50W **360** A4
Berryessa, L. *U.S.A.* 38°31N 122°6W **350** G4
Berryville *U.S.A.* 36°22N 93°34W **356** C8
Berseba *Namibia* 26°0S 17°46E **328** D2
Bershad *Ukraine* 48°22N 29°31E **289** D15
Berthold *U.S.A.* 48°19N 101°44W **352** A3
Berthoud *U.S.A.* 40°19N 105°5W **348** F11
Bertoua *Cameroon* 4°30N 13°45E **324** D2
Bertraghboy B. *Ireland* 53°22N 9°54W **282** C2
Berwick *U.S.A.* 41°3N 76°14W **355** E8
Berwick-upon-Tweed *U.K.* 55°46N 2°0W **284** B6
Berwyn Mts. *U.K.* 52°54N 3°26W **284** E4
Besal *Pakistan* 35°4N 73°56E **315** B5
Besalampy *Madag.* 16°43S 44°29E **329** B7
Besançon *France* 47°15N 6°2E **292** C7
Besar *Indonesia* 2°40S 116°0E **308** E5
Besnard L. *Canada* 55°25N 106°0W **343** B7
Besni *Turkey* 37°41N 37°52E **316** B3
Besor, N. → *Egypt* 31°28N 34°22E **318** D3
Bessarabiya *Moldova* 47°0N 28°10E **289** E15
Bessarabka = Basarabeasca *Moldova* 46°21N 28°58E **289** E15
Bessemer *Ala., U.S.A.* 33°24N 86°58W **357** E11
Bessemer *Mich., U.S.A.* 46°29N 90°3W **352** B8
Bessemer *Pa., U.S.A.* 40°59N 80°30W **354** F4
Beswick *Australia* 14°34S 132°53E **332** B5
Bet She'an *Israel* 32°30N 35°30E **318** C4
Bet Shemesh *Israel* 31°44N 35°0E **318** D4
Betafo *Madag.* 19°50S 46°51E **329** B8
Betancuria *Canary Is.* 28°25N 14°3W **296** F5
Betanzos *Spain* 43°15N 8°12W **293** A1
Bétaré Oya *Cameroon* 5°40N 14°5E **324** C2
Betatao *Madag.* 18°11S 47°52E **329** B8
Bethal *S. Africa* 26°27S 29°28E **329** D4
Bethanien *Namibia* 26°31S 17°8E **328** D2
Bethany *Canada* 44°11N 78°34W **354** B6
Bethany *Mo., U.S.A.* 40°16N 94°2W **352** E6
Bethany *Okla., U.S.A.* 35°31N 97°38W **356** D6
Bethel *Alaska, U.S.A.* 60°48N 161°45W **346** a
Bethel *Conn., U.S.A.* 41°22N 73°25W **355** E11
Bethel *Maine, U.S.A.* 44°25N 70°47W **355** B14
Bethel *Vt., U.S.A.* 43°50N 72°38W **355** C12
Bethel Park *U.S.A.* 40°19N 80°2W **354** F4
Bethlehem = Bayt Lahm *West Bank* 31°43N 35°12E **318** D4
Bethlehem *S. Africa* 28°14S 28°18E **329** D4
Bethlehem *U.S.A.* 40°37N 75°23W **355** F9
Bethulie *S. Africa* 30°30S 25°59E **328** E4
Béthune *France* 50°30N 2°38E **292** A5
Betioky *Madag.* 23°48S 44°20E **329** C7
Betong *Malaysia* 1°24N 111°31E **308** D4
Betong *Thailand* 5°45N 101°5E **311** K3
Betoota *Australia* 25°45S 140°42E **334** D3
Betpaqdala *Kazakhstan* 45°45N 70°30E **300** E8
Betroka *Madag.* 23°16S 46°0E **329** C8
Betsiamites *Canada* 48°56N 68°40W **345** C6
Betsiamites → *Canada* 48°56N 68°38W **345** C6
Betsiboka → *Madag.* 16°3S 46°36E **329** B8
Bettendorf *U.S.A.* 41°32N 90°30W **352** E8
Bettiah *India* 26°48N 84°33E **315** F11
Betul *India* 21°58N 77°59E **312** J10
Betws-y-Coed *U.K.* 53°5N 3°48W **284** D4
Beulah *Mich., U.S.A.* 44°38N 86°6W **352** C10
Beulah *N. Dak., U.S.A.* 47°16N 101°47W **352** B3
Beveren *Belgium* 51°12N 4°16E **287** C4
Beverley *Australia* 32°9S 116°56E **333** F2
Beverley *U.K.* 53°51N 0°26W **284** D7
Beverly *U.S.A.* 42°33N 70°53W **355** D14
Beverly Hills *Calif., U.S.A.* 34°5N 118°24W **351** L8
Beverly Hills *Fla., U.S.A.* 28°55N 82°28W **357** G13
Bevoalavo *Madag.* 25°13S 45°26E **329** D7
Bewas → *India* 23°59N 79°21E **315** H8
Bexhill *U.K.* 50°51N 0°29E **285** G8
Beyānlū *Iran* 36°0N 47°51E **316** C5
Beyneu *Kazakhstan* 45°18N 55°9E **291** E10
Beypazarı *Turkey* 40°10N 31°56E **291** F5
Beyşehir Gölü *Turkey* 37°41N 31°33E **316** B1
Béziers *France* 43°20N 3°12E **292** E5
Bezwada = Vijayawada *India* 16°31N 80°39E **313** L12
Bhabua *India* 25°3N 83°37E **315** G10
Bhachau *India* 23°20N 70°16E **312** H7
Bhadar → *Gujarat, India* 22°17N 72°20E **314** H5
Bhadar → *Gujarat, India* 21°27N 69°47E **314** J3
Bhadarwah *India* 32°58N 75°46E **315** C6
Bhadgaon = Bhaktapur *Nepal* 27°38N 85°24E **315** F11
Bhadohi *India* 25°25N 82°34E **315** G10
Bhadra *India* 29°8N 75°14E **314** E6
Bhadrakh *India* 21°10N 86°30E **313** J15
Bhadran *India* 22°19N 72°6E **314** H5
Bhadravati *India* 13°49N 75°40E **312** N9
Bhag *Pakistan* 29°2N 67°49E **314** E2
Bhagalpur *India* 25°10N 87°0E **315** G12
Bhagirathi → *Uttaranchal, India* 30°8N 78°35E **315** D8
Bhagirathi → *W. Bengal, India* 23°25N 88°23E **315** H13
Bhakkar *Pakistan* 31°40N 71°5E **314** D4
Bhakra Dam *India* 31°30N 76°45E **314** D7
Bhaktapur *Nepal* 27°38N 85°24E **315** F11
Bhamo *Burma* 24°15N 97°15E **313** G20
Bhandara *India* 21°5N 79°42E **312** J11
Bhanpura *India* 24°31N 75°44E **314** G6
Bhanrer Ra. *India* 23°40N 79°45E **315** H8
Bhaptiahi *India* 26°19N 86°44E **315** F12
Bharat = India ■ *Asia* 20°0N 78°0E **312** K11
Bharatpur *Chhattisgarh, India* 23°44N 81°46E **315** H9
Bharatpur *Raj., India* 27°15N 77°30E **314** F7
Bharno *India* 23°14N 84°53E **315** H11
Bharuch *India* 21°47N 73°0E **312** J8
Bhatinda *India* 30°15N 74°57E **314** D6
Bhatpara *India* 22°50N 88°25E **315** H13
Bhattu *India* 29°36N 75°19E **314** E6
Bhaun *Pakistan* 32°55N 72°40E **314** C5
Bhaunagar = Bhavnagar *India* 21°45N 72°10E **312** J8
Bhavnagar *India* 21°45N 72°10E **312** J8
Bhawari *India* 25°42N 73°4E **314** G5
Bhayavadar *India* 21°51N 70°15E **314** J4
Bhera *Pakistan* 32°29N 72°57E **314** C5
Bhikangaon *India* 21°52N 75°57E **314** J6
Bhilai = Bhilainagar-Durg *India* 21°13N 81°26E **313** J12
Bhilainagar-Durg *India* 21°13N 81°26E **313** J12
Bhilsa = Vidisha *India* 23°28N 77°53E **314** H7
Bhilwara *India* 25°25N 74°38E **314** G6
Bhima → *India* 16°25N 77°17E **312** L10
Bhimbar *Pakistan* 32°59N 74°3E **315** C6
Bhind *India* 26°30N 78°46E **315** F8
Bhinga *India* 27°43N 81°56E **315** F9
Bhinmal *India* 25°0N 72°15E **314** G5
Bhiwandi *India* 19°20N 73°0E **312** K8
Bhiwani *India* 28°50N 76°9E **314** E7
Bhogava → *India* 22°26N 72°20E **314** H5
Bhola *Bangla.* 22°45N 90°35E **313** H17
Bholari *Pakistan* 25°19N 68°13E **314** G3
Bhopal *India* 23°20N 77°30E **314** H7
Bhubaneshwar *India* 20°15N 85°50E **313** J14
Bhuj *India* 23°15N 69°49E **314** H3
Bhumiphol Res. *Thailand* 17°20N 98°40E **310** D2
Bhusawal *India* 21°3N 75°46E **312** J9
Bhutan ■ *Asia* 27°25N 90°30E **313** F17
Biafra, B. of = Bonny, Bight of *Africa* 3°30N 9°20E **324** D1
Biak *Indonesia* 1°10S 136°6E **309** E9
Biała Podlaska *Poland* 52°4N 23°6E **289** B12
Białogard *Poland* 54°2N 15°58E **288** A8
Białystok *Poland* 53°10N 23°10E **289** B12
Biaora *India* 23°56N 76°56E **314** H7
Bīārjmand *Iran* 36°6N 55°53E **317** B7
Biaro *Indonesia* 2°5N 125°26E **309** D7
Biarritz *France* 43°29N 1°33W **292** E3
Bias *Indonesia* 8°24S 115°36E **309** J18
Bibai *Japan* 43°19N 141°52E **302** C10
Bibby I. *Canada* 61°55N 93°0W **343** A10
Biberach *Germany* 48°5N 9°47E **288** D5
Bibungwa *Dem. Rep. of the Congo* 2°40S 28°15E **326** C2
Bicester *U.K.* 51°54N 1°9W **285** F6
Bicheno *Australia* 41°52S 148°18E **335** G4
Bichia *India* 22°27N 80°42E **315** H9
Bickerton I. *Australia* 13°45S 136°10E **334** A2
Bida *Nigeria* 9°3N 5°58E **322** G7
Bidar *India* 17°55N 77°35E **312** L10
Biddeford *U.S.A.* 43°30N 70°28W **353** D18
Bideford *U.K.* 51°1N 4°13W **285** F3
Bideford Bay *U.K.* 51°5N 4°20W **285** F3
Bidhuna *India* 26°49N 79°31E **315** F8
Bidor *Malaysia* 4°6N 101°15E **311** K3
Bidyadanga *Australia* 18°45S 121°43E **332** C3
Bié, Planalto de *Angola* 12°0S 16°0E **325** G3
Bieber *U.S.A.* 41°7N 121°8W **348** F3
Biel *Switz.* 47°8N 7°14E **292** C7
Bielefeld *Germany* 52°1N 8°33E **288** B5
Biella *Italy* 45°34N 8°3E **292** D8
Bielsk Podlaski *Poland* 52°47N 23°12E **289** B12
Bielsko-Biała *Poland* 49°50N 19°2E **289** D10
Bien Hoa *Vietnam* 10°57N 106°49E **311** G6
Bienne = Biel *Switz.* 47°8N 7°14E **292** C7
Bienville, L. *Canada* 55°5N 72°40W **344** A5
Biesiesfontein *S. Africa* 30°57S 17°58E **328** E2
Big → *Canada* 54°50N 58°55W **345** B8
Big B. *Canada* 55°43N 60°35W **345** A7
Big Bear City *U.S.A.* 34°16N 116°51W **351** L10
Big Bear Lake *U.S.A.* 34°15N 116°56W **351** L10
Big Belt Mts. *U.S.A.* 46°30N 111°25W **348** C8
Big Bend *Swaziland* 26°50S 31°58E **329** D5
Big Bend △ *U.S.A.* 29°20N 103°5W **356** G3
Big Blue → *U.S.A.* 39°35N 96°34W **352** F5
Big Creek *U.S.A.* 37°11N 119°14W **350** H7
Big Cypress ⌓ *U.S.A.* 26°0N 81°10W **357** H14
Big Desert *Australia* 35°45S 141°10E **335** F3
Big Falls *U.S.A.* 48°12N 93°48W **352** A7
Big Fork → *U.S.A.* 48°31N 93°43W **352** A7
Big Horn Mts. = Bighorn Mts. *U.S.A.* 44°25N 107°0W **348** D10
Big I. *Canada* 61°7N 116°45W **342** A5
Big Lake *U.S.A.* 31°12N 101°28W **356** F4
Big Moose *U.S.A.* 43°49N 74°58W **355** C10
Big Muddy Cr. → *U.S.A.* 48°8N 104°36W **348** B11
Big Pine *U.S.A.* 37°10N 118°17W **350** H8
Big Piney *U.S.A.* 42°32N 110°7W **348** E8
Big Rapids *U.S.A.* 43°42N 85°29W **353** D11
Big Rideau L. *Canada* 44°40N 76°15W **355** B8
Big River *Canada* 53°50N 107°0W **343** C7
Big Run *U.S.A.* 40°57N 78°55W **354** F6
Big Sable Pt. *U.S.A.* 44°3N 86°1W **352** C10
Big Salmon → *Canada* 61°52N 134°55W **342** A2
Big Sand L. *Canada* 57°45N 99°45W **343** B9
Big Sandy *U.S.A.* 48°11N 110°7W **348** B8
Big Sandy → *U.S.A.* 38°25N 82°36W **353** F12
Big Sandy Cr. = Sandy Cr. → *U.S.A.* 41°51N 109°47W **348** F9
Big Sandy Cr. → *U.S.A.* 38°7N 102°29W **348** G12
Big Sioux → *U.S.A.* 42°29N 96°27W **352** D5
Big South Fork ⌓ *U.S.A.* 36°27N 84°47W **357** C12
Big Spring *U.S.A.* 32°15N 101°28W **356** E4
Big Stone City *U.S.A.* 45°18N 96°28W **352** C5
Big Stone Gap *U.S.A.* 36°52N 82°47W **353** G12
Big Stone L. *U.S.A.* 45°18N 96°27W **352** C5
Big Sur *U.S.A.* 36°15N 121°48W **350** J5
Big Timber *U.S.A.* 45°50N 109°57W **348** D9
Big Trout L. *Canada* 53°40N 90°0W **344** B2
Big Trout Lake *Canada* 53°45N 90°0W **344** B2
Biğa *Turkey* 40°13N 27°14E **295** D12

Broads, The U.K. 52°45N 1°30E 284 E9
Broadus U.S.A. 45°27N 105°25W 348 D11
Brochet Canada 57°53N 101°40W 343 B8
Brochet, L. Canada 58°36N 101°35W 343 B8
Brock I. Canada 77°52N 114°19W 341 B8
Brocken Germany 51°47N 10°37E 288 C6
Brockport U.S.A. 43°13N 77°56W 354 C7
Brockton U.S.A. 42°5N 71°1W 355 D13
Brockville Canada 44°35N 75°41W 355 B9
Brockway Mont., U.S.A. 47°18N 105°45W 348 C11
Brockway Pa., U.S.A. 41°15N 78°47W 354 E6
Brocton U.S.A. 42°23N 79°26W 354 D5
Brodeur Pen. Canada 72°30N 88°10W 341 B11
Brodick U.K. 55°35N 5°9W 283 F3
Brodnica Poland 53°15N 19°25E 289 B10
Brody Ukraine 50°5N 25°10E 289 C13
Brogan U.S.A. 44°15N 117°31W 348 D5
Broken Arrow U.S.A. 36°3N 95°48W 356 C7
Broken Bow Nebr., U.S.A. 41°24N 99°38W 352 E4
Broken Bow Okla., U.S.A. 34°2N 94°44W 356 D7
Broken Bow Lake U.S.A. 34°9N 94°40W 356 D7
Broken Hill Australia 31°58S 141°29E 335 E3
Broken Ridge Ind. Oc. 30°0S 94°0E 336 L1
Broken River Ra. Australia 21°0S 148°22E 334 K6
Bromley □ U.K. 51°24N 0°2E 285 F8
Bromo Indonesia 7°55S 112°55E 309 G15
Bromsgrove U.K. 52°21N 2°2W 285 E5
Brønderslev Denmark 57°16N 9°57E 281 H13
Bronkhorstspruit S. Africa 25°46S 28°45E 329 D4
Brønnøysund Norway 65°28N 12°14E 280 D15
Brook Park U.S.A. 41°23N 81°48W 354 E4
Brookhaven U.S.A. 31°35N 90°26W 357 F9
Brookings Oreg., U.S.A. 42°3N 124°17W 348 E1
Brookings S. Dak., U.S.A. 44°19N 96°48W 352 C5
Brooklin Canada 43°55N 78°55W 354 C6
Brooklyn Park U.S.A. 45°6N 93°23W 352 C7
Brooks Canada 50°35N 111°55W 342 C6
Brooks Range U.S.A. 68°0N 152°0W 346 a
Brooksville U.S.A. 28°33N 82°23W 357 G13
Brookton Australia 32°22S 117°0E 333 F2
Brookville U.S.A. 41°10N 79°5W 354 E5
Broom, L. U.K. 57°55N 5°15W 283 D3
Broome Australia 18°0S 122°15E 332 C3
Brora U.K. 58°0N 3°52W 283 C5
Brora → U.K. 58°0N 3°51W 283 C5
Brosna → Ireland 53°14N 7°58W 282 C4
Brothers U.S.A. 43°49N 120°36W 348 E3
Brough U.K. 54°32N 2°18W 284 C5
Brough Hd. U.K. 59°8N 3°20W 283 B5
Broughton Island = Qikiqtarjuaq Canada 67°33N 63°0W 341 C13
Brown, L. Australia 31°5S 118°15E 333 F2
Brown, Pt. Australia 32°32S 133°50E 335 E1
Brown City U.S.A. 43°13N 82°59W 354 C2
Brown Willy U.K. 50°35N 4°37W 285 G3
Brownfield U.S.A. 33°11N 102°17W 356 E3
Browning U.S.A. 48°34N 113°1W 348 B7
Brownsville Oreg., U.S.A. 44°24N 122°59W 348 D2
Brownsville Pa., U.S.A. 40°1N 79°53W 354 F5
Brownsville Tenn., U.S.A. 35°36N 89°16W 357 D10
Brownsville Tex., U.S.A. 25°54N 97°30W 356 J6
Brownville U.S.A. 44°0N 75°59W 355 C9
Brownwood U.S.A. 31°43N 98°59W 356 F5
Browse I. Australia 14°7S 123°33E 332 B3
Bruas Malaysia 4°30N 100°47E 311 K3
Bruay-la-Buissière France 50°29N 2°33E 292 A5
Bruce, Mt. Australia 22°37S 118°8E 332 D2
Bruce Pen. Canada 45°0N 81°30W 354 B3
Bruce Peninsula △ Canada 45°14N 81°36W 354 A3
Bruce Rock Australia 31°52S 118°8E 333 F2
Bruck an der Leitha Austria 48°1N 16°47E 289 D9
Bruck an der Mur Austria 47°24N 15°16E 288 E8
Brue → U.K. 51°13N 2°59W 285 F5
Bruges = Brugge Belgium 51°13N 3°13E 287 C3
Brugge Belgium 51°13N 3°13E 287 C3
Bruin U.S.A. 41°3N 79°43W 354 E5
Brûk, W. el → Egypt 30°15N 33°50E 318 E2
Brûlé Canada 53°15N 117°58W 342 C5
Brumado Brazil 14°14S 41°40W 365 F10
Brumunddal Norway 60°53N 10°56E 280 F14
Bruneau U.S.A. 42°53N 115°48W 348 E6
Bruneau → U.S.A. 42°56N 115°57W 348 E6
Brunei = Bandar Seri Begawan Brunei 4°52N 115°0E 308 C4
Brunei ■ Asia 4°50N 115°0E 308 D4
Brunner, L. N.Z. 42°37S 171°27E 331 E3
Brunssum Neths. 50°57N 5°59E 287 D5
Brunswick = Braunschweig Germany 52°15N 10°31E 288 B6
Brunswick Ga., U.S.A. 31°10N 81°30W 357 F14
Brunswick Maine, U.S.A. 43°55N 69°58W 353 D19
Brunswick Md., U.S.A. 39°19N 77°38W 353 F15
Brunswick Mo., U.S.A. 39°26N 93°8W 352 F7
Brunswick Ohio, U.S.A. 41°14N 81°51W 354 E3
Brunswick, Pen. de Chile 53°30S 71°30W 368 G2
Brunswick B. Australia 15°15S 124°50E 332 C3
Brunswick Junction Australia 33°15S 115°50E 333 F2
Brunt Ice Shelf Antarctica 75°30S 25°0W 277 D2
Brus Laguna Honduras 15°47N 84°35W 360 C3
Brush U.S.A. 40°15N 103°37W 348 F12
Brushton U.S.A. 44°50N 74°31W 355 B10
Brusque Brazil 27°5S 49°0W 367 B6
Brussel Belgium 50°51N 4°21E 287 D4
Brussel ✕ (BRU) Belgium 50°54N 4°29E 287 D5
Brussels = Brussel Belgium 50°51N 4°21E 287 D4
Brussels Canada 43°44N 81°15W 354 C3
Bruthen Australia 37°42S 147°50E 335 F4
Bruxelles = Brussel Belgium 50°51N 4°21E 287 D4
Bryan Ohio, U.S.A. 41°28N 84°33W 353 E11
Bryan Tex., U.S.A. 30°40N 96°22W 356 F6
Bryan, Mt. Australia 33°30S 139°5E 335 E2
Bryansk Russia 53°13N 34°25E 290 D4
Bryce Canyon △ U.S.A. 37°30N 112°10W 349 H7
Bryne Norway 58°44N 5°38E 281 G11
Bryson City U.S.A. 35°26N 83°27W 357 D13
Bsharri Lebanon 34°15N 36°0E 318 A5
Bū Baqarah U.A.E. 25°35N 56°25E 317 E8
Bu Craa W. Sahara 26°45N 12°50W 322 C3
Bū Ḥasā U.A.E. 23°30N 53°20E 317 F7
Bua Fiji 16°48S 178°37E 331 a
Bua Yai Thailand 15°33N 102°26E 310 E4
Buan S. Korea 35°44N 126°44E 307 G14
Buapinang Indonesia 4°40S 121°30E 309 E6
Bubanza Burundi 3°6S 29°23E 326 C2
Bubi → Zimbabwe 22°20S 31°7E 327 G3
Būbiyān Kuwait 29°45N 48°15E 317 D6
Buca Fiji 16°38S 179°52E 331 a
Bucaramanga Colombia 7°0N 73°0W 364 B4
Bucasia Australia 21°2S 149°10E 334 K7
Buccaneer Arch. Australia 16°7S 123°20E 332 C3
Buccoo Reef Trin. & Tob. 11°10N 60°51W 365 J16
Buchach Ukraine 49°5N 25°25E 289 D13
Buchan U.K. 57°32N 2°21W 283 D6
Buchan Ness U.K. 57°29N 1°46W 283 D7
Buchanan Canada 51°40N 102°45W 343 C8
Buchanan Liberia 5°57N 10°2W 322 G3
Buchanan, L. Queens., Australia 21°35S 145°52E 334 C4
Buchanan, L. W. Austral., Australia 25°33S 123°2E 333 E3
Buchanan, L. U.S.A. 30°45N 98°25W 356 F5
Buchanan Cr. → Australia 19°13S 136°33E 334 B2
Buchans Canada 48°50N 56°52W 345 C8
Bucharest = Bucureşti Romania 44°27N 26°10E 289 F14
Bucheon S. Korea 37°28N 126°45E 307 F14
Buchon, Pt. U.S.A. 35°15N 120°54W 350 K6
Buck Hill Falls U.S.A. 41°11N 75°16W 355 E9
Buckeye Lake U.S.A. 39°55N 82°29W 354 G2
Buckhannon U.S.A. 39°0N 80°8W 353 F13
Buckhaven U.K. 56°11N 3°3W 283 E5
Buckhorn L. Canada 44°29N 78°23W 354 B6
Buckie U.K. 57°41N 2°58W 283 D6
Buckingham Canada 45°37N 75°24W 344 C4
Buckingham U.K. 51°59N 0°57W 285 F7
Buckingham B. Australia 12°10S 135°40E 334 A2
Buckinghamshire □ U.K. 51°53N 0°55W 285 F7
Buckle Hd. Australia 14°26S 127°52E 332 B4
Buckleboo Australia 32°54S 136°12E 335 E2
Buckley U.K. 53°10N 3°5W 284 D4
Buckley → Australia 20°10S 138°49E 334 C2
Bucklin U.S.A. 37°33N 99°38W 352 G4
Bucks L. U.S.A. 39°54N 121°12W 350 F5
Bucureşti Romania 44°27N 26°10E 289 F14
Bucyrus U.S.A. 40°48N 82°59W 353 E12
Budalin Burma 22°20N 95°10E 313 H19
Budapest Hungary 47°29N 19°3E 289 E10
Budaun India 28°5N 79°10E 315 E8
Budd Coast Antarctica 68°0S 112°0E 277 C8
Bude U.K. 50°49N 4°34W 285 G3
Budennovsk Russia 44°50N 44°10E 291 F7
Budge Budge = Baj Baj India 22°30N 88°5E 315 H13
Budgewoi Australia 33°13S 151°34E 335 E5
Budjala Dem. Rep. of the Congo 2°50N 19°40E 324 D3
Buellton U.S.A. 34°37N 120°12W 351 L6
Buena Esperanza Argentina 34°45S 65°15W 366 C2
Buena Park U.S.A. 33°52N 117°59W 351 M9
Buena Vista Colo., U.S.A. 38°51N 106°8W 348 G10
Buena Vista Va., U.S.A. 37°44N 79°21W 353 G14
Buena Vista Lake Bed U.S.A. 35°12N 119°18W 351 K7
Buenaventura Colombia 3°53N 77°4W 364 C3
Buenaventura Mexico 29°51N 107°29W 358 B3
Buenos Aires Argentina 34°36S 58°22W 366 C4
Buenos Aires Costa Rica 9°10N 83°20W 360 E3
Buenos Aires □ Argentina 36°30S 60°0W 366 D4
Buenos Aires, L. Argentina 46°35S 72°30W 368 F2
Buffalo Mo., U.S.A. 37°39N 93°6W 352 G7
Buffalo N.Y., U.S.A. 42°53N 78°53W 354 D6
Buffalo Okla., U.S.A. 36°50N 99°38W 356 C5
Buffalo S. Dak., U.S.A. 45°35N 103°33W 352 C2
Buffalo Wyo., U.S.A. 44°21N 106°42W 348 D10
Buffalo → Canada 60°5N 115°5W 342 A5
Buffalo → S. Africa 28°43S 30°37E 329 D5
Buffalo ⌓ U.S.A. 36°14N 92°36W 356 C8
Buffalo Head Hills Canada 57°25N 115°55W 342 B5
Buffalo L. Alta., Canada 52°27N 112°54W 342 C6
Buffalo L. N.W.T., Canada 60°12N 115°25W 342 A5
Buffalo Narrows Canada 55°51N 108°29W 343 B7
Buffalo Springs ⌓ Kenya 0°32N 37°35E 326 B4
Buffels → S. Africa 29°36S 17°3E 328 D2
Buford U.S.A. 34°10N 84°0W 357 D12
Bug = Buh → Ukraine 46°59N 31°58E 291 E5
Bug → Poland 52°31N 21°5E 289 B11
Buga Colombia 4°0N 76°15W 364 C3
Bugala I. Uganda 0°40S 32°20E 326 C3
Buganda Uganda 0°0 31°30E 326 C3
Buganga Uganda 0°3S 32°0E 326 C3
Bugel, Tanjung Indonesia 6°26S 111°3E 309 G14
Bugibba Malta 35°57N 14°25E 297 D1
Bugsuk I. Phil. 8°12N 117°18E 308 C5
Bugulma Russia 54°33N 52°48E 290 D9
Bugun Shara Mongolia 49°0N 104°0E 304 B5
Bugungu ⌓ Uganda 2°17N 31°50E 326 B3
Buguruslan Russia 53°39N 52°26E 290 D9
Buh → Ukraine 46°59N 31°58E 291 E5
Buhera Zimbabwe 19°18S 31°29E 329 B5
Buhl U.S.A. 42°36N 114°46W 348 E6
Builth Wells U.K. 52°9N 3°25W 285 E4
Buir Nur Mongolia 47°50N 117°42E 305 B6
Buji China 22°37N 114°5E 305 F11
Bujumbura Burundi 3°16S 29°18E 326 C2
Bukachacha Russia 52°55N 116°50E 301 D12
Bukama Dem. Rep. of the Congo 9°10S 25°50E 327 D2
Būkān Iran 36°31N 46°12E 316 B5
Bukavu Dem. Rep. of the Congo 2°20S 28°52E 326 C2
Bukene Tanzania 4°15S 32°48E 326 C3
Bukhara = Bukhoro Uzbekistan 39°48N 64°25E 300 F7
Bukhoro Uzbekistan 39°48N 64°25E 300 F7
Bukima Tanzania 1°50S 33°25E 326 C3
Bukit Badung Indonesia 8°49S 115°10E 309 K18
Bukit Kerajaan Malaysia 5°25N 100°15E 311 c
Bukit Mertajam Malaysia 5°22N 100°28E 311 c
Bukit Ni Malaysia 1°22N 104°12E 311 d
Bukit Panjang Singapore 1°23N 103°46E 311 d
Bukit Tengah Malaysia 5°22N 100°25E 311 c
Bukittinggi Indonesia 0°20S 100°20E 308 E2
Bukoba Tanzania 1°20S 31°49E 326 C3
Bukum, Pulau Singapore 1°14N 103°46E 311 d
Bukuya Uganda 0°40N 31°52E 326 B3
Būl, Kuh-e Iran 30°48N 52°45E 317 D7
Bula Indonesia 3°6S 130°30E 309 E8
Bulahdelah Australia 32°23S 152°13E 335 E5
Bulan Phil. 12°40N 123°52E 309 B6
Bulandshahr India 28°28N 77°51E 314 E7
Bulawayo Zimbabwe 20°7S 28°32E 327 G2
Buldan Turkey 38°2N 28°50E 295 E13
Bulgan Mongolia 48°45N 103°34E 304 B5
Bulgar Russia 54°57N 49°4E 290 D8
Bulgaria ■ Europe 42°35N 25°30E 295 C11
Buli, Teluk Indonesia 0°48N 128°25E 309 D7
Buliluyan, C. Phil. 8°20N 117°15E 308 C5
Bulim Singapore 1°22N 103°43E 311 d
Bulkley → Canada 55°15N 127°40W 342 B3
Bull Shoals L. U.S.A. 36°22N 92°35W 356 C8
Bulleringa △ Australia 17°39S 143°56E 334 B3
Bullhead City U.S.A. 35°8N 114°32W 351 K12
Büllingen Belgium 50°25N 6°16E 287 D6
Bullock Creek Australia 17°43S 144°31E 334 B3
Bulloo → Australia 28°43S 142°30E 335 D3
Bulloo L. Australia 28°43S 142°25E 335 D3
Bulls N.Z. 40°10S 175°24E 331 D5
Bulnes Chile 36°42S 72°19W 366 D1
Bulsar = Valsad India 20°40N 72°58E 312 J8
Bultfontein S. Africa 28°18S 26°10E 328 D4
Bulukumba Indonesia 5°33S 120°11E 309 F6
Bulun Russia 70°37N 127°30E 301 B13
Bumba Dem. Rep. of the Congo 2°13N 22°30E 324 D4
Bumbiri I. Tanzania 1°40S 31°55E 326 C3
Bumhpa Bum Burma 26°51N 97°14E 313 F20
Bumi → Zimbabwe 17°0S 28°20E 327 F2
Buna Kenya 2°58N 39°30E 326 B4
Bunaken Indonesia 1°37N 124°46E 309 D6
Bunazi Tanzania 1°3S 31°23E 326 C3
Bunbah, Khalīj Libya 32°20N 23°15E 323 B10
Bunbury Australia 33°20S 115°35E 333 F2
Bunclody Ireland 52°39N 6°40W 282 D5
Buncrana Ireland 55°8N 7°27W 282 A4
Bundaberg Australia 24°54S 152°22E 335 C5
Bundey → Australia 21°46S 135°37E 334 C2
Bundi India 25°30N 75°35E 314 G6
Bundjalung △ Australia 29°16S 153°21E 335 D5
Bundoran Ireland 54°28N 8°16W 282 B3
Bung Kan Thailand 18°23N 103°37E 310 C4
Bungay U.K. 52°27N 1°28E 285 E9
Bungil Cr. → Australia 27°5S 149°5E 335 D4
Bungle Bungle = Purnululu △ Australia 17°20S 128°20E 332 C4
Bungo-Suidō Japan 33°0N 132°15E 303 H6
Bungoma Kenya 0°34N 34°34E 326 B3
Bungotakada Japan 33°35N 131°25E 303 H5
Bungu Tanzania 7°35S 39°0E 326 D4
Bunia Dem. Rep. of the Congo 1°35N 30°20E 326 B3
Bunji Pakistan 35°45N 74°40E 315 B6
Bunkie U.S.A. 30°57N 92°11W 356 F8
Bunnell U.S.A. 29°28N 81°16W 357 G14
Buntok Indonesia 1°40S 114°58E 308 E4
Bunya Mts. △ Australia 26°51S 151°34E 335 D5
Bunyu Indonesia 3°35N 117°50E 308 D5
Buol Indonesia 1°15N 121°32E 309 D6
Buon Brieng Vietnam 13°9N 108°12E 310 F7
Buon Ma Thuot Vietnam 12°40N 108°3E 310 F7
Buong Long Cambodia 13°44N 106°59E 310 F6
Buorkhaya, Mys Russia 71°50N 132°40E 301 B14
Buqayq Si. Arabia 26°0N 49°45E 317 E6
Bur Acaba Somali Rep. 3°12N 44°20E 319 G3
Bûr Safâga Egypt 26°43N 33°57E 316 E2
Bûr Sa'îd Egypt 31°16N 32°18E 323 B12
Bûr Sûdân Sudan 19°32N 37°9E 323 E13
Bura Kenya 1°4S 39°58E 326 C4
Burakin Australia 30°31S 117°10E 333 F2
Burao Somali Rep. 9°32N 45°32E 319 F4
Burāq Syria 33°11N 36°29E 318 B5
Buraydah Si. Arabia 26°20N 43°59E 316 E4
Burbank U.S.A. 34°12N 118°18W 351 L8
Burda India 25°50N 77°35E 314 G6
Burdekin → Australia 19°38S 147°25E 334 B4
Burdur Turkey 37°45N 30°17E 291 G5
Burdwan = Barddhaman India 23°14N 87°39E 315 H12
Bure Ethiopia 10°40N 37°4E 319 E2
Bure → U.K. 52°38N 1°43E 284 E9
Bureya → Russia 49°27N 129°30E 301 E13
Burford Canada 43°7N 80°27W 354 C4
Burgas Bulgaria 42°33N 27°29E 295 C12
Burgeo Canada 47°37N 57°38W 345 C8
Burgersdorp S. Africa 31°0S 26°20E 328 E4
Burges, Mt. Australia 30°50S 121°5E 333 F3
Burghead U.K. 57°43N 3°30W 283 D5
Burgos Spain 42°21N 3°41W 293 A4
Burgsvik Sweden 57°3N 18°19E 281 H18
Burgundy = Bourgogne □ France 47°0N 4°50E 292 C6
Burhaniye Turkey 39°30N 26°58E 295 E12
Burhanpur India 21°18N 76°14E 312 J10
Burhi Gandak → India 25°20N 86°37E 315 G12
Burhner → India 22°43N 80°31E 315 H9
Burias I. Phil. 12°55N 123°5E 309 B6
Burica, Pta. Costa Rica 8°3N 82°51W 360 E3
Burien U.S.A. 47°28N 122°20W 350 C4
Burigi, L. Tanzania 2°2S 31°22E 326 C3
Burigi ⌓ Tanzania 2°20S 31°6E 326 C3
Burin Canada 47°1N 55°14W 345 C8
Buriram Thailand 15°0N 103°0E 310 E4
Burkburnett U.S.A. 34°6N 98°34W 356 D5
Burke → Australia 23°12S 139°33E 334 C2
Burke Chan. Canada 52°10N 127°30W 342 C3
Burketown Australia 17°45S 139°33E 334 B2
Burkina Faso ■ Africa 12°0N 1°0W 322 F5
Burk's Falls Canada 45°37N 79°24W 344 C4
Burleigh Falls Canada 44°33N 78°12W 354 B6
Burley U.S.A. 42°32N 113°48W 348 E7
Burlingame U.S.A. 37°35N 122°21W 350 H4
Burlington Canada 43°18N 79°45W 354 C5
Burlington Colo., U.S.A. 39°18N 102°16W 348 G12
Burlington Iowa, U.S.A. 40°49N 91°14W 352 E8
Burlington Kans., U.S.A. 38°12N 95°45W 352 F6
Burlington N.C., U.S.A. 36°6N 79°26W 357 C15
Burlington N.J., U.S.A. 40°4N 74°51W 355 F10
Burlington Vt., U.S.A. 44°29N 73°12W 355 B11
Burlington Wash., U.S.A. 48°28N 122°20W 350 B4
Burlington Wis., U.S.A. 42°41N 88°17W 352 D9
Burma ■ Asia 21°0N 96°30E 313 J20
Burnaby I. Canada 52°25N 131°19W 342 C2
Burnet U.S.A. 30°45N 98°14W 356 F5
Burney U.S.A. 40°53N 121°40W 348 F3
Burnham U.S.A. 40°38N 77°34W 354 F7
Burnham-on-Sea U.K. 51°14N 3°0W 285 F5
Burnie Australia 41°4S 145°56E 335 G4
Burnley U.K. 53°47N 2°14W 284 D5
Burns U.S.A. 43°35N 119°3W 348 E4
Burns Junction U.S.A. 42°47N 117°51W 348 E5
Burns Lake Canada 54°14N 125°45W 342 C3
Burnside → Canada 66°51N 108°4W 340 C9
Burnside, L. Australia 25°22S 123°0E 333 E3
Burnsville U.S.A. 44°47N 93°17W 352 C7
Burnt, L. Canada 53°35N 64°4W 345 B7
Burnt River Canada 44°41N 78°42W 354 B6
Burntwood → Canada 56°8N 96°34W 343 B9
Burntwood L. Canada 55°22N 100°26W 343 B8
Burqān Kuwait 29°0N 47°57E 316 D5
Burqin China 47°43N 87°0E 304 B3
Burra Australia 33°40S 138°55E 335 E2
Burray U.K. 58°51N 2°54W 283 C6
Burren Ireland 53°9N 9°5W 282 C2
Burren △ Ireland 53°1N 8°58W 282 C3
Burren Junction Australia 30°7S 148°58E 335 E4
Burrinjuck Res. Australia 35°0S 148°36E 335 F4
Burro, Serranías del Mexico 28°56N 102°5W 358 B4
Burrow Hd. U.K. 54°41N 4°24W 283 G4
Burrum Coast △ Australia 25°13S 152°36E 335 D5
Burruyacú Argentina 26°30S 64°40W 366 B3
Burry Port U.K. 51°41N 4°15W 285 F3
Bursa Turkey 40°15N 29°5E 295 D13
Burstall Canada 50°39N 109°54W 343 C7
Burton Ohio, U.S.A. 41°28N 81°8W 354 E3
Burton S.C., U.S.A. 32°26N 80°43W 357 E14
Burton, L. Canada 54°45N 78°20W 344 B4
Burton upon Trent U.K. 52°48N 1°38W 284 E6
Buru Indonesia 3°30S 126°30E 309 E7
Burûn, Râs Egypt 31°14N 33°7E 318 D2
Burundi ■ Africa 3°15S 30°0E 326 C3
Bururi Burundi 3°57S 29°37E 326 C2
Burutu Nigeria 5°20N 5°29E 322 G7
Burwell U.S.A. 41°47N 99°8W 352 E4
Burwick U.K. 58°45N 2°58W 283 C5
Bury U.K. 53°35N 2°17W 284 D5
Bury St. Edmunds U.K. 52°15N 0°43E 285 E8
Buryatia □ Russia 53°0N 110°0E 301 D11
Busan S. Korea 35°5N 129°0E 307 G15
Busango Swamp Zambia 14°15S 25°45E 327 E2
Buşayrah Syria 35°9N 40°26E 316 C4
Būshehr Iran 28°55N 50°55E 317 D6
Būshehr □ Iran 28°20N 51°45E 317 D6
Bushell Canada 59°31N 108°45W 343 B7
Bushenyi Uganda 0°35S 30°10E 326 C3
Bushire = Būshehr Iran 28°55N 50°55E 317 D6
Businga Dem. Rep. of the Congo 3°16N 20°59E 324 D4
Buşra ash Shām Syria 32°30N 36°25E 318 C5
Busselton Australia 33°42S 115°15E 333 F2
Bussum Neths. 52°16N 5°10E 287 B5
Busto Arsizio Italy 45°37N 8°51E 292 D8
Busu Djanoa Dem. Rep. of the Congo 1°43N 21°23E 324 D4
Busuanga I. Phil. 12°10N 120°0E 309 B5
Busungbiu Indonesia 8°16S 114°58E 309 J17
Buta Dem. Rep. of the Congo 2°50N 24°53E 326 B1
Butare Rwanda 2°31S 29°52E 326 C2
Butaritari Kiribati 3°30N 174°0E 336 G9
Bute U.K. 55°48N 5°2W 283 F3
Bute Inlet Canada 50°40N 124°53W 342 C4
Butemba Uganda 1°9N 31°37E 326 B3
Butembo Dem. Rep. of the Congo 0°9N 29°18E 326 B2
Butere Kenya 0°13N 34°30E 326 B3
Butha Qi China 48°0N 122°32E 305 B7
Butiaba Uganda 1°50N 31°20E 326 B3
Butler Mo., U.S.A. 38°16N 94°20W 352 F6
Butler Pa., U.S.A. 40°52N 79°54W 354 F5
Buton Indonesia 5°0S 122°45E 309 E6
Butte Mont., U.S.A. 46°0N 112°32W 348 C7
Butte Nebr., U.S.A. 42°58N 98°51W 352 D4
Butte Creek → U.S.A. 39°12N 121°56W 350 F5
Butterworth = Gcuwa S. Africa 32°20S 28°11E 329 E4
Butterworth Malaysia 5°24N 100°23E 311 c
Buttevant Ireland 52°14N 8°40W 282 D3
Buttfield, Mt. Australia 24°45S 128°9E 333 D4
Button B. Canada 58°45N 94°23W 343 B10
Buttonwillow U.S.A. 35°24N 119°28W 351 K7
Butty Hd. Australia 33°54S 121°39E 333 F3
Butuan Phil. 8°57N 125°33E 309 C7
Butung = Buton Indonesia 5°0S 122°45E 309 E6
Buturlinovka Russia 50°50N 40°35E 291 D7
Buur Hakaba = Bur Acaba Somali Rep. 3°12N 44°20E 319 G3
Buxa Duar India 27°45N 89°35E 315 F13
Buxar India 25°34N 83°58E 315 G10
Buxoro = Bukhoro Uzbekistan 39°48N 64°25E 300 F7
Buxtehude Germany 53°28N 9°39E 288 B5
Buxton U.K. 53°16N 1°54W 284 D6
Buy Russia 58°28N 41°28E 290 C7
Buyant-Uhaa Mongolia 44°55N 110°11E 305 B6
Buyo, L. de Ivory C. 6°16N 7°10W 322 G4
Büyük Menderes → Turkey 37°28N 27°11E 295 F12
Büyükçekmece Turkey 41°2N 28°35E 295 D13
Buzău Romania 45°10N 26°50E 289 F14
Buzău → Romania 45°26N 27°44E 289 F14
Buzen Japan 33°35N 131°5E 303 H5
Buzi → Mozam. 19°50S 34°43E 327 F3
Büzmeýin Turkmenistan 38°3N 58°12E 317 B8
Buzuluk Russia 52°48N 52°12E 290 D9
Buzzards Bay U.S.A. 41°45N 70°37W 355 E14
Bwana Mkubwe Dem. Rep. of the Congo 13°8S 28°38E 327 E2
Bwindi △ Uganda 1°2S 29°42E 326 C2
Byarezina → Belarus 52°33N 30°14E 289 B16
Bydgoszcz Poland 53°10N 18°0E 289 B9
Byelarus = Belarus ■ Europe 53°30N 27°0E 289 B14
Byelorussia = Belarus ■ Europe 53°30N 27°0E 289 B14
Byers U.S.A. 39°43N 104°14W 348 G11
Byesville U.S.A. 39°58N 81°32W 354 G3
Byfield △ Australia 22°52S 150°45E 334 C5
Byford Australia 32°15S 116°0E 333 F2
Bykhaw Belarus 53°31N 30°14E 289 B16
Bykhov = Bykhaw Belarus 53°31N 30°14E 289 B16
Bylas U.S.A. 33°8N 110°7W 349 K8
Bylot Canada 58°25N 94°8W 343 B10
Bylot I. Canada 73°13N 78°34W 341 B12
Byrd, C. Antarctica 69°38S 76°7W 277 C17
Byrock Australia 30°40S 146°27E 335 E4
Byron, C. Australia 28°43S 153°38E 335 D5
Byron Bay Australia 28°43S 153°37E 335 D5
Byrranga, Gory Russia 75°0N 100°0E 301 B11
Byrranga Mts. = Byrranga, Gory Russia 75°0N 100°0E 301 B11
Byske Sweden 64°57N 21°11E 280 D19
Byskeälven → Sweden 64°57N 21°13E 280 D19
Bytom Poland 50°25N 18°54E 289 C10
Bytów Poland 54°10N 17°30E 289 A9
Byumba Rwanda 1°35S 30°4E 326 C3

C

C.W. McConaughy, L. U.S.A. 41°14N 101°40W 352 E3
Ca → Vietnam 18°45N 105°45E 310 C5
Ca Mau Vietnam 9°7N 105°8E 311 H5
Ca Mau, Mui Vietnam 8°38N 104°44E 311 H5
Ca Na Vietnam 11°20N 108°54E 311 G7
Caacupé Paraguay 25°23S 57°5W 366 B4
Caaguazú △ Paraguay 26°5S 55°31W 367 B4
Caála Angola 12°46S 15°30E 325 G3
Caamaño Sd. Canada 52°55N 129°25W 342 C3
Caazapá Paraguay 26°8S 56°19W 366 B4
Caazapá □ Paraguay 26°10S 56°0W 367 B4
Caballeria, C. de Spain 40°5N 4°5E 296 A11
Cabanatuan Phil. 15°30N 120°58E 309 A6
Cabano Canada 47°40N 68°56W 345 C6
Cabazon U.S.A. 33°55N 116°47W 351 M10
Cabedelo Brazil 7°0S 34°50W 365 E12
Cabildo Chile 32°30S 71°5W 366 C1
Cabimas Venezuela 10°23N 71°25W 364 A4
Cabinda Angola 5°33S 12°11E 324 F2

Daikondi = Day Kundī □
  Afghan. 34°0N 66°0E **312** C5

E

390 Eastern Transvaal INDEX TO WORLD MAPS

Eastern Transvaal = Mpumalanga □ *S. Africa* 26°0S 30°0E **329** D5
Easterville *Canada* 53°8N 99°49W **343** C9
Easthampton *U.S.A.* 42°16N 72°40W **355** D12
Eastlake *U.S.A.* 41°40N 81°26W **354** E3
Eastland *U.S.A.* 32°24N 98°49W **356** E5
Eastleigh *U.K.* 50°58N 1°21W **285** G6
Eastmain *Canada* 52°10N 78°30W **344** B4
Eastmain → *Canada* 52°27N 78°26W **344** B4
Eastman *Canada* 45°18N 72°19W **355** A12
Eastman *U.S.A.* 32°12N 83°11W **357** E13
Easton *Md., U.S.A.* 38°47N 76°5W **353** F15
Easton *Pa., U.S.A.* 40°41N 75°13W **355** F9
Easton *Wash., U.S.A.* 47°14N 121°11W **350** C5
Eastport *U.S.A.* 44°56N 67°0W **353** C20
Eastsound *U.S.A.* 48°42N 122°55W **350** B4
Eaton *U.S.A.* 40°32N 104°42W **348** F11
Eatonia *Canada* 51°13N 109°25W **343** C7
Eatonton *U.S.A.* 33°20N 83°23W **357** E13
Eatontown *U.S.A.* 40°19N 74°4W **355** F10
Eatonville *U.S.A.* 46°52N 122°16W **350** D4
Eau Claire *U.S.A.* 44°49N 91°30W **352** C8
Eau Claire, L. à l' *Canada* 56°10N 74°25W **344** A5
Eauripik Rise *Pac. Oc.* 2°0N 142°0E **336** G6
Ebano *Mexico* 22°13N 98°24W **359** C5
Ebbw Vale *U.K.* 51°46N 3°12W **285** F4
Ebeltoft *Denmark* 56°12N 10°41E **281** H14
Ebensburg *U.S.A.* 40°29N 78°44W **354** F6
Eberswalde-Finow *Germany* 52°50N 13°49E **288** B7
Ebetsu *Japan* 43°7N 141°34E **302** C10
Ebey's Landing ⌂ *U.S.A.* 48°12N 122°41W **350** B4
Ebinur Hu *China* 44°55N 82°55E **304** B3
Ebolowa *Cameroon* 2°55N 11°10E **324** D2
Ebonda *Dem. Rep. of the Congo* 2°12N 22°21E **324** D4
Ebro → *Spain* 40°43N 0°54E **293** B6
Ecatepec de Morelos *Mexico* 19°36N 99°3W **359** D5
Eceabat *Turkey* 40°11N 26°21E **295** D12
Ech Chéliff *Algeria* 36°10N 1°20E **322** A6
Echigo-Sammyaku *Japan* 36°50N 139°50E **303** F9
Echizen-Misaki *Japan* 35°59N 135°57E **303** G7
Echo Bay *N.W.T., Canada* 66°5N 117°55W **340** C8
Echo Bay *Ont., Canada* 46°29N 84°4W **344** C3
Echoing → *Canada* 55°51N 92°5W **344** B1
Echternach *Lux.* 49°49N 6°25E **287** E6
Echuca *Australia* 36°10S 144°45E **335** F3
Ecija *Spain* 37°30N 5°10W **293** D3
Eclipse I. *Australia* 35°5S 117°58E **333** G2
Eclipse Is. *Australia* 13°54S 126°19E **332** B4
Eclipse Sd. *Canada* 72°38N 79°0W **341** B12
Ecuador ■ *S. Amer.* 2°0S 78°0W **364** D3
Ed Damazin *Sudan* 11°46N 34°21E **323** F12
Ed Dar el Beida = Casablanca *Morocco* 33°36N 7°36W **322** B4
Ed Debba *Sudan* 18°0N 30°51E **323** E12
Ed Déffa *Egypt* 30°40N 26°30E **323** B11
Ed Dueim *Sudan* 14°0N 32°10E **323** F12
Edam *Canada* 53°11N 108°46W **343** C7
Edam *Neths.* 52°31N 5°3E **287** B5
Eday *U.K.* 59°11N 2°47W **283** B6
Eddrachillis B. *U.K.* 58°17N 5°14W **283** C3
Eddystone *U.K.* 50°11N 4°16W **285** G3
Eddystone Pt. *Australia* 40°59S 148°20E **335** G4
Ede *Neths.* 52°4N 5°40E **287** B5
Edehon L. *Canada* 60°25N 97°15W **343** A9
Edekel, Adrar *Algeria* 23°56N 6°47E **322** D7
Eden *Australia* 37°3S 149°55E **335** F4
Eden *N.C., U.S.A.* 36°29N 79°53W **357** C15
Eden *N.Y., U.S.A.* 42°39N 78°55W **354** D6
Eden *Tex., U.S.A.* 31°13N 99°51W **356** F5
Eden → *U.K.* 54°57N 3°1W **284** C4
Edenburg *S. Africa* 29°43S 25°58E **328** D4
Edendale *S. Africa* 29°39S 30°18E **329** D5
Edenderry *Ireland* 53°21N 7°4W **282** C4
Edenton *U.S.A.* 36°4N 76°39W **357** C16
Edenville *S. Africa* 27°37S 27°34E **329** D4
Eder → *Germany* 51°12N 9°28E **288** C5
Edessa *Greece* 40°48N 22°5E **295** D10
Edgar *U.S.A.* 40°22N 97°58W **352** E5
Edgartown *U.S.A.* 41°23N 70°31W **355** E14
Edge Hill *U.K.* 52°8N 1°26W **285** E6
Edgefield *U.S.A.* 33°47N 81°56W **357** E14
Edgeley *U.S.A.* 46°22N 98°43W **352** B4
Edgemont *U.S.A.* 43°18N 103°50W **352** D2
Edgeøya *Svalbard* 77°45N 22°30E **276** B9
Édhessa = Edessa *Greece* 40°48N 22°5E **295** D10
Edievale *N.Z.* 45°49S 169°22E **331** F2
Edina *U.S.A.* 40°10N 92°11W **352** E7
Edinboro *U.S.A.* 41°52N 80°8W **354** E4
Edinburg *U.S.A.* 26°18N 98°10W **356** H5
Edinburgh *U.K.* 55°57N 3°13W **283** F5
Edinburgh ✕ (EDI) *U.K.* 55°54N 3°22W **283** F5
Edinburgh, City of □ *U.K.* 55°57N 3°17W **283** F5
Edineţ *Moldova* 48°9N 27°18E **289** D14
Edirne *Turkey* 41°40N 26°34E **295** D12
Edison *U.S.A.* 48°33N 122°27W **350** B4
Edithburgh *Australia* 35°5S 137°43E **335** F2
Edmeston *U.S.A.* 42°42N 75°15W **355** D9
Edmond *U.S.A.* 35°39N 97°29W **356** D6
Edmonds *U.S.A.* 47°48N 122°22W **350** C4
Edmonton *Australia* 17°2S 145°46E **334** B4
Edmonton *Canada* 53°30N 113°30W **342** C6
Edmund L. *Canada* 54°45N 93°17W **344** B1
Edmundston *Canada* 47°23N 68°20W **345** C6
Edna *U.S.A.* 28°59N 96°39W **356** G6
Edremit *Turkey* 39°34N 27°0E **295** E12
Edremit Körfezi *Turkey* 39°30N 26°45E **295** E12
Edson *Canada* 53°35N 116°28W **342** C5
Eduardo Castex *Argentina* 35°50S 64°18W **366** D3
Edward → *Australia* 35°5S 143°30E **335** F3
Edward, L. *Africa* 0°25S 29°40E **326** C2
Edward VII Land *Antarctica* 80°0S 150°0W **277** E13
Edwards *Calif., U.S.A.* 34°50N 117°40W **351** L9
Edwards *N.Y., U.S.A.* 44°20N 75°15W **355** B9
Edwards Plateau *U.S.A.* 30°45N 101°20W **356** F4
Edwardsville *U.S.A.* 41°15N 75°56W **355** E9
Edzná *Mexico* 19°39N 90°19W **359** D6
Edzo *Canada* 62°49N 116°4W **342** A5
Eeklo *Belgium* 51°11N 3°33E **287** C3
Eesti = Estonia ■ *Europe* 58°30N 25°30E **281** G21
Effigy Mounds ⌂ *U.S.A.* 43°5N 91°11W **352** D8
Effingham *U.S.A.* 39°7N 88°33W **352** F9
Égadi, Ísole *Italy* 37°55N 12°16E **294** F5
Egan Range *U.S.A.* 39°35N 114°55W **348** G6
Eganville *Canada* 45°32N 77°5W **354** A7
Eger = Cheb *Czech Rep.* 50°9N 12°28E **288** C7
Eger *Hungary* 47°53N 20°27E **289** E11
Egersund *Norway* 58°26N 6°1E **281** G12
Egg L. *Canada* 55°5N 105°30W **343** B7
Éghezée *Belgium* 50°35N 4°55E **287** D4
Egio *Greece* 38°15N 22°5E **295** E10
Eglinton I. *Canada* 75°48N 118°30W **341** B8
Egmont *Canada* 49°45N 123°56W **342** D4
Egmont, C. *N.Z.* 39°16S 173°45E **331** C4
Egmont, Mt. = Taranaki, Mt. *N.Z.* 39°17S 174°5E **331** C5
Egmont △ *N.Z.* 39°17S 174°4E **331** C5
Egra *India* 21°54N 87°32E **315** J12
Eğridir *Turkey* 37°52N 30°51E **291** G5
Eğridir Gölü *Turkey* 37°53N 30°50E **316** B1
Egvekinot *Russia* 66°19N 179°50W **301** C19
Egypt ■ *Africa* 28°0N 31°0E **323** C12
Ehime □ *Japan* 33°30N 132°40E **303** H6
Ehrenberg *U.S.A.* 33°36N 114°31W **351** M12
Eibar *Spain* 43°11N 2°28W **293** A4
Eidsvold *Australia* 25°25S 151°12E **335** D5
Eidsvoll *Norway* 60°19N 11°14E **281** F14
Eifel *Germany* 50°15N 6°50E **288** C4
Eiffel Flats *Zimbabwe* 18°20S 30°0E **327** F3
Eigg *U.K.* 56°54N 6°10W **283** E2
Eighty Mile Beach *Australia* 19°30S 120°40E **332** C3
Eil *Somali Rep.* 8°0N 49°50E **319** F4
Eil, L. *U.K.* 56°51N 5°16W **283** E3
Eildon, L. *Australia* 37°10S 146°0E **335** F4
Eilean Sar = Western Isles □ *U.K.* 57°30N 7°10W **283** D1
Einasleigh *Australia* 18°32S 144°5E **334** B3
Einasleigh → *Australia* 17°30S 142°17E **334** B3
Eindhoven *Neths.* 51°26N 5°28E **287** C5
Eire = Ireland ■ *Europe* 53°50N 7°52W **282** C4
Eiríksjökull *Iceland* 64°46N 20°24W **280** D3
Eirunepé *Brazil* 6°35S 69°53W **364** E5
Eiseb → *Namibia* 20°33S 20°59E **328** C2
Eisenach *Germany* 50°58N 10°19E **288** C6
Eisenerz *Austria* 47°32N 14°54E **288** E8
Eivissa *Spain* 38°54N 1°26E **296** C7
Ejeda *Madag.* 24°20S 44°31E **329** C7
Ejutla *Mexico* 16°34N 96°44W **359** D5
Ekalaka *U.S.A.* 45°53N 104°33W **348** D11
Ekenäs = Tammisaari *Finland* 60°0N 23°26E **281** G20
Eketahuna *N.Z.* 40°38S 175°43E **331** D5
Ekibastuz *Kazakhstan* 51°50N 75°10E **300** D8
Ekoli *Dem. Rep. of the Congo* 0°23S 24°13E **326** C1
Eksjö *Sweden* 57°40N 14°58E **281** H16
Ekuma → *Namibia* 18°40S 16°2E **328** B2
Ekwan → *Canada* 53°12N 82°15W **344** B3
Ekwan Pt. *Canada* 53°16N 82°7W **344** B3
El Aaiún *W. Sahara* 27°9N 13°12W **322** C3
El Abanico *Chile* 37°20S 71°31W **366** D1
El 'Agrûd *Egypt* 30°14N 34°24E **318** E3
El 'Alamein *Egypt* 30°48N 28°58E **323** B11
El 'Aqaba, W. → *Egypt* 30°7N 33°54E **318** E2
El Arīḥā *West Bank* 31°52N 35°27E **318** D4
El 'Arîsh *Egypt* 31°8N 33°50E **318** D2
El 'Arîsh, W. → *Egypt* 31°8N 33°47E **318** D2
El Asnam = Ech Chéliff *Algeria* 36°10N 1°20E **322** A6
El Bayadh *Algeria* 33°40N 1°1E **322** B6
El Bluff *Nic.* 11°59N 83°40W **360** D3
El Cajon *U.S.A.* 32°48N 116°58W **351** N10
El Campo *U.S.A.* 29°12N 96°16W **356** G6
El Capitan *U.S.A.* 37°44N 119°38E **350** H7
El Centro *U.S.A.* 32°48N 115°34W **351** N11
El Cerro *Bolivia* 17°30S 61°40W **364** G6
El Compadre *Mexico* 32°20N 116°14W **351** N10
El Cuy *Argentina* 39°55S 68°25W **368** D3
El Cuyo *Mexico* 21°31N 87°41W **359** C7
El Daheir *Egypt* 31°13N 34°10E **318** D3
El Dere *Somali Rep.* 3°50N 47°8E **319** G4
El Descanso *Mexico* 32°12N 116°58W **351** N10
El Desemboque *Mexico* 30°33N 113°1W **358** A2
El Diviso *Colombia* 1°22N 78°14W **364** C3
El Djouf *Mauritania* 20°0N 9°0W **322** D4
El Dorado *Mexico* 24°17N 107°21W **358** C3
El Dorado *Ark., U.S.A.* 33°12N 92°40W **356** E8
El Dorado *Kans., U.S.A.* 37°49N 96°52W **352** G5
El Dorado *Venezuela* 6°55N 61°37W **364** B6
El Dorado Springs *U.S.A.* 37°52N 94°1W **352** G6
El Escorial *Spain* 40°35N 4°7W **293** B3
El Faiyûm *Egypt* 29°19N 30°50E **323** C12
El Fâsher *Sudan* 13°33N 25°26E **323** F11
El Ferrol = Ferrol *Spain* 43°29N 8°15W **293** A1
El Fuerte *Mexico* 26°25N 108°39W **358** B3
El Gal *Somali Rep.* 10°58N 50°20E **319** E5
El Geneina = Al Junaynah *Sudan* 13°27N 22°45E **323** F10
El Gezira □ *Sudan* 15°0N 33°0E **323** F12
El Giza *Egypt* 30°0N 31°12E **323** C12
El Gogorrón △ *Mexico* 21°49N 100°57W **358** C4
El Goléa *Algeria* 30°30N 2°50E **322** B6
El Golfo de Santa Clara *Mexico* 31°42N 114°30W **358** A2
El Guácharo △ *Venezuela* 10°8N 63°21W **361** D7
El Guache △ *Venezuela* 9°45N 69°30W **361** E6
El Iskandarîya *Egypt* 31°13N 29°58E **323** B11
El Istiwa'iya *Sudan* 5°0N 28°0E **323** G11
El Jadida *Morocco* 33°11N 8°17W **322** B4
El Jardal *Honduras* 14°54N 88°50W **360** D2
El Kef □ *Tunisia* 36°0N 9°0E **323** A7
El Khârga *Egypt* 25°30N 30°33E **323** C12
El Khartûm *Sudan* 15°31N 32°35E **323** E12
El Khartûm Bahrî *Sudan* 15°40N 32°31E **323** E12
El Kuntilla *Egypt* 30°1N 34°45E **318** E3
El Lucero *Mexico* 30°37N 106°31W **358** A3
El Maestrazgo *Spain* 40°30N 0°25W **293** B5
El Mahalla el Kubra *Egypt* 31°0N 31°0E **323** B12
El Malpais ⌂ *U.S.A.* 34°53N 108°0W **349** J10
El Mansûra *Egypt* 31°0N 31°19E **323** B12
El Medano *Canary Is.* 28°3N 16°32W **296** F3
El Milagro *Argentina* 30°59S 65°59W **366** C2
El Minyâ *Egypt* 28°7N 30°33E **323** C12
El Monte *U.S.A.* 34°4N 118°1W **351** L8
El Obeid *Sudan* 13°8N 30°10E **323** F12
El Odaiya *Sudan* 12°8N 28°12E **323** F11
El Oro *Mexico* 19°51N 100°7W **359** D4
El Oued *Algeria* 33°20N 6°58E **322** B7
El Palmar △ *Argentina* 32°10S 58°31W **366** C4
El Palmito, Presa *Mexico* 25°40N 105°30W **358** B3
El Paso *U.S.A.* 31°45N 106°29W **356** F1
El Pinacate y Gran Desierto de Altar = Gran Desierto del Pinacate ⌂ *Mexico* 31°51N 113°32W **358** A2
El Portal *U.S.A.* 37°41N 119°47W **350** H7
El Porvenir *Mexico* 31°15N 105°51W **358** A3
El Prat de Llobregat *Spain* 41°19N 2°5E **293** B7
El Progreso *Honduras* 15°26N 87°51W **360** C2
El Pueblito *Mexico* 29°6N 105°7W **358** B3
El Pueblo *Canary Is.* 28°36N 17°47W **296** F2
El Puerto de Santa María *Spain* 36°36N 6°13W **293** D2
El Qâhira *Egypt* 30°2N 31°13E **323** B12
El Qantara *Egypt* 30°51N 32°20E **318** E1
El Quseima *Egypt* 30°40N 34°15E **318** E3
El Real *Panama* 8°0N 77°40W **364** B3
El Reno *U.S.A.* 35°32N 97°57W **346** C7
El Rey △ *Argentina* 24°40S 64°34W **366** A3
El Rio *U.S.A.* 34°14N 119°10W **351** L7
El Roque, Pta. *Canary Is.* 28°10N 15°25W **296** F4
El Rosarito *Mexico* 28°38N 114°4W **358** B2
El Salto *Mexico* 23°47N 105°22W **358** C3
El Salvador ■ *Cent. Amer.* 13°50N 89°0W **360** D2
El Sauce *Nic.* 13°0N 86°40W **360** D2
El Sueco *Mexico* 29°54N 106°24W **358** B3
El Suweis *Egypt* 29°58N 32°31E **323** C12
El Tamarâni, W. → *Egypt* 30°7N 34°43E **318** E3
El Thamad *Egypt* 29°40N 34°28E **318** F3
El Tigre *Venezuela* 8°44N 64°15W **364** B6
El Tîh, Gebel *Egypt* 29°40N 33°50E **318** F2
El Tofo *Chile* 29°22S 71°18W **366** B1
El Tránsito *Chile* 28°52S 70°17W **366** B1
El Tûr *Egypt* 28°14N 33°36E **316** D2
El Turbio *Argentina* 51°45S 72°5W **368** G2
El Uqsur *Egypt* 25°41N 32°38E **323** C12
El Vergel *Mexico* 26°28N 106°22W **358** B3
El Vigía *Venezuela* 8°38N 71°39W **364** B4
El Wabeira *Egypt* 29°34N 33°6E **318** F2
El Wak *Kenya* 2°49N 40°56E **326** B5
El Wuz *Sudan* 15°5N 30°7E **323** E12
Elat *Israel* 29°30N 34°56E **318** F3
Elâzığ *Turkey* 38°37N 39°14E **316** B3
Elba *Italy* 42°46N 10°17E **294** C4
Elba *U.S.A.* 31°25N 86°4W **357** F11
Elbasan *Albania* 41°9N 20°9E **295** D9
Elbe *U.S.A.* 46°45N 122°10W **350** D4
Elbe → *Europe* 53°50N 9°0E **288** B5
Elbert, Mt. *U.S.A.* 39°7N 106°27W **348** G10
Elberton *U.S.A.* 34°7N 82°52W **357** D13
Elbeuf *France* 49°17N 1°2E **292** B4
Elbing = Elbląg *Poland* 54°10N 19°25E **289** A10
Elbistan *Turkey* 38°13N 37°15E **316** B3
Elbląg *Poland* 54°10N 19°25E **289** A10
Elbow *Canada* 51°7N 106°35W **343** C7
Elbrus *Asia* 43°21N 42°30E **291** F7
Elburz Mts. = Alborz, Reshteh-ye Kūhhā-ye *Iran* 36°0N 52°0E **317** C7
Elche *Spain* 38°15N 0°42W **293** C5
Elcho I. *Australia* 11°55S 135°45E **334** A2
Elda *Spain* 38°29N 0°47W **293** C5
Eldama Ravine *Kenya* 0°3N 35°43E **326** B4
Elde → *Germany* 53°7N 11°15E **288** B6
Eldon *Mo., U.S.A.* 38°21N 92°35W **352** F7
Eldon *Wash., U.S.A.* 47°33N 123°3W **350** C3
Eldora *U.S.A.* 42°22N 93°5W **352** D7
Eldorado *Argentina* 26°28S 54°43W **367** B5
Eldorado *Canada* 44°35N 77°31W **354** B7
Eldorado *Ill., U.S.A.* 37°49N 88°26W **352** G9
Eldorado *Tex., U.S.A.* 30°52N 100°36W **356** F4
Eldoret *Kenya* 0°30N 35°17E **326** B4
Eldred *U.S.A.* 41°58N 78°23W **354** E6
Elea, C. *Cyprus* 35°19N 34°4E **297** D13
Eleanora, Pk. *Australia* 32°57S 121°9E **333** F3
Elefantes → *Africa* 24°10S 32°40E **329** C5
Elektrostal *Russia* 55°41N 38°32E **290** C6
Elemi Triangle *Africa* 5°0N 35°20E **326** B4
Elephant Butte Res. *U.S.A.* 33°9N 107°11W **349** K10
Elephant I. *Antarctica* 61°0S 55°0W **277** C18
Eleuthera *Bahamas* 25°0N 76°20W **360** B4
Elgin *Canada* 44°36N 76°13W **355** B8
Elgin *U.K.* 57°39N 3°19W **283** D5
Elgin *Ill., U.S.A.* 42°2N 88°17W **352** D9
Elgin *N. Dak., U.S.A.* 46°24N 101°51W **352** B3
Elgin *Oreg., U.S.A.* 45°34N 117°55W **348** D5
Elgin *Tex., U.S.A.* 30°21N 97°22W **356** F6
Elgon, Mt. *Africa* 1°10N 34°30E **326** B3
Eliase *Indonesia* 8°21S 130°48E **309** F8
Elim *Namibia* 17°48S 15°31E **328** B2
Elim *S. Africa* 34°35S 19°45E **328** E2
Elista *Russia* 46°16N 44°14E **291** E7
Elizabeth *Australia* 34°42S 138°41E **335** E2
Elizabeth *U.S.A.* 40°39N 74°12W **355** F10
Elizabeth City *U.S.A.* 36°18N 76°14W **357** C16
Elizabethton *U.S.A.* 36°21N 82°13W **357** C13
Elizabethtown *Ky., U.S.A.* 37°42N 85°52W **353** G11
Elizabethtown *N.Y., U.S.A.* 44°13N 73°36W **355** B11
Elizabethtown *Pa., U.S.A.* 40°9N 76°36W **355** F8
Ełk *Poland* 53°50N 22°21E **289** B12
Elk → *Canada* 49°11N 115°14W **342** C5
Elk → *U.S.A.* 34°46N 87°16W **357** D11
Elk City *U.S.A.* 35°25N 99°25W **356** D5
Elk Creek *U.S.A.* 39°36N 122°32W **350** F4
Elk Grove *U.S.A.* 38°25N 121°22W **350** G5
Elk Island △ *Canada* 53°35N 112°59W **342** C6
Elk Lake *Canada* 47°40N 80°25W **344** C3
Elk Point *Canada* 53°54N 110°55W **343** C6
Elk River *Idaho, U.S.A.* 46°47N 116°11W **348** C5
Elk River *Minn., U.S.A.* 45°18N 93°35W **352** C7
Elkedra → *Australia* 21°8S 136°22E **334** C2
Elkhart *Ind., U.S.A.* 41°41N 85°58W **353** E11
Elkhart *Kans., U.S.A.* 37°0N 101°54W **352** G3
Elkhorn *Canada* 49°59N 101°14W **343** D8
Elkhorn → *U.S.A.* 41°8N 96°19W **352** E5
Elkhovo *Bulgaria* 42°10N 26°35E **295** C12
Elkin *U.S.A.* 36°15N 80°51W **357** C14
Elkins *U.S.A.* 38°55N 79°51W **353** F14
Elkland *U.S.A.* 41°59N 77°19W **354** E7
Elko *Canada* 49°20N 115°10W **342** D5
Elko *U.S.A.* 40°50N 115°46W **348** F6
Elkton *U.S.A.* 43°49N 83°11W **354** C1
Ellas = Greece ■ *Europe* 40°0N 23°0E **295** E9
Ellef Ringnes I. *Canada* 78°30N 102°2W **341** B9
Ellen, Mt. *U.S.A.* 44°9N 72°56W **355** B12
Ellenburg *U.S.A.* 44°54N 73°48W **355** B11
Ellendale *U.S.A.* 46°0N 98°32W **352** B4
Ellensburg *U.S.A.* 46°59N 120°34W **348** C3
Ellenville *U.S.A.* 41°43N 74°24W **355** E10
Ellerton *Barbados* 13°7N 59°33W **361** g
Ellery, Mt. *Australia* 37°28S 148°47E **335** F4
Ellesmere, L. *N.Z.* 43°47S 172°28E **331** G4
Ellesmere I. *Canada* 79°30N 80°0W **341** B12
Ellesmere Port *U.K.* 53°17N 2°54W **284** D5
Ellice Is. = Tuvalu ■ *Pac. Oc.* 8°0S 178°0E **330** B10
Ellicottville *U.S.A.* 42°17N 78°40W **354** D6
Elliot *Australia* 17°33S 133°32E **334** B1
Elliot *S. Africa* 31°22S 27°48E **329** E4
Elliot Lake *Canada* 46°25N 82°35W **344** C3
Elliotdale = Xhora *S. Africa* 31°55S 28°38E **329** E4
Ellis *U.S.A.* 38°56N 99°34W **352** F4
Elliston *Australia* 33°39S 134°53E **335** E1
Ellisville *U.S.A.* 31°36N 89°12W **357** F10
Ellon *U.K.* 57°22N 2°4W **283** D6
Ellore = Eluru *India* 16°48N 81°8E **313** L12
Ellsworth *Kans., U.S.A.* 38°44N 98°14W **352** F4
Ellsworth *Maine, U.S.A.* 44°33N 68°25W **353** C19
Ellsworth Land *Antarctica* 76°0S 89°0W **277** D16
Ellsworth Mts. *Antarctica* 78°30S 85°0W **277** D16
Ellwood City *U.S.A.* 40°52N 80°17W **354** F4
Elma *Canada* 49°52N 95°55W **343** D9
Elma *U.S.A.* 47°0N 123°25W **350** D3
Elmalı *Turkey* 36°44N 29°56E **291** G4
Elmhurst *U.S.A.* 41°53N 87°56W **352** E10
Elmira *Canada* 43°36N 80°33W **354** C4
Elmira *U.S.A.* 42°6N 76°48W **354** D8
Elmira Heights *U.S.A.* 42°8N 76°50W **354** D8
Elmore *Australia* 36°30S 144°37E **335** F3
Elmshorn *Germany* 53°43N 9°40E **288** B5
Elmvale *Canada* 44°35N 79°52W **354** B5
Elora *Canada* 43°41N 80°26W **354** C4
Elounda *Greece* 35°16N 25°42E **297** D7
Eloy *U.S.A.* 32°45N 111°33W **349** K8
Elrose *Canada* 51°12N 108°0W **343** C7
Elsie *U.S.A.* 45°52N 123°36W **350** E3
Elsinore = Helsingør *Denmark* 56°2N 12°35E **281** H15
Eltanin Fracture Zone System *S. Ocean* 54°0S 130°0W **277** B14
Eltham *N.Z.* 39°26S 174°19E **331** C5
Eluru *India* 16°48N 81°8E **313** L12
Elvas *Portugal* 38°50N 7°10W **293** C2
Elverum *Norway* 60°53N 11°34E **280** F14
Elvire → *Australia* 17°51S 128°11E **332** C4
Elvire, Mt. *Australia* 29°22S 119°36E **333** E2
Elwell, L. = Tiber Res. *U.S.A.* 48°19N 111°6W **348** B8
Elwood *Ind., U.S.A.* 40°17N 85°50W **353** E11
Elwood *Nebr., U.S.A.* 40°36N 99°52W **352** E4
Elx = Elche *Spain* 38°15N 0°42W **293** C5
Ely *U.K.* 52°24N 0°16E **285** E8
Ely *Minn., U.S.A.* 47°55N 91°51W **352** B8
Ely *Nev., U.S.A.* 39°15N 114°54W **348** G6
Elyria *U.S.A.* 41°22N 82°7W **354** E2
Emāmrūd *Iran* 36°30N 55°0E **317** B7
Embarcación *Argentina* 23°10S 64°0W **366** A3
Embarras Portage *Canada* 58°27N 111°28W **343** B6
Embetsu *Japan* 44°44N 141°47E **302** B10
Embi *Kazakhstan* 48°50N 58°8E **300** E6
Embi → *Kazakhstan* 46°55N 53°28E **291** E9
Embonas *Greece* 36°13N 27°51E **297** C9
Embrun *France* 44°34N 6°30E **292** D7
Embu *Kenya* 0°32S 37°38E **326** C4
Emden *Germany* 53°21N 7°12E **288** B4
Emerald *Australia* 23°32S 148°10E **334** C4
Emerson *Canada* 49°0N 97°10W **343** D9
Emet *Turkey* 39°20N 29°15E **295** E13
Emi Koussi *Chad* 19°45N 18°55E **323** E9
Eminabad *Pakistan* 32°2N 74°8E **314** C6
Emine, Nos *Bulgaria* 42°40N 27°56E **295** C12
Emissi, Tarso *Chad* 21°27N 18°36E **323** D9
Emlenton *U.S.A.* 41°11N 79°43W **354** E5
Emmaus *S. Africa* 29°2S 25°15E **328** D4
Emmaus *U.S.A.* 40°32N 75°30W **355** F9
Emmeloord *Neths.* 52°44N 5°46E **287** B5
Emmen *Neths.* 52°48N 6°57E **287** B6
Emmet *Australia* 24°45S 144°30E **334** C3
Emmetsburg *U.S.A.* 43°7N 94°41W **352** D6
Emmett *Idaho, U.S.A.* 43°52N 116°30W **348** E5
Emmett *Mich., U.S.A.* 42°59N 82°46W **354** D2
Emmonak *U.S.A.* 62°47N 164°31W **346** a
Emo *Canada* 48°38N 93°50W **343** D10
Empalme *Mexico* 27°58N 110°51W **358** B2
Empangeni *S. Africa* 28°50S 31°52E **329** D5
Empedrado *Argentina* 28°0S 58°46W **366** B4
Emperor Seamount Chain *Pac. Oc.* 40°0N 170°0E **336** D9
Emperor Trough *Pac. Oc.* 43°0N 175°30E **336** C9
Emporia *Kans., U.S.A.* 38°25N 96°11W **352** F5
Emporia *Va., U.S.A.* 36°42N 77°32W **353** G15
Emporium *U.S.A.* 41°31N 78°14W **354** E6
Empress *Canada* 50°57N 110°0W **343** C7
Empty Quarter = Rub' al Khālī *Si. Arabia* 19°0N 48°0E **319** D4
Ems → *Germany* 53°20N 7°12E **288** B4
Emsdale *Canada* 45°32N 79°19W **354** A5
Emu *China* 43°40N 128°6E **307** C15
Emu Park *Australia* 23°13S 150°50E **334** C5
'En 'Avrona *Israel* 29°43N 35°0E **318** F4
'En Boqeq *Israel* 31°12N 35°21E **317** D4
'En Gedi *Israel* 31°28N 35°25E **317** D4
En Nahud *Sudan* 12°45N 28°25E **323** F11
Ena *Japan* 35°25N 137°25E **303** G8
Enana *Namibia* 17°30S 16°23E **328** B2
Enard B. *U.K.* 58°5N 5°20W **283** C3
Enare = Inarijärvi *Finland* 69°0N 28°0E **280** B23
Enarotali *Indonesia* 3°55S 136°21E **309** E9
Encampment *U.S.A.* 41°12N 106°47W **348** F10
Encantadas, Serra *Brazil* 30°40S 53°0W **367** C5
Encarnación *Paraguay* 27°15S 55°50W **367** B4
Encarnación de Díaz *Mexico* 21°31N 102°14W **358** C4
Encinitas *U.S.A.* 33°3N 117°17W **351** M9
Encino *U.S.A.* 34°39N 105°28W **349** J11
Encounter B. *Australia* 35°45S 138°45E **335** F2
Endako *Canada* 54°6N 125°2W **342** C3
Endau *Kenya* 1°18S 38°31E **326** C4
Ende *Indonesia* 8°45S 121°40E **309** F6
Endeavour Str. *Australia* 10°45S 142°0E **334** A3
Enderbury I. *Kiribati* 3°8S 171°5W **336** H10
Enderby *Canada* 50°35N 119°10W **342** C5
Enderby Abyssal Plain *S. Ocean* 60°0S 40°0E **277** C5
Enderby I. *Australia* 20°35S 116°30E **332** D2
Enderby Land *Antarctica* 66°0S 53°0E **277** C5
Enderlin *U.S.A.* 46°38N 97°36W **352** B5
Endicott *U.S.A.* 42°6N 76°4W **355** D8
Endwell *U.S.A.* 42°6N 76°2W **355** D8
Endyalgout I. *Australia* 11°40S 132°35E **332** B5
Eneabba *Australia* 29°49S 115°16E **333** E2
Enewetak Atoll *Marshall Is.* 11°30N 162°15E **336** F8
Enez *Turkey* 40°45N 26°5E **295** D12
Enfer, Pte. d' *Martinique* 14°22N 60°54W **360** c
Enfield *Canada* 44°56N 63°32W **345** D7
Enfield *Conn., U.S.A.* 41°58N 72°36W **355** E12
Enfield *N.C., U.S.A.* 36°11N 77°41W **357** C16
Enfield *N.H., U.S.A.* 43°39N 72°9W **355** C12
Engadin *Switz.* 46°45N 10°10E **292** C9
Engaño, C. *Dom. Rep.* 18°30N 68°20W **361** C6
Engaño, C. *Phil.* 18°35N 122°23E **309** A6
Engaru *Japan* 44°3N 143°31E **302** B11
Engcobo = Ngcobo *S. Africa* 31°37S 28°0E **329** E4
Engels *Russia* 51°28N 46°6E **291** D8
Engemann L. *Canada* 58°0N 106°55W **343** B7
Enggano *Indonesia* 5°20S 102°40E **308** F2
England *U.S.A.* 34°33N 91°58W **356** D9
England □ *U.K.* 53°0N 2°0W **285** E5
Englee *Canada* 50°45N 56°5W **345** B8
Englehart *Canada* 47°49N 79°52W **344** C4
Englewood *U.S.A.* 39°38N 104°59W **348** G11
English → *Canada* 49°12N 91°5W **343** C10
English Bazar = Ingraj Bazar *India* 24°58N 88°10E **315** G13
English Channel *Europe* 50°0N 2°0W **285** G6
English Company's Is., The *Australia* 11°50S 136°32E **334** A2
English River *Canada* 49°14N 91°0W **344** C1
Enid *U.S.A.* 36°24N 97°53W **356** C6
Enkhuizen *Neths.* 52°42N 5°17E **287** B5
Enna *Italy* 37°34N 14°16E **294** F6
Ennadai *Canada* 61°8N 100°53W **343** A8
Ennadai L. *Canada* 60°58N 101°20W **343** A8
Ennedi *Chad* 17°15N 22°0E **323** E10
Enngonia *Australia* 29°21S 145°50E **335** D4
Ennis *Ireland* 52°51N 8°59W **282** D3
Ennis *Mont., U.S.A.* 45°21N 111°44W **348** D8
Ennis *Tex., U.S.A.* 32°20N 96°38W **356** E6
Enniscorthy *Ireland* 52°30N 6°34W **282** D5
Enniskillen *U.K.* 54°21N 7°39W **282** B4
Ennistimon *Ireland* 52°57N 9°17W **282** D2
Enns → *Austria* 48°14N 14°32E **288** D8
Eno *Finland* 62°47N 30°10E **280** E24
Enontekiö *Finland* 68°23N 23°37E **280** B20
Enosburg Falls *U.S.A.* 44°55N 72°48W **355** B12

Enriquillo, L. *Dom. Rep.* 18°20N 72°5W **361** C5
Enschede *Neths.* 52°13N 6°53E **287** B6
Ensenada *Argentina* 34°55S 57°55W **366** C4
Ensenada *Mexico* 31°52N 116°37W **358** A1
Ensenada de los Muertos *Mexico* 23°59N 109°51W **358** C2
Ensiola, Pta. de n' *Spain* 39°7N 2°55E **296** B9
Entebbe *Uganda* 0°4N 32°28E **326** B3
Enterprise *Canada* 60°47N 115°45W **342** A5
Enterprise *Ala., U.S.A.* 31°19N 85°51W **357** F12
Enterprise *Oreg., U.S.A.* 45°25N 117°17W **348** D5
Entre Ríos *Bolivia* 21°30S 64°25W **366** A3
Entre Ríos □ *Argentina* 30°30S 58°30W **366** C4
Entroncamento *Portugal* 39°28N 8°28W **293** C1
Enugu *Nigeria* 6°30N 7°30E **322** G7
Enumclaw *U.S.A.* 47°12N 121°59W **350** C5
Éolie, Ís. *Italy* 38°30N 14°57E **294** E6
Epe *Neths.* 52°21N 5°59E **287** B5
Épernay *France* 49°3N 3°56E **292** B5
Ephesus *Turkey* 37°55N 27°22E **295** F12
Ephraim *U.S.A.* 39°22N 111°35W **348** G8
Ephrata *Pa., U.S.A.* 40°11N 76°11W **355** F8
Ephrata *Wash., U.S.A.* 47°19N 119°33W **348** C4
Épinal *France* 48°10N 6°27E **292** B7
Episkopi *Cyprus* 34°40N 32°54E **297** E11
Episkopi *Greece* 35°20N 24°20E **297** D6
Episkopi Bay *Cyprus* 34°35N 32°50E **297** E11
Epsom *U.K.* 51°19N 0°16W **285** F7
Epukiro *Namibia* 21°40S 19°9E **328** C2
Equatoria = El Istiwa'iya *Sudan* 5°0N 28°0E **323** G11
Equatorial Guinea ■ *Africa* 2°0N 8°0E **324** D1
Er Rachidia *Morocco* 31°58N 4°20W **322** B5
Er Rahad *Sudan* 12°45N 30°32E **323** F12
Er Rif *Morocco* 35°1N 4°1W **322** A5
Erāwadī Myit = Irrawaddy → *Burma* 15°50N 95°6E **313** M19
Erāwadī Myitwanya = Irrawaddy, Mouths of the *Burma* 15°30N 95°0E **313** M19
Erbil = Arbīl *Iraq* 36°15N 44°5E **316** B5
Erçek *Turkey* 38°39N 43°36E **316** B4
Erciyaş Dağı *Turkey* 38°30N 35°30E **316** B2
Érd *Hungary* 47°22N 18°56E **289** E10
Erdao Jiang → *China* 42°37N 128°0E **307** C14
Erdek *Turkey* 40°23N 27°47E **295** D12
Erdene = Ulaan-Uul *Mongolia* 44°13N 111°10E **306** B6
Erdenet *Mongolia* 49°2N 104°5E **304** B5
Erdenetsogt *Mongolia* 42°55N 106°5E **306** C4
Erebus, Mt. *Antarctica* 77°35S 167°0E **277** D11
Erechim *Brazil* 27°35S 52°15W **367** B5
Ereğli *Konya, Turkey* 37°31N 34°4E **316** B2
Ereğli *Zonguldak, Turkey* 41°15N 31°24E **291** F5
Erenhot *China* 43°48N 112°2E **306** C7
Eresma → *Spain* 41°26N 4°45W **293** B3
Erfenisdam *S. Africa* 28°30S 26°50E **328** D4
Erfurt *Germany* 50°58N 11°2E **288** C6
Ergani *Turkey* 38°17N 39°49E **316** B3
Ergel *Mongolia* 43°8N 109°5E **306** C5
Ergeni Vozvyshennost *Russia* 47°0N 44°0E **291** E7
Ērgli *Latvia* 56°54N 25°38E **281** H21
Eriboll, L. *U.K.* 58°30N 4°42W **283** C4
Érice *Italy* 38°2N 12°35E **294** E5
Erie *U.S.A.* 42°8N 80°5W **354** D4
Erie, L. *N. Amer.* 42°15N 81°0W **354** D4
Erie Canal *U.S.A.* 43°5N 78°43W **354** C7
Erieau *Canada* 42°16N 81°57W **354** D3
Erigavo *Somali Rep.* 10°35N 47°20E **319** E4
Erikoussa *Greece* 39°53N 19°34E **297** A3
Eriksdale *Canada* 50°52N 98°7W **343** C9
Erimanthos *Greece* 37°57N 21°50E **295** F9
Erimo-misaki *Japan* 41°50N 143°15E **302** D11
Erin Pt. *Trin. & Tob.* 10°3N 61°39W **365** K15
Erinpura *India* 25°9N 73°3E **314** G5
Eriskay *U.K.* 57°4N 7°18W **283** D1
Eritrea ■ *Africa* 14°0N 38°30E **319** D2
Erlangen *Germany* 49°36N 11°0E **288** D6
Erldunda *Australia* 25°14S 133°12E **334** D1
Ermelo *Neths.* 52°18N 5°35E **287** B5
Ermelo *S. Africa* 26°31S 29°59E **329** D4
Ermenek *Turkey* 36°38N 33°0E **316** B2
Ermones *Greece* 39°37N 19°46E **297** A3
Ernakulam *India* 9°59N 76°22E **312** Q10
Erne → *Ireland* 54°30N 8°16W **282** B3
Erne, Lower L. *U.K.* 54°28N 7°47W **282** B4
Erne, Upper L. *U.K.* 54°14N 7°32W **282** B4
Ernest Giles Ra. *Australia* 27°0S 123°45E **333** E3
Erode *India* 11°24N 77°45E **312** P10
Eromanga *Australia* 26°40S 143°11E **335** D3
Erongo *Namibia* 21°39S 15°58E **328** C2
Erramala Hills *India* 15°30N 78°15E **312** M11
Erri-Nundra △ *Australia* 37°28S 148°55E **335** F4
Errigal *Ireland* 55°2N 8°6W **282** A3
Erris Hd. *Ireland* 54°19N 10°0W **282** B1
Erskine *U.S.A.* 47°40N 96°0W **352** B5
Ertis = Irtysh → *Russia* 61°4N 68°52E **300** C7
Erwin *U.S.A.* 36°9N 82°25W **357** C13
Erzgebirge *Germany* 50°27N 12°55E **288** C7
Erzin *Russia* 50°15N 95°10E **301** D10
Erzincan *Turkey* 39°46N 39°30E **316** B3
Erzurum *Turkey* 39°57N 41°15E **316** B4
Es Caló *Spain* 38°40N 1°30E **296** C8
Es Canar *Spain* 39°2N 1°36E **296** B8
Es Mercadal *Spain* 39°59N 4°5E **296** B11
Es Migjorn Gran *Spain* 39°57N 4°3E **296** B11
Es Sahrâ' Esh Sharqîya *Egypt* 27°30N 32°30E **323** C12
Es Sînâ' *Egypt* 29°0N 34°0E **318** F3
Es Vedrà *Spain* 38°52N 1°12E **296** C7
Esambo *Dem. Rep. of the Congo* 3°48S 23°30E **326** C1
Esan-Misaki *Japan* 41°40N 141°10E **302** D10
Esashi *Hokkaidō, Japan* 44°56N 142°35E **302** B11
Esashi *Hokkaidō, Japan* 41°52N 140°7E **302** D10
Esbjerg *Denmark* 55°29N 8°29E **281** J13
Esbo = Espoo *Finland* 60°12N 24°40E **281** F21
Escalante *U.S.A.* 37°47N 111°36W **349** H8
Escalante → *U.S.A.* 37°24N 110°57W **349** H8
Escalón *Mexico* 26°45N 104°20W **358** B4
Escambia → *U.S.A.* 30°32N 87°11W **357** F11
Escanaba *U.S.A.* 45°45N 87°4W **352** C10
Esch-sur-Alzette *Lux.* 49°32N 6°0E **287** E6
Escondido *U.S.A.* 33°7N 117°5W **351** M9
Escuinapa de Hidalgo *Mexico* 22°50N 105°50W **358** C3
Escuintla *Guatemala* 14°20N 90°48W **360** D1
Esenguly *Turkmenistan* 37°37N 53°59E **300** F6
Eşfahān *Iran* 32°39N 51°43E **317** C6
Eşfahān □ *Iran* 32°50N 51°50E **317** C6
Esfarāyen *Iran* 37°4N 57°30E **317** B8
Esfideh *Iran* 33°39N 59°46E **317** C8
Esh Sham = Dimashq *Syria* 33°30N 36°18E **318** B5
Esha Ness *U.K.* 60°29N 1°38W **283** A7
Esher *U.K.* 51°21N 0°20W **285** F7
Eshkol △ *Israel* 31°20N 34°30E **318** D3
Eshowe *S. Africa* 28°50S 31°30E **329** D5
Esigodini *Zimbabwe* 20°18S 28°56E **329** C4
Esil = Ishim → *Russia* 57°45N 71°10E **300** D8
Esira *Madag.* 24°20S 46°42E **329** C8
Esk → *Dumf. & Gall., U.K.* 54°58N 3°2W **283** G5
Esk → *N. Yorks., U.K.* 54°30N 0°37W **284** C7
Eskān *Iran* 26°48N 63°9E **317** E9
Esker *Canada* 53°53N 66°25W **345** B6
Eskifjörður *Iceland* 65°3N 13°55W **280** D7
Eskilstuna *Sweden* 59°22N 16°32E **281** G17
Eskimo Point = Arviat *Canada* 61°6N 93°59W **343** A10
Eskişehir *Turkey* 39°50N 30°30E **291** G5
Esla → *Spain* 41°29N 6°3W **293** B2
Eslāmābād-e Gharb *Iran* 34°10N 46°30E **316** C5
Eslāmshahr *Iran* 35°40N 51°10E **317** C6
Eşme *Turkey* 38°23N 28°58E **295** E13
Esmeraldas *Ecuador* 1°0N 79°40W **364** C3
Esnagi L. *Canada* 48°36N 84°33W **344** C3
España = Spain ■ *Europe* 39°0N 4°0W **293** B4
Espanola *Canada* 46°15N 81°46W **344** C3
Espanola *U.S.A.* 35°59N 106°5W **349** J10
Esparta *Costa Rica* 9°59N 84°40W **360** E3
Esperance *Australia* 33°45S 121°55E **333** F3
Esperance B. *Australia* 33°48S 121°55E **333** F3
Esperance Harbour *St. Lucia* 14°4N 60°55W **361** f
Esperanza *Antarctica* 65°0S 55°0W **277** C18
Esperanza *Argentina* 31°29S 61°3W **366** C3
Esperanza *Puerto Rico* 18°6N 65°28W **361** d
Espichel, C. *Portugal* 38°22N 9°16W **293** C1
Espigão, Serra do *Brazil* 26°35S 50°30W **367** B5
Espinazo, Sierra del = Espinhaço, Serra do *Brazil* 17°30S 43°30W **365** G10
Espinhaço, Serra do *Brazil* 17°30S 43°30W **365** G10
Espinilho, Serra do *Brazil* 28°30S 55°0W **367** B5
Espírito Santo □ *Brazil* 20°0S 40°45W **365** H10
Espíritu Santo *Vanuatu* 15°15S 166°50E **330** C9
Espíritu Santo, B. del *Mexico* 19°20N 87°35W **359** D7
Espíritu Santo, I. *Mexico* 24°30N 110°22W **358** C2
Espita *Mexico* 21°1N 88°19W **359** C7
Espoo *Finland* 60°12N 24°40E **281** F21
Espungabera *Mozam.* 20°29S 32°45E **329** C5
Esquel *Argentina* 42°55S 71°20W **368** E2
Esquimalt *Canada* 48°26N 123°25W **350** B3
Esquina *Argentina* 30°0S 59°30W **366** C4
Essaouira *Morocco* 31°32N 9°42W **322** B4
Essebie *Dem. Rep. of the Congo* 2°58N 30°40E **326** B3
Essen *Belgium* 51°28N 4°28E **287** C4
Essen *Germany* 51°28N 7°2E **288** C4
Essendon, Mt. *Australia* 25°0S 120°29E **333** E3
Essequibo → *Guyana* 6°50N 58°30W **364** B7
Essex *Canada* 42°10N 82°49W **354** D2
Essex *Calif., U.S.A.* 34°44N 115°15W **351** L11
Essex *N.Y., U.S.A.* 44°19N 73°21W **355** B11
Essex □ *U.K.* 51°54N 0°27E **285** F8
Essex Junction *U.S.A.* 44°29N 73°7W **355** B11
Esslingen *Germany* 48°44N 9°18E **288** D5
Estación Camacho *Mexico* 24°25N 102°18W **358** C4
Estación Simón *Mexico* 24°42N 102°35W **358** C4
Estados, I. de Los *Argentina* 54°40S 64°30W **368** G4
Eşţahbānāt *Iran* 29°8N 54°4E **317** D7
Estância *Brazil* 11°16S 37°26W **365** F11
Estancia *U.S.A.* 34°46N 106°4W **349** J10
Estārm *Iran* 28°21N 58°21E **317** D8
Estcourt *S. Africa* 29°0S 29°53E **329** D4
Este △ *Dom. Rep.* 18°14N 68°42W **361** C6
Estelí *Nic.* 13°9N 86°22W **360** D2
Estellencs *Spain* 39°39N 2°29E **296** B9
Esterhazy *Canada* 50°37N 102°5W **343** C8
Estevan *Canada* 49°10N 102°59W **343** D8
Estevan Group *Canada* 53°3N 129°38W **342** C3
Estherville *U.S.A.* 43°24N 94°50W **352** D6
Eston *Canada* 51°8N 108°40W **343** C7
Estonia ■ *Europe* 58°30N 25°30E **281** G21
Estreito *Brazil* 6°32S 47°25W **365** E9
Estrela, Serra da *Portugal* 40°10N 7°45W **293** B2
Estremoz *Portugal* 38°51N 7°39W **293** C2
Estrondo, Serra do *Brazil* 7°20S 48°0W **365** E9
Esztergom *Hungary* 47°47N 18°44E **289** E10
Etah *India* 27°35N 78°40E **315** F8
Étampes *France* 48°26N 2°10E **292** B5
Etanga *Namibia* 17°55S 13°0E **328** B1
Etawah *India* 26°48N 79°6E **315** F8
Etawney L. *Canada* 57°50N 96°50W **343** B9
Etchojoa *Mexico* 26°55N 109°38W **358** B3
eThekwini = Durban *S. Africa* 29°49S 31°1E **329** D5
Ethel *U.S.A.* 46°32N 122°46W **350** D4
Ethelbert *Canada* 51°32N 100°25W **343** C8
Ethiopia ■ *Africa* 8°0N 40°0E **319** F3
Ethiopian Highlands *Ethiopia* 10°0N 37°0E **319** F2
Etive, L. *U.K.* 56°29N 5°10W **283** E3
Etna *Italy* 37°50N 14°55E **294** F6
Etoile *Dem. Rep. of the Congo* 11°33S 27°30E **327** E2
Etosha △ *Namibia* 19°0S 16°0E **328** B2
Etosha Pan *Namibia* 18°40S 16°30E **328** B2
Etowah *U.S.A.* 35°20N 84°32W **357** D12
Etrek *Turkmenistan* 37°36N 54°46E **317** B7
Ettelbruck *Lux.* 49°51N 6°5E **287** E6
Ettrick Water → *U.K.* 55°31N 2°55W **283** F6
Etuku *Dem. Rep. of the Congo* 3°42S 25°45E **326** C2
Etzná-Tixmucuy = Edzná *Mexico* 19°39N 90°19W **359** D6
Eua *Tonga* 21°22S 174°56W **331** c
Euboea = Evia *Greece* 38°30N 24°0E **295** E11
Eucla *Australia* 31°41S 128°52E **333** F4
Euclid *U.S.A.* 41°34N 81°32W **354** E3
Eucumbene, L. *Australia* 36°2S 148°40E **335** F4
Eudora *U.S.A.* 33°7N 91°16W **356** E9
Eufaula *Ala., U.S.A.* 31°54N 85°9W **357** F12
Eufaula *Okla., U.S.A.* 35°17N 95°35W **356** D7
Eufaula L. *U.S.A.* 35°18N 95°21W **356** D7
Eugene *U.S.A.* 44°5N 123°4W **348** D2
Eugowra *Australia* 33°22S 148°24E **335** E4
Eulo *Australia* 28°10S 145°3E **335** D4
Eungella △ *Australia* 20°57S 148°40E **334** C4
Eunice *La., U.S.A.* 30°30N 92°25W **356** F8
Eunice *N. Mex., U.S.A.* 32°26N 103°10W **349** K12
Eupen *Belgium* 50°37N 6°3E **287** D6
Euphrates = Furāt, Nahr al → *Asia* 31°0N 47°25E **316** D5
Eureka *Canada* 80°0N 85°56W **341** B11
Eureka *Calif., U.S.A.* 40°47N 124°9W **348** F1
Eureka *Kans., U.S.A.* 37°49N 96°17W **352** G5
Eureka *Mont., U.S.A.* 48°53N 115°3W **348** B6
Eureka *Nev., U.S.A.* 39°31N 115°58W **348** G6
Eureka *S. Dak., U.S.A.* 45°46N 99°38W **352** C4
Eureka, Mt. *Australia* 26°35S 121°35E **333** E3
Euroa *Australia* 36°44S 145°35E **335** F4
Europa, Île *Ind. Oc.* 22°20S 40°22E **325** J8
Europa, Picos de *Spain* 43°10N 4°49W **293** A3
Europa, Pta. de *Gib.* 36°3N 5°21W **293** D3
Europe 50°0N 20°0E **278** E10
Europoort *Neths.* 51°57N 4°10E **287** C4
Eustis *U.S.A.* 28°51N 81°41W **357** G14
Eutsuk L. *Canada* 53°20N 126°45W **342** C3
Evale *Angola* 16°33S 15°44E **328** B2
Evans *U.S.A.* 40°23N 104°41W **348** F11
Evans, L. *Canada* 50°50N 77°0W **344** B4
Evans City *U.S.A.* 40°46N 80°4W **354** F4
Evans Head *Australia* 29°7S 153°27E **335** D5
Evans Mills *U.S.A.* 44°6N 75°48W **355** B9
Evansburg *Canada* 53°36N 114°59W **342** C5
Evanston *Ill., U.S.A.* 42°3N 87°40W **352** D10
Evanston *Wyo., U.S.A.* 41°16N 110°58W **348** F8
Evansville *U.S.A.* 37°58N 87°35W **352** G10
Evaz *Iran* 27°46N 53°59E **317** E7
Eveleth *U.S.A.* 47°28N 92°32W **352** B7
Evensk *Russia* 62°12N 159°30E **301** C16
Everard, L. *Australia* 31°30S 135°0E **335** E2
Everard Ranges *Australia* 27°5S 132°28E **333** E5
Everest, Mt. *Nepal* 28°5N 86°58E **315** E12
Everett *Pa., U.S.A.* 40°1N 78°23W **354** F6
Everett *Wash., U.S.A.* 47°59N 122°12W **350** C4
Everglades, The *U.S.A.* 25°50N 81°0W **357** J14
Everglades △ *U.S.A.* 25°30N 81°0W **357** J14
Everglades City *U.S.A.* 25°52N 81°23W **357** J14
Evergreen *Ala., U.S.A.* 31°26N 86°57W **357** F11
Evergreen *Mont., U.S.A.* 48°14N 114°17W **348** B6
Evesham *U.K.* 52°6N 1°56W **285** E6
Evia *Greece* 38°30N 24°0E **295** E11
Evje *Norway* 58°36N 7°51E **281** G12
Évora *Portugal* 38°33N 7°57W **293** C2
Evowghlī *Iran* 38°43N 45°13E **316** B5
Évreux *France* 49°3N 1°8E **292** B4
Evros → *Greece* 41°40N 26°34E **295** D12
Évry *France* 48°38N 2°27E **292** B5
Évvoia = Evia *Greece* 38°30N 24°0E **295** E11
Ewe, L. *U.K.* 57°49N 5°38W **283** D3
Ewing *U.S.A.* 42°16N 98°21W **352** D4
Ewo *Congo* 0°48S 14°45E **324** E2
Exaltación *Bolivia* 13°10S 65°20W **364** F5
Excelsior Springs *U.S.A.* 39°20N 94°13W **352** F6
Exe → *U.K.* 50°41N 3°29W **285** G4
Exeter *Canada* 43°21N 81°29W **354** C3
Exeter *U.K.* 50°43N 3°31W **285** G4
Exeter *Calif., U.S.A.* 36°18N 119°9W **350** J7
Exeter *N.H., U.S.A.* 42°59N 70°57W **355** D14
Exmoor *U.K.* 51°12N 3°45W **285** F4
Exmoor △ *U.K.* 51°8N 3°42W **285** F4
Exmouth *Australia* 21°54S 114°10E **332** D1
Exmouth *U.K.* 50°37N 3°25W **285** G4
Exmouth G. *Australia* 22°15S 114°15E **332** D1
Exmouth Plateau *Ind. Oc.* 19°0S 114°0E **336** J3
Expedition △ *Australia* 25°41S 149°7E **335** D4
Expedition Ra. *Australia* 24°30S 149°12E **334** C4
Extremadura □ *Spain* 39°30N 6°5W **293** C2
Exuma Sound *Bahamas* 24°30N 76°20W **360** B4
Eyasi, L. *Tanzania* 3°30S 35°0E **326** C4
Eye Pen. *U.K.* 58°13N 6°10W **283** C2
Eyemouth *U.K.* 55°52N 2°5W **283** F6
Eyjafjörður *Iceland* 66°15N 18°30W **280** C4
Eyre (North), L. *Australia* 28°30S 137°20E **335** D2
Eyre (South), L. *Australia* 29°18S 137°25E **335** D2
Eyre, L. *Australia* 29°30S 137°26E **330** D6
Eyre Mts. *N.Z.* 45°25S 168°25E **331** F2
Eyre Pen. *Australia* 33°30S 136°17E **335** E2
Eysturoy *Færoe Is.* 62°13N 6°54W **280** E9
Eyvānkī *Iran* 35°24N 51°56E **317** C6
Ezine *Turkey* 39°48N 26°20E **295** E12
Ezouza → *Cyprus* 34°44N 32°27E **297** E11

F

F.Y.R.O.M. = Macedonia ■ *Europe* 41°53N 21°40E **295** D9
Faaa *Tahiti* 17°34S 149°35W **331** d
Faaone *Tahiti* 17°40S 149°21W **331** d
Fabala *Guinea* 9°44N 9°5W **322** G4
Fabens *U.S.A.* 31°30N 106°10W **356** F1
Fabriano *Italy* 43°20N 12°54E **294** C5
Fachi *Niger* 18°6N 11°34E **323** E8
Fada *Chad* 17°13N 21°34E **323** E10
Fada-n-Gourma *Burkina Faso* 12°10N 0°30E **322** F6
Faddeyevskiy, Ostrov *Russia* 76°0N 144°0E **301** B15
Fadghāmī *Syria* 35°53N 40°52E **316** C4
Faenza *Italy* 44°17N 11°53E **294** B4
Færoe Is. = Føroyar ☒ *Atl. Oc.* 62°0N 7°0W **280** F9
Făgăras *Romania* 45°48N 24°58E **289** F13
Fagersta *Sweden* 60°1N 15°46E **281** F16
Fagnano, L. *Argentina* 54°30S 68°0W **368** G3
Fahliān *Iran* 30°11N 51°28E **317** D6
Fahraj *Kermān, Iran* 29°0N 59°0E **317** D8
Fahraj *Yazd, Iran* 31°46N 54°36E **317** D7
Faial *Azores* 38°34N 28°42W **322** a
Faial *Madeira* 32°47N 16°53W **296** D3
Fair Haven *U.S.A.* 43°36N 73°16W **353** D17
Fair Hd. *U.K.* 55°14N 6°9W **282** A5
Fair Isle *U.K.* 59°32N 1°38W **286** B6
Fair Oaks *U.S.A.* 38°39N 121°16W **350** G5
Fairbanks *U.S.A.* 64°51N 147°43W **346** a
Fairbury *U.S.A.* 40°8N 97°11W **352** E5
Fairfax *U.S.A.* 44°40N 73°1W **355** B11
Fairfield *Ala., U.S.A.* 33°29N 86°55W **357** E11
Fairfield *Calif., U.S.A.* 38°15N 122°3W **350** G4
Fairfield *Conn., U.S.A.* 41°9N 73°16W **355** E11
Fairfield *Idaho, U.S.A.* 43°21N 114°44W **348** E6
Fairfield *Ill., U.S.A.* 38°23N 88°22W **352** F9
Fairfield *Iowa, U.S.A.* 40°56N 91°57W **352** E8
Fairfield *Tex., U.S.A.* 31°44N 96°10W **356** F6
Fairford *Canada* 51°37N 98°38W **343** C9
Fairhope *U.S.A.* 30°31N 87°54W **357** F11
Fairlie *N.Z.* 44°5S 170°49E **331** F3
Fairmead *U.S.A.* 37°5N 120°10W **350** H6
Fairmont *Minn., U.S.A.* 43°39N 94°28W **352** D6
Fairmont *W. Va., U.S.A.* 39°29N 80°9W **353** F13
Fairmount *Calif., U.S.A.* 34°45N 118°26W **351** L8
Fairmount *N.Y., U.S.A.* 43°5N 76°12W **355** C8
Fairplay *U.S.A.* 39°15N 106°2W **348** G10
Fairport *U.S.A.* 43°6N 77°27W **354** C7
Fairport Harbor *U.S.A.* 41°45N 81°17W **354** E3
Fairview *Canada* 56°5N 118°25W **342** B5
Fairview *Mont., U.S.A.* 47°51N 104°3W **348** C11
Fairview *Okla., U.S.A.* 36°16N 98°29W **356** C5
Fairweather, Mt. *U.S.A.* 58°55N 137°32W **342** B1
Faisalabad *Pakistan* 31°30N 73°5E **314** D5
Faith *U.S.A.* 45°2N 102°2W **352** C2
Faizabad *India* 26°45N 82°10E **315** F10
Fajardo *Puerto Rico* 18°20N 65°39W **361** d
Fajr, W. → *Si. Arabia* 29°10N 38°10E **316** D3
Fakenham *U.K.* 52°51N 0°51E **284** E8
Fakfak *Indonesia* 2°55S 132°18E **309** E8
Faku *China* 42°32N 123°21E **307** C12
Falaise *France* 48°54N 0°12W **292** B3
Falaise, Mui *Vietnam* 19°6N 105°45E **310** C5
Falam *Burma* 23°0N 93°45E **313** H18
Falcó, C. des *Spain* 38°50N 1°23E **296** C7
Falcón, Presa *Mexico* 26°35N 99°10W **359** B5
Falcon Lake *Canada* 49°42N 95°15W **343** D9
Falcon Res. *U.S.A.* 26°34N 99°10W **356** H5
Falconara Marittima *Italy* 43°37N 13°24E **294** C5
Falcone, C. del *Italy* 40°58N 8°12E **294** D3
Falconer *U.S.A.* 42°7N 79°12W **354** D5
Falefa *Samoa* 13°54S 171°31W **331** b
Falelatai *Samoa* 13°55S 171°59W **331** b
Falelima *Samoa* 13°32S 172°41W **331** b
Faleshty = Fălești *Moldova* 47°32N 27°44E **289** E14
Fălești *Moldova* 47°32N 27°44E **289** E14
Falfurrias *U.S.A.* 27°14N 98°9W **356** H5
Falher *Canada* 55°44N 117°15W **342** B5
Faliraki *Greece* 36°22N 28°12E **297** C10
Falkenberg *Sweden* 56°54N 12°30E **281** H15
Falkirk *U.K.* 56°0N 3°47W **283** F5
Falkirk □ *U.K.* 55°58N 3°49W **283** F5
Falkland *U.K.* 56°16N 3°12W **283** E5
Falkland Is. ☒ *Atl. Oc.* 51°30S 59°0W **368** G5
Falkland Sd. *Falk. Is.* 52°0S 60°0W **368** G5
Fall River *U.S.A.* 41°43N 71°10W **355** E13
Fallbrook *U.S.A.* 33°23N 117°15W **351** M9
Fallon *U.S.A.* 39°28N 118°47W **348** G4
Falls City *U.S.A.* 40°3N 95°36W **352** E6
Falls Creek *U.S.A.* 41°9N 78°48W **354** E6
Falmouth *Jamaica* 18°30N 77°40W **360** a
Falmouth *U.K.* 50°9N 5°5W **285** G2
Falmouth *U.S.A.* 41°33N 70°37W **355** E14
Falsa, Pta. *Mexico* 27°51N 115°3W **358** B1
False B. *S. Africa* 34°15S 18°40E **328** E2
Falso, C. *Honduras* 15°12N 83°21W **360** C3
Falster *Denmark* 54°45N 11°55E **281** J14
Falsterbo *Sweden* 55°23N 12°50E **281** J15
Fălticeni *Romania* 47°21N 26°20E **289** E14
Falun *Sweden* 60°37N 15°37E **280** F16
Famagusta *Cyprus* 35°8N 33°55E **297** D12
Famagusta Bay *Cyprus* 35°15N 34°0E **297** D13
Famalé *Niger* 14°33N 1°5E **322** F6
Famatina, Sierra de *Argentina* 27°30S 68°0W **366** B2
Family L. *Canada* 51°54N 95°27W **343** C9
Famoso *U.S.A.* 35°37N 119°12W **351** K7
Fan Xian *China* 35°55N 115°38E **306** G8
Fanad Hd. *Ireland* 55°17N 7°38W **282** A4
Fandriana *Madag.* 20°14S 47°21E **329** C8
Fang *Thailand* 19°55N 99°13E **310** C2
Fangcheng *China* 33°18N 112°59E **306** H7
Fangshan *China* 38°3N 111°25E **306** E6
Fangzi *China* 36°33N 119°10E **307** F10
Fanjakana *Madag.* 21°10S 46°53E **329** C8
Fanjiatun *China* 43°40N 125°15E **307** C13
Fanling *China* 22°30N 114°8E **305** F11
Fannich, L. *U.K.* 57°38N 4°59W **283** D4
Fannūj *Iran* 26°35N 59°38E **317** E8
Fanø *Denmark* 55°25N 8°25E **281** J13
Fano *Italy* 43°50N 13°1E **294** C5
Fanshi *China* 39°12N 113°20E **306** E7
Fao = Al Fāw *Iraq* 30°0N 48°30E **317** D6
Faqirwali *Pakistan* 29°27N 73°0E **314** E5
Far East = Dalnevostochnyy □ *Russia* 67°0N 140°0E **301** C14
Far East *Asia* 40°0N 130°0E **298** E14
Faradje *Dem. Rep. of the Congo* 3°50N 29°45E **326** B2
Farafangana *Madag.* 22°49S 47°50E **329** C8
Farāh *Afghan.* 32°20N 62°7E **312** C3
Farāh □ *Afghan.* 32°25N 62°10E **312** C3
Farahalana *Madag.* 14°26S 50°10E **329** A9
Faranah *Guinea* 10°3N 10°45W **322** F3
Farasān, Jazā'ir *Si. Arabia* 16°45N 41°55E **319** D3
Farasan Is. = Farasān, Jazā'ir *Si. Arabia* 16°45N 41°55E **319** D3
Faratsiho *Madag.* 19°24S 46°57E **329** B8
Fareham *U.K.* 50°51N 1°11W **285** G6
Farewell, C. *N.Z.* 40°29S 172°43E **331** D4
Farewell C. = Nunap Isua *Greenland* 59°48N 43°55W **338** D15
Farghona *Uzbekistan* 40°23N 71°19E **300** E8
Fargo *U.S.A.* 46°53N 96°48W **352** B5
Fār'iah, W. al → *West Bank* 32°12N 35°27E **318** C4
Faribault *U.S.A.* 44°18N 93°16W **352** C7
Faridabad *India* 28°26N 77°19E **314** E6
Faridkot *India* 30°44N 74°45E **314** D6
Faridpur *Bangla.* 23°15N 89°55E **315** H13
Faridpur *India* 28°13N 79°33E **315** E8
Farīmān *Iran* 35°40N 59°49E **317** C8
Farina *Australia* 30°3S 138°15E **335** E2
Fariones, Pta. *Canary Is.* 29°13N 13°28W **296** E6
Farleigh *Australia* 21°4S 149°8E **334** K7
Farmerville *U.S.A.* 32°47N 92°24W **356** E8
Farmingdale *U.S.A.* 40°12N 74°10W **355** F10
Farmington *Canada* 55°54N 120°30W **342** B4
Farmington *Calif., U.S.A.* 37°55N 120°59W **350** H6
Farmington *Maine, U.S.A.* 44°40N 70°9W **353** C18
Farmington *Mo., U.S.A.* 37°47N 90°25W **352** G8
Farmington *N.H., U.S.A.* 43°24N 71°4W **355** C13
Farmington *N. Mex., U.S.A.* 36°44N 108°12W **349** H9
Farmington *Utah, U.S.A.* 40°59N 111°53W **348** F8
Farmington → *U.S.A.* 41°51N 72°38W **355** E12
Farmville *U.S.A.* 37°18N 78°24W **353** G14
Farne Is. *U.K.* 55°38N 1°37W **284** B6
Farnham *Canada* 45°17N 72°59W **355** A12
Farnham, Mt. *Canada* 50°29N 116°30W **342** C5
Faro *Brazil* 2°10S 56°39W **365** D7
Faro *Canada* 62°11N 133°22W **340** C6
Faro *Portugal* 37°2N 7°55W **293** D2
Fårö *Sweden* 57°55N 19°5E **281** H18
Farquhar, C. *Australia* 23°50S 113°36E **333** D1
Farrars Cr. → *Australia* 25°35S 140°43E **334** D3
Farrāshband *Iran* 28°57N 52°5E **317** D7
Farrell *U.S.A.* 41°13N 80°30W **354** E4
Farrokhī *Iran* 33°50N 59°31E **317** C8
Farruch, C. = Ferrutx, C. *Spain* 39°47N 3°21E **296** B10
Fārs □ *Iran* 29°30N 55°0E **317** D7
Farsala *Greece* 39°17N 22°23E **295** E10
Farson *U.S.A.* 42°7N 109°26W **348** E9
Farsund *Norway* 58°5N 6°55E **281** G12
Fartak, Râs *Si. Arabia* 28°5N 34°34E **316** D2
Fartak, Ra's *Yemen* 15°38N 52°15E **319** D5
Fartura, Serra da *Brazil* 26°21S 52°52W **367** B5
Fārūj *Iran* 37°14N 58°14E **317** B8
Farvel, Kap = Nunap Isua *Greenland* 59°48N 43°55W **338** D15
Farwell *U.S.A.* 34°23N 103°2W **356** D3
Faryāb □ *Afghan.* 36°0N 65°0E **312** B4
Fasā *Iran* 29°0N 53°39E **317** D7
Fasano *Italy* 40°50N 17°22E **294** D7
Fastiv *Ukraine* 50°7N 29°57E **289** C15
Fastnet Rock *Ireland* 51°22N 9°37W **282** E2
Fastov = Fastiv *Ukraine* 50°7N 29°57E **289** C15
Fatagar, Tanjung *Indonesia* 2°46S 131°57E **309** E8
Fatehabad *Haryana, India* 29°31N 75°27E **314** E6
Fatehabad *Ut. P., India* 27°1N 78°19E **314** F8
Fatehgarh *India* 27°25N 79°35E **315** F8
Fatehpur *Bihar, India* 24°38N 85°14E **315** G11
Fatehpur *Raj., India* 28°0N 74°40E **314** F6
Fatehpur *Ut. P., India* 25°56N 81°13E **315** G9
Fatehpur *Ut. P., India* 27°10N 81°13E **315** F9
Fatehpur Sikri *India* 27°6N 77°40E **314** F6
Fathom Five ⌂ *Canada* 45°17N 81°40W **354** A3
Fatima *Canada* 47°24N 61°53W **345** C7

Foz do Cunene Angola 17°15S 11°48E 328 B1
Foz do Iguaçu Brazil 25°30S 54°30W 367 B5
Frackville U.S.A. 40°47N 76°14W 355 F8
Fraile Muerto Uruguay 32°31S 54°32W 367 C5
Framingham U.S.A. 42°18N 71°24W 355 D13
Franca Brazil 20°33S 47°30W 365 H9
Francavilla Fontana Italy 40°32N 17°35E 295 D7
France ■ Europe 47°0N 3°0E 292 C5
Frances Australia 36°41S 140°55E 335 F3
Frances → Canada 60°16N 129°10W 342 A3
Frances L. Canada 61°23N 129°30W 342 A3
Franceville Gabon 1°40S 13°32E 324 E2
Franche-Comté □ France 46°50N 5°55E 292 C6
Francis Case, L. U.S.A. 43°4N 98°34W 352 D4
Francisco Beltrão Brazil 26°5S 53°4W 367 B5
Francisco Ignacio Madero Coahuila, Mexico 25°48N 103°18W 358 B4
Francisco Ignacio Madero Durango, Mexico 24°26N 104°18W 358 C4
Francisco Ignacio Madero, Presa Mexico 28°10N 105°37W 358 B3
Francistown Botswana 21°7S 27°33E 329 C4
François Canada 47°35N 56°45W 345 C8
François L. Canada 54°0N 125°30W 342 C3
Francois Peron △ Australia 25°42S 113°33E 333 E1
Francs Pk. U.S.A. 43°58N 109°20W 348 E9
Franeker Neths. 53°12N 5°33E 287 A5
Frank Hann △ Australia 32°52S 120°19E 333 F3
Frankford Canada 44°12N 77°36W 354 B7
Frankfort S. Africa 27°17S 28°30E 329 D4
Frankfort Ind., U.S.A. 40°17N 86°31W 352 E10
Frankfort Kans., U.S.A. 39°42N 96°25W 352 F5
Frankfort Ky., U.S.A. 38°12N 84°52W 353 F11
Frankfort N.Y., U.S.A. 43°2N 75°4W 355 C9
Frankfurt Brandenburg, Germany 52°20N 14°32E 288 B8
Frankfurt Hessen, Germany 50°7N 8°41E 288 C5
Fränkische Alb Germany 49°10N 11°23E 288 D6
Frankland → Australia 35°0S 116°48E 333 G2
Franklin Ky., U.S.A. 36°43N 86°35W 352 G10
Franklin La., U.S.A. 29°48N 91°30W 356 G9
Franklin Mass., U.S.A. 42°5N 71°24W 355 D13
Franklin N.H., U.S.A. 43°27N 71°39W 355 C13
Franklin Nebr., U.S.A. 40°6N 98°57W 352 E4
Franklin Pa., U.S.A. 41°24N 79°50W 354 E5
Franklin Va., U.S.A. 36°41N 76°56W 353 G15
Franklin W. Va., U.S.A. 38°39N 79°20W 353 F14
Franklin B. Canada 69°45N 126°0W 340 C7
Franklin D. Roosevelt L. U.S.A. 48°18N 118°9W 348 B4
Franklin-Gordon Wild Rivers △ Australia 42°19S 145°51E 335 G4
Franklin I. Antarctica 76°10S 168°30E 277 D11
Franklin L. U.S.A. 40°25N 115°22W 348 F6
Franklin Mts. Canada 65°0N 125°0W 340 C7
Franklin Str. Canada 72°0N 96°0W 340 B10
Franklinton U.S.A. 30°51N 90°9W 357 F9
Franklinville U.S.A. 42°20N 78°27W 354 D6
Frankston Australia 38°8S 145°8E 335 F4
Fransfontein Namibia 20°12S 15°1E 328 C2
Frantsa Iosifa, Zemlya Russia 82°0N 55°0E 300 A6
Franz Canada 48°25N 84°30W 344 C3
Franz Josef Land = Frantsa Iosifa, Zemlya Russia 82°0N 55°0E 300 A6
Fraser U.S.A. 42°32N 82°57W 354 D2
Fraser → B.C., Canada 49°7N 123°11W 350 A3
Fraser → Nfld. & L., Canada 56°39N 62°10W 345 A7
Fraser, Mt. Australia 25°35S 118°20E 333 E2
Fraser I. Australia 25°15S 153°10E 335 D5
Fraser Lake Canada 54°0N 124°50W 342 C4
Fraserburg S. Africa 31°55S 21°30E 328 E3
Fraserburgh U.K. 57°42N 2°1W 283 D6
Fraserdale Canada 49°55N 81°37W 344 C3
Fray Bentos Uruguay 33°10S 58°15W 366 C4
Fray Jorge △ Chile 30°42S 71°40W 366 C1
Fredericia Denmark 55°34N 9°45E 281 J13
Frederick Md., U.S.A. 39°25N 77°25W 353 F15
Frederick Okla., U.S.A. 34°23N 99°1W 356 D5
Frederick S. Dak., U.S.A. 45°50N 98°31W 352 C4
Fredericksburg Pa., U.S.A. 40°27N 76°26W 355 F8
Fredericksburg Tex., U.S.A. 30°16N 98°52W 356 F5
Fredericksburg Va., U.S.A. 38°18N 77°28W 353 F15
Fredericktown Mo., U.S.A. 37°34N 90°18W 352 G8
Fredericktown Ohio, U.S.A. 40°29N 82°33W 354 F2
Frederico Westphalen Brazil 27°22S 53°24W 367 B5
Fredericton Canada 45°57N 66°40W 345 C6
Fredericton Junction Canada 45°41N 66°40W 345 C6
Frederikshåb = Paamiut Greenland 62°0N 49°43W 276 C5
Frederikshamn = Hamina Finland 60°34N 27°12E 280 F22
Frederikshavn Denmark 57°28N 10°31E 281 H14
Frederiksted U.S. Virgin Is. 17°43N 64°53W 361 C7
Fredonia Ariz., U.S.A. 36°57N 112°32W 349 H7
Fredonia Kans., U.S.A. 37°32N 95°49W 352 G6
Fredonia N.Y., U.S.A. 42°26N 79°20W 354 D5
Fredrikstad Norway 59°13N 10°57E 281 G14
Free State □ S. Africa 28°30S 27°0E 328 D4
Freehold U.S.A. 40°16N 74°17W 355 F10
Freeland U.S.A. 41°1N 75°54W 355 E9
Freels, C. Canada 49°15N 53°30W 345 C9
Freeman Calif., U.S.A. 35°35N 117°53W 351 K9
Freeman S. Dak., U.S.A. 43°21N 97°26W 352 D5
Freeport Bahamas 26°30N 78°47W 360 A4
Freeport Ill., U.S.A. 42°17N 89°36W 352 D9
Freeport N.Y., U.S.A. 40°39N 73°35W 355 F11
Freeport Ohio, U.S.A. 40°12N 81°15W 354 F3
Freeport Pa., U.S.A. 40°41N 79°41W 354 F5
Freeport Tex., U.S.A. 28°57N 95°21W 356 G7
Freetown S. Leone 8°30N 13°17W 322 G3
Frégate, L. de la Canada 53°15N 74°45W 344 B5
Fregenal de la Sierra Spain 38°10N 6°39W 293 C2
Freibourg = Fribourg Switz. 46°49N 7°9E 292 C7
Freiburg Germany 47°59N 7°51E 288 E4
Freire Chile 38°54S 72°38W 368 D2
Freirina Chile 28°30S 71°10W 366 B1
Freising Germany 48°24N 11°45E 288 D6
Freistadt Austria 48°30N 14°30E 288 D8
Fréjus France 43°25N 6°44E 292 E7
Fremantle Australia 32°7S 115°47E 333 F2
Fremont Calif., U.S.A. 37°32N 121°57W 350 H4
Fremont Mich., U.S.A. 43°28N 85°57W 353 D11
Fremont Nebr., U.S.A. 41°26N 96°30W 352 E5
Fremont Ohio, U.S.A. 41°21N 83°7W 353 E12
Fremont → U.S.A. 38°24N 110°42W 348 G8
French Camp U.S.A. 37°53N 121°16W 350 H5
French Cays = Plana Cays Bahamas 22°38N 73°30W 361 B5
French Creek → U.S.A. 41°24N 79°50W 354 E5
French Guiana ☒ S. Amer. 4°0N 53°0W 365 C8
French Polynesia ☒ Pac. Oc. 20°0S 145°0W 337 J13
Frenchman → N. Amer. 48°31N 107°10W 348 B10
Frenchman Cr. → U.S.A. 40°14N 100°50W 352 E3
Fresco → Brazil 7°15S 51°30W 365 E8
Freshfield, C. Antarctica 68°25S 151°10E 277 C10
Fresnillo Mexico 23°10N 102°53W 358 C4
Fresno U.S.A. 36°44N 119°47W 350 J7
Fresno Res. U.S.A. 48°36N 109°57W 348 B9
Frew → Australia 20°0S 135°38E 334 C2
Frewsburg U.S.A. 42°3N 79°10W 354 D5
Freycinet △ Australia 42°11S 148°19E 335 G4
Freycinet Pen. Australia 42°10S 148°25E 335 G4
Fria Guinea 10°27N 13°38W 322 F3
Fria, C. Namibia 18°0S 12°0E 328 B1
Friant U.S.A. 36°59N 119°43W 350 J7
Frías Argentina 28°40S 65°5W 366 B2
Fribourg Switz. 46°49N 7°9E 292 C7
Friday Harbor U.S.A. 48°32N 123°1W 350 B3
Friedens U.S.A. 40°3N 78°59W 354 F6
Friedrichshafen Germany 47°39N 9°30E 288 E5
Friendship U.S.A. 42°12N 78°8W 354 D6
Friesland □ Neths. 53°5N 5°50E 287 A5
Frigate Seychelles 4°35S 55°56E 325 b
Frio → U.S.A. 28°26N 98°11W 356 G5
Frio, C. Brazil 22°50S 41°50W 362 F6
Friona U.S.A. 34°38N 102°43W 356 D3
Fritch U.S.A. 35°38N 101°36W 356 D4
Frobisher B. Canada 62°30N 66°0W 341 C13
Frobisher Bay = Iqaluit Canada 63°44N 68°31W 341 C13
Frobisher L. Canada 56°20N 108°15W 343 B7
Frohavet Norway 64°0N 9°30E 280 E13
Frome U.K. 51°14N 2°19W 285 F5
Frome → U.K. 50°41N 2°6W 285 G5
Frome, L. Australia 30°45S 139°45E 335 E2
Front Range U.S.A. 40°25N 105°45W 346 C5
Front Royal U.S.A. 38°55N 78°12W 353 F14
Frontera Canary Is. 27°47N 17°59W 296 G2
Frontera Mexico 18°32N 92°38W 359 D6
Fronteras Mexico 30°56N 109°31W 358 A3
Frosinone Italy 41°38N 13°19E 294 D5
Frostburg U.S.A. 39°39N 78°56W 353 F14
Frostisen Norway 68°14N 17°10E 280 B17
Frøya Norway 63°43N 8°40E 280 E13
Frunze = Bishkek Kyrgyzstan 42°54N 74°46E 300 E8
Frutal Brazil 20°0S 49°0W 365 H9
Frýdek-Místek Czech Rep. 49°40N 18°20E 289 D10
Fryeburg U.S.A. 44°1N 70°59W 355 B14
Fu Xian = Wafangdian China 39°38N 121°58E 307 E11
Fu Xian China 36°0N 109°20E 306 G5
Fucheng China 37°50N 116°10E 306 F9
Fuchou = Fuzhou China 26°5N 119°16E 305 D6
Fuchū Japan 34°34N 133°14E 303 G6
Fuencaliente Canary Is. 28°28N 17°50W 296 F2
Fuencaliente, Pta. Canary Is. 28°27N 17°51W 296 F2
Fuengirola Spain 36°32N 4°41W 293 D3
Fuentes de Oñoro Spain 40°33N 6°52W 293 B2
Fuerte → Mexico 25°54N 109°22W 358 B3
Fuerte Olimpo Paraguay 21°0S 57°51W 366 A4
Fuerteventura Canary Is. 28°30N 14°0W 296 F6
Fuerteventura ✕ (FUE) Canary Is. 28°24N 13°52W 296 F6
Fufeng China 34°22N 108°0E 306 G5
Fugou China 34°3N 114°25E 306 G8
Fugu China 39°2N 111°3E 306 E6
Fuhai China 47°2N 87°25E 304 B3
Fuḩaymī Iraq 34°16N 42°10E 316 C4
Fuji Japan 35°9N 138°39E 303 G9
Fuji-Hakone-Izu △ Japan 35°15N 138°45E 303 G9
Fuji-San Japan 35°22N 138°44E 303 G9
Fuji-Yoshida Japan 35°30N 138°46E 303 G9
Fujian □ China 26°0N 118°0E 305 D6
Fujinomiya Japan 35°10N 138°40E 303 G9
Fujisawa Japan 35°22N 139°29E 303 G9
Fujiyama, Mt. = Fuji-San Japan 35°22N 138°44E 303 G9
Fukagawa Japan 43°43N 142°2E 302 C11
Fukien = Fujian □ China 26°0N 118°0E 305 D6
Fukuchiyama Japan 35°19N 135°9E 303 G7
Fukue-Shima Japan 32°40N 128°45E 303 H4
Fukui Japan 36°5N 136°10E 303 F8
Fukui □ Japan 36°0N 136°12E 303 G8
Fukuoka Japan 33°39N 130°21E 303 H5
Fukuoka □ Japan 33°30N 131°0E 303 H5
Fukushima Japan 37°44N 140°28E 302 F10
Fukushima □ Japan 37°30N 140°15E 302 F10
Fukuyama Japan 34°35N 133°20E 303 G6
Fulaga Fiji 19°8S 178°33W 331 a
Fulda Germany 50°32N 9°40E 288 C5
Fulda → Germany 51°25N 9°39E 288 C5
Fulford Harbour Canada 48°47N 123°27W 350 B3
Fullerton Calif., U.S.A. 33°53N 117°56W 351 M9
Fullerton Nebr., U.S.A. 41°22N 97°58W 352 E5
Fulongquan China 44°20N 124°42E 307 B13
Fulton Mo., U.S.A. 38°52N 91°57W 352 F8
Fulton N.Y., U.S.A. 43°19N 76°25W 355 C8
Funabashi Japan 35°45N 140°0E 303 G10
Funafuti = Fongafale Tuvalu 8°31S 179°13E 330 B10
Funchal Madeira 32°38N 16°54W 296 D3
Funchal ✕ (FNC) Madeira 32°42N 16°45W 296 D3
Fundación Colombia 10°31N 74°11W 364 A4
Fundão Portugal 40°8N 7°30W 293 B2
Fundy, B. of Canada 45°0N 66°0W 345 D6
Fundy △ Canada 45°35N 65°10W 345 C6
Funhalouro Mozam. 23°3S 34°25E 329 C5
Funing Hebei, China 39°53N 119°12E 307 E10
Funing Jiangsu, China 33°45N 119°50E 307 H10
Funiu Shan China 33°30N 112°20E 306 H7
Funtua Nigeria 11°30N 7°18E 322 F7
Fuping Hebei, China 38°48N 114°12E 306 E8
Fuping Shaanxi, China 34°42N 109°10E 306 G5
Furano Japan 43°21N 142°23E 302 C11
Furāt, Nahr al → Asia 31°0N 47°25E 316 D5
Fūrg Iran 28°18N 55°13E 317 D7
Furnás Spain 39°3N 1°32E 296 B8
Furnas, Represa de Brazil 20°50S 45°30W 367 A6
Furneaux Group Australia 40°10S 147°50E 335 G4
Furqlus Syria 34°36N 37°8E 318 A6
Fürstenwalde Germany 52°22N 14°3E 288 B8
Fürth Germany 49°28N 10°59E 288 D6
Furukawa Japan 38°34N 140°58E 302 E10
Fury and Hecla Str. Canada 69°56N 84°0W 341 C11
Fusagasuga Colombia 4°21N 74°22W 364 C4
Fushan Shandong, China 37°30N 121°15E 307 F11
Fushan Shanxi, China 35°58N 111°51E 306 G6
Fushun China 41°50N 123°56E 307 D12
Fusong China 42°20N 127°15E 307 C14
Fustic Barbados 13°16N 59°38W 361 g
Futian China 22°32N 114°4E 305 F11
Fuxin China 42°5N 121°48E 307 C11
Fuyang China 33°0N 115°48E 306 H8
Fuyang He → China 38°12N 117°0E 306 E9
Fuyong China 22°40N 113°49E 305 F10
Fuyu Heilongjiang, China 47°49N 124°27E 305 B7
Fuyu Jilin, China 45°12N 124°43E 307 B13
Fuyun China 47°0N 89°28E 304 B3
Fuzhou China 26°5N 119°16E 305 D6
Fyn Denmark 55°20N 10°30E 281 J14
Fyne, L. U.K. 55°59N 5°23W 283 F3

G

Gabela Angola 11°0S 14°24E 324 G2
Gabès Tunisia 33°53N 10°2E 323 B8
Gabès, G. de Tunisia 34°0N 10°30E 323 B8
Gabon ■ Africa 0°10S 10°0E 324 E2
Gaborone Botswana 24°45S 25°57E 328 C4
Gabriels U.S.A. 44°26N 74°12W 355 B10
Gābrīk Iran 25°44N 58°28E 317 E8
Gabrovo Bulgaria 42°52N 25°19E 295 C11
Gāch Sār Iran 36°7N 51°19E 317 B6
Gachsārān Iran 30°15N 50°45E 317 D6
Gadag India 15°30N 75°45E 312 M9
Gadap Pakistan 25°5N 67°28E 314 G2
Gadarwara India 22°50N 78°50E 315 H8
Gadhada India 22°0N 71°35E 314 J4
Gadra Pakistan 25°40N 70°38E 314 G4
Gadsden U.S.A. 34°1N 86°1W 357 D11
Gadwal India 16°10N 77°50E 312 L10
Gaffney U.S.A. 35°5N 81°39W 357 D14
Gafsa Tunisia 34°24N 8°43E 322 B7
Gagaria India 25°43N 70°46E 314 G4
Găgăuzia □ Moldova 46°10N 28°40E 289 E15
Gagnoa Ivory C. 6°56N 5°16W 322 G4
Gagnon Canada 51°50N 68°5W 345 B6
Gagnon, L. Canada 62°3N 110°27W 343 A6
Gahini Rwanda 1°50S 30°30E 326 C3
Gahmar India 25°27N 83°49E 315 G10
Gai Xian = Gaizhou China 40°22N 122°20E 307 D12
Gaidouronisi Greece 34°53N 25°41E 297 E7
Gail U.S.A. 32°46N 101°27W 356 E4
Gaillimh = Galway Ireland 53°17N 9°3W 282 C2
Gaines U.S.A. 41°46N 77°35W 354 E7
Gainesville Fla., U.S.A. 29°40N 82°20W 357 G13
Gainesville Ga., U.S.A. 34°18N 83°50W 357 D13
Gainesville Mo., U.S.A. 36°36N 92°26W 352 G7
Gainesville Tex., U.S.A. 33°38N 97°8W 356 E6
Gainsborough U.K. 53°24N 0°46W 284 D7
Gairdner, L. Australia 31°30S 136°0E 335 E2
Gairloch U.K. 57°43N 5°41W 283 D3
Gairloch, L. U.K. 57°43N 5°45W 283 D3
Gaizhou China 40°22N 122°20E 307 D12
Gaj → Pakistan 26°26N 67°21E 314 F2
Gakuch Pakistan 36°7N 73°45E 315 A5
Galán, Cerro Argentina 25°55S 66°52W 366 B2
Galana → Kenya 3°9S 40°8E 326 C5
Galápagos = Colón, Arch. de Ecuador 0°0 91°0W 362 D1
Galapagos Fracture Zone Pac. Oc. 3°0N 110°0W 337 G17
Galapagos Rise Pac. Oc. 15°0S 95°0W 337 J18
Galashiels U.K. 55°37N 2°49W 283 F6
Galaţi Romania 45°27N 28°2E 289 F15
Galatina Italy 40°10N 18°10E 295 D8
Galax U.S.A. 36°40N 80°56W 353 G13
Galcaio Somali Rep. 6°30N 47°30E 319 F4
Galdhøpiggen Norway 61°38N 8°18E 280 F13
Galeana Chihuahua, Mexico 30°7N 107°38W 358 A3
Galeana Nuevo León, Mexico 24°50N 100°4W 358 A3
Galela Indonesia 1°50N 127°49E 309 D7
Galena U.S.A. 64°44N 156°56W 346 a
Galeota Pt. Trin. & Tob. 10°8N 60°59W 365 K16
Galera Pt. Trin. & Tob. 10°49N 60°54W 361 D7
Galesburg U.S.A. 40°57N 90°22W 352 E8
Galestan △ Iran 37°30N 56°0E 317 B8
Galeton U.S.A. 41°44N 77°39W 354 E7
Galich Russia 58°22N 42°24E 290 C7
Galicia □ Spain 42°43N 7°45W 293 A2
Galilee = Hagalil Israel 32°53N 35°18E 318 C4
Galilee, L. Australia 22°20S 145°50E 334 C4
Galilee, Sea of = Yam Kinneret Israel 32°45N 35°35E 318 C4
Galina Pt. Jamaica 18°24N 76°58W 360 a
Galinoporni Cyprus 35°31N 34°18E 297 D13
Galion U.S.A. 40°44N 82°47W 354 F2
Galiuro Mts. U.S.A. 32°30N 110°20W 349 K8
Galiwinku Australia 12°2S 135°34E 334 A2
Gallan Hd. U.K. 58°15N 7°2W 283 C1
Gallatin U.S.A. 36°24N 86°27W 357 C11
Galle Sri Lanka 6°5N 80°10E 312 R12
Gállego → Spain 41°39N 0°51W 293 B5
Gallegos → Argentina 51°35S 69°0W 368 G3
Galley Hd. Ireland 51°32N 8°55W 282 E3
Gallinas, Pta. Colombia 12°28N 71°40W 364 A4
Gallipoli = Gelibolu Turkey 40°28N 26°43E 295 D12
Gallípoli Italy 40°3N 17°58E 295 D8
Gallipolis U.S.A. 38°49N 82°12W 353 F12
Gällivare Sweden 67°9N 20°40E 280 C19
Galloo I. U.S.A. 43°55N 76°25W 355 C8
Galloway U.K. 55°1N 4°29W 283 F4
Galloway, Mull of U.K. 54°39N 4°52W 283 G4
Galloway ⌂ U.K. 55°3N 4°20W 283 F4
Gallup U.S.A. 35°32N 108°45W 349 J9
Galoya Sri Lanka 8°10N 80°55E 312 Q12
Galt U.S.A. 38°15N 121°18W 350 G5
Galty Mts. Ireland 52°22N 8°10W 282 D3
Galtymore Ireland 52°21N 8°11W 282 D3
Galva U.S.A. 41°10N 90°3W 352 E8
Galveston U.S.A. 29°18N 94°48W 356 G7
Galveston B. U.S.A. 29°36N 94°50W 356 G7
Gálvez Argentina 32°0S 61°14W 366 C3
Galway Ireland 53°17N 9°3W 282 C2
Galway □ Ireland 53°22N 9°1W 282 C2
Galway B. Ireland 53°13N 9°10W 282 C2
Gam → Vietnam 21°55N 105°12E 310 B5
Gamagōri Japan 34°50N 137°14E 303 G8
Gambat Pakistan 27°17N 68°26E 314 F3
Gambhir → India 26°58N 77°27E 314 F6
Gambia ■ W. Afr. 13°25N 16°0W 322 F2
Gambia → W. Afr. 13°28N 16°34W 322 F2
Gambier U.S.A. 40°22N 82°23W 354 F2
Gambier, C. Australia 11°56S 130°57E 332 B5
Gambier, Îs. French Polynesia 23°8S 134°58W 337 K14
Gambier Is. Australia 35°3S 136°30E 335 F2
Gambo Canada 48°47N 54°13W 345 C9
Gamboli Pakistan 29°53N 68°24E 314 E3
Gamboma Congo 1°55S 15°52E 324 E3
Gamka → S. Africa 33°18S 21°39E 328 E3
Gamkab → Namibia 28°4S 17°54E 328 D2
Gamlakarleby = Kokkola Finland 63°50N 23°8E 280 E20
Gammon → Canada 51°24N 95°44W 343 C9
Gammon Ranges △ Australia 30°38S 139°8E 335 E2
Gamtoos → S. Africa 33°58S 25°1E 328 E4
Gan Jiang → China 29°15N 116°0E 305 D6
Ganado U.S.A. 35°43N 109°33W 349 J9
Gananoque Canada 44°20N 76°10W 355 B8
Ganāveh Iran 29°35N 50°35E 317 D6
Gäncä Azerbaijan 40°45N 46°20E 291 F8
Gancheng China 18°51N 108°37E 310 C7
Gand = Gent Belgium 51°2N 3°42E 287 C3
Ganda Angola 13°3S 14°35E 325 G2
Gandajika Dem. Rep. of the Congo 6°46S 23°58E 324 F4
Gandak → India 25°39N 85°13E 315 G11
Gandava Pakistan 28°32N 67°32E 314 E2
Gander Canada 48°58N 54°35W 345 C9
Gander L. Canada 48°58N 54°35W 345 C9
Ganderowe Falls Zimbabwe 17°20S 29°10E 327 F2
Gandhi Sagar India 24°40N 75°40E 314 G6
Gandhinagar India 23°15N 72°45E 314 H5
Gandía Spain 38°58N 0°9W 293 C5
Gando, Pta. Canary Is. 27°55N 15°22W 296 G4
Ganedidalem = Gani Indonesia 0°48S 128°14E 309 E7
Ganga → India 23°20N 90°30E 315 H14
Ganga Sagar India 21°38N 88°5E 315 J13
Gangan → India 28°38N 78°58E 315 E8
Ganganagar India 29°56N 73°56E 314 E5
Gangapur India 26°32N 76°49E 314 F7
Gangaw Burma 22°5N 94°5E 313 H19
Gangdisê Shan China 31°20N 81°0E 315 D9
Ganges = Ganga → India 23°20N 90°30E 315 H14
Ganges Canada 48°51N 123°31W 342 D4
Ganges, Mouths of the India 21°30N 90°0E 315 J14
Ganggyeong S. Korea 36°10N 127°0E 307 F14
Ganghwa S. Korea 37°45N 126°30E 307 F14
Gangneung S. Korea 37°45N 128°54E 307 F15
Gangoh India 29°46N 77°18E 314 E7
Gangotri India 30°50N 79°10E 315 D8
Gangotri △ India 30°50N 79°10E 315 D8
Gangseong S. Korea 38°24N 128°30E 307 E15
Gangtok India 27°20N 88°37E 313 F16
Gangu China 34°40N 105°15E 306 G3
Gangyao China 44°12N 126°37E 307 B14
Gani Indonesia 0°48S 128°14E 309 E7
Ganj India 27°45N 78°57E 315 F8
Gannett Peak U.S.A. 43°11N 109°39W 348 E9
Ganquan China 36°20N 109°20E 306 F5
Gansu □ China 36°0N 104°0E 306 G3
Ganta Liberia 7°15N 8°59W 322 G4
Gantheaume, C. Australia 36°4S 137°32E 335 F2
Gantheaume B. Australia 27°40S 114°10E 333 E1
Gantsevichi = Hantsavichy Belarus 52°49N 26°30E 289 B14
Ganyem = Genyem Indonesia 2°46S 140°12E 309 E10
Ganyu China 34°50N 119°8E 307 G10
Ganzhou China 25°51N 114°56E 305 D6
Gao Mali 16°15N 0°5W 322 E5
Gaomi China 36°20N 119°42E 307 F10
Gaoping China 35°45N 112°55E 306 G7
Gaotang China 36°50N 116°15E 306 F9
Gaoua Burkina Faso 10°20N 3°8W 322 F5
Gaoual Guinea 11°45N 13°25W 322 F3
Gaoxiong = Kaohsiung Taiwan 22°35N 120°16E 305 D7
Gaoyang China 38°40N 115°45E 306 E8
Gaoyou Hu China 32°45N 119°20E 307 H10
Gaoyuan China 37°8N 117°58E 307 F9
Gap France 44°33N 6°5E 292 D7
Gapat → India 24°30N 82°28E 315 G10
Gapuwiyak Australia 12°25S 135°43E 334 A2
Gar China 32°10N 79°58E 304 C2
Gara, L. Ireland 53°57N 8°26W 282 C3
Garabogazköl Aylagy Turkmenistan 41°0N 53°30E 291 F9
Garachico Canary Is. 28°22N 16°46W 296 F3
Garachiné Panama 8°0N 78°12W 360 E4
Garafia Canary Is. 28°48N 17°57W 296 F2
Garagum Turkmenistan 39°30N 60°0E 317 B8
Garah Australia 29°5S 149°38E 335 D4
Garajonay Canary Is. 28°7N 17°14W 296 F2
Garamba △ Dem. Rep. of the Congo 4°10N 29°40E 326 B2
Garanhuns Brazil 8°50S 36°30W 365 E11
Garautha India 25°34N 79°18E 315 G8
Garba Tula Kenya 0°30N 38°32E 326 B4
Garberville U.S.A. 40°6N 123°48W 348 F2
Garbiyang India 30°8N 80°54E 315 D9
Gard → France 43°51N 4°37E 292 E6
Garda, L. di Italy 45°40N 10°41E 294 B4
Garde L. Canada 62°50N 106°13W 343 A7
Garden City Ga., U.S.A. 32°6N 81°9W 357 E14
Garden City Kans., U.S.A. 37°58N 100°53W 352 G3
Garden City Tex., U.S.A. 31°52N 101°29W 356 F4
Garden Grove U.S.A. 33°47N 117°55W 351 M9
Gardēz Afghan. 33°37N 69°9E 314 C3
Gardiner Maine, U.S.A. 44°14N 69°47W 353 C19
Gardiner Mont., U.S.A. 45°2N 110°22W 348 D8
Gardiners I. U.S.A. 41°6N 72°6W 355 E12
Gardner U.S.A. 42°34N 71°59W 355 D13
Gardner Canal Canada 53°27N 128°8W 342 C3
Gardnerville U.S.A. 38°56N 119°45W 350 G7
Gardo Somali Rep. 9°30N 49°6E 319 F4
Garey U.S.A. 34°53N 120°19W 351 L6
Garfield U.S.A. 47°1N 117°9W 348 C5
Garforth U.K. 53°47N 1°24W 284 D6
Gargantua, C. Canada 47°36N 85°2W 353 B11
Gargett Australia 21°9S 148°46E 334 K6
Garibaldi ⌂ Canada 49°50N 122°40W 342 D4
Gariep, L. S. Africa 30°40S 25°40E 328 E4
Garies S. Africa 30°32S 17°59E 328 E2
Garigliano → Italy 41°13N 13°45E 294 D5
Garissa Kenya 0°25S 39°40E 326 C4
Garland Tex., U.S.A. 32°54N 96°38W 356 E6
Garland Utah, U.S.A. 41°45N 112°10W 348 F7
Garm Tajikistan 39°0N 70°20E 300 F8
Garmāb Iran 35°25N 56°45E 317 C8
Garmisch-Partenkirchen Germany 47°30N 11°6E 288 E6
Garmsār Iran 35°20N 52°25E 317 C7
Garner U.S.A. 43°6N 93°36W 352 D7
Garnett U.S.A. 38°17N 95°14W 352 F6
Garo Hills India 25°30N 90°30E 315 G14
Garoe Somali Rep. 8°25N 48°33E 319 F4
Garonne → France 45°2N 0°36W 292 D3
Garoowe = Garoe Somali Rep. 8°25N 48°33E 319 F4
Garot India 24°19N 75°41E 314 G6
Garoua Cameroon 9°19N 13°21E 323 G8
Garrauli India 25°5N 79°22E 315 G8
Garrison Mont., U.S.A. 46°31N 112°49W 348 C7
Garrison N. Dak., U.S.A. 47°40N 101°25W 352 B3
Garrison Res. = Sakakawea, L. U.S.A. 47°30N 101°25W 352 B3
Garron Pt. U.K. 55°3N 5°59W 282 A6
Garry → U.K. 56°44N 3°47W 283 E5
Garry, L. Canada 65°58N 100°18W 340 C9
Garrygala Turkmenistan 38°31N 56°29E 317 B8
Garsen Kenya 2°20S 40°5E 326 C5
Garson L. Canada 56°19N 110°2W 343 B6
Garstang U.K. 53°55N 2°46W 284 D5
Garu India 23°40N 84°14E 315 H11
Garub Namibia 26°37S 16°0E 328 D2

Garut *Indonesia* 7°14S 107°53E **309** G12
Garvie Mts. *N.Z.* 45°30S 168°50E **331** F2
Garwa = Garoua *Cameroon* 9°19N 13°21E **323** G8
Garwa *India* 24°11N 83°47E **315** G10
Gary *U.S.A.* 41°36N 87°20W **352** E10
Garzê *China* 31°38N 100°1E **304** C5
Garzón *Colombia* 2°10N 75°40W **364** C3
Gas-San *Japan* 38°32N 140°1E **302** E10
Gasan Kuli = Esenguly *Turkmenistan* 37°37N 53°59E **300** F6
Gascogne *France* 43°45N 0°20E **292** E4
Gascogne, G. de *Europe* 44°0N 2°0W **292** D2
Gascony = Gascogne *France* 43°45N 0°20E **292** E4
Gascoyne → *Australia* 24°52S 113°37E **333** D1
Gascoyne Junction *Australia* 25°2S 115°17E **333** E2
Gashaka *Nigeria* 7°20N 11°29E **323** G8
Gasherbrum *Pakistan* 35°40N 76°40E **315** B7
Gashua *Nigeria* 12°54N 11°0E **323** F8
Gasparillo *Trin. & Tob.* 10°18N 61°26W **365** K15
Gaspé *Canada* 48°52N 64°30W **345** C7
Gaspé, C. *Canada* 48°48N 64°7W **345** C7
Gaspé Pen. = Gaspésie, Pén. de la *Canada* 48°45N 65°40W **345** C6
Gaspésie, Pén. de la *Canada* 48°45N 65°40W **345** C6
Gaspésie ⌂ *Canada* 48°55N 66°10W **345** C6
Gasteiz = Vitoria-Gasteiz *Spain* 42°50N 2°41W **293** A4
Gastonia *U.S.A.* 35°16N 81°11W **357** D14
Gastre *Argentina* 42°20S 69°15W **368** E3
Gata, C. *Cyprus* 34°34N 33°2E **297** E12
Gata, C. de *Spain* 36°41N 2°13W **293** D4
Gata, Sierra de *Spain* 40°20N 6°45W **293** B2
Gataga → *Canada* 58°35N 126°59W **342** B3
Gatchina *Russia* 59°35N 30°9E **281** G24
Gatehouse of Fleet *U.K.* 54°53N 4°12W **283** G4
Gates *U.S.A.* 43°9N 77°42W **354** C7
Gateshead *U.K.* 54°57N 1°35W **284** C6
Gatesville *U.S.A.* 31°26N 97°45W **356** F6
Gateway ⌂ *U.S.A.* 40°38N 73°51W **355** F11
Gaths *Zimbabwe* 20°2S 30°32E **327** G3
Gatico *Chile* 22°29S 70°20W **366** A1
Gatineau *Canada* 45°29N 75°39W **355** A9
Gatineau → *Canada* 45°27N 75°42W **344** C4
Gatineau △ *Canada* 45°40N 76°0W **344** C4
Gatton *Australia* 27°32S 152°17E **335** D5
Gatun, L. *Panama* 9°7N 79°56W **360** E4
Gatwick, London ✕ (LGW) *U.K.* 51°10N 0°11W **285** F7
Gatyana *S. Africa* 32°16S 28°31E **329** E4
Gau *Fiji* 18°2S 179°18E **331** a
Gauer L. *Canada* 57°0N 97°50W **343** B9
Gauhati = Guwahati *India* 26°10N 91°45E **313** F17
Gauja → *Latvia* 57°10N 24°16E **281** H21
Gaujas △ *Latvia* 57°10N 24°50E **281** H21
Gaula → *Norway* 63°21N 10°14E **280** E14
Gauri Phanta *India* 28°41N 80°36E **315** E9
Gaustatoppen *Norway* 59°48N 8°40E **281** G13
Gauteng □ *S. Africa* 26°0S 28°0E **329** D4
Gāv Koshī *Iran* 28°38N 57°12E **317** D8
Gāvakān *Iran* 29°37N 53°10E **317** D7
Gavāter *Iran* 25°10N 61°31E **317** E9
Gāvbandī *Iran* 27°12N 53°4E **317** E7
Gavdopoula *Greece* 34°56N 24°0E **297** E6
Gavdos *Greece* 34°50N 24°5E **297** E6
Gaviota *U.S.A.* 34°29N 120°13W **351** L6
Gāvkhūnī, Bāţlāq-e *Iran* 32°6N 52°52E **317** C7
Gävle *Sweden* 60°40N 17°9E **280** F17
Gawachab *Namibia* 27°4S 17°55E **328** D2
Gawilgarh Hills *India* 21°15N 76°45E **312** J10
Gawler *Australia* 34°30S 138°42E **335** E2
Gawler Ranges *Australia* 32°30S 135°45E **335** E2
Gaxun Nur *China* 42°22N 100°30E **304** B5
Gay *Russia* 51°27N 58°27E **290** D10
Gaya *India* 24°47N 85°4E **315** G11
Gaya *Niger* 11°52N 3°28E **322** F6
Gaylord *U.S.A.* 45°2N 84°41W **353** C11
Gayndah *Australia* 25°35S 151°32E **335** D5
Gaysin = Haysyn *Ukraine* 48°57N 29°25E **289** D15
Gayvoron = Hayvoron *Ukraine* 48°22N 29°52E **289** D15
Gaza *Gaza Strip* 31°30N 34°28E **318** D3
Gaza □ *Mozam.* 23°10S 32°45E **329** C5
Gaza Strip ■ *Asia* 31°29N 34°25E **318** D3
Gazanjyk = Bereket *Turkmenistan* 39°16N 55°32E **317** B7
Gāzbor *Iran* 28°5N 58°51E **317** D8
Gazi *Dem. Rep. of the Congo* 1°3N 24°30E **326** B1
Gaziantep *Turkey* 37°6N 37°23E **316** B3
Gazimağosa = Famagusta *Cyprus* 35°8N 33°55E **297** D12
Gcoverega *Botswana* 19°8S 24°18E **328** B3
Gcuwa *S. Africa* 32°20S 28°11E **329** E4
Gdańsk *Poland* 54°22N 18°40E **289** A10
Gdańska, Zatoka *Poland* 54°30N 19°20E **289** A10
Gdov *Russia* 58°48N 27°55E **281** G22
Gdynia *Poland* 54°35N 18°33E **289** A10
Gebe *Indonesia* 0°5N 129°25E **309** D7
Gebze *Turkey* 40°47N 29°25E **295** D13
Gedaref *Sudan* 14°2N 35°28E **323** F13
Gediz → *Turkey* 38°35N 26°48E **295** E12
Gedser *Denmark* 54°35N 11°55E **281** J14
Gedung, Pulau *Malaysia* 5°17N 100°23E **311** c
Geegully Cr. → *Australia* 18°32S 123°41E **332** C3
Geel *Belgium* 51°10N 4°59E **287** C4
Geelong *Australia* 38°10S 144°22E **335** F3
Geelvink B. = Cenderwasih, Teluk *Indonesia* 3°0S 135°20E **309** E9
Geelvink Chan. *Australia* 28°30S 114°0E **333** E1
Geesthacht *Germany* 53°26N 10°22E **288** B6
Geidam *Nigeria* 12°57N 11°57E **323** F8
Geikie → *Canada* 57°45N 103°52W **343** B8
Geikie Gorge △ *Australia* 18°3S 125°41E **332** C4
Geistown *U.S.A.* 40°18N 78°52W **354** F6
Geita *Tanzania* 2°48S 32°12E **326** C3
Gejiu *China* 23°20N 103°10E **304** D5
Gel, Meydān-e *Iran* 29°4N 54°50E **317** D7
Gela *Italy* 37°4N 14°15E **294** F6
Gelang Patah *Malaysia* 1°27N 103°35E **311** d
Gelderland □ *Neths.* 52°5N 6°10E **287** B6
Geldrop *Neths.* 51°25N 5°32E **287** C5
Geleen *Neths.* 50°57N 5°49E **287** D5
Gelib *Somali Rep.* 0°29N 42°46E **319** G3
Gelibolu *Turkey* 40°28N 26°43E **295** D12
Gelsenkirchen *Germany* 51°32N 7°6E **288** C4
Gelugur *Malaysia* 5°22N 100°18E **311** c
Gemas *Malaysia* 2°37N 102°36E **311** L4
Gembloux *Belgium* 50°34N 4°43E **287** D4
Gemena *Dem. Rep. of the Congo* 3°13N 19°48E **324** D3
Gemerek *Turkey* 39°15N 36°10E **316** B3
Gemlik *Turkey* 40°26N 29°9E **295** D13
Gemsbok △ *Botswana* 25°5S 21°1E **328** D3
Genadi *Greece* 36°2N 27°56E **297** C9
Genale → *Ethiopia* 6°2N 39°1E **319** F2
General Acha *Argentina* 37°20S 64°38W **366** D3
General Alvear *B. Aires, Argentina* 36°0S 60°0W **366** D4
General Alvear *Mendoza, Argentina* 35°0S 67°40W **366** D2
General Artigas *Paraguay* 26°52S 56°16W **366** B4
General Belgrano *Argentina* 36°35S 58°47W **366** D4
General Bernardo O'Higgins *Antarctica* 63°0S 58°3W **277** C18
General Cabrera *Argentina* 32°53S 63°52W **366** C3
General Cepeda *Mexico* 25°21N 101°22W **358** B4
General Guido *Argentina* 36°40S 57°50W **366** D4
General Juan Madariaga *Argentina* 37°0S 57°0W **366** D4
General La Madrid *Argentina* 37°17S 61°20W **366** D3
General MacArthur *Phil.* 11°18N 125°28E **309** B7
General Martin Miguel de Güemes *Argentina* 24°50S 65°0W **366** A3
General Paz *Argentina* 27°45S 57°36W **366** B4
General Pico *Argentina* 35°45S 63°50W **366** D3
General Pinedo *Argentina* 27°15S 61°20W **366** B3
General Pinto *Argentina* 34°45S 61°50W **366** C3
General Roca *Argentina* 39°2S 67°35W **368** D3
General Santos *Phil.* 6°5N 125°14E **309** C7
General Treviño *Mexico* 26°14N 99°29W **359** B5
General Trías *Mexico* 28°21N 106°22W **358** B3
General Viamonte *Argentina* 35°1S 61°3W **366** D3
General Villegas *Argentina* 35°5S 63°0W **366** D3
Genesee *Idaho, U.S.A.* 46°33N 116°56W **348** C5
Genesee *Pa., U.S.A.* 41°59N 77°54W **354** E7
Genesee → *U.S.A.* 43°16N 77°36W **354** C7
Geneseo *Ill., U.S.A.* 41°27N 90°9W **352** E8
Geneseo *N.Y., U.S.A.* 42°48N 77°49W **354** D7
Geneva = Genève *Switz.* 46°12N 6°9E **292** C7
Geneva *Ala., U.S.A.* 31°2N 85°52W **357** F12
Geneva *N.Y., U.S.A.* 42°52N 76°59W **354** D8
Geneva *Nebr., U.S.A.* 40°32N 97°36W **352** E5
Geneva *Ohio, U.S.A.* 41°48N 80°57W **354** E4
Geneva, L. = Léman, L. *Europe* 46°26N 6°30E **292** C7
Genève *Switz.* 46°12N 6°9E **292** C7
Genil → *Spain* 37°42N 5°19W **293** D3
Genk *Belgium* 50°58N 5°32E **287** D5
Gennargentu, Mti. del *Italy* 40°1N 9°19E **294** D3
Genoa = Génova *Italy* 44°25N 8°57E **292** D8
Genoa *Australia* 37°29S 149°35E **335** F4
Genoa *N.Y., U.S.A.* 42°40N 76°32W **355** D8
Genoa *Nebr., U.S.A.* 41°27N 97°44W **352** E5
Genoa *Nev., U.S.A.* 39°2N 119°50W **350** F7
Génova *Italy* 44°25N 8°57E **292** D8
Génova, G. di *Italy* 44°0N 9°0E **294** C3
Genriyetty, Ostrov *Russia* 77°6N 156°30E **301** B16
Gent *Belgium* 51°2N 3°42E **287** C3
Genteng *Bali, Indonesia* 8°22S 114°9E **309** J17
Genteng *Jawa Barat, Indonesia* 7°22S 106°24E **309** G12
Genyem *Indonesia* 2°46S 140°12E **309** E10
Geochang *S. Korea* 35°41N 127°55E **307** G14
Geographe B. *Australia* 33°30S 115°15E **333** F2
Geographe Chan. *Australia* 24°30S 113°0E **333** D1
Georga, Zemlya *Russia* 80°30N 49°0E **300** A5
George *S. Africa* 33°58S 22°29E **328** E3
George → *Canada* 58°49N 66°10W **345** A6
George, L. *N.S.W., Australia* 35°10S 149°25E **335** F4
George, L. *S. Austral., Australia* 37°25S 140°0E **335** F3
George, L. *W. Austral., Australia* 22°45S 123°40E **332** D3
George, L. *Uganda* 0°5N 30°10E **326** B3
George, L. *Fla., U.S.A.* 29°17N 81°36W **357** G14
George, L. *N.Y., U.S.A.* 43°37N 73°33W **355** C11
George Gill Ra. *Australia* 24°22S 131°45E **332** D5
George Pt. *Australia* 20°6S 148°36E **334** J6
George River = Kangiqsualujjuaq *Canada* 58°30N 65°59W **341** D13
George Sound *N.Z.* 44°52S 167°25E **331** F1
George Town *Australia* 41°6S 146°49E **335** G4
George Town *Bahamas* 23°33N 75°47W **360** B4
George Town *Cayman Is.* 19°20N 81°24W **360** C3
George Town *Malaysia* 5°25N 100°20E **311** c
George V Land *Antarctica* 69°0S 148°0E **277** C10
George VI Sound *Antarctica* 71°0S 68°0W **277** D17
George West *U.S.A.* 28°20N 98°7W **356** G5
Georgetown = Janjanbureh *Gambia* 13°30N 14°47W **322** F3
Georgetown *Australia* 18°17S 143°33E **334** B3
Georgetown *Ont., Canada* 43°40N 79°56W **354** C5
Georgetown *P.E.I., Canada* 46°13N 62°24W **345** C7
Georgetown *Guyana* 6°50N 58°12W **364** B7
Georgetown *Calif., U.S.A.* 38°54N 120°50W **350** G6
Georgetown *Colo., U.S.A.* 39°42N 105°42W **348** G11
Georgetown *Ky., U.S.A.* 38°13N 84°33W **353** F11
Georgetown *N.Y., U.S.A.* 42°46N 75°44W **355** D9
Georgetown *Ohio, U.S.A.* 38°52N 83°54W **353** F12
Georgetown *S.C., U.S.A.* 33°23N 79°17W **357** E15
Georgetown *Tex., U.S.A.* 30°38N 97°41W **356** F6
Georgia □ *U.S.A.* 32°50N 83°15W **357** E13
Georgia ■ *Asia* 42°0N 43°0E **291** F7
Georgia, Str. of *N. Amer.* 49°25N 124°0W **350** A3
Georgia Basin *S. Ocean* 50°45S 35°30W **277** B1
Georgian B. *Canada* 45°15N 81°0W **354** A4
Georgian Bay Islands △ *Canada* 44°53N 79°52W **354** B5
Georgina → *Australia* 23°30S 139°47E **334** C2
Georgina I. *Canada* 44°22N 79°17W **354** B5
Georgioupoli *Greece* 35°20N 24°15E **297** D6
Georgiyevsk *Russia* 44°12N 43°28E **291** F7
Gera *Germany* 50°53N 12°4E **288** C7
Geraardsbergen *Belgium* 50°45N 3°53E **287** D3
Geral, Serra *Brazil* 26°25S 50°0W **367** B6
Geral de Goiás, Serra *Brazil* 12°0S 46°0W **365** F9
Geraldine *U.S.A.* 47°36N 110°16W **348** C8
Geraldton *Australia* 28°48S 114°32E **333** E1
Geraldton *Canada* 49°44N 86°59W **344** C2
Gereshk *Afghan.* 31°47N 64°35E **312** D4
Gerik *Malaysia* 5°50N 101°15E **311** K3
Gering *U.S.A.* 41°50N 103°40W **352** E2
Gerlach *U.S.A.* 40°39N 119°21W **348** F4
Germansen Landing *Canada* 55°43N 124°40W **342** B4
Germantown *U.S.A.* 35°5N 89°49W **357** D10
Germany ■ *Europe* 51°0N 10°0E **288** C6
Germī *Iran* 39°1N 48°3E **317** B6
Germiston *S. Africa* 26°13S 28°10E **329** D4
Gernika-Lumo *Spain* 43°19N 2°40W **293** A4
Gero *Japan* 35°48N 137°14E **303** G8
Gerokgak *Indonesia* 8°11S 114°27E **309** J17
Gerona = Girona *Spain* 41°58N 2°46E **293** B7
Geropotamos → *Greece* 35°3N 24°50E **297** D6
Gerrard *Canada* 50°30N 117°17W **342** C5
Gertak Sanggul *Malaysia* 5°17N 100°12E **311** c
Gertak Sanggul, Tanjung *Malaysia* 5°16N 100°11E **311** c
Gerung *Indonesia* 8°43S 116°7E **309** K19
Geser *Indonesia* 3°50S 130°54E **309** E8
Getafe *Spain* 40°18N 3°43W **293** B4
Gettysburg *Pa., U.S.A.* 39°50N 77°14W **353** F15
Gettysburg *S. Dak., U.S.A.* 45°1N 99°57W **352** C4
Getxo *Spain* 43°21N 2°59W **293** A4
Getz Ice Shelf *Antarctica* 75°0S 130°0W **277** D14
Geyser *U.S.A.* 47°16N 110°30W **348** C8
Geyserville *U.S.A.* 38°42N 122°54W **350** G4
Ghadāmis *Libya* 30°11N 9°29E **323** B8
Ghaggar → *India* 29°30N 74°53E **314** E6
Ghaghara → *India* 25°45N 84°40E **315** G11
Ghaghat → *Bangla.* 25°19N 89°38E **315** G13
Ghagra *India* 23°17N 84°33E **315** H11
Ghagra → *India* 27°29N 81°9E **315** F9
Ghallamane *Mauritania* 23°15N 10°0W **322** D4
Ghana ■ *W. Afr.* 8°0N 1°0W **322** G5
Ghansor *India* 22°39N 80°1E **315** H9
Ghanzi *Botswana* 21°50S 21°34E **328** C3
Ghardaïa *Algeria* 32°20N 3°37E **322** B6
Gharyān *Libya* 32°10N 13°0E **323** B8
Ghat *Libya* 24°59N 10°11E **323** D8
Ghatal *India* 22°40N 87°46E **315** H12
Ghatampur *India* 26°8N 80°13E **315** F9
Ghats, Eastern *India* 14°0N 78°50E **312** N11
Ghats, Western *India* 14°0N 75°0E **312** N9
Ghatsila *India* 22°36N 86°29E **315** H12
Ghaţţī *Si. Arabia* 31°16N 37°31E **316** D3
Ghawdex = Gozo *Malta* 36°3N 14°15E **297** C1
Ghazal, Bahr el → *Chad* 13°0N 15°47E **323** F9
Ghazâl, Bahr el → *Sudan* 9°31N 30°25E **323** G12
Ghaziabad *India* 28°42N 77°26E **314** E7
Ghazipur *India* 25°38N 83°35E **315** G10
Ghaznī *Afghan.* 33°30N 68°28E **314** C3
Ghaznī □ *Afghan.* 32°10N 68°20E **312** C6
Ghent = Gent *Belgium* 51°2N 3°42E **287** C3
Gheorghe Gheorghiu-Dej = Oneşti *Romania* 46°17N 26°47E **289** E14
Ghīnah, Wādī al → *Si. Arabia* 30°27N 38°14E **316** D3
Ghizar → *Pakistan* 36°15N 73°43E **315** A5
Ghotaru *India* 27°20N 70°1E **314** F4
Ghotki *Pakistan* 28°5N 69°21E **314** E3
Ghowr □ *Afghan.* 34°0N 64°20E **312** C4
Ghudāf, W. al → *Iraq* 32°56N 43°30E **316** C4
Ghughri *India* 22°39N 80°41E **315** H9
Ghugus *India* 19°58N 79°12E **312** K11
Ghulam Mohammad Barrage *Pakistan* 25°30N 68°20E **314** G3
Ghūrīān *Afghan.* 34°17N 61°25E **312** B2
Gia Dinh *Vietnam* 10°49N 106°42E **311** G6
Gia Lai = Plei Ku *Vietnam* 13°57N 108°0E **310** F7
Gia Nghia *Vietnam* 11°58N 107°42E **311** G6
Gia Ngoc *Vietnam* 14°50N 108°58E **310** E7
Gia Vuc *Vietnam* 14°42N 108°34E **310** E7
Giamama *Somali Rep.* 0°4N 42°44E **319** G3
Gianitsa *Greece* 40°46N 22°24E **295** D10
Giant Forest *U.S.A.* 36°36N 118°43W **350** J8
Giant Sequoia ⌂ *U.S.A.* 36°10N 118°35W **350** K8
Giants Causeway *U.K.* 55°16N 6°29W **282** A5
Gianyar *Indonesia* 8°32S 115°20E **309** K18
Giarabub = Al Jaghbūb *Libya* 29°42N 24°38E **323** C10
Giarre *Italy* 37°43N 15°11E **294** F6
Gibara *Cuba* 21°9N 76°11W **360** B4
Gibb River *Australia* 16°26S 126°26E **332** C4
Gibbon *U.S.A.* 40°45N 98°51W **352** E4
Gibeon *Namibia* 25°9S 17°43E **328** D2
Gibraltar ☒ *Europe* 36°7N 5°22W **293** D3
Gibraltar, Str. of *Medit. S.* 35°55N 5°40W **293** E3
Gibraltar Range △ *Australia* 29°31S 152°19E **335** D5
Gibson Desert *Australia* 24°0S 126°0E **332** D4
Gibsons *Canada* 49°24N 123°32W **342** D4
Gibsonville *U.S.A.* 39°46N 120°54W **350** F6
Giddings *U.S.A.* 30°11N 96°56W **356** F6
Giebnegáisi = Kebnekaise *Sweden* 67°53N 18°33E **280** C18
Giessen *Germany* 50°34N 8°41E **288** C5
Gīfān *Iran* 37°54N 57°28E **317** B8
Gift Lake *Canada* 55°53N 115°49W **342** B5
Gifu *Japan* 35°30N 136°45E **303** G8
Gifu □ *Japan* 35°40N 137°0E **303** G8
Giganta, Sa. de la *Mexico* 26°0N 111°39W **358** B2
Gigha *U.K.* 55°42N 5°44W **283** F3
Giglio *Italy* 42°20N 10°52E **294** C4
Gijón *Spain* 43°32N 5°42W **293** A3
Gil I. *Canada* 53°12N 129°15W **342** C3
Gila → *U.S.A.* 32°43N 114°33W **349** K6
Gila Bend *U.S.A.* 32°57N 112°43W **349** K7
Gila Bend Mts. *U.S.A.* 33°10N 113°0W **349** K7
Gila Cliff Dwellings ⌂ *U.S.A.* 33°12N 108°16W **349** K9
Gīlān □ *Iran* 37°0N 50°0E **317** B6
Gilbert → *Australia* 16°35S 141°15E **334** B3
Gilbert Is. *Kiribati* 1°0N 172°0E **330** A10
Gilbert River *Australia* 18°9S 142°52E **334** B3
Gilbert Seamounts *Pac. Oc.* 52°50N 150°10W **276** D18
Gilead *U.S.A.* 44°24N 70°59W **355** B14
Gilf el Kebîr, Hadabat el *Egypt* 23°50N 25°50E **323** D11
Gilford I. *Canada* 50°40N 126°30W **342** C3
Gilgandra *Australia* 31°43S 148°39E **335** E4
Gilgil *Kenya* 0°30S 36°20E **326** C4
Gilgit *India* 35°50N 74°15E **315** B6
Gilgit → *Pakistan* 35°44N 74°37E **315** B6
Gili ⌂ *Mozam.* 16°39S 38°27E **327** F4
Gilimanuk *Indonesia* 8°10S 114°26E **309** J17
Gillam *Canada* 56°20N 94°40W **343** B10
Gillen, L. *Australia* 26°11S 124°38E **333** E3
Gilles, L. *Australia* 32°50S 136°45E **335** E2
Gillette *U.S.A.* 44°18N 105°30W **348** D11
Gilliat *Australia* 20°40S 141°28E **334** C3
Gillingham *U.K.* 51°23N 0°33E **285** F8
Gilmer *U.S.A.* 32°44N 94°57W **356** E7
Gilmore, L. *Australia* 32°29S 121°37E **333** F3
Gilroy *U.S.A.* 37°1N 121°34W **350** H5
Gimcheon *S. Korea* 36°11N 128°4E **307** F15
Gimhae *S. Korea* 35°14N 128°53E **307** G15
Gimhwa *S. Korea* 38°17N 127°28E **307** E14
Gimie, Mt *St. Lucia* 13°54N 61°0W **361** f
Gimje *S. Korea* 35°48N 126°45E **307** G14
Gimli *Canada* 50°40N 97°0W **343** C9
Gin Gin *Australia* 25°0S 151°58E **335** D5
Gingin *Australia* 31°22S 115°54E **333** F2
Gingindlovu *S. Africa* 29°2S 31°30E **329** D5
Ginir *Ethiopia* 7°6N 40°40E **319** F3
Giofyros → *Greece* 35°20N 25°6E **297** D7
Giohar *Somali Rep.* 2°48N 45°30E **319** G4
Giona, Oros *Greece* 38°38N 22°14E **295** E10
Gir △ *India* 21°0N 71°0E **314** J4
Gir Hills *India* 21°0N 71°0E **314** J4
Girab *India* 26°2N 70°38E **314** F4
Girâfi, W. → *Egypt* 29°58N 34°39E **318** F3
Girard *Kans., U.S.A.* 37°31N 94°51W **352** G6
Girard *Ohio, U.S.A.* 41°9N 80°42W **354** E4
Girard *Pa., U.S.A.* 42°0N 80°19W **354** E4
Girdle Ness *U.K.* 57°9N 2°3W **283** D6
Giresun *Turkey* 40°55N 38°30E **291** F6
Girga *Egypt* 26°17N 31°55E **323** C12
Giri → *India* 30°28N 77°41E **314** D7
Giridih *India* 24°10N 86°21E **315** G12
Giriftu *Kenya* 1°59N 39°46E **326** B4
Girne = Kyrenia *Cyprus* 35°20N 33°20E **297** D12
Giron = Kiruna *Sweden* 67°52N 20°15E **280** C19
Girona *Spain* 41°58N 2°46E **293** B7
Gironde → *France* 45°32N 1°7W **292** D3
Girraween △ *Australia* 28°46S 151°54E **335** D5
Giru *Australia* 19°30S 147°5E **334** B4
Girvan *U.K.* 55°14N 4°51W **283** F4
Gisborne *N.Z.* 38°39S 178°5E **331** C7
Gisenyi *Rwanda* 1°41S 29°15E **326** C2
Gislaved *Sweden* 57°19N 13°32E **281** H15
Gitega *Burundi* 3°26S 29°56E **326** C2
Githio *Greece* 36°46N 22°34E **295** F10
Giuba → *Somali Rep.* 1°30N 42°35E **319** G3
Giurgiu *Romania* 43°52N 25°57E **289** G13
Giza = El Gîza *Egypt* 30°0N 31°12E **323** C12
Giza Pyramids *Egypt* 29°58N 31°9E **323** C12
Gizab *Afghan.* 33°22N 66°17E **314** C1
Gizhiga *Russia* 62°3N 160°30E **301** C17
Gizhiginskaya Guba *Russia* 61°0N 158°0E **301** C16
Giżycko *Poland* 54°2N 21°48E **289** A11
Gjirokastër *Albania* 40°7N 20°10E **295** D9
Gjoa Haven *Canada* 68°38N 95°53W **340** C10
Gjøvik *Norway* 60°47N 10°43E **280** F14
Glace Bay *Canada* 46°11N 59°58W **345** C8
Glacier △ *Canada* 51°15N 117°30W **342** C5
Glacier △ *U.S.A.* 48°42N 113°48W **348** B7
Glacier Bay ⌂ *U.S.A.* 58°45N 136°30W **342** B1
Glacier Peak *U.S.A.* 48°7N 121°7W **348** B3
Gladewater *U.S.A.* 32°33N 94°56W **356** E7
Gladstone *Queens., Australia* 23°52S 151°16E **334** C5
Gladstone *S. Austral., Australia* 33°15S 138°22E **335** E2
Gladstone *Canada* 50°13N 98°57W **343** C9
Gladstone *U.S.A.* 45°51N 87°1W **352** C10
Gladwin *U.S.A.* 43°59N 84°29W **353** D11
Glagah *Indonesia* 8°13S 114°18E **309** J17
Glåma = Glomma → *Norway* 59°12N 10°57E **281** G14
Gláma *Iceland* 65°48N 23°0W **280** D2
Glamis *U.S.A.* 32°55N 115°5W **351** N11
Glamorgan, Vale of □ *U.K.* 51°28N 3°25W **285** F4
Glasco *Kans., U.S.A.* 39°22N 97°50W **352** F5
Glasco *N.Y., U.S.A.* 42°3N 73°57W **355** D11
Glasgow *U.K.* 55°51N 4°15W **283** F4
Glasgow *Ky., U.S.A.* 37°0N 85°55W **353** G11
Glasgow *Mont., U.S.A.* 48°12N 106°38W **348** B10
Glasgow, City of □ *U.K.* 55°51N 4°12W **283** F4
Glasgow Int. ✕ (GLA) *U.K.* 55°51N 4°21W **283** F4
Glaslyn *Canada* 53°22N 108°21W **343** C7
Glastonbury *U.K.* 51°9N 2°43W **285** F5
Glastonbury *U.S.A.* 41°43N 72°37W **355** E12
Glazov *Russia* 58°9N 52°40E **290** C9
Gleichen *Canada* 50°52N 113°3W **342** C6
Gleiwitz = Gliwice *Poland* 50°22N 18°41E **289** C10
Glen *U.S.A.* 44°7N 71°11W **355** B13
Glen Affric *U.K.* 57°17N 5°1W **283** D3
Glen Canyon *U.S.A.* 37°30N 110°40W **349** H8
Glen Canyon ⌂ *U.S.A.* 37°15N 111°0W **349** H8
Glen Canyon Dam *U.S.A.* 36°57N 111°29W **349** H8
Glen Coe *U.K.* 56°40N 5°0W **283** E3
Glen Cove *U.S.A.* 40°51N 73°38W **355** F11
Glen Garry *U.K.* 57°3N 5°7W **283** D3
Glen Innes *Australia* 29°44S 151°44E **335** D5
Glen Lyon *U.S.A.* 41°10N 76°5W **355** E8
Glen Mor *U.K.* 57°9N 4°37W **283** D4
Glen More ⌂ *U.K.* 57°8N 3°40W **283** D5
Glen Moriston *U.K.* 57°11N 4°52W **283** D4
Glen Robertson *Canada* 45°22N 74°30W **355** A10
Glen Spean *U.K.* 56°53N 4°40W **283** E4
Glen Ullin *U.S.A.* 46°49N 101°50W **352** B3
Glenallen *U.S.A.* 62°7N 145°33W **340** C5
Glenariff △ *Ireland* 55°2N 6°10W **282** A5
Glenbeigh *Ireland* 52°3N 9°58W **282** D2
Glencoe *Canada* 42°45N 81°43W **354** D3
Glencoe *S. Africa* 28°11S 30°11E **329** D5
Glencoe *U.S.A.* 44°46N 94°9W **352** C6
Glencolumbkille *Ireland* 54°43N 8°42W **282** B3
Glendale *Ariz., U.S.A.* 33°32N 112°11W **349** K7
Glendale *Calif., U.S.A.* 34°9N 118°15W **351** L8
Glendale *Zimbabwe* 17°22S 31°5E **327** F3
Glendive *U.S.A.* 47°7N 104°43W **348** C11
Glendo *U.S.A.* 42°30N 105°2W **348** E11
Glenelg → *Australia* 38°4S 140°59E **335** F3
Glenfield *U.S.A.* 43°43N 75°24W **355** C9
Glengad Hd. *Ireland* 55°20N 7°10W **282** A4
Glengarriff *Ireland* 51°45N 9°34W **282** E2
Glenmont *U.S.A.* 40°31N 82°6W **354** F2
Glenmorgan *Australia* 27°14S 149°42E **335** D4
Glenn *U.S.A.* 39°31N 122°1W **350** F4
Glennamaddy *Ireland* 53°37N 8°33W **282** C3
Glenns Ferry *U.S.A.* 42°57N 115°18W **348** E6
Glenorchy *Australia* 42°49S 147°18E **335** G4
Glenore *Australia* 17°50S 141°12E **334** B3
Glenreagh *Australia* 30°2S 153°1E **335** E5
Glenrock *U.S.A.* 42°52N 105°52W **348** E11
Glenrothes *U.K.* 56°12N 3°10W **283** E5
Glens Falls *U.S.A.* 43°19N 73°39W **355** C11
Glenside *U.S.A.* 40°6N 75°9W **355** F9
Glenties *Ireland* 54°49N 8°16W **282** B3
Glenveagh △ *Ireland* 55°3N 8°1W **282** A3
Glenville *U.S.A.* 38°56N 80°50W **353** F13
Glenwood *Canada* 49°0N 54°58W **345** C9
Glenwood *Ark., U.S.A.* 34°20N 93°33W **356** D8
Glenwood *Iowa, U.S.A.* 41°3N 95°45W **352** E6
Glenwood *Minn., U.S.A.* 45°39N 95°23W **352** C6
Glenwood *Wash., U.S.A.* 46°1N 121°17W **350** D5
Glenwood Springs *U.S.A.* 39°33N 107°19W **348** G10
Glettinganes *Iceland* 65°30N 13°37W **280** D7
Glin *Ireland* 52°34N 9°17W **282** D2
Gliwice *Poland* 50°22N 18°41E **289** C10
Globe *U.S.A.* 33°24N 110°47W **349** K8
Głogów *Poland* 51°37N 16°5E **288** C9
Glomma → *Norway* 59°12N 10°57E **281** G14
Glorieuses, Îs. *Ind. Oc.* 11°30S 47°20E **329** A8
Glossop *U.K.* 53°27N 1°56W **284** D6
Gloucester *Australia* 32°0S 151°59E **335** E5
Gloucester *U.K.* 51°53N 2°15W **285** F5
Gloucester *U.S.A.* 42°37N 70°40W **355** D14

Gloucester I. Australia 20°0S 148°30E 334 J6
Gloucester Island △ Australia 20°2S 148°30E 334 J6
Gloucester Point U.S.A. 37°15N 76°30W 353 G15
Gloucestershire □ U.K. 51°46N 2°15W 285 F5
Gloversville U.S.A. 43°3N 74°21W 355 C10
Glovertown Canada 48°40N 54°3W 345 C9
Glusk Belarus 52°53N 28°41E 289 B15
Gmünd Austria 48°45N 15°0E 288 D8
Gmunden Austria 47°55N 13°48E 288 E7
Gniezno Poland 52°30N 17°35E 289 B9
Gnowangerup Australia 33°58S 117°59E 333 F2
Go Cong Vietnam 10°22N 106°40E 311 G6
Gō-no-ura Japan 33°44N 129°40E 303 H4
Goa India 15°33N 73°59E 312 M8
Goa □ India 15°33N 73°59E 312 M8
Goalen Hd. Australia 36°33S 150°4E 335 F5
Goalpara India 26°10N 90°40E 313 F17
Goaltor India 22°43N 87°10E 315 H12
Goalundo Ghat Bangla. 23°50N 89°47E 315 H13
Goat Fell U.K. 55°38N 5°11W 283 F3
Goba Ethiopia 7°1N 39°59E 319 F2
Goba Mozam. 26°15S 32°13E 329 D5
Gobabis Namibia 22°30S 19°0E 328 C2
Gobi Asia 44°0N 110°0E 306 C6
Gobō Japan 33°53N 135°10E 303 H7
Gochas Namibia 24°59S 18°55E 328 C2
Godalming U.K. 51°11N 0°36W 285 F7
Godavari → India 16°25N 82°18E 313 L13
Godavari Pt. India 17°0N 82°20E 313 L13
Godbout Canada 49°20N 67°38W 345 C6
Godda India 24°50N 87°13E 315 G12
Goderich Canada 43°45N 81°41W 354 C3
Godfrey Ra. Australia 24°0S 117°0E 333 D2
Godhavn = Qeqertarsuaq Greenland 69°15N 53°38W 276 C5
Godhra India 22°49N 73°40E 314 H5
Godoy Cruz Argentina 32°56S 68°52W 366 C2
Gods → Canada 56°22N 92°51W 344 A1
Gods L. Canada 54°40N 94°15W 344 B1
Gods River Canada 54°50N 94°5W 343 C10
Godthåb = Nuuk Greenland 64°10N 51°35W 339 C14
Goeie Hoop, Kaap die = Good Hope, C. of S. Africa 34°24S 18°30E 328 E2
Goéland, L. au Canada 49°50N 76°48W 344 C4
Goélands, L. aux Canada 55°27N 64°17W 345 A7
Goeree Neths. 51°50N 4°0E 287 C3
Goes Neths. 51°30N 3°55E 287 C3
Goffstown U.S.A. 43°1N 71°36W 355 C13
Gogama Canada 47°35N 81°43W 344 C3
Gogebic, L. U.S.A. 46°30N 89°35W 352 B9
Gogra = Ghaghara → India 25°45N 84°40E 315 G11
Gogriâl Sudan 8°30N 28°8E 323 G11
Gohana India 29°8N 76°42E 314 E7
Goharganj India 23°1N 77°41E 314 H7
Goi → India 22°4N 74°46E 314 H6
Goiânia Brazil 16°43S 49°20W 365 G9
Goiás Brazil 15°55S 50°10W 365 G8
Goiás □ Brazil 12°10S 48°0W 365 F9
Goio-Erê Brazil 24°12S 53°1W 367 A5
Gojō Japan 34°21N 135°42E 303 G7
Gojra Pakistan 31°10N 72°40E 314 D5
Gökçeada Turkey 40°10N 25°50E 295 D11
Gökova Körfezi Turkey 36°55N 27°50E 295 F12
Gokteik Burma 22°26N 97°0E 313 H20
Gokurt Pakistan 29°40N 67°26E 314 E2
Gokwe Zimbabwe 18°7S 28°58E 329 B4
Gola India 28°3N 80°32E 315 E9
Golakganj India 26°8N 89°52E 315 F13
Golan Heights = Hagolan Syria 33°0N 35°45E 318 C4
Golāshkerd Iran 27°59N 57°16E 317 E8
Golchikha Russia 71°45N 83°30E 276 B12
Golconda U.S.A. 40°58N 117°30W 348 F5
Gold U.S.A. 41°52N 77°50W 354 E7
Gold Beach U.S.A. 42°25N 124°25W 348 E1
Gold Coast W. Afr. 4°0N 1°40W 322 H5
Gold Hill U.S.A. 42°26N 123°3W 348 E2
Gold River Canada 49°46N 126°3W 342 D3
Golden Canada 51°20N 116°59W 342 C5
Golden B. N.Z. 40°40S 172°50E 331 D4
Golden Gate U.S.A. 37°48N 122°29W 349 H2
Golden Gate Highlands △ S. Africa 28°40S 28°40E 329 D4
Golden Hinde Canada 49°40N 125°44W 342 D3
Golden Lake Canada 45°34N 77°21W 354 A7
Golden Spike ⌓ U.S.A. 41°37N 112°33W 348 F7
Golden Vale Ireland 52°33N 8°17W 282 D3
Goldendale U.S.A. 45°49N 120°50W 348 D3
Goldfield U.S.A. 37°42N 117°14W 349 H5
Goldsand L. Canada 57°2N 101°8W 343 B8
Goldsboro U.S.A. 35°23N 77°59W 357 D16
Goldsmith U.S.A. 31°59N 102°37W 356 F3
Goldthwaite U.S.A. 31°27N 98°34W 356 F5
Goleniów Poland 53°35N 14°50E 288 B8
Golestān □ Iran 37°20N 55°25E 317 B7
Golestānak Iran 30°36N 54°14E 317 D7
Goleta U.S.A. 34°27N 119°50W 351 L7
Golfito Costa Rica 8°41N 83°5W 360 E3
Golfo Aranci Italy 40°59N 9°38E 294 D3
Goliad U.S.A. 28°40N 97°23W 356 G6
Golpāyegān Iran 33°27N 50°18E 317 C6
Golra Pakistan 33°37N 72°56E 314 C5
Golspie U.K. 57°58N 3°59W 283 D5
Goma Dem. Rep. of the Congo 1°37S 29°10E 326 C2
Gomal Pass Pakistan 31°56N 69°20E 314 D3
Gomati → India 25°32N 83°11E 315 G10
Gombari Dem. Rep. of the Congo 2°45N 29°3E 326 B2
Gombe Nigeria 10°19N 11°2E 323 F8
Gombe → Tanzania 4°38S 31°40E 326 C3
Gomel = Homyel Belarus 52°28N 31°0E 289 B16
Gomera Canary Is. 28°7N 17°14W 296 F2
Gómez Palacio Mexico 25°34N 103°30W 358 B4
Gomīshān Iran 37°4N 54°6E 317 B7
Gomogomo Indonesia 6°39S 134°43E 309 F8
Gomoh India 23°52N 86°10E 315 H12
Gompa = Ganta Liberia 7°15N 8°59W 322 G4
Gonābād Iran 34°15N 58°45E 317 C8
Gonaïves Haiti 19°20N 72°42W 361 C5
Gonarezhou △ Zimbabwe 21°32S 31°55E 327 G3
Gonâve, G. de la Haiti 19°29N 72°42W 361 C5
Gonâve, Île de la Haiti 18°51N 73°3W 361 C5
Gonbad-e Kāvūs Iran 37°20N 55°25E 317 B7
Gonda India 27°9N 81°58E 315 F9
Gondal India 21°58N 70°52E 314 J4
Gonder Ethiopia 12°39N 37°30E 319 E2
Gondia India 21°23N 80°10E 312 J12
Gondola Mozam. 19°10S 33°37E 327 F3
Gönen Turkey 40°6N 27°39E 295 D12
Gongbei China 22°12N 113°32E 305 G10
Gonghe China 36°18N 100°32E 304 C5
Gongju S. Korea 36°27N 127°7E 307 F14
Gongming China 22°47N 113°53E 305 F10
Gongolgon Australia 30°21S 146°54E 335 E4
Gongzhuling China 43°30N 124°40E 307 C13
Goniri Nigeria 11°30N 12°15E 323 F8
Gonzales Calif., U.S.A. 36°30N 121°26W 350 J5
Gonzales Tex., U.S.A. 29°30N 97°27W 356 G6
González Mexico 22°48N 98°25W 359 C5
González Chaves Argentina 38°2S 60°5W 366 D3
Good Hope, C. of S. Africa 34°24S 18°30E 328 E2
Gooderham Canada 44°54N 78°21W 354 B6
Goodhouse S. Africa 28°57S 18°13E 328 D2
Gooding U.S.A. 42°56N 114°43W 348 E6
Goodland U.S.A. 39°21N 101°43W 352 F3
Goodlands Mauritius 20°2S 57°39E 325 d
Goodlow Canada 56°20N 120°8W 342 B4
Goodooga Australia 29°3S 147°28E 335 D4
Goodsprings U.S.A. 35°49N 115°27W 351 K11
Goole U.K. 53°42N 0°53W 284 D7
Goolgowi Australia 33°58S 145°41E 335 E4
Goomalling Australia 31°15S 116°49E 333 F2
Goomeri Australia 26°12S 152°6E 335 D5
Goonda Mozam. 19°48S 33°57E 327 F3
Goondiwindi Australia 28°30S 150°21E 335 D5
Goongarrie, L. Australia 30°3S 121°9E 333 F3
Goongarrie △ Australia 30°7S 121°30E 333 F3
Goonyella Australia 21°47S 147°58E 334 C4
Goose → Canada 53°20N 60°35W 345 B7
Goose Creek U.S.A. 32°59N 80°2W 357 E14
Goose L. U.S.A. 41°56N 120°26W 348 F3
Gop India 22°5N 69°50E 314 H3
Gopalganj India 26°28N 84°30E 315 F11
Göppingen Germany 48°42N 9°39E 288 D5
Gorakhpur India 26°47N 83°23E 315 F10
Goražde Bos.-H. 43°38N 18°58E 295 C8
Gorda, Pta. Canary Is. 28°45N 18°0W 296 F2
Gorda, Pta. Nic. 14°20N 83°10W 360 D3
Gordan B. Australia 11°35S 130°10E 332 B5
Gordon U.S.A. 42°48N 102°12W 352 D2
Gordon → Australia 42°27S 145°30E 335 G4
Gordon L. Alta., Canada 56°30N 110°25W 343 B6
Gordon L. N.W.T., Canada 63°5N 113°11W 342 A6
Gordonvale Australia 17°5S 145°50E 334 B4
Goré Chad 7°59N 16°31E 323 G9
Gore Ethiopia 8°12N 35°32E 319 F2
Gore N.Z. 46°5S 168°58E 331 G2
Gore Bay Canada 45°57N 82°28W 344 C3
Gorey Ireland 52°41N 6°18W 282 D5
Gorg Iran 29°29N 59°43E 317 D8
Gorgān Iran 36°55N 54°30E 317 B7
Gorgona, I. Colombia 3°0N 78°10W 364 C3
Gorham U.S.A. 44°23N 71°10W 355 B13
Goriganga → India 29°45N 80°23E 315 E9
Gorinchem Neths. 51°50N 4°59E 287 C4
Goris Armenia 39°31N 46°22E 291 G8
Gorízia Italy 45°56N 13°37E 294 B5
Gorkiy = Nizhniy Novgorod Russia 56°20N 44°0E 290 C7
Gorkovskoye Vdkhr. Russia 57°2N 43°4E 290 C7
Gorleston U.K. 52°35N 1°44E 285 E9
Görlitz Germany 51°9N 14°58E 288 C8
Gorlovka = Horlivka Ukraine 48°19N 38°5E 291 E6
Gorman U.S.A. 34°47N 118°51W 351 L8
Gorna Dzhumayo = Blagoevgrad Bulgaria 42°2N 23°5E 295 C10
Gorna Oryakhovitsa Bulgaria 43°7N 25°40E 295 C11
Gorno-Altay □ Russia 51°0N 86°0E 300 D9
Gorno-Altaysk Russia 51°50N 86°5E 300 D9
Gornyatski Russia 67°32N 64°3E 290 A11
Gornyy Russia 44°57N 133°59E 302 B6
Gorodenka = Horodenka Ukraine 48°41N 25°29E 289 D13
Gorodok = Horodok Ukraine 49°46N 23°32E 289 D12
Gorokhov = Horokhiv Ukraine 50°30N 24°45E 289 C13
Goromonzi Zimbabwe 17°52S 31°22E 327 F3
Gorong, Kepulauan Indonesia 3°59S 131°25E 309 E8
Gorongosa △ Mozam. 18°50S 34°29E 329 B5
Gorongose → Mozam. 20°30S 34°40E 329 C5
Gorongoza Mozam. 18°44S 34°2E 327 F3
Gorongoza, Sa. da Mozam. 18°27S 34°2E 327 F3
Gorontalo Indonesia 0°35N 123°5E 309 D6
Gorontalo □ Indonesia 0°50N 122°20E 309 D6
Gort Ireland 53°3N 8°49W 282 C3
Gortis Greece 35°4N 24°58E 297 D6
Goryeong S. Korea 35°44N 128°15E 307 G15
Gorzów Wielkopolski Poland 52°43N 15°15E 288 B8
Gosford Australia 33°23S 151°18E 335 E5
Goshen Calif., U.S.A. 36°21N 119°25W 350 J7
Goshen Ind., U.S.A. 41°35N 85°50W 353 E11
Goshen N.Y., U.S.A. 41°24N 74°20W 355 E10
Goshogawara Japan 40°48N 140°27E 302 D10
Goslar Germany 51°54N 10°25E 288 C6
Gospič Croatia 44°35N 15°23E 288 F8
Gosport U.K. 50°48N 1°9W 285 G6
Gosse → Australia 19°32S 134°37E 334 B1
Göta älv → Sweden 57°42N 11°54E 281 H14
Göta kanal Sweden 58°30N 15°58E 281 G16
Götaland Sweden 57°30N 14°30E 281 H16
Göteborg Sweden 57°43N 11°59E 281 H14
Gotha Germany 50°56N 10°42E 288 C6
Gothenburg = Göteborg Sweden 57°43N 11°59E 281 H14
Gothenburg U.S.A. 40°56N 100°10W 352 E3
Gotland Sweden 57°30N 18°33E 281 H18
Gotō-Rettō Japan 32°55N 129°5E 303 H4
Gotska Sandön Sweden 58°24N 19°15E 281 G18
Gōtsu Japan 35°0N 132°14E 303 G6
Gott Pk. Canada 50°18N 122°16W 342 C4
Göttingen Germany 51°31N 9°55E 288 C5
Gottwaldov = Zlín Czech Rep. 49°14N 17°40E 289 D9
Goubangzi China 41°20N 121°52E 307 D11
Gouda Neths. 52°1N 4°42E 287 B4
Goudouras, Akra Greece 34°59N 26°6E 297 E8
Gouin, Rés. Canada 48°35N 74°40W 344 C5
Goulburn Australia 34°44S 149°44E 335 E4
Goulburn Is. Australia 11°40S 133°20E 334 A1
Goulimine Morocco 28°56N 10°0W 322 C3
Goundam Mali 16°27N 3°40W 322 E5
Gourits → S. Africa 34°21S 21°52E 328 E3
Gournes Greece 35°19N 25°16E 297 D7
Gourock U.K. 55°57N 4°49W 283 F4
Gouverneur U.S.A. 44°20N 75°28W 355 B9
Gouvia Greece 39°39N 19°50E 297 A3
Governador Valadares Brazil 18°15S 41°57W 365 G10
Governor's Harbour Bahamas 25°10N 76°14W 360 A4
Govindgarh India 24°23N 81°18E 315 G9
Gowan Ra. Australia 25°0S 145°0E 334 D4
Gowanda U.S.A. 42°28N 78°56W 354 D6
Gower U.K. 51°35N 4°10W 285 F3
Gowna, L. Ireland 53°51N 7°34W 282 C4
Goya Argentina 29°10S 59°10W 366 B4
Goyder Lagoon Australia 27°3S 138°58E 335 D2
Goyllarisquisga Peru 10°31S 76°24W 364 F3
Goz Beïda Chad 12°10N 21°20E 323 F10
Gozo Malta 36°3N 14°15E 297 C1
Graaff-Reinet S. Africa 32°13S 24°32E 328 E3
Gračac Croatia 44°18N 15°57E 288 F8
Gracias a Dios, C. Honduras 15°0N 83°10W 360 D3
Graciosa Azores 39°4N 28°0W 322 a
Graciosa, I. Canary Is. 29°15N 13°32W 296 E6
Grado Spain 43°23N 6°4W 293 A2
Grady U.S.A. 34°49N 103°19W 349 J12
Grafham Water U.K. 52°19N 0°18W 285 E7
Grafton Australia 29°38S 152°58E 335 D5
Grafton N. Dak., U.S.A. 48°25N 97°25W 352 A5
Grafton W. Va., U.S.A. 39°21N 80°2W 353 F13
Graham Canada 49°20N 90°30W 344 C1
Graham U.S.A. 33°6N 98°35W 356 E5
Graham, Mt. U.S.A. 32°42N 109°52W 349 K9
Graham Bell, Ostrov = Greem-Bell, Ostrov Russia 81°0N 62°0E 300 A7
Graham I. Canada 53°40N 132°30W 342 C2
Graham Land Antarctica 65°0S 64°0W 277 C17
Grahamstown S. Africa 33°19S 26°31E 328 E4
Grahamsville U.S.A. 41°51N 74°33W 355 E10
Grain Coast W. Afr. 4°20N 10°0W 322 H3
Grajagan Indonesia 8°35S 114°13E 309 K17
Grajagan, Teluk Indonesia 8°40S 114°18E 309 K17
Grajaú Brazil 5°50S 46°4W 365 E9
Grajaú → Brazil 3°41S 44°48W 365 D10
Grampian U.S.A. 40°58N 78°37W 354 F6
Grampian Highlands = Grampian Mts. U.K. 56°50N 4°0W 283 E5
Grampian Mts. U.K. 56°50N 4°0W 283 E5
Grampians, The Australia 37°15S 142°20E 335 F3
Gran Canaria Canary Is. 27°55N 15°35W 296 G4
Gran Chaco S. Amer. 25°0S 61°0W 366 B3
Gran Desierto del Pinacate ⌓ Mexico 31°51N 113°32W 358 A2
Gran Paradiso Italy 45°33N 7°17E 292 D7
Gran Sasso d'Itália Italy 42°27N 13°42E 294 C5
Granada Nic. 11°58N 86°0W 360 D2
Granada Spain 37°10N 3°35W 293 D4
Granada U.S.A. 38°4N 102°19W 348 G12
Granadilla de Abona Canary Is. 28°7N 16°33W 296 F3
Granard Ireland 53°47N 7°30W 282 C4
Granbury U.S.A. 32°27N 97°47W 356 E6
Granby Canada 45°25N 72°45W 355 A12
Granby U.S.A. 40°5N 105°56W 348 F11
Grand → Canada 42°51N 79°34W 354 D5
Grand → Mo., U.S.A. 39°23N 93°7W 352 F7
Grand → S. Dak., U.S.A. 45°40N 100°45W 352 C3
Grand Bahama I. Bahamas 26°40N 78°30W 360 A4
Grand Baie Mauritius 20°0S 57°35E 325 d
Grand Bank Canada 47°6N 55°48W 345 C8
Grand Bassam Ivory C. 5°10N 3°49W 322 G5
Grand-Bourg Guadeloupe 15°53N 61°19W 360 b
Grand Canal = Da Yunhe → China 39°10N 117°10E 307 E9
Grand Canyon U.S.A. 36°3N 112°9W 349 H7
Grand Canyon △ U.S.A. 36°15N 112°30W 349 H7
Grand Canyon-Parashant ⌓ U.S.A. 36°30N 113°45W 349 H7
Grand Cayman Cayman Is. 19°20N 81°20W 360 C3
Grand Centre Canada 54°25N 110°13W 343 C6
Grand Coulee U.S.A. 47°57N 119°0W 348 C4
Grand Coulee Dam U.S.A. 47°57N 118°59W 348 C4
Grand Erg de Bilma Niger 18°30N 14°0E 323 E8
Grand Falls Canada 47°3N 67°44W 345 C6
Grand Falls-Windsor Canada 48°56N 55°40W 345 C8
Grand Forks Canada 49°0N 118°30W 342 D5
Grand Forks U.S.A. 47°55N 97°3W 352 B5
Grand Gorge U.S.A. 42°21N 74°29W 355 D10
Grand Haven U.S.A. 43°4N 86°13W 352 D10
Grand I. Mich., U.S.A. 46°31N 86°40W 352 B10
Grand I. N.Y., U.S.A. 43°0N 78°58W 354 D6
Grand Island U.S.A. 40°55N 98°21W 352 E4
Grand Isle La., U.S.A. 29°14N 90°0W 357 G9
Grand Isle Vt., U.S.A. 44°43N 73°18W 355 B11
Grand Junction U.S.A. 39°4N 108°33W 348 G9
Grand L. N.B., Canada 45°57N 66°7W 345 C6
Grand L. Nfld. & L., Canada 49°0N 57°30W 345 C8
Grand L. Nfld. & L., Canada 53°40N 60°30W 345 B7
Grand L. U.S.A. 29°55N 92°47W 356 G8
Grand Lake U.S.A. 40°15N 105°49W 348 F11
Grand Manan I. Canada 44°45N 66°52W 345 D6
Grand Marais Mich., U.S.A. 46°40N 85°59W 353 B11
Grand Marais Minn., U.S.A. 47°45N 90°25W 344 C1
Grand-Mère Canada 46°36N 72°40W 344 C5
Grand Portage U.S.A. 47°58N 89°41W 352 B9
Grand Prairie U.S.A. 32°44N 96°59W 356 E6
Grand Rapids Canada 53°12N 99°19W 343 C9
Grand Rapids Mich., U.S.A. 42°58N 85°40W 353 D11
Grand Rapids Minn., U.S.A. 47°14N 93°31W 352 B7
Grand St-Bernard, Col du Europe 45°50N 7°10E 292 D7
Grand Staircase-Escalante ⌓ U.S.A. 37°25N 111°33W 349 H8
Grand Teton U.S.A. 43°54N 110°50W 348 E8
Grand Teton △ U.S.A. 43°50N 110°50W 348 E8
Grand Union Canal U.K. 52°7N 0°53W 285 E7
Grande → Jujuy, Argentina 24°20S 65°2W 366 A2
Grande → Mendoza, Argentina 36°52S 69°45W 366 D2
Grande → Bolivia 15°51S 64°39W 364 G6
Grande → Bahia, Brazil 11°30S 44°30W 365 F10
Grande → Minas Gerais, Brazil 20°6S 51°4W 365 H8
Grande, B. Argentina 50°30S 68°20W 368 G3
Grande, Rio → N. Amer. 25°58N 97°9W 356 J6
Grande Anse Seychelles 4°18S 55°45E 325 b
Grande Baleine, R. de la → Canada 55°16N 77°47W 344 A4
Grande Cache Canada 53°53N 119°8W 342 C5
Grande Comore Comoros Is. 11°35S 43°20E 325 a
Grande-Entrée Canada 47°30N 61°40W 345 C7
Grande Prairie Canada 55°10N 118°50W 342 B5
Grande-Rivière Canada 48°26N 64°30W 345 C7
Grande-Terre Guadeloupe 16°20N 61°25W 360 b
Grande-Vallée Canada 49°14N 65°8W 345 C6
Grande Vigie, Pte. de la Guadeloupe 16°32N 61°27W 360 b
Grandfalls U.S.A. 31°20N 102°51W 356 F3
Grands-Jardins ⌓ Canada 47°41N 70°51W 345 C5
Grandview Canada 51°10N 100°42W 343 C8
Grandview U.S.A. 46°15N 119°54W 348 C4
Graneros Chile 34°5S 70°45W 366 C1
Grangemouth U.K. 56°1N 3°42W 283 E5
Granger U.S.A. 41°35N 109°58W 348 F9
Grangeville U.S.A. 45°56N 116°7W 348 D5
Granisle Canada 54°53N 126°13W 342 C3
Granite City U.S.A. 38°42N 90°8W 352 F8
Granite Falls U.S.A. 44°49N 95°33W 352 C6
Granite L. Canada 48°8N 57°5W 345 C8
Granite Mt. U.S.A. 33°5N 116°28W 351 M10
Granite Pk. U.S.A. 45°10N 109°48W 348 D9
Graniteville U.S.A. 44°8N 72°29W 355 B12
Granity N.Z. 41°39S 171°51E 331 D3
Granja Brazil 3°7S 40°50W 365 D10
Granollers Spain 41°39N 2°18E 293 B7
Grant U.S.A. 40°50N 101°43W 352 E3
Grant, Mt. U.S.A. 38°34N 118°48W 348 G4
Grant City U.S.A. 40°29N 94°25W 352 E6
Grant I. Australia 11°10S 132°52E 332 B5
Grant Range U.S.A. 38°30N 115°25W 348 G6
Grantham U.K. 52°55N 0°38W 284 E7
Grantown-on-Spey U.K. 57°20N 3°36W 283 D5
Grants U.S.A. 35°9N 107°52W 349 J10
Grants Pass U.S.A. 42°26N 123°19W 348 E2
Grantsville U.S.A. 40°36N 112°28W 348 F7
Granville France 48°50N 1°35W 292 B3
Granville N. Dak., U.S.A. 48°16N 100°47W 352 A3
Granville N.Y., U.S.A. 43°24N 73°16W 355 C11
Granville Ohio, U.S.A. 40°4N 82°31W 354 F2
Granville L. Canada 56°18N 100°30W 343 B8
Graskop S. Africa 24°56S 30°49E 329 C5
Grass → Canada 56°3N 96°33W 343 B9
Grass Range U.S.A. 47°2N 108°48W 348 C9
Grass River ⌓ Canada 54°40N 100°50W 343 C8
Grass Valley Calif., U.S.A. 39°13N 121°4W 350 F6
Grass Valley Oreg., U.S.A. 45°22N 120°47W 348 D3
Grasse France 43°38N 6°56E 292 E7
Grassflat U.S.A. 41°0N 78°6W 354 E6
Grasslands △ Canada 49°11N 107°38W 343 D7
Grassy Australia 40°3S 144°5E 335 G3
Graulhet France 43°45N 1°59E 292 E4
Gravelbourg Canada 49°50N 106°35W 343 D7
's-Gravenhage Neths. 52°7N 4°17E 287 B4
Gravenhurst Canada 44°52N 79°20W 354 B5
Gravesend Australia 29°35S 150°20E 335 D5
Gravesend U.K. 51°26N 0°22E 285 F8
Gravois, Pointe-à- Haiti 18°15N 73°56W 361 C5
Grayling U.S.A. 44°40N 84°43W 353 C11
Grays U.K. 51°28N 0°21E 285 F8
Grays Harbor U.S.A. 46°59N 124°1W 348 C1
Grays L. U.S.A. 43°4N 111°26W 348 E8
Grays River U.S.A. 46°21N 123°37W 350 D3
Graz Austria 47°4N 15°27E 288 E8
Greasy L. Canada 62°55N 122°12W 342 A4
Great Abaco I. = Abaco I. Bahamas 26°25N 77°10W 360 A4
Great Artesian Basin Australia 23°0S 144°0E 334 C3
Great Australian Bight Australia 33°30S 130°0E 333 F5
Great Bahama Bank Bahamas 23°15N 78°0W 360 B4
Great Barrier I. N.Z. 36°11S 175°25E 331 B5
Great Barrier Reef Australia 18°0S 146°50E 334 B4
Great Barrier Reef ⌓ Australia 20°0S 150°0E 334 B4
Great Barrington U.S.A. 42°12N 73°22W 355 D11
Great Basalt Wall △ Australia 19°52S 145°43E 334 B4
Great Basin U.S.A. 40°0N 117°0W 348 G5
Great Basin △ U.S.A. 38°56N 114°15W 348 G6
Great Bear → Canada 65°0N 124°0W 340 C7
Great Bear L. Canada 65°30N 120°0W 340 C8
Great Belt = Store Bælt Denmark 55°20N 11°0E 281 J14
Great Bend Kans., U.S.A. 38°22N 98°46W 352 F4
Great Bend Pa., U.S.A. 41°58N 75°45W 355 E9
Great Blasket I. Ireland 52°6N 10°32W 282 D1
Great Britain Europe 54°0N 2°15W 278 E5
Great Camanoe Br. Virgin Is. 18°30N 64°35W 361 e
Great Codroy Canada 47°51N 59°16W 345 C8
Great Divide, The = Great Dividing Ra. Australia 23°0S 146°0E 334 C4
Great Divide Basin U.S.A. 42°0N 108°0W 348 E9
Great Dividing Ra. Australia 23°0S 146°0E 334 C4
Great Driffield = Driffield U.K. 54°0N 0°26W 284 C7
Great Exuma I. Bahamas 23°30N 75°50W 360 B4
Great Falls U.S.A. 47°30N 111°17W 348 C8
Great Fish = Groot-Vis → S. Africa 33°28S 27°5E 328 E4
Great Guana Cay Bahamas 24°0N 76°20W 360 B4
Great Harbour Deep Canada 50°25N 56°32W 345 B8
Great Himalayan △ India 31°30N 77°30E 314 D7
Great Inagua I. Bahamas 21°0N 73°20W 361 B5
Great Indian Desert = Thar Desert India 28°0N 72°0E 314 F5
Great Karoo S. Africa 31°55S 21°0E 328 E3
Great Khingan Mts. = Da Hinggan Ling China 48°0N 121°0E 305 B7
Great Lake Australia 41°50S 146°40E 335 G4
Great Lakes N. Amer. 46°0N 84°0W 347 A10
Great Malvern U.K. 52°7N 2°18W 285 E5
Great Miami → U.S.A. 39°7N 84°49W 353 F11
Great Ormes Head U.K. 53°20N 3°52W 284 D4
Great Ouse → U.K. 52°48N 0°21E 284 E8
Great Palm I. Australia 18°45S 146°40E 334 B4
Great Pedro Bluff Jamaica 17°51N 77°44W 360 a
Great Pee Dee → U.S.A. 33°21N 79°10W 357 E15
Great Plains N. Amer. 47°0N 105°0W 346 A6
Great Ruaha → Tanzania 7°56S 37°52E 326 D4
Great Sacandaga L. U.S.A. 43°6N 74°16W 355 C10
Great Saint Bernard Pass = Grand St-Bernard, Col du Europe 45°50N 7°10E 292 D7
Great Salt Desert = Kavīr, Dasht-e Iran 34°30N 55°0E 317 C7
Great Salt L. U.S.A. 41°15N 112°40W 348 F7
Great Salt Lake Desert U.S.A. 40°50N 113°30W 348 F7
Great Salt Plains L. U.S.A. 36°45N 98°8W 356 C5
Great Sand Dunes ⌓ U.S.A. 37°48N 105°45W 349 H11
Great Sandy △ Australia 26°13S 153°2E 335 D5
Great Sandy Desert Australia 21°0S 124°0E 332 D3
Great Sandy Desert U.S.A. 43°35N 120°15W 346 B2
Great Sangi = Sangihe, Pulau Indonesia 3°35N 125°30E 309 D7
Great Sea Reef Fiji 16°15S 179°0E 331 a
Great Skellig Ireland 51°47N 10°33W 282 E1
Great Slave L. Canada 61°23N 115°38W 342 A5
Great Smoky Mts. △ U.S.A. 35°40N 83°40W 357 D13
Great Snow Mt. Canada 57°26N 124°0W 342 B4

Hachiōji Japan 35°40N 139°20E 303 G9
Hackensack U.S.A. 40°52N 74°4W 355 F10
Hackettstown U.S.A. 40°51N 74°50W 355 F10
Hadali Pakistan 32°16N 72°11E 314 C5
Hadarba, Ras Sudan 22°4N 36°51E 323 D13
Hadarom □ Israel 31°0N 35°0E 318 E4
Ḥadd, Ra's al Oman 22°35N 59°50E 319 C6
Haddington U.K. 55°57N 2°47W 283 F6
Hadejia Nigeria 12°30N 10°5E 322 F7
Ḥadera Israel 32°27N 34°55E 318 C3
Ḥadera, N. → Israel 32°28N 34°52E 318 C3
Haderslev Denmark 55°15N 9°30E 281 J13
Hadhramaut = Ḥaḍramawt Yemen 15°30N 49°30E 319 D4
Hadībоh Yemen 12°39N 54°2E 319 E5
Hadong S. Korea 35°5N 127°44E 307 G14
Ḥaḍramawt Yemen 15°30N 49°30E 319 D4
Ḥadrānīyah Iraq 35°38N 43°14E 316 C4
Hadrian's Wall U.K. 55°0N 2°30W 284 B5
Haeju N. Korea 38°3N 125°45E 307 E13
Haenam S. Korea 34°34N 126°35E 307 G14
Haenertsburg S. Africa 24°0S 29°50E 329 C4
Haerhpin = Harbin China 45°48N 126°40E 307 B14
Hafar al Bāṭin Si. Arabia 28°32N 45°52E 316 D5
Ḥafirat al 'Aydā Si. Arabia 26°26N 39°12E 316 E3
Ḥafit Oman 23°59N 55°49E 317 F7
Hafizabad Pakistan 32°5N 73°40E 314 C5
Haflong India 25°10N 93°5E 313 G18
Haft Gel Iran 31°30N 49°32E 317 D6
Hagalil Israel 32°53N 35°18E 318 C4
Hagen Germany 51°21N 7°27E 288 C4
Hagerman U.S.A. 33°7N 104°20W 349 K11
Hagerman Fossil Beds ⌂ U.S.A. 42°48N 114°57W 348 E6
Hagerstown U.S.A. 39°39N 77°43W 353 F15
Hagersville Canada 42°58N 80°3W 354 D4
Hagfors Sweden 60°3N 13°45E 281 F15
Hagi Japan 34°30N 131°22E 303 G5
Hagolan Syria 33°0N 35°45E 318 C4
Hagondange France 49°16N 6°11E 292 B7
Hags Hd. Ireland 52°57N 9°28W 282 D2
Hague, C. de la France 49°44N 1°56W 292 B3
Hague, The = 's-Gravenhage Neths. 52°7N 4°17E 287 B4
Haguenau France 48°49N 7°47E 292 B7
Hai Duong Vietnam 20°56N 106°19E 310 B6
Haicheng China 40°50N 122°45E 307 D12
Haidar Khel Afghan. 33°58N 68°38E 314 C3
Haidarâbâd = Hyderabad India 17°22N 78°29E 312 L11
Haidargarh India 26°37N 81°22E 315 F9
Haifa = Ḥefa Israel 32°46N 35°0E 318 C4
Haikou China 20°1N 110°16E 310 B8
Ḥā'il Si. Arabia 27°28N 41°45E 316 E4
Ḥā'il □ Si. Arabia 26°40N 41°40E 316 E4
Hailar China 49°10N 119°38E 305 B6
Hailey U.S.A. 43°31N 114°19W 348 E6
Haileybury Canada 47°30N 79°38W 344 C4
Hailin China 44°37N 129°30E 307 B15
Hailuoto Finland 65°3N 24°45E 280 D21
Hainan □ China 19°0N 109°30E 310 C7
Hainan Dao China 19°0N 109°30E 310 C7
Hainan Str. = Qiongzhou Haixia China 20°10N 110°15E 310 B8
Hainaut □ Belgium 50°30N 4°0E 287 D4
Haines Alaska, U.S.A. 59°14N 135°26W 342 B1
Haines Oreg., U.S.A. 44°55N 117°56W 348 D5
Haines City U.S.A. 28°7N 81°38W 357 G14
Haines Junction Canada 60°45N 137°30W 342 A1
Haiphong Vietnam 20°47N 106°41E 310 B6
Haiti ■ W. Indies 19°0N 72°30W 361 C5
Haiya Sudan 18°20N 36°21E 323 E13
Haiyang China 36°47N 121°9E 307 F11
Haiyuan China 36°35N 105°52E 306 F3
Haizhou China 34°37N 119°7E 307 G10
Haizhou Wan China 34°50N 119°20E 307 G10
Hajdúböszörmény Hungary 47°40N 21°30E 289 E11
Hajipur India 25°45N 85°13E 315 G11
Ḥajjah Yemen 15°42N 43°36E 319 D3
Ḥājjī Muḥsin Iraq 32°35N 45°29E 316 C5
Ḥājjīābād Iran 28°19N 55°55E 317 D7
Ḥājjīābād-e Zarrīn Iran 33°9N 54°51E 317 C7
Hajnówka Poland 52°47N 23°35E 289 B12
Hakansson, Mts. Dem. Rep. of the Congo 8°40S 25°45E 327 D2
Hakkâri Turkey 37°34N 43°44E 316 B4
Hakken-Zan Japan 34°10N 135°54E 303 G7
Hakodate Japan 41°45N 140°44E 302 D10
Hakos Namibia 23°13S 16°21E 328 C2
Haku-San Japan 36°9N 136°46E 303 F8
Haku-San △ Japan 36°15N 136°45E 303 F8
Hakui Japan 36°53N 136°47E 303 F8
Hala Pakistan 25°43N 68°20E 312 G6
Ḥalab Syria 36°10N 37°15E 316 B3
Ḥalabjah Iraq 35°10N 45°58E 316 C5
Halaib Sudan 22°12N 36°30E 323 D13
Halaib Triangle Africa 22°30N 35°20E 323 D13
Ḥālat 'Ammār Si. Arabia 29°10N 36°4E 316 D3
Halbā Lebanon 34°34N 36°6E 318 A5
Halberstadt Germany 51°54N 11°3E 288 C6
Halcombe N.Z. 40°8S 175°30E 331 D5
Halcon Phil. 13°0N 121°30E 309 B6
Halde Fjäll = Haltiatunturi Finland 69°17N 21°18E 280 B19
Halden Norway 59°9N 11°23E 281 G14
Haldimand Canada 42°59N 79°52W 354 D5
Haldwani India 29°31N 79°30E 315 E8
Hale → Australia 24°56S 135°53E 334 C2
Halesowen U.K. 52°27N 2°3W 285 E5
Halesworth U.K. 52°20N 1°31E 285 E9
Haleyville U.S.A. 34°14N 87°37W 357 D11
Half Dome U.S.A. 37°44N 119°32E 350 H7
Halfmoon Bay N.Z. 46°50S 168°5E 331 G2
Halfway → Canada 56°12N 121°32W 342 B4
Halia India 24°50N 82°19E 315 G10
Haliburton Canada 45°3N 78°30W 354 A6
Halifax Australia 18°32S 146°22E 334 B4
Halifax Canada 44°38N 63°35W 345 D7
Halifax U.K. 53°43N 1°52W 284 D6
Halifax U.S.A. 40°25N 76°55W 354 F8
Halifax B. Australia 18°50S 147°0E 334 B4
Halifax I. Namibia 26°38S 15°4E 328 D2
Halīl → Iran 27°40N 58°30E 317 E8
Halkida Greece 38°27N 23°42E 295 E10
Halkirk U.K. 58°30N 3°29W 283 C5
Hall Beach = Sanirajak Canada 68°46N 81°12W 341 C11
Hall Pen. Canada 63°30N 66°0W 341 C13
Hall Pt. Australia 15°40S 124°23E 332 C3
Halland Sweden 57°8N 12°47E 281 H15
Hallāniyat, Jazā'ir al Oman 17°30N 55°58E 319 D6
Hallasan S. Korea 33°22N 126°32E 307 H14
Halle Belgium 50°44N 4°13E 287 D4
Halle Germany 51°30N 11°56E 288 C6
Hällefors Sweden 59°47N 14°31E 281 G16
Hallett Australia 33°25S 138°55E 335 E2
Hallettsville U.S.A. 29°27N 96°57W 356 G6
Hallim S. Korea 33°24N 126°15E 307 H14
Hallingdalselva → Norway 60°23N 9°35E 280 F13
Hallock U.S.A. 48°47N 96°57W 352 A5
Halls Creek Australia 18°16S 127°38E 332 C4
Halls Gap Australia 37°8S 142°34E 335 F3
Hallsberg Sweden 59°5N 15°7E 281 G16
Hallstead U.S.A. 41°58N 75°45W 355 E9
Halmahera Indonesia 0°40N 128°0E 309 D7
Halmstad Sweden 56°41N 12°52E 281 H15
Hälsingborg = Helsingborg Sweden 56°3N 12°42E 281 H15
Hälsingland Sweden 61°40N 16°5E 280 F17
Halstead U.K. 51°57N 0°40E 285 F8
Haltiatunturi Finland 69°17N 21°18E 280 B19
Halton □ U.K. 53°22N 2°45W 284 D5
Haltwhistle U.K. 54°58N 2°26W 284 C5
Ḥālūl Qatar 25°40N 52°40E 317 E7
Halvad India 23°1N 71°11E 314 H4
Ḥalvān Iran 33°57N 56°15E 317 C8
Ham Tan Vietnam 10°40N 107°45E 311 G6
Ham Yen Vietnam 22°4N 105°3E 310 A5
Hamab Namibia 28°7S 19°16E 328 D2
Hamada Japan 34°56N 132°4E 303 G6
Hamadān Iran 34°52N 48°32E 317 C6
Hamadān □ Iran 35°0N 49°0E 317 C6
Ḥamāh Syria 35°5N 36°40E 316 C3
Hamamatsu Japan 34°45N 137°45E 303 G8
Hamar Norway 60°48N 11°7E 280 F14
Hamâta, Gebel Egypt 24°17N 35°0E 316 E2
Hambantota Sri Lanka 6°10N 81°10E 312 R12
Hamber ⌂ Canada 52°20N 118°0W 342 C5
Hamburg Germany 53°33N 9°59E 288 B5
Hamburg Ark., U.S.A. 33°14N 91°48W 356 E9
Hamburg N.Y., U.S.A. 42°43N 78°50W 354 D6
Hamburg Pa., U.S.A. 40°33N 75°59W 355 F9
Ḥamḍ, W. al → Si. Arabia 24°55N 36°20E 316 E3
Hamden U.S.A. 41°23N 72°54W 355 E12
Häme Finland 61°38N 25°10E 280 F21
Hämeenlinna Finland 61°0N 24°28E 280 F21
Hamelin Pool Australia 26°22S 114°20E 333 E1
Hameln Germany 52°6N 9°21E 288 B5
Hamerkaz □ Israel 32°15N 34°55E 318 C3
Hamersley Ra. Australia 22°0S 117°45E 332 D2
Hamhŭng N. Korea 39°54N 127°30E 307 E14
Hami China 42°55N 93°25E 304 B4
Hamilton Australia 37°45S 142°2E 335 F3
Hamilton Canada 43°15N 79°50W 354 C5
Hamilton N.Z. 37°47S 175°19E 331 B5
Hamilton U.K. 55°46N 4°2W 283 F4
Hamilton Ala., U.S.A. 34°9N 87°59W 357 D11
Hamilton Mont., U.S.A. 46°15N 114°10W 348 C6
Hamilton N.Y., U.S.A. 42°50N 75°33W 355 D9
Hamilton Ohio, U.S.A. 39°24N 84°34W 353 F11
Hamilton Tex., U.S.A. 31°42N 98°7W 356 F5
Hamilton → Queens., Australia 23°30S 139°47E 334 C2
Hamilton → S. Austral., Australia 26°40S 135°19E 335 D2
Hamilton City U.S.A. 39°45N 122°1W 350 F4
Hamilton I. Australia 20°21S 148°56E 334 J6
Hamilton Inlet Canada 54°0N 57°30W 345 B8
Hamilton Mt. U.S.A. 43°25N 74°22W 355 C10
Hamina Finland 60°34N 27°12E 280 F22
Hamirpur H.P., India 31°41N 76°31E 314 D7
Hamirpur Ut. P., India 25°57N 80°9E 315 G9
Hamju N. Korea 39°51N 127°26E 307 E14
Hamlet U.S.A. 34°53N 79°42W 357 D15
Hamley Bridge Australia 34°17S 138°35E 335 E2
Hamlin = Hameln Germany 52°6N 9°21E 288 B5
Hamlin N.Y., U.S.A. 43°17N 77°55W 354 C7
Hamlin Tex., U.S.A. 32°53N 100°8W 356 E4
Hamm Germany 51°40N 7°50E 288 C4
Ḥammār, Hawr al Iraq 30°50N 47°10E 316 D5
Hammerfest Norway 70°39N 23°41E 280 A20
Hammond Ind., U.S.A. 41°38N 87°30W 352 E10
Hammond La., U.S.A. 30°30N 90°28W 357 F9
Hammond N.Y., U.S.A. 44°27N 75°42W 355 B9
Hammondsport U.S.A. 42°25N 77°13W 354 D7
Hammonton U.S.A. 39°39N 74°48W 353 F16
Hampden N.Z. 45°18S 170°50E 331 F3
Hampshire □ U.K. 51°7N 1°23W 285 F6
Hampshire Downs U.K. 51°15N 1°10W 285 F6
Hampton N.B., Canada 45°32N 65°51W 345 C6
Hampton Ont., Canada 43°58N 78°45W 354 C6
Hampton Ark., U.S.A. 33°32N 92°28W 356 E8
Hampton Iowa, U.S.A. 42°45N 93°13W 352 D7
Hampton N.H., U.S.A. 42°57N 70°50W 355 D14
Hampton S.C., U.S.A. 32°52N 81°7W 357 E14
Hampton Va., U.S.A. 37°2N 76°21W 353 G15
Hampton Bays U.S.A. 40°53N 72°30W 355 F12
Hampton Tableland Australia 32°0S 127°0E 333 F4
Hamyang S. Korea 35°32N 127°42E 307 G14
Han Pijesak Bos.-H. 44°5N 18°57E 295 B8
Hanak Si. Arabia 25°32N 37°0E 316 E3
Hanamaki Japan 39°23N 141°7E 302 E10
Hanang Tanzania 4°30S 35°25E 326 C4
Hanau Germany 50°7N 8°56E 288 C5
Hanbogd = Ihbulag Mongolia 43°11N 107°10E 306 C4
Hancheng China 35°31N 110°25E 306 G6
Hancock Mich., U.S.A. 47°8N 88°35W 352 B9
Hancock N.Y., U.S.A. 41°57N 75°17W 355 E9
Handa Japan 34°53N 136°55E 303 G8
Handa I. U.K. 58°23N 5°11W 283 C3
Handan China 36°35N 114°28E 306 F8
Handeni Tanzania 5°25S 38°2E 326 D4
Handwara India 34°21N 74°20E 315 B6
Hanegev Israel 30°50N 35°0E 318 E4
Hanford U.S.A. 36°20N 119°39W 350 J7
Hanford Reach ⌂ U.S.A. 46°40N 119°30W 348 C4
Hang Chat Thailand 18°20N 99°21E 310 C2
Hang Dong Thailand 18°41N 98°55E 310 C2
Hangang → S. Korea 37°50N 126°30E 307 F14
Hangayn Nuruu Mongolia 47°30N 99°0E 304 B4
Hangchou = Hangzhou China 30°18N 120°11E 305 C7
Hanggin Houqi China 40°58N 107°4E 306 D4
Hanggin Qi China 39°52N 108°50E 306 E5
Hangu China 39°18N 117°53E 307 E9
Hangzhou China 30°18N 120°11E 305 C7
Hangzhou Wan China 30°15N 120°45E 305 C7
Hanhongor Mongolia 43°55N 104°28E 306 C3
Hania = Chania Greece 35°30N 24°4E 297 D6
Ḥanīdh Si. Arabia 26°35N 48°38E 317 E6
Ḥanīsh Yemen 13°45N 42°46E 319 E3
Hankinson U.S.A. 46°4N 96°54W 352 B5
Hankö Finland 59°50N 22°57E 281 G20
Hanksville U.S.A. 38°22N 110°43W 348 G8
Hanle India 32°42N 79°4E 315 C8
Hanmer Springs N.Z. 42°32S 172°50E 331 E4
Hann → Australia 17°26S 126°17E 332 C4
Hann, Mt. Australia 15°45S 126°0E 332 C4
Hanna Canada 51°40N 111°54W 342 C6
Hanna U.S.A. 41°52N 106°34W 348 F10
Hannah B. Canada 51°40N 80°0W 344 B4
Hannibal Mo., U.S.A. 39°42N 91°22W 352 F8
Hannibal N.Y., U.S.A. 43°19N 76°35W 355 C8
Hannover Germany 52°22N 9°46E 288 B5
Hanoi Vietnam 21°5N 105°55E 310 B5
Hanover = Hannover Germany 52°22N 9°46E 288 B5
Hanover Canada 44°9N 81°2W 354 B3
Hanover S. Africa 31°4S 24°29E 328 E3
Hanover N.H., U.S.A. 43°42N 72°17W 355 C12
Hanover Ohio, U.S.A. 40°4N 82°16W 354 F2
Hanover Pa., U.S.A. 39°48N 76°59W 353 F15
Hanover, I. Chile 51°0S 74°50W 368 G2
Hans Lollik I. U.S. Virgin Is. 18°24N 64°53W 361 e
Hansdiha India 24°36N 87°5E 315 G12
Hansi India 29°10N 75°57E 314 E6
Hanson, L. Australia 31°0S 136°15E 335 E2
Hantsavichy Belarus 52°49N 26°30E 289 B14
Hanumangarh India 29°35N 74°19E 314 E6
Hanzhong China 33°10N 107°1E 306 H4
Hanzhuang China 34°33N 117°23E 307 G9
Haora India 22°34N 88°18E 315 H13
Haparanda Sweden 65°52N 24°8E 280 D21
Happy U.S.A. 34°45N 101°52W 356 D4
Happy Camp U.S.A. 41°48N 123°23W 348 F2
Happy Valley-Goose Bay Canada 53°15N 60°20W 345 B7
Hapsu N. Korea 41°13N 128°51E 307 D15
Hapur India 28°45N 77°45E 314 E7
Ḥaql Si. Arabia 29°10N 34°58E 318 F3
Har Indonesia 5°16S 133°14E 309 F8
Har-Ayrag Mongolia 45°47N 109°16E 306 B5
Har Hu China 38°20N 97°38E 304 C4
Har Us Nuur Mongolia 48°0N 92°0E 304 B4
Har Yehuda Israel 31°35N 34°57E 318 D3
Ḥaraḍ Si. Arabia 24°22N 49°0E 319 C4
Haranomachi Japan 37°38N 140°58E 302 F10
Harare Zimbabwe 17°43S 31°2E 327 F3
Harazé Chad 9°57N 20°48E 323 G10
Harbin China 45°48N 126°40E 307 B14
Harbor Beach U.S.A. 43°51N 82°39W 354 C2
Harbour Breton Canada 47°29N 55°50W 345 C8
Harda India 22°27N 77°5E 314 H7
Hardangerfjorden Norway 60°5N 6°0E 281 F12
Hardangervidda Norway 60°7N 7°20E 280 F12
Hardap ⌂ Namibia 24°29S 17°45E 328 C2
Hardap Dam Namibia 24°32S 17°50E 328 C2
Hardenberg Neths. 52°34N 6°37E 287 B6
Harderwijk Neths. 52°21N 5°38E 287 B5
Hardey → Australia 22°45S 116°8E 332 D2
Hardin U.S.A. 45°44N 107°37W 348 D10
Harding S. Africa 30°35S 29°55E 329 E4
Harding Ra. Australia 16°17S 124°55E 332 C3
Hardisty Canada 52°40N 111°18W 342 C6
Hardoi India 27°26N 80°6E 315 F9
Hardwar = Haridwar India 29°58N 78°9E 314 E8
Hardwick U.S.A. 44°30N 72°22W 355 B12
Hardy, Pen. Chile 55°30S 68°20W 368 H3
Hardy, Pte. St. Lucia 14°6N 60°56W 361 f
Hare B. Canada 51°15N 55°45W 345 B8
Hareid Norway 62°22N 6°1E 280 E12
Harer Ethiopia 9°20N 42°8E 319 F3
Hargeisa Somali Rep. 9°30N 44°2E 319 F3
Hari → Indonesia 1°16S 104°5E 308 E2
Haria Canary Is. 29°8N 13°32W 296 E6
Haridwar India 29°58N 78°9E 314 E8
Harim, Jabal al Oman 25°58N 56°14E 317 E8
Haringhata → Bangla. 22°0N 89°58E 313 J16
Harīr, W. al → Syria 32°44N 35°59E 318 C4
Harīrūd → Asia 37°24N 60°38E 317 B9
Härjedalen Sweden 62°22N 13°5E 280 E15
Harlan Iowa, U.S.A. 41°39N 95°19W 352 E6
Harlan Ky., U.S.A. 36°51N 83°19W 353 G12
Harlech U.K. 52°52N 4°6W 284 E3
Harlem U.S.A. 48°32N 108°47W 348 B9
Harlingen Neths. 53°11N 5°25E 287 A5
Harlingen U.S.A. 26°12N 97°42W 356 H6
Harlow U.K. 51°46N 0°8E 285 F8
Harlowton U.S.A. 46°26N 109°50W 348 C9
Harnai Pakistan 30°6N 67°56E 314 D2
Harney Basin U.S.A. 43°0N 119°30W 348 E4
Harney L. U.S.A. 43°14N 119°8W 348 E4
Harney Peak U.S.A. 43°52N 103°32W 352 D2
Härnösand Sweden 62°38N 17°55E 280 E17
Haroldswick U.K. 60°48N 0°50W 283 A8
Harp L. Canada 55°5N 61°50W 345 A7
Harper Liberia 4°25N 7°43W 322 H4
Harrai India 22°37N 79°13E 315 H8
Harrand Pakistan 29°28N 70°3E 314 E4
Harricana → Canada 50°56N 79°32W 344 B4
Harriman U.S.A. 35°56N 84°33W 357 D12
Harrington Harbour Canada 50°31N 59°30W 345 B8
Harris U.K. 57°50N 6°55W 283 D2
Harris, L. Australia 31°10S 135°10E 335 E2
Harris, Sd. of U.K. 57°44N 7°6W 283 D1
Harris Pt. Canada 43°6N 82°9W 354 C2
Harrisburg Ill., U.S.A. 37°44N 88°32W 352 G9
Harrisburg Nebr., U.S.A. 41°33N 103°44W 352 E2
Harrisburg Pa., U.S.A. 40°16N 76°53W 354 F8
Harrismith S. Africa 28°15S 29°8E 329 D4
Harrison Ark., U.S.A. 36°14N 93°7W 356 C8
Harrison Maine, U.S.A. 44°7N 70°39W 355 B14
Harrison Nebr., U.S.A. 42°41N 103°53W 352 D2
Harrison, C. Canada 54°55N 57°55W 345 B8
Harrison L. Canada 49°33N 121°50W 342 D4
Harrisonburg U.S.A. 38°27N 78°52W 353 F14
Harrisonville U.S.A. 38°39N 94°21W 352 F6
Harriston Canada 43°57N 80°53W 354 C4
Harrisville Mich., U.S.A. 44°39N 83°17W 354 B1
Harrisville N.Y., U.S.A. 44°9N 75°19W 355 B9
Harrisville Pa., U.S.A. 41°8N 80°0W 354 E5
Harrodsburg U.S.A. 37°46N 84°51W 353 G11
Harrogate U.K. 54°0N 1°33W 284 C6
Harrow □ U.K. 51°35N 0°21W 285 F7
Harrowsmith Canada 44°24N 76°40W 355 B8
Harry S. Truman Res. U.S.A. 38°16N 93°24W 352 F7
Harsīn Iran 34°18N 47°33E 316 C5
Harstad Norway 68°48N 16°30E 280 B17
Harsud India 22°6N 76°44E 314 H7
Hart U.S.A. 43°42N 86°22W 352 D10
Hart, L. Australia 31°10S 136°25E 335 E2
Hartbees → S. Africa 28°45S 20°32E 328 D3
Hartford Conn., U.S.A. 41°46N 72°41W 355 E12
Hartford Ky., U.S.A. 37°27N 86°55W 352 G10
Hartford S. Dak., U.S.A. 43°38N 96°57W 352 D5
Hartford Vt., U.S.A. 43°40N 72°20W 355 C12
Hartford Wis., U.S.A. 43°19N 88°22W 352 D9
Hartford City U.S.A. 40°27N 85°22W 353 E11
Hartland Canada 46°20N 67°32W 345 C6
Hartland Pt. U.K. 51°1N 4°32W 285 F3
Hartlepool U.K. 54°42N 1°13W 284 C6
Hartlepool □ U.K. 54°42N 1°17W 284 C6
Hartley Bay Canada 53°25N 129°15W 342 C3
Hartmannberge Namibia 17°0S 13°0E 328 B1
Hartney Canada 49°30N 100°35W 343 D8
Harts → S. Africa 28°24S 24°17E 328 D3
Hartselle U.S.A. 34°27N 86°56W 357 D11
Hartshorne U.S.A. 34°51N 95°34W 356 D7
Hartstown U.S.A. 41°33N 80°23W 354 E4
Hartsville U.S.A. 34°23N 80°4W 357 D14
Hartswater S. Africa 27°34S 24°43E 328 D3
Hartwell U.S.A. 34°21N 82°56W 357 D13
Harunabad Pakistan 29°35N 73°8E 314 E5
Harvand Iran 28°25N 55°43E 317 D7
Harvey Australia 33°5S 115°54E 333 F2
Harvey Ill., U.S.A. 41°36N 87°50W 352 E10
Harvey N. Dak., U.S.A. 47°47N 99°56W 352 B4
Harwich U.K. 51°56N 1°17E 285 F9
Haryana □ India 29°0N 76°10E 314 E7
Haryn → Belarus 52°7N 27°17E 289 B14
Harz Germany 51°38N 10°44E 288 C6
Hasa Si. Arabia 25°50N 49°0E 317 E6
Ḥasā, W. al → Jordan 31°4N 35°29E 318 D4
Ḥasanābād Iran 32°8N 52°44E 317 C7
Ḥasb, W. → Iraq 31°45N 44°17E 316 D5
Hasdo → India 21°44N 82°44E 315 J10
Hashimoto Japan 34°19N 135°37E 303 G7
Hashtjerd Iran 35°52N 50°40E 317 C6
Haskell U.S.A. 33°10N 99°44W 356 E5
Haskovo = Khaskovo Bulgaria 41°56N 25°30E 295 D11
Haslemere U.K. 51°5N 0°43W 285 F7
Hasselt Belgium 50°56N 5°21E 287 D5
Hassi Messaoud Algeria 31°51N 6°1E 322 B7
Hässleholm Sweden 56°10N 13°46E 281 H15
Hastings N.Z. 39°39S 176°52E 331 C6
Hastings U.K. 50°51N 0°35E 285 G8
Hastings Mich., U.S.A. 42°39N 85°17W 353 D11
Hastings Minn., U.S.A. 44°44N 92°51W 352 C7
Hastings Nebr., U.S.A. 40°35N 98°23W 352 E4
Hastings Ra. Australia 31°15S 152°14E 335 E5
Hat Yai Thailand 7°1N 100°27E 311 J3
Hatanbulag = Ergel Mongolia 43°8N 109°5E 306 C5
Hatay Turkey 36°14N 36°10E 316 B3
Hatch U.S.A. 32°40N 107°9W 349 K10
Hatchet L. Canada 58°36N 103°40W 343 B8
Hateruma-Shima Japan 24°3N 123°47E 303 M1
Hatfield P.O. Australia 33°54S 143°49E 335 E3
Hatgal Mongolia 50°26N 100°9E 304 A5
Hathras India 27°36N 78°6E 314 F8
Hatia Bangla. 22°30N 91°5E 313 H17
Hato Mayor Dom. Rep. 18°46N 69°15W 361 C6
Hatta India 24°7N 79°36E 315 G8
Hatta U.A.E. 24°45N 56°4E 317 E8
Hattah Australia 34°48S 142°17E 335 E3
Hattah-Kulkyne △ Australia 34°16S 142°33E 335 E3
Hatteras, C. U.S.A. 35°14N 75°32W 357 D17
Hattiesburg U.S.A. 31°20N 89°17W 357 F10
Hatvan Hungary 47°40N 19°45E 289 E10
Hau Duc Vietnam 15°20N 108°13E 310 E7
Haugesund Norway 59°23N 5°13E 281 G11
Haukipudas Finland 65°12N 25°20E 280 D21
Haultain → Canada 55°51N 106°46W 343 B7
Hauraki G. N.Z. 36°35S 175°5E 331 B5
Haut Atlas Morocco 32°30N 5°0W 322 B4
Hautes Fagnes = Hohes Venn Belgium 50°30N 6°5E 287 D6
Hauts Plateaux Algeria 35°0N 1°0E 322 B6
Havana = La Habana Cuba 23°8N 82°22W 360 B3
Havana U.S.A. 40°18N 90°4W 352 E8
Havant U.K. 50°51N 0°58W 285 G7
Havasor = Kığzı Turkey 38°18N 43°25E 316 B4
Havasu, L. U.S.A. 34°18N 114°28W 351 L12
Havel → Germany 52°50N 12°3E 288 B7
Havelian Pakistan 34°2N 73°10E 314 B5
Havelock Canada 44°26N 77°53W 354 B7
Havelock N.Z. 41°17S 173°48E 331 D4
Havelock U.S.A. 34°53N 76°54W 357 D16
Haverfordwest U.K. 51°48N 4°58W 285 F3
Haverhill U.K. 52°5N 0°28E 285 E8
Haverhill U.S.A. 42°47N 71°5W 355 D13
Haverstraw U.S.A. 41°12N 73°58W 355 E11
Havirga Mongolia 45°41N 113°5E 306 B7
Havířov Czech Rep. 49°46N 18°20E 289 D10
Havlíčkův Brod Czech Rep. 49°36N 15°33E 288 D8
Havre U.S.A. 48°33N 109°41W 348 B9
Havre-Aubert Canada 47°12N 61°56W 345 C7
Havre-St.-Pierre Canada 50°18N 63°33W 345 B7
Haw → U.S.A. 35°36N 79°3W 357 D15
Hawai'i U.S.A. 19°30N 155°30W 346 b
Hawai'i □ U.S.A. 19°30N 156°30W 346 b
Hawaiian Is. Pac. Oc. 20°30N 156°0W 346 b
Hawaiian Ridge Pac. Oc. 24°0N 165°0W 337 E11
Hawarden U.S.A. 43°0N 96°29W 352 D5
Hawea, L. N.Z. 44°28S 169°19E 331 F2
Hawera N.Z. 39°35S 174°19E 331 C5
Hawick U.K. 55°26N 2°47W 283 F6
Hawk Junction Canada 48°5N 84°38W 344 C3
Hawke B. N.Z. 39°25S 177°20E 331 C6
Hawker Australia 31°59S 138°22E 335 E2
Hawke's Bay Canada 50°36N 57°10W 345 B8
Hawkesbury Canada 45°37N 74°37W 344 C5
Hawkesbury I. Canada 53°37N 129°3W 342 C3
Hawkesbury Pt. Australia 11°55S 134°5E 334 A1
Hawkinsville U.S.A. 32°17N 83°28W 357 E13
Hawley Minn., U.S.A. 46°53N 96°19W 352 B5
Hawley Pa., U.S.A. 41°28N 75°11W 355 E9
Ḥawrān, W. → Iraq 33°58N 42°34E 316 C4
Hawsh Mūssá Lebanon 33°45N 35°55E 318 B4
Hawthorne U.S.A. 38°32N 118°38W 348 G4
Hay Australia 34°30S 144°51E 335 E3
Hay → Australia 24°50S 138°0E 334 C2
Hay → Canada 60°50N 116°26W 342 A5
Hay, C. Australia 14°5S 129°29E 332 B4
Hay I. Canada 44°53N 80°58W 354 B4
Hay L. Canada 58°50N 118°50W 342 B5
Hay-on-Wye U.K. 52°5N 3°8W 285 E4
Hay River Canada 60°51N 115°44W 342 A5
Hay Springs U.S.A. 42°41N 102°41W 352 D2
Haya = Tehoru Indonesia 3°23S 129°30E 309 E7
Hayachine-San Japan 39°34N 141°29E 302 E10
Hayastan = Armenia ■ Asia 40°20N 45°0E 291 F7
Haydān, W. al → Jordan 31°29N 35°34E 318 D4
Hayden U.S.A. 40°30N 107°16W 348 F10
Haydon Australia 18°0S 141°30E 334 B3
Hayes U.S.A. 44°23N 101°1W 352 C3
Hayes → Canada 57°3N 92°12W 344 A1
Hayes Creek Australia 13°43S 131°22E 332 B5
Hayle U.K. 50°11N 5°26W 285 G2
Hayling I. U.K. 50°48N 0°59W 285 G7
Haymen I. Australia 20°3S 148°52E 334 J6
Hayrabolu Turkey 41°12N 27°5E 295 D12
Hays Canada 50°6N 111°48W 342 C6
Hays U.S.A. 38°53N 99°20W 352 F4
Haysyn Ukraine 48°57N 29°25E 289 D15
Hayvoron Ukraine 48°22N 29°52E 289 D15
Hayward Calif., U.S.A. 37°40N 122°4W 350 H4
Hayward Wis., U.S.A. 46°1N 91°29W 352 B8
Haywards Heath U.K. 51°0N 0°5W 285 G7
Hazafon □ Israel 32°40N 35°20E 318 C4
Hazar Turkmenistan 39°34N 53°16E 291 G9
Hazārān, Kūh-e Iran 29°35N 57°20E 317 D8
Hazard U.S.A. 37°15N 83°12W 353 G12
Hazaribag India 23°58N 85°26E 315 H11
Hazaribag Road India 24°12N 85°57E 315 G11
Hazelton Canada 55°20N 127°42W 342 B3
Hazelton U.S.A. 46°29N 100°17W 352 B3
Hazen U.S.A. 47°18N 101°38W 352 B3
Hazlehurst Ga., U.S.A. 31°52N 82°36W 357 F13
Hazlehurst Miss., U.S.A. 31°52N 90°24W 357 F9
Hazlet U.S.A. 40°25N 74°12W 355 F10
Hazleton U.S.A. 40°57N 75°59W 355 F9
Hazlett, L. Australia 21°30S 128°48E 332 D4
Hazro Turkey 38°15N 40°47E 316 B4
Head of Bight Australia 31°30S 131°25E 333 F5
Headlands Zimbabwe 18°15S 32°2E 327 F3

Healdsburg U.S.A. 38°37N 122°52W 350 G4
Healdton U.S.A. 34°14N 97°29W 356 D6
Healesville Australia 37°35S 145°30E 335 F4
Heany Junction Zimbabwe 20°6S 28°54E 329 C4
Heard I. Ind. Oc. 53°0S 74°0E 275 G13
Hearne U.S.A. 30°53N 96°36W 356 F6
Hearst Canada 49°40N 83°41W 344 C3
Heart → U.S.A. 46°46N 100°50W 352 B3
Heart's Content Canada 47°54N 53°27W 345 C9
Heath, Pte. Canada 49°8N 61°40W 345 C7
Heathrow, London ✕ (LHR) U.K. 51°28N 0°27W 285 F7
Heavener U.S.A. 34°53N 94°36W 356 D7
Hebbronville U.S.A. 27°18N 98°41W 356 H5
Hebei □ China 39°0N 116°0E 306 E9
Hebel Australia 28°58S 147°47E 335 D4
Heber U.S.A. 32°44N 115°32W 351 N11
Heber Springs U.S.A. 35°30N 92°2W 356 D8
Hebgen L. U.S.A. 44°52N 111°20W 348 D8
Hebi China 35°57N 114°7E 306 G8
Hebrides U.K. 57°30N 7°0W 278 D4
Hebrides, Sea of the U.K. 57°5N 7°0W 283 D2
Hebron = Al Khalīl West Bank 31°32N 35°6E 318 D4
Hebron Canada 58°5N 62°30W 341 D13
Hebron N. Dak., U.S.A. 46°54N 102°3W 352 B2
Hebron Nebr., U.S.A. 40°10N 97°35W 352 E5
Hecate Str. Canada 53°10N 130°30W 342 C2
Heceta I. U.S.A. 55°46N 133°40W 342 B2
Hechi China 24°40N 108°2E 304 D5
Hechuan China 30°2N 106°12E 304 C5
Hecla U.S.A. 45°53N 98°9W 352 C4
Hecla I. Canada 51°10N 96°43W 343 C9
Hede Sweden 62°23N 13°30E 280 E15
Hedemora Sweden 60°18N 15°58E 281 F16
Heerde Neths. 52°24N 6°2E 287 B6
Heerenveen Neths. 52°57N 5°55E 287 B5
Heerhugowaard Neths. 52°40N 4°51E 287 B4
Heerlen Neths. 50°55N 5°58E 287 D5
H̱efa Israel 32°46N 35°0E 318 C4
H̱efa □ Israel 32°40N 35°0E 318 C4
Hefei China 31°52N 117°18E 305 C6
Hegang China 47°20N 130°19E 305 B8
Hei Ling Chau China 22°15N 114°2E 305 G11
Heichengzhen China 36°24N 106°3E 306 F4
Heidelberg Germany 49°24N 8°42E 288 D5
Heidelberg S. Africa 34°6S 20°59E 328 E3
Heilbron S. Africa 27°16S 27°59E 329 D4
Heilbronn Germany 49°9N 9°13E 288 D5
Heilongjiang □ China 48°0N 126°0E 305 B7
Heilunkiang = Heilongjiang □ China 48°0N 126°0E 305 B7
Heimaey Iceland 63°26N 20°17W 280 E3
Heinola Finland 61°13N 26°2E 280 F22
Heinze Kyun Burma 14°25N 97°45E 310 E1
Heishan China 41°40N 122°5E 307 D12
Heishui China 42°8N 119°30E 307 C10
Hejaz = Ḩijāz Si. Arabia 24°0N 40°0E 316 E3
Hejian China 38°25N 116°5E 306 E9
Hejin China 35°35N 110°42E 306 G6
Hekımhan Turkey 38°50N 37°55E 316 B3
Hekla Iceland 63°56N 19°35W 280 E4
Hekou China 22°30N 103°59E 304 D5
Helan Shan China 38°30N 105°55E 306 E3
Helen Atoll Pac. Oc. 2°40N 132°0E 309 D8
Helena Ark., U.S.A. 34°32N 90°36W 357 D9
Helena Mont., U.S.A. 46°36N 112°2W 348 C7
Helendale U.S.A. 34°44N 117°19W 351 L9
Helensburgh U.K. 56°1N 4°43W 283 E4
Helensville N.Z. 36°41S 174°29E 331 B5
Helenvale Australia 15°43S 145°14E 334 B4
Helgeland Norway 66°7N 13°29E 280 C15
Helgoland Germany 54°10N 7°53E 288 A4
Heligoland = Helgoland Germany 54°10N 7°53E 288 A4
Heligoland B. = Deutsche Bucht Germany 54°15N 8°0E 288 A5
Hell Hole Gorge △ Australia 25°31S 144°12E 334 D3
Hella Iceland 63°50N 20°24W 280 E3
Hellas = Greece ■ Europe 40°0N 23°0E 295 E9
Hellertown U.S.A. 40°35N 75°21W 355 F9
Hellespont = Çanakkale Boğazı Turkey 40°17N 26°32E 295 D12
Hellevoetsluis Neths. 51°50N 4°8E 287 C4
Hellín Spain 38°31N 1°40W 293 C5
Hells Canyon ⌓ U.S.A. 45°30N 117°45W 348 D5
Hell's Gate △ Kenya 0°54S 36°19E 326 C4
Helmand □ Afghan. 31°20N 64°0E 312 D4
Helmand → Afghan. 31°12N 61°34E 312 D2
Helmeringhausen Namibia 25°54S 16°57E 328 D2
Helmond Neths. 51°29N 5°41E 287 C5
Helmsdale U.K. 58°7N 3°39W 283 C5
Helmsdale → U.K. 58°8N 3°43W 283 C5
Helong China 42°40N 129°0E 307 C15
Helper U.S.A. 39°41N 110°51W 348 G8
Helsingborg Sweden 56°3N 12°42E 281 H15
Helsingfors = Helsinki Finland 60°10N 24°55E 281 F21
Helsingør Denmark 56°2N 12°35E 281 H15
Helsinki Finland 60°10N 24°55E 281 F21
Helston U.K. 50°6N 5°17W 285 G2
Helvellyn U.K. 54°32N 3°1W 284 C4
Helwân Egypt 29°50N 31°20E 323 C12
Hemel Hempstead U.K. 51°44N 0°28W 285 F7
Hemet U.S.A. 33°45N 116°58W 351 M10
Hemingford U.S.A. 42°19N 103°4W 352 D2
Hemis △ India 34°10N 77°15E 314 B7
Hemmingford Canada 45°3N 73°35W 355 A11
Hempstead N.Y., U.S.A. 40°42N 73°37W 355 F11
Hempstead Tex., U.S.A. 30°6N 96°5W 356 F6
Hemse Sweden 57°15N 18°22E 281 H18
Henan □ China 34°0N 114°0E 306 H8
Henares → Spain 40°24N 3°30W 293 B4
Henashi-Misaki Japan 40°37N 139°51E 302 D9
Henderson Argentina 36°18S 61°43W 366 D3
Henderson Ky., U.S.A. 37°50N 87°35W 352 G10
Henderson N.C., U.S.A. 36°20N 78°25W 357 C15
Henderson Nev., U.S.A. 36°2N 114°58W 351 J12
Henderson Tenn., U.S.A. 35°26N 88°38W 357 D10
Henderson Tex., U.S.A. 32°9N 94°48W 356 E7
Henderson I. Pac. Oc. 24°22S 128°19W 337 K15
Hendersonville N.C., U.S.A. 35°19N 82°28W 357 D13
Hendersonville Tenn., U.S.A. 36°18N 86°37W 357 C11
Hendījān Iran 30°14N 49°43E 317 D6
Hendorābī Iran 26°40N 53°37E 317 E7
Hengcheng China 38°18N 106°28E 306 E4
Hengdaohezi China 44°52N 129°0E 307 B15
Hengelo Neths. 52°16N 6°48E 287 B6
Henggang China 22°39N 114°12E 305 F11
Hengmen China 22°33N 113°35E 305 F10
Hengqin Dao China 22°7N 113°34E 305 G10
Hengshan China 37°58N 109°5E 306 F5
Hengshui China 37°41N 115°40E 306 F8
Hengyang China 26°59N 112°22E 305 D6
Henley-on-Thames U.K. 51°32N 0°54W 285 F7
Henlopen, C. U.S.A. 38°48N 75°6W 353 F16
Hennenman S. Africa 27°59S 27°1E 328 D4
Hennessey U.S.A. 36°6N 97°54W 356 C6
Henri Pittier △ Venezuela 10°26N 67°37W 361 D6
Henrietta U.S.A. 33°49N 98°12W 356 E5
Henrietta, Ostrov = Genriyetty, Ostrov Russia 77°6N 156°30E 301 B16
Henrietta Maria, C. Canada 55°9N 82°20W 344 A3
Henry U.S.A. 41°7N 89°22W 352 E9
Henryetta U.S.A. 35°27N 95°59W 356 D7
Henryville Canada 45°8N 73°11W 355 A11
Hensall Canada 43°26N 81°30W 354 C3
Hentiesbaai Namibia 22°8S 14°18E 328 C1
Hentiyn Nuruu Mongolia 48°30N 108°30E 305 B5
Henty Australia 35°30S 147°3E 335 F4
Henzada Burma 17°38N 95°26E 313 L19
Heppner U.S.A. 45°21N 119°33W 348 D4
Hepworth Canada 44°37N 81°9W 354 B3
Hequ China 39°20N 111°15E 306 E6
Héraðsflói Iceland 65°42N 14°12W 280 D6
Héraðsvötn → Iceland 65°45N 19°25W 280 D4
Heraklion = Iraklio Greece 35°20N 25°12E 297 D7
Herald Cays Australia 16°58S 149°9E 334 B4
Herāt Afghan. 34°20N 62°7E 312 B3
Herāt □ Afghan. 35°0N 62°0E 312 B3
Herbert Canada 50°30N 107°10W 343 C7
Herbert → Australia 18°31S 146°17E 334 B4
Herberton Australia 17°20S 145°25E 334 B4
Herbertsdale S. Africa 34°1S 21°46E 328 E3
Herceg-Novi Montenegro 42°30N 18°33E 295 C8
Herchmer Canada 57°22N 94°10W 343 B10
Herðubreið Iceland 65°11N 16°21W 280 D5
Hereford U.K. 52°4N 2°43W 285 E5
Hereford U.S.A. 34°49N 102°24W 356 D3
Herefordshire □ U.K. 52°8N 2°40W 285 E5
Herentals Belgium 51°12N 4°51E 287 C4
Herford Germany 52°7N 8°39E 288 B5
Herington U.S.A. 38°40N 96°57W 352 F5
Herkimer U.S.A. 43°2N 74°59W 355 D10
Herlong U.S.A. 40°8N 120°8W 350 E6
Herm U.K. 49°30N 2°28W 285 H5
Hermann U.S.A. 38°42N 91°27W 352 F8
Hermannsburg Australia 23°57S 132°45E 332 D5
Hermanus S. Africa 34°27S 19°12E 328 E2
Hermidale Australia 31°30S 146°42E 335 E4
Hermiston U.S.A. 45°51N 119°17W 348 D4
Hermite, I. Chile 55°50S 68°0W 368 H3
Hermon U.S.A. 44°28N 75°14W 355 B9
Hermon, Mt. = Shaykh, J. ash Lebanon 33°25N 35°50E 318 B4
Hermosillo Mexico 29°10N 111°0W 358 B2
Hernád → Hungary 47°56N 21°8E 289 D11
Hernandarias Paraguay 25°20S 54°40W 367 B5
Hernandez U.S.A. 36°24N 120°46W 350 J6
Hernando Argentina 32°28S 63°40W 366 C3
Hernando U.S.A. 34°50N 90°0W 357 D10
Herndon U.S.A. 40°43N 76°51W 354 F8
Herne Germany 51°32N 7°14E 287 C7
Herne Bay U.K. 51°21N 1°8E 285 F9
Herning Denmark 56°8N 8°58E 281 H13
Heroica Caborca = Caborca Mexico 30°37N 112°6W 358 A2
Heroica Nogales = Nogales Mexico 31°19N 110°56W 358 A2
Heron Bay Canada 48°40N 86°25W 344 C2
Heron I. Australia 23°27S 151°55E 334 C5
Herradura, Pta. de la Canary Is. 28°26N 14°8W 296 F5
Herreid U.S.A. 45°50N 100°4W 352 C3
Herrin U.S.A. 37°48N 89°2W 352 G9
Herriot Canada 56°22N 101°16W 343 B8
Herschel I. Canada 69°35N 139°5W 276 C1
Hershey U.S.A. 40°17N 76°39W 355 F8
Herstal Belgium 50°40N 5°38E 287 D5
Hertford U.K. 51°48N 0°4W 285 F7
Hertfordshire □ U.K. 51°51N 0°5W 285 F7
's-Hertogenbosch Neths. 51°42N 5°17E 287 C5
Hertzogville S. Africa 28°9S 25°30E 328 D4
Hervey B. Australia 25°0S 152°52E 334 C5
Herzliyya Israel 32°10N 34°50E 318 C3
Ḩeşār Fārs, Iran 29°52N 50°16E 317 D6
Ḩeşār Markazī, Iran 35°50N 49°12E 317 C6
Heshui China 35°48N 108°0E 306 G5
Heshun China 37°22N 113°32E 306 F7
Hesperia U.S.A. 34°25N 117°18W 351 L9
Hesse = Hessen □ Germany 50°30N 9°0E 288 C5
Hessen □ Germany 50°30N 9°0E 288 C5
Hetch Hetchy Aqueduct U.S.A. 37°29N 122°19W 350 H5
Hettinger U.S.A. 46°0N 102°42W 352 B2
Heuksando S. Korea 34°40N 125°30E 307 G13
Heunghae S. Korea 36°12N 129°21E 307 F15
Heuvelton U.S.A. 44°37N 75°25W 355 B9
Hewitt U.S.A. 31°28N 97°12W 356 F6
Hexham U.K. 54°58N 2°4W 284 C5
Hexigten Qi China 43°18N 117°30E 307 C9
Ḩeydarābād Iran 30°33N 55°38E 317 D7
Heysham U.K. 54°3N 2°53W 284 C5
Heywood Australia 38°8S 141°37E 335 F3
Heze China 35°14N 115°20E 306 G8
Hi, Ko Thailand 7°44N 98°22E 311 a
Hi Vista U.S.A. 34°45N 117°46W 351 L9
Hialeah U.S.A. 25°51N 80°16W 357 J14
Hiawatha U.S.A. 39°51N 95°32W 352 F6
Hibbing U.S.A. 47°25N 92°56W 352 B7
Hibbs B. Australia 42°35S 145°15E 335 G4
Hibernia Reef Australia 12°0S 123°23E 332 B3
Hickman U.S.A. 36°34N 89°11W 352 G9
Hickory U.S.A. 35°44N 81°21W 357 D14
Hicks, Pt. Australia 37°49S 149°17E 335 F4
Hicks L. Canada 61°25N 100°0W 343 A9
Hicksville U.S.A. 40°46N 73°32W 355 F11
Hida-Gawa → Japan 35°26N 137°3E 303 G8
Hida-Sammyaku Japan 36°30N 137°40E 303 F8
Hidaka-Sammyaku Japan 42°35N 142°45E 302 C11
Hidalgo □ Mexico 20°30N 99°0W 359 C5
Hidalgo, Presa M. Mexico 26°30N 108°35W 358 B3
Hidalgo del Parral Mexico 26°56N 105°40W 358 B3
Hierro Canary Is. 27°44N 18°0W 296 G1
Higashiajima-San Japan 37°40N 140°10E 302 F10
Higashiōsaka Japan 34°39N 135°37E 303 G7
Higgins U.S.A. 36°7N 100°2W 356 C4
Higgins Corner U.S.A. 39°2N 121°5W 350 F5
High Bridge U.S.A. 40°40N 74°54W 355 F10
High Island Res. China 22°22N 114°21E 305 G11
High Level Canada 58°31N 117°8W 342 B5
High Point U.S.A. 35°57N 80°0W 357 D15
High Prairie Canada 55°30N 116°30W 342 B5
High River Canada 50°30N 113°50W 342 C6
High Tatra = Tatry Slovak Rep. 49°20N 20°0E 289 D11
High Veld Africa 27°0S 27°0E 320 J6
High Wycombe U.K. 51°37N 0°45W 285 F7
Highland □ U.K. 57°17N 4°21W 283 D4
Highland Park U.S.A. 42°11N 87°48W 352 D10
Highmore U.S.A. 44°31N 99°27W 352 C4
Highrock L. Man., Canada 55°45N 100°30W 343 B8
Highrock L. Sask., Canada 57°5N 105°32W 343 B7
Higüey Dom. Rep. 18°37N 68°42W 361 C6
Hiiumaa Estonia 58°50N 22°45E 281 G20
Ḩijāz Si. Arabia 24°0N 40°0E 316 E3
Hijo = Tagum Phil. 7°33N 125°53E 309 C7
Hikari Japan 33°58N 131°58E 303 H5
Hiko U.S.A. 37°32N 115°14W 350 H11
Hikone Japan 35°15N 136°10E 303 G8
Hikurangi Gisborne, N.Z. 37°55S 178°4E 331 C6
Hikurangi Northland, N.Z. 35°36S 174°17E 331 A5
Hildesheim Germany 52°9N 9°56E 288 B5
Hill → Australia 30°23S 115°3E 333 F2
Hill City Idaho, U.S.A. 43°18N 115°3W 348 E6
Hill City Kans., U.S.A. 39°22N 99°51W 352 F4
Hill City Minn., U.S.A. 46°59N 93°36W 352 B7
Hill City S. Dak., U.S.A. 43°56N 103°35W 352 D2
Hill Island L. Canada 60°30N 109°50W 343 A7
Hillaby, Mt. Barbados 13°12N 59°35W 361 g
Hillcrest Barbados 13°13N 59°31W 361 g
Hillcrest Center U.S.A. 35°23N 118°57W 351 K8
Hillegom Neths. 52°18N 4°35E 287 B4
Hillsboro Kans., U.S.A. 38°21N 97°12W 352 F5
Hillsboro N. Dak., U.S.A. 47°26N 97°3W 352 B5
Hillsboro Ohio, U.S.A. 39°12N 83°37W 353 F12
Hillsboro Oreg., U.S.A. 45°31N 122°59W 350 E4
Hillsboro Tex., U.S.A. 32°1N 97°8W 356 E6
Hillsborough Grenada 12°28N 61°28W 361 D7
Hillsborough U.S.A. 43°7N 71°54W 355 C13
Hillsborough Channel Australia 20°56S 149°15E 334 J7
Hillsdale Mich., U.S.A. 41°56N 84°38W 353 E11
Hillsdale N.Y., U.S.A. 42°11N 73°32W 355 D11
Hillsport Canada 49°27N 85°34W 344 C2
Hillston Australia 33°30S 145°31E 335 E4
Hilo U.S.A. 19°44N 155°5W 346 b
Hilton U.S.A. 43°17N 77°48W 354 C7
Hilton Head Island U.S.A. 32°13N 80°45W 357 E14
Hilversum Neths. 52°14N 5°10E 287 B5
Himachal Pradesh □ India 31°30N 77°0E 314 D7
Himalaya Asia 29°0N 84°0E 315 E11
Himatnagar India 23°37N 72°57E 314 H5
Himeji Japan 34°50N 134°40E 303 G7
Himi Japan 36°50N 136°55E 303 F8
Ḩimş Syria 34°40N 36°45E 318 A5
Ḩimş □ Syria 34°30N 37°0E 318 A6
Hinche Haiti 19°9N 72°1W 361 C5
Hinchinbrook I. Australia 18°20S 146°15E 334 B4
Hinchinbrook Island △ Australia 18°14S 146°6E 334 B4
Hinckley U.K. 52°33N 1°22W 285 E6
Hinckley U.S.A. 46°1N 92°56W 352 B7
Hindaun India 26°44N 77°5E 314 F7
Hindmarsh, L. Australia 36°5S 141°55E 335 F3
Hindu Bagh Pakistan 30°56N 67°50E 314 D2
Hindu Kush Asia 36°0N 71°0E 312 B7
Hindupur India 13°49N 77°32E 312 N10
Hines Creek Canada 56°20N 118°40W 342 B5
Hinesville U.S.A. 31°51N 81°36W 357 F14
Hinganghat India 20°30N 78°52E 312 J11
Hingham U.S.A. 48°33N 110°25W 348 B8
Hingir India 21°57N 83°41E 315 J10
Hingoli India 19°41N 77°15E 312 K10
Hinna = Imi Ethiopia 6°28N 42°10E 319 F3
Hinnøya Norway 68°35N 15°50E 280 B16
Hinojosa del Duque Spain 38°30N 5°9W 293 C3
Hinsdale U.S.A. 42°47N 72°29W 355 D12
Hinthada = Henzada Burma 17°38N 95°26E 313 L19
Hinton Canada 53°26N 117°34W 342 C5
Hinton U.S.A. 37°40N 80°54W 353 G13
Hios Greece 38°27N 26°9E 295 E12
Hirado Japan 33°22N 129°33E 303 H4
Hirakud Dam India 21°32N 83°45E 313 J13
Hiran → India 23°6N 79°21E 315 H8
Hirapur India 24°22N 79°13E 315 G8
Hirara Japan 24°48N 125°17E 303 M2
Hiratsuka Japan 35°19N 139°21E 303 G9
Hiroo Japan 42°17N 143°19E 302 C11
Hirosaki Japan 40°34N 140°28E 302 D10
Hiroshima Japan 34°24N 132°30E 303 G6
Hiroshima □ Japan 34°50N 133°0E 303 G6
Hisar India 29°12N 75°45E 314 E6
Hisb, Sha'ib = Ḩasb, W. → Iraq 31°45N 44°17E 316 D5
Ḩismá Si. Arabia 28°30N 36°0E 316 D3
Hispaniola W. Indies 19°0N 71°0W 361 C5
Hīt Iraq 33°38N 42°49E 316 C4
Hita Japan 33°20N 130°58E 303 H5
Hitachi Japan 36°36N 140°39E 303 F10
Hitchin U.K. 51°58N 0°16W 285 F7
Hitiaa Tahiti 17°36S 149°18W 331 d
Hitoyoshi Japan 32°13N 130°45E 303 H5
Hitra Norway 63°30N 8°45E 280 E13
Hiva Oa French Polynesia 9°45S 139°0W 337 H14
Hixon Canada 53°25N 122°35W 342 C4
H̱iyyon, N. → Israel 30°25N 35°10E 318 E4
Hjalmar L. Canada 61°33N 109°25W 343 A7
Hjälmaren Sweden 59°18N 15°40E 281 G16
Hjørring Denmark 57°29N 9°59E 281 H13
Hjort Trench S. Ocean 58°0S 157°30E 277 B10
Hkakabo Razi Burma 28°25N 97°23E 313 E20
Hlobane S. Africa 27°42S 31°0E 329 D5
Hluhluwe S. Africa 28°1S 32°15E 329 D5
Hluhluwe ⌓ S. Africa 22°10S 32°5E 329 C5
Hlyboka Ukraine 48°5N 25°56E 289 D13
Ho Ghana 6°37N 0°27E 322 G6
Ho Chi Minh City = Thanh Pho Ho Chi Minh Vietnam 10°58N 106°40E 311 G6
Ho Thuong Vietnam 19°32N 105°48E 310 C5
Hoa Binh Vietnam 20°50N 105°20E 310 B5
Hoa Da Vietnam 11°16N 108°40E 311 G7
Hoa Hiep Vietnam 11°34N 105°51E 311 G5
Hoai Nhon Vietnam 14°28N 109°1E 310 E7
Hoang Lien Son Vietnam 22°0N 104°0E 310 A4
Hoanib → Namibia 19°27S 12°46E 328 B2
Hoare B. Canada 65°17N 62°30W 341 C13
Hoarusib → Namibia 19°3S 12°36E 328 B2
Hobart Australia 42°50S 147°21E 335 G4
Hobart U.S.A. 35°1N 99°6W 356 D5
Hobbs U.S.A. 32°42N 103°8W 349 K12
Hobbs Coast Antarctica 74°50S 131°0W 277 D14
Hobe Sound U.S.A. 27°4N 80°8W 357 H14
Hoboken U.S.A. 40°44N 74°3W 355 F10
Hobro Denmark 56°39N 9°46E 281 H13
Hoburgen Sweden 56°55N 18°7E 281 H18
Hochfeld Namibia 21°28S 17°58E 328 C2
Hodaka-Dake Japan 36°17N 137°39E 303 F8
Hodeida = Al Ḩudaydah Yemen 14°50N 43°0E 319 E3
Hodgeville Canada 50°7N 106°58W 343 C7
Hodgson Canada 51°13N 97°36W 343 C9
Hódmezővásárhely Hungary 46°28N 20°22E 289 E11
Hodna, Chott el Algeria 35°26N 4°43E 322 A6
Hodonín Czech Rep. 48°50N 17°10E 289 D9
Hoek van Holland Neths. 52°0N 4°7E 287 C4
Hoengseong S. Korea 37°29N 127°59E 307 F14
Hoeryong N. Korea 42°30N 129°45E 307 C15
Hoeyang N. Korea 38°43N 127°36E 307 E14
Hof Germany 50°19N 11°55E 288 C6
Hofmeyr S. Africa 31°39S 25°50E 328 E4
Höfn Iceland 64°15N 15°13W 280 D6
Hofors Sweden 60°31N 16°15E 281 F17
Hofsjökull Iceland 64°49N 18°48W 280 D4
Hōfu Japan 34°3N 131°34E 303 G5
Hogan Group Australia 39°13S 147°1E 335 F4
Hogarth, Mt. Australia 21°48S 136°58E 334 C2
Hoge Kempen △ Belgium 51°6N 5°35E 287 C5
Hoggar = Ahaggar Algeria 23°0N 6°30E 322 D7
Hogsty Reef Bahamas 21°41N 73°48W 361 B5
Hoh → U.S.A. 47°45N 124°29W 350 C2
Hoh Xil Shan China 35°0N 89°0E 304 C3
Hohenwald U.S.A. 35°33N 87°33W 357 D11
Hoher Rhön = Rhön Germany 50°24N 9°58E 288 C5
Hohes Venn Belgium 50°30N 6°5E 287 D6
Hohhot China 40°52N 111°40E 306 D6
Hoi An Vietnam 15°30N 108°19E 310 E7
Hoi Xuan Vietnam 20°25N 105°9E 310 B5
Hoisington U.S.A. 38°31N 98°47W 352 F4
Hōjō Japan 33°58N 132°46E 303 H6
Hokianga Harbour N.Z. 35°31S 173°22E 331 A4
Hokitika N.Z. 42°42S 171°0E 331 E3
Hokkaidō □ Japan 43°30N 143°0E 302 C11
Hola Kenya 1°29S 40°2E 326 B4
Holakas Greece 35°57N 27°53E 297 D9
Holbrook Australia 35°42S 147°18E 335 F4
Holbrook U.S.A. 34°54N 110°10W 349 J8
Holden U.S.A. 39°6N 112°16W 348 G7
Holdenville U.S.A. 35°5N 96°24W 356 D6
Holdrege U.S.A. 40°26N 99°23W 352 E4
Holetown Barbados 13°11N 59°38W 361 g
Holguín Cuba 20°50N 76°20W 360 B4
Hollams Bird I. Namibia 24°40S 14°30E 328 C1
Holland Mich., U.S.A. 42°47N 86°7W 352 D10
Holland N.Y., U.S.A. 42°38N 78°32W 354 D6
Holley U.S.A. 43°14N 78°2W 354 C6
Hollidaysburg U.S.A. 40°26N 78°24W 354 F6
Hollis U.S.A. 34°41N 99°55W 356 D5
Hollister Calif., U.S.A. 36°51N 121°24W 350 J5
Hollister Idaho, U.S.A. 42°21N 114°35W 348 E6
Holly Hill U.S.A. 29°16N 81°3W 357 G14
Holly Springs U.S.A. 34°46N 89°27W 357 D10
Hollywood U.S.A. 26°0N 80°8W 357 J14
Holman Canada 70°44N 117°44W 340 B8
Hólmavík Iceland 65°42N 21°40W 280 D3
Holmen U.S.A. 43°58N 91°15W 352 D8
Holmes Reefs Australia 16°27S 148°0E 334 B4
Holmsund Sweden 63°41N 20°20E 280 E19
Holroyd → Australia 14°10S 141°36E 334 A3
Holstebro Denmark 56°22N 8°37E 281 H13
Holsworthy U.K. 50°48N 4°22W 285 G3
Holton Canada 54°31N 57°12W 345 B8
Holton U.S.A. 39°28N 95°44W 352 F6
Holtville U.S.A. 32°49N 115°23W 351 N11
Holwerd Neths. 53°22N 5°54E 287 A5
Holy I. Anglesey, U.K. 53°17N 4°37W 284 D3
Holy I. Northumberland, U.K. 55°40N 1°47W 284 B6
Holyhead U.K. 53°18N 4°38W 284 D3
Holyoke Colo., U.S.A. 40°35N 102°18W 348 F12
Holyoke Mass., U.S.A. 42°12N 72°37W 355 D12
Holyrood Canada 47°27N 53°8W 345 C9
Homa Bay Kenya 0°36S 34°30E 326 C3
Homalin Burma 24°55N 95°0E 313 G19
Homand Iran 32°28N 59°37E 317 C8
Homathko → Canada 51°0N 124°56W 342 C4
Hombori Mali 15°20N 1°38W 322 E5
Home B. Canada 68°40N 67°10W 341 C13
Home Hill Australia 19°43S 147°25E 334 B4
Home Reef Tonga 18°59S 174°47W 331 c
Homedale U.S.A. 43°37N 116°56W 348 E5
Homer Alaska, U.S.A. 59°39N 151°33W 346 a
Homer La., U.S.A. 32°48N 93°4W 356 E8
Homer City U.S.A. 40°32N 79°10W 354 F5
Homestead Australia 20°20S 145°40E 334 C4
Homestead U.S.A. 25°28N 80°29W 357 J14
Homestead ⌓ U.S.A. 40°17N 96°50W 352 E5
Homoine Mozam. 23°55S 35°8E 329 C6
Homs = Ḩimş Syria 34°40N 36°45E 318 A5
Homyel Belarus 52°28N 31°0E 289 B16
Hon Chong Vietnam 10°25N 104°30E 311 G5
Hon Hai Vietnam 10°0N 109°0E 311 G7
Hon Me Vietnam 19°23N 105°56E 310 C5
Honan = Henan □ China 34°0N 114°0E 306 H8
Honbetsu Japan 43°7N 143°37E 302 C11
Honcut U.S.A. 39°20N 121°32W 350 F5
Honda, Bahía Cuba 22°54N 83°10W 360 B3
Hondeklipbaai S. Africa 30°19S 17°17E 328 E2
Hondo Japan 32°27N 130°12E 303 H5
Hondo U.S.A. 29°21N 99°9W 356 G5
Hondo, Río → Belize 18°25N 88°21W 359 D7
Honduras ■ Cent. Amer. 14°40N 86°30W 360 D2
Honduras, G. de Caribbean 16°50N 87°0W 360 C2
Hønefoss Norway 60°10N 10°18E 281 F14
Honesdale U.S.A. 41°34N 75°16W 355 E9
Honey L. U.S.A. 40°15N 120°19W 350 E6
Honfleur France 49°25N 0°13E 292 B4
Hong → Vietnam 22°0N 104°0E 304 D5
Hong Gai Vietnam 20°57N 107°5E 310 B6
Hong He → China 32°25N 115°35E 306 H8
Hong Kong □ China 22°11N 114°14E 305 G11
Hong Kong I. China 22°16N 114°12E 305 G11
Hong Kong Int. ✕ (HKG) China 22°19N 113°57E 305 G10
Hongcheon S. Korea 37°44N 127°53E 307 F14
Hongjiang China 27°7N 109°59E 305 D5
Hongliu He → China 38°0N 109°50E 306 F5
Hongor Mongolia 45°45N 112°50E 306 B7
Hongsa Laos 19°43N 101°20E 310 C3
Hongseong S. Korea 36°37N 126°38E 307 F14
Hongshui He → China 23°48N 109°30E 305 D5
Hongtong China 36°16N 111°40E 306 F6
Honguedo, Détroit d' Canada 49°15N 64°0W 345 C7
Hongwon N. Korea 40°0N 127°56E 307 E14
Hongze Hu China 33°15N 118°35E 307 H10
Honiara Solomon Is. 9°27S 159°57E 330 B8
Honiton U.K. 50°47N 3°11W 285 G4
Honjō Japan 39°23N 140°3E 302 E10
Honningsvåg Norway 70°59N 25°59E 280 A21
Honolulu U.S.A. 21°19N 157°52W 346 b
Honshū Japan 36°0N 138°0E 305 C8
Hood, Mt. U.S.A. 45°23N 121°42W 348 D3
Hood, Pt. Australia 34°23S 119°34E 333 F2
Hood River U.S.A. 45°43N 121°31W 348 D3
Hoodsport U.S.A. 47°24N 123°9W 350 C3
Hoogeveen Neths. 52°44N 6°28E 287 B6
Hoogezand-Sappemeer Neths. 53°9N 6°45E 287 A6
Hooghly = Hugli → India 21°56N 88°4E 315 J13
Hooghly-Chinsura = Chunchura India 22°53N 88°27E 315 H13
Hook Hd. Ireland 52°7N 6°56W 282 D5
Hook I. Australia 20°4S 149°0E 334 J6
Hook of Holland = Hoek van Holland Neths. 52°0N 4°7E 287 C4
Hooker U.S.A. 36°52N 101°13W 356 C4
Hooker Creek = Lajamanu Australia 18°23S 130°38E 332 C5

Hoonah U.S.A. 58°7N 135°27W 342 B1
Hooper Bay U.S.A. 61°32N 166°6W 346 a
Hoopeston U.S.A. 40°28N 87°40W 352 E10
Hoopstad S. Africa 27°50S 25°55E 328 D4
Hoorn Neths. 52°38N 5°4E 287 B5
Hoover U.S.A. 33°24N 86°49W 357 E11
Hoover Dam U.S.A. 36°1N 114°44W 351 K12
Hooversville U.S.A. 40°9N 78°55W 354 F6
Hop Bottom U.S.A. 41°42N 75°46W 355 E9
Hope Canada 49°25N 121°25W 342 D4
Hope Ariz., U.S.A. 33°43N 113°42W 351 M13
Hope Ark., U.S.A. 33°40N 93°36W 356 E8
Hope, L. S. Austral., Australia 28°24S 139°18E 335 D2
Hope, L. W. Austral., Australia 32°35S 120°15E 333 F3
Hope, Pt. U.S.A. 68°21N 166°47W 338 C3
Hope I. Canada 44°55N 80°11W 354 B4
Hope Town Bahamas 26°35N 76°57W 360 A4
Hope Vale Australia 15°16S 145°20E 334 B4
Hopedale Canada 55°28N 60°13W 345 A7
Hopedale U.S.A. 42°8N 71°33W 355 D13
Hopefield S. Africa 33°3S 18°22E 328 E2
Hopei = Hebei □ China 39°0N 116°0E 306 E9
Hopelchén Mexico 19°46N 89°51W 359 D7
Hopetoun Vic., Australia 35°42S 142°22E 335 F3
Hopetoun W. Austral., Australia 33°57S 120°7E 333 F3
Hopetown S. Africa 29°34S 24°3E 328 D3
Hopewell U.S.A. 37°18N 77°17W 353 G15
Hopkins, L. Australia 24°15S 128°35E 332 D4
Hopkinsville U.S.A. 36°52N 87°29W 352 G10
Hopland U.S.A. 38°58N 123°7W 350 G3
Hoquiam U.S.A. 46°59N 123°53W 350 D3
Hordern Hills Australia 20°15S 130°0E 332 D5
Horinger China 40°28N 111°48E 306 D6
Horlick Mts. Antarctica 84°0S 102°0W 277 E15
Horlivka Ukraine 48°19N 38°5E 291 E6
Hormak Iran 29°58N 60°51E 317 D9
Hormoz Iran 27°35N 55°0E 317 E7
Hormoz, Jaz.-ye Iran 27°8N 56°28E 317 E8
Hormozgān □ Iran 27°30N 56°0E 317 E8
Hormuz, Kūh-e Iran 27°27N 55°10E 317 E7
Hormuz, Str. of The Gulf 26°30N 56°30E 317 E8
Horn Austria 48°39N 15°40E 288 D8
Horn → Canada 61°30N 118°1W 342 A5
Horn, Cape = Hornos, C. de Chile 55°50S 67°30W 368 H3
Horn Head Ireland 55°14N 8°0W 282 A3
Horn I. Australia 10°37S 142°17E 334 A3
Horn Plateau Canada 62°15N 119°15W 342 A5
Hornavan Sweden 66°15N 17°30E 280 C17
Hornbeck U.S.A. 31°20N 93°24W 356 F8
Hornbrook U.S.A. 41°55N 122°33W 348 F2
Horncastle U.K. 53°13N 0°7W 284 D7
Hornell U.S.A. 42°20N 77°40W 354 D7
Hornell L. Canada 62°20N 119°25W 342 A5
Hornepayne Canada 49°14N 84°48W 344 C3
Hornings Mills Canada 44°9N 80°12W 354 B4
Hornitos U.S.A. 37°30N 120°14W 350 H6
Hornos, C. de Chile 55°50S 67°30W 368 H3
Hornsea U.K. 53°55N 0°11W 284 D7
Horobetsu = Noboribetsu Japan 42°24N 141°6E 302 C10
Horodenka Ukraine 48°41N 25°29E 289 D13
Horodok Khmelnytskyy, Ukraine 49°10N 26°34E 289 D14
Horodok Lviv, Ukraine 49°46N 23°32E 289 D12
Horokhiv Ukraine 50°30N 24°45E 289 C13
Horqin Youyi Qianqi China 46°5N 122°3E 307 A12
Horqueta Paraguay 23°15S 56°55W 366 A4
Horse Cr. → U.S.A. 41°57N 103°58W 348 F12
Horse I. Canada 53°20N 99°6W 343 C9
Horse Is. Canada 50°15N 55°50W 345 B8
Horsefly L. Canada 52°25N 121°0W 342 C4
Horseheads U.S.A. 42°10N 76°49W 354 D8
Horsens Denmark 55°52N 9°51E 281 J13
Horsham Australia 36°44S 142°13E 335 F3
Horsham U.K. 51°4N 0°20W 285 F7
Horta Azores 38°32N 28°38W 322 a
Horten Norway 59°25N 10°32E 281 G14
Horton U.S.A. 39°40N 95°32W 352 F6
Horton → Canada 69°56N 126°52W 340 C7
Horwood L. Canada 48°5N 82°20W 344 C3
Ḥoseynābād Khuzestān, Iran 32°45N 48°20E 317 C6
Ḥoseynābād Kordestān, Iran 35°33N 47°8E 316 C5
Hoshangabad India 22°45N 77°45E 314 H7
Hoshiarpur India 31°30N 75°58E 314 D6
Hospet India 15°15N 76°20E 312 M10
Hoste, I. Chile 55°0S 69°0W 368 H3
Hot Thailand 18°8N 98°29E 310 C2
Hot Creek Range U.S.A. 38°40N 116°20W 348 G5
Hot Springs Ark., U.S.A. 34°31N 93°3W 356 D8
Hot Springs S. Dak., U.S.A. 43°26N 103°29W 352 D2
Hot Springs △ U.S.A. 34°31N 93°3W 356 D8
Hotagen Sweden 63°59N 14°12E 280 E16
Hotan China 37°25N 79°55E 304 C2
Hotazel S. Africa 27°17S 22°58E 328 D3
Hotchkiss U.S.A. 38°48N 107°43W 348 G10
Hotham, C. Australia 12°2S 131°18E 332 B5
Hoting Sweden 64°8N 16°15E 280 D17
Hotte, Massif de la Haiti 18°30N 73°45W 361 C5
Hottentotsbaai Namibia 26°8S 14°59E 328 D1
Hou Hai China 22°32N 113°56E 305 F10
Houei Sai Laos 20°18N 100°26E 310 B3
Houffalize Belgium 50°8N 5°48E 287 D5
Houghton Mich., U.S.A. 47°7N 88°34W 352 B9
Houghton N.Y., U.S.A. 42°25N 78°10W 354 D6
Houghton L. U.S.A. 44°21N 84°44W 353 C11
Houghton-le-Spring U.K. 54°51N 1°28W 284 C6
Houhora Heads N.Z. 34°49S 173°9E 331 A4
Houlton U.S.A. 46°8N 67°51W 353 B20
Houma U.S.A. 29°36N 90°43W 357 G9
Housatonic → U.S.A. 41°10N 73°7W 355 E11
Houston Canada 54°25N 126°39W 342 C3
Houston Mo., U.S.A. 37°22N 91°58W 352 G8
Houston Tex., U.S.A. 29°45N 95°21W 356 G7
Hout → S. Africa 23°4S 29°36E 329 C4
Houtkraal S. Africa 30°23S 24°5E 328 E3
Houtman Abrolhos Australia 28°43S 113°48E 333 E1
Hovd □ Mongolia 48°2N 91°37E 304 B4
Hove U.K. 50°50N 0°10W 285 G7
Hovenweep ⌂ U.S.A. 37°20N 109°0W 349 H9
Hoveyzeh Iran 31°27N 48°4E 317 D6
Hövsgöl Mongolia 43°37N 109°39E 306 C5
Hövsgöl Nuur Mongolia 51°0N 100°30E 304 A5
Howar, Wadi → Sudan 17°30N 27°8E 323 E11
Howard Australia 25°16S 152°32E 335 D5
Howard Pa., U.S.A. 41°1N 77°40W 354 F7
Howard S. Dak., U.S.A. 44°1N 97°32W 352 C5
Howe U.S.A. 43°48N 113°0W 348 E7
Howe, C. Australia 37°30S 150°0E 335 F5
Howe, West Cape Australia 35°8S 117°36E 333 G2
Howe I. Canada 44°16N 76°17W 355 B8
Howell U.S.A. 42°36N 83°56W 353 D12
Howick Canada 45°11N 73°51W 355 A11
Howick S. Africa 29°28S 30°14E 329 D5
Howick Group Australia 14°20S 145°30E 334 A4
Howitt, L. Australia 27°40S 138°40E 335 D2
Howland I. Pac. Oc. 0°48N 176°38W 336 G10
Howrah = Haora India 22°34N 88°18E 315 H13
Howth Ireland 53°23N 6°6W 282 C5
Howth Hd. Ireland 53°22N 6°4W 282 C5
Höxter Germany 51°46N 9°22E 288 C5
Hoy U.K. 58°50N 3°15W 283 C5
Høyanger Norway 61°13N 6°4E 280 F12
Hoyerswerda Germany 51°26N 14°14E 288 C8
Hoylake U.K. 53°24N 3°10W 284 D4
Hpa-an = Pa-an Burma 16°51N 97°40E 313 L20
Hpunan Pass Burma 27°30N 96°55E 313 F20
Hradec Králové Czech Rep. 50°15N 15°50E 288 C8
Hrodna Belarus 53°42N 23°52E 289 B12
Hrodzyanka Belarus 53°31N 28°42E 289 B15
Hron → Slovak Rep. 47°49N 18°45E 289 E10
Hrvatska = Croatia ■ Europe 45°20N 16°0E 288 F9
Hrymayliv Ukraine 49°20N 26°5E 289 D14
Hsenwi Burma 23°22N 97°55E 313 H20
Hsiamen = Xiamen China 24°25N 118°4E 305 D6
Hsian = Xi'an China 34°15N 109°0E 306 G5
Hsinchu Taiwan 24°48N 120°58E 305 D7
Hsinhailien = Lianyungang China 34°40N 119°11E 307 G10
Hsüchou = Xuzhou China 34°18N 117°10E 307 G9
Hu Xian China 34°8N 108°42E 306 G5
Hua Hin Thailand 12°34N 99°58E 310 F2
Hua Xian Henan, China 35°30N 114°30E 306 G8
Hua Xian Shaanxi, China 34°30N 109°48E 306 G5
Huab → Namibia 20°52S 13°25E 328 B2
Huachinera Mexico 30°9N 108°55W 358 A3
Huacho Peru 11°10S 77°35W 364 F3
Huade China 41°55N 113°59E 306 D7
Huadian China 43°0N 126°40E 307 C14
Huahine, Î. French Polynesia 16°46S 150°58W 337 J12
Huai Had △ Thailand 16°52N 104°17E 310 D5
Huai He → China 33°0N 118°30E 305 C6
Huai Nam Dang △ Thailand 19°30N 98°30E 310 C2
Huai Yot Thailand 7°45N 99°37E 311 J2
Huai'an Hebei, China 40°30N 114°20E 306 D8
Huai'an Jiangsu, China 33°30N 119°10E 307 H10
Huaibei China 34°0N 116°48E 306 G9
Huaide = Gongzhuling China 43°30N 124°40E 307 C13
Huaidezhen China 43°48N 124°50E 307 C13
Huainan China 32°38N 116°58E 305 C6
Huairen China 39°48N 113°20E 306 E7
Huairou China 40°20N 116°35E 306 D9
Huaiyang China 33°40N 114°52E 306 H8
Huaiyin China 33°30N 119°2E 307 H10
Huaiyuan China 32°55N 117°10E 307 H9
Huajuapán de León Mexico 17°48N 97°46W 359 D5
Hualapai Peak U.S.A. 35°5N 113°54W 349 J7
Huallaga → Peru 5°15S 75°30W 364 E3
Huambo Angola 12°42S 15°54E 325 G3
Huan Jiang → China 34°28N 109°0E 306 G5
Huan Xian China 36°33N 107°7E 306 F4
Huancabamba Peru 5°10S 79°15W 364 E3
Huancane Peru 15°10S 69°44W 364 G5
Huancavelica Peru 12°50S 75°5W 364 F3
Huancayo Peru 12°5S 75°12W 364 F3
Huanchaca Bolivia 20°15S 66°40W 364 H5
Huang Hai = Yellow Sea China 35°0N 123°0E 307 G12
Huang He → China 37°55N 118°50E 307 F10
Huang Xian China 37°38N 120°30E 307 F11
Huangling China 35°34N 109°15E 306 G5
Huanglong China 35°30N 109°59E 306 G5
Huangshan China 29°42N 118°25E 305 D6
Huangshi China 30°10N 115°3E 305 C6
Huangsongdian China 43°45N 127°25E 307 C14
Huanren China 41°23N 125°20E 307 D13
Huantai China 36°58N 117°56E 307 F9
Huánuco Peru 9°55S 76°15W 364 E3
Huaraz Peru 9°30S 77°32W 364 E3
Huarmey Peru 10°5S 78°5W 364 F3
Huascarán, Nevado Peru 9°7S 77°37W 364 E3
Huasco Chile 28°30S 71°15W 366 B1
Huasco → Chile 28°27S 71°13W 366 B1
Huasna U.S.A. 35°6N 120°24W 351 K6
Huatabampo Mexico 26°50N 109°38W 358 B3
Huauchinango Mexico 20°12N 98°3W 359 C5
Huautla de Jiménez Mexico 18°8N 96°51W 359 D5
Huayin China 34°35N 110°5E 306 G6
Hubbard Ohio, U.S.A. 41°9N 80°34W 354 E4
Hubbard Tex., U.S.A. 31°51N 96°48W 356 F6
Hubbart Pt. Canada 59°21N 94°41W 343 B10
Hubei □ China 31°0N 112°0E 305 C6
Hubli India 15°22N 75°15E 312 M9
Huch'ang N. Korea 41°25N 127°2E 307 D14
Hucknall U.K. 53°3N 1°13W 284 D6
Huddersfield U.K. 53°39N 1°47W 284 D6
Hudiksvall Sweden 61°43N 17°10E 280 F17
Hudson Canada 50°6N 92°9W 344 B1
Hudson Mass., U.S.A. 42°23N 71°34W 355 D13
Hudson N.Y., U.S.A. 42°15N 73°46W 355 D11
Hudson Wis., U.S.A. 44°58N 92°45W 352 C7
Hudson Wyo., U.S.A. 42°54N 108°35W 348 E9
Hudson → U.S.A. 40°42N 74°2W 355 F10
Hudson, C. Antarctica 68°21S 153°45E 277 C20
Hudson Bay Nunavut, Canada 60°0N 86°0W 341 D11
Hudson Bay Sask., Canada 52°51N 102°23W 343 C8
Hudson Falls U.S.A. 43°18N 73°35W 355 C11
Hudson Mts. Antarctica 74°32S 99°20W 277 D16
Hudson Str. Canada 62°0N 70°0W 341 C13
Hudson's Hope Canada 56°0N 121°54W 342 B4
Hue Vietnam 16°30N 107°35E 310 D6
Huehuetenango Guatemala 15°20N 91°28W 360 C1
Huejúcar Mexico 22°21N 103°13W 358 C4
Huelva Spain 37°18N 6°57W 293 D2
Huentelauquén Chile 31°38S 71°33W 366 C1
Huerta, Sa. de la Argentina 31°10S 67°30W 366 C2
Huesca Spain 42°8N 0°25W 293 A5
Huetamo Mexico 18°35N 100°53W 358 D4
Hugh → Australia 25°1S 134°1E 334 D1
Hughenden Australia 20°52S 144°10E 334 C3
Hughesville U.S.A. 41°14N 76°44W 355 E8
Hugli → India 21°56N 88°4E 315 J13
Hugo Colo., U.S.A. 39°8N 103°28W 348 G12
Hugo Okla., U.S.A. 34°1N 95°31W 356 D7
Hugoton U.S.A. 37°11N 101°21W 352 G3
Hui Xian = Huixian China 35°27N 113°12E 306 G7
Hui Xian China 33°50N 106°4E 306 H4
Hui'anbu China 37°28N 106°38E 306 F4
Huichapan Mexico 20°23N 99°39W 359 C5
Huichon N. Korea 40°10N 126°16E 307 D14
Huifa He → China 43°0N 127°50E 307 C14
Huila, Nevado del Colombia 3°0N 76°0W 364 C3
Huimin China 37°27N 117°28E 307 F9
Huinan China 42°40N 126°2E 307 C14
Huinca Renancó Argentina 34°51S 64°22W 366 C3
Huining China 35°38N 105°0E 306 G3
Huinong China 39°5N 106°35E 306 E4
Huiting China 34°5N 116°5E 306 G9
Huixian China 35°27N 113°12E 306 G7
Huixtla Mexico 15°9N 92°28W 359 D6
Huize China 26°24N 103°15E 304 D5
Hukawng Valley Burma 26°30N 96°30E 313 F20
Hukuntsi Botswana 23°58S 21°45E 328 C3
Ḥulayfā' Si. Arabia 25°58N 40°45E 316 E4
Hulin He → China 45°0N 122°10E 307 B12
Hull = Kingston upon Hull U.K. 53°45N 0°21W 284 D7
Hull Canada 45°26N 75°43W 355 A9
Hull → U.K. 53°44N 0°20W 284 D7
Hulst Neths. 51°17N 4°2E 287 C4
Hulun Nur China 49°0N 117°30E 305 B6
Huma, Tanjung Malaysia 5°29N 100°16E 311 c
Humacao Puerto Rico 18°9N 65°50W 361 d
Humahuaca Argentina 23°10S 65°25W 366 A2
Humaitá Brazil 7°35S 63°1W 364 E6
Humaitá Paraguay 27°2S 58°31W 366 B4
Humansdorp S. Africa 34°2S 24°46E 328 E3
Humbe Angola 16°40S 14°55E 328 B1
Humber → U.K. 53°42N 0°27W 284 D7
Humboldt Canada 52°15N 105°9W 343 C7
Humboldt Iowa, U.S.A. 42°44N 94°13W 352 D6
Humboldt Tenn., U.S.A. 35°50N 88°55W 357 D10
Humboldt → U.S.A. 39°59N 118°36W 348 G4
Humboldt Gletscher = Sermersuaq Greenland 79°30N 62°0W 276 B4
Hume U.S.A. 36°48N 118°54W 350 J8
Hume, L. Australia 36°0S 147°5E 335 F4
Humen China 22°50N 113°40E 305 F10
Humenné Slovak Rep. 48°55N 21°50E 289 D11
Humphreys, Mt. U.S.A. 37°17N 118°40W 350 H8
Humphreys Peak U.S.A. 35°21N 111°41W 349 J8
Humptulips U.S.A. 47°14N 123°57W 350 C3
Hūn Libya 29°2N 16°0E 323 C9
Hun Jiang → China 40°50N 125°38E 307 D13
Húnaflói Iceland 65°50N 20°50W 280 D3
Hunan □ China 27°30N 112°0E 305 D6
Hunchun China 42°52N 130°28E 307 C16
Hundewali Pakistan 31°55N 72°38E 314 D5
Hundred Mile House Canada 51°38N 121°18W 342 C4
Hunedoara Romania 45°40N 22°50E 289 F12
Hung Yen Vietnam 20°39N 106°4E 310 B6
Hunga Ha'apai Tonga 20°41S 175°7W 331 c
Hungary ■ Europe 47°20N 19°20E 289 E10
Hungary, Plain of Europe 47°0N 20°0E 278 F10
Hungerford Australia 28°58S 144°24E 335 D3
Hŭngnam N. Korea 39°49N 127°45E 307 E14
Hunjiang China 41°54N 126°26E 307 D14
Hunsberge Namibia 27°45S 17°12E 328 D2
Hunsrück Germany 49°56N 7°27E 288 D4
Hunstanton U.K. 52°56N 0°29E 284 E8
Hunter U.S.A. 42°13N 74°13W 355 D10
Hunter I. Australia 40°30S 144°45E 335 G3
Hunter I. Canada 51°55N 128°0W 342 C3
Hunter Ra. Australia 32°45S 150°15E 335 E5
Hunters Road Zimbabwe 19°9S 29°49E 327 F2
Hunterville N.Z. 39°56S 175°35E 331 C5
Huntingburg U.S.A. 38°18N 86°57W 352 F10
Huntingdon Canada 45°6N 74°10W 344 C5
Huntingdon U.K. 52°20N 0°11W 285 E7
Huntingdon U.S.A. 40°30N 78°1W 354 F6
Huntington Ind., U.S.A. 40°53N 85°30W 353 E11
Huntington N.Y., U.S.A. 40°52N 73°26W 355 F11
Huntington Oreg., U.S.A. 44°21N 117°16W 348 D5
Huntington Utah, U.S.A. 39°20N 110°58W 348 G8
Huntington W. Va., U.S.A. 38°25N 82°27W 353 F12
Huntington Beach U.S.A. 33°40N 118°5W 351 M9
Huntly N.Z. 37°34S 175°11E 331 B5
Huntly U.K. 57°27N 2°47W 283 D6
Huntsville Canada 45°20N 79°14W 354 A5
Huntsville Ala., U.S.A. 34°44N 86°35W 357 D11
Huntsville Tex., U.S.A. 30°43N 95°33W 356 F7
Hunyani → Zimbabwe 15°57S 30°39E 327 F3
Hunyuan China 39°42N 113°42E 306 E7
Hunza → India 35°54N 74°20E 315 B6
Huo Xian = Huozhou China 36°36N 111°42E 306 F6
Huong Khe Vietnam 18°13N 105°41E 310 C5
Huonville Australia 43°0S 147°5E 335 G4
Huozhou China 36°36N 111°42E 306 F6
Hupeh = Hubei □ China 31°0N 112°0E 305 C6
Ḥūr Iran 30°50N 57°7E 317 D8
Ḥuraymīla Si. Arabia 25°8N 46°8E 316 E5
Hurd, C. Canada 45°13N 81°44W 354 A3
Hure Qi China 42°45N 121°45E 307 C11
Hurghada Egypt 27°15N 33°50E 323 C12
Hurley N. Mex., U.S.A. 32°42N 108°8W 349 K9
Hurley Wis., U.S.A. 46°27N 90°11W 352 B8
Huron Calif., U.S.A. 36°12N 120°6W 350 J6
Huron Ohio, U.S.A. 41°24N 82°33W 354 E2
Huron S. Dak., U.S.A. 44°22N 98°13W 352 C4
Huron, L. U.S.A. 44°30N 82°40W 354 B2
Huron East Canada 43°37N 81°18W 354 C3
Hurricane U.S.A. 37°11N 113°17W 349 H7
Hurungwe ⌂ Zimbabwe 16°7S 29°5E 327 F2
Hurunui → N.Z. 42°54S 173°18E 331 E4
Húsavík Iceland 66°3N 17°21W 280 C5
Huşi Romania 46°41N 28°7E 289 E15
Hustadvika Norway 63°0N 7°0E 280 E12
Hustontown U.S.A. 40°3N 78°2W 354 F6
Hutchinson Kans., U.S.A. 38°5N 97°56W 352 F5
Hutchinson Minn., U.S.A. 44°54N 94°22W 352 C6
Hutte Sauvage, L. de la Canada 56°15N 64°45W 345 A7
Hutton, Mt. Australia 25°51S 148°20E 335 D4
Huy Belgium 50°31N 5°15E 287 D5
Huzhou China 30°51N 120°8E 305 C7
Hvammstangi Iceland 65°24N 20°57W 280 D3
Hvar Croatia 43°11N 16°28E 294 C7
Hvítá → Iceland 64°30N 21°58W 280 D3
Hwacheon-Cheosuji S. Korea 38°5N 127°50E 307 E14
Hwang Ho = Huang He → China 37°55N 118°50E 307 F10
Hwange Zimbabwe 18°18S 26°30E 327 F2
Hwange △ Zimbabwe 19°0S 26°30E 328 B4
Hyannis Mass., U.S.A. 41°39N 70°17W 353 E18
Hyannis Nebr., U.S.A. 42°0N 101°46W 352 E3
Hyargas Nuur Mongolia 49°0N 93°0E 304 B4
Hydaburg U.S.A. 55°15N 132°50W 342 B2
Hyde Park U.S.A. 41°47N 73°56W 355 E11
Hyden Australia 32°24S 118°53E 333 F2
Hyder U.S.A. 55°55N 130°5W 342 B2
Hyderabad India 17°22N 78°29E 312 L11
Hyderabad Pakistan 25°23N 68°24E 314 G3
Hydra Greece 37°20N 23°28E 295 D10
Hyères France 43°8N 6°9E 292 E7
Hyères, Îs. d' France 43°0N 6°20E 292 E7
Hyesan N. Korea 41°20N 128°10E 307 D15
Hyland → Canada 59°52N 128°12W 342 B3
Hymia India 33°40N 78°2E 315 C8
Hyndman Peak U.S.A. 43°45N 114°8W 348 E6
Hyōgo □ Japan 35°15N 134°50E 303 G7
Hyrum U.S.A. 41°38N 111°51W 348 F8
Hysham U.S.A. 46°18N 107°14W 348 C10
Hythe U.K. 51°4N 1°5E 285 F9
Hyūga Japan 32°25N 131°35E 303 H5
Hyvinge = Hyvinkää Finland 60°38N 24°50E 280 F21
Hyvinkää Finland 60°38N 24°50E 280 F21

I

I-n-Gall Niger 16°51N 7°1E 322 E7
Iaco → Brazil 9°3S 68°34W 364 E5
Iakora Madag. 23°6S 46°40E 329 C8
Ialomiţa → Romania 44°42N 27°51E 289 F14
Iaşi Romania 47°10N 27°40E 289 E14
Ib → India 21°34N 83°48E 315 J10
Iba Phil. 15°22N 120°0E 309 A6
Ibadan Nigeria 7°22N 3°58E 322 G6
Ibagué Colombia 4°20N 75°20W 364 C3
Ibar → Serbia 43°43N 20°45E 295 C9
Ibaraki □ Japan 36°10N 140°10E 303 F10
Ibarra Ecuador 0°21N 78°7W 364 C3
Ibb Yemen 14°2N 44°10E 319 E3
Ibembo Dem. Rep. of the Congo 2°35N 23°35E 326 B1
Ibenga → Congo 2°19N 18°9E 324 D3
Ibera, L. Argentina 28°30S 57°9W 366 B4
Iberian Peninsula Europe 40°0N 5°0W 278 H5
Iberville Canada 45°19N 73°17W 355 A11
Iberville, Lac d' Canada 55°55N 73°15W 344 A5
Ibiá Brazil 19°30S 46°30W 365 G9
Ibiapaba, Sa. da Brazil 4°0S 41°30W 365 D10
Ibicuí → Brazil 29°25S 56°47W 367 B4
Ibicuy Argentina 33°55S 59°10W 366 C4
Ibiza = Eivissa Spain 38°54N 1°26E 296 C7
Ibo Mozam. 12°22S 40°40E 327 E5
Ibonma Indonesia 3°29S 133°31E 309 E8
Ibotirama Brazil 12°13S 43°12W 365 F10
Ibrāhīm → Lebanon 34°4N 35°38E 318 A4
'Ibrī Oman 23°14N 56°30E 317 F8
Ibu Indonesia 1°35N 127°33E 309 D7
Ibusuki Japan 31°12N 130°40E 303 J5
Ica Peru 14°0S 75°48W 364 F3
Iça → Brazil 2°55S 67°58W 364 D5
Icacos Pt. Trin. & Tob. 10°3N 61°57W 365 K15
Içana Brazil 0°21N 67°19W 364 C5
Içana → Brazil 0°26N 67°19W 364 C5
İçel Turkey 36°51N 34°36E 316 B2
Iceland ■ Europe 64°45N 19°0W 280 D4
Iceland Basin Atl. Oc. 61°0N 19°0W 276 C7
Icelandic Plateau Arctic 64°0N 10°0W 276 C7
Ich'ang = Yichang China 30°40N 111°20E 305 C6
Ichchapuram India 19°10N 84°40E 313 K14
Icheon S. Korea 37°17N 127°27E 307 F14
Ichhawar India 23°1N 77°1E 314 H7
Ichihara Japan 35°28N 140°5E 303 G10
Ichikawa Japan 35°43N 139°54E 303 G9
Ichilo → Bolivia 15°57S 64°50W 364 G6
Ichinohe Japan 40°13N 141°17E 302 D10
Ichinomiya Japan 35°18N 136°48E 303 G8
Ichinoseki Japan 38°55N 141°8E 302 E10
Icod Canary Is. 28°22N 16°43W 296 F3
Icy C. U.S.A. 70°20N 161°52W 338 B3
Ida Grove U.S.A. 42°21N 95°28W 352 D6
Idabel U.S.A. 33°54N 94°50W 356 E7
Idaho □ U.S.A. 45°0N 115°0W 348 D6
Idaho City U.S.A. 43°50N 115°50W 348 E6
Idaho Falls U.S.A. 43°30N 112°2W 348 E7
Idalia △ Australia 24°49S 144°36E 334 C3
Idar-Oberstein Germany 49°43N 7°16E 288 D4
Idensalmi = Iisalmi Finland 63°32N 27°10E 280 E22
Idfû Egypt 24°55N 32°49E 323 D12
Ídhra = Hydra Greece 37°20N 23°28E 295 F10
Idi Indonesia 5°2N 97°37E 308 C1
Idi, Oros = Psiloritis, Oros Greece 35°15N 24°45E 297 D6
Idiofa Dem. Rep. of the Congo 4°55S 19°42E 324 E3
Idlib Syria 35°55N 36°36E 316 C3
Idria U.S.A. 36°25N 120°41W 350 J6
Idutywa = Dutywa S. Africa 32°8S 28°18E 329 E4
Ieper Belgium 50°51N 2°53E 287 D2
Ierapetra Greece 35°1N 25°44E 297 E7
Iesi Italy 43°31N 13°14E 294 C5
Ifakara Tanzania 8°8S 36°41E 324 F7
'Ifāl, W. al → Si. Arabia 28°7N 35°3E 316 D2
Ifanadiana Madag. 21°19S 47°39E 329 C8
Ife Nigeria 7°30N 4°31E 322 G6
Iffley Australia 18°53S 141°12E 334 B3
Iforas, Adrar des Africa 19°40N 1°40E 322 E6
Ifould, L. Australia 30°52S 132°6E 333 F5
Iganga Uganda 0°37N 33°28E 326 B3
Igarapava Brazil 20°3S 47°47W 365 H9
Igarka Russia 67°30N 86°33E 300 C9
Igatimi Paraguay 24°5S 55°40W 367 A4
Iggesund Sweden 61°39N 17°10E 280 F17
Iglésias Italy 39°19N 8°32E 294 E3
Igloolik Canada 69°20N 81°49W 341 C11
Igluligaarjuk = Chesterfield Inlet Canada 63°30N 90°45W 340 C10
Iglulik = Igloolik Canada 69°20N 81°49W 341 C11
Ignace Canada 49°30N 91°40W 344 C1
İğneada Burnu Turkey 41°53N 28°2E 295 D13
Igoumenitsa Greece 39°32N 20°18E 295 E9
Iguaçu → Brazil 25°36S 54°36W 367 B5
Iguaçu, Cat. del Brazil 25°41S 54°26W 367 B5
Iguaçu △ Brazil 25°30S 54°0W 367 B5
Iguaçu Falls = Iguaçu, Cat. del Brazil 25°41S 54°26W 367 B5
Iguala Mexico 18°21N 99°32W 359 D5
Igualada Spain 41°37N 1°37E 293 B6
Iguassu = Iguaçu → Brazil 25°36S 54°36W 367 B5
Iguatu Brazil 6°20S 39°18W 365 E11
Iguazú △ Argentina 25°42S 54°22W 367 B5
Iguidi, Erg Africa 27°0N 7°0W 322 C4
Iharana Madag. 13°25S 50°0E 329 A9
Ihbulag Mongolia 43°11N 107°10E 306 C4
Iheya-Shima Japan 27°4N 127°58E 303 L3
Ihosy Madag. 22°24S 46°8E 329 C8
Ihotry, Farihy Madag. 21°56S 43°41E 329 C7
Ii Finland 65°19N 25°22E 280 D21
Ii-Shima Japan 26°43N 127°47E 303 L3
Iida Japan 35°35N 137°50E 303 G8
Iijoki → Finland 65°20N 25°20E 280 D21
Iisalmi Finland 63°32N 27°10E 280 E22
Iiyama Japan 36°51N 138°22E 303 F9
Iizuka Japan 33°38N 130°42E 303 H5
Ijâfene Mauritania 20°40N 8°0W 322 D4
Ijebu-Ode Nigeria 6°47N 3°58E 322 G6
IJmuiden Neths. 52°28N 4°35E 287 B4
Ijo älv = Iijoki → Finland 65°20N 25°20E 280 D21
IJssel → Neths. 52°35N 5°50E 287 B5
IJsselmeer Neths. 52°45N 5°20E 287 B5

Kandangan *Indonesia* 2°50S 115°20E **308** E5
Kandanghaur *Indonesia* 6°21S 108°6E **309** G13
Kandanos *Greece* 35°19N 23°44E **297** D5
Kandavu = Kadavu *Fiji* 19°0S 178°15E **331** a
Kandavu Passage = Kadavu Passage *Fiji* 18°45S 178°0E **331** a
Kandhkot *Pakistan* 28°16N 69°8E **314** E3
Kandhla *India* 29°18N 77°19E **314** E7
Kandi *Benin* 11°7N 2°55E **322** F6
Kandi *India* 23°58N 88°5E **315** H13
Kandiaro *Pakistan* 27°4N 68°13E **314** F3
Kandla *India* 23°0N 70°10E **314** H4
Kandos *Australia* 32°45S 149°58E **335** E4
Kandreho *Madag.* 17°29S 46°6E **329** B8
Kandy *Sri Lanka* 7°18N 80°43E **312** R12
Kane *U.S.A.* 41°40N 78°49W **354** E6
Kane Basin *Greenland* 79°1N 70°0W **338** B12
Kāne'ohe *U.S.A.* 21°25N 157°48W **346** b
Kang *Botswana* 23°41S 22°50E **328** C3
Kang Krung △ *Thailand* 9°30N 98°50E **311** H2
Kangān *Fārs, Iran* 27°50N 52°3E **317** E7
Kangān *Hormozgān, Iran* 25°48N 57°28E **317** E8
Kangar *Malaysia* 6°27N 100°12E **311** J3
Kangaroo I. *Australia* 35°45S 137°0E **335** F2
Kangaroo Mts. *Australia* 23°29S 141°51E **334** C3
Kangasala *Finland* 61°28N 24°4E **280** F21
Kangāvar *Iran* 34°40N 48°0E **317** C6
Kangdong *N. Korea* 39°9N 126°5E **307** E14
Kangean, Kepulauan *Indonesia* 6°55S 115°23E **308** F5
Kangean Is. = Kangean, Kepulauan *Indonesia* 6°55S 115°23E **308** F5
Kanggye *N. Korea* 41°0N 126°35E **307** D14
Kangikajik *Greenland* 70°7N 22°0W **276** B6
Kangiqliniq = Rankin Inlet *Canada* 62°30N 93°0W **340** C10
Kangiqsualujjuaq *Canada* 58°30N 65°59W **341** D13
Kangiqsujuaq *Canada* 61°30N 72°0W **341** C12
Kangiqtugaapik = Clyde River *Canada* 70°30N 68°30W **341** B13
Kangirsuk *Canada* 60°0N 70°0W **341** D13
Kangkar Chemaran *Malaysia* 1°34N 104°12E **311** d
Kangkar Sungai Tiram *Malaysia* 1°35N 103°55E **311** d
Kangkar Teberau *Malaysia* 1°32N 103°51E **311** d
Kangping *China* 42°43N 123°18E **307** C12
Kangra *India* 32°6N 76°16E **314** C7
Kangrinboqe Feng *China* 31°0N 81°25E **315** D9
Kangto *China* 27°50N 92°35E **313** F18
Kanha △ *India* 22°15N 80°40E **315** H9
Kanhar → *India* 24°28N 83°8E **315** G10
Kaniama *Dem. Rep. of the Congo* 7°30S 24°12E **326** D1
Kaniapiskau = Caniapiscau → *Canada* 56°40N 69°30W **345** A6
Kaniapiskau, L. = Caniapiscau, L. *Canada* 54°10N 69°55W **345** B6
Kanin, Poluostrov *Russia* 68°0N 45°0E **290** A8
Kanin Nos, Mys *Russia* 68°39N 43°32E **290** A7
Kanin Pen. = Kanin, Poluostrov *Russia* 68°0N 45°0E **290** A8
Kaniva *Australia* 36°22S 141°18E **335** F3
Kanjut Sar *Pakistan* 36°7N 75°25E **315** A6
Kankaanpää *Finland* 61°44N 22°50E **280** F20
Kankakee *U.S.A.* 41°7N 87°52W **352** E10
Kankakee → *U.S.A.* 41°23N 88°15W **352** E9
Kankan *Guinea* 10°23N 9°15W **322** F4
Kankendy = Xankändi *Azerbaijan* 39°52N 46°49E **316** B5
Kanker *India* 20°10N 81°40E **313** J12
Kankroli *India* 25°4N 73°53E **314** G5
Kannapolis *U.S.A.* 35°30N 80°37W **357** D14
Kannauj *India* 27°3N 79°56E **315** F8
Kannod *India* 22°45N 76°40E **312** H10
Kano *Nigeria* 12°2N 8°30E **322** F7
Kan'onji *Japan* 34°7N 133°39E **303** G6
Kanowit *Malaysia* 2°14N 112°20E **308** D4
Kanoya *Japan* 31°25N 130°50E **303** J5
Kanpetlet *Burma* 21°10N 93°59E **313** J18
Kanpur *India* 26°28N 80°20E **315** F9
Kansas □ *U.S.A.* 38°30N 99°0W **352** F4
Kansas → *U.S.A.* 39°7N 94°37W **352** F6
Kansas City *Kans., U.S.A.* 39°7N 94°38W **352** F6
Kansas City *Mo., U.S.A.* 39°6N 94°35W **352** F6
Kansenia *Dem. Rep. of the Congo* 10°20S 26°0E **327** E2
Kansk *Russia* 56°20N 95°37E **301** D10
Kansu = Gansu □ *China* 36°0N 104°0E **306** G3
Kantaphor *India* 22°35N 76°34E **314** H7
Kantharalak *Thailand* 14°39N 104°39E **310** E5
Kantli → *India* 28°20N 75°30E **314** E6
Kantō □ *Japan* 36°15N 139°30E **303** F9
Kantō-Sanchi *Japan* 35°59N 138°50E **303** G9
Kanturk *Ireland* 52°11N 8°54W **282** D3
Kanuma *Japan* 36°34N 139°42E **303** F9
Kanus *Namibia* 27°50S 18°39E **328** D2
Kanye *Botswana* 24°55S 25°28E **328** C4
Kanzenze *Dem. Rep. of the Congo* 10°30S 25°12E **327** E2
Kanzi, Ras *Tanzania* 7°1S 39°33E **326** D4
Kao *Tonga* 19°40S 175°1W **331** c
Kao Phara *Thailand* 8°3N 98°22E **311** a
Kaohsiung *Taiwan* 22°35N 120°16E **305** D7
Kaokoveld *Namibia* 19°15S 14°30E **328** B1
Kaolack *Senegal* 14°5N 16°8W **322** F2
Kaoshan *China* 44°38N 124°50E **307** B13
Kapaa *U.S.A.* 22°5N 159°19W **346** b
Kapadvanj *India* 23°5N 73°0E **314** H5
Kapan *Armenia* 39°18N 46°27E **316** B5
Kapanga *Dem. Rep. of the Congo* 8°30S 22°40E **324** F4
Kapchagai = Qapshaghay *Kazakhstan* 43°51N 77°14E **300** E8
Kapedo *Kenya* 1°10N 36°6E **326** B4
Kapela = Velika Kapela *Croatia* 45°10N 15°5E **288** F8
Kapema *Dem. Rep. of the Congo* 10°45S 28°22E **327** E2
Kapenguria *Kenya* 1°14N 35°7E **326** B4
Kapfenberg *Austria* 47°26N 15°18E **288** E8
Kapiri Mposhi *Zambia* 13°59S 28°43E **327** E2
Kāpīsā □ *Afghan.* 35°0N 69°20E **312** B6
Kapiskau → *Canada* 52°47N 81°55W **344** B3
Kapit *Malaysia* 2°0N 112°55E **308** D4
Kapiti I. *N.Z.* 40°50S 174°56E **331** D5
Kaplan *U.S.A.* 30°0N 92°17W **356** F8
Kapoe *Thailand* 9°34N 98°32E **311** H2
Kapoeta *Sudan* 4°50N 33°35E **323** H12
Kaposvár *Hungary* 46°25N 17°47E **289** E9
Kapowsin *U.S.A.* 46°59N 122°13W **350** D4
Kapps *Namibia* 22°32S 17°18E **328** C2
Kapsabet *Kenya* 0°12N 35°6E **326** B4
Kapsan *N. Korea* 41°4N 128°19E **307** D15
Kapsukas = Marijampolė *Lithuania* 54°33N 23°19E **281** J20
Kaptai L. *Bangla.* 22°40N 92°20E **313** H18
Kapuas → *Indonesia* 0°25S 109°20E **308** E3
Kapuas Hulu, Pegunungan *Malaysia* 1°30N 113°30E **308** D4
Kapuas Hulu Ra. = Kapuas Hulu, Pegunungan *Malaysia* 1°30N 113°30E **308** D4
Kapulo *Dem. Rep. of the Congo* 8°18S 29°15E **327** D2
Kapunda *Australia* 34°20S 138°56E **335** E2
Kapuni *N.Z.* 39°29S 174°8E **331** C5
Kapurthala *India* 31°23N 75°25E **314** D6
Kapuskasing *Canada* 49°25N 82°30W **344** C3
Kapuskasing → *Canada* 49°49N 82°0W **344** C3
Kaputar, Mt. *Australia* 30°15S 150°10E **335** E5
Kaputir *Kenya* 2°5N 35°28E **326** B4
Kara *Russia* 69°10N 65°0E **300** C7
Kara Bogaz Gol, Zaliv = Garabogazköl Aylagy *Turkmenistan* 41°0N 53°30E **291** F9
Kara-Kala = Garrygala *Turkmenistan* 38°31N 56°29E **317** B8
Kara Kalpak Republic = Qoraqalpoghistan □ *Uzbekistan* 43°0N 58°0E **300** E6
Kara Kum = Garagum *Turkmenistan* 39°30N 60°0E **317** B8
Kara Sea *Russia* 75°0N 70°0E **300** B7
Karabiğa *Turkey* 40°23N 27°17E **295** D12
Karabük *Turkey* 41°12N 32°37E **291** F5
Karaburun *Turkey* 38°41N 26°28E **295** E12
Karabutak = Qarabutaq *Kazakhstan* 49°59N 60°14E **300** E7
Karacabey *Turkey* 40°12N 28°21E **295** D13
Karacasu *Turkey* 37°43N 28°35E **295** F13
Karachey-Cherkessia □ *Russia* 43°40N 41°30E **291** F7
Karachi *Pakistan* 24°50N 67°0E **314** G2
Karad *India* 17°15N 74°10E **312** L9
Karaganda = Qaraghandy *Kazakhstan* 49°50N 73°10E **300** E8
Karagayly = Qaraghayly *Kazakhstan* 49°26N 76°0E **300** E8
Karaginskiy, Ostrov *Russia* 58°45N 164°0E **301** D17
Karagiye, Vpadina *Kazakhstan* 43°27N 51°45E **291** F9
Karagiye Depression = Karagiye, Vpadina *Kazakhstan* 43°27N 51°45E **291** F9
Karagola Road *India* 25°29N 87°23E **315** G12
Karaikal *India* 10°59N 79°50E **312** P11
Karaikkudi *India* 10°5N 78°45E **312** P11
Karaj *Iran* 35°48N 51°0E **317** C6
Karak *Malaysia* 3°25N 102°2E **311** L4
Karakalpakstan = Qoraqalpoghistan □ *Uzbekistan* 43°0N 58°0E **300** E6
Karakelong *Indonesia* 4°35N 126°50E **309** D7
Karakitang *Indonesia* 3°14N 125°28E **309** D7
Karakol *Kyrgyzstan* 42°30N 78°20E **300** E8
Karakoram Pass *Asia* 35°33N 77°50E **315** B7
Karakoram Ra. *Pakistan* 35°30N 77°0E **315** B7
Karakuwisa *Namibia* 18°56S 19°40E **328** B2
Karalon *Russia* 57°5N 115°50E **301** D12
Karama *Jordan* 31°57N 35°35E **318** D4
Karaman *Turkey* 37°14N 33°13E **316** B2
Karamay *China* 45°30N 84°58E **304** B3
Karambu *Indonesia* 3°53S 116°6E **308** E5
Karamea Bight *N.Z.* 41°22S 171°40E **331** D3
Karamnasa → *India* 25°31N 83°52E **315** G10
Karān *Si. Arabia* 27°43N 49°49E **317** E6
Karand *Iran* 34°16N 46°15E **316** C5
Karanganyar *Indonesia* 7°38S 109°37E **309** G13
Karangasem *Indonesia* 8°27S 115°37E **309** J18
Karanjia *India* 21°47N 85°58E **315** J11
Karasburg *Namibia* 28°0S 18°44E **328** D2
Karasino *Russia* 66°50N 86°50E **300** C9
Karasjok *Norway* 69°27N 25°30E **280** B21
Karasuk *Russia* 53°44N 78°2E **300** D8
Karasuyama *Japan* 36°39N 140°9E **303** F10
Karatau, Khrebet = Qarataū *Kazakhstan* 43°30N 69°30E **300** E7
Karatax Shan *China* 35°57N 81°0E **304** C3
Karatsu *Japan* 33°26N 129°58E **303** H5
Karaul *Russia* 70°6N 82°15E **300** B9
Karauli *India* 26°30N 77°4E **314** F7
Karavostasi *Cyprus* 35°8N 32°50E **297** D11
Karawang *Indonesia* 6°30S 107°15E **309** G12
Karawanken *Europe* 46°30N 14°40E **288** E8
Karayazı *Turkey* 39°41N 42°9E **291** G7
Karazhal = Qarazhal *Kazakhstan* 48°2N 70°49E **300** E8
Karbalā' *Iraq* 32°36N 44°3E **316** C5
Karcag *Hungary* 47°19N 20°57E **289** E11
Karcha → *Pakistan* 34°45N 76°10E **315** B7
Karchana *India* 25°17N 81°56E **315** G9
Karditsa *Greece* 39°23N 21°54E **295** E9
Kärdla *Estonia* 59°0N 22°45E **281** G20
Kareeberge *S. Africa* 30°59S 21°50E **328** E3
Kareha → *India* 25°44N 86°21E **315** G12
Kareima *Sudan* 18°30N 31°49E **323** E12
Karelia □ *Russia* 65°30N 32°30E **280** D25
Karelian Republic = Karelia □ *Russia* 65°30N 32°30E **280** D25
Karera *India* 25°32N 78°9E **314** G8
Kārevāndar *Iran* 27°53N 60°44E **317** E9
Kargasok *Russia* 59°3N 80°53E **300** D9
Kargat *Russia* 55°10N 80°15E **300** D9
Kargi *Kenya* 2°31N 37°34E **326** B4
Kargil *India* 34°32N 76°12E **315** B7
Kargopol *Russia* 61°30N 38°58E **290** B6
Karhal *India* 27°1N 78°57E **315** F8
Karīān *Iran* 26°57N 57°14E **317** E8
Karianga *Madag.* 22°25S 47°22E **329** C8
Kariba *Zimbabwe* 16°28S 28°50E **327** F2
Kariba, L. *Zimbabwe* 16°40S 28°25E **327** F2
Kariba Dam *Zimbabwe* 16°30S 28°35E **327** F2
Kariba Gorge *Zambia* 16°30S 28°50E **327** F2
Karibib *Namibia* 22°0S 15°56E **328** C2
Karijini △ *Australia* 23°8S 118°15E **332** D2
Karimata, Kepulauan *Indonesia* 1°25S 109°0E **308** E3
Karimata, Selat *Indonesia* 2°0S 108°40E **308** E3
Karimata Is. = Karimata, Kepulauan *Indonesia* 1°25S 109°0E **308** E3
Karimnagar *India* 18°26N 79°10E **312** K11
Karimun Kecil, Pulau *Indonesia* 1°8N 103°22E **311** d
Karimunjawa, Kepulauan *Indonesia* 5°50S 110°30E **308** F4
Karin *Somali Rep.* 10°50N 45°52E **319** E4
Karīt *Iran* 33°29N 56°55E **317** C8
Kariya *Japan* 34°58N 137°1E **303** G8
Kariyangwe *Zimbabwe* 18°0S 27°38E **329** B4
Karjala *Finland* 62°0N 30°25E **280** F24
Karkaralinsk = Qarqaraly *Kazakhstan* 49°26N 75°30E **300** E8
Karkheh → *Iran* 31°2N 47°29E **316** D5
Karkinitska Zatoka *Ukraine* 45°56N 33°0E **291** E5
Karkinitskiy Zaliv = Karkinitska Zatoka *Ukraine* 45°56N 33°0E **291** E5
Karkuk = Kirkūk *Iraq* 35°30N 44°21E **316** C5
Karleby = Kokkola *Finland* 63°50N 23°8E **280** E20
Karlovac *Croatia* 45°31N 15°36E **288** F8
Karlovo *Bulgaria* 42°38N 24°47E **295** C11
Karlovy Vary *Czech Rep.* 50°13N 12°51E **288** C7
Karlsbad = Karlovy Vary *Czech Rep.* 50°13N 12°51E **288** C7
Karlshamn *Sweden* 56°10N 14°51E **281** H16
Karlskoga *Sweden* 59°28N 14°33E **281** G16
Karlskrona *Sweden* 56°10N 15°35E **281** H16
Karlsruhe *Germany* 49°0N 8°23E **288** D5
Karlstad *Sweden* 59°23N 13°30E **281** G15
Karlstad *U.S.A.* 48°35N 96°31W **352** A5
Karmi'el *Israel* 32°55N 35°18E **318** C4
Karnak *Egypt* 25°43N 32°39E **323** C12
Karnal *India* 29°42N 77°2E **314** E7
Karnali → *Nepal* 28°45N 81°16E **315** E9
Karnaphuli Res. = Kaptai L. *Bangla.* 22°40N 92°20E **313** H18
Karnaprayag *India* 30°16N 79°15E **315** D8
Karnataka □ *India* 13°15N 77°0E **312** N10
Karnes City *U.S.A.* 28°53N 97°54W **356** G6
Karnische Alpen *Europe* 46°36N 13°0E **288** E7
Kärnten □ *Austria* 46°52N 13°30E **288** E8
Karoi *Zimbabwe* 16°48S 29°45E **327** F2
Karon, Ao *Thailand* 7°51N 98°17E **311** a
Karonga *Malawi* 9°57S 33°55E **327** D3
Karoo △ *S. Africa* 32°18S 22°27E **328** E3
Karoonda *Australia* 35°1S 139°59E **335** F2
Karor *Pakistan* 31°15N 70°59E **314** D4
Karora *Sudan* 17°44N 38°15E **323** E13
Karpasia *Cyprus* 35°32N 34°15E **297** D13
Karpathos *Greece* 35°37N 27°10E **295** G12
Karpinsk *Russia* 59°45N 60°1E **290** C11
Karpogory *Russia* 64°0N 44°27E **290** B7
Karpuz Burnu = Apostolos Andreas, C. *Cyprus* 35°42N 34°35E **297** D13
Karratha *Australia* 20°53S 116°40E **332** D2
Kars *Turkey* 40°40N 43°5E **291** F7
Karsakpay *Kazakhstan* 47°55N 66°40E **300** E7
Karshi = Qarshi *Uzbekistan* 38°53N 65°48E **300** F7
Karsiyang *India* 26°56N 88°18E **315** F13
Karsog *India* 31°23N 77°12E **314** D7
Kartala *Comoros Is.* 11°45S 43°21E **325** a
Kartaly *Russia* 53°3N 60°40E **300** D7
Kartapur *India* 31°27N 75°32E **314** D6
Karthaus *U.S.A.* 41°8N 78°9W **354** E6
Karufa *Indonesia* 3°50S 133°20E **309** E8
Karuma ⌓ *Uganda* 2°5N 32°15E **326** B3
Karumba *Australia* 17°31S 140°50E **334** B3
Karumo *Tanzania* 2°25S 32°50E **326** C3
Karumwa *Tanzania* 3°12S 32°38E **326** C3
Kārūn → *Iran* 30°26N 48°10E **317** D6
Karungu *Kenya* 0°50S 34°10E **326** C3
Karviná *Czech Rep.* 49°53N 18°31E **289** D10
Karwan → *India* 27°26N 78°4E **314** F8
Karwar *India* 14°55N 74°13E **312** M9
Karwi *India* 25°12N 80°57E **315** G9
Kasache *Malawi* 13°25S 34°20E **327** E3
Kasai → *Dem. Rep. of the Congo* 3°30S 16°10E **324** E3
Kasai-Oriental □ *Dem. Rep. of the Congo* 5°0S 24°30E **326** D1
Kasaji *Dem. Rep. of the Congo* 10°25S 23°27E **327** E1
Kasama *Zambia* 10°16S 31°9E **327** E3
Kasan *N. Korea* 41°18N 126°55E **307** D14
Kasandra Kolpos *Greece* 40°5N 23°30E **295** D10
Kasane *Namibia* 17°34S 24°50E **328** B3
Kasanga *Tanzania* 8°30S 31°10E **327** D3
Kasanka △ *Zambia* 11°34S 30°15E **327** E3
Kasaragod *India* 12°30N 74°58E **312** N9
Kasba L. *Canada* 60°20N 102°10W **343** A8
Kāseh Garān *Iran* 34°5N 46°2E **316** C5
Kasempa *Zambia* 13°30S 25°44E **327** E2
Kasenga *Dem. Rep. of the Congo* 10°20S 28°45E **327** E2
Kasese *Uganda* 0°13N 30°3E **326** B3
Kasewa *Zambia* 14°28S 28°53E **327** E2
Kasganj *India* 27°48N 78°42E **315** F8
Kashabowie *Canada* 48°40N 90°26W **344** C1
Kashaf *Iran* 35°58N 61°7E **317** C9
Kāshān *Iran* 34°5N 51°30E **317** C6
Kashechewan *Canada* 52°18N 81°37W **344** B3
Kashgar = Kashi *China* 39°30N 76°2E **304** C2
Kashi *China* 39°30N 76°2E **304** C2
Kashimbo *Dem. Rep. of the Congo* 11°12S 26°19E **327** E2
Kashipur *India* 29°15N 79°0E **315** E8
Kashiwazaki *Japan* 37°22N 138°33E **303** F9
Kashk-e Kohneh *Afghan.* 34°55N 62°30E **312** B3
Kashkū'īyeh *Iran* 30°31N 55°40E **317** D7
Kāshmar *Iran* 35°16N 58°26E **317** C8
Kashmir *Asia* 34°0N 76°0E **315** C7
Kashmor *Pakistan* 28°28N 69°32E **314** E3
Kashun Noerh = Gaxun Nur *China* 42°22N 100°30E **304** B5
Kasiari *India* 22°8N 87°14E **315** H12
Kasimov *Russia* 54°55N 41°20E **290** D7
Kasinge *Dem. Rep. of the Congo* 6°15S 26°58E **326** D2
Kasiruta *Indonesia* 0°25S 127°12E **309** E7
Kaskaskia → *U.S.A.* 37°58N 89°57W **352** G9
Kaskattama → *Canada* 57°3N 90°4W **343** B10
Kaskinen *Finland* 62°22N 21°15E **280** E19
Kaskö = Kaskinen *Finland* 62°22N 21°15E **280** E19
Kaslo *Canada* 49°55N 116°55W **342** D5
Kasmere L. *Canada* 59°34N 101°10W **343** B8
Kasongo *Dem. Rep. of the Congo* 4°30S 26°33E **326** C2
Kasongo Lunda *Dem. Rep. of the Congo* 6°35S 16°49E **324** F3
Kasos *Greece* 35°20N 26°55E **295** G12
Kassalâ *Sudan* 15°30N 36°0E **323** E13
Kassel *Germany* 51°18N 9°26E **288** C5
Kassiopi *Greece* 39°48N 19°53E **297** A3
Kasson *U.S.A.* 44°2N 92°45W **352** C7
Kastamonu *Turkey* 41°25N 33°43E **291** F5
Kasteli *Greece* 35°29N 23°38E **297** D5
Kastelli *Greece* 35°12N 25°20E **297** D7
Kasterlee *Belgium* 51°15N 4°59E **287** C4
Kastoria *Greece* 40°30N 21°19E **295** D9
Kasulu *Tanzania* 4°37S 30°5E **326** C3
Kasumi *Japan* 35°38N 134°38E **303** G7
Kasungu *Malawi* 13°0S 33°29E **327** E3
Kasungu △ *Malawi* 12°53S 33°9E **327** E3
Kasur *Pakistan* 31°5N 74°25E **314** D6
Kata Archanes *Greece* 35°15N 25°10E **297** D7
Kata Tjuta *Australia* 25°20S 130°50E **333** E5
Kataba *Zambia* 16°5S 25°10E **327** F2
Katahdin, Mt. *U.S.A.* 45°54N 68°56W **353** C19
Katako Kombe *Dem. Rep. of the Congo* 3°25S 24°20E **326** C1
Katale *Tanzania* 4°52S 31°7E **326** C3
Katanda *Katanga, Dem. Rep. of the Congo* 7°52S 24°13E **326** D1
Katanda *Nord-Kivu, Dem. Rep. of the Congo* 0°55S 29°21E **326** C2
Katanga □ *Dem. Rep. of the Congo* 8°0S 25°0E **326** D2
Katangi *India* 21°56N 79°50E **312** J11
Katanning *Australia* 33°40S 117°33E **333** F2
Katavi △ *Tanzania* 6°51S 31°3E **326** D3
Katavi Swamp *Tanzania* 6°50S 31°10E **326** D3
Katerini *Greece* 40°18N 22°37E **295** D10
Katghora *India* 22°30N 82°33E **315** H10
Katha *Burma* 24°10N 96°30E **313** G20
Katherîna, Gebel *Egypt* 28°30N 33°57E **316** D2
Katherine *Australia* 14°27S 132°20E **332** B5
Katherine Gorge *Australia* 14°18S 132°28E **332** B5
Kathi *India* 21°47N 74°3E **314** J6
Kathiawar *India* 22°20N 71°0E **314** H4
Kathikas *Cyprus* 34°55N 32°25E **297** E11
Kathmandu = Katmandu *Nepal* 27°45N 85°20E **315** F11
Kathua *India* 32°23N 75°34E **314** C6
Katihar *India* 25°34N 87°36E **315** G12
Katima Mulilo *Zambia* 17°28S 24°13E **328** B3
Katimbira *Malawi* 12°40S 34°0E **327** E3
Katingan = Mendawai → *Indonesia* 3°30S 113°0E **308** E4
Katiola *Ivory C.* 8°10N 5°10W **322** G4
Katmandu *Nepal* 27°45N 85°20E **315** F11
Katni *India* 23°51N 80°24E **315** H9
Kato Chorio *Greece* 35°3N 25°47E **297** D7
Kato Korakiana *Greece* 39°42N 19°45E **297** A3
Káto Pyrgos *Cyprus* 35°11N 32°41E **297** D11
Katompe *Dem. Rep. of the Congo* 6°2S 26°23E **326** D2
Katong *Singapore* 1°18N 103°53E **311** d
Katonga → *Uganda* 0°34N 31°50E **326** B3
Katoomba *Australia* 33°41S 150°19E **335** E5
Katowice *Poland* 50°17N 19°5E **289** C10
Katrine, L. *U.K.* 56°15N 4°30W **283** E4
Katrineholm *Sweden* 59°9N 16°12E **281** G17
Katsepe *Madag.* 15°45S 46°15E **329** B8
Katsina *Nigeria* 13°0N 7°32E **322** F7
Katsumoto *Japan* 33°51N 129°42E **303** H4
Katsuura *Japan* 35°10N 140°20E **303** G10
Katsuyama *Japan* 36°3N 136°30E **303** F8
Kattavia *Greece* 35°57N 27°46E **297** D9
Kattegat *Denmark* 56°40N 11°20E **281** H14
Katumba *Dem. Rep. of the Congo* 7°40S 25°17E **326** D2
Katwa *India* 23°30N 88°5E **315** H13
Katwijk *Neths.* 52°12N 4°24E **287** B4
Kaua'i *U.S.A.* 22°3N 159°30W **346** b
Kauai Channel *U.S.A.* 21°45N 158°50W **346** b
Kaudom ⌓ *Namibia* 18°45S 20°51E **328** B3
Kaufman *U.S.A.* 32°35N 96°19W **356** E6
Kauhajoki *Finland* 62°25N 22°10E **280** E20
Kaukauna *U.S.A.* 44°17N 88°17W **352** C9
Kaukauveld *Namibia* 20°0S 20°15E **328** C3
Kaunakakai *U.S.A.* 21°6N 157°1W **346** b
Kaunas *Lithuania* 54°54N 23°54E **281** J20
Kaunia *Bangla.* 25°46N 89°26E **315** G13
Kautokeino *Norway* 69°0N 23°4E **280** B20
Kauwapur *India* 27°31N 82°18E **315** F10
Kavacha *Russia* 60°16N 169°51E **301** C17
Kavala *Greece* 40°57N 24°28E **295** D11
Kavalerovo *Russia* 44°15N 135°4E **302** B7
Kavali *India* 14°55N 80°1E **312** M12
Kavār *Iran* 29°11N 52°44E **317** D7
Kavi *India* 22°12N 72°38E **314** H5
Kavimba *Botswana* 18°2S 24°38E **328** B3
Kavīr, Dasht-e *Iran* 34°30N 55°0E **317** C7
Kavīr △ *Iran* 34°40N 52°0E **317** C7
Kavos *Greece* 39°23N 20°3E **297** B4
Kaw *Fr. Guiana* 4°30N 52°15W **365** C8
Kawagama L. *Canada* 45°18N 78°45W **354** A6
Kawagoe *Japan* 35°55N 139°29E **303** G9
Kawaguchi *Japan* 35°52N 139°45E **303** G9
Kawambwa *Zambia* 9°48S 29°3E **327** D2
Kawanoe *Japan* 34°1N 133°34E **303** G6
Kawardha *India* 22°0N 81°17E **315** J9
Kawasaki *Japan* 35°31N 139°43E **303** G9
Kawasi *Indonesia* 1°38S 127°28E **309** E7
Kawawachikamach *Canada* 54°48N 66°50W **345** B6
Kawerau *N.Z.* 38°7S 176°42E **331** C6
Kawhia *N.Z.* 38°4S 174°49E **331** C5
Kawhia Harbour *N.Z.* 38°5S 174°51E **331** C5
Kawio, Kepulauan *Indonesia* 4°30N 125°30E **309** D7
Kawthaung *Burma* 10°5N 98°36E **311** H2
Kawthoolei = Kayin □ *Burma* 18°0N 97°30E **313** L20
Kawthule = Kayin □ *Burma* 18°0N 97°30E **313** L20
Kaya *Burkina Faso* 13°4N 1°10W **322** F5
Kayah □ *Burma* 19°15N 97°15E **313** K20
Kayan → *Indonesia* 2°55N 117°35E **308** D5
Kaycee *U.S.A.* 43°43N 106°38W **348** E10
Kayeli *Indonesia* 3°20S 127°10E **309** E7
Kayenta *U.S.A.* 36°44N 110°15W **349** H8
Kayes *Mali* 14°25N 11°30W **322** F3
Kayin □ *Burma* 18°0N 97°30E **313** L20
Kayoa *Indonesia* 0°1N 127°28E **309** D7
Kayomba *Zambia* 13°11S 24°2E **327** E1
Kayseri *Turkey* 38°45N 35°30E **316** B2
Kaysville *U.S.A.* 41°2N 111°56W **348** F8
Kazachye *Russia* 70°52N 135°58E **301** B14
Kazakhstan ■ *Asia* 50°0N 70°0E **300** E7
Kazan *Russia* 55°50N 49°10E **290** C8
Kazan → *Canada* 64°2N 95°29W **343** A9
Kazan-Rettō *Pac. Oc.* 25°0N 141°0E **336** E6
Kazanlŭk *Bulgaria* 42°38N 25°20E **295** C11
Kazatin = Kozyatyn *Ukraine* 49°45N 28°50E **289** D15
Kāzerūn *Iran* 29°38N 51°40E **317** D6
Kazi Magomed = Qazimämmäd *Azerbaijan* 40°3N 49°0E **317** A6
Kazuma Pan △ *Zimbabwe* 18°20S 25°48E **327** F2
Kazuno *Japan* 40°10N 140°45E **302** D10
Kazym → *Russia* 63°54N 65°50E **300** C7
Kea *Greece* 37°35N 24°22E **295** F11
Keady *U.K.* 54°15N 6°42W **282** B5
Kearney *U.S.A.* 40°42N 99°5W **352** E4
Kearny *U.S.A.* 33°3N 110°55W **349** K8
Kearsarge, Mt. *U.S.A.* 43°22N 71°50W **355** C13
Keban *Turkey* 38°50N 38°50E **291** G6
Keban Barajı *Turkey* 38°41N 38°33E **316** B3
Kebnekaise *Sweden* 67°53N 18°33E **280** C18
Kebri Dehar *Ethiopia* 6°45N 44°17E **319** F3
Kebumen *Indonesia* 7°42S 109°40E **309** G13
Kechika → *Canada* 59°41N 127°12W **342** B3
Kecskemét *Hungary* 46°57N 19°42E **289** E10
Kėdainiai *Lithuania* 55°15N 24°2E **281** J21
Kedarnath *India* 30°44N 79°4E **315** D8
Kedgwick *Canada* 47°40N 67°20W **345** C6
Kediri *Indonesia* 7°51S 112°1E **308** F4
Kedros Oros *Greece* 35°11N 24°37E **297** D6
Keeler *U.S.A.* 36°29N 117°52W **350** J9
Keeley L. *Canada* 54°54N 108°8W **343** C7
Keeling Is. = Cocos Is. *Ind. Oc.* 12°10S 96°55E **336** J1
Keelung = Chilung *Taiwan* 25°3N 121°45E **305** D7
Keene *Canada* 44°15N 78°10W **354** B6
Keene *Calif., U.S.A.* 35°13N 118°33W **351** K8
Keene *N.H., U.S.A.* 42°56N 72°17W **355** D12
Keene *N.Y., U.S.A.* 44°16N 73°46W **355** B11
Keep River △ *Australia* 15°49S 129°8E **332** C4
Keeper Hill *Ireland* 52°45N 8°16W **282** D3
Keerweer, C. *Australia* 14°0S 141°32E **334** A3
Keeseville *U.S.A.* 44°29N 73°30W **355** B11
Keetmanshoop *Namibia* 26°35S 18°8E **328** D2
Keewatin *Canada* 49°46N 94°34W **343** D10
Keewatin → *Canada* 56°29N 100°46W **343** B8
Kefalonia *Greece* 38°15N 20°30E **295** E9
Kefamenanu *Indonesia* 9°28S 124°29E **309** F6
Kefar Sava *Israel* 32°11N 34°54E **318** C3
Keffi *Nigeria* 8°55N 7°43E **322** G7
Keflavík *Iceland* 64°2N 22°35W **280** D2
Keg River *Canada* 57°54N 117°55W **342** B5
Kegaska *Canada* 50°9N 61°18W **345** B7
Kehancha *Kenya* 1°11S 34°37E **326** C3
Keighley *U.K.* 53°52N 1°54W **284** D6
Keila *Estonia* 59°18N 24°25E **281** G21
Keimoes *S. Africa* 28°41S 20°59E **328** D3
Keitele *Finland* 63°10N 26°20E **280** E22
Keith *Australia* 36°6S 140°20E **335** F3
Keith *U.K.* 57°32N 2°57W **283** D6

KwaZulu Natal □ S. Africa 29°0S 30°0E 329 D5
Kweichow = Guizhou □ China 27°0N 107°0E 304 D5
Kwekwe Zimbabwe 18°58S 29°48E 327 F2
Kwidzyn Poland 53°44N 18°55E 289 B10
Kwilu → Dem. Rep. of the Congo 3°22S 17°22E 324 E3
Kwinana Australia 32°15S 115°47E 333 F2
Kwoka Indonesia 0°31S 132°27E 309 E8
Kwun Tong China 22°19N 114°13E 305 G11
Kyabra Cr. → Australia 25°36S 142°55E 335 D3
Kyabram Australia 36°19S 145°4E 335 F4
Kyaikto Burma 17°20N 97°3E 310 D1
Kyakhta Russia 50°30N 106°25E 301 D11
Kyambura ⌓ Uganda 0°7S 30°9E 326 C3
Kyancutta Australia 33°8S 135°33E 335 E2
Kyaukpadaung Burma 20°52N 95°8E 313 J19
Kyaukpyu Burma 19°28N 93°30E 313 K18
Kyaukse Burma 21°36N 96°10E 313 J20
Kyburz U.S.A. 38°47N 120°18W 350 G6
Kyelang India 32°35N 77°2E 314 C7
Kyenjojo Uganda 0°40N 30°37E 326 B3
Kyle Canada 50°50N 108°2W 343 C7
Kyle Dam Zimbabwe 20°15S 31°0E 327 G3
Kyle of Lochalsh U.K. 57°17N 5°44W 283 D3
Kymijoki → Finland 60°30N 26°55E 280 F22
Kymmene älv = Kymijoki → Finland 60°30N 26°55E 280 F22
Kyneton Australia 37°10S 144°29E 335 F3
Kynuna Australia 21°37S 141°55E 334 C3
Kyō-ga-Saki Japan 35°45N 135°15E 303 G7
Kyoga, L. Uganda 1°35N 33°0E 326 B3
Kyogle Australia 28°40S 153°0E 335 D5
Kyŏngju = Gyeongju S. Korea 35°51N 129°14E 307 G15
Kyŏngsŏng N. Korea 41°35N 129°36E 307 D15
Kyonpyaw Burma 17°12N 95°10E 313 L19
Kyōto Japan 35°0N 135°45E 303 G7
Kyōto □ Japan 35°15N 135°45E 303 G7
Kyparissovouno Cyprus 35°19N 33°10E 297 D12
Kyperounda Cyprus 34°56N 32°58E 297 E11
Kypros = Cyprus ■ Asia 35°0N 33°0E 297 E12
Kyrenia Cyprus 35°20N 33°20E 297 D12
Kyrgyzstan ■ Asia 42°0N 75°0E 300 E8
Kyro älv = Kyrönjoki → Finland 63°14N 21°45E 280 E19
Kyrönjoki → Finland 63°14N 21°45E 280 E19
Kystatyam Russia 67°20N 123°10E 301 C13
Kythira Greece 36°8N 23°0E 295 F10
Kythréa Cyprus 35°15N 33°29E 297 D12
Kyunhla Burma 23°25N 95°15E 313 H19
Kyuquot Sound Canada 50°2N 127°22W 342 D3
Kyūshū Japan 33°0N 131°0E 303 H5
Kyūshū □ Japan 33°0N 131°0E 303 H5
Kyushu-Palau Ridge Pac. Oc. 20°0N 136°0E 336 E5
Kyūshū-Sanchi Japan 32°35N 131°17E 303 H5
Kyustendil Bulgaria 42°16N 22°41E 295 C10
Kyusyur Russia 70°19N 127°30E 301 B13
Kyyiv Ukraine 50°30N 30°28E 289 C16
Kyyivske Vdskh. Ukraine 51°0N 30°25E 289 C16
Kyzyl Russia 51°50N 94°30E 301 D10
Kyzyl Kum Uzbekistan 42°30N 65°0E 300 E7
Kyzyl-Kyya Kyrgyzstan 40°16N 72°8E 300 E8
Kyzyl-Orda = Qyzylorda Kazakhstan 44°48N 65°28E 300 E7

L

La Alcarria Spain 40°31N 2°45W 293 B4
La Amistad △ Cent. Amer. 9°28N 83°18W 360 E3
La Asunción Venezuela 11°2N 63°53W 364 A6
La Baie Canada 48°19N 70°53W 345 C5
La Banda Argentina 27°45S 64°10W 366 B3
La Barca Mexico 20°17N 102°34W 358 C4
La Barge U.S.A. 42°16N 110°12W 348 E8
La Belle U.S.A. 26°46N 81°26W 357 H14
La Biche → Canada 59°57N 123°50W 342 B4
La Biche, L. Canada 54°50N 112°3W 342 C6
La Brea Trin. & Tob. 10°15N 61°37W 365 K15
La Calera Chile 32°50S 71°10W 366 C1
La Campana △ Chile 32°58S 71°14W 366 C1
La Canal = Sa Canal Spain 38°51N 1°23E 296 C7
La Carlota Argentina 33°30S 63°20W 366 C3
La Ceiba Honduras 15°40N 86°50W 360 C2
La Chaux-de-Fonds Switz. 47°7N 6°50E 292 C7
La Chorrera Panama 8°53N 79°47W 360 E4
La Cocha Argentina 27°50S 65°40W 366 B2
La Concepción Panama 8°31N 82°37W 360 E3
La Concordia Mexico 16°5N 92°38W 359 D6
La Coruña = A Coruña Spain 43°20N 8°25W 293 A1
La Crescent U.S.A. 43°50N 91°18W 352 D8
La Crete Canada 58°11N 116°24W 342 B5
La Crosse Kans., U.S.A. 38°32N 99°18W 352 F4
La Crosse Wis., U.S.A. 43°48N 91°15W 352 D8
La Cruz Costa Rica 11°4N 85°39W 360 D2
La Cruz Mexico 23°55N 106°54W 358 C3
La Désirade Guadeloupe 16°18N 61°3W 360 b
La Digue Seychelles 4°20S 55°51E 325 b
La Esmeralda Paraguay 22°16S 62°33W 366 A3
La Esperanza Cuba 22°46N 83°44W 360 B3
La Esperanza Honduras 14°15N 88°10W 360 D2
La Estrada = A Estrada Spain 42°43N 8°27W 293 A1
La Fayette U.S.A. 34°42N 85°17W 357 D12
La Fé Cuba 22°2N 84°15W 360 B3
La Follette U.S.A. 36°23N 84°7W 357 C12
La Grande U.S.A. 45°20N 118°5W 348 D4
La Grande → Canada 53°50N 79°0W 344 B5
La Grande Deux, Rés. Canada 53°40N 76°55W 344 B4
La Grande Quatre, Rés. Canada 54°0N 73°15W 344 B5
La Grande Trois, Rés. Canada 53°40N 75°10W 344 B4
La Grange Calif., U.S.A. 37°42N 120°27W 350 H6
La Grange Ga., U.S.A. 33°2N 85°2W 357 E12
La Grange Ky., U.S.A. 38°24N 85°22W 353 F11
La Grange Tex., U.S.A. 29°54N 96°52W 356 G6
La Guaira Venezuela 10°36N 66°56W 364 A5
La Habana Cuba 23°8N 82°22W 360 B3
La Independencia Mexico 16°15N 92°1W 359 D6
La Isabela Dom. Rep. 19°58N 71°2W 361 C5
La Junta U.S.A. 37°59N 103°33W 348 H12
La Laguna Canary Is. 28°28N 16°18W 296 F3
La Libertad = Puerto Libertad Mexico 29°55N 112°43W 358 B2
La Libertad Guatemala 16°47N 90°7W 360 C1
La Ligua Chile 32°30S 71°16W 366 C1
La Línea de la Concepción Spain 36°15N 5°23W 293 D3
La Loche Canada 56°29N 109°26W 343 B7
La Louvière Belgium 50°27N 4°10E 287 D4
La Lune Trin. & Tob. 10°3N 61°22W 365 K15
La Malbaie Canada 47°40N 70°10W 345 C5
La Malinche △ Mexico 19°15N 98°3W 359 D5
La Mancha Spain 39°10N 2°54W 293 C4
La Martre, L. Canada 63°15N 117°55W 342 A5
La Mesa Mexico 32°30N 116°57W 351 N10
La Mesa U.S.A. 32°46N 117°1W 351 N9
La Mesilla U.S.A. 32°16N 106°48W 349 K10
La Misión Mexico 32°6N 116°53W 358 A1
La Moure U.S.A. 46°21N 98°18W 352 B4
La Negra Chile 23°46S 70°18W 366 A1
La Oliva Canary Is. 28°36N 13°57W 296 F6
La Orotava Canary Is. 28°22N 16°31W 296 F3
La Oroya Peru 11°32S 75°54W 364 F3
La Palma Canary Is. 28°40N 17°50W 296 F2
La Palma Panama 8°15N 78°0W 360 E4
La Palma del Condado Spain 37°21N 6°38W 293 D2
La Paloma Chile 30°35S 71°0W 366 C1
La Pampa □ Argentina 36°50S 66°0W 366 D2
La Paragua Venezuela 6°50N 63°20W 364 B6
La Paz Entre Ríos, Argentina 30°50S 59°45W 366 C4
La Paz San Luis, Argentina 33°30S 67°20W 366 C2
La Paz Bolivia 16°20S 68°10W 364 G5
La Paz Honduras 14°20N 87°47W 360 D2
La Paz Mexico 24°10N 110°18W 358 C2
La Paz Centro Nic. 12°20N 86°41W 360 D2
La Pedrera Colombia 1°18S 69°43W 364 D5
La Pérade Canada 46°35N 72°12W 345 C5
La Perla Mexico 28°18N 104°32W 358 B4
La Perouse Str. Asia 45°40N 142°0E 302 B11
La Pesca Mexico 23°46N 97°47W 359 C5
La Piedad Mexico 20°21N 102°0W 358 C4
La Pine U.S.A. 43°40N 121°30W 348 E3
La Plata Argentina 35°0S 57°55W 366 D4
La Pocatière Canada 47°22N 70°2W 345 C5
La Porte U.S.A. 29°40N 95°1W 356 G7
La Purísima Mexico 26°10N 112°4W 358 B2
La Push U.S.A. 47°55N 124°38W 350 C2
La Quiaca Argentina 22°5S 65°35W 366 A2
La Restinga Canary Is. 27°38N 17°59W 296 G2
La Rioja Argentina 29°20S 67°0W 366 B2
La Rioja □ Argentina 29°30S 67°0W 366 B2
La Rioja □ Spain 42°20N 2°20W 293 A4
La Robla Spain 42°50N 5°41W 293 A3
La Roche-en-Ardenne Belgium 50°11N 5°35E 287 D5
La Roche-sur-Yon France 46°40N 1°25W 292 C3
La Rochelle France 46°10N 1°9W 292 C3
La Roda Spain 39°13N 2°15W 293 C4
La Romaine Canada 50°13N 60°40W 345 B7
La Romana Dom. Rep. 18°27N 68°57W 361 C6
La Ronge Canada 55°5N 105°20W 343 B7
La Rumorosa Mexico 32°34N 116°6W 351 N10
La Sabina = Sa Savina Spain 38°44N 1°25E 296 C7
La Salle U.S.A. 41°20N 89°6W 352 E9
La Santa Canary Is. 29°5N 13°40W 296 E6
La Sarre Canada 48°45N 79°15W 344 C4
La Scie Canada 49°57N 55°36W 345 C8
La Selva Beach U.S.A. 36°56N 121°51W 350 J5
La Serena Chile 29°55S 71°10W 366 B1
La Seu d'Urgell Spain 42°22N 1°23E 293 A6
La Seyne-sur-Mer France 43°7N 5°52E 292 E6
La Soufrière St. Vincent 13°20N 61°11W 361 D7
La Spézia Italy 44°7N 9°50E 292 D8
La Tagua Colombia 0°3N 74°40W 364 C4
La Tortuga Venezuela 11°0N 65°22W 361 D6
La Trinité Martinique 14°43N 60°58W 360 c
La Tuque Canada 47°30N 72°50W 344 C5
La Unión Chile 40°10S 73°0W 368 E2
La Unión El Salv. 13°20N 87°50W 360 D2
La Unión Mexico 17°58N 101°49W 358 D4
La Urbana Venezuela 7°8N 66°56W 364 B5
La Vache Pt. Trin. & Tob. 10°47N 61°28W 365 K15
La Vall d'Uixó Spain 39°49N 0°15W 293 C5
La Vega Dom. Rep. 19°20N 70°30W 361 C5
La Vela de Coro Venezuela 11°27N 69°34W 364 A5
La Venta Mexico 18°5N 94°3W 359 D6
La Vergne U.S.A. 36°1N 86°35W 357 C11
Laas Caanood = Las Anod Somali Rep. 8°26N 47°19E 319 F4
Labasa Fiji 16°30S 179°27E 331 a
Labdah = Leptis Magna Libya 32°40N 14°12E 323 B8
Labe = Elbe → Europe 53°50N 9°0E 288 B5
Labé Guinea 11°24N 12°16W 322 F3
Laberge, L. Canada 61°11N 135°12W 342 A1
Labinsk Russia 44°40N 40°48E 291 F7
Labis Malaysia 2°22N 103°2E 311 L4
Laborie St. Lucia 13°45N 61°2W 361 f
Laboulaye Argentina 34°10S 63°30W 366 C3
Labrador Canada 53°20N 61°0W 345 B7
Labrador City Canada 52°57N 66°55W 345 B6
Labrador Sea Atl. Oc. 57°0N 54°0W 341 D14
Lábrea Brazil 7°15S 64°51W 364 E6
Labuan Malaysia 5°20N 115°14E 308 C5
Labuan, Pulau Malaysia 5°21N 115°13E 308 C5
Labuha Indonesia 0°30S 127°30E 309 E7
Labuhan Indonesia 6°22S 105°50E 309 G11
Labuhanbajo Indonesia 8°28S 119°54E 309 F6
Labuk, Telok Malaysia 6°10N 117°50E 308 C5
Labyrinth, L. Australia 30°40S 135°11E 335 E2
Labytnangi Russia 66°39N 66°21E 300 C7
Lac-Bouchette Canada 48°16N 72°11W 345 C5
Lac Édouard Canada 47°40N 72°16W 344 C5
Lac La Biche Canada 54°45N 111°58W 342 C6
Lac la Martre = Wha Ti Canada 63°8N 117°16W 340 C8
Lac La Ronge ⌓ Canada 55°9N 104°41W 343 B7
Lac-Mégantic Canada 45°35N 70°53W 345 C5
Lac Thien Vietnam 12°25N 108°11E 310 F7
Lacanau France 44°58N 1°5W 292 D3
Lacantún → Mexico 16°36N 90°39W 359 D6
Laccadive Is. = Lakshadweep Is. India 10°0N 72°30E 275 D13
Lacepede B. Australia 36°40S 139°40E 335 F2
Lacepede Is. Australia 16°55S 122°0E 332 C3
Lacerdónia Mozam. 18°3S 35°35E 327 F4
Lacey U.S.A. 47°7N 122°49W 350 C4
Lachania Greece 35°58N 27°54E 297 D9
Lachhmangarh India 27°50N 75°4E 314 F6
Lachi Pakistan 33°25N 71°20E 314 C4
Lachine Canada 45°26N 73°42W 344 C5
Lachlan → Australia 34°22S 143°55E 335 E3
Lachute Canada 45°39N 74°21W 344 C5
Lackagh Hills Ireland 54°16N 8°10W 282 B3
Lackawanna U.S.A. 42°50N 78°50W 354 D6
Lackawaxen U.S.A. 41°29N 74°59W 355 E10
Lacolle Canada 45°5N 73°22W 355 A11
Lacombe Canada 52°30N 113°44W 342 C6
Lacona U.S.A. 43°39N 76°10W 355 C8
Laconia U.S.A. 43°32N 71°28W 355 C13
Ladakh Ra. India 34°0N 78°0E 315 C8
Ladismith S. Africa 33°28S 21°15E 328 E3
Lādīz Iran 28°55N 61°15E 317 D9
Ladnun India 27°38N 74°25E 314 F6
Ladoga, L. = Ladozhskoye Ozero Russia 61°15N 30°30E 280 F24
Ladozhskoye Ozero Russia 61°15N 30°30E 280 F24
Lady Elliott I. Australia 24°7S 152°42E 334 C5
Lady Grey S. Africa 30°43S 27°13E 328 E4
Ladybrand S. Africa 29°9S 27°29E 328 D4
Ladysmith Canada 49°0N 123°49W 350 B3
Ladysmith S. Africa 28°32S 29°46E 329 D4
Ladysmith U.S.A. 45°28N 91°12W 352 C8
Lae Papua N. G. 6°40S 147°2E 330 B7
Laem Hin Khom Thailand 9°25N 99°56E 311 b
Laem Khat Thailand 8°6N 98°26E 311 a
Laem Nga Thailand 7°55N 98°27E 311 a
Laem Ngop Thailand 12°10N 102°26E 311 F4
Laem Phan Wa Thailand 7°47N 98°25E 311 a
Laem Pho Thailand 6°55N 101°19E 311 J3
Laem Phrom Thep Thailand 7°45N 98°19E 311 a
Laem Riang Thailand 8°7N 98°27E 311 a
Laem Sam Rong Thailand 9°35N 100°4E 311 b
Laem Son Thailand 7°59N 98°16E 311 a
Laem Yamu Thailand 7°59N 98°26E 311 a
Laerma Greece 36°9N 27°57E 297 C9
Læsø Denmark 57°15N 11°5E 281 H14
Lafayette Ind., U.S.A. 40°25N 86°54W 352 E10
Lafayette La., U.S.A. 30°14N 92°1W 356 F8
LaFayette Tenn., U.S.A. 36°31N 86°2W 357 C11
Laferte → Canada 61°53N 117°44W 342 A5
Lafia Nigeria 8°30N 8°34E 322 G7
Lafleche Canada 49°45N 106°40W 343 D7
Lagan → U.K. 54°36N 5°55W 282 B6
Lagarfljót → Iceland 65°40N 14°18W 280 D6
Lagdo, Rés. de Cameroon 8°40N 14°0E 323 G8
Lågen → Oppland, Norway 61°8N 10°25E 280 F14
Lågen → Vestfold, Norway 59°3N 10°3E 281 G14
Laghouat Algeria 33°50N 2°59E 322 B6
Lagoa do Peixe △ Brazil 31°12S 50°55W 367 C5
Lagoa Vermelha Brazil 28°13S 51°32W 367 B5
Lagonoy G. Phil. 13°35N 123°50E 309 B6
Lagos Nigeria 6°25N 3°27E 322 G6
Lagos Portugal 37°5N 8°41W 293 D1
Lagos de Moreno Mexico 21°21N 101°55W 358 C4
Lagrange = Bidyadanga Australia 18°45S 121°43E 332 C3
Lagrange B. Australia 18°38S 121°42E 332 C3
Laguna Brazil 28°30S 48°50W 367 B6
Laguna U.S.A. 35°2N 107°25W 349 J10
Laguna, Sa. de la Mexico 23°35N 109°55W 358 C3
Laguna Beach U.S.A. 33°33N 117°47W 351 M9
Laguna de la Restinga △ Venezuela 10°58N 64°0W 361 D6
Laguna del Laja △ Chile 37°27S 71°20W 366 D1
Laguna del Tigre △ Guatemala 17°32N 90°56W 360 C1
Laguna Limpia Argentina 26°32S 59°45W 366 B4
Lagunas Chile 21°0S 69°45W 366 A2
Lagunas Peru 5°10S 75°35W 364 E3
Lagunas de Chacahua △ Mexico 16°0N 97°43W 359 D5
Lagunas de Montebello △ Mexico 16°4N 91°42W 359 D6
Lahad Datu Malaysia 5°0N 118°20E 309 C5
Lahad Datu, Telok Malaysia 4°50N 118°20E 309 D5
Lahan Sai Thailand 14°25N 102°52E 310 E4
Lahanam Laos 16°16N 105°16E 310 D5
Lahar India 26°12N 78°57E 315 F8
Laharpur India 27°43N 80°56E 315 F9
Lahat Indonesia 3°45S 103°30E 308 E2
Lahewa Indonesia 1°22N 97°12E 308 D1
Lāhījān Iran 37°10N 50°6E 317 B6
Lahn → Germany 50°19N 7°37E 288 C4
Laholm Sweden 56°30N 13°2E 281 H15
Lahore Pakistan 31°32N 74°22E 314 D6
Lahri Pakistan 29°11N 68°13E 314 E3
Lahti Finland 60°58N 25°40E 280 F21
Lahtis = Lahti Finland 60°58N 25°40E 280 F21
Laï Chad 9°25N 16°18E 323 G9
Lai Chau Vietnam 22°5N 103°3E 310 A4
Laila = Layla Si. Arabia 22°10N 46°40E 319 C4
Laingsburg S. Africa 33°9S 20°52E 328 E3
Lainioälven → Sweden 67°35N 22°40E 280 C20
Lairg U.K. 58°2N 4°24W 283 C4
Laisamis Kenya 1°36N 37°48E 326 B4
Laishui China 39°23N 115°45E 306 E8
Laiwu China 36°15N 117°40E 307 F9
Laixi China 36°50N 120°31E 307 F11
Laiyang China 36°59N 120°45E 307 F11
Laiyuan China 39°20N 114°40E 306 E8
Laizhou China 37°8N 119°57E 307 F10
Laizhou Wan China 37°30N 119°30E 307 F10
Laja → Mexico 20°55N 100°46W 358 C4
Lajamanu Australia 18°23S 130°38E 332 C5
Lajes Brazil 27°48S 50°20W 367 B5
Lak Sao Laos 18°11N 104°59E 310 C5
Lakaband Pakistan 31°2N 69°15E 314 D3
Lake U.S.A. 44°33N 110°24W 348 D8
Lake Alpine U.S.A. 38°29N 120°0W 350 G7
Lake Andes U.S.A. 43°9N 98°32W 352 D4
Lake Arthur U.S.A. 30°5N 92°41W 356 F8
Lake Bindegolly △ Australia 28°0S 144°12E 335 D3
Lake Cargelligo Australia 33°15S 146°22E 335 E4
Lake Charles U.S.A. 30°14N 93°13W 356 F8
Lake City Colo., U.S.A. 38°2N 107°19W 348 G10
Lake City Fla., U.S.A. 30°11N 82°38W 357 F13
Lake City Mich., U.S.A. 44°20N 85°13W 353 C11
Lake City Minn., U.S.A. 44°27N 92°16W 352 C7
Lake City Pa., U.S.A. 42°1N 80°21W 354 D4
Lake City S.C., U.S.A. 33°52N 79°45W 357 E15
Lake Cowichan Canada 48°49N 124°3W 342 D4
Lake District △ U.K. 54°30N 3°21W 284 C4
Lake Elsinore U.S.A. 33°38N 117°20W 351 M9
Lake Eyre △ Australia 28°40S 137°31E 335 D2
Lake Gairdner △ Australia 31°41S 135°51E 335 E2
Lake George U.S.A. 43°26N 73°43W 355 C11
Lake Grace Australia 33°7S 118°28E 333 F2
Lake Harbour = Kimmirut Canada 62°50N 69°50W 341 C13
Lake Havasu City U.S.A. 34°27N 114°22W 351 L12
Lake Hughes U.S.A. 34°41N 118°26W 351 L8
Lake Isabella U.S.A. 35°38N 118°28W 351 K8
Lake Jackson U.S.A. 29°3N 95°27W 356 G7
Lake King Australia 33°5S 119°45E 333 F2
Lake Lenore Canada 52°24N 104°59W 343 C8
Lake Louise Canada 51°30N 116°10W 342 C5
Lake Malawi △ Malawi 14°2S 34°53E 327 E3
Lake Mburo △ Uganda 0°33S 30°56E 326 C3
Lake Mead ⌓ U.S.A. 36°30N 114°22W 351 K12
Lake Meredith ⌓ U.S.A. 35°50N 101°50W 356 D4
Lake Mills U.S.A. 43°25N 93°32W 352 D7
Lake Nakura △ Kenya 0°21S 36°8E 326 C4
Lake Placid U.S.A. 44°17N 73°59W 355 B11
Lake Pleasant U.S.A. 43°28N 74°25W 355 C10
Lake Providence U.S.A. 32°48N 91°10W 356 E9
Lake Roosevelt ⌓ U.S.A. 48°5N 118°14W 348 B4
Lake St. Peter Canada 45°18N 78°2W 354 A6
Lake Superior ⌓ Canada 47°45N 84°45W 344 C3
Lake Torrens △ Australia 30°55S 137°40E 335 E2
Lake Village U.S.A. 33°20N 91°17W 356 E9
Lake Wales U.S.A. 27°54N 81°35W 357 H14
Lake Worth U.S.A. 26°37N 80°3W 357 H14
Lakeba Fiji 18°13S 178°47W 331 a
Lakeba Passage Fiji 18°0S 178°45W 331 a
Lakefield Canada 44°25N 78°16W 354 B6
Lakefield △ Australia 15°24S 144°26E 334 B3
Lakehurst U.S.A. 40°1N 74°19W 355 F10
Lakeland Australia 15°49S 144°57E 334 B3
Lakeland U.S.A. 28°3N 81°57W 357 G14
Lakemba = Lakeba Fiji 18°13S 178°47W 331 a
Lakeport Calif., U.S.A. 39°3N 122°55W 350 F4
Lakeport Mich., U.S.A. 43°7N 82°30W 354 C2
Lakes Entrance Australia 37°50S 148°0E 335 F4
Lakeside Calif., U.S.A. 32°52N 116°55W 351 N10
Lakeside Nebr., U.S.A. 42°3N 102°26W 352 D2
Lakeside Ohio, U.S.A. 41°32N 82°46W 354 E2
Lakeview U.S.A. 42°11N 120°21W 348 E3
Lakeville U.S.A. 44°39N 93°14W 352 C7
Lakewood Colo., U.S.A. 39°42N 105°4W 348 G11
Lakewood N.J., U.S.A. 40°6N 74°13W 355 F10
Lakewood N.Y., U.S.A. 42°6N 79°19W 354 D5
Lakewood Ohio, U.S.A. 41°28N 81°47W 354 E3
Lakewood Wash., U.S.A. 47°11N 122°32W 350 C4
Lakha India 26°9N 70°54E 314 F4
Lakhimpur India 27°57N 80°46E 315 F9
Lakhnadon India 22°36N 79°36E 315 H8
Lakhnau = Lucknow India 26°50N 81°0E 315 F9
Lakhonpheng Laos 15°54N 105°34E 310 E5
Lakhpat India 23°48N 68°47E 314 H3
Lakin U.S.A. 37°57N 101°15W 352 G3
Lakitusaki → Canada 54°21N 82°25W 344 B3
Lakki Greece 35°24N 23°57E 297 D5
Lakki Pakistan 32°36N 70°55E 314 C4
Lakonikos Kolpos Greece 36°40N 22°40E 295 F10
Lakor Indonesia 8°15S 128°17E 309 F7
Lakota Ivory C. 5°50N 5°30W 322 G4
Lakota U.S.A. 48°2N 98°21W 352 A4
Laksar India 29°46N 78°3E 314 E8
Laksefjorden Norway 70°45N 26°50E 280 A22
Lakselv Norway 70°2N 25°0E 280 A21
Lakshadweep Is. India 10°0N 72°30E 275 D13
Lakshmanpur India 22°58N 83°3E 315 H10
Lakshmikantapur India 22°5N 88°20E 315 H13
Lala Musa Pakistan 32°40N 73°57E 314 C5
Lalaghat India 24°30N 92°40E 313 G18
Lalago Tanzania 3°28S 33°58E 326 C3
Lalapanzi Zimbabwe 19°20S 30°15E 327 F3
L'Albufera Spain 39°20N 0°27W 293 C5
Lalganj India 25°52N 85°13E 315 G11
Lalgola India 24°25N 88°15E 315 G13
Lālī Iran 32°21N 49°6E 317 C6
Lalibela Ethiopia 12°3N 39°0E 319 E2
Lalin China 45°12N 127°0E 307 B14
Lalín Spain 42°40N 8°5W 293 A1
Lalin He → China 45°32N 125°40E 307 B13
Lalitapur Nepal 27°40N 85°20E 315 F11
Lalitpur India 24°42N 78°28E 315 G8
Lalkua India 29°5N 79°31E 315 E8
Lalsot India 26°34N 76°20E 314 F7
Lam Vietnam 21°21N 106°31E 310 B6
Lam Pao Res. Thailand 16°50N 103°15E 310 D4
Lamaing Burma 15°25N 97°53E 310 E1
Lamar Colo., U.S.A. 38°5N 102°37W 348 G12
Lamar Mo., U.S.A. 37°30N 94°16W 352 G6
Lamas Peru 6°28S 76°31W 364 E3
Lambaréné Gabon 0°41S 10°12E 324 E2
Lambasa = Labasa Fiji 16°30S 179°27E 331 a
Lambay I. Ireland 53°29N 6°1W 282 C5
Lambert's Bay S. Africa 32°5S 18°17E 328 E2
Lambeth Canada 42°54N 81°18W 354 D3
Lambomakondro Madag. 22°41S 44°44E 329 C7
Lambton Shores Canada 43°10N 81°56W 354 C3
Lame Deer U.S.A. 45°37N 106°40W 348 D10
Lamego Portugal 41°5N 7°52W 293 B2
Lamèque Canada 47°45N 64°38W 345 C7
Lameroo Australia 35°19S 140°33E 335 F3
Lamesa U.S.A. 32°44N 101°58W 356 E4
Lamia Greece 38°55N 22°26E 295 E10
Lamington △ Australia 28°13S 153°12E 335 D5
Lamma I. China 22°12N 114°7E 305 G11
Lammermuir Hills U.K. 55°50N 2°40W 283 F6
Lamoille → U.S.A. 44°38N 73°13W 355 B11
Lamon B. Phil. 14°30N 122°20E 309 B6
Lamont Canada 53°46N 112°50W 342 C6
Lamont Calif., U.S.A. 35°15N 118°55W 351 K8
Lamont Wyo., U.S.A. 42°13N 107°29W 348 E10
Lampa Peru 15°22S 70°22W 364 G4
Lampang Thailand 18°16N 99°32E 310 C2
Lampasas U.S.A. 31°4N 98°11W 356 F5
Lampazos de Naranjo Mexico 27°1N 100°31W 358 B4
Lampedusa Medit. S. 35°36N 12°40E 294 G5
Lampeter U.K. 52°7N 4°4W 285 E3
Lampione Medit. S. 35°33N 12°20E 294 G5
Lampman Canada 49°25N 102°50W 343 D8
Lampung □ Indonesia 5°30S 104°30E 308 F2
Lamta India 22°8N 80°7E 315 H9
Lamu Kenya 2°16S 40°55E 326 C5
Lamy U.S.A. 35°29N 105°53W 349 J11
Lan Xian China 38°15N 111°35E 306 E6
Lāna'i U.S.A. 20°50N 156°55W 346 b
Lanak La China 34°27N 79°32E 315 B8
Lanak'o Shank'ou = Lanak La China 34°27N 79°32E 315 B8
Lanark Canada 45°1N 76°22W 355 A8
Lanark U.K. 55°40N 3°47W 283 F5
Lanbi Kyun Burma 10°50N 98°20E 311 G2
Lancang Jiang → China 21°40N 101°10E 304 D5
Lancashire □ U.K. 53°50N 2°48W 284 D5
Lancaster Canada 45°10N 74°30W 355 A10
Lancaster U.K. 54°3N 2°48W 284 C5
Lancaster Calif., U.S.A. 34°42N 118°8W 351 L8
Lancaster Ky., U.S.A. 37°37N 84°35W 353 G11
Lancaster N.H., U.S.A. 44°29N 71°34W 355 B13
Lancaster N.Y., U.S.A. 42°54N 78°40W 354 D6
Lancaster Ohio, U.S.A. 39°43N 82°36W 353 F12
Lancaster Pa., U.S.A. 40°2N 76°19W 355 F8
Lancaster S.C., U.S.A. 34°43N 80°46W 357 D14
Lancaster Wis., U.S.A. 42°51N 90°43W 352 D8
Lancaster Sd. Canada 74°13N 84°0W 341 B11
Lancelin Australia 31°0S 115°18E 333 F2
Lanchow = Lanzhou China 36°1N 103°52E 306 F2
Lanciano Italy 42°14N 14°23E 294 C6
Lancun China 36°25N 120°10E 307 F11
Land Between the Lakes ⌓ U.S.A. 36°25N 88°0W 357 C11
Landeck Austria 47°9N 10°34E 288 E6
Lander U.S.A. 42°50N 108°44W 348 E9
Lander → Australia 22°0S 132°0E 332 D5
Landes France 44°0N 1°0W 292 D3
Landi Kotal Pakistan 34°7N 71°6E 314 B4
Landisburg U.S.A. 40°21N 77°19W 354 F7
Landmannalaugar Iceland 63°59N 19°4W 280 E4
Land's End U.K. 50°4N 5°44W 285 G2
Landsborough Cr. → Australia 22°28S 144°35E 334 C3
Landshut Germany 48°34N 12°8E 288 D7
Lanesboro U.S.A. 41°57N 75°34W 355 E9
Lanett U.S.A. 32°52N 85°12W 357 E12
Lang Qua Vietnam 22°16N 104°27E 310 A5
Lang Shan China 41°0N 106°30E 306 D4

Monte Lindo → Paraguay 23°56S 57°12W 366 A4
Monte Patria Chile 30°42S 70°58W 366 C1
Monte Quemado Argentina 25°53S 62°41W 366 B3
Monte Rio U.S.A. 38°28N 123°0W 350 G4
Monte Santu, C. di Italy 40°5N 9°44E 294 D3
Monte Vista U.S.A. 37°35N 106°9W 349 H10
Monteagudo Argentina 27°14S 54°8W 367 B5
Montebello Canada 45°40N 74°55W 344 C5
Montebello Is. Australia 20°30S 115°45E 332 D2
Montecito U.S.A. 34°26N 119°40W 351 L7
Montecristo Italy 42°20N 10°19E 294 C4
Montego Bay Jamaica 18°28N 77°55W 360 a
Montélimar France 44°33N 4°45E 292 D6
Montello U.S.A. 43°48N 89°20W 352 D9
Montemorelos Mexico 25°12N 99°49W 359 B5
Montenegro Brazil 29°39S 51°29W 367 B5
Montenegro ■ Europe 42°40N 19°20E 295 C8
Montepuez Mozam. 13°8S 38°59E 327 E4
Montepuez → Mozam. 12°32S 40°27E 327 E5
Monterey U.S.A. 36°37N 121°55W 350 J5
Monterey B. U.S.A. 36°45N 122°0W 350 J5
Montería Colombia 8°46N 75°53W 364 B3
Monteros Argentina 27°11S 65°30W 366 B2
Monterrey Mexico 25°40N 100°19W 358 B4
Montes Azules ⌓ Mexico 16°21N 91°3W 359 D6
Montes Claros Brazil 16°30S 43°50W 365 G10
Montesano U.S.A. 46°59N 123°36W 350 D3
Montesilvano Italy 42°29N 14°8E 294 C6
Montevideo Uruguay 34°50S 56°11W 367 C4
Montevideo U.S.A. 44°57N 95°43W 352 C6
Montezuma U.S.A. 41°35N 92°32W 352 E7
Montezuma Castle ⌓ U.S.A. 34°39N 111°45W 349 J8
Montgomery U.K. 52°34N 3°8W 285 E4
Montgomery Ala., U.S.A. 32°23N 86°19W 357 E11
Montgomery Pa., U.S.A. 41°10N 76°53W 354 E8
Montgomery W. Va., U.S.A. 38°11N 81°19W 353 F13
Montgomery City U.S.A. 38°59N 91°30W 352 F8
Monticello Ark., U.S.A. 33°38N 91°47W 356 E9
Monticello Fla., U.S.A. 30°33N 83°52W 357 F13
Monticello Ind., U.S.A. 40°45N 86°46W 352 E10
Monticello Iowa, U.S.A. 42°15N 91°12W 352 D8
Monticello Ky., U.S.A. 36°50N 84°51W 353 G11
Monticello Minn., U.S.A. 45°18N 93°48W 352 C7
Monticello Miss., U.S.A. 31°33N 90°7W 357 F9
Monticello N.Y., U.S.A. 41°39N 74°42W 355 E10
Monticello Utah, U.S.A. 37°52N 109°21W 349 H9
Montijo Portugal 38°41N 8°54W 293 C1
Montilla Spain 37°36N 4°40W 293 D3
Montluçon France 46°22N 2°36E 292 C5
Montmagny Canada 46°58N 70°34W 345 C5
Montmartre Canada 50°14N 103°27W 343 C8
Montmorillon France 46°26N 0°50E 292 C4
Monto Australia 24°52S 151°6E 334 C5
Montongbuwoh Indonesia 8°33S 116°4E 309 K19
Montoro Spain 38°1N 4°27W 293 C3
Montour Falls U.S.A. 42°21N 76°51W 354 D8
Montoursville U.S.A. 41°15N 76°55W 354 E8
Montpelier Idaho, U.S.A. 42°19N 111°18W 348 E8
Montpelier Vt., U.S.A. 44°16N 72°35W 355 B12
Montpellier France 43°37N 3°52E 292 E5
Montréal Canada 45°30N 73°33W 355 A11
Montreal → Canada 47°14N 84°39W 344 C3
Montreal L. Canada 54°20N 105°45W 343 C7
Montreal Lake Canada 54°3N 105°46W 343 C7
Montreux Switz. 46°26N 6°55E 292 C7
Montrose U.K. 56°44N 2°27W 283 E6
Montrose Colo., U.S.A. 38°29N 107°53W 348 G10
Montrose Pa., U.S.A. 41°50N 75°53W 355 E9
Monts, Pte. des Canada 49°20N 67°12W 345 C6
Montserrat ☒ W. Indies 16°40N 62°10W 361 C7
Montuïri Spain 39°34N 2°59E 296 B9
Monywa Burma 22°7N 95°11E 313 H19
Monza Italy 45°35N 9°16E 292 D8
Monze Zambia 16°17S 27°29E 327 F2
Monze, C. Pakistan 24°47N 66°37E 314 G2
Monzón Spain 41°52N 0°10E 293 B6
Mooers U.S.A. 44°58N 73°35W 355 B11
Mooi → S. Africa 28°45S 30°34E 329 D5
Mooi River S. Africa 29°13S 29°50E 329 D4
Moonah → Australia 22°3S 138°33E 334 C2
Moonda, L. Australia 25°52S 140°25E 334 D3
Moonie Australia 27°46S 150°20E 335 D5
Moonie → Australia 29°19S 148°43E 335 D4
Moonta Australia 34°6S 137°32E 335 E2
Moora Australia 30°37S 115°58E 333 F2
Moorcroft U.S.A. 44°16N 104°57W 348 D11
Moore → Australia 31°22S 115°30E 333 F2
Moore, L. Australia 29°50S 117°35E 333 E2
Moore Park Australia 24°43S 152°17E 334 C5
Moore Res. U.S.A. 44°20N 71°53W 355 B13
Moore River △ Australia 31°7S 115°39E 333 F2
Moorea French Polynesia 17°30S 149°50W 331 d
Moorefield U.S.A. 39°4N 78°58W 353 F14
Moorfoot Hills U.K. 55°44N 3°8W 283 F5
Moorhead U.S.A. 46°53N 96°45W 352 B5
Moorpark U.S.A. 34°17N 118°53W 351 L8
Moorreesburg S. Africa 33°6S 18°38E 328 E2
Moorrinya △ Australia 21°42S 144°58E 334 C3
Moose → Canada 51°20N 80°25W 344 B3
Moose → U.S.A. 43°38N 75°24W 355 C9
Moose Creek Canada 45°15N 74°58W 355 A10
Moose Factory Canada 51°16N 80°32W 344 B3
Moose Jaw Canada 50°24N 105°30W 343 C7
Moose Jaw → Canada 50°34N 105°18W 343 C7
Moose Lake Canada 53°46N 100°8W 343 C8
Moose Lake U.S.A. 46°27N 92°46W 352 B7
Moose Mountain ⌓ Canada 49°48N 102°25W 343 D8
Moosehead L. U.S.A. 45°38N 69°40W 353 C19
Mooselookmeguntic L. U.S.A. 44°55N 70°49W 355 B14
Moosilauke, Mt. U.S.A. 44°3N 71°40W 355 B13
Moosomin Canada 50°9N 101°40W 343 C8
Moosonee Canada 51°17N 80°39W 344 B3
Moosup U.S.A. 41°43N 71°53W 355 E13
Mopane S. Africa 22°37S 29°52E 329 C4
Mopeia Velha Mozam. 17°30S 35°40E 327 F4
Mopipi Botswana 21°6S 24°55E 328 C3
Mopoi C.A.R. 5°6N 26°54E 326 A2
Mopti Mali 14°30N 4°0W 322 F5
Moqor Afghan. 32°50N 67°42E 314 C2
Moquegua Peru 17°15S 70°46W 364 G4
Mora Sweden 61°2N 14°38E 280 F16
Mora Minn., U.S.A. 45°53N 93°18W 352 C7
Mora N. Mex., U.S.A. 35°58N 105°20W 349 J11
Moradabad India 28°50N 78°50E 315 E8
Morafenobe Madag. 17°50S 44°53E 329 B7
Moramanga Madag. 18°56S 48°12E 329 B8
Moran Kans., U.S.A. 37°55N 95°10W 352 G6
Moran Wyo., U.S.A. 43°50N 110°31W 348 E8
Moranbah Australia 22°1S 148°6E 334 C4
Morant Bay Jamaica 17°53N 76°25W 360 a
Morant Cays Jamaica 17°22N 76°0W 360 C4
Morant Pt. Jamaica 17°55N 76°12W 360 a
Morar India 26°14N 78°14E 314 F8
Morar, L. U.K. 56°57N 5°40W 283 E3
Moratuwa Sri Lanka 6°45N 79°55E 312 R11
Morava → Serbia 44°36N 21°4E 295 B9
Morava → Slovak Rep. 48°10N 16°59E 289 D9
Moravia U.S.A. 42°43N 76°25W 355 D8
Moravian Hts. = Českomoravská Vrchovina Czech Rep. 49°30N 15°40E 288 D8
Morawa Australia 29°13S 116°0E 333 E2
Morawhanna Guyana 8°30N 59°40W 364 B7
Moray □ U.K. 57°31N 3°18W 283 D5
Moray Firth U.K. 57°40N 3°52W 283 D5
Morbi India 22°50N 70°42E 314 H4
Morden Canada 49°15N 98°10W 343 D9
Mordovian Republic = Mordvinia □ Russia 54°20N 44°30E 290 D7
Mordvinia □ Russia 54°20N 44°30E 290 D7
Morea Greece 37°45N 22°10E 278 H10
Moreau → U.S.A. 45°18N 100°43W 352 C3
Morebeng S. Africa 23°30S 29°55E 329 C4
Morecambe U.K. 54°5N 2°52W 284 C5
Morecambe B. U.K. 54°7N 3°0W 284 C5
Moree Australia 29°28S 149°54E 335 D4
Morehead U.S.A. 38°11N 83°26W 353 F12
Morehead City U.S.A. 34°43N 76°43W 357 D16
Morel → India 26°13N 76°36E 314 F7
Morelia Mexico 19°42N 101°7W 358 D4
Morella Australia 23°0S 143°52E 334 C3
Morella Spain 40°35N 0°5W 293 B5
Morelos Mexico 26°42N 107°40W 358 B3
Morelos □ Mexico 18°45N 99°0W 359 D5
Moremi ⌓ Botswana 19°18S 23°10E 328 B3
Morena India 26°30N 78°4E 314 F8
Morena, Sierra Spain 38°20N 4°0W 293 C3
Moreno Valley U.S.A. 33°56N 117°14W 351 M10
Moresby I. Canada 52°30N 131°40W 342 C2
Moreton I. Australia 27°10S 153°25E 335 D5
Moreton Island △ Australia 27°2S 153°24E 335 D5
Morey Spain 39°44N 3°20E 296 B10
Morgan U.S.A. 41°2N 111°41W 348 F8
Morgan City U.S.A. 29°42N 91°12W 356 G9
Morgan Hill U.S.A. 37°8N 121°39W 350 H5
Morganfield U.S.A. 37°41N 87°55W 352 G10
Morganton U.S.A. 35°45N 81°41W 357 D14
Morgantown U.S.A. 39°38N 79°57W 353 F14
Morgenzon S. Africa 26°45S 29°36E 329 D4
Morghak Iran 29°7N 57°54E 317 D8
Morhar → India 25°29N 85°11E 315 G11
Mori Japan 42°6N 140°35E 302 C10
Moriarty U.S.A. 34°59N 106°3W 349 J10
Morice L. Canada 53°50N 127°40W 342 C3
Morinville Canada 53°49N 113°41W 342 C6
Morioka Japan 39°45N 141°8E 302 E10
Moris Mexico 28°10N 108°32W 358 B3
Morlaix France 48°36N 3°52W 292 B2
Mornington Australia 38°15S 145°5E 335 F4
Mornington, I. Chile 49°50S 75°30W 368 F1
Mornington I. Australia 16°30S 139°30E 334 B2
Moro Pakistan 26°40N 68°0E 314 F2
Moro → Pakistan 29°42N 67°22E 314 E2
Moro G. Phil. 6°30N 123°0E 309 C6
Morocco ■ N. Afr. 32°0N 5°50W 322 B4
Morogoro Tanzania 6°50S 37°40E 326 D4
Morogoro □ Tanzania 8°0S 37°0E 326 D4
Moroleón Mexico 20°8N 101°12W 358 C4
Morombe Madag. 21°45S 43°22E 329 C7
Moron Argentina 34°39S 58°37W 366 C4
Morón Cuba 22°8N 78°39W 360 B4
Morón de la Frontera Spain 37°6N 5°28W 293 D3
Morona → Peru 4°40S 77°10W 364 D3
Morondava Madag. 20°17S 44°17E 329 C7
Morongo Valley U.S.A. 34°3N 116°37W 351 L10
Moroni Comoros Is. 11°40S 43°16E 325 a
Moroni U.S.A. 39°32N 111°35W 348 G8
Morotai Indonesia 2°10N 128°30E 309 D7
Moroto Uganda 2°28N 34°42E 326 B3
Moroto, Mt. Uganda 2°30N 34°43E 326 B3
Morpeth U.K. 55°10N 1°41W 284 B6
Morphou Cyprus 35°12N 32°59E 297 D11
Morphou Bay Cyprus 35°15N 32°50E 297 D11
Morrilton U.S.A. 35°9N 92°44W 356 D8
Morrinhos Brazil 17°45S 49°10W 365 G9
Morrinsville N.Z. 37°40S 175°32E 331 B5
Morris Canada 49°25N 97°22W 343 D9
Morris Ill., U.S.A. 41°22N 88°26W 352 E9
Morris Minn., U.S.A. 45°35N 95°55W 352 C6
Morris N.Y., U.S.A. 42°33N 75°15W 355 D9
Morris Pa., U.S.A. 41°35N 77°17W 354 E7
Morris, Mt. Australia 26°9S 131°4E 333 E5
Morris Jesup, Kap Greenland 83°40N 34°0W 338 A16
Morrisburg Canada 44°55N 75°7W 355 B9
Morristown Ariz., U.S.A. 33°51N 112°37W 349 K7
Morristown N.J., U.S.A. 40°48N 74°29W 355 F10
Morristown N.Y., U.S.A. 44°35N 75°39W 355 B9
Morristown Tenn., U.S.A. 36°13N 83°18W 357 C13
Morrisville N.Y., U.S.A. 42°53N 75°35W 355 D9
Morrisville Pa., U.S.A. 40°13N 74°47W 355 F10
Morrisville Vt., U.S.A. 44°34N 72°36W 355 B12
Morro, Pta. Chile 27°6S 71°0W 366 B1
Morro Bay U.S.A. 35°22N 120°51W 350 K6
Morro del Jable Canary Is. 28°3N 14°23W 296 F5
Morro Jable, Pta. de Canary Is. 28°2N 14°20W 296 F5
Morrocoy △ Venezuela 10°48N 68°13W 361 D6
Morrosquillo, G. de Colombia 9°35N 75°40W 360 E4
Morrumbene Mozam. 23°31S 35°16E 329 C6
Morshansk Russia 53°28N 41°50E 290 D7
Morteros Argentina 30°50S 62°0W 366 C3
Mortlach Canada 50°27N 106°4W 343 C7
Mortlake Australia 38°5S 142°50E 335 F3
Morton Tex., U.S.A. 33°44N 102°46W 356 E3
Morton Wash., U.S.A. 46°34N 122°17W 350 D4
Moruga Trin. & Tob. 10°4N 61°16W 365 K15
Morundah Australia 34°57S 146°19E 335 E4
Moruya Australia 35°58S 150°3E 335 F5
Morvan France 47°5N 4°3E 292 C6
Morven Australia 26°22S 147°5E 335 D4
Morvern U.K. 56°38N 5°44W 283 E3
Morwell Australia 38°10S 146°22E 335 F4
Morzhovets, Ostrov Russia 66°44N 42°35E 290 A7
Moscos Is. Burma 14°0N 97°30E 310 E1
Moscow = Moskva Russia 55°45N 37°37E 290 C6
Moscow Idaho, U.S.A. 46°44N 117°0W 348 C5
Moscow Pa., U.S.A. 41°20N 75°31W 355 E9
Mosel → Europe 50°22N 7°36E 292 A7
Moselle = Mosel → Europe 50°22N 7°36E 292 A7
Moses Lake U.S.A. 47°8N 119°17W 348 C4
Mosgiel N.Z. 45°53S 170°21E 331 F3
Moshaweng → S. Africa 26°35S 22°50E 328 D3
Moshchnyy, Ostrov Russia 60°1N 27°50E 281 F22
Moshi Tanzania 3°22S 37°18E 326 C4
Moshupa Botswana 24°46S 25°29E 328 C4
Mosjøen Norway 65°51N 13°12E 280 D15
Moskenesøya Norway 67°58N 13°0E 280 C15
Moskenstraumen Norway 67°47N 12°45E 280 C15
Moskva Russia 55°45N 37°37E 290 C6
Mosomane Botswana 24°2S 26°19E 328 C4
Mosonmagyaróvár Hungary 47°52N 17°18E 289 E9
Mosquera Colombia 2°35N 78°24W 364 C3
Mosquero U.S.A. 35°47N 103°58W 349 J12
Mosquitia Honduras 15°20N 84°10W 360 C3
Mosquito Coast = Mosquitia Honduras 15°20N 84°10W 360 C3
Mosquito Creek L. U.S.A. 41°18N 80°46W 354 E4
Mosquito L. Canada 62°35N 103°20W 343 A8
Mosquitos, G. de los Panama 9°15N 81°10W 360 E3
Moss Norway 59°27N 10°40E 281 G14
Moss Vale Australia 34°32S 150°25E 335 E5
Mossaka Congo 1°15S 16°45E 324 E3
Mossbank Canada 49°56N 105°56W 343 D7
Mossburn N.Z. 45°41S 168°15E 331 F2
Mosselbaai S. Africa 34°11S 22°8E 328 E3
Mossendjo Congo 2°55S 12°42E 324 E2
Mossgiel Australia 33°15S 144°5E 335 E3
Mossman Australia 16°21S 145°15E 334 B4
Mossoró Brazil 5°10S 37°15W 365 E11
Mossuril Mozam. 14°58S 40°42E 327 E5
Most Czech Rep. 50°31N 13°38E 288 C7
Mosta Malta 35°55N 14°26E 297 D1
Mostaganem Algeria 35°54N 0°5E 322 A6
Mostar Bos.-H. 43°22N 17°50E 295 C7
Mostardas Brazil 31°2S 50°51W 367 C5
Mostiska = Mostyska Ukraine 49°48N 23°4E 289 D12
Mosty = Masty Belarus 53°27N 24°38E 289 B13
Mostyska Ukraine 49°48N 23°4E 289 D12
Mosul = Al Mawşil Iraq 36°15N 43°5E 316 B4
Motagua → Guatemala 15°44N 88°14W 360 C2
Motala Sweden 58°32N 15°1E 281 G16
Motaze Mozam. 24°48S 32°52E 329 C5
Moth India 25°43N 78°57E 315 G8
Motherwell U.K. 55°47N 3°58W 283 F5
Motihari India 26°30N 84°55E 315 F11
Motozintla de Mendoza Mexico 15°22N 92°14W 359 D6
Motril Spain 36°31N 3°37W 293 D4
Mott U.S.A. 46°23N 102°20W 352 B2
Motueka N.Z. 41°7S 173°1E 331 D4
Motueka → N.Z. 41°5S 173°1E 331 D4
Motul Mexico 21°6N 89°17W 359 C7
Mouchalagane → Canada 50°56N 68°41W 345 B6
Moudros Greece 39°50N 25°18E 295 E11
Mouila Gabon 1°50S 11°0E 324 E2
Moulamein Australia 35°3S 144°1E 335 F3
Moule à Chique, C. St. Lucia 13°43N 60°57W 361 f
Mouliana Greece 35°10N 25°59E 297 D7
Moulins France 46°35N 3°19E 292 C5
Moulmein Burma 16°30N 97°40E 313 L20
Moulouya, O. → Morocco 35°5N 2°25W 322 B5
Moultrie U.S.A. 31°11N 83°47W 357 F13
Moultrie, L. U.S.A. 33°20N 80°5W 357 E14
Mound City Mo., U.S.A. 40°7N 95°14W 352 E6
Mound City S. Dak., U.S.A. 45°44N 100°4W 352 C3
Moundou Chad 8°40N 16°10E 323 G9
Moundsville U.S.A. 39°55N 80°44W 354 G4
Moung Cambodia 12°46N 103°27E 310 F4
Mount Airy U.S.A. 36°31N 80°37W 357 C14
Mount Albert Canada 44°8N 79°19W 354 B5
Mount Aspiring △ N.Z. 44°19S 168°47E 331 F2
Mount Barker S. Austral., Australia 35°5S 138°52E 335 F2
Mount Barker W. Austral., Australia 34°38S 117°40E 333 F2
Mount Bellew Bridge Ireland 53°28N 8°31W 282 C3
Mount Brydges Canada 42°54N 81°29W 354 D3
Mount Burr Australia 37°34S 140°26E 335 F3
Mount Carmel = Ha Karmel △ Israel 32°45N 35°5E 318 C4
Mount Carmel Ill., U.S.A. 38°25N 87°46W 352 F10
Mount Carmel Pa., U.S.A. 40°47N 76°26W 355 F8
Mount Clemens U.S.A. 42°35N 82°53W 354 D2
Mount Coolon Australia 21°25S 147°25E 334 C4
Mount Darwin Zimbabwe 16°47S 31°38E 327 F3
Mount Desert I. U.S.A. 44°21N 68°20W 353 C19
Mount Dora U.S.A. 28°48N 81°38W 357 G14
Mount Edziza ⌓ Canada 57°30N 130°45W 342 B2
Mount Elgon △ E. Afr. 1°4N 34°42E 326 B3
Mount Field △ Australia 42°39S 146°35E 335 G4
Mount Fletcher S. Africa 30°40S 28°30E 329 E4
Mount Forest Canada 43°59N 80°43W 354 C4
Mount Frankland △ Australia 31°47S 116°37E 332 F2
Mount Gambier Australia 37°50S 140°46E 335 F3
Mount Garnet Australia 17°37S 145°6E 334 B4
Mount Holly U.S.A. 39°59N 74°47W 355 G10
Mount Holly Springs U.S.A. 40°7N 77°12W 354 F7
Mount Hope N.S.W., Australia 32°51S 145°51E 335 E4
Mount Hope S. Austral., Australia 34°7S 135°23E 335 E2
Mount Isa Australia 20°42S 139°26E 334 C2
Mount Jewett U.S.A. 41°44N 78°39W 354 E6
Mount Kaputar △ Australia 30°16S 150°10E 335 E5
Mount Kenya △ Kenya 0°7S 37°21E 326 C4
Mount Kilimanjaro △ Tanzania 3°2S 37°19E 326 C4
Mount Kisco U.S.A. 41°12N 73°44W 355 E11
Mount Laguna U.S.A. 32°52N 116°25W 351 N10
Mount Larcom Australia 23°48S 150°59E 334 C5
Mount Lofty Ranges Australia 34°35S 139°5E 335 E2
Mount Magnet Australia 28°2S 117°47E 333 E2
Mount Maunganui N.Z. 37°40S 176°14E 331 B6
Mount Molloy Australia 16°42S 145°20E 334 B4
Mount Morgan Australia 23°40S 150°25E 334 C5
Mount Morris U.S.A. 42°44N 77°52W 354 D7
Mount Pearl Canada 47°31N 52°47W 345 C9
Mount Penn U.S.A. 40°20N 75°54W 355 F9
Mount Perry Australia 25°13S 151°42E 335 D5
Mount Pleasant Iowa, U.S.A. 40°58N 91°33W 352 E8
Mount Pleasant Mich., U.S.A. 43°36N 84°46W 353 D11
Mount Pleasant Pa., U.S.A. 40°9N 79°33W 354 F5
Mount Pleasant S.C., U.S.A. 32°47N 79°52W 357 E15
Mount Pleasant Tenn., U.S.A. 35°32N 87°12W 357 D11
Mount Pleasant Tex., U.S.A. 33°9N 94°58W 356 E7
Mount Pleasant Utah, U.S.A. 39°33N 111°27W 348 G8
Mount Pocono U.S.A. 41°7N 75°22W 355 E9
Mount Rainier △ U.S.A. 46°55N 121°50W 350 D5
Mount Revelstoke △ Canada 51°5N 118°30W 342 C5
Mount Robson ⌓ Canada 53°0N 119°0W 342 C5
Mount St. Helens ⌓ U.S.A. 46°14N 122°11W 350 D4
Mount Selinda Zimbabwe 20°24S 32°43E 329 C5
Mount Shasta U.S.A. 41°19N 122°19W 348 F2
Mount Signal U.S.A. 32°39N 115°37W 351 N11
Mount Sterling Ill., U.S.A. 39°59N 90°45W 352 F8
Mount Sterling Ky., U.S.A. 38°4N 83°56W 353 F12
Mount Surprise Australia 18°10S 144°17E 334 B3
Mount Union U.S.A. 40°23N 77°53W 354 F7
Mount Upton U.S.A. 42°26N 75°23W 355 D9
Mount Vernon Ill., U.S.A. 38°19N 88°55W 352 F9
Mount Vernon Ind., U.S.A. 37°56N 87°54W 352 G10
Mount Vernon N.Y., U.S.A. 40°54N 73°49W 355 F11
Mount Vernon Ohio, U.S.A. 40°23N 82°29W 354 F2
Mount Vernon Wash., U.S.A. 48°25N 122°20W 350 B4
Mount William △ Australia 40°56S 148°14E 335 G4
Mountain Ash U.K. 51°40N 3°23W 285 F4
Mountain Center U.S.A. 33°42N 116°44W 351 M10
Mountain City Nev., U.S.A. 41°50N 115°58W 348 F6
Mountain City Tenn., U.S.A. 36°29N 81°48W 357 C14
Mountain Dale U.S.A. 41°41N 74°32W 355 E10
Mountain Grove U.S.A. 37°8N 92°16W 352 G7
Mountain Home Ark., U.S.A. 36°20N 92°23W 356 C8
Mountain Home Idaho, U.S.A. 43°8N 115°41W 348 E6
Mountain Iron U.S.A. 47°32N 92°37W 352 B7
Mountain Pass U.S.A. 35°29N 115°35W 351 K11
Mountain View Ark., U.S.A. 35°52N 92°7W 356 D8
Mountain View Calif., U.S.A. 37°23N 122°5W 350 H4
Mountain View Hawai'i, U.S.A. 19°33N 155°7W 346 b
Mountain Zebra △ S. Africa 32°14S 25°27E 328 E4
Mountainair U.S.A. 34°31N 106°15W 349 J10
Mountlake Terrace U.S.A. 47°47N 122°18W 350 C4
Mountmellick Ireland 53°7N 7°20W 282 C4
Mountrath Ireland 53°0N 7°28W 282 D4
Moura Australia 24°35S 149°58E 334 C4
Moura Brazil 1°32S 61°38W 364 D6
Moura Portugal 38°7N 7°30W 293 C2
Mourdi, Dépression du Chad 18°10N 23°0E 323 E10
Mourilyan Australia 17°35S 146°3E 334 B4
Mourne → U.K. 54°52N 7°26W 282 B4
Mourne Mts. U.K. 54°10N 6°0W 282 B5
Mournies Greece 35°29N 24°1E 297 D6
Mouscron Belgium 50°45N 3°12E 287 D3
Moussoro Chad 13°41N 16°35E 323 F9
Moutong Indonesia 0°28N 121°13E 309 D6
Movas Mexico 28°10N 109°25W 358 B3
Moville Ireland 55°11N 7°3W 282 A4
Mowandjum Australia 17°22S 123°40E 332 C3
Moy → Ireland 54°8N 9°8W 282 B2
Moya Comoros Is. 12°18S 44°18E 325 a
Moyale Kenya 3°30N 39°0E 326 B4
Moyen Atlas Morocco 33°0N 5°0W 322 B4
Moyne, L. Le Canada 56°45N 68°47W 345 A6
Moyo Indonesia 8°10S 117°40E 308 F5
Moyobamba Peru 6°0S 77°0W 364 E3
Moyyero → Russia 68°44N 103°42E 301 C11
Moyynqum Kazakhstan 44°12N 71°0E 300 E8
Moyynty Kazakhstan 47°10N 73°18E 300 E8
Mozambique = Moçambique Mozam. 15°3S 40°42E 327 F5
Mozambique ■ Africa 19°0S 35°0E 327 F4
Mozambique Chan. Africa 17°30S 42°30E 329 B7
Mozdok Russia 43°45N 44°48E 291 F7
Mozdūrān Iran 36°9N 60°35E 317 B9
Mozhnābād Iran 34°7N 60°6E 317 C9
Mozyr = Mazyr Belarus 51°59N 29°15E 289 B15
Mpanda Tanzania 6°23S 31°1E 326 D3
Mphoengs Zimbabwe 21°10S 27°51E 329 C4
Mpika Zambia 11°51S 31°25E 327 E3
Mpulungu Zambia 8°51S 31°5E 327 D3
Mpumalanga S. Africa 29°50S 30°33E 329 D5
Mpumalanga □ S. Africa 26°0S 30°0E 329 B5
Mpwapwa Tanzania 6°23S 36°30E 326 D4
Mqanduli S. Africa 31°49S 28°45E 329 E4
Msaken Tunisia 35°49N 10°33E 323 A8
Msambansovu Zimbabwe 15°50S 30°3E 327 F3
M'sila → Algeria 35°30N 4°29E 322 A6
Msoro Zambia 13°35S 31°50E 327 E3
Mstislavl = Mstsislaw Belarus 54°0N 31°50E 289 A16
Mstsislaw Belarus 54°0N 31°50E 289 A16
Mtama Tanzania 10°17S 39°21E 327 E4
Mtamvuna → S. Africa 31°6S 30°12E 329 E5
Mthatha S. Africa 31°36S 28°49E 329 E4
Mtilikwe → Zimbabwe 21°9S 31°30E 327 G3
Mtito Andei Kenya 2°41S 38°10E 326 C4
Mtubatuba S. Africa 28°30S 32°8E 329 D5
Mtwalume S. Africa 30°30S 30°38E 329 E5
Mtwara-Mikindani Tanzania 10°20S 40°20E 327 E5
Mu Gia, Deo Vietnam 17°40N 105°47E 310 D5
Mu Ko Chang △ Thailand 11°59N 102°22E 311 G4
Mu Us Shamo China 39°0N 109°0E 306 E5
Muang Chiang Rai = Chiang Rai Thailand 19°52N 99°50E 310 C2
Muang Khong Laos 14°7N 105°51E 310 E5
Muang Lamphun Thailand 18°40N 99°2E 310 C2
Muang Mai Thailand 8°5N 98°21E 311 a
Muang Pak Beng Laos 19°54N 101°8E 310 C3
Muar Malaysia 2°3N 102°34E 311 L4
Muarabungo Indonesia 1°28S 102°52E 308 E2
Muaraenim Indonesia 3°40S 103°50E 308 E2

418 Nakhichevan INDEX TO WORLD MAPS

Nakhichevan = Naxçıvan Azerbaijan 39°12N 45°15E 316 B5
Nakhichevan Rep. = Naxçıvan □ Azerbaijan 39°25N 45°26E 316 B5
Nakhl Egypt 29°55N 33°43E 318 F2
Nakhl-e Taqī Iran 27°28N 52°36E 317 E7
Nakhodka Russia 42°53N 132°54E 302 C6
Nakhon Nayok Thailand 14°12N 101°13E 310 E3
Nakhon Pathom Thailand 13°49N 100°3E 310 F3
Nakhon Phanom Thailand 17°23N 104°43E 310 D5
Nakhon Ratchasima Thailand 14°59N 102°12E 310 E4
Nakhon Sawan Thailand 15°35N 100°10E 310 E3
Nakhon Si Thammarat Thailand 8°29N 100°0E 311 H3
Nakhon Thai Thailand 17°5N 100°44E 310 D3
Nakhtarana India 23°20N 69°15E 314 H3
Nakina Canada 50°10N 86°40W 344 B2
Nakodar India 31°8N 75°31E 314 D6
Naktong → S. Korea 35°7N 128°57E 307 G15
Nakuru Kenya 0°15S 36°4E 326 C4
Nakuru, L. Kenya 0°23S 36°5E 326 C4
Nakusp Canada 50°20N 117°45W 342 C5
Nal Pakistan 27°40N 66°12E 314 F2
Nal → Pakistan 25°20N 65°30E 314 G1
Nalázi Mozam. 24°3S 33°20E 329 C5
Nalchik Russia 43°30N 43°33E 291 F7
Nalgonda India 17°6N 79°15E 312 L11
Nalhati India 24°17N 87°52E 315 G12
Naliya India 23°16N 68°50E 314 H3
Nallamalai Hills India 15°30N 78°50E 312 M11
Nalubaale Dam Uganda 0°30N 33°5E 326 B3
Nam Can Vietnam 8°46N 104°59E 311 H5
Nam-ch'on N. Korea 38°15N 126°26E 307 E14
Nam Co China 30°30N 90°45E 304 C4
Nam Dinh Vietnam 20°25N 106°5E 310 B6
Nam Du, Hon Vietnam 9°41N 104°21E 311 H5
Nam Nao △ Thailand 16°44N 101°32E 310 D3
Nam Ngum Res. Laos 18°35N 102°34E 310 C4
Nam-Phan Vietnam 10°30N 106°0E 311 G6
Nam Phong Thailand 16°42N 102°52E 310 D4
Nam Tha Laos 20°58N 101°30E 310 B3
Nam Tok Thailand 14°21N 99°4E 310 E2
Namacunde Angola 17°18S 15°50E 328 B2
Namacurra Mozam. 17°30S 36°50E 329 B6
Namak, Daryācheh-ye Iran 34°30N 52°0E 317 C7
Namak, Kavir-e Iran 34°30N 57°30E 317 C8
Namakzār, Daryācheh-ye Iran 34°0N 60°30E 317 C9
Namaland Namibia 26°0S 17°0E 328 C2
Namanga Kenya 2°33S 36°47E 326 C4
Namangan Uzbekistan 41°0N 71°40E 300 E8
Namapa Mozam. 13°43S 39°50E 327 E4
Namaqualand S. Africa 30°0S 17°25E 328 E2
Namasagali Uganda 1°2N 33°0E 326 B3
Namber Indonesia 1°2S 134°49E 309 E8
Nambour Australia 26°32S 152°58E 335 D5
Nambouwalu = Nabouwalu Fiji 17°0S 178°45E 331 a
Nambucca Heads Australia 30°37S 153°0E 335 E5
Nambung △ Australia 30°30S 115°5E 333 F2
Namcha Barwa China 29°40N 95°10E 304 D4
Namche Bazar Nepal 27°51N 86°47E 315 F12
Namchonjŏm = Nam-ch'on N. Korea 38°15N 126°26E 307 E14
Namecunda Mozam. 14°54S 37°37E 327 E4
Namenalala Fiji 17°8S 179°9E 331 a
Nameponda Mozam. 15°50S 39°50E 327 F4
Nametil Mozam. 15°40S 39°21E 327 F4
Namew L. Canada 54°14N 101°56W 343 C8
Namgia India 31°48N 78°40E 315 D8
Namib Desert Namibia 22°30S 15°0E 328 C2
Namib-Naukluft ⌂ Namibia 24°40S 15°16E 328 C2
Namibe Angola 15°7S 12°11E 325 H2
Namibe □ Angola 16°35S 12°30E 328 B1
Namibia ■ Africa 22°0S 18°9E 328 C2
Namibwoestyn = Namib Desert Namibia 22°30S 15°0E 328 C2
Namlea Indonesia 3°18S 127°5E 309 E7
Namoi → Australia 30°12S 149°30E 335 E4
Nampa U.S.A. 43°34N 116°34W 348 E5
Namp'o N. Korea 38°52N 125°10E 307 E13
Nampō-Shotō Japan 32°0N 140°0E 303 J10
Nampula Mozam. 15°6S 39°15E 327 F4
Namrole Indonesia 3°46S 126°46E 309 E7
Namse Shankou China 30°0N 82°25E 315 E10
Namsen → Norway 64°28N 11°37E 280 D14
Namsos Norway 64°29N 11°30E 280 D14
Namtok Chat Trakan △ Thailand 17°17N 100°40E 310 D3
Namtok Mae Surin △ Thailand 18°55N 98°2E 310 C2
Namtsy Russia 62°43N 129°37E 301 C13
Namtu Burma 23°5N 97°28E 313 H20
Namtumbo Tanzania 10°30S 36°4E 327 E4
Namu Canada 51°52N 127°50W 342 C3
Namuka-i-Lau Fiji 18°53S 178°37W 331 a
Namur Belgium 50°27N 4°52E 287 D4
Namur □ Belgium 50°17N 5°0E 287 D4
Namuruputh Kenya 4°34N 35°57E 326 B4
Namutoni Namibia 18°49S 16°55E 328 B2
Namwala Zambia 15°44S 26°30E 327 F2
Namwon S. Korea 35°23N 127°23E 307 G14
Namyang N. Korea 42°57N 129°52E 307 C15
Nan Thailand 18°48N 100°46E 310 C3
Nan → Thailand 15°42N 100°9E 310 E3
Nan-ch'ang = Nanchang China 28°42N 115°55E 305 D6
Nanaimo Canada 49°10N 124°0W 342 D4
Nanam N. Korea 41°44N 129°40E 307 D15
Nanango Australia 26°40S 152°0E 335 D5
Nanao Japan 37°0N 137°0E 303 F8
Nanchang China 28°42N 115°55E 305 D6
Nanching = Nanjing China 32°2N 118°47E 305 C6
Nanchong China 30°43N 106°2E 304 C5
Nancy France 48°42N 6°12E 292 B7
Nanda Devi India 30°23N 79°59E 315 D8
Nanda Devi △ India 30°30N 79°50E 315 D8
Nanda Kot India 30°17N 80°5E 315 D9
Nandan Japan 34°10N 134°42E 303 G7
Nanded India 19°10N 77°20E 312 K10
Nandewar Ra. Australia 30°15S 150°35E 335 E5
Nandi = Nadi Fiji 17°42S 177°20E 331 a
Nandigram India 22°1N 87°58E 315 H12
Nandurbar India 21°20N 74°15E 312 J9
Nandyal India 15°30N 78°30E 312 M11
Nanga-Eboko Cameroon 4°41N 12°22E 324 D2
Nanga Parbat Pakistan 35°10N 74°35E 315 B6
Nangade Mozam. 11°5S 39°36E 327 E4
Nangapinoh Indonesia 0°20S 111°44E 308 E4
Nangarhār □ Afghan. 34°20N 70°0E 312 B7
Nangatayap Indonesia 1°32S 110°34E 308 E4
Nangeya Mts. Uganda 3°30N 33°30E 326 B3
Nangong China 37°23N 115°22E 306 F8
Nanhuang China 36°58N 121°48E 307 F11
Nanjeko Zambia 15°31S 23°30E 327 F1
Nanjing China 32°2N 118°47E 305 C6
Nanjirinji Tanzania 9°41S 39°5E 327 D4
Nankana Sahib Pakistan 31°27N 73°38E 314 D5
Nanking = Nanjing China 32°2N 118°47E 305 C6
Nankoku Japan 33°39N 133°44E 303 H6
Nanlang China 22°30N 113°32E 305 G10
Nanning China 22°48N 108°20E 304 D5
Nannup Australia 33°59S 115°48E 333 F2
Nanpara India 27°52N 81°33E 315 F9
Nanpi China 38°2N 116°45E 306 E9
Nanping China 26°38N 118°10E 305 D6
Nanripe Mozam. 13°52S 38°52E 327 E4
Nansei-Shotō = Ryūkyū-rettō Japan 26°0N 126°0E 303 M3
Nansen Basin Arctic 84°0N 50°0E 276 A10
Nansen Sd. Canada 81°0N 91°0W 341 A10
Nansha China 22°45N 113°34E 305 F10
Nanshan I. S. China Sea 10°45N 115°49E 308 B5
Nansio Tanzania 2°3S 33°4E 326 C3
Nantes France 47°12N 1°33W 292 C3
Nanticoke U.S.A. 41°12N 76°0W 355 E8
Nanton Canada 50°21N 113°46W 342 C6
Nantong China 32°1N 120°52E 305 C7
Nantou China 22°32N 113°55E 305 F10
Nantucket I. U.S.A. 41°16N 70°5W 353 E18
Nantwich U.K. 53°4N 2°31W 284 D5
Nanty Glo U.S.A. 40°28N 78°50W 354 F6
Nanuku Passage Fiji 16°45S 179°15W 331 a
Nanuque Brazil 17°50S 40°21W 365 G10
Nanusa, Kepulauan Indonesia 4°45N 127°1E 309 D7
Nanutarra Roadhouse Australia 22°32S 115°30E 332 D2
Nanyang China 33°11N 112°30E 306 H7
Nanyuki Kenya 0°2N 37°4E 326 B4
Nao, C. de la Spain 38°44N 0°14E 293 C6
Naococane, L. Canada 52°50N 70°45W 345 B5
Napa U.S.A. 38°18N 122°17W 350 G4
Napa → U.S.A. 38°10N 122°19W 350 G4
Napanee Canada 44°15N 77°0W 354 B8
Napanoch U.S.A. 41°44N 74°22W 355 E10
Nape Laos 18°18N 105°6E 310 C5
Nape Pass = Keo Neua, Deo Vietnam 18°23N 105°10E 310 C5
Napier N.Z. 39°30S 176°56E 331 C6
Napier Broome B. Australia 14°2S 126°37E 332 B4
Napier Pen. Australia 12°4S 135°43E 334 A2
Napierville Canada 45°11N 73°25W 355 A11
Naples = Nápoli Italy 40°50N 14°15E 294 D6
Naples U.S.A. 26°8N 81°48W 357 H14
Napo → Peru 3°20S 72°40W 364 D4
Napoleon N. Dak., U.S.A. 46°30N 99°46W 352 B4
Napoleon Ohio, U.S.A. 41°23N 84°8W 353 E11
Nápoli Italy 40°50N 14°15E 294 D6
Napopo Dem. Rep. of the Congo 4°15N 28°0E 326 B2
Naqb, Ra's an Jordan 29°48N 35°44E 318 F4
Naqqāsh Iran 35°40N 49°6E 317 C6
Nara Japan 34°40N 135°49E 303 G7
Nara Mali 15°10N 7°20W 322 E4
Nara □ Japan 34°30N 136°0E 303 G8
Nara Canal Pakistan 24°30N 69°20E 314 G3
Nara Visa U.S.A. 35°37N 103°6W 349 J12
Naracoorte Australia 36°58S 140°45E 335 F3
Naradhan Australia 33°34S 146°17E 335 E4
Naraini India 25°11N 80°29E 315 G9
Naranjos Mexico 21°21N 97°41W 359 C5
Narasapur India 16°26N 81°40E 313 L12
Narathiwat Thailand 6°30N 101°48E 311 J3
Narayanganj Bangla. 23°40N 90°33E 313 H17
Narayanpet India 16°45N 77°30E 312 L10
Narberth U.K. 51°47N 4°44W 285 F3
Narbonne France 43°11N 3°0E 292 E5
Nardīn Iran 37°3N 55°59E 317 B7
Nardò Italy 40°11N 18°2E 295 D8
Narembeen Australia 32°7S 118°24E 333 F2
Narendranagar India 30°10N 78°18E 314 D8
Nares Str. Arctic 80°0N 70°0W 338 A13
Naretha Australia 31°0S 124°45E 333 F3
Narew → Poland 52°26N 20°41E 289 B11
Nari → Pakistan 28°0N 67°40E 314 F2
Narin Afghan. 36°5N 69°0E 312 A6
Narindra, Helodranon' i Madag. 14°55S 47°30E 329 A8
Narita Japan 35°47N 140°19E 303 G10
Nariva Swamp Trin. & Tob. 10°26N 61°4W 365 K15
Narmada → India 21°38N 72°36E 314 J5
Narnaul India 28°5N 76°11E 314 E7
Narodnaya Russia 65°5N 59°58E 290 A10
Narok Kenya 1°55S 35°52E 326 C4
Narooma Australia 36°14S 150°4E 335 F5
Narowal Pakistan 32°6N 74°52E 314 C6
Narrabri Australia 30°19S 149°46E 335 E4
Narran → Australia 28°37S 148°12E 335 D4
Narrandera Australia 34°42S 146°31E 335 E4
Narrogin Australia 32°58S 117°14E 333 F2
Narromine Australia 32°12S 148°12E 335 E4
Narrow Hills ⌂ Canada 54°0N 104°37W 343 C8
Narsimhapur India 22°54N 79°14E 315 H8
Narsinghgarh India 23°45N 76°40E 314 H7
Naruto Japan 34°11N 134°37E 303 G7
Narva Estonia 59°23N 28°12E 290 C4
Narva → Russia 59°27N 28°2E 281 G23
Narva Bay = Narva Laht Estonia 59°35N 27°35E 281 G22
Narva Laht Estonia 59°35N 27°35E 281 G22
Narvik Norway 68°28N 17°26E 280 B17
Narwana India 29°39N 76°6E 314 E7
Naryan-Mar Russia 67°42N 53°12E 290 A9
Narym Russia 59°0N 81°30E 300 D9
Naryn Kyrgyzstan 41°26N 75°58E 300 E8
Nasa Norway 66°29N 15°23E 280 C16
Nasau Fiji 17°19S 179°27E 331 a
Nasca = Nazca Peru 14°50S 74°57W 364 F4
Naseby N.Z. 45°1S 170°10E 331 F3
Naselle U.S.A. 46°22N 123°49W 350 D3
Naser, Buheirat en Egypt 23°0N 32°30E 323 D12
Nashua Mont., U.S.A. 48°8N 106°22W 348 B10
Nashua N.H., U.S.A. 42°45N 71°28W 355 D13
Nashville Ark., U.S.A. 33°57N 93°51W 356 E8
Nashville Ga., U.S.A. 31°12N 83°15W 357 F13
Nashville Tenn., U.S.A. 36°10N 86°47W 357 C11
Nasik India 19°58N 73°50E 312 K8
Nasirabad India 26°15N 74°45E 314 F6
Nasirabad Pakistan 28°23N 68°24E 314 E3
Nasiriyah = An Nāşirīyah Iraq 31°0N 46°15E 316 D5
Naskaupi → Canada 53°47N 60°51W 345 B7
Naşrābād Iran 34°8N 51°26E 317 C6
Naşriān-e Pā'īn Iran 32°52N 46°52E 316 C5
Nass → Canada 55°0N 129°40W 342 C3
Nassau Bahamas 25°5N 77°20W 360 A4
Nassau U.S.A. 42°31N 73°37W 355 D11
Nassau, B. Chile 55°20S 68°0W 368 H3
Nasser, L. = Naser, Buheirat en Egypt 23°0N 32°30E 323 D12
Nässjö Sweden 57°39N 14°42E 281 H16
Nastapoka → Canada 56°55N 76°33W 344 A4
Nastapoka, Is. Canada 56°55N 76°50W 344 A4
Nata Botswana 20°12S 26°12E 328 C4
Nata → Botswana 20°14S 26°10E 328 C4
Natal Brazil 5°47S 35°13W 365 E11
Natal Indonesia 0°35N 99°7E 308 D1
Natal Drakensberg ⌂ S. Africa 29°27S 29°30E 329 D4
Naţanz Iran 33°30N 51°55E 317 C6
Natashquan Canada 50°14N 61°46W 345 B7
Natashquan → Canada 50°7N 61°50W 345 B7
Natchez U.S.A. 31°34N 91°24W 356 F9
Natchitoches U.S.A. 31°46N 93°5W 356 F8
Natewa B. Fiji 16°35S 179°40E 331 a
Nathalia Australia 36°1S 145°13E 335 F4
Nathdwara India 24°55N 73°50E 314 G5
Nati, Pta. Spain 40°3N 3°50E 296 A10
Natimuk Australia 36°42S 142°0E 335 F3
Nation → Canada 55°30N 123°32W 342 B4
National City U.S.A. 32°40N 117°5W 351 N9
Natitingou Benin 10°20N 1°26E 322 F6
Natividad, I. Mexico 27°52N 115°11W 358 B1
Natkyizin Burma 14°57N 97°59E 310 E1
Natron, L. Tanzania 2°20S 36°0E 326 C4
Natrona Heights U.S.A. 40°37N 79°44W 354 F5
Natukanaoka Pan Namibia 18°40S 15°45E 328 B2
Natuna Besar, Kepulauan Indonesia 4°0N 108°15E 308 D3
Natuna Is. = Natuna Besar, Kepulauan Indonesia 4°0N 108°15E 308 D3
Natuna Selatan, Kepulauan Indonesia 2°45N 109°0E 308 D3
Natural Bridge U.S.A. 44°5N 75°30W 355 B9
Natural Bridges ⌂ U.S.A. 37°36N 110°0W 349 H9
Naturaliste, C. Tas., Australia 40°50S 148°15E 335 G4
Naturaliste, C. W. Austral., Australia 33°32S 115°0E 330 E4
Naturaliste Plateau Ind. Oc. 34°0S 112°0E 336 L3
Nau Qala Afghan. 34°5N 68°5E 314 B3
Naugatuck U.S.A. 41°30N 73°3W 355 E11
Naujaat = Repulse Bay Canada 66°30N 86°30W 341 C11
Naumburg Germany 51°9N 11°47E 288 C6
Nauru ■ Pac. Oc. 1°0S 166°0E 330 B9
Naushahra = Nowshera Pakistan 34°0N 72°0E 312 C8
Naushahro Pakistan 26°50N 68°7E 314 F3
Naushon I. U.S.A. 41°29N 70°45W 355 E14
Nausori Fiji 18°2S 178°32E 331 a
Nauta Peru 4°31S 73°35W 364 D4
Nautanwa India 27°20N 83°25E 315 F10
Naute ⌂ Namibia 26°55S 17°57E 328 D2
Nautla Mexico 20°13N 96°47W 359 C5
Nava Mexico 28°25N 100°45W 358 B4
Navadwip India 23°34N 88°20E 315 H13
Navahrudak Belarus 53°40N 25°50E 289 B13
Navajo Res. U.S.A. 36°48N 107°36W 349 H10
Navalmoral de la Mata Spain 39°52N 5°33W 293 C3
Navan = An Uaimh Ireland 53°39N 6°41W 282 C5
Navarin, Mys Russia 62°15N 179°5E 276 C16
Navarino, I. Chile 55°0S 67°40W 368 H3
Navarra □ Spain 42°40N 1°40W 293 A5
Navarre U.S.A. 40°43N 81°31W 354 F3
Navarro → U.S.A. 39°11N 123°45W 350 F3
Navasota U.S.A. 30°23N 96°5W 356 F6
Navassa I. W. Indies 18°30N 75°0W 361 C5
Naver → U.K. 58°32N 4°14W 283 C4
Navibandar India 21°26N 69°48E 314 J3
Navidad Chile 33°57S 71°50W 366 C1
Naviraí Brazil 23°8S 54°13W 367 A5
Naviti Fiji 17°7S 177°15E 331 a
Navlakhi India 22°58N 70°28E 314 H4
Năvodari Romania 44°19N 28°36E 289 F15
Navoi = Nawoiy Uzbekistan 40°9N 65°22E 300 E7
Navojoa Mexico 27°6N 109°26W 358 B3
Navolato Mexico 24°47N 107°42W 358 C3
Navsari India 20°57N 72°59E 312 J8
Navua Fiji 18°12S 178°11E 331 a
Nawa Kot Pakistan 28°21N 71°24E 314 E4
Nawab Khan Pakistan 30°17N 69°12E 314 D3
Nawabganj Ut. P., India 26°56N 81°14E 315 F9
Nawabganj Ut. P., India 28°32N 79°40E 315 E8
Nawabshah Pakistan 26°15N 68°25E 314 F3
Nawada India 24°50N 85°33E 315 G11
Nawakot Nepal 27°55N 85°10E 315 F11
Nawalgarh India 27°50N 75°15E 314 F6
Nawanshahr India 32°33N 74°48E 315 C6
Nawar, Dasht-i- Afghan. 33°52N 68°0E 314 C3
Nawoiy Uzbekistan 40°9N 65°22E 300 E7
Naxçıvan Azerbaijan 39°12N 45°15E 316 B5
Naxçıvan □ Azerbaijan 39°25N 45°26E 316 B5
Naxos Greece 37°8N 25°25E 295 F11
Nay, Mui Vietnam 12°55N 109°23E 308 B3
Nāy Band Būshehr, Iran 27°20N 52°40E 317 E7
Nāy Band Khorāsān, Iran 32°20N 57°34E 317 C8
Nayakhan Russia 61°56N 159°0E 301 C16
Nayarit □ Mexico 22°0N 105°0W 358 C4
Nayau Fiji 18°6S 178°10E 331 a
Nayoro Japan 44°21N 142°28E 302 B11
Nayyāl, W. → Si. Arabia 28°35N 39°4E 316 D3
Nazaré Brazil 13°2S 39°0W 365 F11
Nazareth = Nazerat Israel 32°42N 35°17E 318 C4
Nazareth U.S.A. 40°44N 75°19W 355 F9
Nazas Mexico 25°14N 104°8W 358 B4
Nazas → Mexico 25°12N 104°12W 358 B4
Nazca Peru 14°50S 74°57W 364 F4
Nazca Ridge Pac. Oc. 20°0S 80°0W 337 K19
Naze Japan 28°22N 129°27E 303 K4
Naze, The U.K. 51°53N 1°18E 285 F9
Nazerat Israel 32°42N 35°17E 318 C4
Nāzīk Iran 39°1N 45°4E 316 B5
Nazilli Turkey 37°55N 28°15E 295 F13
Nazko Canada 53°1N 123°37W 342 C4
Nazko → Canada 53°7N 123°34W 342 C4
Nazret Ethiopia 8°32N 39°22E 319 F2
Nchanga Zambia 12°30S 27°49E 327 E2
Ncheu Malawi 14°50S 34°47E 327 E3
Ndala Tanzania 4°45S 33°15E 326 C3
Ndalatando Angola 9°12S 14°48E 324 F2
Ndareda Tanzania 4°12S 35°30E 326 C4
Ndélé C.A.R. 8°25N 20°36E 324 C4
Ndjamena Chad 12°10N 14°59E 323 F8
Ndola Zambia 13°0S 28°34E 327 E2
Ndomo ⌂ S. Africa 26°52S 32°15E 329 D5
Ndoto Mts. Kenya 2°0N 37°0E 326 B4
Nduguti Tanzania 4°18S 34°41E 326 C3
Neagh, Lough U.K. 54°37N 6°25W 282 B5
Neah Bay U.S.A. 48°22N 124°37W 350 B2
Neale, L. Australia 24°15S 130°0E 332 D5
Neales → Australia 28°8S 136°47E 335 D2
Neapoli Greece 35°15N 25°37E 297 D7
Near Is. U.S.A. 52°30N 174°0E 346 a
Neath U.K. 51°39N 3°48W 285 F4
Neath Port Talbot □ U.K. 51°42N 3°45W 285 F4
Nebine Cr. → Australia 29°27S 146°56E 335 D4
Nebitdag = Balkanabat Turkmenistan 39°30N 54°22E 317 B7
Nebo Australia 21°42S 148°42E 334 C4
Nebraska □ U.S.A. 41°30N 99°30W 352 E4
Nebraska City U.S.A. 40°41N 95°52W 352 E6
Nébrodi, Monti Italy 37°54N 14°35E 294 F6
Necedah U.S.A. 44°2N 90°4W 352 C8
Nechako → Canada 53°55N 122°42W 342 C4
Neches → U.S.A. 29°58N 93°51W 356 G8
Neckar → Germany 49°27N 8°29E 288 D5
Necochea Argentina 38°30S 58°50W 366 D4
Nederland = Netherlands ■ Europe 52°0N 5°30E 287 C5
Needles Canada 49°53N 118°7W 342 D5
Needles U.S.A. 34°51N 114°37W 351 L12
Needles, The U.K. 50°39N 1°35W 285 G6
Ñeembucú □ Paraguay 27°0S 58°0W 366 B4
Neemuch = Nimach India 24°30N 74°56E 314 G6
Neenah U.S.A. 44°11N 88°28W 352 C9
Neepawa Canada 50°15N 99°30W 343 C9
Neftçala Azerbaijan 39°19N 49°12E 317 B6
Neftekumsk Russia 44°46N 44°50E 291 F7
Nefyn U.K. 52°56N 4°31W 284 E3
Negapatam = Nagappattinam India 10°46N 79°51E 312 P11
Negara Indonesia 8°22S 114°37E 309 J17
Negaunee U.S.A. 46°30N 87°36W 352 B10
Negele Ethiopia 5°20N 39°36E 319 F2
Negev Desert = Hanegev Israel 30°50N 35°0E 318 E4
Negombo Sri Lanka 7°12N 79°50E 312 R11
Negotin Serbia 44°16N 22°37E 295 B10
Negra, Pta. Mauritania 22°54N 16°18W 322 D2
Negra, Pta. Peru 6°6S 81°10W 364 E2
Negrais, C. = Maudin Sun Burma 16°0N 94°30E 313 M19
Negril Jamaica 18°22N 78°20W 360 a
Negro → Argentina 41°2S 62°47W 368 E4
Negro → Brazil 3°0S 60°0W 364 D7
Negro → Uruguay 33°24S 58°22W 366 C4
Negros Phil. 9°30N 122°40E 309 C6
Neguac Canada 47°15N 65°5W 345 C6
Nehalem → U.S.A. 45°40N 123°56W 350 E3
Nehāvand Iran 35°56N 49°31E 317 C6
Nehbandān Iran 31°35N 60°5E 317 D9
Nei Monggol Zizhiqu □ China 42°0N 112°0E 306 D7
Neiafu Tonga 18°39S 173°59W 331 c
Neiges, Piton des Réunion 21°5S 55°29E 325 c
Neijiang China 29°35N 104°55E 304 D5
Neilingding Dao China 22°25N 113°48E 305 G10
Neillsville U.S.A. 44°34N 90°36W 352 C8
Neilton U.S.A. 47°25N 123°53W 348 C2
Neiqiu China 37°15N 114°30E 306 F8
Neiva Colombia 2°56N 75°18W 364 C3
Neixiang China 33°10N 111°52E 306 H6
Nejanilini L. Canada 59°33N 97°48W 343 B9
Nejd = Najd Si. Arabia 26°30N 42°0E 319 B3
Nekā Iran 36°39N 53°19E 317 B7
Nekemte Ethiopia 9°4N 36°30E 319 F2
Neksø Denmark 55°4N 15°8E 281 J16
Nelia Australia 20°39S 142°12E 334 C3
Neligh U.S.A. 42°8N 98°2W 352 D4
Nelkan Russia 57°40N 136°4E 301 D14
Nellore India 14°27N 79°59E 312 M11
Nelson Canada 49°30N 117°20W 342 D5
Nelson N.Z. 41°18S 173°16E 331 D4
Nelson U.K. 53°50N 2°13W 284 D5
Nelson Ariz., U.S.A. 35°31N 113°19W 349 J7
Nelson Nev., U.S.A. 35°42N 114°49W 351 K12
Nelson → Canada 54°33N 98°2W 343 C9
Nelson, C. Australia 38°26S 141°32E 335 F3
Nelson, Estrecho Chile 51°30S 75°0W 368 G2
Nelson Forks Canada 59°30N 124°0W 342 B4
Nelson House Canada 55°47N 98°51W 343 B9
Nelson L. Canada 55°48N 100°7W 343 B8
Nelson Lakes △ N.Z. 41°55S 172°44E 331 D4
Nelspoort S. Africa 32°7S 23°0E 328 E3
Nelspruit S. Africa 25°29S 30°59E 329 D5
Néma Mauritania 16°40N 7°15W 322 E4
Neman = Nemunas → Lithuania 55°25N 21°10E 281 J19
Nemeiben L. Canada 55°20N 105°20W 343 B7
Nemiscau Canada 51°18N 76°54W 344 B4
Nemiscau, L. Canada 51°25N 76°40W 344 B4
Nemunas → Lithuania 55°25N 21°10E 281 J19
Nemuro Japan 43°20N 145°35E 302 C12
Nemuro-Kaikyō Japan 43°30N 145°30E 302 C12
Nen Jiang → China 45°28N 124°30E 307 B13
Nenagh Ireland 52°52N 8°11W 282 D3
Nenasi Malaysia 3°9N 103°23E 311 L4
Nene → U.K. 52°49N 0°11E 285 E8
Nenjiang China 49°10N 125°10E 305 B7
Neno Malawi 15°25S 34°40E 327 F3
Neodesha U.S.A. 37°25N 95°41W 352 G6
Neora Valley △ India 27°0N 88°45E 315 F13
Neosho U.S.A. 36°52N 94°22W 352 G6
Neosho → U.S.A. 36°48N 95°18W 356 C7
Nepal ■ Asia 28°0N 84°30E 315 F11
Nepalganj Nepal 28°5N 81°40E 315 E9
Nepalganj Road India 28°1N 81°41E 315 E9
Nephi U.S.A. 39°43N 111°50W 348 G8
Nephin Ireland 54°1N 9°22W 282 B2
Nephin Beg Range Ireland 54°0N 9°40W 282 C2
Neptune U.S.A. 40°13N 74°2W 355 F10
Nerang Australia 27°58S 153°20E 335 D5
Nerastro, Sarīr Libya 24°20N 20°37E 323 D10
Nerchinsk Russia 52°0N 116°39E 301 D12
Néret, L. Canada 54°45N 70°44W 345 B5
Neretva → Croatia 43°1N 17°27E 295 C7
Neringa Lithuania 55°20N 21°5E 281 J19
Neris → Lithuania 55°8N 24°16E 281 J21
Neryungri Russia 57°38N 124°28E 301 D13
Nescopeck U.S.A. 41°3N 76°12W 355 E8
Ness, L. U.K. 57°15N 4°32W 283 D4
Ness City U.S.A. 38°27N 99°54W 352 F4
Nesterov Ukraine 50°4N 23°58E 289 C12
Nesvizh = Nyasvizh Belarus 53°14N 26°38E 289 B14
Netanya Israel 32°20N 34°51E 318 C3
Netarhat India 23°29N 84°16E 315 H11
Nete → Belgium 51°7N 4°14E 287 C4
Netherdale Australia 21°10S 148°33E 334 K6
Netherlands ■ Europe 52°0N 5°30E 287 C5
Netherlands Antilles ☑ W. Indies 12°15N 69°0W 364 A5
Netrang India 21°39N 73°21E 314 J5
Nettilling L. Canada 66°30N 71°0W 341 C12
Netzahualcóyotl, Presa Mexico 17°8N 93°35W 359 D6
Neubrandenburg Germany 53°33N 13°15E 288 B7
Neuchâtel Switz. 47°0N 6°55E 292 C7
Neuchâtel, Lac de Switz. 46°53N 6°50E 292 C7
Neufchâteau Belgium 49°50N 5°25E 287 E5
Neumayer Antarctica 71°0S 68°30W 277 D17
Neumünster Germany 54°4N 9°58E 288 A5
Neunkirchen Germany 49°20N 7°9E 288 D4
Neuquén Argentina 38°55S 68°0W 368 D3
Neuquén □ Argentina 38°0S 69°50W 366 D2
Neuruppin Germany 52°55N 12°48E 288 B7
Neuse → U.S.A. 35°6N 76°29W 357 D16
Neusiedler See Austria 47°50N 16°47E 289 E9
Neustrelitz Germany 53°21N 13°4E 288 B7
Neva → Russia 59°56N 30°20E 290 C5
Nevada Iowa, U.S.A. 42°1N 93°27W 352 D7
Nevada Mo., U.S.A. 37°51N 94°22W 352 G6
Nevada □ U.S.A. 39°0N 117°0W 348 G5
Nevada City U.S.A. 39°16N 121°1W 350 F6
Nevado, Cerro Argentina 35°30S 68°32W 366 D2
Nevado de Colima = Volcán de Colima △ Mexico 19°30N 103°40W 358 D4

Ritter, Mt. U.S.A. 37°41N 119°12W 350 H7
Rittman U.S.A. 40°58N 81°47W 354 F3
Ritzville U.S.A. 47°8N 118°23W 348 C4
Riva del Garda Italy 45°53N 10°50E 294 B4
Rivadavia B. Aires, Argentina 35°29S 62°59W 366 D3
Rivadavia Mendoza, Argentina 33°13S 68°30W 366 C2
Rivadavia Salta, Argentina 24°5S 62°54W 366 A3
Rivadavia Chile 29°57S 70°35W 366 B1
Rivas Nic. 11°30N 85°50W 360 D2
River Cess Liberia 5°30N 9°32W 322 G4
River Jordan Canada 48°26N 124°3W 350 B2
Rivera Argentina 37°12S 63°14W 366 D3
Rivera Uruguay 31°0S 55°50W 367 C4
Riverbank U.S.A. 37°44N 120°56W 350 H6
Riverdale U.S.A. 36°26N 119°52W 350 J7
Riverhead U.S.A. 40°55N 72°40W 355 F12
Riverhurst Canada 50°55N 106°50W 343 C7
Rivers Canada 50°2N 100°14W 343 C8
Rivers Inlet Canada 51°42N 127°15W 342 C3
Riversdale S. Africa 34°7S 21°15E 328 E3
Riverside U.S.A. 33°59N 117°22W 351 M9
Riverton Australia 34°10S 138°46E 335 E2
Riverton Canada 51°1N 97°0W 343 C9
Riverton N.Z. 46°21S 168°0E 331 G2
Riverton U.S.A. 43°2N 108°23W 348 E9
Riviera U.S.A. 35°4N 114°35W 351 K12
Riviera di Levante Italy 44°15N 9°30E 292 D8
Riviera di Ponente Italy 44°10N 8°20E 292 D8
Rivière-au-Renard Canada 48°59N 64°23W 345 C7
Rivière-du-Loup Canada 47°50N 69°30W 345 C6
Rivière-Pentecôte Canada 49°57N 67°1W 345 C6
Rivière-Pilote Martinique 14°26N 60°53W 360 c
Rivière St-Paul Canada 51°28N 57°45W 345 B8
Rivière-Salée Martinique 14°31N 61°0W 360 c
Rivne Ukraine 50°40N 26°10E 289 C14
Rívoli Italy 45°3N 7°31E 292 D7
Rivoli B. Australia 37°32S 140°3E 335 F3
Riyadh = Ar Riyāḍ Si. Arabia 24°41N 46°42E 316 E5
Riyadh al Khabrā' Si. Arabia 26°2N 43°33E 316 E4
Rize Turkey 41°0N 40°30E 291 F7
Rizhao China 35°25N 119°30E 307 G10
Rizokarpaso Cyprus 35°36N 34°23E 297 D13
Rizzuto, C. Italy 38°53N 17°5E 294 E7
Rjukan Norway 59°54N 8°33E 281 G13
Road Town Br. Virgin Is. 18°27N 64°37W 361 e
Roan Plateau U.S.A. 39°20N 109°20W 348 G9
Roanne France 46°3N 4°4E 292 C6
Roanoke Ala., U.S.A. 33°9N 85°22W 357 E12
Roanoke Va., U.S.A. 37°16N 79°56W 353 G14
Roanoke → U.S.A. 35°57N 76°42W 357 D16
Roanoke I. U.S.A. 35°53N 75°39W 357 D17
Roanoke Rapids U.S.A. 36°28N 77°40W 357 C16
Roatán Honduras 16°18N 86°35W 360 C2
Robāt Sang Iran 35°35N 59°10E 317 C8
Robāṭkarīm Iran 35°25N 50°59E 317 C6
Robāṭkarīm □ Iran 35°26N 50°59E 317 B6
Robbins I. Australia 40°42S 145°0E 335 G4
Robe → Australia 21°42S 116°15E 332 D2
Robert Lee U.S.A. 31°54N 100°29W 356 F4
Robertsdale U.S.A. 40°11N 78°6W 354 F6
Robertsganj India 24°44N 83°4E 315 G10
Robertson S. Africa 33°46S 19°50E 328 E2
Robertson I. Antarctica 65°15S 59°30W 277 C18
Robertson Ra. Australia 23°15S 121°0E 332 D3
Robertstown Australia 33°58S 139°5E 335 E2
Roberval Canada 48°32N 72°15W 345 C5
Robeson Chan. N. Amer. 82°0N 61°30W 276 A4
Robesonia U.S.A. 40°21N 76°8W 355 F8
Robinson U.S.A. 39°0N 87°44W 352 F10
Robinson → Australia 16°3S 137°16E 334 B2
Robinson Ra. Australia 25°40S 119°0E 333 E2
Robinvale Australia 34°40S 142°45E 335 E3
Roblin Canada 51°14N 101°21W 343 C8
Roboré Bolivia 18°10S 59°45W 364 G7
Robson Canada 49°20N 117°41W 342 D5
Robson, Mt. Canada 53°10N 119°10W 342 C5
Robstown U.S.A. 27°47N 97°40W 356 H6
Roca, C. da Portugal 38°40N 9°31W 293 C1
Roca Partida, I. Mexico 19°1N 112°2W 358 D2
Rocas, I. Brazil 4°0S 34°1W 365 D12
Rocha Uruguay 34°30S 54°25W 367 C5
Rochdale U.K. 53°38N 2°9W 284 D5
Rochefort Belgium 50°9N 5°12E 287 D5
Rochefort France 45°56N 0°57W 292 D3
Rochelle U.S.A. 41°56N 89°4W 352 E9
Rocher River Canada 61°23N 112°44W 342 A6
Rochester U.K. 51°23N 0°31E 285 F8
Rochester Ind., U.S.A. 41°4N 86°13W 352 E10
Rochester Minn., U.S.A. 44°1N 92°28W 352 C7
Rochester N.H., U.S.A. 43°18N 70°59W 355 C14
Rochester N.Y., U.S.A. 43°10N 77°37W 354 C7
Rock → Canada 60°7N 127°7W 342 A3
Rock, The Australia 35°15S 147°2E 335 F4
Rock Creek U.S.A. 41°40N 80°52W 354 E4
Rock Falls U.S.A. 41°47N 89°41W 352 E9
Rock Hill U.S.A. 34°56N 81°1W 357 D14
Rock Island U.S.A. 41°30N 90°34W 352 E8
Rock Port U.S.A. 40°25N 95°31W 352 E6
Rock Rapids U.S.A. 43°26N 96°10W 352 D5
Rock Sound Bahamas 24°54N 76°12W 360 B4
Rock Springs Mont., U.S.A. 46°49N 106°15W 348 C10
Rock Springs Wyo., U.S.A. 41°35N 109°14W 348 F9
Rock Valley U.S.A. 43°12N 96°18W 352 D5
Rockall Atl. Oc. 57°37N 13°42W 278 D3
Rockdale Tex., U.S.A. 30°39N 97°0W 356 F6
Rockdale Wash., U.S.A. 47°22N 121°28W 350 C5
Rockeby = Mungkan Kandju △ Australia 13°35S 142°52E 334 A3
Rockefeller Plateau Antarctica 76°0S 130°0W 277 E14
Rockford U.S.A. 42°16N 89°6W 352 D9
Rockglen Canada 49°11N 105°57W 343 D7
Rockhampton Australia 23°22S 150°32E 334 C5
Rockingham Australia 32°15S 115°38E 333 F2
Rockingham N.C., U.S.A. 34°57N 79°46W 357 D15
Rockingham Vt., U.S.A. 43°11N 72°29W 355 C12
Rockingham B. Australia 18°5S 146°10E 334 B4
Rocklake U.S.A. 48°47N 99°15W 352 A4
Rockland Canada 45°33N 75°17W 355 A9
Rockland Idaho, U.S.A. 42°34N 112°53W 348 E7
Rockland Maine, U.S.A. 44°6N 69°7W 353 C19
Rockland Mich., U.S.A. 46°44N 89°11W 352 B9
Rocklin U.S.A. 38°48N 121°14W 350 G5
Rockly B. Trin. & Tob. 11°9N 60°46W 365 J16
Rockmart U.S.A. 34°0N 85°3W 357 D12
Rockport Mass., U.S.A. 42°39N 70°37W 355 D14
Rockport Tex., U.S.A. 28°2N 97°3W 356 G6
Rocksprings U.S.A. 30°1N 100°13W 356 F4
Rockville Conn., U.S.A. 41°52N 72°28W 355 E12
Rockville Md., U.S.A. 39°5N 77°9W 353 F15
Rockwall U.S.A. 32°56N 96°28W 356 E6
Rockwell City U.S.A. 42°24N 94°38W 352 D6
Rockwood Canada 43°37N 80°8W 354 C4
Rockwood Maine, U.S.A. 45°41N 69°45W 353 C19
Rockwood Tenn., U.S.A. 35°52N 84°41W 357 D12
Rocky Ford U.S.A. 38°3N 103°43W 348 G12
Rocky Gully Australia 34°30S 116°57E 333 F2
Rocky Harbour Canada 49°36N 57°55W 345 C8
Rocky Island L. Canada 46°55N 83°0W 344 C3
Rocky Lane Canada 58°31N 116°22W 342 B5
Rocky Mount U.S.A. 35°57N 77°48W 357 D16
Rocky Mountain △ U.S.A. 40°25N 105°45W 348 F11
Rocky Mountain House Canada 52°22N 114°55W 342 C6
Rocky Mts. N. Amer. 49°0N 115°0W 348 B6
Rocky Point Namibia 19°3S 12°30E 328 B2
Rod Pakistan 28°10N 63°5E 312 E3
Roda Greece 39°48N 19°46E 297 A3
Rødbyhavn Denmark 54°39N 11°22E 281 J14
Roddickton Canada 50°51N 56°8W 345 B8
Rodez France 44°21N 2°33E 292 D5
Ródhos = Rhodes Greece 36°15N 28°10E 297 C10
Rodia Greece 35°22N 25°1E 297 D7
Rodney Canada 42°34N 81°41W 354 D3
Rodney, C. N.Z. 36°17S 174°50E 331 B5
Rodopos Greece 35°34N 23°45E 297 D5
Rodriguez Ind. Oc. 19°45S 63°20E 275 E13
Roe → U.K. 55°6N 6°59W 282 A5
Roebling U.S.A. 40°7N 74°47W 355 F10
Roebourne Australia 20°44S 117°9E 332 D2
Roebuck B. Australia 18°5S 122°20E 332 C3
Roermond Neths. 51°12N 6°0E 287 C6
Roes Welcome Sd. Canada 65°0N 87°0W 341 C11
Roeselare Belgium 50°57N 3°7E 287 D3
Rogachev = Ragachow Belarus 53°8N 30°5E 289 B16
Rogagua, L. Bolivia 13°43S 66°50W 364 F5
Rogatyn Ukraine 49°24N 24°36E 289 D13
Rogers U.S.A. 36°20N 94°7W 356 C7
Rogers City U.S.A. 45°25N 83°49W 353 C12
Rogersville Canada 46°44N 65°26W 345 C6
Roggan → Canada 54°24N 79°25W 344 B4
Roggan L. Canada 54°8N 77°50W 344 B4
Roggeveen Basin Pac. Oc. 31°30S 95°30W 337 L18
Roggeveldberge S. Africa 32°10S 20°10E 328 E3
Rogoaguado, L. Bolivia 13°0S 65°30W 364 F5
Rogojampi Indonesia 8°19S 114°17E 309 J17
Rogue → U.S.A. 42°26N 124°26W 348 E1
Rohnert Park U.S.A. 38°16N 122°40W 350 G4
Rohri Pakistan 27°45N 68°51E 314 F3
Rohri Canal Pakistan 26°15N 68°27E 314 F3
Rohtak India 28°55N 76°43E 314 E7
Roi Et Thailand 16°4N 103°40E 310 D4
Roja Latvia 57°29N 22°43E 281 H20
Rojas Argentina 34°10S 60°45W 366 C3
Rojo, C. Mexico 21°33N 97°20W 359 C5
Rokan → Indonesia 2°0N 100°50E 308 D2
Rokiškis Lithuania 55°55N 25°35E 281 J21
Rolândia Brazil 23°18S 51°23W 367 A5
Rolla Mo., U.S.A. 37°57N 91°46W 352 G8
Rolla N. Dak., U.S.A. 48°52N 99°37W 352 A4
Rolleston Australia 24°28S 148°35E 334 C4
Rollingstone Australia 19°2S 146°24E 334 B4
Roma Australia 26°32S 148°49E 335 D4
Roma Italy 41°54N 12°28E 294 D5
Roma Sweden 57°32N 18°26E 281 H18
Roma-Los Saenz U.S.A. 26°24N 99°1W 356 H5
Romain, C. U.S.A. 33°0N 79°22W 357 E15
Romaine → Canada 50°18N 63°47W 345 B7
Roman Romania 46°57N 26°55E 289 E14
Romang Indonesia 7°30S 127°20E 309 F7
Romāni Egypt 30°59N 32°38E 318 E1
Romania ■ Europe 46°0N 25°0E 289 F12
Romano, Cayo Cuba 22°0N 77°30W 360 B4
Romans-sur-Isère France 45°3N 5°3E 292 D6
Romblon Phil. 12°33N 122°17E 309 B6
Rome = Roma Italy 41°54N 12°28E 294 D5
Rome Ga., U.S.A. 34°15N 85°10W 357 D12
Rome N.Y., U.S.A. 43°13N 75°27W 355 C9
Rome Pa., U.S.A. 41°51N 76°21W 355 E8
Romney U.S.A. 39°21N 78°45W 353 F14
Romney Marsh U.K. 51°2N 0°54E 285 F8
Rømø Denmark 55°10N 8°30E 281 J13
Romorantin-Lanthenay France 47°21N 1°45E 292 C4
Romsdalen Norway 62°25N 7°52E 280 E12
Romsey U.K. 51°0N 1°29W 285 G6
Ron Vietnam 17°53N 106°27E 310 D6
Rona U.K. 57°34N 5°59W 283 D3
Ronan U.S.A. 47°32N 114°6W 348 C6
Roncador, Cayos Colombia 13°32N 80°4W 360 D3
Roncador, Serra do Brazil 12°30S 52°30W 365 F8
Ronda Spain 36°46N 5°12W 293 D3
Rondane Norway 61°57N 9°50E 280 F13
Rondônia □ Brazil 11°0S 63°0W 364 F6
Rondonópolis Brazil 16°28S 54°38W 365 G8
Rong, Koh Cambodia 10°45N 103°15E 311 G4
Ronge, L. la Canada 55°6N 105°17W 343 B7
Rønne Denmark 55°6N 14°43E 281 J16
Ronne Ice Shelf Antarctica 77°30S 60°0W 277 D18
Ronsard, C. Australia 24°46S 113°10E 333 D1
Ronse Belgium 50°45N 3°35E 287 D3
Roodepoort S. Africa 26°11S 27°54E 329 D4
Roof Butte U.S.A. 36°28N 109°5W 349 H9
Rooiboklaagte → Namibia 20°50S 21°0E 328 C3
Rooniu, Mt. Tahiti 17°49S 149°12W 331 d
Roorkee India 29°52N 77°59E 314 E7
Roosendaal Neths. 51°32N 4°29E 287 C4
Roosevelt U.S.A. 40°18N 109°59W 348 F9
Roosevelt → Brazil 7°35S 60°20W 364 E6
Roosevelt, Mt. Canada 58°26N 125°20W 342 B3
Roosevelt I. Antarctica 79°30S 162°0W 277 D12
Roper → Australia 14°43S 135°27E 334 A2
Roper Bar Australia 14°44S 134°44E 334 A1
Roque Pérez Argentina 35°25S 59°24W 366 D4
Roquetas de Mar Spain 36°46N 2°36W 293 D4
Roraima □ Brazil 2°0N 61°30W 364 C6
Roraima, Mt. Venezuela 5°10N 60°40W 364 B6
Røros Norway 62°35N 11°23E 280 E14
Rosa Zambia 9°33S 31°15E 327 D3
Rosa, L. Bahamas 21°0N 73°30W 361 B5
Rosa, Monte Europe 45°57N 7°53E 292 D7
Rosalia U.S.A. 47°14N 117°22W 348 C5
Rosamond U.S.A. 34°52N 118°10W 351 L8
Rosario Argentina 33°0S 60°40W 366 C3
Rosário Brazil 3°0S 44°15W 365 D10
Rosario Baja Calif., Mexico 30°0N 115°50W 358 B1
Rosario Sinaloa, Mexico 22°58N 105°53W 358 C3
Rosario Paraguay 24°30S 57°35W 366 A4
Rosario de la Frontera Argentina 25°50S 65°0W 366 B3
Rosario de Lerma Argentina 24°59S 65°35W 366 A2
Rosario del Tala Argentina 32°20S 59°10W 366 C4
Rosário do Sul Brazil 30°15S 54°55W 367 C5
Rosarito Mexico 32°20N 117°2W 351 N9
Roscoe U.S.A. 41°56N 74°55W 355 E10
Roscommon Ireland 53°38N 8°11W 282 C3
Roscommon □ Ireland 53°49N 8°23W 282 C3
Roscrea Ireland 52°57N 7°49W 282 D4
Rose → Australia 14°16S 135°45E 334 A2
Rose Belle Mauritius 20°24S 57°36E 325 d
Rose Blanche-Harbour Le Cou Canada 47°38N 58°45W 345 C8
Rose Hill Mauritius 20°14S 57°27E 325 d
Rose Pt. Canada 54°11N 131°39W 342 C2
Rose Valley Canada 52°19N 103°49W 343 C8
Roseau Dominica 15°17N 61°24W 361 C7
Roseau U.S.A. 48°51N 95°46W 352 A6
Rosebery Australia 41°46S 145°33E 335 G4
Rosebud S. Dak., U.S.A. 43°14N 100°51W 352 D3
Rosebud Tex., U.S.A. 31°4N 96°59W 356 F6
Roseburg U.S.A. 43°13N 123°20W 348 E2
Rosehearty U.K. 57°42N 2°7W 283 D6
Roseires Res. Sudan 11°51N 34°23E 323 F12
Roseland U.S.A. 38°25N 122°43W 350 G4
Rosemary Canada 50°46N 112°5W 342 C6
Rosenberg U.S.A. 29°34N 95°49W 356 G7
Rosenheim Germany 47°51N 12°7E 288 E7
Roses, G. de Spain 42°10N 3°15E 293 A7
Rosetown Canada 51°35N 107°59W 343 C7
Roseville Calif., U.S.A. 38°45N 121°17W 350 G5
Roseville Mich., U.S.A. 42°30N 82°56W 354 D2
Rosewood Australia 27°38S 152°36E 335 D5
Roshkhvār Iran 34°58N 59°37E 317 C8
Rosignano Maríttimo Italy 43°24N 10°28E 294 C4
Rosignol Guyana 6°15N 57°30W 364 B7
Roşiori de Vede Romania 44°9N 25°0E 289 F13
Roskilde Denmark 55°38N 12°3E 281 J15
Roslavl Russia 53°57N 32°55E 290 D5
Rosmead S. Africa 31°29S 25°8E 328 E4
Ross Australia 42°2S 147°30E 335 G4
Ross N.Z. 42°53S 170°49E 331 E3
Ross Dependency Antarctica 76°0S 170°0W 277 D12
Ross I. Antarctica 77°30S 168°0E 277 D11
Ross Ice Shelf Antarctica 80°0S 180°0E 277 E12
Ross L. U.S.A. 48°44N 121°4W 348 B3
Ross-on-Wye U.K. 51°54N 2°34W 285 F5
Ross River Australia 23°44S 134°30E 334 C1
Ross River Canada 62°30N 131°30W 342 A2
Ross Sea Antarctica 74°0S 178°0E 277 D11
Rossall Pt. U.K. 53°55N 3°3W 284 D4
Rossan Pt. Ireland 54°42N 8°47W 282 B3
Rossano Italy 39°36N 16°39E 294 E7
Rossburn Canada 50°40N 100°49W 343 C8
Rosseau Canada 45°16N 79°39W 354 A5
Rosseau, L. Canada 45°10N 79°35W 354 A5
Rosses, The Ireland 55°2N 8°20W 282 A3
Rossignol, L. Canada 52°43N 73°40W 344 B5
Rossignol L. Canada 44°12N 65°10W 345 D6
Rossiya = Russia ■ Eurasia 62°0N 105°0E 301 C11
Rossland Canada 49°6N 117°50W 342 D5
Rosslare Ireland 52°17N 6°24W 282 D5
Rosslare Harbour Ireland 52°15N 6°20W 282 D5
Rosso Mauritania 16°40N 15°45W 322 E2
Rossosh Russia 50°15N 39°28E 291 D6
Røssvatnet Norway 65°45N 14°5E 280 D16
Røst Norway 67°32N 12°0E 280 C15
Rosthern Canada 52°40N 106°20W 343 C7
Rostock Germany 54°5N 12°8E 288 A7
Rostov Don, Russia 47°15N 39°45E 291 E6
Rostov Sverdlovsk, Russia 57°14N 39°25E 290 C6
Roswell Ga., U.S.A. 34°2N 84°22W 357 D12
Roswell N. Mex., U.S.A. 33°24N 104°32W 349 K11
Rotan U.S.A. 32°51N 100°28W 356 E4
Rother → U.K. 50°59N 0°45E 285 G8
Rothera Antarctica 67°20S 63°0W 277 C17
Rotherham U.K. 53°26N 1°20W 284 D6
Rothes U.K. 57°32N 3°13W 283 D5
Rothesay Canada 45°23N 66°0W 345 C6
Rothesay U.K. 55°50N 5°3W 283 F3
Roti Indonesia 10°50S 123°0E 309 F6
Roto Australia 33°0S 145°30E 335 E4
Rotondo, Mte. France 42°14N 9°8E 292 E8
Rotoroa, L. N.Z. 41°55S 172°39E 331 D4
Rotorua N.Z. 38°9S 176°16E 331 C6
Rotorua, L. N.Z. 38°5S 176°18E 331 C6
Rotterdam Neths. 51°55N 4°30E 287 C4
Rotterdam U.S.A. 42°48N 74°1W 355 D10
Rottnest I. Australia 32°0S 115°27E 333 F2
Rottumeroog Neths. 53°33N 6°34E 287 A6
Rottweil Germany 48°9N 8°37E 288 D5
Rotuma Fiji 12°25S 177°5E 330 C10
Roubaix France 50°40N 3°10E 292 A5
Rouen France 49°27N 1°4E 292 B4
Rouleau Canada 50°10N 104°56W 343 C8
Round I. Mauritius 19°51S 57°45E 325 d
Round Mountain U.S.A. 38°43N 117°4W 348 G5
Round Mt. Australia 30°26S 152°16E 335 E5
Round Rock U.S.A. 30°31N 97°41W 356 F6
Roundup U.S.A. 46°27N 108°33W 348 C9
Rousay U.K. 59°10N 3°2W 283 B5
Rouses Point U.S.A. 44°59N 73°22W 355 B11
Rouseville U.S.A. 41°28N 79°42W 354 E5
Rousse = Ruse Bulgaria 43°48N 25°59E 295 C12
Roussillon France 42°30N 2°35E 292 E5
Rouxville S. Africa 30°25S 26°50E 328 E4
Rouyn-Noranda Canada 48°20N 79°0W 344 C4
Rovaniemi Finland 66°29N 25°41E 280 C21
Rovereto Italy 45°53N 11°3E 294 B4
Rovigo Italy 45°4N 11°47E 294 B4
Rovinj Croatia 45°5N 13°40E 288 F7
Rovno = Rivne Ukraine 50°40N 26°10E 289 C14
Rovuma = Ruvuma → Tanzania 10°29S 40°28E 327 E5
Row'ān Iran 35°8N 48°51E 317 C6
Rowena Australia 29°48S 148°55E 335 D4
Rowley Shoals Australia 17°30S 119°0E 332 C2
Roxas Phil. 11°36N 122°49E 309 B6
Roxboro U.S.A. 36°24N 78°59W 357 C15
Roxborough Trin. & Tob. 11°15N 60°35W 365 J16
Roxburgh N.Z. 45°33S 169°19E 331 F2
Roxbury U.S.A. 40°6N 77°39W 354 F7
Roxby Downs Australia 30°43S 136°46E 335 E2
Roy Mont., U.S.A. 47°20N 108°58W 348 C9
Roy N. Mex., U.S.A. 35°57N 104°12W 349 J11
Roy Utah, U.S.A. 41°10N 112°2W 348 F7
Royal Bardia △ Nepal 28°20N 81°20E 315 E9
Royal Canal Ireland 53°30N 7°13W 282 C4
Royal Chitawan △ Nepal 26°30N 84°30E 315 F11
Royal Leamington Spa U.K. 52°18N 1°31W 285 E6
Royal Natal △ S. Africa 28°43S 28°51E 329 D4
Royal Tunbridge Wells U.K. 51°7N 0°16E 285 F8
Royale, Isle U.S.A. 48°0N 88°54W 352 B9
Royan France 45°37N 1°2W 292 D3
Royston U.K. 52°3N 0°0 285 E7
Rozdilna Ukraine 46°50N 30°2E 289 E16
Rozhyshche Ukraine 50°54N 25°15E 289 C13
Rtishchevo Russia 52°18N 43°46E 290 D7
Ruacaná Namibia 17°27S 14°21E 328 B1
Ruaha △ Tanzania 7°41S 34°30E 326 D3
Ruahine Ra. N.Z. 39°55S 176°2E 331 C6
Ruapehu N.Z. 39°17S 175°35E 331 C5
Ruapuke I. N.Z. 46°46S 168°31E 331 G2
Ruâq, W. → Egypt 30°0N 33°49E 318 F2
Rub' al Khālī Si. Arabia 19°0N 48°0E 319 D4
Rubeho Mts. Tanzania 6°50S 36°25E 326 D4
Rubh a' Mhail U.K. 55°56N 6°8W 283 F2
Rubha Hunish U.K. 57°42N 6°20W 283 D2
Rubha Robhanais = Lewis, Butt of U.K. 58°31N 6°16W 283 C2
Rubicon → U.S.A. 38°53N 121°4W 350 G5
Rubio Venezuela 7°43N 72°22W 364 B4
Rubondo △ Tanzania 2°18S 31°58E 326 C3
Rubtsovsk Russia 51°30N 81°10E 300 D9
Ruby L. U.S.A. 40°10N 115°28W 348 F6
Ruby Mts. U.S.A. 40°30N 115°20W 348 F6
Rubyvale Australia 23°25S 147°42E 334 C4
Rūd Sar Iran 37°8N 50°18E 317 B6
Rudall Australia 33°43S 136°17E 335 E2
Rudall → Australia 22°34S 122°13E 332 D3
Rudall River △ Australia 22°38S 122°30E 332 D3
Rudewa Tanzania 10°7S 34°40E 327 E3
Rudnyy Kazakhstan 52°57N 63°7E 300 D7
Rudolfa, Ostrov Russia 81°45N 58°30E 300 A6
Rudyard U.S.A. 46°14N 84°36W 353 B11
Ruenya → Africa 16°24S 33°48E 327 F3
Ruffling Pt. Br. Virgin Is. 18°44N 64°27W 361 e
Rufiji → Tanzania 7°50S 39°15E 326 D4
Rufino Argentina 34°20S 62°50W 366 C3
Rufunsa Zambia 15°4S 29°34E 327 F2
Rugby U.K. 52°23N 1°16W 285 E6
Rugby U.S.A. 48°22N 100°0W 352 A4
Rügen Germany 54°22N 13°24E 288 A7
Ruhengeri Rwanda 1°30S 29°36E 326 C2
Ruhnu Estonia 57°48N 23°15E 281 H20
Ruhr → Germany 51°27N 6°43E 288 C4
Ruhuhu → Tanzania 10°31S 34°34E 327 E3
Ruidoso U.S.A. 33°20N 105°41W 349 K11
Ruivo, Pico Madeira 32°45N 16°56W 296 D3
Rujm Tal'at al Jamā'ah Jordan 30°24N 35°30E 318 E4
Ruk Pakistan 27°50N 68°42E 314 F3
Rukhla Pakistan 32°27N 71°57E 314 C4
Ruki → Dem. Rep. of the Congo 0°5N 18°17E 324 E3
Rukwa □ Tanzania 7°0S 31°30E 326 D3
Rukwa, L. Tanzania 8°0S 32°20E 326 D3
Rulhieres, C. Australia 13°56S 127°22E 332 B4
Rum = Rhum U.K. 57°0N 6°20W 283 E2
Rum Jordan 29°39N 35°26E 318 F4
Rum Cay Bahamas 23°40N 74°58W 361 B5
Rum Jungle Australia 13°0S 130°59E 332 B5
Ruma △ Kenya 0°39S 34°18E 326 C3
Rumāḥ Si. Arabia 25°29N 47°10E 316 E5
Rumania = Romania ■ Europe 46°0N 25°0E 289 F12
Rumaylah Iraq 30°47N 47°37E 316 D5
Rumbêk Sudan 6°54N 29°37E 323 G11
Rumford U.S.A. 44°33N 70°33W 355 B14
Rumia Poland 54°37N 18°25E 289 A10
Rumoi Japan 43°56N 141°39E 302 C10
Rumonge Burundi 3°59S 29°26E 326 C2
Rumson U.S.A. 40°23N 74°0W 355 F11
Rumuruti Kenya 0°17N 36°32E 326 B4
Runan China 33°0N 114°30E 306 H8
Runanga N.Z. 42°25S 171°15E 331 E3
Runaway, C. N.Z. 37°32S 177°59E 331 B6
Runaway Bay Jamaica 18°27N 77°20W 360 a
Runcorn U.K. 53°21N 2°44W 284 D5
Rundu Namibia 17°52S 19°43E 328 B2
Rungwa Tanzania 6°55S 33°32E 326 D3
Rungwa → Tanzania 7°36S 31°50E 326 D3
Rungwa ⌂ Tanzania 6°53S 34°2E 326 D3
Rungwe Tanzania 9°11S 33°32E 327 D3
Rungwe, Mt. Tanzania 9°8S 33°40E 324 F6
Runton Ra. Australia 23°31S 123°6E 332 D3
Ruokolahti Finland 61°17N 28°50E 280 F23
Ruoqiang China 38°55N 88°10E 304 C3
Rupa India 27°15N 92°21E 313 F18
Rupar India 31°2N 76°38E 314 D7
Rupat Indonesia 1°45N 101°40E 308 D2
Rupen → India 23°28N 71°31E 314 H4
Rupert U.S.A. 42°37N 113°41W 348 E7
Rupert → Canada 51°29N 78°45W 344 B4
Rupert B. Canada 51°35N 79°0W 344 B4
Rupert House = Waskaganish Canada 51°30N 78°40W 344 B4
Rupsa India 21°37N 87°1E 315 J12
Rurrenabaque Bolivia 14°30S 67°32W 364 F5
Rusambo Zimbabwe 16°30S 32°4E 327 F3
Rusape Zimbabwe 18°35S 32°8E 327 F3
Ruschuk = Ruse Bulgaria 43°48N 25°59E 295 C12
Ruse Bulgaria 43°48N 25°59E 295 C12
Rush Ireland 53°31N 6°6W 282 C5
Rushan China 36°56N 121°30E 307 F11
Rushden U.K. 52°18N 0°35W 285 E7
Rushmore, Mt. U.S.A. 43°53N 103°28W 352 D2
Rushville Ill., U.S.A. 40°7N 90°34W 352 E8
Rushville Ind., U.S.A. 39°37N 85°27W 353 F11
Rushville Nebr., U.S.A. 42°43N 102°28W 352 D2
Russas Brazil 4°55S 37°50W 365 D11
Russell Canada 50°50N 101°20W 343 C8
Russell Kans., U.S.A. 38°54N 98°52W 352 F4
Russell N.Y., U.S.A. 44°27N 75°9W 355 B9
Russell Pa., U.S.A. 41°56N 79°8W 354 E5
Russell Cave ⌂ U.S.A. 34°59N 85°49W 357 D12
Russell L. Man., Canada 56°15N 101°30W 343 B8
Russell L. N.W.T., Canada 63°5N 115°44W 342 A5
Russellkonda India 19°57N 84°42E 313 K14
Russellville Ala., U.S.A. 34°30N 87°44W 357 D11
Russellville Ark., U.S.A. 35°17N 93°8W 356 D8
Russellville Ky., U.S.A. 36°51N 86°53W 352 G10
Russia ■ Eurasia 62°0N 105°0E 301 C11
Russian → U.S.A. 38°27N 123°8W 350 G3
Russkoye Ustie Russia 71°0N 149°0E 276 B15
Rustam Pakistan 34°25N 72°13E 314 B5
Rustam Shahr Pakistan 26°58N 66°6E 314 F2
Rustavi Georgia 41°30N 45°0E 291 F8
Rustenburg S. Africa 25°41S 27°14E 328 D4
Ruston U.S.A. 32°32N 92°38W 356 E8
Rutana Burundi 3°55S 30°0E 326 C3
Ruteng Indonesia 8°35S 120°30E 309 F6
Ruth U.S.A. 43°42N 82°45W 354 C2
Rutherford U.S.A. 38°26N 122°24W 350 G4
Rutland U.S.A. 43°37N 72°58W 355 C12
Rutland □ U.K. 52°38N 0°40W 285 E7
Rutland Water U.K. 52°39N 0°38W 285 E7
Rutledge → Canada 61°4N 112°0W 343 A6
Rutledge L. Canada 61°33N 110°47W 343 A6
Rutog China 33°27N 79°42E 304 C2
Rutshuru Dem. Rep. of the Congo 1°13S 29°25E 326 C2
Ruvu Tanzania 6°49S 38°43E 326 D4
Ruvu → Tanzania 6°23S 38°52E 326 D4
Ruvuba △ Burundi 3°3S 29°33E 326 C2
Ruvuma □ Tanzania 10°20S 36°0E 327 E4
Ruvuma → Tanzania 10°29S 40°28E 327 E5
Ruwais U.A.E. 24°5N 52°50E 317 E7
Ruwenzori Africa 0°30N 29°55E 326 B2
Ruwenzori △ Uganda 0°20N 30°0E 326 B2
Ruya → Zimbabwe 16°27S 32°5E 329 B5
Ruyigi Burundi 3°29S 30°15E 326 C3
Ružomberok Slovak Rep. 49°3N 19°17E 289 D10
Rwanda ■ Africa 2°0S 30°0E 326 C3

434 Severo-Zapadnyy
INDEX TO WORLD MAPS

Severo-Zapadnyy □ *Russia* 65°0N 40°0E **300 C4**
Severodvinsk *Russia* 64°27N 39°58E **290 B6**
Severomorsk *Russia* 69°5N 33°27E **280 B25**
Severouralsk *Russia* 60°9N 59°57E **290 B10**
Sevier → *U.S.A.* 39°4N 113°6W **348 G7**
Sevier Desert *U.S.A.* 39°40N 112°45W **348 G7**
Sevier L. *U.S.A.* 38°54N 113°9W **348 G7**
Sevilla *Spain* 37°23N 5°58W **293 D2**
Seville = Sevilla *Spain* 37°23N 5°58W **293 D2**
Sevlievo *Bulgaria* 43°2N 25°6E **295 C11**
Sewani *India* 28°58N 75°39E **314 E6**
Seward *Alaska, U.S.A.* 60°7N 149°27W **346 a**
Seward *Nebr., U.S.A.* 40°55N 97°6W **352 E5**
Seward *Pa., U.S.A.* 40°25N 79°1W **354 F5**
Seward Peninsula *U.S.A.* 65°30N 166°0W **346 a**
Sewell *Chile* 34°10S 70°23W **366 C1**
Sewer *Indonesia* 5°53S 134°40E **309 F8**
Sewickley *U.S.A.* 40°32N 80°12W **354 F4**
Sexsmith *Canada* 55°21N 118°47W **342 B5**
Seychelles ■ *Ind. Oc.* 5°0S 56°0E **325 b**
Seyðisfjörður *Iceland* 65°16N 13°57W **280 D7**
Seydişehir *Turkey* 37°25N 31°51E **291 G5**
Seydvān *Iran* 38°34N 45°2E **316 B5**
Seyhan → *Turkey* 36°43N 34°53E **316 B2**
Seym → *Ukraine* 51°27N 32°34E **291 D5**
Seymour *Australia* 37°2S 145°10E **335 F4**
Seymour *S. Africa* 32°33S 26°46E **329 E4**
Seymour *Conn., U.S.A.* 41°24N 73°4W **355 E11**
Seymour *Ind., U.S.A.* 38°58N 85°53W **353 F11**
Seymour *Tex., U.S.A.* 33°35N 99°16W **356 E5**
Sfântu Gheorghe *Romania* 45°52N 25°48E **289 F13**
Sfax *Tunisia* 34°49N 10°48E **323 B8**
Sha Tau Kok *China* 22°33N 114°13E **305 F11**
Sha Tin *China* 22°23N 114°12E **305 G11**
Shaanxi □ *China* 35°0N 109°0E **306 G5**
Shaba = Katanga □ *Dem. Rep. of the Congo* 8°0S 25°0E **326 D2**
Shaba ⌓ *Kenya* 0°38N 37°48E **326 B4**
Shaballe = Scebeli, Wabi → *Somali Rep.* 2°0N 44°0E **319 G3**
Shabogamo L. *Canada* 53°15N 66°30W **345 B6**
Shabunda *Dem. Rep. of the Congo* 2°40S 27°16E **326 C2**
Shache *China* 38°20N 77°10E **304 C2**
Shackleton Fracture Zone *S. Ocean* 60°0S 60°0W **277 B18**
Shackleton Ice Shelf *Antarctica* 66°0S 100°0E **277 C8**
Shackleton Inlet *Antarctica* 83°0S 160°0E **277 E11**
Shādegān *Iran* 30°40N 48°38E **317 D6**
Shadi *India* 33°24N 77°14E **315 C7**
Shadrinsk *Russia* 56°5N 63°32E **300 D7**
Shadyside *U.S.A.* 39°58N 80°45W **354 G4**
Shafter *U.S.A.* 35°30N 119°16W **351 K7**
Shaftesbury *U.K.* 51°0N 2°11W **285 F5**
Shagram *Pakistan* 36°24N 72°20E **315 A5**
Shah Alizai *Pakistan* 29°25N 66°33E **314 E2**
Shah Bunder *Pakistan* 24°13N 67°56E **314 G2**
Shahabad *Punjab, India* 30°10N 76°55E **314 D7**
Shahabad *Raj., India* 25°15N 77°11E **314 G7**
Shahabad *Ut. P., India* 27°36N 79°56E **315 F8**
Shahadpur *Pakistan* 25°55N 68°35E **314 G3**
Shahbā' *Syria* 32°52N 36°38E **318 C5**
Shahdād *Iran* 30°30N 57°40E **317 D8**
Shahdād, Namakzār-e *Iran* 30°20N 58°20E **317 D8**
Shahdadkot *Pakistan* 27°50N 67°55E **314 F2**
Shahdol *India* 23°19N 81°26E **315 H9**
Shahe *China* 37°0N 114°32E **306 F8**
Shahganj *India* 26°3N 82°44E **315 F10**
Shahgarh *India* 27°15N 69°50E **314 F3**
Shahjahanpur *India* 27°54N 79°57E **315 F8**
Shahpur *India* 22°12N 77°58E **314 H7**
Shahpur *Baluchistan, Pakistan* 28°46N 68°27E **314 E3**
Shahpur *Punjab, Pakistan* 32°17N 72°26E **314 C5**
Shahpur Chakar *Pakistan* 26°9N 68°39E **314 F3**
Shahpura *Mad. P., India* 23°10N 80°45E **315 H9**
Shahpura *Raj., India* 25°38N 74°56E **314 G6**
Shahr-e Bābak *Iran* 30°7N 55°9E **317 D7**
Shahr-e Kord *Iran* 32°15N 50°55E **317 C6**
Shāhrakht *Iran* 33°38N 60°16E **317 C9**
Shahrig *Pakistan* 30°15N 67°40E **314 D2**
Shahukou *China* 40°20N 112°18E **306 D7**
Shaikhabad *Afghan.* 34°2N 68°45E **314 B3**
Shajapur *India* 23°27N 76°21E **314 H7**
Shajing *China* 22°44N 113°48E **305 F10**
Shakargarh *Pakistan* 32°17N 75°10E **314 C6**
Shakawe *Botswana* 18°28S 21°49E **328 B3**
Shaker Heights *U.S.A.* 41°28N 81°32W **354 E3**
Shakhty *Russia* 47°40N 40°16E **291 E7**
Shakhunya *Russia* 57°40N 46°46E **290 C8**
Shaki *Nigeria* 8°41N 3°21E **322 G6**
Shaksam Valley *Asia* 36°0N 76°20E **315 A7**
Shallow Lake *Canada* 44°36N 81°5W **354 B3**
Shalqar *Kazakhstan* 47°48N 59°39E **300 E6**
Shaluli Shan *China* 30°40N 99°55E **304 C4**
Shām *Iran* 26°39N 57°21E **317 E8**
Shām, Bādiyat ash *Asia* 32°0N 40°0E **316 C3**
Shamâl Sînî □ *Egypt* 30°30N 33°30E **318 E2**
Shamattawa *Canada* 55°51N 92°5W **344 A1**
Shamattawa → *Canada* 55°1N 85°23W **344 A2**
Shamīl *Iran* 27°30N 56°55E **317 E8**
Shāmkūh *Iran* 35°47N 57°50E **317 C8**
Shamli *India* 29°32N 77°18E **314 E7**
Shammar, Jabal *Si. Arabia* 27°40N 41°0E **316 E4**
Shamo = Gobi *Asia* 44°0N 110°0E **306 C6**
Shamo, L. *Ethiopia* 5°45N 37°30E **319 F2**
Shamokin *U.S.A.* 40°47N 76°34W **355 F8**
Shamrock *U.S.A.* 35°13N 100°15W **356 D4**
Shamva *Zimbabwe* 17°20S 31°32E **327 F3**
Shan □ *Burma* 21°30N 98°30E **313 J21**
Shan Xian *China* 34°50N 116°5E **306 G9**
Shanchengzhen *China* 42°20N 125°20E **307 C13**
Shāndak *Iran* 28°28N 60°27E **317 D9**
Shandon *U.S.A.* 35°39N 120°23W **350 K6**
Shandong □ *China* 36°0N 118°0E **307 G10**
Shandong Bandao *China* 37°0N 121°0E **307 F11**
Shang Xian = Shangzhou *China* 33°50N 109°58E **306 H5**
Shanga *Nigeria* 11°12N 4°33E **322 F6**
Shangalowe *Dem. Rep. of the Congo* 10°50S 26°30E **327 E2**
Shangani *Zimbabwe* 19°41S 29°20E **329 B4**
Shangani → *Zimbabwe* 18°41S 27°10E **327 F2**
Shangbancheng *China* 40°50N 118°1E **307 D10**
Shangdu *China* 41°30N 113°30E **306 D7**
Shanghai *China* 31°15N 121°26E **305 C7**
Shanghe *China* 37°20N 117°10E **307 F9**
Shangnan *China* 33°32N 110°50E **306 H6**
Shangqiu *China* 34°26N 115°36E **306 G8**
Shangrao *China* 28°25N 117°59E **305 D6**
Shangshui *China* 33°42N 114°35E **305 C6**
Shangzhi *China* 45°22N 127°56E **307 B14**
Shangzhou *China* 33°50N 109°58E **306 H5**
Shanhetun *China* 44°33N 127°15E **307 B14**
Shanklin *U.K.* 50°38N 1°11W **285 G6**
Shannon *N.Z.* 40°33S 175°25E **331 D5**
Shannon → *Ireland* 52°35N 9°30W **282 D2**
Shannon ✈ (SNN) *Ireland* 52°42N 8°57W **282 D3**
Shannon, Mouth of the *Ireland* 52°30N 9°55W **282 D2**
Shannon △ *Australia* 34°35S 116°25E **333 F2**
Shannonbridge *Ireland* 53°17N 8°3W **282 C3**
Shansi = Shanxi □ *China* 37°0N 112°0E **306 F7**
Shantar, Ostrov Bolshoy *Russia* 55°9N 137°40E **301 D14**
Shantipur *India* 23°17N 88°25E **315 H13**
Shantou *China* 23°18N 116°40E **305 D6**
Shantung = Shandong □ *China* 36°0N 118°0E **307 G10**
Shanxi □ *China* 37°0N 112°0E **306 F7**
Shanyang *China* 33°31N 109°55E **306 H5**
Shanyin *China* 39°25N 112°56E **306 E7**
Shaoguan *China* 24°48N 113°35E **305 D6**
Shaoxing *China* 30°0N 120°35E **305 D7**
Shaoyang *China* 27°14N 111°25E **305 D6**
Shap *U.K.* 54°32N 2°40W **284 C5**
Shapinsay *U.K.* 59°3N 2°51W **283 B6**
Shaqra' *Si. Arabia* 25°15N 45°16E **316 E5**
Shaqrā' *Yemen* 13°22N 45°44E **319 E4**
Sharafkhāneh *Iran* 38°11N 45°29E **316 B5**
Sharbot Lake *Canada* 44°46N 76°41W **355 B8**
Shari *Japan* 43°55N 144°40E **302 C12**
Sharjah = Ash Shāriqah *U.A.E.* 25°23N 55°26E **317 E7**
Shark B. *Australia* 25°30S 113°32E **333 E1**
Shark Bay ⌓ *Australia* 25°30S 113°30E **333 E1**
Sharm el Sheikh *Egypt* 27°53N 34°18E **323 C12**
Sharon *Mass., U.S.A.* 42°7N 71°11W **355 D13**
Sharon *Pa., U.S.A.* 41°14N 80°31W **354 E4**
Sharon Springs *Kans., U.S.A.* 38°54N 101°45W **352 F3**
Sharon Springs *N.Y., U.S.A.* 42°48N 74°37W **355 D10**
Sharp Pt. *Australia* 10°58S 142°43E **334 A3**
Sharpe L. *Canada* 54°24N 93°40W **344 B1**
Sharpsville *U.S.A.* 41°15N 80°29W **354 E4**
Sharqi, Al Jabal ash *Lebanon* 33°40N 36°10E **318 B5**
Sharya *Russia* 58°22N 45°20E **290 C8**
Shashemene *Ethiopia* 7°13N 38°33E **319 F2**
Shashi *Botswana* 21°15S 27°27E **329 C4**
Shashi *China* 30°25N 112°14E **305 C6**
Shashi → *Africa* 21°14S 29°20E **327 G2**
Shasta, Mt. *U.S.A.* 41°25N 122°12W **348 F2**
Shasta L. *U.S.A.* 40°43N 122°25W **348 F2**
Shatsky Rise *Pac. Oc.* 34°0N 157°0E **336 D7**
Shatt al Arab *Asia* 29°57N 48°34E **317 D6**
Shaunavon *Canada* 49°35N 108°25W **343 D7**
Shaver L. *U.S.A.* 37°9N 119°18W **350 H7**
Shaw → *Australia* 20°21S 119°17E **332 D2**
Shaw I. *Australia* 20°30S 149°2E **334 J7**
Shawanaga *Canada* 45°31N 80°17W **354 A4**
Shawangunk Mts. *U.S.A.* 41°35N 74°30W **355 E10**
Shawano *U.S.A.* 44°47N 88°36W **352 C9**
Shawinigan *Canada* 46°35N 72°50W **344 C5**
Shawmari, J. ash *Jordan* 30°35N 36°35E **318 E5**
Shawnee *U.S.A.* 35°20N 96°55W **356 D6**
Shay Gap *Australia* 20°30S 120°10E **332 D3**
Shaybārā *Si. Arabia* 25°26N 36°47E **316 E3**
Shaykh, J. ash *Lebanon* 33°25N 35°50E **318 B4**
Shaykh Miskīn *Syria* 32°49N 36°9E **318 C5**
Shaykh Sa'īd *Iraq* 32°34N 46°17E **316 C5**
Shchūchīnsk *Kazakhstan* 52°56N 70°12E **300 D8**
She Xian *China* 36°30N 113°40E **306 F7**
Shebele = Scebeli, Wabi → *Somali Rep.* 2°0N 44°0E **319 G3**
Sheboygan *U.S.A.* 43°46N 87°45W **352 D10**
Shediac *Canada* 46°14N 64°32W **345 C7**
Sheelin, L. *Ireland* 53°48N 7°20W **282 C4**
Sheep Haven *Ireland* 55°11N 7°52W **282 A4**
Sheep Range *U.S.A.* 36°35N 115°15W **351 J11**
Sheerness *U.K.* 51°26N 0°47E **285 F8**
Sheet Harbour *Canada* 44°56N 62°31W **345 D7**
Sheffield *U.K.* 53°23N 1°28W **284 D6**
Sheffield *Ala., U.S.A.* 34°46N 87°41W **357 D11**
Sheffield *Mass., U.S.A.* 42°5N 73°21W **355 D11**
Sheffield *Pa., U.S.A.* 41°42N 79°3W **354 E5**
Sheikhpura *India* 25°9N 85°53E **315 G11**
Shekhupura *Pakistan* 31°42N 73°58E **314 D5**
Shekou *China* 22°30N 113°55E **305 G10**
Shelburne *N.S., Canada* 43°47N 65°20W **345 D6**
Shelburne *Ont., Canada* 44°4N 80°15W **354 B4**
Shelburne *U.S.A.* 44°23N 73°14W **355 B11**
Shelburne B. *Australia* 11°50S 142°50E **334 A3**
Shelburne Falls *U.S.A.* 42°36N 72°45W **355 D12**
Shelby *Mich., U.S.A.* 43°37N 86°22W **352 D10**
Shelby *Mont., U.S.A.* 48°30N 111°51W **348 B8**
Shelby *N.C., U.S.A.* 35°17N 81°32W **357 D14**
Shelby *Ohio, U.S.A.* 40°53N 82°40W **354 F2**
Shelbyville *Ill., U.S.A.* 39°24N 88°48W **352 F9**
Shelbyville *Ind., U.S.A.* 39°31N 85°47W **353 F11**
Shelbyville *Ky., U.S.A.* 38°13N 85°14W **353 F11**
Shelbyville *Tenn., U.S.A.* 35°29N 86°28W **357 D11**
Sheldon *U.S.A.* 43°11N 95°51W **352 D6**
Sheldrake *Canada* 50°20N 64°51W **345 B7**
Shelikhova, Zaliv *Russia* 59°30N 157°0E **301 D16**
Shell Lakes *Australia* 29°20S 127°30E **333 E4**
Shellbrook *Canada* 53°13N 106°24W **343 C7**
Shellharbour *Australia* 34°31S 150°51E **335 E5**
Shelter I. *U.S.A.* 41°4N 72°20W **355 E12**
Shelton *Conn., U.S.A.* 41°19N 73°5W **355 E11**
Shelton *Wash., U.S.A.* 47°13N 123°6W **350 C3**
Shen Xian *China* 36°15N 115°40E **306 F8**
Shenandoah *Iowa, U.S.A.* 40°46N 95°22W **352 E6**
Shenandoah *Pa., U.S.A.* 40°49N 76°12W **355 F8**
Shenandoah *Va., U.S.A.* 38°29N 78°37W **353 F14**
Shenandoah → *U.S.A.* 39°19N 77°44W **353 F15**
Shenandoah △ *U.S.A.* 38°35N 78°22W **353 F14**
Shenchi *China* 39°8N 112°10E **306 E7**
Shendam *Nigeria* 8°49N 9°30E **322 G7**
Shendî *Sudan* 16°46N 33°22E **323 E12**
Shengfang *China* 39°3N 116°42E **306 E9**
Shenjingzi *China* 44°40N 124°30E **307 B13**
Shenmu *China* 38°50N 110°29E **306 E6**
Shenqiu *China* 33°25N 115°55E **306 H8**
Shensi = Shaanxi □ *China* 35°0N 109°0E **306 G5**
Shenyang *China* 41°48N 123°27E **307 D12**
Shenzhen *China* 22°32N 114°5E **305 F10**
Shenzhen ✈ (SZX) *China* 22°41N 113°49E **305 F10**
Shenzhen Shuiku *China* 22°34N 114°8E **305 F11**
Shenzhen Wan *China* 22°27N 113°55E **305 G10**
Sheo *India* 26°11N 71°15E **314 F4**
Sheopur Kalan *India* 25°40N 76°40E **314 G7**
Shepetivka *Ukraine* 50°10N 27°10E **289 C14**
Shepetovka = Shepetivka *Ukraine* 50°10N 27°10E **289 C14**
Shepparton *Australia* 36°23S 145°26E **335 F4**
Sheppey, I. of *U.K.* 51°25N 0°48E **285 F8**
Shepton Mallet *U.K.* 51°11N 2°33W **285 F5**
Sheqi *China* 33°12N 112°57E **306 H7**
Sher Qila *Pakistan* 36°7N 74°2E **315 A6**
Sherborne *U.K.* 50°57N 2°31W **285 G5**
Sherbro I. *S. Leone* 7°30N 12°40W **322 G3**
Sherbrooke *N.S., Canada* 45°8N 61°59W **345 C7**
Sherbrooke *Qué., Canada* 45°28N 71°57W **355 A13**
Sherburne *U.S.A.* 42°41N 75°30W **355 D9**
Shergarh *India* 26°20N 72°18E **314 F5**
Sherghati *India* 24°34N 84°47E **315 G11**
Sheridan *Ark., U.S.A.* 34°19N 92°24W **356 D8**
Sheridan *Wyo., U.S.A.* 44°48N 106°58W **348 D10**
Sheringham *U.K.* 52°56N 1°13E **284 E9**
Sherkin I. *Ireland* 51°28N 9°26W **282 E2**
Sherkot *India* 29°22N 78°35E **315 E8**
Sherman *U.S.A.* 33°38N 96°36W **356 E6**
Sherpur *India* 25°34N 83°47E **315 G10**
Sherridon *Canada* 55°8N 101°5W **343 B8**
Sherwood Forest *U.K.* 53°6N 1°7W **284 D6**
Sherwood Park *Canada* 53°31N 113°19W **342 C6**
Sheslay → *Canada* 58°48N 132°5W **342 B2**
Shethanei L. *Canada* 58°48N 97°50W **343 B9**
Shetland □ *U.K.* 60°30N 1°30W **283 A7**
Shetland Is. *U.K.* 60°30N 1°30W **283 A7**
Shetrunji → *India* 21°19N 72°7E **314 J5**
Sheung Shui *China* 22°31N 114°7E **305 F11**
Shey-Phoksundo △ *Nepal* 29°30N 82°45E **315 E10**
Sheyenne → *U.S.A.* 47°2N 96°50W **352 B5**
Shibām *Yemen* 15°59N 48°36E **319 D4**
Shibata *Japan* 37°57N 139°20E **302 F9**
Shibecha *Japan* 43°17N 144°36E **302 C12**
Shibetsu *Japan* 44°10N 142°23E **302 B11**
Shibogama L. *Canada* 53°35N 88°15W **344 B2**
Shibushi *Japan* 31°25N 131°8E **303 J5**
Shickshinny *U.S.A.* 41°9N 76°9W **355 E8**
Shickshock Mts. = Chic-Chocs, Mts. *Canada* 48°55N 66°0W **345 C6**
Shidao *China* 36°50N 122°25E **307 F12**
Shido *Japan* 34°19N 134°10E **303 G7**
Shiel, L. *U.K.* 56°48N 5°34W **283 E3**
Shield, C. *Australia* 13°20S 136°20E **334 A2**
Shīeli *Kazakhstan* 44°20N 66°15E **300 E7**
Shiga □ *Japan* 35°20N 136°0E **303 G8**
Shiguaigou *China* 40°52N 110°15E **306 D6**
Shihchiachuangi = Shijiazhuang *China* 38°2N 114°28E **306 E8**
Shihezi *China* 44°15N 86°2E **304 B3**
Shijiazhuang *China* 38°2N 114°28E **306 E8**
Shikarpur *India* 28°17N 78°7E **314 E8**
Shikarpur *Pakistan* 27°57N 68°39E **314 F3**
Shikohabad *India* 27°6N 78°36E **315 F8**
Shikoku □ *Japan* 33°30N 133°30E **303 H6**
Shikoku-Sanchi *Japan* 33°30N 133°30E **303 H6**
Shikotsu-Ko *Japan* 42°45N 141°25E **302 C10**
Shikotsu-Tōya △ *Japan* 44°4N 145°8E **302 C10**
Shiliguri *India* 26°45N 88°25E **313 F16**
Shiliu = Changjiang *China* 19°20N 108°55E **310 C7**
Shilka *Russia* 52°0N 115°55E **301 D12**
Shilka → *Russia* 53°20N 121°26E **301 D13**
Shillelagh *Ireland* 52°45N 6°32W **282 D5**
Shillington *U.S.A.* 40°18N 75°58W **355 F9**
Shillong *India* 25°35N 91°53E **313 G17**
Shilo *West Bank* 32°4N 35°18E **318 C4**
Shilou *China* 37°0N 110°48E **306 F6**
Shimabara *Japan* 32°48N 130°20E **303 H5**
Shimada *Japan* 34°49N 138°10E **303 G9**
Shimane □ *Japan* 35°0N 132°30E **303 G6**
Shimanovsk *Russia* 52°15N 127°30E **301 D13**
Shimba Hills ⌓ *Kenya* 4°14S 39°25E **326 C4**
Shimizu *Japan* 35°0N 138°30E **303 G9**
Shimla *India* 31°2N 77°9E **314 D7**
Shimodate *Japan* 36°20N 139°55E **303 F9**
Shimoga *India* 13°57N 75°32E **312 N9**
Shimoni *Kenya* 4°38S 39°20E **326 C4**
Shimonoseki *Japan* 33°58N 130°55E **303 H5**
Shimpuru Rapids *Namibia* 17°45S 19°55E **328 B2**
Shin, L. *U.K.* 58°5N 4°30W **283 C4**
Shinano-Gawa → *Japan* 36°50N 138°30E **303 F9**
Shināş *Oman* 24°46N 56°28E **317 E8**
Shīndand *Afghan.* 33°12N 62°8E **312 C3**
Shinglehouse *U.S.A.* 41°58N 78°12W **354 E6**
Shingū *Japan* 33°40N 135°55E **303 H7**
Shingwidzi *S. Africa* 23°5S 31°25E **329 C5**
Shinjō *Japan* 38°46N 140°18E **302 E10**
Shinkolobwe *Dem. Rep. of the Congo* 11°10S 26°40E **324 G5**
Shinshār *Syria* 34°36N 36°43E **318 A5**
Shinyanga *Tanzania* 3°45S 33°27E **326 C3**
Shinyanga □ *Tanzania* 3°50S 34°0E **326 C3**
Shio-no-Misaki *Japan* 33°25N 135°45E **303 H7**
Shiogama *Japan* 38°19N 141°1E **302 E10**
Shiojiri *Japan* 36°6N 137°58E **303 F8**
Shipchenski Prokhod *Bulgaria* 42°45N 25°15E **295 C11**
Shiping *China* 23°45N 102°23E **304 D5**
Shippagan *Canada* 47°45N 64°45W **345 C7**
Shippensburg *U.S.A.* 40°3N 77°31W **354 F7**
Shippenville *U.S.A.* 41°15N 79°28W **354 E5**
Shiprock *U.S.A.* 36°47N 108°41W **349 H9**
Shiqma, N. → *Israel* 31°37N 34°30E **318 D3**
Shiquan *China* 33°5N 108°15E **306 H5**
Shiquan He = Indus → *Pakistan* 24°20N 67°47E **314 G2**
Shīr Kūh *Iran* 31°39N 54°3E **317 D7**
Shiragami-Misaki *Japan* 41°24N 140°12E **302 D10**
Shirakawa *Fukushima, Japan* 37°7N 140°13E **303 F10**
Shirakawa *Gifu, Japan* 36°17N 136°56E **303 F8**
Shirane-San *Gumma, Japan* 36°48N 139°22E **303 F9**
Shirane-San *Yamanashi, Japan* 35°42N 138°9E **303 G9**
Shiraoi *Japan* 42°33N 141°21E **302 C10**
Shīrāz *Iran* 29°42N 52°30E **317 D7**
Shire → *Africa* 17°42S 35°19E **327 F4**
Shiretoko-Misaki *Japan* 44°21N 145°20E **302 B12**
Shirinab → *Pakistan* 30°15N 66°28E **314 D2**
Shiriya-Zaki *Japan* 41°25N 141°30E **302 D10**
Shiroishi *Japan* 38°0N 140°37E **302 F10**
Shirshov Ridge *Pac. Oc.* 58°0N 170°0E **336 B8**
Shīrvān *Iran* 37°30N 57°50E **317 B8**
Shirwa, L. = Chilwa, L. *Malawi* 15°15S 35°40E **327 F4**
Shivpuri *India* 25°26N 77°42E **314 G7**
Shixian *China* 43°5N 129°50E **307 C15**
Shiyan *China* 22°42N 113°56E **305 F10**
Shiyan Shuiku *China* 22°42N 113°54E **305 F10**
Shizuishan *China* 39°15N 106°50E **306 E4**
Shizuoka *Japan* 34°57N 138°24E **303 G9**
Shizuoka □ *Japan* 35°15N 138°40E **303 G9**
Shklov = Shklow *Belarus* 54°16N 30°15E **289 A16**
Shklow *Belarus* 54°16N 30°15E **289 A16**
Shkodër *Albania* 42°4N 19°32E **295 C8**
Shkumbini → *Albania* 41°2N 19°31E **295 D8**
Shmidta, Ostrov *Russia* 81°0N 91°0E **301 A10**
Shō-Gawa → *Japan* 36°47N 137°4E **303 F8**
Shoal L. *Canada* 49°33N 95°1W **343 D9**
Shoal Lake *Canada* 50°30N 100°35W **343 C8**
Shōdo-Shima *Japan* 34°30N 134°15E **303 G7**
Sholapur = Solapur *India* 17°43N 75°56E **312 L9**
Shōmrōn *West Bank* 32°15N 35°13E **318 C4**
Shoreham by Sea *U.K.* 50°50N 0°16W **285 G7**
Shori → *Pakistan* 28°29N 69°44E **314 E3**
Shorkot Road *Pakistan* 30°47N 72°15E **314 D5**
Shoshone *Calif., U.S.A.* 35°58N 116°16W **351 K10**
Shoshone *Idaho, U.S.A.* 42°56N 114°25W **348 E6**
Shoshone L. *U.S.A.* 44°22N 110°43W **348 D8**
Shoshone Mts. *U.S.A.* 39°20N 117°25W **348 G5**
Shoshong *Botswana* 22°56S 26°31E **328 C4**
Shoshoni *U.S.A.* 43°14N 108°7W **348 E9**
Shouguang *China* 37°52N 118°45E **307 F10**
Shouyang *China* 37°54N 113°8E **306 F7**
Show Low *U.S.A.* 34°15N 110°2W **349 J8**
Shqipëria = Albania ■ *Europe* 41°0N 20°0E **295 D9**
Shreveport *U.S.A.* 32°31N 93°45W **356 E8**
Shrewsbury *U.K.* 52°43N 2°45W **285 E5**
Shri Mohangarh *India* 27°17N 71°18E **314 F4**
Shrirampur *India* 22°44N 88°21E **315 H13**
Shropshire □ *U.K.* 52°36N 2°45W **285 E5**
Shū *Kazakhstan* 43°36N 73°42E **300 E8**
Shuangcheng *China* 45°20N 126°15E **307 B14**
Shuanggou *China* 34°2N 117°30E **307 G9**
Shuangliao *China* 43°29N 123°30E **307 C12**
Shuangshanzi *China* 40°20N 119°8E **307 D10**
Shuangyang *China* 43°28N 125°40E **307 C13**
Shuangyashan *China* 46°28N 131°5E **305 B8**
Shuguri Falls *Tanzania* 8°33S 37°22E **327 D4**
Shuiye *China* 36°7N 114°8E **306 F8**
Shujalpur *India* 23°18N 76°46E **314 H7**
Shukpa Kunzang *India* 34°22N 78°22E **315 B8**
Shulan *China* 44°28N 127°0E **307 B14**
Shule *China* 39°25N 76°3E **304 C2**
Shumagin Is. *U.S.A.* 55°7N 160°30W **346 a**
Shumen *Bulgaria* 43°18N 26°55E **295 C12**
Shumikha *Russia* 55°10N 63°15E **300 D7**
Shuo Xian = Shuozhou *China* 39°20N 112°33E **306 E7**
Shuozhou *China* 39°20N 112°33E **306 E7**
Shūr → *Fārs, Iran* 28°30N 55°0E **317 D7**
Shūr → *Kermān, Iran* 30°52N 57°37E **317 D8**
Shūr → *Yazd, Iran* 31°45N 55°15E **317 D7**
Shūr Āb *Iran* 34°23N 51°11E **317 C6**
Shūr Gaz *Iran* 29°10N 59°20E **317 D8**
Shūrāb *Iran* 33°43N 56°29E **317 C8**
Shūrjestān *Iran* 31°24N 52°25E **317 D7**
Shurugwi *Zimbabwe* 19°40S 30°0E **327 F3**
Shūsf *Iran* 31°50N 60°5E **317 D9**
Shūshtar *Iran* 32°0N 48°50E **317 D6**
Shuswap L. *Canada* 50°55N 119°3W **342 C5**
Shuyang *China* 34°10N 118°42E **307 G10**
Shūzū *Iran* 29°52N 54°30E **317 D7**
Shwebo *Burma* 22°30N 95°45E **313 H19**
Shwegu *Burma* 24°15N 96°26E **313 G20**
Shweli → *Burma* 23°45N 96°45E **313 H20**
Shymkent *Kazakhstan* 42°18N 69°36E **300 E7**
Shyok *India* 34°13N 78°12E **315 B8**
Shyok → *Pakistan* 35°13N 75°53E **315 B6**
Si Chon *Thailand* 9°0N 99°54E **311 H2**
Si Kiang = Xi Jiang → *China* 22°5N 113°20E **305 D6**
Si Lanna △ *Thailand* 19°17N 99°12E **310 C2**
Si-ngan = Xi'an *China* 34°15N 109°0E **306 G5**
Si Prachan *Thailand* 14°37N 100°9E **310 E3**
Si Racha *Thailand* 13°10N 100°48E **310 F3**
Si Xian *China* 33°30N 117°50E **307 H9**
Siachen Glacier *Asia* 35°20N 77°30E **315 B7**
Siahaf → *Pakistan* 29°3N 68°57E **314 E3**
Siahan Range *Pakistan* 27°30N 64°40E **312 F4**
Siaksriindrapura *Indonesia* 0°51N 102°0E **308 D2**
Sialkot *Pakistan* 32°32N 74°30E **314 C6**
Siam = Thailand ■ *Asia* 16°0N 102°0E **310 E4**
Sian = Xi'an *China* 34°15N 109°0E **306 G5**
Sian Ka'an ⌓ *Mexico* 19°35N 87°40W **359 D7**
Siantan *Indonesia* 3°10N 106°15E **308 D3**
Sīāreh *Iran* 28°5N 60°14E **317 D9**
Siargao I. *Phil.* 9°52N 126°3E **309 C7**
Siari *Pakistan* 34°55N 76°40E **315 B7**
Siasi *Phil.* 5°34N 120°50E **309 C6**
Siau *Indonesia* 2°50N 125°25E **309 D7**
Šiauliai *Lithuania* 55°56N 23°15E **281 J20**
Sibâi, Gebel el *Egypt* 25°45N 34°10E **316 E2**
Sibang *Indonesia* 8°34S 115°13E **309 K18**
Sibay *Russia* 52°42N 58°39E **290 D10**
Sibayi, L. *S. Africa* 27°20S 32°45E **329 D5**
Šibenik *Croatia* 43°48N 15°54E **294 C6**
Siberia = Sibirskiy □ *Russia* 58°0N 90°0E **301 D10**
Siberia *Russia* 60°0N 100°0E **276 D13**
Siberut *Indonesia* 1°30S 99°0E **308 E1**
Sibi *Pakistan* 29°30N 67°54E **314 E2**
Sibil = Oksibil *Indonesia* 4°59S 140°35E **309 E10**
Sibiloi △ *Kenya* 4°0N 36°20E **326 B4**
Sibirskiy □ *Russia* 58°0N 90°0E **301 D10**
Sibirtsevo *Russia* 44°12N 132°26E **302 B5**
Sibiti *Congo* 3°38S 13°19E **324 E2**
Sibiu *Romania* 45°45N 24°9E **289 F13**
Sibley *U.S.A.* 43°24N 95°45W **352 D6**
Sibolga *Indonesia* 1°42N 98°45E **308 D1**
Sibsagar *India* 27°0N 94°36E **313 F19**
Sibu *Malaysia* 2°18N 111°49E **308 D4**
Sibuco *Phil.* 7°20N 122°10E **309 C6**
Sibuguey B. *Phil.* 7°50N 122°45E **309 C6**
Sibut *C.A.R.* 5°46N 19°10E **324 C3**
Sibutu *Phil.* 4°45N 119°30E **309 D5**
Sibutu Passage *E. Indies* 4°50N 120°0E **309 D5**
Sibuyan I. *Phil.* 12°25N 122°40E **309 B6**
Sibuyan Sea *Phil.* 12°30N 122°20E **309 B6**
Sicamous *Canada* 50°49N 119°0W **342 C5**
Siccus → *Australia* 31°55S 139°17E **335 E2**
Sichuan □ *China* 30°30N 103°0E **304 C5**
Sicilia *Italy* 37°30N 14°30E **294 F6**
Sicily = Sicilia *Italy* 37°30N 14°30E **294 F6**
Sicily, Str. of 37°35N 11°56E **294 F4**
Sicuani *Peru* 14°21S 71°10W **364 F4**
Sidari *Greece* 39°47N 19°41E **297 A3**
Siddhapur *India* 23°56N 72°25E **314 H5**
Siddipet *India* 18°5N 78°51E **312 K11**
Sideros, Akra *Greece* 35°19N 26°19E **297 D8**
Sidhauli *India* 27°17N 80°50E **315 F9**
Sidhi *India* 24°25N 81°53E **315 G9**
Sidi-bel-Abbès *Algeria* 35°13N 0°39W **322 A5**
Sidi Ifni *Morocco* 29°29N 10°12W **322 C3**
Sidlaw Hills *U.K.* 56°32N 3°2W **283 E5**
Sidley, Mt. *Antarctica* 77°2S 126°2W **277 D14**
Sidmouth *U.K.* 50°40N 3°15W **285 G4**
Sidmouth, C. *Australia* 13°25S 143°36E **334 A3**
Sidney *Canada* 48°39N 123°24W **350 B3**
Sidney *Mont., U.S.A.* 47°43N 104°9W **348 C11**
Sidney *N.Y., U.S.A.* 42°19N 75°24W **355 D9**
Sidney *Nebr., U.S.A.* 41°8N 102°59W **352 E2**
Sidney *Ohio, U.S.A.* 40°17N 84°9W **353 E11**
Sidney Lanier, L. *U.S.A.* 34°10N 84°4W **357 D12**
Sidoarjo *Indonesia* 7°27S 112°43E **309 G15**
Sidon = Saydā *Lebanon* 33°35N 35°25E **318 B4**
Sidra, G. of = Surt, Khalīj *Libya* 31°40N 18°30E **323 B9**
Siedlce *Poland* 52°10N 22°20E **289 B12**
Sieg → *Germany* 50°46N 7°6E **288 C4**
Siegen *Germany* 50°51N 8°0E **288 C5**
Siem Pang *Cambodia* 14°7N 106°23E **310 E6**
Siem Reap = Siemreab *Cambodia* 13°20N 103°52E **310 F4**
Siemreab *Cambodia* 13°20N 103°52E **310 F4**
Siena *Italy* 43°19N 11°21E **294 C4**
Sieradz *Poland* 51°37N 18°41E **289 C10**

V

Verner Canada 46°25N 80°8W 344 C3
Verneukpan S. Africa 30°0S 21°0E 328 E3
Vernon Canada 50°20N 119°15W 342 C5
Vernon U.S.A. 34°9N 99°17W 356 D5
Vernonia U.S.A. 45°52N 123°11W 350 E3
Vero Beach U.S.A. 27°38N 80°24W 357 H14
Véroia = Veria Greece 40°34N 22°12E 295 D10
Verona Canada 44°29N 76°42W 355 B8
Verona Italy 45°27N 10°59E 294 B4
Versailles France 48°48N 2°7E 292 B5
Vert, C. Senegal 14°45N 17°30W 322 F2
Verulam S. Africa 29°38S 31°2E 329 D5
Verviers Belgium 50°37N 5°52E 287 D5
Veselovskoye Vdkhr. Russia 46°58N 41°25E 291 E7
Vesoul France 47°40N 6°11E 292 C7
Vesterålen Norway 68°45N 15°0E 280 B16
Vestfjorden Norway 67°55N 14°0E 280 C16
Vestmannaeyjar Iceland 63°27N 20°15W 280 E3
Vestspitsbergen Svalbard 78°40N 17°0E 276 B8
Vestvågøya Norway 68°18N 13°50E 280 B15
Vesuvio Italy 40°49N 14°26E 294 D6
Vesuvius, Mt. = Vesuvio Italy 40°49N 14°26E 294 D6
Veszprém Hungary 47°8N 17°57E 289 E9
Vetlanda Sweden 57°24N 15°3E 281 H16
Vetlugu → Russia 56°36N 46°4E 290 C8
Vettore, Mte. Italy 42°49N 13°16E 294 C5
Veurne Belgium 51°5N 2°40E 287 C2
Veys Iran 31°30N 49°0E 317 D6
Vezhen Bulgaria 42°50N 24°20E 295 C11
Vi Thanh Vietnam 9°42N 105°26E 311 H5
Viacha Bolivia 16°39S 68°18W 364 G5
Viamão Brazil 30°5S 51°0W 367 C5
Viana Brazil 3°13S 44°55W 365 D10
Viana do Alentejo Portugal 38°17N 7°59W 293 C2
Viana do Castelo Portugal 41°42N 8°50W 293 B1
Vianden Lux. 49°56N 6°12E 287 E6
Viangchan = Vientiane Laos 17°58N 102°36E 310 D4
Vianópolis Brazil 16°40S 48°35W 365 G9
Vianos Greece 35°2N 25°21E 297 D7
Viaréggio Italy 43°52N 10°14E 294 C4
Vibo Valéntia Italy 38°40N 16°6E 294 E7
Viborg Denmark 56°27N 9°23E 281 H13
Vic Spain 41°58N 2°19E 293 B7
Vicenza Italy 45°33N 11°33E 294 B4
Vich = Vic Spain 41°58N 2°19E 293 B7
Vichada → Colombia 4°55N 67°50W 364 C5
Vichy France 46°9N 3°26E 292 C5
Vicksburg U.S.A. 33°45N 113°45W 351 M13
Victor India 21°0N 71°30E 314 J4
Victor U.S.A. 42°58N 77°24W 354 D7
Victor Harbor Australia 35°30S 138°37E 335 F2
Victoria Argentina 32°40S 60°10W 366 C3
Victoria Canada 48°30N 123°25W 350 B3
Victoria Chile 38°13S 72°20W 368 D2
Victoria China 22°17N 114°9E 305 G11
Victoria Malta 36°3N 14°14E 297 C1
Victoria Seychelles 4°38S 55°28E 325 b
Victoria Kans., U.S.A. 38°52N 99°9W 352 F4
Victoria Tex., U.S.A. 28°48N 97°0W 356 G6
Victoria □ Australia 37°0S 144°0E 335 F3
Victoria → Australia 15°10S 129°40E 332 C4
Victoria, Grand L. Canada 47°31N 77°30W 344 C4
Victoria, L. Africa 1°0S 33°0E 326 C3
Victoria, L. Australia 33°57S 141°15E 335 E3
Victoria, Mt. Burma 21°14N 93°55E 313 J18
Victoria Beach Canada 50°40N 96°35W 343 C9
Victoria de Durango = Durango Mexico 24°3N 104°39W 358 C4
Victoria de las Tunas = Las Tunas Cuba 20°58N 76°59W 360 B4
Victoria Falls Zimbabwe 17°58S 25°52E 327 F2
Victoria Harbour Canada 44°45N 79°45W 354 B5
Victoria I. Canada 71°0N 111°0W 340 B8
Victoria L. Canada 48°20N 57°27W 345 C8
Victoria Ld. Antarctica 75°0S 160°0E 277 D11
Victoria Nile → Uganda 2°14N 31°26E 326 B3
Victoria River Australia 16°25S 131°0E 332 C5
Victoria Str. Canada 69°31N 100°30W 340 C9
Victoria West S. Africa 31°25S 23°4E 328 E3
Victoriaville Canada 46°4N 71°56W 345 C5
Victorica Argentina 36°20S 65°30W 366 D2
Victorville U.S.A. 34°32N 117°18W 351 L9
Vicuña Chile 30°0S 70°50W 366 C1
Vicuña Mackenna Argentina 33°53S 64°25W 366 C3
Vidal U.S.A. 34°7N 114°31W 351 L12
Vidal Junction U.S.A. 34°11N 114°34W 351 L12
Vidalia U.S.A. 32°13N 82°25W 357 E13
Vidin Bulgaria 43°59N 22°50E 295 C10
Vidisha India 23°28N 77°53E 314 H7
Vido Greece 39°38N 19°55E 297 A3
Vidzy Belarus 55°23N 26°37E 281 J22
Viedma Argentina 40°50S 63°0W 368 E4
Viedma, L. Argentina 49°30S 72°30W 368 F2
Vielsalm Belgium 50°17N 5°54E 287 D5
Vieng Pou Kha Laos 20°41N 101°4E 310 B3
Vienna = Wien Austria 48°12N 16°22E 288 D9
Vienna Ill., U.S.A. 37°25N 88°54W 352 G9
Vienna Mo., U.S.A. 38°11N 91°57W 352 F8
Vienne France 45°31N 4°53E 292 D6
Vienne → France 47°13N 0°5E 292 C4
Vientiane Laos 17°58N 102°36E 310 D4
Vientos, Paso de los Caribbean 20°0N 74°0W 361 C5
Vieques Puerto Rico 18°8N 65°25W 361 d
Vierge Pt. St. Lucia 13°49N 60°53W 361 f
Vierzon France 47°13N 2°5E 292 C5
Vietnam ■ Asia 19°0N 106°0E 310 C6
Vieux Fort St. Lucia 13°46N 60°58W 361 f
Vigan Phil. 17°35N 120°28E 309 A6
Vigévano Italy 45°19N 8°51E 292 D8
Vigia Brazil 0°50S 48°5W 365 D9
Viglas, Akra Greece 35°54N 27°51E 297 D9
Vigo Spain 42°12N 8°41W 293 A1
Vihowa Pakistan 31°8N 70°30E 314 D4
Vihowa → Pakistan 31°8N 70°41E 314 D4
Vijayawada India 16°31N 80°39E 313 L12
Vijosë → Albania 40°37N 19°24E 295 D8
Vík Iceland 63°25N 19°1W 280 E4
Vikeke = Viqueque E. Timor 8°52S 126°23E 309 F7
Viking Canada 53°7N 111°50W 342 C6
Vikna Norway 64°55N 10°58E 280 D14
Vila da Maganja Mozam. 17°18S 37°30E 327 F4
Vila da Ribeira Brava C. Verde Is. 16°32N 24°25W 322 b
Vila do Bispo Portugal 37°5N 8°53W 293 D1
Vila Franca de Xira Portugal 38°57N 8°59W 293 C1
Vila Gamito Mozam. 14°12S 33°0E 327 E3
Vila Gomes da Costa Mozam. 24°20S 33°37E 329 C5
Vila Machado Mozam. 19°15S 34°14E 327 F3
Vila Mouzinho Mozam. 14°48S 34°25E 327 E3
Vila Nova de Gaia Portugal 41°8N 8°37W 293 B1
Vila Real Portugal 41°17N 7°48W 293 B2
Vila-real de los Infantes Spain 39°55N 0°3W 293 C5
Vila Real de Santo António Portugal 37°10N 7°28W 293 D2
Vila Vasco da Gama Mozam. 14°54S 32°14E 327 E3
Vila Velha Brazil 20°20S 40°17W 367 A7
Vilagarcía de Arousa Spain 42°34N 8°46W 293 A1
Vilaine → France 47°30N 2°27W 292 C2
Vilanandro, Tanjona Madag. 16°11S 44°27E 329 B7
Vilanculos Mozam. 22°1S 35°17E 329 C6
Vilanova i la Geltrú Spain 41°13N 1°40E 293 B6
Vilcheka, Zemlya Russia 80°30N 60°30E 276 A11
Vileyka Belarus 54°30N 26°53E 289 A14
Vilhelmina Sweden 64°35N 16°39E 280 D17
Vilhena Brazil 12°40S 60°5W 364 F6
Viliya = Neris → Lithuania 55°8N 24°16E 281 J21
Viljandi Estonia 58°28N 25°30E 281 G21
Vilkitskogo, Proliv Russia 78°0N 103°0E 301 B11
Vilkovo = Vylkove Ukraine 45°28N 29°32E 289 F15
Villa Abecia Bolivia 21°0S 68°18W 366 A2
Villa Ana Argentina 28°28S 59°40W 366 B4
Villa Ángela Argentina 27°34S 60°45W 366 B3
Villa Bella Bolivia 10°25S 65°22W 364 F5
Villa Cañás Argentina 34°0S 61°35W 366 C3
Villa Colón Argentina 31°38S 68°20W 366 C2
Villa Constitución Argentina 33°15S 60°20W 366 C3
Villa de Arriaga Mexico 21°56N 101°20W 358 C4
Villa de María Argentina 29°55S 63°43W 366 B3
Villa de Méndez Mexico 25°7N 98°34W 359 B5
Villa Dolores Argentina 31°58S 65°15W 366 C2
Villa Frontera Mexico 26°56N 101°27W 358 B4
Villa Guillermina Argentina 28°15S 59°29W 366 B4
Villa Hayes Paraguay 25°5S 57°20W 366 B4
Villa Hidalgo Mexico 24°15N 99°26W 359 C5
Villa Iris Argentina 38°12S 63°12W 366 D3
Villa María Argentina 32°20S 63°10W 366 C3
Villa Mazán Argentina 28°40S 66°30W 366 B2
Villa Montes Bolivia 21°10S 63°30W 366 A3
Villa Ocampo Argentina 28°30S 59°20W 366 B4
Villa Ocampo Mexico 26°27N 105°31W 358 B3
Villa Ojo de Agua Argentina 29°30S 63°44W 366 B3
Villa San José Argentina 32°12S 58°15W 366 C4
Villa San Martín Argentina 28°15S 64°9W 366 B3
Villa Unión Mexico 23°12N 106°14W 358 C3
Villacarlos Spain 39°53N 4°17E 296 B11
Villacarrillo Spain 38°7N 3°3W 293 C4
Villach Austria 46°37N 13°51E 288 E7
Villafranca de los Caballeros Spain 39°34N 3°25E 296 B10
Villagrán Mexico 24°29N 99°29W 359 C5
Villaguay Argentina 32°0S 59°0W 366 C4
Villahermosa Mexico 17°59N 92°55W 359 D6
Villajoyosa Spain 38°30N 0°12W 293 C5
Villalba Spain 43°26N 7°40W 293 A2
Villanueva U.S.A. 35°16N 105°22W 349 J11
Villanueva de la Serena Spain 38°59N 5°50W 293 C3
Villanueva y Geltrú = Vilanova i la Geltrú Spain 41°13N 1°40E 293 B6
Villarreal = Vila-real de los Infantes Spain 39°55N 0°3W 293 C5
Villarrica Chile 39°15S 72°15W 368 D2
Villarrica Paraguay 25°40S 56°30W 366 B4
Villarrobledo Spain 39°18N 2°36W 293 C4
Villavicencio Argentina 32°28S 69°0W 366 C2
Villavicencio Colombia 4°9N 73°37W 364 C4
Villaviciosa Spain 43°32N 5°27W 293 A3
Villazón Bolivia 22°0S 65°35W 366 A2
Ville-Marie Canada 47°20N 79°30W 344 C4
Ville Platte U.S.A. 30°41N 92°17W 356 F8
Villena Spain 38°39N 0°52W 293 C5
Villeneuve-d'Ascq France 50°38N 3°9E 292 A5
Villeneuve-sur-Lot France 44°24N 0°42E 292 D4
Villiers S. Africa 27°2S 28°36E 329 D4
Villingen-Schwenningen Germany 48°3N 8°26E 288 D5
Villmanstrand = Lappeenranta Finland 61°3N 28°12E 280 F23
Vilna Canada 54°7N 111°55W 342 C6
Vilnius Lithuania 54°38N 25°19E 281 J21
Vilvoorde Belgium 50°56N 4°26E 287 D4
Vilyuy → Russia 64°24N 126°26E 301 C13
Vilyuysk Russia 63°40N 121°35E 301 C13
Viña del Mar Chile 33°0S 71°30W 366 C1
Vinarós Spain 40°30N 0°27E 293 B6
Vincennes U.S.A. 38°41N 87°32W 352 F10
Vincent U.S.A. 34°33N 118°11W 351 L8
Vinchina Argentina 28°45S 68°15W 366 B2
Vindelälven → Sweden 63°55N 19°50E 280 E18
Vindeln Sweden 64°12N 19°43E 280 D18
Vindhya Ra. India 22°50N 77°0E 314 H7
Vineland U.S.A. 39°29N 75°2W 353 F16
Vinh Vietnam 18°45N 105°38E 310 C5
Vinh Linh Vietnam 17°4N 107°2E 310 D6
Vinh Long Vietnam 10°16N 105°57E 311 G5
Vinh Yen Vietnam 21°21N 105°35E 310 B5
Vinita U.S.A. 36°39N 95°9W 356 C7
Vinkovci Croatia 45°19N 18°48E 295 B8
Vinnitsa = Vinnytsya Ukraine 49°15N 28°30E 289 D15
Vinnytsya Ukraine 49°15N 28°30E 289 D15
Vinson Massif Antarctica 78°35S 85°25W 277 D16
Vinton Calif., U.S.A. 39°48N 120°10W 350 F6
Vinton Iowa, U.S.A. 42°10N 92°1W 352 D7
Vinton La., U.S.A. 30°11N 93°35W 356 F8
Viqueque E. Timor 8°52S 126°23E 309 F7
Virac Phil. 13°30N 124°20E 309 B6
Virachey Cambodia 13°59N 106°49E 310 F6
Virachey △ Cambodia 14°14N 106°55E 310 E6
Virago Sd. Canada 54°0N 132°30W 342 C2
Viramgam India 23°5N 72°0E 314 H5
Viranşehir Turkey 37°13N 39°45E 316 B3
Virawah Pakistan 24°31N 70°46E 314 G4
Virden Canada 49°50N 100°56W 343 D8
Vire France 48°50N 0°53W 292 B3
Vírgenes, C. Argentina 52°19S 68°21W 368 G3
Virgin → U.S.A. 36°28N 114°21W 349 H6
Virgin Gorda Br. Virgin Is. 18°30N 64°26W 361 e
Virgin Is. (British) ☑ W. Indies 18°30N 64°30W 361 e
Virgin Is. (U.S.) ☑ W. Indies 18°20N 65°0W 361 e
Virgin Islands △ U.S. Virgin Is. 18°21N 64°43W 361 C7
Virginia S. Africa 28°8S 26°55E 328 D4
Virginia U.S.A. 47°31N 92°32W 352 B7
Virginia □ U.S.A. 37°30N 78°45W 353 G14
Virginia Beach U.S.A. 36°44N 76°0W 353 F16
Virginia City Mont., U.S.A. 45°18N 111°56W 348 D8
Virginia City Nev., U.S.A. 39°19N 119°39W 350 F7
Virginia Falls Canada 61°38N 125°42W 342 A3
Virginiatown Canada 48°9N 79°36W 344 C4
Viroqua U.S.A. 43°34N 90°53W 352 D8
Virovitica Croatia 45°51N 17°21E 294 B7
Virpur India 21°51N 70°42E 314 J4
Virton Belgium 49°35N 5°32E 287 E5
Virudunagar India 9°30N 77°58E 312 Q10
Virunga △ Dem. Rep. of the Congo 0°5N 29°38E 326 B2
Vis Croatia 43°4N 16°10E 294 C7
Visalia U.S.A. 36°20N 119°18W 350 J7
Visayan Sea Phil. 11°30N 123°30E 309 B6
Visby Sweden 57°37N 18°18E 281 H18
Viscount Melville Sd. Canada 74°10N 108°0W 341 B9
Visé Belgium 50°44N 5°41E 287 D5
Višegrad Bos.-H. 43°47N 19°17E 295 C8
Viseu Brazil 1°10S 46°5W 365 D9
Viseu Portugal 40°40N 7°55W 293 B2
Vishakhapatnam India 17°45N 83°20E 313 L13
Visnagar India 23°45N 72°32E 314 H5
Viso, Mte. Italy 44°38N 7°5E 292 D7
Visokoi I. Antarctica 56°43S 27°15W 277 B1
Vista U.S.A. 33°12N 117°14W 351 M9
Vistula = Wisła → Poland 54°22N 18°55E 289 A10
Vitebsk = Vitsyebsk Belarus 55°10N 30°15E 290 C5
Viterbo Italy 42°25N 12°6E 294 C5
Viti Levu Fiji 17°30S 177°30E 331 a
Vitigudino Spain 41°1N 6°26W 293 B2
Vitim Russia 59°28N 112°35E 301 D12
Vitim → Russia 59°26N 112°34E 301 D12
Vitória Brazil 20°20S 40°22W 365 H10
Vitória da Conquista Brazil 14°51S 40°51W 365 F10
Vitória de São Antão Brazil 8°10S 35°20W 365 E11
Vitoria-Gasteiz Spain 42°50N 2°41W 293 A4
Vitsyebsk Belarus 55°10N 30°15E 290 C5
Vittória Italy 36°57N 14°32E 294 F6
Vittório Véneto Italy 45°59N 12°18E 294 B5
Viveiro Spain 43°39N 7°38W 293 A2
Vivian U.S.A. 32°53N 93°59W 356 E8
Viwa Fiji 17°10S 177°58E 331 a
Vizcaíno, Desierto de Mexico 27°30N 113°45W 358 B2
Vizcaíno, Sierra Mexico 27°30N 114°0W 358 B2
Vize Turkey 41°34N 27°45E 295 D12
Vizianagaram India 18°6N 83°30E 313 K13
Vlaardingen Neths. 51°55N 4°21E 287 C4
Vladikavkaz Russia 43°0N 44°35E 291 F7
Vladimir Russia 56°15N 40°30E 290 C7
Vladimir Volynskiy = Volodymyr-Volynskyy Ukraine 50°50N 24°18E 289 C13
Vladivostok Russia 43°10N 131°53E 302 C5
Vlieland Neths. 53°16N 4°55E 287 A4
Vlissingen Neths. 51°26N 3°34E 287 C3
Vlorë Albania 40°32N 19°28E 295 D8
Vltava → Czech Rep. 50°21N 14°30E 288 D8
Vo Dat Vietnam 11°9N 107°31E 311 G6
Voe U.K. 60°21N 1°16W 283 A7
Vogelkop = Doberai, Jazirah Indonesia 1°25S 133°0E 309 E8
Vogelsberg Germany 50°31N 9°12E 288 C5
Voghera Italy 44°59N 9°1E 292 D8
Vohibinany Madag. 18°49S 49°4E 329 B8
Vohilava Madag. 21°4S 48°0E 329 C8
Vohimarina = Iharana Madag. 13°25S 50°0E 329 A9
Vohimena, Tanjon' i Madag. 25°36S 45°8E 329 D8
Vohipeno Madag. 22°22S 47°51E 329 C8
Voi Kenya 3°25S 38°32E 326 C4
Voiron France 45°22N 5°35E 292 D6
Voisey B. Canada 56°15N 61°50W 345 A7
Vojmsjön Sweden 65°0N 16°24E 280 D17
Vojvodina □ Serbia 45°20N 20°0E 295 B9
Volborg U.S.A. 45°51N 105°41W 348 D11
Volcán de Colima △ Mexico 19°30N 103°40W 358 D4
Volcano Is. = Kazan-Rettō Pac. Oc. 25°0N 141°0E 336 E6
Volcans △ Rwanda 1°30S 29°26E 326 C2
Volda Norway 62°9N 6°5E 280 E12
Volga = Privolzhskiy □ Russia 56°0N 50°0E 300 D6
Volga → Russia 46°0N 48°30E 291 E8
Volga Hts. = Privolzhskaya Vozvyshennost Russia 51°0N 46°0E 291 D8
Volgodonsk Russia 47°33N 42°5E 291 E7
Volgograd Russia 48°40N 44°25E 291 E7
Volgogradskoye Vdkhr. Russia 50°0N 45°20E 291 D8
Volkhov → Russia 60°8N 32°20E 290 B5
Volkovysk = Vawkavysk Belarus 53°9N 24°30E 289 B13
Volksrust S. Africa 27°24S 29°53E 329 D4
Volochanka Russia 71°0N 94°28E 301 B10
Volodymyr-Volynskyy Ukraine 50°50N 24°18E 289 C13
Vologda Russia 59°10N 39°45E 290 C6
Volos Greece 39°24N 22°59E 295 E10
Volosovo Russia 59°27N 29°32E 281 G23
Volovets Ukraine 48°43N 23°11E 289 D12
Volozhin = Valozhyn Belarus 54°3N 26°30E 289 A14
Volsk Russia 52°5N 47°22E 290 D8
Volta → Ghana 5°46N 0°41E 320 F4
Volta, L. Ghana 7°30N 0°0 322 G6
Volta Redonda Brazil 22°31S 44°5W 367 A7
Voltaire, C. Australia 14°16S 125°35E 332 B4
Volterra Italy 43°24N 10°51E 294 C4
Volturno → Italy 41°1N 13°55E 294 D5
Volzhskiy Russia 48°56N 44°46E 291 E7
Vomo Fiji 17°30S 177°15E 331 a
Vondrozo Madag. 22°49S 47°20E 329 C8
Vopnafjörður Iceland 65°45N 14°50W 280 D6
Vories Sporades Greece 39°15N 23°30E 295 E10
Vorkuta Russia 67°48N 64°20E 290 A11
Vormsi Estonia 59°1N 23°13E 281 G20
Voronezh Russia 51°40N 39°10E 291 D6
Võrts Järv Estonia 58°16N 26°3E 281 G22
Võru Estonia 57°48N 26°54E 281 H22
Vosges France 48°20N 7°10E 292 B7
Voss Norway 60°38N 6°26E 280 F12
Vostok Antarctica 78°30S 106°50E 277 D8
Vostok I. Kiribati 10°5S 152°23W 337 J12
Votkinsk Russia 57°0N 53°55E 290 C9
Votkinskoye Vdkhr. Russia 57°22N 55°12E 290 C10
Votsuri-Shima Japan 25°45N 123°29E 303 M1
Vouga → Portugal 40°41N 8°40W 293 B1
Vouxa, Akra Greece 35°37N 23°32E 297 D5
Voyageurs △ U.S.A. 48°32N 93°0W 352 A7
Voynitsa Russia 65°10N 30°20E 280 D24
Vozhe, Ozero Russia 60°45N 39°0E 290 B6
Voznesensk Ukraine 47°35N 31°21E 291 E5
Voznesenye Russia 61°0N 35°28E 290 B6
Vrangelya, Ostrov Russia 71°0N 180°0E 301 B19
Vranje Serbia 42°34N 21°54E 295 C9
Vratsa Bulgaria 43°15N 23°30E 295 C10
Vrbas → Bos.-H. 45°8N 17°29E 294 B7
Vrede S. Africa 27°24S 29°6E 329 D4
Vredefort S. Africa 27°0S 27°22E 328 D4
Vredenburg S. Africa 32°56S 18°0E 328 E2
Vredendal S. Africa 31°41S 18°35E 328 E2
Vrindavan India 27°37N 77°40E 314 F7
Vrisses Greece 35°23N 24°13E 297 D6
Vršac Serbia 45°8N 21°20E 295 B9
Vryburg S. Africa 26°55S 24°45E 328 D3
Vryheid S. Africa 27°45S 30°47E 329 D5
Vu Liet Vietnam 18°43N 105°23E 310 C5
Vukovar Croatia 45°21N 18°59E 295 B8
Vulcan Canada 50°25N 113°15W 342 C6
Vulcan Romania 45°23N 23°17E 289 F12
Vulcaneşti Moldova 45°41N 28°18E 289 F15
Vulcano Italy 38°24N 14°58E 294 E6
Vulkaneshty = Vulcaneşti Moldova 45°41N 28°18E 289 F15
Vunduzi → Mozam. 18°56S 34°1E 327 F3
Vung Tau Vietnam 10°21N 107°4E 311 G6
Vunidawa Fiji 17°50S 178°21E 331 a
Vunisea Fiji 19°3S 178°10E 331 a
Vwaza ⌂ Malawi 10°58S 33°25E 327 E3
Vyartsilya Russia 62°8N 30°45E 280 E24
Vyatka = Kirov Russia 58°35N 49°40E 290 C8
Vyatka → Russia 55°37N 51°28E 290 C9
Vyatskiye Polyany Russia 56°14N 51°5E 290 C9
Vyazemskiy Russia 47°32N 134°45E 301 E14
Vyazma Russia 55°10N 34°15E 290 C5
Vyborg Russia 60°43N 28°47E 280 F23
Vychegda → Russia 61°18N 46°36E 290 B8
Vychodné Beskydy Europe 49°20N 22°0E 289 D11
Vyg-ozero Russia 63°47N 34°29E 290 B5
Vylkove Ukraine 45°28N 29°32E 289 F15
Vynohradiv Ukraine 48°9N 23°2E 289 D12
Vyrnwy, L. U.K. 52°48N 3°31W 284 E4
Vyshniy Volochek Russia 57°30N 34°30E 290 C5
Vyshzha = imeni 26 Bakinskikh Komissarov Turkmenistan 39°22N 54°10E 317 B7
Vyškov Czech Rep. 49°17N 17°0E 289 D9
Vytegra Russia 61°0N 36°27E 290 B6

W

W.A.C. Bennett Dam Canada 56°2N 122°6W 342 B4
Wa Ghana 10°7N 2°25W 322 F5
Waal → Neths. 51°37N 5°0E 287 C5
Waalwijk Neths. 51°42N 5°4E 287 C5
Wabakimi △ Canada 50°43N 89°29W 344 B2
Wabana Canada 47°40N 53°0W 345 C9
Wabasca → Canada 58°22N 115°20W 342 B5
Wabasca-Desmarais Canada 55°57N 113°56W 342 B6
Wabash U.S.A. 40°48N 85°49W 353 E11
Wabash → U.S.A. 37°48N 88°2W 352 G9
Wabigoon L. Canada 49°44N 92°44W 343 D10
Wabowden Canada 54°55N 98°38W 343 C9
Wabuk Pt. Canada 55°20N 85°5W 344 A2
Wabush Canada 52°55N 66°52W 345 B6
Waco U.S.A. 31°33N 97°9W 356 F6
Waconichi, L. Canada 50°8N 74°0W 344 B5
Wad Hamid Sudan 16°30N 32°45E 323 E12
Wad Medanî Sudan 14°28N 33°30E 323 F12
Wad Thana Pakistan 27°22N 66°23E 314 F2
Wadai Africa 12°0N 19°0E 320 E5
Wadayama Japan 35°19N 134°52E 303 G7
Waddeneilanden Neths. 53°25N 5°10E 287 A5
Waddenzee Neths. 53°6N 5°10E 287 A5
Waddington U.S.A. 44°52N 75°12W 355 B9
Waddington, Mt. Canada 51°23N 125°15W 342 C3
Waddy Pt. Australia 24°58S 153°21E 335 C5
Wadebridge U.K. 50°31N 4°51W 285 G3
Wadena Canada 51°57N 103°47W 343 C8
Wadena U.S.A. 46°26N 95°8W 352 B6
Wadeye Australia 14°28S 129°52E 332 B4
Wadhams Canada 51°30N 127°30W 342 C3
Wādī as Sīr Jordan 31°56N 35°49E 318 D4
Wadi Halfa Sudan 21°53N 31°19E 323 D12
Wadi Rum △ Jordan 29°30N 35°20E 318 F4
Wadsworth Nev., U.S.A. 39°38N 119°17W 348 G4
Wadsworth Ohio, U.S.A. 41°2N 81°44W 354 E3
Waegwan S. Korea 35°59N 128°23E 307 G15
Wafangdian China 39°38N 121°58E 307 E11
Wafrah Si. Arabia 28°33N 47°56E 316 D5
Wageningen Neths. 51°58N 5°40E 287 C5
Wager B. Canada 65°26N 88°40W 341 C11
Wagga Wagga Australia 35°7S 147°24E 335 F4
Waghete Indonesia 4°10S 135°50E 309 E9
Wagin Australia 33°17S 117°25E 333 F2
Wagner U.S.A. 43°5N 98°18W 352 D4
Wagon Mound U.S.A. 36°1N 104°42W 349 H11
Wagoner U.S.A. 35°58N 95°22W 356 D7
Wah Pakistan 33°45N 72°40E 314 C5
Wahai Indonesia 2°48S 129°35E 309 E7
Wahiawā U.S.A. 21°30N 158°2W 346 b
Wâḥid Egypt 30°48N 32°21E 318 E1
Wahnai Afghan. 32°40N 65°50E 314 C1
Wahoo U.S.A. 41°13N 96°37W 352 E5
Wahpeton U.S.A. 46°16N 96°36W 352 B5
Waiau → N.Z. 42°47S 173°22E 331 E4
Waibeem Indonesia 0°30S 132°59E 309 E8
Waigeo Indonesia 0°20S 130°40E 309 E8
Waihi N.Z. 37°23S 175°52E 331 B5
Waihou → N.Z. 37°15S 175°40E 331 B5
Waika Dem. Rep. of the Congo 2°22S 25°42E 326 C2
Waikabubak Indonesia 9°45S 119°25E 309 F5
Waikaremoana, L. N.Z. 38°49S 177°9E 331 C6
Waikari N.Z. 42°58S 172°41E 331 E4
Waikato → N.Z. 37°23S 174°43E 331 B5
Waikerie Australia 34°9S 140°0E 335 E3
Waikokopu N.Z. 39°3S 177°52E 331 C6
Waikouaiti N.Z. 45°36S 170°41E 331 F3
Wailingding Dao China 22°6N 114°2E 305 G11
Wailuku U.S.A. 20°53N 156°30W 346 b
Waimakariri → N.Z. 43°24S 172°42E 331 E4
Waimate N.Z. 44°45S 171°3E 331 F3
Wainganga → India 18°50N 79°55E 312 K11
Waingapu Indonesia 9°35S 120°11E 309 F6
Waini → Guyana 8°20N 59°50W 364 B7
Wainwright Canada 52°50N 110°50W 343 C6
Waiouru N.Z. 39°28S 175°41E 331 C5
Waipara N.Z. 43°3S 172°46E 331 E4
Waipawa N.Z. 39°56S 176°38E 331 C6
Waipiro N.Z. 38°2S 178°22E 331 C7
Waipoua Forest N.Z. 35°39S 173°33E 331 A4
Waipu N.Z. 35°59S 174°29E 331 A5
Waipukurau N.Z. 40°1S 176°33E 331 D6
Wairakei N.Z. 38°37S 176°6E 331 C6
Wairarapa, L. N.Z. 41°14S 175°15E 331 D5
Wairoa N.Z. 39°3S 177°25E 331 C6
Waitaki → N.Z. 44°56S 171°7E 331 F3
Waitangi N.Z. 35°16S 174°5E 331 A5
Waitara N.Z. 38°59S 174°15E 331 C5
Waitomo Caves N.Z. 38°16S 175°7E 331 C5
Waitsburg U.S.A. 46°16N 118°9W 348 C4
Waiuku N.Z. 37°15S 174°45E 331 B5
Wajima Japan 37°30N 137°0E 303 F8
Wajir Kenya 1°42N 40°5E 326 B5
Wakasa Japan 35°20N 134°24E 303 G7
Wakasa-Wan Japan 35°40N 135°30E 303 G7
Wakatipu, L. N.Z. 45°5S 168°33E 331 F2
Wakaw Canada 52°39N 105°44W 343 C7
Wakaya Fiji 17°37S 179°0E 331 a